The Metallurgy of Steel

BY

HENRY MARION HOWE, A. M. (HARVARD), S. B.

VOLUME I.

THE SCIENTIFIC PUBLISHING COMPANY
27 PARK PLACE, NEW YORK

1890

To SIR LOWTHIAN BELL., Bart., F. R. S., D. C. L.. M. S.,

Fellow of the Royal Academy of Science of Stockholm,

Magister Magnus in Ignibus,

As a token of the author's admiration,

this volume is dedicated.

PREFACE TO THE FIRST VOLUME.

The present work is the final outcome of a desire on the part of its publishers to give metallurgists an account of our American steel works.

A quarter of a century has elapsed since the appearance of Percy's classical work on iron and steel. Though we have had meanwhile, beside many other works, the really admirable handbooks of Bauerman and of Ledebur, and though Bell has discussed in a masterly way many of the problems connected with the metallurgy of iron, and especially with the blast-furnace process, it has seemed to me that this was a fitting time to post our ledger and strike a trial-balance: to offer in accessible form, and more fully than these distinguished writers have, the data which make up our present knowledge of the metallurgy of steel, and, above all, to discuss these data and to seek their true teachings.

In order that the work might the sooner become available to the readers of the ENGINEERING AND MINING JOURNAL it was first published in the pages of that paper. This plan has several serious defects, the chief of which is that the earlier parts of the volume have to stand as they were written, some of them nearly three years ago: for, once electrotyped, I cannot readily modify them in accordance with later discoveries, and with changes of opinion to which these discoveries as well as further research, discussion, and reflection have naturally led me. It is also because of this mode of publishing that the tables and figures are not numbered quite consecutively.

I cannot sufficiently thank my American fellow-metallurgists for their great kindness and generosity in supplying me with information and with drawings, for their patience in answering my many questions, and for their liberality in allowing me to study their practice minutely and to take notes of it. I am under a special debt of gratitude to Mr. Robert Forsyth, engineer of the Illinois Steel Company, and Mr. William Metcalf, of the firm of Miller, Metcalf & Parkin, who, besides giving me endless information, have each examined a chapter of this volume, Mr. Forsyth the chapter on apparatus for the Bessemer process, Mr. Metcalf that on the crucible process: and to Messrs. Hunt and Clapp, of the Pittsburgh Testing Laboratory, who have most generously made many chemical analyses for this volume gratuitously. I also thank most heartily Mr. W. R. Walker, of the Union Steel Company, now the Illinois Steel Company; Messrs. John Fritz, Maunsel White and George Jenkins, of the Bethlehem Iron Company; Messrs. F. A. Emmerton and Thomas Crow, of the Joliet Steel Company, now the Illinois Steel Company; Mr. Philip W. Moen, of the Washburn & Moen Manufacturing Company; Messrs. W. R. Jones and James Gayley, of the Edgar Thomson Steel Works; Mr. S. T. Wellman, of the Otis Iron and Steel Company; Dr. Thomas M. Drown, of the Massachusetts Institute of Technology; Mr. F. W. Wood, of the Pennsylvania Steel Company; Messrs. Joseph Morgan, Jr., T. T. Morrell, and John Coffin, of the Cambria Iron Company; Mr. E. S. Moffat, of the Lackawanna Iron and Coal Company; Mr. J. M. Sherrerd, of the Troy Steel and Iron Company; Messrs. E. C. Potter, John C. Parkes and J. C. Walker, of the North Chicago Rolling Mill Company, now the Illinois Steel Company; Mr. Phineas Barnes, of the American Iron Company; Mr. G. H. Billings, of the late Norway Steel and Iron Company; Mr. W. F. Downs, of the Dixon Crucible Company, and Mr. E. Gibbon Spilsbury, of the Trenton Iron Company.

With regard to the cost of metallurgical processes I have in general given the quantities of material and the amount of labor needed for given work, rather than the actual cost in dollars and cents: for the former, though far from constant, change much less than the latter, being almost free from one important cause of variation, changes in the current prices of these materials themselves and of labor. Given the quantities of material and of labor needed, one who knows the market rates at a given spot can calculate the cost: while if the actual cost for given conditions alone is given, the cost under other conditions and where the prices of materials and labor are different cannot be determined readily. Again, while the managers of works are often willing that the quantities of materials which they use should be known, they for obvious reasons prefer that the costs should not.

Seeking to lighten the labor of others who may wish to examine the matter in greater detail, or who may wish to verify my statements, I have given many references which it would profit most readers but little to examine. Indeed, many of my references are given merely to indicate that my statements have solid foundation. In a few cases I have been unable to consult works to which others have referred, and which I had good reason to believe contained important matter bearing on the subject in hand. With like aim, I have not hesitated to refer to them, nor, where the same paper has appeared even in the same form in different works, to refer to several of them simultaneously, so that those who could not consult one might find the matter in another. With a few exceptions in the earlier pages, where several authorities are quoted together, the first is the one whose statements I have used.

Such a work as this cannot, of course, be carried out without much compilation: but by far the greater part of the labor has been expended in the original work of discussing the data thus compiled, and in acquiring wholly new data, whether by experimental research, or in prolonged examination of the processes described. For instance, there are about two hundred tables in this volume; of these all but about twenty (and most of these twenty are very small) are either wholly original, or consist mainly or wholly, not of matter published by others, but of numbers calculated therefrom.

Uniform accuracy in publishing so much varied and practically original numerical matter is not to be expected The author will be very grateful to any one who will point out to him numerical or other errors.

Many of the more important tables have been calculated twice, wholly independently, and often by different methods. In many other cases effective checks have been used Not a few numerical errors, hitherto handed down from text-book to text-book, have been detected and corrected. Whenever possible, numerical and other data have been verified from the original memoirs, at one or another of the several important libraries which have been accessible. Where statements have seemed improbable or vague verification or explanation has been sought and often obtained from their authors.

The numberless determinations of tensile strength and elastic limit quoted have, for uniformity, been reduced from tons and kilogrammes to pounds per square inch, the measure habitually used in this country. Temperatures are in general given both in Fahrenheit and Centigrade.

In describing old experiments and abandoned processes, I have not aimed to give matter of historic interest, but rather that which might be useful, whether in deterring others from repeating unnecessary or hopeless experiments, or in guiding them should processes, once unsuccessful, become commercially possible through changed conditions.

The task of deciding what information about present practice to give, and what to withhold, has been a delicate one. First we must recognize that the practice, the experience, the knowledge of a metallurgist or of a company is distinctly property and that communicating to others against the wishes of its owner may be quite as much robbery morally as if it were legally punishable. Indeed, in that it sneaks behind the cloak of law, it is contemptible as well. But beyond this there is a certain amount of information which, once published by others, or once a matter of general knowledge, may be regarded as more or less public property. In deciding what part of this to publish one has to weigh against the duty of making one's work as useful as possible, one's regards for the wishes of those whose liberality in giving other information has laid on him a burden of gratitude.

I have sought to steer between these shoals on either hand, by giving all information as to practice which seems useful and which I have permission to give, while trying to conceal the identity of the establishment at which it exists. The important thing for the reader, be he practitioner or student, is to know that certain practice exists or is possible; for the manufacturer that it be not known as his particular practice. Probably even the close-mouthed Krupp would object relatively little to having his practice known, provided it were not known as his, but as that of the shadowy X, Y, or Z.

An exception is made in case of the plans of certain works which, repeatedly published, are already clearly public property; and in a few cases, such as the great output of certain Bessemer works, in which the results, due to his administrative skill, are a matter of pride to the manager, and in which he certainly prefers to receive publicly his just credit.

BOSTON, January, 1890. H. M. H.

TABLE OF CONTENTS

CHAPTER I.

CLASSIFICATION AND CONSTITUTION OF STEEL.

CHAPTER II.

CARBON AND IRON, HARDENING, TEMPERING, AND ANNEALING.

CHAPTER III.

IRON AND SILICON.

CHAPTER IV.

IRON AND MANGANESE.

CHAPTER V.

IRON AND SULPHUR.

CHAPTER VI.

IRON AND PHOSPHORUS.

EFFECT OF PHOSPHORUS ON THE PHYSICAL PROPERTIES OF IRON.

CHAPTER VII.

CHROMIUM, TUNGSTEN, COPPER.

CHAPTER VIII.

THE METALS OCCURRING BUT SPARINGLY IN IRON.

CHAPTER IX.

IRON AND OXYGEN.

CHAPTER X.

NITROGEN, HYDROGEN, CARBONIC OXIDE.

IRON AND HYDROGEN.

IRON AND CARBONIC OXIDE.

CHAPTER XI.

THE ABSORPTION AND ESCAPE OF GAS FROM IRON.

PUNCHING AND SHEARING.

CHAPTER XV.

DIRECT PROCESSES.

DESCRIPTION OF DIRECT PROCESSES.

CHAPTER XVI.

CHARCOAL-HEARTH PROCESSES.

CHAPTER XVII.

THE CRUCIBLE STEEL PROCESS.

CHEMISTRY OF THE CRUCIBLE PROCESS.

CHAPTER XVIII.

APPARATUS FOR THE BESSEMER PROCESS.

APPENDIX I—SPECIAL STEELS.

APPENDIX II—ANTI-RUST COATINGS.

APPENDIX III—LEAD-QUENCHING.

TABLE OF CONTENTS.

LIST OF ILLUSTRATIONS.

LIST OF TABLES.

THE METALLURGY OF STEEL.

CHAPTER I.

Classification and Constitution of Steel.

§ 1. Metallurgy.—The art of extracting metals from their ores and other combinations and of fashioning them.

Steel has (1) a specific sense, and (2) in English and French a generic sense which harmonizes poorly with its specific meaning.

(A) In its specific sense steel is a compound of iron possessing, or capable of possessing, decided hardness simultaneously with a valuable degree of toughness when hot or when cold, or both. It includes primarily compounds of iron combined with from say 0·30 to 2 per cent of carbon, which can be rendered decidedly soft and tough or intensely hard by slow and rapid cooling respectively, and secondarily compounds of iron with chromium, tungsten, manganese, titanium, and other elements, compounds which like carbon steel possess intense hardness with decided toughness.

This specific sense was formerly the sole one, in all lands; it is the legitimate and dominant one to-day in Teutonic and Scandinavian countries, and it would be in this country also, could the little band, which stoutly opposed the introduction of the present anomaly and confusion into our nomenclature, have resisted the momentum of an incipient custom as successfully as they silenced the arguments of their opponents.

The following scheme classifies iron in accordance with this specific meaning:

Classification of International Committee of 1876, of the American Institute of Mining Engineers.

	Malleable.		Non-malleable.
	Can not be hardened by sudden cooling. IRON.	Can be hardened by sudden cooling. STEEL.	
Cast when molten into a malleable mass.	Ingot iron. Flusseisen. Fer fondu.	Ingot steel. Fluss Stahl. Acier fondu.	Cast-iron.
Aggregated from pasty particles without subsequent fusion.	Weld iron. Sweisseisen, Fer soudé.	Weld steel. Schweiss Stahl Acier soudé.	

(B) Generic Sense.—While these species are universally recognized they are not usually grouped in accordance with the above scheme in English speaking countries and France, where "steel" is used generically to include not only the species "steel," but "ingot iron," as well. Most of the "boiler-plate steel" of to-day and much structural material, which is unquestionably steel in its now established generic sense, belong to the species "ingot iron." So firmly has this sense of the word become established that unfortunately it were vain to oppose it.

Freedom from intermingled slag, etc., is not only, I believe, a better recognized, but intrinsically a more valuable basis for discrimination between weld and ingot metal, as it implies the possession of definite properties, than Holley's historical basis of having been cast when molten into a malleable mass; since metal which is not metallic when cast may, by subsequent treatment, be made to resemble so closely that which is as to justify classing them together. We should recognize inherent properties rather than the accident of birth or previous conditions.

"Iron" and "steel" are employed so ambiguously and inconsistently, that it is to-day impossible to arrange all varieties under a simple and consistent classification. The following scheme expresses the current meanings as accurately as may be:

Present American and British Classification. (1890)

	Malleable.			Non-malleable
	Can not be hardened by sudden cooling, AND contains intermingled slag or similar matter. IRON.	Can be hardened by sudden cooling, OR is both malleable and hard, OR is free from intermixed slag and similar matter. STEEL.		
Is free from slag, etc.		Ingot iron.	Ingot steel.	Cast-iron.
Contains slag or similar matter.	Wrought or Weld iron.		Weld steel.	

Highly carbureted non-siliciferous non-malleable castings are to-day rendered malleable by semi-decarburization and are then called steel castings; this is just *if* they resemble castings of similar composition and initially malleable more closely than they resemble cast-iron; their malleableness, freedom from slag, etc., and their power of being hardened then entitle them to be called steel. Ordinary malleable-iron castings can hardly be embraced in this scheme, but form a separate division.

The attempt to call mitis castings "wrought-iron," is to be deprecated; it can only more hopelessly confuse matters. They are clearly ingot-iron.

Steel is cross-classified in many ways; for example, after the element which gives the iron its increased hardness, as carbon,—tungsten,—chromium-steel, etc.; according to the hardness or degree of carburization, as mild steel, hard steel, etc.; according to the mode of manufacture, as open-hearth, crucible steel, etc., and otherwise.

§ 2. The constitution of steel is somewhat obscure. The former view that nitrogen or other gases played an essential part in its nature has, probably, no important supporters.

I conceive it to consist (A) of a matrix of iron which is sometimes (as in ingot-iron and annealed steel), comparatively, or even quite pure, and sometimes (as in hardened steel, manganese steel, etc.) chemically combined with a portion, or even the whole of the other elements which are present, probably in indefinite ratios, its mechanical properties being greatly affected by them; and (B) of a number of independent entities which we may style "minerals," chemical compounds of the elements present, including iron, which crystallize within the matrix, and by their mechanical properties, shape, size, and mode of distribution, also profoundly affect the mechanical properties of the composite mass, though probably less profoundly than do changes of corresponding magnitude in the composition of the matrix. This conception is based on the following phenomena and analogies.

When a crystalline rock, consisting let us say of a mixture of quartz, mica, and feldspar is fused, its constituents which, prior to fusion, had existed as separate entities, coalesce, and form, apparently, one homogeneous magma. Just as an ordinary aqueous solution may be regarded as a single complex chemical combination, each element of which is directly combined with every other one present, so such a fused magma may be regarded as a single polybasic silicate of iron, lime, magnesia, etc.

[In the common, narrow view, solutions are not chemical combinations, because the most familiar chemical unions (1) occur in definite proportions, (2) are attended with thermal or electric phenomena, and (3) yield a product whose physical properties differ widely from those of its components, while solutions occur in all ratios, usually without marked thermal and electric phenomena, and yield products whose properties are intermediate between those of their components. Many philosophic chemists, however, believing with Hegel that the identification of different substances with the formation of a new one is the essence of chemical union, and that the three common characteristics I have mentioned are simply accidents of certain familiar chemical unions, consider solutions as true chemical unions, though less stable than many of the typical ones. They believe that in solutions, though the chemical force is not the overwhelming one, though it does not dominate the purely physical forces, such as cohesion, as completely as in the more stable chemical unions, yet it is always present. They point out that many solutions exhibit some one at least of the three characteristics of the common stable chemical unions to so marked a degree as to lead us to believe that on further examination most and perhaps all solutions will be found to exhibit some of them; and that the apparent absolute homogeneousness of solutions in itself suffices to distinguish them from mixtures, for apparently absolutely no concentration by gravity occurs in them.

(1) Thus, though solutions occur in many ratios, they probably do not in all, since some solutions, if diluted beyond a certain degree, cease to be homogeneous, separation by gravity occurs, they become mixtures. Moreover, if we regard all the components of a single crystal as mutually combined, then many strong undoubted typical chemical combinations occur in continuously varying indefinite ratios, as in the co-crystallization of antimony and zinc, of ferrous and cupric sulphates, of gold and tin, in homogeneous well-defined crystals.

(2) Many solutions do exhibit marked thermal phenomena; witness the evolution of heat on mixing sulphuric acid and water; its absorption when sal-ammoniac is dissolved.

(3) It is the fact of the unlikeness of the compound to the mean of its components, not the degree of that unlikeness, which should be regarded as the prominent characteristic of chemical compounds. But many solutions are strikingly unlike the mean of their components. Thus the specific gravity of many saline solutions is far greater than the mean specific gravity of salt and dissolving water; some salts indeed dissolve without at all increasing the volume of the water. In other cases, dilution causes vivid chromatic changes; for example, brown cupric chloride forms with a little water an emerald green liquor; with more water, it turns blue. If these solutions be admitted to be chemical unions, how can we bar out the rest, which certainly are true identifications of different substances, and which may, on close examination, prove to possess the familiar but non-essential characteristics of the stronger compounds? If we admit solutions, how can we exclude fused alloys, slags, molten rocks when homogeneous? That each contains distinct separable entities when solidified, does not show that it does when molten.]

When such a fused magma as I have described solidifies, its properties will depend very greatly on the conditions under which solidification occurs, and probably on other conditions now unguessed. These properties are influenced not alone by the mineral species which form during solidification, but by the shape and size of the individual crystals, by the degree of cohesion between the adjacent crystals of dissimilar minerals, and by the manner in which they are interlaced; in short, by structure. Now, not only does the structure, but the very nature of the minerals themselves depend on unknown conditions. We cannot tell, for instance, whether a given lot of CaO, Al_2O_3, Na_2O, and SiO_2, will form oligoclase or a mechanical mixture of anorthite and quartz (the composition of some oligoclase differs from that of some anorthite only in having a little more silica); whether a given lot of CaO, MgO, and SiO_2, will form hornblend, or pyroxene (they are often of identical composition). Many other cases could be cited of minerals of identical composition, but different physical properties: opal and quartz, calcite and aragonite, and the olefines, which, though of identical composition, include very dissimilar compounds, (1) the wax-like ozocerite, (2) the liquid pittoliums, and (3), olefiant gas itself. It is, moreover, impossible to predict what changes in the mineral species which compose a crystalline rock, and in the form and arrangement of their crystals, will be effected, into what new minerals its component elements will be induced to rearrange themselves, by a given change in its ultimate composition.

The ultimate composition of a crystalline rock may indeed give us a rough idea of its physical properties. A highly siliceous rock will be specifically light and probable hard and vitreous; a rock containing much lead, no matter what the state of combination of that lead may be, will ordinarily be heavy. The addition of magnesia and ferric oxide might be shown by experience to change the hard feldspar to the soft cleaving mica. But it is clear that any attempt at an accurate prediction of the physical properties of a crystalline rock from its ultimate composition must be futile. They must either be ascertained by direct test, or inferred from a study of its proximate composition, which must be determined by whatever means are available, and of the arrangement of its component minerals, the size, etc., of their individual crystals, etc.

In the present state of our knowledge it seems probable that the conditions in a solidifying steel ingot, and perhaps in many other alloys and similar compounds, resemble those in a solidifying crystalline rock. For we find that the chemical condition of the components of the solidified steel and the size and probably the shape and arrangement of its individual crystals are affected according to now unknown laws by changes in its ultimate composition, and by the conditions which precede and accompany its solidification and cooling.

The influence of the conditions of cooling on the chemical condition of the components of the solid steel is well exemplified by the case of carbon. If a highly carbureted steel is long exposed to a high temperature while cooling, graphite crystallizes out as a distinct, readily recognized "mineral," if I may so speak; if the molten steel be cooled with sufficient rapidity, no graphite is formed, but the whole of the carbon passes into a condition in which it renders the metal brittle. If we cool the steel slowly from a red heat, most of the carbon forms a carbide, probably of definite composition, Fe_3C, which, distributed uniformly in minute crystals through the matrix of iron, strengthens and hardens the mass, but much less than does the carbon when in the condition induced by sudden cooling.

These variations in the condition of carbon are accompanied by closely corresponding variations in its chemical behavior on the application of solvents. So too, if we may judge from marked differences in its behavior under the action of solvents and from apparently closely corresponding differences in the mechanical properties of the metal which contains it, not only is the chemical condition of phosphorus different in different steels, but that of different portions of phosphorus in the same piece of steel differs greatly. Similar differences probably exist with the other elements found in steel.

The influence of the conditions of cooling on the structure of steel is readily recognized. Slow, undisturbed cooling induces coarse crystallization; if the metal be vigorously hammered during slow cooling, the structure becomes much finer; if the cooling be sudden, extremely fine structure results. That other and now unguessed conditions profoundly alter both the mineral species and the structure of steel, and that changes in ultimate composition modify both species and structure of steel, as of crystalline rock, in most complex ways, is indicated by the utterly anomalous relations between the ultimate composition and the mechanical properties of steel. This anomalousness, which has puzzled so many, is readily explained by the close resemblance between the conditions of the formation of rock and of ingot, which not only shows us why we do not discover these relations, but that in all probability *we never can* from ultimate composition. The lithologist who attempted to-day to deduce the mechanical properties of a granite from its ultimate composition would be laughed at. Are our metallurgical chemists in a much more reasonable position?

The complex way in which slight changes in ultimate composition may induce disproportionate changes in the proximate composition of the mineral species making up the solid steel, and through them its mechanical properties, is readily seen on reflection. If between the elements of the molten mass there exists a certain balance which just permits the formation of certain compounds during solidification, the introduction of a minute quantity of a certain element, say manganese, might just upset this balance and give rise to the formation of quite a different set of compounds, which might have radically different effects on the properties of the metal. While, were the original composition somewhat and perhaps but slightly different, then the addition of the same quantity of manganese might not in the least alter the kind or proportion of the different mineral species which make up the solid mass.

If, pointing out that ·02 per cent phosphorus sensibly alters the ductility of steel, you ask how this effect can be due to so minute a quantity of a simply intermingled mineral, I answer: (1) That we have just seen how minute changes in ultimate composition may profoundly alter the proximate composition. One per cent of salt distributed through gneiss would destroy its weather resisting powers; 5 per cent of mica would give it strong cleavage; so 5, or even 1 per cent of a mineral whose presence in steel might be due to an addition of say ·02 per cent of phosphorus, might profoundly alter its properties. We note among the hydrocarbons compounds whose physical properties differ greatly, yet whose ultimate composition is very similar, nay even identical. (2) That if 0·0002 per cent of iodine gives starch liquor a perceptible color it is not surprising that 100 times as large a quantity of phosphorus should perceptibly affect the properties of the iron matrix with which we may fancy that it directly combines. (3) That even so minute a quantity of phosphorus as ·02 per cent may so affect the conditions of solidification, for example by altering the fluidity of the matrix at some critical temperature at which crystallization occurs, as to greatly affect the size, shape and mode of arrangement of the crystals of some of the minerals present, and of the matrix itself.

If now it is asked why, if these so-called minerals form in steel during solidification, we never see them, I reply (1), that the component minerals of many crystalline rocks are only discernible under the microscope, and even then only because they happen to be more or less transparent, to differ from each other in color, and to have crystalline forms which have been accurately determined by the study of large crystals; (2) that we have hardly begun to look for them in steel; (3), that under favorable circumstances, we do find what appear to be distinct minerals in steel (graphite, Fe_3C, TiC in definite crystals) and to so great an extent as to render it probable that these or similar minerals usually exist, but that being opaque, so nearly alike in color, and in such minute and uniformly distributed particles, they escape observation. In considering segregation, we shall see that when steel contains considerable quantities of manganese, phosphorus, sulphur, etc., what are probably distinct minerals, perhaps even of definite chemical composition, form, now concentrating in the center of the ingot, now liquating from its exterior according to the existing conditions.

If these views be correct, then, no matter how accurate

and extended our knowledge of ultimate composition, and how vast the statistics on which our inferences are based, if we attempt to predict mechanical properties from them accurately we become metallurgical Wigginses. For while we may predict that siliceous rocks will usually be vitreous, July hot, April rainy, and phosphoric steel brittle, yet when we go farther and predict accurately, we state what is not inferable from our premises. It may, and sometimes does, snow in July; Christmas may be warmer than Easter; the more siliceous may be less vitreous than the less siliceous rock; and the more phosphoric steel tougher than the less phosphoric one.

And here it may be observed that the intimate knowledge which the public and many non-metallurgical engineers attribute to metallurgists as to the effects of composition on physical properties has, I believe, no existence in fact. Many steel-metallurgists persuade themselves from wholly insufficient data that they have discovered the specific quantitative effects of this or that element; in other, and I trust few cases, in metallurgy as in medicine, the charlatan feigns profound knowledge, dreading the effect on his client of acknowledged though unavoidable ignorance. Many an experienced steel-maker has confidently assured me of such and such specific effects, producing when challenged a few analyses unconsciously culled from those which opposed his view, and shown, on comparison with a larger number, to be without special significance.

When we confront him with cases which upset his theory, he calmly replies that if we had only determined the sulphur as well, all would have been clear; if by bad luck this, too, is known, he thinks, probably, that nitrogen or carbonic oxide may affect matters; or possibly he attaches great weight to oxygen, which he can always fall back on, triumphantly remarking that when we can determine this element the problem will be solved.

Again, it it is our ignorance of the effects of the rare metals, titanium, vanadium, or what not. And if all these and all gases were fully known he would probably sigh for exact determinations of some millionths of osmium, boron, or rubidium. Certain he is that chemistry can explain all if you will only give him time. So it may, but not the chemistry that he knows; ultimate analysis never will; proximate analysis may, but by methods which are not yet even guessed at, and in the face of fearful obstacles.

How often do we look for the coming of the master mind which can decipher our undecipherable results and solve our insoluble equations, while if we will but rub our own dull eyes and glance from the petty details of our phenomena to their great outlines their meaning stands forth unmistakably; they tell us that we have followed false clues, and paths which lead but to terminal morasses. In vain do we flounder in the sloughs and quagmires at the foot of the rugged mountain of knowledge seeking a royal road to its summit. If we are to climb, it must be by the precipitous paths of proximate analysis, and the sooner we are armed and shod for the ascent, the sooner we devise weapons for this arduous task, the better.

By what methods ultimate composition is to be determined is for the chemist rather than the metallurgist to discover. But, if we may take a leaf from lithology, if we can sufficiently comminute our metal (ay, there's the rub!), by observing differences in specific gravity (as in ore dressing), in rate of solubility under rigidly fixed conditions, in degree of attraction by the magnet, in cleavage, luster, and crystalline form under the microscope, in readiness of oxidation by mixtures of gases in rigidly fixed proportions and at fixed temperatures, we may learn much.

Will the game be worth the candle? Given the proximate composition, will not the mechanical properties of the metal be so greatly influenced by slight and undeterminable changes in the crystalline form, size, and arrangement of the component minerals, so dependent on trifling variations in manufacture, as to be still only roughly deducible?

CHAPTER II.

Carbon and Iron.—Hardening, Tempering, and Annealing.

§ 3. Iron combines with carbon in all proportions up to about seven per cent, absorbing it readily when in contact at or above a red heat with carbonaceous matter, such as charcoal, graphite, and even diamond, or with cast-iron, or steel. About 4·6 per cent of carbon appears sufficient to saturate pure iron.[a]

The presence of manganese raises the point of saturation of carbon in iron, while silicon lowers it. Sulphur is thought to lower the saturation point for molten iron, but rather to raise that for solid iron—*i.e.*, to diminish the *total carbon* which iron can take up, but to increase the proportion of that total carbon which during cooling remains chemically combined, in both these ways opposing the formation of graphite.

Carbon has a remarkable power of diffusing itself through iron, tending to become uniformly distributed, not only through the different portions of a given piece of iron, but between separate pieces of iron which are in contact with each other. Thus Bell[b] raised the percentage of carbon contained in wrought-iron from 0·04 to 0·39 by heating it in contact with cast-iron. Abel,[c] by heating steel disks 0·01 inch thick between wrought-iron plates reduced their carbon from about 1 per cent to 0·1. This diffusing power of carbon is not confined to iron. Marsden[d] states that amorphous carbon in impalpable powder in contact with porcelain at a temperature above redness gradually diffuses into the porcelain and ultimately permeates it throughout. These facts, of course, clear up

[a] Rammelsberg (*Metallurgical Review*, I., p. 176) is said to have found in Wootz 7·867 per cent carbon wholly combined, 0·136 silicon, and 0·002 sulphur. But this is surely an error.

[b] "Principles of the Manufacture of Iron and Steel," p. 160.

[c] *Iron*, 1883, I., p. 76.

[d] *Jour. Iron and Steel Inst.*, 1881, I., p. 233.

the mysteries which formerly hung about the cementation of steel.

§ 4. The Total Carbon, or *Saturation Point for Carbon.*—The quantity of carbon with which molten iron can combine (= combined + graphitic carbon of the solidified iron), depends chiefly on the percentage of silicon, sulphur, and manganese which it contains. The former two elements lower the saturation point for carbon, while manganese raises it.

Chemically pure iron can apparently only combine with about 4·63 per cent of carbon. Thus E. Riley [a] exposed pure iron imbedded in charcoal for two days to a steel-melting temperature. It absorbed only a little more than 4 per cent carbon; 4·63 was the highest percentage of carbon that either Dick or Hochstätter[b] obtained by melting sometimes pure, sometimes nearly pure iron, with an excess of carbon in Percy's laboratory. That this is about the point of saturation with almost pure iron is suggested by the fact that when in these experiments the iron contained this amount, its upper surface was covered with graphite apparently extruded before solidification, even when the iron was rapidly cooled.

§ 5. Manganese raises the point of saturation for carbon—that is, permits higher total carbon. Thus ferro-manganese (see Table 20) often contains above 5·5 per cent, and occasionally 7 per cent. Ledebur[c] considers that, with increasing manganese, the saturation point for carbon rises as follows:

Manganese	10 to 20	35	50	65	80	90
Corresponding saturation point for carbon	5	5·5	6	6·5	7	7·3

§ 6. Silicon probably lowers the saturation point for carbon. Thus, in Fig. 1 we note that the total carbon for those irons which are apparently saturated with it (*i. e.* those which have the highest "total carbon" spots for given silicon) closely follow the broken line $C + \frac{12}{28} Si = 6$.

As 12 and 28 are the atomic weights of carbon and silicon, we may believe with Stöckman[d] that silicon ordinarily displaces carbon atomically from irons already saturated with it. Yet the above formula does not represent absolute saturation, since we find that in Nos. 28 and 29 in Table 1, the value $C + \frac{12}{28}$ Si rises to 7·08 and 7·39. In No. 11, in Table 20, this value reaches 7·02.

Thus sulphur and manganese oppose each other, the one lowering, the other raising the saturation point for carbon. This is illustrated by Nos. 20, 25, 24 and 26, Table 1, which though rich in manganese have only 3 per cent carbon or less, while in non-siliciferous ferro-manganese the carbon usually runs up to 4, 5 or even 6 per cent.

§ 7. Sulphur in large quantity appears to lower the saturation point for carbon. Thus Weston[e] adding small quantities of FeS to graphitic cast-iron with 4·5 per cent C, obtained irons whose carbon, always much less than in the initial iron, fell as their sulphur rose, thus:

Sulphur	2·12	1·08	1·318 (?)
Carbon	3·17	3·00	2·60

That the sulphur by its presence actually expelled carbon is indicated by the fact that graphite separated from the iron apparently while molten, in certain cases floating on its surface.

That moderate amounts of sulphur (0·45 per cent), do not necessarily lower the saturation point for carbon, is shown by Karsten's experiment. Melting gray iron (with 3·31 of graphite and ·625 combined = 3·94 total C and ·03 per cent S) with sulphur, part of the iron united with the sulphur to form a sulphide which did not coalesce with the remainder of the iron: the carbon of the latter, by the elimination of part of its iron, rose to 5·488 C (wholly combined), though its sulphur had risen to 0·45 per cent. It is not probable that the high carbon content of this iron was due to the presence of a large quantity of manganese, for the carbon of the initial iron was almost wholly graphitic; had it been manganiferous its carbon would have been combined. It appears that therefore 0·45 per cent S had actually raised the saturation point for C. (For the effect of sulphur on the *condition* of carbon see § 20.)

§ 8. The Condition of Carbon in Iron.—Carbon may exist in iron (A) mechanically mixed with it as graphite, or (B) in chemical combination with the iron, or (C) in chemical combination with some third element contained in the iron, or (D) in solution, if we admit that solution differs from combination.

A. Graphite occurs most characteristically in highly carburized cast-iron, long exposed to a temperature approaching fusion. As its tenacity is very low, it has little influence on the physical properties of the iron beyond destroying its continuity, thus lowering its tensile and compressive strength and ductility.

B. Chemically Combined with Iron.—Carbon exists in combination with the iron in at least two perfectly distinct modifications. Let us first review the evidence which shows that they are really distinct.

Evidence of Two Conditions of Combination of Carbon and Iron.

§ 9. Chemical Evidence.—Faraday in 1822 first showed that steel, which, when suddenly cooled, dissolved completely in hydrochloric acid, when annealed left a carbonaceous residue when thus dissolved.[f]

Caron obtained like results. Rinman, in 1865, observing that the quantity of carbon remaining undissolved when one and the same steel was attacked by cold HCl differed greatly, being greatest in unworked steel, and smallest in hardened steel (which sometimes yielded little or no carbonaceous residue) named the carbon which dissolved *hardening carbon*, because chiefly found in hardened steel, and that which did not *cement carbon*, because he found it chiefly in cement or blister steel.

Karsten[g] recognized that, in addition to the condition of graphite and that of combination seen in hardened steel, carbon existed in a third state, which he regarded as a polycarbide of unknown composition. From his description of its properties and the conditions under which it was formed, it is probable that his polycarbide was identical with Rinman's cement carbon.

Abel, whose results are by far the most valuable, by dissolving different steels in a "chromic" solution (obtained by adding sulphuric acid to an aqueous solution of potassium-bichromate),[h] whether after annealing, hardening, or tempering, obtained varying quantities of a heavy,

[a] *Jour. Iron and Steel Inst.*, 1877, I., p. 162.
[b] Percy: "Iron and Steel," p. 113-114.
[c] "Handbuch der Eisenhuttenkunde," p. 233.
[d] *Stahl und Eisen*, 1883, IV.; *Jour. Iron and St. Inst.*, 1883, pp. 41 [illegible]
[e] Percy: "Iron and Steel," p. 135.
[f] Percy: "Iron and Steel."
[g] *Idem*, p. 128.
[h] *Iron*, 1883, I., p. 76, and 1885, I., p. 116.

gray-black, spangly carbide of iron as a carbonaceous insoluble residue, attracted by the magnet, and of nearly constant composition, closely approaching that of the formula Fe_3C. The steels examined were almost free from graphite. The proportion of the total combined carbon found in this insoluble carbide varied from 4·7 per cent in hardened steel to 92·8 per cent in certain annealed steel, *i. e.*, in hardened steel nearly all the carbon was soluble in his chromic solvent, in annealed steel hardly any of it was. Unannealed steel yielded slightly less Fe_3C than that which had been annealed, while tempered steel yielded an amount intermediate between that of hardened and that of annealed steel, the proportion of carbide in tempered steel being in general higher the more strongly and the longer the steel had been heated before tempering.

The carbide, whose composition was similar, not only in the same steel after different treatment (hardening, annealing and tempering), but in different steels as well, contained a small quantity of water (carbon-hydrate?), say 0·77 to 3·23 per cent, probably arising from the partial decomposition of the carbide by the chromic solvent.

The carbide Fe_3C is dissolved by hot HCl nearly, or perhaps quite completely. The impossibility of discriminating sharply between it and the small quantity of graphite (?) with which it is mixed, together with the slight decomposition of the carbide itself by the chromic solvent by which it is separated from the mass of the iron, are probably the chief causes of the slight variations observed in its composition. When obtained by means of a chromic solution whose strength was not so great as to largely decompose the carbide itself, it contained from 6·39 C to 8·09 C, a varying proportion of which was probably graphite. Fe_3C should contain 6·57 C.

Müller, on dissolving Bessemer steel in dilute sulphuric acid, obtained a carbide of iron as a pyrophoric residue containing 6·01 to 7·38 per cent C, and thus closely resembling Abel's Fe_3C.

Müller's carbide residue, however, only contained from 19 to 73 per cent of the total carbon of the steel, while Abel's had a much larger proportion, and differed from Müller's in not being pyrophoric.[a]

To sum up, many investigators have distinguished two modifications of combined carbon, a more and a less readily soluble modification. Both clearly differ from graphite in being soluble in boiling hydrochloric acid. The less soluble of the two is insoluble or partly so in dilute cold acids, sulphuric, hydrochloric, and according to Woodcock, in nitric, as well as in Abel's chromic solution. The more readily soluble of the two dissolves completely in these solvents. To fix our ideas, I shall, after Rinman, provisionally call the more soluble *hardening* carbon, as it predominates in hardened steel, and the less soluble, *cement* carbon, and I shall speak of the combination between cement carbon and iron as Abel's carbide, Fe_3C. In adopting these names as those best known, I recognize fully that each of these modifications may actually comprise several yet undistinguished varieties, and that the less readily soluble portions obtained by different experimenters and by different solvents may not be identical. Still, each of these two modifications has strongly distinctive characteristics, and, if it be subdivisible into varieties, the varieties of each species possess in common a similar chemical behavior, and similar effects on the properties of the iron which contains them.

So, too, I adopt the formula Fe_3C provisionally, recognizing that the cement carbon which it contains may not exist in the iron as Fe_3C, but merely in a condition which on solution yields Fe_3C, but that none the less it differs in this respect, as in its comparative insolubility, from hardening carbon.

§ 10. MICROSCOPIC EVIDENCE.—With a power of 650 linear, Sorby,[b] a very trustworthy observer, finds in unhardened steel a mass of crystals, say 0.001 inch in diameter, with their faces covered with fine striæ, say $\frac{1}{30000}$ inch apart, due to the fact that each crystal is composed of minute parallel layers of two wholly different substances, a softer one in layers about $\frac{1}{40000}$ inch thick, and a very hard, brittle one, in layers about $\frac{1}{80000}$ inch thick, interstratified with the first: and he has apparently completely satisfied himself by very prolonged investigation that the materials which compose these alternate layers are of widely different physical properties. His very brief paper does not give his evidence in detail, but he says (apparently as a sample of it) "in partially decarbonized white cast-iron" these "plates are sufficiently thick to show perfectly well that the hard plates are continuous with portions of the original hard white constituent, and the soft plates continuous with the soft malleable iron free from carbon, produced by decarbonization. These two substances differ greatly."

The soft layers he regards as composed of soft carbonless iron: we may provisionally regard the hard ones as composed of Fe_3C; and for brevity, I shall refer to them by this name, recognizing that they have not yet been directly proved to be Fe_3C. He finds that at a very high temperature these components unite to form an intermediate compound (*i. e.*, the C becomes hardening C?), which by long exposure to a lower but still high temperature (annealing) splits up again into the former parallel layers, or if exposed long enough to this temperature they "segregate into comparatively thick and irregular plates" (of Fe_3C?) "and aggregations of pure Fe;" while if suddenly cooled (as in hardening) from a very high temperature, the intermediate compound apparently has not time to split up, at least he finds no evidence that it has, and no trace of what I have supposed to be Fe_3C. Apparently this intermediate compound, formed at a high temperature, split up at a lower one, but retained undecomposed by sufficiently rapid cooling, is Fe united with hardening C. The hard plates (Fe_3C) are absent from practically carbonless iron, and increase in quantity under like conditions as the combined carbon increases.

§ 11. ACCORD OF CHEMICAL, MICROSCOPIC, AND PHYSICAL PHENOMENA.—Microscopic and chemical evidence here agree in detecting a substance (Fe_3C) absent from wrought and ingot-iron and hardened steel, found in greatest quantity in annealed steel, clearly differing from pure Fe, from the Fe and C of hardened steel, and from graphite. Considering now steel of say 1 per cent total combined carbon in its hardened, tempered, and annealed

[a] *Iron*, 1885, L., p. 116, and *Zeits. Ver. Deutsch. Ingen.*, XXII., 385, 1878.

[b] *Journal of the Iron and Steel Institute*, 1886, p. 142.

states, together with ingot iron, we may condense the results of observations into the following table:

Product.	Chemical analysis shows				Microscope shows		Physical tests show hardness and strength.
	Fe_3C.	Combination of Fe with hardening C.			Fe_3C?	Other iron	
		Fe.	C.	Summa*			
Hardened steel.	0·0	99	1	100	0	100	highest
Tempered "	7·5±	92	0·5	92·5	....	......	next highest
Annealed "	15·0±	85	0	85	33±	67±	much lower
Softest Ingot-iron	almost none.	99·95	0·05	100	0	100	lowest

These four products—(1) hardened, (2) tempered, (3) annealed steel, and (4) ingot iron, are composed of four elements, sometimes singly present, sometimes mixed, viz.:

1. Pure carbonless iron, very soft.
2. Fe_3C, reported by Sorby as very hard and brittle.
3. A compound of Fe with hardening C in the ratio of about 99 : 1, almost the sole component of hardened steel, naturally supposed to be very hard and strong.
4. A similar compound with the ratio 92 Fe : 0·5 C = 99·43 Fe : 0·54 C. Having only about half the hardening C which the preceding compound has, it is naturally supposed to be much less hard and strong.

Now HARDENED STEEL, composed almost solely of compound 3, should be, as it is, extremely hard and strong. TEMPERED STEEL, a mixture of 92·5 per cent of the much softer and weaker substance, No. 4, as matrix with 7·5 per cent of the hard brittle substance, No. 2, should be, as it is, much less strong and hard, the presence of only 7·5 per cent of the hard Fe_3C by no means compensating for the reduced strength and hardness of the matrix.

ANNEALED STEEL, consisting of a matrix of soft carbonless iron, which constitutes 85 per cent of the mass, with 15 per cent of the hard brittle Fe_3C crystallized within it, should be, as it is, still much softer and weaker, as even 15 per cent of Fe_3C mechanically interspersed, no matter how hard we may suppose it, could not be expected to bring up the strength and hardness of ingot iron to that of tempered steel. Fifteen per cent of quartz disseminated through steatite can not bring the hardness of the whole up to that of feldspar, though it certainly will raise it, as a comparatively small amount of tough hornblende in granite raises the toughness of the mass sensibly.

SOFT INGOT IRON, finally, should be, as it is, the softest and weakest of all, for it consists almost solely of substance 1, pure carbonless iron. This remarkable accord between the results of chemical, microscopic, and physical examination; the wonderful difference between the physical properties of hardened and unhardened steel, corresponding as it does to such marked differences in the characters of their respective components as revealed by the microscope, and in the chemical behavior of their combined C; the correspondence between the intermediate strength of tempered steel and the chemical behavior of its combined C; the chemical and the almost certain microscopic isolation of a definite compound of Fe with C found copiously in annealed steel, but practically absent from hardened steel and soft iron; these, taken together, leave in my mind no shadow of a doubt that we have in steel at least two distinct states of combination of carbon which exercise widely different effects on the properties of the metal. The supposition that the brittle Fe_3C is simply mechanically mixed with the remainder of the iron is wholly compatible with the malleableness of the whole; we have a parallel case in a copper ingot which Percy describes,[a] which was malleable, though it contained 22 per cent of tungsten, which he states was certainly simply mechanically diffused through the copper.

* This is the sum of the hardening carbon plus the iron united with it, and excludes the Fe_3C.

§ 12. EVIDENCE OF OTHER COMBINATIONS OF CARBON WITH IRON.—Dudley[b] in certain cast-irons distinguishes besides graphite two forms of carbon, one combined with iron to form a gray carbide, the other apparently quite distinct from this carbide. To the latter he gives the name *strength carbon*. Unfortunately he has neither determined the quantity nor the composition of this carbide. Whether either of the forms of combined carbon which he distinguishes are identical with those distinguished by Abel in steel is uncertain. As they have not been recognized in steel, they are not of especial moment for our present purpose.

The endeavors of several investigators to prove the existence of other definite combinations of iron and carbon have not been supported by sufficient evidence to command general acquiescence. Tunner (Ledebur, Handbuch, p. 240), regarded the combined carbon as in the condition of Fe_4C, which in iron with but little carbon was mixed with pure iron. Gurlt regarded gray cast-iron as an octocarbide mixed with graphite, and white cast-iron as a tetracarbide, formed at a low heat and resolved at a higher one into octocarbide and graphite.

§ 13. COMPOUNDS OF C WITH ELEMENTS OTHER THAN IRON.—S. A. Ford on dissolving cast-iron in boiling HCl in an atmosphere of CO_2 obtains a flocculent yellowish residue,[c] decomposed by hot potash solution with separation of a black varnishlike mass (separated carbon?). He regards it as a compound of carbon and silicon.

Shimer,[d] on dissolving cast-iron in HCl, finds in the residue minute non-magnetic cubes, usually perfect, $\frac{1}{1800}$ to $\frac{1}{1000}$ inch thick; Sp. Gr. 5·1; soluble in HNO_3; unaffected by HCl, (apparently) by strong boiling caustic potassa, and by prolonged heating at bright redness in H; and consisting of TiC, with 12 per cent of apparently mechanically mixed foreign matter.

§ 14. THERMAL RELATIONS OF THE COMPOUNDS OF CARBON AND IRON.—Osmund's[e] results indicate that when iron and carbon unite heat is evolved, as in the formation of so many other chemical compounds. They suggest, though equivocally, that more heat is evolved when carbon combines with iron in the cement state than when it unites with it in the hardening state. Troost and Hautefenille's[f] results appear to directly contradict these, and indicate that the combination of iron and carbon is attended by absorption of heat, as in the formation of explosive compounds. The matter appears to need further investigation. Osmund's results are as follows:

RISE OF TEMPERATURE, ON DISSOLVING IRON.

Percentage of carbon.		0·17	0·54	1·17 tool steel.	4·10 white cast-iron
Absolute rise of temperature in degrees centigrade.	Annealed	2·151	2·111	1·895	1.410
	Cold-forged	2·217	2·207	2·018	......
	Hardened	......	2·222	2·056	1·632
Rise of temperature relative to that of the annealed state.	Annealed	1	1	1	1
	Cold-forged	1·045	1·045	1·065	......
	Hardened	......	1·052	1·084	1·150

a *Journal of the Iron and Steel Institute*, 1883, Vol. I., p. 34.
b *Trans. Am. Inst. Mining Engineers*, XIV., 1886, p. 798.
c *Idem*, XIV., 1886, p. 939.
d *Idem*, 1887, XV.
e *Comptes Rendus*, C., 1885, pp. 1228, 1231.
f *Metallurgical Review*, Vol. I., p. 177.

Both in annealed and hardened steel the higher the carbon the less heat is evolved when the metal is dissolved in a calorimeter, hence it is inferred that splitting up the union between iron and carbon causes an absorption of heat, and consequently that their union had been accompanied by evolution of heat.

In each case the hardened metal, with its carbon largely in the hardening state, gives out more heat than when annealed, and with its carbon chiefly in the cement condition. This might be thought to imply that the passage of carbon from the cement to the hardening state was accompanied by absorption of heat, were it not (1) that the heat evolved by cold-forged steel exceeds that evolved by annealed steel almost as much as that evolved by hardened steel does; and Abel has shown that cold-forging does not cause carbon to pass to the hardening state: and (2) that the excess of heat evolved from hardened over that evolved from annealed steel is far from being proportional to the percentage of carbon. In case of cold-forged steel this excess is the same whether 0·17 or 0·54 per cent C is present, and in the case of hardened steel it is only 60 per cent greater with 1·17 than with 0·54 per cent C. These anomalies suggest that the variations in the evolution of heat caused by hardening, annealing, etc., are due to some other effect than the variations in the condition of carbon.

Troost and Hautefeuille found that carburetted iron evolved more heat when dissolved than iron nearly free from carbon.

§ 15. The Distribution of the Carbon between the graphitic, cement, and hardening conditions, *i. e.*, the proportion of the total C found in each state, depends chiefly, 1, on the total amount of carbon present; 2, on the conditions under which the iron has been exposed to a high temperature and subsequently cooled; 3, on the presence of certain other elements, notably sulphur, silicon, and manganese; 4, perhaps on other imperfectly understood conditions. Akerman, Caron and Barba consider that pressure causes carbon to pass from the cement to the hardening condition even at low temperatures; but this conclusion is not warranted by their evidence, and is strongly opposed by Abel's[a] demonstration that in ordinary cold-rolled steel almost all the carbon is in the cement state in spite of the enormous pressure which arises in cold rolling. (See § 56.)

In general the formation of graphite is favored by a high total percentage of carbon, by long exposure to a very high temperature (say 1,500° C.), and by the presence of silicon; and it is opposed by the presence of sulphur and manganese. The formation of cement carbon is favored by slow cooling, and that of hardening carbon by rapid cooling, from a red heat.

§ 16. Effect of Total Percentage of Carbon.—Graphite vs. Combined Carbon. Under like conditions, the more carbon is present the larger apparently is the proportion of the total which escapes from combination and becomes graphitic. Witness the readiness with which under favorable conditions 70 per cent, and even occasionally 90 per cent of the total carbon becomes graphitic in highly carburetted cast-iron. In steel with say 1 per cent carbon we can still find graphite, but the amount is small, while the separation of graphite from ingot iron would probably be difficult if not impossible.

Cement vs. Hardening Carbon.—The conditions under which carbon passes from the cement to the hardening condition and back are so complex that the influence of the total percentage of carbon on the proportion of the combined carbon which passes into the cement and the hardening state respectively is masked by the influence of other variables. It probably cannot be traced without further experimental evidence. The softness of graphitic cast-iron suggests that, when the total carbon is very high, the combined carbon passes rather into the cement than the hardening state. The graphite indeed lessens the strength and hardness of the iron as a whole, but we can hardly ascribe to it the softness of the individual crystals which we observe; these it simply encompasses. But the occurrence of the carbon in such iron in the cement state may be due to other causes than the total percentage of carbon; for example, to the presence of silicon, slow cooling, etc.

§ 17. Effects of Silicon, Sulphur and Manganese on the Proportion of Graphite to Total Combined Carbon.—In general, silicon forces carbon out of combination and into the graphitic state; manganese and sulphur (and perhaps phosphorus) have the opposite effect, favoring the retention in the combined state of all the carbon which the iron contains.

§ 18. Silicon appears not only to oppose the union of carbon with molten iron, but (at least when present in quantities exceeding 1·37 per cent) to oppose to a still higher degree its union with solid iron, to force the carbon out of combination and into the graphitic state. Graphitic cast-irons generally contain much silicon; if this be removed they become white, and their graphite is converted into combined carbon. Thus, in the Bell-Krupp purifying process (pig washing), if a highly graphitic iron be melted and brought in contact with iron-oxide, nearly the whole of its silicon is oxidized before any considerable percentage of carbon has been. If the iron be removed and allowed to solidify after but a brief contact with the oxide, it is found to have become perfectly white.

In the old finery process the same conversion of gray into white iron occurs. It may be observed in the Bessemer process, in which the iron, after it has been blown but a few minutes, during which much of its silicon but very little of its carbon is removed, becomes white. A spiegel with 5·39 per cent Mn and 0·37 Si, which Percy melted in a clay crucible, took up 2·91 per cent Si from the crucible and became gray.[b]

If we examine cast-irons which are tolerably well saturated with carbon and silicon we find that, as the silicon rises the total carbon (which is the percentage with which the iron combines when molten) falls, while the combined carbon (the percentage which the iron is able to retain in combination after solidifying) falls still more rapidly, at least when the silicon exceeds 1·37 per cent. Hence the ratio of graphite to combined carbon rises rapidly with the rising silicon, so rapidly indeed that, for a while, the absolute percentage of graphite actually rises, in spite of the decline in the total carbon, though later the graphite in turn declines. Some of these effects may be traced in Table 1 and Fig. 1. We may consider them under two heads, (A) Turner's results and (B) the others. Considering the latter first, we note that passing in Table 1 from

[a] *Trans. Institution Mechanical Engineers*, 1881, p. 691.

[b] Akerman: *Engineering and Mining Journal*, I., 1875, p. 388.

TABLE 1.—SILICON AND CARBON.

	c 1	a 2	c 3	a 4	c 5	a 6	a 7	a 8	a 9	a 10	c 11	c 12	a 13	d 14	a 15	h 16
Combined carbon	.....	1·6	.....	1·90	.....	1·85	1·71	0·56	0·68	0·80	.....	.....	0·20	.....	0·37	0·79
Graphite	.....	0·38	.....	0·10	.....	0·24	0·50	1·62	1·19	1·43	.....	.....	1·81	.....	1·66	2·59
Total carbon	5·59	1·98	5·79	2·00	5·69	2·09	2·21	2·18	1·87	2·23	4·68	4·55	2·01	3·65	2·03	3·38
Silicon	0·12	0·19	0·43	0·45	0·87	0·96	1·27	1·96	2·31	2·00	3·30	3·35	3·92	4·98	4·74	5·12
Manganese	70·10	0·1[illegible]	68·64	0·21	75·76	0·26	.....	0·60	0·75	0·76	44·04	48·20	0·84	27·13	0·95	0·77
Phosphorus	.....	0·3[illegible]	.....	0·33	.....	0·33	0·3[illegible]	0·28	0·25	0·34	.....	.....	0·38	.....	0·30	1·12
Sulphur	.....	0·3[illegible]	.....	0·05	.....	0·04	[illegible]	0·03	0·0[illegible]	0·04	.....	.....	0·03	.....	0·05	0·17

	h 17	h 18	h 19	d 20	a 21	c 22	d 23	c 24	b 25	d 26	a 27	f 28	e 29	g 30	g 31
Combined carbon	0·71	0·00	0·58	.....	0·38	.....	.....	.....	0·00	.....	0·69	.....	.....	0	0
Graphite	2·68	2·88	2·38	.....	1·48	.....	.....	.....	1·94	.....	1·12	0·60	.....	0	0
Total carbon	3·39	2·88	2·96	3·01	1·86	2·42	2·13	2·72	1·94	1·74	1·81	.....	0·79	0	0
Silicon	5·18	5·47	5·92	6·72	7·33	8·33	8·81	9·12	9·50	9·75	9·80	15·10	15·38	20	23
Manganese	0·53	1·54	1·69	25·70	1·56	2·11	28·80	21·36	1·20	30·14	1·05	.....	8·42	.....	.....
Phosphorus	1·12	0·60	0·14	.....	0·29	.....	.....	.....	0·11	.....	0·21	.....	0·11	.....	.....
Sulphur	0·23	0·04	0·03	.....	0·03	.....	.....	.....	0·02	.....	0·04	.....	0·09	.....	.....

a, T. Turner, *Jour. Iron and St. Inst.*, 1886, I., p. 174; b, Zaboudsky, *Idem*, 1884, I., p. 298; c, *Idem*, 1883, II., p. 780; d, Stöckman, *Idem*, 1883, I., p. 415; e, Percy, *Idem*, 1877, I., p. 164; f, Lawrence Smith, *Idem*, 1880, I., p. 332; g, E. Riley, *Idem*, 1883, I., p. 121; h, E. Hart, *Am. Inst. Min. Engrs.*, V., p. 164.

left to right, the silicon gradually increases; the combined carbon diminishes; the total carbon diminishes after the silicon reaches 6 per cent; the graphite at first increases as the combined carbon diminishes, but later on as the total carbon in turn diminishes the graphite declines.

The effects thus caused by increasing silicon do not appear here with perfect regularity, since they are in some cases obscured by those of manganese and other variables which will shortly be referred to. In Fig. 1 these results are graphically shown. In each instance in which both total and combined carbon are given, I have joined their spots with a line, whose length indicates the percentage of graphite present; this, in irons approximately saturated with carbon and silicon probably reaches a maximum with about 4 to 5 per cent Si. In Fig. 1 the graphite evidently declines as the silicon rises above 6 per cent.

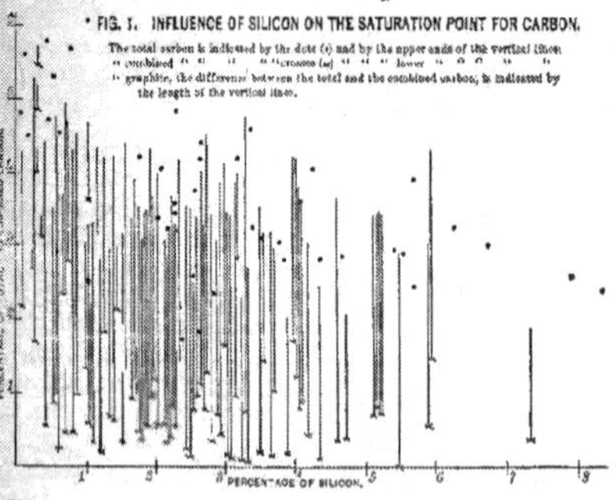

FIG. 1. INFLUENCE OF SILICON ON THE SATURATION POINT FOR CARBON.

The total carbon is indicated by the dots (•) and by the upper ends of the vertical lines. " combined " " " " crosses (×) " " " lower " " " " " graphite, the difference between the total and the combined carbon, is indicated by the length of the vertical lines.

TURNER'S RESULTS.—By melting together in various proportions cast-irons whose compositions (including total C) were closely alike, excepting that one was rich in silicon, while the other had but little,[a] Turner obtained a series of irons in which silicon was practically the only variable. Unlike the other results here given, Turner's throw no light on the effect of silicon on the total quantity of carbon which iron will take up, since his irons were far from saturated with carbon; but they show the effect of varying percentages of silicon on the distribution of carbon between the graphitic and combined states in irons whose total carbon is practically constant.

[a] *Jour. Iron and Steel Inst.*, 1886, I., p. 174.

The curve[b] in Fig. 1 shows his results, which indicate that as silicon rises from 0 to 1 per cent the percentage of carbon held in combination rises; but that as silicon rises from 1 per cent to about 5 per cent it causes the carbon to become more and more largely graphitic; and finally, that as it rises from about 5 per cent to about 10 per cent the proportion of carbon remaining in combination again increases; but as this final apparent rise of combined carbon is due wholly, or nearly so, to a single instance (No. 27), little weight should be attached to it, especially as we find that the total carbon in the other instances continues to decline regularly as the Si rises from 5 per cent to 10 per cent.

Had Turner added silicon to an iron initially saturated with carbon, even the smallest addition would probably have diminished the total carbon and have caused the formation of graphite. His results are, however, valuable as showing that when the total carbon is far below the point of saturation the addition of moderate quantities of silicon may actually increase the proportion of that carbon which remains in combination; the silicon may rise from ·19 to ·96 per cent without increasing the proportion of carbon which becomes graphitic.

§ 19. MANGANESE promotes the union of carbon with iron both in the molten and solid states. Thus we find that highly manganiferous cast-irons (spiegel and ferro-manganese) not only contain much more carbon than others, but that their carbon is ordinarily almost wholly in combination. Thus silicon and manganese oppose each other; the former lowers, the latter raises the saturation point for carbon in molten iron, (*i. e.*, the maximum attainable total C), as well as the saturation point in solid iron, *i. e.*, the proportion of carbon which can remain combined during solidification and cooling. Whether under given conditions a cast-iron of given total carbon becomes graphitic or white on solidification depends greatly on the relative proportions of carbon, silicon, and manganese which it contains. Thus Pourcel obtained cast-iron with 15 per cent Mn, but actually gray (*i. e.*, graphitic), owing to the presence of a large percentage of silicon, though had the silicon been absent a much smaller percentage of manganese would have sufficed to make the iron perfectly white (*i. e.*, to have held all the carbon in combination).

Conversely Ledebur[c] affirms that with 60 per cent

[b] This is a "first derived curve" which I have obtained from Turner's results by taking them in groups of three (1st, 2d, 3d, then 2d, 3d, 4th, etc.), and plotting the center of gravity of each group.

[c] "Handbuch der Eisenhuttenkunde," p. 236.

Mn, iron may contain about 5 per cent C, wholly in combination, even in the presence of more than 2·5 per cent Si, a quantity which but for the manganese would render the greater part of the carbon graphitic.

§ 20. SULPHUR, though it appears like silicon to lower the saturation point for carbon in molten iron, and thus to lower the total carbon, yet like manganese prevents the formation of graphite; from which we may infer that, while silicon lessens the power of carbon to unite with iron even more in the solid than in the molten state, so that part of the carbon taken up by the molten iron is separated out as graphite on the solidification of siliciferous irons, sulphur limits the power of molten quite as much as of solid iron to combine with carbon, so that the whole of the carbon taken up by a sulphurous iron when molten is retained in combination during solidification.

The effect of sulphur in preventing the formation of graphite is illustrated by the common observation that while white cast-iron has often more than 0·3 per cent S, we rarely find more than 0·15 per cent S in gray iron, and it is stated that the sulphur in No. 1[a] Bessemer cast-iron cannot exceed ·05 to ·07 per cent. I have, however, analyses of No. 1 iron with 0·12, 0·13, 0·14, and even 0·18 per cent S.

Since the high blast-furnace temperature and the refractory calcareous slags which accompany the formation of graphitic cast-iron at once increase (by temperature) the amount of silicon and diminish (by basicity of slag) the amount of sulphur which passes into the cast-iron, and since the presence and absence of a considerable amount of silicon in gray and white irons respectively suffice to account for the separation of graphite from the one and the retention of the carbon in combination in the other, it might be thought that sulphur did not directly prevent the carbon of white iron from becoming graphitic, but that the presence of sulphur and the freedom from graphite of white iron merely resulted from a common cause, namely, the condition of the blast-furnace. But that sulphur may directly prevent the formation of graphite and cause the retention of all the carbon in the combined state is indicated by experiments of Karsten, and of Smith and Weston in Percy's laboratory, in which adding sulphur to graphitic gray iron turned it white, the carbon in general passing wholly into combination. In one case the iron contained 5·49 per cent of combined carbon, together with 0·446 per cent S. The presence of silicon of course limits the power of sulphur to retain carbon in the state of combination.

§ 21. PHOSPHORUS is thought to prevent the separation of graphite, but to a much less degree than sulphur and manganese.

§ 22. CEMENT VS. HARDENING CARBON.—It is not yet possible to distinguish the effects of silicon, manganese, sulphur, and phosphorus on the proportion of the combined carbon which passes into the cement and the hardening conditions respectively; indeed, it is not unlikely that, when these elements are present in considerable quantity, they form ternary or even more complex compounds with part of the iron and carbon, so that part, or possibly all, of the carbon is neither in the cement nor the hardening condition as now understood.

§ 23. THE EFFECT OF TEMPERATURE ON THE CONDITION OF CARBON.—The graphite-forming tendencies appear to reach a maximum at a temperature approaching whiteness, the tendencies to form cement carbon at a temperature near dull redness; while where these tendencies fall to their minima, the tendencies to form hardening carbon seem to reach two corresponding distinct maxima, one at or above a white heat, and a second at a rather low yellow heat, the W of Brinnell. They appear to be complementary to the graphite-forming tendencies at very high temperatures, and to the cement-forming tendencies at lower ones. The existence of these two maxima suggests that what we call hardening carbon may really comprise two or more distinct compounds, all considerably harder than pure iron, and hence not easily distinguished from each other. Each of the supposed maxima of tendencies to form hardening carbon may be simply the maximum tendency to form some one of these as yet undistinguished compounds.

The accompanying attempt to sketch the relative strength of the tendencies to form graphite, hardening and cement carbon at different temperatures, far from attempting accuracy, is necessarily conjectural. It may serve to elucidate a working hypothesis which places the facts thus far observed in an easily remembered scheme.

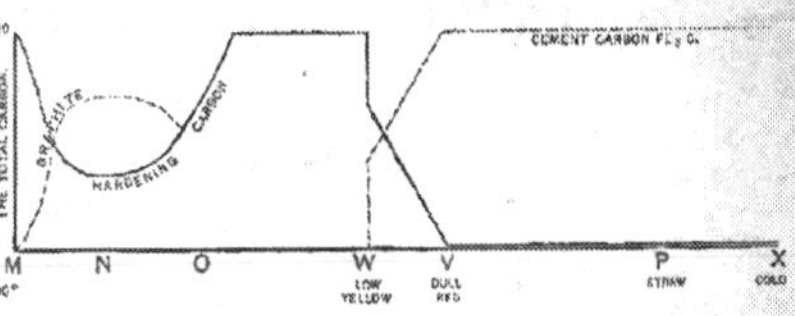

Fig. 2.—Supposed influence of temperature on the relative strength of the tendencies to form graphite, hardening, and cement carbon.

In melted iron all the carbon must be present in solution or combination, or partly in each condition. Were any of it present as graphite it would rise to the surface on account of its lower specific gravity, and would be found concentrated there on solidification; whereas it is nearly uniformly distributed through the iron after solidifying, showing that the graphite is formed after solidification has set in. This appears to be often imperfectly understood, since we hear metallurgists speaking of the oxidation of graphite, as distinguished from combined carbon, in the Bessemer process. It is utterly inconceivable that graphite should exist as such in molten iron; indeed, it would be hard to frame definitions of chemical combination and solution which would not between them necessarily include all the carbon in molten iron; and carbon in either combination or solution can be no more properly spoken of as graphite than can the carbon in beef. If further evidence be needed, witness the way in which graphite separates from molten iron when it is supersaturated with carbon (as by the introduction of silicon); the graphite here rises to the surface of the molten metal as "kish."

§ 24. THE TENDENCY TO THE FORMATION OF GRAPHITE appears to reach a maximum at a temperature N slightly below fusion. Witness the formation of graphite when highly carbureted cast-iron is slowly cooled; that is, when it occupies a long time in passing through the range of

[a] Riley: *Jour. Iron and St. Inst.*, 1871, I., p. 107.

temperature most favorable to the formation of graphite, and the conversion of white into graphitic gray cast-iron by prolonged exposure to a temperature slightly below fusion.

[Karsten indeed states that white cast-iron can only be rendered graphitic by superheating far above its melting point, with subsequent slow cooling. This is, however, opposed to common experience and to the statements of many distinguished observers. Forquignon,[a] by exposing white iron, whose carbon was wholly combined, to a temperature of about 1000 degrees C. in vacuo for several days, converted the greater part of its carbon into graphite, the total percentage of carbon being unaltered. Bell,[b] by heating white iron in a hot-blast oven for thirteen days raised its graphite from 0·374 to 1·70 per cent, the total carbon being nearly unchanged.]

The net tendency to form graphite rather than combined carbon appears to be stronger at this temperature N than at either higher or lower ones,[c] since by either raising or lowering the temperature, part of the graphite formed at temperature N may unite chemically with the iron. Thus if, after rendering cast-iron highly graphitic by prolonged exposure to a temperature somewhat below fusion, we further raise its temperature, the graphite recombines, so that by the time it is melted the carbon is again wholly combined. Whether the recombination occurs suddenly when a certain temperature is reached, or whether every increment of temperature is accompanied by a corresponding degree of recombination of carbon, is not known; but analogy points to the latter as the more probable supposition.

That this recombination occurs, at least in part, before fusion, is shown by the fact that graphitic cast-iron with but little combined carbon (the combined C in No. 1 gray iron is occasionally as low as 0·30 per cent) has a vastly lower melting point than graphiteless steel with the same percentage of combined carbon. The melting point of the iron can not be lowered by the carbon while graphitic (graphite, infusible itself, is an inert foreign body), but only on its passing into combination and thus increasing the percentage of combined carbon, which must evidently commence, in the case of a comparatively fusible cast-iron, with initially only 0·30 combined C, at a temperature far below the melting point corresponding to this degree of carburization.

On the other hand, if an iron, saturated with graphite by long exposure to temperature N, be long exposed to a somewhat lower temperature, say O, part of its graphite is apparently changed into combined carbon.[d] Indeed wrought-iron may be carburized by long heating in contact with cast-iron or even steel, which play the rôle of the charcoal of the cementation furnace.

The passage of carbon from the graphitic to the combined state, and the reverse, comparatively rapid at elevated temperatures, becomes much slower as the temperature descends towards redness; and it is stated that it can not take place below a red heat,[e] at least in case of cast-iron.

Superheating beyond the melting point indirectly favors the formation of graphite during solidification, since the superheated metal, in cooling in the mold down to the melting point, raises the temperature of its walls so that the metal after solidification cools more slowly than it otherwise would, that is, it remains for a longer time at temperatures near N. A high blast-furnace temperature also indirectly favors the formation of graphite during solidification by increasing the percentage of silicon in the cast-iron, and usually by diminishing that of sulphur. Whether at a temperature far above the melting point the chemical condition of the carbon becomes altered in a way that *directly* increases its readiness to become graphitic during solidification, *i. e.*, whether an iron melting at 1600 degrees, superheated to 2000 degrees, and again cooled to 1700 degrees before pouring into its mold, would become more graphitic on solidification than it would had it been initially cast into that same mold at 1700 degrees without previous superheating, is not clear, though it is clear from Bell's[f] experiments that this superheating in certain cases permanently raises the grade of the iron. He superheated white cast-iron far beyond its melting point: it became gray. On remelting and rapidly cooling it still remained gray.

§ 23. EFFECT OF TEMPERATURE ON THE RELATIVE PROPORTIONS OF CEMENT AND HARDENING CARBON.—We may obtain considerable information as to the distribution of carbon between the cement and hardening states at different temperatures by examining iron which has been cooled from those temperatures so suddenly as to give little time for change of chemical condition; *i. e.*, by preserving the chemical *status quo*.

In Table 2 I have condensed Abel's more important results bearing on this question. It gives the percentage of the total carbon found as Fe_3C (plus an insignificant quantity of graphite) in different steels after different treatment.

We here note that in annealed steel practically all the carbon is in the cement state, while in hardened steel hardly any of it is, from which we infer that it is in the hardening state. In tempered steel an intermediate pro-

[a] *Journal of the Iron and Steel Inst.*, 1884, p. 626.

[b] "Principles of the Manufacture of Iron and Steel," p. 150.

[c] According to this view, if graphitic cast-iron, saturated with graphite by long exposure to temperature N, were suddenly cooled from N by immersion in water, it should be more graphitic than if we allowed it to cool slowly from this point, since the sudden cooling should preserve the chemical constitution and prevent the subsequent recombination of graphite. This at first seems opposed to experience, since suddenly cooling graphitic iron from even a temperature as low as N is known to lower its grade, to make it more close grained. But this objection is more apparent than real. From Bell's researches it is probable that sudden cooling from N, while it makes the grain of the cast-iron closer and makes it *look* less graphitic, does not diminish the amount of graphite it contains seriously, if at all.

The grade of iron is not dependent solely on its composition, but also on its rate of cooling. Witness Bell's experiment of allowing a large mass of iron to cool slowly. The interior which cooled very slowly was mottled, the edges white, while certain portions were gray; yet the percentage of both combined and graphitic carbon was practically constant throughout the block. Indeed, white iron has occasionally more graphite than No. 1 gray iron: thus Bell reports instances in which white iron had 2·2 per cent graphite, while No. 1 iron had only 0·10 per cent.

In the second place, under ordinary conditions the cast-iron cools so rapidly from the melting point to N that sufficient time is not given for the graphite-forming tendencies to completely assert themselves, so that by the time the iron is cooled down to N it is far from being saturated with graphite. Hence, in ordinary slow cooling below N, say from N to O, graphite would continue forming to a considerable further extent without reaching the somewhat lower percentage corresponding to saturation at O; while this further separation of graphite would be checked if the iron were very suddenly cooled from N

[d] Percy: "Iron and Steel," p. 127.

[e] Akerman: *Journal of the Iron and Steel Inst.*, 1879, p. 508.

[f] *Journal of the Iron and Steel Inst.*, 1871, p. 297. Bell, however, goes too far in inferring that the quantity of graphite and combined carbon do not *affect* the grade of iron. They clearly do not exclusively control it, but it is exceedingly probable that they affect it; that is, the grade is a function of composition jointly with other variables. (Bell: "Manufacture of Iron and Steel," p. 158.)

TABLE 2.—CARBON FOUND AS Fe_3C PER 100 OF TOTAL CARBON PRESENT.

CONDITION OF STEEL.	Dannemora blister steel. (C, 0·01 to 0·04; Si, 0·006, Mn, 0·009)	Ingot steel. (C, 0·995 to 1·12).
Annealed	87·4 to 92·8	87·5
Unannealed	81·5 to 95·8	
Previously hardened steel tempered at a blue heat	16·1 to 31·9	
Do, after 15 minutes exposure to a blue heat	....	15·4 to 22·0 } average 33·0
Do., after 6 hours exposure to a blue heat	....	41·9 to 42·9 }
Do., tempered at a straw heat	33·8 to 59·2; aver. 46·5	
Do., after 15 minutes exposure to a straw heat	....	30·3 to 32·5 } average 30·9
Do., after 6 hours exposure to a straw heat	....	31·2 to 36·0 }
Hardened steel	....	4·7

portion is in the cement state, and on the whole rather more in blue than in straw-tempered steel, which harmonizes with the greater softness of the former. Further, after prolonged exposure to a tempering heat, whether blue or straw, we find more cement carbon than after brief exposure, which indicates that the passage of carbon from the hardening to the cement state is not instantaneous at these temperatures.

In melted iron and steel the carbon is probably in a state closely related to hardening carbon, since on sudden cooling from fusion we find it chiefly in the hardening state.

At temperatures below fusion the tendency to form hardening carbon rapidly diminishes, as shown by the formation of graphite; but we infer that it again increases as the temperature falls below O (Fig. 2), reaching a maximum at W, again diminishing as the temperature descends to V, and below this remaining nearly constant. That it rises as the temperature falls from N to O, we infer from the gradual recombination of part of the graphite formed at N, if the iron be long exposed to O. That it reaches a maximum at W and again diminishes, we infer from the fact that steel hardened at W has all or nearly all of its carbon in the hardening state, but that if after exposing steel to a red heat we cool it to any temperature T, at or below V, so slowly that the carbon has ample time to distribute itself between the hardening and cement states in the proportions corresponding to equilibrium for T, and then suddenly cool it from T, we find its carbon in the cement state (as inferred from the fact that the steel is then almost as soft as if thoroughly annealed), no matter how violent the cooling be.

Conversely, if we quench previously annealed steel bars of identical physical properties from successively higher temperatures we find that they do not (as Chernoff has shown), become materially harder than when annealed, until a temperature V is reached; but as the quenching temperature rises above V, the resulting hardness increases abruptly, quickly reaching a maximum.

I have verified this statement experimentally by heating one end of a previously annealed steel bar to dull redness, the remainder being heated by conduction from the hot end. It was exposed for about four hours to practically *uniform conditions*, as all but the hot end, which was kept by a constant flame at constant temperature, was buried in lime. The bar was then quenched in a very rapid stream of water. Examining the hardness by the method of indentation, I found that the portions which had not been visibly red-hot were not appreciably harder than the cool end, which had not been materially heated (it hardly felt warm in the hand), and which was therefore still annealed

Now if, at any temperature materially below redness, any important proportion of the carbon tended to pass into the hardening state, it would clearly have done so in some portion of my bar, since each successive portion of the bar was, immediately before quenching, exposed for hours to a temperature practically constant for each such portion, but progressively diminishing as we pass from portion to portion, and from the hot towards the cool end of the bar, and embracing every degree of temperature between redness and 70° F. On quenching, I should have found some portion of my bar harder than the annealed end; as I did not, I infer that there is no such tendency.

Slightly varying the experiment, I leisurely heated one end of a steel bar to whiteness, the remainder being heated by conduction. On quenching it, and determining its hardness by indentation, I found that where the temperature had been below V. (which is in the neighborhood of dull redness), the steel was not measurably harder than when annealed; but that as the quenching temperature rose above V, the hardness increased very abruptly, quickly reaching glass hardness, so that I was unable to effect any indentation with an exceedingly hard knife-edge. By carrying the pressure high enough, the glass-hard steel bar would fly violently in pieces, but without being visibly indented; the knife edge was not visibly affected.

Other phenomena indicate an important chemical change at a temperature between W and V. Iron undergoes a very sudden expansion at or in the neighborhood of this range, and its thermo-electric behavior is abnormal; moreover, "the temporary magnetism of saturated iron at this temperature suddenly vanishes from a foregoing very large value." [a]

Am I asked to reconcile the hypothesis that the carbon tends throughout the range of temperature between V (Fig. 2) and X to pass with equal completeness into the cement state with the fact that blue-tempered is softer than straw-tempered steel? I reply that, though the tendency exists throughout this range, it is held in check by what we may term chemical inertia or viscosity; that at 60 degrees this tendency is as completely checked as is the tendency of hydrogen and oxygen to combine; that when we raise the temperature and relax this viscosity the carbon does actually pass into the cement state, and the more fully the more completely we relax it; *i. e.*, the higher we raise the temperature. When we reach a straw heat, viscosity is so far relaxed that a considerable portion of the carbon previously imprisoned in the hardening state is able to pass into the cement state, and our steel is greatly softened. At a blue heat still more of the carbon is able to overcome chemical inertia, and our steel is still farther softened, while just below visible redness this viscosity appears to completely depart and the carbon passes wholly into the *cement state*. This hypothesis

[a] Barus and Strouhal, "Bulletin U. S. Geological Survey," No. 14, p. 99; Tait, *Trans. Roy. Soc. Edinburgh*, XXVII., 1872-3, p. 125; Gore, *Phil. Mag.*, XXXVII., p. 59, 1869; *Ibid.*, XL., p. 170, 1870; Baur, Wie. Ann., XL., p. 408, 1880.

harmonizes with the fact that though hardened steel is softened by heating to temperatures below redness, and the more so the higher this temperature be (provided it does not exceed V.), yet annealed steel is not hardened by such heating, whether followed by sudden or slow cooling. For the softening of hardened steel by this heating means that its carbon passes into the cement state; the fact that annealed steel is not hardened by this treatment means that carbon in the cement state remains there: both point to the cement state as the one towards which the carbon tends at these temperatures.

That the transfer of carbon from the hardening to the cement state may occur at very low temperatures is suggested by the reported fact that table knives[a] gradually lose their hardness if they are habitually washed in hot water. It is the experience of many that razors used cold last for a greater number of years than those which are habitually heated for shaving, though for other reasons the razor while hot may cut better than when cold.

The views I have given harmonize with Jarolimek's observation that steel may be somewhat hardened by quenching from a red heat in molten zinc, which melts at 752 degrees F., but not as much as if quenched in water; while steel thus hardened is again annealed by prolonged immersion in melted zinc.

After exposing steel to temperature W, and allowing its carbon to pass completely into the hardening state, if we could cool it absolutely instantaneously we would retain all its carbon in that state; the steel would acquire its maximum theoretical hardness. Cooling can never be instantaneous; more or less carbon will pass into the cement state, towards which it tends at temperatures below V, the steel will lose something of its maximum theoretical hardness, and it will lose the more, roughly speaking, the slower this cooling be. Cooled in water, which, thanks to its low boiling point, high specific heat, conductivity, and mobility, cools the steel very suddenly, it loses very little, it acquires nearly its maximum theoretical hardness. Cooled in air it loses much, for the air, thanks to its low specific gravity, specific heat and conductivity, cools it but slowly. Momentarily immersed in molten zinc and immediately withdrawn, and its cooling finished in air, it cools with intermediate rapidity, and hence has, when cold, an intermediate degree of hardness, because the zinc, thanks to its high specific gravity and high thermal conductivity, for an instant, though hot, withdraws heat very rapidly—more rapidly than air—from the steel, which is so much hotter. Prolonged immersion in molten zinc, however (*i.e.*, *prolonged exposure* to a temperature near V), enables the carbon to pass largely to the cement state; the steel becomes softer than after the previous momentary immersion followed by air cooling; it is softened by the very medium which had partially hardened it.

§ 26. EFFECTS OF CARBON ON THE MECHANICAL PROPERTIES OF IRON. IN GENERAL.—For given proportion between the percentages of graphitic, cement, and hardening carbon, as the carbon increases the tensile strength, elastic limit, elastic ratio, and compressive strength increase within limits; the fusibility, hardness, and hardening power increase, perhaps without limit; while the malleableness and ductility, both hot and cold, and the welding power diminish, apparently without limit. The modulus of elasticity appears nearly independent of the percentage of carbon, at least within the limits carbon zero to carbon 2·00 per cent.

For reasons given in § 2, it is not to be expected that mere equality in the carbon content would, even were the composition otherwise identical, insure like mechanical properties, nor that like changes in composition would entail like changes in these properties. Yet we might reasonably hope that, since carbon influences them so greatly, the innumerable published observations might have enabled us to determine accurately its average effects. Unfortunately this is far from being the case. Its average effects have been determined independently by many observers, some of whom have deduced them from very extended data. Their results are dishearteningly discordant.

§ 27. TENSILE STRENGTH.—Though we have more information on the effects of carbon on tensile strength than on the other properties, yet even here our results are very conflicting.

The views of several writers are summed up in the following table:

TABLE 3.—EFFECT OF CARBON ON TENSILE STRENGTH.[e]

Writer.	Kind of steel.	Tensile strength. Lbs. per sq. inch.			
Deshayes[d]	Unannealed steel	$T = 42{,}668 + 25{,}601\,C + 51{,}202\,C^2$.			
Thurston[a]	Unannealed " [f]	$T = 60{,}000 + 70{,}000\,C$.			
"	Annealed " [f]	$T = 50{,}000 + 60{,}000\,C$.			
Bauschinger[a]	Bessemer "	$T = 61{,}870\,(1 + C^2)$.			
Weyrauch[a]	Minimum values	$T = 52{,}625\,(1 + C)$.			
Salom[b]	Ordinary "	$T = 45{,}000 + 100{,}000\,C$.			
Gatewood[c]	When carbon is from ..	·10 to ·2	·2 to ·3	·3 to ·4	·4 to ·5
	It increases tensile strength at the rate of	65,000	70,000	76,000	83,000
	When carbon is from ..	·5 to ·6	·6 to ·7	·7 to ·8	·8 to ·9
	It increases tensile strength at the rate of	91,000	100,000	109,000	117,000
	When carbon is from ..	·9 to 1·	1 to 1·1	1·1 to 1·2	
	It increases tensile strength at the rate of	117,000	100,000	60,000	

[a] Thurston: "Materials of Engineering," II., p. 420-1. [b] *Trans. American Inst. Mining Engineers*, XIV., p. 127. [c] Asst. Naval Constructor R. Gatewood, private communication. [d] *Annales des Mines*, 1879, p. 339. [e] C = the percentage of carbon present. [f] Minimum values.

These formulæ, as may be seen in Fig. 3, where their curves are plotted, are very discordant. Comparing them with each other, and with about 1500 cases, which I have plotted (many of which are given in Fig. 3), and which are gathered from many sources, the more firmly rivets the conviction that ultimate composition can no more in steel than in lithology or organic chemistry be an accurate and trustworthy index of physical properties, since in the one as in the others we find identical ultimate composition with very different properties.

Thus I find that with the same, or nearly the same carbon, the tensile strength varies in one case from 47,000 to 137,000 pounds per square inch; in another from 48,000 to 135,000, and in a third from 73,000 to 170,000; nor do I find any difference in the other variables sufficient to account for these enormous discrepancies. Nor, if we go a step farther and almost completely eliminate other variables, do we find concordant results. Thus Gatewood[b] reports three sets of most valuable results, whose salient features I have grouped in the following table.

In each of these three sets of tests the conditions appear to have been fairly constant, the only important variable being the carbon. The compositions were in other respects nearly constant, if we except the variations in manganese (which I shall endeavor to show has probably little effect

[a] Ledebur: "Handbuch der Eisenhüttenkunde," p. 646.

[b] *Op cit.*

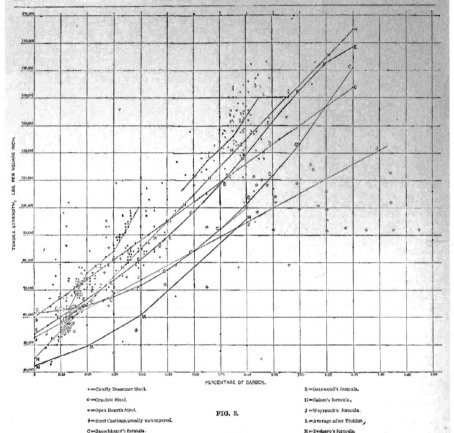

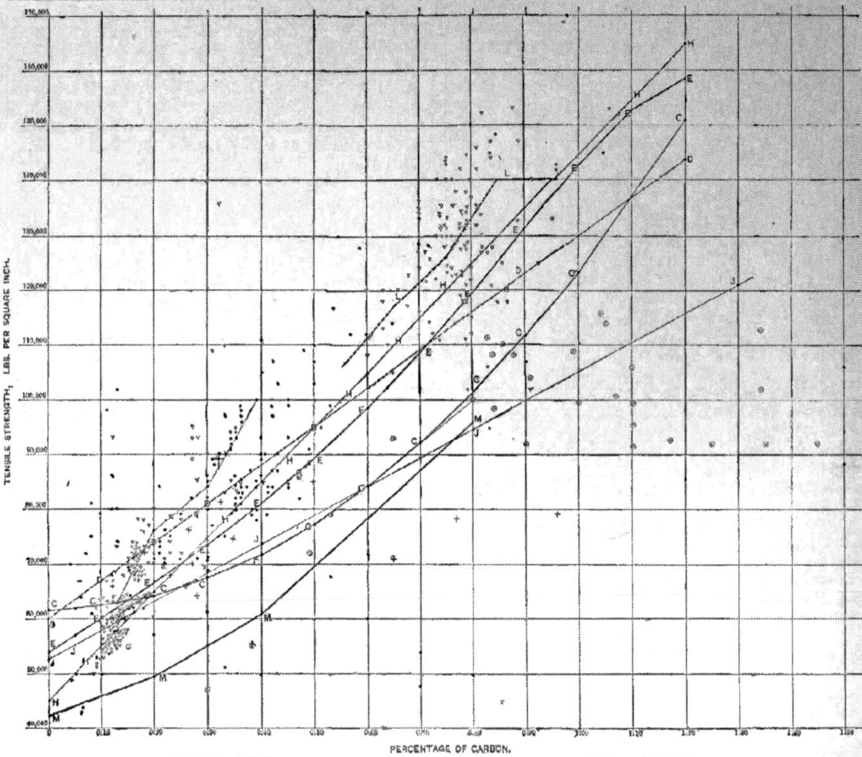

• = Chiefly Bessemer Steel.
⊛ = Crucible Steel.
▾ = Open Hearth Steel.
+ = Steel Castings, usually untempered.
C = Bauschinger's formula.
D = Thurston's formula.
E = Gatewood's formula.
H = Salom's formula.
J = Weyrauch's formula.
L = Average after Trollius.
M = Deshayes's formula.

FIG. 3.

TABLE 4.—SUMMARY OF GATEWOOD'S CARBON RESULTS.

STEEL.	Number of heats.	Composition. Carbon. Maximum.	Carbon. Minimum.	Manganese. Maximum.	Manganese. Minimum.	Manganese. Average.	Phosphorus. Average.	Physical properties. Average Increase (+) or Decrease (—) per 1 per cent carbon. Tensile strength. Pounds per square inch.	Elongation. Per cent.
Chester...	130	·22	·10	·73	·20	·38	·05	+138,750	—42·5
Norway..	339	·31	·11	·64	·17	·38	·06	+ 41 900	— 7·8
Cambria..	120	·24	·09	·90	·18	·45+	·085 ±	+ 65,500	—13·3

on the tensile strength), as were the methods of testing and of preparing the test pieces. The inferences from these sets of observations, among the most valuable ever presented in view of their number and the constancy of their conditions, should be concordant; they are utterly discordant. Thus the effect of carbon on tensile strength indicated by the Cambria results is 50 per cent greater, and that indicated by the Chester tests over 200 per cent greater than that of the Norway; its effect on elongation is nearly twice as great in the Cambria and more than five times as great in the Chester as in the Norway steel. I hold that these results indicate either a degree of carelessness and ignorance in the conduct of these tests hardly credible in these well (and in two cases admirably) ordered establishments, and on the part of the apparently intelligent inspectors; or, more probably, in view of like differences in the effects of carbon deduced from the enormous mass of results published by other observers, that the effects of carbon are not quantitatively constant.

In Fig. 4 Gatewood's results are graphically represented. While between the Cambria and the sinuous Nor-

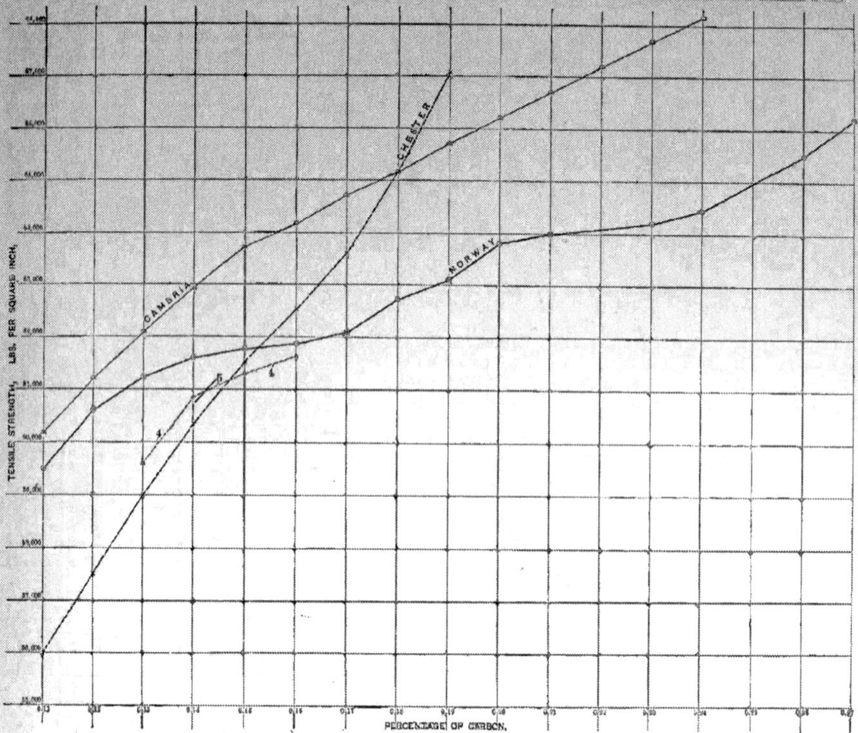

a=Cambria. 4=Δ=Chester, Heat Nos. 870 & 767.

a=Norway. **FIG. 4.** 5=Curve derived from 4.

x=Chester.

way curve, whose sinuosities have been artificially reduced by derivation, there is an approach to parallelism, both are abruptly crossed by the Chester curve. As each of these latter curves represents a greater number of heats than the Cambria, they rudely shake our faith in it. Curve 4, which I have derived from the results obtained at Chester after a change of *personnel* had removed apparent causes of discrepancy, is more nearly parallel with the others than the original Chester curve, but it implies an increment of 73,812 pounds tensile strength per square inch per increase of one per cent carbon, or nearly twice as much as is implied by the Norway curve.

The most important lesson of these results is that we must use the most extreme caution in drawing inferences even from extended data as to the effects of composition on physical properties.

The Cambria curve is so smooth that, representing as it does 130 results, even the experienced observer would be tempted to rely on its teachings. Yet here, as in so many similar cases, if we extend our observations they overthrow our apparently well established conclusions; these, then, should be considered authoritative only when based on an enormous number of observations, on steel from many sources and made under different conditions, since coincidences between composition and properties often result, not from the causal relation between them, but from some common unsuspected cause, whose effects may be eliminated by comparing steel produced by different methods and under different conditions.

In Fig. 3 we note that the spots lie in a band which rises and rapidly widens as the carbon rises till it reaches, say, 1 per cent. The comparatively few cases whose carbon is between 1 and 1·5 per cent indicate that the tensile strength reaches its maximum with carbon about 1 per cent, which accords with common observation. The formulæ of Thurston, Gatewood and Salom run fairly through the most thickly dotted region, Thurston's being too high for low carbon steel (ingot iron), while Salom's is too low for carbon below 0·10. Troilius' figures are rather high, and those of Weyrauch and Bauschinger much too low except for low carbon steel.

While we can not accurately quantify the effects of carbon, I believe that for ordinary unhardened merchantable steel, the tensile strength is likely to lie between the following pretty wide limits:

TABLE 5.—EFFECTS OF CARBON ON TENSILE STRENGTH.

Carbon. Per cent		0·5	0·10	0·15	0·20	0·30	0·40	0·50	0·60	0·80	1·00	1·60
Tensile strength Lbs. per sq. in.	Upper Limit...	66,000	70,000	75,000	80,000	90,000	100,000	110,000	120,000	150,000	170,000	115,000
	Lower Limit...	50,000	50,000	55,000	60,000	065,00	70,000	75,000	80,000	90,000	90,000	96,000

§ 28. DUCTILITY.—The effects of the percentage of carbon on the elongation, for our purposes the most available measure of ductility because the most frequently recorded, are obscured by other variables even more strikingly than are its effects on tensile strength. Thus we find that in exceptional cases the elongation varies from 2·3 to 32 per cent with constant carbon; in another case from 0· to 20·3 per cent; nor, if we turn from exceptional cases to ordinary ones, do we find a closer approach to uniformity in elongation than in tensile strength. Thus in the Chester, Norway, and Cambria lots of steel investigated by Gatewood, and already referred to under tensile strength, we find that the loss of elongation per increase of ·01 per cent carbon is ·425, ·078 and 0·133 per cent respectively. (See Table 4.) I have plotted the results of over a thousand determinations with elongation as ordinate, carbon as abscissa, as shown in Fig. 5. We note that the thickly dotted region lies in a broad band, gradually declining as the carbon increases, its width showing that, where carbon is below 0·5, the elongation for given carbon in common merchantable steel often varies by 20 per cent of the initial length. With increasing carbon the elongation at first declines slowly, say from C 0· to C 0·2 per cent, then more rapidly till the carbon reaches say 0·5 per cent, and after this it again declines more slowly. I find that the empirical formulæ

$$(A): E = 33 - 60\,(C^2 + 0{\cdot}1);\ \text{and}$$
$$(B): E = 12 - 11{\cdot}9\ \sqrt[3]{C - 0{\cdot}5}$$

(In which E = per cent elongation in 8″ and C = per cent carbon)

give curves plotted in the diagram and running well through the most thickly dotted region, (A) applying when C is below 0·5 per cent; (B) when it is between 0·5 per cent and 1 per cent. Above 1 per cent the elongation diminishes very slowly. The following table gives the upper and lower limits which, judging from these instances, we are likely to meet:

TABLE 6.—EFFECT OF CARBON ON ELONGATION.

Carbon.		0·10	0·20	0·3	0·40	0·50	0·60	0·70	0·80
Elongation...	By formula...	26·4	24·6	21·6	17·4	12·	6·48	5·04	4·06
	Usual upper limit...	29·6	33·2	23·0	21·0	.....	13·0	7·5	6·9
	Usual lower " ...	17·5	15·3	12·0	.....	7·5	.....	2·5	1·5

Deshayes, from study of an enormous number of European steels, proposes the formulæ[a]—

Elongation = 35 — 30 C, and

Elongation = 42 — 36 C, (here C = the percentage of carbon), for the percentage of elongation measured in 7·8 and 3·9 inches respectively.

There is little in the results I have plotted, either as to elongation or tensile strength, to support the popular belief that the properties of Bessemer steel correspond with those of open-hearth steel of lower carburization, which I incline to regard as a superstition, though without more prolonged study of our statistics, we can not wholly discredit it. The many cases in which the elongation and tensile strength of crucible steel fall, the one above, the other below the limits usual in Bessemer and open-hearth steel for given carbon, give color to the less often expressed belief that the properties of crucible steel of given carburization correspond to those of Bessemer and open-hearth steel of lower carburization. I also notice a fact which has not heretofore been brought to my attention, that the elongation and tensile strength of steel castings of given carbon, like those of crucible steel, correspond with those of Bessemer and open-hearth steel of lower carbon. While this may be due to plotting an insufficient number of cases, it occurs to me that this similar behavior of crucible steel and of steel castings may be due to their both containing more silicon than Bessemer and open-hearth steel, silicon opposing the effects of carbon.[b] The greater freedom from phosphorus of crucible steel and often of steel castings is another possible explanation.

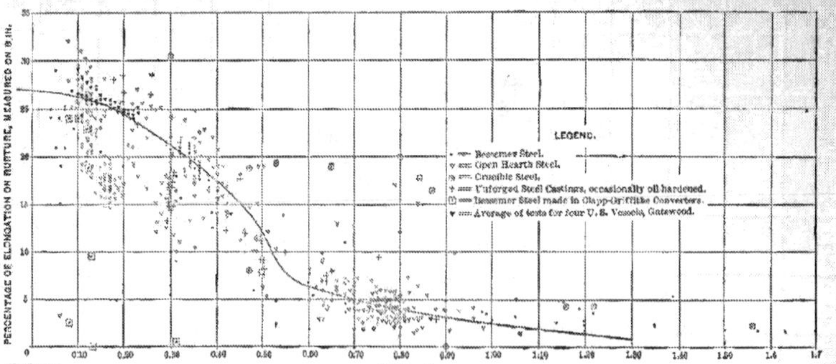

Carbon %. FIG. 5.

[a] *Annales des Mines*, 1879, p. 330.

[b] Müller, J. I. and S. I., 1882, I., p. 374, concludes that Si has an effect opposite to that here suggested, raising the tensile strength.

§ 28A. ELONGATION AND TENSILE STRENGTH.—I here insert a table showing the usual upper and lower limits of tensile strength for given elongation in steel:

TABLE 6A.—TENSILE STRENGH AND ELONGATION.

Elongation, per cent		4	6	8	10	12	14	16	18
Usual limits of tensile strength, Lbs. per sq. in.	Upper	150,000	138,000	130,000	122,000	115,000	108,000	102,000	99,000
	Lower	110,000	102,000	91,000	88,000	80,000	75,000	73,000	64,000

Elongation, per cent		20	22	24	26	28	30	32
Usual limits of tensile strength, Lbs. per sq. in.	Upper	95,000	88,000	80,000	77,000	74,000	71,000	70,000
	Lower	59,000	56,000	52,000	51,000	51,000	50,000	50,000

§ 29. MODULUS OF ELASTICITY.—The effect of carbon on the modulus is probably very slight. Deshayes,[a] from an analysis of a great number of cases, concluded that the modulus was constant for all steel, under identical conditions of previous mechanical treatment, etc.

In Table 7 I have condensed the results of many observations and of the values given by different authorities for the modulus. While apparently only based on 52 cases it really represents a much greater number, since in certain cases a given unit of the 52 represents the average of many results.

Omitting one apparently abnormal case (reported by Cloud 45,000,000 pounds) we find that the average modulus is practically the same for each of the groups arbitrarily made.

Certain writers believe that the modulus rises slightly as the carbon increases from 0, reaching a maximum with carbon 0·30 to 0·35, and again declining as the carbon rises above 0·35; but if there is any such variation it is so slight as to be of no importance.

When the carbon passes some point now unknown the modulus begins to decline, since we find it much lower in cast-iron than in steel.

TABLE 7.—MODULUS OF ELASTICITY OF INGOT METAL AS AFFECTED BY THE PERCENTAGE OF CARBON.

	C 0 to 0·15	C 0·15 to 0·25	C 0·25 to 0·35	C 0·35 to 0·75	C 0·75 to 1·00	C 1·00 to 1·36
No. of cases...	14	12	4	8	6	8
	Lbs. per sq. in.	Lbs. per sq. in.	Lbs. per sq. in.	Lbs. per sq. in.	Lbs. per sq. in.	Lbs. per sq. in.
Maximum...	30,185,000	27,300,000	(45,000,000 ?) a 30,750,000 b	31,350,340	29,238,000	31,880,630
Minimum...	22,000,000	24,576,000	24,830,000	23,558,000	28,000,000	25,266,000
Average...	27,407,000	26,327,000	(32,762,000 ?) a 28,083,000 b	27,800,000	26,011,000	28,292,500

a, including one abnormal case. b, omitting one abnormal case.

Abbot gives the modulus and other physical properties[b] of 10 steel castings. If we may infer their carbon from either their tensile strength or elongation, the very considerable variations in the modulus are but faintly influenced by the degree of carburization. If we number them according to their moduli, No. 1 having the highest, then, taken in the order of tensile strength, they stand thus: 3, 1, 2, 10, 4, 7, 5, 6, 9, 8, the modulus being on the whole rather higher in those with highest tensile strength. If arranged in the order of elongation, the first having the highest elongation, they stand thus: 5, 3, 1, 9, 4, 10, 2, 7, 6, 8. Those with the highest modulus have on the whole the highest elongation, yet, the highest modulus but one accompanies an elongation of only 2 per cent. Arranged in order of their elastic limit they stand thus: 3, 1, 2, 4, 7, 6, 10, 5, 8, 9.

§ 30. The COMPRESSIVE STRENGTH rises with increasing carbon within limits at present unknown. From Kirkaldy's data, I have calculated (Table 7A) the effect of increments of carbon on elastic and ultimate compressive strength. The results are so harmonious as to inspire confidence, though the data are so scanty that inferences from them can not be considered conclusive.

(1.) While the compressive strength increases constantly for all lengths as the carbon rises to 1·2, it increases most rapidly with the rise from C 0·3 to C 0·6 per cent. In some cases the compressive strength is but little greater, and in one case actually less with C 1·2 than with C 0·9 per cent.

(2.) The longer the piece (*i. e.*, the greater the ratio of length to diameter) the greater in general is the gain of ultimate compressive strength with increasing carbon; while the gain of elastic compressive strength seems to be about the same for one length as for another.

TABLE 7A.—COMPRESSIVE STRENGTH AS INFLUENCED BY CARBON.

Number.	Description.		Carbon.	Percentage of excess of compressive strength over that of steel of 0·3 carbon. Length = 1 diameter. Pr ct.	Length = 2 diameters. Pr ct.	Length = 4 diameters. Pr ct.	Length = 8 diameters. Pr ct.	Compressive strength. Lbs. per sq. in. Length = 1 diameter.	Length = 8 diameters.
1...	Mean of results by Kirkaldy, Fagersta steel, series A2.	Ultimate compressive strength.	1·2		40	63	115		102,173
2...			0·9		43	44	106		95,207
3...			0·6		29	29	79		84,827
			0·3		0	0	0		47,513
4...		Elastic compressive strength.	1·2	64	51	52	52	64,000	61,666
5...			0·9	61	40	43	44	62,666	58,000
6...			0·6	54	37	30	31	60,000	52,666
			0·3	0	0	0	0	39,000	40,666

§ 31. THE HARDNESS of steel, as measured by its resistance to abrasion or by the indentation made by given pressure on given indenting knife edge, etc., rises with rising carbon, and especially as the percentage of carbon in the hardening state increases; it certainly continues to increase beyond that degree of carburization which corresponds with the maximum tensile strength and probably beyond that corresponding with maximum compressive strength, as measured by the resistance of columns to bulging, buckling and skewing. Steel wire-dies of 1·7 per cent C wear, according to Metcalf,[c] much more rapidly than those of 2·37 or 2·80 per cent C, while tensile strength appears to reach its maximum with about 1 per cent C.

I know of no data which enable us to quantify the effects of carbon on hardness.

§ 32. THE FUSIBILITY increases with the carbon, probably without limit. It is generally stated that graphitic iron has a higher melting point[d] than graphiteless iron of otherwise identical composition, and identical total carbon. It is probably more accurate to say that graphitic iron melts at the same temperature, but *more slowly*, as at the melting point of graphiteless iron the graphite of graphitic iron probably gradually completely combines, so that the iron eventually becomes graphiteless and melts.

HARDENING, TEMPERING, AND ANNEALING.

§ 33. DEFINITIONS.—1. STEEL IS HARDENED (in the specific sense of the word) by sudden cooling from a high temperature, usually at or above redness, *e. g.*, by plunging it in water, oil, etc.

2. *To temper* (to qualify, to soften) in its specific sense means to mitigate, to partly remove, to moderate the effects of previous hardening. It is usually performed by gently reheating the previously hardened steel, but to a

[a] *Annales des Mines*, 1879, p. 312.
[b] *Trans. Am. Inst. Mining Engineers*, XIV., p. 353, 1886.
[c] *Trans. Am. Inst. Mining Engineers*, IX., p. 549.
[d] Ledebur "Handbuch," p. 240.

TABLE 8.—PERCENTAGE OF EXCESS (+) OR DEFICIT (−) OF ELASTIC AND ULTIMATE TENSILE STRENGTH AND OF ELONGATION OF UNANNEALED AND OF HARDENED IRON AND STEEL FORGINGS ABOVE THOSE OF THE SAME IRON WHEN ANNEALED.

I. Number.	II. Reference.	III. C.	IV. Si.	V. Mn.	VI. P.	VII. Description.	VIII. Quenching temperature.	Per cent. of excess of ultimate tensile strength. IX. In the unannealed steel.	X. When hardened in Water	XI. Coal tar.	XII. Tallow.	XIII. Oil.	Per cent. of excess of elongation. XIV. In the unannealed steel.	XV. When hardened in Water	XVI. Coal tar.	XVII. Tallow.	XVIII. Oil.	P. c. excess of elastic tensile strength. XIX. In the unannealed steel.	XX. When hardened in Water	XXI. Oil.	Properties of the annealed steel. Tensile strength.	Elongation. Per cent.	Elastic limit.
0·5	H M	·07	......	......	......	Norway wrought-iron	Full redness	......	+ 5	......	......	......	......	− 58	......	......	......	......	......	......	54,200	22·1	
1	S	·07	......	......	......	Charcoal-hearth iron	Redness	+0·3	+ 7	......	......	......	......	......	......	......	......	......	......	......	47,552		
2	S	·07	......	......	......	" " "	"	......	+ 41	......	......	......	......	− 79	......	......	......	......	......	......	44,877	9	
3	S	·06	......	......	......	" " "	"	......	+ 40	......	......	......	......	− 47	......	......	......	......	......	......	44,063	19	
4	D	·05@·15	·01@·02	·05@·12	·02@·09	Average of 5 Bessemer steels	Not stated	+ 2	+ 76	......	......	......	− 5	− 56	......	......	......	+ 4	+31	......	52,540	32·2	35,134
5	H	·15	·02	·41	·08	Open-hearth steel	Red heat	− 4	+ 28	Brine + 45	......	+36	− 2	− 30	Brine − 35	......	−29	......	......	......	58,510	28·5	
6	D	·14@·28	·03@·04	·09@·10	·01@·02	Average 2 open-hearth steels	Not stated	+ 8	+ 58	......	......	......	+11	− 45	......	......	......	− 9	+36	......	40,413	33	30,364
7	S	·20	......	......	......	Puddled iron	Redness	......	+ 48	......	......	......	......	......	......	......	......	......	......	......	46,780		
8	D	·10@·30	·02@·06	·17@·27	·08	Average of 5 Bessemer steels	Not stated	+11	+ 66	......	......	......	−15	− 50	......	......	......	+17	+32	......	54,244	31·6	36,123
9	D	·19@·30	·02@·04	·09@·86	·09	" " "	"	+ 5	+ 55	......	......	......	− 3	− 51	......	......	......	−12	+31	......	59,214	29·9	38,116
10	D	·17@·22	·02@·06	·14@·37	·03	" 2 open-hearth "	"	+ 6	+ 42	......	......	......	− 6	− 40	......	......	......	+ 9	+21	......	55,096	32·4	26,584
11	S	·33	......	......	......	Bessemer steel	Redness	+27	+ 55	......	......	......	−12	− 82	......	......	......	......	......	......	51,250	19	
12	K	·40 ?	......	......	......	Homogeneous metal, off 1 bar	High	......	− 19	......	......	+58	......	−100	......	......	−89	......	......	......			
							Medium	......	......	......	......	+45	......	......	......	......	−23	......	......	......			
							Low	......	......	......	......	+11	......	......	......	......	− 5	......	......	......	82,100	22	
13	K	·40 ?	......	......	......	Gun steel		......	......	......	......	+55	......	......	......	......	−38	......	......	+20	79,520	11·9	40,144
14	S	·49	......	......	......	Bessemer steel	Redness	−11	+30	......	......	+30	......	......	......	......	......	......	......	......	77,000		
14·5	H M	·39	......	......	......	Pittsburgh open-hearth steel	Yellow	......	+27	......	......	......	......	−97·4	......	......	......	......	......	......	92,900	31·2	
15	S	·78	......	......	......	......	"	......	......	......	......	+63	......	......	......	......	......	......	......	......	90,801		
16	K	1·00 ?	......	......	......	Cast-steel	High	......	−26	......	......	+76	......	−100	......	......	−53	......	......	......	121,716	7	
17	"	"	......	......	......	"	Medium	......	......	+40	+50	+55	......	......	− 22	− 65	−65	......	......	......	119,172	7·7	
18	"	"	......	......	......	"	Low	......	......	+13	+14	+29	......	......	− 15	− 30	−50	......	......	......	120,918	16	
19	"	"	......	......	......	" off 1 bar	High	......	......	......	......	+79	......	......	......	......	−78	......	......	......	106,062	15	
							Low	......	......	......	+ 6	+24	......	......	......	+ 20	−38	......	......	......			
20	"	"	......	......	......	Bessemer steel	Not stated	......	......	......	......	+71	......	......	......	......	−98	......	......	......	123,165	5·2	
21	"	"	......	......	......	" "	"	......	......	......	......	+65	......	......	......	......	−96	......	......	......	113,221	2·7	
22	"	"	......	......	......	" "	"	......	......	......	......	+57	......	......	......	......	−97·5	......	......	......	110,588	7·8	
23	"	"	......	......	......	Rivet steel	"	......	......	......	......	+65	......	......	......	......	−61	......	......	......	122,262	9·2	
24	"	"	......	......	......	"	"	......	......	......	......	+78	......	......	......	......	−70	......	......	......	101,421	3·3	
25	"	"	......	......	......	"	"	......	......	......	......	+71	......	......	......	......	−52	......	......	......	102,309	12·5	
26	"	"	......	......	......	"	"	......	......	......	......	+41	......	......	......	......	− 8	......	......	......	116,788	11·8	
27	"	"	......	......	......	"	"	......	......	......	......	+58	......	......	......	......	−15	......	......	......	101,422	12·0	
28	"	"	......	......	......	"	"	......	−25	......	......	......	......	−100	......	......	......	......	......	......	108,649	12·5	
29	S	1·29	......	......	......	Steel	Redness	+11	......	......	......	+119	......	......	......	......	......	......	......	......	89,000		
							Strongly Heated	......	......	......	......	+14	......	......	......	......	......	......	......	......			

NOTE.—For references, see end of Table 19.

very much lower temperature than that employed in hardening, and then cooling generally suddenly, but sometimes slowly. I shall use the word exclusively in this sense, though it is often and not incorrectly employed generically to designate any sudden cooling, whether from an excessively high or a moderate temperature.

3. *Annealing.*—While tempering somewhat moderates the effects of previous hardening, annealing aims to nearly completely eliminate them, as well as to remove the stresses caused by previous cold working. It is ordinarily effected by slow cooling from a high temperature, at or above redness. Thus steel is in its hardest and most brittle state when hardened, in its softest and toughest when annealed, and in an intermediate condition when tempered.

4. *Quenching* may be employed to designate generically any sudden cooling.

I will describe first for those who run the methods and effects of quenching and annealing, and then seek the rationale of these operations for those who think.

§ 34. METHODS AND EFFECTS—HARDENING.—The general effect of hardening is to increase the hardness, to raise the elastic limit, to diminish the ductility and specific gravity, and, if the cooling be not extremely sudden, to raise the tensile strength. It is said to raise the modulus of elasticity.

The degree to which these properties are affected depends chiefly (A) on the temperature from which cooling occurs, (B) on the composition of the steel, and (C) on the rapidity of cooling, which in turn depends chiefly (C_1), on the shape and size of the piece, and (C_2) on the medium employed for hardening.

APPARENT EXCEPTIONS to the statement of the effects of hardening just made are found in quenching previously cold-rolled and cold-drawn steel, and previously unforged and unannealed steel-castings.

ADDENDUM TO TABLE 8.—Percentage of excess, etc., of tensile strength, etc., of open-hearth fire-box plate steel of five sixteenths inch thickness, when unannealed and when hardened over those of the same metal when annealed. Carbon, 0·2 per cent; manganese, 0·36 per cent; silicon, 0·008 per cent; phosphorus, 0·035 per cent; sulphur, 0·017 per cent. Test strips were all from one plate of open hearth fire-box steel, all 1¾ inch wide by 96 inches long, one end extending uninjured above testing machine grips, which were subsequently bent.

I. Number.	II. Reference.	III. C.	IV. Si.	V. Mn.	VI. P.	VII. Description.	VIII. Quenching temperature.	Percentage of excess of tensile strength. IX. In the unannealed steel.	X. When hardened in Water	XI. Brine.	XII. Coal tar.	XIII. Oil.	Percentage of excess of elongation. XIV. In the unannealed steel.	XV. When hardened in Water	XVI. Brine.	XVII. Coal tar.	XVIII. Oil.	P. c. excess of elastic tensile strength. XIX. In the unannealed steel.	XX. When hardened in Water	XXI. Oil.	Properties of the annealed steel. XXII. Tensile strength	XXIII. Elongation %.	XXIV. Elastic limit.
29·5	...	...	...	...	...	Calculated from A. E. Hunt's data, in the discussion of a paper on "Steel," etc., by W. Metcalf, American Society of Civil Engineers, April 4, 1887.	Dark orange	−10	+16	+92	......	+ 3	− 4	−31	−47	......	−18	− 1	−36	+ 9	82,150	30·4	32,600
							Medium "	......	+19	+38	......	+ 8	......	−34	−58	......	−16	......	+40	+15			
							Bright "	......	− 5	+44	......	+ 7	......	−29	−50	......	−27	......	+37	+12			
							Lemon	......	+12	+80	......	+12	......	−31	−62	......	−40	......	+51	+21			
							Light lemon	......	+29	+45	......	+24	......	−47	−54	......	−48	......	+57	+24			
							Low white	......	+31	+82	......	+28	......	−67	−48	......	−58	......	+89	+42			
							Scintillating white		54	2		− 6	..	−92	−94	...	98	..	115	+18			

TABLE NO. 9.

PERCENTAGE OF EXCESS OF TENSILE STRENGTH, ETC. OF UNANNEALED AND OF OIL HARDENED UNFORGED CASTINGS OVER THOSE OF THE SAME CASTINGS WHEN ANNEALED.

I.	II. Reference.	III. C.	IV. Si.	V. Mn.	VI. Description. Unforged Castings.	VII. Quenching temperature.	VIII. Per cent excess of tensile strength. Unannealed.	IX. Cooled in oil.	X. Cooled in oil and slightly annealed.	XI. Per cent excess of elongation. Unannealed.	XII. Cooled in oil.	XIII. Cooled in oil and slightly annealed.	XIV. Per cent excess of elastic strength. Unannealed.	XV. Cooled in oil.	XVI. Cooled in oil and slightly annealed.	Properties of the annealed casting. Tensile strength, Pounds per square inch.	Elongation.	Elastic limit. Lbs. per square inch.
30	P	·18±	·20	·42	Terre Noire open-hearth castings.......	Cherry red.	......	+28	......	......	—17	......	......	+64	......	69,987	28.80	32,995
31	P	·18+	·21	·68	" " "	" "	......	+9	......	......	—34	......	......	+32	......	71,545	24·30	33,846
32	P	·18±	·23	·61	" " "	" "	......	+31	......	......	—27	......	......	+48	......	64,960	26·7	28.448
33	E	·26	·26	·41	Terre Noire castings..................	Not stated.	—4	......	+15	—55	......	—39	—18	......	+33	69,864	25·5	33.370
34	E	·26	·26	·41	" " "	" "	+1	......	+16	—48	......	—14	—10	......	+62	66,080	26·5	27,264
35	U	·30	......	......	Newburn Steel Works..................	......	+6	......	......	—33	......	......	......	......	......	70,112	24·0	......
36	E	·32	·30±	·48	Terre Noire castings..................	Not stated.	+5	......	+25	—31	......	—49	—11	......	+74	76,964	21·5	28,684
38	E	·42	·27	·75	" " "	" "	—23	......	+1	—34	......	—6	—5	......	+5	103,660	9·8	35,926
39	E	·42	·27	·75	" " "	" "	—15	......	+5	—77	......	—14	—15	......	+5	103,518	14·0	52,398
40	E	·45	·35	1·1	" " "	" "	—19	......	+15	—84	......	—54	—10	......	+32	105,080	17·5	48,280
41	U	·50	......	......	Newburn Steel Works..................	" "	+1	......	......	—76	......	......	......	......	......	96,544	8·6	......
42	P	·50±	·39±	·88±	Terre Noire castings..................	Cherry red.	......	......	+9	......	......	—19	......	......	+40	108,891	9·0	47.645
43	P	·50±	·39±	·66±	" " "	" "	......	......	+18	......	......	—52	......	......	+32	108,371	11·5	51,520
44	P	·50±	·30±	·88±	" " "	" "	......	......	+11	......	......	+1	......	......	+27	113,792	7·7	51.900
45	P	·50±	·39±	·88+	" " "	" "	......	......	+1	......	......	—26	......	......	+21	113,075	11·8	51.206
46	P	.50+	·39±	·88±	" " "	" "	......	......	+11	......	......	—25	......	......	+38	107,385	9·3	48,384
47	P	.50+	·39±	·88±	" " "	" "	......	......	+2	......	......	—5	......	......	+13	110.947	7·9	51,206
48	P	.50±	·39±	·88±	" " "	" "	......	......	+7	......	......	—14	......	......	+24	99,568	8·1	48,205
49	E	.55	·40	1·05	" " "	Not stated.	—20	......	+8	—59	......	—34	0	......	+14	103,660	9·8	35,926
50	P	.56±	·34±	·94±	" " "	Cherry red.	......	......	+9	......	......	—10	......	......	+7	103,107	6·2	54,432
51	P	.56±	·34±	·94±	" " "	" "	......	......	+17	......	......	+70	......	......	+13	103,107	4·0	51,475
52	P	.56±	·34±	·94±	" " "	" "	......	......	+9	......	......	—6	......	......	0	103,824	13·0	51,475
53	E	·63	·55	·95	" " "	Not stated.	—34	......	+47	—83	......	—90	—13	......	+51	111,470	7·0	51,830
54	E	·63	·55	·95	" " "	" "	—23	......	+53	—72	......	—87	—10	......	+45	108,660	7·5	41,748
55	U	·77	·48	·67	Newburn Steel Works..................	......	—2	......	......	—100	......	......	......	......	......	84,000	1·5	......
56	U	·96	·62	·64	" " "	......	+6	......	......	—100	......	......	......	......	......	78,176	1·3	......

NOTE.—For references see end of table. Excesses +; Deficits —.

NOTE.—The percentages of increase of elongation columns XI. to XIII., are per 100 of elongation of the unannealed piece, not per 100 of its length.

The net result of highly heating them (say to a cherry red), with subsequent quenching is usually to soften and toughen them, often with a great increase of tensile strength. (Thus the numbers in column X. of Table 9 are invariably algebraically larger than the corresponding numbers in col. VIII.: those in col. XIII. are algebraically larger than the corresponding ones in col. XI., with three exceptions, doubtless due to experimental errors, or to heterogeneousness of the steel). But this is because the coarse structure of the castings and the brittleness which cold-working gives iron and other metals depart when the metal is heated; and the brittleness which quenching causes is less intense than that which previously existed.

In Tables 8, 9, 10, 11, and 16A I have analyzed the results of many experiments on hardening; this enables me to present its specific quantitative effects more fully I believe than has heretofore been done.[a]

A. TENSILE STRENGTH.—In general, moderately rapid cooling raises the tensile strength. Violent cooling may lower it, especially in the case of high-carbon steel and when the quenching temperature is high.

a. WATER-HARDENING cools steel very rapidly. With low-carbon steel (say with carbon below 0·5 per cent) water-hardening from a moderate temperature raises the tensile strength greatly (see cases 1 to 14, and 71; in these 13 cases the tensile strength is raised on an average 47 per cent). Water-hardening low-carbon steel from a high temperature, however, in the only case I have met (No. 12) lowers the tensile strength (by 19 per cent).

Water-hardening high-carbon steel (with C above, say, 0·75 per cent), whether from a high or low temperature, either lowers the tensile strength (see cases 16, 23, and 75, in which it is lowered by from 25 to 58 per cent); or at most raises it very slightly (case 76, in which it is raised by 2 per cent).[b]

(b) OIL HARDENING almost invariably raises the tensile strength, even when the quenching-temperature and the carbon are both high, sometimes more than doubling it.

In 62 cases of oil-hardening which I have analyzed the tensile strength is raised on the average 35%, and is lowered in only one of them (No. 76); in this a high-carbon steel (1·12% C) is quenched from a very high temperature.

If both the carbon and the quenching temperature be low, water-hardening may give slightly higher tensile strength than oil-hardening. (See case 5.) But in the great majority of cases oil-hardening gives much higher tensile strength than water-hardening. In 4 cases (Nos. 12, 16, 19, and 29) in which the same steel is oil-hardened from both high and low temperatures, I find that where the carbon is moderately low the high quenching-temperature gives the greatest tensile strength; where the carbon is high (1·22%) low-temperature quenching gives the highest tensile strength.

Coal tar and tallow in cases 17, 18, and 19 raise the tensile strength less than oil.

These facts appear to point to the conclusion that to get the highest tensile strength with very low-carbon steel we must cool rapidly, quenching in water from a high temperature; for steel of say 0·4 C we must harden more moderately, using oil, but still a rather high quenching temperature; for high-carbon steel (say 1·25%) we must cool gently, from a low temperature and in oil.

[a] See also addendum to Table 8.

[b] This statement refers only to the cases which I have met. I do not mean to imply that water-hardening never greatly increases the tensile strength of high-carbon steel; indeed, it would probably largely increase the tensile strength of pieces of large cross-section, even if their carbon were decidedly high, and especially if the quenching temperature were low, since they cool comparatively slowly even in cold water. The following paragraphs are written in the same spirit.

TABLE 10.

PERCENTAGE OF EXCESS OF TENSILE STRENGTH, ETC., OF HARDENED IRON AND STEEL FORGINGS OVER THOSE OF THE SAME MATERIAL WHEN UNANNEALED.

Number.	Reference.	C.		Temperature from which quenched.	Per cent increase of tensile strength. Quenched in Water.	Per cent increase of tensile strength. Quenched in Oil.	Increase of elongation per 100 of the elongation of the unannealed bar. Quenched in Water.	Increase of elongation per 100 of the elongation of the unannealed bar. Quenched in Oil.	Per cent increase of elastic tensile strength. Quenched in Water.	Per cent increase of elastic tensile strength. Quenched in Oil.	Properties of the unannealed steel. Tensile strength lbs. per sq. in.	Properties of the unannealed steel. Elongation per cent.	Properties of the unannealed steel. Elastic limit lbs. per sq. in.
57	T	·01	Weld iron	Not stated.	+7·8	......	−12	......	......	......	51,202	......	......
58	T	·08±	Basic Bessemer steel	"	+38·5	......	−55	......	......	......	63,900	......	......
59	B	·1	......	"	......	+23	......	−4	......	+83	56,000	34·	23,000
60	H	·15	Terre Noire steel	"	+22·	+20	−42	−12	+64	+81	51,520	32·5	24,640
61	A	·27	" " open-hearth steel	"	......	+36	......	−45	......	+16	79,904	24·	51,404
62	A	·31	" " " " "	"	......	+33	......	?	......	+17	84,774	25·25	53,676
63	A	·31	" " " " "	"	......	+30	......	−44	......	+23	78,381	23·5	47,426
64	B	·34	......	"	......	+12	......	+14	......	......	74,800	20·	35,800
65	N	·35?	Krupp steel for gun hoops	"	......	+39	......	−26	......	+15	77,952	7·4	36,960
66	N	·38?	Creusot gun steel	"	......	+27	......	−31	......	+45	78,460	18·7	36,900
67	N	·40?	Krupp gun steel	"	+17·	+50	−79	−95	......	......	92,515	21·	......
68	B	·41	......	"	......	+32	......	−30	......	+109	72,800	23·	31,300
69	A	·45	Terre Noire open-hearth steel	"	......	+47	......	−51	......	+58	73,556	24·5	37,846
70	A	·47	" " " " "	"	......	+62	......	......	......	+108	86,762	21·4	41,204
71	N	·49	Terre Noire	"	+78·	+60	−90	−52	+100	+80	67,200	24·8	33,600
72	N	·71	" "	"	broke in quenching	+77	broke in quenching	−60	broke in quenching	+161	87,360	10·	40,320
73	N	·87	" "	"		+30		−88		+190	109,760	8·4	44,800
74	O	1·05	Cambria open-hearth steel	"	......	+30	......	+13	......	+44	145,400	5·5	82,810
75	S	1·05	Bessemer steel, Högbo	"	−(58·+)	+48	−100	−100	......	......	97,783	8·9	......
76	S	1·16	Uchatius steel, Wikmanshyttan	Slightly heated	+2·	......	−100	......	......	......	139,840	4·6	......
				Strongly "	......	−(61+)	......	−100	......	......	......	......	......

NOTE.—Excesses +, deficits —.

REFERENCES TO TABLES 8, 9, AND 10.

A, Akerman, *Jour. of the Iron and Steel Institute*, 1879, II., p. 539. B, W. Armstrong, *Engineering*, 1882, II., p. 351. D, Dellvik, *Jour. Iron and Steel Inst.*, 1879, II., p. 538. E, Euverte, *Jour. Iron and Steel Inst.*, 1877, I., p. 245. H, Hunt, *Trans. Amer. Inst. Mining Engineers*, XII., p. 311. K, Kiraldy, "Experiments on Wrought Iron and Steel," 1866, p. 164. N, "Proc. U. S. Naval Institute," X., p. 561. O, "Report of U. S. Senate Select Committee on Ordnance and War Ships," 1886, p. 310. P, Holley, *Metallurgical Review*, II., p. 220, May, 1878. S, Styffe, *Iron and Steel*, Sandberg's Translation, p. 137. T, Tetmajer, *Jour. of the Iron and Steel Inst.*, 1885, II., p. 700. U, Spencer and Sons, *Jour. of the Iron and Steel Inst.*, 1883, I., p. 304. ? After the percentage of carbon indicates that it is not given by the authority quoted, but is simply inferred from the tensile strength. V, It is probable, but not certain, that the casting was slightly reheated after cooling in oil. H M, Experiments by the Author.

(B) ELONGATION.—Analyzing 81 recorded cases (some water, some oil-hardened), I find that 60 of them lose 25% or more of their elongation on hardening, 35 lose 50% or more, and 13 of them lose 90% or more. In each of 19 cases of water-hardening the elongation is considerably lowered, the mean loss being 63% (of the original elongation). In 52 out of 56 cases of oil-hardening the elongation is lowered, but on the whole considerably less than by water-hardening; the mean loss of elongation by oil-hardening is 45%. In only one out of seven cases in which the effect of both water and oil-hardening on the same steel is given does the oil-hardening reduce the elongation more than water-hardening. The elongation of steel high in carbon is on the whole reduced by hardening rather more than that of steel low in carbon. But in the cases which I have collected the loss of ductility by high-carbon steel on hardening exceeds the loss which low-carbon steel undergoes much less than is generally supposed. Thus in 34 cases in which the C is 0·40% or below, the mean loss of elongation by hardening is 41%; in 47 cases whose C is between 0·4% and 1·16% the mean loss of elongation by hardening is 40%.

Cases 2, 3, 4, 6, 8, 9, 10, and 20, whose C does not exceed 0·30%, each lose 40% or more of their elongation on hardening. Case 2, with only 0·07% C, loses 79% of its elongation.

Hardening from a high temperature generally, though not invariably, lowers the elongation more than low-temperature quenching.

(C) THE ELASTIC LIMIT is almost invariably raised by hardening, and usually more than the tensile strength is. In examining 44 recorded cases I do not find one in which the elastic limit is lowered by hardening, and but one in which it is not raised. In these 44 cases the effect of hardening on the tensile strength is also determined. In 29 of them the elastic limit is raised more than the tensile strength, being raised on the average by 47% while the tensile strength in the same cases is raised on the average by only 32%.

On the whole hardening appears to raise the elastic limit of high rather more than that of low carbon steel, though by no means invariably. Thus in 20 cases whose C is 0·4 % or less the mean elevation of elastic limit is 42%; in 24 cases with C above 0·40, the mean elevation is 50%; yet cases 59 and 60, with C 0·1% and 0·15% respectively, have their elastic limit raised by oil-hardening 83% and 81%.

D. HARDNESS.—While we have little quantitative information as to the effects of hardening on the hardness of steel, we may say roughly that the higher the initial temperature, the more rapid the cooling and the higher the percentage of carbon, the harder does the steel become. The effect of varying temperatures is illustrated by Metcalf's experiment.* One end of a steel bar is heated to dazzling whiteness, the remainder being heated by conduction from the hot end. If it be quenched in water with its different portions thus at different temperatures, we find that the part which had been scintillatingly hot will now scratch glass, and has a coarse, very lustrous, yellowish fracture. That which was simply white-hot is nearly as hard as glass, with a coarse but less yellow fracture. Those which had been at a high yellow, an orange, and a high red-heat are successively softer and tougher, with successively finer fractures, which are in all three fiery. That which had been at a cherry-red heat is very strong and much less brittle than the preceding, with the finest fracture of all; it is well hardened, *e. g.*, for cutting tools, though, of course, requiring subsequent tempering. That which had shown a low-red color is tougher and softer yet, but still hard enough for tap-teeth; its edges show a very fine fracture, its center is somewhat coarser. The portion which had not been visibly red-hot is not materially hardened, and is consequently softer than any of the others, and has the same

* Metallurgical Review, I., p. 246.

fracture as the unhardened steel, which is decidedly coarser than that of the portion quenched from cherry-redness.

Extending Metcalf's experiment to lower temperatures and quantitatively determining the hardness of the different portions of the bar by the method of indentation, I found that the hardness was not measurably above that of the annealed steel until the quenching-temperature reached a point in the neighborhood of a dull red, but that passing above this point the hardness very suddenly increased, soon reaching an apparent maximum.

While the ductility and tensile strength are somewhat more affected by a given quenching in high than in low-carbon steel, the hardness proper is incomparably more affected in the former than in the latter. Indeed, a quenching which in high-carbon steel replaces decided toughness with glass-hardness, does not sensibly increase the hardness proper of ingot and weld iron.

Thus on quenching wrought-iron from a white heat I was unable to detect quantitatively by the method of indentation any increase of hardness, though its ductility was somewhat impaired, and though, as we see in Table 8, its tensile strength may be affected by quenching nearly as much as that of high carbon steel.

§ 35. Conditions of Hardening. A. Temperature.—The specific effects of different quenching-temperatures on the properties of steel have already been indicated. It is thought that, at least in the case of tool steels, the best general results are obtained by employing the lowest quenching-temperature which suffices to give the required hardening, as needlessly high temperatures impart a coarseness of structure and consequent brittleness which can not be wholly effaced by subsequent treatment, while no compensating advantage accrues. In general, the hardness proper is not increased unless the quenching-temperature be at least as high as a dull cherry-red heat; and it is stated that the lower the carbon the higher must the quenching-temperature be to produce decided hardening. Thus tool steels with say 1% C often require only a low red-heat for quenching; gun-steels with say 0·4% C are said to acquire the most advantageous hardening by quenching from a salmon or even a strong yellow heat. (Cf. Pp. 175, 191, bottom.)

Quenching from lower temperatures, however, probably affects the tensile strength and apparently diminishes the ductility, though much less than high-temperature quenching.

B. Heating for Hardening.—The method used should depend largely on the shape, size and number of the pieces to be heated. The smith's forge, though largely used, is far from advantageous. Molten lead appears to afford the most uniform heating, but its use is insalubrious. Small pieces may be heated in a reverberatory furnace, by contact with hot iron of appropriate shape, in a gas flame, etc. Where many small pieces are to be hardened they may be inclosed in an iron pipe, box or pan filled with charcoal dust, and placed in a smith's forge, a reveberatory furnace, etc. A pan or open box offers the advantage that the pieces can be stirred about and thus heated uniformly.

Large pieces must of course be heated in reverberatory furnaces, often of shapes specially adapted to the pieces to be heated; *e. g.*, long gun tubes are heated one at a time in very narrow rectangular vertical furnaces, in which a single tube stands on end. One side of the furnace is hinged so that the tube may be very rapidly removed sidewise, to be immediately plunged in a deep tank of oil.

C. Rapidity and Media of Cooling.—In general the more rapid the cooling the harder and more brittle is the steel; rapidity of cooling up to a certain point increases the tensile strength, but if the cooling be exceedingly rapid the tensile strength may be very greatly lowered, and the steel may even be broken by the hardening itself. Apparently the lower the carbon the more rapid and violent should the cooling be to give the highest tensile strength.

The hardness and brittleness of hardened steel are influenced far more by the rapidity with which the steel cools from a cherry-red heat to 400° C. than by the rapidity of cooling below 400° C., though the latter is not without influence on the resulting hardness. Thus red-hot steel is somewhat hardened by brief immersion in melted zinc (zinc melts at 412° C.), followed by moderately rapid cooling in the air, while if the steel be left immersed in the zinc the hardness thus acquired is again lost.

Mercury cools steel with the greatest rapidity; water, rapeseed oil, tallow and coal-tar follow in the order here given. Urine and brine are said to cool steel more rapidly, and soapy water less rapidly than pure water. A thin layer of oil on the surface of the water retards the cooling. Oil-hardening almost always gives both higher tensile strength and higher elongation than water-hardening. But it must be remembered that even oil hardened steel has almost, if not quite, invariably lower elongation than the same steel when annealed, and in an overwhelming majority of cases even lower elongation than when unannealed.

For castings and most forgings of steel with less than 0·75% C, such as guns, marine shafts, and armor plate, tensile strength is more important than hardness, hence they are habitually hardened in oil. For cutting tools, hardness is more important than strength, hence they are ordinarily hardened in water. Once heated the pieces should be promptly quenched; there should be plenty of the cooling medium, so that its temperature may not be considerably raised by the heat it receives from the steel; the piece should be moved about in the bath. This not only hastens the cooling by exposing the steel to fresh portions of the bath, and by mechanically removing the steam from the surface, but also equalizes the rate of cooling of the different portions of the piece. For large pieces a running stream may be needed for these ends, and Jarolimek advises a spray of water for hardening, as giving the greatest hardness with the smallest consumption of water. When large pieces (gun tubes, castings, etc.) are to be cooled in oil, the oil may be cooled by worms or water jackets, through which cold water circulates, as a running stream of oil might be inconvenient.

Clearly, under otherwise like conditions, a more rapidly cooling medium will be needed to produce a given rapidity of cooling in thick than in thin pieces. For instance, while to attain given stiffness, thin springs (*e. g.*, those of locks), are hardened by quenching in oil from a cherry-red, thick springs are given a similar stiffness and hardness by water-hardening, as water abstracts heat far more rapidly than oil; while those of intermediate thickness are given like qualities by quenching in water covered with a film of oil, which abstracts heat with a rapidity intermediate between that of oil and water.

§ 36. PRECAUTIONS.—If we plunge a red-hot cylinder of steel into water, the exterior at first cools much more rapidly than the interior: the outer shell is in the position of a thin, highly heated cylinder slipped over a cold inner cylinder, which it is barely able to contain while hot. The outer cylinder is strained and may be burst by its own contraction, resisted by the interior which it is unable to compress. If we have a square rod, instead of a cylindrical one, the resistance of the interior, which cools and contracts comparatively slowly, to the initially rapid contraction of the exterior, may cause the exterior to bulge, to become convex to approach the cylindrical shape, in which the ratio of surface to volume reaches the minimum. If we have an unsymmetrical piece (*e. g.*, an eccentric), the more rapid early cooling of the outside may warp it out of shape.

In these cases cracking, convexing and warping are due to the fact that, immediately after immersion, the exterior cools more rapidly than the interior. With pieces of other shapes similar cracks, distortions, warpings may arise from the endeavor of the more slowly cooling portions to cool and contract after the more rapidly cooling ones have already become cool and rigid. In short, we must endeavor to avoid dissimilar rates of cooling and contraction in different portions of the piece. These may be partially or even wholly guarded against by the following expedients:

A. BY ACCELERATING THE COOLING OF THE MORE SLOWLY COOLING PARTS; *e. g.*, we may dish, panel, or perforate the central portions of thick flat pieces; and we may perforate cylindrical and prismatic pieces longitudinally, or cut longitudinal furrows on their surfaces, in each case aiming to hasten the cooling of the central portion of the piece. When one portion of the piece is much thicker, and hence tends to cool more slowly than the rest, we may dip that portion into the cooling medium first.

B. BY RETARDING THE COOLING OF THE MORE RAPIDLY COOLING PARTS; *e. g.*, to the periphery of flat pieces, and to other portions which tend to cool too fast, we may, before hardening, fit pieces of iron, or even wire gauze; the scale from rolling or forging purposely left on such pieces has a similar but of course milder effect. When, as in eccentrics, holes occur in the periphery of flat pieces, there is great liability to cracking, since the outer rim is then in the condition of a band shrunk upon a cylinder and nearly filed through at one point; the contractility of the band is here resisted by such a small area of cross-section that fracture is likely to occur. So, too, when sharp re-entering angles occur on the exterior of a piece, it is apt to crack, just as a piece of cloth tears across where notched. So, too, where holes occur near the inner border of annular and similar pieces, or where re-entering angles (key-seats, etc.) occur on their inner border, fracture is likely to occur. Such holes, notches, re-entering angles, etc., should be avoided as far as possible, and where they occur it is important to retard the cooling of the metal immediately surrounding them, as by inserting in the hole or nick a piece of hot fire-clay or iron, by wrapping wire in the corners of key-seats, etc., before hardening, etc.

C. BY VARYING INITIAL TEMPERATURES.—In certain cases, such as taps, we may heat the more rapidly cooling portion (here the exterior) to a somewhat higher temperature than the interior, to partially equalize their temperatures during cooling. And in general the more slowly cooling portions should certainly not be initially hotter than the more rapidly cooling parts, as this would exaggerate the contraction which they undergo after the latter have become cold and rigid. Per contra, we must carefully avoid overheating and burning the corners and thin portions of the piece, as the steel may thus be readily and irreparably injured.

IN PARTIAL DIPPING, where only a portion of the piece is to be hardened, it should be moved up and down in the water. Otherwise, an aggravated case of æliochronous cooling arises, as we have a sharp line of demarcation at the water's surface between the immersed and rapidly cooling parts and the non-immersed and slowly cooling ones.

DIRECTION OF IMMERSION.—Long and narrow or thin pieces should be immersed lengthwise; otherwise the aeliochronous contraction will warp the piece; *e. g.*, if a thick rod be immersed not lengthwise, but sidewise, the side first immersed cooling and contracting first will become concave for the instant; the upper side cooling and contracting after the first has become cold, will not exactly compensate for this initial curvature, and the piece when cold will still be somewhat curved.

§ 38. TEMPERING.—Hardened steel is too brittle for most purposes; hence it is generally somewhat toughened by tempering, by slightly re-heating it. The higher the temperature to which the steel is heated in tempering the tougher does it become, with a corresponding loss of hardness, but, at least in certain cases, with considerable gain in tensile strength. Steel when tempered, though much more ductile than when hardened, is far less ductile than when annealed.

TABLE 11.—EFFECTS OF TEMPERING.

	Open-hearth steel of 0·15 C.[a]		Cast steel of 1·00 ± C.[b]	
	Tensile strength. Lbs. per sq. in.	Elongation %.	Tensile strength. Lbs. per sq. in.	Elongation.
Hardened in water	72,760@ 76,690	25·@ 25·75	90,049	0·
Tempered at straw heat	66,385	27·	100,98[illegible]	0·
" " spring temper heat	....	....	104,888	0·7
" " blue heat	59,790@ 60,580	32·	112,119	0·7
Annealed	58,600@ 58,480	36·5	121,716	7·0

[a] A. E. Hunt, in Transactions Am. Inst. Mining Engineers, XII, p. 311.
[b] Kirkaldy experiments on wrought-iron and steel, p. 165.

§ 39. HEATING FOR TEMPERING.—The hardened steel must be re-heated uniformly. If slowly heated the steel is said to become tougher than if rapidly heated, without corresponding loss of strength and hardness. Though the smith's forge is largely used for heating steel for tempering it is utterly unfitted for this purpose. According to the size and shape of the piece to be tempered we may heat it by contact with hot iron bars, plates, rings, etc., or by radiation from them; on the surface of melted lead or other fusible metal; in hot sand,[a] in burning charcoal, in reverberatory furnaces, etc. When, as in the case of drills, only the point is hardened and tempered, after hardening the still hot shank heats the point by conduction.

In all these cases the temperature of the steel is indi-

[a] Ede; the Treatment of Steel, Miller, Metcalf & Parkin, p. 69.

cated, with sufficient accuracy for practical purposes, by the color[a] of the film of oxide which forms on the surface of the steel (see Table 12), which on this account must be brightened before it is re-heated, and the steel must be withdrawn from the heat the instant the desired tint appears, lest it become too hot and hence too soft.

TABLE 12.—TEMPERATURES, ETC., FOR TEMPERING STEEL.

Oxide tint.	Temperature.		Appearance of oil bath.[b]	Corresponding uses of the tempered steel.	% C. in steel for which each temper is employed.
	Cent.	Fah.			
White............	....	....	....	Tungsten steel.[c] HARDEST.	Tungsten steel
Pale yellow.......	220	428	....	Lancets.	
Straw............	230	446	....	Razors, surgical instruments, engravings,[b] taps,[b] dies,[b] cutters[b]	1·5%[c]
	232	450	First smoke.		
Golden yellow....	243	469	....	Razors, penknives, hammers,[d] taps, reamers and dies, for wrought and cast-iron, copper, brass, etc.,[d] cold chisels for cutting steel[d]	1·3%[c]
Brown............	255	491	....	Cold chisels, shears, scissors, hatchets.	
	260	500	Strong dark smoke		
Brown, dappled with purple....	265	509	....	Axes, planes, lathe tools for copper.[d]	
	276	530	Abundant black smoke.		
Purple............	277	531	....	Table knives, large shears, wood turning and cutting tools,[d] cold chisels for soft cast iron.[d]	
Violet............	....	....	....	Cold chisels for brass.[d]	0·9[c]
Bright blue......	288	550	....	Swords, coiled springs.	
Full blue........	293	559	....	Fine saws, augers, etc.	
	304	580	Can be lighted, but does not continue to burn..	....	0·8[c]
Dark blue	316	600	....	Hand and pitsaws, cold chisels for wrought-iron and copper.[d]	
			Lights spontaneously........	Spiral springs.[b]	
Just visibly red in the dark......	....	....	Burns rapidly....	Clockmakers' purposes.[b] SOFTEST.	

[b] Ede: Treatment of Steel, Miller, Metcalf and Parkin. [c] Böker: Journ. Iron and Steel Inst., 1886, I., p. 334. [d] Thurston: Materials of Engineering, II., p. 326.

When many pieces are to be similarly tempered they are advantageously heated in oil or tallow, the behavior of the oil then roughly indicating the temperature (see Table 12).

Thus Ede recommends that springs of all kinds, immersed in oil or smeared with it, be heated till the oil burns on them with a white flame, when they are immediately quenched in cool oil. If they are heated in the oil, it is necessary to remove them from it to ascertain whether they are hot enough to permit the oil to burn persistently on their surfaces, *i. e*, to "blaze."

The temperatures appropriate for tempering for various purposes, and the indications by which they are recognized are given in Table 12. They vary considerably with different steels, in a way imperfectly understood. The oxide tints too are said to differ with different steels, and it is not unlikely that a long exposure to a given temperature produces a deeper tint than a brief one; *e. g.*, a golden-yellow may indicate either a brief exposure to 243° C., or a longer exposure to say 230°. But this too is probably of little practical moment, as the toughening effect of a given temperature appears to increase with the length of exposure to that temperature.

If the tempered piece be too hard, that is, if it has not been heated strongly enough, it may be further softened by re-heating to a slightly higher temperature, and without repeating the hardening proper. If, however, it be too soft, that is, if it has been too highly heated in tempering, it must be hardened again by sudden cooling from a high temperature (*e. g.*, a cherry-red heat).

§ 40. COOLING.—Ede[b] states that the properties of steel are the same whether rapidly or slowly cooled after heating for tempering, *i. e.*, the tempering is due to the reheating, not to the subsequent cooling; but as a matter of convenience the tempered steel is usually promptly cooled in water or oil. My preliminary experiments indicate that steel slowly cooled from a blue heat is slightly tougher than if suddenly cooled. Drills, etc., whose points are heated for tempering by conduction from the hot shank of the drill, must of course be plunged in water the moment that their point shows the desired temper, as otherwise the point would become overheated by conduction.

§ 41. OTHER METHODS OF HARDENING AND TEMPERING.—The ordinary method here described may seem irrational in that it first gives the steel undesirable hardness and brittleness, part of which has to be subsequently removed. Its advantage is that it employs readily recognized and regulated temperatures and rates of cooling, so that the degree of hardness obtained is fairly under control. By the oxide tints the temperature reached in tempering may be very closely controlled, and if the temperature from which the steel is initially hardened can not be so closely recognized, this is of slight importance, since the effect of considerable variations in this temperature is slight. Two of its disadvantages are (A) that the violent cooling employed in hardening often cracks costly pieces, and (B) the subsequent tempering chiefly softens the exterior, which in the case of cutting tools needs the greatest hardness. Hence plans for dispensing with subsequent tempering by directly hitting the desired degree of hardness by the hardening operation itself, which gives the exterior the greatest hardness, leaving the interior somewhat tougher, have been proposed.

They all appear to have two serious disadvantages. 1st, the degree of hardness cannot be so nicely regulated by a single operation as by hardening combined with subsequent tempering. 2nd, we apparently obtain a higher combination of strength with ductility by hardening followed by tempering than is attainable with a single operation, since the tempering does not appear to lessen the tensile strength and hardness imparted by the preceding hardening as much as it restores the ductility which the hardening had removed. On account of these drawbacks they have met with little favor even for cutting tools; while for softer steels, *e. g.*, for ordnance, armor plate, castings, etc., they seem still less fitted, since here their advantage of giving the exterior greater hardness than the interior counts for naught.

A. CARON[c] recommended hardening not in cold but in warm water, which would cool the steel more slowly, and harden it less violently. But this does not appear to

[a] If steel be heated in vacuo, these colored films do not form, which indicates that they are of oxide. (Roberts: Trans. Inst. Mechanical Engineers, 1881, p. 710.)

[b] Treatment of Steel, Miller, Metcalf & Parkin, p. 69.

[c] Metallurgical Review, I., p. 158.

give uniform results, as the degree of hardness acquired is influenced by the size and shape of the piece, the rapidity with which it is moved under the water and by other variables little under control, more than by the temperature of the water.

B. Interrupted Cooling is recommended by Jarolimek.[a] Observing that the degree of hardness depends chiefly on the rapidity with which the steel passes from a red heat to one slightly below redness, while tempering depends on exposure to a much lower temperature, he would harden by immersing the red-hot steel in the comparatively dense center of a spray of water till the red color disappeared, then allow it to cool at a comparatively slow but (as he claims) controllable rate, by removing it to the outer and rarer portions of the spray, or if it be very small and would cool very rapidly, by removing it completely, so that it may cool in the air.

C. Ordinary Hardening without Subsequent Tempering is employed for uses which demand great hardness but for which toughness is not needed, *e. g.*, where friction alone is to be resisted. Thus hardened steel bushings,[b] rings, collars, plug gauges as well as lathe tools[c] for cutting very hard cast-iron and unannealed steel may be used untempered.

In other cases where great stiffness is required, as in some spiral springs which must sustain a heavy load but which require but little play, the desired hardness and stiffness may be attained by hardening alone without subsequent tempering, by employing a steel lower in carbon than would be suitable were it to be tempered after hardening.

§ 42. Gun Tubes and jackets are generally oil-hardened, though it is said that Krupp's[f] are not. The quenching temperature varies from a blood-red (Woolwich[d]), to a strong yellow heat (Terre-Noire[e]), a salmon heat being employed in the best American practice. The higher the carbon and the more the piece has been forged before hardening the lower should the quenching temperature be. In the Russian[f] practice it is said that the piece is left but from 10 to 15 minutes in the oil; at Terre-Noire, and I believe at Woolwich, and in the best American practice it is allowed to cool in the oil, which is sometimes cooled by circulation.

Usually the hardened tube or jacket is next tempered by heating it to a temperature which varies from 500° Fahr. (Woolwich), to a cherry-red (Terre-Noire), the tempering temperature being generally highest where the hardening temperature has been highest, *i. e.*, where the carbon is lowest. At Woolwich the jackets are tempered in the act of shrinking them upon the tube, and it is said that the tubes are not tempered, except in as far as they are heated by the contact with the hot jackets. To remove the brittleness due to hardening, the piece is almost invariably either subsequently annealed or tempered.

In shrinking the coils upon the tubes at Woolwich[d] the jacket is, according to Maitland, heated to 500° or 600° F., and slipped over the tube, the shrinkage in the case of 12·5″ guns varying from 0 to $\frac{1}{150}$ of the diameter. The upper end of the jacket is kept hot by a ring of gas or a hot cylinder of iron, while the other end is cooled by a ring of water, which is gradually raised as the cooling proceeds. This is done, lest both ends of the jacket should simultaneously cool and grip the tube, since then its subsequent contraction would subject the jacket to abnormal longitudinal tensile stress.

The initial oil-quenching of gun tubes, etc., is frequently spoken of as tempering or even toughening, but as in the cases which I have observed, the tensile strength is raised and the elongation is lowered by this quenching, it appears to me a true hardening and not a tempering. (See Cases 13, 65, 66, and 67, Tables 8, 9, 10.) The temperature at which the hardened tube or jacket is tempered is usually governed by an examination of its physical properties. If, after hardening, it appears abnormally hard, the tempering temperature is raised higher than would otherwise be desirable. If it appears unexpectedly soft it is less strongly reheated for tempering. The reheated piece is at some works again suddenly cooled (*e. g.*, Terre-Noire, where it is reimmersed in oil, in which it is allowed to cool). In others it cools slowly, which naturally renders it somewhat softer and tensilely weaker than when suddenly cooled.

§ 43. Hardening Special Steels.—Mushet's "special" (tungsten) steel, Park Bro. & Co.'s "imperial" steel, Miller, Metcalf & Parkin's "hardened" steel, and Hadfield's "manganese" steel are used for cutting-tools without previous quenching of any kind. The steel is forged at a strong red heat to the desired shape and then allowed to cool slowly in the air; after grinding on an emery wheel (it is hardly cut by a file) it is ready for use. Chrome steel is quenched in water from dull redness. See further §§ 86, 138 and 139.

§ 45. Annealing effaces more or less completely the effects of previous hardening; it increases the ductility and specific gravity, and it generally lowers the elastic limit. As gentle hardening raises the tensile strength while violent hardening may lower it, so annealing, while it generally lowers the tensile strength, may raise it, if it has been previously lowered by violent hardening or otherwise. Annealing removes hardness and brittleness arising from cold working and aeliochronous[g] contraction (as in steel castings) as effectually as those caused by quenching. Important steel castings are generally thoroughly annealed in this country. It is sometimes specified that steel marine boiler and ship plates shall be annealed. The most careful of marine boiler makers (*e. g.*, Cramp & Sons) anneal boiler plates after severe, but not after light flanging, etc. Locomotive and stationary boiler plates are not annealed in this country, even after the most severe punishment, *e. g.*, flanging, punching, drifting, etc. In European ship-yards steel was formerly very largely annealed after undergoing any trying work. Annealing appears to be much less frequently resorted to to-day. (Cf. p. 179.)

Heating for Annealing.—The steel should be heated uniformly, and to this end without direct contact with the flames.

Temperature for Annealing.—The most advantageous temperature for all kinds of steel appears to be a bright cherry-red, or for tool steels (with say 1% C) per-

a Metallurgical Review, I., p. 158.
b Ede, Op. cit.
c Thurston: Materials of Engineering, II. p. 326.
d Maitland: Jour. Iron and Steel Inst., 1881, II., pp. 433–6.
e Pourcel; Op. Cit. P., 1882, II., p. 513.
f Benét: Proceedings U. S. Naval Inst., X., p. 561.

g I suggest the adjective aeliochronous or aeliotachic to express the fact that the cooling and contraction, even if equal in amount, occur at different rates in different portions of the piece.

haps a slightly lower one. If the steel be long exposed to a much higher temperature (say a light red or orange heat) it assumes a coarsely crystalline structure, which it retains on cooling, and its toughness and strength are greatly impaired. High-carbon steels (*e. g.*, tool steel) appear to assume this crystalline structure at a much lower temperature than steels with less carbon.

COOLING.—The more slowly the steel is cooled, within reasonable limits, the softer and tougher does it in general become. But slow cooling from a cherry-red to a temperature slightly below visible redness increases the toughness and softness far more than slowness of cooling from this temperature down. Hence for many purposes which do not demand extreme toughness it suffices to cool the steel slowly till the red color disappears and then quench it in water. Indeed low-carbon steel which has been rendered hard and brittle (*e. g.*, by cold-rolling or drawing, by punching, shearing, etc.), and steel castings, may be rendered far less hard and brittle by simply heating to redness and quenching, especially if oil-quenched, but still usually less ductile than if slowly cooled.

It is, however, probable that phosphoriferous steels acquire their greatest ductility by only moderately slow cooling. Thus Styffe[a] gives an instance in which weld iron, with 0·26% P, is much tougher as well as somewhat stronger after quenching in water than even after ordinarily slow cooling, in the former case having a tensile strength of 66,769 lbs., and an elongation of 25%, against a tensile strength of 61,758 lbs., and an elongation of only 6·5% after ordinary cooling.

A thorough annealing may be obtained by cooling the heated steel in ashes, lime, or other slow conductor of heat, or by permitting it to cool slowly in the furnace in which it is heated, by drawing its fire and closing all apertures. Many important steel castings are thus annealed. At many American works, however, boiler and ship-plates, etc., are annealed (?) by heating them (often under conditions which insure irregular heating) to a red heat, then allowing them to cool on the mill floor, exposed to draughts, and often in contact with cold iron plates; in view of this the incredulity of many engineers about the benefits of annealing is hardly surprising. Indeed, unless to remove really violent stresses (*e. g.*, after punching and shearing very thick pieces with rather high carbon) annealing should not be resorted to, unless it can be performed carefully, as it may simply exaggerate the effects of previous rapid cooling and cool-rolling which it aims to remove: (*e. g.*, in case 21 of Table 16 the tensile strength is actually higher and the elongation lower after the annealing than before; yet on carefully annealing steel of the same kind, case No. 20, *idem*, it became softer and tougher.

§ 46. QUANTITATIVE EFFECTS OF ANNEALING. A. HARDENED STEEL.—The effects of annealing hardened steel are almost exactly the reverse of those of hardening annealed steel; and as most of the quantitative effects of hardening, detailed above, refer to the difference between the tensile strength and ductility in the hardened and annealed states respectively, it is not necessary to repeat them here. The reader is referred to the preceding paragraphs, and to Tables 8 and 9.

B. UNHARDENED STEEL.—The rolling and hammering of steel is often finished at so low a temperature as to considerably raise its tensile strength and diminish its ductility, and these effects are often reinforced by the comparatively rapid cooling which it undergoes after leaving the rolls or hammer, under exposure to draughts of air and often in contact with cold plates. These effects are largely removed by annealing, which thus increases the ductility and diminishes the tensile strength of ordinary commercial steel like those of hardened steel, but to a much lower degree, which varies greatly, depending as it does not alone on the efficiency of the annealing, but more especially on the degree to which these properties had previously been affected by cool forging and rapid cooling.

The efficiency of the annealing depends chiefly (1), on the *annealing temperature*, and (2) on the *rapidity of cooling*, and hence on the *cooling medium*. The effect of cool-forging and rapid cooling depends chiefly on (3) the *cross section* of the steel, since thin pieces not only are finished at a lower temperature but cool more rapidly after leaving the rolls than thick pieces, and (4) on the *percentage of carbon*.

1. ANNEALING-TEMPERATURE.—The higher the annealing temperature, if it be not so high as to give rise to crystalline structure, the more efficient it is. Thus in Table 14, annealing the same steel from a bright cherry-red affects the ultimate and elastic tensile strength about 50% more, and the ductility about twice as much as annealing from a dark cherry-red. Steels of 1 per cent and of ·12 per cent carbon appear to acquire their highest ductility when annealed from bright cherry-redness and from an orange color respectively. With higher annealing temperatures both tensile strength and ductility decline: if even ingot iron be slowly cooled from scintillating whiteness its ductility may be almost wholly destroyed.

2. RAPIDITY OF COOLING.—In the same table we note that lime-cooling affects the tensile strength and elastic limit much more, and the ductility on the whole somewhat more than cooling in oil, which is a much better conductor of heat than lime, and cools the steel faster. The intrinsic value of the steel, if we may measure it by the product of the tensile strength into the elongation, is somewhat greater after the slower lime-annealing than after oil-cooling, though this might not hold true with pieces of other cross-sections and of different carbon.

3. CROSS SECTION.—Since thin steel becomes colder while being forged and cools more rapidly after forging than thicker steel, we should naturally expect to find that the stresses set up by cool forging and rapid cooling would be greater in thin than in thick steel, and hence that the former would be more affected by annealing. And as regards tensile strength, this is apparently the case. Thus, comparing together Cases 1 with 6, 2 with 7, 3 with 8, and 4 with 9, in Table 16, we note that the tensile strength of the former of each pair (representing 2-inch square bars) is diminished by annealing more than that of the latter (which represents the average of 2-inch square and of larger bars).

So too in Table 15 we see that, with a rough approach to uniformity, the smaller the cross-section of the finished piece the more the tensile strength is lowered by annealing. But as regards ductility we find the very opposite. Thus in Table 15 columns C and D we see that the thicker

[a] Iron and Steel, p. 132, No. 31; and p. 136, Nos. 33 to 35.

TABLE 14.

INFLUENCE OF THE TEMPERATURE OF ANNEALING. INCREASE (+) OR DECREASE (—) OF TENSILE STRENGTH, ETC., CAUSED BY ANNEALING, PER 100 OF ORIGINAL.

	Tensile strength. Lbs. per sq. in.	Elastic limit. Lbs. per sq. in.	Elongation. Per cent.	Reduction of area. Per cent.
	Initial (unannealed).			
Steel of 0·30 per cent carbon	74,950	43,320	20	35
	Percentage of increase on annealing.			
Calculated from A. F. Hill's data. Annealed from black heat	— 6	— 6	+ 15	+ 9
" " " dark cherry-red	— 16	— 18	+ 40	+ 26
" " " bright "	— 23	— 20	+ 80	+ 51

EFFECT OF DIFFERENT ANNEALING MEDIA.

	Tensile strength. Lbs. per sq. in.	Elastic limit. Lbs. per sq. in.	Elongation. Per cent.	Reduction of area. Per cent.	Efficiency. Number.
	Initial (unannealed).				
Carbon 0·40	98,200	50,180	15·3	30	1,425,960
	Percentage of increase on annealing.				
Calculated from A. F. Hill's data, annealed from dark cherry-red, in Lime	— 14	— 17	+ 49	+ 29	+ 25
" " " Oil	— 11	— 9	+ 82	+ 36	+ 17

TABLE 15.

EFFECTS OF ANNEALING AS INFLUENCED BY VARYING CROSS SECTION. CALCULATED FROM KIRKALDY'S DATA, "EXPERIMENTS ON FAGERSTA STEEL," SERIES C^1 C^2 C^3, AND B^1 B^2 B^3 AND B^4.

Increase (+) or decrease (—) of tensile strength, elongation, etc., caused by annealing ordinary Bessemer steel bars, per 100 of the original.

No.		Size of Bars.	A Tensile Strength. H	A Tensile Strength. R	B Elastic Limit. H	B Elastic Limit. R	C Elongation. H	C Elongation. R	D Reduction of Area. R	E Efficiency Number. H	E Efficiency Number. R
1	Mean of results obtained with steel of 1·0, 0·5, and 0·15 per cent C.	½″ × ½″	—15·1	—12·		—16·	+ 27·	— 6·	+ 25·	+ 9·	— 16·
2		1″ × 1″	— 8·7	— 6·		—12·	+ 11·	— 7·	+ 32·	+ 2·	— 13·
3		1½″ × 1½″	— 3·5	— 2·		—12·	+ 65·	+ 40·	+ 78·	+ 59·	+ 30·
4		2″ × 2″	— 2·7	— 2·		—14·	+ 75·	+ 60·	+ 24·	+ 72·	+ 22·
5		2½″ × 2½″	— 7·6	— 3·		—18·	+111·	+160·	+289·	+107·	+153·
6		3″ × 3″	— 2·9	— 4·		—15·	+188·	+ 97·	+161·	+184·	+ 87·
7	Mean of results obtained with steel of 0·8, 0·6, 0·4, and 0·2 per cent C.	2″ × 2″	—7·7		......		+ 45·		+ 57·	+ 32·	
8		3″ × 3″	—6·4		......		+ 64·		+ 96·	+ 54·	
9		4″ × 4″	—3·7		......		+ 38·		+ 43·	+ 34·	
10		5″ × 5″	—4·7		......		+ 22·		+ 46·	+ 13·	
11		6″ × 6″	—0·3		......		+189·a		+169·a	+108·a	

NOTE.—The percentages of increase of elongation and of reduction of area, cols. C and D are per 100 of elongation, etc., of the unannealed steel, and not per 100 of its length, etc.

a = These figures are exaggerated by one abnormal result. H = hammered. R = rolled.

the steel, the more does annealing increase its elongation and contraction. Since then, thick pieces have their tensile strength diminished less and their ductility increased more by annealing than thin ones, our data suggest that annealing benefits thick more than thin pieces, an important conclusion, which I have not hitherto seen set forth. The effect of annealing on the elastic limit appears to be independent of the cross section.

4. CARBON.—Under apparently like conditions, the tensile strength is sometimes lowered more in high than in low-carbon steel, while as often the low-carbon steel is the most affected. Thus, in Cases 1 to 10 of Table 16, the high-carbon steel is the most affected. In Cases 11 to 18, the low-carbon steel is rather more affected than the high, while in Cases 23 to 26 the low-carbon steel has its tensile strength and elastic limit in every case affected more than high-carbon steel. But, almost without exception, under like conditions, the higher the carbon the more the ductility is increased by annealing, the effect of the annealing on the ductility generally rising very rapidly with increasing carbon. Thus, in Table 16, the higher is the C, under like conditions the higher algebraically are the numbers in columns 6 and 7. Since, then, with increasing carbon the effect of annealing in raising the ductility rises more rapidly and constantly than does its effect in lowering the tensile strength, it follows that, if we may measure the intrinsic value of steel by the product of its tensile strength into its elongation, the higher the carbon the more beneficial in general is annealing. I am not aware that this deduction has heretofore being pointed out. Thus, in all the comparable cases in Table 16, with one exception, due in turn to a single abnormal observation, the higher the carbon the greater algebraically is the percentage of increase of the efficiency number.[a]

The few cases given in columns IX. and XIV. of Table 8 throw little light on these questions, as the other variables vary so much as to mask the effects of varying C, while in each set of cases in Table 16 we have practically constant conditions.

5. HAMMERING VS. ROLLING.—Comparing in Table 16 the figures of cases 11 to 14 (hammered) with the corresponding ones of cases 15 to 18 (rolled steel), we note that in the majority of cases the hammered steel is affected by annealing more than the rolled steel. But this is no doubt chiefly, perhaps wholly due to the fact that this particular hammer worked more slowly than these particular rolls, hence finished the piece at a lower temperature, and thus induce to a greater degree those effects which annealing removes. This does not necessarily indicate that hammered steel is in general more affected by annealing than rolled steel, except in so far as hammers in general may work more slowly than rolls. It points to no occult difference between the effects of the hammer and the rolls.

§ 47. UNFORGED STEEL CASTINGS.—The cases before us show how the coarse structure and the stresses which exist in unannealed castings weaken them, besides very

[a] Efficiency number = elongation × tensile strength, pounds per square inch.

TABLE 16.—EFFECTS OF ANNEALING AS INFLUENCED BY THE PERCENTAGE OF CARBON.

Description of Steel.	Increase (+) or decrease (—) of tensile strength, etc., caused by annealing, per 100 of the original.							Properties of the steel before annealing.			
	No.	Per cent Carbon.	Tensile strength.	Elastic limit.	Elongation.	Reduction of area.	Efficiency number.	Tensile strength. Lbs. per sq. in.	Elastic limit.	Elongation. Per cent.	Reduction. Per cent.
Two-inch square Fagersta Bessemer steel bars hammered from 6-inch square ingots [a]	1	·80	—12·7	—29·	+ 150·	+153·	+13[illegible]	93,034	66,500	2·2	3·2
	2	·60	— 6·2	— 2·9	+ 25·	+ 63·	+ 17·	97,887	47,700	10·2	28·4
	3	·40	— 5·6	— 7·0	+ 0·	+ 9·8	+ 0·7	75,013	39,200	17·0	[illegible]·5
	4	·20	— 6·0	— 6·0	— 1·3	+ 4·6	— 7·3	59,940	35,200	22·5	61·3
Average of the four preceding	5	....	— 7·6	—11·2	+ 4?·	+ 57·6	....	....	....	....	....
Average of results from 6-inch square ingots and bars 5 in., 4 in., 3 in., and 2 in. square hammered from them. Fagersta Bessemer steel [a]	6	·80	— 7·1	—22·3	+ 70·	+ 70·	+ 58·	75,989	53,457	....	....
	7	·60	— 1·5	— 4·4	+ 110·4	+196·4	+119·7	75,639	41,713	....	....
	8	·40	4·1	— 7·1	+ 21·	+ 48·	+ 16·	65,001	31,048	....	....
	9	·20	— 3·7	— 8·2	+ 16·	+ 49·	+ 13·	56,401	27,800	....	....
Average of the four preceding	10	....	— 4·18	—11·86	....	....	....	68,250	38,738	....	....
Average of results from bars 3 in., 2½ in., 2 in., 1½ in., 1 in., and ½ in. square, hammered from Fagersta Bessemer steel ingots [a]	11	1·00	— 3·3	—23·6	+ 88·	+ 50·	+189·	99,223	73,383	2·6	6·2
	12	0·30	— 6·9	—23·4	+ 19·	+ 28·	+ 29·	81,207	48,850	13·1	[illegible]·8
	13	0·15	—11·6	—29·5	+ 5·	+ 21·	— 2·	60,884	40,033	20·	57·9
Average of the three preceding	14	....	— 7·2	—24·5	....	....	....	80,421	54,280	11·0	31·4
Average of results from bars similar to the last set (Nos. 11 to 14), but rolled instead of being hammered [a]	15	1·00	— 5·0	—28·3	+ 58·	+ 75·	+140·	105,784	67,900	3·1	6·7
	16	0·30	— 3·7	— 8·6	+ 3·	+ 69·	+ 15·	79,470	39,283	11·5	20·6
	17	0·15	— 6·8	—10·9	+ 3·	+ 20·	— 2·	56,843	28,317	26·2	56·4
Average of the three preceding	18	....	— 5·0	—14·8	....	....	....	80,099	45,167	13·6	27·9
Five lots of Chester open-hearth steel plates, 0·48 and 0·74 inches thick. Gatewood, p. 1?1 [b] — Maximum	19	0·145	— 7·42	....	+ 23·16	....	....	66,500	....	28·05	....
Minimum	19	0·145	— 1·38	....	+ 2·68	....	....	63,067	....	19·93	....
Average	19	0·145	— 5·17	....	+ 12·52	....	....	....	....	....	....
Three carefully annealed open-hearth steel plates. *Idem*, p. 165 [b]	20	0·18 to	— 4·7 to	....	+ 6·3 to	....	+ 0·1 to	....	....	....	....
	20	0·23	— 8·5	....	+ 8·4	....	+ 5·	....	....	....	....
Steel plates representing 60 per cent of 35 casts, annealed carelessly [b]	21	0·20±	+ 5·	....	— 4·	....	....	....	....	....	....
Steel bars 1·5x0·5x12 inches, calculated from A. F. Hill's data [c]	22	0·50	— 6·	—14·	+ 23·	....	+ 15·	97,200	56,700	12·	....
	23	0·40	—13·	—15·	+ 29·	....	+ 13·	90,900	49,300	17·	....
	24	0·30	—22·	—25·	+ 21·	....	— 7·	76,400	48,100	24·	....
Steel bars, previously hardened by shearing from plates [c]	25	0·50	+12·	+19·	+ 131·	....	....	82,930	49,960	5·2	....
	25	0·40	+14·	+25·	+ 101·	....	....	75,400	41,250	6·3	....
	25	0·30	+23·	+43·	+ 79·	....	....	69,376	31,290	11·3	....
Steel bars, previously hardened by cold hammering [c]	26	0·50	— 1·	— 9·	+1057·	....	....	91,810	71,630	0·7	....
	26	0·40	— 2·	—19·	+ 513·	....	....	87,560	64,180	2·3	....
	26	0·30	— 3·	—27·	+ 394·	....	....	85,380	63,790	2·4	....

NOTE.—The percentage of increase of elongation and of reduction of area, columns 6 and 7, are per 100 of the elongation, etc., of the unannealed steel, and not per 100 of its length. These results are calculated by the author from the data given by the following writers: [a] Kirkaldy, "Experiments on Fagersta Steel." [b] Gatewood, "Report of the Naval Advisory Board on Mild Steel," U. S. Navy Department, 1886. [c] A. F. Hill, Transactions of the American Institute of Mining Engineers, XI., p. 248, 1883. [d] these two results are exaggerated by one abnormal case. Except where specified the steel was in the ordinary condition, and had undergone no treatment after leaving the rolls or hammer.

greatly diminishing the ductility. Thus in columns VIII., XI., and XIV. of Table 9 we see that the elongation of the unannealed casting is always, and its elastic limit and tensile strength are almost always below those of the same casting when annealed.

Moreover, we observe that as the carbon increases (*i. e.*, as we pass down the columns) there is on the whole a decided decrease in the algebraic value of the numbers in columns VIII. and XI.; *i. e.*, the higher the carbon the more are both tensile strength and elongation increased by annealing, which means that in castings as in forgings annealing is the more beneficial the higher is the carbon.

PUNCHED AND SHEARED STEEL.—The stresses in punched, sheared and flanged boiler-plate steel are greatly relieved by simply heating to redness and quenching in oil or boiling water,[a] but perhaps less than by slow cooling. Cases 25 and 26, Table 16, show a greater increase of efficiency number on annealing ·50 carbon than ·30 carbon steel. This agrees with the observation made concerning the effect of annealing on other high *vs.* low-carbon steel. The effects of annealing on punched and sheared steel will be discussed with the effects of punching, etc.

EFFECT OF ANNEALING ON THE MODULUS OF ELASTICITY.—The indications are at present not only meager, but contradictory. On the one hand, it is stated that hardening raises the modulus, which would imply that annealing should lower it; and analyzing Kirkaldy's results on 10 plates of 0·15 C we find that annealing lowers it from 37,300,000 to 32,260,000 lbs., or by say 14%. On the other hand, from an examination of results obtained with Cambria steel (C ·09@·24) Gatewood[b] concludes that the modulus of this steel, in the condition in which it ordinarily leaves the rolls, is raised by about 1,000,000 lbs. by annealing.

§ 48. NET EFFECT OF HARDENING PLUS ANNEALING.—Though annealing counteracts the effects of hardening it does not necessarily obliterate them, and, while giving the metal even greater ductility than it had before hardening, it may not completely remove the increase of tensile strength conferred by hardening, so that by judiciously managing these two operations we may simultaneously increase both tensile strength and ductility. This is illustrated in Table 16 A. Here in one instance we have a simultaneous gain of 33% in tensile strength, 25 % in elongation and 77 % in reduction. The cases here given all represent steel forgings. Steel castings, whose tensile strength and ductility are lowered by coarse structure and internal stress, might undergo a still greater simultaneous gain of tensile strength and ductility when hardened and subsequently annealed.

THE RATIONALE OF HARDENING AND ANNEALING.

§ 49. IN THE PREVALENT VIEW sudden cooling affects the physical properties of steel by preserving the chemical condition which existed at a red heat.

The following discussion recognizes in addition certain purely physical effects of sudden cooling, to which in common with its chemical features it ascribes the changes in the properties of the metal. The changes in hardness proper it ascribes mainly to chemical, those in tensile strength and ductility jointly to chemical and ph·sical origin. Let him pass it by who seeks easy reading; my feeble light can but faintly illumine these obscure depths.

I recognize three distinct proximate effects of sudden

[a] Barnaby: Jour. Iron and Steel Inst., 1882, I., p. 208-9.
[b] Rept. U. S. Naval Advisory Bd. on Mild Steel, 1886, p. 136.

TABLE 16 A.—GAIN (+) OR LOSS (—) OF TENSILE STRENGTH, ETC., DUE TO HARDENING PLUS ANNEALING PER 100 OF THOSE OF THE STEEL BEFORE HARDENING.

Gain of tensile strength	— 1·2	+ 9·2	— 1·6	+ 11·	+ 2·	+ 13·	+ 15·	+ 10·	+ 38·	+ 26·	+ 16·	+ 7·	— 8·	+ 8·	+ 30·	+ 13·
Gain of elongation	+ 47·	+ 35·	+ 52·	+ 44·	+ 95·	+ 11·	+ 28·	+ 32·	+ 25·	— 28·	— 4·	+ 10·	+ 16·	+ 5·	+ 3·	+ 30·
Gain of reduction of area	+ 113·	+ 102·	+ 173·	+ 82·	+ 145·	+ 83·	+ 86·	+ 71·	+ 77·	— 21·	+ 33·	+ 8·	+ 69·	+ 47·	+ 44·	+ 158·
Gain of efficiency number	+ 46·	+ 47·	+ 49·	+ 60·	+ 99·	+ 25·	+ 47·	+ 45.	+ 66·	— 11·	+ 11·	+ 18·	— 25·	+ 13·	— 24·	47·
Original tensile strength	82,709	71,722	82,058	76,129	89,555	78,144	83,850	82,709	79,568	81,811	97,539	100,759	95,098	94,100	89,000	86,135
Original elongation	18·5	18·	17·	16·5	11·5	19·	17	17·	15·5	23·5	17·	15·	12·5	19·5	18·5	11·5
Original reduction of area	22·50	23·61	10·59	25·30	16·83	21·85	22·56	24·31	22·86	37·52	26·73	29·72	13·0	32·0	27·0	12·0

Proc. U. S. Naval Inst., No. 40, 1887, pp. 62 and 118. Gain and loss of elongation and of reduction of area are per 100 of the elongation and reduction of the unhardened steel, and not per 100 of its dimensions.

cooling. Others, Neptune-like, may perturb our phenomena. Superimposed they produce resultant effects on each mechanical property, and the ratio which the resultant for one (*e. g.*, tensile strength) bears to that for another (*e. g.*, hardness[a]), under different conditions differs very greatly, not merely in amount but actually in sign. Our present data do not permit us to determine the value of each proximate effect quantitatively; I merely seek their signs and, where possible, a rough estimation of their relative values.

Hardening differs from annealing essentially in being a more rapid cooling. A rapid cooling may affect the physical properties of steel,

(1.) By maintaining in the cooled steel the chemical condition of the metal, and especially that of its carbon, which existed at a high temperature; this should increase its hardness and tensile strength but lower its ductility.

(2.) By causing the outside to cool much faster than the inside, which may act in two ways:

(A.) By setting up stresses which if moderate increase the tensile strength, but if intense lower it, and, whether slight or severe, lower the ductility. By compressing the exterior they may increase the superficial density and hardness.

(B.) By causing a pressing or kneading together of the different layers, somewhat resembling that of forging, which should increase both the tensile strength and ductility.

(3.) By preventing the coarse crystallization which occurs when the metal is long exposed to a high temperature, and perhaps by breaking it up in some measure if already acquired. In this way both tensile strength and ductility should be increased.

The following table sums these effects up, + indicating that a property is increased, — that it is diminished by sudden, as compared with slow cooling:

EFFECTS OF SUDDEN COOLING.

PROXIMATE EFFECTS.	Ultimate effects on the physical properties of steel.		
	Tensile strength.	Ductility.	Hardness.
1. It preserves the chemical *status quo*	+	—	+
2. It causes dissimilar rates of contraction:			
A. These set up stresses	±	—	+
B. They knead the particles together	+	+	+ ?
3. It prevents coarse crystallization	+	+	?

Annealing, *i. e.*, slow cooling, by offering the opposite set of conditions, effaces more or less completely all the effects of sudden cooling, except (2 B.) those due to the kneading together of the particles, which it is probably powerless to remove.

None of the proximate effects diminishes hardness; hence steel is always harder when quickly than when slowly cooled. But the signs in the ductility and tensile strength columns are sometimes +, sometimes —; hence, sudden cooling renders steel stronger or weaker, tougher or more brittle, according to the special conditions of the case. It is certain that the relation between the effects of sudden cooling on tensile strength, ductility and hardness respectively differ greatly with the special conditions of cooling, *i. e.*, the shape and size of the piece, its percentage of carbon, the temperature from which quenching occurs, the cooling medium, etc. Hence, while the usual effect of sudden cooling is to make steel stronger and more brittle, it may, under exceptional conditions, render it at once weaker and more brittle, and under others at once stronger and tougher than if slowly cooled. And while slow cooling usually renders steel tougher and tensilely weaker, it may, under exceptional conditions, render it both weaker and more brittle, and under others both tougher and stronger.

Let us now consider in detail these proximate effects of sudden cooling and their relations to its ultimate effects.

§ 50. SUDDEN COOLING AFFECTS THE MECHANICAL PROPERTIES OF STEEL BY PRESERVING THE CHEMICAL STATUS QUO.

In §§ 23-25 I gave reasons for believing that at or about cherry-redness the carbon of steel passes almost wholly into the hardening state, combining with the whole of the matrix of iron present to form a compound which, when cold, is intensely hard and much stronger and more brittle than pure iron, and which is preserved by sudden cooling. Hence quenching from redness hardens, strengthens makes brittle. That at a lower temperature, V, it tends to pass into the cement state, crystallizing within the matrix of iron as a definite carbide, Fe_3C, giving the composite mass a degree of hardness, strength and brittleness intermediate between those of hardened steel and of pure iron; hence slow cooling, implying long exposure to temperatures near V, softens, toughens, weakens. That at temperatures below V this tendency remains, but that, if by sudden cooling the carbon has been imprisoned in the hardening state, it is prevented by chemical inertia from escaping into the cement state as long as the metal remains cold; yet that this inertia is gradually relaxed, the change to the cement state gradually occurs, and the hardness, strength and brittleness due to quenching from redness are gradually more and more completely removed as the suddenly cooled steel is reheated, till, when V is reached, their removal is complete. Chemistry thus explains much, but, as I shall now try to show, not all.

[a] In this discussion I use hardness in its strictest sense of power to resist indentation, which, though usually accompanied by rigidity and brittleness, stands in no fixed relation to them.

§ 51. SUDDEN COOLING AFFECTS THE PHYSICAL PROPERTIES OF STEEL BY CAUSING DISSIMILAR RATES OF CONTRACTION.

I. THROUGH CAUSING INTERNAL STRESSES.—Let us consider these stresses and their effects on (A) specific gravity, (B) tensile strength, (C) ductility, and (D) hardness.

A. EFFECT ON SPECIFIC GRAVITY.—Consider a round bar while being quenched. The exterior first cools, contracts, becomes rigid, its dimensions being determined by the size of the still comparatively hot, expanded, mobile interior. The resistance of the interior to the return of the exterior to the dimensions which it had before heating acts on that exterior precisely as a tensile stress does on a body at constant temperature. If very powerful it strains it beyond its elastic limit, it takes a permanent set, it is permanently distended. The stress may exceed the ultimate strength of the outer layers, which then crack, the piece breaks in hardening. The interior continues to contract; its adhesion to the now rigid distended exterior prevents its own complete return to its initial dimensions; it may, in its struggle to reach them, somewhat compress the exterior, but not enough to efface the distention previously caused. The piece, as a whole, remains somewhat enlarged, its specific gravity is lowered.

The final state of external compression and internal tension is readily verified by slitting a hardened steel bar in two, lengthwise, in a planing machine; each half becomes curved, concave on the planed side.[a]

That the low specific gravity of hardened steel, while perhaps in part due to the preservation by sudden cooling of chemical combinations, which are lighter than the composite mass of iron plus the carbide Fe_3C of which annealed steel mainly consists, is largely due to mechanical distention, is further indicated by the experiments of Barus and Stronhal. On progressively removing annular layer after layer from the exterior of a hardened steel bar, 3 cm. in diameter, whose sp. gr. after hardening was 7·7744, the sp. gr. of the residual core increased with surprising regularity, as, by the removal of more and more of the shell it was permitted to contract further and further, until, when its diameter had fallen to 1·38 cm., or a little less than half its initial size, its sp. gr. had risen to 7·8009, or approximately half way towards that which it had before hardening, which had been 7·8337.[b]

After the cooling has progressed slightly and the outside has contracted more than the still comparatively slowly cooling and disproportionally distended interior, it is no longer able to contain it and at the same time to preserve its original shape. It is therefore shortened and bulged,[c] thus slightly approaching the spherical shape, in which the minimum of exterior holds the maximum of interior; and this distortion is not wholly effaced by the subsequent contraction of the interior. I have elsewhere offered, with confirmatory experiments, this explanation of the shortening and the increase in diameter of round bars on sudden cooling.[d]

B. EFFECT ON TENSILE STRENGTH.—Studying the effect of sudden cooling on the tensile strength of a round bar, we may, for our present purpose, consider it as composed of a nest of concentric cylindrical spiral springs, firmly, but not absolutely rigidly attached to each other at many points along their length. If to an annealed bar, which in this view would consist of such a nest of springs initially free from internal stress, we apply a powerful longitudinal tensile stress, grasping as usual the skin of the bar (*i. e.*, the outermost spring), owing to the pliancy of the interstratal connections the outer spring must clearly bear an undue proportion of the stress, and indeed each spring will bear a slightly greater proportion than the one next within it. This will cause the system to break down piecemeal under a stress which would be impotent if uniformly resisted by all the springs. This effect is more readily grasped if we conceive a very thick short bar, *e. g.*, a disk 6 feet in diameter and 6 inches long, subjected to stress parallel with its axis and applied to its circumference.

A suddenly cooled bar in this view consists of such a set of springs, but with the outer ones in initial compression, the inner ones in tension, owing to the residual stress due to contraction at dissimilar rates. Extraneous tensile stress applied by grasping the outer spring (as happens when such a bar is pulled apart in the testing machine), is not resisted by the outer springs until they have elongated by as much as they were initially compressed, the inner springs meanwhile supporting the whole extraneous stress in addition to their initial residual stress. This condition, the opposite of that in the annealed bar, tends to favor the outer springs at the expense of the inner ones. Residual stress, then, if moderate, should increase the tensile strength of the system, by tending to equalize the stress borne by the several springs, through counteracting the effects of interstratal yielding; and when it becomes just intense enough to exactly balance them, the tensile strength should reach its maximum, again declining as with still more sudden cooling the still more powerful residual stress throws an excessive proportion of stress on the inner springs.

C. EFFECT ON DUCTILITY.—While the effect of stress on ductility may not be so readily traced, yet the simile of the springs may at least partially explain it. When extraneous tensile stress is applied to the outermost of such a nest of connected concentric springs initially free from stress, and thus resembling an annealed bar, the outer spring first reaches its elastic limit, undergoes permanent elongation, breaks; the particles which connect it with the next inner spring similarly permanently elongate, then break, then the next spring elongates and breaks, etc. After the outer spring breaks (and it may break at many points in its length), its broken fragments, still transmitting the stress to the intact springs within it, are, owing to the elongation which each of these undergoes both before and after its individual rupture, progressively drawn apart

[a] Use of Steel, Barba, Holley, p. 10. I have verified this experimentally.

The internal distortion and consequent stresses set up in large steel castings by the difference in the rates of cooling and contraction of their different portions (a difference which, thanks to the high melting-point of the metal, and the comparatively low temperature of the mould, may be very great), are sometimes so extreme that the particles of the metal, even with the mobility which they acquire at a full red heat, may not be able to travel and to flow far enough to completely efface them. A large casting from which much cutting has to be done, even if carefully annealed before the cutting begins, will often spring much out of shape when part of the metal has been cut away, proving the existence even after annealing of internal stresses, whose equilibrium is destroyed by cutting away a portion of the metal which had sustained them. Hence the importance of annealing such pieces after rough machining.

[b] Am. Jour. of Science XXXI., p. 386; Jour. Iron and St. Inst., 1886, I, p. 372.

[c] Journal Iron and Steel Inst., 1879, II., p. 428, Caron, Barba, op. cit., p. 10.

[d] Trans. Am. Inst. Mining Engineers, XIV., p. 400.

more and more up to the instant when the final parting of the last spring occurs, so that part of the elongation of each spring is superadded to that of those outside it, and the system, as a whole, is greatly elongated.

So, too, as the fragments of each broken spring are drawn apart longitudinally, the remaining area of cross-section of the system is simply that of the still unbroken inner springs, and we get great reduction of area.

If, however, as in the case of a bar of hardened steel, the inner springs are under such initial tensile stress that they break simultaneously with the outer ones, we have none of the cumulative action, the superadding of the elongation of one layer to that of the next which occurs with our annealed bar; we get but little elongation, and, since the final area is not diminished by the drawing asunder of successive outer layers, but little reduction of area. Nor, if the initial stresses be so severe that the inner springs break before the outer ones, will the elongation of the system be increased by the addition of the elongation of one spring to that of another, such as arises when the outer spring breaks first, as is clear on reflection. If the tensile stress were applied through the inner spring, then as the fracture gradually extended outward from spring to spring the two fragments of each broken spring would continue to transmit the tensile stress to the spring next outside them, and, being always under tensile stress, they might be continually drawn farther and farther apart, and the final fracture might be deeply cup-shaped. But as the stress is transmitted along the outer spring, there is nothing to draw apart the fragments of the successively broken inner ones; their elongation is not superadded to that of the outer one, and the total elongation of the piece is simply that of the outer spring, which breaks last.

A simile pushed too far always misleads. This one may, I hope, portray certain features of what occurs during rupture, not, of course, with complete accuracy, yet closely enough to facilitate our present study. Dissatisfied with it, I offer it for lack of a better.

D. Effect on Hardness.—The state of violent compression in which the exterior of a quenched bar is left may be expected to force its particles more closely together, and thus to partially account for the hardness of the external layers. The powerful compression which steel undergoes in cold-forging does actually harden its exterior.

To test this I had one portion of an unhardened steel bar of $1\frac{3}{16}''$ diameter reduced to $\frac{3}{4}''$ diameter when cold, by a single draught through a die (Billings cold-drawing process). A portion of the same bar which had not been thus treated, was accurately turned to the same diameter. The hardness of the cold-drawn portion, as measured by indentation, was very perceptibly greater than that of the turned portion. I doubt whether the difference could be detected by the file.

II. Dissimilar Rates of Contraction Produce a Kneading Effect.—The different rates at which the concentric layers of a steel bar contract during sudden cooling, owing to their different rates of cooling, must occasion more or less interstratal motion, rubbing together, interlacing, pressure, tension; and since we find that such internal motion, whether as in kneading dough, putty or clay, arising chiefly from compression; or, as in forging metals, from both compression and tension;[a] or, as in pulling molasses candy, chiefly from tension, appears to increase the intermolecular cohesion, to raise both tensile strength and toughness, we may reasonably ascribe to this feature of sudden cooling a strengthening and toughening effect. And if by more thorough interlacing it increases the intermolecular cohesion, the resistance to displacement, we may suppose that this increases the hardness as measured by indentation.

§ 52. Sudden Cooling vs. Coarse Crystallization. Though as explained in § 243, p. 172, as we heat steel farther and farther above W its grain grows coarser and coarser, yet on heating it to W itself pre-existing crystallization is broken up, and the grain becomes very fine or even porcelanic. During slow cooling from W, however, a certain amount of crystallization occurs. So, too, forging breaks up crystallization more or less completely: but if forging cease while the temperature is considerably above W, crystallization again sets in, and tends to become the coarser the higher the temperature. Sudden cooling, whether after heating to W or after forging, in that it shortens the exposure to temperatures at which crystallization occurs, limits crystallization, and crystallization clearly lessens both strength and ductility, the more so the coarser it becomes. This effect of sudden cooling is especially marked where the crystallizing tendency is strongest, *e. g.* in large masses and in phosphoric iron. In some phosphoric irons the tendency to coarse crystallization is so strong that they are actually tougher after sudden than after slow cooling. (See §§ 45 and 126.) In sudden cooling interstratal movements must arise, since neighboring layers must cool and contract at very different rates, and forging must cause similar interstratal movements. These, like the agitation of any solidifying crystallizing mass, should not only prevent the formation of large crystals with extended surfaces of weak cohesion, but even break them up when once formed.

§ 53. Effects of Tempering and Annealing.—Let us now consider how the effects of sudden cooling which have just been discussed are removed or weakened by tempering and annealing, and how the latter operation removes the effects of cold-working.

1. Chemical Action.—As explained in §§ 23 and 50, the heating which occurs in tempering and annealing relaxes chemical inertia so as to permit the carbon to pass from the hardening state, in which it has been previously imprisoned by sudden cooling, to the cement state, to a degree which, within limits, increases with the temperature reached; hence, the higher this heating the softer the steel becomes.

2. Removal of the Effects of Contraction at Dissimilar Rates.—We have seen that contraction at dissimilar rates, owing to sudden cooling, should produce two quite distinct mechanical effects, (A) internal stresses, (B) a kneading or forcing together of the particles of the metal. There is both reason to expect that cold-forging, punching, etc., should, and evidence that they do, produce both these effects, though not in the same relative proportion. Cold-working in moderation, as in cold-rolling and wire-drawing, increases the tensile strength very

[a] That forging acts very largely by tension is suggested by the fact that cold-forging makes iron lighter and not denser. Langley found that repeated cold-hammering lowered the specific gravity of a steel bar from 7·828 to 7·817 and then to 7·780. ("The Treatment of Steel," p. 42.) So, too, in a case reported by Percy (Journ. Iron and St. Inst., 1886, I., p. 63), cold-drawing appears to have lowered the specific gravity of wire from 7·8102± to 7·8112.

greatly while lowering the ductility. In excess, as in punching and shearing, it lowers both tensile strength and ductility, sometimes wholly destroying the latter. As shown in § 51, these are the results which should be expected from the stresses which sudden cooling should set up, which from the nature of the case should closely resemble those of cold forging, which must leave the exterior in a state of compression, the interior in one of tension.

A. REMOVAL OF INTERNAL STRESS.—The action of tempering and annealing in removing internal stress can, I think, be most readily grasped by regarding the metal not as an ideal solid, but merely as an extremely viscous liquid, approaching the condition of lead or of molasses candy. A remembrance of the readiness with which cold steel flows under the action of car wheels, of the punch, etc., may help us to grasp this idea. If the particles of the metal be subjected, even when cold, to sufficient stress, they may yield to it and flow, and thus diminish the stress. Just as in the case of molasses candy, this flow may continue until the stress is so far relieved that it just fails to produce any further flow, when the particles gradually come to rest in equilibrium under the maximum stress which, with their existing viscosity, they can sustain without flow; or, if the stress and the flow which it induces exceed a certain amount, the viscosity of the metal exceeds its cohesion, and, unable to flow farther, it breaks. Evidently, the more we heat either candy or steel the less viscous does it become, the more readily does it yield to stress, whether external, as that of hammering, etc., or internal, as that induced by previous sudden cooling or cold-forging. If hardened or cold-forged steel be heated to a red or yellow heat (say 900° to 1100° C.) its viscosity is so much diminished, its particles become so mobile that they flow under the stress which they had defied when cold, and almost completely relieve and efface it. If we would avoid setting up new stresses in place of those which we have dispelled we must allow our steel to cool so slowly that its different portions will contract practically uniformly: our steel becomes annealed: but it is clear that the true annealing, the relief of stress, was effected by the heating, and that the slow cooling is merely to avoid undoing the annealing already accomplished.

If the hardened or cold-worked steel be heated, not to a red but merely to a straw heat (say 230° C.), its particles are rendered mobile, but far less so than by the much higher heating employed for annealing: if heated a little higher than a straw-heat, say to blueness (290° C.), they become still somewhat more mobile. This increased mobility relieves previously induced stresses, and the brittleness which they had caused is thus removed to a greater or less degree as the temperature reached be higher or lower: the steel is tempered. The temperature to which steel is heated for tempering, though it suffices to relieve the more intense stresses, is so low, and hence the contraction which occurs when the tempered steel is again cooled is so slight, that, even if the steel be suddenly cooled no serious stresses are likely to arise.[a] Hence rapid cooling is usually employed for convenience.

As heating hardened steel softens and toughens it by transferring carbon to the cement state, it may appear superfluous to call in the relief of stress simultaneously effected to help explain annealing; but in § 54 cogent reasons are given for believing that both the chemical effect of sudden cooling and its physical effect in causing stress give strength and brittleness. And the same reasoning indicates that both the chemical and physical effects of reheating contribute powerfully to its weakening and toughening effect.

B. REMOVAL OF THE EFFECT OF THE KNEADING ACTION.—As shown in § 54, the effect of the kneading action due to dissimilar rates of contraction is probably not wholly, if at all, removed by subsequent annealing.

3. REMOVAL OF THE EFFECT OF HARDENING ON CRYSTALLIZATION.—See § 52.

4. THE TEMPERATURE AT WHICH ANNEALING BEGINS.—Annealing appears to begin at surprisingly low temperatures. The gradual deterioration of cutlery even at temperatures below 100° C is referred to in § 25. So, too, the thermo-electric power,[b] which appears to increase so constantly as stress diminishes that it has been regarded as an index of stress (indeed, they may stand in the causal relation), increases even when steel is exposed to a temperature no higher than 66° C., though very gradually. During three hours of exposure to this temperature the rise of the thermo-electric power continues at an almost constant rate. At 100° C. it rises more rapidly, rising as much in ten minutes at this temperature as it increases in three hours at 66°. At 185° C. the rise is still more abrupt, and at 330° it rises so abruptly as to seem to jump instantly to its maximum. At each temperature there is a maximum, or normal thermo-electric power, and hence, probably, a maximum degree to which stress is relieved, which during continued exposure to that temperature are approached asymptotically. The higher the temperature the higher is the normal (maximum) thermo-electric power, the lower is the corresponding normal state of stress which is thus approached, and the more rapidly are they approached, *i. e.*, the faster and more fully is stress effaced.

The stresses due to sudden cooling appear (as already explained) to lower the density. Langley found that the density of steel, slightly lowered by quenching from 100° C., was restored by re-exposure to 100° with subsequent slow cooling.[a]

Similar changes occur in other metals at low temperatures; thus Matthiessen and Barus and Strouhal[c] found that the conductivity of hard-drawn silver and German silver was changed, from which it is inferred that the stress due to hard-drawing was diminished, by continued boiling in water.

It is not certain how far the changes effected at these low temperatures are due to relief of stress and how far to the escape of part of the carbon from the hardening to the cement state.

Abel's results show that at a straw heat the condition of carbon changes quite rapidly. But the changes which occur at 100° C. we naturally ascribe to the relief of stress, because it is easy to understand how stress should be relieved at this low temperature, especially since we find

[a] That slight stress may arise even in quenching from 100° C. is indicated by an experiment of Langley's. (The Treatment of Steel, p. 42.) A cold-hammered steel bar was heated to 100° C. and slowly cooled; its sp. gr. then was 7·816. When again heated to 100 and quenched in cold water its sp. gr. fell to 7·790, but it rose again to 7·817 on again heating to 100, and cooling slowly. Other trials gave closely similar results.

[b] Barus and Strouhal: Bulletin of the U. S. Geological Survey, No. 14, pp. 54-55.

[c] *Idem*, pp. 93-4.

similar changes occurring at 100° in silver and in German silver, while a change in the condition of carbon at such low temperatures would certainly be more unexpected.

§ 54. ACTUAL INFLUENCE OF THE SEVERAL PROXIMATE EFFECTS OF HARDENING, TEMPERING AND ANNEALING.—Let us now consider how far the changes in each of the physical properties of steel are due to each of the proximate effects of these operations.

I. TENSILE STRENGTH AND DUCTILITY.—I believe that the changes in these properties are chiefly due to corresponding changes in the condition of carbon, not only because of the fair correspondence between them but because the changes in tensile strength and ductility are the more marked the higher the percentage of carbon is. But this indication is slightly equivocal, for, owing to the high elastic limit of high-carbon steel its particles come to rest under stress which would be impossible in low-carbon steel, because the particles of this metal would flow when exposed to it: it is therefore possible, though I think highly improbable, that high-carbon steel gains more strength and ductility when hardened than that which contains less carbon, solely because it is capable of retaining more intense residual stresses. Be this as it may, several facts conspire to show that change in the chemical condition of carbon is not the sole cause of these changes in tensile strength and ductility.

A. The tensile strength of almost carbonless iron may be much increased by sudden cooling. (See Tables 8, 9, and 10, § 34.) The tensile strength of Cases 2 and 3, in Table 8, is increased 41 and 40 % respectively, and their elongation is lowered by 79 and 47 % by water-quenching, though they contain but ·07 and ·03 % of carbon respectively.

I heated to whiteness two pieces of wrought-iron cut from the same bar: one was slowly cooled, the other quenched in cold water. The slowly cooled bar had 47,600 lbs. tensile strength, 25 % elongation in 2 inches, and 15 % reduction of area, against 42,700 lbs., 6 % and 3 % for the quenched bar. Now if a change in the condition of carbon (from which the bar was almost free) sufficient to account for this great change in the properties of the iron was induced by sudden cooling, that change would have simultaneously greatly affected the hardness, which is so closely dependent on the condition of carbon: but I was unable to detect, by the method of indentation, any difference in hardness.

B. Though the changes in the condition of carbon and in tensile strength and ductility at first appear to follow similar laws, yet closer observation appears to reveal marked discrepancies. Thus for given quenching temperature, known to be high enough to transfer the carbon to the hardening state, the more sudden and violent the cooling the more completely doubtless is the carbon retained in that state. But the tensile strength seems to follow quite another law, reaching a maximum with moderately sudden cooling, and again rapidly declining if the cooling becomes more sudden. This occurs even in steel with comparatively little carbon. (See cases 12, 14, and 16, Table 8.) Still again, since on quenching the exterior of a bar cools more suddenly than the interior, the carbon in it should be the more completely retained in the hardening state: yet, as shown by the experiment which I will shortly describe the interior of a hardened bar is sometimes vastly stronger tensilely than the outside.

My experiments indicate, though not conclusively, that quenching from temperatures which are not quite high enough to transfer carbon to the hardening state, while it does not affect the hardness may strongly influence tensile strength and ductility. Should further investigation corroborate this, it would still further illustrate the discrepancies between the behavior of carbon and the changes in these properties.

I believe that the tensile strength and ductility are greatly influenced by the stresses set up by sudden cooling and relieved by subsequent heating (as set forth in § 51, I, B and C), for the following reasons. If these stresses act in the manner which I have supposed, then, if we cut a hardened steel bar into a series of concentric cylinders and thereby partially relieve these stresses, the sum of the tensile strength of the detached cylinders should differ materially from that of the undivided bar.

Let P = the tensile strength per square inch of the undivided bar.
A = the area of its cross-section.
p^1 = the tensile strength per square inch of the central core after dividing the bar.
p^2 = that of the cylinder adjoining this core.
p^3, p^4, etc. = those of the other cylinders.
a^1, a^2, a^3, etc. = the areas of their cross-sections.

Then, if my hypothesis is true, $P \times A$ would not usually equal $\Sigma p \times a$. The same hypothesis implies that for given conditions a stress of one certain degree of intensity, S, should produce the maximum tensile strength for the undivided bar, greater than that produced by either more or less intense stress: and hence that if the stress in the undivided bar were greater than S, since subdividing it into cylinders would, by lessening the stress, bring it nearer to S, $\Sigma p \times a$ would be greater than $P \times A$. Were the stress in the hardened bar less than S then $\Sigma p \times a < P \times A$. Furthermore, if, even after subdividing the bar the stresses still residual in the detached annuli were greater than S, then, since the stresses in the comparatively slowly cooling central core should be less intense than in the exterior layers, p^1 should be greater than p^2, p^2 greater than p^3, etc. If my hypothesis were false, and if the gain of strength by hardening were wholly due to some chemical feature of hardening, as, for instance, to its preserving the *status quo* or to some chemical change caused by the sudden change of temperature or by the accompanying stress, then such subdivision of the bar should not be expected to alter the chemical condition of its members, and in this case we should find that $\Sigma p \times a = P \times A$. Moreover, since this chemical feature should be more marked in the rapidly cooling exterior than in the comparatively slowly cooling core, we should usually find that $p^1 < p^2$, $p^2 < p^3$, etc. If, for instance, the increase of tensile strength were wholly due to its retaining carbon in the hardening state, since this retention would evidently be more complete in the exterior of the bar than in the interior the outside should be the strongest, as it actually is the hardest.

To test the matter, I cut a ¾-inch round steel bar (No. 14·5 in Table 8), containing 0·39% carbon, into five equal pieces. All were heated nearly to whiteness in a muffle, under identical conditions. One was slowly cooled, the others quenched very rapidly by agitation in cold water.

This quenching appeared so violent as to set up stresses much greater than S, and the steel became so hard that it could be machined only with extreme difficulty. One of the hardened bars received no further treatment. A second had its exterior turned down in a lathe to a diameter of 0·565 inches; a third was in the same way reduced to a diameter of 0·259 inches; while a fourth had its interior removed by drilling holes across it radially, and then filing their sides away till only thin segments of the exterior remained. This was done at two points in the length of the piece, enabling me to determine the strength of the exterior twice. The following results were obtained:[a]

	Tensile strength, Lbs. per sq. in.	Elongation %.	In.
The annealed bar, 0·784″ diameter	92,900	31·2	2″
The hardened bar, 0·74″ diameter	118,000	0·8	2″
Core of the hardened bar, 0·565″ diameter	141,000	0·0	2″
Core of the hardened bar, 0·259″ diameter	248,000	3·0	0·5″
Segments of the exterior shell of the hardened bar: 1st experiment	165,000	....	....
Segments of the exterior shell of the hardened bar: 2d experiment	167,000	....	....

Thus the sum of the tensile strength of the several detached portions greatly exceeds that of the undivided bar, and the strength rises as we approach the center; or, algebraically, $\Sigma p \times a > P \times A$: $p^1 > p^2$; $p^2 > p^3$, etc. These facts, taken in conjunction with Abel's discovery that pressure applied to cold steel does not change the condition of its carbon, almost amount to a mathematical demonstration that the tensile strength of hardened steel is powerfully affected by factors other than chemical condition. And while they do not demonstrate the truth of my hypothesis, since they may be shown to accord with other suppositions, yet as they are in themselves surprising, hitherto unsuspected so far as I know, incompatible with the other explanations offered, but experimentally verified corollaries to it, they certainly support it powerfully. So does the fact, predictable from it, that while moderately sudden cooling raises the tensile strength, violently sudden cooling lowers it. So does the fact that cold working, which may be expected to set up stresses like those ascribed to sudden cooling, produces closely similar results, always lowering ductility, and, if moderate (as in ordinary cold-rolling), raising the tensile strength, but if violent (as in punching and shearing) actually lowering it. So does the observation, so far as it is complete, that sudden cooling strengthens and renders brittle only those metals in which it is capable of setting up severe stresses. These it can only create in metals which, with at least moderately high coefficient of expansion, combine low thermal conductivity with high modulus of elasticity and high elastic limit. Metals with high thermal conductivity cool and hence contract at an almost uniform rate throughout their cross-section: this removes the cause of stress. If the modulus be low, given distortion from dissimilar rates of contraction produces but little stress. If the elastic limit be low severe stress cannot exist, because the metal flows under the growing stress and relieves it before it can become severe. Gold, silver, copper and many of its alloys have very high thermal conductivity with in general low modulus and low elastic limit. Now, with repeated experiments, undertaken to elucidate this point, I find that the rate of cooling from dull cherry-redness does not appreciably affect the tensile strength or ductility of silver, copper or brass, nor the tensile strength of gold or German silver: and, while I found the last two metals somewhat less ductile after sudden than after slow cooling, the difference was within the limits of experimental error.

I know of no direct evidence that the supposed kneading effect of sudden cooling actually increases the tensile strength and ductility. The progressive strengthening and toughening caused by repeated quenchings each followed by an annealing indeed seem at first to point to such a kneading effect, since most of the other effects of sudden cooling should be removed by subsequent annealing, while the kneading effect might be expected to persist through reheating to a moderate temperature. This, however, is far from conclusive. Reheating to W breaks up coarse crystallization; but Coffin finds that, in case of soft steel, repeated reheatings to W may be needed to break it up completely. Thus the beneficial action of our repeated quenchings and annealings may be due to progressive destruction of pre-existing coarse crystallization rather than to our supposed kneading effect. (§ 245, p. 175.)

That in so far as sudden cooling checks a tendency to coarse crystallization it tends to increase ductility is rendered very probable by the fact that when, as in the case of phosphoric iron, this tendency is very strong, sudden cooling gives greater ductility than slow cooling. It is extremely probable that it in the same way tends to increase the tensile strength, though this is not easily shown except in extreme cases. Bessemer,[b] by enabling a mass of wholly decarburized molten ingot metal to cool so slowly that after five or six days it was still very hot, found when it was cold that it had resolved itself into cubical crystals, some of them with edges over 0·25 inches long: the individual crystals were highly malleable; but the mass as a whole was so incoherent that, holding it in the hand, showers of detached crystals were readily broken off by blows from a 2-lb. hammer—the slow cooling had destroyed both strength and ductility.

Similar effects are probably producible in other metals. Some inconclusive trials seemed to show that while, as already stated, if copper has been heated to a temperature not above dull redness, its strength and ductility are almost independent of the rate at which it has then been cooled, and while these properties are not seriously affected by heating it almost to its melting point (say 1,000° C.), provided it be then suddenly cooled, yet that if it be slowly cooled from 1,000° it becomes very weak, brittle and coarsely crystalline: its strength, ductility and silky fracture are completely restored by quenching from redness, its coarse crystallization obliterated, perhaps, by interstratal motion too slight to produce serious stress. Were this confirmed we would refer these effects to coarse crystallization, because it occurs, because it is a competent cause, and

[a] The strength of the inner core, 248,000 pounds per square inch, is indeed extraordinary, and I should discredit it if I saw any possibility of error. But as I tested the steel myself and have carefully verified my calculations, I am forced to believe that we here have stress of a degree of intensity especially favorable to high tensile strength, such as exists in hard-drawn wire, whose tensile strength rises to 432,000 pounds per square inch (Percy: Journ. Iron and Steel Inst., 1886, I., p. 70). Wire with 0·828% carbon is reported with 344,960 pounds tensile strength (idem), and thin hardened steel plates are quoted with 314,800 pounds tensile strength. (Emery: Report of U. S. Senate Select Committee on Ordnance and War Ships, 1886, p. 468). The fact here brought out that the tensile strength of a steel bar may be less than half that of a test piece cut from its center, and may be much less than the mean tensile strength of test pieces cut from various portions of it, may be of practical importance in ascertaining the tensile strength of large hardened pieces, such as gun hoops. It may be demonstrated, but it should not be assumed, that the annealing to which such pieces are generally submitted after hardening removes this source of error.

[b] Journal of the Iron and Steel Institute, 1885, I., p. 200.

because change of stress and of chemical condition (the other recognized functions of the rate of cooling) can hardly produce such effects in this metal.

Riche found that bronzes with 20% tin and 80% copper were tougher after sudden than after slow cooling.[a]

II. The changes in hardness are probably almost wholly due to corresponding changes in the chemical condition of carbon. (A). The degree of hardness imparted by sudden cooling, instead of rising gradually and uniformly with the quenching temperature, remains practically nil till a temperature approaching dull redness is reached, when, with slight further increase in quenching temperature, it leaps rapidly to a maximum, thus apparently closely following the changes in the chemical condition of carbon. (B). Thin bars, cooling more suddenly than thick ones, also, I believe, are hardened more by quenching. (C). The increase of hardness caused by quenching is roughly proportional to the percentage of carbon in the metal, being practically nil for practically carbonless iron. The supposition that the latter fact is chiefly due to the more intense stress, the more powerful kneading and the more complete prevention of coarse crystallization caused by sudden cooling in high- than in low-carbon steel appears improbable, though these factors may intensify the effects of the changes in the condition of carbon.

That the hardness caused by sudden cooling is not due chiefly to the stresses which it sets up is very probable, because both exterior and interior are hardened, though under opposite kinds of stress: because thin bars, though their stresses should be less severe, are, I believe, hardened more than thick ones: and because, though violent stresses probably arise when practically carbonless iron is quenched (as inferred from its loss of ductility) it is not rendered appreciably harder, at least in certain cases.[b]

The protection from coarse crystallization afforded by quenching hardly appears a competent cause of the hardness simultaneously produced: and the facts that a copper rod, which (as described in § 54, I.), was so slowly cooled as to become coarsely crystalline, weak and brittle, did not differ in hardness from similar but quenched and fine-grained ones, and that the coarse crystallization induced in practically carbonless iron by slow cooling is accompanied by no apparent change of hardness, go to show that it is not the true cause.

§ 54. A. Apparent Anomaly.—I find manganese steel very slightly softer (as measured by indentation), and it is said to be decidedly tougher, after sudden than after slow cooling. We know as yet too little of its thermal conductivity and modulus of elasticity to discern whether this toughening is due mainly to the prevention of coarse crystallization, or to the formation at a high temperature of some chemical compound which, preserved by sudden cooling, is tougher and softer than some other compounds into which it is resolved at some lower temperature during slow cooling: but we may conjecture that the softening due to sudden cooling arises in this latter way.

§ 55. Other Explanations of Hardening. (Cf. Pp. 187-9).

Diamond Theory.—This explanation, hardly competent to explain a single phenomenon of hardening and utterly incompatible with many of them, merits notice solely because its discussion and even commendation by those who should have gauged it better has given it fictitious value. Briefly, sudden cooling has been supposed to harden steel by converting its carbon into diamond. It is certain that hardened steel does not contain diamond, because none is found in the residue from dissolving it even in dilute acids. The readiness with which hardened steel of 0·4 carbon is cut by steel of higher carbon, which will not scratch stones which are incomparably softer than diamond, hardly points to the presence of the gem. Diamond powder imbedded in a soft matrix should destroy the edge of the best steel tool. A soluble substance cut by steel is not diamond.

Now, sudden cooling may triple the tensile strength of steel which contains but 0·4% carbon, while wholly destroying its great ductility. If it is conceivable that a skeleton of diamond dust could produce these two effects simultaneously on a matrix of soft ingot-iron, of whose mass it formed but 0·4% (raising the tensile strength perchance by preventing flow), can it, in view of the evidence negativing the presence of diamond, be regarded as a probable explanation, with such *veræ causæ* at hand as the preceding sections have set forth? The evidence supporting the diamond hypothesis is too inconclusive to merit reproduction.

Occluded Gases.—It has been suggested that at a high temperature, or during sudden cooling, steel expels occluded cases, gradually reabsorbing them as the temperature descends in slow cooling: that suddenly cooled steel is hard because it has had no opportunity to reabsorb the gases expelled when it was hot or during sudden cooling, that slowly cooled steel is soft because it has had this opportunity.

Roberts[c] has demolished this theory by heating steel wire in vacuo, suddenly cooling part of it by immersion in mercury, but slowly cooling the remainder. The suddenly cooled part was glass-hard, the slowly cooled part soft. No gases were expelled during the sudden cooling. Clearly suddenness of cooling and not absorption and expulsion of gases cause the phenomena observed.

§ 56. Åkerman's Theory.[d]—Of a very different order is the explanation learnedly and ingeniously expounded by this illustrious metallurgist. Recognizing that residual stress may lower tensile strength, he appears to attribute the changes in hardness, ductility and structure as well as the chief changes in tensile strength caused by sudden cooling not to its maintaining by its suddenness the chemical *status quo*, not to its giving no opportunity for coarse crystallization, not to its kneading action which as I believe increases intermolecular cohesion, prevents and even breaks up coarse crystallization, but directly and, as I understand him, solely to its compression as such, which, in his view, forces carbon into the hardening state, thereby increasing strength and hardness, but diminishing ductility, and breaks up coarse structure.

Compression would, I think, be quite incompetent to explain the phenomena, even if it were known to have the power of transferring carbon to the hardening state; and what evidence there is indicates that it has this power to but a slight extent if at all.

(1.) If compression causes the passage of carbon into the hardening state and thus hardens steel, it must be

[a] Thurston: Materials of Engineering, III., p. 485.

[b] See my experiment described in § 54, I., A.

[c] Trans. Inst. Mechanical Engineers, 1881, p. 700; Engineering, 1881, p. 646.

[d] Journal of the Iron and Steel Institute, 1879, II., pp. 504-521.

compression at a rather high temperature, for no appreciable hardening is produced, no matter how suddenly the steel is cooled, unless the quenching temperature be above a certain limit, which we may provisionally call 500° C. Now if the exterior were compressed at a temperature sensibly above 500° it would be so plastic as to bulge or buckle: no trace of buckling has ever been observed, so far as I am aware, yet the exterior hardens more than any other portion.

(2.) Many cases suggest themselves in which no compression can occur, yet in which steel is hardened. A steel cylinder, around which a fine steel wire is so tightly stretched as to be in extreme tension, is heated and quenched. The wire, as it cools so much faster than the cylinder, must remain in tension at least as long as it is above 500°. Doubtless it would still be hardened. Its inner particles are doubtless compressed by the resistance of the cylinder to its contraction: nevertheless its net condition is tension: the tension to which it is exposed vastly outweighs the compression. (3.) The exterior of a steel bar during sudden cooling undergoes tension at a high temperature, followed by compression at a lower one: the interior undergoes compression at a high temperature followed by tension at a low one. Yet both interior and exterior are rendered harder. Are we asked to believe that both sets of conditions force carbon into the hardening state? (4.) If we suppose that it is compression at some critical temperature which forces carbon into the hardening state, then it is clear that in a bar of certain proportions there must be a region which at the critical temperature will be neither in compression nor tension: such a region would not on this theory be hardened: actually every portion is. (5.) The difference between the rates of cooling and contraction of adjacent layers during sudden cooling would be greater, and consequently the pressure would be greater, in thick than in thin bars: on Åkerman's theory the thick bar should be rendered harder than the thin one, while actually the reverse is true, which accords with the *status quo* explanation, since the thin bar must cool faster than the thick one, and hence more perfectly preserve the chemical condition which existed at redness.

So much for its competence to explain the phenomena. Now for the evidence that compression forces carbon into the hardening state.

1. Caron found that hot iron hammered on an anvil covered with charcoal powder became far more steely on its face than if simply heated in contact with charcoal. Since (1), the hammering may have promoted the absorption of carbon by bringing the charcoal into more intimate contact with the iron and not by pressure as such, and since (2) if we admit that pressure does favor the absorption of carbon, it does not follow that it favors the passage of previously combined carbon into the hardening state, I attach little weight to this.

2. CARON[a] found in blister steel in the state in which it came from the cementing furnace somewhat less hardening carbon than when hammered; when rolled it had an intermediate amount, and when hardened very much more. This is inferred from the quantities of (cement) carbon insoluble in dilute acid which he found, which were:

In unforged blister steel	1·624
" the same hammered	1·243
" the same hardened	0·240

[a] Comptes Rendus, LVI., p. 45.

It is inferred that the pressure of hammering determined the passage of carbon into the hardening state. It appears much more probable that the slight excess of hardening carbon in the hammered over that in the unhammered and probably pretty well annealed blister steel is due to the comparatively rapid cooling which the hammered steel underwent because of its reduced cross-section, and because of its contact with the cold faces of hammer and anvil.[b]

Against this inconclusive evidence we have the greater hardness of outside than inside, and of small than of thick bars when quenched—*i. e.*, the most thorough hardening where we have least compression: and further, the fact that cold-forging does not transfer carbon to the hardening state. Thus Abel,[c] examining discs of the same steel, some hardened, some annealed, and some cold-rolled without subsequent treatment, found the carbon unattacked by chromic acid solution (cement carbon) as follows:

	Carbon unattacked by chromic solution.	
	Per 100 of steel.	Per 100 of total carbon present.
In the cold-rolled steel	1·039%	94 %
In the annealed steel	0·830%	97 %
In the hardened steel	0·178%	17 ± %

To show that quenching works by compression, Åkerman adduces the resemblance of the effects of quenching to those of hot-forging in removing the courseness of structure of burnt iron and the brittleness consequent to it, and to those of cold-forging, in raising tensile strength and elastic limit, in lowering ductility and in giving fine structure. I find it easier to ascribe these resemblances not to compression alone, nor, indeed, chiefly, but also to the other features which these operations have in common, kneading action, interstratal motion and residual stress.

§ 57. RAPIDITY OF COOLING EFFECTED BY DIFFERENT MEDIA.—In general, the greater the specific gravity, specific heat, mobility, latent heat of gasification, coefficient of expansion and thermal conductivity, and the lower the boiling point and the initial temperature of the cooling medium, the more suddenly will the immersed metal cool. Mercury cools steel extremely rapidly because it is extremely heavy (*i. e.*, the surface of the steel is exposed to a great mass of it) and decidedly mobile: water cools it rapidly because, while very mobile, it has high specific heat and latent heat of gasification and low boiling point. Oil cools steel slowly because it is comparatively light and viscid, and has low specific heat and high boiling point. A low boiling point favors rapid cooling, for, as a liquid cannot rise above its boiling point, if this be low it always remains cool. If water contains soap, or is covered with an oil film, it cools steel less energetically, the soap, we may surmise, temporarily forming a coating on the steel as the

[b] Osmond's observations, published since Akerman's paper, might at first be thought to accord with Akerman's view (see § 14). He found that iron and steel, when cold-forged, just as when hardened by quenching, evolved when dissolved more heat than the same steel after annealing: whence it might be inferred that cold-forging produced the same chemical results as quenching. It is however on further examination very improbable, I think, that the similar behavior of cold-forged and quenched steel is due to similar condition of carbon. For we find that cold-forging increases the evolution of heat from steel with only 0·17% carbon as much as it does that of steel with 0·54%, and nearly as much as when the carbon is 1·17%; and quenching too affects the heat evolution of steel but slightly more when 1·17% carbon is present than when there is but 0·54%. Now if the increased evolution of heat on dissolving cold-forged steel were due to a change in the condition of carbon caused by cold-forging, then the increase should be thrice as great with 0·54% carbon as when only 0·17% carbon is present.

[c] Trans. Institution Mechanical Engineers, 1881, p. 708.

water which had dissolved it is gasified, the oil perhaps adhering to the steel as a thin film when it is immersed.

The rapidity with which water cools steel is lessened by the formation of a layer of steam between it and the steel, which has low conductivity, specific heat and specific gravity. Hence Jarolimek suggested that steel be dipped slowly, so that the steam, forming only near the surface, may escape readily, and so that the steel, once it enters the water, may cool the quicker. For hardening certain pieces, he advises a spray of water, through the interstices between whose drops the steam may readily escape. These methods appear to be of limited application and value; they have not come into extended use, at least in this country. He further advises hardening in a stream of water, which hastens cooling not only by exposing fresh surfaces of water to the metal but also by dragging away the steam.[d]

CHAPTER III.

IRON AND SILICON.

§ 60. SUMMARY.—Silicon alloys with iron in all ratios, at least up to 30%, being readily reduced from silica by carbon in the presence of iron. It rarely, if ever, exists in iron in the graphitoidal state. It diminishes the power of iron to combine with carbon, not only when molten (thus diminishing the total carbon content), but more especially at a white heat, thus favoring the formation of graphite during slow cooling. (See § 18.) It increases the fusibility and fluidity of iron: it lessens the formation of blowholes: by reducing iron oxide it apparently removes one cause of redshortness: it hinders at high temperatures the oxidation of iron and probably of the elements combined with it. Its effect on the welding power of steel is in dispute. If like carbon it confers the power of hardening on sudden cooling it is to an unimportant extent. It is thought by the majority to increase tensile strength slightly, and to render steel brittle and redshort: but it very often does not have this effect. Silicon steels with 1 to 2, or even 2·5 silicon, sometimes excellent for cutting hard steel, have been made.

§ 61. ABSORPTION OF SILICON.—Iron absorbs silicon greedily, uniting with it in all proportions at least up to 30%, and apparently the more readily the higher the temperature, absorbing it even at a red heat when imbedded in sand[a] and charcoal. Ferro-silicons of the following compositions have been made:

No.	% Silicon.	Made by	Obtained by heating together.
1	30·8	Hahn.	Ferrous chloride, salt, sodium and silico-fluoride of sodium.
2	21·71	E. Riley.	Iron oxide, quartz, charcoal in excess; steel-melting heat, 48 hours.
3	20·17	Hahn.	Ferrous chloride, salt, silicon, sodium, and fluorite.
4	18·77	Percy.	Sulphide of iron, silica, and charcoal.
5	18·	E. Riley.	Silicate of iron with charcoal: steel-melting heat, 48 hours.

1. Hahn, Ann. Chem. Pharm. CXXIX., 1864. Exposed 2 hours to nickel-melting heat: light bronze to gray; extraordinarily brittle; fracture homogeneous, non-crystalline; feebly attracted by magnet; Sp. Gr. 6·269. 2. E. Riley, Journ. Chem. Soc., 1872, XXV., p. 562. 3. Hahn, loc. cit.: completely fused after 2½ hours exposure to the strongest heat; extremely brittle. 4. Percy, Iron and Steel, p. 88: hard and brittle. 5. E. Riley, loc. cit.

Though silica can neither be reduced by iron[b] alone nor by carbon alone, it is readily reduced by carbon if iron be present to alloy with the resulting silicon, which, under these conditions, is readily reduced even from the walls of clay and graphite crucibles, from acid slags, and even from basic ones if the temperature be excessively high. (Carbon also reduces silica in presence of copper or silver.) Nor is the presence of free carbon necessary, for the carbon initially contained in iron reduces silicon[c] from the walls of clay and still more readily from those of graphite crucibles,[e] the graphite of the latter doubtless contributing towards the reducing action. The manganese of manganiferous irons also seems to reduce silicon[f] from the walls of crucibles and even from those of cupola furnaces,[e] with oxidation and scorification of the manganese. (Cf. § 268 D.)

Caron[g] melted cast-iron containing 0·99% silicon in crucibles, (A) alone and (B) with 6% metallic manganese. Melted alone its silicon fell to 0·88, and on a second fusion to 0·80. Melted with 6% manganese the silicon rose to 1·3% and on a second fusion without further addition to 1·66%, with heavy loss of manganese. (See § 81.)

So readily is silicon reduced in presence of iron, that Troost and Hautefeuille,[h] melting cast-steel containing ·10% silicon and 1·54% carbon in a siliceous crucible, found that, after two hours fusion, it contained ·80% silicon and only ·70% carbon. They also found that fused cast-iron in prolonged contact with porcelain lost carbon and gained silicon, till the latter metalloid in some cases reached 8%. Müller,[i] melting white cast-iron in a graphite crucible raised its silicon from ·07 to 1·07%, and its carbon from 3·59 to 3·64% while its manganese fell from 2·04 to 1·86%.

§ 62. REMOVAL OF SILICON.—Silicon may be oxidized, according to Caron, by both carbonic acid and carbonic oxide: it is removed from molten iron very rapidly by atmospheric air and by simple contact with iron oxide, magnesia, and other bases.

The oxidation of silicon in presence of carbon and manganese will be specially considered later.

For every temperature and set of conditions a certain balance between the oxidized and unoxidized silicon and carbon corresponds to equilibrium: if the oxygen be not distributed according to this balance, it will redistribute itself till the balance is approached, provided the temperature be high enough to permit a transfer. (1) The higher the temperature, (2) the more oxidized and the less unoxidized silicon be present, (3) the less oxidized and the more unoxidized carbon be present, the more completely will oxygen combine with carbon in preference to silicon: the opposite conditions favor the union of oxygen with silicon rather than with carbon. The presence of bases strengthens, that of metallic iron weakens the affinity of silicon for oxygen. At temperatures even as low as the

a Karsten, Eisenhüttenkunde, I., p. 477; Eng. and Mining Jl., 1875, I., p. 287.
b Percy: Iron and Steel, p. 91.
c Comptes Rendus, LXXVI., p. 183: Journ. Iron and St. Inst., 1885, I., pp. 290, 295.
d Metallurgical Review, I., p. 153.
e Eng. and Mining Jl., 1888, II., p. 367.
f Ledebur: Handbuch, p. 241; Percy: Iron and Steel, p. 139.
g Comptes Rendus, 56, p. 828.
h Comptes Rendus, LXXVI., 1873, p. 483.
i Stahl und Eisen, 1885, V., p. 181: Journ. Iron and St. Inst., 1885, I., p. 294.

melting point of steel with 1·7% carbon (say 1600° C.), carbon may deoxidize silicon: at the highest temperature of the Bessemer process, the affinity of carbon for oxygen greatly outweighs that of silicon.

§ 63. THE CONDITION OF SILICON IN IRON.—Silicon, like carbon and boron, exists in three states, viz., amorphous, graphitoidal and diamond-like. It behaves towards aluminium and zinc as carbon does towards cast-iron, dissolving in these metals when melted, and separating out in a crystalline form when they solidify. It was formerly thought that silicon frequently occurred in the graphitoidal state in iron: but recent investigations show that it rarely, if ever, does so under ordinary conditions. It is true that Percy, whose observations led him to believe that silicon separates graphitically during the slow cooling of gray iron, thought that he found unmistakable evidence of the existence of separated silicon[a] in kish, *i. e.*, the graphitic mass which separates from cast-iron supersaturated with carbon. Sorby,[b] with a very high-power microscope, finds beautiful triangles, rhombs and crosses in cast-iron, sometimes ruby-red, sometimes dark, which he believes are separated silicon: but no reasons are given to support this view. Richter[c] thought that he had found silicon in defined crystals in cast-iron: Henry[c] thought he had found it in crystals in the graphite of cast-iron: Blair[d] asserts that kish is quite as frequently graphitoidal silicon as graphite, without, however, adducing evidence. In brief, I cannot find that graphitoidal silicon has ever been unmistakably identified in iron.

Now Snelus, Jordan, Morton, and Turner have vainly sought it, nor did Abel find it during a prolonged examination of cast-irons. Were it frequently present it would hardly have been missed by all these investigators, though we cannot infer that it may not form under exceptionally favorable conditions. But as iron has the power of combining with much more silicon (30%) than cast-iron proper ever contains, the separation of graphitoidal silicon would be most surprising. The reason why graphite separates so readily from cast-iron is that iron, when manganese is absent, is only able to unite chemically with a small quantity of carbon.[e]

The occurrence of crusts and druses of silica[f] and of silicates on the exterior and in the vugs of cast-iron and in the hearths of blast-furnaces is not, as has frequently been supposed, *prima facie* evidence of the extrusion and subsequent oxidation of graphitoidal silicon, since the silicon may have escaped from the iron in combination with some other element and have become subsequently oxidized. Passing by siliciuretted hydrogen and chloride and fluoride of silicon, all volatile and possible though improbable causes of the siliceous druses, sulphide of silicon (SiS_2) may be considered as a not unlikely cause. According to Frémy[g] and Ledebur it is formed by the reaction of sulphur, carbon and silica, at a white heat, or by passing bisulphide of carbon over a mixture of carbon and silica. It is volatile at a high temperature, and in moist air is rapidly oxidized to silica, with formation of sulphuretted hydrogen. Colson[h] finds two volatile compounds of silicon, SiS and SiSO, formed by passing bisulphide of carbon over silicon at a high temperature. Sulphide and silicide of iron may not, however, directly react upon each other, since Percy[i] on melting them together obtained two distinct and almost unaltered layers. Crusts of silicates (not silica) are probably, in my opinion, often due to the liquation of silicides from the solidifying cast-iron and their subsequent oxidation.

Silica and silicates mechanically intermixed and arising from the oxidation of silicon previously combined with iron often exist in ingot metal: readily mistaken for silicon, their effects have been attributed to it. Pourcel,[j] volatilizing the iron in certain steel castings with chlorine, obtains "a network of silicate of iron preserving the original form of the pieces." A cloud of siliceous dust escaped when steel, prepared by Turner by adding ferro-silicon to unrecarburized basic Bessemer steel, was broken in the testing machine: its fracture revealed many small pipes partly filled with a whitish siliceous powder: dissolved in acids it yielded white flakes of silica unlike the ordinary gelatinous variety.[k]

§ 64. EFFECT OF SILICON ON TENSILE STRENGTH AND DUCTILITY.—It is generally thought to increase tensile strength,[l] though slightly: the prevalent views as to its effects on ductility, usually ill-founded, differ widely. Probably a large majority of metallurgists think that it diminishes ductility, especially under shock, and far more for given increase of tensile strength than carbon does,[m] and that its effect is the stronger the more carbon is present. Interested patentees have proclaimed that even ·02% of silicon seriously affects ductility, and have deceived many of narrow experience. Others think that up to ·5 or even ·7% it increases tensile strength without at all diminishing ductility[n] and is highly beneficial. Many insist that it makes steel very redshort, many that it can only be tolerated when accompanied by much manganese: both views are contradicted by others.

§ 65. DETAILED EVIDENCE AS TO THE EFFECTS OF SILICON ON DUCTILITY AND FORGEABLENESS.—I here offer examples of siliceous steels which are ductile and non-red-

---

[a] Percy: Iron and Steel, pp. 131, 511.

[b] Journ. Iron and St. Inst., 1886, I., p. 114.

[c] Idem., 1871, p. 36.

[d] Idem, 1886, I., p. 82.

[e] Snelus, sifting the finer from the coarser portions of the borings of graphitic cast-iron, found a larger proportion of the friable graphite in the fine than in the coarse portions, but no similar concentration of silicon occurred, whence he inferred that it was all chemically combined. (Journ. Iron and St. Inst., 1871, p. 31.) Turner and Jordan (Idem, 1886, I., p. 172) vainly sought silicon in the residue from dissolving siliceous cast iron, nor were they able to separate it from comminuted cast iron with the magnet. Morton (Idem, 1874, I., p. 102) examined No. 1 Bessemer and white iron, each with nearly 5% silicon, by several apparently decisive chemical methods, but was unable to detect free silicon, though he specially sought it.

[f] Journ. Iron and St. Inst., 1886, I., pp. 82, 97, 98: 1871, I., p. 14: Trans. Am. Inst. Mining Engineers XII., p. 612: Percy op. cit. p. 507.

[g] Comptes Rendus, 1852: Ledebur, Handbuch, p. 248.

[h] Comptes Rendus, Vol. 94, p. 1526: Ledebur loc. cit.

[i] Iron and Steel, p. 95.

[j] Journ. Iron and St. Inst., 1877, I., p. 44.

[k] Journ. Chem. Soc., 1887, p. 142.

[l] Deshayes (Private communication, April 13, 1887, and Classement et emploi des aciers) considers that ·01% silicon raises the tensile strength by 142· pounds per square inch.

[m] Snelus (Journ. Iron and St. Inst., 1871, I., p. 24) says that about ·1% silicon makes Bessemer steel hard and brittle when cold; in "Chemistry Applied to the Arts and Manufactures," he says that it makes steel both redshort and coldshort especially if carbon be present, so that while ·3% silicon may not make steel particularly brittle when less than ·1% carbon is present, yet with ·4 to ·5% carbon even ·2% silicon produces decided redshortness and coldshortness, and ·5% would be dangerous. Hackney (Inst. Civ. Engrs., XLII., p. 35) considers that for given increase of hardness silicon increases brittleness so much more than carbon that more than ·1 or ·2% is unsafe in rail steel. Akerman (Journ. Iron and St. Inst., 1878, II., p. 379) considers the belief that silicon diminishes resistance to shock completely confirmed. Deshayes believes that ·01% silicon diminishes the elongation in 3·9 inches by ·0[illegible].

[n] Müller: Journ. Iron and St. Inst., 188[illegible], I., p. 374.

short (A to G): results of statistical examinations, indicating that silicon does not affect ductility (H to J): facts implying that it does (K to M): an attempt to reconcile them (N to Q): and a résumé (R).

(A) SILICON STEEL.—In Table 19, § 66, good steels with from ·54 to 2·07 and even 7·4% silicon are quoted: at many points within these limits, then, silicon is not incompatible with good quality.

(B) CRUCIBLE STEEL will be admitted to be excellent steel, certainly better than ordinary Bessemer and open-hearth steel and ordinarily more ductile for given tensile strength: yet it generally contains far more silicon than they do. Taking 35 examples of tool steel, tested by D. Smith,[a] we find the silicon between ·07 and 1·28, and in many cases above ·20%. Arranging them in the order of merit for cutting tools the percentages of silicon are as follows: Best ·17 and 1·28; ·14 and ·19; ·29; ·10 and ·13; ·31; ·21 and ·23; ·37; ·20; ·09; ·10; ·19; ·14; ·10 and ·25; ·27; ·07 and ·11—worst. This should finally dispose of the notion that silicon is only tolerable when carbon is very low, since none of these steels have less than 0·70%, and most of them have over 1% carbon.

(C) STEEL CASTINGS, when annealed, considering their disadvantage in not having been forged, compare very favorably with forgings in tensile strength and ductility; yet their silicon is much higher than that of ordinary forgings, running usually from 0·20 to 0·55, or even 0·6%, and that, too, with carbon as high as ·96% (see Table 9). It is often said that silicon may do for castings, but certainly not for forgings: and that, moreover, we cannot usually anneal forgings, while these castings have to be annealed to give them toughness. The annealing is needed not to counteract the effects of silicon, but those of irregular contraction and coarse structure: and the proof of this is that if we forge one of these castings it remains tough, even without annealing. (See Table 17 A.)

(D) EXAMPLES OF GOOD SILICEOUS STEELS are given in Table 17, all sufficiently forgeable to be rolled into rails, sufficiently tough to endure in the track in some cases remarkably well, in all at least well enough to escape attention, and how much better we know not.

Did silicon always increase brittleness and redshortness as much as it is thought to, neither 12 nor 18 (with but ·22 manganese to counteract redshortness) could have been rolled, and they and others would have broken under the straightening press. You who hold that high silicon is only permissible with certain percentages of certain other elements, mark well how in Tables 17 and 19 the carbon is now high, now low, now nil; and how, be it high or low, it is now joined to high, now to low manganese: mark too No. 12, with high silicon carbon and phosphorus.

TABLE 17.—SILICIFEROUS RAILS OF AT LEAST TOLERABLE QUALITY.

	1	2	3	4	5	6	7	8	9	12	13	16	17	18
	f	a	a	f	f	f	f	f	f	f	f	c	d	e
Carbon	·30	·41	·16	·24	·29	·23	·17	·52	·10	·45	....	·36	·48	under ·30
Silicon	·62	·84	·55	·32	·81	·79	·84	·97	·59	·76	·85	·47	·45	·53
Sulphur	·025	·08	·01	·02	·06	·06	·02	·05	·02	·06	·19	....	....	·01
Phosphorus	·033	·11	·056	·09	·16	·13	·08	·11	·06	·15	·10	·19	·08	·07
Manganese	1·50	1·48	1·85	·73	·76	·91	1·14	2·06	1·84	·75	1·61	·57	·78	·23

a = redshort. c = extraordinarily good rail, R. W. Hunt, Trans. Am. Inst. Mining Engineers, IX., p. 536. d = tough good rail, Dudley, idem, p. 341. e = very tough rail, Sachs, Journ. Iron and St. Inst., 1882, II., p. 583. f = private notes.

MÜLLER[b] states that at one German works the composition of steel rails lay for over three years between the following limits:

Carbon.	Silicon.	Manganese.	Phosphorus.	Sulphur.	Copper.
0·10 to 0·15	0·3 to 0·6	0·8 to 1·0	0·12 to 0·15	·03	·05

He quotes the mechanical properties of 64 excellent rails, whose composition apparently lies between the limits just given as follows:

40	Had tensile strength from	71,111 to 78,225	Lbs. per sq. in.	8 had from 34·4 to 40	% contraction of area.
9		78,225 " 85,337		20 " " 40· " 50	
15		85,337 " 92,183		27 " " 50· " 60	
				14 " " 60· " 69	

He quotes steel with carbon 0·14, silicon 0·435, manganese 0·828, and phosphorus 0·15, which combines 100,000 pounds tensile strength with 24% elongation. Such ductility in steel with 0·15 phosphorus is rather surprising: hence if silicon has affected its ductility at all it has probably increased it.

Table 18 gives many siliceous steels which combine high tensile strength and ductility.

(E) SPECIAL EXPERIENCE.—The open-hearth steel, justly famed for its excellence, made at an eastern U. S. mill, is often decidedly siliceous, the spring grade usually containing from ·10 to ·30% silicon. Indeed, certain customers, on receiving steel with less than the usual percentage of silicon, complain of brittleness, though ignorant of its composition.

(F) GUN STEEL, surely, for given tensile strength, should have the highest attainable resistance to shock: yet it is often purposely siliceous (Table 19). The decision of the Swedish ordnance commission, apparently reached after thorough study, that gun-barrel steel should have ·25 to ·40% silicon is of weight.[c]

TABLE 17A.—SILICIFEROUS GUN STEELS.

No.	Carbon.	Silicon.	Manganese.	Phosphorus.	Sulphur	Copper.	Tensile strength, Lbs. per sq. in.	Elastic limit, Lbs. per sq. in.	Elongation.	Reduction of area.
1	·72	·23	·53	·11	·02	......	98,000	42,668	15·7	43·3
2	·47	·44	·41	·08	·04	......	96,759	36,000	18·8	44·7
3	·45	·85	·54	·61	tr	......	83,000	32,713	27·	51·
4	·40	·32	·61	·04	·02	......	88,800	56,000	22·	50·2
5	·35@·45	·25@·40	·4@·6	·06 or less	......	......	......	......	......	......
6	·60	·19	·18	tr	......	·27	......	......	......	......

1. Gun barrels for Russian army, forged. 2. Gun barrels for Swedish Government, from Witten-upon-Ruhr: considered admirable. 3 and 4. Bofors open-hearth steel for guns. 5. Composition considered best suited for gun barrels by Swedish Ordnance Commission. The preceding from Gautier, Journal Iron and Steel Inst., 1881, II., p. 452. 6. Krupp gun steel, Kern, Metallurgical Review, II., p. 519.

(G) MRAZEK concluded that the redshortness attributed to silicate was due to silicate mixed with the iron: he found that metallic silicon added in certain proportions to iron did not alter its properties (in any respect?).[d]

(H) RAYMOND,[e] analyzing by the method of least squares Dudley's data of the composition and wearing power of 64 rails, finds that silicon increases the wearing power, thus having an effect opposite to that of carbon and phosphorus.

(I) P. G. SALOM, analyzing Dudley's data by the same method, finds that phosphorus and carbon greatly diminish elongation while increasing tensile strength, but that silicon increases both tensile strength and ductility.

(J) STATISTICAL EXAMINATION.—The results of an analysis of 354 sets of observations of tensile strength and ductility, drawn from many sources with no selection beyond the rejection of tungsten and chrome steels, are

[a] Thurston: Materials of Engineering, II., pp. 434-6.
[b] Glaser's Annalen, X., Nos. 9 and 10. Journ. Iron and St. Inst., 1882, I, p. 374.
[c] Journ. Iron and St. Inst., 1881, II., p. 459.
[d] Gautier: Journ. Iron and St. Inst., 1877, I., p. 43.
[e] Trans. Am. Inst. Mining Engineers, IX., p. 607.

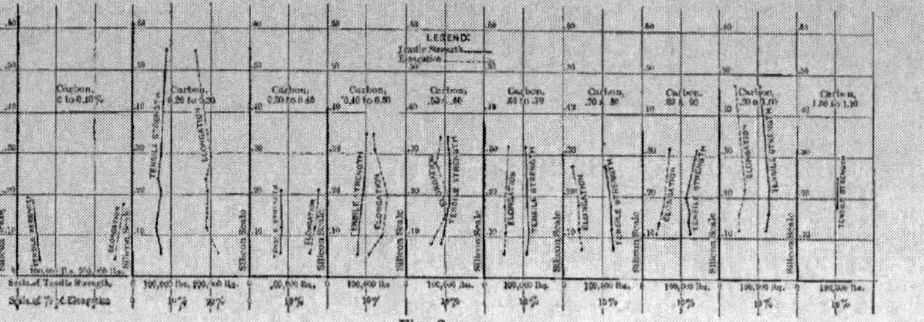

Fig. 6.

TABLE 18.—EFFECT OF SILICON ON TENSILE STRENGTH AND ELONGATION.

Carbon.	Si 0·00@0·05 No. of cases.	Tensile strength	Elongation.	Si 0·05@0·10 No. of cases.	Tensile strength	Elongation.	Si ·10@·15 No. of cases.	Tensile strength	Elongation.	Si ·15@·20 No. of cases.	Tensile strength	Elongation.	Si ·20@·30 No. of cases.	Tensile strength	Elongation
0@·10	22	59,181	27·	...	...	...	1	51,000	...	2	46,000	29·	1	55,000	25·
·10@·20	11	66,626	26·							...	...	...	5	74,000	24·4
·20@·30	11	70,000	23·	5	60,800	21·	2	80,000	17·	2	60,900	16·	7	67,000	21·
·30@·40	83	73,000	16·5	14	84,000	15·6	3	86,800	19·2	...	...	...	5	83,400	19·2
·40@·50	12	81,600	6·6	9	83,900	15·3	1	71,000	29·	2	97,500	18·	3	101,300	12·3
·50@·60	4	88,500	3·	...	...	...	1	83,000	20·	2	114,800	6·7	1	130,000	14·
·60@·70	6	100,400	4·	11	117,400	6·7	8	121,500	6·3	5	115,500	5·6	5	100,000	8·
·70@·80	9	126,000	4·4	29	124,400	4·3	14	130,200	4·8	14	125,600	8·9	9	131,300	3·4
·80@·90	1	142,000	3·	3	118,700	4·5	7	128,000	5·	8	120,900	5·0	2	139,000	8·
·90@1·00	1	184,000	2·	3	127,800	3	...	...	...	4	136,200	7·2	2	130,000	5·
1·00@1·10	..	...	...	...	...	...	2	99,000	..	1	123,000	8·	2	96,500	...
1·10@1·20	..	...	...	1	95,000	...	1	100,000	...	1	106,000	...	2	127,500	3·5
1·20@1·30	..	...	...	...	...	...	...	...	...	...	...	...	...	...	...
1·30@1·40	..	...	...	1	92,000	...	.	...	...	...	...	...	1	135,000	7·
1·40@1·50	..	...	...	1	92,000	...	..	...	...	...	...	...	...	...	..

Carbon.	Si ·30@·40 No. of cases.	Tensile strength	Elongation.	Si ·40@·50 No. of cases.	Tensile strength	Elongation.	Si ·50@·60 No. of cases.	Tensile strength	Elongation.	Si ·60@·70 No. of cases.	Tensile strength	Elongation.	Si ·70@·80 No. of cases.	Tensile strength	Elongation.
0@·10	...	...	...	...	...	...	...	...	...	...	...	...	...	...	...
·10@·20	..	...	...	4	83,700	15·5	...	...	...	...	...	...	...	...	...
·20@·30	1	70,000	8·	...	...	...	1	87,000	21·	...	...	...	1	110,000	10·
·30@·40	2	75,000	13·5	...	...	...	..	...	...	..	...	...	.	...	...
·40@·50	11	102,000	11·3	8	98,700	16	..	...	...	...	...	...	...	...	...
·50@·60	4	107,000	8·2	1	104,000	10·	..	...	...	...	...	...	...	...	...
·60@·70	...	...	...	...	...	...	2	107,500	7·	...	...	...	...	...	...
·70@·80	...	...	...	3	79,000	1·8	..	...	...	..	...	...	...	...	...
·80@·90	1	140,000	12·	1	147,000	6	...	...	...	...	...	...	...	...	...
·90@1·00	1	140,000	10·	...	...	...	...	...	...	3	81,000	1·1	...	...	...
1·00@1·10	1	114,000	...	...	...	...	...	...	...	...	...	...	...	...	...
1·10@1·20	...	...	...	...	...	...	...	...	...	...	...	...	...	...	...
1·20@1·30	1	113,000	...	...	...	...	...	...	...	...	...	...	...	...	...
1·30@1·40	...	...	...	...	...	...	...	...	...	...	...	...	...	...	...
1·40@1·50	...	...	...	...	...	...	...	...	...	...	...	...	...	...	...

given in Table 18, and graphically in Fig. 6,[a] with silicon as ordinate, tensile strength and elongation as abscissæ. I first divide the cases into groups of nearly constant carbon, each of which has a separate diagram: and these again into sub-groups of nearly constant silicon. Each curve in Fig. 6 and each horizontal line in Table 18 represent one primary group with (nearly) constant carbon but varying silicon: each spot on the curves and each number in the table represent one sub-group with carbon and silicon both nearly constant.

This method, while not quantitatively accurate, would, when applied to so many cases whose silicon varies so widely, reveal the effects of silicon qualitatively, were they weighty, constant and cumulative, just as it unmistakably reveals those of carbon. Passing in any line from left to right tensile strength rises almost uninterruptedly till carbon passes 1·00, when it declines: elongation falls almost continuously.[b] But no constant effect can be traced to silicon: passing down some columns tensile strength rises and elongation falls, both slightly: but in as many the reverse occurs. The curves too, generally nearly vertical, turn as often to left as right.

This result indicates, not that silicon never injures ductility but that, if it does, it also promotes it as often and as much. An analysis of more extended data is desirable.

[a] The curves are derived by plotting a curve for each column of Table 18, attaching to each spot a weight proportional to the number of cases it represents, finding the center of gravity of each group of three consecutive spots (1st, 2d, 3d, then 2d, 3d, 4th, etc.), and drawing new curves through these centers of gravity.

Slight discrepancies exist between the curves for carbon ·70 to ·80 and ·60 to ·70, and the corresponding numbers in Table 18, due to my incorporating additional matter into the table after these curves had been engraved.

[b] This method of analysis applied to steels with varying phosphorus reveals the effects of this element on ductility very clearly (Table 27 and Fig. 8, § 123).

Now for the evidence that silicon makes iron brittle and redshort.

(K) FOR HOLLEY'S[c] conclusion, that silicon injures wrought-iron, I find little warrant in his data, the results obtained by the U. S. Board for Testing Metals. True, the worst of his irons has the highest silicon, but then it also has almost the highest phosphorus: he has several excellent irons with high silicon, which is therefore compatible with excellence. Arranged in order of elongation their silicon percentages are—Greatest elongation, 0·10: ·07: ·14: ·17: ·16: ·16: ·20: ·11: ·16: ·14: ·15: ·16: ·27—lowest elongation.

(L) TURNER'S EXPERIMENTS[d] do not in my opinion justify his conclusions that silicon increases redshortness and tensile strength but diminishes static ductility. Adding varying quantities of ferro-silicon to apparently different lots of unrecarburized basic Bessemer steel, he obtained steels with from ·009 to ·4% silicon, almost free from other elements, and in certain cases very redshort. In view of our almost complete ignorance of the composition of the redshort ones, and of the facts that some of them received less ferro-silicon than some of the non-redshort ones, and that much larger percentages of silicon do not, in normal manufacture, cause redshortness, the observed variations in redshortness are more naturally ascribed to variations in the percentage of oxygen in the unrecarburized steel than to variations in the silicon of the recarburized metal. Further, the non-coalescing, non-rising silicates which, thanks to the almost total lack of manganese, should and apparently did form, are more probable

[c] Trans. Am. Inst. Mining Engineers, VI., p. 101.

[d] Journ. Chem. Soc., 1887, p. 129.

causes of redshortness than is silicon." His testing machine results, if more numerous, might indicate that silicon raises tensile strength: but they are too scanty and discordant[b] to even faintly suggest that it lowers static ductility.

(M) THE PREVALENT BELIEF of Anglo-Saxon steel makers, voiced by Snelus who says "all steel makers are aware that if the silicon rises to over ·2% the carbon must be kept down to about ·35%, or the rail will ordinarily be brittle"[c] cannot be so easily dismissed: yet, as it is at least largely based not on systematic but casual observation, it may prove a superstition.

Now to reconcile this belief with the facts I have detailed.

(N) SILICON A CONCOMITANT, NOT A CAUSE OF BRITTLENESS AND REDSHORTNESS.—Forsyth (I know no more competent observer), informs me that in the Bessemer process a considerable percentage of silicon introduced with the recarburizing additions affects the ductility and forgeableness of the steel but slightly, while the same percentage of silicon if residual, *i. e.* if remaining in the blown steel from that initially in the cast-iron, would be fatal. This indicates that the residual silicon does not cause the brittleness, but that both spring from a common source: this may be the high temperature which almost necessarily accompanies high residual silicon. Many steel makers report that ingots crack in rolling if cast unduly hot, but that if the steel be cooled before casting it rolls soundly, even if unduly hot when blown.

(O) DIRECT AND INDIRECT EFFECTS OF SILICON.—As the indirect effect of silicon in increasing soundness and continuity (§ 67) should increase tensile strength and ductility, and as our statistics indicate that its net effect on these properties is nil, it may be that it directly diminishes them, masking its indirect effect. But that if this be its direct effect it is either not constant and cumulative or slight, is shown by the excellence of many of the siliciferous steels quoted.

(P) SILICA is often mistaken for silicon: who knows how far it is responsible for this metalloid's bad name?

(Q) CHEMICAL CONDITION.—Finally, I suspect that silicon enters into different combinations in steel, some promoting, some injuring ductility and forgeableness. Its passage into one or another of these states may follow, in an obscure and complex way (to be revealed by proximate rather than ultimate analysis), even trivial changes in ultimate composition and treatment.

RÉSUMÉ.—We have on the one hand the widespread dread of silicon among the most competent judges: on the other the belief of many high authorities in its harmlessness, the failure of statistical examination to show that it causes brittleness, and the numberless instances of good and often admirable siliceous steels, the percentages of whose carbon and manganese vary within very wide limits, and apparently without law. Making all reasonable allowance for the discrepancies between static ductility as revealed by the testing machine and the power to resist shock, no doubt can remain that very many highly siliceous steels are in every sense ductile.

[a] That at least some of the steel held silica or silicates is shown by the escape of a cloud of siliceous dust on breaking one piece.

[b] Numbered in order of silicon content, 1 having the least, and arranged in order of elongation, they stand 1 (highest), 3, 6, 8, 5, 2, 4, 7 (lowest). Arranged in order of reduction of area, they stand 1 (highest), 3, 6, 8, 2, 5, 4, 7 (lowest).

[c] Jour. Iron and Steel Inst., 1882, II., p. 584.

Let each one reconcile these facts in his own way. While we can hardly with our present light reach final conclusions, yet, after making all reasonable allowance for the belief that silicon is often considered a cause when it is merely a concomitant of brittleness and redshortness and for its being a scapegoat for the sins of silica, in view of the profound and widespread belief in its hurtfulness, I believe it on the whole probable that it often and under certain conditions causes brittleness, especially under shock, and perhaps also redshortness: but that in many and probably in the great majority of cases it is harmless, and that it may sometimes even increase ductility, be it directly, be it indirectly by promoting soundness and continuity. If only occasionally injurious it could readily acquire a bad name. I regard its influence as dependent on its chemical condition, on which we have no light: it is very probable that it more often injures high- than low-carbon steel, and that the presence of an abundance of manganese counteracts its tendency to cause redshortness.

In brief, the presence of silicon does not prove but suggests brittleness, and calls for unusually rigorous tests.

It probably slightly increases tensile strength, chiefly by increasing the continuity.

TABLE 19.—SILICON STEELS.

	Silicon.	Carbon.	Manganese.	Phosphorus.	Sulphur.	Ductility.		Welding power.	
						Cold.	Hot.		
1	7·4	tr	·0	...	...	Brittle	Good	Perfect	Forges readily at white, with care at red heat.
2	2·44	·4	·83	·08	·06	...	...	...	Tensile strength, 107,500 lbs.; elongation, 8%.
3	2·07	...	...	...	...	Tough	Very good	...	Efficient for cutting tools.
4	2·0	...	...	...	...	Coldshort	Rather poor	...	
5	1·5	·13	·76	...	...	...	Very good	...	Very strong.
6	1·5±	...	...	...	...	...	...	Perfect (?)	
7	1·38	·84	·41	...	...	Good	...	...	Tensile strength, 114,240 lbs.; elastic limit, 82,720 lbs.; elongation, 5%.
8	1·34	1·28	·48	·045	·07	...	...	...	Good; stands all tests usual for good tool steel.
9	1·25	1·20	·01	·005	tr	...	...	...	Best cutting steel tested by U. S. B'd to test metals.
10	1·02	·28	·004	...	...	...	Forges at red	None	
11	·54	·26	0	...	...	Soft and tough	Good	High	

1. Mrazek, Journ. Iron and St. Inst., 1877, I., p. 48: Proc. Inst. Civ. Eng., 1876, XLIV., p. 376. Made by fusing iron wire, sodium, silica, and fluorite in Hessian crucible. Exceedingly brittle cold, hardens slightly on quenching from redness: contains little or no manganese. 2. Snelus, Journ. Chem. Soc., 1887, p. 182. 3. Riley, Idem. 1872, XXV., p. 562: Journ. Iron and St. Inst., 1872, I., pp. 274-7. 4. Hupfeld, coldshort, malleable with difficulty: Journ. Iron and St. Inst., 1882, I., p. 376. 5. Mrazek, Idem, 1877, I., p. 44. 6. Hadfields: Weeks, Trans. Am. Inst. Mining Engrs., XIV., p. 988. 7. Hardisty, Steel for Guns and Projectiles, p. 6. 8. Mushet's "titanium" steel, quite free from titanium. Riley, Journ. Chem. Soc., 1872, XXV., p. 562. 9. Thurston, Mat's. of Engineering, II., p. 486. 10. Mrazek, Proc. Inst. Civ. Eng., 1876, XLIV., p. 316. 11. Idem, soft and tough cold, forges at both red and white, welds easily, though free from manganese.

§ 66. SILICON STEEL, in one case with over 7% silicon, has been made by several metallurgists. It is reported that hard steel with 1 to 2% silicon is or has been made on a commercial scale in Sheffield. Riley[d] reports steel with 2·07% silicon, which endured well when used for turning the skin from cast-steel wheels, a most trying task, forged admirably with particularly sharp edges, and was decidedly tough, as shown by the edge of the tool turning up slightly. Other instances are given in Table 19, of which the most remarkable is Mrazek's with 7·4% silicon, which forged readily and welded perfectly! Silicon steel is said to have an adhesive scale, and a fine or indeed, if the silicon be very high, an earthy fracture.[e]

While it is too early to speak positively, silicon steel does not appear to promise as well as tungsten, chromium and manganese steels, though it may prove advantageous

[d] Journ. Chem. Soc., 1872, XXV., p. 562: Journ. Iron and St. Inst., 1872, I., p. 274-7.

[e] Müller: Journ. Iron and St. Inst., 1882, I., p. 376.

to add silicon to them for certain purposes. For several years iron was puddled in this country with so-called "codorus" or "silicon" ore, which had no other effect than to afford a bulky slag in the puddling furnace. The *venders of the ore impudently called this puddled iron* "silicon steel," though both free from silicon (the average silicon in six samples which I took was, by Wuth's determination, 0·07%) and clearly no more steel than any other puddled iron is. I had the good fortune to investigate this swindling manufacture twice and to expose it to two prominent consumers. Holley sang of it—

"There was an old man of Codôrus, who said he took out the phosphôrus,
So the iron he puddled, and with chemicals muddled,
But the puddling took out the phosphôrus."

§ 67. Effect of Silicon on Soundness.—Silicon promotes soundness in ingots and other castings by restraining the formation of blowholes, and by reducing iron oxide, and it thus indirectly restrains redshortness. Indeed, Sandberg[a] considers that 0·10% silicon is the smallest amount permissible for rolling rails, angles, etc., as with less the steel cracks in rolling, a striking example of how the most experienced may be deceived: for in many American works the silicon in rail steel habitually lies between ·02 and ·03%, yet the proportion of second quality rails does not rise above 3% and is frequently below 1% for months.

Investigating[b] the question of silicon in soft steel I find that in ordinary American Bessemer practice it rarely rises over 0·02%, and is occasionally as low as 0·004 (these extremely small amounts are rarely accurately determined). Yet this steel, practically free from silicon, with only say ·09 to ·12% carbon and with manganese ·30 to ·40% is rolled into plates as thin as No. 12 W. G., in certain cases without edging passes, and without serious cracking. Silicon therefore is not essential to sound rolling. It was formerly thought that silicon prevented blowholes in steel by restraining the formation of carbonic oxide, silicon being oxidized in preference to carbon. But since Müller has shown that blowholes are due to nitrogen and hydrogen, we must infer that silicon acts by increasing the solubility of these gases in the solid steel, so that it is able to retain in solution while solidifying the gas which it had dissolved while molten. Silicon eliminates iron oxide from steel by reducing part of it and itself forming silica which combines with the remainder of the oxide, to form a silicate which escapes by rising to the surface more or less completely according to its condition of aggregation (cf. effects of manganese on soundness).

§ 69. Fusibility.—Silicon appears to increase the fusibility of iron, though, at least when abundantly present, less than the same percentage of carbon does. Thus Mrazek found that iron with 7·4% silicon was intermediate in fusibility between steel of 0·75% carbon and cast-iron of 5% carbon. It is probable that it lowers the melting point of steel also, since the experience of the makers of open-hearth steel (say with silicon 0·15 to 0·40), is that siliciferous steel cannot in forging be safely exposed to so high a temperature as that which has but little silicon, all other conditions being alike. Further investigation may, however, show that this is merely a superstition.

Fluidity.—Silicon is said to give very great fluidity: hence the highly siliciferous Scotch irons are greatly prized for making fine sharp castings, and are used even for the manufacture of elaborate cast-iron jewelry, chains, brooches, etc.[c]

Oxidation.—Silicon appears to indirectly retard the oxidation of iron at high temperatures and of the other elements combined with it. Thus Åkerman[d] points out that in the Bessemer process the more silicon the iron contains the less completely is the oxygen of the air consumed. So too siliciferous cast-irons do not sparkle while running, while if, as in Krupp's process (pig-washing) the cast-iron be almost completely deprived of its silicon, it effervesces in the air as it runs from the furnace with extreme brilliancy, which is perhaps enhanced by the reaction of small suspended particles of iron-oxide on the carbon present.

This effect of silicon is probably an indirect one: when present, by absorbing part of the oxygen to which the iron is exposed, it diminishes *pro tanto* the oxidation of carbon, restraining the formation of carbonic oxide and carbonic acid and the ebullition which their escape causes and which in itself hastens oxidation by increasing the surface exposure. Its influence on the solubility of carbonic oxide in iron may contribute to these phenomena.

§ 70. The welding power of iron and steel does not appear to be lessened more, if indeed as much, by silicon as by carbon. In addition to Mrazek's steel with 7·4% silicon and Hadfield's with over 1·5% silicon, both said to weld perfectly, we have the results obtained by the U. S. Testing Board which, in my opinion, do not indicate that silicon affects the welding power of weld iron. Of 13 irons examined, one with 0·16 silicon (the highest in silicon but 4) welded the second best. On the other hand three of the irons highest in silicon welded worst. Placing them in the order of the excellence of welding their silicon was as follows: Best welding,[e]—0·14: ·16: ·07: ·16: ·14: ·17: ·15: ·16: ·10: ·16: ·20: ·17: ·27—worst welding.

§ 71. Effect of Silicon on Cast-Iron.—Silicon affects the properties of cast-iron in two ways, by forcing carbon out of combination and into the graphitic state, and by its own direct specific effects. The latter may be traced in the changes in the properties of the metal which accompany variations in the percentage of silicon when this element does not reach an amount high enough to affect the condition of the carbon present. Under these conditions Turner's results[f] indicate that silicon makes cast-iron softer, and increases its tensile and crushing strength while lowering its specific gravity. They are as follows:

Sp. gr.	Relative hardness.	Tensile strength. Lbs. per sq. inch.	Modulus of elasticity.	Crushing strength.	Total carbon.	Graphite.	Combined carbon.	Silicon.
7·72	72·	22,720	25,790,000	168,700	1·98	0·38	1·60	0·19
7·67	52·	27,580	28,670,000	204,800	2·00	0·10	1·90	0·45
7·63	42·	28,490	31,180,000	207,300	2·09	0·24	1·85	0·96
7·47	....	31,440	23,500,000	183,900	2·21	0·50	1·71	1·37

As the silicon rises beyond 1·4 the percentage of graphite at first increases rapidly, then falls off slowly: while tensile and compressive strength both decline uninterruptedly. While experience shows that no one set of observations on the effects of foreign elements on iron is conclusive, Turner's results are so harmonious as to inspire confidence.

a Trans. Am. Inst. Mining Engineers, X., p. 469.
b Trans. Am. Inst. Mining Engineers, XV., to appear.
c Abel, Jour. Iron and Steel Inst., 1886, I., p. 197.
d Engineering and Mining Journal, 1875, I., p. 311.
e Trans. Am. Inst. Mining Engineers, VI., p. 116.
f Journ. Iron and St. Inst., 1886, I., p. 174.

CHAPTER IV.

IRON AND MANGANESE.

§ 75. SUMMARY.—Manganese alloys with iron in all ratios, being reduced from its oxides by carbon at a white heat, and the more readily the more metallic iron is present to combine with it. It is easily removed from iron by oxidation, being oxidized even by silica, and partly in this way partly in others it restrains the oxidation of the iron, while sometimes restraining sometimes permitting the oxidation of the other elements combined with it. It is also apparently removed from iron by volatilization. Its presence increases the power of carbon to combine with iron at very high temperatures (say 1400° C.), and restrains its separation as graphite at lower ones. (See carbon.) By preventing ebullition during solidification and the formation of blowholes, by reducing or removing oxide and silicate of iron, by bodily removing sulphur from cast-iron and probably from steel, by counteracting the effects of the sulphur which remains as well as of iron-oxide, phosphorus, copper, silica and silicates, and perhaps in other ways, it prevents hot-shortness, both red and yellow. (It does not however counteract the coldshortness caused by phosphorus.) These effects are so valuable that it is to-day well nigh indispensable, though admirable steel was made before its use was introduced by Josiah Marshall Heath.[a]

It is thought to increase tensile strength slightly, hardness proper, and fluidity, to raise the elastic limit, and, at least when present in considerable quantity, to diminish fusibility. It is generally thought to diminish ductility: evidence will be offered tending to show that its effects in this respect have been exaggerated. While 1·5 to 2·5% of manganese is nearly universally admitted to cause brittleness, steel with 8% of manganese is astonishingly ductile: with further increase of manganese the ductility again diminishes. Steel with 8 to 10% manganese, though extremely tough, is so hard as to be employed without quenching for cutting-tools. It is denied and asserted with equal positiveness that manganese confers the power of becoming harder when suddenly cooled, but it is generally thought to make steel crack when quenched.

OXIDE of manganese gives slags a strong characteristic green color and considerable fluidity, and makes them so strongly corrosive that their effect on the linings of open-hearth, cupola and other melting furnaces must be guarded against.

§ 76. COMBINING POWER.—There appears to be no limit to the extent to which manganese can combine with iron: the higher the percentage of manganese in the alloy the higher is the temperature needed in the blast-furnace for its production. These alloys contain considerable carbon, but are often almost completely free from silicon, of which they sometimes contain but 0·06%. Ferro-manganese containing more than 90% manganese often crumbles to powder in the air.

The analyses of several siliciferous ferro-manganeses are given in Table 1. Most of the compositions in Table 20 are normal.

a Percy: Iron and Steel, p. 840.

§ 77. VOLATILITY.—Manganese appears to volatilize with considerable rapidity at a white heat. Thus Jordan[b] states that at a French blast-furnace 10% of the manganese charged could not be accounted for by the contents of metal, slag and dust. The fumes, white at first, turned red on burning. Much reddish gas escaped from the tap hole. Further, ferromanganese of 84·9% manganese lost 4% of its manganese on being exposed to the heat of a wind furnace for 2½ hours in a brasqued crucible, in which scorification can hardly have occurred.

§ 78. EFFECT ON FUSIBILITY.—A large percentage of manganese, as in ferromanganese, raises the melting point of iron: but smaller percentages may lower it, for a small addition of a less to a more fusible body (*e. g.*, of lead to tin, or silver to lead, or bisilicate of magnesia to that of lime) often produces one more fusible than either.

§ 79. MANGANESE AND BLOWHOLES.—Be it by increasing the solubility of gases in steel, so that it retains while solidifying the gas which it dissolved when molten, be it by preventing the oxidation of carbon and the formation of carbonic oxide, manganese like silicon, though probably less thoroughly, hinders the formation of blowholes. Ingots containing but ·005% of silicon and which but for manganese would be exceedingly porous, are rendered by it comparatively solid.

§ 80. MANGANESE AND OXIDATION.—As the oxidation and deoxidation of manganese in the presence of carbon and silicon will be fully discussed in a later chapter, I here confine myself chiefly to a few generalizations.

While manganese is reduced from its oxides by carbon at a white heat even in the absence of iron, thus revealing an affinity for oxygen weaker than that of silicon: yet, be it because its affinity for iron is weaker than that of silicon, be it because acid slags seize and hold its oxide, when both are combined with iron manganese is often more readily oxidized than silicon, especially in the presence of acid slags, and often causes the reduction of silicon from the walls of cupola furnaces and of crucibles.

Manganese added to molten oxygenated iron removes its oxygen as oxide or silicate of manganese. It not only thus cures but may even prevent oxygenation: in certain cases when added to molten iron it is thought to permit the oxidation of carbon and silicon while preventing that of iron, or at least preventing the redshortness which we attribute to oxygenation. So too the presence of manganese in solidified steel appears to hinder its oxygenation in heating and forging: hence an otherwise needlessly large amount of manganese (say ·5%) is often purposely left in soft steel which is liable to fall into careless hands.

Manganese appears to act upon oxygenated iron in two distinct ways, (1) by reducing iron oxide, (2) by forming a readily separating double silicate of iron and manganese: it may act in both ways simultaneously.

(1) While iron oxide if present in molten steel remains diffused or dissolved through the mass of the metal and renders it redshort, behaving as cuprous oxide does towards metallic copper, silicate and probably oxide of

b Metallurgical Review, II., p. 155. Rev. Indust., July 3, 1878.

TABLE 20.—SPIEGELEISEN AND FERROMANGANESE.

	1.	2.	3.	5.	6.	7.	8.	9.	10.	11.	12.	13.	14.	15.	16.	17.	18.	19.	20.	21.	22.	23.
	B	B	B	A	A	J	F	D1	A	E5	E1	E2	E3	D2	E1	C	E4	G	C	H	C	C
Carbon	4·28	4·38	4·39	4·10	4·01	3·9	4·73	4·55	4·40	5·65	4·91	5·56	5·31	1·85	6·21	6·51	6·94	6·50		6·57		
Silicon	·31	·62	·79	0·23	0·27	·5	·65	·18	0·60	10·90	·99	·06	2·52	·08	0·25	·31	·02	·53	·51	·61a	·51	·51
Phosphorus	·56	·59	·52	·06	·08	·08	·64	·08	·08	·18	·24	trace	·38	·47	·06	·17	·24	·17@·20	·14	·20@·25	·47	·17
Sulphur				·08	·03	trace		·06	·01		·003	trace	trace		trace	·06		0				
Manganese	5·87	6·91	6·12	11·12	12·00	12·3	18·24	13·56	14·11	20·50	28·35	35·48	50·06	55·23	9·64	74·5	76·95	80·00	83·8	86·95	87·2	87·5
Copper				·25	·34			·00	·17													

References.—A, Siegen; Jour. Iron and St. Inst., 1880, II., p. 765. B, unknown, Idem, 1885, I., p. 369. C, unknown, private notes. D1, Terre-Noire, private notes. D2, U. S., Idem. E1, Reschitza. E2, Oberhausen. E3, Hoerde. E4, Kurbert. E5, Terre-Noire, all from Ledebur, Handbuch, p. 317. F, Franklinite, New Jersey, private notes. G, Edgar Thomson steel-works, J. H. Cremer, private communication. H, the same, J. Gayley, private communication. J, Dowlais, Journ. Iron and Steel Inst., 1874, I., p. 78. a In 100 consecutive casts of ferromanganese containing over 80% manganese, the silicon averages 0·131%.

manganese escape from the iron by rising to the surface of the molten mass. Hence, as in the Bessemer and open-hearth processes of making steel the metal under ordinary conditions becomes slightly oxygenated, manganese is usually added at the completion of these processes, in the form of a manganiferous cast-iron (spiegeleisen, ferro-manganese); it reduces the iron oxide and is itself oxidized and scorified. It has been assumed that this reaction between the manganese and iron oxide is expressed accurately by the formula—

$$Fe_3O_4 + Mn = MnO + 3FeO.$$

and *Ford supports this view by showing that, assuming the unrecarburized steel to contain 0·24% oxygen as magnetic oxide, in the practice at the Edgar Thomson Steel Works the amount of manganese, 0·18%, removed from the metal corresponds closely to this formula. But this coincidence is purely accidental. Indeed, from his statement it is not clear that his assumption that the steel contained ·24% oxygen, on which the whole rests, is any thing more than guess. It is highly probable that in the presence of so vast an excess of metallic iron the oxygen exists as ferrous rather than as magnetic oxide: moreover the quantity of manganese which is removed by the reaction varies very greatly, as will be shown by examples in due time. Further still, its removal is largely and probably chiefly due to the action, not of iron oxide contained in the metal, but of the supernatant slag. This is shown by an experiment at an American Bessemer mill, in which simply preventing the metal from coming into contact with the slag after the addition of the ferro-manganese greatly diminished the loss of manganese. In their ordinary practice on adding 1% of 80% ferromanganese to the blown steel in the ladle, 58% of the manganese thus added was removed: but in a special charge made under otherwise like conditions the steel was separated from the slag before adding the ferromanganese, by pouring it from the ladle through the nozzle in its bottom into a second ladle, in which 1% of ferromanganese was added, and from which the steel was subsequently teemed into molds in the ordinary way. In this case only 21% of the manganese added was removed from the steel. I here summarize these results:

	Ferromanganese of 80% Mn added to blown steel.		Manganese removed.		Composition of steel.			
	Parts "ferro" per 100 of steel.	Manganese added per 100 of steel.	Per 100 of steel.	Per 100 of manganese added.	Carbon.	Manganese.	Silicon.	Sulphur.
Single pouring	1·	0·80	0·23	58·	·015	·336	·011	·002
Double pouring	1·	0·80	0·12	21·	·009	·638	·016	·002

Müller found that 0·354% manganese was removed in a spiegel reaction of the acid Bessemer process in which slag was present: that in the basic Bessemer process 0·380% manganese was eliminated when slag was present, but that, when the slag was wholly removed before recarburizing, only from 0 to 0·064% of manganese was expelled.[b]

(2) Manganese appears to free molten steel from minute mechanically suspended particles of slag which cause red-shortness, by forming a double silicate of manganese and iron, which, by coalescing more readily than the simple silicate of iron, rises more completely to the surface. Thus Pourcel,[c] volatilizing by chlorine the iron of two pieces of steel, to the first of which when molten he had added silicon alone, to the second both silicon and manganese, obtains from the first a residual network of silicate of iron, while the second volatilizes completely, leaving no residuum.

This is usually confusedly explained by saying that the double silicate is more fusible than the simple one. But the simple silicates of iron, such as would form under these conditions, fuse at temperatures vastly below that of the molten steel, and if they were not melted they would still rise to the surface just as quickly as if they were. Does cork rise less rapidly through water because it is a solid? What the manganese does is either to make a silicate which is specifically lighter than the simple silicate of iron, or more probably one which more readily coalesces into globules so large that their upward motion is but little impeded by the friction of the surrounding steel.

§ 81. MANGANESE *vs.* SULPHUR.—Manganese not only counteracts the redshortness caused by sulphur but in some cases actually removes this metalloid from iron, sometimes (probably because sulphide of manganese like sulphide of calcium is less soluble in metallic iron than sulphide of iron is) by forming some compound rich in sulphur and manganese which liquates or separates by gravity, and perhaps sometimes by carrying oxygen to the sulphur. Thus Åkerman[d] quotes a manganiferous slag from a Swedish blast-furnace with 1·4% sulphur, while the accompanying cast-iron had but some hundredths of one per cent of sulphur. Parry[e] found 2% sulphur in manganiferous blast-furnace slags: when the slags were less manganiferous they contained less sulphur, while the cast-iron contained more.

Here sulphide of manganese appears to enter the slag like sulphide of lime, and like sulphide of iron, which Le Play[f] found in considerable quantities in ferruginous copper-smelting slags. Other sulphides, especially that of zinc, dissolve in slags. Åkerman considers that manganese drags sulphur into the blast-furnace slag even more powerfully than calcium does.

* Trans. Am. Inst Mining Engineers, IX., p. 396.

[b] Stahl und Eisen, 1883, pp. 446-453: idem, 1884, p. 71. Zeit. Vereins Deutsc. Ing., XXII., p. 385.

[c] Journ. Iron and St. Inst., 1877, I., p. 44.

[d] Eng. and Mining Jl., 1875, 2, p. 214.

[e] Perry, Iron and Steel, p. 89.

[f] Description des Procédés Métallurgiques employés dans le Pays de Galles, p. 212.

In three sets of experiments (1) on phosphoric, (2) on sulphurous and (3) on siliceous cast-iron respectively, each melted (A) alone and (B) with metallic manganese, Caron found that the addition of manganese energetically expelled sulphur, increased the percentage of silicon (by reducing it from the walls of the crucible) but had little effect on phosphorus. His results follow :[a]

		Phosphoric cast-iron.		Sulphurous cast-iron.		Siliceous cast-iron.	
		% phosphorus.	% manganese.	% sulphur.	% manganese.	% silicon.	% manganese.
	The initial cast-irons	0·88	.....	1·15	.....	0·98	.....
1..	The initial iron remelted without addition	0·82	.....	1·14	.....	0·88	.....
2..	The initial iron remelted with 6% metallic manganese	0·80	4·28	0·34[a]	3·92	1·30	4·77
3..	No. 1 remelted a second time without further addition	0·79	.....	1·05	.....	0·80	.....
4.	No. 2 remelted a second time without further addition	0·78	3·74	0·10	2·81	1·66	2·98
5..	No. 3 remelted for the third time without further addition	0·78	.....	0·96	.....	.....	.....
6..	No. 4 remelted for the third time without further addition	0·76	1·62	0·08	1·73	.....	.....
7..	The initial iron melted with 10% ferric oxide	0·76	.....	1·08	.....	0·61	.....
8..	The initial iron melted with 10% ferric oxide and 6% metallic manganese	0·74	1·57	0·07	1·22	0·37	5·59
9..	No. 7 remelted a second time with 10% ferric oxide	.....	.....	.....	.....	0·52	.....
10..	No. 8 remelted a second time with 10% ferric oxide (no further addition of manganese)	.....	.....	.....	.....	0·13	1·10

a This figure is given in the original as 1·15 : but this is evidently a misprint, as Caron remarks : "We see from these results that by a simple fusion in a crucible with access of air manganese removes more than 7-10ths of the sulphur which the cast-iron contains (on voit, d'après ces résultats que, par une simple fusion dans un creuset où l'air a accès, le manganese enlève à la fonte plus des 7-10 du soufre qu'elle contient)." Nevertheless the original figure is copied, blindly it seems, in most text-books. The iron after fusion with manganese must have had less than 0·34 of sulphur, which is 3-10ths of that initially present.

E. Riley,[b] on melting a cast-iron which contained ·207% sulphur with 10% of ferromanganese found, that the sulphur fell to 0·035%. Percy[c] considers that the manganese, in Caron's experiments, expelled sulphur by carrying oxygen to it.: while I venerate his opinions, the facts that just about enough manganese was lost to form the sulphide, MnS, with the expelled sulphur, that manganese has the power of dragging sulphur into blast-furnace slags, apparently as sulphide of manganese, very much as iron and calcium do, and that manganese and sulphur so often appear to segregate together in iron, coupled with Walrand's results incline me to believe that in Caron's case also much at least of the sulphur escaped in combination with manganese.

Walrand, after melting 300 parts of sulphurous cast-iron in one crucible and 24 parts of spiegeleisen of 16% manganese under lime in another, poured the cast-iron into the spiegel, and stirred the mixture for a minute, when an insupportable odor of sulphurous acid arose from the supernatant slag: the sulphur of the cast-iron fell from 0·50 to 0·06.[d] The manganese could not have carried oxygen to the sulphur so rapidly as to have caused the almost instantaneous expulsion of the latter which appears to have occurred: sulphur and manganese probably combined and rose to the surface together, when, exposed to the air, the sulphur became rapidly oxidized.

Under favorable conditions drop-like masses separate from liquid cast-iron and float on its surface: in these Ledebur[e] finds much more sulphur and manganese than in the mass of the iron.

	Carbon.	Silicon.	Phosphorus.	Sulphur.	Manganese.	Iron.	Oxygen. (Difference.)
Segregation	3·618	1·589	0·475	0·223	5·188	87·092	1·328
Mother metal	3·408	2·196	.....	0·050	2·520	.....	0·609

When steels which contain any considerable quantity of sulphur also contain so much manganese that this metal segregates to an extent which can be detected, the segregated portion is in general, in the many cases which I have examined, richer also in sulphur than the mother metal, indicating that a compound containing both sulphur and manganese has segregated.

Besides bodily removing sulphur from iron, manganese counteracts the effects of that which remains. This it may do by giving the particles of the metal greater mobility and plasticity at forging heats: or by combining directly with the sulphur to form a sulphide of manganese, which would only affect the iron as an intermixed foreign substance. The fact that sulphurous irons are ordinarily far more malleable at a yellow than at a red heat favors the former view: but both explanations may be true, and the readiness with which sulphide of manganese segregates from iron under favorable circumstances lends probability to the second explanation. We may suppose that sulphide of manganese (with perhaps also other metals) forms, which, owing to its small quantity and to the viscosity of the inclosing steel does not aggregate into masses sufficiently large to be readily recognized except under the most favorable conditions.

§ 62. Influence of Manganese on the Effects of Phosphorus, Copper and Silicon.—The special variety of hot-shortness thought to be due to phosphorus, like that caused by sulphur, is counteracted by manganese, but probably rather by its making the steel plastic and thus counteracting the tendency to crystallize which phosphorus causes, than by its forming phosphide of manganese and thus preventing the direct action of phosphorus on the matrix of iron: for, were the latter the case, then, since phosphorus tends strongly to segregate in steel, we should find manganese accompanying it in its segregations, just as it accompanies sulphur: but, examining many cases of segregation in cast-iron and in steel which is both phosphoric and manganiferous, I find little to suggest cosegregation of phosphorus and manganese. In Caron's experiment just cited manganese expelled sulphur but not phosphorus.

The redshortness due to copper and the hot-shortness thought to be due to silicon are also remedied by the presence of manganese. As the tendency of iron to crystallize becomes very strong as it approaches the melting point, as it is at this temperature that phosphorus seems to render steel non-malleable, and as phosphorus lowers the melting point and increases the tendency to crystallize at all temperatures, it has been thought that its hot-shortening effect was due to its lowering the melting point, and that manganese counteracted its effects by raising the melting point. As sulphurous irons are malleable at a high but brittle at a low (red) heat while phosphoric irons are malleable at a red but brittle at a high heat, and as manganese counteracts the effects of both, and as it moreover counteracts hot-shortness no matter at what temperature and from what cause it may arise, whether from phosphorus, sulphur, copper, silicon, iron oxide, suspended silicate of iron or blowholes, we may ascribe its effects to its directly increasing the plasticity of the steel at all temperatures at and above redness, to its even increasing the range of temperature through which plasticity prevails, on the one hand raising the melting point, on the other lowering the point at which plasticity gives way to rigidity.

a Comptes Rendus, LVI., p. 828, 1863.
b Journal of the Iron and Steel Institute, 1877, I., 105.
c Iron and Steel, p. 137.
d Revue Universelle, X., 1881, 2, p. 407.
e Handbuch der Eisenhüttenkunde, p. 257.

§ 83. QUANTITATIVE EFFECTS OF MANGANESE ON HOT-SHORTNESS.—Most of the manganese that is added to steel passes immediately into the slag. If the metal contains sulphur or phosphorus in important amount it is desirable that a considerable quantity of metallic manganese should remain unscorified to counteract their effects: and even in metal practically free from sulphur and phosphorus the presence of a little residual manganese is important, but whether through any direct action or merely because it is a guarantee that all oxide of iron has been reduced is not clear: I incline to the latter view, because admirable non-redshort iron was made before the employment of manganese.

It is at present impossible to state the quantities of manganese required to counteract the effects of given quantities of sulphur and phosphorus. In order to completely reduce iron oxide once formed in steel it is probably necessary to add so much manganese that the quantity which remains after the reduction of the iron oxide is in many cases far more than is needed to counteract the sulphur and phosphorus present. Thus at an American Bessemer works steel with carbon ·07, sulphur ·05, phosphorus ·05 and manganese about ·35%, was regularly made. One charge was allowed to remain in the converter long after being blown and after the addition of ferromanganese, till ebullition had nearly ceased. It was then poured and formed sound non-redshort ingots, which had only 0·18% manganese. It is so extremely difficult to decide how far the quantity of manganese which we find it necessary to leave in the steel in any particular case is merely residual from the excess which we have to add to completely reduce iron oxide or remove iron silicate as in the case just described, how far it is simply a guarantee that reoxidation has not occurred, how far it is needed to counteract sulphur, phosphorus, silicon and copper and to prevent blowholes, nay even how far it is simply suspended oxide or silicate of manganese (of which the last portions may remove themselves by gravity but slowly), than an attempt to quantify its effects in any of these respects must with our present data be fruitless, except perhaps in the case of steel containing so much sulphur or phosphorus that the quantity of residual manganese needed to counteract them is clearly more than is needed for other purposes. The difficulty of such an attempt is shown by a study of Table 21. Not to needlessly multiply cases, how can we reconcile the fact that steel of composition 48 in repeated trials rolled badly, at least at one time, unless its manganese was above 0·80%, with the fact that No. 7, with less than ¼th as much manganese but with more than twice as much phosphorus can be rolled at all? If you answer that No. 7 has not enough carbon to vitalize its phosphorus, how can we meet the fact that No. 12 with only 1-3rd as much manganese but with more phosphorus and thrice as much carbon, and No. 22 with about half as much manganese but with more phosphorus and twice as much carbon as No. 48 can be rolled at all? If it be answered that silicon is so extremely hurtful an impurity that Nos. 7, 12 and 22 are enabled to roll by having slightly less of it than No. 48, how is it that No. 28 (Table 21) with four times as much of this terrible silicon, with twice as much phosphorus and 30% more carbon can be rolled with only 80% of the manganese which No. 48 is known to require? How can No. 12 (in Table 17) with more carbon, with 9 times as much silicon, with twice as much phosphorus, and with more sulphur be rolled with less manganese than No. 48 (Table 21) requires? How can No. 16 (Table 21), an extraordinarily good rail, with the same carbon, with 6 times as much silicon, with 50% more phosphorus be rolled with only 70% as much manganese as No. 48 demands? The problem is at present insoluble.

Wendel[a] proposed the formula—

$$Mn = \cdot 8(C + 0\cdot 5Si) + 4P.$$

(in which the figures refer to percentages) as giving the quantity of residual manganese needed to insure sound rolling. This formula, doubtless useful for Wendel's special conditions, is not of general application. Here steel with but a fraction of the manganese which it calls for rolls admirably: there steel with twice as much manganese as it prescribes rolls badly.

Thus in Table 21 we find many cases of apparently well-rolling steel with less than half, and others with but 1-4th (2 cases), 1-7th (4 cases), 1-9th, and even 1-20th, and in Table 29 (No. 48) 1-17th of the manganese which this formula demands, while among the badly-rolling ones are several with much more and three with actually twice as much manganese as it requires. Nor does the formula fit the facts much better if we apply it only to steels comparatively free from sulphur and phosphorus, for which it was particularly designed. Indeed it is the practice at some admirable works to diminish the manganese as the carbon increases instead of increasing it as Wendel's formula demands. As we have neither a scientific basis for calculating the quantity of residual manganese needed to prevent hot-shortness under given conditions, nor even

[a] Trans. Am. Inst. Mining Engineers, IV., p. 364.

TABLE 21.—MANGANESE AND FORGEABLENESS.

	Steel known or supposed to forge tolerably well.																					
No.	1.	2.	3.	5.	6.	8.	9.	10.	11.	12.	13.	15.	16.	17	18	19.	21.	22.	25.	26.	27.	28.
	G f	E	E	G f	J	J		E		H	J	F	J	F	F			F		a A		J
Carbon	·13	1·33	·86	·17	·10	·15	·14	·87	·20	1·03	·19	·10	·20	·15	1·00	·13	·47	·40	·23	...	·45	·48
Silicon	·14	·01	·02	trace	·008	·006	·002	·29	·19	·02	·006	·005	·009	·018	·03	...	·44	·04	...	...	...	·32
Phosphorus	·16	·02	·033	·02	·23	·04	·26	·03	·08	·09	·20	......	·18	·10	·04	·24	·03	·10	·18	...	·25	·17
Sulphur	·00	trace	trace	trace	......	......	...	·05	·08	......	......	......	......	......	......	..	·01	·04	......	·10	......	...
Manganese	·60	·05	·08	·15	·18	·19	·19	·18	·21	·23	·23	·28	·31	·34	·35	·63	·41	·50	·60	·68	·68	·67

	Steel known or supposed to forge tolerably well.											Steel known to forge badly.											
No.	30.	33.	34.	35.	38.	39.	40.	41.	42.	43.	45	46	47.	48.	49	50.	51	52.	53.	54.	55.	56	57.
	F	F	F	F	F	J	c D	F	F	F	F	A	D d	D	d B	d B	d B	F	F	F	e F	F	e
Carbon	·39	·40	·37	·40	·33	·23	·35	·03	·07	·34	·34	......	·35	·35	·29	·23	·30	·47	·70	·78	·38	·52	·41
Silicon	·28	·10	·67	·04	·07	·08	·09	·03	·05	·07	·04	......	·08	·03	...	...	...	·64	·60	·58	·08	·87	·04
Phosphorus	......	·07	·12	·09	·07	·07	·08	·06	......	·14	·13	......	·08	·08	·50	·52	·51	·11	·06	·06	·24	·11	·15
Sulphur	......	·07	·05	·05	·06	......	·05	·08	·10	·10	·07	·201	·05	·05	·08	·09	·03	·06	·018	·01	·07	·05	·01
Manganese	·71	·65	·90	·95	·96	·97	·92@1·10	1·05	1·70	1·14	1·63	·50	<·60	·06@·8	·84	·90	·93	1·48	1·84	1·85	1·87	2·08	2·09
Copper	......	......	......	......	......	......	......	0·05	6·65	......	......	......	......	......	......	......	......	......	......	......	......	......	..
Percentage of second quality rails		0·4	4·0	2·1	0·66	......	......	3	5	10@15	10@15	.	......	......		..			......	......	......	......	......

a Slightly redshort. c. Rolled well. d. Rolled very badly. e. Rolled badly but not excessively so. f Wrought-iron. A. Ledebur, Handbuch, p. 27? B. Wendel, Trans. Am. Inst. Mining Engrs., IV., p. 360. D. Cabot, idem, X., p. 462. E. Metcalf, idem, IX., p. 549. F. Private notes. G. Bell, Principles of Manufacture of Iron and Steel. H. Troilus, Notes on the Chemistry of Iron. J. Beck-Guerhard, Jour. Iron and Steel Inst., 1886, I, p. 294. [illegible]

TABLE 22.—MANGANESE AND SULPHUR IN STEEL KNOWN OR BELIEVED TO HAVE FORGED AT LEAST TOLERABLY WELL.

No.	IJ 1.	JM 2.	JM 3.	JM 4.	BC 7.	IJ 10.	BD 12.	BEG 15	X 17.	BHL 18.	BEG 19.	BK 20.	BC 21.	BD 22.	IC 24.	BD 25.	BEF 28.	BD 30.	BD 32.	A 33.	BD 36.	BD 37.	A 38.	N 44.
Carbon	1·30	1·08	1·11	1·32	·22	2·80	·47	·07	·84	·15	·06	·27	·36	·06	2·37	·08	....	·07	·07	·45	·60	·08	·52	·41
Silicon	·01	·21	·23	·07	·00	·14	·47	....	·38	·01	·04	·00	·13	....	·20	·08	·08	·02	·02	·06	·04	·01	·08	....
Manganese	·05	·08	·05	·05	·36	·26	·41	·75	2·06	·28	·30	1·00	1·05	·85	·18	·67	·86	·66	·59	·92	·91	·60	1·04	·87
Phosphorus	·02	·02	·02	·01	·09	·02	·06	·05	·40	·04	·10	·09	·09	·08	·03	·08	·05	·08	·08	·05	·09	·08	·05	·08
Sulphur	0	0	0	0	·02	·03	·04	·05	·06	·06	·07	·07	·08	·08	·09	·10	·11	·12	·14	·14	·15	·15	·17	·22

A. Bell, Manufacture of Iron and Steel, pp. 414-415: Bessemer rails. B. Private notes. C. British. D. Bessemer, Western U. S. E. Bessemer, Eastern U. S. F. Somewhat redshort. G. Rolled admirably. H. U. S. open-hearth. I. Metcalf, Trans. Am. Inst. Mining Engineers, IX., p. 549. J. Crucible steel. K. Cammel's armor plate. L. Boiler plate. M. Thurston, Mat's of Engineering, p. 464. N. Morrell, Metallurgical Review, II., p. 198.

trustworthy empirical formulæ, the steel maker has to proceed tentatively when under unusual conditions. The examples of well and ill-rolling steels in Table 21, arranged in the order of their manganese contents, may serve as rough guides: other examples occur in Tables 17, 22, 28, 29 and 30.

Table 22 gives the compositions of many steels with sulphur from 0 to 0·22%. They are selected from a vast number at hand, primarily to show how small a quantity of manganese may suffice to restrain the redshortness conferred by sulphur, at least so fully as under favorable conditions to permit the rolling of T rails with thin flanges. We may infer from this table that for this purpose it is only necessary that the manganese should equal say 4·5 times the sulphur present, even when the latter rises to 0·16%. But the percentage of manganese required for other reasons may greatly exceed that which the sulphur present calls for. Moreover as the sulphur rises, even if the manganese rises proportionally, the redshortness and the difficulty of forging increase. But, after seeing so many apparently trustworthy empirical formulæ prove worthless under altered conditions, it would be rash to conclude that 4·5 parts of manganese are always needed or always suffice to counteract one part of sulphur.

§ 84. INFLUENCE OF MANGANESE ON TENSILE STRENGTH AND DUCTILITY.—Manganese may affect these properties in iron both indirectly, by restraining the formation of blowholes, and directly by entering into chemical union with the metal. Moreover, the manganese present may not all be directly alloyed with iron but may exist in variable proportions as oxide, silicate, or sulphide, of unknown and inconstant composition, and the effect of each of these substances on iron doubtless not only differs from those of the others but also itself varies with varying conditions. We should therefore hardly expect careful scrutiny to support the popular belief that the effects of manganese are constant and cumulative, and I for one should expect its influence to vary greatly under varying, and perhaps but slightly varying, conditions: and the evidence at hand indicates, I think, that it does thus vary.

In so far as it prevents blowholes it doubtless increases both tensile strength and ductility. But few discriminate between its direct and indirect effects: still less have its different direct effects been distinguished from each other: the opinions held chiefly regard its net effect. Some day we may make these discriminations clearly: to-day it is impossible. But it is of practical moment to learn whether its net effect is on the average good or bad: or, failing this, whether it is usually or often so strongly marked that it should be taken into account.

Formerly regarded by nearly all as merely a necessary evil, it has largely lived down its bad repute. In 1872 four distinguished steel metallurgists gave me the figures ·5, ·5, ·75 and 1% respectively as the highest amount of manganese which should be tolerated in Bessemer rail steel under any conditions whatsoever. To-day rail steel occasionally contains as much as 2·1% manganese and frequently as much as 1·55%. In 1872 Holley thought manganese could not safely rise above ·5%: in 1878 he reported the admirable qualities of steel castings with ·94% manganese. Not a few now regard manganese in moderation as harmless or even beneficial: very many have been prejudiced against it, often unconsciously, by their personal interest in the standing of open-hearth steel, which is ordinarily less manganiferous than Bessemer steel. But, making all allowances for prejudice, many intelligent and unbiassed metallurgists dread it and echo Siemens's illogical complaint that it is but a cloak for impurities.

I now present evidence as to its effects on tensile strength and ductility.

A. SALOM,[a] analyzing by the method of least squares Dudley's data as to the composition, tensile strength and ductility of 64 rails, finds that manganese increases both tensile strength and ductility, but by an insignificant amount.

B. RAYMOND,[b] similarly analyzing Dudley's data as to wear, finds that manganese has no effect.

C. THE AUTHOR'S ANALYSIS.—It may justly be objected to these deductions that they are based on utterly insufficient data, the number of cases being very small, and that the other variables vary so greatly as to mask the effects of variations of manganese. Gatewood[c] has presented incomparably more valuable data, both numerous and with but trifling variations in the variables other than carbon and manganese. They indicate that manganese has no important constant effect on either tensile strength or ductility, at least within the limits manganese 0·20 to 0·60 and carbon ·12 to ·22%. Of these I have analyzed two sets, the Chester steel, with 130 cases, with carbon between 0·10 and 0·22 (in 110 of these the carbon is between ·12 and ·17), the manganese varying from ·20 to ·73: and the Norway, with no less than 369 heats, whose carbon varies from ·11 to ·31 (in 355 of them it lies between 0·12 and 0·22) and whose manganese varies from ·17 to ·64.

An analysis of the first set indicated that between these limits manganese raised the tensile strength at the rate of 16,430 pounds per square inch per 1% (or 164 lbs. per ·01% manganese), or about one fourth as much as the same percentage of carbon does. The second set yields far more valuable results, because its cases are far more numerous, and because certain tedious precautions were employed in its analysis which were omitted in the study of the first set.

I divide the 369 cases into primary groups, each with constant carbon, and determine the average manganese for each group. These are subdivided into secondary groups

[a] Trans. Am. Inst. Mining Engineers, XIII., p. 157.
[b] Idem, IX., p. 607.
[c] Rept. Nav. Advisory Bd. on Mild Steel, 1886.

each with constant manganese as well as carbon. Noting the amounts by which the manganese and the tensile strength of each group differ from those of the primary group in which it lies, we assume that the deviations of tensile strength are so far due to those of manganese that, if we eliminate the effects of other variables by taking the mean of a large number of cases, we shall discover the relation between manganese and tensile strength. To this end I combine into tertiary groups all those secondary groups whose manganese differs by like algebraic amount from the average manganese of their primary groups, and I find the average deviation of the tensile strength, etc., of the members of each tertiary group from the average tensile strength, etc., of their primary groups. If now within the limits of manganese 0·17 and ·64, and carbon ·12 and ·22, manganese has, as is generally believed, an effect which is largely independent of other variables, and which is constant and cumulative, taking such a large number of cases of steel produced and tested under like conditions, with all other variables reduced to their narrowest limits, then the average deviations of the tensile strength, etc., of these tertiary groups should bear a traceable relation to the corresponding deviations of manganese, and plotting them as I have done with deviations of tensile strength, etc., as ordinates, deviations of manganese as abscissæ, we should obtain a curve of some degree of regularity. Actually the resulting zigzag for tensile strength is perfectly hopeless: it does not even suggest that the effect of manganese is on the whole either to increase or to diminish tensile strength.

Here and there a group shows much higher tensile strength than its neighbors, but these excesses are not referable to any simple principle, and they are probably due to other causes than variation in manganese. Fig. 7,

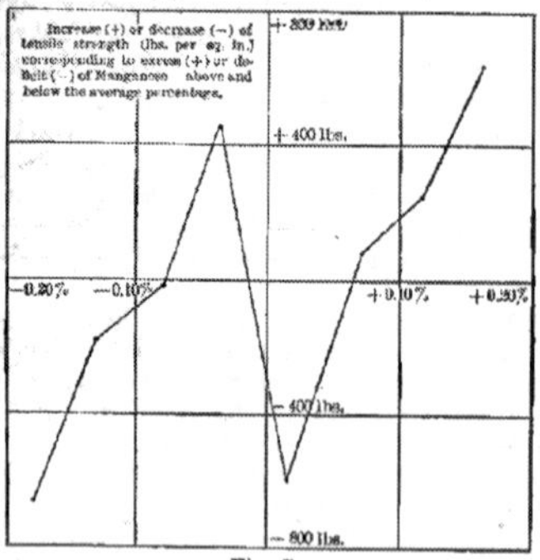

Fig. 7.

which shows a curve derived from the tertiary groups by combining them by fives into quaternary groups and plotting the centers of gravity of the latter, indicates either that the effects of manganese on tensile strength are not constant, but sometimes positive sometimes negative, or that they are so insignificant as to be completely masked by trifling variations of other variables.

The indications as to the effects of manganese on ductility (as measured by elongation) are more conclusive: the elongation of each tertiary group so closely approximates the average of its primary group that, combining the tertiary groups by fives, the elongation of the quaternary groups thus produced in no case differs by as much as 0·5% from the elongation of their primary groups, suggesting that, if manganese does directly cause brittleness, it is balanced by its indirect effect of increasing ductility by promoting continuity.

D. Deshayes from examination of the Terre-Noire steels concludes that, when the manganese is in the neighborhood of 0·5%, an increase of 0·1% of manganese raises the tensile strength about 1-3rd as much as 0·1% of carbon does, or say from 2560 to 2845 lbs. per sq. in.: that it raises the elastic limit slightly more than the tensile strength; that it diminishes the permanent elongation on rupture, but by only about 1-6th or 1-7th as much as carbon does, an increment of 0·1% manganese diminishing the elongation by hardly 0·5%.[a]

The effects which he attributes to manganese are so slight that they may easily be due to variations of other variables: and as I have neither his data nor his method of analyzing them I know not how much weight to attach to his conclusions. They on the whole harmonize with the results of our other evidence, in indicating that the net effects of manganese within moderate limits are comparatively unimportant as regards tensile strength, and insignificant as regards elongation.

E. I have known the rails of a western Bessemer mill to contains 2·1% manganese when the carbon was below ·30%: at another it frequently reaches 1·55% with ·35% carbon. Table 17 gives three cases in which the manganese varies from 1·85% with ·76% carbon to 2·08% with ·52% carbon, in rails.

F. An eminent but dogmatic authority states that manganese in tool steel must not exceed 0·2%: yet very good tool steel with ·5[b] and even ·78%[c] manganese is recorded. I have a trustworthy analysis of Jessop's best saw steel with manganese 0·45, carbon 1·06, silicon ·19 and phosphorus ·024.

G. Steel castings of admirable quality are often highly manganiferous: *e. g.*, No. 40, table 9, with 1·10 manganese, ·45 carbon, and ·35 silicon, with 105,080 lbs. tensile strength and 17·5% elongation: the same table gives many other tough and strong castings with from ·94 to 1·08% manganese.

H. Excellent boiler plate steel which passes the rigorous government tests often has more than ·55, and occasionally as much as ·64% manganese.

I. Experienced makers of soft open-hearth steel report that the addition of a moderate amount of manganese, with simultaneous diminution of carbon, greatly increases the ductility of steel containing ·24% carbon, and nearly free from manganese.

Résumé.—Let each reader reconcile these facts with the prevalent dread of manganese as best he may: his conclusions will not injure the facts: neither will mine, which are as follows. The statistical examinations A to D indicate that, on the average, the net effects of manganese on tensile strength and ductility are slight. G shows that if ·9 to 1·1% manganese ever seriously injures static ductility,

[a] Annales des Mines, 1870, p. 549.
[b] Thurston, Materials of Engineering, II., p. 435.
[c] Engineering and Mining Journal, 1875, II., p. 383.

there are many cases in which it does not. The fact that rails (E) with 1·55% manganese and ·35 carbon very often successfully pass the straightening press and that those with over 2% manganese and ·53% carbon occasionally do, indicates that, if manganese renders steel brittle under shock, this effect is either slight or exceptional or non-cumulative, while H indicates that it is slight. F indicates that, if say ·45% or less of manganese lessens the power of steel to hold a cutting edge, this effect is not constant: and the presence of ·45% manganese in the crucible saw steel of a maker whose product has and apparently deserves the very highest reputation, indicates that if it tends to produce this effect this tendency can be safely combated.

While the evidence is too fragmentary to warrant final conclusions, it certainly strongly suggests that the present dread of manganese is largely a superstition: that while 1 or 2% of manganese is probably liable to cause decided brittleness, its effects have been grossly exaggerated, and that Dudley's[a] conjecture that 5 parts of manganese cause as much brittleness as one part of phosphorus is very wide of the mark.

§86. MANGANESE STEEL.—While the small amounts of manganese in ordinary commercial steel increase its forgeableness and within certain limits its brittleness, yet when so much manganese is present that its effects outweigh those of carbon and that it forms a true manganese steel, the alloy becomes extraordinarily tough and difficultly forgeable: it possesses a combination of hardness and toughness which should be of value for tools which cut by impact, and which is not otherwise attainable so far as I know, at least in any material available for the arts. Several attempts to utilize its remarkable properties have been made of late, and others are to be expected.

The extreme brittleness of tungsten steel often prevents us from availing ourselves of its intense hardness, which equals that of any steel within my knowledge: manganese, which gives such toughness and hardness, holds out promise as a means of remedying this defect, and indeed tungsten steel often contains from 1 to 2·5% of manganese. But as both tungsten and manganese steel are difficultly forgeable, this defect would probably still restrict its use.

The open-hearth cutlery steel of a western United States mill in two cases contained

Manganese.	Carbon.	Silicon.
1·25	·35	·08
1·00	·45	·09

But this can hardly be classed as a true manganese steel. N. Washburn, at Allston, Mass., is reported to have made railway car wheels of steel containing 7% manganese and 0·6% carbon, and to have suspended his manufacture solely for legal considerations.

Far better known is Hadfield's[b] manganese steel, which contains from 7 to 30% manganese. The following specimens of his steel have been described:

I.[b] Manganese, 9.8; carbon, 0.72; silicon, 0·37; sulphur, 0·06; phosphorus, 0·08. Elongation in 8 inches, (1) 22%, (2) 28·9%; tensile strength, (1) 106,490, (2) 119,054 lbs. per sq. in.

II.[b] 9 to 10% manganese: can be machined, but with difficulty. With more manganese the steel can hardly be cut by carbon steel.

III.[c] 12·5% manganese. Hard-drawn wire, tensile strength 246,480 lbs. per sq. in. The same annealed 107,-520 lbs., with 20%± elongation. Modulus of elasticity 23,890,000 lbs. per sq. in., or about 85% of that of carbon steel.

IV.[d] 17·5% manganese, 0·8% carbon. Hardly cut in a lathe by carbon steel. When quenched in water it could be bent double without cracking.

V.[b] 18% manganese. Could be forged, but with difficulty.

I found a specimen of manganese steel readily forgeable between dull and light redness: at a yellow or very dull red heat it was tender, and below the latter temperature extremely so. Cold-forging raises its tensile strength but makes it brittle. Its toughness is restored by heating it. I find it slightly softer and it is said to be much tougher after sudden than after slow cooling.

Its electric conductivity is very low, 12% of that of iron (1·8% of that of copper?) according to Barrett.[e] It is but very slightly magnetic: Bottomley[c] found that, after being submitted to the most powerful magnetizing force, its permanent magnetism was but 0·02% of that of ordinary steel, while Barrett found that its induced magnetization in a uniform field was but 0·3% of that of iron: but for the high cost of manganese this property would commend this steel for the plating of iron vessels, which, if built of this wonderful material, would have little deviation of the compass.

It is stated by interested persons to be exceedingly fluid, to solidify with but little contraction, and without blowholes, and to be, even without forging, "harder, stronger, denser and tougher" than most forged steel.

Brustlein[f] states that it welds with great facility.

Concerning manganese steel see further Appendix I.

CHAPTER V.

IRON AND SULPHUR.

§ 90. SUMMARY.—Sulphur unites with iron probably in all proportions up to 53·3%, being readily absorbed from many sources. It may however be prevented from combining with iron and even expelled from it by many agents (*e. g.*, basic slags, carbon, silicon, manganese, oxygen, water, ferric oxide). Certain of these in the blast-furnace prevent the sulphur present from combining with the cast-iron, and in the conversion of cast-iron into malleable iron, whether by puddling, by pig-washing or by the basic process much of the sulphur of the cast-iron is expelled. It causes cast-iron to retain its carbon in the combined state. Carbon and sulphur and perhaps also silicon and sulphur are mutually exclusive within limits. Sulphur makes mal-

[a] Trans. Am. Inst. Mining Engineers, 1879, VII., p. 197.

[b] Weeks., Trans. Am. Inst. Mining Engineers, XIII., p. 233; also XV.

[c] The Electrician, Jan. 7, 1887.

[d] S. Wellman, private communication.

[e] The Electrician, loc. cit.

[f] Journal Iron and St. Inst., 1886, II., p. 775.

leable iron redshort and interferes with its welding, but these effects are largely effaced by the presence of manganese. It is thought to make malleable iron slightly *tougher and softer* when cold, but to make cast-iron harder, though this latter effect is at least in part due to its causing it to retain the carbon in the combined state. It increases the fusibility of cast-iron but makes it thick and sluggish when molten and gives rise to blowholes during its solidification.

§ 91. COMBINATION.—Sulphur unites readily with iron in many proportions (the sulphides Fe_8S, Fe_2S, FeS, Fe_2S_3, Fe_7S_8 and FeS_2 = Fe 46·7%, S 53·3% are recognized), being greedily absorbed by it, as the following paragraphs show, from sulphurous fuel and even from sulphurous gases, from the sulphates of baryta and lime, and probably from other sulphates. Ferrous sulphide (FeS with 36·36% sulphur) appears to dissolve in non-carburetted iron or to unite with it in the igneous way in all proportions: Percy,[a] melting ferrous sulphide and iron together in various proportions, obtained completely fused and apparently homogeneous products.

Willis states that in the open-hearth process 30% of the sulphur contained as sulphate of baryta in some ore that was added was absorbed by the steel.[b] Finkener found that when metallic iron and lime sulphate were exposed to a white heat *in vacuo* the mass was fused, an oxide and sulphide formed (whether any iron sulphide formed is not stated).[c] This indicates that, in the presence of an acid slag, *e. g.*, in the open-hearth process, metallic iron would take up sulphur from lime sulphate.

Odelstjerna and Forsberg[d] found that steel in the open-hearth furnace absorbed from 0·015 (0·15 ?) to 0·3% sulphur from the producer gas, as proved by repeated experiments, and crucially by desulphurizing this gas by adding in the gas-producers 7 parts of crushed lime to 100 of coal, when the absorption of sulphur by the steel ceased. Hardisty[e] states that he has often found ·01 to ·02% more sulphur in open-hearth steel than could be accounted for by the iron charged.

Finkener,[f] heating iron in an atmosphere of sulphurous acid found that the iron absorbed sulphur, and was in part simultaneously oxidized.

M. White informs me that repeated investigations at the Bethlehem Iron Works have shown more sulphur in the Bessemer ingots than is contained in the cast-iron when it runs into the convertor; this excess, amounting to say 0·008%, is probably absorbed by the steel from the sides of the ladles, which in turn probably absorb bisulphide of carbon from the producer gas with which they are heated.

§ 92. THE CONDITION OF SULPHUR IN IRON.—Several facts suggest that in solid iron sulphur, at least in part and under favorable conditions, exists not in simple uniform combination with the matrix of metal, but as a sulphide, probably of indefinite composition, dissolved or suspended in particles usually so minute as to escape detection. It tends strongly to segregate or even to liquate from cast-iron: it is often very irregularly distributed through sulphurous steel. Snelus, sifting the borings of cast-iron, found the finer and more graphitic portions unduly sulphurous.[g] When cast-iron is dissolved in hydrochloric acid "even after all the iron is dissolved and the solution boiled for some time, sulphuretted hydrogen is still given off"—especially in case of siliceous cast-iron.[h]

§ 93. REMOVAL OF SULPHUR. Fortunately sulphur is readily removed from iron by many reagents, lime, magnesia, the alkalies (and their basic silicates), carbon, silicon and manganese, which all probably remove it as sulphide, since their sulphides, unlike that of iron, are but slightly soluble in the metal: ferric oxide, atmospheric oxygen, steam and alkaline nitrates, which oxidize and expel it as sulphurous and sulphuric acids: and heat alone, which decomposes sulphates of iron (*e. g.*, in roasting iron ores) volatilizing the sulphur as sulphuric acid. Further, manganese counteracts the effects of moderate amounts of sulphur retained by the iron.

A. CARBON removes sulphur from ferrous sulphide and apparently from cast-iron and steel, probably in both cases as bisulphide of carbon, CS_2, which forms when sulphur and carbon meet at a red heat. Very inflammable, it burns in the air to carbonic and sulphurous acids. Hochstätter[i] in Percy's laboratory, exposing sulphide of iron (which had about 20% sulphur and was therefore nearly ferrous sulphide) with charcoal in covered brasqued crucibles to a white heat, expelled 21·13% of the sulphur initially present, obtaining a sulphide with about 33 34% of sulphur and a small quantity of highly siliciferous metallic iron (iron 89·53, silicon 9·41). The expulsion of sulphur is attributable to the carbon present.

That sulphur is expelled from cast-iron by carbon is indicated by Smith's experiment in Percy's laboratory. Exposing white cast-iron to a steel-melting heat in a graphite crucible with an excess of charcoal, collecting and remelting the resulting buttons under charcoal, he found that the sulphur which was initially 0·78% had fallen to 0·34%, and the iron had become mottled. Similarly both Smith and Weston in Percy's laboratory melted gray cast-iron with ferrous sulphide in such small proportion that it was wholly either decomposed or absorbed by the cast-iron. A very considerable proportion of sulphur was in general expelled.[j] Their results are here summarized.

TABLE 23 A.—FUSION OF CAST-IRON WITH FERROUS SULPHIDE.

No.	Observer.	In the mixture of cast-iron and FeS before fusion. Carbon.	Sulphur.	In the fused product. Carbon. Comb'd	Graphite	Total.	Sulphur.	Loss on fusion. Carbon.	Sulphur.	Grade of the product.
1	Smith, Weston.	3·84	4·38	....	....	3·17	2·12	·67	2·26	White, no graphite separated.
2		4·16	2·23	2·48	1·41	3·9	1·68	·26	0·55	" graphite separated.
3		4·31	1·24	....	....	3·6	1·31(?)	·71	....	" " "
4		4·30	0·75	....	....	....	0·72	....	....	Mottled
5		....	2·48	....	....	....	·78	....	1·90	White
6		....	·78	....	....	....	·34	..	·44	Mottled,
7		....	·90	....	....	....	·09	..	·81	Graphite separated.
8		....	1·60	....	....	....	2·13	..	·52	White " "

1 to **4** inclusive. Non-sulphurous graphitic cast-iron, prepared by heating sheet-iron in chemically pure charcoal, was melted with sulphide of iron containing 29·3% sulphur. **5.** Gray cast-iron melted under plate glass in clay crucible with the same sulphide. The crucible was perfectly closed, so that nothing can have fallen in: yet a considerable quantity of pulverulent graphitic matter was found between metal and slag. **6.** The white cast-iron produced in 5 remelted in a graphite crucible with a great excess of charcoal. **7.** Another variety of gray cast-iron was melted under plate glass in a clay crucible with the same sulphide. A considerable quantity of graphitic matter was found between metal and slag. **8.** Gray iron, about No. 2 in grade, was melted in a clay crucible under a plug of charcoal with the same sulphide: graphitic matter was found on the surface of the button.

[a] Percy, Iron and Steel, p. 33.
[b] Journal Iron and St. Inst., 1880, I., p. 91.
[c] Wedding, Basische Bessemer oder Thomas Process, p. 155.
[d] Journal Iron and St. Inst., 1886, I., pp. 125, 337; Iron Age, April 8, 1886 p. 11.
[e] Journ. Iron and St. Inst., 1886, I., p. 128.
[f] Wedding, Der basische Bessemer oder Thomas-process, p. 155.
[g] Journ. Iron and St. Inst., 1871, I., p. 40.
[h] E. Riley, Journ. Chem. Soc., 1872, XXV., p. 540.
[i] Percy, Iron and Steel, p. 34.
[j] Percy, Op. Cit., pp. 133 to 136.

So too Riley obtained graphitic cast-iron free from sulphur by fusion in a highly sulphurous gas-carbon crucible, the excess of carbon present apparently either preventing the absorption of sulphur from the crucible walls or actually expelling it when absorbed.[a]

In cementation (carburization of malleable iron by prolonged heating in contact with charcoal) the sulphur has been observed to fall from ·577 (?) to ·017[b]: from ·055 to ·019[c]: from ·04 to ·02, and, in case of white cast-iron heated for 35 days in charcoal from ·101 to ·036. Ledebur[d] thinks that bisulphide of carbon is probably evolved from solidifying sulphurous cast-iron.

In view of these facts Karsten's[e] statement that sulphide of iron with the minimum of sulphur remains unchanged when exposed to carbon for an hour at the strongest white heat, but takes up some carbon, is hard to explain. The experiments of Percy's laboratory are so conclusive that we must conclude either that Karsten was mistaken or that the special conditions of his experiments prevented the expulsion of sulphur.

B. Mutual Exclusiveness of Sulphur and Carbon.—The experiments of Table 22 A not only show that carbon when present in excess, as in cementation and in fusion in carbonaceous crucibles, expels sulphur, and that, under favorable but little known conditions even the comparatively moderate quantity of carbon in gray cast-iron may so completely expel sulphur that, as in case 7, it falls from ·90 to ·09%, but also that, as noticed in § 20, sulphur in turn expels carbon, probably in part by dragging it off as bisulphide of carbon, partly by lowering the saturation point of the iron for carbon. Indeed, No. 7 indicates that even when so little as ·09 per cent of sulphur remains it may cause the graphitic separation from molten gray iron of part of the carbon which it had previously retained, or that it may at least prevent the reabsorption of the graphite expelled before the sulphur had fallen to so low a proportion. While part of the carbon thus expelled probably escapes as bisulphide, it is clear that the expulsion of a part is due to the effect of sulphur in lowering the saturation point of the iron for carbon: for not only is much more carbon expelled in every case than is needed to form bisulphide with the sulphur simultaneously eliminated, but in many cases a layer of graphite occurs on the surface of the resulting button of iron, which itself is perfectly white; and moreover, as in No. 4 (and also No. 3?) a heavy loss of carbon may occur even when no sulphur is removed. The expelled carbon which in these experiments remains as graphite, because protected by a layer of glass, would doubtless be oxidized under ordinary conditions.

We safely attribute these effects to the presence of sulphur, for when, in an experiment parallel with No. 8, gray cast-iron was melted under glass in a clay crucible at an excessively high temperature and under the same conditions as prevailed in these experiments except that no sulphide was added, the fracture of the iron remained dark gray, and no indication of white iron arose.

In the experiments which we have been considering a little sulphur is added to an excess of iron: both sulphur and carbon are partly expelled, but (if we exclude the trifling quantity of graphite formed) a single product with a moderate amount of carbon and sulphur arises. Under other and imperfectly defined conditions, *e. g.* when a large quantity of sulphide comes into contact with cast-iron at a high temperature, two products arise, sulphide of iron and metallic iron, which do not mix.

Thus, in Hochstätter's experiment above, siliciferous iron did not mix with iron sulphide from which it had been reduced by an excess of carbon: so too Karsten,[f] bringing sulphur and cast-iron together, obtained two products, sulphide of iron and a cast-iron containing but 0·446% of sulphur. In Karsten's experiment by successive additions of sulphur more and more of the iron was removed from the cast-iron and converted into sulphide, and as the carbon was not proportionally removed the metal grew richer in carbon till it became saturated (which appears to have occurred when the carbon rose above 5·5%). After this the excess of carbon separated as graphite, which collected between the layers of metal and sulphide. Karsten's statement that the cast-iron thus obtained in presence of 5·5% carbon held ·45% of sulphur harmonizes poorly with the other results which I give above, and, so far as I know, with common observation. As we know that very many of the older determinations of sulphur, even by most careful chemists, were excessively high, we may reasonably doubt whether this iron actually contained anything like this quantity of sulphur.

From what has been said it appears (1) that iron which is not highly carburetted unites with sulphuretted irons and even with iron sulphides, and (2) that highly carburetted irons unite with sulphuretted irons when the latter are distinctly metallic (a partial expulsion of sulphur or carbon or both usually occurring when the percentage of these elements exceeds a now unknown limit): yet (3) highly carburetted irons do not, at least under certain conditions, unite with any large quantity iron sulphides so rich in sulphur as to be no longer metallic but matte-like; and cast-iron may even remain in contact with such an iron matte without becoming exceedingly rich in sulphur. The behavior of metallic iron toward its sulphide here resemble that of metallic lead and copper toward theirs.

C. Silicon.—Silicon like carbon appears to expel sulphur from iron to a certain limited extent, though probably not enough to be of importance commercially, as a high proportion of silicon may coexist with sufficient sulphur to ruin iron for most purposes.

Thus Hochstätter[g] found, in Percy's laboratory, that though silica at a white heat had no effect on ferrous sulphide, yet if carbon were present to reduce the silica to silicon (*e. g.* as when silica, ferrous sulphide and carbon were raised to a white heat in a graphite crucible) the ferrous sulphide was decomposed, its sulphur largely expelled (as sulphurous acid ?) and a ferro-silicon resulted, whose composition in three cases was as follows:

Iron by loss	80·23	83·28	81·53
Silicon	18·77	15·33	16·76
Sulphur	1·00	1·40	1·71
Sulphur expelled per 100 of that initially present	97·46	96·28	92·82

According to Turner sulphur and silicon appear to mutually exclude each other much as sulphur and carbon

[a] Journ. Iron and St. Inst., 1877, I, p. 162.
[b] Percy, Iron and Steel, p. 773.
[c] Ledebur, Handbuch der Eisenhüttenkunde, p. 954.
[d] Idem, p. 251.
[e] Percy, Op. Cit., p. 136; Karsten, Eisenhüttenkunde, I., p. 429.
[f] Percy, Iron and Steel, p. 131.
[g] Percy, Iron and Steel, p. 88.

do: he finds that the addition of sulphur to siliceous iron causes the separation of graphitic matter containing silicon: the addition of silicon to an iron containing sulphur causes the separation of graphitic matter rich in sulphur.[a]

D. THE ALKALIES AND ALKALINE EARTHS, potash, soda, lime, magnesia baryta (and alumina?), rapidly and almost completely remove sulphur from ferrous sulphide and from cast-iron as alkaline or earthy sulphide: as these sulphides are readily soluble in many silicates, while apparently almost insoluble in metallic iron, the employment in the blast-furnace of basic slags (a portion of whose base is readily taken up by the sulphur) almost completely prevents sulphur from entering the cast-iron. This action, for which Ledebur suggests the general formula $FeS + CaO + C = Fe + CaS + CO$ is so complete that at the Clarence blast-furnaces only from 2·5 to 5% of the sulphur in the materials charged enters the cast-iron.[b] The presence of free lime, etc., is not necessary to the removal of sulphur, since basic silicates of lime, magnesia, etc., also remove it: the more basic the slag and the more there is of it the more thoroughly is the sulphur removed; lime appears to remove it far more energetically than magnesia. These facts are illustrated by experiments of Åkerman and Ledebur.[c] Åkerman with otherwise identical conditions obtained from the same ore iron with ·09, ·04 and ·01% sulphur by reducing it with addition of 15% silica, 5% carbonate of lime and 20% carbonate of lime respectively. The readiness with which sulphur is removed from cast-iron by basic

	Akerman, ore smelted with			Ledebur; iron with 2·33% sulphur smelted with			
	15% quartz.	5% limestone.	20% limestone.	200% of calcareous singulo-silicate slag.	200% of calcareous bisilicate slag.	200% o magnesian singulo-silicate slag.	200% of magnesian bisilicate slag.
% sulphur in resulting iron........	·09	·04	·01	·079	·357	·260	·39
% sulphur in resulting slag	......	......	......	1·445	·681	1·069	·29

slags is shown by Ledebur's results obtained on melting cast-iron containing 2·33% sulphur with different slags. The singulosilicates (the more basic) took up far more sulphur than the bisilicate slags, and the calcareous far more than the magnesian, the iron retaining ·079% sulphur when melted with the calcareous singulo- and ·357 with the calcareous bi-silicate: ·26% with the magnesian singulo- and ·39% with the magnesian bi-silicate. The greater desulphurizing power of lime than of magnesia is illustrated by the Illinois blast-furnace practice, in which the substitution of calcite for dolomite materially diminished the percentage of sulphur contained in the cast-iron.

That the power of basic silicates to remove sulphur increases with the temperature is suggested not alone by the fact that, *cæteris paribus*, the hotter the blast-furnace the freer the cast-iron from sulphur (here the larger proportion of fuel and the more basic slags which ordinarily accompany high temperature might be regarded as the cause of the accompanying freedom from sulphur), but by large scale experiments of Bell.[d] Fusing iron oxide with soda waste (which contains 17% ± sulphur with calcium and lime) at a low temperature, his product had as much as 32% sulphur with 4% oxygen: at a higher temperature nearly all the iron was recovered as cast-iron, containing only 1 to 2% of sulphur. Unfortunately Bell does not recite his conditions so fully as to make it clear that the more complete expulsion of sulphur was due directly to the higher temperature rather than to some accompanying condition.

The presence of basic slags in cupola-furnace fusion may in this way not only restrain the absorption of sulphur from the fuel, but even largely eliminate sulphur from cast-iron.[e] Walrand,[f] melting sulphurous cast-iron both in basic and in siliceous cupolas with from 10 to 20% of lime, found that in both the greater portion of the sulphur was removed during the fusion. Rollet[g] reports that a simple fusion in a cupola-furnace with basic slag removes 85 to 90% of the sulphur of but moderately sulphurous cast-irons, and 90 to 95 and occasionally 98% of that of highly sulphurous ones, containing 0·5% of sulphur or more. If the cupola be water-jacketed the lining may, according to Rollet be either acid or basic: but if unjacketed its lining must be basic. The slag may contain as much as 2 % of silica.

Both Rollet and Walrand employ fluor-spar: it probably assists desulphurization by liquefying the slag: but that it is not essential is shown by the fact that its almost complete omission (line 3) did not interfere with desulphurization. Table 23 summarizes their results.

TABLE 23.—DESULPHURIZATION IN CUPOLA MELTING.

No.	Number of heats.	Cupola acid or basic.	Additions per 100 of cast-iron average.				% Sulphur average.		% Manganese average.		% Phosphorus.		% Carbon.		% Silicon.	
			Spiegel.	Lime.	Fluor spar.	Coke.	Before fusion.	After fusion.	Before fusion.	After fusion.	Before.	After.	Before.	After.	Before.	After.
1	12	Basic	8±	10±	6·0±	10·8	·62	·10		.....	.....	.....	.....	.....	.....	.....
2.....	1	"	0	15	8	12	·58	·17	·80	·26	.....	.....	.....	.....	.....	.....
3.....	1	"	9	10	0·8	18	·71	·10	.	.....	.....	.....	.....	.....	.....	.....
4.....	1	"	7	13	1·3	13	·74	·17	.....	.....	.....	.....	.....	.....	.....	.....
5.....	4	Acid	8	17·5	4·5	19	·76	·08	1·40	1·32	.....	.....	.....	.....	.....	.....
6.....	4	Acid	9		6·2	14	·49	·07	1·40	1·20	.....	.....	.....	.....	.....	.....
7.....	...	Basic	...	.....	.....	.....	·22	·01	1·36	·81	·07	·06	3·50	3·50	·90	·38
8.....	...	"	...	7·2@33	2·4@4·8	18	·37	·01	tr.	tr.	·35	·07	2·90	3·08	·65	·06
9.....	....	"	....	.....	.....	...	·52	·04	tr.	tr.	1·90	·41	2·50	3·50	·45	·19

Nos. 1 to 6, Walrand; 7 to 9, Rollet.

E. MANGANESE like the metals of the alkaline earths appears to have the power of removing sulphur as sulphide, since manganiferous blast-furnace slags often contain a large amount of sulphur. Thus Parry reports finding not less than 2% sulphur in these slags when manganiferous, while when less manganiferous they contained less sulphur and the accompanying cast-iron had so much the more. Åkerman[h] indeed considers that manganese removes sulphur in this way even more powerfully than calcium does, so that under like conditions the richer the slags are in manganese the richer are they also in sulphur.

In other cases manganese causes the segregation and liquation of compounds rich in manganese and sulphur from cast-iron and steel. The addition of spiegeleisen to molten sulphurous cast-iron causes an immediate removal of sulphur. (See § 81.)

F. HYDROGEN does not, according to Percy,[i] decompose ferrous sulphide: yet Boussingault[j] states that Bonis observed a continuous evolution of sulphuretted hydrogen, which persistently blackened acetate of lead paper, on

[a] Journ. Iron and St. Inst., 1886, I., p. 184.
[b] Bell, Principles of the Manufacture of Iron and Steel, p. 164.
[c] Ledebur, Handbuch der Eisenhüttenkunde, p. 240.
[d] Bell, loc. cit.
[e] Jour. Iron and St. Inst., 1880, I., p. 213.
[f] Revue Universelle, X., p. 408, 1881.
[g] Stahl und Eisen, III., p. 305, 1883. From Bulletin de la Société de l'Industrie Minérale.
[h] Ledebur, Handbuch de Eisenhüttenkunde, p. 258.
[i] Iron and Steel, p. 33.
[j] Comptes Rendus, 52, p. 1,009.

passing hydrogen over different steels at a red heat, which indicates that hydrogen gradually removes sulphur from steel. Either this action is very slight, or it is confined to certain conditions of exposure, since not only does the atmospheric hydrogen ordinarily fail to remove any notable quantity of sulphur in the Bessemer process, but Forsyth,[a] blowing simply enormous volumes of steam along with air in Bessemerizing cast-iron, found that no removal of sulphur occurred: yet here hydrogen must have been abundantly present, since the steam must have been decomposed by the molten iron.

G. STEAM energetically decomposes ferrous sulphide with the formation of sulphuretted hydrogen and sulphurous acid as well as hydrogen, the latter being formed perhaps directly, perhaps by the action of water on the iron oxide previously formed (say $2FeS + 4H_2O = 2\,FeO + SO_2 + H_2S + 6H$).

It is stated that sulphur may be expelled from cast-iron by steam, *e.g.* that when cast-iron which, when cast in pigs has 0·05% sulphur, is granulated in water it is freed from this element,[c] and that the steam from damp sand-molds expels sulphur from cast-iron as sulphuretted hydrogen.[d] It is further stated that prolonged immersion in water even at the ordinary temperature, and even simple exposure to moist air for years partially removes sulphur from iron Boussingault[e] found that steam gradually removed sulphur from steel at a red heat. Exposing cast-steel (acier fondu, not *molten* steel as Lenox Smith[f] translates it) in a porcelain tube at a red heat to steam, a persistent odor of sulphuretted hydrogen arose, which continued during the whole course of the experiment (8 h. 50 min.) and acetate of lead paper was persistently blackened by it. So too Parry[g] stated that jets of steam blown upon the cinder in the puddling furnace caused the removal of some sulphur from the metal and of a great deal of sulphur from the cinder. Evidently in case of cast-irons with but little sulphur this action does not occur to an important extent at high temperatures unless under special conditions, since the employment of steam in the Bessemer process does not remove sulphur.

In Parry's case the steam may have caused the removal of sulphur from the iron indirectly, by decomposing the ferrous sulphide of the slag, and thus increasing the power of that slag to take up fresh portions of sulphur from the metal. This accords well with his statement that much more sulphur was removed from slag than metal, and with the familiar removal of sulphur from blast furnace slags with the accompanying odor of sulphuretted hydrogen by steam evolved from the moist ground over which they flow. This suggests the possibility of increasing the expulsion of sulphur in the basic Bessemer process by the injection of steam along with the blast: by desulphurizing the slag it might increase its desulphurizing power.

H. FERRIC OXIDE, FERROUS SULPHATE AND ATMOSPHERIC OXYGEN.—In the roasting of pyritous ores part of their sulphur is volatilized without oxidation: part is directly oxidized to sulphurous acid and thus volatilized, be it by the atmospheric oxygen or by the ferric oxide of the ore itself ($FeS + 3,O = FeO + SO_2$,[h] and $FeS + 10Fe_2O_3 = 7Fe_3O_4 + SO_2$[i]): part, especially at low temperatures, is converted into ferrous sulphate, which at higher ones in part reacts on still undecomposed ferrous sulphide with expulsion of sulphur as sulphurous acid (say $FeS + 3FeSO_4 = 4FeO + 4SO_2$, in this way sulphur may be completely expelled according to Berthier), and is in part decomposed with complete expulsion of its sulphur as sulphurous and sulphuric acids ($2FeSO_4 = Fe_2SO_6 + SO_2$ and $FeSO_3 = Fe_2O_3 + SO_3$[j]).

The sulphur of cast-iron may also be oxidized and expelled by ferric oxide, as is shown by its rapid expulsion in pig-washing (the Bell-Krupp process), in the basic open-hearth process and in puddling, in which say 60 to 90, 40 to 90 and 50 to 60% respectively of the sulphur may be removed, partly at least as ferrous sulphide, since as much as 7% of this substance occurs in puddling slags.

I. ALKALINE NITRATES as in the Heaton process (in which molten cast-iron is brought into contact with nitrate of soda) rapidly remove sulphur from cast-iron. Thus Prof. Miller reports that by this process the sulphur was reduced from 0·113 to ·018%. Snelus[k] reports 1·225% "sulphuric acid" in the slag of the Heaton process. Gruner[l] found that from 85 to 94% of the sulphur of cast-iron containing 0·34% sulphur, and from 67 to 100% of that contained in a cast-iron with ·09% sulphur was expelled by this process; the slag had in one case 0·60% sulphur and 0·70% sulphuric acid.

§ 94. REDSHORTNESS.—Sulphur has the specific effect of making iron exceedingly brittle at a red heat and of destroying its welding power. Its effects are in general most marked at a dull-red heat, and irons which crack at this temperature owing to the presence of a small percentage of sulphur may often be readily forged at higher temperatures, while when cold they are as malleable and indeed often more malleable than non-sulphurous irons. If however the percentage of sulphur is considerable, the iron is no longer malleable even at temperatures above redness. Manganese counteracts these effects of sulphur. (See § 81.) The redshortness imparted by a given percentage of sulphur is probably independent of the percentage of carbon which accompanies it: but more sulphur can usually be tolerated in steel rich in carbon than in others because such steel usually contains much manganese also.

Eggertz[m] found that at a red heat weld iron with 0·02% sulphur cracked when punched through, and with 0·03% sulphur cracked at the corners when being drawn out. But I doubt if the effects of ·03 per cent of sulphur would ordinarily be serious: Bell[n] quotes iron rails, whose manufacture calls for great malleableness, with 0·124 sulphur though without manganese. Their composition was, carbon ·10, silicon trace, sulphur ·124, phosphorus ·303, manganese trace. Another had ·08 sulphur with ·11 manganese.

[a] Trans. Am. Inst. Mining Engineers, XII., p. 265.
[b] Balling, Compendium der Metallurgischen Chemie, p. 52. Percy, Iron and Steel, p. 33; Watts, Dictionary of Chemistry, III., p. 400.
[c] Akerman, Eng. and Mining Jl., 1875, I., p. 352.
[d] Ledebur, Op. Cit., p. 251.
[e] Comptes Rendus, 52, p. 1,008.
[f] Manufacture of Steel, Gruner, Smith, p. 76.
[g] Percy, Op. Cit., p. 667
[h] Balling, Op. Cit., p. 46.
[i] Percy, Op. Cit., p. 35.
[j] Balling, Op. Cit., pp. 36–40.
[k] Journ. Iron and St. Inst., 1871, II., p. 186.
[l] Annales des Mines, 1869, XVI.
[m] Eng. and Mining Jl., 1875, I., p. 458: Jernkontorets Annalen, 1860, p. 15.
[n] Manufacture of Iron and Steel, p. 198. Journal Iron and St. Inst., 1877, II., p. 325.

The older determinations of sulphur are not to be trusted, since precautions to prevent its absorption from the coal gas were too often omitted: they gave the sulphur in weld iron, even when apparently of good quality, as high as 0·60 and even ·757%. Rejecting these old analyses and all other doubtful ones, I find that among 86 cases of weld iron, drawn from many sources, the maximum sulphur is 0·124%; many are reported as quite free from sulphur, while the average is only ·017%: but as a majority of the cases represent unusually good irons the average here given is somewhat below that of commercial irons. Eleven iron rails[a] given by Bell average ·045 sulphur.

Ingot metal it is thought may contain a much larger percentage of sulphur than can be tolerated in weld metal, be it because the sulphur in the former is less liable to be locally concentrated, be it because it contains far more manganese, whose presence counteracts sulphur. The highest percentages of sulphur which I have met in rail steel are given in Table 24.

TABLE 24.—SULPHUROUS RAIL STEEL.

	Carbon.	Silicon.	Phosphorus.	Sulphur.	Manganese.	Slag.	Copper.	
1..	·757	·048	·099	·178	·881	·024	·078	Segregation } Good rail.
2..	·673	·041	·098	·133	·856	·022	·074	Mother metal } Good rail.
3..	·865	·043	·124	·217	·915	·040	·077	Segregation } Same rail, *a*
4..	·686	·041	·098	·148	·910	·022	·075	Mother metal } Same rail, *a*
5..	·806	·009	·240	·148	·887	·021	·018	Segregation } Bad rail.
6..	·273	·008	·194	·187	·884	·029	·011	Mother metal } Bad rail.
7..	·41	....	·09	·22	·97	...	....	French rail.
8..	·45	·10	·18	·15	1·31	....	....	British rails.
9..	·41	·11	·05	·15	1·46	....	....	British rails.
10..	·52	·08	·05	·17	1·04	...	....	British rails.
11..	·52	·12	·05	·18	1·01	....	....	British rails.
12..	·39	·14	·06	·16	·69	....	·04	Slightly redshort.
13..	·26	·14	·04	·20	·50	....	·05	Very redshort.
14..	·31	·07	·04	·21	·49	...	·06	Total wreck.
15..	·22	·09	·03	·23	·44	...	·07	Fell in pieces.
16..	·48	·07	·12	·22	1·35	*b*	....	
17..	·54	....	·12	·24	1·56	*c*	....	
18..	·43	·07	·13	·30	1·61		....	
19..	·29	....	....	·46	....	....	....	

Nos. **1** to **6**, Forsyth Western U. S. rails, private communication. **7**, Morrell, Metallurgical Review, II., p. 193. **8** to **11**, Bell, Manufacture of Iron and Steel, p. 414. **12** to **15**, Wasum, Stahl und Eisen, 1882, p. 192. **16** to **19**, R. W. Lodge, private communication, Feb., 1887; rails made at an Illinois mill. *a*, These analyses are from the opposite end of the rail from which analyses 1 and 2 come. *b*, This heat of steel yielded 60% of "lost" (*i. e.*, worthless) rails and 35% of second quality rails: it was so redshort that some of the ingots fell to pieces in the blooming roll-train. *c*, This heat yielded 78% of first quality rails, 13% of second quality and 9% of "lost" rails.

Some European rails appear to be much richer in sulphur than those made in this country: thus while W. Richards[b] admits that 0·20% sulphur makes steel very redshort, Thomas[c] states that this amount can be tolerated, and E. Riley[d] has known rails with 0·27 sulphur to pass the mechanical tests required. But with these high percentages of sulphur the steel is so redshort that it must be rolled at a very high temperature. Instances in which the sulphur in rails exceeds ·18% are so rare that they might be thought to represent, not the average composition of the whole rail, but merely that of some segregated spot. I am, however, convinced that analyses 7, 16, 17, 18 and 19, with from ·22 to ·62% of sulphur, represent the mother metal, since the observers privately inform me that the borings were taken from the upper portion of the head of the rail, while segregations, if present, occur at the junction of head and web, *i.e.*, near what has been the center of cross-section of the ingot. (These analyses are from thin-flanged T rails.)

Sandberg,[e] whose opportunities for observation are excellent, states that, in about 800 instances, rail steel (presumably largely British) contained usually from ·03 to ·06% sulphur: 20% of the cases had less than ·03% sulphur and 24% of them had more than ·06%. The rail steel of our Eastern mills has usually from ·03 to ·06% sulphur: that of our Western mills has usually somewhat more, occasionally as much as ·10, ·12 and even exceptionally ·14%. When sulphur is under ·08 its effects are probably almost completely effaced by the presence of ·8% manganese, since with this composition the redshortness is so slight that T rails, the formation of whose thin flanges necessitates great malleableness, can be rolled with so little cracking that at some mills only 0·4% of the rails made are of second quality (*i. e.* have cracked flanges).

In some of the western mills however, especially when high phosphorus accompanies high sulphur, as much as 10%, and at one mill occasionally even 15% of the rails have been of second quality. From the evidence I judge that if the sulphur often rises above 0·08 a considerable percentage (say 2 to 4%) of second quality rails is liable to be made, if above 0·11% the number of second quality rails is liable to be excessive, and if it be as high as 0·18% the number is likely to be ruinous.

Pieces of a shape which can be produced without necessitating such extreme malleableness as the formation of the thin flanges of T rails requires may contain more sulphur: and we may suspect that the rails quoted by Riley as containing 0·27% of sulphur were not of the thin flanged T, but of the comparatively easily rolled double-headed pattern. But it is rare to find more than 0·12 sulphur in any steel. Crucible tool steel has ordinarily less than 0·01% (though Metcalf quotes wire dies with 0·09%).[f] Nail plate has usually from 0·05 to 0·10, boiler plate from 0·02 to 0·08%.

Manganese counteracts the effects of sulphur, as described in § 81, where it is stated that in many cases 4·5 parts by weight of manganese so far counteract the effects of 1 part of sulphur as to permit the rolling of flanged T rails.

§ 95. WELDING.—Sulphur also interferes with the welding power of iron; but we have little quantitative information as to its effect in this respect. The U. S. testing board found that ·046% sulphur in wrought-iron (the highest percentage which they encountered) did not affect its welding.[g] Harbord reports basic open-hearth steel with carbon ·13, sulphur ·125 and manganese ·51% and another lot with carbon ·16, sulphur ·20 and manganese ·78% which welded perfectly; this is most surprising, even if we make great allowance for the elastic sense in which "perfect welding" is often used.[h]

§ 96. TENSILE STRENGTH AND DUCTILITY.—The redshortness caused by sulphur may diminish tensile strength and ductility by breaking up the continuity through cracks, perhaps internal and beyond detection. But apart from this let us consider its direct effects. In moderate quantity sulphur makes weld-iron tougher, and it is generally thought to have the same effect on ingot metal: though the evidence is neither decisive in kind nor in amount, it favors this view. Many American experts with preconceived and tenaciously held belief that manganese like phosphorus makes steel brittle, yet finding in western rails percentages of manganese with

a Manufacture of Iron and Steel, p. 428.
b Journ. Iron and St. Inst., 1880, I., p. 100.
c Idem, p. 110.
d Idem., p. 197.
e Trans. Am. Inst. Min. Eng., X., p. 410, 1882: Journ. Iron and St. Inst., 1882, I., p. 258.

f Trans. Am. Inst. Mining Engineers, IX., p. 549.
g Holley, Trans. Am. Inst. Mining Engineers, VI., p. 111.
h Journ. Iron and St. Inst., 1886, II., pp. 701–703 and 725.

phosphorus which, in their view, should make them so brittle that they should break under the straightening press, explain their ductility by supposing that the sulphur, which is often high in western rails, makes steel tough, counteracting the manganese and phosphorus. But unfortunately this, like other explanations based on limited knowledge, will not stand the least scrutiny: for we find many western rails with abnormally high manganese and phosphorus, with high carbon yet with very little sulphur, which are still tough. So here the explainers must fall back on hydrogen or ozone or whatever they can think of which is undeterminable. In Table 25 are collected a few cases of rails whose composition should, if the ordinary views be correct, be extremely brittle, whose sulphur is low, in many cases extremely low, yet which at least are not extremely brittle: indeed, some of them are extremely tough.

TABLE 25.—GOOD RAILS WITH HIGH PHOSPHORUS AND MANGANESE BUT LOW SULPHUR.

№	1	2	3	4	5	6	7	8	9	10	11	12	13	14
Carbon	·84	·37	·45	·68	·85	·40	·42	·68	·42	·70	·52	·79	·83	1
Silicon	·01	·05	·06	·07	·05	·06	·04	·06	·05	·58	·87	·60	·08	·49
Manganese	1·63	1·60	1·28	1·45	1·58	1·68	1·38	1·57	1·39	1·85	2·98	1·51	1·87	·74
Phosphorus	·15	·14	·14	·15	·14	·12	·13	·12	·13	·06	·11	·06	·24	·144
Sulphur	·07	·07	·04	·05	·06	·06	·03	·028	·098	·013	·05	·015	·07	·055

Nos. 1 to 9 inclusive, rails from U. S. ores rolled at a western U. S. mill. Nos. 10 to 13 rails rolled from imported blooms at another western mill. Private communications. 14, Müller, Journ. Iron and St. Inst., 1882, I., p. 375.

Important light might have been thrown on the effect of sulphur on strength, ductility and wearing power had Dudley and Beck-Guerhard, in their investigations into the relations between composition and the physical properties of rail steel, determined the sulphur in the rails observed: this they unfortunately neglected to do, pleading that sulphur is so very objectionable to the railmaker that the consummer need not trouble himself about it, as if it were not extremely possible that variations of sulphur below the maximum which the railmaker can permit might not affect the wearing power, both directly and indirectly, and help to explain the inconsistencies in their results. A high percentage of sulphur may indirectly have a most potent effect on wear, by necessitating finishing the rail at an excessively high temperature.

Morrell,[a] when comparing by his wearing-test apparatus steel No. 7 of Table 24 with Cambria steel with much less sulphur but of otherwise closely similar composition (viz, carbon ·44, manganese ·53, phosphorus ·079, sulphur ·02), found that the rail rich in sulphur lost weight much more rapidly than the other, in one case 80% faster. As far as this goes it indicates that sulphur makes steel *softer*, but it throws no strong light on toughness and tensile strength, because one swallow makes no summer, and because, though toughness usually accompanies softness and low tensile strength, there is no necessary relation between them. Kerpely[b] from prolonged examination considers that sulphur softens steel: E. Williams[c] considers that it toughens it: Parry[d] is unequivocally of the opinion that it strengthens it: Adamson[e] thinks that it renders it brittle, but he appears to have something like a monopoly of this opinion.

§ 97. SULPHUR IN CAST-IRON.—Sulphur is generally thought to make cast-iron hard and brittle. The Finspong (Swedish) gun cast-iron has from 0·10 to 0·15% of sulphur intentionally imparted to it by the addition of pyrites. But whether the hardness is directly caused by the presence of the sulphur is doubtful, for it is well known that sulphur has the specific effect of causing carbon to be retained in the combined state, which in itself of course greatly increases the hardness of the iron.[f]

CHAPTER VI.

IRON AND PHOSPHORUS.

§ 100. SUMMARY.—PHOSPHORUS, the steelmaker's bane, unites with iron probably in all proportions at least up to 26%, being readily absorbed by it, especially at high temperatures and when under deoxidizing conditions, from acid phosphates and silico-phosphates. Fortunately it is readily removed from iron, especially under strongly oxidizing conditions, by contact with strong bases (oxides of iron and manganese, the alkalies and alkaline earths) and by basic silicates and even silico-phosphates, by alkaline carbonates and nitrates and by fluor spar. It is volatilized under many conditions, *e. g.*, when phosphates are heated with carbon (the presence of metallic iron more or less completely prevents this volatilization): and when molten phosphoric cast-iron is brought in contact with alkaline nitrates or (probably) with fluor spar. In the blast-furnace, however, phosphorus is not effectively volatilized, for any which volatilizes immediately recondenses. Hence in the blast-furnace nearly all the phosphorus passes into the metal, though a little is found in the slag if the deoxidizing conditions be weak. In puddling 90%, and in the basic Bessemer process 96 to 99% or even more of the phosphorus initially present may be removed under favorable conditions.

Phosphorus probably has little effect on tensile strength under gently applied load: but phosphoric iron is readily broken by jerky, shock-like or vibratory stresses, sometimes when quite trifling:—it is treacherous. It sometimes affects iron but slightly, sometimes under apparently like conditions profoundly:—it is capricious. It usually increases the elastic limit, thus raising the elastic ratio, an index of brittleness. It diminishes also the elongation and contraction on rupture, two other measures of ductility, affecting this property like tensile strength much more under shock than under quiescent stress. Carbon greatly intensifies these effects of phosphorus, and silicon may intensify them, but certainly to a very much smaller degree if at all. Low temperature is thought to intensify them, but I find no evidence to support this opinion, *i. e.* to show that there is more difference between the ductility of phosphoric and that of non-phosphoric

[a] Metallurgical Review, II., p. 193.
[b] Idem, II., p. 521.
[c] Journ. Iron and Steel Inst., 1880, I., p. 190.
[d] Idem, p. 198.
[e] Idem, p. 197.
[f] Akerman, Eng. and Mining Jl., 1875, I., p. 158; Turner, Jour. Iron and St. Inst., 1886, I., p. 184: Ledebur, Handbuch, p. 251.

steel at very low temperatures than at 70° F. Rapid cooling and forging during cooling, by preventing the coarse crystallization to which phosphoric iron strongly inclines, oppose the effects of phosphorus on ductility. It is certain that phosphorus does not always diminish the hot-malleableness of iron, at least at moderate temperatures; but, by increasing the tendency to coarse crystallization, it probably diminishes malleableness at very high temperatures, and especially when the iron has slowly cooled without forging from a very high temperature to a somewhat lower though still high one, as this seems to be the condition most favorable to coarse crystallization. It is thought to increase the welding power and to slightly lower the modulus of elasticity: what evidence I find opposes the latter view.

§ 101. The Condition of Phosphorus in Iron.—In ingot metal phosphorus exists chiefly if not exclusively as phosphide: but in weld metal it probably exists both as phosphide and as phosphate, *i. e.* as part of the mechanically intermixed slag, in which condition it is reasonable to suppose that its effect on the mechanical properties of the metal should be comparatively slight. Many, and perhaps an indefinite number of phosphides of indefinite composition may exist in iron, for we find wide differences between the chemical behavior of different portions of phosphorus even in one and the same piece of iron, and apparently equally wide discrepancies between the effect of a given quantity of phosphorus on the physical properties of different irons. The differences in the chemical behavior of phosphorus are exemplified by the fact that, on dissolving some steels in chlorhydric acid, part of the phosphorus escapes as phosphoretted hydrogen, part is found as phosphoric acid, part apparently as some lower oxygen acid, while still another part is insoluble.

The existence in solid iron of a definite phosphide of iron, Fe_3P, and probably that of a definite phosphide of manganese, Mn_2P_3, is well established. Hvoslef,[a] on melting the non-magnetic phosphide Fe_2P under borax, obtained the magnetic phosphide Fe_3P, while Percy, by digesting in cupric chloride a phosphide prepared by the action of lumps of phosphorus on red-hot iron, obtained a crystalline phosphide with 85% iron, corresponding closely to Fe_3P, which should contain 84·4% phosphorus. These facts suggest that iron and phosphorus preferentially combine in this particular ratio. Shimer's[b] investigations indicated the presence of such a phosphide in cast-iron, though, as he had been unable to completely free it from titanium carbide, he had not definitely determined its composition.

Less than a month later L. Schneider[c] described the phosphide Fe_3P, which he isolated from eight different samples of cast-iron by digestion in cupric chloride, as a crystalline, dark gray, strongly magnetic, friable substance, with metallic lustre, almost insoluble in dilute acids, rapidly dissolved by nitric acid and by aqua regia, and dissolved by hot concentrated chlorhydric acid with evolution of phosphoretted hydrogen. Three of the cast-irons examined contained a considerable amount of manganese: one of these yielded a slightly manganiferous magnetic phosphide, the others yielded highly manganiferous and non-magnetic phosphides. These three manganiferous phosphides corresponded very closely to the formula xFe_3P,yMn_3P_2.

The composition of these eight phosphides is surprisingly close to the calculated composition, especially as other substances insoluble in cupric chloride would be expected to accompany the phosphide. I here summarize Schneider's results.

Phosphides Obtained by Schneider on Digesting Cast-Iron in Cupric Chloride.

		1.	2.	3.	4	5.	6.	7.	8.
In the cast-iron	Manganese	0·2	....	2·47	0	·07	4·83	18·15	38·7
	Phosphorus	2·5	1·45	0·36	1·48	0·91	2·01	3·4	0·38
In the phosphide per 100 of iron in it.	Manganese	....	....	....	....	....	5·7	52·2	54·4
	Phosphorus	18·6	18·5	18·2	18·2	18·5	20·5	37·7	38·8
Discrepancy between phosphorus found and calculated		0·15	0·15	0·25	0·25	0·05	0·00	0·60	0·10

The presence of phosphates in weld iron, long reasonably suspected because the metal contains a considerable quantity of the slag which accompanies its production and which ordinarily contains phosphates, and because the properties of weld metal are often but slightly affected by the presence of a considerable quantity of phosphorus, is shown to be exceedingly probable by the fact that when weld metal is volatilized with chlorine a large proportion of its phosphorus remains in the non-volatile residue.

There is however little reason to expect the presence of an important quantity of phosphate in ingot metal, excepting perhaps that made by the basic process, (A) because the slag which accompanies its production is ordinarily nearly or quite free from both phosphates and phosphides; (B) because the metal itself ordinarily contains but a trifling quantity of such slag, often less than 0·02%; (C) because the slag which accompanies the production of the metal is ordinarily acid, and we find that metallic iron greedily reduces and absorbs the phosphorus from acid slags; and (D) because if phosphorus were present as phosphate, *i. e.* as a simply mechanically intermixed foreign substance, we should reasonably expect that it would gradually separate from the molten ingot metal by gravity: while in fact phosphoric steel may lie for hours in tranquil fusion in the open-hearth furnace apparently without the loss of the smallest trace of phosphorus. But in spite of these obstacles Dudley would explain the difference (of whose existence I endeavor to show in § 129 there is no evidence) between the forging properties of Bessemer steel made (*A*) in the Clapp-Griffiths and (*B*) in the common converter by the existence of phosphorus as phosphate in the former.[d] But as he offers no evidence we may dismiss his plea. Cheever would explain the different chemical behavior of different portions of phosphorus in the same piece of steel, and the different effects of phosphorus on the physical properties of different steels, by the existence of both phosphates and phosphides, though these differences are as fully and more simply explained by the existence of different phosphides. He argues that,[e] because certain definite phosphides of iron are difficultly soluble while certain phosphates dissolve readily, and because part of the phosphorus found in ingot iron and steel is readily soluble, therefore this portion exists as phosphate, a conclusion certainly not warranted by the premises. The fact that certain phosphides dissolve with difficulty does not prove

[a] Journ. Prakt. Chemie, LXX., p. 149.

[b] "Titanium Carbide in Pig-Iron," read in October, 1886, before the Am. Inst Mining Engineers.

[c] Oesterreich. Zeitschrift, 1886, p. 735, No. 45.

[d] Trans. Am. Inst. Mining Engineers, XIV., 1886, p. 938.

[e] Op. Cit., XV., 1887, to appear.

that none dissolve readily. Indeed, a phosphide of manganese, Mn_3P_2, whose presence is far more probable than that of a phosphate, is thought to be readily soluble. To clear the matter up he volatilizes several irons with chlorine, and examines the non-volatile residue for phosphorus, at the same time treating other portions of the same irons with several weak solvents, cupric sulphate, ferric chloride, cold dilute chlorhydric acid, etc. I here summarize the more important features of his results:[a]

Metal.	Phosphorus existing as phosphate per 100 of total phosphorus.	
	As indicated by ignition in chlorine.	As indicated by weak solvents.
Cast-iron	0	50 ±
Weld iron	98 ± to 100	73
Blown and unrecarburized Bessemer steel (Clapp-Griffiths vessels)	2 ±	38 ±
Do. ordinary vessels	26 ±	87 ±
Bessemer steel (Clapp-Griffiths converters)	5@15 ±	87@91 ±
Bessemer steel, ordinary converters	14@40 ±	75 ±

When the many necessary precautions are observed and when we know that oxygen is wholly absent, phosphorus found in the residue from ignition in chlorine may be held to have existed in the metal as phosphate. The liability to err in this method is, however, very great, and here several facts raise suspicion of error. (1) The proportion of the total phosphorus apparently existing as phosphate is often very much lower in unrecarburized than in recarburized metal: (2) all or nearly all the phosphorus of weld metal appears as phosphate: and (3) the indications afforded by the weak solvents are largely directly opposed to those of the chlorine treatment. The solvents indicate that much or most of the phosphorus of the cast-iron is phosphate, chlorine shows that none of it is: the solvents indicate that nearly all the phosphorus of the decarburized metals, of the steels and of the weld irons is phosphate, chlorine indicates that little of it is. To abandon the original ground and assume that it is the phosphides that dissolve readily and the phosphates that resist, helps little: for then the solvents would show that say half the phosphorus of the cast-iron is phosphate, while chlorine shows that none is. Cheever's results diminish the improbability of the existence of important quantities of phosphate in ingot metal: in my opinion evidence less tainted with suspicion is needed to convert it into a probability. Note that a smaller proportion of the phosphorus of Clapp-Griffiths than of other Bessemer steel appears as phosphate.

SEGREGATION.—Phosphorus has a strong tendency to segregate in phosphoric steel; this may give rise to erroneous determinations unless special precautions are taken. I append a *few* cases observed by Forsyth.

SEGREGATION OF PHOSPHORUS.

	A	B	A	B	A	B	A	B
Carbon	·60	·31	·70	·25	·89	·30	·20	·25
Silicon	·09	·00	....	....	·08	·08	·01	·02
Phosphorus	·20	·11	·38	·04	·23	·14	·24	·19
Manganese	·79	·68	1·22	·97	·95	·71	·59	·69

A = Segregation. B = Mother metal.
Private communication Jan. 27, 1886.

§ 102. UNION OF PHOSPHORUS AND IRON—DIRECT COMBINATION.—Phosphorus, when dropped on red-hot iron, is greedily absorbed: but Percy[b] was unable in this way to make iron take up more than 8·4% phosphorus, forming a beautifully crystalline substance, approaching the composition Fe_6P.

[a] Private communication, Feb. 22, June 27, 1887.
[b] Percy, Iron and Steel, p. 60.

COMBINATION UNDER DEOXIDIZING CONDITIONS.—Under strongly deoxidizing conditions iron can take up a large percentage of phosphorus, certainly 26%. Thus Brackelsberg, melting lime phosphate with ferric oxide and coal in a carbonaceous crucible, obtained iron phosphide with 26·36% phosphorus. This was the highest percentage which he succeeded in obtaining, even though a great excess of phosphate was present and though the conditions were strongly deoxidizing.

In the blast-furnace iron readily absorbs a large percentage of phosphorus. Lord[c] quotes cast-iron made in Ohio with 4·9% phosphorus, though a high percentage of phosphorus does not appear to have been aimed at.

At Hoerde in Westphalia ferro-phosphorus with 20% phosphorus is made in the blast-furnace from apatite and slag of the basic Bessemer process.[d]

§ 103. ACTION OF SLAGS (Phosphates and Silicates).—Under certain conditions metallic iron takes up phosphorus from the phosphates of lime, iron, etc., and from their silico-phosphates, especially in presence of carbon, silicon and manganese: under other conditions these compounds remove phosphorus from metallic iron.

Which of these actions will occur and the extent to which it will occur depends primarily on the basicity of these phosphates and silicates and on the strength of the existing oxidizing or deoxidizing conditions, (I include the presence of carbon, silicon and manganese in the iron itself as a deoxidizing condition), and secondarily on the temperature, on the percentage of phosphorus which the iron contains, and on the proportion of iron oxide to lime, etc., among the bases, ferruginous slags probably removing phosphorus more energetically than calcareous ones of like basicity. *In general, intimate mixture with a highly basic and preferably ferruginous slag under strong oxidizing conditions and at a relatively low temperature favors the removal of phosphorus from iron: the opposite conditions oppose it.* These factors must all be taken into account to fully comprehend the phenomena of the absorption of phosphorus by iron and its removal. Carbon, manganese and silicon in iron oppose the removal of phosphorus by being preferentially oxidized, and by reducing the phosphoric acid formed by its oxidation. Yet in puddling, in pig-washing and in the basic Bessemer process we see that dephosphorization sometimes progresses to a considerable extent while the iron still contains much manganese, silicon and carbon: indeed in pig washing 93% of the initial phosphorus may be removed while the iron yet retains 90% of its initial carbon.

§ 104. BASICITY OF SLAG.—The influence of this factor is most clearly seen by comparing cases in which all other conditions are nearly alike, of which the most striking are found in the Bessemer process. In the acid lined converter the necessarily siliceous slags almost completely prevent the removal of phosphorus. Bell,[e] overblowing a charge of phosphoric cast-iron in an acid converter converted about 25% of its iron into oxide, yet the phosphorus in the metal increased (owing to the elimination of part of the iron and the concentration of the whole of the phosphorus in the remainder) from 1·33 to 1·66%, simply because, even after scorifying so much iron, his slag

[c] Trans. Am. Inst. Mining Engineers, XII., p. 506.
[d] Journal Iron and St. Inst., 1880, II., p. 754.
[e] Jour. Iron and St. Inst., 1877, I., p. 117.

remained acid, having 45·38 silica (the oxygen ratio of base to acid being 1 : 1·94, a bisilicate). In the basic Bessemer process, however, all other conditions remain almost precisely the same, except that a basic slag is substituted for an acid one, which permits us to dephosphorize the metal practically completely. Berthier[a] taught that by the use of lime in the blast-furnace phosphorus may be prevented from uniting with the cast-iron—"because this earth tends to remove phosphorus from the iron—to form phosphate of lime."

The perspicacious Gruner is credited with being the first to point out that, since phosphorus can in general only be eliminated from iron in contact with a basic slag, the necessarily acid slag of the ordinary Bessemer converter bars its removal: this he stated in 1857,[b] repeating in 1869[c] that "when the slags contain 40% silica the bases no longer retain phosphoric acid: phosphide of iron is continuously regenerated" and in 1870[d] "the proportion of silica should not exceed 30%, for beyond this the iron phosphate is decomposed anew by the carbon."[e]

While slag with over 60% of silica may retain small quantities of phosphoric acid though in contact with metallic iron, and while a considerable proportion of phosphorus may be removed from iron which is in contact with slags holding over 30% of silica together with even as much as 6% of phosphoric acid (*e. g.* slag 47 in Table 26), yet it is probably true that nothing approaching complete dephosphorization can be accomplished in presence of slags containing as much as 30% silica. W. Richards[f] states that phosphorus will not leave iron rapidly in the basic Bessemer process unless the silica in the slag be below 20%, and that the most complete dephosphorization is obtained when it is below 15%: Gilchrist corroborates this, as do the many published analyses of metal and slag of this process.

a Traité de la Voie Sèche, II., p. 276.

b Bulletin de L'Industrie Minerale, II., p. 190 : Journ. Iron and St. Inst., 1883, II., p. 661.

c Annales des Mines, 1869, XVI., p. 200.

d Idem, 1870.

e It has been stated that he considered temperature as serious an obstacle to dephosphorization as acidity of slag : but a perusal of his writings leaves no doubt in my mind that he regarded a basic slag as the first requisite, and considered temperature as an important element chiefly because of the difficulty of maintaining basic linings at high temperatures. (Idem, 1869, p. 272).

f Journal Iron and St. Inst., 1879, I., pp. 159-201.

As the silica of the slag falls below 30% the completeness with which phosphorus can be removed from the iron rapidly increases. Among a host of recorded cases of the treatment of iron containing a considerable portion of phosphorus, the following are the most complete instances which I have met of dephosphorization for given silica in the accompanying slag :

Process.	Basic.	Puddling.	Basic.	Puddling.	Basic.	Basic.
Percentage of silica in slag ...	31·7	27·77	24·[illegible]	20·27	16·60	10·5
Percentage of phosphoric acid in slag..................	5·98	9·19	8·06	5·[illegible]	13·94	2·05
Percentage of phosphorus initially in metal	1·42	....	1·27	·47	....	....
Percentage of phosphorus in metal accompanying this slag....................	0·54	·23	0·15	·07	·02	·008
Oxygen ratio of base : acid ...	1 : 1·10	1 : 0·88	1 : 0·88	1 : 0·75	1 : 0·6[illegible]	1 : 0·31
Oxygen ratio of total bases : oxide of iron.	1 : 0·25	1 : 0·79	1 : 0·18	1 : 0·83	1 : 0·14	1 : 0·30
Number in Table 26...	47	32	38	21	31	2

Nos. 39, 44, 45, 46, 49, 50, 52, 53 and 54 Table 26 further illustrate the fact that slags containing from 36 to 44% of silica may yet hold phosphoric acid in the presence of metallic iron, which in certain cases contains considerable carbon; *e. g.*, No. 52 (basic Bessemer slag), in which the slag has 44·8% silica with 2·3% phosphoric acid, though in contact with metal holding 3% of carbon. Further, certain of them illustrate the removal of phosphorus from iron when in contact with slags holding more than 30% of silica.

§ 105. Basicity of Silicates Compared with that of Phosphates.—In comparing the influence of the basicity of phosphates on their dephosphorizing power with that of silicates, we may either select phosphates and silicates of like percentage of acid, *e. g.*, comparing phosphates of 30% phosphoric acid with silicates of 30% silica : or those of like atomic ratio of base to acid, *e. g.*, comparing tricalcic phosphate with tricalcic silicate : or finally those with like oxygen ratio of base to acid, *e. g.*, comparing the metallurgical bi-silicate of lime with what may by analogy be called the bi-phosphate, 2·5-CaO, P_2O_5.

Our scanty data do not permit accurate comparisons : yet, whatever standard we employ, phosphates appear to have much greater dephosphorizing power than silicates of like basicity.

Hilgenstock found that apparently practically carbonless iron absorbed phosphorus abundantly from tricalcic phosphate, and that it even took up a little from tetracalcic phosphate: Finkener observed that it took up none from triferrous phosphate, but that it absorbed a little from phosphates which were but slightly more acid, even from one with 2·9 equivalents of base to one of acid. But a

Table 25 A.—Composition, etc., of Pure Phosphates and Silicates.

Names.		Composition.					
Chemical.	Metallurgical.	Formula.	Percentage composition.				Oxygen ratio. Base ÷ Acid.
			P_2O_5.	SiO_2.	CaO.	FeO.	
Phosphates :							
Mono-(meta)-calcic phosphate	Quinquiphosphate of lime	$CaO, P_2O_5 = CaP_2O_6$	71·70	......	28·30	......	1 : 5
Di-(pyro)- " "		$2CaO, P_2O_5 = Ca_2P_2O_7$	55·91	......	44·09	......	1 : 2·5
	Biphosphate "		50·39	......	49·61	......	1 : 2
Tri-(ortho)- " " (nearly apatite)		$3CaO, P_2O_5 = Ca_3P_2O_8$	45·81	......	54.19	......	1 : 1·7
	Sesquiphosphate "		43·19	......	56·81	......	1 : 1·5
Tetra-calcic "		$4CaO, P_2O_5 = Ca_4P_2O_9$	38·81	......	61·19	......	1 : 1·25
Penta-calcic "	Singulophosphate "	$5CaO, P_2O_5 = Ca_5P_2O_{10}$	33·64	......	66·36	......	1 : 1
Mono-(meta)-ferrous "	Ferrous quinquiphosphate	$FeO, P_2O_5 = FeP_2O_6$	66·34	......	......	33·66	1 : 5
Di-(pyro)- " "		$2FeO, P_2O_5 = Fe_2P_2O_7$	49·65	......	......	50·35	1 : 2·5
	" biphosphate		44·00	......	......	55·90	1 : 2
Tri-(ortho)-ferrous " (vivianite less water)		$3FeO, P_2O_5 = Fe_3P_2O_8$	39·44	......	......	60·56	1 : 1·7
	" sesquiphosphate		37·15	......	......	62·84	1 : 1·5
Tetra-ferrous "		$4FeO, P_2O_5 = Fe_4P_2O_9$	33·03	......	......	66·96	1 : 1·25
Penta- " "	" singulophosphate	$5FeO, P_2O_5 = Fe_5P_2O_{10}$	28·28	......	......	71·71	1 : 1
Silicates :							
Sesquisilicate (gyrolite less water)	Trisilicate of lime	$2CaO, 3SiO_2 = Ca_2Si_3O_8$	......	61·64	38·36	......	1 : 3
Mono-(meta)-calcic silicate (Wollastonite)	Bisilicate "	$CaO, SiO_2 = CaSiO_3$	......	51·72	48·27	......	1 : 2
	Sesquisilicate "	$4CaO, 3SiO_2 = Ca_4Si_3O_{10}$	......	44·53	55·46	......	1 : 1·5
Dicalcic "	Singulosilicate of lime	$2CaO, SiO_2 = Ca_2SiO_4$	......	34·82	65·17	......	1 : 1
Tricalcic "		$3CaO, SiO_2 = Ca_3SiO_5$	......	26·31	73·63	......	1 : 0·67
Tetracalcic "	Subsilicate "	$4CaO, SiO_2 = Ca_4SiO_6$	......	21·11	78·88	......	1 : 0·5
	Ferrous trisilicate	$2FeO, 3SiO_2 = Fe_2Si_3O_8$	......	55·78	......	44·40	1 : 3·0
Monoferrous " (Grunerite)	" bisilicate	$FeO, SiO_2 = FeSiO_3$	......	45·45	......	54·54	1 : 2·0
	" sesquisilicate	$4FeO, 3SiO_2 = Fe_4Si_3O_{10}$	......	38·44	......	61·55	1 : 1·5
Diferrous " (Fayalite)	" singulosilicate	$2FeO, SiO_2 = Fe_2SiO_4$	......	29·35	......	70·64	1 : 1
Triferrous "		$3FeO, SiO_2 = Fe_3SiO_5$	......	21·73	......	7[illegible]·26	1 : 0·67
Tetraferrous "	" subsilicate	$4FeO, SiO_2 = Fe_4SiO_6$	......	17·23	......	82·76	1 : 0·5

TABLE 26.—DEPHOSPHORIZATION VS. SLAG BASICITY.

No.	2.	3.	4.	6.	7.	8.	9.	10.	11.	12.	13.	14.	15.	16.	17.	18.	19.	20.	21.	23.	24.	25.	26.	27.
Process	B.B.	B.B.	Pud.	B.B.	B.B.	Pud.	B.B.	S.d.	P.w.	B.B.	B.B.	Ref.	B.B.	B.B.	B.B.	B.B.	B.B.	B.B.	Pud.	B.o.	B.B.	B.B.	Pud.	Pud.
Reference	S.	E.	Q.	F.	C.	R.	F.	I.	N.	F.	E.	P.	D.	E.	C.	C.	G.	E.	K.	H.	D.	E.	I.	L.
Silica	10·5	6·60	12·75	9·50	9·72	15·79	13·81	18·80	9·5	11·16	10·47	15·47	11·88	9·	11·82	12·28	2·45	15·	20·97	10·60	12·78	13·	6·73	15·75
Phosphoric acid	2·85	5·79	3·13	2·76	10·98	1·86	7·38	8·46	11·5	12·43	10·88	4·11	12·	14·5	12·41	12·08	22·23	12·2	8±	23·65	16·08	12·5	2·77	·29
Ferrous oxide	49·00	34·87	67·02	7·24	3·58	69·52	5·70	49·24	70·3	5·90	49·11	76·31	8·24	15·48	4·45	9·42	15·10	12·21	61·30	8·87	4·87	17·5	56·87	63·2
Ferric oxide	11·42	22·39	14·30	1·56	3·81	9·21	1·30	7·05		1·75	6·82	.....	3·16	3·19	0·57	1·61	5·74	1·17	5·30	9·99	4·06	·94	6·86	3·55
Lime	25·0	27·48	0·18	59·35	49·75	.....	57·83	tr.	1·9	60·21	26·74	1·95	51·	35·6	63·32	48·38	46·82	40·08	2·12	45·87	41·31	35·48	.....	.....
Magnesia	.....	.....	0·18	5·01	6·42	.....	6·99	.....	0·8	9·84	.....	.....	4.74	9·5	4·37	5·60	1·14	10·67	2·04	9·12	7·79	11·7	.....	.....
Oxide of manganese	.....	1·40	·53	5·16	5·02	2·81	5·20	.....	2·1	4·40	.....	·93	3·50	4·98	1·93	5·32	2·75	1·76	.....	4·26	3·35	8·79	.....	.....
Alumina	.....	.....	2·35	tr.	2·21	.....	tr.	20·4	4·1	tr.	1·88	.....	2·85	1·35	·39	2·31	2·85	2·2	2·91	1·65	1·12	1·11	.....	.....
Miscellaneous	S. ·26	.....	S. ·05	.....	CaS. 2·96	.....	.....	S. 0·41	.....	.....	.....	S. ·68	CaS. 3·15	.....	.....	CaS. 2·84	.....	.....	.....	.....	.....	.....	TiO_2 15·5	TiO_2 10·49
Oxygen ratio: Base: acid	1:0·81?	1:0·87	1:0·41	1:0·47	1:0·50	1:0·5	1:0·51	1:·58	1:0·56	1:0·39	1:0·60	1:0·60	1.0·81	1:0·62	1:0·62	1:0·68	1:0·57	1:0·74	1:0·75	1:0·76	1:0·79	1:0·92	1:0·84	1:0·86
Oxygen ratio: Total bases+iron oxides	1:0·79?	1.0·69	1:0·81	1:0·09	1:0·14	1:0·8	1:0·08	1:0·57	1:0·85	1:0·11	1:0·57	1:0·96	1:0·18	1:0·21	1:0·06	1:0·12	1:0·24	1:0·15	1:0·83	1:0·87	1:0·11	1:0·19	1:1·	1:1
Phosphorus: In initial metal	.....	1·46	·49	1·04	1·23	.....	0·90	.....	2·23	1·04	1·19	.....	1·40	1·45?	1·28	1·37	2·6@3·2	1·45?	·47	3·32	2·18	1·45?	1·49	·65
Phosphorus: In metal accompanying this slag	·093	b. ·04	·06	·06	·02	·23	·05	·07	·08	·06	·13	·82	·07	·04	·48	·06	·02@·04	·04	·07	·04	·15	·08	·45	·29

No.	28.	29.	30.	31.	32.	33.	34.	37.	39.	40.	41.	43.	44.	45.	46.	47.	48.	49.	50.	50a.	51.	52.	53.	54.	60.
Process	B.B.	B.B.	B.B.	B.B.	Pud.	B.B.	P.w.	B.B.	B.B.	B.B.	Ref.	Pud.	Ref.	Ref.	B.B.	B.B.	B.B.	Ref.	B.B.	S.d.	A.B.	B.B.	B.B.	B.B.	B.f.
Reference	B.	B.	E.	E.	R.	E.	N.	E.	E	E.	P.	L.	O.	P.	E.	R.	T.	O.	F.	J.	A.	S.	E.	E.	X.
Silica	17·8	21·1	24·09	18·6	27·77	19·50	10·40	22·20	36·5	14·4	28·41	11·87	31·05	30·31	36·09	31·7	36·39	33·33	39·8	20·80	45·08	44·8	38·7	31·0	68·2
Phosphoric acid	13·68	10·56	8·56	18·94	2·19	11·11	20·00	7·46	1·04	17·86	4·14	2·10	2·79	2·56	2·11	5·93	3·12	2·26	1·10	4·94	.....	2·3	2·26	4·14	2·21
Ferrous oxide	18·39	18·89	14·6±	12·2±	59·93	24·22	41·0	51·93	8·09±	18·16	57·80	52·05	43·36	51·33	3·55	15·64	8·97	56·11	6·4	40·20	47·19	.....	.....	.....	5·12
Ferric oxide	2·09	1·71	3·24	.....	4·51	4·88		4·08	.....	5·28	2·57	8·86	10·08	8·66	0·49	2·35	·46	.....	0·71	.....	2·96	.....	.....	.....	.....
Lime	34·73	29·44	37·00	.....	.....	36·12	7·3	10·52	.....	37·49	2·90	.....	1·56	1·56	33·42	32·9	39·5	1·19	37·86	2·68	1·40	14·8	18·8	25·1	19·12
Magnesia	9·56	7·33	0·30	.....	.....	.....	0·7	.....	.....	.....	0·24	.....	·85	·73	0·38	0·26	8·39	0·30	0·26	.....	tr.	.....	.....	.....	4·67
Oxide of Mn	6·24	12·40	8·22	.....	5·29	1·40	10·8	3·07	.....	3·71	3·90	.....	5·06	4·96	9·90	4·50	11·09	2·71	7·21	·50	2·02	.....	.....	.....	.....
Alumina	2·26	3·68	3·57	.....	.....	1·19	2·00	.....	.....	1·30	2·47	.....	4·37	5·73	4·69	4·06	1·30	5·75	6·43	15·36	·51	.....	.....	.....	3·60
Miscellaneous	.....	.....	.....	.....	.....	.....	.....	.....	.....	.....	S. ·05	TiO_2 14·80	S. ·08	.....	S. ·09	S. ·05	.....	S. ·17	.....	.....	.....	S. ·80	.....	.....	.....
Oxygen ratio: Base: acid	1:0·80	1:0·87	1:0·88	1:0·88	1:0·88	1:0·92	1:0·93	1:0·98	1:1·±	1:1·	1:1·	1:1·04	1:1·06	1:1·1	1:1·19	1:1·19	1:1·26	a. 1:1·45	a. 1:1·52	a. 1:1·84	a. 1:1·94	.....	.....	.....	.....
Oxygen ratio: Total bases+iron oxides	1:0·12	1:0·18	1:0·13	1:0·14	1:0·78	1:0·88	1:0·55	1:0·80	1:0·94±	1:0·92	1:0·85	1:1·	1:0·04	1:0·8	1:0·08	1:0·25	.....	0:0·91	1:0·116	.....	1:0·95	.....	.....	.....	.....
Phos.: In initial metal	1·5±	1·5±	1·27	.....	.....	1·89	2·92	1·19	.....	1·19	1,47	1·04	.....	.....	1·21	1·42	.....	.....	1·21	.....	.....	3·0	1·44	1·44	.....
Phos.: In metal accompanying this slag	·06	·15	·15	·02	·23	·20	·77	·13	1·25	·29	·54	·23	.....	.....	1·11	0·64	.....	.....	1·11	.....	1·60	·86	1·28	1·07	.....

A. Bell, Journ. Iron and St. Inst., 1877, I., p. 117. Acid Bessemer process. **B.** Ditto, Principles of the Manufacture of Iron and Steel, p. 403. Basic Bessemer. **C.** Massenez, Jour. Iron and St. Inst., 1880, II., p. 475. Basic Bessemer. **D.** Wedding, idem, p. 559. Basic Bessemer. **E.** Thomas and Gilchrist, idem, 1879, I., p. 128. Basic Bessemer. **F.** Pink, idem, 1880, I., p. 61. Basic Bessemer. **G.** Engineering and Mining Jl., 1888, II., p. 17. Basic Bessemer. **H.** Iron Age, Aug. 6th, 1885, p. 37. **H1.** Tunner. Metallurg. Review, I., p. 578. Siemens direct process, 1st tapping. **I.** Bell, Journ. Iron and St. Inst., 1877, I., p. 1?2. Siemens direct process. **J.** Siemens, idem, p. 357. Siemens direct process. **K.** Schilling, puddling, Ledebur, Handbuch der Eisenhüttenkunde, pp. 798, 800. **L.** Snelus, Jour. Iron and St. Inst., 1872, I., p. 259. Puddling. **M.** Percy, Iron and Steel, p. 668. Puddling. **N.** Holley, Trans. Am. Inst. Min. Eng. Krupp's pig washing. **O.** Bell, Principles Manuf. Iron and Steel, p. 394. Refinery. **P.** Ditto, pp. 364, 359. Refinery. **Q.** Ditto, p. 390. Puddling. **R.** Louis, Jour. Iron and St. Inst., 1879, I., p. 222. Puddling. **S.** Sachs, idem, 1879, I., p. 244, 140. Basic Bessemer. **T.** Finkener. Ledebur, Handbuch der Eisenhüttenkunde, p. 924. Basic Bessemer. **U.** Ehrenwerth, Stahl und Eisen, 1880, 10, p. 637. Basic Bessemer. **V.** Harbord, Journ. Iron and St. Inst., 1886, II., p. 700. Basic open-hearth. **W.** Ledebur, Handbuch, pp. 797, 800. Puddling. **X.** Kerl, Grundriss der Eisenhüttenkunde, p. 167. Blast furnace. **Y.** Harbord, Loc. cit.

a. Excluding alumina. *b.* Metal accompanying similar slag. A.B. Acid Bessemer. B.B. Basic Bessemer. B.o. Basic open-hearth. Pud. Puddling. Ref. Refinery. S.d. Siemens direct process. B.f. Blast furnace. P.w. Pig washing.

slag which is to actively absorb phosphorus must be considerably more basic than one which is barely able to hold in the presence of non-carburetted iron the phosphorus which it already has. Hence we may infer that about 3·5 atomic equivalents of ferrous oxide or 4·5 of lime to one of phosphoric acid are needed to permit complete dephosphorization, and, at a rough guess, we may say that 2·75 equivalents of ferrous oxide or 3·5 of lime to one of phosphoric acid should permit dephosphorization to proceed till the metal retains but 0·6 of phosphorus.

It is true that Stead found that almost pure carburetted iron absorbed but 0·1% of phosphorus when melted between layers of (tribasic?) lime phosphate in a lime-lined crucible, which at first seems discordant with Hilgenstock's statements concerning the absorption of phosphorus. But we do not know how much lime was absorbed by Stead's initial lime phosphate from the lime lining. In this way his slag may easily have become even more basic than tetracalcic phosphate. In this view there seems to be little justification for Mathesius' statement* that Hilgenstock's results are directly contradicted by Stead's, and by his own, in which an extremely basic lime-phosphate extracted phosphorus from ferro-phosphorus, and that they are therefore attributable to experimental error.

In Hilgenstock's experiments metallic iron was melted in contact with tricalcic phosphate and an excess of earthy base: it invariably took up phosphorus, and considerably more when this excess consisted of the comparatively inert magnesia than when an excess of lime was employed.

* Stahl und Eisen, VI., p. 643, 1886, No. 10.

As, by the absorption of part of the basic excess present, and by the reduction of part of their acid by the metallic iron, the final composition of his phosphates was doubtless more basic than their initial composition, his results leave little doubt that, even in the absence of carbon, metallic iron may absorb phosphorus from phosphate which is at least as basic as tricalcic phosphate and probably more basic yet, and to a moderate degree from slags at least as basic as tetra-phosphate. As Finkener's experiments were performed in an iron boat in an atmosphere of nitrogen it is probable that his ferrous-phosphates remained approximately of their initial basicity in those cases in which the iron absorbed no phosphorus from them, and at most became but slightly more basic, by the substitution of iron oxide for phosphoric acid, in those in which the metal absorbed phosphorus. Their results are summarized in Table 26 A: they will be again referred to.

Turning now to the silicates, I have already stated that slags with over 30% of silica do not in general permit us to reduce the phosphorus in iron below ·60% ±: such silicates may then be roughly likened to a 3·5-basic lime phosphate or a 2·75-basic ferrous phosphate in dephosphorizing power. Slag 21 Table 26, already referred to, with 25·± % acid, of which 4-5ths are silica, and whose bases are chiefly iron oxides, permits almost complete dephosphorization: we may then roughly liken it to calcic phosphate with 4·5 equivalents of base to one of acid, or to ferrous phosphate with 3·5 equivalents of base to one of acid. This is summarized in Table 26 B.

These figures suggest that, as regards influence on de-

TABLE 26 A.—ABSORPTION OF PHOSPHORUS FROM PHOSPHATES BY METALLIC IRON, ETC.

Number.	Observer.	Conditions of experiment. Kind of vessel, etc.	Time, Hours.	Temperature.	Metal, etc., employed.	Phosphate employed.	Resulting metal. Composition. P. %	Mn. %	Fe %	Description.
1	Hilgenstock	Lime-lined.			Iron, apparently non-carburetted	Tricalcic	0·37			
2	"	Magnesia-lined			" " "	"	0·72			
3	"	"				"	1·08			
4	"	Lined with dolomite				"	0·86			
5	"	With neutral lining				" with great excess of lime	0·27			
6	"	" " "				Tricalcic, with a small excess of lime	0·37			
7	"	Lined with tricalcic phosphate melted with lime				Tricalcic, previously melted with lime	0·27			
8	Stead	Lime-lined.	1	White	5 g. of ferro-manganese of 71·5% Mn.	1·5 g. of manganese-phosphate	1·00	57·6		
9	"	" "	1	"	1 part ferro-manganese	1 part tricalcic, the mixture covered with excess of tricalcic (?) phosphate	1·00	68·6		
10	"	" "	1	"	5 g. of nearly pure carburetted iron	2 layers of tricalcic phosphate, enclosing the iron.	0·1(?)			"The button showed an absorption of only 0·1% of phosphorus."
11	Hilgenstock	Basic-lined			Apparently non-carburetted iron, containing 0·04% of phosphorus	Tetracalcic	0·088			
12	"	" "			Pure carburetted iron	"	0·56			
13	"	" "			Ferro-manganese	"	1·10			
14	Finkener	Iron boat in atmosphere of nitrogen			Apparently non-carburetted iron, 1 part	Triferrous, 1 part. 3 FeO, P_2O_5	0·			No iron phosphide formed. Sintered.
15	"	Iron boat in atmosphere of nitrogen			" " " 2 parts.	Triferrous, 1 part, Diferrous, 1 " = 2·5 FeO, P_2O				Iron phosphide formed. Completely fused.
16	"	Iron boat in atmosphere of nitrogen			" " " 4 "	Triferrous 3 parts, Diferrous 1 " = 2·75 FeO, P_2O_5				Dilute sulphuric acid evolved but little phosphoretted hydrogen, i. e., a little phosphorus was reduced by the iron. Sintered.
17	"	Iron boat in atmosphere of nitrogen				Triferrous 9 parts, Diferrous 1 " =2·9 FeO, P_2O_5				
18	"	Atmosphere of carbonic oxide		White	None	Triferrous phosphate				No important action.
19	"	Atmosphere of nitrogen, nickel boat		"	Cast-iron with 3·8% carbon; just enough to unite with the oxygen present as carbonic oxide	Triferrous phosphate				Completely reduced to iron phosphide.
20	"	Atmosphere of carbonic oxide, metallic boat		"	Ferric oxide	" " in proportion to yield iron with 8% phosphorus if wholly reduced				Completely reduced to iron phosphide.
21	Brackelsberg	Brasqued crucible	1	"	None	55 parts diferrous phosphate, 85·5 parts diferric phosphate, 10·4 parts ferric oxide	24·55		75·45	Completely reduced to iron phosphide, phosphorus partly volatilized. No slag.
22	"	" "		"	"	5 g. tricalcic (?) phosphate 8·85 g. ferric oxide	24·58		75·32	The phosphide contained about 85% of the phosphorus initially present.
23	"	Carbonless crucible (?)		"	2·5 g. very soft iron wire	4·7 g. tricalcic (?) phosphate	10·88		89.12	The reduction of the phosphorus must have been effected chiefly by the iron

HILGENSTOCK, Stahl und Eisen, VI., p. 583, 1886; Rev. Univ., XX., 3, p. 661, 1886; Iron Age, Sept. 2, 1886, p. 15. STEAD, Ehrenwerth, Oest. Zeit. für Berg- und Hüttenwesen, XXIX., p. 104, 1881. FINKENER, Wedding, Der Basische Bessemer-oder Thomas-Process, pp. 153-4. BRACKELSBERG, Stahl und Eisen, V., pp. 545-548, 1885, 10.

TABLE 26 B.

	Silicates. Base.	% Silica.	Atomic ratio, base to acid.	Oxygen ratio, base to acid.	Phosphates. % Phosphoric acid.	Atomic ratio, base to acid.	Oxygen ratio, base to acid.	Basicity ratios, Phosphate ÷ Silicate, for like dephosphorizing power. Percentage ratio.	Atomic ratio.	Oxygen ratio.
Most acid slag in whose presence phosphorus can be reduced to 8·69%	Lime	30	2·5	1 : 0·8	42	3·5	1 : 1·43	1·40	1·40	1·79
	Iron	36	1·944	1 : 1·022	41·8	2·75	1 : 1·82	1·39	1·42	1·77
Most acid slag in whose presence phosphorus can be almost completely removed.	Lime				36	4·5	1 : 1·11			
	Iron	25	2·49	1 : 0·83	36·6	3·5	1 : 1·48	1·41	1·41	1·66

phosphorizing power of slags, 1% of silica should be counted as equal to 1·4± of phosphoric acid: one atomic equivalent of silica as 1·4± of phosphoric acid: and that, if we employ the oxygen ratio of base to acid, 1 of oxygen in silica should count as 1·7± in phosphoric acid. These numbers, however, rest on a very doubtful basis, and can at best serve as very rough and makeshift guides.

Ehrenwerth[a] considers that to prevent absorption of phosphorus by metal from slag ("rephosphorization") on recarburizing in the basic Bessemer process, it is only necessary that the slag should contain enough earthy base to form subsilicate with the silica present and tribasic phosphate with the phosphoric acid, but that rephosphorization will occur unless this condition is satisfied: but he seems to lose sight of the oxides of iron and manganese, which, if we look beyond this single process to puddling and the basic open-hearth, we find are at least as efficient in retaining phosphorus in the slag as are the earthy bases. In the basic open-hearth process permanent dephosphorization may be effected with slags which have far from enough earthy base to satisfy Ehrenwerth's formula, *e. g.* a slag mentioned by Harboard which contains 12% of silica and 13·3 of phosphoric acid, yet only 15·2% of lime with 5·75% of other earthy bases: but its 43·1% of ferrous oxide permits it to almost completely dephosphorize the metal, the phosphorus having fallen from 3·56 to 0·07%. Here the conditions on recarburizing appear to be identical with those of the basic Bessemer process.

[a] Oest. Zeitschrift, für Berg- und Hüttenwesen, 1881, p. 120.

§ 106. FERRUGINOUS VS. CALCAREOUS PHOSPHATES AND SILICO-PHOSPHATES.—As the removal of phosphorus from metal to slag requires its oxidation and conversion into phosphoric acid, ferruginous slags, themselves sources and carriers of oxygen, dephosphorize iron much more energetically than calcareous ones when, as in the puddling, pig-washing and basic open-hearth processes, the oxidation of the phosphorus has to be effected by the slag itself, and when there is but little contact between metal and air. But how does their dephosphorizing power compare when, as in the basic Bessemer process, intimate admixture of air permits rapid oxidation of phosphorus, so that we do not have to rely on the slag for our oxygen supply? Let us compare first slags of like basicity, then those of similar percentage composition.

The evidence which I have met indicates that pure phosphates of iron yield up their phosphorus to metallic iron less readily, whence we infer that they absorb it from iron more greedily, than pure lime phosphates of like basicity: that is, that under like conditions an equilibrium between the tendency of phosphorus to pass into slag and its opposite tendency to pass into the metal is reached with iron slags when they are more phosphoric and in general more acid than is the case with lime slags. Hilgenstock's experiments just referred to indicate that the latter, when tetrabasic with oxygen ratio of base to acid 1 : 1·25, and perhaps even when more basic than this, still yield up a little phosphorus to metallic iron: while Finkener's results indicate that with iron phosphates an oxygen ratio of 1 : 1·67, as in triferrous phosphate, barely suffices to prevent the absorption of phosphorus by metal from slag. (These statements may only hold true of the particular conditions of the experiments on which they are based.)

For similar percentage composition lime slags are more basic than iron slags, measuring basicity atomically or by the oxygen ratio of base to acid. Thus ferrous-silicate with 30% silica is a singulo-silicate, lime silicate with the same percentage of silica is between a singulo and a subsilicate, their oxygen ratios being 1:1 and 1:0.8 respectively. It might be inferred that lime slags would have greater power of removing phosphorus from iron than ferruginous slags of corresponding percentage composition, and that a given degree of dephosphorization could be attained with a higher percentage of silica in the accompanying slags when calcareous than when ferruginous. But, as suggested by Table 26 B, the greater basicity of lime slags appears to be approximately balanced by the greater readiness with which phosphorus is removed by metallic iron from lime than from iron phosphates of like basicity. At least, in the study of a great number of cases I have neither been able to convince myself that calcareous slags remove phosphorus from iron more fully than ferruginous ones of like percentage composition or the reverse. The slags of the basic Bessemer process, sometimes almost free from iron oxide, and essentially silico-phosphates of lime, permit extremely thorough dephosphorization: witness No. 23 of Table 26, which holds 23·05% of phosphoric acid though but 6·16% of iron oxide, while the accompanying metal has but 0·04% of phosphorus. Among the six cases of maximum dephosphorization for given silica lately quoted we find that three are of ferruginous and three of calcareous slags. "Honors are easy."

The preceding statement is not designed to apply to conditions which are so strongly deoxidizing as to tend to nearly completely reduce the phosphates—unless indeed silica be present to relieve the phosphoric acid from duty. When ferrous phosphates are heated with a deoxidizing agent, as in experiments 19 to 20, Table 26 A, both iron and phosphorus are completely reduced. But, though lime phosphates, even in the absence of silica readily yield a portion of their phosphorus to metallic iron, and a very large portion to the joint influence of iron and carbon, their complete dephosphorization is doubtless far more difficult than that of iron phosphates, unless indeed an abundance of silica be present to displace phosphoric acid from the lime phosphate: for the irreducible lime retains its diminishing stock of acid with ever increasing stubbornness, while the base of the iron phosphate is deoxized *pari passu* with its acid. But that a very large proportion of the phosphorus of pure lime phosphates may be reduced by iron and carbon jointly is shown by experiment 22, Table 26 A, in which on heating (tri?) calcic phosphate in a graphite crucible with ferric oxide and carbon, about 8 % of its phosphorus appears to have been reduced and to have entered the metallic iron formed.

§ 107. Strength of Oxidizing Conditions.—That the intensity of the existing oxidizing or deoxidizing tendencies plays as important a part as the basicity of the slag, is shown by several independent considerations.

(A). Blast-Furnace. While under the strongly oxidizing conditions of the refinery, the puddling furnace and the basic Bessemer converter part of the phosphorus may remain in the slags even if they be comparatively acid (sesqui-silicates), under the strongly deoxidizing conditions of the blast-furnace the whole of the phosphorus may remain combined with the metallic iron even if the slags be extremely basic (sub-silicates).

Thus in Table 26 the comparatively acid slags 44, 45 and 49 (refinery), 32 (puddling), 50 A (Siemens direct) and 46, 47, 48, 50 and 52 (basic Bessemer) all hold phosphoric acid (*e. g.*, 5·93 phosphoric acid with 31·7 silica) though most of them are approximately sesqui-silicates. Yet in the manufacture of ferro-manganese in the blast-furnace the slags, though extremely basic, are reported as often absolutely free from phosphorus, even in the extreme case quoted by Pourcel[a] of a slag with only 18% silica; though this slag is more basic even than a sub-silicate, (oxygen ratio = 1 : 0·37 ±), the whole of the phosphorus unites with the cast-iron. If it be objected that the comparatively low temperature of the refinery furnace favors the scorification of phosphorus, we have in Table 26 the comparatively acid slags of the basic Bessemer process Nos. 50 and 47 with 38·8 silica (oxygen ratio of base to acid 1 : 1·52 = a sesqui-silicate) yet holding 1·13 phosphoric acid, and with 31·7 silica (oxygen ratio = 1 : 1·19) holding 5·93 phosphoric acid.

It appears, moreover, that as long as the strength of the reducing action of the blast-furnace is approximately constant, (as inferred from constancy of the composition of the charge and of the percentage of ferrous oxide in the slag), practically constant amounts of phosphorus pass into metal and slag respectively, even though the temperature may alter considerably, as inferred from alteration in the grade of the cast-iron produced, which, as Bell has shown, appears to be primarily a function of the temperature and only secondarily a function of the reducing action. If, however, the reducing action be weakened, as inferred from the production of ferruginous (scouring) slag, the percentage of phosphorus in the slag rapidly increases, remaining roughly proportional to the percentage of ferrous

a Journ. Iron and St. Inst., 1879, II., p. 378.

oxide which it contains.[a] This is illustrated by slag 60 with 63·2% silica, 5·12% ferrous oxide and 2·21 phosphoric acid.

(B). POURCEL'S EXPERIMENT.[b]—On melting cast-iron in contact with basic phosphoric slags, *A* in a dolomite-lined and *B* in a carbon-lined crucible, Pourcel found that when melted with carbon, but under conditions otherwise less favorable to the absorption of phosphorus, the cast-iron took up over six times as much phosphorus as when melted without carbon. White cast-iron was melted during 2 hours with additions which yielded the following substances:

	Phosphorus in metal. Initial.	Final.	Slag. SiO_2.	P_2O_5.	FeO.	CaO.	MgO.	Al_2O_3.
Fusion in carbon crucible....	·06	·64	10·9	17·3	17·	43·	7·5	4·6
" " dolomite "	·06	·10	14·30	10·44	?	58· ±	10·6 ±	5·5 ±

NOTE.—With the fusion in the carbon crucible the composition which the slag had before fusion is given: with the fusion in the dolomite crucible I give the final composition of the slag, which is far more instructive. The latter slag held initially 16% of silica and 9·40% of phosphoric acid.

The slag accompanying the fusion with carbon was one which under otherwise like conditions would yield up its phosphorus to iron much less readily than the other, since, though initially slightly more acid, reckoning its basicity from phosphoric acid and silica together, yet (A) it contained so little silica as to be practically a strongly dephosphorizing slag (see § 105) and (B) its final composition must have been far more basic than the slag in the fusion without carbon, since its phosphoric acid was almost completely reduced by the iron.

§ 108. REDUCING ACTION OF THE CARBON, ETC., OF THE IRON.—The carbon and still more powerfully the manganese present in metallic iron increase its tendency to absorb phosphorus from slag, and its power to resist dephosphorizing influences. Thus Finkener found that while apparently non-carburetted iron did not take up phosphorus from triferrous phosphate when heated alone with it in a stream of nitrogen, yet, when cast-iron with 3·8% carbon was heated with this phosphate under apparently like conditions, in such proportions that the carbon of the cast-iron just sufficed to form carbonic oxide with the whole of the oxygen of the phosphate, complete deoxidation occurred, and the iron took up the phosphorus of the phosphate.[c] (Experiments 14 and 19, Table 26 A.)

Hilgenstock, too, found that, after fusion with powdered tetracalcic phosphate, non-carburetted iron held but ·088 to ·084% of phosphorus, while ferromanganese and pure carburetted iron absorbed 1·10 and 0·80% of this element respectively. (Experiments 11, 12 and 13, Table 26 A.)

Experiments of Stead's illustrate the greater power of ferromanganese than of ordinary cast-iron to reduce phosphorus from slags. He placed the mixtures indicated in experiments 8, 9 and 10 in Table 26 A (1, ferromanganese with phosphate of manganese, 2, ferromanganese with phosphate of lime, and, 3, nearly pure carburetted iron with phosphate of lime) each in a lime-lined crucible, and inclosed all three in a large graphite crucible, surrounded them with powdered lime, and heated them to whiteness for an hour. After fusion the ferromanganese held in both instances 1% of phosphorus, the initially nearly pure cast-iron held but 0·1%.

Certain European writers go so far as to state dogmatically, but without the least foundation in fact, that phosphorus cannot be removed from iron in the basic Bessemer process until *the whole of the silicon and carbon have* been oxidized, *i. e.* not until the "after-blow." They here overstate the influence of an undoubted principle. I append a few instances, which could be multiplied, in which a very considerable quantity of phosphorus has been scorified, though the metal from which it has been removed and with which the slag is in contact contains much carbon, and in certain cases much silicon as well.

Process.	Phosphorus in initial metal.	Composition of resulting metal. Carbon.	Silicon.	Manganese.	Phosphorus.	Sulphur.	Composition of accompanying slag. Phosphoric acid.	Silica.	
Basic Bessemer..................	2·18	3·12	·15	·50	2·22	·06	8·12	36·90	Wedding, Basische Bessemer, pp. 139, 141.
"	1·28	·70	tr	·80	1·28	·20	8·46	21·25	Massenet, Journ. Iron and St. Inst., 1888, II., pp. 478-48
"	1·86	1·30	tr	·23	1·10	·35	7·74	28·25	(Massenet, idem)
"	....	1·25	·11	....	·81	·27	7·90	25	Snelus, Idem, 1879, I., p. 344.
" "	2·50 ±	·09	·07	·36	·12	·15	....	....	Locality withheld. Private Notes.
" "	1·45 +	2·21	tr	·25	1·17	·54	2·22	22·69	Stahl und Eisen, VI., p. 637, 1886.
Puddling	1·49	2·63	·82	....	·91	·10	....	....	Snelus, Op. Cit., 1872, I., p. 259.
Pig washing..................	1·35	3·25	·02	....	·029	·01	....	....	Bell, Idem, 1877, II., p. 337.
" "	0·74	3·32	·02	·06	·11	·03	....	....	Holley, Trans. Am. Inst. Min. Eng., VIII., p. 158.

In the basic Bessemer process the retention of the phosphorus till after nearly all the carbon has been removed, has been explained by the supposition that the slag, though apparently strongly basic from the start, is not effectively so: that is to say that much of the lime remains in lumps uncombined with silica and inert till near the end of the operation, when, with rise of temperature and protracted violent stirring, it gradually combines: and many observations accord with this view.

The experience at Creusot and Athus shows that, in the basic process as in pig-washing, nearly all the phosphorus may be removed before any considerable percentage of carbon has been oxidized, by simply making the slag *effectively* basic, *e. g.* by liquefying it through the addition of fluor spar. By this means the phosphorus in the metal was in one case reduced from 2·3 to 0·22% during the first period, and before the carbon began to burn rapidly, the slag then carrying 18% of phosphoric acid. As explained in § 112, this was not due to volatilization of phosphorus or silicon.[d]

Stead found that when powdered lime was blown through the metal in the basic Bessemer converter, and therefore, owing to its fine state of division and intimate exposure to freshly formed phosphoric acid, at once became an active component of the slag, the phosphorus was removed before the carbon, of which a large quantity remained after complete dephosphorization.[e]

In the basic open-hearth process, all the bases of whose more ferruginous and fusible slags rapidly become effective, dephosphorization may progress far while *the metal* still holds a great deal of carbon. Thus Harbord quotes a case in which phosphorus fell from 2·3% to ·30%, while the metal retained ·84% of carbon and ·08 of silicon.[f]

Finally, in pig-washing under favorable conditions 95%

[a] Percy, Iron and Steel, p. 512.
[b] Journ. Iron and St. Inst., 1881, I., p. 324.
[c] Wedding, der Basische Bessemer oder Thomas process, pp. 153-4.
[d] Iron Age, February 25, 1886, p. 7.
[e] Journ. Iron and St. Inst., 1886, II., p. 717.
[f] Idem, pp. 701-3.

of the phosphorus present may be removed while 95% of the carbon remains[a]; and in other cases we find that cast-iron containing initially 3·637% carbon and 1·351% phosphorus holds, after washing, 3·25% carbon with ·089% phosphorus, 3·209% carbon with ·085% of phosphorus, etc.[b]

§ 109. Effect of Temperature.—Of all the evidence adduced to show that high temperature favors the retention of phosphorus by metallic iron, that of the puddling furnace and of Bell's experiments alone appear to me conclusive, the retention of phosphorus in the other cases which I have met appearing explicable on other grounds.

In puddling by far the highest temperature is reached at the very end of the operation. This high temperature appears to cause the iron to reabsorb from the slag part of the phosphorus which it has previously given up to it. Thus Bell found that while the iron granules just before balling contained in two cases 0·09 and 0·10% phosphorus respectively, the bar iron made from them had 0·15 and 0·145% phosphorus.[c] To clinch the matter he exposed to an intensely high temperature and in contact with the slag with which they had been puddled, two lots of granules which had purposely been puddled at an unusually low temperature. In one case the percentage of phosphorus in the metal rose from ·068 to 0·145 when thus superheated; in the other it rose in 30 minutes from ·086 to ·122%, and in 160 minutes to 0·255%. In each case the samples analyzed were first freed from adhering slag by fusion with alkaline carbonates.

It has long been surmised that high temperature favors the retention of phosphorus by iron. Its retention in the Bessemer process was in 1865 chiefly ascribed by Wedding to the high temperature of that operation. But, since the development of the basic Bessemer process, in which phosphorus may be practically completely eliminated at an exalted temperature and with extreme rapidity, it is absolutely certain that the influence of temperature is wholly subordinate to the united influence of the composition of the slag and the intensity of the oxidizing conditions. Pourcel in 1879, even after the success of the basic process, eloquently but vainly insisted that temperature was more potent than slag-composition.[d]

In his blast-furnace experience he finds that gray iron always contains under like conditions more phosphorus than white, 0·6 *vs.* 0·3%. As gray iron is made at a higher temperature and with more basic slags than white, he infers that the effect of temperature in favoring the retention of phosphorus by iron here outweighs that of slag-basicity in eliminating it.

As this experience is not general (Bell[e] does not find that iron made at a low temperature has less phosphorus than that made at a higher, under otherwise like conditions) the higher phosphorus in gray than in white iron is to be attributed to some special accompanying condition rather than to temperature. High fuel ratio (*i. e.* large proportion of the reducing agent) rather than high temperature as such is probably the *vera causa:* for it is, I believe, the general experience that the amount of phosphorus in cast-iron is more closely proportional to the strength of the reducing conditions (as inferred from the percentage of ferrous oxide in the slag) than to the blast-furnace temperature (which is inferable from the grade of the iron): though of course high temperature and strong reducing conditions usually, though not always, accompany each other. With such a *vera causa* at hand, it seems superfluous to call in temperature here as a dominant factor.

§ 110. Effect of the Initial Percentage of Phosphorus in the Iron.—It is altogether probable that, when iron already contains much phosphorus, it absorbs this element less readily from slags with which it is in contact, and yields it up to them more readily than when it has but little. This is shown by the familiar fact that while comparatively acid slags remove the first portions of phosphorus from phosphoric cast-iron, yet the last traces of phosphorus can only be removed in contact with extremely basic ones. Thus basic-Bessemer slags 47 and 54 in Table 26 with 31·7 and 31·0% of silica have 5·93 and 4·14% of phosphoric acid, while the accompanying metal has ·61 and 1·07% of phosphorus: yet, so far as my observation goes, such acid slags can only remove phosphorus from iron which has a comparatively large percentage of this element. At least among the many recorded cases of basic Bessemer, puddling, refinery, pig-washing and Siemens-direct-process slags I find none containing more than 30% silica which accompanies iron whose phosphorus, if initially much above 0·50%, has fallen below this point.

So too, while blast-furnace slags rarely contain an important quantity of phosphoric acid, yet if the cast-iron be extremely phosphoric the slag is habitually rich in phosphoric acid. The following instances illustrate this:[f]

Silica in slag	34·58	36·42	36·94	37·89
Phosphoric acid in slag	6·00	4·45	3·65	3·34
Phosphorus in cast-iron	16·20	14·36	17·50	14·68
Silicon in cast-iron	0·19	0·98	0·30	0·19

Even extremely acid slags (*e. g.* with 64% silica and midway between bi- and trisilicate, oxygen ratio = 1 : 2·57) may retain a small quantity of phosphoric acid when in contact with highly phosphoriferous iron. Thus Brackelsberg,[g] melting phosphate of iron in a carbon lined crucible with a small quantity of acid slag, obtained iron with 22·27% phosphorus and a slag which, in spite of holding 64·31% silica, contained 0·59% phosphoric acid. Yet this was not because the iron was saturated with phosphorus, for in other experiments iron was obtained with 26·36% of this metalloid.

§ 111. Effect of Carbonic Oxide.—While this gas unaided cannot reduce phosphorus from triferrous phosphate, yet in the presence of metallic iron it does reduce this salt, and it probably reduces phosphorus from phosphoriferous slags in general, even when strongly basic.

Thus Finkener found that, while no important action occurred when triferrous phosphate alone was exposed to carbonic oxide at a white heat; yet when it was mixed with ferric oxide in such proportion that if the whole were reduced an iron with 3% phosphorus should result, they were wholly deoxidized when exposed to a white heat in an atmosphere of carbonic oxide. (Experiments 18 and 20, Table 26 A.)[h]

a Bell, Principles of the Manufacture of Iron and Steel, p. 401.
b Bell, Journal Iron and St. Inst., 1877, II., p. 337.
c Journ. Iron and Steel Inst., 1877, II., p. 330: Manuf. Iron and Steel, p. 408.
d Idem, pp. 342-4.
e Manufacture of Iron and Steel, p. 416.
f Stahl und Eisen, VI., 10, p. 642, 1886.
g Idem, 1885, p. 546.
h Wedding, Der Basische Bessemer oder Thomas Process, pp. 155-4.

That carbonic oxide reduces phosphorus from even apparently strongly basic ferruginous slags is indicated by experiments by Pourcel.[a] After melting cast-iron containing 2·5% carbon and 0·5% phosphorus in an ordinary apparently acid-lined open-hearth furnace, he skimmed the slag, laying bare the surface of the metal, which he next exposed to the action of hot air, by cutting off the gas supply, thus giving it a roasting comparable to the roasting of blister copper.

(A). Carbonic oxide was evolved; at the end of 15 minutes, during which a layer of slag formed, no phosphorus had been removed from the iron.

(B). The conditions were the same as in (A) except that the evolution of carbonic oxide as prevented by adding ferro-silicon (with silicon 10%, manganese 20%). After 15 minutes, during which a slag formed as before, the metal had lost 0·15% phosphorus, containing only 0·35 instead of 0·50%. The slag contained phosphoric acid.

(C). In another case the conditions of (B) were reproduced: after a while evolution of carbonic oxide recommenced: the phosphoric slag was left on the metal. After 15 minutes more, during which both gas and air entered the furnace, it was found that the metal had reabsorbed all the phosphorus removed during experiment (B), having now 0·5% phosphorus.

(D). By thrice repeating experiment (B) the phosphorus in the metal fell from 0·5 to 0·24.

Now we infer that the slag was basic; for, if acid dephosphorization would not have occurred in (B): it could readily be basic even in an acid lined furnace if the initial slag were first skimmed, since such quiet may prevail that the silica which the slag at its periphery takes up from the walls would only slowly diffuse toward the centre of the slag layer. All conditions appear to have been closely alike except that in (A) and (C) carbonic oxide was evolved, but not in (B) and (D). The rephosphorization in (C) can hardly have been due simply to the agitation caused by the escape of carbonic oxide: for, though this would indeed increase the contact between slag and carburetted metal, thus strengthening the tendency to reduce phosphorus, it would simultaneously and probably to the same extent increase the exposure of slag to atmospheric oxygen, the source of the oxidizing tendencies. And as the resultant of the reducing action of the metal and the oxidizing action of the atmosphere is shown by (B) to oxidize phosphorus, mere agitation, while it would hasten the chemical action, should not reverse the direction of the resultant of two chemical forces which it stimulates apparently in an equal degree.

The reducing effectof carbonic oxide in C appears to have been more energetic than that of the carbon, silicon and manganese added in B: the reducing action during B was strengthened by the presence of more carbon, silicon and manganese than were present in A and C, yet it was not strong enough to prevent oxidation of phosphorus: but when, as in A and C it was strengthened by the escape of carbonic oxide, it sufficed not only to prevent oxidation of phosphorus but to reduce this metalloid back from the slag. While under favorable conditions of contact carbon, silicon and manganese would probably reduce phosphorus far more energetically than carbonic oxide, the latter is more effective in this case because of its extensive contact as it bubbles through the slag. This explanation accords with experiments 18 and 19, Table 26 A, in which the carbon of cast-iron completely reduced the phosphorus from triferrous phosphate, on which exposure to an atmosphere of carbonic oxide had no important effect. In pig-washing it has been observed that the conditions which permit abundant evolution of carbonic oxide cause reduction of phosphorus from the slag, which, as in the case just explained, can hardly be due agitation as such.

In the basic Bessemer process the tendency of the carbonic oxide to reduce phosphorus from the slag as it rushes through it may be largely masked during the blow by the simultaneous rapid oxidation of phosphorus occurring at the bottom of the bath of metal, where atmospheric oxygen is in great excess. But it is observed that in recarburizing the blown metal, the oxidizing action of the blast having ceased, conditions which permit copious evolution of carbonic oxide (*e. g.* the employment of a recarburizer with much carbon, spiegeleisen instead of ferro-manganese) cause reabsorption of phosphorus by the metal. But this may be in part due to the agitation caused by the escape of carbonic oxide, which brings the slag into more extended contact with the metal which is now (owing to the addition of the spiegeleisen) richer in carbon, manganese and silicon than during the immediately preceding period, when its phosphorus was being oxidized and scorified.

§ 112. FLUOR SPAR is said to expel phosphorus together with silicon and carbon from iron, the phosphorus partly as fluoride of phosphorus PF_3 (a colorless, inflammable, fuming liquid, readily volatilized), partly as phosphate of lime. Its employment in the basic Bessemer process causes the phosphorus to leave the iron rapidly during the early part of the operation, but this is ascribed to its effect in fluxing the lime and rendering the slag *effectively* basic. Without fluor spar the lime is thought to melt and combine with the slag but slowly.[b]

Henderson[c] states that, in 1869, heating and melting white cast-iron during an hour in a clay crucible lined with magnesia with an inner lining of fluor spar, its phosphorus was reduced from 0·75% to 0·02%, the carbon being simultaneously wholly eliminated. Employing fluor spar in puddling in common ore-lined puddling furnaces, he found that much of the silicon was volatilized (as fluoride, SiF_4 ?), and that the slags were abnormally free from silica and phosphoric acid. Readily condensed fumes were given off by the puddled balls. So too on running cast-iron upon fluor spar dense fumes arose; most of the silicon and part of the phosphorus were eliminated, yet no slag formed; hence it is inferred that silicon and phosphorus volatilized as fluorides. The resulting iron was porous and filled with a white substance.

In another experiment also phosphorus appears to have been volatilized by fluor spar. 2,287 pounds of cast-iron, containing initially 1·14% of phosphorus, held but 0·17% after fusion with 82 pounds of fluor spar in an ore-lined open-hearth furnace, the accompanying slag containing 2·84%. Of the 25·7 pounds of phosphorus in the initial metal, but 11·49 remained, 4·39 in metal and 7·1 in slag: to volatilize the missing 14·21 pounds as the fluoride PF_3

[a] Journ. Iron and St. Inst., 1879, II., pp. 370-383.

[b] Revue Universelle, X., 1881, p. 418; Iron Age, February 25, 1886, p. 7.

[c] James Henderson, private communication.

25·5 pounds of fluorine are needed, while 39·9 pounds of this element, or a great excess, are supplied by the 28 pounds of fluor spar present.[a] If these experiments are to be trusted they appear to show that fluor spar under certain conditions volatilizes phosphorus as fluoride.

It is not easy to harmonize these results with those obtained in Percy's laboratory, except on the rather violent assumption that cast-iron retains its phosphorus much less tenaciously than the phosphide of iron Fe_2P. This substance, which contains 23±% phosphorus, was melted in a brasqued crucible with fluor spar: from the fact that the weight of the metal changed less than 0·5 grain it is inferred that little or no phosphorus was volatilized.[b] So too in the basic Bessemer process, though the employment of fluor spar hastens dephosphorization, it appears to be by assisting the scorification of phosphorus rather than by volatilizing it: at least the slags contain a large percentage of phosphorus: one is reported with 18% phosphoric acid. Further, the quantity of air required for oxidizing the phosphorus and other elements, as inferred from the length of the blow and revolutions of the engine, does not appear to have been lessened by the addition of fluor spar, which would certainly indicate that the phosphorus, taking up the oxygen of the blast, was removed as phosphate.[c]

Henderson's statements can be reconciled with these by supposing that under strongly oxidizing conditions, like those of the basic Bessemer process, phosphorus tends rather to form phosphate than fluoride; but that under the gently oxidizing conditions of the basic open-hearth it more readily forms fluoride. But how they can be reconciled with Percy's results I know not.

To sum up, fluor spar appears to favor dephosphorization,

1. By liquefying the slag, thus enabling it to assimilate the lime present, part of which might otherwise remain unmolten and inert, and thus rendering the slag effectively basic.

2. Probably by volatilizing silicon from the metal, thus diminishing the formation of silica and thereby increasing the basicity of the slag.

3. In certain cases, *e. g.* when the conditions are not strongly oxidizing, by volatilizing phosphorus as fluoride.

§ 113. Rationale of the Action of Slags.—In the puddling and other processes in which the metal, whose phosphorus and other elements are removed by oxidation, is protected from the air by a layer of slag, the iron oxides of the slag carry oxygen from the air to the metalloids: their remarkable power of carrying oxygen, of determining the oxidation of elements with which they are in contact, is shown in many metallurgical operations. In roasting sulphide ores with salt the mere addition of ferric oxide prevents the sulphur present from escaping as sulphurous anhydride, and determines its complete oxidation to sulphuric acid and thus the formation of sulphate of soda.

Doubtless in the basic Bessemer process also part of the oxidation of phosphorus is due to the action of iron oxide: but it is by no means certain that phosphorus may not be directly oxidized by the atmospheric oxygen as well. This however is of little practical moment: but what is of moment is that a large quantity of phosphorus may in this process be eliminated without the permanent oxidation and loss of much iron. If the phosphorus is oxidized only through iron oxide, then clearly this oxide plays a part like that of the oxides of nitrogen in the manufacture of sulphuric acid, carrying oxygen from the air to the phosphorus, the presence of a small quantity of iron oxide sufficing to oxidize a large quantity of phosphorus.

If I understand Ehrenwerth aright, he considers it ridiculous[d] to suppose that phosphorus can pass directly to phosphate of lime in this process without the intervention of iron oxide: but I think this belief deserves more toleration. Thus, basic Bessemer slag No. 17, Table 26, contains 12·41% of phosphoric acid and 63·33% of lime, with only 5·02% of iron oxide. Now it may be that the whole of the phosphoric acid which forms unites at first with iron oxide, and that this iron oxide is displaced so rapidly by lime and picks up a new lot of phosphoric acid so suddenly that for a considerable length of time it does not rise above 5·02%: but this implies so rapid a decomposition of iron phosphate and so instantaneous a transfer of its iron oxide to fresh portions of phosphoric acid throughout such enormous masses of material, that those who find it easier to believe that some, at least, of the phosphoric acid unites directly with the great excess of lime present, do not deserve ridicule. Indeed, Mathesius' observation[e] that, when phosphoric iron was melted with lime and charcoal in a graphite crucible with careful exclusion of oxiding influences, nearly half of its phosphorus was slagged, apparently without the intervention of iron oxide, would seem to rob this idea of the humor which Ehrenwerth found in it; the removal of phosphorus from the interior of solid cast-iron bars by mere immersion in fused alkaline carbonates (§ 114) may not intensify his mirth.

How large a quantity of phosphorus may be oxidized by a small quantity of iron oxide is shown by slags 23 (basic open-hearth) and 17 (basic Bessemer), Table 26. The latter, with 12·41 phosphoric acid has but 5·02% iron oxide: the former has 23·05 phosphoric acid with but 6·16% iron oxide. The oxygen ratio of iron oxide to phosphoric acid in these two cases is 1 : 6·25 and 1 : 9·95 respectively. Gilchrist[f] mentions basic Bessemer slag with 5 to 6% iron and 13 to 15% phosphoric acid. It is clear that the phosphoric acid is at least in part combined with lime in these slags. The oxygen ratio of base to acid is 1 : 1·67 in tribasic (ortho) phosphate (*e. g.* apatite, pyromorphite, vivianite, annabergite, etc., the most acid natural phosphates mentioned by Dana), and 1 : 5·0 in monobasic (meta) phosphate (ultra acid phosphate). Now if the whole of the phosphoric acid in slag 23 is combined with iron oxide and none of it with lime, we have an astonishingly acid iron phosphate in contact while molten with an as astonishingly basic lime silicate, the oxygen ratio of base to acid in these two compounds being 1 : 9·95 and 1 : 0·29 repectively. It is hard to believe that two such substances can coexist in the fused mass as independent entities.

a Henderson, Iron Age, Jan 11, 1885, p. 35.
b Percy, Iron and Steel, p. 67.
c Iron Age, February 25, 1886, p. 7.
d "Etwas drolligen Idee." Oesterreich. Zeit. für Berg- und Hüttenwesen, 1881, p. 102.
e Stahl und Eisen, VI., 10, pp. 641-3, 1886.
f Journ. Iron and St. Inst., 1879, I., p. 200.

From similar reasoning I unhesitatingly conclude that some of the phosphoric acid of certain molten basic Bessemer slags is in part combined with iron oxide: this granted, we distrust arguments intended to prove that the phosphoric acid of these slags is in general exclusively combined with earthy bases, and completely divorced from the oxides of iron. In puddling thorough dephosphorization may occur with slags free from lime, *e. g.* slag 4, Table 26, p. 58, which has 3·12% phosphoric acid with but 0·18% lime and 0·18% magnesia, the accompanying metal having but ·06% phosphorus. In the basic Bessemer process also dephosphorization may occur when the slag contains so little lime that it is very probable that the phosphoric acid must be largely combined with iron oxide, *e. g.* slag 37, which with 7·46 phosphoric acid has but 10·52 lime. To assume that all the phosphoric acid in this slag is combined with lime and that its iron oxides exist wholly as silicates, would imply the coexistence in the fused mass of an acid lime phosphate in contact with a basic iron silicate, the oxygen ratio of base to acid in these two compounds being respectively 1 : 1·4 and 1 : 0·88 respectively. It is far more reasonable to suppose that the phosphoric acid is here combined with both lime and iron oxide.

Pourcel endeavors to show that phosphorus exists in the slag of the basic process as iron phosphate by stating that, when certain of these slags are heated in an atmosphere of hydrogen, they lose a quantity of oxygen equal to that contained in the phosphoric acid and iron oxide present, while hydrogen is inert on pure phosphate of lime.[a] This is far from cogent, for no evidence is offered to show that the loss of oxygen was not from silicates of iron, manganese, etc.

Stead endeavors to prove that phosphorus exists as phosphate of lime and not of iron in these slags by showing that, when they are fused after heating in an atmosphere of hydrogen, malleable (*i. e.* non-phosphoric) buttons of iron are obtained, which indicates that the hydrogen reduced iron but not phosphorus.[b] This tends to show that the phosphorus does not in this particular instance exist as iron phosphate: but it is by no means conclusive.

Gilchrist[c] mentions a fact which strongly indicates the existence of lime phosphates in the solidified basic Bessemer slag. Lime phosphate is soluble in sulphurous acid, but not when digested with ammonium sulphide or fused with sodium chloride. Iron phosphate is insoluble in sulphurous acid but soluble when digested in ammonium sulphide or fused with sodium chloride. Now the phosphoric acid of certain basic Bessemer slags is completely soluble in sulphurous acid, but almost insoluble when digested in ammonium sulphide or fused with sodium chloride. Yet the phosphorus of certain double phosphates of iron and lime or in certain silico-phosphates of iron may possess the specific properties shown by the phosphoric acid of these slags. Hilgenstock[d] finds distinct crystals of tetracalcic phosphate in the vugs, and bunches of it in the solid portion of basic Bessemer slags, which is conclusive.

It appears most philosophic to regard a fused slag as a single complex chemical compound, a polybasic silico-phosphate, in which each element is chemically united with every other element present, and in which there are no separate entities such as phosphates of lime and silicates of iron. In this view the evidence of Pourcel, Stead and Gilchrist is beside the mark, and merely throws light on the compounds which form and perhaps segregate and crystallize out when the mass solidifies and passes from the condition of homogeneous magma to that of a heterogeneous mechanical mixture of salts, sulphides and oxides, each crystallizing and assuming an individual existence as the falling temperature reaches its particular freezing point.

This view is powerfully supported by the phenomena of the devitrification of glass, and by that of obsidian in nature.[e] In certain cases different portions of what was originally an apparently homogeneous magma has in solidifying cooled at a rate which, comparatively rapid in one portion, diminishes by most minute gradations, little by little, trace by trace, till in another and distant portion it has been so unutterably slow that complete refrigeration may have occupied centuries. Here we can follow every gradation from the transparent homogeneous glass, whose rapid cooling has preserved the *status quo* and prevented every trace of differentiation and crystallization, through the first hardly perceptible incipiency of widely scattered microscopic hair crystals of some mineral which has barely had time to isolate itself at its exalted freezing point from the enclosing magma. Thence through stages in which the crystalline enclosures encroach on the vitreous mother mass more and more, ever increasing in size and number as we reach portions which have cooled more and more slowly, till now the crystals predominate, now the amorphous glassy patches are seen among them only here and there, and at last we reach the completely devitrified crystalline mass, composed of many differentiated, dissimilar interlaced minerals. Is it not most philosophic to hold that these independent entities were wholly integrated in the initial magma; that their presence in it was wholly potential; that, unborn and even unconceived, their existence was hardly more actual than that of the grandson of the boy who will be born a month hence is to-day?

§ 113 A. Dephosphorization in Cupola Furnaces.—According to Rollet[f] a simple fusion in a cupola furnace with a slag which after dephosphorization should not hold

[a] Journ. Iron and St. Inst., 1879, 2, p. 384. [b] Idem, p. 1880, I., p. 112.

[c] Journ. Iron and St. Inst., 1879, I., p. 200.

[d] Stahl und Eisen, VI., p. 525, 1886, No. 8. Revue Universelle, XX., p. 457, No. 2, and p. 655, No. 3, 1886. Groddeck and Brockmann find in basic Bessemer slag two varieties of crystals of tetracalcic phosphate, one in brown, rectangular, very thin, friable, transparent tables with vitreous luster: the other blue, minute, tabular or prismatic crystals, apparently of the rhombic system. (Revue Universelle, XX., 2, p. 458, 1886.) Stead and Ridsdale find these in this slag, but they always find 10 to 11% of silica in the blue ones. They also find crystals of four other species, some of which have been referred to by Hilgenstock and by Groddeck and Brockmann, three of them consisting almost wholly of bases nearly free from acid, the fourth chiefly of tetracalcic phosphate with some 10% of silicates. (Journ. Iron and St. Inst., 1887, I., to appear: also 1886, II., p. 715.) The discovery of so basic a phosphate has elicited a degree of surprise surprising in view of the existence of a crystallized native phosphate which may be considered as tetrabasic (wagnerite, $4(\frac{5}{6}MgO + \frac{1}{6}MgF), P_2O_5$) and of many in which the oxygen ratio of base to acid is far greater than in tetracalcic phosphate, if, as is usual, ferric oxide be regarded as a base, *e. g.* dufrenite and cacoxenite, $2Fe_2O_3P_2O_5 + 3{\cdot}5H_2O$ and $2Fe_2O_3,P_2O_5 + 12H_2O$, and borickite, $5(Fe_2O_3,2CaO), 2P_2O_5 + 15H_2O$. Among our slags we find many which have more than four equivalents of base to one of acid, *e. g.* final basic Bessemer slag No. 6, Table 26, essentially a silico-phosphate of lime, which has over 7 equivalents of base to one of acid. Those who regard such substances as chemically integral when molten will not wonder at the isolation of tetrabasic phosphates, but rather regard it as supporting their views.

[e] Hague and Iddings, Bulletin U. S. Geol. Survey, No. 17, p. 10; Am. Journ. Science, XXVI., 1883.

[f] Stahl und Eisen, III., 5, p. 805, 1883.

more than 18% of phosphoric acid plus silica, removes much or most of the phosphorus of cast-iron. When cast-iron was thus fused its phosphorus in three instances fell from ·07 to ·058%, from ·35 to ·068%, and from 1·95 to ·415%. Other details of these cases are given in lines 7, 8 and 9, Table 23, p. 51.

§ 114. FUSED ALKALINE CARBONATES (Eaton process) gradually and sometimes almost completely remove phosphorus together with carbon and silicon from the interior of planed bars of cast-iron immersed in them.

Of several cases reported by T. M. Drown[a] the following shows the most complete dephosphorization. The iron itself showed no trace of oxidation; in other cases however oxidation occurred.

	Outer layer 1-16″ thick.?	Second layer 1-16″ thick.?	Third layer 1-16″ thick.?	Interior.	Original.
Carbon	0·057	0·166	0·942	3·293	3·56
Silicon	0·374	0·807	1·281	1·362	1·38
Phosphorus	0·015	0·201	0·776	0·911	0·87

The removal of phosphorus and silicon from the interior of solid bars by the action of alkaline carbonates on their exterior is interesting and surprising.

§ 115. ALKALINE NITRATES (Heaton process) expel phosphorus from molten iron very rapidly. As this process was actually carried out the dephosphorization was far from complete, as it was restrained by the senseless addition of sand, and by insufficiency of niter; but the use of a larger and under most conditions prohibitory proportion of nitrate would probably have rendered it thorough. The nitric acid, expelled from the nitrate by the heat of the molten iron, oxidizes its phosphorus energetically; while the soda, passing into the slag, renders it more basic and thus increases its power of retaining phosphoric acid. In two cases Gruner[b] found that 58 and 33% of the phosphoric acid contained in cast-iron, which contained initially 1·57 and 1·2% phosphorus respectively, was removed by this process, including 16 and 27% respectively which was volatilized. In six other cases he found it reduced from 1·06 to from 0·23 to 0·30%[c]; Miller found it reduced from 1·45 to 0·30%; but Snelus[d] found that hardly any phosphorus was removed from cast-iron holding about 0·5% of this element.

§ 116. MANGANESE, whether (1) in metal or (2) in slag, is thought to favor dephosphorization, because its oxides attack phosphorus more energetically than those of iron, and because its phosphates yield up their phosphorus to metallic iron and the carbon, manganese, etc., which it holds less readily than iron phosphates do. (1). Manganese remaining in the metal as it often does at the end of the basic Bessemer and open-hearth processes, prevents the metal from absorbing oxygen; hence its presence in the cast-iron employed for these processes is doubtless an advantage.

(2). Oxide of manganese in the slag, like other bases, assists dephosphorization: but it appears probable that dephosphorizing power can be obtained as fully and, with the usual relations of prices, far more cheaply by lime or iron oxide. It was formerly thought that, in pig-washing, the costly oxides of manganese would effect more thorough dephosphorization than iron oxides alone; experience indicates that, if they here offer any advantage over iron oxide, it is very slight and not commensurate with their higher cost. In this process Bell employs iron oxide alone, Krupp the mixed oxides of iron and manganese. I find that in six cases Bell removes 77, 93, 93, 88, 92 and 96% of the initial phosphorus, while Krupp removes 74, 63, 81, 72, 48 and 72% in six cases: but this is rather misleading, as Krupp may have stopped his operation unnecessarily early. A comparison of the ratio of

$$\frac{\%\text{ of initial phosphorus removed}}{\%\text{ of initial carbon removed}}$$

is more instructive. I find that for 6 cases of washing without oxide of manganese (Bell) this ratio was 3·5: 9·3: 8·5: 7·3: 9·2: and 1·6, or on the average 6·6: while when oxide of manganese is employed (Krupp) it was 18·4: 5·9: 6·5: 6·8: and 6·5, the mean being 8·8. While the mean ratio of $\frac{\text{dephosphorization}}{\text{decarburization}}$ is thus slightly higher when oxide of manganese is employed, too few results have been published to permit trustworthy conclusions. Thus, dropping one case from each we find that the mean ratio becomes 7·6 without and 6·4 with oxide of manganese, which would suggest that oxide of manganese opposed dephosphorization. Actually at American pig-washing works 85 to 90% of the initial phosphorus is ordinarily removed with the use of iron oxide only, leaving say ·01 to ·03 phosphorus in the washed metal. (See pig-washing.)

§ 117. INTERREACTION OF SULPHIDE AND PHOSPHIDE OF IRON.—These substances when melted do not unite. They appear to react on each other but slightly, the phosphide taking up a very little sulphur, the sulphide a little iron and sometimes a little phosphorus. When, however, lime phosphate is melted with pyrites and silica in the presence of carbon, much of the phosphorus and most of the sulphur may be volatilized, and a phosphide of iron with a little sulphur results.

Thus Hochstätter,[e] in Percy's laboratory, melted in clay crucibles the two phosphides Fe_6P, containing 8% of phosphorous, and Fe_2P, containing 23·3±%, separately, both with ferrous sulphide containing 39·4% of sulphur, and with an excess of sulphur. Each phosphide when melted with sulphur took up a little of this element, while a thin layer of iron sulphide was formed: when fused with ferrous sulphide, one phosphide became richer, the other poorer in phosphorus: they both took up a little sulphur, and were overlain by iron sulphide. The iron sulphide resulting from the fusion of the phosphide Fe_6P with ferrous sulphide contained no trace of phosphorus: that resulting from the fusion of the phosphide Fe_2P with ferrous sulphide contained a considerable amount of phosphorus in its lower part. I here summarize these results.

[a] Trans. Am. Inst. Mining Engineers, 1879, VII., p. 147. The thickness of these layers is not positively stated, but is inferred from the context to have been about 1-16″.

[b] Gruner, Annales des Mines, 1869, XVI., p. 260.

[c] Idem, 1870, XVII., p. 330.

[d] Journ. of the Iron and St. Inst., 1871, II., p. 185.

[e] Percy, Iron and Steel, p. 66.

Composition of initial phosphide.			Fused with	Composition of Products.				Character of Resulting Sulphide.
				Iron Sulphide.	Iron Phosphide.			
Phosphorus.	Iron.	Formula.		Phosphorus.	Phosphorus.	Sulphur.	Iron.	
8 ±	92 ±	Fe_6P	Sulphur	......	8·45	3·19	89·54	A thin layer of iron sulphide, not analyzed.
23·3 ±	76·67	Fe_2P	"	......	......	4·82	......	" " " "
8 ±	92 ±	Fe_6P	FeS	0·00	10·75	1·25	87·84	Sulphide, free from phosphorus.
23·3 ±	76·67 ±	Fe_2P	FeS	A considerable amount.	19·19	4·92	75·75	Much sulphide; the lower part had a considerable amount of phosphorus.

Brackelsberg[a] melted 8 parts of lime phosphate, 4·6 of pyrite, 4·0 of silica and 2·8 of alumina in a carbonaceous crucible. Had the phosphorus been completely reduced the iron resulting would have had 45·41% phosphorus: actually it had 24·98% phosphorus with 2·31% sulphur. The accompanying slag had 48·75% silica, 5·48 phosphoric acid and 1·98% sulphur. A very large proportion of the phosphorus was here volatilized, together with a still larger part of the sulphur.

§ 118. Volatilization.—Besides phosphorus itself, its chlorides, fluoride, phosphoretted hydrogen, PH_3, phosphorous oxide, P_2O_3, and phosphoric acid readily volatilize, the latter subliming below a red heat. Hence phosphorus is volatilized as such by heating acid phosphate of lime, *e. g.*, mono-phosphate, in contact with charcoal: if sand be added the whole of the phosphorus may be expelled: $2CaP_2O_6 + 2SiO_2 + 10C = 2CaSiO_3 + 10CO + 4P$.

Phosphorus may be partially volatilized from tricalcic phosphate by heating it in contact with iron oxide and carbon: and from iron phosphates by heating them (A) in contact with carbon, either alone or in presence of silicates: and (B) in contact with silica. In the latter case it is probably expelled as phosphoric acid. Thus Bell[b] decomposed mono-ferrous phosphate, whose oxygen ratio of base: acid is 1 : 5, by heating it contact with half its weight of silica at a bright red heat for five hours, whereby 4·2% of its initial phosphorus was expelled (say $FeP_2O_6 + SiO_2 = FeSiO_3 + P_2O_5$). He then cooled and pulverized it, next exposing it for two hours to a steel melting heat, whereby 13·4% more, or altogether 17·6% of the initial phosphorus was volatilized.

It is stated that if diferrous phosphate is heated in a crucible with 25% of powdered charcoal, half its phosphorus is volatilized, and iron phosphide, Fe_2P, containing 21·7±% of phosphorus, is formed:[c] say $14C + 2Fe_2P_2O_7 = Fe_2P + 14CO + 2P$.

So too Brackelsberg volatilized phosphorus from much less acid iron phosphates by the action of carbon alone. He melted a mixture of ferrous and ferric phosphates (oxygen ratio base : acid = 1 : 1·38) in carbon crucibles, A alone, B with a little acid slag. The iron was almost, and in one case quite, fully deoxidized, and contained from 21·99 to 24·56% phosphorus. The accompanying acid slag contained a little phosphoric acid, but most of the excess of phosphorus above that which the iron was capable of absorbing, or from 14·3 to 18·73% of the total phosphorus present, was volatilized, or at least was not accounted for. I here summarize his results.

Phosphorus Volatilized on Melting Iron Phosphate (Oxygen Ratio Base : Acid = 1 : 1·38) in Brasqued Crucibles.[a]

	Weight of products.		Composition of products.									Loss % of initial Phosphorus.
			Metal.			Slag.						
	Metal %.	Slag %.	Iron.	Phosphorus.	Silicon.	Silica.	Al_2O_3.	FeO.	CaO.	MgO	P_2O_5.	
(1) Iron phosphate melted alone..	....	....	75.45	24·65	....	....	....	....	..	....	....	14·3
(2) Iron phosphate melted with acid slag..........	2·00	2·10	76·5	21·99	1·71	54·88	0.13[b]	......	38·79	1·40	·68	18·73
(3) Iron phosphate melted with acid slag..........	2·16	4·59	76·96	22·27	0·87	64·81	20·12	3·06	11·35	0·21	0·59	16·08
(4) Iron phosphate melted with acid slag..........	2·06	2.9	73·94	25·06	0·94	45·79	4·38	0·02	47.23	0·70	0·25	15·80

a Brackelsberg, Stahl und Eisen, V., 1885, p. 548. b Alumina and ferric oxide

In two fusions at the Stockholm School of Mines,[d] in which iron ore was melted with carbonaceous matter in crucibles, (*A*) apparently with acid slag and (*B*) apparently with basic slag, a considerable quantity of phosphorus was volatilized, viz.: about 1-3d and 1-10th respectively of that initially present in the ore. I here summarize the results.

Volatilization of Phosphorus.—Akerman.

Charge.			Products.							
Ore.	Flux.		Slag.			Metal.			Total	Loss of phosphorus per 100 of ore.
% P in ore	Kind	Wt. per 100 of ore.	Wt. per 100 of ore.	Phosphorus in slag per 100 of Slag.	Phosphorus in slag per 100 of Ore.	Wt. per 100 of ore.	Phosphorus in metal per 100 of Metal.	Phosphorus in metal per 100 of Ore.	Phosphorus in slag + metal per 100 of ore.	
1·62	SiO_2	78	168	0·068	0·01	66·9	1·57	1·41	1·65	0·57
0·89	lime	256	33·75	·026	·009	56·	1·41	0·730	0·738	0·093

Gruner[e] found that in the Heaton process, (treatment of molten cast-iron with nitrate of soda) phosphorus was copiously volatilized, especially if the accompanying slags were acid.

But no important effective volatilization of phosphorus is to be looked for in the blast-furnace, for any phosphorus which volatilized would be immediately recondensed by the cooler ore above. Bell,[f] accurately controlling his materials, found that of 1·578 parts of phosphorus per 100 of cast-iron entering his blast-furnaces from all sources, 1·441 parts were accounted for by the cast-iron and 0·147 by the slag, or together 1·588, *i. e.*, the two sides balance to within 0·6% of the total phosphorus.

The volatilizing effect of fluor spar is discussed on p. 63.

§ 122. Effect of Phosphorus on Tensile Strength and Elastic Limit.—Disastrous as are the effects of phosphorus on ductility, it affects tensile strength under quiescent load comparatively slightly: indeed it is uncertain whether moderate amounts of phosphorus, say 0·25% or less, sensibly affect this property. Certain facts indeed suggest that, as phosphorus rises from 0 to about 0·12%, it raises the tensile strength of low-carbon steel: but our evidence as to the influence of larger proportions of phosphorus, say from 0·12 to 0·25%, is contradictory. Table 27 and Figure 8 give the results of an analysis[g] of 435 cases of more or less phosphoric steel selected at random: they accord closely with the data furnished by Gatewood[h] as to the properties of 619 specimens of steel, so that they are in a sense based on over 1,000 cases. The tensile strength curves in the seven right-hand diagrams are nearly vertical, indicating that phosphorus does not affect this property: but in the three left-hand diagrams, and to a slighter extent in those including carbon ·2 to ·3%, these curves as they rise at first incline to the right, but reverse at about phosphorus 0·12% and then incline to the left. This may be accidental, or it may truly indicate that, in low-carbon steels, rising phosphorus at first raises but later diminishes tensile strength and that this effect becomes weaker as carbon increases. This accords fairly with the statements of Ledebur, Kent and Salom, and possibly with Åkerman's experience, but not with that of Deshayes except as regards low-carbon steel.

a Stahl und Eisen, V., 1885, p. 548.
b Manufacture of Iron and Steel, p. 397.
c Percy, Iron and Steel, p. 62.
d Akerman, Eng. and Mining Jl., 1875, I., p. 475.
e Annales des Mines, 1869, XVI., p. 200.
f Journ. Iron and St. Inst., 1871, II., p. 283.
g This analysis was made as described in § 65 J.
h Report of U. S. Naval Advisory Bd. on Mild Steel, 1886, pp. 188 to 190.

TABLE 27.—EFFECT OF PHOSPHORUS ON TENSILE STRENGTH AND ELONGATION.

% Carbon.	P. 0@·03 No. of cases.	Tensile strength	Elongation.	P. ·03@·06 No. of cases.	Tensile strength	Elongation.	P. ·06@·09 No. of cases.	Tensile strength	Elongation.
0@·05	3	51,400	33·5				3	51,000	23·5
·05@·10	5	49,360	33·8	7	65,514	30·9	4	58,750	26·3
·10@·15	4	55,000	29·6	55	59,640	27·4	10	61,900	27·6
·15@·20	3	55,666	32·2	37	62,786	25·6	7	64,221	24·3
·20@·25	4	58,250	30·6	6	64,216	23·8	11	71,709	21·
·25@·30	1	62,500	27·5	8	68,253	21·7	16	78,981	19·5
·30@·40	2	69,450	18·3	11	73,000	23·	48	87,794	19·
·40@·50	8	88,285	18·8	11	88,328	15·9	10	86,940	15·6
·50@·60				2	115,500	8·4	4	95,250	14·9
·60@·70	3	87,466	4·8				2	104,000	7·8
·70@·80				1	127,000	5			
·80@·90	2	112,750	8·9	2	124,800	4·2	2	103,500	3·8
·90@1·00	2	120,350	10·6	1	170,400	2·1	2	130,900	5·1
1·00@1·10	2	125,250	5·3	1	98,300	8·5			
1·10@1·20	3	131,000	7·1						
1·20@1·30									
1·30@1·40	1	135,300	7·3	1	123,200	2·5			

% Carbon.	P. ·09@·12 No. of cases.	Tensile strength	Elongation.	P. ·12@·15 No. of cases.	Tensile strength	Elongation.	P. ·15@·20 No. of cases.	Tensile strength	Elongation.
0@·05	1	70,000	25·						
·05@·10	2	56,180	27·				1	55,000	25·5
·10@·15	3	84,766	19·5	2	79,000	22	1	77,000	10·0
·15@·20	3	82,200	18·	4	80,075	24	2	77,500	17·
·20@·25	4	81,000	20·1	5	79,160	32	1	77,800	19·
·25@·30	8	79,887	15·0	1	66,000	14	3	76,333	17·
·30@·40	22	82,440	18·	13	81,937	16·2	5	82,980	11·6
·40@·50	9	89,006	14·	7	75,425	13	6	90,833	11·0
·50@·60	3	95,793	11·5	9	76,000	1·5			
·60@·70	1	119,000	6·0				1	68,000	1·6
·70@·80									
·80@·90	1	104,000	9·4						
·90@1·00									
1·00@1·10									
1·10@1·20									
1·20@1·30									
1·30@1·40									

% Carbon.	P. ·20@·25 No. of cases.	Tensile strength	Elongation.	P. ·25@·30 No. of cases.	Tensile strength	Elongation.	P. ·30@·40 No. of cases.	Tensile strength	Elongation.
0@·05									
·05@·10				2	32,000	9·0			
·10@·15	3	69,600	11·1	2	81,000	21·0	1	74,500	18·3
·15@·20	1	72,000	16	3	69,500	12·5	2	74,500	6·1
·20@·25	3	76,833	13	1	72,000	4·1	4	76,875	9·4
·25@·30	3	78,600	19	2	80,550	21·	1	90,000	25
·30@·40	3	79,866	10·8	1	72,900	20·4	4	83,750	19·7
·40@·50	2	100,750	8·5	2	81,500	1·9			
·50@·60	3	103,333	4·3	1	98,500	8·2			
·60@·70									
·70@·80									
·80@·90									
·90@1·00									
1·00@1·10									
1·10@1·20									
1·20@1·30									
1·30@1·40									

Fig. 8

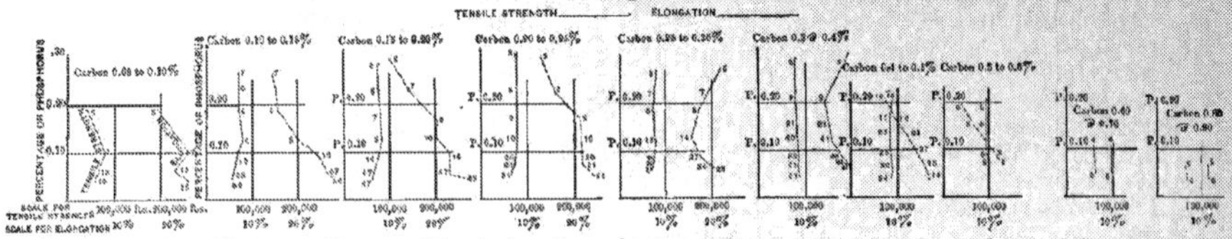

LEDEBUR[a] states that a small proportion of phosphorus has slight effect on tensile strength, but that a large proportion lowers it: the second of these statements agrees roughly with my left-hand diagrams. Kent plotted the tensile strength (ordinate) and carbon (abscissa) of 42 steels with from ·06 to ·18% of carbon; 26 had ·03%, 16 had ·10% of phosphorus. The latter formed a group above the low-phosphorus group, and nowhere overlapped it;[b] this agrees fully with the easterly inclination of my low-carbon tensile strength lines. Salom,[c] analyzing by the method of least squares Dudley's 64 rail steels, with carbon from ·19 to ·62% and phosphorus from ·026 to ·158%, found that phosphorus did not affect tensile strength appreciably. My curves, teaching that when carbon is above 0·20% phosphorus affects tensile strength slightly, agree with this. Åkerman[d] thinks that phosphorus rather raises tensile strength. Studying more than 1,000 phosphoric steels (Nos. 1 to 3, Table 28), whose carbon averages ·325% and whose phosphorus averages from ·26 to ·348%, Deshayes[e] concludes that ·1% of phosphorus raises the tensile strength by 2,129 pounds per square inch, or about one-fourth as much as the same proportion of carbon. This disagrees with Ledebur's view, with Salom's results and with my curves, which suggest that when carbon is as high as in Deshayes' steels phosphorus should not affect tensile strength. We may infer that, when above say 0·12%, phosphorus probably has no important constant effect, for if it had the analyses of statistics should yield concordant results.

Phosphorus however usually raises the elastic limit and thus the elastic ratio, an index of brittleness: indeed the elastic limit and breaking strength of phosphoric steels occasionally coincide (see cases 14, 17, Heaton, and 22-23, Clapp-Griffiths, table 28).

The effect of phosphorus on the elastic ratio, as on elongation and contraction, is very capricious. We occasionally find highly phosphoric steels with very low elastic ratio, *e. g.* steels 10, 12, Terre Noire, and 43, 47, 49, 50 and 51, tested in Russia, in Table 28, whose elastic ratio lies between 0·37 and 0·63.

Phosphoric steels are, however, liable to break under very slight tensile stress if suddenly or vibratorily applied or shock-like.

§ 123. EFFECT OF PHOSPHORUS ON DUCTILITY.—Phosphorus diminishes the ductility of steel under a gradually applied load, as measured by its elongation, contraction and elastic ratio when ruptured in the ordinary testing machine: but it diminishes its toughness under shock to a still greater degree, and this it is that unfits phosphoric steels for most purposes. The influence of ·01% of phosphorus is perceptible, that of ·20% is generally fatal in ingot metal: (see § 130).

A. Static Ductility.—The effect of phosphorus on static ductility appears to be very capricious, for we find many cases of highly phosphoric steel which show excellent elongation, contraction and even fair elastic ratio, while side by side with them are others produced under apparently identical conditions but statically brittle.

Thus two Heaton bars (15 and 18, table 28) have high contraction and good elongation; four, apparently made under like conditions, have no contraction, and three of these but slight elongation. No. 22 (Clapp-Griffiths), with carbon ·31, phosphorus ·40%, is almost as brittle as glass; 3 and 12 (Terre-Noire), with as high or higher carbon, and nearly or quite as high phosphorus (carbon, 32 with phosphorus ·35%, and carbon ·31, with phosphorus ·40%) are admirably ductile statically. 28 and 29 (Clapp-Griffiths) are statically rather brittle and not tensilely strong; the preceding and following cases are fairly ductile with the same tensile strength. 34 (Heaton) is both strong and ductile; 35 to 39 are brittle, though made under apparently like conditions, and with no corresponding difference in their composition.

But while we find small groups of cases of statically

a Handbuch der Eisenhüttenkunde, p. 245.
b Private communication, Aug. 22, 1887. With another form of test pieces these groups overlapped at one point.
c Trans. Am. Inst. Min. Eng., XIII., p. 157, 1885.
d Eng. and Min. Jl., 1875, I., p. 475.
e Annales des Mines, 7 Ser., XV., pp. 351-2, 1870.

ductile phosphoric steel, yet if we examine sufficiently large groups the static brittleness caused by this element is plainly seen. To illustrate this I present in Table 27 and graphically in Fig. 8 the results of an analysis of 435 cases of more or less phosphoric steel. The direction of the broken lines in Fig. 8 reveals the effect of phosphorus. In 8 out of 10 large groups, each with approximately constant carbon but varying phosphorus, the ductility lines point west of north, showing that with rising phosphorus the elongation declines. In two of these (carbon ·60 to ·70 and ·80 to ·90) the westward obliquity of the elongation curve is but slight: little weight attaches however to these two curves, since they represent but 7 cases each. Furthermore, the two curves (carbon ·25 to ·30 and carbon ·30 to ·40) which at first do not appear to show the influence of phosphorus, since, though in their lower portion pointing nearly northwest, their upper portions point N. N. E., on further examination corroborate the teaching of the other curves. For their westerly-pointing parts are really the ones which deserve weight, since they represent many cases, while their easterly-pointing portions represent comparatively few, the orientation of the upper part of the carbon ·30 to ·40 curve being wholly due to 5 cases, while its westerly pointing portion represents 104 cases. These curves are obtained as described in § 65, J.

Abnormally low contraction and high elastic ratio as compared with the elongation are said to characterize phosphoric steels: and from a careful examination of a large number of cases I believe that this combination of properties is much commoner in phosphoric than in other steels. Thus, in Table 28 the contraction of Heaton steels Nos. 13, 14, 16 and 17, and of Clapp-Griffiths steels Nos. 23, 24, 26, 28 and 29 is abnormally low for their elongation: while in Heaton steels 13 to 18 and Clapp-Griffiths steels 22, 23, 31, 32 and 33 we find abnormally high elastic ratio for the elongation. But these cannot be set down as constant characteristics, for in Terre-Noire open-hearth steels 1, 2, 3, 10, 11 and 12, in Heaton steels 15 and 18, and in Clapp-Griffiths Bessemer steels 25 and 34 the relation between contraction and elongation is fairly normal.

B. Ductility Under Shock.—If any relation between composition and physical properties is established by experience, it is that of phosphorus in making steel brittle under shock. And it appears reasonably certain, though exact data sufficing to demonstrate it are not at hand, that phosphoric steels are liable to be very brittle under shock even though they may be tolerably ductile statically. The effects of phosphorus on shock-resisting power, though probably more constant than its effects on static ductility, are still decidedly capricious.

This and the capricious behavior of phosphorus under the action of solvents, harmonize with the belief that the state of chemical combination in which it exists in steel, the mineral species which it helps to compose, depends upon imperfectly understood conditions, such as those of cooling. It may exist now as part of the matrix, whose properties it thus profoundly affects, now as a distinct phosphide, whose composition and properties, and through these its effects on the physical properties of the composite mass as a whole, may differ greatly.

TABLE 28—PHOSPHORIC STEELS.

No.	C.	Si.	Mn.	P.	S.	Tensile strength.	Elastic limit.	Elongation.	In.	Contraction.	
								%		%	
1	·32	...	1·7	·31	...	72,300	54,000	14·68	8"	23·86	Terre Noire, 1874. Mean of over 1,000 cases.
2	·34	...	·58	·26	...	72,600	47,600	23·45	8"	45·66	
3	·32	...	·87	·25	...	68,100	51,000	19·95	8"	41·56	
10	·31	tr.	·75	·28	tr.	80,560	48,600	22·7	4"	47·0	Terre Noire, 1878.
11	·27	tr.	·80	·27	tr.	80,000	50,000	21·5	4"	44·9	
12	·31	tr.	·89	·40	tr.	83,200	55,600	22·1	4"	40·7	
13	·49	·10	...	·30	·2	93,800	91,900	2·8	8"	6·	Heaton process, Fairbairn, Gruner.
14	·57	·12	...	·26	·01	93,800	102,000	3·1	8"	0·	
15	·53	·10	...	·24	·01	113,130	107,800	9·4	8"	30	
16	·54	·10	...	·24	·01	104,800	36,800	2·8	8"	0·	
17	·54	·12	...	·28	·0	98,000	96,000	9·4	8"	0·	
18	·47	·09	...	·33	·0	104,300	92,300	10·4	8"	43·	
19	·10	tr.	·88	·32	·08	79,449	58,500	24·		47·0	Clapp-Griffiths Bessemer steel.
20	·12	tr.	·81	·43	·03	86,250	67,150	18·75	...	31·8	
21	·12	tr.	·77	·55	·05	79,736	59,050	23·50	...	35·5	
22	·31	tr.	...	·46	...	77,460	?	0·62	...	6·	
23	·08	tr.	·30	·72	·08	73,200	69,130	2·25	...	2·6	
24	·13	tr.	·73	·85	...	101,540	71,090	9·50	...	9·44	
25	Phosphorus not given, but supposed to be high.					74,758	56,078	26·25	8"	48·8	Clapp-Griffiths Bessemer steel.
26						60,063	55,000	28·0	8"	26·9	
27						80,270	56,290	22·75	8"	30·6	
28						80,423	58,290	17·5	8"	14·8	
29						78,730	58,413	14·25	8"	15·8	
30	...	...	...	...	...	80,943	58,570	21·0	8"	36·4	
31	...	...	...	...	...	79,870	58,570	26·25	8"	36·4	
32	·03	·01	·48	·30	·09	80,670	60,240	23·0	8"	32·5	
33	...	...	...	...	...	79,700	59,850	28·25	8"	37·6	
34	·33	·14	...	·28	·08	110,800	...	12·5	...	29·	Heaton steel. Gruner.
35	·55	·13	...	·25	·06	116,400	...	4·0	...	4·	
36	·35	...	...	...	...	110,100	...	6·0	...	0·	
37	·81	...	...	...	...	113,800	...	8·1	...	5·	
38	·39	·11	...	·34	tr.	84,000	...	1·8	...	8·	
39	·48	·17	...	·60	·03	112,500	...	3·2	...	6·	
40	·18	...	·18 Cr.	·54	...	90,700	...	4·6	...	...	Chrome (?) steel.
41	·18	...	·20 Cr.	·66	...	89,600	...	24·	...	...	
42	·28	...	·27 Cr.	·70	...	112,700	...	5·7	...	...	
43	·26	...	·32 Cr.	·70	...	165,300	...	4·7	...	...	
44	·30	...	·14 Cr.	·90	...	97,700	...	19·3	...	...	
45	·36	...	·16 Cr.	·98	...	99,500	...	3·2	...	...	
46	·28	·01	·93	·58	?	90,700	58,300	24·6	...	44·1	Steel rails examined by a Russian Commission.
47	·24	·02	·40	·32	?	77,500	25,900	21·1	...	51·3	
48	·28	·08	·99	·67	?	...	...	22·2	...	58·0	
49	·23	·01	·62	·24	?	73,900	32,700	12·5	...	19·1	
50	·18	·01	·26	·26	?	80,000	28,000	10·5	...	16·5	
51	·15	·01	·19	·34	?	79,800	32,700	15·7	...	47·5	
52	·24	tr.	...	·29	...	82,700	...	26·9	...	36·1	Steel rails examined by a Russian Commission.
53	·28	·02	...	·29	...	78,100	...	12·8	...	28·6	
54	·30	·01	...	·35	...	104,600	...	11·0	...	16·9	
55	·25	tr.	...	·32	...	74,300	...	32·5	...	50·	

1, 2 and **3**. Terre Noire, 1874, Annales des Mines, 1878, p. 361, mean of over 1,000 cases.
10, 11 and **12**. Terre Noire, 1878. Idem, p. 872.
13 to **18**. Made by the Heaton process at Langley Mills, tested by Fairbairn. Annales des Mines, 1870, XVII., pp. 851 to 861.
19 to **24**. Clapp-Griffiths Bessemer steel. R. W. Hunt, Trans. Am. Inst. Mining Engrs., XIV., pp. 140-141, 1886.
25 to **33**. Clapp-Griffiths Bessemer steel. R. W. Hunt, Trans. Am. Inst. Mining Engrs., XIII., pp. 756-7, 1885.
34 to **39**. Heaton steel, Gruner. Annales des Mines, 1869, XVI.
40 to **45**. Chrome steel. Brown. Journ. Iron and St. Inst., 1879, II., p. 358. Trustworthiness doubtful.
46 to **51**. Rails employed in Russia. Beck-Guerhard. Idem, 1886, I., p. 254. Trustworthiness doubtful.
52 to **55**. Rails tested in Russia. Jouraffsky. Idem, 1880, I., p. 192, Appendix E. Trustworthiness doubtful.

§ 124. INFLUENCE OF CARBON ON THE EFFECTS OF PHOSPHORUS.—General experience, and especially the results obtained by Slade in 1869 and subsequently by Tessié du Motay, at Terre-Noire, and by R. W. Hunt, have abundantly shown that the influence of phosphorus is the more severe the more carbon is simultaneously present, so that while the effects of 0·10% of phosphorus on the ductility of steel which contains less than 0·10% carbon may escape notice in rough testing, yet if the steel contain 1% carbon the effects of 0·01% and perhaps even of 0·005% phosphorus may be detected. This influence of carbon on the effects of phosphorus is illustrated by Fig. 8. We note that the degree of obliquity of the elongation lines is on the whole only slightly greater for the low than for the high carbon steels, and roughly speaking indicates that an increment of 0·10% of phosphorus diminishes the elongation by about 6% of the initial length of the test piece. This loss would cut down the elongation of a low-carbon steel (initially free from phosphorus) from say 31 to 25% of the length of the test piece, or by about 20% of the original elongation, a loss which might easily be masked by the effects of other variables: but it would lower the elongation of a high-carbon steel from say 8 to 2%, or by 75% of its original value, enough to change a valuable to an utterly worthless material.

Tables 28 and 29 give many instances of tough phosphoric steels low in carbon.

§ 125. Influence of Silicon on the Effect of Phosphorus.—It is often stated that silicon like carbon greatly exaggerates the effects of phosphorus; but what evidence I find very strongly opposes this view, and supports Ledebur's[a] statement that it does not. Thus the first of the Trenton phosphoric steels in table 29 has 0·17% silicon, 0·15 phosphorus and 0.16 carbon, yet is "excellent soft boiler plate:" No. 50 has ·05 silicon, ·27 phosphorus and ·12 carbon and is "remarkably tough boiler plate." These data are from a most conscientious observer, Mr. F. J. Slade.

So among the Heaton steels one with nearly the highest silicon (0·16% in No. 15) is more ductile than those of otherwise similar composition but with much less silicon.

§ 126. Structure, Conditions of Cooling and Ductility.—Phosphorus tends to induce a coarsely crystalline structure, which is plausibly regarded as a proximate cause the brittleness of phosphoric metal. As slow, undisturbed cooling favors coarse crystallization, while sudden cooling and agitation impede it, whether in solidification from aqueous solution, from magma of molten rock, or from fused or pasty metal or glass, it is not surprising that these same conditions respectively favor and oppose both coarse crystallization and brittleness in phosphoric steel. We have seen that sudden cooling tends to induce brittleness in ordinary steel by preserving a brittle compound of iron and carbon which is broken up by slow cooling, and by inducing severe internal stresses (see §§ 51 C, 34 B). But in phosphoric iron the net effect of sudden cooling is sometimes at least to increase ductility, since its toughening effect in preventing coarse crystallization outweighs its opposite effect of internal stress and of preserving a brittle iron-carbon compound. Thus, while in tables 8, 9, 10, 11, non-phosphoric steels are tougher after slow than after sudden cooling, in the following instance[b] phosphoric weld iron became much tougher on sudden cooling. It is probable that this applies to other irons with much phosphorus but comparatively little carbon.

		Tensile strength.	Elongation.	Contraction.	Carbon.	Phosphorus.
Swedish charcoal-hearth weld iron.	Unannealed.......	61,753	6·5	6	·07	·26±
	Quenched in water from redness....	68,700	25%	34%	·07	·26±

So too, when phosphoric iron is heated, it appears especially desirable to continue forging it until its temperature has fallen so low that the tendency to coarse crystallization is no longer to be feared.

§ 127. Influence of Cold on the Effects of Phosphorus.—Steel is far more brittle under shock when very cold (say 0° F.) than at the ordinary temperature, and it is generally believed that cold increases the brittleness of phosphoric more than that of non-phosphoric steel. The most direct evidence on this point that I have met is that of a Russian commission;[c] it strongly opposes this belief, though the commission does not state so.

In their tests two pieces from each of 33 steel rails were submitted, one at 16° to 20° C. (61° to 68° F.) the other artificially cooled to from —16° to —21° C. (+ 5° to — 6° F.), to the drop test under identical conditions. Twenty-four of those tested cold broke: only three of those tested when warm broke. All the rails with over 0·14 phosphorus broke when cold: but as the three fractures which occurred during the warm tests were also of phosphoric rails, this merely shows that, warm or cold, phosphorus causes brittleness. The difference between the cold-resistance to shock of the phosphoric and of the non-phosphoric rails was certainly not greater, and perhaps even less than that which would be expected at 70° F. Thus three non-phosphoric rails broke more readily and three moderately phosphoric rails broke at least as readily when cold as five of the phosphoric ones: these non-phosphoric ones with ·07, ·08 and ·10% phosphorus and ·40, ·5, and ·38% carbon respectively broke at the first blow under a drop of 8·5 feet: the three moderately phosphoric ones, with ·13% phosphorus or less and ·33% carbon or less, broke at the second blow under the same fall: while of the five phosphoric ones with ·15, ·15, ·18, ·20 and ·27% phosphorus and ·50, ·31, ·41, ·41 and ·21% of carbon respectively, the first resisted two blows of 8·5 feet and one of 9·5 feet, and the others each resisted one blow. Further, many of the rails which did not break had more phosphorus than some of those which did. Thus, eight which did not break had from ·1 to ·14% of phosphorus: while four of those which broke had ·1% or less.

Unfortunately grave doubts exist as to the trustworthiness of these results: *e. g.* they credit the Seraing rails with containing ·18 to ·20% of phosphorus, though cast-iron which could yield such phosphoric steel had never been employed at these works.[d]

The fact that, of 100 steel rails with ·25% phosphorus laid by Sandberg in Sweden, not one broke during the first six years, though the temperature occasionally fell to—30° F., weighs against the belief that cold increases the brittleness of phosphoric more than that of other steel.[e]

§ 128. Illusions Concerning the Neutralization of Phosphorus.—The capriciousness of the effects of phosphorus and the fact that its effect on the ductility of low-carbon steel is so slight as to be easily masked, coupled with the fact, if fact it be, that statically ductile phosphoric steel may be brittle under shock, has led to the discovery every few years, and probably to the subsequent extreme annoyance of the discoverers, of methods of neutralizing phosphorus, or of special conditions or processes by which it is rendered harmless. If the investigator of a new process for making excellent though phosphoric steel confines his attention to low-carbon steel, or to this with a small number of static (not dynamic) tests of high-carbon steel, and especially if he is ignorant of the fate of his predecessors, he readily falls into the trap, and pronounces absolutely worthless processes to be of enormous value. And here I think it wise to deviate from the plan of this work and to introduce a little ancient history, because it clarifies our atmosphere, enables us to view more clearly an apparatus to-day much noised about, and justifies the extreme skepticism as to its reputed merits which I have shown, precipitating on my head the wrath of the true believers, those men of childlike and religious faith.

(A). In 1869 the Heaton Process, which partially dephosphorized cast-iron, yielding steel with from say 0·23

a Handbuch der Eisenhüttenkunde, 1883, p. 247.

b Styffe, Iron and Steel, pp. 132, 136.

c Jourafsky, Journ. Iron and St. Inst., 1880, I., p. 192.

d Greiner, Journ. Iron and St. Inst., 1880, I., p. 198.

e Trans. Am. Inst. Mining Engrs., IX., p. 598, 1881.

to 0·30 phosphorus, was vigorously promoted. Actually the percentage of phosphorus which it left in the steel was simply fatal: yet no less distinguished and competent authorities than Sir Wm. Fairbairn, Robert Mallet and Prof. Miller after personal investigation highly commended process and product.

Fairbairn, examining six bars of Heaton steel with from 0·23 to 0·30% phosphorus, and comparing them with the best Sheffield crucible steel, reported that under transverse flexure the Heaton steel showed a very marked superiority over the others: that it was evidently specially adapted to *resisting force of impact!* That its elongation was notably above the mean of the other bars: that in short it compared advantageously with the steel of the other makers (the best Sheffield makers). This was not a joke, but a serious professional opinion by an illustrious engineer. How Fairbairn deduced such views from his tests, whose results were published, must remain a mystery. Gruner showed their true meaning.

(B). Professor Miller, examining Heaton steel, reported that the quantity of phosphorus which it retained (0·29%) was obviously not such as to injure its quality! That it resisted many severe tests, being bent and hammered sharply around both cold and at red and yellow heats without cracking, and that it welded satisfactorily. This steel contained 0·29% phosphorus, 0·99 carbon, 0·15 silicon, 0·09% manganese.

(C). Mallet reported that this process yielded excellent steel from highly phosphoric cast-iron, from which no "process, *not even Bessemer's!*" (which, with the intuition of true genius, he saw was better adapted to phosphoric iron than puddling, conversion, and crucible melting) "enables steel of commercial value to be produced at all."

(D). Tessié du Motay,[a] about four years later, appears to have rediscovered the already pretty well known fact that a large amount of phosphorus can be tolerated in steel, provided the carbon be low, which was rather amusing to American as well as to well informed European metallurgists, as F. J. Slade[b] had in 1869 made a considerable quantity of good phosphoric steel, low in carbon. I append a few analyses of it.

Table 29.—Trenton Phosphoric Steel, 1869.

	Carbon.	Silicon.	Manganese.	Phosphorus.	Sulphur.	Date.	Quality, etc.
46..	·16	·17	·14	·153	·063	Dec 29, 1869	Excellent soft boiler plate.
47..	·12	·015	·06	·113	·008	Oct. 20, 1869	" " " "
48..	·12	·025	·07	·275	·007	Oct. 19, 1869	" " " "
49..	·125	....	....	·314	....	Nov. 26, 1869	Remarkably tough.
50..	·19	·052	....	·272	....	" " "	" " boiler plate.
51..	·21	....	....	·345	....	" " "	" " bar.

Great excitement was manifested generally on the continent when it was announced in 1874 that Terre Noire had solved the phosphoric steel problem, where, Euverte stated, it had been proved that a steel with 0·30 phosphorus and 0·15 carbon was very malleable and fit for making rails of good quality.[c]

(E). The Sherman process, which would neutralize but not remove phosphorus from steel, was thoroughly exposed by Menelaus,[d] Snelus and others in 1871, and by Euverte in 1876, and shown to have no effect whatsoever. Yet many eminent and experienced manufacturers, including Crawshay of Cyfarthfa and I believe the Firminy Iron Works, in spite of these exposures are said to have had complete faith in this ridiculous operation, and actually adopted it: and in 1877 it still had such vitality that large scale experiments with it were carried out in Boston under Holley's inspection, who of course again exposed its worthlessness.

(F). Richard Brown was permitted in 1879 to read before the Iron and Steel Institute[e] a paper in which he claimed that, if bichromate of potash were blown through the steel in the Bessemer converter, the metal would be soft and malleable even if it contained 1·5% phosphorus, and among other evidence produced cases 40 to 45 in table 28 to support his statements. I mention this process for no merit of its own, but to show what rubbish, provided it claim to neutralize phosphorus, may be accepted by a board so really wise as that of this institute, and, as I am credibly informed, so conservative as to refuse Thomas for some time the privilege of describing the basic process in its journal.

(G). Clapp-Griffiths Converter.—The last to fall into this trap is no less competent a person than the very experienced and judicious Capt. R. W. Hunt, who lauds the excellent quality of phosphoric low-carbon Bessemer steel made in the Clapp-Griffiths converter: and, though I do not find that he says so in so many words, he evidently thinks that, for given composition, phosphoric steel produced in this converter is incomparably superior to steel of identical composition produced in the ordinary converter, but, as is perfectly patent on examination, without proper ground for such a conclusion. Passing by the surprising fact that this steel, even with 1·10% phosphorus, rolls in a "practical manner" which will be considered under the effects of phosphorus on hotshortness, and taking only his strongest cases, he reports steel with 0·08 carbon and 0·30 phosphorus to 0·12 carbon and 0·55 phosphorus which shows good static ductility; and one with 0·13 carbon and 0·85 phosphorus which shows fair static ductility for its tensile strength. He reports but one case with over 0·13 carbon, No. 22 Table 28, and this was surprisingly brittle. In short he too has rediscovered for the Nth time that phosphorus affects the ductility of low-carbon steel relatively little, and, so far as I can see, nothing more.

Let us now examine his results in detail and see whether they indicate that his phosphoric steel is really less brittle than that of other observers, and whether therefore there is any ground for supposing that the use of this converter any more than of Sherman's and Brown's nostrums even partially neutralizes phosphorus. The three most noticeable cases which he reports are numbers 21, 24 and 30 in Table 28. If they are no better than other steels of like composition, we need not examine his poorer cases.

No. 21 (Clapp-Griffiths) with 0·12 carbon and 0·55 phosphorus, has actually less ductility and much less tensile strength than No. 41 (Brown), though the latter has both more phosphorus and more carbon, and should therefore be more brittle. No. 24 (C. G.) has about 4% more tensile strength but less than half of the elongation of No. 44 (Brown), though the latter has somewhat more phosphorus and much more carbon, and should therefore be

[a] Journ. Iron and St. Inst., 1874, I., p. 232.
[b] Raymond, Trans. Am. Inst. Mining Engineers, 1875, III., p. 182.
[c] Jour. Iron and St. Inst., Loc. Cit.
[d] Idem, 1871, I., p. 452.
[e] Idem, 1879, II., p. 355.

more brittle. No. 30 (C. G.) has the same elongation but decidedly less tensile strength than No. 41 (Brown), though the latter exceeds it somewhat in phosphorus and very much more carbon, and should therefore be decidedly more brittle. I frankly confess, however, that while I have no ground for doubting Brown's results beyond their inherent improbability, and while I find them harmonious and observe that they show the characteristics of phosphoric steel reported by others, I do not know how trustworthy they are.

There is, however, every reason to trust the Terre Noire results 3, 12 and 15. The only Clapp-Griffiths steel directly comparable with these without making any allowances whatsoever is No. 22, which has the same carbon and phosphorus as Terre Noire No. 12, yet is astonishingly brittle while the Terre Noire steel is admirably ductile: the former has 0·62% elongation and 0·00 contraction: the Terre Noire has 26% elongation with 46·7% contraction. But comparing the best Clapp-Griffiths steels with the Terre Noire and making any reasonable allowance for differences in composition, I can not find that the former are superior to the latter. Clapp-Griffiths 21 and 30 have less elongation and decidedly less contraction and tensile strength than Terre Noire 12, which with about 4-5ths as much phosphorus has 2·5 to 3 times as much carbon. Now I for one should expect this Terre Noire (12) steel to be more brittle than the Clapp-Griffiths (21 and 30), because with but little less phosphorus it has so very much more carbon, which so greatly exaggerates the effect of phosphorus. Or, to look at it a little differently, if 0·40% phosphorus in Terre Noire steel No. 12 has absolutely no effect on its ductility (its elongation is 13% above the usual upper limit for elongation for steels of this carbon: see Table 6 § 28), I am not surprised to learn that 0·50 and 0·55% phosphorus in Clapp-Griffiths steel 21 and 30 permits their elongation to remain within 20% of (but below) the usual upper limit for their carbon: nor do I see that it redounds to the credit of the Clapp-Griffiths converter that ·85% phosphorus in No. 24 Clapp-Griffiths steel drags the elongation down 64% below the usual upper limit and actually 48% below the usual lower limit for elongation for its carbon. (See Table 6, § 28.) Making similar allowances I find these best Clapp-Griffiths steels no better if as good as Terre Noire 2 and 3, which, be it remembered, are not picked, but represent the averages of hundreds of heats.

Again Clapp-Griffiths Nos. 21 and 30 have about the same elongation but much less contraction than the Russian rail No. 48, though they have at once decidedly less phosphorus and only half as much carbon as it: while No. 48 (Russian) with twice as much carbon and within 21% as much phosphorus has 2·5 times as great elongation and over 6 times as great contraction as the Clapp-Griffiths No. 24. I think these facts imply that phosphorus has affected the Clapp-Griffiths far more than the Russian steel. The Russian results are, however, so tainted with suspicion that I attach no weight to them.

The Trenton steels are not closely comparable with the Clapp-Griffiths steels, because their elongation and contraction are not given, and because their phosphorus is much below that of the three most surprising specimens of Clapp-Griffiths steel. But the fact that No. 51, Trenton, with ·21% of carbon and ·345% of phosphorus, was "remarkably tough" is liable to cool the ardor of the worshipers of Clapp-Griffiths.

In short, carefully comparing the Clapp-Griffiths steels with those of identical composition among the Terre Noire, Heaton, R. Brown and Russian phosphoric steels, and making liberal allowances when their compositions are not identical, I find in each of the last three classes instances as good, and among the R. Brown, Russian and Terre Noire steels instances decidedly better than the best Clapp-Griffiths cases as regards ductility: while the worst Clapp-Griffiths cases are much worse than the worst Terre Noire, and about the same as the worst Heaton. And I am profoundly convinced that no unbiased person, bearing in mind the capriciousness of the effects of phosphorus on ductility and its much greater effect on high than on low-carbon steel, can find any warrant in the data at hand for believing that phosphorus is one whit less injurious in Clapp-Griffiths than in other steel, or that its effects are neutralized by the Clapp-Griffiths converter to a higher degree or in any other way than that which is equally open to the ordinary Bessemer and open-hearth processes, nay has long been practiced in them, and which consists essentially in keeping the carbon and probably the other foreign elements low.

This error neither surprises us nor reflects on Captain R. W. Hunt if we remember that he was apparently in ignorance of many of the results previously obtained with phosphoric steel, and that such eminent observers as Fairbairn, Mallet, Miller and Tessié du Motay, dazzled by the false glitter of this tinsel, mistook it for gold much as he has. Nor does the adoption of the converter by several manufacturers vouch for its efficacy: the history of metallurgy, aye and of recent metallurgy, is simply strewn with the corpses of foredoomed processes which the "genuine practical" manufacturer has adopted to his sorrow: he is as fallible as others.

§ 129. Phosphorus and Forgeableness.—Iron in general cannot be forged at a temperature closely bordering on its melting point, and slow cooling without forging from this temperature to a lower but still exalted one induces coarse crystallization and a consequent lack of cohesion which renders iron extremely tender in forging. As phosphorus appears to lower the melting point of iron, and as it greatly exaggerates the tendency to coarse crystallization, it is not surprising that phosphoric iron and steel must be forged lightly when at very high temperatures, and are prone to crack and even fall to pieces.

It is the general belief that at lower temperatures, say from a yellow to a dull red heat, the influence of phosphorus on forgeableness is relatively very slight: there are those who even consider moderately phosphoric steels as unusually easy to forge. I shall shortly endeavor to show that it is uncertain whether the highest proportion of phosphorus ordinarily met with in commercial steel has any serious influence on its forgeableness under the usual conditions of manufacture. Such uncertainty could hardly exist were its influence serious and constant.

The following evidence shows that while in many cases it has been possible to forge highly phosphoric steel with care, in others in which the high percentage of phosphorus appears to be the sole abnormal condition, forging has been impossible. The evidence is discordant, steel with ·88% of phosphorus rolling well, while that with ·24, ·38 and ·52% rolls badly. This harmonizes with the capricious effects of this element on ductility, and calls to mind the marked differences observed in its chemical behavior during solution by acids. (See §§ 101, 123.)

(1). 1·10% PHOSPHORUS. R. W. Hunt[a] found that Bessemer (Clapp-Griffiths) steel with 1·10% of phosphorus, ·004 of silicon, ·5 of manganese, and ·05 of sulphur rolled in a "practical manner." He seems to regard this as due to some influence of the Clapp-Griffiths converter, but as steel with 0·4, 0·88 and 0·98% phosphorus had previously been successfully rolled, as I know of no evidence that steel of this composition produced in non-Clapp-Griffiths converters will not roll in a "practical manner," and as I know that much Clapp-Griffiths steel with moderate amounts of phosphorus has cracked badly in rolling, I find little ground for his belief.

(2). ·98% PHOSPHORUS. M. White has shown me a small bar, about ½" × ¾", which he assures me contains 0·98% phosphorus and was rolled from a 2" × 2" ingot. It evidently had cracked a great deal in rolling, yet it had rolled and held together.

(3). 88% PHOSPHORUS. Z. S. Durfee states that steel with ·88% of phosphorus hammered and worked "beautifully" when above a low red heat.[b]

(4). ·40% PHOSPHORUS. E. Williams in 1856 or 1857 found Bessemer steel with ·40 phosphorus non-hotshort, or at least rolled it into perfectly sound rails.[c]

(5). ·35% PHOSPHORUS. It is stated that steel with this percentage of phosphorus was rolled into rails for the South Austrian Railway with perfect ease.[d]

(6). ·35% PHOSPHORUS. Slade informs me that the Trenton phosphoric steel (see § 128, D.) with phosphorus from ·11 to ·35% (in one case phosphorus ·27 with only ·07 manganese ·12 carbon ·02 silicon) rolled *perfectly*, with the reductions employed for other steel, at any heat not above an orange color; "It would not fly even when heated to a true white heat, but after having been brought to this heat it was redshort when the temperature fell to an orange color, but all right again when down to a blood red."[e] I have observed this in non-phosphoric low-carbon steel as well: I should attribute it to the extraordinary lack of manganese rather than to the presence of phosphorus.

(7). ·524% PHOSPHORUS. Wendel found that Bessemer steel with ·498 to ·524% of phosphorus but otherwise of normal composition fell to pieces in rolling, whether a high or low temperature were employed. As he subsequently found the same behavior in steel with but ·20% phosphorus, some may doubt that the phosphorus was the cause, or at least that it was the sole cause of the hotshortness.[f]

(8). ·38% PHOSPHORUS. The Sherman phosphoric steel rolled at Boston in 1877, containing ·24 to ·38 of phosphorus, rolled badly: after diligent inquiry I fail to learn whether it was unforgeable at all temperatures or only at high ones.

(9). The Terre Noire phosphoric steel is rumored to have cracked very badly when rolled into rails.

So much for excessive proportions of phosphorus: how is it with the comparatively small proportion actually employed commercially, say from 0 to 0·17%? Percy considers that phosphorus does not interfere with hot malleableness: Ledebur that it does not except at very high temperatures.[g] It is a general belief or perhaps superstition among American Bessemer men that phosphorus makes steel hotshort, an increase of 0·01% phosphorus being considered by some sufficient to produce this effect: yet I learn from a most competent authority at an Illinois works, which has probably turned out as much phosphoric steel (say phosphorus 0·10 to 0·17) as any in the country, that the most careful observation does not show that an increase of phosphorus from 0·10 to 0·14 has ever affected the hot-malleableness of their steel. And from the chemist of another Illinois works famed for its phosphoric steel and for the cracked flanges of its rails, I learn that prolonged investigations designed to discover the relations between composition and the rolling properties of their steel, not only established no relation between phosphorus and hotshortness, but did not even make him believe that phosphorus ever caused bad rolling.

Others may have convincing evidence: I for one consider it improbable that the proportion of phosphorus which, in view of its causing brittleness, is permissible in commercial steel, has an important effect on forging power.

WELDING is thought to be favored by the presence of phosphorus: the United States test board[h] found that, arranging the welded wrought-iron chains in order of merit, their phosphorus was as follows: Best, 0·23%: ·18: ·07: ·20: ·18: ·19: ·17: ·19: ·17: ·25: ·15%, worst welding.

THE MODULUS OF ELASTICITY of six phosphoric Heaton steels tested by Fairbairn (Nos. 13 to 18, Table 28) was normal, maximum 30,000,000; minimum 26,580,000; average 28,603,000. Phosphorus is currently reported to diminish the modulus; but, finding no evidence to support this view I regard it as a popular superstition. If it were true, then phosphoric steels with their high elastic limit should be very springy.

§ 130. PERCENTAGE OF PHOSPHORUS PERMISSIBLE FOR VARIOUS USES.—As the effects of phosphorus are intensified by the presence of carbon, and probably also by undisturbed slow cooling, so the proportion of this element which can be tolerated in steel for a given purpose must vary greatly; it is hard to give rules of wide applicability.

A. WELD VS. INGOT METAL.—The effects of phosphorus are considered much more severe in ingot than in weld metal, partly because the sum of the other foreign elements (carbon, silicon, manganese) is usually very much greater in the former, and possibly partly because the slag intercalated in weld metal mechanically lessens brittleness by creating a condition slightly approaching that of a wire rope, *i. e.*, by giving pliancy and interrupting the growth of incipient cracks. But I attach little weight to this hypothesis, for had the slag this effect to a notable degree, then the modulus of elasticity of weld metal should be much lower than that of ingot metal, *i. e.*, it should be less stiff. Actually their moduli are practically identical. Finally, as phosphorus appears to make steel brittle by inducing coarse crystallization, the intercalated slag may partially counteract it by directly obstructing the growth

[a] Trans. Am. Inst. Min. Engrs., XIV., pp. 140-1, 1886.
[b] Eng. and Mining Jl., 1874, I., p. 358.
[c] Journ. Iron and St. Inst., 1880, II., p. 574.
[d] Idem, 1875, I., p. 347.
[e] Private Communication, Jan. 12th, 1887.
[f] Trans. Am. Inst. Min. Eng., IV., p. 300, 1876.
[g] Handbuch der Eisenhüttenkunde, p. 247.
[h] Trans. Am. Inst. Mining Engrs., 1878, VI., p. 116.

of large crystalline faces, and by offering so many points from which crystallization simultaneously commences that the crystalline faces interrupt each other before attaining injurious size.

The comparatively mild effect of phosphorus on weld metal is sometimes explained by supposing that much of it here exists as phosphate in the slag: this may explain it in part, but probably in small part. We find ductile weld irons containing 0·24% of phosphorus and but 0·5% of slag: if this is of the composition of common tap cinder it is not likely to hold more than 10% of phosphoric acid, which would account for but 0·025 of phosphorus per 100 of metal. Indeed, the slag produced in puddling such iron may hold as little as 1·7% of phosphoric acid, which would account for but 0·004% of phosphorus. Few published analyses of tap cinder show over 8% of phosphoric acid; but one out of 42 analyses of wrought-iron given by Holley shows more than 1·7% of slag, which, if holding 8% of phosphoric acid, would account for but 0·07% of phosphorus.

KARSTEN thought that 0·3 phosphorus in weld metal did not cause coldshortness: that with 0·5 phosphorus iron might yet be worked, and that even with 0·6 it might be bent to a right angle, but that with 0·8 phosphorus it was decidedly coldshort. Yet Eggertz found 1″ sq. bars of weld iron with 0·25 to 0·3 phosphorus very coldshort, which again illustrates the capriciousness of phosphorus, if indeed both these observers are right.

RAILS.—Weld iron rails often have 0·45 phosphorus, and 0·4% is not thought to be injurious. Bell gives one with 0·67%. American steel rails, which ordinarily contain 0·3 to 0·5 carbon, rarely have more than 0·16 phosphorus. The unsurpassed Bethlehem rails have but ·07 phosphorus, and those of other Eastern mills rarely contain more than ·09 or 0·095%. The highest proportion which I have met in a steel rail with over 0·3 carbon is 0·24%, together with carbon ·38: silicon ·03 sulphur ·07 and manganese ·87. This I believe was a European rail. Rails 2 and 2a in Table 30, the former a bad the latter an excellent rail, both have 0·24 phosphorus. I know of American steel rails with 0·14 phosphorus and say ·35 carbon which were pronounced "excellent" by their purchasers.

For 851 cases of steel rails examined by Sandberg the normal limits for phosphorus appeared to be ·05 and ·10%. No less than 29% of them, however, had more than ·10% of phosphorus, and 11% of them less than ·05% of this metalloid.[a]

If we can believe Beck-Guerhard (I cannot) Russian rails have as much as 0·67 phosphorus. Table 28 gives six phosphoric rails reported by him, of which the most remarkable have ·28 carbon with ·33 phosphorus (No. 46), and ·23 carbon with ·67 phosphorus (No. 48). Though behaving well under static stress, their track record is surprising. No. 48 was greatly damaged after 41 months' service, during which 12 tons (737 poods) had passed over it. Another, No. 47, broke after 2 months' service, during which a total weight of 900 lbs. (25 poods) had passed over it, presumably a hand car.[b] Unless the pood has some other meaning than that assigned it by the text and the encyclopædias (about ·017 ton), Russian train-dispatchers are to be envied. *Dudley* would limit the phosphorus in rails to 0·10%.[c] *Boiler plate* steel has ordinarily not above ·04 to ·05 phosphorus: yet I know one instance of boiler plate made at an American works whose reputation for this product is probably unequaled, which contained ·07 phosphorus, and many other cases of admirable boiler plate with this amount.

Steel boiler plates of this composition are in very extensive use, and are mercilessly punched and flanged cold without subsequent annealing or reaming, and it is next to certain that they actually behave admirably in service, for otherwise more frequent failures of steel boilers in manufacture or use would have occurred. Boiler plate with 0·31% phosphorus and 0·12 carbon has moreover been pronounced "remarkably tough" by so conscientious an engineer as F. J. Slade, (see § 128 D.); but this was manufactured in such small quantity that we can draw little inference as to its trustworthiness under the trying condition of actual service. The effects of phosphorus are so capricious that we cannot infer complete trustworthiness from a few instances of good behavior.

CUTTING TOOLS should apparently be very free from phosphorus (say with not over ·03%). Indeed the reputed superiority of tool steel made from Dannemora ore is by many attributed to its freedom from phosphorus. Of 18 tool steels tested by Smith, the only three with over ·03 phosphorus were among the worst, their value being from 40 to 60% of the maximum: yet one steel with ·024 phosphorus had the best record in slotting; and its average for all cutting purposes was 81% of the maximum. The value was measured by the weight of the shavings which a tool would turn, plane, etc., without dressing.[d]

I am informed that the saws of one of the most celebrated American makers formerly contained as much as 0·09% of phosphorus, but that their quality has been materially improved by limiting the phosphorus to ·027, and raising the carbon from ·90 to 1·10%.

TABLE 30.—PHOSPHORUS IN VARIOUS IRONS AND STEELS. (SEE TABLES 28 AND 29.)

	Carbon.	Silicon.	Manganese.	Phosphorus.	Sulphur.		Purpose, etc.
1.	.....	.....	.....	·16	....	Ingot metal.	Rails, usual upper limit for phosphorus.
2.	·25	·05	·24	·24	·04		Bad German rail. Pourcel, Trans. Am. Inst. Mining Engrs., XI., p. 201
2a	·21	·65	·33	·24	·08		Rail removed after 12 years wear on an American railway. R. W. Lodge, private communication.
3.	·16	·04	·60	·07	·06		Boiler plate, usual upper limit for phosphorus.
4.	·15	...	·67	·10	..		Wire rods, common.
5.	·12	..	·67	·10	..		Structural steel, common.
6.	·10	·01	·37	·10@·12	·05		Nail plate, common.
7.	0·90	·80	·35	·09	....		Saws, formerly made by a celebrated maker.
8.	1·10	·30	·35	·027	..		" now " " the same "
9.	·16	·18	·07	·67	·07	Weld iron.	Iron rails, unusually phosphoric, p. 428 — Bell, Manuf. Iron and Steel.
10.	·04	·12	...	·195	·01		Best Yorkshire boiler plate. p. 434 — Bell, Manuf. Iron and Steel.
11.	·13	·14	0	·16	0		" " railroad axles. p. 434 — Bell, Manuf. Iron and Steel.

§ 131. PHOSPHORUS UNITS.—For conciseness Dudley would measure the brittleness due to a given percentage of carbon, silicon or manganese in terms of that caused by ·01% phosphorus: he suggests provisionally assigning to ·02% silicon, ·03% carbon and ·05% of manganese respectively an effect equivalent to that of 0·01 phosphorus, and conveniently designates each of these quantities as a phosphorus unit.[e] When we discover what quantity of each

[a] Trans. Am. Inst. Min. Eng., X., 1882, p. 410.

[b] The Secretary of the Iron and Steel Institute assures me that the incomprehensible numbers which I have quoted are those given by the Russian Commission, and not misprints. (Private communication.)

[c] Trans. Am. Inst. Mining Engrs., IX., p. 356.

[d] Report U. S. Board on Testing Iron, etc., 1881, II., p. 593; Thurston, Matls. of Engineering, II., p. 434.

[e] Trans. Am. Inst. Min. Engrs., VII., p. 197, 1879.

of these elements is equivalent to ·01% of phosphorus, this clever conception will be of great value, and it may be very useful to-day if cautiously employed. But, as the values assigned to the phosphorus unit are purely conjectural, it is liable to be wildly misleading if used beyond the narrow limits for which its talented author designed it.

Thus, while four irons with 0·60% carbon, ·40 silicon, 1% manganese and ·20% phosphorus respectively and containing nothing beyond iron and one impurity, might possibly be equally brittle, it is extremely improbable that, if an iron initially contained 0·50% carbon and nothing else it would be rendered as brittle by an addition of 1% manganese or of ·5% manganese + ·20 silicon, or of ·40 manganese + ·16 silicon + ·12% carbon as by an addition of ·20% phosphorus.

CHAPTER VII.

Chromium, Tungsten, Copper.

[*For later information see Appendix I.*]

§ 136. Iron and Chromium.

Summary.—In 1820 Berthier[a] publicly described chrome steel, whose value he recognized, and his method of preparing it, substantially that employed to-day. Chromium appears to combine with iron in all proportions, probably often tending to form heterogeneous compounds: to be readily oxidized when thus alloyed: to raise the saturation point for carbon: to increase the hardness, especially that of the hardened steel, and perhaps also the tensile strength and elastic limit: and to lessen the welding power. It does not confer on carbonless iron the power of being hardened by sudden cooling: it does not diminish but perhaps increases this power conferred by carbon simultaneously present: it does not very seriously diminish hot malleableness or ductility under impact or under quiescent load. Chromic oxide is liable to cause flaws in chrome steel, which is more easily burnt than chromeless steel.

Chrome steel is rather hard when annealed and intensely so when quenched: is readily forged: is not peculiarly brittle: will not truly weld, but can be made to cohere (even to wrought-iron it is said) with a tenacity valuable for many purposes. Its manufacture is a promising field, but only for those competent to control it scientifically.

§ 137. Their Metallurgical Chemistry.

A. Ferro-Chrome.—Chromium appears to combine with iron readily and in all proportions, at least up to 80%. Ferro-chrome, *i. e.* highly chromiferous iron, may be readily prepared as stated by Berthier,[b] by very strongly heating the mixed oxides of iron and chromium in brasqued crucibles, adding charcoal powder if oxide of chromium predominates, and fluxes (*e. g.* borax and glass) to scorify earthy matter and to prevent oxidation: the presence of iron or of its oxides facilitates the reduction of the chromium, which demands a higher temperature than that of iron. This is said to be substantially the method employed at Brooklyn[c] and at Unieux (France), where chrome steel has been for years produced on a large scale. It has also been made at Sheffield. Of late 12% ferro-chrome produced in the Cowles electric furnace has been offered for sale. Ferro-chrome has also been made in the blast-furnace at Terre-Noire, but it is stated with not over 40% chromium.

B. Chrome Steel also is made to-day substantially by Berthier's process, by simply melting ferro-chrome with wrought-iron or steel in plumbago crucibles.[c]

C. Oxidation.—Chromium, even when alloyed with iron, is very readily oxidized. In puddling chromiferous cast-iron its chromium is largely scorified, and, by forming a thick slag, prevents the puddled ball from welding (this appears distinctly due to the oxide of chromium in the slag and not to the metallic chromium in the metal). Thus Riley found that adding 11% of cast-iron which contained about 7% of chromium greatly delayed the puddling of good gray forge iron: the chromium was found in the slag soon after fusion. Equal parts of this chromiferous cast-iron and of hematite pig puddled with difficulty, and the slag was so viscid that the puddled balls could not be formed into blooms.[d]

The Bessemer process, possibly because its slags are acid, seems less prone to remove chromium than puddling. At one time the acid-Bessemer steel of Harrisburg had occasionally as much as 0·59% of chromium.[e]

The readiness with which chromium oxidizes has suggested the use of ferro-chrome instead of spiegeleisen as a recarburizer for the Bessemer process. But its efficacy is very doubtful. The oxides of manganese arising from the reaction between the oxygen of the blown steel and the manganese of the spiegeleisen are fusible and scorifiable: they coalesce and rise to the surface of the molten metal. Chromic oxide, infusible and well-nigh unscorifiable, would probably remain mixed with the steel, break up its continuity and impair its forgeableness. Indeed, even in the crucible process, in which chromium has comparatively little chance to oxidize, chromic oxide, formed while the steel is molten, is liable to cause deep ineradicable veins in chrome steel, especially if its carbon be low or its chromium high.[f] Even in heating chrome steel a very strong and adherent scale forms which renders welding next to impossible.

Chromium is said to hasten the rusting of iron.

D. Carbon, Silicon, Sulphur.—Chromium raises the saturation point for carbon, probably even more powerfully than manganese does: ferro-chromes Nos. 1 and 11 in Table 31 have 11 and 6·2% carbon with 80 and 18% chromium respectively. Like manganese it prevents the separation of graphite.

Ferro-chrome often contains over 2% of silicon. Chromium does not necessarily exclude sulphur from iron, for ferro-chrome 3, Table 31, with 67·15% chromium has 0·3% sulphur.

E. Kern.—I find neither result nor promise in his proposal to substitute chrome iron ore and calcined limestone for ferro-manganese in the crucible process.[g]

[a] Annales des Mines, 1st series, VI., p. 573; Ann. Chim. Phys., 2d series, XVII., p. 55.

[b] Percy, Iron and Steel, p. 185.

[c] Ferro-chrome is said to be made at Brooklyn by melting finely pulverized chrome ore with charcoal in common graphite crucibles, about 45% of ferro-chrome resulting, which holds 80% of chromium and 3% of carbon. From 0·25 to 2% of this product is melted with Swedish or bloomary wrought-iron in 70 lb. charges in crucibles in common crucible furnaces, which melt 6 rounds per 24 hours with a consumption of 2 lbs. of anthracite to 1 of steel: (Stahl und Eisen, II., p. 165, 1882).

[d] E. Riley, Journal of the Iron and Steel Institute, 1877. I., p. 104.

[e] A. S. McCreath, private communication, March 19, 1887.

[f] Brustlein, Journal of the Iron and Steel Inst., 1886. II., p. 770. After prolonged study I cannot quite assure myself that I understand the passage on which this statement is based.

[g] Metallurgical Review, I., p. 489.

TABLE 31.—COMPOSITION OF FERRO-CHROME.

No.	1.	2.	3.	4.	5.	6.	7.	8.	9	10.	11.	12.
Chromium %	60	75±	67·	60	54±	48@52	42 ±	30 ±	27±	25	18 ±	16 ±
Carbon %	11	....	5·4	....	....	7@8	7·8±	4·7±	....	3·8	6·2±	2·1±
Silicon %	....	....	8·30	....	....	often > 2	2·1±	....	....	0·4	0·5	0·4
Scratches glass	....	yes	....	yes	yes	....	....	....	yes	....	....	....
Pulverizable	....	yes	....	yes	yes	....	....	....	yes	....	....	....
Magnet attracts	no	no	....	....	no	....	....	....	yes	....	....	....

1. Unieux. **2.** Percy, Iron and Steel, p. 186: imperfectly fused: yellowish gray white: center filled with minute acicular crystals. Attacked with difficulty by acids. **3.** Boussingault. Journ. Iron and St. Inst., 1886, II., p. 818. **4.** Berthier, Percy, loc. cit.: well rounded button: full of large bubbles lined with prismatic crystals: whiter than platinum: attacked with great difficulty even by nitro-hydrochloric acid. **5.** Percy, loc. cit. **6.** Usual composition of Unieux ferro-chrome. **7.** Unieux, silky when chilled. **8.** Unieux: when slowly cooled a mass of needles. **9.** Percy, loc. cit., well-fused: tin-white, finely granular, attacked with difficulty by acids. **10.** Unieux: fracture white, acicular. **11.** Unieux: fracture brilliant acicular when slowly cooled, silky when chilled. **12.** Unieux: fracture when slowly cooled gray, small square facets: silky when chilled. Unieux specimens from Brustlein, Journ. Iron and St. Inst., 1886, II., p. 770.

§ 138. INFLUENCE OF CHROMIUM ON THE PHYSICAL PROPERTIES OF IRON.

A. TENSILE STRENGTH.—It is usually stated that chromium raises the tensile strength. What evidence I have collected while it does not disprove certainly does not warrant this statement. Plotting in Figure 3, § 27, those steels of Table 32 whose composition and tensile strength are given, with tensile strength as ordinate, carbon as abscissa, I find that in six cases the tensile strength about equals the normal strength of chrome-less steels of like percentage of carbon, in three cases it is slightly higher and in three slightly lower. Of the three with unusually high tensile strength, one (No. 1) has 4% of chromium: a calculation based on this instance alone gives chromium but slight influence, about 400 pounds increase of tensile strength per 0·1% of chromium per square inch. The second (No. 7 unhardened) is rather stronger than the average of chromeless steel of like carbon content, but the difference is too slight to build on, especially as a hardened piece from the same bar was decidedly weak. The percentage of chromium of the third (No. 13, with ·25% of chromium) is so low that we hesitate to ascribe to it the high tensile strength of the steel. These cases are here summarized.[a]

Tensile strength compared with other steels of like carbon content.

	High.			Normal.						Low.		
Number in Table 32	1	7 unhardened.	13	2	4	6	9	12	29	7 hardened.	8	9·5
Chromium	4·00	0·53	0·25	2·2	1·2	·22@·64	·38	·29	?	·53	·50	·38
Carbon	1·10	1·03	0·70	0·6	0·84	·81@·99	·90	1·32	·7±	1·03	·91	·84

From the other instances, Nos. 16 to 28, no safe inferences can be drawn: so much "chrome steel" contains little or no chromium that we cannot safely assume its presence where it is not explicitly given. Excepting tungsten steel No. 10, Table 34, § 141, I know of none whose tensile strength, when not raised by hardening or cold-forging, equals that of chrome steel No. 21 (187,915 pounds per square inch). It is not explicitly stated that this had not been hardened, but this is to be inferred from the context. The strength of the hardened bars Nos. 3 (199,000 pounds), 18 (202,900 pounds) and 30 (213,842 pounds) is decidedly

[a] I here leave No. 5 out of consideration, not knowing which of the compositions given corresponds to the tensile strength. For none of them would the tensile strength be high.

TABLE 32.—CHROME STEEL.

Number.	Observer, source, etc.	Composition. Chromium.	Combined carbon.	Graphite.	Manganese.	Silicon.	Tungsten.	Physical properties. Tensile strength. Lbs. per sq. in.	Elastic limit. Lbs. per sq. in.	Elongation %	Elongation In.	Reduction of area %	Bent before breaking. Degrees.	Diameter of piece. Inches.
1	Unieux, unhardened, Brustlein	4·	1·10					177,800	177,000±	7·5				
1·5	Faraday and Stodart; very hard, extremely malleable	2·0±	1·[illegible]											
2	Unieux, unhardened (same steel, Brustlein)	2·2	0·6					103,000	67,500	19·		67+		
3	" annealed after oil hardening (same steel, Brustlein)	2·2	0·6					199,000	199,000	8·				
4	" Brustlein	1·2	·84					88,180	55,900	7·				
4·5	Faraday and Stodart; hard, forged well	·99±	1·[illegible]											
5	A. A. Blair and D. Smith, P	·45@·92	·84@1·10	·01@·03	·06	1·28		115,922						
6	" " F	·22@·64	·81@·99	·01@·02				104,756						
7	Brooklyn Adamantine, Hunt and Clapp and the author	·53	1·03		·17	·05		157,000 a 116,000 b		0·6 0·6	4″ 4″	0 0	2·5 15·5	·58 octagon. ·58 "
8	Döhlen, Ledebur	·50	·91					122,300		15·7				
9	Brooklyn, very hard, Hunt and Clapp and the author	·38	·90		1·39	·03	·98	134,000		2·	4″	0	40°	·48 square.
9·5	A. A. Blair and D. Smith, G	·38	·84	·01	·29	·09		110,572						
10	Brooklyn, St. Louis Bridge (?) Blair	·38	·94											
11	" " " (?) "	·38	·98											
12	" Hunt and Clapp and the author	·29	1·32		·15	·15	·73	124,000 a 127,000 b		6· 9·	3·5″ 3·5″	4 2	1·5 5·5	·63 round. ·63 "
13	" 1A, " " " "	·25	·70					145,400		5·5		19	25 a 30 c	
14	Brooklyn, St. Louis Bridge (?), Blair	0	·60											
15	" " " "	0	·31											
16	Unieux, unhardened (same bar, Barbier, Boussingault)							108,700	95,446	15·		50	60	·86 octagon.
17	" quenched from yellow							191,000		1·2		2		
18	" " " bright cherry							202,900		2·		6		
19	" " " cherry							104,260	62,306	14·		63		
20	" " " dark red							100,000	55,000	17·		63		
21	Brooklyn, West Point test, strongest bar							187,915						
22	" " weakest "							168,765						
23	" Kirkaldy's test							166,800	97,000	7·6		39·		
24	" "							129,630	71,000	5·2		50·		
25	" "							126,970	63,000	7·2		59·		
26	" "							194,390	54,000	11		47·		
27	Unieux, private communication							157,090				57·		
28	" " "							152,200				57·		
29	" annealed (same bar, Brustlein)		·7±					102,200	59,300	19·5	8″	68·		
30	" oil hardened and annealed (same bar, Brustlein)		·7±					213,300	189,000	6·2	3″	29·2		
31	Brooklyn, Thurston	1·04	·63	·01	·05	·15								
32	" "	·92	·44	·01	·02	·11								
33	" "	·61	·46	0	·08	·13								

1. Unhardened, Unieux. **1·5.** Faraday and Stodart. Forged well, with no disposition to crack: hard, as malleable as pure iron, gave a very fine damask. The composition here given is inferred from their statements that they melted together 1600 grs. of steel, whose carbon is roughly assumed at 1%, and 48 grs. of pure chromium; and further that "in all the experiments made in the laboratory the button produced was weighed, and if it fell short of the weight of both metals put into the crucible it was rejected as imperfect." Phil. Trans. Royal Soc., 1822, pp. 267, 258. **2** and **3.** Unieux, 2 unhardened, 3 the same steel annealed from bright redness after oil hardening. **4.** Unieux. **4·5.** Faraday and Stodart, loc. cit., good, forged well, with no disposition to crack; hard, but not so hard as No. 1·5. The remarks concerning No. 1·5 apply to No. 4·5, mutatis mutandis. **5** and **6.** Rept. of U. S. Bd. to Test Iron, etc., II., p. 590. Thurston, Mat'ls of Engineering, II., p. 484. **7.** Brooklyn "Adamantine" chrome steel, a, unhardened, b, quenched in oil from dull redness. Hunt and Clapp and the author. **8.** Döhlen, Ledebur, Handbuch, p. 261. **9.** One of the hardest brands of Brooklyn chrome steel, Hunt and Clapp and the author. **9·5.** Rept. U. S. Bd. to Test Iron, II., p. 590. **10** and **11.** A. A. Blair. Said to be from staves of St. Louis Bridge: private communication, May 30, 1887. **12** and **13.** Brooklyn chrome steel. Hunt and Clapp and the author. 13 is styled "No. 1A." a, Unhardened; b, hardened in oil from dull redness. **14** and **15.** Brooklyn (?) chrome steel, said to be from staves of St. Louis Bridge. A. A. Blair, private communication, May 30, 1887. **16** to **20.** Unieux. 16, hardened; 17, quenched from yellow; 18, from bright cherry; 19, from cherry; 20, from dark red (sombre). **21** strongest, and **22** weakest of three bars of Brooklyn chrome steel tested at West Point foundry. No. 21, in two trials, gave 176,020 and 198,910 pounds, and after being heated, 168,530 and 193,210 pounds tensile strength; No. 22, in the same way, gave before heating 173,720 and 163,790 pounds, and after heating 174,540 and 190,910 pounds, tensile strength per square inch. **24** to **26.** Kirkaldy, circular of Brooklyn Chrome Steel Co. **27, 28.** Unieux. Private communication from J. Holtzer et Cie. **29, 30.** Unieux: 29, annealed; 30, oil-quenched, and annealed from dark redness. **31** to **33.** Brooklyn, Thurston, Mat'ls of Engineering, II., p. 907.

UNIEUX STEELS.—Excepting Nos. 27, 28, and 31 to 33, described by Brustlein and Boussingault, Ann. de Chim. et Phys., 5th Ser., XV., and Jour. Iron and St. Inst., 1886, II., p. 807.

BROOKLYN CHROME STEELS.—Nos. 7, 9, 12, and 13, obtained by the author from the makers or their Boston agents, and tested by him: Messrs. Hunt and Clapp, of Pittsburgh, Pa., have been so kind as to analyze these at [illegible] for this work. In the bending test, these steels were held firmly in a vise and struck with moderate force with a sledge till they broke. The bending was measured after fracture.

a. As received from the makers. b. After quenching in oil from dull redness. c. After annealing from cherry redness. Several chromiferous phosphoric steels are described in Table 28.

high: but we have too few recorded cases of the tensile strength of hardened high-carbon steel to justify our terming it extraordinary, or the inference that it has been raised by chromium. § 54, I, gives cases in which the tensile strength of hardened steel rises to 248,000 and 314,800 pounds, and that of wire to 432,000 pounds: hardened steel No. 20, Table 6, has 211,072 pounds tensile strength, and hardened steel of Park Bro. & Co. is reported with 227,500[a] pounds tensile strength. These four are apparently chromeless.

B. The elastic limit, it is stated, is raised by chromium even more than the tensile strength: this however is only true of one of the cases which I have met, No. 1, Table 33, with 4% chromium, whose elastic limit is nearly identical with its tensile strength, 177,000 pounds per square inch. The elastic ratio of the others is either normal or (as in Nos. 18 and 19) unusually low.

C. Ductility.—If we compare the steels in Table 32 with the numbers given in Table 6A, § 28A, we find that, considering their tensile strength, the elongation of three of them, Nos. 4, 7 and 9, is decidedly low, that of eleven of them is about normal, and that of four of them, Nos. 1, 2, 8 and 23, is decidedly high. In a later chapter combinations of tensile strength with elongation which equal if they do not greatly excel these will be given. Comparing them with Table 6 and Figure 5, § 23, we note that, considering their carbon content, the elongation of three, Nos. 2, 8 and 12, is high, that of two, 4 and 7, is low, while that of the remaining ones whose composition is given is about normal. There is little in these numbers to suggest that chromium either favors or precludes an unusually high combination of strength and toughness.

As regards ductility under shock our data are equally contradictory. Boussingault, who investigated chrome steel perhaps more thoroughly than any other pecuniarily disinterested person, considered that its resistance to impact was far greater than that of other steels.[b] He cites an octagonal bar (No. 23, Table 32), whose inscribed diameter was 0·87 inch: when notched 0·08 inch deep and grasped in a vise with this notch ·08 inch above its jaws, it bent 60° under 20 blows of an eleven-pound sledge before breaking. This is certainly good resistance: unfortunately it is not stated that it was positively known to contain chromium. Holtzer's twelve-inch chrome steel projectiles shattered a hard sixteen-inch Brown compound steel armor plate, and were found entire at the back.[c] Here too we are not positively informed that they contained an important quantity of chromium. Unfortunately in other cases chrome steel has shown poor resistance to impact. I found that four Brooklyn chrome steels, 7, 9, 12 and 13, Table 32, bent from 1·5° to 40° under the blows of a sledge before breaking: none behaved well, two behaved wretchedly. A bar of chromeless Pittsburgh crucible cutlery steel of about 1% carbon, 0·4 inches square, bent 93·5° under like conditions before breaking.

McCreath informs me (partly from memory) that, at the Pennsylvania Steel Works, Bessemer rails with from ·12 to ·54% chromium passed the drop test when their carbon was from ·25 to ·30%, but often broke under it when their carbon was from ·40 to ·50%: *e. g.*, one with ·41 chromium and ·28 carbon passed: two with ·59 and ·41 chromium and ·50 + and 28 + carbon respectively broke.[d] Here too chromium appears to have injured the shock-resisting power.

D. Hardness, Hardening and Annealing.—Chromium is said to increase the hardness of iron both in the ordinary condition and when hardened. Unhardened chrome steels are slightly harder and more difficult to cut than chromeless steels of like carbon content, and their hardness increases with the percentage of chromium. Steel with 4·24%[e] chromium scratched glass (presumably when unhardened). Ferro-chromes 2, 4 and 5, Table 33, with 54 to 76% chromium scratched glass.

Chromium does not appear to give iron the power of becoming harder when suddenly cooled. At Unieux ingot iron with 1% chromium could still be easily filed after quenching from cherry-redness.[e] Wire with 1·24% chromium and 0·31% carbon acquired no more elasticity on oil-quenching than similar metal without chromium.[f] But chromium does not prevent metal which also contains carbon from hardening. Steel 13, Table 32, when unhardened was slightly harder than ordinary unhardened tool steel. Quenched in running cold water from blood-redness it was much softer than Mushet's tungsten steel, and could be filed, though with difficulty. Quenched from an orange heat it had a porcelanic fracture, scratched glass, was very slightly indented by Mushet's tungsten steel, but slightly indented imperial (Tungsten) steel, Hadfield's manganese steel and glass-hard cutlery carbon steel. It could be filed, but with great difficulty: even Mushet's steel is slightly attacked by the file.[g]

Steels 5, 6 and 9·5, Table 32, tested in competition with fourteen lots of the best American and British steels, though not notably harder than their competitors judging from the pressure required to produce the first perceptible compression, on the whole excelled them in efficiency as cutting tools, as gauged by the weight of standard iron cut by each under fixed conditions without re-sharpening. The greatest weight cut by the best chromeless steel was but 80·99% of that cut by the best chrome steel, No. 5: while No. 6 also slightly excelled the best carbon steels. The chrome steel No. 9·5 was excelled by five of the chromeless steels, the best of which excelled it by 22%.[h] Unfortunately they were not compared with tungsten steels which probably excel them.

Eight specimens of chrome steel (which include Nos. 23 to 26, Table 33) gave Kirkaldy the following results:[i]

Crushing strength	Elastic.		Ultimate.	
Length	8 diams.	12 diams.	8 diams.	12 diams.
Lbs. per sq. in.	73,000@196,000	60,900@97,900	90,411@184,144	77,041@103,890

This combination of tensile and compressive strength with static ductility is certainly extremely good, but not enough examples are at hand to justify our pronouncing it extraordinary: 63,000 and 112,320 lbs. per square inch (8 diameters) were the highest elastic and ultimate com-

[a] W. S. Shock, quoted in Trautwine's Civil Engineer's Pocket Book, p. 179, 1872.

[b] Ann. Chim. et Phys., 5th ser., XV.

[c] Engineering, April 1st, 1887, p. 306.

[d] Private communication, March 19th, 1887.

[e] Percy, Iron and Steel, p. 187.

[f] Boussingault, Journal of the Iron and Steel Inst., 1886, II., p. 811.

[g] J. H. H. Corbin (Silliman's Jl., 1869, 2d. Ser., XLVIII., p. 348) reports that Brooklyn chrome steel with 1·66% chromium and ·98% carbon was as hard as quartz when hardened and as felspar when unhardened; I have never met steel which would scratch quartz.

[h] Rep. U. S. Board on Testing Iron, etc., II., p. 592: Thurston, Matls. of Engineering, II., p. 434.

[i] Circular of Chrome Steel Co., 1874.

pressive strength which Kirkaldy found in Fagersta Bessemer steel of 1·2% of carbon.[a]

FOR HARDENING, the lowest quenching temperature which will give sufficient hardness should be employed, which appears to be the highest compatible with preserving a fine fibrous fracture. It may be accurately ascertained by heating a bar differentially by conduction from one end, quenching, and examining the fracture at different points. The point where a fine fiber replaces a coarse granular one, an index of too high temperature, was at the proper temperature when quenched. This temperature is near dull redness. If chrome steel which is to be hardened has for forging been heated beyond its proper quenching temperature, it should cool in air below that point and be again heated to it, lest the interior be too hot at the instant of quenching: the Chrome Steel Company states that thus alone can chrome steel be injured. For annealing it should be heated to barely visible redness (a higher temperature might lead to detrimental coarse crystallization), and if practicable it should cool extremely slowly.

The foregoing are the instructions of the Brooklyn Chrome Steel Company.

E. FORGING.—From what information I can obtain and from the results of my own incomplete trials I judge that chrome steels forge more readily than tungsten steels, and, when they do not contain more than about ·50% of chromium, nearly as well as ordinary carbon steels of like percentage of carbon.

Faraday and Stodart found that chrome steel with 1±% chromium (and presumably about 1% carbon) forged well, and one with 3±% chromium (and presumably 1±% carbon) "was as malleable as pure iron."[b] Brustlein states that chrome steel forges quite as well as ordinary carbon steel, but is more easily burnt under oxidizing conditions at a yellow heat:[c] the Brooklyn Chrome Steel Company states that it may be forged like any other good steel:[d] Rolland that it works advantageously at a temperature approaching whiteness.[e] Even with 12% of chromium and 2% of carbon iron may be forged.[f] Brooklyn chrome steels 7, 9, 12 and 38 forged well between a light yellow and a dull red heat, in some cases even enduring light blows at slightly scintillating whiteness. I here condense my observations, adding for comparison some results obtained with tungsten steel. See Table 34A, § 141.

TABLE 32A.—FORGING TEMPERATURES OF BROOKLYN CHROME STEEL.

Nos. in Table 32.	Composition.				Temperature.							
	Chromium.	Carbon.	Manganese.	Tungsten.	Scintillating white.	White.	Light yellow.	Yellow.	Full red.	Cherry red.	Dull red.	Black.
7	·58	1·06	·17	......	Crumbles badly...	Crumbles badly...	Forges well......	Forges well...	Forges well...	Forges well...	Forges......	Hammer hardens and cracks.
9	·38	·90	1·99	·98	Crumbles......	Crumbles a little..	Forges	Forges well...	....	....	....	
12	·29	1·32	·15	·78	Crumbles a little..	Forges pretty well	Forges well......	....	....	....	....	
13	·25	·70	....	......	"	"	"	Forges well...	Forges well...	Forges well...	Forges......	Forges a little.
Mushet's tungsten steel 7·8					....	....	Cracks........	Forges well...	" ...	" ...	Cracks......	Hammer hardens.

F. WELDING.—The Chrome Steel Co. state that chrome steel "welds readily either to iron or to itself, and will not separate at the weld:" but here the suspicion of interest arises. Brustlein, who as the (I believe) chief European maker of chrome steel should not knowingly depreciate it, admits that it is "difficult, if not impossible, to weld two pieces of steel which contain a notable proportion of chromium," owing to the formation of an unscorifiable scale of oxide.[g] With repeated trials at different temperatures and closely following the maker's directions a skillful blacksmith was unable to weld for me steel No. 13, which contains but 0·25% of chromium. It would stick together and could be bent back and forth at dull redness without separating: but on twisting the steel when cold it parted at the weld, the perfectly bright clean surfaces showing that no true weld had occurred. The pieces, however, adhered with a tenacity sufficient for many purposes. We would naturally expect this tenacity to decrease with increasing proportion of chromium, and from Brustlein's statements I infer that it does, and probably rapidly.

G. HOMOGENEOUSNESS.—Several facts indicate that chrome steel is liable to be exceedingly heterogeneous. The tensile strength of two test pieces cut from the same bar of Brooklyn chrome steel tested at West Point differed by 21,990 pounds: that of two others, cut from the same bar after heating, differed by 24,680 pounds.[h]

The specific gravity of two pieces cut from another test bar varied from 7·8556 to 7·8161, or by ·0395. In carbon steel a variation of about 0·25% of carbon would be required to produce such a difference in tensile strength, and of about 0·50% of carbon to produce such a variation in specific gravity. For comparison I here tabulate a few instances of deviation of specific gravity.

Difference between the mean sp. gr. of the heaviest and lightest of 18 lots of tool steel: [i]	0·0508
Difference between sp. gr. of steel ingots of 1·079 and 0·529% of carbon: [j]	0·036
Difference between the sp. gr. of hammered bars of 1·079 and 0·529% of carbon: [j]	0·019
Difference in sp. gr. due to hardening steel of 1·005% carbon from redness: [i]	0·087
Maximum variation in pieces cut from the same piece of Bessemer steel: Miller: [k]	0·015
Do. do. for open-hearth steel: Kent: [k]	0·0081
Greatest difference between two pieces cut from the same bar of Brooklyn chrome steel, West Point	0·0395

Only moderate differences, however, existed between the specific gravities of duplicate pieces cut from the other bars of chrome steel tested.

On etching the polished surface of bar 13, Table 32, with dilute sulphuric acid, irregular bright white spots appeared, 0·12 inch in diameter and less, apparently unacted on by the acid. On digestion with acid these spots grew into projecting lumps, as the surrounding matrix was dissolved. These may be segregations rich in chromium: certain chromium-iron alloys resist acids. This segregation is a possible explanation of the apparent chromeless-

[a] Kiraldy's Experiments on Fagersta Steel, Series A2, test B 1083.
[b] Phil. Trans. Royal Society, 1822, p. 207.
[c] Journ. Iron and St. Inst., 1886, II., pp. 775, 820.
[d] Circular.
[e] Ann. Mines, 1878, 13, p. 152.
[f] Brustlein, Journ. Iron and St. Inst., 1886, II., p. 774.
[g] Idem, p. 776.
[h] Circular of Chrome Steel Company.
[i] Rept. U. S. Bd. on Testing Iron, etc., II., p. 592.
[j] Metcalf, Treatment of Steel, p. 87.
[k] Miller, Trans. Am. Inst. Mining Engineers, XIV., p. 583, 1886.

ness of "chrome steel." If so segregated as to escape ordinary sampling, how beneficial chromium must be!

II. FUSIBILITY.—Chromium raises the melting point of iron: with more than 68% of chromium ferro-chromes are "with difficulty fusible at the highest temperatures of the blast-furnace."[a] Chrome steel must be teemed at a very high temperature, since according to Boussingault it solidifies incomparably faster than other steels.

MAGNETISM.—Even with 65% chromium ferro-chrome is according to Brustlein attracted by the magnet: Percy however found that one with 54·6%± chromium was not thus attracted.

STRUCTURE: DAMASKING.—Chromium tends to produce an acicular structure in iron, especially if the metal be slowly cooled and if it be also rich in carbon.[b] Thus No. 8 in Table 31 "is a mass of minute needles": No. 11 is brilliantly acicular, yet the fracture of No. 12 shows only small square facets, though it differs from No. 11 chiefly in having much less carbon.

A slight application of dilute sulphuric acid to the polished surface of chrome steel produces at least in certain cases a very beautiful damask, which Berthier observed, and which Faraday and Stodart[c] ascribed to the elongation of the crystals by forging. I cannot develop this damask on steel 13, nor could J. H. H. Corbin produce it on a Brooklyn chrome steel containing 1·66% chromium and 0·98% carbon.[d]

The fracture of chrome steel in the normal condition (*i. e.*, neither hardened nor annealed) closely resembles that of chromeless steel of the same carbon content: when quenched it becomes extremely fine, and if the steel be the rich in chromium porcelanic, like that of tungsten steel. If long exposed to a yellow oxidizing fire it acquires a coarse, square, crystalline structure and becomes worthless.

§ 139. THE STATUS OF CHROME STEEL.—The admirable properties of chrome steel, its combination of hardness with forgeableness, long ago attracted Faraday, Berthier, Percy and Boussingault. There seems to be little doubt that, where extreme hardness coupled with a fair degree of forgeableness is required, it is preferable to carbon steel. Now how is it that a material with such valuable properties, in spite of the eclat due to its adoption for the Illinois and St. Louis bridge (!) finds itself to-day, some sixteen years after that event, in little demand and in ill favor? I have little doubt that this is because its manufacture, which demands unusual skill and intelligence, has in the past largely fallen into incompetent hands: and that the poor management of this promising industry has for a time deprived the world of a most valuable material, both directly and indirectly by giving it a bad name.

Though, owing to the proneness of chromium to oxidize, the manufacture of chrome steel calls for unusually close chemical control, it is stated that at Brooklyn no competent control is exercised, and that the ferro-chrome is not even analyzed, a like quantity of it being employed, irrespective of its composition, to produce steel of given quality. This is a very serious charge, but one for which my observations made during a recent visit quite prepared me. The irregularity and chromelessness of chrome steel is a matter of frequent complaint. Many experienced chemists have found either no chromium or the merest traces in chrome steel sold in the American and I believe also in the British market. Among these are Abel,[e] Snelus,[f] A. E. Hunt[g] and A. A. Blair.[h] G. W. Maynard[i] with repeated careful analyses could find no chromium in the chrome steel of the St. Louis bridge: Hunt could find none even in the slag from the Brooklyn Chrome Steel Works.

What now is chrome steel? Finding no satisfactory definition I suggest this:—"Steel whose physical properties are influenced more by the chromium than by the other non-ferrous elements which it contains." Our present knowledge does not permit close discriminations: but I may safely say that while steels 1 to 4·5 and 31 to 33 in Table 32 are chrome steels, 12 to 15 clearly are not, their name to the contrary notwithstanding, and that numbers 7 to 11 occupy debatable ground.

Beyond this the grossly exaggerated statements of the properties of chrome steel which have been widely circulated, are well calculated to lead to disappointment and improper treatment even where true chrome steel is supplied, and still more when chromeless steel masquerades in its place.[j]

The present limited employment of chrome steel, coupled with the prevalent belief that the Illinois and St. Louis bridge was built of it, would lead us to regard it as a material of the past, not of the future, and to believe that, in spite of the skill and experience acquired by the manufacture of enormous structural masses, in spite of the control gained over its quality in producing such vast quantities with rigidly specified properties, it had not been able to hold its own, but had been driven by carbon steel from

[a] Boussingault, op. cit., p. 281.

[b] From Brustlein's statements the opposite might be inferred: but Boussingault's statement on this point appears unequivocal. Op. cit., p. 815.

[c] Loc. cit.

[d] Op. cit.

[e] Am. Journ. Science, 3d Series, XIII., p. 424, 1877.

[f] Journ. Iron and St. Inst., 1874, I., p. 87.

[g] Private communication.

[h] Private communication.

[i] Journ. Iron and St. Inst., 1874, I., p. 88.

[j] I reluctantly feel compelled to call attention to a most astonishing report by three officials of the U. S. Navy, one of them a chief engineer, widely disseminated through the circular of the Chrome Steel Co. There is hardly a statement in it which can be reconciled with those of other and competent observers. They state (1) that "chrome steel is not a carbon steel but an alloy of chromium with iron": in the great majority of the analyses of American chrome steel which I have seen the carbon exceeds the chromium. 2. "It is of a uniform texture in large or small masses." The indications are that it is unusually heterogeneous. 3. "It is exceedingly tough when hardened": so it is, just about as tough as glass. The four varieties which I have examined are, when hardened, as brittle as other hardened steel. 4. "It will do from three to four times more work in all the various kinds of tools than carbon steel." The elaborate tests of D. Smith show that while it on the whole slightly excels carbon steel in efficiency when employed for cutting, in many cases carbon steel excels it: *e. g.* in drilling, carbon steel of one lot excelled the three chrome steels with which it was compared, excelling two of them by about 100%. 5. "It can be welded and worked at the same degree of heat and with the same ease that wrought-iron can—without danger of ever being destroyed by overheating." This statement is simply incredible and is opposed by Brustlein's observations and my own, and by the instructions of the Chrome Steel Company to forge the steel like that of any other good brand, and, in welding, to tap it lightly and increase the force of the blows gradually as it is liable to fly. If it welded as easily as wrought-iron such instructions would be superfluous.

In a less widely circulated version of their report they state that "chromium is a non-oxidizable metal." Actually chromium when hot decomposes aqueous vapor, and, under certain conditions, oxidizes with great facility, taking fire in the air even at a heat below redness. I am fully persuaded that no steel ever possessed the combination of qualities which they describe, and that such exaggerations are calculated to restrict rather than to extend the use of this valuable substance, by leading would-be employers to injure it by too severe usage, and in other obvious ways. A single proved misstatement is but too apt to inspire disgust and complete incredulity.

ground already won. I gladly refute this story: no such retreat has occurred: the bridge was built of chromeless steel.[a]

To sum up, I believe that the employment of chrome steel has been greatly restricted by the unfortunate reputation which it has acquired through irregularity in its composition and through exaggerated statements of its valuable properties, leading to too severe treatment, disappointment, disgust. These have been intensified by the extensive sale as "chrome steel" of material which has either no chromium or too little to entitle it to this name: applied to this these exaggerations are the more exaggerated and prejudicial.

Fain would I praise, not censure. I am induced to write the foregoing by the hope that a plain statement of these sufficient reasons for the present disappointing status of chrome steel, due not to its faults but to its unfortunate treatment, may contribute to its acquiring the far better position to which I am confident that it is entitled. That it will rapidly approach this I am encouraged to believe by what I can learn of the spirit of its makers in France, Jacob Holtzer et Cie.

§ 140. THE FUTURE OF THE SPECIAL STEELS.—This of the past: what of the future? Chrome steel appears to lie between carbon and manganese steels on the one hand and tungsten steel on the other. More costly, harder and less easily forged than the former, it is cheaper, when hot more forgeable and when cold more ductile and less hard than the latter:[b] manganese steel however excels it in toughness.

Three natural fields suggest themselves for chrome steel. First, where extreme hardness is needed and where tungsten and manganese steels are excluded by the difficulty of forging them, as in the case of cutting tools and abrasion-resisting pieces of complex form. Second, where extreme hardness must be coupled with fair resistance to shock, as in the case of armor piercing projectiles: here tungsten steel appears to be excluded by its brittleness and badly handicapped by its cost: but manganese steel, incomparably tougher and but slightly softer than hardened chrome steel, may offer it serious competition, while some tungsten-manganese steel, borrowing extreme hardness from tungsten and toughness from manganese, may prove a yet more formidable competitor. The combined hardness and toughness of manganese steel should pre-eminently fit it for armor plate. Third, where extreme hardness in the finished piece or in some portion of it must be combined with the power of being toughened or softened by annealing, as in the case of pieces which must be machined or engraved, or of which one part must be very hard and another very tough. Here the fact that tungsten and manganese steels can be but slightly softened by annealing appears to exclude them.

It is very doubtful whether the tensile strength of chrome and tungsten steels, high as it often is, is greater than that attainable in carbon steel; and, as the latter for given tensile strength is certainly less treacherous and brittle than tungsten steel, and probably both more uniform in composition and more homogeneous than chrome steel, the employment of these special steels where tensile strength alone or chiefly is sought, is hardly to be looked for. Manganese steel, however, may commend itself where unusual tensile strength coupled with great toughness is demanded.

Naturally where we can sacrifice but a little of the forgeableness of chrome steel we may add tungsten to gain hardness, or manganese to gain toughness. (See Nos. 9 and 12, Table 32.) But too little evidence of the effect of crossing these alloys exists to permit definite statements.

In the past the employment of these steels has been restricted by irregularity in their composition and by ignorance on the part of both maker and user of the composition best suited to special purposes. The solution of the difficult problem of adapting to their uses these alloys, whose properties seem to vary with their composition according to most complex and unguessed laws, has been chiefly entrusted to men utterly unfitted for it by nature and training. Groping in the dark, often with neither adequate chemical nor physical testing, their jealousy and narrowness have too often thrown Chinese walls around their establishments, keeping knowledge out far more than in. Each crucible steel maker, hugging his own ignorance lest his trivial secrets or his lack of them should leak out, often refused to advance lest his neighbor should advance too. The introduction of the special steels has been further hampered by their need of special treatment at the hands of the smith, ever loth to learn, for learning confesses previous ignorance. As none of them can for general purposes compete with carbon steel, he has in general been called on to employ them only in special cases, so isolated that he remains skilless in their use. But the light of a brighter day o'ertops our Chinese walls: technical schools train steel makers of a different spirit, and investigators who can not be restrained from learning and telling: artisans' schools and the rapidly increasing specialization of artisan's labor will give us smiths of a different type. To-day the forces which make for the use of special steels wax, the old opposing ones wane.

I here endeavor to indicate roughly to the eye the rela-

[a] The Chrome Steel Co., referring in their circular to this bridge say "Capt. J. B. Eads did adopt our 'chrome steel' for this wonderful structure, as the only steel made that would withstand the requisite pulling and thrusting stress, as will be seen by his (Eads') report to that company, dated October, 1871." I find no warrant for this statement in Eads' report. He indeed expresses his preference for chrome steel, but, expressly stating (p. 12) that he "did not feel justified in assuming that crucible carbon steel of the qualities and forms required could not be readily made, when he was assured of the contrary by some of the most eminent steel-makers of America" and by the managers of Krupp's and of Petin Godet & Co.'s works, he says (p. 11) that "it seemed but fair to state the qualities which the steel should possess, without prescribing the method of manufacture": *i. e.*, the contractors were simply required to supply steel of given properties, and were at liberty to supply either carbon or chrome steel. Actually they supplied chromeless steel, which was accepted. Eads had evidently been completely deceived on the subject, for he states (p. 11) that chromium "has little or no affinity for oxygen, while carbon has a great affinity for it, and, by the application of heat it is liable to be burnt out of the steel;" while in fact all the evidence goes to show that chromium in steel is much more oxidizable than carbon. Eads further states that the company which was to manufacture steel for the bridge had bought the right to make chrome steel for it, and had assured him that no other kind would be made. This assurance, a word which seems to fit this case, was not kept. Mr. W. F. Durfee informs me (private communication, June 15th, 1887) that "there was no chromium used in the materials for the St. Louis bridge, which was all made under my supervision, with the exception of the sheet steel envelope of the tubes. This was made by Park Brothers of Pittsburgh, and I have been assured that no chromium was used in that. Before I assumed the charge of the works there had been some experiments made with chrome steel, and the company had purchased the right to use it, and these facts have probably given rise to the story that the bridge was made of chrome steel, which is *not a fact*." (The italics are his.) I here call attention to Maynard's failure to find chromium in this steel, and to analyses 14 and 15 Table 32, by Blair, of steel said to be from this bridge.

[b] Tungsten steel is certainly harder than much of the chrome steel of commerce, but I do not know that highly chromiferous steel may not be as hard or even harder than tungsten steel.

tive toughness, hardness, etc., of these three special steels and of hard high-carbon steel. With our present knowledge such statements must be somewhat conjectural.

TABLE 32 B.

Hardness......	*TUNGSTEN!!!*	CHROME!!ª	CARBON!	*Manganese(?)*
Toughness.....	*MANGANESE!!!*	CARBON	*Chromium*	Tungsten
Tensile strength	*(CARBON!!*	*CHROMIUM!!*	*TUNGSTEN!?)*	*Manganese*
Forging power.	*CARBON!!!*	*Chromium*	Manganese?	Tungsten
Welding "	*Carbon*	....	Chromium	Tungsten
Annealing "	*CARBON!!!*	CHROMIUM!	Manganese	Tungsten
Cheapness.....	*CARBON.*	MANGANESE	CHROMIUM	*Tungsten*

ª It is not intended to assert that rich chrome steel may not be as hard as tungsten steel.

§ 141. IRON AND TUNGSTEN were first alloyed by the brothers d'Elhuyar in 1783, and later by Berthier. Though metal sold at one time as tungsten steel contained no tungsten, it is certain that it is now largely employed in the manufacture of the harder grades of crucible steel. Mushet's "Special," "Imperial" and "Crescent Hardened" are brands of tungsten steel now sold in the American markets.

COMBINATION.—Tungsten, itself exceedingly infusible, unites with iron apparently in all proportions, at least up to 80%. Ferro-tungsten is apparently readily obtained, often as a dark, heavy, slightly sintered mass, by long and strongly heating wolframite, (FeMn) WO_4, or scheelite, $CaWO_4$, preferably with iron or iron oxide, in brasqued crucibles, after roasting to expel sulphur and arsenic, washing, and finally pulverizing. It has been made in the blast-furnace, but a demand for its production on so large a scale in the near future seems hardly probable. When made from wolframite it inevitably and not undesirably contains manganese. As tungsten raises the melting point of iron, alloys with more than 40% of it are rarely made. Ferro-tungsten has been reported for sale in the European markets with 20 to 50 (?) % tungsten and 1·5 to 6% manganese.

Tungsten steel is made by the crucible process, ferro-tungsten of known composition being added to the ordinary charge. Instead of this Mushet recommended a mixture of roasted wolframite and pitch, which could hardly give so uniform a product.

Bernoulli prepared tungsten steel by melting tungstic anhydride, WO_3, with turnings of gray cast-iron, whose graphite he found reduced tungsten to the metallic state, though combined carbon alone did not.ª

CONDITION OF TUNGSTEN.—Ferro-tungstens appear to consist of a matrix of iron within which various alloys are crystallized. Schneider, digesting ferro-tungsten No. 6, Table 35, in hydrochloric acid (which dissolved about 60% of the whole, though only traces of its tungsten), obtained a residue, magnetically separable into two portions: one, constituting 90% of the whole, contained 24 to 31% iron and 1·4 to 1·6% carbon; was not attracted by the magnet; gained about 26% in weight when heated in air; but was again readily reduced by hydrogen to an alloy whose iron was insoluble in hydrochloric acid. The other, containing 68·1% iron, 4·1% carbon and 27% tungsten, was attracted by the magnet. He appears to consider these residual substances as mechanical mixtures of iron and tungsten: but their easy magnetic separation from each other and the fact that, after oxidation and subsequent reduction, the iron of one remained insoluble in acid, strongly suggest chemical union.ᵇ

ª Poggendorff's Annalen, 1860, CXI., p. 581.
ᵇ Oest. Zeitschrift: 1885, XXXIII., p. 257. Stahl und Eisen, 1885, p. 332.

TABLE 33.—FERRO-TUNGSTEN.

	1.	2.	3.	4.	5.	6.
Tungsten............	37	77·8	53·1	29·12	34·25	28·15
Iron............	63	16·4	43·4	67·03	60	68·86
Manganese............	......	5·8	3·5	but little	4·20	0·99
Silicon............	......	......	......	·61	......	0·23
Carbon............	......	......	......	4·27	3·65	1·85
Phosphorus............	......	......	......	......	·14	0·008

1. Brilliant, hard, lamellar, more brittle than common iron; **2.** hard, brittle, lamellar; fuses only in the highest heat of furnace, and **3.** platinum gray, hard, brittle, lamellar completely fusible. Berthier, Percy, Iron and Steel, p. 190. **4** Hanover, examined by Ledebur; **5.** Terre-Noire, according to Kerpeley; Ledebur, Handbuch, p. 262. **6.** Austrian Alpine Mining Co., Journ. Iron and St. Inst., 1884, I., p. 230. Oest. Zeit., XXXIII., p. 257. This is incorrectly quoted in Stahl und Eisen, V., p. 332, as "68·1 W, 28·2 Fe."

TABLE 34.—TUNGSTEN STEEL.

Source, etc.	Composition.						Tensile strength. Pounds per square inch.	Elongation, %.
	W.	Fe.	C.	Si.	Mn.	P.		
1. Schneider..................	11·06	......	2·15	·26	1·48	·007	....	....
2. Mushet's special..................	9·99	......	1·34	0·33	1·04	·04	....	....
3. " "..................	7·81	......	1·93	·09	·19	...	140,400	6
4. English..................	8·95	......	1·70	0·32	1·26	...	....	....
5. "Crescent Hardened," Pittsburgh. ...	0·73	...	2·96	·05	2·06	..	70,100 a 94,000 b	0
6. "Imperial," Pittsburgh	0·38	......	1·6	·16	2·71	....	....	....
7. " (another bar)..................	....	....	....	....	...	....	87,000 91,600	0
8. Ledebur..................	5·87	....	·42	·76	2·57	...	....	....
9. "	8·74	....	·86	·78	2·46	...	....	....
10. Styrian..................	8·40	....	1·20	·21	·38	...	190,000	0·75
11. Bochum..................	3·06	95·85	....	..	tr	....	....	....
12. "	2·71	96·37		.	tr	....	....	....
13. "	1·94	....	1·49	·19	·44	....	....	....
14. De Feuffe..................	......	....	....	.	...	....	158,900	....
15. " "	......	....	....	.	....	....	160,500	....

1. L. Schneider, Oest. Zeit., 1885, XXXIII., p. 257; Journ. Iron and St. Inst., 1884, I., p. 230. **2.** Hard English Mushet's Steel, Metallurgical Rev., II., p. 441. **3.** The same, tested by the author. **4.** Ledebur, Handbuch, p. 263. **5.** Made by Miller, Metcalf & Parkin, tested by the author. **6** and **7.** Made by Park Bros. & Co. and tested by the author. **8**, **9** and **10.** Ledebur, loc. cit. **11** and **12.** Percy, Iron and Steel, p. 194. **13.** Ledebur, loc. cit. **14** and **15.** Rev. Univ., 1866, p. 58. a. As received from the makers. b. Quenched in oil from very dull redness.

I have to thank Messrs. Hunt and Clapp, Pittsburgh, Pa., for the compositions of numbers 5, 6 and 7, which they kindly analyzed for this work.

EFFECTS ON THE PHYSICAL PROPERTIES OF IRON. TENSILE STRENGTH.—While steels 3, 10, 14 and 15 in Table 34 suggest that tungsten raises the tensile strength, steels 5 and 7, which differ from 3 and 10 chiefly in having much more manganese, are decidedly weak.

HARDNESS.—Tungsten renders iron intensely hard. Mushet's steel, No. 3 Table 34, is the hardest which I have met, indenting hardened chrome steel No. 13, Table 32. It is slowly and slightly attacked by a very sharp file. I found hardened chrome steel slightly harder than Crescent hardened steel and Imperial steel (both unhardened and tungstiferous). All these readily scratch glass. These two tungsten steels as already pointed out differ chiefly from Mushet's in composition in having more manganese. The specimens of Mushet's steel which I have examined do not scratch quartz, but a rich ferro-tungsten made by Bernoulli is said to have scratched quartz readily. Tungsten steel is thought harder than chrome steel: but I do not know that it has been proved to be harder than rich chrome steel. Weight for weight tungsten probably does not increase the hardness as much as carbon, and perhaps not as much as chromium; Metcalf found that dies with 1·37% carbon and ·78% tungsten wore much faster than tungstenless ones with 2·37% carbon.ᶜ Steel may however contain a much larger proportion of tungsten (at least 10%) than of carbon without losing its power of being forged.

DUCTILITY.—Tungsten steel is exceedingly brittle. When bars 3, 5 and 7 were grasped in a vise and struck with a sledge with gradually increasing force, though they appeared to be resilient, they broke without the least perceptible set, and in certain cases flew into many small pieces at the point of fracture like glass. It is hence not only unfit for structural purposes, but even for tools subject to shock, such as rock-drills, cold-chisels,

ᶜ Trans. Am. Inst. Mining Engrs., IX., p. 549, 1881

etc. Even the chattering of a lathe is said to be liable to crack it:[a] yet it is successfully used for the knives of nail-cutting machines. The chief normal use of these steels is for the tools of lathes, planers, etc., designed for heavy cuts.

FORGING AND WELDING.—Tungsten steel can be forged only between a cherry-red and a low yellow heat, and then with a difficulty which restricts its use to pieces of simple shape. I here condense the results of my observations in forging it. Only general conclusions can be drawn from these tests, as the smith was not skilled in the use of tungsten steel. The "Crescent" appeared to forge better than the "Imperial" at a low yellow, the "Imperial" better than the "Crescent" at a dull red. This may have been because the Crescent contains more carbon, because of unobserved differences in the conditions of forging, or because of some peculiarities of these particular bars. The general lesson, the limited range of forging temperature, is unmistakeable.

molten or solid: but when these metals are mixed in more nearly equal quantities they often tend to split up into alloys, on the one hand more ferruginous and on the other more cupriferous. These may or may not be of definite composition: they separate more or less completely by gravity, the copper concentrating downwards. Thus Riche[c] found in an alloy made from 94·1% of copper and 5·9% of iron, microscopic gray spots: melting 90% of copper with 10% of pure iron he obtained an ingot which, after prolonged fusion at a high temperature, had four times as much iron in its upper as in its lower portion: while Percy,[d] in an alloy containing 80% of iron (with 20% of copper?) found copper-red particles, which, especially towards the bottom of the mass, were occasionally visible to the naked eye. These were probably in Riche's case a more ferruginous, and in Percy's a more cupreous alloy. When the segregated portion becomes more considerable its particles coalesce and the separation is more complete. But even when the proportions of the

TABLE 84 A.—FORGING PROPERTIES OF TUNGSTEN STEEL.

	Composition.			Temperature.					
	W.	Mn.	C.	Light yellow.	Yellow	Orange.	Full red.	Low red.	Black
Mushet........	7·81	0·19	1·90	Cracks badly......	Forges	Bends well	Bends and hammers close together without cracking	Cracks in bending.	
Crescent	6·78	2·66	2·08	Crumbles badly....	Bends fairly.......	... .	Bends well	Breaks when bent at blood red	Cracks after 4 or 6 light blows.
Imperial.	6·38a	2·11a	1·6a	....	Forges but cracks in bending........	....	....	Bent double and hammered close at very dull red without cracking	Forges better than the preceding

a This is the composition of a bar similar to the one forged.

Imperial steel is said to be weldable, but with extreme difficulty: I doubt if it can be truly welded by ordinary methods. Prof. Elihu Thomson, by his electric welding process, welded for me small bars of both Mushet's and Imperial steel so perfectly that I could not, by the most severe tests, detect the point of juncture: Mushet's steel, twisted till it flew apart, revealed no trace of the welded surface.

HARDENING.—Even slightly tungstiferous steels are said to be very prone to crack in hardening. I can detect no increase of hardness on quenching Mushet's steel. I found two bars of Imperial steel slightly softer after sudden than after slow cooling; it here resembles manganese steel; indeed it has a notable proportion of manganese. Mushet's, "Crescent Hardened" and "Imperial" steels are employed without quenching, which indeed would be dangerous. Quenched or unquenched they readily scratch glass, but not quartz: as their hardness is not impaired by heat, they may be driven much faster than carbon steel when used as machine cutting tools.

DETERIORATION.—Chernoff states that after a few heatings tungsten steel becomes oxidized and loses its special properties.[b]

MAGNETIZATION.—Tungsten steel is said to be exceptionally retentive of magnetization.

§ 142. IRON AND COPPER. A. COMBINING POWER.—It is stated that iron and copper unite in all proportions. The alloys of iron with a little copper and of copper with a little iron appear to be homogeneous and stable whether

two metals are nearly equal, this separation does not always occur, or at least is not always perceptible. Thus Percy (loc. cit.) could detect no segregation in an alloy containing 20% of iron (and 80% of copper?) These facts suggest that copper and iron unite chemically in many but not in all proportions, and hence that if either copper or iron be added to a homogeneous alloy of both, a new homogeneous alloy arises if the new composition permits: if not, the metals rearrange themselves in alloys of some chemically possible composition, separating more or less completely by gravity, perhaps during, perhaps prior to solidification.

The presence of carbon still further diminishes the tendency of copper and iron to unite. If copper and carburetted iron be intimately mixed they again separate almost completely, apparently the more fully the more carbon is present. Thus Mushet found that, though 5% of copper formed on apparently homogeneous alloy with steel, yet when the copper reached 10% minute segregations appeared; if 25% of copper were present much of it sank to the bottom and occurred in knots and streaks. With white cast-iron the tendency to segregation was stronger: if 5% of copper were added to gray cast-iron, copper-colored specks concentrated at the bottom of the ingot, with 9% of copper deep-red leaves separated, and with 10·7% a separate copper button formed beneath the cast-iron.[e] Melting 10% of cast-iron with 90% of copper, Riche[f] found uncombined iron at the top of the ingot: while at Perm[g] (Urals) ferruginous copper ore smelted in blast-furnaces 19 feet high yielded 4 parts of copper containing about

a A. Willis (Journ. Iron and St. Inst., 1880, I., p. 92) considers that tungsten hardens steel without making it brittle: and M. Böker (Stahl und Eisen, VI., p. 42), states that it enables us to obtain steel of greater hardening power together with increased toughness. If this be true at all, it can only apply to comparatively small percentages of tungsten: the four tungsten steels which I have examined are astonishingly brittle.

b Revue Universelle, 1877, I., p., 400.

c Thurston, Matls. of Engineering, III., p. 184.

d Iron and Steel, p. 150.

e L. & E. Philosophical Magazine, 3d series, VI., p. 81, 1835.

f Thurston, loc. cit.

g Rivot, Principes Généraux du Traitement des Minerals, I., p. 89, and Percy, Iron and Steel, p. 153.

10% of iron, and 3 parts of cast-iron containing 12·6% of copper and 3·03% of carbon. This cast-iron, when remelted, yielded an upper stratum of iron with 0·25 to 2% of copper and a lower one, tapped from beneath the upper, and consisting of copper with 20% of iron. So too Percy,[a] melting spiegeleisen of 8% of manganese with pure copper in luted clay crucibles, obtained cast-iron containing 2·5% of copper together with copper containing 3·67 to 4·87% of iron and 1·16 to 2·82% of manganese. The iron salamanders obtained in copper smelting occasionally contain as little as 1·5%[b] of copper, and I have produced black copper with not over 3 to 4% of iron in contact with these salamanders.

Owing to its low affinity for oxygen all the copper contained in iron ore must necessarily be reduced in the blast-furnace: but if much copper is present most of it may be expected separate by gravity, so that the iron would not hold more than perhaps 2% of it. But the copper which it retains should adhere tenaciously to the iron through all stages in its manufacture, and should concentrate in the steel, which might thus have 2·5% of copper, necessitating great dilution.

Effects of Copper: Redshortness.—The chief effect of copper, like that of sulphur, is to render steel redshort and to destroy its welding power: but its influence has been greatly exaggerated. Steel may contain 0·85 and according to Choubly 0·96% of copper without serious redshortness, and W. W. Scranton[c] habitually makes Bessemer T rails with 0·51 to 0·66%, which he states are so non-redshort that, in spite of their thin flanges and the exceptionally low temperature at which they are finished, only from 1·25 to 2·5% of them are sufficiently cracked to be classed as second quality. Eggertz[d] indeed stated that 0·5% of copper rendered steel worthless, but it is evident from Table 35 that this can only be true under special conditions if at all. I know not what percentage of copper is required to produce redshortness, but 2% appears to destroy hot-malleableness completely, for Billings,[e] melting 2% of copper with a remarkably pure weld-iron, found the resulting alloy so redshort that in forging it crumbled into grains: and Mushet reports steel melted with 5% of copper as "useless for forge purposes."[f]

The evidence as to the effects of copper on weld metal are less harmonious. The illustrious Karsten[g] found that 0·286% of copper (remaining from 1% introduced into the charcoal refining hearth) sensibly affected the welding power of weld metal: Stengel[h] reports that puddled iron with 0·018 sulphur and 0·21% of copper was slightly redshort; of thirteen wrought-irons for chain cables tested by the U. S. Board to test metals one with 0·32 to 0·43% of copper stood lowest but one in welding power.[1] Clearly these weld metals are injured far more than ingot metal is by the same proportion of copper. In other cases the influence of copper is less severe than in the preceding, though still perhaps more severe than on ingot metal. Thus, of the only two other cupreous irons among the thirteen just referred to, one with 0·17% of copper stood highest but one in welding power, and one with 0·31% stood well in this respect. So too Eggertz reports that 0·5% of copper produces only traces of redshortness in weld metal.[d] Holley suggests that the excellent welding of the iron with 0·31 copper may possibly be due to the simultaneous presence of ·34 nickel and ·11 cobalt.[1] These incomplete data suggest that the influence of less than 0·2% of copper is not likely to be appreciable in weld iron, that of ·30% not necessarily injurious, and that of ·34% at least occasionally serious.

Influence of Manganese.—Whether manganese counteracts the effects of copper like those of sulphur is not known: but from the fact that Nos. 3, 6, 7, 13 and 14 in Table 31 are not redshort, though they have ·85, ·35, ·31, ·96 and ·48% of copper respectively with but ·51, ·07, trace ·46 and ·53% of manganese, it is not probable that the presence of this metal is as imperative in cupreous as in sulphurous iron and steel. No. 14 shows that the co-existence of much phosphorus and copper does not necessarily cause redshortness.

Other Effects of Copper.—It is not known whether the highest proportion of copper which commercial iron contains has any sensible effect beyond those just discussed. We have the following information concerning the alloys of copper with iron. All refer to alloys of practically carbonless iron with pure copper, except Mushet's, which were of steel (apparently crucible steel) with copper, and possibly Rinman's.

% Cu.	Description of the alloys.	
2±	Extremely redshort: weak when cold	a
5±	Useless for forge purposes: cannot take an edge	b
9±	Hard and brittle	b
16·7	Apparently stronger than the two preceding	b
20±	Extremely brittle, crystalline granular, fracture pale coppery gray	c
35	Separated: bottom of soft malleable copper	b
41·75	Very brittle; fracture uneven and crystalline; strongly magnetic	c
50±	Very brittle and fine-grained: strongly magnetic	c
67 to 80	Harder but not appreciably less ductile than copper (?)	d
80±	Less ductile than the following one: strongly magnetic	c
88·4±	Decidedly redshort: much harder and tougher than copper	c
94±	Extremely ductile: stronger than copper	c
94	Harder than copper; magnetic	d

a, Billings, loc. cit.; b, Mushet, loc. cit.; c, Percy, loc. cit.; d, Rinman, Matls. of Engineering, Thurston, III., p. 183; e, Liebe, Mem.

While the alloys of copper with a little iron hold out some promise (sterro-metal, a brass with 1·77 to 4% iron and 0·15 to 1·5% tin has much higher tensile strength than brass proper) alloying iron with small quantities of copper is not an alluring field.

a Op. cit., p. 140.

b Kerl, Grundriss der Metallhüttenkunde, p. 171.

c Private communication.

d Wagners Jahresbericht, 1862, p. 9.

e Trans. Am. Inst. Mining Engineers, V., p. 450, 1877.

f Phil. Mag., loc. cit.

g Percy, Iron and Steel, p. 148.

h Idem, p. 151.

1 Trans. American Inst. Mining Engrs., VI., p. 101, 1879.

Table 35.—Effect of Copper on Hot-Malleableness.

Cupriferous steel known to be non-redshort.

No.	Cu.	C.	Si.	Mn.	P.	S.	Reference.	Rolled into.	Behavior in rolling.
1	·45	·28	·14	·78	·06	·06	A	Rails	Perfect.
2	·66	·23	·09	·71	·05	·04	A	"	Almost perfect; the end made from the top of the ingot cracked slightly.
3	·85	·31	·05	·51	·06	·11	A	"	Very good; slight cracks which closed up later.
4	·85	·68	·19	·16	tr	.....	B	Krupp's gun steel	Presumably very good.
5	·80	·46	·11	·18	0	...	B	" " "	" " "
6	·35	·52	·09	·07	0		B	" " "	" " "
7	·31	·08	·17	tr	·25	·005	C	Wrought-iron for chain cables	Welded well. Others of similar composition welded rather poorly.
8	·17	·02	·14	·09	·15	·007	C	" " " "	Welded admirably.
9	·662	·37	·05	·10	.....	·19	D	Bessemer steel rails	Rolled well.
10	·51@ ·66	·33@ ·38	·03@ ·08	1·05@ 1·26	·05@ ·06	·05@ ·10	D	" " "	Steel within these limits gave 1·25 to 2·5% of second quality rails.
11	·21	.....	·038	.....	.....	·02	E	Puddled iron	Some tendency to redshortness.
12	·80						F	Open-hearth steel	Extremely slight redshortness.
13	·96	·40	·15	·46	·07	·04	G	Steel	Perfect.
14	·48	·54	·12	·43	·19	[illegible]	G	"	Perfect.

A = Wasum, Stahl und Eisen, 1884, p. 1[illegible]. B = Kern, Metallurgical Review, II., p. 240. C = Holley, Transactions of the American Institute of Mining Engineers, VI., p. 115. D = W. W. Scranton, private communication. E = Stengel, Percy, Iron and Steel, p. 151. F = Wilks, Journal Iron and Steel Inst., 1880, I., p. 95. G = Choubley, idem, 188[illegible], I., p. 248.

CHAPTER VIII.

The Metals Occurring but Sparingly in Iron.

§ 145. A. Zinc.—The alloys of this metal with a little iron appear to be tolerably stable. In galvanizing, *i. e.* zincing iron, the molten zinc gradually attacks the iron vessels, and a zinc-iron alloy collects at the bottom.[a] Several analyses of it give from 3 to 9·4% of iron. The alloys of iron with a little zinc are extremely unstable, evolving their zinc when heated, readily and apparently completely.

Parry's experiments prove that the vapor of zinc and of other metals may be temporarily absorbed but is apparently feebly retained by iron. Cast-iron, previously heated in vapor of zinc, cobalt, cadmium, bismuth and magnesium (each separately), after being cooled, cleaned with acid and filed bright, gave metallic sublimates when re-heated in vacuo. Gray cast-iron, when fused in closed crucibles with zinc, bismuth and tin (each separately) became white, and, on heating in vacuo after cleaning with acid, gave distinct sublimates. Gray and white cast-irons made from zinciferous ores gave faint sublimates when heated in vacuo. Some of the zinc and cobalt sublimates were spectroscopically shown to contain these metals: the others were not examined. In one case iron gained ·05% in weight when heated in zinc vapor.[b]

In cast-iron made from zinciferous ores Percy found no zinc and Karsten but traces.[c] In smelting zinciferous iron ores in Virginia, green zinc flames escape for days at a time from the tap-hole and from the cinder-notch. Metallic zinc escapes through the cracks in the hearth,[d] and here as well as in smelting zinc residues for spiegeleisen (Franklinite) at Newark,[e] N. J., pieces of zinc sometimes float on both slag and iron as they run from the furnace, burning with a green flame and leaving deposits of zinc oxide. Occasionally, at Newark, after about a ton of cadmia has passed through the furnace, the "cast" is covered with zinc oxide, and the casting-house is filled with zinc fume: yet after removing the crust of sand and zinc oxide no zinc can be found in the cast-iron[e] on which zinc has been seen burning, and among many analyses of the slag I learn of but one which shows zinc. An old analysis of New Jersey spiegeleisen (1860±) gives 0·3% of zinc:[f] this is probably an error: it is said that both sampling and analysis were formerly improperly conducted.

As metallic zinc volatalizes far below the temperature at which iron and slag escape from the blast-furnace, its floating and burning on the cast-iron at first suggests that a zinc-iron alloy forms in the furnace, somewhat as in Parry's experiment, owing to the pressure of the zinc vapor, but decomposes and evolves its zinc when the pressure falls on its escape from the furnace. But the true explanation doubtless is that the metallic zinc, volatilized within the furnace, in escaping through the walls condenses in the damp clay stoppings of tap-hole and cinder-notch[g]: indeed, metallic zinc will often drip out when these stoppings are picked at, and in one case it is reported to have collected in a little pool beneath the tap-hole, and to have boiled furiously when the cast-iron ran upon it, burning the men.[e] A little of this condensed metallic zinc, picked up by the cast-iron or slag, would naturally float and burn as described.

Zinc added by G. H. Billings to pure molten ingot iron volatilized till but traces remained: the resulting ingot was slightly redshort,[h] perhaps owing to lack of manganese.

Zinc appears to render iron brittle at a red heat.[i] Thus a piece of tough galvanized iron wire was heated to redness so quickly that the coating of zinc melted and apparently penetrated into the interior of the metal instead of volatilizing. On attempting to bend it while hot it readily broke off short, exhibiting a uniform blue-gray fracture —as though the zinc had penetrated into the interior of the iron. When again cooled it became tough, and, on reheating it long enough to completely volatilize the zinc, its hot-shortness ceased.[j] It is stated that iron wire in molten zinc will often break off short, though the part outside the bath remains tough.

Ledebur[k] has verified the observation that molten gray cast-iron becomes hard and inclined to whiteness if zinc be immersed in it, though little if any zinc is retained. This is possibly due to the expulsion of silicon.

The consideration of sterro-metal, a brass with 1.77 to 4% of iron, belongs rather to the metallurgy of copper than of steel.

B. Tin and Iron unite readily, as the firm union effected in making tin-plate shows, and in all proportions, forming apparently homogeneous alloys: but tin, or more probably a highly stanniferous alloy, liquates when alloys containing more than about 35% of tin are heated to or slightly above the melting point of this metal, till the more or less definite alloy Fe_4Sn holding about 35% of tin remains.[l]

Luckily tin occurs but very rarely in iron ores, for it destroys the ductility and forgeableness of iron. Some think it even more deleterious, weight for weight, than phosphorus. About 0·52% of tin, added to the charge in the puddling furnace according to Sterling's patent, caused copious white fumes and rendered the iron, which also emitted white fumes, extremely difficult to forge and weld.[l] Karsten[l] found that ·19% of tin made charcoal weld iron very brittle at a strong (*i. e.* welding?) heat, and extremely cold-short: Billings[m] found that ·73% of it rendered a very tough ingot iron decidedly cold-short, and so hot-short that at a white heat it flew under the hammer into particles so minute as to scintillate. Cast-iron melted with 2 to 5% of tin is reported as very hard and fragile; with 5% producing a bell of pretty good tone: with 9·09% as fusible, extremely fluid, non-rusting, whiter than cast-iron, acquiring a beautiful polish and having as

a Percy, Iron and Steel, p. 153. Ledebur, Handbuch, p. 267.
b Journ. Iron and St. Inst., 1874, I., p. 96.
c Percy, loc. cit.
d H. Firmstone, Trans. Am. Inst. Mining Engineers, VII., p. 93, 1879.
e Geo. C. Stone, private communications, July 25–28, 1887.
f Kerl, Grundriss der Eisenhüttenkunde, p. 42.
g H. Firmstone, private communication, July 29, 1887.

h Trans. Am. Inst. Mining Engrs., V., p. 454, 1877.
i Kerl, Grundriss der Eisenhüttenkunde, p. 24.
j W. H. Johnson, Proc. Royal Society, XXIII., p. 172, 1875.
k Loc. cit. Cf. Parry's experiment above.
l Percy, Iron and Steel, p. 161.
m Trans. Am. Inst. Min. Engrs., V., p. 450, 1877.

good a tone as bell-metal. The tin-iron alloys thus interest the iron founder more than the steel maker. Descriptions of a few better known alloys are here condensed.

TABLE 35.—TIN IRON ALLOYS.

			% Tin.	
1.	Nöllner		a 50·8c	
2.	Deville and Caron		a 67·8c	
3.	Berthier		a 50	Grayish white, very brittle, fracture granular.
4.	Berthier, Percy		a 35·1	Brittle, pulverizable, magnetic.
5.	Hervé		9·2	Hard and brittle, slightly granular.
6.	G. H. Billings		b 6·70	Very cold-short, extremely red and white short.
7.	Karsten		a 9·18	Very tender at strong heat, difficult weldable, extremely cold short.
8.		Calculated composition. c	a 90·9	Apparently uniform: very malleable.
9.			a 75·9	Pretty homogeneous, semi-malleable.
10.	Rinman		a 9·09	Very hard brittle, dense: rust-proof, fusible, very fluid, can be slightly polished.
11.	Percy		a 5·	A bell of this alloy had a pretty good tone.
			a 2·to 5·	Very hard, fragile, low tenacity.

a Percy, Iron and Steel, p. 180. b Billings, Trans. Am. Inst. Mining Engrs., V., p. 450. c Calculated composition.

C. IRON AND LEAD.—It is apparently possible but extremely difficult to alloy these metals, and no valuable properties have been notedin their alloys. I know of no successful attempt to alloy them directly. By reducing litharge with an excess of pure iron at a very high temperature Karsten obtained an iron containing on an average 2·06% of lead: Biewend obtained an iron containing 3·24% of lead by heating a slag rich in lead and iron in a brasqued crucible: beneath an iron blast-furnace a crystallized alloy containing 88·76% of lead and 11·14% of iron has been found. The wrought-iron ladles used in Pattinsonizing eventually become permeated with lead.[a]

Percy was unable, either by Karsten's method or otherwise, to obtain a decided alloy of lead and iron. Lead added by Billings to molten ingot iron completely volatilized, traces only remaining.[b] Metallic lead usually contains a minute quantity of iron.

The lead of plumbiferous iron ores separates in the blast-furnace hearth from the cast-iron, carrying with it any silver present, and thus sometimes forming an important bye-product.

TITANIUM, a metal so oxidizable that it decomposes boiling water, often occurs in gray cast-iron,[c] existing at least in part as carbide, much as suspected by Riley in 1872. (See § 13). It has been found in spiegeleisen; it is said to occur rarely or never in other white cast-iron, but the complete absence of graphite from the very titaniferous cast-iron quoted below strongly suggests whiteness. Nor is it found in commercial wrought-iron and steel, for it is inevitably oxidized along with the other electro-positive elements of the cast-iron from which they are made: indeed it can probably only be introduced into any malleable variety of iron (except possibly the most highly carburetted steels) by a *tour de force*, nor is there reason to believe that if introduced it would be beneficial. It is indeed possible, though apparently extremely difficult, to obtain titaniferous steel by melting titanic acid and iron or iron oxide with charcoal in crucibles: Sefström[d] thus obtained a very hard but malleable iron with 4·78% of titanium: it may even be questioned whether this metal did not closely approach cast-iron. Though many competent chemists have sought it, I find no other record of its detection in wrought-iron or steel. A titaniferous "plate iron"[e] quoted by A. H. Allen turns out to be nothing but cast-iron, probably white or nearly white, containing

Combined carbon	2·70	Silicon	1·09	Sulphur	·068	Manganese	1·37
Graphite	tr	Titanium	4·18	Phosphorus	·061	Iron	90·53

Faraday and Stodart stated that though their crucibles sufficed for fusing rhodium and (imperfectly) platinum, they could not bear the temperature needed for reducing titanium.[f] In an undoubted sample of Mushet's "Titanic steel" which I obtained personally from the maker's American agents, and which was stamped as such, neither Shimer nor H. L. Wells could detect titanium, though they have made its determination a special study.[g]

Percy[h] states that chemists of skill and repute have failed to find titanium in "titanic steel": and later Riley,[i] Greenwood[j] and others have found this steel free from titanium. (Cf. Appendix I.)

§ 146. A. ARSENIC behaves towards iron much as sulphur does.

COMBINATION.—They unite readily and in all proportions. Iron heated in contact with alkaline arsenite and charcoal, or arsenious acid and nitrogenous animal matter, acquires an arsenical case-hardening. Ordinary cast-iron occasionally contains small unimportant quantities of arsenic: but non-European irons have occasionally contained large quantities. Thus Berthier found 9·8% (with 1·5% carbon) and 27% (with 1% carbon) in cannon-balls from Algiers, free from sulphur, manganese, copper and silicon. The former was easily pulverized; the latter, still more fragile, could be split diametrically, revealing a fracture like that of marcasite nodules.[k] Percy found 16·2% arsenic in a cannon-ball from Sinope.[l]

In roasting mispickel-bearing ores the arsenic is expelled in large part, but not completely, as part forms non-volatile arsenate of iron, which is reduced in the blast-furnace. Simple heating to whiteness does not completely expel arsenic. It is not known whether arsenic can be scorified by other metals as sulphur is by manganese in iron-smelting. Even the violently oxidizing conditions of the basic Bessemer process do not always completely remove arsenic, for Ledebur found ·013% of it in a basic rail.[m]

Parry found that hot iron readily absorbed vapor of arsenic, which it retained on heating in vacuo. Iron behaves in the same way towards phosphorus, but after absorbing vapors of zinc, cobalt and certain other metals it again evolves them on heating in vacuo. Riley, however, observed a strong smell of arsenic on working arsenical steel, which indicates that his metal, unlike Parry's, evolves its arsenic at least in part when heated.[n]

EFFECTS.—Arsenic appears to lower the saturation point for carbon: to give iron a white fracture, to destroy its power of welding, and make it redshort and sometimes brittle at higher temperatures: a larger proportion of arsenic renders iron coldshort also. We have few quantitative data as to its effects: Lundin's analyses, too scanty to build on, indicate that in wrought-iron they begin to be

a Percy, Iron and Steel, p. 168.

b Trans. Am. Inst. Mining Engineers, V., p. 454, 1877.

c Riley, Journ. Chem. Soc., 1872, XXV., p. 562; Journ. Iron and St. Inst., 1880, I., p. 190.

d Ledebur, Handbuch der Eisenhüttenkunde, p. 265.

e Iron and St. Inst., 1880, I., p. 190: A. H. Allen, private communication, May 23d, 1887.

f Phil. Trans. Royal Society, 1822, p. 254.

g Private communications, P. W. Shimer and H. L. Wells, April 7th and May 14th, 1887. Wells states that his method (by hydrogen peroxide) would probably detect ·01 and would certainly detect ·02% of titanium.

h Iron and Steel, p. 158.

i Journ. Chem. Soc., XVI., p. 387; 1872, XXV., p. 562.

j Greenwood, Steel and Iron, p. 396.

k Annales des Mines, 3rd Ser., XI., 1837, p. 501.

l Percy, Iron and Steel, p. 76.

m Stahl und Eisen, 1884, IV., p. 640.

n Compare § 145 A. Journ. Iron and St. Inst., 1874, I., pp. 96, 97, 101.

serious at some point between ·045 and ·09%. Here are his results.[a]

Arsenic.	Sulphur.		Quality of the wrought-iron.
	By silver plate.	By barium chloride.	
·09%	0·08%	0·042%	Very unforgeable.
·045	0·015	0·023	The best in every respect.

Here the amount of sulphur is too trifling to have caused redshortness. Riley reports that steel so arsenical as to smell strongly of this metal when forged, yet worked pretty well, but was brittle and useless.[b] The wrought-iron of Alais, rendered unweldable by arsenic, has been successfully made into open-hearth steel.[c]

B. Antimony unites with iron readily, and probably in all proportions; even a minute quantity of it makes iron hard and both red- and cold-short. Fortunately it is not often present in iron ores. It is not wholly removed in the manufacture of wrought-iron, nor on exposing antimony-bearing iron to a steel-melting heat. Of 1% of antimony added by Karsten to cast-iron in the charcoal hearth, the bar-iron produced contained ·23%.[d] Of 1% added by G. H. Billings[e] to almost pure molten ingot-iron, enough remained after 20 minutes' exposure to a steel-melting heat to ruin the metal.

Karsten's weld iron with ·23% antimony was extremely red- and cold-short: another bar iron, in which he found ·114% of antimony, was worthless. Billings' antimonial iron was decidedly cold-short, and so redshort that it crumbled to pieces whether hammered or rolled.

C. Bismuth.—Of 1% of this metal added by Karsten to cast-iron while being refined in the charcoal hearth, ·081% was retained by the bar iron: its sole effect was to make the iron work "raw."[f] Of 0·5% added by Billings to molten ingot iron only traces remained in the solidified metal, which was decidedly red-short. It contained ·08% of carbon.[g] Hot iron absorbs vapor of bismuth, evolving it when heated in vacuo.[h]

D. Vanadium occurs occasionally in cast-iron, in which Riley[i] has found 0·086% of it; Sefström discovered it in the bar-iron and refinery slags from the Taberg (Swedish) ores.[j] I know no data concerning its influence.

According to Witz and Osmond[k] it concentrates in certain slags, notably in those the basic Bessemer process; these taken collectively contain large quantities of this rare metal, whose recovery they propose.

§ 147. Molybdenum produces with iron alloys analogous to those of iron with tungsten, according to Berthier, one with 2% of molybdenum being fusible, extremely hard and brittle, but tenacious:[l] yet Billings found that 1% of this metal rendered good iron extremely redshort and utterly worthless.[m] Some Mansfeld copper-smelting salamanders consist chiefly of iron-molybdenum alloys; as much as 28·40% of molybdenum is reported in them.[n]

§ 148. Nickel and Cobalt are frequently present in cast-iron, though rarely if ever in important amount, and are retained when it is converted into wrought-iron and steel.

A. Nickel alloys with iron readily and probably in all proportions: meteoric iron usually contains from 1 to 20% of it.[o] The largest amount which I have met in a commercial iron is ·35%, which, together with ·11% cobalt and ·31% copper, had no traceable effect on the weld iron which contained it, unless, as Holley pointed out, it counteracted the copper present: for the metal welded well. (See § 142.)

Effects.—Nickel appears to make iron redshort: in certain proportions and under certain conditions, both undefined, it appears to make it brittle. Billings[p] found an alloy with ·66% nickel and ·72% carbon redshort; and one with ·732 nickel and ·07 carbon very redshort, the difference being attributed to its lower carbon content: both were forgeable at higher temperature: one with 6% nickel and but little carbon was extremely redshort. These alloys were almost absolutely free from elements other than those here mentioned.

The following proportions of nickel have been found in iron: **0·35%**[q]: 0·66%[r]: 1%[s]: **3%**,[t] as malleable as pure iron: 5%[s]: **6%**,[r] almost as ductile and tenacious as pure iron: **6·36%**[u]: **7 to 8%**[u]: **7·87%**[u]: **8·21%**[u]: 8·3%,[v] semi-ductile: 10%[t] more brittle than pure iron. The irons whose proportion of nickel is here given in heavy faced type are ductile, the rest appear to be at least comparatively brittle. The influence of nickel appears to be very capricious: why 0·66, 1, and 5% of it should greatly impair ductility while 0·35, 3, and 6% do not, is not known.

Meteoric irons with 6·36, 7·87 and 8·21% nickel are reported as hard to file, and one with 8·59% nickel as easily filed.[u] The nickel-iron alloys are reported to rust less easily than iron: Faraday and Stodart found this true of an alloy of iron with 10% of nickel, but not to the extent previously alleged: while 10% of nickel alloyed with steel greatly accelerated rusting. (Cf. Appendix I.)

B. Cobalt.—Of the effects of cobalt on iron we have still less knowledge. Billings found ingot-iron with ·33 cobalt (but otherwise almost perfectly pure) solid, tough and decidedly weak when cold, and somewhat redshort.[w] As it contained no manganese its redshortness may have been due to what we call oxygenation. Alloys of 53·29 and 12·79% cobalt, with 46·71 and 87·21% iron respectively, made in Percy's laboratory were brittle.[x] Hot iron absorbs vapor of cobalt, evolving it when heated in vacuo.[y]

§ 149. Iron and Aluminium may according to Deville be alloyed in all proportions; among others the following alloys have been described.

[a] Stahl und Eisen, 1884, p. 485, from Jernkontorets Ann., 1884, II.
[b] Journ. Iron and Steel Inst., 1874, I., p. 101.
[c] Idem, 1885, I., p. 272.
[d] Percy, Iron and Steel, p. 169.
[e] Trans. Am. Inst. Mining Engrs., 1887, V., p. 453.
[f] Percy, Iron and Steel, p. 170.
[g] Trans. Am. Inst. Mining Engineers, V., p. 453, 1877.
[h] Cf. § 145 A.
[i] Riley, Journ. Chem. Soc., XVII., p. 21, 1864; XXV., p. 544, 1872.
[j] Watts. Dict. Chem., V., p. 983.
[k] Journ. Iron and St. Inst., 1882, II., p. 770, from Comptes Rendus, XCV., I., p. 42.
[l] Percy, Iron and Steel, p. 195.
[m] Trans. Am. Inst. Mining Engrs., V., p. 454, 1877.
[n] Kerl. Grundriss der Metall-Hüttenkunde, p. 171.
[o] System of Mineralogy, J. D. Dana, p. 18.
[p] Trans. Am. Inst. Mining Engrs., V., p. 448, 1877.
[q] Holley, Trans. Am. Inst. Mining Engrs., VI., p. 115.
[r] G. H. Billings, Idem, V., p. 448.
[s] Percy, Iron and Steel, p. 171.
[t] Faraday and Stodart, Percy, Iron and Steel, p. 171.
[u] Boussingault and De Rivero, Meteoric Irons, "The Useful Metals and Their Alloys," p. 272.
[v] Berthier.
[w] Trans. Am. Inst. Mining Engrs., V., p. 454.
[x] Percy, Iron and Steel, p. 173.
[y] Compare § 145 A.

TABLE 37.—ALLOYS OF IRON AND ALUMINIUM.

No.	Observer.	Composition. Al.	C.	Si.	Properties, etc.
1...	Faraday and Stodart	·0128 / ·0695	......	......	Wootz.
2...	Gruner........	·86	2·30	2·26	Cast-iron.
3.	G. H. Billings........	·52	·20	......	Solid, homogeneous, forges well at red heat, crumbles at yellow.
4...	Rogers........	·86	......	......	Resembled best Bombay wootz.
5...	Mrazek........	2·82	·16	5·35	
6...	Faraday........	3·41	......	......	White, close-grained, very brittle.
7...	Calvert and Johnson..	12·00	......	......	Very hard, but forgeable and weldable; rusts.

1. Quarterly Jour. of Science, etc., 7, p. 288; Percy, Iron and Steel, p. 183. **2.** Ledebur, Handbuch der Eisenhüttenkunde, p. 265, from Annales des Mines, XV., p. 185. Cast-iron from Champigneulle. **3.** Trans. Am. Inst. Mining Engrs., V., p. 452, 1877. Produced by fusing 12 parts of emery, 18 of alumina, 1 of pulverized charcoal and 56 of pure iron turnings; after heating to whiteness for 48 hours, the crucible was heated in an open-hearth steel-melting furnace. **4.** Rogers, "Aluminium, its History, etc." Richards, p. 281, from Moniteur Ind., 1859, No. 2370. **5.** Ledebur, loc. cit. Obtained by fusing iron wire with sodium, silica and cryolite. **6.** Quarterly Journ. of Science, etc., 9, p. 320; Percy, Iron and Steel, p. 183. Obtained by intensely heating pure alumina with pure highly carburetted iron in a close crucible. Close granular texture. **7.** Obtained by heating to whiteness 8 equivalents of chloride of aluminium, 48 of fine iron filings and 8 of lime: it was extremely hard and rusted when exposed to damp air, but could be forged and welded. Philosophical Magazine, X., p. 242, 1855; Percy, op. cit., p. 181. "Aluminium," Richards, p. 219.

A. ALUMINIUM AND WOOTZ.—As Faraday found from ·0128 to ·0695% of aluminium in wootz,[a] and as he obtained a product with "all the appreciable characters of wootz" by melting "good steel" with enough of an iron-aluminium alloy to yield by calculation, ·40% of aluminium,[b] he ascribed the damask of wootz to the presence of aluminium.[a] But the wootz-like character of his product was probably accidental, if not imaginary, for Henry, a most trustworthy analyst, Karsten and Rammelsberg find no aluminium in wootz.

The alloys of iron with a larger proportion of aluminium appear to be brittle, and hold out little promise.

B. MITIS CASTINGS.—Without special additions non-carburetted iron evolves gas so copiously in setting that its castings are very porous: its freezing point is so high that, even when cast at the highest temperature ordinarily attainable, it sets so rapidly that it can only be cast into rather thick forms: yet, if ·05 to ·1% of aluminium be added just before teeming, it yields solid castings of astonishingly attenuated shapes, and still retains its great ductility. So says P. Ostberg, and one most trustworthy metallurgist assures me that a slight addition of aluminium does check the escape of gas from non-carburetted iron, and another that it renders it extremely fluid.[c] Indeed, the remarkable castings which Ostberg has exhibited, and which he assures us have not been annealed, combine the ductility of the most carbonless iron with the thinness and solidity of the most carburetted and brittle castings. Such additions of aluminium, however, appear to render molten carburetted iron thicker rather than thinner.[c]

Note that we have two distinct effects, increased fluidity, and increased solidity and freedom from blowholes. These are not necessarily connected, or dependent on the same proximate cause.

What now is the rationale of these effects of aluminium? Ostberg states that the addition of ·05 to ·1% of aluminium lowers the melting point by say 300 to 500° F.: hence the thin castings. Further, that it is while being raised from its melting point to a temperature enough higher to permit casting that steel acquires the gases which it later evolves while setting, and that the addition of aluminium immediately after fusion, depressing the melting point, enables us to teem at once, and so nearly eliminates the opportunity for absorbing gases. Finally, aluminium renders the metal so fluid that it releases what gas it has, which, in his view, appears to be entangled as in a net. He speaks, however, with a degree of positiveness which neither his nor our present knowledge justifies, and which awakens suspicion.[d] I vainly request his evidence: without it such statements carry no weight.

Now (1) it is not shown that the melting point is actually lowered in the mitis process; (2) there is, moreover, reason to doubt that aluminium even tends to produce this specific effect of lowering the melting point; and (3) were it known to lower the melting point too little of it is present to plausibly explain a fall of the melting point sufficient to account for the startling effects produced. (4) Finally, a fall in the melting point is incompetent to explain all the phenomena. In brief, our aluminium is not shown to be qualitatively competent and is shown to be almost certainly quantitatively incompetent to explain the phenomena in this particular way. The following paragraphs evidence these statements seriatim.

1. A rise in the metal's temperature explains the phenomena quite as easily as a fall in its melting point.

2. I vainly seek in the writings of Deville, Faraday and Calvert and Johnson, who have all investigated the iron-aluminium alloys, any intimation that aluminium lowers the melting point of iron in this remarkable way, a point which these in two cases illustrious observers would hardly overlook. Moreover, as just stated, the addition of ferro-aluminium to molten carburetted steel appears to stiffen it, doubtless by diluting its heat.

3. On diligent inquiry among those best informed, I learn of no determination of aluminium in mitis castings,

[a] Quarterly Journal of Science, Literature and the Arts, 9, p. 320, 1820.

[b] Idem, 7, p. 288, 1819: Percy, Iron and Steel, p. 183. Metallurgical Review, I., p. 175.

[c] Trans. Am. Inst. Mining Engrs., XIV., p. 773, 1886. R. W. Davenport has personally conducted direct comparative tests under rigidly similar conditions, which leave no doubt as to this effect of aluminium. A large charge of unrecarburized, non-carburetted, wild, effervescing ingot iron, holding about 0·08% of carbon, was tapped from an open-hearth furnace simultaneously into two similar ladles, into each of which small red-hot lumps of ferromanganese were thrown at the same time, introducing 0·7 of manganese per 100 of steel, while one ladle also received 1 of ferro-aluminium, or sufficient to introduce ·064% of aluminium, ·024% of silicon and 0·01% of manganese. After a few minutes both lots were teemed into similar sand castings of a few hundred pounds weight each, and into common ingot molds. The aluminium-treated steel lay perfectly dead and "piped" in the ingot molds, and yielded a practically solid sand casting: the other rose in the molds and had to be stoppered, and yielded a very porous sand casting.

On another occasion he added 1% of ferro-aluminium, or enough to yield ·04 of aluminium and ·10 of silicon per 100 of metal, to both oxygenated rising metal obtained by melting wrought-iron alone in crucibles, and to crucible steel which, owing to the presence of carbon and manganese, evolved no important quantity of gas. This addition prevented the evolution of gas from the former, making it pipe when teemed, and appeared to thin it, or at least it poured easily; but it appeared to stiffen the latter and to make it hard to pour. In no case, however, has he been able to find aluminium in the castings themselves. (Private communication, Sept. 10th, 1887.)

[d] He states unreservedly that to gradually heat steel above its melting point as in "killing" is most injurious: that practically no gases are absorbed by solid steel, (though Parry has observed by direct measurement that gray cast-iron absorbed 14 times its own volume of hydrogen at bright redness and 22 times its volume at whiteness; the volume of gas being measured at the usual temperature Journ. Iron and St. Inst., 1874, I., p. 91): and that increasing the fluidity of molten iron causes it to evolve its gases. Here he asserts now what is probably false, now what is only conjecturable or at best probable. His further statement that, apparently in two or three years, the mitis inventors have had time to conduct the most exhaustive and elaborate experiments with every conceivable metal, metalloid and alloy, certainly does not indicate a careful weighing of words. The previous protracted labors of many a physicist and metallurgist, probably collectively representing scores of years, had been able to conquer exhaustively but a fraction of this ground. As Davenport finds that silicon gives at least approximately as good results as aluminium, some may infer that Ostberg regards silicon as in some sort inconceivable.

though several complete analyses by Riley are given;[a] here indeed the presence of aluminium might have been purposely suppressed. Competent chemists have vainly sought it in them; Davenport could find it in no instance; and I am credibly informed that Ostberg admits that it has never been detected. The effects described are produced even when only 0·06% of aluminium is added. Now the proportion of aluminium actually present in common steel often varies from 0 to 0·034%, without producing any noticeable effect: are we to believe that the further addition of another 0·03% is to so intensely affect the properties of the metal? It may indeed be questioned whether even this amount remains in the mitis casting: for aluminium, though difficult to oxidize at low temperatures, oxidizes readily at higher ones, and it may well be oxidized by the oxygen of the oxygenated metal which forms the basis of these castings.[b]

If it be present why does no one find it? The analytical methods are not perfected? Perhaps not for 0·001% of aluminium. But so eminent an analyst as A. A. Blair, who has given the subject special attention, informs[c] me that he considers it impossible that 0·03% of aluminium should escape detection when properly sought in iron or steel, and that the limit of error should not exceed a few thousandths of one per cent. Can we believe that enough aluminium remains to influence the physical properties appreciably? Must we not rather conclude that it is almost or quite wholly scorified? and if scorified, can we believe that the fact of its former brief presence can alter the melting point after its departure? The supposition appears to me very improbable.

4. A fall in the melting point, by increasing the fluidity, enables the gases present to escape? Then when, as in Davenport's experiment, already boiling metal receives ferro-aluminium, it should immediately boil the more tumultuously: actually it at once grows quiet. Hence the ferro-aluminium clearly acts by enabling the metal to retain in solution gas which otherwise would have continued to escape, and not by promoting its release. And this is a direct consequence of a lowered melting point? Or perhaps of the conjunction of some planets?

Davenport's Explanation[d] is that the aluminium attacks the oxygen present in the oxygenated metal, its combustion raising the temperature.[e] This is indeed qualitatively competent to explain why oxygenless carburetted steel is stiffened while oxygenated metal is thinned by ferro-aluminium; and as the addition of 0·06% of aluminium might remove 0·47% of ferrous oxide by such a reaction as

$$2Al + 6FeO = 3FeO, Al_2O_3 + 3Fe$$

and as the removal of this quantity of ferrous oxide might well check the evolution of gas, it may be regarded as quantitatively competent to explain the quieting effect.

But is the combustion of the small quantity of aluminium employed quantitatively competent to raise the temperature of the metal enough to account for its increased fluidity? Calculemus. Thomsen calculates that aluminium, in uniting with oxygen and water to form aluminium hydrate thus, Al_2, O_3, $3H_2O$, generates 388,920 calories, or about 7,097 calories per kilo of aluminium.[f] This may be more or less than the heat generated by the oxidation of aluminium to alumina: but assuming that it equals it, our 0·06% of aluminium would generate 425·8 calories per 100 kg of metal, which would raise the temperature by 27°, were we to assume its specific heat as 0·16, or say one eighteenth as much as it rises in the Bessemer process.

The heat which is thus evolved is on the one hand lessened by that absorbed by the simultaneous deoxidation of the iron, whose oxygen the aluminium seizes, and on the other increased by that evolved by the union of alumina with the residual ferrous oxide. Moreover, by stopping the escape of gas, the aluminium prevents a small quantity of heat from becoming latent through vaporization. Finally, the radiation of heat is somewhat slower from a quiescent than from a bubbling liquid, as they know who stir their soup. All things considered, it may not be unreasonable to claim that, directly and indirectly, our ·06% of aluminium may raise the temperature of our steel by from 25° to 30° C. (77° to 86° F.) which may be considered sufficient to account for the increase of fluidity, which was probably not great: for Davenport speaks of it very guardedly as "an apparent increase" only. A rise of 100° C. (180° F.), which would imply the combustion of only 0·22% of aluminium, might well account even for the extreme thinness of Ostberg's castings: and this quantity may easily have been added to them.

Now the attenuated castings testify that the ingot iron which composes them was unusually far above its freezing point when cast; either its freezing point was lowered (Ostberg's theory) or its temperature raised by the aluminium (Davenport's). The former theory is hardly tenable: the latter is made to account for all the phenomena by a series of assumptions which, while in no case preposterous, perhaps not even unreasonable, still by no means command acceptance. It seems to me improbable, though possible, that the oxidation of so small a quantity of aluminium would cause such a rise in temperature. I doubt if as much as 426 calories would be available for raising the temperature of the iron, and I think it probable that the specific heat of this iron at its melting point is considerably above that here taken. These are grave difficulties which Davenport's explanation has to contend with. It appears to me decidedly the less improbable of the two: but the true explanation may be yet unguessed.

C. Aluminium in Commercial Iron.—Though the direct reduction of alumina by the usual reducing agents, hydrogen and carbon, is extremely difficult, Faraday and Billings seem to have effected its reduction in presence of a great excess of iron by means of carbon. Hence the frequent presence of small quantities of aluminium in commercial cast iron is hardly surprising. Difficultly oxidized below redness, at higher temperatures it behaves like silicon: and, like silicon, a little of it may survive the oxi-

[a] Pamphlet of the United States Mitis Company, containing what purports to be a paper read by T. Nordenfelt before the British Iron and Steel Institute, May, 1886: yet strangely enough I have been unable to find in the journal of that society any reference to such a paper: the words "Mitis" and "Nordenfelt" are not even indexed in its journal for 1885 and 1886. Ostberg (loc. cit.) refers to this paper as "read before the British Iron and Steel Institute."

[b] According to Deville aluminium does not decompose metallic oxides at a red heat; an alloy of aluminium and copper yields cupric oxide when heated in a muffle; an alloy of lead and aluminium can be cupelled. But above redness aluminium takes the properties of silicon and reduces the oxides of copper and lead, yielding aluminates.

[c] Private communication, September 29th, 1887.

[d] Private communication, ante cit.

[e] Even initially clean wrought-iron might easily absorb enough oxygen from the furnace gases during melting to account for the oxidation of the aluminium.

[f] Thermochemische Untersuchungen, III., p. 239.

dizing processes of refining and be found in the resulting steel or wrought-iron. A. A. Blair has examined very many irons and steels for aluminium, which he reports "nearly always exists as such in steel," but he has never found more than a few thousandths of one per cent, say ·032%. He has been unable to connect its presence with any peculiarity in the properties of the metal, or with any particular mode of manufacture.[a]

Percy quotes and questions an analysis of cast-iron containing 0·97% of aluminium.[b] Part of the aluminium of cast-iron probably exists as alumina in slag. Karsten detected but traces of aluminium in iron and steel, and those rarely.[c] Alumina, which he added to cast-iron which was being refined in the charcoal hearth, was wholly slagged.[d]

§ 150. MERCURY does not amalgamate with iron directly, hot or cold, but, by immersing sodium amalgam in ferrous sulphate solution and probably by other indirect means, iron amalgams apparently of feeble stability may be formed.[e]

§ 151. Faraday and Stodart stated that "the metals which form the most valuable alloys with steel are silver, platina, rhodium, iridium and osmium, and palladium."[f] The scanty subsequent investigations into this group of alloys have not tended to confirm their statement. With to-day's knowledge of the influence of other elements on iron they would probably have interpreted their observations quite differently.

(A.) IRON AND PLATINUM appear to combine readily in all proportions, platinum melting even below the fusing point of steel when in contact with that metal. Their alloys are considered of no technical importance, Faraday and Stodart to the contrary notwithstanding. Melting Indian steel and 0·99% of platinum they obtained an alloy which, though not so hard as that obtained by melting the same steel with 0·2% of silver, was considerably tougher, and they prophesied its extensive use in spite of the cost of platinum.[g] Their prophecy is not yet fulfilled.

They obtained alloys of steel (A) with 50% of platinum, beautiful, with the finest imaginable color for a mirror, taking a high polish, non-tarnishing and malleable; (B) with 11% of platinum, taking a high polish, finely damasked, and free from rust after many months exposure.[h] They were probably in error in attributing the excellent qualities of platinum as of silver steel to the presence of the noble metal.

Billings found that platinum increased the hardness of steel less, but diminished its forgeableness more, than a like proportion of carbon did. A pure ingot iron with ·08% carbon and ·82% of platinum was extremely redshort and white-short: otherwise pure steel with 4% of platinum and nearly 2% of carbon was slightly redshort, and inferior in quality to steel of like composition less the platinum.[i]

B. PALLADIUM in steel in the ratio 1 : 100 produces according to Faraday and Stodart an alloy "truly valuable," especially for instruments demanding a perfectly smooth edge.[j]

RHODIUM, uniting with iron in all proportions, forms with steel alloys "perhaps the most valuable of all" according to Faraday and Stodart, remarkably hard, forgeable, and hardening without cracking. Steel with 50% of rhodium has when polished "the most exquisite beauty" and "the finest imaginable color" for mirrors, and long resists tarnishing.[j]

C. OSMIUM-IRIDIUM-iron alloys of the following compositions have been prepared.

3% osmium-iridium with pure iron; forgeable, long resists rusting, distinctly blue, hardens when quenched from redness, though no carbon could be detected in it. Faraday and Stodart.[k] Calculated composition.

2·98% osmium-iridium with Swedish iron containing not more than ·07% of carbon. Very homogeneous, not hardened by quenching; Boussingault.[l]

2·98% iridium replaced the osmium-iridium of the preceding alloy with like results; Boussingault.[l]

Note that osmium-iridium conferred the power of hardening on Faraday's alloy, but not on Boussingault's.

D. GOLD alloys with iron: of the value of its alloys with steel Faraday and Stodart were doubtful.

E. SILVER does not alloy with iron readily if at all. On exposing steel and 0·62% of silver foil to a white heat for three hours in a crucible filled with crushed glass, Faraday and Stodart found the silver fused and adhering to the steel, but none had combined. After many trials they found that steel would take up but 0·2% of silver: when more was present part was found as a metallic dew lining the interior of the crucible, and the fused button itself was a mere mechanical mixture of the two metals. But 0·2% of silver appeared to unite perfectly with the steel, yielding a product harder than either the best cast-steel or wootz, and with no disposition to crack in forging or hardening.[m] They thought that silver greatly benefited steel, but were probably completely deceived.

Of 0·5% of silver added by Billings to molten ingot metal only traces were found in the solidified ingot, while globules of silver were found above it.[n] Of 1·5% of silver added by Karsten to cast-iron in the charcoal refinery, but ·034% was retained by the bar iron, which was unsound, laminar and very redshort.[o]

IRON WITH THE METALS OF THE ALKALINE EARTHS.—It is very doubtful whether any class of iron made by ordinary methods can contain calcium, magnesium, barium or strontium as such: nor is it certain that any of these metals can be alloyed with iron even experimentally. The small quantities occasionally reported probably exist as oxide or silicate in the mechanically held slag. Gay Lussac and Thenard were unable to reduce calcium, barium or strontium from their oxides by heating with charcoal and iron: Berzelius failed to reduce calcium in this way, though he obtained "indications" of an alloy of iron and magnesium.[p]

---

a Private communication, May 10, 1887: Rept. of U. S. Board Test on Testing Metals, II., p. 590. Am. Jl. Science, XIII., p. 424, 1877; Thurston, Matls. of Engineering, II., p. 434.

b Percy, Iron and Steel, p. 542.

c Percy, Iron and Steel, p. 185.

d Corbin (Silliman's Journal, 2d Ser., XLVIII., p. 348, 1869), reports 2·38% aluminium with 1·66% chromium and ·98% carbon in chrome steel; but this is hardly credible. Blair finds no more aluminium in chrome than in other steels.

e Percy, op. cit. p. 174.

f Phil. Trans. Royal Society, 1822, p. 254.

g Idem, p. 257.

h Percy, Iron and Steel, p. 177. These are the calculated compositions.

i Trans. Am. Inst. Mining Engrs., V., p. 452, 1887.

j Percy, Iron and Steel, p. 180, from Phil. Trans., 1822, p. 256. Calculated composition.

k Percy, Iron and Steel, p. 181.

l Journ. Iron and Steel Inst., 1886, II., p. 812, from Ann. de Chimie et Phys., 5th Ser., XV.

m Phil. Trans. Royal Society, 1822, p. 255.

n Trans. Am. Inst. Mining Engineers, V., p. 454, 1877.

o Percy, Iron and Steel, p. 175.

p Percy, Iron and Steel, p. 196. A famous analysis of spiegeleisen by Fresenius

Hot iron absorbs vapor of magnesium, evolving it when heated in vacuo.[a]

POTASSIUM AND SODIUM, however, are reduced from their hydrates by iron at a white heat, and from their carbonates by carbon: hence their reduction in the blast-furnace and their retention by the metal through the refining processes is not impossible on a priori grounds, especially if the refining be accompanied by basic slags. By strongly heating iron-filings with bitartrate of potash, alloys containing 74·6 and 81·4% of iron and 25·4 and 18·58% of potassium respectively have been produced, which closely resemble wrought-iron, can be forged and welded, are so hard as to be barely filcable, and oxidize rapidly in air or water.[f] By long exposing iron turnings at a high temperature to vapor of potassium Gay-Lussac and Thenard obtained a flexible iron-potassium alloy, which was occasionally soft, sectile and even scratched with the nail.[g] These metals have, however, rarely been detected in iron, perhaps because rarely sought. Their influence on commercial iron is unknown, if indeed it exists.

CHAPTER IX.

IRON AND OXYGEN.

§ 155. THE OXIDES OF IRON.

A. SUBOXIDE.—Bell obtained strong indications of the existence of an oxide lower than ferrous oxide, perhaps of the composition Fe_2O.[b]

B. FERROUS OXIDE, FeO, though it may be isolated according to Debray by passing equal volumes of carbonic acid and oxide over red-hot ferric oxide, and though according to Liebig it may be obtained mixed with spongy iron by igniting ferrous oxalate in a closed vessel, yet absorbs oxygen with such avidity that it is not easily produced.[c] A powerful base, its silicates and phosphates are of great importance in the slags of iron metallurgy. Ferrous silicate is formed with evolution of oxygen by the action of silica on ferric oxide at high temperatures[d]: stable at moderately high temperatures, at extremely high ones it readily absorbs oxygen from the air.

C. FERRIC OXIDE, Fe_2O_3, frequently giving up its oxygen to organic matter even at ordinary temperatures, at higher ones becomes a strong oxidizing agent, being reduced to magnetic oxide with evolution of oxygen when heated alone to its very high melting point, and at apparently much lower temperatures when heated in contact with metallic iron. It is readily and completely reduced by hydrogen, by carbon and by ammonia: its reduction by carbonic oxide is probably never quite complete unless carbon intervenes, though the contrary is generally stated, for Bell found that both spongy iron and ferric oxide when heated at bright redness and cooled in this gas yielded a product containing from ·8 to 1% of the oxygen required to form ferric oxide.[e] Even large lumps of ferric oxide may be nearly if not quite completely reduced by contact with lump carbon, the carbonic oxide formed by the surface action doubtless penetrating, then carrying oxygen from the interior oxide outwards, being again reduced to carbonic oxide by the surrounding carbon, and so on. In the interior of lumps of ore which had been heated in lump charcoal, I have found particles of malleable spongy iron so placed that they had been apparently (though not certainly) completely surrounded by gangue, and so cut off from contact with outer iron which was being deoxidized.

Both at high and low temperatures ferric oxide, like alumina, at least occasionally acts as an acid. Percy completely melted mixtures of ferric oxide and lime, twice obtaining masses of interlacing acicular crystals containing 73·39% of ferric oxide and 24·5% of lime ($Fe_2O_3CaO = Fe_2CaO_4$), which may be regarded as magnetic oxide whose ferrous oxide is replaced by lime.[h] The neutral carbonates of potash and of soda are not decomposed by heat alone: but their carbonic acid is expelled when they are strongly heated with ferric oxide.[i] A compound of the formula $4CaO,\ Fe_2O_3 = Ca_4Fe_2O_7$ may be precipitated from certain solutions as a snow-white powder, though containing nearly 50% of ferric oxide.[j]

D. IRON RUST, consisting essentially of hydrated iron oxide, varies in composition with the conditions under which it forms. According to Mallet[k] it tends in proportion to the duration of reaction to approach the formula $2Fe_2O_3,\ 3H_2O$ (limonite), mixed with more or less (usually less) ferrous carbonate, $FeCO_3$, and when very old it appears to lose water and approach the composition of hematite, Fe_2O_3. When formed far beneath the surface of water it consists of black hydrated magnetic oxide.[l] Iron rust often contains minute quantities of ammonia.

E. FERROSO-FERRIC OXIDES.—Oxides of many and perhaps all compositions intermediate between ferrous and ferric oxide form: magnetic oxide $Fe_3O_4 = Fe_2O_3,\ FeO$, and probably scale oxide $Fe_8O_9 = 6FeO,\ Fe_2O_3$ are of definite composition: the others may be viewed as chemical compounds of ferrous and ferric oxide in continuously varying proportions.

These oxides are in general unstable, on slight provocation taking up oxygen or letting it go, and passing readily from a lower to a higher state of oxidation or vice versa: they thus act as carriers of oxygen, assisting oxidation in oxidizing operations and reduction in reducing ones. This is probably true of their silicates also.

THE MAGNETIC is in many respects the most stable oxide of iron. At ordinary temperatures it resists the action of

gave ·063 potassium, traces of sodium, ·045 magnesium, ·091 calcium and traces of lithium. (Kerl, Grundriss der Eisenhüttenkunde, p. 42.) Karsten found ·1774 calcium in wrought-iron, which was deficient in weldability and tenacity, though neither red- nor coldshort. (Percy, Iron and Steel, p. 197.) Kerl quotes seven cast-irons which contain from ·02 to ·46% of calcium and from ·00 to ·25% of magnesium. (Op. cit., pp. 27 to 43.) Percy quotes but doubts an analysis of cast-iron with ·07% aluminium, 1·37% calcium and 0·43% magnesium. (Iron and Steel, p. 542.) Concerning slag in cast-iron see foot-note to § 188.

[a] Compare § 145, A.

[b] Journ. Iron and St. Inst., I., 1871, p. 106.

[c] Watts, Dictionary of Chemistry, 1871, III., p. 393.

[d] Percy, Iron and Steel, p. 20.

[e] Jour. Iron and St. Inst., 1871, I., p. 113.

[f] Calvert and Johnson, Phil. Mag., 4th Series, X., p. 242, 1855.

[g] Percy, Iron and Steel, p. 190.

[h] Metallurgy, Fuel, New Edition, 1875, p. 78.

[i] Percy, Iron and Steel, p. 17.

[j] Idem, p. 19.

[k] Rept. British Ass., 1843, p. 11.

[l] Percy, Iron and Steel, p. 28.

the weather and of many reagents. A coating of this oxide, such as is produced in blueing, Barffing, etc., protects metallic iron from rusting, while ferric oxide on the one hand hastens the rusting of iron with which it is in contact, and ferrous oxide on the other itself rapidly absorbs oxygen. While at moderately high temperatures, as when ignited in air, magnetic oxide is converted into ferric oxide, at still higher ones it is spontaneously formed by the decomposition of ferric oxide by heat alone.

The facts that magnetic oxide is so comparatively stable: that ferrous oxide is so powerful a base: that in certain cases both at high and low temperatures ferric oxide acts as an acid, and in certain of them forms compounds similar to magnetic oxide, (*e. g.*, the compound Fe_2CaO_4 already described), and in others even isomorphous with it (*e. g.*, franklinite Fe_2ZnO_4 = ZnO, Fe_2O_3): that the sesquioxides analogous to ferric oxide, viz. alumina and chromic oxide, form with ferrous oxide compounds isomorphous with magnetic oxide, (ceylonite Al_2FeO_4 = FeO, Al_2O_3 and chrome iron ore Cr_2FeO_4 = FeO, Cr_2O_3), in the latter of which chromic oxide may reasonably be regarded as an acid: that ferric oxide and alumina often replace part of the chromic acid in this mineral: and that in other cases both alumina and chromic oxide act as acids, strongly suggest that in magnetic oxide we have a true salt, a ferrite, ferric oxide its rather mild acid, ferrous oxide its powerful base. This view harmonizes with the fact that, when magnetic oxide is attacked in a closed vessel by not more than enough hydrochloric acid to dissolve its ferrous oxide, the latter alone dissolves, hydrochloric acid appearing to displace ferric oxide much as it would carbonic acid.

F. Scale Oxide.—Fe_8O_9 = 6FeO, Fe_2O_3. Exposed to air or to furnace gases at a red or higher heat, iron acquires a coating intermediate in composition between ferrous and ferric oxides, often divisible into two or three layers more or less arbitrarily chosen: the outer is always the most highly oxidized, the inner though probably of indefinite composition sometimes approximates the formula Fe_8O_9. The following percentages of ferric oxide in iron scale have been published, chiefly by Percy:[a] The heavy faced figures represent the compositions Fe_8O_9 and Fe_3O_4.

Table 40.—Percentage of Ferric Oxide in Iron Scale.

26·19 inner layer.	36·80*	47·67 middle layer.	89·27 velvet scale.
27·04 Fe_8O_9	37·49 all layers.	59·41 " "	98·63 outer layer.
27·98 inner layer.	40·51 middle layer.	59·60 " "	95·80 " "
35·77 outer "	48·77 inner "	**68·97** Fe_3O_4	99·63 " "

* G. W. Maynard, Trans. Am. Inst. Mining Engrs., X., p. 281, 1882.

G. Ferric Acid, FeO_3, though never isolated, may be supposed to exist in the ferrates of the alkalies and of baryta, which form in the dry and the wet way. It is conceivable that similar salts may form in metallurgical operations.

§ 156. Oxygen in Commercial Iron.—Even when cold iron can probably retain but a fraction of one per cent of hydrogen or of carbonic oxide, which are readily expelled and which modify it comparatively little.

Of nitrogen it can permanently hold more than 11%, which alters its properties more profoundly: sometimes readily evolving at least a portion of it, *e. g.* on boring, at others it retains it far more tenaciously, but it always releases it at a white heat completely or nearly completely. In ferric acid iron may be conceived to unite with over 46% of oxygen, of which it retains 27·6% at the highest temperatures, which completely obliterates its metallic nature. Though the properties of iron are thus more deeply affected by oxygen and nitrogen than by hydrogen and carbonic oxide, yet it is by a much larger percentage of the former two, and it is not clear that, weight for weight they affect it more than the latter two: indeed in this respect the glass-hardness produced by ·26% of hydrogen (No. 29, Table 56, § 170) probably outweighs in intensity the effect of the same proportion of any other element.

The ratio of the chemical to the physical force concerned in the retention of these substances appears to be lowest in case of hydrogen and carbonic oxide and comparatively high in case of at least that part of the nitrogen which forms the white brittle nitride: while the union of iron with oxygen is typically chemical. Hence it is not to be expected that oxygen would be given off, nor is it as the three other gases are when metallic iron is heated in vacuo, or when it solidifies in casting: and I find it in but two of the many recorded analyses of gases obtained on boring, (No. 13, porous steel, and No. 34, from a blister in puddled iron, in Table 54, § 171). The following table gives the proportion of oxygen found in commercial and unrecarburized iron, etc. Further details of the composition of certain of these irons are given in Table 43.

§ 157. Effect of Oxygen.—At the end of the Bessemer process the metal usually absorbs a certain proportion of oxygen, which renders it unforgeable, and which is removed by addition of carbon, manganese, etc., though under certain conditions unrecarburized Bessemer metal is so free from oxygen as to be forgeable. It is stated that more than ·1% of oxygen appreciably affects forgeableness, but that in smaller proportion it is often harmless: I do not, however, think that we have evidence sufficient to warrant precise statements. That a small quantity of oxygen does not necessarily cause redshortness is shown by the fact that steel No. 5, Tables 42 and 70 A, after receiving 2% of ferromanganese was non-redshort, though it still retained some ·025% of oxygen, as calculated from the data of the spiegel reaction which occurred when it was further recarburized with spiegeleisen, and which was accompanied by flame and rather active boiling.[b]

When carelessly heated ingot and weld iron may absorb oxygen, of which Tucker finds ·063% in burnt steel: but "burning," while often accompanied by absorption of oxygen, apparently consists essentially in structural change due to overheating, which may be almost completely effaced by purely physical means (cautious heating and forging). The oxygen which causes redshortness in unrecarburized and in burnt steel is not to be confounded with the comparatively inert oxygen of the slag mechanically held in weld iron (·5% of oxygen is thus reported, No. 13, Table 41).

§ 158. Oxygen in Molten Iron.—Molten iron like molten copper can retain a small quantity of oxygen, which has been assumed to exist as magnetic oxide, though in the presence of so vast an excess of metallic iron ferrous oxide would be more naturally expected. Indeed, part or all of the oxygen may, like hydrogen or carbon, be united with the whole of the metal. The quantity of oxygen which molten

[a] Iron and Steel, pp. 21 et seq.

[b] Müller, Stahl und Eisen, IV., p. 72, 1884.

TABLE 41.—OXYGEN IN COMMERCIAL IRON AND UNRECARBURIZED STEEL.

No.	Observer.	Mode of determination.	Description of metal.	Oxygen. %	Oxygen. Volumes per vol. metal.
1..	Ledebur..	Ignition in hydrogen	Unrecarburized basic Bessemer metal not fully dephosphorized..	·068	3·91
2..	"	" " "	Do. do., fully dephosphorized. ..	·111@·126	6·38@7·24
3..	Bender...	" " "	Unrecarburized fully decarburized acid Bessemer metal........	·34	19·55
4..	" ...	Spiegel-reaction method.	The same sample as No. 3......	·398 (·958)	....
5..	King. ...	Spiegel-reaction method........	Unrecarburized fully decarburized acid Bessemer metal.....	·438± (0·79±)	....
6.	Müller...	Spiegel-reaction method.....	Do do	·086 (·394)	....
7..	" ...	Do. do., slag not present	Unrecarburized basic Bessemer metal fully dephosphorized...	·03@·25 (·09@·28)	....
8	" ...	Do. do. slag present	Do. do	0·38 (1·76@1·79)	....
9..	Tucker...	Fusion with charcoal	Unrecarburized oxygenated basic (?) Bessemer metal	·68@1·74	39·@100·
10..	Ledebur..	Not stated	Unrecarburized basic Bessemer metal dephosphorized	·171@·244	9·88@14.
11..	Tucker..	Fusion with charcoal	Burnt steel	·063	3·62
12..	Percy .	Ignition in hydrogen	Oxygenated iron.	·017	1·00
13..	Ledebur..	" " "	Wrought-iron................	·507@·524	29·15@30·18
14..	" ..	" " "	Commercial steel	·032	1·84
15..	Kern....	" " "	" "	·025@·037	1·44@2·13
15·5	Parry	Not stated	Bessemer "	·18@·557	....
16	Ledebur..	Ignition in hydrogen.	Cast-iron...................	0	0
17..	" ..	....	Burnt weld iron....	·177	....
18.	Parry	Not stated.........	Overblown burnt steel	2·04 ?	....

1 and **2**. 15 grammes of the metal previously dried in nitrogen at 200° C, are heated to redness in a current of hydrogen for 45 minutes: the water formed is collected by phosphoric anhydride and weighed. (Stahl und Eisen, *II.*, p. 198, 1882: *Journ. Iron and St. Inst.*, 1882, *I.*, p. 388.)

3 and **4.** Unrecarburized Bessemer metal is heated in hydrogen, and the water thus formed is caught in chloride of calcium. This is checked by the loss of weight which the iron simultaneously undergoes, ·383% after allowing for loss of sulphur. It is further checked by the loss of manganese, carbon and silicon occurring on recarburizing, which represents the action of ·398±% of oxygen, of which a portion may have been furnished by the atmosphere or by the slag. See No. 10 in Tables 42, 43, 70 A. (Dingler's Polyt. Journal, CCV., p. 531, 1872; from Berg- und Hütt. Zeit., 1872, No. 31.)

5. In calculating these results I have been obliged to assume the composition of the ferro-manganese employed: but, as it amounted to only ·22% of the product, the error thus introduced is unimportant. Trans. Am. Inst. Mining Engineers, IX., p. 238, 1881. See No. 11 in Tables 42, 43, 70 A.

6. (Zeit. Vereins Deutscher Ing., XXII., p. 385.) See No. 9 in Tables 42, 43, 70 A. The metal was recarburized in the usual way.

7. To prevent the action of the slag and to lessen that of the atmospheric oxygen, the metal was completely separated from the slag and recarburized in common ingot moulds. See Nos. 1 to 4, Tables 42, 43, 70 A. (Stahl und Eisen, IV., pp. 72-3, 1884.)

8. The after-blown metal was recarburized in the converter with 2% of ferro-manganese, and then transferred to common ingot moulds, separated from slag and further recarburized. I have been obliged to assume that the ferro-manganese contained the same proportion of manganese as in other experiments of Müller, viz.: 70%. See Nos. 5 and 6, Tables 43, 42, 70 A. (Stahl und Eisen, IV., pp. 72-3, 1884.)

9. The metal is melted in a crucible brasqued with pure charcoal, and the oxygen inferred from the loss of weight, after allowing for the change in the percentage of carbon. (Journ. Iron and Steel Inst., 1881, p. 205.)

10. 3 specimens of after-blown basic Bessemer metal taken from the converter held ·244, 187 and ·171% of oxygen. See Nos. A B C in Table 43. (Handbuch der Eisenhüttenkunde, I., p. 276).

11. Same conditions as No. 9.

12. Oxygenated iron was prepared by melting in a clay crucible pure ferric oxide mixed with a quantity of lamp-black theoretically sufficient to reduce 82.2% of it. 150 grains of the resulting very soft file-clogging product were ignited in hydrogen during 30 minutes, and the resulting water caught and weighed. (Percy, Iron and Steel, p. 15.)

13, 14. Same conditions as No. 1.

15. About 100 grammes of steel in lumps of 10 to 15 grammes each, were ignited in dry nitrogen for an hour, the oxygen evolved being caught in pyrogallic acid and weighed. 5 specimens yielded ·034 ·037, ·025, ·040 and ·031% of oxygen. (Chemical News, XXXVI., p. 20, 1877.)

15·5. It is not definitely stated whether these represent unrecarburized or recarburized commercial steel. If, as is strongly suggested by the context, they refer to the latter, they must be taken very guardedly, especially as Parry does not describe his method of determining oxygen. (Journ. Iron and St. Inst., 1881, I., p. 190.)

16. Conditions and reference the same as for number 1.

17. Jahrbuch Berg- und Huttenwesen Königr. Sachsen, 1858, p. 21; Handbuch der Eisenhüttenkunde, p. 276. See No. E, Table 43.

18. "Overblown burnt steel gave 7·4% iron oxide." As Parry evidently regards the oxide present as magnetic oxide, this implies 2·04% of oxygen. Overblown steel is one thing: burnt steel quite another: "overblown burnt" steel literally means steel which had been overblown, and later had been burnt: I think however that Parry here refers to simply overblown metal. Journ. Iron and St. Inst., 1881, I., p. 190.

The numbers in parentheses are calculated on the assumption that manganese reacts thus: $Mn + O = MnO$. The corresponding unenclosed numbers are calculated on the assumption that it reacts thus: $Mn + Fe_3O_4 = 3FeO + MnO$. In both cases the silicon is assumed to react thus;— $Si + 3FeO = 2Fe + FeSiO_3$.

iron can retain when, as in the "after blow"[b] of the basic Bessemer process, it has an opportunity to saturate itself, is a question of practical importance. Very different proportions are found by the same analytical method in different specimens of after-blown steel; the proportions found by different methods in different specimens differ still more widely, from ·034 indicated by Müller's data and ·111% found by Ledebur, to 1·74% found by Tucker. "Overblown burnt steel," whatever that may be, gave Parry 7·4% of iron oxide, apparently magnetic, which would imply 2·04% of oxygen.[a] His method of determination is not stated. Sources of error inherent in these methods can apparently account for so small a part of these differences that we may reasonably conclude not that our methods are defective (indeed in cases 3 and 4, Table 41, dissimilar methods applied to the same sample give harmonious results), but that the proportion of oxygen even in after-blown[b] steel varies within wide limits. We know not whether this is because even in after-blowing the metal saturates itself but slowly with oxygen, or because the power of retaining oxygen varies with the temperature and other variables.

DISCUSSION OF ANALYTICAL METHODS AND RESULTS.[c]—In the SPIEGEL-REACTION METHOD we deduce the proportion of oxygen in the blown metal from the quantity of manganese, carbon and silicon which are oxidized when a recarburizer is added to it. In seven spiegel reactions described by Müller and in two which I have calculated from data of Bender and King, from ·034 to ·782% of oxygen react, if we assume that the manganese acts thus;

$$\text{hypothesis A; } Mn + FeO = Fe + MnO:$$

and from ·089 to 1·78% if we assume that it acts thus;

$$\text{hypothesis B; } Mn + Fe_3O_4 = 3FeO + MnO.$$

The apparent percentage of oxygen found by this method is liable to be exaggerated by the oxidizing action of the slag and of the atmosphere, and to be depressed by the mechanical retention of silica and of oxide of manganese by the solidified metal, for these substances would be mistaken in analysis for unoxidized silicon and manganese. When the former source of error is eliminated by completely removing the slag and recarburizing in ingot moulds, Müller's data in three cases imply from ·034 to ·254% of oxygen on hypothesis A, and from ·089 to ·281% on hypothesis B: when it is not eliminated I find from ·086 to ·782% of oxygen on hypothesis A, and from ·394 to 1·78% on hypothesis B. Table 42 summarizes these calculations.

Müller's reaction 9 on hypothesis A gives but ·086 and on hypothesis B but ·394% of oxygen: here the oxidizing action of the slag had full play: these numbers exceed those in which it was eliminated (Müller's reactions 1, 2 and 4) by so little that we may infer that its influence may be slight, at least in the acid Bessemer process.

Let us now consider the influence of the second of the above sources of error. The quantity of silica and of oxide of manganese which forgeable steel can retain is probably small. In Müller's reaction 1 only ·042% of silicon is present in blown metal plus recarburizer, so that the depressing effect of silica may here be neglected. If the recarburized steel retained even as much as 1% of oxide of manganese this would depress the apparent oxygen by only 0·22%: so that we may safely conclude that this specimen of blown steel had not much more than ·14 + ·22 = ·36% of oxygen.

Were the recarburized steel to retain a portion of its oxygen unacted on by the recarburizer, this would constitute a third source of error, depressing the apparent below the true percentage of oxygen. But in the cases here presented error from this source is probably not serious, as each steel retains after recarburizing from ·48 to 1·60% of silicon, manganese and carbon collectively, with which a large quantity of oxygen could hardly coexist.

It is as yet uncertain whether in the spiegel-reaction

a No. 18, Table 41.

b In the basic Bessemer process as usually conducted, after the nearly complete removal of the carbon, silicon and manganese, much phosphorus still remains: by continuing the operation this in turn is oxidized, and this portion of the process is termed the "after-blow."

c The methods here discussed are briefly described in the note to Table 41.

TABLE 42.—OXYGEN IN OXYGENATED BESSEMER METAL, AS INFERRED FROM THE SPIEGEL REACTION.

[Hypothesis A; the reactions are assumed to be $Mn + O = MnO$; $Si + 3FeO = 2Fe + FeSiO_3$; $C + O = CO$.
" B; " " " $Mn + Fe_3O_4 = 3FeO + MnO$; $Si + 3FeO = 2Fe + FeSiO_3$; $C + O = CO$.]

These cases are numbered to correspond to those in Table 70A and 43.

	1.			2.			4.			5.			6.		
Observer	Müller.			Müller.			Müller.			Müller.			Müller.		
	Mn C and Si removed by reaction.	O corresponding By hypothesis A.	O corresponding By hypothesis B.	Mn C and Si removed by reaction.	O corresponding By hypothesis A.	O corresponding By hypothesis B.	Mn C and Si removed by reaction.	O corresponding By hypothesis A.	O corresponding By hypothesis B.	Mn C and Si removed by reaction.	O corresponding By hypothesis A.	O corresponding By hypothesis B.	Mn C and Si removed by reaction.	O corresponding By hypothesis A.	O corresponding By hypothesis B.
Manganese removed	·007	·002	·008	·331	·009	·036	·064	·019	·074	1·89	·40	1·61	1·88	0·40	1·58
Carbon	·059	·073	·073	·030	·040	·040	·020	·027	·027	·12	·16	·16	·10	·13	·13
Sum		·075	·081		·049	·076		·046	·101		·56	1·77		·53	1·71
Silicon removed	·025	·043	·043	·120	·205	·205	·007	—·012	—·012	·01	·02	·02	·03	·05	·05
Total oxygen implied		·118	·124		·254	·281		·034	·089		·58	1·79		·58	1·76

	7.			9.			10.			11.		
Observer	Müller.			Müller.			Bender.			King.		
	Mn C and Si removed by reaction.	O corresponding By hypothesis A.	O corresponding By hypothesis B.	Mn C and Si removed by reaction.	O corresponding By hypothesis A.	O corresponding By hypothesis B.	Mn C and Si removed by reaction.	O corresponding By hypothesis A.	O corresponding By hypothesis B.	Mn C and Si removed by reaction.	O corresponding By hypothesis A.	O corresponding By hypothesis B.
Manganese removed	·289	·113	·451	·354	·103	·411	·620@·67	·188	·748	·95	·27	1·10
Carbon	·027	·036	·036	·081	·108	·108	·19±	·253	·253	·17	·22	·22
Sum		·149	·487		·211	·519		·441	1·001		·49	1·32
Silicon removed	·373	·633	·633	—·073	—·125	—·125	—·025±	—·043	—·043	·05	·09	·09
Total oxygen implied		·782	1·120		·086	·394		·398	·958		·58	1·40

1, 2 and **4**, oxygenated basic Bessemer metal, recarburized in iron moulds to avoid the action of the slag. 1 was recarburized with spiegeleisen, 2 with ferro silicon, 4 with ferro-silico-manganese. **5** and **6**, oxygenated basic Bessemer metal is first recarburized with 2% of ferro-manganese in the converter, and then more fully recarburized in iron moulds, to avoid the action of the slag, No. 5 receiving spiegeleisen, No. 6 ferro-silicon. Assuming that the ferro-manganese holds 70% of manganese and 6% of carbon, we find that the following quantities of carbon, silicon and manganese were removed on the addition of the first and second recarburizers respectively.

	Number 5. C%	Si%	Mn%	Number 6. C%	Si%	Mn%
On adding ferro-manganese there is removed	·1 ±		1·4 ±	·1 ±		1·4 ±
On adding the second recarburizer there is removed	·019	·011	—·011	·002	·062	—·036
Total, approximately	·119	·011	1·389	·102	·062	1·364

7, oxygenated basic Bessemer metal is recarburized with ferro-silicon and ferro-manganese in the ladle, to diminish the action of the slag. **9, 10,** and **11**, acid Bessemer metal is recarburized, probably in the usual way with spiegeleisen added in the converter.

manganese acts in accordance with hypothesis A or B or with some third formula, or sometimes according to one sometimes according to another. Hypothesis A gains color from the fact that the results obtained by Bender with the hydrogen method accord with it: to hold hypothesis B we must assume that Bender by the hydrogen method found only about one-third of the oxygen present. This however is rather slender foundation for hypothesis A, and neither hypothesis is excluded by the other results recorded in Table 41.[a] We are also in doubt as to the formula in accordance with which silicon is oxidized, though we probably err little in assuming that it is

$$3FeO + Si = 2\,Fe + FeSiO_3.$$

Till these formulæ are known the spiegel-reaction method can only give us a rough notion of the percentage of oxygen present when the quantity of manganese reacting is large: but when, as in Nos. 1, 2 and 4, very little manganese reacts, its results should not be far wrong. It is difficult to believe that in these cases anything approaching the 1·74% of oxygen found by Tucker can have been present.

HYDROGEN METHOD.—It may be held that in the 30 to 60 minutes usually employed hydrogen is not likely to completely remove oxygen from the interior of the particles of even fine iron filings: we are led to hope that this source of error need not be serious by the fact that the hydrogen method gave Bender (Nos. 3 and 4, Table 41) almost the same result as the spiegel-reaction method: but these two methods here support each other but feebly. In view of the small percentage of oxygen found by the latter method in Müller's reactions 1 and 4, which cannot be far wrong, serious suspicion of Ledebur's hydrogen-method results (No. 2, Table 41), low as they are, is hardly justified.

TUCKER'S METHOD.—The proportion of oxygen found by this method in afterblown steel, 1·8 to 1·74%, is much higher than those which I have met obtained by the hydrogen method, or by the spiegel reaction method if interpreted by hypothesis A: but the latter method on hypothesis B finds, in Müller's reactions 5 and 6, 1·79 and 1·76% of oxygen.

Of the three sources of error which suggest themselves in connection with Tucker's method none is likely to have had serious influence. 1. Its results might possibly be slightly depressed by absorption of gases from the atmosphere: but they are so high that suspicion of having been depressed does not arise. 2. They might be exaggerated by the expulsion from the molten metal of hydrogen, nitrogen, carbonic oxide and sulphur initially present along with the oxygen: but the proportion of sulphur in afterblown basic steel is small, and the largest recorded proportions of the three other substances which I have met in commercial irons, say ·01, ·06 and ·05% respectively, would collectively affect Tucker's high results but slightly, would explain but a fraction of the difference between his and Ledebur's. 3. They might possibly be exaggerated by the removal of manganese, silicon, etc.: but these elements are almost completely absent from afterblown steel. Further, the facts that when applied to steel reasonably believed to be approximately free from oxygen it indicated the presence of but ·02% of that element; that, applied to steel mixed with a known weight of oxide, its results "left nothing to be desired"; and that they are harmonious, ·064, ·062 and ·066% of oxygen in a sample of burnt steel, and 1·71, 1·74 and 1·69% in one of blown metal, furnish positive evidence of good character. Hence I infer that the steels treated by Tucker probably contained an unusual proportion of oxygen: it is hardly conceivable that the steel in which he found from 1·69 to 1·74% of oxygen should actually have held anything like as little as those in which the spiegel-reaction method finds at most ·080 and ·124%, and those in which the hydrogen method finds but ·11@·12%, making all possible allowances and supposing that all the possible errors combined to swell the apparent percentage in one case and to depress it in the others.

TO SUM UP, while none of these methods inspires abso-

[a] This question could easily be settled by recarburizing different portions of the same afterblown metal (1) with pure carburetted iron, (2) with very rich ferro-manganese and (3) with very rich ferro-silicon.

lute trust, we yet have strong reasons for believing that the results of Tucker's method closely approximate the truth, and no serious reason for believing that those of the hydrogen method, or of the spiegel-reaction method when but little manganese and silicon react, are far wrong. But, when much manganese enters into the reaction, the uncertainty as to whether hypothesis A or B be correct leaves the latter method no pretence to accuracy.

§ 159. OXYGEN WITH CARBON.—Though carbon silicon and manganese remove oxygen from molten steel, a small proportion of these elements and of oxygen may coexist: it is stated that ·1 to ·2% of carbon and as much manganese can exist with some hundredths of one per cent of oxygen, while the coexistence of very considerable quantities of oxygen and a little carbon is illustrated by Table 43. Müller describes thoroughly blown steel which contained ·605% of silicon: that it simultaneously contained oxygen is inferred from the violent development of carbonic oxide on subsequently adding spiegeleisen to it.[a]

[a] Iron, 1883, p. 18.

TABLE 43.—OXYGEN WITH CARBON, ETC., IN IRON.
(This table is numbered to correspond with Tables 70 A and 42.)

Number.	Description.	Mode of determining oxygen.	Composition. O.	C.	Si.	Mn.	P.	S.	Cu.	Ni. and Co.
A..	Afterblown basic metal......	....	·244	·037	·001	0	·098	·059	·046	·061
B..	" " " Ledebur.	....	·187	·123	0	tr	·077	·081	·065	·149
C..	" " "	....	·171	·050	0	0	·083	·057	·061	·110
1..	" " " Müller...	Spiegel-reaction.	·179a	·039	·016	·158	....	....	....	....
2..	" " " "	" "	·254a	·038	·008	·189	....	....	....	....
4	" " " "	" "	·084a	·037	·021	·212	....	....	....	....
7..	" " " "	" "	·182a	·062	·002	·053	·078	....	....	....
9..	Decarburized acid Bessemer metal; Müller	" "	·066a	·046	·122	·248	....	....	....	....
10..	Decarburized acid Bessemer metal; Bender	" "	·098a	·08	....	....	....	....	....	....
11..	Decarburized acid Bessemer metal; King..........	" "	·438a	·004	·040	·16	....	....	....	....
D..	Partly recarburized basic Bessemer metal; Müller..........	" "	·041	·039	·014	·858	....	....	....	....
E..	Weld metal; Ledebur..........	....	·177	·052	0	0	·223	tr	·430	·157

a Calculated on hypothesis A; on hypothesis B the percentage of oxygen is larger. See heading to Table 42.

A, B, C, Handbuch der Eisenhüttenkunde, p. 276. Nos. 1 to 11, see corresponding numbers in Table 70 A. D, Stahl und Eisen, IV., p. 73, 1884.

§ 160. CORROSION OF IRON.—The readiness with which iron oxidizes, familiar to all through its exasperating proneness to rust, deemed a token and penalty for the blood it

TABLE 44.—LOSS OF IRON BY CORROSION, IN POUNDS PER SQUARE FOOT OF SURFACE PER ANNUM.

Number.	Observer.	Metal.	Exposed to weather.	Immersed in cold pure sea water. Unconfined.	Immersed in cold pure sea water. Confined.	Immersed in cold foul sea water. Sewage-bearing.	Immersed in cold foul sea water. Bilge water.	Immersed in hot sea water. P. and O. steamer.	Immersed in hot sea water. Boiler with zinc.	Immersed in hot sea water. Boiler impure water.	Immersed in hot sea water. Pure sea water at 46° C., 115° F.	Immersed in fresh water. Pure river.	Immersed in fresh water. Foul river.	Immersed in cold sea water in voltaic contact with Bright wrought-iron.	Immersed in cold sea water in voltaic contact with Scale-bearing iron.	Immersed in cold sea water in voltaic contact with Copper.	Immersed in cold sea water in voltaic contact with Bronze.	In acidulated water.
1..	Mallet.	Green sand,	·059	·069	....	·078	....	....	....	....	·068	·01	·028	....	....	·22	·35	....
2..	"	Chilled, Cast-iron	·08	·073	....	·064	....	....	....	....	·117	·01	·029	....	....	....	....	....
3..	"	Planed,	·098	·098	....	·258	....	....	....	....	·270	·012	·080	....	....	....	....	....
4.	"	Painted.	·015	·082	....	·188	....	....	....	....	·848	·010	·066	....	....	....	....	....
5.	"	Standard,	·081	·089	....	·128	....	....	....	....	·277	·021	·067	....	....	·44	·58	....
6..	"	Aver. of 17, Wrought-iron.	·138	·121	....	·215	....	....	....	....	....	·018	·158	....	....	....	....	....
7..	"	Zinced.	0	·089	....	·088	....	....	....	....	....	·005	·041	....	....	....	....	....
8..	"	Steel, average of 7..........	·117	·107	....	·214	....	....	....	....	....	·013	·128	....	....	....	....	....
11..	Andrews.	Cast-iron..........	....	....	·065	....	....	....	....	....	....	....	....	·086	·064	·129	....	....
12..	"	"	....	....	·024	....	....	....	....	....	....	....	....	·080	....	....	....	....
13..	"	Wrought-iron	....	....	·023	....	....	....	....	....	....	....	....	....	·053	·118	....	....
14..	"	" "	....	....	·019	....	....	....	....	....	....	....	....	....	....	....	....	....
15..	"	Bessemer,	....	....	·022	....	....	....	....	....	....	....	....	·065	·059	·108	....	....
16..	"	Open-hearth, Soft steel....	....	....	·021	....	....	....	....	....	....	....	....	·098	·073	·074	....	....
17..	"	Crucible.	....	....	·031	....	....	....	....	....	....	....	....	·088	·081	·109	....	....
18..	"	Bessemer,	....	....	·027	....	....	....	....	....	....	....	....	·098	·060	·111	....	....
19..	"	Open-hearth, Hard steel....	....	....	·024	....	....	....	....	....	....	....	....	·081	·076	·117	....	....
20..	"	Crucible.	....	....	·025	....	....	....	....	....	....	....	....	....	....	....	....	....
23..	Parker.	Landore,	·206	·208	....	....	·480	·294	·120	·666	....	....	....	....	....	....	....	....
24..	"	Brown, Soft steel.	·254	·215	....	....	·560	·310	·147	·765	....	....	....	....	....	....	....	....
27..	"	Bolton,	·214	·195	....	....	·544	·260	·117	·785	....	....	....	....	....	....	....	....
28..	"	Steel Co. of Scotland.	·222	·207	....	....	·509	·258	·182	·729	....	....	....	....	....	....	....	....
29..	"	Taylor,	·169	·168	....	....	·475	164	·061	·609	....	....	....	....	....	....	....	....
30..	"	Leeds.	·155	·198	....	....	·527	·191	·068	·657	....	....	....	....	....	....	....	....
31..	"	Bowling, Wrought-iron....	·156	·225	....	....	·518	·193	·062	·698	....	....	....	....	....	....	....	....
32..	"	Farnley,	·167	·178	....	....	·573	·217	·069	·705	....	....	....	....	....	....	....	....
33	"	Lowmoor,	·166	·212	....	....	·589	·209	·087	607	....	....	....	....	....	....	....	....
34..	Gruner.	Grey,	28@·87	1·45	....	....	....	....	....	....	....	....	....	....	....	....	....	10·81
35..	"	" Cast-iron....	"	2·07	....	....	....	....	....	....	....	....	....	....	....	....	....	11·12
36	"	Spiegeleisen,	"	2·90	....	....	....	....	....	....	....	....	....	....	....	....	....	1·37
37..	"	Charcoal.	"	....	....	....	....	....	....	....	....	....	....	....	....	....	....	1
38..	"	Soft steel..........	·56@·75	·41@·83	....	....	....	....	....	....	....	....	....	....	....	....	....	·12@·50
39..	"	" "			....	....	....	....	....	....	....	....	....	....	....	....	....	1@1·27
40..	"	Manganese steel annealed...			....	....	....	....	....	....	....	....	....	....	....	....	....	2
41..	"	" " hardened.			....	....	....	....	....	....	....	....	....	....	....	....	....	5·12
42..	Farquharson.	Wrought-iron..........	....	·118	....	....	....	....	....	....	....	....	....	·22	....	....	....	....
43..	"	Soft steel	....	·126	....	....	....	....	....	....	....	....	....	·046	....	....	....	....
44..	Thwaite's averages.	Wrought-iron..........	·188	·121	....	·215	....	....	....	....	....	....	....	....	....	....	....	....
45..	"	Steel, miscellaneous..........	·157	·107	....	·214	....	....	....	....	....	....	....	....	....	....	....	....
46..	"	Cast-iron	·064	·070	....	·072	....	....	....	....	....	....	....	....	....	....	....	....
47..	"	" galvanized..........	·022	·089	....	·088	....	....	....	....	....	....	....	....	....	....	....	....

1 to **8**. Five apparently exactly similar sets of specimens, each consisting of 11 pieces of green-sand castings, 5 × 5 × 1, apparently retaining their skin, 6 of them unprotected (No. 1), 5 of them painted or varnished (No. 4); 5 specimens of unprotected chilled cast-iron 5 × 5 × 1, four of them differing from four of the preceding only in being chilled (No. 2); 1 of unprotected gray cast-iron (No. 3) with its skin removed by planing; and 1 of unprotected wrought-iron (No. 5) about 5 × 3 × 0·875. These were exposed as follows. (1) In clear sea water at 46° to 58° F. for 732 days: (2) In foul sea water, close to the mouth of the Great Kingston main sewer at 46° to 58° F. for 732 days. (3) In pure sea water at 115° F., for 117 days: (4) In clear unpolluted water of the River Liffey, at 53° to 68° F. for 732 days: (5) In foul river water with much organic matter, in the same river at Dublin, the bottom soft putrid mud, temperature 56° to 61° F., for 732 days: (6) To the weather on the summit of an exposed building in Dublin, for 539 days. In addition these were simultaneously exposed to condition (1) 64 pieces of unprotected green-sand cast-iron, apparently retaining their skin, and mostly either 5″ × 5″ × 1″ or 5″ × 5″ × 0.25″ (No. 1); and to all the conditions except (3) apparently exactly similar sets each consisting of 17 pieces of wrought-iron of various kinds (No. 6), 7 of steel (No. 8) (blister, shear, spring, etc., apparently all of high-carbon steel) and one of galvanized wrought-iron (No. 7), all except the last apparently unprotected. Moreover, bars of the "standard" wrought-iron (No. 5) were immersed in cold sea water in contact with copper, zinc, and various brasses and bronzes (*i. e.* copper-zinc and copper-tin alloys). [Tables III. and VII., pp. 286, 299, Rept. British Assn., 1840; Tables I. to XIII. inclusive, pp. 30 to 51. Idem, 1843.]

11 to **20**. Thomas Andrews, Proc. Inst. Civ. Engrs., LXXXII., p. 281, 1885. In these experiments the metal was immersed in confined cold sea water in glass or wooden vessels, the sea water being generally changed every month and the loss by evaporation being frequently made good by addition of distilled water. In every case the rusting proceeded very much more slowly than in the experiments of other observers in which the water was unconfined. This suggests that, by the reaction between the metal and the sea water, the latter rapidly loses its corrosive power. Should this be true, it might possibly be taken advantage of by preventing the circulation of the sea water surrounding important submerged structures. The simple immersion in cold sea water lasted 378 days: that in contact with bright wrought iron plates lasted 770 days: those in contact with scale-bearing iron plates and with copper plates each 112 days. These are the periods at the end of which the results in Table 44 were obtained. In certain cases the experiments were further prolonged, with results on the whole similar to those here given. If I understand him correctly, the results in the column headed "Scale-bearing iron" are the losses suffered by bright iron, etc., when a bright plate of each kind was galvanically connected with *a* similar but scale-bearing plate of the same metal, each of these couples being immersed in a separate jar, and all being coupled together in series.

23 to **33**. Parker, Journ. Iron and St. Inst., 1881, I., p. 39. On each of six glass-coated rods were placed 22 discs 4·5 inches in diameter and about 0·05 inch thick. Each set contained one bright and one scale-bearing disc from each of seven lots of wrought-iron and of four lots of mild steel, from 11 different makers. The results obtained with two lots of "common" wrought-iron are omitted in the table. One set was suspended for 455 days on a London roof: a second was attached under water to the Brighton pier for 437 days: a third was submerged for 240 days in bilge water in an Eastern trading vessel. Three sets were submerged in marine boilers, one of which contained zinc and was blown off as seldom as possible; the immersion lasted 361 days: the second was in a "Peninsular and Oriental" steamship, and was blown out at each terminal port and filled afresh with salt water; the immersion lasted 264 days: the third was in a steam collier using Tyne water, probably acidulated by local chemical works; the immersion lasted 336 days. In this boiler corrosion was extremely rapid, both for iron and steel.

34 to **41**. Gruner, Revue Universelle, XIII., p. 659, 1883. Twenty-eight polished plates of steel and cast-iron of different degrees of hardness and purity, each 3·937 inches square, were exposed under three sets of conditions. One set was exposed to moist air for 29 days, a second was immersed in sea water for 9 days, a third was immersed in water acidulated with 0·5% of concentrated sulphuric acid for three days. In air chrome steels corroded more and tungsten steel less than common steel. In sea water hardened steels corroded less than the same steels when annealed, the soft steels less than the manganese and chrome steels, and tungsten steel less than common steel of like carbon content. It will be noticed that in these experiments the corrosion is very much more rapid than in the others, possibly because the exposures were so brief. These results are so unexpected that if published by a less trustworthy author they might be questioned.

42, **43**. Farquharson, Journ. Iron and St. Inst., 1882, I., p. 204: Proc. Inst. Nav. Architects April, 1882. His results differ from those of Andrews in that the rusting of steel was greatly retarded while in Andrews' experiments it was very slightly hastened by contact with wrought-iron. In both the rusting of wrought-iron is hastened by contact with steel. Six plates of wrought-iron and six of steel were immersed in sea water in Portsmouth harbor, England, for six months, three of each being simply immersed, the remaining three being coupled together in pairs, each wrought-iron plate being coupled to one of steel. The steel was apparently soft.

44 to **47**. Averages deduced by R. H. Thwaite from several thousand results of Mallet, Calvert and others. Journ. Iron and St. Inst., 1880, II., p. 568.

The composition of Parker's and Andrews' steels is given in Table 47, § 164.

has shed, in general increases with its heterogeneousness, with the fineness of its subdivision, and with the temperature. It is affected by contact with substances of different potential, zinc and highly zinciferous brasses retarding, bronzes, copper, tin, lead and iron scale hastening corrosion. While it is doubtless affected by the metal's composition, we have as yet very little information as to what compositions favor and what oppose corrosion. Skin-bearing cast-iron resists corrosion better than wrought-iron and steel, and the hard close-grained cast-irons better than the softer and more open ones. If its skin be removed, however, cast-iron cannot yet be said to resist corrosion better than malleable iron. Nor can we say which class of malleable iron resists corrosion best: soft steel plates are thought to retain their scale more tenaciously than wrought-iron, which hastens their corrosion: if this be removed there is probably no important difference in the rates at which they corrode.

Individual peculiarities of the specimens experimented on and slight differences in the conditions affect the rapidity corrosion to an astonishing degree; this necessitates extreme caution in drawing inferences from even direct comparative tests: accurate conclusions can only be drawn from the averages of many determinations. Moreover, the relative corrosion of two classes of iron under one set of conditions gives no safe indication as to what it will be under another set.

The chief ulterior sources of the oxidation of iron are atmospheric oxygen, free or dissolved in water, its own oxides (sometimes as in puddling and pig washing ulterior sources, sometimes as in Bessemerizing mere carriers of oxygen), and more rarely water.

Table 44 condenses the results obtained by several experimenters, as regards the rate of corrosion of various classes of iron under different conditions.

§ 161. Influence of Surface Exposure; Pyrophorism.—Finely divided iron, *e. g.* that prepared by reducing precipitated ferric oxide by hydrogen, is said to be pyrophoric when quite cold; that made in Percy's laboratory, however, would only ignite when sensibly warm to the hand, and sometimes only when heated above 100° C. Dropped into hot air it burns brilliantly. In pure water from which air is excluded it is not oxidized at 21° C (70° F.) and it is said to begin to oxidize at 55° C. (131° F.).[a]

§ 162. Influence of Temperature.—*Pure dry oxygen*, inert on compact iron at 21° C. (70° F.) is said to begin to oxidize it appreciably at or above 200° C. (392° F.): at redness they unite with vivid incandescence.

Atmospheric oxygen at a white heat burns iron vividly, with marked rise of temperature, especially if blown upon it. At a still higher temperature compact iron scintillates as it burns in air.

Pure water deprived of air appears to be absolutely inert even on finely divided iron at 21° C. (70° F.),[b] and on compact iron even at 100° C.[c] Steam converts iron superficially into magnetic oxide[d] even at about the melting point of lead, and at and above redness this action goes on rapidly.

Common pure fresh water, containing dissolved air, in very shallow open vessels attacks iron more rapidly at 100° C. than at a lower temperature according to Mallet: but, presumably in comparatively deep vessels to which air has less ready access, it corrodes fastest between 79° and 88° C. (175 and 190° F.),[e] probably because at higher temperatures the water contains comparatively little carbonic acid and free oxygen.

Ordinary sea water does not appear to corrode iron materially faster when hot or even boiling than when cold (Table 44),[e] perhaps because when hot it can dissolve but very little air. In many direct comparative tests hot sea water corrodes iron faster, in many others slower than cold sea water. In one set of exposures (Parker's) every one of the nine specimens which were immersed in boiling sea water in a boiler containing zinc, corroded much less rapidly than the exactly similar ones in cold pure sea water, and even much slower than those simply exposed to the weather. It is not clear how the zinc acted here: the usual conditions of galvanic action, actual contact or connection through some metallic conductor, were lacking, for the iron discs were completely insulated: there was no communication between iron and zinc save through the sea water itself, which indeed is a much better conductor than fresh water.[f] The corrosion of the zinc may have satisfied the more actively corroding components of the water, or the salts of zinc may have themselves retarded the corrosion of the iron.

If, as Mallet implies,[g] hot sea water attacks galvanized iron more energetically than cold, it is probably because it is the more destructive towards its zinc coating.

§ 163. Influences of Different Media. A n General.—Neither pure oxygen nor water nor carbonic acid alone, nor oxygen with carbonic oxide appears able to start rusting at the ordinary temperature. But either oxygen and water or carbonic acid and water can start it. The action of deposited and indeed of liquid water in general is far more energetic than that of vapor of water, and the degree of concentration of the carbonic acid and oxygen influence the power of starting rust. Thus the diluted oxygen and carbonic acid of the atmosphere when in conjunction with liquid water are able to start rusting, but apparently not when simply acting with the undeposited aqueous vapor of the atmosphere; either pure oxygen or pure carbonic acid may produce slight rusting with aqueous vapor even when no water appears to be deposited; while with liquid water pure oxygen energetically attacks iron at the ordinary temperature. In ordinary cases rusting is probably induced by the joint action of the atmospheric

[a] Percy, Iron and Steel, p. 13.

This pyrophorism has been ascribed to the condensation of hydrogen employed for deoxidizing in the pores of the spongy iron, which, like spongy platinum, is thought to determine the union of this gas with atmospheric oxygen: nor is this disproved, as has been thought, by the fact that the mixture of spongy iron and ferrous oxide which is obtained by igniting ferrous oxalate in closed vessels, is also pyrophoric: for, if this be free from hydrogen, may not its pyrophorism be ascribed to the finely divided unstable ferrous oxide which it contains? The influence of surface exposure is perhaps illustrated by the fact that while finely divided iron ceases to be pyrophoric if previous to exposure to the air it is heated beyond 427° C., yet if intimately and uniformly mixed with 3% of silica or alumina, which should protect its porosity, it is pyrophoric even if reduced at a red heat.

[b] Percy, Iron and Steel, p. 26.

[c] Mallet, Rept. Brit. Ass., 1840, p. 229.

[d] Idem, 1843, p. 12. It is not stated whether this occurs when the steam is wholly free from air.

[e] Mallet states, Idem, 1840, p. 226, that cast-iron corrodes more rapidly at 46° C. (115° F.) than at 8°@14° C. (46° @ 58° F.). I cannot reconcile this with his numerical results (Table 44). Eight out of 12 specimens of cast-iron, of which 11 apparently retained their skin, oxidized more rapidly in cold than hot sea water, the average loss being 30% greater in the former.

[f] The electric resistance of distilled water is about 3,300 times as great as that of a saturated solution of sodium chloride.

[g] Idem, 1843, p. 12.

oxygen and carbonic acid with deposited or ordinary liquid water. These two gases are usually present in both fresh and salt water: if they be absent iron immersed in water remains bright indefinitely.

Thus Percy found that bright iron gave no sign of rusting even after one or two years, when immersed in boiled distilled water in a sealed tube containing hydrogen, and that the fractures of iron in the often opened cases of the London museum of practical geology remained perfectly bright during twelve years, which he ascribes to the complete prevention of dew by the method employed for warming the museum.[a] Mallet too found that fresh water deprived of air did not corrode iron in a closed vessel, even at 100° C.[b]

Calvert, exposing clean iron blades for four months under different conditions, obtained the following results:[c]

TABLE 45.—CALVERT'S EXPERIMENTS ON RUSTING.

In dry oxygen and ammonia	No oxidation.
" damp " "	"
" dry oxygen alone	"
" damp oxygen	In three experiments only one blade slightly oxidized.
" dry carbonic acid	No oxidation.
" damp carbonic acid	In 4 out of 6 cases a slight precipitate of iron carbonate formed.
" dry carbonic acid and oxygen	No oxidation.
" damp carbonic acid and oxygen	Oxidation most rapid, a few hours sufficing; iron turned dark-green, then brown-ochre.

In a bottle containing distilled water and oxygen, the submerged portion of a clean iron blade rapidly rusted, the protruding part remained for weeks unoxidized: but when the oxygen was mixed with carbonic acid the protruding part as well rapidly "showed the result of chemical action."

The influence of air on rusting is further indicated by the facts, elsewhere alluded to, that hot sea water, in spite of being hot and in spite of its high electric conductivity, usually corrodes iron no faster than when cold, apparently because it has so little solvent power for air: and that Mallet's experiments convinced him (1) that fresh water corrodes iron most rapidly at from 175° to 190° F., which is approximately the temperature at which it releases its dissolved air most rapidly; (2) that the rate of corrosion in water is directly proportional to the volume of dissolved air for given temperature; and (3) that for given initial proportion of dissolved air, the rate of corrosion in still water is inversely as the depth of immersion within limits, as is naturally the proportion of air which diffuses downward to replace that consumed by the corrosion.[d]

Rust ordinarily contains but little carbonic acid, (Calvert found but ·9 and ·617% of iron carbonate in two specimens), whose role in the oxidation of iron is not clear. It may simply start the rust: or the iron may first form carbonate, which later turns to hydrated ferric oxide.

B. SUBAERIAL RUSTING, as we have seen, is probably not induced by the atmospheric oxygen and carbonic acid without the intervention of deposited water: but once started it appears to proceed without further deposition of water, iron rust being so strongly electro-negative as to determine oxidation, and acid fumes, sulphuretted hydrogen, chlorine, etc., suffice to start it without deposition of water.

[a] Percy, Iron and Steel, pp. 26, 27.

[b] Mallet, Rept. Brit. Ass., 1840, p. 229.

[c] Journ. Iron and St. Inst., 1871, I., p. 515, fr. Trans. Manchester Lit. and Phil. Soc.

[d] Mallet, Rept. Brit. Ass., 1840, pp. 228–9. It is not clear how far these conclusions are based on direct comparative tests, and how far on general observation and a priori reasoning.

While subaerial rusting is probably very much slower than subaqueous in cold dry climates, yet as the amount of corrosion is probably nearly proportional to the time that the iron is actually wet by the weather, as dew, rain and snow appear to be very highly charged with oxygen and carbonic acid, and as the thinness of the film of water on objects exposed to the weather is so favorable to rapid rusting, (iron covered with a thin film of water or "wet and dry" rusts very much faster than when deeply immersed), it is hardly surprising that Table 44 contains many instances of corrosion by pure sea, and by both pure and foul fresh water, which are less than the corresponding weather corrosions. But as this wet and dry condition which favors the corrosion of iron so greatly is not especially injurious to coatings applied to protect it, so when zinced, painted or varnished, iron appears from Mallet's experiments (4 and 7, Table 44) to rust much less when exposed to the weather even in damp climates than when immersed in sea water, but yet usually more than in pure river water.

Iron ships are found to corrode more deeply along the water line than where constantly wet or constantly dry, illustrating the power of this wet and dry state to accelerate rusting.

C. SUBAQUEOUS RUSTING.—The much smaller proportion of air and carbonic acid which sea water usually contains tends to render it less corrosive than common fresh water; but this is probably in most cases outweighed by influence of the higher electric conductivity and of the saline contents of sea water.[e]

The ratio of its corrosive action to that of fresh water on various kinds of wrought-iron, cast-iron and steel, according to Mallet's numerous direct determinations, while it occasionally rises to 20 : 1 and falls to 2·5 : 1, yet in general lies with rather surprising regularity between about 6 : 1 and 9 : 1.

D. SEWAGE, ETC., according to Mallet's experiments, greatly increases the corrosive action of fresh water, and rather more for wrought than for cast-iron. It also increases that of sea water on irons other than skin-bearing cast-iron, but much less than in case of fresh-water. Owing to this, foul fresh water corrodes unprotected wrought-iron and steel and galvanized wrought-iron faster, and both painted and planed cast-iron nearly as fast as pure sea water. So too while the presence of sewage

[e] Mallet states, op. cit., 1840, pp. 233–4, that the relative corroding power of sea water is increased, in the case of wrought-iron, by the fact that the coating of rust which forms in it is comparatively pulverulent, while that which forms in fresh water adheres more tenaciously, acting as a cloak to hinder further oxidation: and that while this is also true of cast-iron, it is to a much smaller degree, since the fresh water oxide coating adheres to it much less tenaciously than to wrought iron. On the other hand, according to the same writer, the relative corroding power of fresh as compared with sea water on galvanized iron is increased by the greater power of the former to perforate its zinc coating. Indeed, in one set of experiments he found that cast- and wrought-iron and steel, when in voltaic contact with zinc, were all corroded faster by fresh than by sea water, the former holding one volume of air and carbonic acid in eight, the latter one in seventy. (Op. cit., p. 255.) It will, however, be noted that this is not true of the zinced wrought-iron No. 7, Table 44.

In comparing the ratio of the corrosive action of sea water to that of fresh water, as given by Mallet in Table 44, we observe that it is 7·5 : 1 in case of galvanised wrought-iron, and in case of ungalvanized cast-iron wrought-iron and steel respectively about 7·5 : 1, 8·9 : 1 and 8 : 1. In brief the difference between the rate of corrosion in fresh and in salt water is about the same for one class of iron as in another. It is true that in earlier and briefer exposures Mallet found that this ratio was about 4 : 1 to 6 : 1 for cast- and 8 : 1 for wrought-iron, i. e. that the sea water was especially severe on the latter metal. But these results refer to but a single pair of exposures of wrought-iron, while those in Table 44 lines 5 and 6 refer to 18 pairs of exposures, and carry weight proportionally.

invariably greatly hastens the corrosion of both cast and wrought-iron in fresh river water, yet it affects skin-bearing cast-iron much less than most other varieties, increasing its corrosion about threefold, while it raises that of painted and of planed cast-iron about six and sevenfold respectively, that of galvanized wrought-iron about eightfold, and that of unprotected wrought-iron and steel about eleven- and tenfold. Turning now to sea water, we find that in 13 out of Mallet's 22 pairs of immersions of skin-bearing cast-iron of which only 11 are given in Table 44, the presence of sewage retards corrosion, and on an average the foul sea water corrodes it less rapidly than the clear. Sewage however about doubles the corrosive action of sea water on painted and on planed cast-iron, on galvanized and on unprotected wrought-iron, and on unprotected steel, increasing the corrosion by from 43 to 158 per cent.

The preceding paragraph refers to Mallet's results, which are on the whole corroborated by those of Parker (28 to 33, Table 44) and C. O. Thompson. Parker's 11 wrought-irons and steels are invariably corroded faster by bilge than by pure sea water, on an average nearly thrice as fast. Thompson found that while the waste of gas works did not appear to increase the corrosive action of pond water initially somewhat polluted by stables, etc., sewage increased it 37% in case of wrought-iron and 76% in case of cast-iron. Here sewage hastens the corrosion of cast more than of wrought-iron, the reverse of Mallet's results.[a]

E. SULPHUROUS ACID.—W. Kent found in the rust of railway bridges, whose iron is reported to corrode very rapidly, traces of chlorine, much soot, carbonic, sulphuric and traces of sulphurous acid, supposed to arise from the products of the combustion of pyritiferous coal in the locomotive. As carbon is electro-negative to iron and apt to condense passing vapors, he attributes to it and to carbonic and sulphurous acids the rapid corrosion. He further found that an aqueous solution of sulphurous acid, in a closed vessel, corroded iron energetically, forming ferrous sulphate.[b]

§ 164. INFLUENCE OF THE COMPOSITION OF IRON.—The influence of other elements combined with iron on its oxidation at high temperatures will be considered later.

It is stated[c] that at ordinary temperatures combined carbon, and probably silicon and to a smaller extent phosphorus, retard the corrosion of iron. Manganese is said to increase the rusting tendency of malleable iron, but to diminish that of cast-iron. But it seems to me very doubtful whether such sweeping statements are justified by the present state of our knowledge.

To study the effect of combined carbon, I number the irons of each of several sets of experiments in order of their combined carbon, 1 having the most, and place them in Table 46 in order of the rapidity of corrosion, the fastest corroding standing first. Were it true that corrosion is inversely as the combined carbon, they should stand in inverted sequence, say 6, 5, 4, 3, 2, 1. To illustrate simultaneously the relative corrodibility of cast and malleable iron the former appears in heavy-faced type.

In not one of these 16 sets do the numbers happen to stand in inverted sequence, and this might easily happen if they were arranged at random. Indeed, comparing the sum of the first half of the digits of each case with that of the last half (*e. g.* in case number 1 comparing $3+4=7$ with $1+2=3$) we find that in eight out the sixteen cases of this table their first half is less than their last; and adding together all of these first halves we find that their gross sum is less than that of the last halves. To one rash enough to draw an inference from such conflicting data, this would mean that combined carbon hastened corrosion.[d]

The eight cases in which the last half of the digits exceeds the first include the immersions with scale-bearing and copper plates, one case of immersion in acidulated water, and all but one of the cases of simple immersion in cold sea and bilge water.

It is impossible to explain away these facts by the influence of manganese and silicon. Thus number 16 Table 44 is numbered 7th in order of combined carbon among Andrews' irons in Table 46. As it has decidedly high manganese and very low combined carbon it should be one of the quickest to corrode, while actually it is the slowest. Many another anomaly, "grateful—comforting," will reward the patient digger.

TABLE 46.—COMBINED CARBON AND RAPIDITY OF CORROSION.

No.	Observer.	Exposed to or immersed in	Numbered after proportion of combined carbon, 1 highest, placed in order of corrosion, fastest first.
1	Parker	Exposure to London air	3, 4, 1, 2.
2	Gruner	Exposure to air	(2, 3) **1**.a
3	"	Cold sea water, simple immersion	**1** (2, 3).a
4	Mallet	" " " "	**11, 6, 8, 7, 3, 9, 1, 5, 10, 2, 4.**
5	Andrews	" " " "	**1**, 5, 3, 2, **4**, 3, 8, 7.
6	Parker	" " " "	3, 2, 4, 1.
7	"	Cold bilge water, " "	3, 1, 4, 2.
8	"	Suspended in marine boiler	1, 3, 4, 2.
9	"	" " "	3, 4, 2, 1.
10	"	" " "	3, 4, 1, 2.
11	Andrews	Cold sea water, in contact with bright wrought-iron	5, 6, 7, **1**, 8, 3, **4**.
12	"	Cold sea water, in contact with scale-bearing iron	6, 8, **1**, 5, 3, 7.
13	"	Cold sea water, in contact with copper plates	**1**, 3, 5, 6, 8, 7.
14	Adamson	Acidulated water	3, 1, 2.
15		" "	**5, 3, 4, 6, 2, 1.**
16	Gruner	" "	2, **1**, 3.a
17	Parker	Mean of all conditions	3, 4, 1, 2.
18	Andrews	" " "	**1**, 6, 3, 5, 8, 7.

a. Gruner does not give the combined carbon of his irons, but three, spiegeleisen, hard manganese steel and soft steel, are selected, since there can be little doubt that of these the spiegeleisen has the most and the soft steel the least combined carbon.

Heavy-faced type represents cast-iron. Where two numbers are placed in parentheses I do not know which of the two corrodes fastest.

The numbers in line 12 are derived from the specimens 11 to 20 of Table 44, but refer to exposures prolonged beyond the point at which the results in column 16 of Table 44, "scale bearing iron," were obtained.

Line 14, Jour. Iron and St. Inst., 1878, II., p. 396.
Line 15, Ledebur, Handbuch, p. 279.

The following tables, calculated from the results of Parker and of Andrews, are thought to bring out the anomalous relation between corrosion and composition:

TABLE 47.—PARKER'S AND ANDREWS' EXPERIMENTS ON RUSTING.

Parker's experiments.	Percentage of						Relative corrosion mean of all conditions.
	Carbon.	Silicon.	Manganese.	Phosphorus.	Sulphur.	Copper.	
Landore steel	·18	·013	·04	·077	·074	·015	1·00
Brown & Co.'s steel	·12	tr	·11	·058	·077	tr	1·19
Bolton & Co.'s steel	·19	060	·52	041	·068	tr	1·05
Steel of Steel Co. of Scotland	·10	·032	·36	·067	·080	tr	1·07

	Andrews' experiments.	Percentage of						Relative loss by corrosion in sea water, wrought-iron = 100.				
		Graphite.	Combined carbon.	Silicon.	Manganese.	Phosphorus.	Sulphur.	Simple immersion.	Immersion in galvanic circuit with Bright wrought-iron.	Scale-bearing iron.	Copper plates.	Mean.
1	Soft Bessemer steel	....	·15	·01	·54	·06	·11	·944	1·802	·971	·791	5 1·081
2	Soft open-hearth steel	....	·17	·07	·63	·08	·12	1·004	1·489	·764	·861	4 1·029
3	Soft cast-steel		·46	·07	·18	·21	·02	1·200	1·332	1·216	1·031	7 1·215
4	Hard Bessemer steel	....	·51	·07	1·15	·09	·11	1·189	1·284	1·126	1·60	2 1·144
5	Hard open-hearth steel	....	·72	·08	1·24	·14	·10	1·032	1·325	1·183	1·016	1 ·971
6	Hard cast-steel	..	1·41	·12	·34	·0-	·06	1·136	....	....	....	6 1·180
7	Cast-iron	1·50	2·01	·41	0·65	0·45	·25	....	1·572	1·128	1·036	3 1·264

[a] Trans. Am. Inst. Mining Engineers, IX., p. 368, 1881.
[b] Journ. Franklin Inst., XCIX., p. 437, 1875.
[c] Ledebur, Handbuch der Eisenhüttenkunde, p. 278.
[d] Reversing the order of Gruner's doubtful numbers, 2 and 3, would reverse the balance.

Not to needlessly multiply cases, note how No. 7 of Andrews' which, greatly excelling all others in both combined carbon and silicon and with but a moderate proportion of manganese should corrode the slowest of all, actually corrodes the fastest when in contact with copper, and when in contact with bright wrought-iron; and is one of the most corrodible under the third set of conditions.

Numbering the irons of Table 47 in order of their manganese, 1 having the most, and arranging them in order of corrosion, the fastest-rusting first, then if as is believed manganese hastens rusting, they should stand in sequence, say 1, 2, 3, 4, etc. Actually they are more nearly in inverted than in direct sequence. Parker's stand 4, 3, 2, 1; Andrews' stand 3, 7, 2, 6, 1, 4, 5.

Doubtless composition does influence the rapidity of corrosion; but we may surmise that structure and proximate rather than ultimate composition are the important factors. The local pitting of steel plates, the most dangerous form of corrosion, indicates the local segregation of readily corroding compounds, or, if I may so style them, electro-positive "minerals": Mallet indeed concluded that the homogeneousness of cast-iron influenced its rate of corrosion far more than did its chemical composition.[a]

STRUCTURE.—Experience in the management of chemical manufacturing works, in which the very rapid corrosion of all iron work due to the presence of acid fumes and to various similar causes gives unusual opportunities for observation, seems to indicate clearly that hard, compact, close-grained cast-iron resists corrosion better than the softer, open, dark gray irons;[b] numbers 2 and 3 better than number 1. Mallet indeed reaches the opposite conclusion from his small scale tests,[c] but I find little justification for his belief. Taking the average of all his conditions of exposure (hot, cold and foul sea water, pure and foul fresh water, and damp air), his number 1 irons in both series corrode about 30% faster than those of lower grade under identical conditions.

In pure sea water the rates of corrosion are nearly identical in his experiments, the average corrosion in four exposures of number 1 iron being about 4% greater than that in fourteen exposures of harder iron. It is uncertain whether the greater corrodibility of the softer irons is due chiefly to structure, to composition, or to composition as governing structure, or to the greater resisting power of their skin.

SIZE.—Immersing 26 pairs of specimens of cast-iron, each consisting of one block 5 inches × 5 inches × 1 inch, and of a similar one 5 inches × 5 inches × 0·25 inch, in pure sea water for 387 days, Mallet found that the thin piece in every case corroded faster, and generally very much faster, than its companion. On reimmersing them for 732 days, in 21 out of the 26 pairs the thin piece still corroded faster than the thick, but the difference was less marked than before, while in five pairs the thick piece corroded somewhat the faster. He attributed this to the greater heterogeneousness of the thin piece: but the slow cooling of the thick piece should give better opportunity for segregation during solidification, and the difference seems more naturally attributable to a difference in the structure of the metal, or in the thickness or adhesiveness or corrodibility of its skin, due to different rates of cooling.

§ 165. CAST-IRON VS. STEEL AND WROUGHT-IRON.—In general cast-iron corrodes much less readily than malleable iron, but this is certainly in large part and perhaps wholly due to its tenaciously held skin. Thus in Table 44 Mallet's skin-bearing cast-irons under all conditions corrode less than his wrought-iron and steels, though in pure river water the difference is comparatively slight. But the planed cast-irons of Mallet, Andrews and Gruner on the whole corrode rather faster than unprotected wrought-iron and steel. Mallet and Gruner indeed find that planed cast-iron corrodes more slowly than malleable iron when simply exposed to the weather; but it corrodes on the whole decidedly faster than malleable iron in cold sea water, whether simply immersed or in voltaic contact with copper or with scale-bearing wrought-iron. In three out of the four groups in figure 9 the corrosion of cast-iron outstrips that of malleable iron.

In Gruner's experiments the planed cast-iron corrodes in sea water from about 2 to 3·5 times as fast, and in acidulated water from 0·8 to 14 times as fast as the fastest corroding carbon steel.

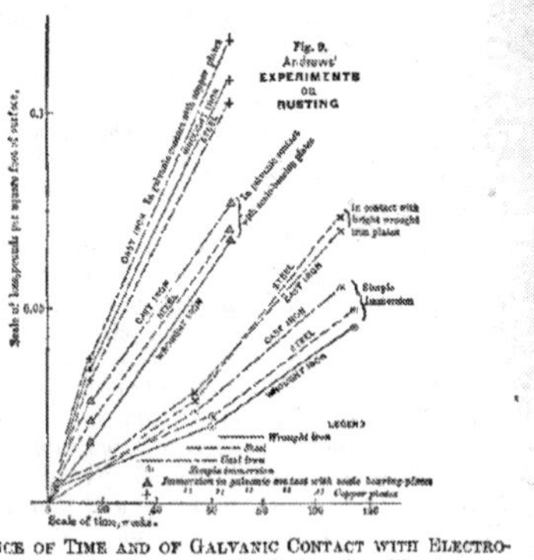

INFLUENCE OF TIME AND OF GALVANIC CONTACT WITH ELECTRO-NEGATIVE SUBSTANCES ON RUSTING IN SEA WATER.

§ 166. THE RELATIVE CORROSION OF WROUGHT-IRON AND STEEL is a question whose economic importance, I hope, justifies the length at which I shall consider it. I first present the results of experiments on a small scale, then those of actual experience in use in land and marine boilers, ships' hulls, etc.

As already indicated, there is probably no important difference in the rate at which these two classes of iron corrode under ordinary conditions. It is true that our

[a] Op. cit., 1843, p. 4. Mallet considered that chilled cast-iron corroded faster than that cast in green sand: and this he attributed to the heterogeneousness of the former, citing in support of this the fact that its rusting was tubercular, which he considers an unfailing index of heterogeneousness (Idem, 1840, p. 234). In earlier and briefer exposures chilled iron nearly always corroded much faster than similar unchilled iron in foul sea water; but I am inclined to attribute this to individual peculiarities of certain of the specimens. For in the same series there was little difference between the rates of corrosion of chilled and unchilled irons, otherwise similar, in pure sea water, and in river water pure or foul: while in the later series, whose results are given in Table 44, we find that even in foul sea water the chilled iron corroded slower than the unchilled; and that in cold pure sea water and in river water, whether fresh or foul, their corrosion was closely similar, while chilled iron corroded about twice as fast in hot sea water yet only half as fast in damp air as similar unchilled iron.

[b] Several very experienced and intelligent managers of chemical works assure me that their experience fully agrees with this statement. It seems to be true both of corrosion by air slightly charged with acid fumes, and by brine.

[c] Op cit., 1843, p. 5.

small scale tests indicate that under certain conditions steel corrodes much faster than iron; but at least under some of these this is opposed by experience on a large scale. It is to be observed, however, that if, as is probable, the two metals corrode equally per square foot of surface per annum, steel suffers more per unit of strength. A steel plate of the same strength as an iron one is considerably thinner; and if each loses the same thickness in the same time, the steel plate becomes finally considerably weaker than the iron one. Hence, where serious corrosion is to be expected, it is not prudent, in substituting steel for wrought-iron, to reduce the thickness proportionally to the increased strength of the metal. And where transverse as well as tensile stress is to be resisted, it is also to be remembered that a steel piece, whose cross-section is such that it is tensilely just as strong as a thicker one of wrought-iron, is by no means as strong transversely.

While it would hardly have been surprising had a decided difference in the corrodibility of these two classes of iron been proved to exist, I do not know that there is any strong reason to expect such a difference on a priori grounds. We have seen that there is comparatively little difference between the corrodibility of wrought- and of skinless cast-iron, though their compositions differ so greatly. As steel resembles wrought-iron much more closely in composition than cast-iron, no serious difference in corrodibility need be expected on the score of composition. Beyond this, wrought-iron differs from steel in having a small quantity of slag mechanically intercalated, which if anything should hasten its corrosion. Beyond this there appears to be a decided difference in their structure, due at least in part to the presence of that slag in the one and its absence from the other. But I do not know that this difference is of a kind which should be expected to affect corrodibility.

It appears tolerably certain that the mild steel of to-day compares more favorably with wrought-iron in corrodibility than that formerly made. This may be due to former neglect to remove its scale, or to present greater regularity in the proportion of manganese and perhaps of other elements which tend to segregate, and which, if even occasionally present in excessive proportions would, by assisting segregation, lead to the formation of spots differing in potential from the mass of the metal, and thus leading to aggravated local corrosion. Or, again, carelessness in recarburizing may have formerly led to heterogeneousness and difference of potential.

A. Small scale tests indicate that in cold sea water, whether pure or foul, and whether it be simply immersed in it or in galvanic contact with bright wrought-iron, with scale-bearing iron, or with copper, as well as in pure fresh water, steel corrodes at about the same rate as wrought-iron. The data are not always harmonious: but where they are discordant those which point to steel as the more corrodible are so far offset by others pointing in the opposite direction as to strongly suggest that there is no important difference. But in hot sea water, *e. g.* in marine boilers, and when exposed to the weather, our small scale tests indicate that steel is decidedly the more corrodible of the two: while our rather scanty data concerning the effect of acidulated water and sewage-bearing river water point rather to wrought-iron as somewhat the more corrodible. This is summed up in Table 47 A.

Table 47 A.—Relative Corrosion of Wrought-Iron and Steel, Small Scale Tests.

Conditions of exposure.	Relative corrodibility.	Quality of evidence.
A. In pure cold sea water—		
1. Simple immersion	Corrode nearly equally	Abundant and tolerably harmonious.
2. Steel and bright wrought-iron in galvanic contact	Probably little difference	Contradictory.
3. In galvanic contact with scale-bearing iron	Nearly identical	Scanty; tolerably harmonious.
3. In galvanic contact with copper	" "	" " "
B. Hot sea water	Steel much the more corrodible, perhaps by 10%	Very harmonious, tolerably abundant.
C. Exposed to the weather	Soft steel corrodes decidedly faster than wrought-iron	Harmonious scanty.
D. In foul sea water	Nearly identical	Harmonious; moderately abundant.
E. In pure fresh water	" "	Rather scanty.
F. In foul " "	Steel rather the less corrodible	" "
G. In acidulated "	Steel decidedly the less corrodible	Scanty.

In extensive experiments by D. Phillips[a] mild steel appeared to corrode much more rapidly than wrought-iron in marine boilers, but his results are so tainted with suspicion that I do not produce them here, believing that very little weight should be attached to them. Bessemer[b] points out that were steel to corrode in practice at the rate stated by Phillips, a boiler plate three-eighths of an inch thick would be completely destroyed in 8·5 years, the coat of paint alone remaining, a result it is needless to say directly contradicted by abundant experience. Indeed, it is stated that when Phillips' experiments were prolonged, the committee which had them in charge concluded that there was no difference in the rates of corrosion of wrought-iron and mild steel.[c]

In other and apparently more trustworthy experiments, Phillips exposed plates of wrought-iron and steel, each carefully insulated with glass, and here his results agree in general more nearly with those of other observers, the corrosion of the two metals being nearly identical in cold sea and rain water, while that of steel exceeded that of wrought-iron on exposure to the weather, though in a much higher proportion than in Parker's experiments.

Detailed Evidence.—Let us now briefly run through the evidence.[d]

1. Simple Immersion in Cold Sea Water.—The results obtained by Mallet, Andrews, Parker, and Farquharson, and Thwaites' averages agree fairly in showing that both metals corrode at about the same rate. The greatest difference is in Andrews' results, in which steel corrodes about 19% faster than wrought-iron; but as only two specimens of wrought-iron are here represented, and as the difference in large part is due to the exceptionally rapid corrosion of one out of the six specimens of steel, it is referable to individual peculiarities. In Mallet's results wrought-iron corrodes 11% faster than steel. Parker's (and apparently Farquharson's) results refer to

[a] Proc. Inst. Civ. Eng., LXV., p. 73. Engineering, 1881, I., p. 813.

It appears that in certain cases copper plates were present with the steel and wrought-iron ones experimented on by Phillips, and the latter metals were often held by uninsulated brass or copper rods, yet the influence of these electro-negative metals was ignored. Further, in the experiments conducted with hot water, the steel plates were placed above the wrought-iron ones, and consequently in hotter water, which might be expected to corrode more energetically. What trust can we put in such work? The untrustworthiness of his methods and results was fully exposed by Abel, Siemens and others, in the discussion which followed the reading of his paper.

[b] Journ. Iron and St. Inst., 1881, I., p. 76.

[c] Wright, Engineer-in-Chief of the Admiralty, Proc. Inst. Civ. Eng., LXV., p. 104.

[d] In the following discussion some discrepancies will be observed between the numbers given and those which might be deduced from Table 44. This is because the numbers in that table give only the more important results obtained by the several observers, while those in the following discussion often refer to a larger number of results, which include those in this table.

soft steel, Mallet's to hard steel, and Andrews' partly to each.

2. UNDER GALVANIC ACTION IN COLD SEA WATER there is little reason to suspect an important difference between the corrodibility of wrought-iron and steel. The cases in which steel corrodes the faster are pretty well offset by others in which wrought-iron is the more corrodible.

a. When wrought-iron and steel are galvanically connected in cold sea water, Andrews' results indicate that the steel corrodes slightly faster than the wrought-iron, and both metals decidedly faster than when simply immersed. Farquharson's results indicate just the reverse, that the corrosion of steel, slightly more rapid than that of wrought-iron when insulated, is almost completely arrested by connection with wrought-iron, the rapidity of rusting of the latter being nearly doubled. This appears opposed to common experience, and may be due to some peculiarity of the material employed. Andrews' ten sets of experiments harmonize among themselves, as do Farquharson's three sets.

b. When similarly immersed in galvanic contact with copper, Andrews' results indicate that wrought-iron rusts about 10% faster than steel. Similar result were obtained by a longer exposure of 68 weeks, during which steel lost by rusting about 6% less than wrought-iron. But this difference is so slight that it may easily have been due to some individual peculiarity.

c. When similarily immersed in contact with scale-bearing plates, Andrews' results in Table 44 indicate that steel corrodes faster than wrought-iron: but when their exposure was farther prolonged this result was reversed, and the corrosion of the wrought-iron exceeded that of the steel by about 9%.

3. IN SIMPLE IMMERSION IN COLD WATER OTHER THAN PURE SEA WATER there appears to be little difference between the corrosion of these two metals. In pure river water, in sewage-bearing sea water and in bilge water they corrode at approximately equal rates, and in the case of foul river water alone does any important difference arise, wrought-iron here corroding 22% faster than the hard steels of Mallet's experiments.

4. IN SIMPLE IMMERSION IN HOT SEA WATER soft steel appears to corrode decidedly faster in Parker's experiments than wrought-iron. although when the same steels and wrought-irons were immersed in pure cold sea water and in bilge water the two metals corroded at practically uniform rates. In two of his boilers the slowest corroding steel corroded 8% and 34% faster respectively than the fastest corroding wrought-iron, while in the third boiler but one of the wrought-irons corroded faster than the slowest corroding steel. The average corrosion of the four steels exceeds that of the seven wrought-irons by 22, 34 and 98% in the three boilers; the average of these three excesses is 51%. The difference here is too marked and too constant to be readily accounted for by individual peculiarities, and certainly seems to indicate that soft steel corrodes faster than wrought-iron in hot sea water.

5. ON EXPOSURE TO THE WEATHER Mallet's hard steels corrode more slowly than his wrought-irons: while Parker's soft steels uniformly corrode faster than his wrought-irons, on an average 41% faster, the slowest rusting steel corroding 22% faster than the fastest rusting wrought-iron. As Mallet's wrought-irons, which were exposed in Dublin, corrode at a rate not very different from that at which Parker's did in London, this would go to show that in the weather hard steels corrode more slowly than soft, though such an inference should be used cautiously.

6. IN ACIDULATED WATER.—In addition to Gruner's results in Table 44, those in Table 47 B are offered.

TABLE 47 B.—CORROSION BY ACIDULATED WATER.

		Composition.						Relative loss. Wrought-iron = 100.
		Graph.	Com. car.	Si.	Mn.	P.	S.	
1.	Bessemer steel	......	·33	·06	1·01	·07	·02	25·
2.	" "		·11	·05	0·50	·04	·03	9·
3.	Tool steel	......	1·00	......	......	......	...	75·
4.	Spiegeleisen	......	4·5	..	10·	......	...	16·
5.	White cast-iron	......	3·0			·78	...	22·
6.	Dark grey cast-iron	3·5	tr	2·5	1·5	·80	...	31·
7.	Grey cast-iron	3.	0·5	1·8	1·0	·26	....	43·
8.	Steel	......	......	..	......	..	....	128·
9.		......	......		......	......	...	98·

1 and **2.** Adamson, Journ. Iron and St. Inst., 1878, II., p. 398. **3** to **7.** Ledebur, Handbuch der Eisenhüttenkunde, p. 279, Berg und Hütten. Zeitung, 1877, p. 280.

8. H. M. Boies, private communication, Aug. 8th, 1885. Four plates, one each of steel and wrought-iron unprotected and one of each galvanized ("coated with zinc or something of the kind") were suspended in boilers using Lackawanna River water for from one to two months, at the Rushdale Powder Mills, Pennsylvania. This water is reported to contain sulphuric acid, from the mine water of the adjacent anthracite mines, and is extremely corrosive. Each plate was immersed twice, with results which I here condense, in loss per 100 of weight of the original plates per annum. Note that while the unprotected steel at first corroded faster than the wrought-iron, the tables were turned later. It would be rash to draw conclusions from such data as to which metal was the more corrodible.

Loss per cent. per annum.	First Immersion.	Second Immersion.
Steel unprotected	25	50
Wrought-iron unprotected	35	28
Steel zinced	9·5	4·7
Wrought-iron zinced	11	5·5

9. Bars of wrought-iron and steel were immersed during 8·5 months in the acid water issuing from the pits of the Bonifacius Coal Mining Company, and the loss by corrosion ascertained. Iron Age, August 18th, 1887.

As far as this evidence goes it tends to show that wrought-iron is attacked by acidulated water faster than steel.

B. CORROSION IN ACTUAL PRACTICE.—It may justly be objected to the preceding evidence that it is based on comparatively small scale experiments, that it is often contradictory, and that no one of the sets of conditions accurately represents those of actual use. Since in such a question as this experience on a large scale is the court of last resort, let us see what its verdict is.

Steel boilers used by Platt Brothers for over twenty years (presumably with fresh water) did not corrode noticeably except while temporarily fed with acid-bearing water.[a] Walker for years vainly sought difference of behavior in boilers whose flues were part iron, part steel.[b] Denny reported that but one steel vessel built by his firm had shown a symptom of corrosion.[c] The periodical examination by Lloyd's surveyors of the majority of their 1100 marine steel boilers, indicates that, though reported to corrode more irregularly, they on the whole resist corrosion about as well as their iron ones.[d] Steel vessels are reported afloat after over 20 years, and after 14 and 15 they have shown no unusual corrosion.[e] The inner side of steel plates of the Stad Vlissinger, though inaccessible, unscraped and unpainted, appeared after about ten years' service in quite as good condition as when new.[f] At Seraing steel boilers after about seven years' use are reported to have deteriorated less than iron ones; indeed no pitting or corrosion could be detected, and no important repairs had been made.[g]

On the other hand, not a few cases of very serious corrosion of soft steel are reported. In one case steel marine

[a] Jour. Iron and St. Inst., 1881, I., p. 67.
[b] Idem, p. 70.
[c] Idem, p. 63.
[d] Idem, p. 52–71.
[e] Martell, Jeans, Steel, p. 743.
[f] Parker, Journal Iron and St. Inst., 1879, I., pp. 75, 76.
[g] Engineering, 1879, I., p. 40, Report by Lloyd's surveyor.

boiler tubes lost about 70% of their weight in nine months, while the adjoining iron tubes were almost uninjured:[a] in another, three steel tubes in an iron marine boiler, whose other tubes were of iron, pitted so badly that they had to be removed after about a fortnight's use.[a] The steel plated Tromblon pitted so rapidly and was so nearly perforated in several places that it was deemed prudent, nine months after launching, to remove her from the water till actually needed for service, though during that brief time she had been thrice docked and painted. The steel plates of the Epée too corroded fast and deep, but it was possible to keep her afloat in the brackish comparatively cool waters of L'Orient.[b] In spite of unusually careful removal of scale from the Iris, she showed signs of corrosion after a brief stay in the Mediterranean,[c] and another steel vessel corroded seriously in the warm brackish Irrawaddy.[d]

Not satisfied with this evidence, which belongs chiefly to a period when mild steel was a comparatively new and untried material, I have endeavored to ascertain the present views of those whose position should enable them to form the most valuable opinions, and, to this end, I have addressed the chief American and many of the chief British shipbuilders, many American makers and users of locomotive boilers, and others. If a really important difference between the corrodibility of the wrought-iron and steel, which are used to so great an extent under identical conditions, existed, it would not be likely to escape observation on our best railways, where the lives of the boilers and fire-boxes are carefully ascertained, and a decided majority of those consulted might be expected to agree as to which was the more corrodible. If on the other hand no such important difference existed, we should expect that, while owing to personal prejudices, to individual peculiarities of the particular specimens of metal employed, to unweighed differences in the conditions of trial, some would consider the one, some the other metal the more corrodible, the majority should either be undecided, or believe that the two metals corroded at approximately the same rate. This was so fully the case as to raise a very strong presumption that there is no very serious difference in the corrodibility of these two classes of iron. Still, while fashion in opinion is not sufficiently strong to conceal a really serious difference, such a difference for instance as Parker found in the corrodibility of wrought-iron and steel in his small scale tests in marine boilers, 51%, yet it might well cover up smaller differences, say of ten per cent or even more.

A condensed statement of the answers received is presented in Table 47 C.

Discussion of Opinions.—I intend to publish elsewhere a more elaborate statement of the replies received than would be appropriate here, and I will now indicate only a few points of possible importance.

In the case of locomotive boilers several believed confidently that steel was less corrodible than iron: but in case of marine boilers and hulls none were of this opinion: and in general the answers were more favorable to steel in the former than in the latter class. This appears to harmonize to a certain extent with the results of small scale tests, in which hot sea water appeared to be relatively unfavorable to steel.

Table 47 C.—Relative Corrosion of Wrought-Iron and Steel. Summary of Replies to Circular of Enquiry.

Opinions as to the relative corrodibility of soft steel and wrought-iron.	Locomotive boilers, etc.				Marine boilers and hulls.				
	Fire box.	Tender in contact with coal.	Not stated.	Total.	Marine boilers.	Hulls.	Not stated.	Total.	Grand total.
Steel more corrodible than wrought-iron—									
A. Decided opinion	...	2	1	3	...	...	...	...	3
B. Impression	1	1	..	2		1	...	1	3
C. Steel more corrodible, yet steel boilers last longer than iron	...	...	1	1	..	...	...	..	1
No difference in corrodibility—									
A. Decided opinion	...	...	2	2	1	1	3	4	6
B. Impression	1	...	5	6	...	...	1	1	7
C. No difference observed in corrosion, yet steel boilers last longer than iron	..	...	1	1	...	...	...	...	1
Steel less corrodible than wrought-iron—									
A. Decided opinion	...	..	7	7	..	...	...	..	7
C. Steel much more desirable, but not stated whether it lasts longer	...	...	1	1	...	...	..	..	1
No opinion	...	...	5	5	...	...	3	3	8
Summary—									
Steel more corrodible	...	...	...	6	..	...	...	1	7
No difference	...	...	..	9	...	..	...	5	14
Steel less corrodible	...	...	...	8	...	...	...	0	8
No opinion	...	...	...	5	...	...	..	3	8

Again, while several confidently believed that steel was the less corrodible, yet only one was decidedly of the opposite opinion, the three others who regarded steel as the more corrodible merely entertaining an impression, or at most a belief which was not a confident one, so far as could be inferred from their letters.

An exception to this is found in the case of steel when exposed to moist coal, in the tender of the locomotive: here two were decidedly of the opinion that steel corroded faster than wrought-iron, and another had the same impression, while no opinion to the contrary was expressed. The number who expressed this opinion was so small, however, that I attach no great weight to it, but rather regard it as suggesting further inquiry. It will be remembered that in our small scale tests steel was less corrodible than wrought-iron in acidulated water.

To my mind the most valuable opinion is that of Mr. Wm. Parker, whose position as chief engineer-surveyor of Lloyd's register gives very exceptional opportunities for observation. He states positively that steel is no more corrodible than wrought-iron.[e]

Several of those who stated that they found no difference in the corrosion of wrought-iron and steel in hot and cold sea water, qualified their statements by adding "provided the scale be first removed by pickling or otherwise" or words to that effect. There appears to be a belief that scale is more likely to be injurious to steel than wrought-iron, and many ship-builders habitually pickle steel plates on this account.

Two who did not think steel less corrodible than iron, yet believed that steel boilers outlived wrought-iron ones.

Although no question was raised as to the general merits

a Parker, Journal Iron and St. Inst., 1879, I., pp. 75, 76.

b M. B. Fontaine, Engineering, XXXI., p. 450, 1881, from Trans. Inst. Nav. Architects.

c Journ. Iron and Steel Inst., 1881, I., p. 69.

d Engineering, XXXI., p. 415, 1881.

e "Experience has proved that steel *does resist corrosion* equally as well as iron, and it is used almost exclusively in the manufacture of marine boilers." "Ninety-nine out of every *100 boilers constructed under the inspection of this society's surveyors* are made of steel. In fact, the use of iron for marine boiler making is a thing of the past. The introduction of mild steel has allowed the working pressures of boilers to be more than doubled." Private communication, Aug. 10th, 1887.

Similar views are expressed by Mr. B. Martell, also of Lloyd's Register, who says (Trans. Inst. Nav. Architects, XXVII., p. 58, 1886) "constant attention has been given to this subject (corrosion) by the surveyors to Lloyd's Register, as the vessels have from time to time come under examination. The general opinion expressed by them is that, so far as corrosion is concerned, mild steel is not more injuriously affected than iron, provided the mill scale be first cleaned off the surfaces before coating the steel."

of these two classes of iron, many asserted, and often in very strong terms, the very great general superiority of steel over wrought-iron, and not a single opinion to the contrary was expressed, which is certainly striking, considering that I had no knowledge in general as to the views of the persons addressed, and hence exercised no selection, conscious or unconscious, in favor of either metal.

The very rapid increase in the use of steel for ship-building, and in the ratio of steel to iron vessels built, illustrated by the following table, goes to show that ship-builders and users no longer consider that steel is at a serious disadvantage as regards corrosion.

TABLE 47 D.—STEEL AND IRON VESSELS CLASSED AT LLOYD'S REGISTER.[a]

Year		1878.	1879.	1880.	1881.	1882.	1883.	1884.	1885.
Steel..	Number	7	9	23	28	63	109	92	118
	Tons	4,170	16,600	85,373	42,407	136,641	166,128	192,457	165,437
Iron..	Number	425	348	386	453	525	614	315	260
	Tons	517,602	479,969	430,994	696,724	851,075	383,774	961,201	290,429
Ratio steel : iron, tons		1 : 118·	1 : 29·4	1 : 18·	1 : 16·4	1 : 6·77	1 : 5·61	1 : 4·90	1 : 1·76

[a] Trans. Inst. Nav. Architects, XXVII., p. 55, 1886. The last line is calculated from the data there given. Vessels built on the continent, in America and the colonies are excluded.

From our small scale tests it might be expected that the contact of wrought-iron and steel, like that of any dissimilar classes of iron, would hasten the corrosion of one if not both. And in some instances this has been the case; it is sometimes the wrought-iron, sometimes the steel whose corrosion is accelerated. Thus Martell found that, after a year's exposure to sea water, the steel plating of a vessel riveted with wrought-iron had, in the immediate neighborhood of the rivets, corroded more than the rivets: while Denny reports that, in case of a steel vessel, the forgings and certain covering plates of whose rudder were of iron, the iron had corroded rather seriously, while the steel with which it was in contact had not corroded at all.[a]

In the manufacture of screws a tendency on the part of soft Bessemer steel to rust has prevented certain manufacturers from substituting this material for wrought-iron. It seems that the discoloration in general does not appear immediately after cutting the threads, but begins a few hours or days afterwards, and increases with time. The cause is obscure. It has been suggested that the steel may be harder than the wrought-iron, and thus become slightly hotter when the thread is cut, a slight oxidation then occurring, which increases later. The screws do not become sensibly warm: yet at the instant of cutting the very skin may be hot enough to oxidize, the temperature being reduced so instantaneously by conduction that the warmth cannot be detected. Oxidation thus started may increase later. But the fact that the surface of the steel screw is left somewhat rougher by the cutting tool than that of the iron one seems sufficient to account for the facts. From the rough surface of the steel the liquid in which the screws are cut would not be so completely removed: remaining slightly moist, rusting might ensue. Indeed, there is probably little doubt that a smooth polished iron surface in general rusts less readily than a rough one.[b]

§ 166 A. There is a belief that the best kinds of wrought-iron corrode more easily than the commoner kinds, and some of our small scale evidence supports this belief, but by no means conclusively. If there were a really important difference in favor of the common wrought-iron, then we should expect that it would nearly always corrode faster than the purer kinds, which is far from true. Mallet indeed found that the admirable Swedish and Low-moor wrought-iron corroded faster than the common varieties in sewage-bearing sea water and when exposed to the weather: but, on the other hand, in river water and pure sea water the reverse occurred. So, too, in Parker's experiments, in which two kinds of common and five of best wrought-iron were exposed to six different sets of conditions, while the mean corrosion of the common was less than that of the best irons under five of the six sets of conditions, yet the difference was always slight, from 5 to 17%, and in four out of these five sets at least one of the best irons corroded more slowly than at least one of the common irons. In the sixth set the common iron corroded slightly faster than the best. Were we to strike a mean of all of Parker's and Mallet's results, it might be in favor of the common irons: but, in view of the characteristics of our evidence, such an average carries little weight unless based on a vastly greater number of observations than we possess.

§ 167. INFLUENCE OF DIFFERENCE OF POTENTIAL.—The contact of more electro-positive substances, such as zinc, retards, that of more electro-negative ones, such as tin, lead, copper, magnetic and ferric oxides, accelerates the rusting of iron. Hence while galvanizing even if defective hinders the rusting even of exposed spots, tinning and coating with magnetic oxide probably greatly hasten the corrosion of unprotected portions.

A. *Galvanizing.* In lines 6 and 7 of Table 44 we note that galvanizing reduces the corrosion of wrought iron under all conditions of exposure, by from about 60% in case of foul sea and pure river water to nearly 75% in case of foul river water, completely preventing it in case of exposure to the weather. Taking all the conditions together, the galvanized wrought-iron may be considered as resisting corrosion much better than even skin-bearing cast-iron.

B. *Segregations* within the metal itself, as already pointed out, probably greatly hasten corrosion, by creating difference of potential.

C. INFLUENCE OF MAGNETIC OXIDE.—The magnetic and similar oxides of which iron scale consists, whose stability is illustrated by the resistance of native magnetite, iron sands, etc., to the oxidizing action of the atmosphere, and of fresh and salt water even when periodically wet and dried by the tide for countless centuries, protect iron which they coat from oxidation, but hasten that of naked iron. Their protective action is shown in the comparatively slow rusting of Russia iron, of blued iron, and of castings which retain their original skin. An effective form is the comparatively thick coating of oxide produced on a very great scale by repeatedly heating iron to redness alternately in an atmosphere of carbonic oxide plus nitrogen and in one of mixed carbonic oxide, carbonic acid and nitrogen (Bower's process), or better still, by prolonged heating to redness in steam, which, though it acts more slowly, is said by some to create a more tenacious and impervious skin (Barff's process). The coating of oxide produced in this way under favorable conditions is impervious, adheres well, and is a powerful protection.[c]

[a] Proc. Inst. Nav. Architects, XXIII., pp. 146-7, 1882.

[b] Private communications, T. M. Drown and Russell and Erwin, December 6th, 10th and 17th, 1887.

[c] Percy, Journ. Iron and St. Inst., 1877, II., p. 456: Bower, Idem, 1881, I., p. 166: Trans. Am. Inst. Mining Engrs., XI., p. 329, 1883: Kidder, paper before Chem. Soc. of Washington, 1883: Stahl und Eisen, IV., p. 98, 1884.

All the parts of the Springfield United States rifles, excepting those which are case-hardened, the barrels and the lock parts, are coated with magnetic oxide by Buffington's process of suspending them for five minutes or more in pure molten niter containing manganic oxide, at a temperature sufficing to ignite sawdust.[a] It was for a time applied to gun barrels also, but even the very moderate temperature employed sometimes twisted them.

It has, however, been repeatedly shown that iron scale is strongly electro-negative to iron, and that, while it hinders the corrosion of those portions of the iron which it actually covers, its presence greatly hastens the corrosion of naked iron, whether in adjacent portions of the same piece or in separate pieces with which it is galvanically connected. It thus acts like copper, but less intensely. Andrews, immersing in confined cold sea water bright plates of wrought-iron, cast-iron and steel, each coupled galvanically to a similar but scale-bearing plate, detected by the galvanometer a rapidly diminishing electromotive force, from about one third to about one fourth of that existing under like conditions between similar bright plates and copper plates.[b] In experiments in Portsmouth Harbor, England, the galvanometer showed active galvanic action between scale-covered and naked portions of the same plate immersed in sea water. When cylinders of naked and Barffed (*i. e.* artificially scale-coated) iron, galvanically connected by platinum, were immersed by J. H. Kidder in pure sea water, a decided current was indicated by the galvanometer.[c]

In Andrews' experiments, which I here summarize, contact with scale-bearing plates appeared to about quadruple the corrosion of bright plates, affecting it about three fifths as much as contact with copper plates did. Note, in these harmonious results, that contact with scale-bearing plates hastens corrosion in every case, increasing it from 3·3 to 4·7 fold. To facilitate comparison I have reduced the results to a uniform time of exposure of one year.

TABLE 48.—INFLUENCE OF IRON SCALE: CORROSION IN CONFINED COLD SEA WATER. ANDREWS.

Number.	Metal.	Loss of scaleless steel and iron by corrosion, per square foot of surface per annum.				
		In simple insulated immersion, 56 weeks	Immersed in galvanic circuit.			
			Each plate connected with a bright wrought-iron plate 56 weeks.	Each plate connected with a similar but scale bearing plate. For 4 weeks.	Each plate connected with a similar but scale bearing plate. For 16 weeks.	Each plate connected with a copper plate for 16 weeks.
1.	Wrought-iron	·015	...	·055	·063	·113
2.	Soft Bessemer steel	·014	·026	·052	·059	·108
3.	Soft open-hearth "	·017	·027	·061	·078	·074
4.	Soft cast steel	·020	·027	·049	·081	·109
5.	Hard Bessemer steel	·018	·025	·082	·060	·111
6.	Hard open-hearth "	·016	·019	·067	·078	·117
7.	Cast-iron	·021	·030	·068	·086	·122
..	Mean	·017	·026	·061	·070	·107

Bright and scale-bearing discs, cut from the same plates and each completely insulated, were exposed by W. Parker under identical conditions for from 38 to 65 weeks to London air, cold sea and bilge water, and in marine boilers, each set containing 22 discs (lines 23 to 33, Table 44). During exposure the scale-bearing plates lost part and in some cases all their scale. The degree to which the remaining scale hastened the rusting of the portions thus left exposed was estimated by dividing the total loss of weight per square foot of finally scaleless surface, by the total time of exposure. This however brings the apparent much below the true influence of the scale: for much of the scale doubtless fell off some time after immersion began, so that actually much less than the total time of immersion was available for the corrosion of the portions thus left bare. But even if we make no allowance for this exaggeration of the apparent time, the corrosion of the naked portions of these plates still appears on the whole greater than that of the scaleless plates. In the case of exposure to London air and of the marine boilers without zinc this exaggeration of the apparent time of exposure masks the effects of scale. I here condense his results.

TABLE 49.—RATIO OF THE APPARENT RATE OF CORROSION OF THE NAKED PORTION OF SCALE-BEARING TO THAT OF SCALELESS DISCS. PARKER.[d]

	In cold water.		In London air.	In marine boilers.			
	Sea.	Bilge.		With zinc.	Without zinc, a	Without zinc, a	Mean.
Maximum	3·3	1·2	1·1	3·1	1·2	1·1	...
Minimum	0·6	0·5	0·5	0·3	0·9	0·5	...
Average	2·12	·87	·88	1·65	1·08	·77	1·23

a, a. In these two instances the scale was either wholly or nearly wholly *removed* during exposure.

Fig. 9 also illustrates the influence of scale. The corrosion curves for galvanic contact with copper and with scale bearing iron are convex towards the vertical axis, thus harmonizing with the observed progressive diminution of electromotive force, while the concavity of the other curves illustrates the accelerated corrosion under simple immersion or contact with bright plates.

Actual experience seems to fully bear out the results of these experiments, and it is considered very important to remove the scale from the plates of iron ships, and to that end they are sometimes pickled.

D. *Copper, Brass, etc.* As copper is electro-negative to iron under ordinary circumstances, while zinc is electro-positive, so we find that while the contact of zinc and of the most zinciferous brasses retards rusting, that of copper and of the common brasses rich in copper hastens it, the brasses very rich in copper being apparently as injurious as copper itself; that of the bronzes (copper-tin alloys) hastens it still more, and that of pure tin more yet. Mallet found that a brass consisting of 75% of zinc and 25% of copper protected cast-iron from corrosion as well as pure zinc, while it was not so rapidly corroded itself as zinc is; whence he inferred that it would form a more permanent protection than zinc. He found that during an immersion of from 15 to 66 days in pure sea water, the corrosion of cast-iron was increased by galvanic contact as follows:

Brasses containing less than 31% of copper *retard* corrosion.	
Copper and brasses containing 31% of copper or more increase corrosion by	19 to 61%
Bronzes increase rusting by	62 to 237%
Tin increases rusting by	364%

E. *Iron on Iron.* As there is a decided difference of potential between different sorts of irons, so their mutual contact hastens the corrosion of the more electro-positive while retarding that of the more electro-negative. Thus, immersing similar blocks of very hard dense bright gray and of soft "highly carbonaceous" dark gray cast-iron for 25 months in jars of confined sea water, A separately, and B with the hard in galvanic contact with the soft, Mallet found that the average depth of removal of metal by corrosion was as follows:

Depth of corrosion on simple immersion	hard iron ·007" soft iron ·01"
Depth of corrosion when immersed in mutual contact	" " ·00233" " " ·03"

The net effect of the contact is to greatly increase corro-

[a] Buffington, Annual Rept. Chf. Ordnance U. S. Army, 1884, p. 77; private communication, Nov. 15, 1887. Weightman, Trans. Am. Soc. Mechanical Engineers, 1884: Iron Age, June 11, 1885, p. 1.

[b] Minutes Proc. Inst. Civ. Eng., LXXXII., p. 300, 1885.

[c] Paper read before the Chemical Society of Washington, April 10, 1885.

[d] Journ. Iron and St. Inst., 1881, I., p. 49.

sion, as the soft iron now loses nearly twice as much as both together lost when separately immersed. See p. 100.

§ 168. PROTECTIVE COATINGS, ETC.—Finding no data as to the relative protection against rusting afforded by galvanizing, tinning, barffing, etc., I have begun some experiments to fill the gap. Their final results will appear in an appendix; those obtained shortly after immersion follow. In comparing these protective coatings, two chief points are to be considered, the thoroughness and permanence with which they exclude air and moisture, and thus mechanically prevent oxidation, and their galvanic effect. Thus, while a coating of tin or of magnetic oxide, being electro-negative to iron, hastens, while one of zinc retards the corrosion of unprotected portions, yet the former may be so much more impervious and enduring than the latter that their mechanical advantage may outweigh their galvanic disadvantage. As far as my inquiries have gone, workers of tinned and zinced iron consider zincing as a much better and more enduring protection than tinning: and my results agree to a certain extent with their belief. Of the twenty-three galvanized pieces tested, fifteen of which were sheared from sheets of galvanized iron, and therefore had no zinc on their edges, one only showed rust, after an exposure of from 16 to 18 days: the edges of all the sheared pieces, even of those in sea water, remaining perfectly bright after 18 days immersion. All of the fifteen sheared tin pieces, including those in distilled water, had rusted at the end of 24 hours: while all the unsheared pieces, *i. e.* those which were completely covered with tin, had rusted after 17 hours immersion when in sea water, and after 8 days when in Cochituate water

But when we come to the actual loss of weight (Lines 9 to 11, Table 47 F) we find little difference between the galvanized and tinned pieces. The very considerable loss of weight which the galvanized pieces undergo in Cochituate and distilled water, indicates that a considerable proportion of their zinc is pretty rapidly removed. As with its removal the conditions must change greatly, longer exposures are needed before we can decide as to the relative protection afforded by zinc and tin.

During the brief immersions of my experiments the other classes of iron rusted much more than either galvanized or tinned iron: whether the same will hold true in all cases after prolonged immersion remains to be seen. While to judge by the eye bright iron appears to rust much more rapidly than the others, becoming completely or nearly completely covered with rust in about twelve hours, though a large part of the surface of the Russia and black irons remained free from rust after 18 days, yet the actual loss of weight by corrosion does not differ very greatly among these three classes; the black iron on the whole corrodes somewhat faster than the bright and the Russia.

Judging from the proportion of surface covered with rust, the barffed iron appears on the whole to resist rusting better than any of the others, excepting the galvanized and the tinned. Though I cannot state confidently that the barffed iron corroded less rapidly than the Russia in sea water, in Cochituate water the difference was marked, the Russia iron always showing signs of rust in from one to eight hours after immersion, while of the barffed pieces one began to rust after 16·5 hours, another after 47 hours, and the other two were free from rust after 16 days immersion.

The few pieces of blued iron experimented on rusted with extraordinary rapidity, becoming about one-third covered with rust in 8·5 hours, even in distilled water.

The nickeled pieces also rusted very rapidly, but the rusting appeared to be confined to certain spots: and, in several cases after a nickeled piece had become much rusted, on removing the rust with a cloth and rubbing the piece I was unable to discover with the naked eye the spot at which the rust had formed.

The barffed pieces undergo tubercular rusting, the corrosion being confined to certain spots, at which the rust piles itself up in little knobs. The tinned pieces also occasionally developed tubercles of rust, but to a much less marked degree.

TABLE 47 F.—CORROSION OF GALVANIZED AND TINNED IRON, ETC.

	Simple immersion in.	Thin sheet iron. Galvanized.	Thin sheet iron. Tinned.	Thin sheet iron. Russia.	Thin sheet iron. Black.	Thin sheet iron. Bright.	Barffed lumps.	Tinned nails.	Galvanized staples.	Blued screws.	Nickeled screws.
Length of time immersed when rusting was first observed.	Sea water.	…	25·5 hrs.	5·5 hrs.	0·67 hrs.	3·25 hrs.	4·5 hrs.	17 hrs.	15 days.	…	17 hrs.
	Cochituate (Boston) water.	…	25·5 hrs.	7·67 hrs.	3·25 hrs.	1 hr.	16·5 hrs.	46 hrs.	…	…	10·5 hrs.
	Distilled water.	…	24 hrs.	1 hr.	1 hr.	1 hr.	…	…	…	1·5 hrs.	1·5 (?) hrs.
Percentage of upper surface covered with rust after 18 days	Sea water.	All perfectly bright, including edges.	4	27	10	100	…	…	…	…	…
	Cochituate.		3	20	62	99·5	…	…	…	…	…
	Distilled.		5	14	27	100	…	…	…	…	…
Appearance after 16 days immersion	Sea.	…	…	…	…	…	Much tubercular rust.	Ends badly rusted.	Almost perfectly clean.	…	Heads completely covered with rust, or nearly so.
	Cochituate.	…	…	…	…	…	Tubercular rusting.	Slightly spotted.	Perfectly clean.	…	Heads much rusted.
Loss of weight, lbs. per sq. ft. of surface per annum	Sea water.	0·00013	0·036	0·136	0·138	0·148	…	…	…	…	…
	Cochituate water.	0·062	0·042	0·143	0·275	0·177	…	…	…	…	…
	Distilled water.	0·041	0·030	0·128	0·187	0·109	…	…	…	…	…

The pieces were in all cases immersed in confined water, in shallow, open porcelain vessels, the water standing about ·37 inch above the iron, and the loss by evaporation being compensated for by adding distilled water, usually every alternate day. The different pieces did not touch each other.

THIN SHEET IRON.—In each of the three menstrua five pieces each of galvanized, tinned and Russia iron, four or five of black iron, and two of bright sheet iron, each 0·5 inches square, were immersed.

OTHER PIECES.—Four galvanized iron staples, 4 and 5 tinned nails, 4 and 9 barffed lumps, and 4 nickeled screws were immersed in "Cochituate" and in sea water: and 3 nickeled and 8 blued screws in distilled water.

Cochituate water is Boston city water.

Previous to immersion the pieces were simply wiped clean.

The pieces of sheet-iron lay horizontally, or nearly so, and were raised above the bottom of the vessel by thin wooden strips. In nearly every case the upper side of these pieces rusted very much more than the under side.

CHAPTER X.

Nitrogen, Hydrogen, Carbonic Oxide.

§ 170. Condition of these Substances in Iron.—They may exist in three if not four fairly distinct conditions: (1) in chemical combination of the ordinary type: (2) in solution: (3) in adhesion: (4) mechanically retained in pores which are at least microscopically visible, and hence set free when the metal is comminuted. In the first three conditions these substances are distinctly no more gaseous than water and ice are: in the fourth they are gaseous.

Some of these terms are vague enough: in this classification I purposely avoid the still more equivocal ones alloying and occlusion: alloying is included under the first three conditions, but occlusion may be held to imply any of the four or a combination of any or all of them.

The first condition may be exemplified by the oxygen of iron oxide in minute particles dissolved or suspended in solid iron, or of cuprous oxide in molten copper: the second by hydrogen or sulphur apparently united with the whole of the mass of molten iron which contains it: the third, in which physical probably greatly preponderates over chemical force, by the oxygen and nitrogen condensed on the surface of glass tubes, from which barometer makers remove them with the greatest difficulty, or by ammonia or carbonic acid absorbed by charcoal: the fourth by bubbles of air in ice, or of carbonic acid escaping from champagne. For many readers the first three classes are resolvable into two: for many of us either hold that solutions differ only in degree from typical chemical unions, or maintain that solution and adhesion are one. I will not even assert that I have in the foregoing examples correctly stated the conditions of the elements. We can as yet rarely if ever fully discriminate, in the case of nitrogen, hydrogen, etc., in iron, between these first three conditions: for our purposes they may be regarded as a single group, the non-gaseous or condensed state, clearly distinguished from the fourth or gaseous condition.

We must free ourselves from the popular misconception that these substances can only exist either in chemical union of the common type, *i. e.* in definite ratio, or as gas. The case of charcoal, which at atmospheric pressure absorbs as much as 90 times its own volume of ammonia, may assist us. In view of the similar retention of gases by glass, we safely hold that the charcoal and ammonia are not in chemical union of the ordinary type: nor is the ammonia present as a gas, for in this case its pressure should burst the charcoal. So too electro-deposited iron may hold 248 times its own volume of hydrogen, about half of which escapes when the metal is exposed to the air at the ordinary temperature. Palladium absorbs 980 times its own volume of hydrogen, whose density is thought to be thereby increased about 10,000 times, so that it doubtless exists either as a liquid or solid.

While we readily understand how solid or even pasty iron may mechanically retain a very considerable quantity of hydrogen, nitrogen, etc., in the gaseous condition, it is almost inconceivable that molten iron should hold an important quantity. Ice may be as spongy as you please, but water can retain but few and minute gas bubbles.

These substances pass back and forth, from the condition of a gas mechanically held in blowholes to the non-gaseous condition of adhesion, so readily that, while the two conditions are very unlike, it is extremely difficult in the case of gas present in solid iron to decide how much exists in each state. If we would collect the mechanically held hydrogen by exhausting the metal, part of that in adhesion probably becomes gasified the instant that the pressure of the initially gaseous portion begins to decline. Nay, even the mechanical action of the drill with which we seek the larger cavities may gasify part of the hydrogen in adhesion. And, if there be a real difference of kind between adhesion and solution, hydrogen probably slides back and forth between these states also on slight provocation.

We readily see how hydrogen, nitrogen, etc., in chemical combination or solution may affect the properties of iron: we may also conceive that, when in adhesion, they may have a powerful influence, owing to the ease with which they become gasified. If as is probable, the metal contains numberless microscopic or even intermolecular pores, when we distort it we change their size. Part of the hydrogen in adhesion may be supposed to gasify and rush into those which we thus temporarily enlarge, as fast as this enlargement lowers the pressure of the gas already in them. This increased quantity of gas may subsequently oppose our effort to return the metal to its initial shape, and perhaps the more powerfully the larger the quantity of hydrogen in adhesion. The ·01% of hydrogen often present in iron might in this way influence its properties greatly, more perhaps than if in chemical combination; for, if gasified, its volume would be ten times that of the steel at atmospheric pressure. This is not brought forward as the actual condition of things, but merely as an illustration of the way in which hydrogen, nitrogen, etc., in adhesion might be conceived to act, and as showing that it is conceivable that they might influence the properties of iron without being chemically combined with it. A possible example will be presented in § 178.

But a given weight of hydrogen, etc., probably produces by far the most severe effects when it passes from the condensed to the gaseous state while the metal is plastic. Unable to free itself it collects, producing cavities or blowholes: if these occupy but one-twentieth of the volume of the metal they may make it perfectly useless; yet they could be caused by gas which formed but 0·00005% of the metal by weight, or one part in 2,000,000. We can hardly believe that so minute a quantity in chemical combination could sensibly affect the properties of the metal.

The gases present in iron may be classified according to the time of their escape as follows:

I. Gasified while the metal is so liquid that no trace of their passage remains.

II. Still retained at that time, or formed later by reactions.

A. Gasified during plasticity: form blowholes (and pipes ?)

1. Escape gradually from the blowholes through the walls of the cooling ingot.
2. Redissolve in the metal.
3. Remain in pores and blowholes.

B. Remain dissolved after plasticity has ceased or not formed till then.

1. May be extracted by heating in vacuo.
2. Cannot be extracted by heat alone.

This classification will be considered at length in § 200. Clearly rigid discrimination between these classes is difficult if not impossible. That gasified from the interior of the ingot while it is still liquid (class I.) may be prevented from escaping by the already rigid exterior, and become mixed with the gases of class II., A, evolved from the earlier solidifying crust. Again, as we can never lay bare all the microscopic pores, the gas removed from solution by heating in vacuo (class B 1) may be contaminated with that present in pores (class A 3.)

Let us now consider nitrogen, hydrogen and carbonic oxide in iron separately, reserving for a later chapter the study of the conditions under which they form blowholes by being gasified in the plastic metal.

The following tables condense the results obtained by several investigators of the quantity and composition of gas evolved by iron under various conditions.

§ 172. Iron and Nitrogen.—Iron in its ordinary condition combines with pure[a] [b] dry nitrogen only with great difficulty: but it readily absorbs this gas when heated in ammonia, and nascent iron may unite even with pure nitrogen, *e. g.* when this gas is passed over iron oxide while it is being reduced either by hydrogen or carbon.[b]

Commercial iron contains small quantities of nitrogen, which has been determined by several investigators, either by converting it into ammonia, or by collecting and measuring it after expelling it from the iron either by chemical means, by heating it in vacuo, or by simply comminuting it. Their more important results are summarized in Table 58.

Of these 6 and 7 should represent the total nitrogen: 12 should give only that which is at least partly physically retained and which is not in strong chemical union with the iron: heating in hydrogen should only give that which is in chemical combination, since nitrogen and hydrogen do not unite unless at least one of them be nascent: while heating in vacuo might or might not give the chemically combined nitrogen. Dissolving in acid might perhaps convert both the physically and the chemi-

a Ledebur, Handbuch der Eisenhüttenkunde, p. 275.
b Frémy, Comptes Rendus, LII, p 323, 1861. Percy, Iron and Steel, p. 58.

Table 54.—Gas Obtained by Boring Cold Steel, Iron, etc., Under Water, etc.

Number.	Description of Metal.	Observer.	Recarburizing, etc.: Recarburized or not	Forged or not	Composition of metal: C.	Mn.	Si.	Behavior of metal in casting, etc. Degree of: Scattering.	Rising.	Solidity.	Composition of gases: H.	N.	CO.	CO_2	O.	Vol. gas per vol. iron.	Drill sharp or dull.
1	Bessemer rail steel a	M	Yes	No		·7@·9	·4@·6		Rises quietly	Porous	90·8	9·8	0			·48	S.
2	" spring steel, bored under oil a	M	Yes	"		do.	do.	Frothed		Few small holes	81·9	18·1	0			·21	"
3	" metal oxygenated a	M	Not	"		do(?).	do(?).			Many large blow-holes	88·9	10·5	0·7			·80	"
4	The same charge recarburized a	M	Yes	"		do.	do.		Rose quietly		77·	23·	0			·45	"
5	Bessemer rail steel, from iron No. 36 a	M	Yes	"		do.	do.		Slight		76·7	23·3	0			·29	"
6	" metal oxygenated a	M	Not	"							79·4	17·9	1·3			·44	"
7	" ingot iron a	M	Yes	"			·25 +		Did not rise	Few blow holes	68·8	30·5	0			·165	"
8	" rail steel (interrupted blowing) a	M	Not	"			·25 +			Very porous	78·1	20·8	0·9			·51	"
9	Forged rail steel initially porous a	M	Yes	Yes		·7@·9	·4@·6			Perfectly solid	52·2	48·1	0			·05	"
10	" " " " " a	M	"	"		do.	do.			" "	54·9	45·5	0			·078	"
11	Unforged rail steel a	M	"	No		·6 +	·25 +			Solid	92·4	5·9	1·4			·17	"
12	Same steel forged a	M	"	Yes		·6 +	·25 +			"	75·4	23·3	1·3			·65	"
13	Porous steel b	S			·33	·69	·10			Porous	86·6	13·8	·62		·37	·54	"
14	" " b	S			·45	·40	·04			"	85·3	14·6	0			·78	"
15	" " b	S			·17	·89	·09			"	87·21	11·15	1·65			·25	"
16	Solid steel b	S			·42	1·08	1·0			Solid	67·1	33·3	1·6			·21	"
17	" " same piece as No. 16, dull drill b	S			·42	1·08	1·0			"	88·7	10·3	0			11·	D.
21	Basic Bessemer steel recarburized with ferro-manganese c	M	Yes		Low			Scatters	Moderately	Many blow-holes	80·4	14·8	6·6			·86	S.
22	Basic Bessemer steel by interrupted blowing c	M	No		"			Scatters little	Rises slowly	Few blow-holes	64·5	35·4	0			·20	"
23	" " " recarburized with ferro-manganese and ferro-silicon c	M	Yes		"				" gently	Moderately porous	86·4	12·7	0·4			·22	"
24	Basic Bessemer steel, recarburized with ferro-silicon c	M	"		"				" "	Very few blow-holes	54·7	45·3	0			·06	"
30	Open-hearth steel, unrecarburized (oxygenated?) a	M	Not								67·	30·3	2·2			·35	"
33	Blister in basic Bessemer ingot iron e	M									43·	28·5	27·2	1·6	0		
34	Blister in puddled plate iron d	F											70·42	20·85	·85	·85±	
36	Bessemer pig, direct from cupola a	M								No blow-holes	86·5	9·2	4·8			·15	S.
36.5	The same blown a few seconds a	M									81·1	14·8	4·1			·23	"
37	Bessemer pig direct from cupola a	M									88·3	14·2	2·5			·35	"
38	" " hematite, English a	M								No blow-holes	52·1	44·	3·9			·085	"
39	" " German a	M									69·2	35·5	2·8			·10	"
40	Solid gray foundry pig, sharp drill b	S								Solid	52·5	44·3				·73	"
41	Same pig, dull drill b	S								"	54·5	45·5				8·	D.

In most of these experiments the gas was obtained by boring cold metal under water, as shown in figure 16, § 217. The columns headed "degree of scattering, rising and solidity" refer to the behavior of the metal before and during solidification, and to the porosity of the cold solidified metal.

The metal was in general bored with a sharp drill, but in two cases, Numbers 17 and 41, the cutting edge was previously removed from the drill, which then ground instead of cutting a hole in the metal, releasing very much more gas than the sharp drill, but of essentially the same composition.

Müller's drill was so wide that it cut out the greater part of the cross section of the ingot.

3. Müller unquestionably includes this among the steels which contain ·4 to ·6% of silicon and ·7 to ·9% of manganese: but as Number 4 is also included in this class, it is possible that Number 3 may have been included accidentally.

6. Unrecarburized Bessemer metal. When this metal was subsequently recarburized with spiegeleisen a violent reaction ensued, and perfectly solid rail steel was produced.

7. Obtained by interrupting the process: *i. e.* not fully blown.

21. Soft, recarburized with 2·5% of 85% ferro-manganese.

23. Recarburized with 5% of 14% ferro-silicon and 2·5% of 70% ferro-manganese.

24. Recarburized with 6% of 14% ferro-silicon.

33. Basic Bessemer ingot iron. It behaved normally in the roughing rolls, in which it reduced to an |——| section. On reheating it blistered to an extraordinary degree, the web swelling out on both sides till it was wider than the flanges. When cooled it was bored under water, and the gas was found to be below the atmospheric pressure, so that it had to be removed by an aspirator. A duplicate analysis in another laboratory gave like results. The absence of oxygen shows that the gas was not contaminated with air.

34. In rolling puddled plate iron about three-eighths of an inch thick (10 mm.) in the finishing rolls, a blister arose, nearly equal on both sides of the plate. It was bored under water, and 100 cc. gas extracted, while the volume of the blister itself was 189 cc.

a = Müller, Iron, 1888, p. 51.
b = Idem, p. 115.
c = Müller, Stahl und Eisen 1883, p. 446; Iron, 1883, p. 244.
d = A. Friedman, Stahl und Eisen, 1880, p. 629, Journ. Iron and St. Inst., 1885, II., p. 645.
e = Müller, Stahl und Eisen, II., p. 79, 1885.

TABLE 55.—GAS ESCAPING FROM HOT IRON, BEFORE, DURING AND SHORTLY AFTER SOLIDIFICATION.

Number.	Description of metal.	When collected.	Authority.	Recarburized or not.	Composition of metal. C.	Si.	Mn.	P.	Degree of Scattering.	Rising.	Solidity.	Composition of gases. CO.	H.	N.	CO₂.	O.	Collected from
61.	Bessemer rail steel	From mould	M	Yes	·33@·38	·13@·25	·52@·8	·06@·08	Quiet	No rising	Perfectly solid	37·3	47·3	7·9	7·5	...	Above
62.	" spring steel	"	"	"	·48@·58	·15@·25	·8@·9	·06@·08	"	" "	" "	51·0	33·5	8·6	7·9		to
63	" " "	"	"	"	do.	do.	do.	do.	"	" "	" "	41·7±	19·1±	37·9±	0·4±	...	Below
64	" " "	"	"	"	do.	do.	do.	do.	"	" "	" "	45·9	41·4	9·9	2·8		
65.	" rail steel, first mould	From first mould	"	"					"	" "	" "	38·7	51·3	7·2	2·8		
66.	" " " same cast, 17 min. later	" last "	"	"					"	" "	" "	48·4	40·9	6·8	3·1		
67	Bessemer spring steel, first mould	" first "	"	"					"	" "	" "	48·9	44·5	2·5	4·5		
68.	" " " same cast, 21 min. later	" last "	"	"					"	" "	" "	42·5	36·5	17·1	3·7		
69.	Bessemer steel rising slightly		"	"						Rises slightly		63·4	31·3	2·2	3·4	...	Above
70.	" " " excessively, ingots cut up		"	"						Rises excessively		31·5	39·2	21·6	7·7		"
71.	Bessemer steel rising excessively		"	"						Rises excessively		70·7	20·7	6·5	2·1		"
72.	" " Darlington.a		S	"								12·5	82·5	5·0	0		Below
73.	" " oxygenated		M	No					Scatters	Rises	A zone of blowholes.	18·6	54·2	24·9	2·3		
74.												18·1	52·9	26·3	2·2		
75.	Basic steel, soft, recarburized with 2% of 95% ferro-manganese		M	Yes	·06@·1	tr.	·45@·55	·05@·1				61·5	2·2	36·4	0	...	Below
76.			"	"	do.	do.	do.	do.				57·5	4·7	38·0	0		"
77.	do		"	"	do.	do.	do.	do.				76·6	6·1	17·3	0		"
78.	do		"	"	do.	do.	do.	do.				57·7±	4·8±	30·5±			"
79.	do		"	"	do.	do.	do.	do.				50·9	5·1	43·2	0·8		"
80.	do		"	"	do.	do.	do.	do.				77·3	6·4	16·0	0·4		"
81.	Basic rail steel recarburized with 8% of spiegel		"	"	·25	do.	do.	do.				68·	16·2	11·0	4·8	...	Above
82.	Basic rail steel recarburized with 18% of spiegel	4th mould	"	"					Restless	Rose quickly		56·5	33·0	8·6	1·9		"
83.	Basic steel, same cast as the preceding	Last mould 9 mins. later	"	"					"	"		62·	34·2	1·0	2·8		"
84.	" ingot iron	During teeming	"	"								77·9	5·7	14·7	1·7	...	Below
85.	Same cast as the preceding	During solidification	"	"								62·6	12·6	23·2	1·6		Above
86.	Basic rail steel	During teeming	"	"								91·7	8·2	0·5	0·6	...	Below
87.	Same cast as the preceding	During solidification	"	"								54·1	38·6	3·5	8·8	...	Above
88.	Basic steel unrecarburized (interrupted blowing)		"	No								3·5	71·9	18·1	2·		"
89	Basic steel unrecarburized, two samples from one ingot		"	"								27·3 35·0	43·5 38·4	26·2 22·5	8· 4·1		" "
90.	Basic steel recarburized with 5% of ferro-silicon of 14% and 2·5% of 70% ferro-manganese	First ingot At end of teeming	" "	Yes "		·011 do.		·515 do.	Quiet "	Rose "	 Zone of blowholes.	64·6 44·1	18·9 41·6	14·4 10·6	2·1 3·7		
91.	Basic steel recarburized nearly like the preceding in the ladle		"	"	·115	·102	·944	·097	Perfectly quiet	Rose slowly		34·7 30·5	58·0 63·8	4·1 1·9	3·2 1·5		
92.	Bessemer steel, gas from soaking pit.a		S	"								12·89 12·90	27·21 20·47	59·91 66·63			
93	" " gas escaping from converter during violent spiegel reaction		M	"								82·6 78·55	2·8 2·52	14·3 16·38	0·09 0·85	0 1·82	
94.	Bessemer steel, gas under slag in converter (Stead)		"									47·8	19·6	31·4	2·5		
95	Half blown Bessemer metal (beginning of boil)		"	No					Frothed much		Solid	68·4 46·8	50·2 50·1	9·2 1·2	2·2 1·9		
96.	Open-hearth steel, unrecarburized, red-short		"	"					Active gas production	Rising	A zone of blowholes.	48·0 46·1	50·1 43·6	15·4 6·9	1·5 3·4		
97.	Bessemer pig-iron } Melted in a common cupola: gases evolved in common cast-iron ingot moulds.		"	...	3·688	1·69	1·93		Evolves much gas		Solid	37·3	58·3	0·5	3·9	...	Above
98	Spiegeleisen		"	...	4·150	·258	7·37		Evolves much gas		"	48·7	49·3	0·5	1·8		"
99.	Basic pig-iron		"	...	3·690	·908	·736	3·095	Less gas than 98		"	39·8	48·8	10·0	3·6	...	Above
100.	Gray pig-iron, British		C									57·0	33·7	8·4			
101.	Charcoal pig-iron, grayish		"									49·2	38·6	12·2			

a The context strongly suggests, but I do not find that it positively states, that the metal which evolved this gas was Bessemer steel.

In Müller's experiments, excepting 93 and perhaps 95, gas was collected either on filling the mould with molten metal from BELOW (bottom casting), by employing a mould closed at the top with a small aperture, in which a thin iron pipe appears to have been inserted; or else on teeming from ABOVE, quickly filling the mould above the metal with clean quartz, and closing it with a luted plate containing a cork with the collecting tube. The mode of collecting is indicated in the last column.

84 and **86.** The gas was collected while the mould was being filled from below, and the collecting tube was removed as soon as the mould was full.

85 and **87.** Here he did not begin to collect the gas till the steel became still, when he filled a tube from above by means of sand.

92. This is the corrected composition, allowance being made for a considerable quantity of air initially present in the soaking pit. The quantity of air is arrived at by assuming that the carbonic acid of the uncorrected analysis escaped from the steel as carbonic oxide, and was subsequently oxidized to carbonic oxide by atmospheric oxygen. A further correction is needed, for part of the atmospheric oxygen was doubtless consumed in burning hydrogen, and its accompanying atmospheric nitrogen exaggerates the apparent proportion of nitrogen escaping from the steel; but Messrs. Pattinson and Stead found no way of estimating the quantity of nitrogen which should be thus deducted for this correction. It is furthermore possible that part of the carbonic acid and oxide present may have arisen from the oxidation of particles of fuel dust falling into the soaking pit.

94. "Mr. Stead analyzed in 1880 the gas liberated in the converter under the slag crust of Bessemer steel." Müller.

100, 101. A hollow cast-iron cone, open below, connecting at its apex with a copper tube, and previously brought to a red heat, is plunged into molten cast-iron in a large ladle. The cast-iron which penetrates into the interior of the cone solidifies, and gives off gas copiously, which is collected through the copper tube under water or mercury.

AUTHORITIES.—M. = Müller, Stahl und Eisen, 1883, p. 444; Iron, 1883, pp. 116, 245; 1884, p. 138.
S = Stead, Journal Iron and Steel Institute, 1882, II., p. 672.
C = Cailletet, Comptes Rendus, LXI., 1865, p. 850.

cally held nitrogen into ammonia.a These two classes probably overlap: indeed, from the fact that what we may consider the total nitrogen in some specimens (Nos. 6 and 7) does not greatly exceed either that which is apparently chiefly physically (12) or that which is probably chemically combined in others (3, 4, 5,) we may conjecture that nearly all the nitrogen is held in part by chemical in part by physical force, and that these forces are so weak that if either be paralyzed (as the physical force is by attrition in No. 12) the other is unable to retain the nitrogen which their allied strength had held captive.

a That nitrogen present in iron, but not chemically combined, should form ammonia when the metal is dissolved by acid implies that under these conditions nascent hydrogen would unite with non-nascent nitrogen. A possibly similar case may be presented by the ammonia present in iron rust formed in damp air, which may be conceived to be formed by the union of the non-nascent atmospheric nitrogen with the nascent hydrogen set free by the decomposition of the water which rusts the iron. But this is not conclusive, for the ammonia may be acquired already from the atmosphere, which always contains this alkali. The same view is supported by the fact that Boussingault obtained apparently from the same steel nearly as much nitrogen (·049%) by dissolving in acid as by heating with cinnabar (·057%), since the latter treatment should expel both the chemically and the mechanically retained nitrogen. (Comptes Rendus, LIII, p. 10, 1861.) His observation (idem, p. 7) that ammonia was not formed when nitrogen was passed through a cold solution, in which zinc was being dissolved by sulphuric acid, in such a manner that the gas was in continual contact with the metallic surfaces from which hydrogen was escaping: and that, when iron was substituted for zinc, the total quantity of ammonia formed was no more than when iron was thus dissolved in the absence of nitrogen, oppose this view. Non-nascent nitrogen and hydrogen do not unite to form ammonia, even when heated together with spongy platinum. But if either or both of these gases be nascent they form ammonia very readily.

Table 58 does not include almost incredible results such as Schafhäutl's, (he found from ·18 to 1·20% nitrogen in iron) which are readily explained by the great difficulties in the determination of this element. The analytical results in lines 2 to 7, obtained by four distinguished observers, by five different methods, most of them with elaborate and effective precautions, agree as closely as do the quantities of other elements (*e. g.* phosphorus, manganese, etc.) found by unquestionable methods in different specimens of iron. Confirmed as they are by the discovery of similar quantities of nitrogen by the wholly independent methods of heating in vacuo and of boring under water, they leave little or no doubt that commercial irons ordinarily contain minute quantities of nitrogen, rarely exceeding say 0·04%.

Stuart and Baker[a] thought they had proved that nitrogen was rarely present in iron. Seeking it in many specimens by attempting to convert it into ammonia through heating them to full redness in hydrogen, they found in the great majority of cases absolutely no nitrogen, in only two cases over 0·0051% and in only one as much as 0·015%. (I here exclude their preliminary and distrusted results.) The evidence of its existence is, however, so powerful that the results obtained by these experimenters tend rather to disprove the value of their method than the presence of nitrogen, for it is by no means certain that, at so high a temperature as they employed, hydrogen would convert the minute quantity of nitrogen present into ammonia. Bouis' observation that this method acts only superficially, and cannot be employed quantitatively unless the metal be very finely divided or the process very long continued, accords with this view.

§ 173. NITROGENIZED IRON.—Berthollet and after him several others, notably Despretz and Frémy, observed that iron was altered in appearance by being heated in a stream of ammonia. It absorbs nitrogen, but not hydrogen as proved by Frémy, becomes white, brittle to friable, much lighter (its specific gravity occasionally falls to 5), less readily attacked by air or moisture, easily and permanently magnetizable, and acquires a brilliant fracture; the nitride of iron thus formed, which is reported to be of definite composition, is not decomposed by a red heat, nor attacked by oxygen except at high temperatures, but is readily decomposed at a gentle heat by dry hydrogen with formation of ammonia and pure iron.[b]

[a] Journ. Chem. Soc., XVII., p. 300, 1864.

[b] Frémy, Comptes Rendus, LII., p. 323, 1861; Percy, Iron and Steel, p. 53.

TABLE 56.—GASES EVOLVED FROM IRON WHILE HEATED IN VACUO.

Number.	Observer.	Description of metal.	Treatment previous to heating in vacuo. Heated. No. of Hours	In atmosphere of	At temperature of	Evolution of gases in vacuo. Conditions of heating in vacuo. Hours	Temperature.	Composition of gas evolved. CO.	H.	N.	CO_2.	O.	Volume of gas evolved per volume of metal. CO.	H.	N.	CO_2	O.	Total
1	T.&H.	Spiegeleisen	Not previously treated.			......	800°	·0	91·5	8·5	·0	......	·0	0·38	·035	·0	......	0·42
2	P.	″	″	″	″	8	Low red.	17·87	81·10	·0±	·94	·0	·35	1·62	·0±	·018	......	2·00
3	″	White cast-iron	″	″	″	6·5	......	2·82	84·	6·58	6·80	......	·04	1·63	·18	·186	......	2·
4	″	Gray ″	″	″	″	9·	......	5·26	89·7	8·25	1·60	......	1·09	18·8	0·68	0·34	......	21·
5	″	″ ″	″	″	″	24·	Good red.	7·70	91·2	·0±	1·	......	1·46	17·33	·0±	0·15	......	19·
6	″	″ ″	″	″	″	76	Red to white.	42·37	57·32	......	......	......	54·84	72·76	......	......	......	127·6
7	″	″ ″	″	″	″	53·5	White.	59·78	47·21	......	......	......	65·10	58·81	......	......	......	128·5
8	″	″ ″ wrapped in	″	″	″	36·	Rising to high.	17·56	82·54	......	......	......	15·95	74·95	......	......	......	90·80
9	″	″ ″ platinum	″	″	″	59·	Rising to full heat.	24·44	75·55	......	......	......	47·50	146·39	......	......	......	194·3
10	″	″ ″	″	″	″	165·	......	58·73	60·28	......	......	......	185·	205·	......	......	......	340·
11	T.&H.	Charcoal ″	″	″	″	100·	800°	16·76	74·07	5·58	3·59	......	·04	·18	·014	·008	......	·21
12	P.	Gray ″	......	Hydrogen.	White.	24·	......	9·09	90·90	......	......	......	2·	20·	......	......	......	22·
13	″	″ ″	24·	″	Bright red	......	......	2	80·	......	......	......	·30	13·4	......	......	......	15·
14	T.&H.	Charcoal ″ Same piece	48·	″	800° C.	......	......	2·35	94·42	8·22	......	......	·016	·63	·02	·0	......	·67
15	″	″ ″ as No. 11	48·	Carbonic oxide	800° C.	......	......	86·93	8·81	4·15	......	......	·21	·02	·01	......	......	·24
16	″	Cast steel	Not previously treated.			190·	800°	63·65	22·72	11·36	2·27	......	·02	·007	·008	·001	......	·031
17	″	″ Same piece as No.	48·	Hydrogen.	800°.	......	......	11·53	82·05	6·42	......	......	·018	·092	·007	·0	......	·112
18	″	″ 16	48·	Carbonic oxide	800°.	......	......	62·50	25·00	12·4	......	......	·029	·012	·006	......	......	·047
19	P.	Soft steel	Not previously treated.			2·	......	24·35	62·61	6·49	16·55	......	3·16	0·83	·34	2·15	......	13·
20	″	Bessemer steel	″	″	″	60·	1000° ± C.	52·8	45·6	......	1·6	......	37·23	32·15	......	1·13	......	76·5
21	Z.	Soft open-hearth steel	″	″	″	......	......	7·9	57·3	34·7	......	......	·43	3·12	1·90	......	......	5·45
22	″	Puddled iron	″	″	″	......	......	44·07	24·5	31·42	......	......	2·18	1·21	1·55	......	......	4·95
23	P.	Wrought-iron	″	″	″	2·	......	34·26	54·1	1·72	0·32	......	·08	1·08	·08	·10	......	2·
24	G.	″ wire	″	″	″	2·	Red.	67·±	......	......	......	......	5·29	......	......	......	......	7·94
25	″	″ ″	″	″	″	1·	......	......	......	......	14·6	......	......	......	......	1·08	......	7·27
26	″	″ ″	″	″	″	7·	Red.	......	......	......	......	......	......	......	......	......	......	12·55
27	″	Horse-shoe nails	″	″	″	4·5	Red.	52·7	30·4	11·5	5·2	......	1·39	·80	·80	·13	......	2·65
28	″	Meteoric iron	″	″	″	2·5	Redness	4·46±	85·68±	9·86±	......	......	0·12	2·44	0·28	......	......	2·85
29	C.	Electrolytic iron (0·26% hydrogen)	″	″	″	......	......	·0	100·	·0	·0	......	......	......	......	......	......	236@248
30	T.&H.	Wrought-iron	″	″	″	100·	800° C.	58·98	23·78	5·95	11·89	......	·167	·068	·017	·034	......	·286
31	″	″ same as No. 30.	48·	Hydrogen.	800° C.	......	......	4·31	71·94	13·75	......	......	·009	·154	·051	·0	......	·214
32	P.	″	34·5	″	Red.	......	Red.	·0	100·	......	·0	......	......	10·5	......	......	......	10·5
33	G.	″ Wire, same piece	......	″	″	1·	Low red	8·	92·	......	......	......	0·04	0·46	......	......	......	0·50
34	″	″ as No. 26	......	Carbonic oxide	″	2·	″ ″	89·9	......	......	......	......	4·15	......	......	......	......	4·59
35	P.	″	63·	″	......	......	......	100	......	......	......	......	8·2	......	......	......	......	8·2
36	T.&H.	″ same as No. 31.	48·	″	800° C.	......	......	97·85	1·43	0·72	......	......	·21	·003	·002	......	......	·23
37	R.	″	......	......	......	......	......	......	100·	......	......	......	......	10·	......	......	......	10·

The iron from which gas was extracted was sometimes in its natural state, and had sometimes been previously heated in hydrogen or carbonic oxide. In no case is there evidence that, even after being heated in vacuo for many days, the escape of gas had wholly ceased: further heating would probably have extracted still more gas.

Troost and Hautefeuille thrice heated in vacuo cylinders of cast-iron, cast-steel and wrought-iron, each weighing 500 grammes, during 100 hours at 800° C., first in their natural state, next after heating during 48 hours in hydrogen at 800° C., and then after similar heating in carbonic oxide, examining the gas evolved at each heating. A similar cylinder of spiegeleisen was similarly heated in vacuo, but only in its natural state.

Graham similarly heated meteoric iron, horse-shoe nails and fine wrought-iron wire, 21 to 22 gauge, in vacuo in its natural state. Wire number 26, 33 and 34, which all refer to the same specimen, was heated in vacuo thrice, as in the experiments of Troost and Hautefeuille, *i. e.* first in its natural state till it seemed "nearly exhausted," then after heating and gradual cooling in hydrogen and free exposure to air "to get rid of any loosely attached hydrogen," and then after similar heating in carbonic oxide.

Parry performed similar experiments on iron sometimes in clean lumps, sometimes in borings.

1. Troost and Hautefeuille, Comptes Rendus, LXXX., 1875, p. 909. **2. 3** and **4.** Parry, Journal Iron and St. Inst., 1872, II., p. 240. **5.** Idem, 1873, I., p. 430. **6.** Idem, 1874, I., p. 93. Temperature rose from red to white: iron unchanged in appearance. **7.** Idem. **8.** Idem, wrapped in platinum: temperature rose from dull red to "high heat." **9.** Idem, wrapped in platinum. Temperature rose from red through full red to "full heat of furnace." **10.** Idem, 1881, I., p. 189: during first 129 hours ratio carbonic oxide: hydrogen = 0·0, during last 36 hours = 0·213. **11.** Troost and H., op. cit., LXXVI., 1878, p. 568. Most of the carbonic oxide comes off in the first few hours; the hydrogen is retained more tenaciously. **12.** Parry, op. cit., 1873, I., p. 430. **13.** Idem, 1874, I., p. 93. **14.** Troost and H., op. cit., p. 564. This specimen before saturation with hydrogen had been exhausted, with results as described in No. 11. **15.** Idem: this specimen, before saturation with carbonic oxide, had been exhausted with results as described in No. 11. **16, 17,** and **18.** Idem. These results obtained with one specimen which, before saturation for Nos. 17 and 18 had been exhausted with results as described in No. 16. **19.** Parry, op. cit., 1871, II., p. 240. **20.** Idem, 1881, I., p. 186. Contains ·08% silicon, ·35 carbon, ·72 manganese, 1·02 magnetic oxide (?) = 0·281% oxygen. **21.** Zyromski, Stahl und Eisen, 1884, p. 535. Journ. Iron and St. Inst., 1884, II., p. 625. Contains ·05% carbon, trace silicon, trace sulphur, ·024% phosphorus, ·288% manganese. **22.** Idem. Puddled iron from same materials as No. 20. Contains ·82 carbon, ·046 silicon, trace sulphur, ·078 phosphorus, ·20 manganese. **23.** Parry, op. cit., 1872, II., p. 240. **24, 25, 26.** Graham, Journ. Chem. Soc., 1867, XX., p. 285. **27** and **28.** Graham, Chem. News, XV., 1867, p. 275. **29.** Iron deposited by electrolysis from ferrous chloride. Cailletet, Comptes Rendus, LXXX., 1875, p. 319. **30** and **31.** Troost and H., loc. cit. Before saturation with hydrogen for No. 31 it had been exhausted with results given in No. 30. **32.** Parry, op. cit., 1873, I., p. 430. Before being saturated with hydrogen it had been exhausted in vacuo for 7 days. **33.** Graham, Journ. Chem. Soc., loc. cit. Before being saturated with hydrogen the wire had been exhausted in vacuo with results given in No. 26. After saturation with hydrogen the wire became white, like galvanized iron. A repeat experiment gave similar results. **34.** Idem. Before exposure to carbonic oxide it had been saturated with hydrogen, and subsequently exhausted with results given in No. 33. **35.** Parry, op. cit., 1878, I., p. 430. **36.** Troost and H., loc. cit. Before exposure to carbonic oxide it had been exhausted with results given in No. 31. **37.** W. Chandler Roberts.

TABLE 57.—ABSORPTION OF GASES BY IRON.

Number.	Observer.	No. in Table 54.	Description of metal.	Treatment before exposure to the gas absorbed: Heated. Hours.	In.	Temperature.	Absorption of gases. Conditions during absorption. Hours.	In.	Temperature.	Gas absorbed. Vol. gas per vol. iron. H.	CO.	Measured directly or inferred from volume subsequently evolved in vacuo.
41..	P	..	Gray cast-iron	Apparently previously heated in vacuo			......	Hydrogen	......	22·4	......	Direct.
42..	"		" " "				......	"	......	13·2	......	"
43..	"	12	" " "				......	"	White	20·	......	"
44..	"		" " "	......	Vacuo	1400°C ‡	18	"	"	22·	......	"
45..	"	15	" " "	......	"	1400°C ‡	24	"	Bright red	13·2	......	"
46..	"	10	" " "	165	"	......	......	"	......	20·	......	"
47..	T and H	14	Cast-iron	190	"	800°C	48	"	800° C	0·63	0·016	Indirect.
50..	"	17	Cast-steel	190	"	800°C	48	"	800° C	0·69	0·013	"
51..	P	20	Bessemer steel	......	"	......	24	"	......	10·84	......	Direct.
52..	"	32	Wrought-iron	163	"	......	24·5	"	Red ‡	13·	......	"
53..	T and H	31	" "	190	"	800°C	48	"	800°C	0·15	0·069	Indirect.
54..	G	33	" " wire	7	"	Red	....	"	Red	·46	......	"
60..	P	10	Gray cast-iron (see No. 46)	165	"	......	......	Carbonic oxide	......	......	0·	Direct.
61..	T and H	11	Charcoal cast-iron (see No. 47)	190	"	800°C	48	"	800°C	0·02	0·21	Indirect.
63..	"	16	Cast-steel (see No. 50)	190	"	800°C	48	"	800°C	0·01	·08	"
65..	"	30	Wrought-iron (see No. 53)	190	"	800°C	48	"	800°C	0·003	·21	"
66..	P	35	" "	......	"	......	68	"	......	......	4·56	Direct.
67..	G	26	" " wire (see No. 54)	1	"	Low red	......	"	Red	......	4·15	Indirect.

Parry measured the absorption of hydrogen and carbonic oxide by iron, by heating the metal, which at least in certain cases had been previously heated or even fused in vacuo, in a closed tube in contact with a known volume of gas. The diminution of volume could then be read. In case of hydrogen this is supposed to be due to absorption. In case of carbonic oxide it is assumed in this table that this gas was absorbed as such: but, as will be shown later, its disappearance may be due to its decomposition, with the absorption of its oxygen and carbon separately.

The indirect determinations were made by first heating the metal in vacuo, in some cases till it appeared to be nearly exhausted, then heating it in an atmosphere of hydrogen or carbonic oxide, and then later again heating it in a vacuo. The gas now evolved is analyzed, and is supposed to have been absorbed from the atmosphere of gas in which the metal had just been heated. Its composition in general supports this view.

The conditions of these indirect determinations are described in the reference to Table 54, some of whose data are reproduced here, to bring all the cases of absorption together. **41, 42, 43,** Parry, Journ. Iron and St. Inst., 1873, II., p. 431. **44, 45,** Idem, 1874, I., p. 94. Temperature above the melting point of the iron. **46,** idem, 1881, I., p. 190. **47,** Troost and Hautefeuille, Comptes Rendus, LXXVI., 1873, p. 563. **50,** idem, p. 564. **51,** Parry, op. cit., 1881, I., p. 190. **52,** idem, 1873, I., p. 431. **53,** Troost and Haut., loc. cit. **54,** Graham, Journ. Chem. Soc., XX., 1867, p. 285. The wire became white like galvanized iron. **60,** Parry, op. cit., 1881, I., p. 190. This iron had previously been saturated with hydrogen, with results as in No. 46. **61, 63** and **65,** Troost and Haut., loc. cit. These pieces had been previously saturated with hydrogen, and then exhausted, with results as given in numbers 47, 50 and 53 respectively. **66,** Parry, op. cit., 1873, I., 431. **67,** Graham, loc. cit. This wire had previously been saturated with hydrogen and then exhausted, as per No. 54.

TABLE 58.—NITROGEN IN COMMERCIAL IRON.

	Observer.		Mode of extracting nitrogen.	Cast-iron. %	Cast-iron. Vols.	Steel. %	Steel. Vols.	Wrought-iron. %	Wrought-iron. Vols.
1..	Stuart and Baker	Expansion and measurement. Conversion into ammonia.	Heating in hydrogen	0@·015	0@·95	0@·01	0@·65	......	......
2..	Bouis		" " "	0@·001	·065	·0002@·01	·013 @·554	·0009	......
3..	Allen		Solution with acid	·004@·0088	·20@·64	·0008@·0172	·41 @1·12	·0094@·0148	·61@·97
4..	Boussingault		" " "	......	......	·022 @ ·042	1·44 @2·74	·0075	·49
5..	Marchand		Heating with soda-lime	·009	·58	·014	·81	......	......
6..	"		" " cupric oxide	·0180	1·24	·0169	1·24	......	......
7..	Boussingault		" " cinnabar	......	......	·057	3·72	......	......
8..	Graham		" in vacuo	......	......	......	......	·00459	·80
9..	Troost and Hautefeuille		" " "	·00021@·00061	·014@·04	·000346	·008	·00026	·017
10..	Parry		" " "	0@·010	0@·68	·0129	·84	·000459	·03
11..	Zyromski		" " "	......	......	·020	1·50	·034	1·66
12..	Stead		Boring cold metal	·042	2·73	·0178	1·13	......	......
13..	Müller		Escape during solidification	......	......	·0019?	·125?	......	......
14	"		Boring cold metal	·0002@·0007	·01@·05	·0002@·0016	·01@1·13	......	......

1, Pure hydrogen passed over the metal at full redness: the ammonia formed was absorbed in sulphuric acid. Their results average 0·0033% nitrogen. Journ. Chem. Soc., XVII., 1864, p. 390. **2,** Comptes Rendus, LII., p. 1,195, 1861. Percy, Iron and Steel, p. 55. Two streams of the same perfectly dried hydrogen are passed independently through two red-hot porcelain tubes in the same furnace, one containing the iron, the other empty and serving as a check. The removal of nitrogen appears to be only superficial: on filing the iron after exposure to hydrogen the fresh surfaces again give off nitrogen. Bouis results appear to be incorrectly given in at least one standard text-book, the weights of nitrogen which he gives being mistaken for percentages: this magnifies some of his numbers 203 times. Yet his text leaves no doubt that the high figures ordinarily quoted are incorrectly attributed to him. **3,** Journ. Iron and St. Inst., 1879, II., p. 436 and 1880, I., p. 181. Iron is dissolved in hydrochloric acid with complete exclusion of air: the solution is distilled after adding excess of lime: ammonia is determined in the distillate by Nessler's test. The nitrogen recovered must have come from the iron, for analyses of zinc and of iron freshly reduced by hydrogen gave absolutely no ammonia whether in presence or absence of air: blank analyses gave minute quantities of ammonia, which were deducted. **4,** Comptes Rendus, 1861, LXIII., p. 77. Percy, Iron and Steel, p. 56. Method same as the last, except that the ammonia is determined by sulphuric acid. This method gave 2·635 nitrogen in nitrogenized iron, in which the cinnabar method found 2·669. **5** and **6,** Percy, Iron and Steel, p. 52. **7,** Idem, p. 58. **8, 9, 10,** See Table 56. **11,** Stahl und Eisen, IV., p. 534, 1884. **12,** Iron, 1888, p. 115. **13,** Idem, 1884, p. 133. Müller found from 1 to 1·5 volumes of gas escaping from Bessemer steel during solidification, whose composition was not determined. The percentage of nitrogen in gas escaping under similar conditions varied from 2·2 to 48% (see Table 55): assuming it at 10% merely to get a rough idea of the quantity of nitrogen thus escaping, we have 0·125 volumes per volume of steel. **14,** See Table 54

The percentages of nitrogen found by several investigators in iron thus nitrogenized are here given.

TABLE 59.—NITROGENIZED IRON OBTAINED BY HEATING IN AMMONIACAL GAS.

No.	Observer.	Substance heated.	Nitrogen absorbed. Vol.	%	How determined.
1...	Despretz	Iron	754·385	11·538	By gain of weight.
2...	Frémy	Ferrous chloride at bright redness	663·22	9·8	By loss on heating in hydrogen.
3...	"	Iron at redness, 26 hrs	640·92	9·8	
4...	Boussingault	......	173·964	2·66	As ammonia.
5...	Percy	Thin iron wire, 90 mins	28·776	0·44	By gain of weight.
6...	H. N. Warren	Puddled iron	00·2616 to 32·70	0·004 to 5	By Nessler's test.

1. Percy, Iron and Steel, p. 51. **2.** Idem, p. 53. **2** and **3.** Comptes Rendus, LII., 1861, p. 325; Percy, op. cit., p. 54. **4.** Comptes Rendus, LIII., p. 10, 1861, Percy, op. cit., p. 57. **5.** Percy, op. cit., p. 55. **6.** Chem. News, LV., p. 155, 1887.

Percy's wire, number 5, though it apparently had taken up but 0·44% of nitrogen, had turned white, was remarkably brittle, and had a very brilliant fracture. Bars of the finest puddled iron nitrogenized by Warren (included in number 6, Table 59), after taking up 0·5% nitrogen became so brittle that they broke transversely on falling from a height of 6 feet. A bar of the same iron which had absorbed but 0·004% nitrogen is reported as breaking with a decidedly crystalline structure: one with 0·01% nitrogen is reported as still more crystalline and apparently somewhat more brittle. Unfortunately Warren reports no numerically comparable tests of strength and ductility.

§ 174. INFLUENCE OF NITROGEN IN COMMERCIAL IRON.—As 9% of nitrogen suffices to render iron friable, and as even 0·44% appears to render it "remarkably brittle," it is by no means unlikely that the 0·04% occasionally found in commercial iron may materially affect it. Metcalf[a] ascribes the lustrous fracture of Bessemer steel and its reported relatively low ductility compared with crucible steel of otherwise identical composition, to the presence of nitrogen absorbed from the enormous volumes of air blown through the metal at high pressure during manufacture. If merely a coincidence, it is a striking one that Allen (Table 58) finds twice as much nitrogen in pneumatic as in crucible steel[b]: but his results are too few to decide the question. The nascent iron which alone ab-

[a] Trans. Am. Inst. Mining Engrs., IX., p. 548, 1881.

[b] Journ. Iron and St. Inst., 1880, I., p. 188. He obtained the following percentages of nitrogen in several specimens of steel: acid Bessemer, ·0164; basic Bessemer, ·0115; open hearth, ·0107, ·0098; blister, ·0148, ·0156; double shear, ·0139; crucible, ·0082.

sorbs nitrogen from the atmosphere, may be furnished by the reduction of iron-oxide by carbon, etc., in the Bessemer process.

IRON AND HYDROGEN.[a]

§ 175. SUMMARY.—Hydrogen is usually present in both solid and molten iron, abundantly if measured by volume, sparingly if measured by weight: commercial iron probably does not usually contain much more than 0·01%. Parry has indeed found 0·22% of hydrogen in commercial iron: but numerical relations in his results and the wide discrepancy between them and those of other observers indicate that they are erroneous. Certain facts suggest that iron cannot retain permanently more than about 0·17% or 154 volumes of this gas, but it can temporarily acquire at least ·26%.

The hydrogen in iron usually and perhaps always exists in part at least as gas, and sometimes as ammonia gas: but a part at least in certain cases probably exists in some non-gaseous state. It appears to be always easily expelled, and hence is probably not in strong chemical union with the metal.

Heated in hydrogen or exposed when cold to nascent hydrogen iron absorbs a minute quantity of this gas, exposure to the nascent gas reducing the metal's flexibility surprisingly, in view of the minute quantity of gas absorbed, probably not over ·01%. The flexibility is restored and at least part of the hydrogen is expelled rapidly by heating, and slowly by simple rest. It is uncertain whether the hydrogen usually present in commercial iron affects it sensibly.

Hydrogen escapes from iron when heated in vacuo, when bored under water, oil or mercury, and during solidification, in the latter case producing blowholes. It is usually accompanied by nitrogen and, except when the metal is bored under water, etc., by carbonic oxide. From fresh fractures of ingots and other castings, and sometimes even from rails, a strong smell of ammonia sometimes escapes, which unquestionably proceeds from the metal itself: and occasionally the escape of ammonia and hydrogen from the fracture is so rapid as to be distinctly audible.

§ 176. *The presence of hydrogen in iron.*

A. Its Absorption.—Melting cast-iron in vacuo, in order to remove the gas initially present, and then without removing it from his apparatus and while it was still hot exposing it to a known volume of hydrogen, Parry found by direct measurement that it absorbed from 13·2 to 22·4 volumes[b] of this gas.

In a similar way he found that malleable iron, after more or less complete exhaustion in vacuo, reabsorbed from 10·5 to 13 volumes of hydrogen (see Table 57).

No other observer, so far as I know, has directly measured the volume of gas absorbed by iron, though Troost and Hautefeuille and Graham have estimated it by first exhausting the iron by heating in vacuo, then heating and cooling it in hydrogen, and noting the quantity emitted on again heating in vacuo: this varied from ·09 to ·63 volumes per volume of iron. The gas now evolved contained a larger and usually a much larger proportion of hydrogen than that originally extracted. Graham found a low, Parry a relatively high temperature most favorable to the absorption of hydrogen.[c]

B. Hydrogen a usual constituent of commercial iron. So far as my inquiries have gone hydrogen has always been found when properly sought in commercial iron,[d] but, neglecting Parry's results for the moment, in very small quantities. The largest quantities found by each of several observers in previously untreated commercial iron are given in Table 60.

TABLE 60.—MAXIMUM HYDROGEN FOUND BY SEVERAL OBSERVERS IN SOLID IRON PREVIOUSLY UNTREATED.

			Cast-iron.		Wrought-iron.		Steel.	
			Vols. per vol. iron.	%	Vols. per vol. iron.	%	Vols. per vol. iron.	%
1.	Troost and Hautefeuille	Heated in vacuo.	0·177	·00019	·065	·00007	·007	·000008
2.	Graham		....	......	6·8	·0008	....	......
3	Zyromski		....	......	1·21	·0013	3·12	·0034
4.	Parry		265·	·223	1·09	·0012	22·35	·025
5.	F. Fox	Combustion.	....	......	....	......	5·01a	·0058
6.	Ledebur		2·6	·0028	....	......	1·6	·0017
7.	Stead (dull drill)	Boring under water.	8·3	·0088	....	......	9·76	·0106
8.	Müller		·29	·0003	....	......	·23	·0003

a Other experiments with this same steel gave 0·1 volume of hydrogen. I have deducted for probable error as inferred from blank analyses.

The results obtained by Troost and Hautefeuille, Graham, Zyromski, Parry, Stead and Müller are further described in Tables 54 and 56.

Ledebur (Wagner's Jahresbericht, 1883, XXIX., p. 46, Stahl und Eisen, 1882, p. 591) oxidized ferro-silicon and ingot iron with dry air in a porcelain tube, first thoroughly drying the tube while the iron was in it by heating to 300° or 400° C. in a stream of dry nitrogen. The water formed by the oxidation of the hydrogen of the iron was caught and weighed. Fox (Thesis for the degree of Master of Science, Mass. Inst. Technology, 1886) in a long and careful investigation in Drown's laboratory, made some twenty determinations of the hydrogen in cast-iron and steel, by oxidizing the metal, mixed with copper oxide or chromate of lead in porcelain tubes, by means of dry oxygen, catching and weighing the water formed. When employing chromate of lead he obtained 14 volumes of hydrogen from cast-iron; but he suspected that the result was exaggerated by hydrogen evolved by this reagent, though precautions apparently sufficient were employed. That the iron was completely oxidized is inferred from the fact that the carbonic acid escaping during combustion corresponded closely to the total carbon independently determined by trustworthy methods.

The results obtained by these observers by the combustion method must be accepted reservedly. In the first place, we do not know that this method will remove the hydrogen from iron. It is possible, though indeed extremely improbable, that the hydrogen initially occluded by the iron may not become oxidized by the oxygen employed, but may remain occluded in the resulting iron oxide: for we do not know that iron oxide has not as great or even greater power for occluding hydrogen than metallic iron has. Indeed, some of Fox's results suggest that it has greater occluding power. Thus, a steel which in one combustion yielded 5 volumes of hydrogen, in another gave but 0·1 volume, or very much less than Parry, Zyromski, Graham and Stead extract in vacuo or by boring. We have in the second place the danger of leakage at the many joints or through the cracks or pores of the porcelain tubes, and of the introduction of unoxidized hydrogen or some of its volatile compounds along with the air: they might well pass the apparatus employed for drying the air, become oxidized with the iron and swell the results. Hence the air or oxygen employed should, before admission to the combustion tube, be heated with copper oxide and dried. As the weight of hydrogen found was generally and that of the water caught occasionally less than one milligramme, trifling errors would seriously vitiate the results. A similar source of error is the hydrogen initially occluded by the porcelain tubes and other portions of the apparatus and slowly evolved; how tenaciously this adheres may be inferred from the fact that when, as in Bunsen and Roscoe's photometer, it is necessary to obtain even in so non-absorptive a body as a glass vessel, an atmosphere absolutely free from oxygen and nitrogen, the vessel must be swept for several days with other gases (in this case chlorine and hydrogen. Roscoe, in Watt's Dictionary, II., p. 805).

Fox found that thoroughly dried oxygen, when swept through an otherwise empty redhot porcelain tube, persistently yielded small quantities of water, 3·5 mmgms. during the first hour, 0·7 mmgms. per hour from the 12th to the 14th hour.

While the results obtained by these combustions might well be too high, it seems decidedly improbable that they should be too low.

In the combustion methods employed by Ledebur and Fox the slight changes in the weight of their phosphoric anhydride tubes, following the protracted passage of gas, might be attributed to experimental error rather than to the absorption of water actually formed by the oxidation of hydrogen escaping from the metal under treatment. Indeed, with elaborate precautions, Fox found that these tubes always gained weight, even when the combustion tubes contained no iron, though the increase of weight was invariably greater when iron was under treatment. In heating in vacuo, too, there is a chance that hydrogen should enter the apparatus through faulty joints or through the pores of the apparatus, rendered permeable by the high temperature. Had we to rely on these methods alone the usual existence of hydrogen in iron might well be questioned.

But wholly independent methods corroborate its pres-

a Tables 54 to 57 and Chapter XI. contain additional facts and further discussion concerning hydrogen and iron.

b Throughout this work the volume of gas is supposed to be measured at 0° C. and 76 cc. barometric pressure, unless otherwise stated.

c Journ. Iron and Steel Inst., 1874, I., p. 95.

d On heating iron wire in dry nitrogen for 20 minutes at a "bright glow," Ledebur found no weighable quantity of hydrogen: but it is doubtful if so brief a heating in nitrogen should be expected to extract a weighable quantity of his gas. (Stahl und Eisen, VII., p. 693, 1887.)

ence. Troost and Hautefeuille observed that, when iron after tranquil fusion in hydrogen was suddenly solidified with fall of pressure, gas was visibly evolved. Müller finds that the gas evolved by iron on solidifying in the air is chiefly hydrogen. This is the chief constituent of the gaseous contents of the blowholes found after solidification.

By increasing the pressure during solidification and by the addition of silicon, manganese or aluminium before solidification, the escape of this hydrogen can be prevented, and it is probable that it remains after solidification in the cold iron. The indirectly and more especially the directly measured absorption of hydrogen by solid iron and the frequent evolution of ammonia from common cold steel, so abundant as to force itself on the attention of numerous unexpectant observers, prove that solid iron can contain hydrogen: and the hydrogen almost always found on boring cold iron under water, oil or mercury, leaves no doubt that iron usually contains this gas.

While part of the hydrogen found on boring cold steel doubtless exists as gas in visible cavities, which indeed sometimes contain it in such quantities that, when bored from below under water, gas bubbles out from the bore hole when the point of the drill pierces the first blowholes, yet in some cases hydrogen is released on boring solid steel quite free from visible cavities. Moreover, by triturating the metal with a dull drill over 69 times as much hydrogen has been obtained as when the same metal was cut in the ordinary way with a sharp drill. (16-17, Table 54.)

While the trituration may increase the evolution of hydrogen simply by laying bare innumerable microscopic but not intermolecular cavities, it seems probable that a considerable part of the hydrogen extracted by trituration exists in the iron in some non-gaseous state; and in such a state the gas which escapes from molten iron certainly exists before its escape.

Now the quantity of hydrogen which is found on boring under water and which unquestionably comes from the iron, does not differ more from that found in other specimens of iron by combustion and heating in vacuo (except Parry's results) than do the proportions of manganese or of carbon in different specimens of iron. This is no proof that the results obtained by these latter methods are correct, but it shows that they are not in themselves improbable.

The combustion method should give the total hydrogen: indeed the errors to which it is liable should exaggerate the proportion of this gas. But, if part of the hydrogen were united with the iron by some strong chemical tie, heating in vacuo and boring might not release it, and we might expect that the results thus obtained would be below those of the combustion method. The fact that they are not suggests that most and perhaps all the hydrogen is but feebly held by the metal. The fact that the marked effects apparently produced by the absorption of nascent hydrogen are removed by heating and rest, which simultaneously expel hydrogen, points in the same direction. (§ 178.)

C. Parry's Results.—In eight out of the twelve cases in which he extracts hydrogen from previously untreated iron, he recovers more, usually much more and in one case 21 times as much hydrogen as has been recovered by any other observer by any method whatsoever within my knowledge.[a] In the remaining four cases the length of exposure, if stated, was comparatively short: so that the inference might be justified that, had he employed his usual prolonged exposures, he would probably in every case have extracted much more hydrogen than any one else.

He found that, while the flow of gas from iron heated in vacuo gradually slackened at constant temperature, and could be completely checked by lowering the temperature say from whiteness to redness, yet it always started up afresh on raising the temperature, "and this continued up to the highest heat attainable." In no case was there satisfactory evidence that the metal was completely freed from hydrogen, even after seven days heating in vacuo.[b]

There is little reason to doubt that he, like others, actually extracted some hydrogen from the iron itself: but the great difference between his results and those of others suggests that a large portion of his gas may have come from some source other than his iron. Shall we accept or reject his results? Shall we believe that a comparatively short heating in vacuo suffices to extract nearly all the hydrogen present, or that it extracts but a small fraction of the hydrogen, and that this gas is actually evolved by the iron at a rapid rate even after days of heating?

Against his results we have his own candid admission[c] that it appears to the last degree improbable that cast-iron contains the large quantity of hydrogen shown: the fact that the iron from which he extracted these large volumes of hydrogen would reabsorb but a relatively small proportion[c]: the fact that there appears to be a chance for hydrogen to enter his apparatus, which might be suspected of permeability at the high temperatures employed: and that, as just stated, when he employed a long exposure he obtained much higher results than other observers, even when they employed methods which, unlike his, would naturally be expected to extract the whole of the hydrogen present. I see but two ways of reconciling his results with theirs. These are to suppose either that he usually happened on irons very exceptionally rich in hydrogen: or that the methods employed by Fox and Ledebur recover but a fraction of the hydrogen present: and neither of these suppositions is probable. A further difficulty, that of supposing that the large quantity of carbonic oxide and hydrogen which he finds, sometimes amounting together to nearly one per cent, should be overlooked in ordinary analyses, the sum of whose results still usually very nearly equals 100%, cannot be passed over lightly.

In favor of his results we have the following facts.

1. The nearly and often quite complete absence of nitrogen from his gases indicates that they are not of atmospheric origin: and the absence of carbonic acid argues that they do not arise from the flame used for heating the tubes, which should yield carbonic acid and nitrogen, and this carbonic acid would probably only be partially reduced by the iron under treatment. To this it may be objected that hydrogen is so diffusive that it might enter rapidly where nitrogen and carbonic acid could enter but slowly,

[a] Cf. Tables 56 and 60.
[b] Journ. Iron and St. Inst., 1881, I., p. 189.
[c] Idem, 1874, I., p. 100.

and that the carbonic oxide which Parry finds with his hydrogen may arise from reaction within the tube.[a] Moreover, the hydrogen might arise from the tubes themselves.

2. There is a rough accord between the quantity of gas extracted on the one hand, and the temperature and length of exposure on the other. But to this it may be objected justly that, if the gas arose from leakage or diffusion or any source other than the iron, its quantity would still increase with the temperature and duration of the experiment.

3. On exhausting platinum by this same method Parry's results agreed with Graham's.

4. Parry is a very intelligent chemist, of prolonged experience in the analysis of iron, and, according to such information as I can obtain, exceptionally conscientious and trustworthy.

5. With his longer exposures and higher temperatures we should expect him to extract whatever hydrogen was present more completely than others who heat iron in vacuo. This latter consideration does not explain why he gets more hydrogen than Ledebur and Fox, who appear to have completely oxidized their specimens. Its force is also much weakened by the fact that the very prolonged exposures to a vacuum employed by Troost and Hautefeuille extracted but a minute fraction of the quantity of hydrogen that Parry found. That at about the melting point of copper, say 1000° C., and in 60 hours (Number 20, Table 56) he should extract nearly 5000 times as much hydrogen per volume of steel as they did in 190 hours at 800° C. (Number 16, idem) is surprising, and perhaps more than surprising.

6. Parry states that the gas is certainly not due to leakage: that experiments with empty tubes do not indicate that it can enter by diffusion: and that his rubber connections do not evolve gas at 70,° (probably C.).

This is a vital point. Were his tubes impermeable or not?[b]

It seems to me quite clear that Parry satisfied himself that there was no leakage through the joints, but did not satisfy himself that the portions of his apparatus other than the joints were also impermeable. His language implies that experiments with empty tubes were not decisive.

Looking beneath the surface, let us see whether the numerical relations between his various results support or oppose the belief that all or nearly all his gas came from his iron. Leaving out of consideration his exposures of 6·5 hours and less, because at the beginning of an exposure a very large quantity of gas would be expected to be given off by the metal, we have six experiments in which the quantity of gas and of metal are given, and in which the exposures lasted 24 hours or longer. If now the whole of the gas came from the metal, we might expect that the volume of gas per gramme of metal would gradually diminish with the progress of the exhaustion, so that the longer the exposure the less gas would be given off per hour per gramme of metal, and so that, were we to number the experiments by the length of exposure, 1 having the longest, and place them in the order of the volume of gas emitted per hour per gramme of metal, the most rapid emission first, they should stand thus; 6, 5, 4, 3, 2, 1. Now they actually stand in a very different order, viz.: 3, 5, 4, 1, 2, 6, the shortest exposure yielding the least gas per hour. (Lines 9 and 10, Table 60 A.) Here the sum of the first half of the digits is but little larger than that of the last.

TABLE 60 A.—ANALYSIS OF PARRY'S RESULTS, SPECIMENS HEATED 24 HOURS OR MORE.

Number.							
	I. Relation between weight of metal and volume of gas per volume of metal.						
	Number in Table 56	9.	6.	7.	8.	20.	5.
1..	Volume of gas per volume of metal	194	127·6	123·5	90·8	79·5	19
2..	Weight of metal, grammes	3·33	10	4·5	5·1	10	41·
3..	No. by weight of metal. 1. Heaviest	5	2	4	3	2	1
	II. Relation between volume of gas per hour and weight of metal.						
4..	Number in Table 56	9.	8.	7.	6.	20.	5.
5..	Volume of gas per hour, cc.	1·64	1·95	1·59	2·41	1·51	4·79
6..	Vol. of gas per hour per gr. metal, cc.	·493	·382	·353	·241	·151	·117
7..	No. by weight of metal. 1. Heaviest.	5	3	4	2	2	1
8..	Hours exposure	59	36	52·5	76	60	24
	Relation between volume of gas per gramme of metal per hour and length of exposure.						
9..	Vol. of gas per hour per gr. metal	·493	·382	·353	·241	·151	·117
10..	No. by length of exposure. 1. Longest	3	5	4	1	2	6

The actual differs so much from the expected sequence that it certainly does not argue for the belief that the whole of the gas came from the metal: nor, on the other hand does it differ enough to argue strongly against this belief.

Whether the gas came wholly from the metal or partly from metal and partly from other sources, the total volume of gas per hour should increase with the weight of metal; and, numbering the experiments according to the weight of metal, 1 having the most, and placing them in order of the total volume of gas per hour, the largest volume first, they should stand 1, 2, 2, 3, 4, 5: actually the order in which they stand, viz.: 1, 2, 3, 5, 4, 2, while it differs from the expected sequence, hardly differs enough to suggest that no important part comes from the metal. But this sequence of course throws no light on the question whether an important part also comes from some other source.

If, however, the gas came wholly from the metal, then, numbering the experiments according to the weight of metal as before and placing the numbers in the order of the volume of gas per hour per gramme of metal, no especial order should be looked for. But, if the gas came in large part from some other source, then the less metal the more gas per hour per gramme of metal should be found: and, if numbered and placed as just stated, the largest volume first, they should stand 5, 4, 3, 2, 2, 1; and this is almost

[a] See § 188 B.

[b] This is so important a matter that I quote at length several of Parry's remarks bearing on it. "A good heat could be applied without danger from leakage or fusion of tubes." (Journ. Iron and St. Inst., 1873, II., p. 241.) "At a full red heat a vacuum could always be obtained, but, on raising the heat, gas again came off. The cause of this continuous evolution of gas has not yet been ascertained. It has been proved that it is not due to leakage." (Idem, 1873, I., p. 430.) "On fusing gray pig iron in vacuo it was found impossible to maintain a good vacuum for any length of time, gas in small quantity being continually evolved: that this continuous evolution of gas *did not appear* to be due to leakage, for the quantity of gas evolved *increased in proportion to the weight of iron used.*" *The italics* are mine. (Idem, 1874, I., p. 92.) It will be shown shortly that the relation between the quantity of gas and that of iron gives good reason to suspect that much of the gas obtained came from some source other than the iron. "It is certain that the gas is not due to leakage, and must be derived either from the iron or tubes, or by diffusion from the gas flame through the substance of the tube, this latter, considering the precautions taken, being very improbable, and is not confirmed by experiments with empty tubes." (Idem, p. 100.) "It is, moreover, very possible that no exhausted vessel heated from the exterior remains perfectly gas-tight at the high temperature which appears necessary, although actual results with empty tubes so far disprove this. To remove all uncertainty arising from possible leakage, the author proposes heating the metal (inclosed in an exhausted glass globe) by means of the electric current." (Idem, p. 1881, I., p. 192.) This would indeed be a crucial as well as an extremely easy test. I commend it to metallurgical investigators.

exactly their order, which is 5, 6, 4, 2, 2, 1 (line 7, Table 60 A). Here the sequence would be perfect but for the transposition of 4 and 3, which is far from surprising: for number 4 had a longer exposure than number 3, which might well diminish its volume of gas per hour by a greater amount than the very slight difference, less than 8%, in the volume of gas per hour per gramme of metal of these two experiments.

If we go a step farther and, ignoring the quantity of gas evolved during the first part of the exhaustion, consider only that evolved later, we obtain a similar sequence, viz.: 4, 5, 3, 2, 2, 1. Here, too, transposing two adjoining numbers gives us the perfect sequence.

Again, even if much gas came from some source other than the metal, the quantity of gas obtained during the first part of the exhaustion should increase with the weight of metal treated, for doubtless some gas comes from the metal itself. But if, as we suspect, the metal itself is soon exhausted, and the gas obtained later comes from some other source, then the total volume of gas per hour obtained during the latter part of the exhaustion should bear no relation to the weight of the metal: and it bears none. Still confining ourselves to these six cases, and ignoring the volume of gas evolved during the first recorded division of each experiment, we find that in three experiments (5, 6 and 20, Table 56), in which from 10 to 41 grammes of metal were treated, from 0·42 to 2·15 cc. of gas were obtained per hour, or on an average 1·28 cc.: while in the other three (7, 8 and 9) only from 3·33 to 5·16 grammes of metal were treated, yet more gas than before was obtained, viz.: from 1·3 to 2·16 cc., or, on an average, 1·59 cc. This probably cannot be explained away by differences in the temperature of the experiments, for comparing those portions of the experiments in which a given temperature prevailed I find no indication that after the first hours the greater weight of metal evolved more gas than the lesser. Thus at redness the greater weights of iron evolve from ·42 to 3·1 cc. per hour, the lighter weights from 1·2 to 5·2 cc. At whiteness the heavy weights evolve in the only recorded case 2·1 cc. per hour, while the light weights evolve from 1·79 to 2·59 cc. per hour.

In regard to the sequences just discussed we have this dilemma: either these numbers stand so close to the expected sequences by a chance conspiracy of the other conditions: or a considerable proportion of the gas which Parry found came from some source other than the metal, and the latter seems in itself rather the more probable supposition. Add the weight of the fact that the quantity of gas evolved after the first hours seems quite independent of the weight of metal treated, of the intrinsic improbability of Parry's results, and of the fact that no other observer has been able to obtain by any method anything beginning to approach these quantities of gas, and the balance of probabilities inclines very strongly to this latter supposition. The balance may of course be reversed by additional facts which Mr. Parry may now have or may discover later.

D. Saturation Point for Hydrogen in Iron.—Several facts indicate that the proportion of hydrogen which iron can retain permanently is small measured by weight.

a. From glass-hard electrolytic iron Cailletet extracted from 238·5 to 250 volumes of hydrogen by heating in vacuo.[a] During 15 days exposure in an open tube, apparently at the ordinary temperature, it appeared to lose about 94 volumes of this gas. In water at 60° to 70° C. (140° to 158° F.) it gave off gas tumultuously. If, ignoring Parry's results, we consider that on heating in vacuo Cailletet extracted all or nearly all the hydrogen present, it appears that under these conditions iron is unable to retain more than 250 — 94 = 156 volumes of hydrogen, = 0·17%. If we accept Parry's results, we must admit that even his prolonged heating may not have extracted all the hydrogen. But it would be generous, I think, to admit that, in his seven-day heating, Parry extracted only half the hydrogen: but let us admit it. Let us go farther, and admit that after Cailletet had heated his iron in vacuo it still retained twice as much hydrogen as Parry extracted from his iron in seven days. With this extreme admission, Cailletet's iron appears able to retain on exposure to the air for 15 days only 250 + 2 × 205 — 94 = 566 volumes or 0·615% of hydrogen.

b. It is probable, however, that common commercial steel is actually nearly saturated with hydrogen, and that, if Cailletet's iron had been long enough exposed to the air a far greater proportion of its hydrogen would have escaped than left it in his fifteen-day exposure. The small quantity of hydrogen, 1·9 to 4·8 volumes (·0021 to ·0052%) which Ledebur found in iron after exposure to nascent hydrogen probably escapes on simple exposure to the air: at least, its effects disappear, and they are made to disappear by the very treatment (gentle heating) by which Ledebur extracts this hydrogen from the iron. This is of course simply suggestive, not conclusive.

Again, on solidifying, most classes of iron evolve more or less hydrogen, which indicates that they are then saturated. That this expulsion continues after solidification has well advanced is shown by the presence of hydrogen in the blowholes of iron. Unless the iron were saturated it would not expel this hydrogen; nay, it would rather reabsorb that present in the blowholes.

If this view that common commercial irons contain nearly or quite as much hydrogen as they are capable of holding permanently be true, and if the results in Table 60 give the whole or nearly the whole of the hydrogen in iron, it would follow that, while their capacity for hydrogen varied greatly, none of those tested are able to hold much over say 10 volumes (0·01%) of this gas if we reject Parry's results. If we accept them, and admit as above that his seven-day heatings extract but half the hydrogen, it would follow that none of the irons tested can contain much over 410 volumes (0·446%).

E. Ammonia from Steel.—Regnard[b] observed that the fresh fractures of all or nearly all the 3·1 inch square ingots from certain heats of open-hearth steel emitted a sound of escaping gas, and an ammoniacal smell whose intensity seemed proportionate to the quantity of gas escaping. Soap water placed on the fresh fracture was thrown into thousands of microscopic bubbles, whose total volume sometimes exceeded 1 cc. (0·06 cubic inches), and which formed chiefly in the center of the fracture. The gas from more than a hundred fractures when collected in test tubes burned with a hardly visible flame, detonated if mixed with air, and was almost pure

[a] Comptes Rendus, LXXX., 1875, p. 319.
[b] Idem, LXXXIV., p. 260, 1877.

hydrogen. If, as is probable, the gas was collected over water, it may be inferred that the steel emitted a mixture of hydrogen and ammonia, the latter being absorbed by the water. These phenomena did not occur with porous and soft steel, and were prevented by annealing, which probably permitted the imprisoned hydrogen to escape by diffusion.

Barré,[a] by smell and litmus paper, recognized ammonia escaping from the fracture of both open-hearth and Bessemer steel; and, without knowledge of these facts, Forsyth[b] at Chicago and Emmerton[b] at Joliet independently observed the unmistakable evolution of ammonia on breaking certain Bessemer steel rails under the hammer. Here we may suppose that the greater thickness of the ingots prevented the hydrogen from escaping during heating so completely as it appears to have from Regnard's thin ingots.

Finally, Goetz reports that the fresh fractures of large steel castings, especially those of large risers which have a shrinkage hole at the fracture, nearly always evolve a smell of ammonia, which has been so strong as to draw the attention of the workmen. The presence of ammonia is proved by the white fumes formed on the approach of hydrochloric acid, and by the formation of chloride of ammonium when the air in the neighborhood of the fracture is drawn through hydrochloric acid. On evaporating this to dryness chloride of ammonium is found. In the shrinkage hole itself he reports "a regular pocket" of ammonia. The smell is noticed even when the fracture is perfectly solid, "not a pin-hole in it": and the fumes, though less noticeable, appear when the steel is cut in a lathe. Like Regnard, he has not noticed the escape of ammonia from soft castings, and he finds it most pronounced when the steel contains from ·3 to ·38% of carbon, ·9 to 1·% of manganese, and ·3% of silicon. When but little silicon is present little and sometimes no odor can be detected.[c] The low silicon suggests porosity, and recalls Regnard's observation that porous steel evolved no ammonia. The close agreement between the observations of Regnard and Goetz is the more striking as the latter was unacquainted with the former's work.

From these observations and especially from the "pockets of ammonia" in large cavities described by Goetz, it is probable that ammonia is formed in the cooling steel, the hydrogen in its pores acting on nitrogen combined with the metal or escaping from it. (See § 172, p. 106.)

§ 178. INFLUENCE OF HYDROGEN.

A. *Non-nascent Hydrogen.*—So far as I know, no marked change in the properties of iron has been observed to follow the removal of hydrogen by heating in vacuo. Graham observed that iron wire Number 54, Table 57, after taking up apparently but 0·46 volumes or ·0005% of hydrogen, became white like galvanized iron. Bouis observed that after being heated for some hours in hydrogen iron became very crystalline, brittle, and of a steel-like appearance.[d] Further observations are needed.

B. *Exposure to nascent hydrogen*[e] greatly diminishes the flexibility[f] of wrought-iron and steel, and to a much smaller degree that of cast-iron,[i] and the transverse strength of steel[i] and probably of the other varieties of iron. The elongation of the metal is often simultaneously diminished, though usually to a very much smaller degree, and it is in general affected in a way which is much less clearly understood; while the tensile strength and modulus of elasticity are affected but slightly, if at all.

The fracture of metal which has been thus exposed, if moistened while still warm from the effort of breaking, froths and gives off copious gas bubbles for 30 or 40 seconds, and even the unbroken metal evolves gas bubbles when first immersed in water, especially if the latter be warm.[g] The frothing power is destroyed,[g] and the flexibility nearly, and perhaps quite completely restored, very rapidly by heating the metal, slowly by simple exposure to the atmosphere at ordinary temperatures.

Some or all of these effects are produced when iron is immersed *A* in hydrochloric, sulphuric,[g h i] or acetic[g] acid, in the two former even if extremely dilute: *B* in mine water[j]: *C* if employed as the hydrogen pole (cathode) in electrolyzing common water,[g h] caustic soda,[g] hydrochloric,[g] sulphuric,[h] or indeed any acid,[h] or neutral salts,[h] the iron becoming very brittle though wholly uncorroded; while if employed as the oxygen pole (anode) it is greatly corroded but does not become brittle.[g h] Moreover, the metal exhibits the characteristic frothing after employment as cathode, but not after acting as anode.[g] *D* If exposed to the weather.[i] *E* In electrolytically deposited iron some at least of these effects are greatly exaggerated.

That these effects are due to exposure to nascent hydrogen and not to corrosion, is shown by several facts, *e. g.*, *A* That, as just stated, in iron electrodes they are directly as the exposure to hydrogen but inversely as the corrosion. *B* That they are hastened and intensified by means which increase the evolution of nascent hydrogen: among these we have the passage of an electric current, and the contact of the iron with metallic zinc.[h i] The latter intensifies the brittleness, both in case of immersion in acidulated water and of exposure to the weather,[i] though it simultaneously diminishes the corrosion of the metal. Indeed, acidulated water renders iron brittle much faster if scraps of zinc be dropped into it, even if the two metals do not touch, and evidently because of the hydrogen rapidly evolved by the zinc.[h] *C* That heating and rest which expel hydrogen also remove these effects.[g h i] *D* That on filing away the exterior of the metal the interior is found brittle.[i] *E* That immersion in nitric acid, which does not under ordinary conditions liberate hydrogen by its action on iron, does not render the metal brittle, though it rapidly corrodes it.[g]

That the nascent state is essential to these phenomena is indicated by the fact that when a violent stream of

---

[a] Wagner's Jahresbericht, XXIII., p. 95, 1877.

[b] Private communications, 1886.

[c] G. W. Goetz, of the Otis Works, Cleveland, Ohio, private communications, Nov. 18th and Dec. 17th, 1887: also quoted by Wedding, Stahl und Eisen, VII., p. 513, 1887.

[d] Comptes Rendus, LII., p. 1195, 1861.

[e] For our information on this subject we are chiefly indebted to W. H. Johnson (Proc. Royal Society, XXIII., p. 168, 1875), D. E. Hughes (Journ. Soc. Telegraph Engineers, 1880, IX., p. 163), and A. Ledebur (Stahl und Eisen, VII., p. 681, 1887). Johnson's results have been strangely overlooked, though they appear to me much more important than those of Hughes, which have attracted wide attention. Indeed, I do not find that Ledebur even refers to Johnson's work in his own admirable paper, though he gives a résumé of all the literature of the subject that he has found.

Johnson anticipated most of the results and deductions of Ledebur and Hughes.

[f] *I. e.*, the power of being bent back and forth without breaking.

[g] Johnson, loc. cit.

[h] Hughes, loc. cit.

[i] Ledebur, loc. cit.

[j] Strob, Journ. Teleg. Engrs., aute, cit.

TABLE 61.—INFLUENCE OF EXPOSURE TO NASCENT HYDROGEN.

Number.	Observer.	Number of pairs of tests.	Description of iron experimented on.	Exposure to nascent hydrogen. Immersed or exposed to	Days.	In contact with zinc.	Subsequent treating before testing. Heated—yes or no.	Hours.	Temperature.	Allowed to rest, days.	Effect of exposure. Tensile strength, etc., of the bar after treatment per 100 of initial tensile strength, etc. Tensile strength.	Modulus of elasticity.	Elongation.	Flexibility.	Transverse strength.	Breaking load.	Maximum bending.
1	L.	8	Iron wire from ·065 to ·14 inch diameter	In dilute sulphuric acid, strength, 1:100	1·	No	No.	......	......	8	99·51	100·2	80·0	78·4			
2	"	8	"	" 1:40	0·96	No	No.	......	......	0	102·1	108·5	79·4	43·9			
3	"	8	" "	" 1:40	0·12	Yes	No.	......	......	0	**98·9**	**98·9**	{(96·7) **110·0**} a	**39·0**			
4	"	8	" "	" 1:40	0·12	Yes	No.	......	......	4	**102·9**	**106·8**	**73·3**	**71·3**			
5	"	8	" "	" 1:40	0·17	Yes	Yes	0·25	Cherry red	......	{(**100·7**) **103·9**} a	**104·7**	**94·4**	**90·1**			
6	"	8	Iron wires from ·08 to ·14 inch diameter	In very dilute sulphuric acid	0·42	Yes	No.	......	......	0	**99·4**	**99·3**	**67·3**	**23·7**			
7	"	8	"	In dilute sulphuric acid, 1:200	4·	No.	......	......	......	......	98·6	94·8	92·1	26·2			
8	"	6	"	In very dilute sulphuric acid	0·42	Yes	......	......	......	29	**96·0**	**97·6**	**79·4**	**62·5**			
9	"	8	" "	In acid mine water	3·	......	......	......	......	......	84·9	84·9	84·3	58·5			
10	"	8	" "	" "	0·96	......	......	......	......	......	81·6	83·0	65·1	65·8			
11	"	8	" "	" "	1·	......	......	......	......	......	82·5	82·4	69·5	86·8			
12	"	8	" "	Exposed to the weather	62·	No	......	......	......	......	94·0	96·0	55·0	55·1			
13	"	6	" "	"	14·	Yes	......	......	......	......	**98·8**	**99·5**	**91·9**	**66·9**			
14	"	2	Oil-hardened bars of spring steel, ·87 inch sqr.	In dilute sulphuric acid	1·	No	......	......	......	......	......	......	......	......	70·8		
15	"	2	"	"	1·	Yes	......	......	......	......	......	......	......	......	**60·5**		
16	"	...	Spiral springs, oil-hardened	......		......	......	......	......	......	......	......	......	......	......	79·0	
17a	"	...	U springs hardened	In dilute sulphuric acid	1·	......	......	......	......	......	......	......	......	......	......	84·9	
17b	"	...	" "	" " "	1·	......	......	......	......	......	......	......	......	......	......	52·4	
17c	"	...	" "	" " "	1·	......	Yes	......	......	......	......	......	......	......	......	85·4	
18a	"	8	Cast-iron bars, ·2 inch square	In dilute sulphuric acid, 1:50	1·	......	......	......	......	......	......	......	......	......	100·2	......	100·9
18b	"	10	"	" 4:50	9·	......	......	......	......	......	......	......	......	......	89·0	......	88·7
18c	"	10	U-shaped cast-iron bars	" 4:50	9·	......	......	......	......	......	......	......	......	......	80·1	......	81·2
19a	J.	6	Bright, *i. e.*, hard drawn solid steel wire, 0·227% carbon	In very dilute hydrochloric acid	0·21	......	No.	......	......	......	98·1	......	108·7				
19b	"	6	"	"	0·21	......	Yes	12·	100° C	......	104·5	......	130·1				
19c	"	6	"	"	0·21	......	Yes	168·	100° C	......	109·9	......	206·0				
20a	"	6	Harden'd and tempered hard cast-steel wire, about ·68 carbon	In sulphuric acid	0·5	......	No.	......	......	......	80·8	......	88·7				
20b	"	6	"	" "	0·5	......	Yes	240·	100@200°C	......	98·9	......	123·1				
21a	"	2	" "	" "	0·04	......	No.	......	......	......	99·7	......	100·0				
21b	"	2	" "	" "	0·04	......	Yes	24·	100@200°C	......	105·2	......	78·8				
21·5	H.	7	Soft iron wire, 0·06 inch diameter	In sulphuric acid, about 1:50	1·	No	No.	0·	......	......	......	......	......	16·9			
	"	5	The same galvanized	"	1·	No	"	0·	......	......	......	......	......	17·4			
	"	6	" same Barffed	"	1·	No	"	0·	......	......	......	......	......	24·8			
											Effect of heating. Tensile strength, etc., of the iron after exposure to hydrogen and reheating, per 100 of the tensile strength of similarly exposed iron not reheated.						
22	J.	12	Annealed iron wire	In hydrochloric acid	0·04	......	Yes	12@48·	......	......	100·49	......	103·9				
23	"	8	Bright iron wire	" "	0·04	......	Yes	12@48·	......	......	100·27	......	141·5				
24	"	9	Annealed mild steel wire	" " very dilute	0·21	......	Yes	12·	100°±	......	104·77	......	76·5				
25	"	6	Bright charcoal iron wire	In sulphuric acid	0·5	......	Yes	120·	......	......	106·62	......	807·7				
26	"	6	"	In hydrochloric acid	0·5	......	Yes	120·	......	......	105·85	......	826·2				

Heavy-faced figures indicate that the iron was in contact with zinc.

The numbers in this table represent not the absolute tensile strength, etc., but the tensile strength, etc., of the iron after exposure to hydrogen per 100 of the tensile strength, etc., of similar but unexposed pieces.

The eight wires for Numbers 1 to 5 inclusive appear to have been cut from the same eight mine ropes, which had already been in use: and though in each individual test the same wire was tested before and after exposure to nascent hydrogen, yet it does not appear that the same eight wires were used for the different experiments. The eight wires employed for each of experiments 6 to 13 were cut from the same eight coils of previously unused wire. These experiments are thus more closely comparable.

ZINCING.—In certain experiments the wires were in contact with metallic zinc. In Ledebur's experiments contact was effected by casting a zinc block weighing about one pound around one end of the wire: in every case this prevented the corrosion of the wire completely or nearly so.

OBSERVER.—L. = Ledebur, Stahl und Eisen, VII., p. 682. 1887. J. = W. H. Johnson, Proc. Royal Soc. XXIII., p. 168, 1875. H. = the author.

The flexibility is measured by the number of times that the piece could be bent back and forth through 180°, about round cornered iron pieces, before fracture.

a In each of these cases the numbers deduced directly from Ledebur's averages are exaggerated by one abnormal result. Omitting this we obtain the numbers given in parenthesis.

1. Not previously cleaned with ether: 2. previously cleaned with ether.

3 A violent evolution of gas over the whole surface of the wire, which remained completely white, and was not in the least eaten with acid.

7. The wires were considerably but not very seriously (deutlich, doch nicht sehr erheblich) corroded.

9, 10, 11 9 and 10 immersed in acid water from one mine, 11 in that from another mine. The wire became coated with salts in each case. In 9 and 11 the wire was much corroded by the water, in 10 less corroded than in 9.

12. The wires were not previously freed from grease. They became much covered with rust.

13 The wires rusted considerably, but much less than in Number 12.

14 and **15** Spring steel, with 0·65 carbon, oil-hardened and spring-tempered. Loaded to breaking in the middle, between supports 17·7 inches apart.

16 Spiral springs, made from steel of 0·9 carbon, 0·31 inch in diameter, were oil-hardened and tempered. Those which had not been exposed to acid broke into 2 or 3 pieces: those which had been so exposed broke into from 10 to 12 pieces.

17. U springs were hardened in water, tempered to spring hardness and loaded to breaking. One was not treated with acid, the remaining three were treated for 24 hours with sulphuric acid. A was loaded to breaking without further treatment, B after being hammered, C after being heated, again hardened, and tempered.

18 Bars 0·197 inch square, were fixed at one end and loaded at the other to breaking, at a distance of 9·78 inches from the fixed end.

21·5. A single coil of wire was cut into many pieces. Some of these were galvanized, others were Bower-Barffed, and the remainder were not coated. They were then simultaneously immersed in dilute sulphuric acid for 24 hours. The flexibility was determined by bending the wire back and forth till fracture occurred. The wire was held in iron jaws with rounded edges.

hydrogen was bubbled for an hour through water containing wire, and when the latter was exposed to hydrogen for hours in a glass tube at the ordinary temperature, no brittleness arose.[a]

The great loss of flexibility and elongation which simple exposure to the weather produces, even when the almost undiminished tensile strength indicates that but little rusting has occurred, may seriously affect iron engineering structures: and it is surmised that coating with zinc to prevent the action of the weather will merely aggravate the evil.[b] That iron should lose nearly half its elongation and flexibility on simple exposure for 62 days,

[a] Johnson, loc. cit.

[b] Ledebur, loc. cit.

though but little corroded, is certainly disquieting. The fact that pieces nearly an inch thick are rapidly rendered brittle in acid, and are probably affected by the weather much as thinner ones are, is not reassuring. (Experiments 14 and 15.) Further investigations to learn the extent of injury to large pieces by the weather, and to discover whether certain classes of iron may not resist this action better than others, seems desirable. It is not improbable that the tendency of the absorbed hydrogen to escape ultimately balances its absorption,[a] and so prevents the effects of the weather from being cumulative beyond a certain point.

We may now consider in more detail the specific effects of exposure to hydrogen, as given in Table 61.

The tensile strength and modulus of elasticity are not in general seriously affected, unless the cross section of the piece is diminished by actual corrosion, as in numbers 9, 10 and 11. The only exception to this is number 20 A, and here the conditions are complicated by the fact that the wire before immersion was hardened and tempered. On exposure its tensile strength falls to 80·8% of the original, but rises again to 98·9% on reheating, which suggests that the iron had not become corroded.

In the six experiments, numbers 3, 4, 5, 6, 8 and 13 (comprising 92 individual tests for each property) in which unexposed iron is compared with that which had been exposed to hydrogen but which had been at least partially protected from corrosion by contact with zinc, the average loss of tensile strength is but 0·017% of the original, while there is a gain of 1·05% in modulus elasticity.

The elongation is, on the whole, affected somewhat more than the tensile strength, the average loss in these six experiments being 10·62% (14·5% if we omit one abnormal result). The elongation ratios are very high in numbers 19 B, 19 C, 20 B, 25 and 26, perhaps because here the elongation of the wire unexposed to hydrogen had been depressed by the stresses induced by previous hard-drawing or hardening. It may be that these stresses are released by the subsequent heating which expels the hydrogen, and that their release brings the elongation of the wire exposed to hydrogen and reheated, above that of the wire before exposure to hydrogen. (Cf. § 51, C, § 53, 2, A, pp. 29–31). Indeed, the high elongation ratio of number 19 A, which is hard-drawn wire exposed to hydrogen without subsequent heating, suggests that the hydrogen has in some way released these stresses. But the effects of exposure to hydrogen and of subsequent rest and heating on the elongation are so often extremely anomalous, that it is not improbable that this property is influenced by some important factor which has escaped detection.

The *flexibility*, however, is the property which appears to be most affected, usually falling more, and often very much more than the other properties tested. In average of the six cases in which the iron was in contact with zinc the flexibility falls by 34·42%.

The transverse strength of spring steel and the carrying power of steel springs are also greatly diminished by exposure to hydrogen, falling by from 14·6 to 47·6%.

The hardness is affected if at all to a degree which usually escapes observation. According to Stroh it is not affected in the least.[b] But, by sufficient exposure to hydrogen, as when iron is electrolytically deposited, glass-hardness is acquired.

In numbers 2, 3, 6 and 7 the effects of exposure to hydrogen, unobscured by heating, rest, or visible corrosion, are especially striking, the tensile strength and modulus being practically unaffected, on an average falling by only 1·5% and 0·87% respectively, while the elongation falls by 7·8% (13·62% omitting one abnormal result) and the flexibility by 66·27%.

Contact with Zinc.—In experiments 2 and 3 the conditions are alike, except that in the latter the iron was in contact with zinc, and was exposed to hydrogen for a much shorter time: the same is true of experiments 12 and 13. In the first pair the loss of elongation is greater (if we except one abnormal result), and that of flexibility very much greater per day of exposure when zinc is present. Indeed, the total loss of flexibility is greater in the short exposure with zinc than in the long one without it. In the second pair also the presence of zinc increases the loss of flexibility per diem.

In the former pair of experiments the zinc appears to have slightly diminished, in the latter pair to have slightly protected the tensile strength and modulus of elasticity. But an examination of the details of the experiments leaves little doubt that the changes in the tensile strength and modulus of elasticity are apparent only, and are due to those slight differences in the properties of different portions of the same piece which are to be expected.

It might be inferred that the contact of electro-negative substances, such as iron scale, would lessen just as that of zinc intensifies the effect of exposure to nascent hydrogen. To test this as well as Ledebür's inference that coating with zinc like other contact with that metal should intensify these effects, I have cut a single coil of wire into many pieces, some of which were galvanized, some Bower-Barffed, and some employed without protective coating. As the important question is whether these coatings influence the degree of brittleness caused by exposure to the weather, several of each set are now under exposure: the results will appear in an appendix. In order to obtain immediate indications others were immersed in dilute acid (number 21·5, Table 61): the results do not support Ledebur's inference, but they tend to show that Barffing does lessen the effects of exposure to nascent hydrogen.

Heating, even if brief, removes the effects of exposure to hydrogen (the loss of elongation sometimes excepted), nearly and sometimes quite completely. Johnson states that the metal regains its original toughness in twelve hours at 200° C., and that no bubbles can then be seen on moistening its fracture: Hughes that its flexibility is completely restored by heating to cherry redness for a few seconds in a spirit lamp: while Lebebur (3 and 5, Table 61) finds that in 15 minutes at cherry redness in a stream of producer gas made from charcoal, the elongation usually rises, while the flexibility, which exposure to hydrogen had depressed to 39% of the original, rises on heating to 90·1% of the original. In 17 b and c heating restores to a spring much of the carrying power which it had lost by exposure to hydrogen.

In six out of Johnson's nine experiments heating raises, and twice it more than triples the elongation which had been diminished by hydrogen; yet in the remaining three

[a] Johnson, loc. cit.

[b] Journ. Teleg. Engrs., IX., p. 172, 1880.

cases, collectively representing the results of fifteen pairs of comparative tests, heating the wire after exposure to hydrogen lowers the elongation.

These surprising results may be regarded as additional illustrations of the wide difference between the effects of hydrogen on elongation and on flexibility: for Johnson states unreservedly that heating restores the original toughness: and his remarks leave little doubt that he uses toughness as nearly identical with flexibility, as something to be gauged by the bending power, and as having little connection with ductility as measured by elongation.[a]

Influence of Rest.—The flexibility and possibly the elongation are restored more or less completely by simple rest. In experiments 3 and 4 the conditions are alike, except that in 4 the wire is allowed to rest before testing it: so with experiments 6 and 8. In both cases there is a surprising restoration of flexibility: the elongation, however, falls. In experiments 6 and 8, which are closely comparable, the elongation is less after than before the four weeks rest in five out of the eight cases. Johnson found that wire "regained its original toughness" (*i. e.* flexibility?) after resting three days at about 16° C. (61° F.), and Dittmar states that the brittleness due to pickling is so far removed by simple rest that the wire can be drawn with complete satisfaction.[b] Yet Hughes states that the effects of exposure to hydrogen do not disappear at ordinary temperatures. Ledebur's results are so harmonious that it is probable that Hughes did not thoroughly examine the effect of rest on flexibility. In all of the eight cases in which similar wires were tested after and before rest, and in five out of the eight in which dissimilar wires were tested, Ledebur found a very marked, and in a sixth a decided restoration of flexibility.

Cold working, according to Brustlein, expels the hydrogen from wire rendered brittle by immersion in acid[c]: but Ledebur found that the carrying power of steel U springs thus immersed was not restored by hammering. (17 b, Table 61).

Proportion of Hydrogen Absorbed.—If these effects are really due to the absorption of hydrogen it might be anticipated that heating and rest, which remove the effects, would also expel the hydrogen, though they might simply transfer it from a noxious to a relatively harmless state without expelling it. Johnson found indications that the gas whose gradual escape from iron was shown by the protracted frothing accelerated by heating, was hydrogen; and Roberts, Ledebur, and Fox have extracted from iron which had been immersed in acid the quantities of hydrogen given in the accompanying table.

Observer.	Method.	Hydrogen, volumes.	Hydrogen %.
W. C. Roberts a	Heating in vacuo	10·0	0·0109
F. Fox, Jr. b	Combustion in dry oxygen	9·5	0·0103
Ledebur c	Heating in steam of nitrogen	1·93@4·78	0·0021@0·0052

a "By experiment I found that, on heating the steel wires" (after exposure to nascent hydrogen) "in vacuo, it is possible to remove from them at least ten times their volume of hydrogen, the latter being quite pure and not contaminated with hydrocarbon, provided care is taken to extract any natural gas occluded by the wire during the metallurgical process involved in the manufacture." "The amount of natural gas varies from three to ten volumes." Roberts, Journ. Teleg. Engrs., IX., pp. 168-9, 1880. It is not absolutely clear whether ten volumes is the total quantity of gas which he extracts from hydrogenized wire, or whether he extracted a larger quantity, and after making allowance for natural gas regards ten volumes as the quantity due to exposure to hydrogen.

b Loc. cit.

c Loc. cit. He reasonably objects to the method of heating in vacuo that, as we cannot first warm the iron for fear of expelling the absorbed hydrogen, we cannot be sure that it is free from moisture; that this moisture on heating in vacuo is liable to be decomposed by the iron with the liberation of hydrogen, thus exaggerating the apparent proportion of this gas evolved by the metal. Employing a rapid stream of nitrogen we remove the moisture rapidly, and thus diminish its opportunity of being decomposed by the metal. This method, applied to wire which had not been exposed to nascent hydrogen, extracted no trace of this gas.

The quantity of hydrogen thus extracted is so minute as to suggest[d] that its absorption has merely accompanied not caused the intense effects described. If, however, the influence of an element on iron depends not on the weight but number of equivalents present,[e] our 0·002% of hydrogen might indeed affect iron as intensely as 0·002 × 31 ÷ 1 = ·062% of phosphorus. Indeed, that one part of hydrogen should so greatly affect the properties of fifty thousand of iron would hardly surprise him who already knew how greatly one of phosphorus affects five thousand of iron, as much as this latter fact would surprise one who was ignorant of the influence of small quantities of impurities on the metals in general.

If the hydrogen absorbed be the direct cause of these effects, its influence is clearly far out of proportion to that of the much larger quantities of this gas in the irons of Table 60, which suggests that hydrogen may exist in two or more conditions in iron. It is conceivable that the hydrogen absorbed when nascent exists in iron in a state resembling that of adhesion, whose possible effects have been conjectured in § 170.

§ 180. Deoxidation by Hydrogen.—Bell's experiments indicate that hydrogen and carbonic oxide begin to reduce iron oxide at about the same temperature, the reduction of Cleveland ore by hydrogen beginning at between 199° and 227° C.[f] (390° and 440° F.), and by carbonic oxide at 199° C., the latter gas reducing precipated ferric oxide at 141° C.[g] (285° F.). But, as might be inferred from its power to reduce not only carbonic acid but carbonic oxide, hydrogen reduces iron oxide far more energetically than carbonic oxide does, as is indicated by the following

Results of Bell's Experiments on Calcined Cleveland Ore. Table 62.

No.	Composition of reducing gas by volume.			Temperature.	Hours exposed.	Oxygen removed per 100 of initial oxygen.	
	H.	CO.	CO_2.			Per hour.	Total.
1f	10·7	0·	89·3	427°@525° C.	1·5	45·	68·
2f	0·	100·	0·	427° C. = 800° F.	7·0	1·34	9·4
3f	7·8	62·6	29·6a	450° C. ± = 842° F. ±	10·5	1·11	11·7
4f	0·	76·4	23·6	427° C.	10·5	0·65	6·8
5f	10·7	89·3	0·	Very bright red.	1·	70·	70·
6h	0·	100·	0·	Bright red.	3·75	24·	90·

a Excluding 46·4% nitrogen.

In No. 1 the rapidity of reduction by the mixture of hydrogen and carbonic oxide exceeds that of reduction by pure carbonic oxide in No. 2 far more than can be accounted for by the difference in temperature. In No. 3, even in presence of a larger proportion of an oxidizing gas, carbonic acid, the addition of hydrogen to carbonic oxide accelerates deoxidation.

The same holds true at higher temperatures: thus in 5 and 6 the addition of 10·7% of hydrogen to carbonic oxide at a red heat hastens reduction.

a "No exact and easily applied test has yet been devised by which we can obtain with precision a numerical result expressing the relative toughness of any of two samples—this difficulty is fortunately not met with in the examination of the change in elasticity and tensile strength; for the breaking weight and maximum elongation—can be pretty easily ascertained." Op. cit., p. 175.

b Ledebur, loc. cit., from Zeit. Vereins Deutsch. Ingen., 1887, p. 331.

c Stahl und Eisen, III., p. 252, 1883.

d Abel, Journ. Teleg. Eng., ante cit.

e Ledebur, loc. cit.

f Principles of the Manufacture of Iron and Steel, pp. 310 to 314.

g Jour. Iron and St. Inst., 1871, I., p. 98.

h Idem, p. 103.

IRON AND CARBONIC OXIDE.

§ 181. SUMMARY.—Carbonic oxide reduces iron oxide, but never quite completely: indeed at high temperatures it oxidizes metallic iron slightly, especially spongy iron. Carbonic acid oxidizes hot metallic iron energetically. Mixtures of these gases occupy an intermediate position, their reducing power rising with the proportion of carbonic oxide and within limits with falling temperature.

While oxidizing iron nickel and cobalt, and while reducing their oxides, carbonic oxide impregnates them with carbon, probably at all temperatures above 200° C., but most rapidly between 400° and 500° C. This action almost ceases at bright redness. Compact metallic iron absorbs but little carbon from pure carbonic oxide, but receives it more readily if a little carbonic acid be present. Spongy iron acquires much more and partially reduced oxide still more carbon, the former acquiring as much as 158, the latter as much as 808 parts per 100 of iron. Carbonic acid opposes, and if as much as 50% of it be present, completely prevents carbon deposition.

Iron evolves and sometimes absorbs carbonic oxide, both when solid and when molten: but trifling quantities are usually found on boring cold metal under water, yet sufficient to prove that it can exist undecomposed for a considerable length of time, in the cavities of the iron while still hot; indeed, in distinct blisters it is found in considerable quantity. In some cases its apparent absorption by iron is due to its decomposition, the iron absorbing its carbon and oxygen separately. There is evidence which strongly indicates, or at least very strongly suggests, that in other cases carbonic oxide as such dissolves in iron: but, with perhaps one exception, there seems to be room for a difference of opinion as to whether any or all of this collectively is quite conclusive. It may be later shown that carbonic oxide influences the properties of iron: I know of no present evidence that it does.

TABLE 63.—TEMPERATURES WHICH LIMIT THE ACTION OF CARBONIC OXIDE AND CARBONIC ACID.

Expt. No.		Cent.	Fahr.
18	Carbonic oxide begins to reduce precipitated ferric oxide at about.	141°	285°
17	" " Cleveland ore at about.	199	390
289	" " deposit carbon, reactions (1) and (5)	200@221	392@430
20	" removes 49% of the oxygen of precipitated ferric oxide in six hours at	232@254	450@489
241	Deposited carbon begins to react on iron oxide at or below	249@265	480@509
72	Carbonic acid begins to oxidize metallic iron between	299@417	570@783
798-9	" oxidizes soft but not hard coke at	417	783
286	Carbonic oxide begins to oxidize spongy iron at or below	417	783
201@228	Carbon deposition is most rapid between	400@430	752@842
196	Hard coke is oxidized by carbonic acid at	bright redness.	
229	Carbon deposition almost ceases at	very bright redness.	

NOTE.—These are the temperatures found by Bell. The numbers in the first column are those of his experiments as given in the Journal of the Iron and Steel Institute, 1871, 1872.

§ 182. REDUCTION AND OXIDATION BY CARBONIC OXIDE AND ACID.—Carbonic oxide reduces iron oxide at all temperatures above 141°C. as far as observed (Table 63), at a rate which increases with the temperature at least up to bright redness,[a] and with the rapidity of the current of gas, and is greatly influenced by the structure of the oxide. It is however unable to completely deoxidize it, but slightly oxidizes metallic iron, slowly if compact,[b] comparatively rapidly if spongy, perhaps thus:

(1); $Fe + xCO = FeO_x + xC$.

[a] Bell, Jour. Iron and St. Inst., 1871, I., p. 182, states that deoxidation is at a maximum at about 417°C. If "at a maximum" means most rapid or most thorough, I am at a loss to reconcile this statement with his experimental results.

[b] That iron wire is oxidized by carbonic oxide and simultaneously absorbs carbon was shown by its turning blue and straw-colored after heating in this gas, and by its yielding black flakes (carbon) when dissolved in hydrochloric acid; the same wire when not previously exposed to carbonic oxide yielded no such flakes. In another case, after exposure to carbonic oxide, the solution obtained by brief contact of strong hydrochloric acid gave an intense blue with ferrocyanide of potassium, indicating the formation of an oxide higher than ferrous oxide. (Bell Journ. Iron and St. Inst., 1871, I., pp. 163–4).

The influence of temperature is illustrated by Table 64, and by numbers 11, 12 and 13, and 19 and 21 in Table 65, in which gases of given composition deoxidize ferric oxide more fully at a higher temperature than in the same or a longer period at a lower one.

The influence of rapidity of current is shown by Table 67, in which the swift current removes on an average 1·76, and in one case 4 times as much oxygen as the slow one.

The influence of structure also is exemplified in Table 67. Of two specimens of the same ore but of different structure exposed together, one lost six times as much oxygen as the other; ferric oxide obtained by calcining ferrous sulphate lost 4·7 times as much as spathic ore exposed beside it. The influence of structure is also shown in Table 64, but less clearly, as it is here sometimes masked by the effects of other variables.

TABLE 64.—REMOVAL OF OXYGEN PER 100 OF ORIGINAL BY CARBONIC OXIDE.

Temperature		210@254° C.	419° C. ±	Low red.	Bright red.
Cleveland ore	Total	13·66	3·4 @50·6	63·	90 a
	Per hour	6·26@8·66	1·34@6·4	7·9	24·
Precipitated ferric oxide	Total	49·3	48·2 @80	....	99·
	Per hour	8·2	8·2 @18·3	....	19·8

a Nearly 99 %.

Pure carbonic acid oxidizes metallic iron and its low oxides energetically, if in sufficient excess probably eventually producing ferric oxide.

(2); $Fe + xCO_2 = FeO_x + xCO$,

(3); $FeO_x + yCO_2 = FeO_{x+y} + yCO$.

It thus appears that when iron, oxygen and carbon, however initially combined, are together exposed to a high temperature, the oxygen tends to distribute itself between the carbon and iron in proportions corresponding to equilibrium for the existing conditions, such as temperature, proportion of iron to carbon present, etc. This is true whether the mixture consists initially of metallic iron, carbonic acid and oxide, or of iron oxide and carbon, or whatever it be. For instance, if a mixture of equal volumes of carbonic acid and oxide be exposed at full redness to ferrous oxide, which contains 28·57 of oxygen per 100 of iron, no action occurs; neither takes nor yields oxygen; they are in equilibrium. If however the gases contain 60% of carbonic acid they yield oxygen to ferrous oxide, if only 40% they take oxygen from it: if the iron oxide has more oxygen than ferrous oxide it gives up, if less it absorbs oxygen from this mixture of equal volumes of carbonic acid and oxide. In each case the transfer of oxygen proceeds till a new equilibrium is reached.

In Table 65 the full-faced figures indicate approximately certain of these sets of conditions of equilibrium: that is, the proportion of oxygen retained by 100 of iron when exposed to certain mixtures of carbonic oxide and acid till they have ceased or nearly ceased to react. Unfortunately in but a few cases has the composition both of the gas and of the iron oxide which are in mutual equilibrium been directly determined: but in several others where one is given the other can be more or less closely estimated.

In figure 10 the five points p to p^4 indicate by their distance from the horizontal axis the percentage of oxygen which iron oxide must hold in order to stand in equilibrium with the five corresponding mixtures of carbonic acid and oxide at bright redness. Of these p, p^3 and p^4 command confidence, for in these cases the fact that the gases gave to spongy iron the same percentage of oxygen

TABLE 65.—REDUCTION, OXIDATION AND CARBON DEPOSITION BY CARBONIC OXIDE AND ACID.

Number.	No. of Bell's experiment.	Conditions of exposure. Material.	Hours.	Temperature.	After exposure to the gas the metal held per 100 of iron. % carbon.	% Oxygen. At low temp'ratures.	At medium temperatures.	At high temperatures.	Composition of gas by volume. Before exposure. CO.	CO_2.	After exposure. CO.	CO_2.	Remarks.
1 ...	340	Cleveland sponge	0·75	417.	0·	18·45	.....	.....	14·	86·			
2 ...	90	" ore	0·5	Red.	.....	.....	.....	**40·3**	14·	86·	14·—	86·+	Equilibrium nearly reached.
3 ...	91	" sponge	0·75	Bright red.	.....	.....	.....	**37·3**	14·	86·	14·+	86·—	
4 ...	73-8	Sponge	.....	Low red.	.....	.....	.....	.....	0·	100	40·	60·	
5 ...	74-330	Cleveland sponge	0·5	417.	0·	0·	.....	.....	50·5	49·5			
6 ...	232	Precipitated ferric oxide	6·0	Fairly red.	0·	.....	**29·06**	.....	50	50·	50·	50·	Equilibrium reached with FeO.
7 ...	218	Cleveland ore	5·5	Bright "	0	.....	.....	**28·59**	50	50·			
8 ...	89	Precipitated sponge	13·0	" "	.....	.....	.....	**28·5**	50·	50·	50·	50·	
9 ...	88	Cleveland ore	5·5	" "	.....	.....	.....	**28**	50·	50·	50·	50·	
10 ...	87	Sponge	.....	" "	.....	.....	.....	**28·59**	50·	50·	.....	.....	
11 ...	261	Ferric oxide from nitrate	10·5	410.	6·4	26·7	.....	.....	67·	33·			
12 ...	101	Ferric oxide	11·5	417.	.....	26·6	.....	.....	67·	33·			
13 ...	263-109	Precipitated ferric oxide	6·	Very dull red.	1·5	.....	28·2	.....	67·	33·	.....	.....	Equilibrium reached.
14 ...	79	Cleveland sponge	11·5	Bright red.	.....	.....	.....	**3·5**	59·7	36·9	63·8	30·9	
15 ...	330	" "	7·	" "	0·	.....	.....	**5·14**	66·7	36·3			
16 ...	Dumas	Iron turnings	.....	Cherry red.	.....	.....	.....	.....	0·	100·	64·29	34·84	CO_2 max. 41·86; CO_2 min. 31·81
17 ...		" " and alloys	.....	" "	.....	.....	.....	.....	0·	100·	68·74	31·01	38·66; 25·56
18 ...		" " " "	.....	Almost white.	.....	.....	.....	.....	0·	100·	71·71	27·94	35·82; 16·39
19 ...	105-260	Precipitated ferric oxide	5·	416·	9·8	16·2	.....	.....	73·	23·6			
20 ...	334	Cleveland sponge	0·5	417·	0·	1·81	.....	.....	72·5	27·5			
21 ...	108-434	Precipitated ferric oxide	5·	Low red.	0·9	.....	4·2	.....	75·4	23·6			
22 ...	77	Cleveland sponge	0·5	Full red.	.....	.....	.....	1·31	73·	27·			
23 ...	338	Sponge	2·5	.....	·36	.....	.....	9·02	91·8	3·2	.....	.....	Equilibrium reached.
24 ...	80	Cleveland sponge	7	Nearly white.	.....	.....	.....	**5·1**	63·5	36·5	83·2	10·	
25 ...	72	Sponge	0·66	417·	2·6		.....	.....	0·	100·	96·	4·	
26 ...	345	"	5·5	238@248·	3·8		.....	.....	100·	0·	.....	.....	Carbon deposited.
27 ...	342	"	9	417·	138·	.....	.....	.....	100·	0·			
28 ...	331-6	"	4·5	417·	20·3	**2·2**	.....	.....	100·	0·			
29 ...	332	"	1	Very dull red.	23·3	.....	.....	.....	100·	0·			
30 ...	335	"	2·5	Low red.	12·75	.....	**0·84**	.....	100·	0·			
32 ...	348	Cleveland sponge	3·	Red	2·43	.....	.....	·40	100·	0·	.....	.....	Equilibrium reached
33 ...	337	Precipitated sponge	4·	Bright red.	·30	.....	.....	**·38**	100·	0·	.....	.....	
34 ...	291-370	Precipitated ferric oxide	5·	" "	·24	.....	.....	**·43**	100·	0·	.....	.....	
35 ...	286-372	Precipitated sponge	4·	" "	·35	.....	.....	**·30**	100·	0·	.....	.....	Equilibrium reached.
36 ...	285-371	" "	1·	" "	·32	.....	.....	·49	100·	0·	.....	.....	
37 ...	93-4	Sponge	4·	" "	.....	.....	.....	**·34**	100·	0·	100·	0·	Equilibrium reached.
38 ...	343	Iron wire	3·17	18@282	.....	tr.	.....	.....	100·	0·	.....	.....	
39 ...	244	" "	4·	Bright red.	0·17±a	.....	.....	0·13±a	100·	0·			

The horizontal rule lines divide these experiments into six groups, in each of which the final composition of the gases is nearly constant. Comparing one group with another gives at a glance the influence of the proportion of carbonic acid to carbonic oxide.

The column head "% of oxygen" is split into three, in each of which the temperature of exposure is approximately constant. The temperature is more accurately given in the column headed "temperature:" but this grouping, combined with the grouping by the horizontal lines, shows at a glance the influence of temperature. In any one of the horizontal groups, e. g. lines 11 to 18, on passing from left to right the proportion of oxygen acquired declines; and as the carbonic acid is approximately constant in each group, this decline is readily attributed to the rise of temperature.

"Precip. sponge" = precipitated ferric oxide reduced by hydrogen.

"Cleveland sponge" = Cleveland ore thus reduced.

Full-faced figures indicate that the exposure had been so long that equilibrium had probably been nearly reached.

"Equilibrium reached" in the last column indicates that successive analyses or other data prove that action had ceased.

a These numbers are doubtful.

I give these results at greater length than would otherwise be expedient, because no digested statement of them exists elsewhere so far as I am aware, and the labor of mining the raw but precious material from its labyrinthine deposit is usually prohibitory.

I am at a loss to reconcile certain of these results. Thus, in No. 5, equal parts of carbonic acid and oxide are inert on Cleveland sponge: yet other mixtures with less carbonic acid, and even as in No. 32 pure carbonic oxide itself, oxidize this same substance.

that they left in iron oxide, proves that their action was complete on both. p^1 and p^2, however, were obtained simply by treating spongy iron, and not checked by reducing iron oxide with the same gases: hence the suspi-

Figure 10

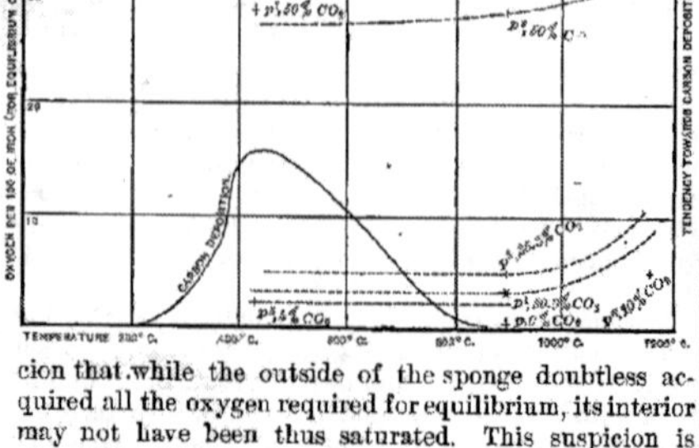

cion that while the outside of the sponge doubtless acquired all the oxygen required for equilibrium, its interior may not have been thus saturated. This suspicion is strengthened by the fact that p^1 and p^2 are much lower than the position of p^3 would lead us to expect.

§ 183. INFLUENCE OF TEMPERATURE ON THE CONDITIONS OF EQUILIBRIUM BETWEEN THE OXIDES OF IRON AND OF CARBON.—Bell's experiments indicate that, under the conditions we are studying, *i. e.*, *when carbonic acid or oxide or both are exposed to iron or its oxide, the relative affinity of iron for oxygen as compared with that of carbonic oxide rises with rising temperature.*[a] I do not consider the evidence either harmonious or abundant enough to prove this, but it points strongly toward it. For instance, a mixture of these gases which at one temperature is inert toward a given iron oxide, or which even takes oxygen from it, at a higher temperature yields oxygen to it. Thus in numbers 14 and 24, Table 65, mixtures of carbonic acid and oxide of initially almost identical composition were exposed to spongy iron (1) at bright redness and (2) just below whiteness. At redness equilibrium was reached when enough oxygen had passed from carbonic acid to iron to lower the proportion of this gas to 30·9% and to give the iron 3·5%[b] of oxygen (p^1, figure 10): at just below whiteness (p^6), however, this transfer of

[a] This supposition that the relative affinity of carbon for its second equivalent of oxygen as compared with that of iron for oxygen, decreases with rising temperature, does not exclude the belief that its affinity for its first equivalent as compared with that of iron rises with rising temperature: in other words, while a given low oxide of iron may deoxidize carbonic acid the more readily, and be deoxidized by carbonic oxide the less readily the higher the temperature, yet with rising temperature it may be deoxidized by carbon itself the more readily.

[b] These numbers refer to the proportion of oxygen per 100 of iron.

oxygen went much farther, ceasing only when the proportion of carbonic acid had fallen to 10% and when the iron had taken up 5·1%[b] of oxygen, the carbonic acid thus having lost and the iron having gained more oxygen than at the lower temperature. On slightly lowering the temperature in the latter experiment part of the oxygen which at the higher temperature had just left carbonic acid for iron immediately returned to the carbonic oxide, and the proportion of carbonic acid rose again to 13·4%, again to fall when the temperature again rose. In both these experiments it is known that equilibrium was reached, for further exposure of from one to two hours caused no further transfer of oxygen.

Returning now to figure 10, in which we have already plotted at p^2 the equilibrium which the last paragraph states was obtained at bright redness with 30·9% of carbonic acid, we may plot in it as p^6 the equilibrium obtained just below whiteness between iron oxide with 5·1% of oxygen and a mixture of 89·2% of carbonic oxide with 10 of carbonic acid (No. 24, Table 65), interpreting "just below whiteness" as about 1160° C.

If now we were to determine the different percentages of oxygen which iron oxide must hold at each of several temperatures in order to remain in equilibrium with a mixture of say equal volumes of carbonic acid and oxide, and plot corresponding points, a curve would be formed which we may term the 50% carbonic acid equilibrium curve: similar curves might be plotted for equilibrium with other proportions of carbonic acid. As the temperature rises above bright redness the tendency of oxygen to leave carbonic acid for iron increases; hence the proportion of oxygen which iron oxide must contain in order to resist this tendency in presence of a given mixture of gases, and to stand in equilibrium with it, must also rise. Hence these equilibrium curves rise as we pass to the right from redness, somewhat as sketched. Indeed, it is clear that the 30·9% curve must rise somewhat rapidly from p^1 to clear the 10% curve at p^6, though perhaps less abruptly than in the sketch, for we have seen that p^1 may have been plotted too low.

Searching carefully I find little to locate these curves to the left of bright redness: that little, however, indicates that, while the curves do not reverse and rise as we pass to the left, they probably fall much less suddenly than between 1,200° and 900° C. No. 25, Table 65, shows that at 417° C. the 4% carbonic acid curve is at least as high as p^5, which implies that the 30·9% curve must flatten in passing from 900° to 417° C. No. 7, Table 65, proves that the 50° curve does not pass higher than p^7 at 417° C., hence that it does not rise, but probably falls as the temperature descends from 900° to 417° C. No. 28, in which pure carbonic oxide confers about five times as much oxygen on spongy iron at 417° as in any of the experiments at redness, at first suggests that between these points the tendency of oxygen to leave carbon for iron or the relative affinity of iron for oxygen, falls with rising temperature, *i. e.* that a given percentage of carbonic acid stands in equilibrium with a higher oxide of iron at the low than at the higher temperature, and thus that our equilibrium curves rise as the temperature falls from 900° to 417°, instead of descending as sketched. But this is fallacious: at these low temperatures carbonic acid is rapidly generated, as will be shortly shown: the large deposition of carbon recorded in No. 28 shows how much carbonic acid must have been formed: this, not the low temperature, is probably the direct cause of the greater absorption of oxygen by the iron.

§ 184. Influence of the Proportion of Iron to Carbon on the Conditions of Equilibrium.—Clearly a small quantity of carbonic oxide or acid or both can but slightly alter the degree of oxidation of iron, for, when but a little oxygen has been transferred a mixture of these gases is reached which is inert towards the existing compound of iron and oxygen. Nor, conversely, can a small surface of iron or of its oxide greatly affect the proportion of carbonic oxide to acid. Thus Dumas found (No. 16, Table 65) that carbonic acid was so imperfectly reduced in passing over iron turnings that the issuing gas held at least 31·8% by volume of carbonic acid and sometimes as much as 41·86%[a]: for the iron became so oxidized, at least superficially, that it was inert on this mixture of gases. On increasing the exposed surface by filling the interstices with iron filings, the proportion of carbonic acid fell to from 16·39 to 36·66% (No. 17 and 18, idem); while when Bell passed this gas at snail-pace over spongy iron, which offers still more surface, the first issuing portions were almost completely reduced, holding but 4% of carbonic acid.[b] (No. 25, Table 65.)

A sufficient excess of surface of iron, such as is offered when a minute quantity of gas is evolved in a solidifying ingot, would probably not only completely reduce carbonic acid to carbonic oxide, but might even completely deoxidize the latter gas by reaction (1), absorbing both its carbon and oxygen.

§ 185. Carbon Impregnation.—While oxidizing iron and reducing its oxides, carbonic oxide simultaneously impregnates them with carbon, probably at all temperatures above 200° C., but most rapidly between 400° and 450°: at and above bright redness permanent deposition almost ceases. Carbon is deposited on metallic iron containing at most a trace of oxygen, on ferric oxide which has lost but 1·36% of its initial oxygen, and which contains no iron in the metallic state, and on all intermediate compounds: the deposition usually progresses with deoxidation, but in no fixed ratio. It is far more rapid with a swift than with a slow current of gas. The carbon deposits now in blotches, now uniformly; here bursting the iron oxide into powder, there without changing its form.[c] On iron oxide 808 parts of carbon, and on metallic iron 158 parts, per 100 of metal, have been deposited.[d] The reactions may be:

(1) $Fe + xCO = FeO_x + xC$,

(4) $FeO_x + yCO = FeO_{x-y} + yCO_2$,

(5) $FeO_x + yCO = FeO_{x+y} + yC$,

(6) $2CO = C + CO_2$.

Under altered conditions, and especially at higher temperatures, deposited carbon is oxidized by carbonic acid and iron oxide, thus:—

(7) $CO_2 + C = 2CO$,

(8) $FeO_{x+y} + yC = FeO_x + yCO$.

The action of carbonic acid probably begins at about 417° C.[e]: that of iron oxide certainly begins at or perhaps

[a] Comptes Rendus, LXXV., p. 511: Watt's Dict. Chem., 2d Supp., p. 360.
[b] Journ. Iron and St. Inst., 1871, I., p. 108.
[c] Bell, idem, p. 135.
[d] Idem, p. 162.
[e] Idem, p. 193.

even below 265° C.[a] (Table 63). A mixture of 60% by volume of carbonic oxide with 40 of carbonic acid still deposits a little carbon, but the presence of 50% of carbonic acid completely arrests the deposition, or at least the permanent deposition of carbon.[b] This, coupled with the fact that carbon is permanently deposited on almost pure ferric oxide, suggests that the oxygen of this substance attacks deposited carbon less energetically than carbonic acid does.

The tendencies to deposit carbon and to reoxidize the carbon thus deposited exist simultaneously, and one or the other action takes place till equilibrium between them is reached.[c] But, in general, the higher the temperature and the larger the proportion of oxygen (free or combined) present, the stronger, relatively speaking, is the tendency to oxidize the deposited carbon.

To the deposition of carbon in the blast furnace we probably owe not only much of the carbon of the cast-iron[d] but also the removal of the last 1% of the initial oxygen, which carbonic oxide alone is powerless to expel.[e]

Carbon is also deposited by carbonic oxide on nickel and cobalt and their oxides at all temperatures between 417° C. and low redness, with simultaneous partial oxidation of the metals and reduction of their oxides, but not on spongy platinum, copper, or lead, nor on the oxides of zinc, tin, manganese or chromium, nor on asbestos, pumice-stone[f] or other inert substance. It is true that carbonic oxide is also decomposed by heat alone at a very high temperature,[g] its constituents combining when the temperature again declines: but in the presence of iron, nickel, cobalt and their oxides it is decomposed at a relatively low temperature, and its elements do not recombine during slow cooling.

I will now indicate a little more fully the evidence on which some of these statements are based: it is derived almost wholly from Bell's famous researches.

That carbon deposition is the rule, not the exception, between 200° C. and dull redness is indicated by the experiments of Table 65.

The influence of temperature is illustrated by Table 65, Nos. 11, 13 and 15; 19 and 21; and 27 to 36; and better by Table 66, and is indicated graphically in figure 10. Mark in Table 66 how Cleveland ore received but 1·85% of

TABLE 66.—INFLUENCE OF TEMPERATURE AND STRUCTURE ON CARBON IMPREGNATION.[a]

Temperature C.	Carbon deposited by carbonic oxide per 100 of metallic iron.							
	On Cleveland ore.	Hours exposed to CO.	On Lancashire ore.	Hrs. exposed to CO.	On Fe_2O_3 on pumice.	Hrs. exposed to CO.	On iron sponge.	Hrs. exposed to CO.
	% C.		% C.		% C.		% C.	
213 to 221	1·85	20.5	...	...	...	...	...	...
415 ±	4·686	7·5	65·3@581	7·5	770@808	9	158	9
	0·3	7					20·3	4·5
Higher but not red	86·13	12	...	...	...	...	...	...
Red to bright red	2·8	21	...	...	...	...	0·30	4
Very bright red	0·3	4·5	...	...	...	...	...	...

[a] Condensed from Bell, Idem, pp. 130 to 199.

carbon in 20·5 hours at 213° C., and no less than 86·13% in a shorter time at a higher temperature: and how at bright redness carbon deposition was so nearly arrested that but 0·3% was deposited in 4·5 hours. Note how spongy iron, which took up 20·3% and 158% of carbon at about 417°, acquired but 0·3% at bright redness. Gruner, too, found that carbon deposition ceased if the temperature rose to redness.[h]

Though carbon deposits much more slowly at 213° than at 417° C., it is quite possible that as much might eventually deposit at the former as at the latter temperature, granted time and carbonic oxide enough. This, however, would imply that there was a limit to the amount of carbon which can be absorbed, and it is not clear that there is any such limit: deposition may go on indefinitely.

A. *The Deposition of Carbon on Metallic Iron* is illustrated by Nos. 27 to 39 in Table 65. That the presence of metallic iron is not necessary to this deposition is shown by the fact that Cleveland ore absorbed 0·11% of carbon when it had lost but 2·84 of oxygen per 100 of ferric oxide (9·48% of its total oxygen). Here, and in another case in which 1·69% of carbon was absorbed, the absence of metallic iron was directly proved by attacking the ore with iodine and cold water, which dissolved no iron, though it readily dissolves any which is in the metallic state.[i]

Though carbon deposits rapidly on iron sponge (Nos. 27 and 29, Table 65), it deposits very slowly on compact iron (Nos. 38–9, idem). In § 188, B, instances are given in which at most but little decomposition of carbonic oxide can have occurred when this gas was exposed to hot compact iron. Gruner found that perfectly pure dry carbonic oxide deposited carbon on ferrous oxide, but hardly at all on metallic iron: if mixed with a little carbonic acid, however, it deposited carbon on metallic iron as well.[h] Bell's carbonic oxide too should have been pure, for it was prepared from ferrocyanide of potassium, was passed through potash and nitrate of silver, and produced no turbidity in lime water (op. cit. p. 97).

B. *The Influence of Carbonic Acid* on carbon impregnation is readily traced in Table 65. Here when less than 25% of carbonic acid is present the deposition of carbon is usually recorded, its absence never: when more than 33% of this gas is present the absence of deposited carbon is frequently recorded, its presence never. In various other experiments Bell never observed carbon deposition from gas containing as much as 50% of carbonic acid: when 25·6 and 33% of this gas with 75 and 67% of carbonic oxide respectively was present, some forms of oxide of iron received carbon, others did not. While blast furnace gases which, excluding their nitrogen, consisted of 29·6% of carbonic acid with 70·4% of carbonic oxide, deposited on Cleveland ore from trace to 1·28 parts of carbon per 100 of iron, those with 16% of carbonic acid deposited from 1·96 to 3·11% of carbon in from one hour to four days.[j]

C. *That deposited carbon is attacked by iron oxide at 249° to 265° C.* was proved by Bell. Iron oxide, previously partly reduced and richly impregnated with carbon by ignition in carbonic oxide, was heated to this temperature in a sealed tube filled with nitrogen, when carbonic acid and oxide were evolved.[k]

[a] Idem, pp. 137–8.

[b] Idem, pp. 140, et seq.

[c] It is probably more accurate to say that both reactions occur simultaneously, one outstripping the other till equilibrium is attained, after which they just balance each other.

[d] Idem, p. 189.

[e] Idem, p. 182.

[f] Idem, pp. 172 to 183.

[g] Deville, Leçons sur la Dissociation.

[h] Watts, Dict. Chem., 2d Supp., p. 259, from Comptes Rend., LXXIII., 281.

[i] Bell, op. cit., pp. 105, 107, expts. 858–9.

[j] Op. cit., pp. 140 to 143 and 154.

[k] Idem, pp. 137–8, expts. 241–2.

D. *That it is attacked by carbonic acid at about* 417° is probable, for at this temperature this gas rapidly attacks soft and sometimes slightly affects hard coke.[a] But deposited carbon in Cleveland iron ore, whose iron had been removed by digestion in acid and which therefore held only carbon and gangue, was not acted on by carbonic acid at 260° C.[b]

That deposited carbon is competent to account for the carbon which cast-iron acquires in the blast-furnace Bell proved by melting, in a well closed crucible, iron oxide which previous exposure to carbonic oxide had impregnated with 8% of carbon, and had reduced till it held but 0·74% of oxygen: a button holding 1% of carbon resulted. Moreover, in the interior and at 50 feet below the throat of a furnace in blast, and also in cavities due to excessive wear in the lower part of extinguished furnaces, he found lumps of fuel and flux, but none of ore, which was replaced by "a powdery substance consisting of partially reduced ore" and of carbon.[c] Ore exposed to the furnace gases absorbs carbon till it bursts. Now the carbon thus intimately mixed with the ore seems a more probable source of the carbon of the cast-iron, and more competent to remove the last traces of oxygen from the iron than the comparatively scattered lumps of fuel, though these doubtless contribute. That the iron is finally completely deoxidized is shown by the usual absence of ferrous oxide from the slag.

The fact that, at given temperature, the most readily reducible oxides absorb the most carbon, and that carbon deposition progresses with deoxidation, though in no fixed ratio and indeed not invariably, is illustrated by Table 67. Numbering its cases in order of the quantity of carbon deposited, 1 having the most, and placing them in the order of deoxidation, the most thoroughly reduced first, they stand thus:—3, 1, 4, 8, 2, 6, 16, 10, 7, 21, 19, 12, 5, 13, 14, 9, 11, 18, 20, 15, 22, 17, 23, 24. The sum of the digits of the first eight cases in this list is 50, that of the second eight 100, that of the last eight 150. This law does not, however, hold good with varying temperature. As we rise from 200° to about 500° C. both reduction and carbon impregnation accelerate: with further rise of the temperature reduction is further hastened, but carbon deposition is checked.

E. *The exact nature of the reactions* in the deposition of carbon is not known. Metals which like iron are reduced by carbonic oxide, but which unlike it are not oxidized by this gas or by carbonic acid, do not induce carbon deposition as far as is known: this suggests that it is connected with the oxidation of iron by one or both of these gases by reactions like (1) and (5), rather than that it is due to mere dissociation of carbonic oxide by (6), which indeed may be regarded as the resultant of (4) and (5). Gruner's observation that with a minute quantity of oxygen or carbonic acid carbon was deposited on metallic iron, but that hardly any was deposited by pure carbonic oxide, favors the belief that this action is connected with oxidation.[d]

F. *The influence of structure* is prominent in Tables 66 and 67. In the latter, one of two specimens of Cleveland ore, differing only in structure, and exposed side by side, absorbed 63 times as much carbon as the other: artificial ferric oxide absorbed 122 times as much as spathic ore exposed beside it. The results in Table 66 are still more striking, though not so exactly comparable, for the exposures were not simultaneous. Observe how at about the same temperature and in about the same time Lancashire ore absorbed more than 100 times, and artificial oxide nearly 200 times as much carbon as Cleveland ore. In another case[e] artificial ferric oxide absorbed at 420° C. 480 times as much carbon as Cleveland ore exposed beside it in the same vessel, to wit 111 *vs.* 0·3 per 100 of iron.

G. *The influence of speed of current* is illustrated by Table 67. Here on an average the fast current deposits 5.26 times as much and in one case actually 118 times as much carbon as the slow current, under otherwise like conditions, be it because it offers more carbonic oxide, be it because it more thoroughly sweeps away the heavy carbonic acid which tends to linger and obstruct, be it because the accelerated action, by raising the temperature, still further accelerates itself.

TABLE 67.—INFLUENCE OF STRUCTURE AND OF SPEED OF CURRENT ON REDUCTION AND CARBON IMPREGNATION BY PURE CARBONIC OXIDE.a

Effect.	Gas current.	Exposed together for 6 hours at 410° C.						Simultaneously exposed at 410° C.					
		Cleveland ore in different physical conditions.						Fe_2O_3 from $FeSO_4$	Pp'ted Fe_2O_3	Lancashire ore.	Cleveland ore.	Elba ore.	Spathic calcined.
O. removed % of initial..	Slow	14·0	81·7	86·4	18·0	18·4	7·4	69·9	49·3	88·0	37·2	16·9	18·0
	Fast	90·5	48·2	85·7	56·5	55·6	80·8	72·6	60·6	71·0	59·7	18·2	42·6
C. deposited per 100 Fe..	Slow	20·0	44·3	46·7	96·4	16·4	5·7	90·9	78·7	60·1	12·6	8·6	2·8
	Fast	71·5	125·6	196·8	253·5	140·6	89·4	476·5	235·4	270·5	22·3	4·9	8·9

a Condensed from Bell, Journ. Iron and St. Inst., 1871, I., pp. 144, 150.

§ 188. DOES CARBONIC OXIDE EXIST AS SUCH IN IRON?—(1) That it should is perhaps not improbable, certainly not impossible on a priori grounds: (2) that it does occasionally in the blisters of solid iron is certain: that it exists in combination, solution or adhesion, *i. e.* in a non-gaseous state, in both (3) molten and (4) solid iron is on the whole probable. I will now substantiate these statements, admitting first that we may not now and may never have positive evidence that carbonic oxide or indeed any other compound exists *as such* dissolved or chemically combined with another body, or as to the grouping in which the separate elements of a single ternary or more complex substance are chemically combined *inter se.* We can, however, pile up cumulative evidence pointing one way or the other.

(1) The difficulty which some have had in understanding how a metal can unite chemically with an oxidized substance like carbonic oxide, or at least dissolve it, seems to evaporate when we recall the presence of iron oxide in molten iron, of copper oxide in molten copper, of many sulphides in molten slags, and the stubborn retention of small quantities of nitrogen and hydrogen in charcoal after intense and prolonged heating. Moreover Graham has shown that gold and silver absorb and evolve carbonic oxide and acid.[f] We have seen that the dissociation of carbonic oxide at a red heat by iron, etc., is probably connected

a Idem, p. 193, expt. 448, 1871 II., p. 331, expts. 708-9,

b Idem, 1871, II., pp. 330-1, expts. 706-7,

c Idem, 1871, I., pp. 186-9,

d Loc. cit.

e Idem, p. 182, Expts. 201, 205.

f E. g. he found that 4·88 cc. of previously untreated gold cornets gave out when heated to redness in vacuo 2·1 volumes of gas, or 10·25 cc., consisting of 6·7 cc. carbonic oxide, 1·5 cc. carbonic acid, 1·58 cc. hydrogen and 0·44 cc. nitrogen. The same cornets after soaking in carbonic oxide gave out 1·6 vc. of occluded gas, composed of 1·4 cc. of carbonic oxide and 0·2 of carbonic acid. Silver was found to occlude ·486 volumes of carbonic oxide and ·150 of carbonic acid. (Journ. Chem. Soc., 1867, pp. 281, 283.)

with the oxidizing action of this gas or of carbonic acid, and that spongy platinum, copper and lead do not dissociate it: hence it is probable that it is carbonic oxide itself and not merely its dissociated elements that the gold and silver absorb.

But can carbonic oxide exist in hot iron without being decomposed? Will not the iron rob it of its oxygen? Not necessarily completely. The larger the proportion of surface of iron to carbonic oxide the more completely, probably, is the gas decomposed by iron. Thus we have seen that compact iron (No. 39, Table 65) took up but 0·17% of carbon and not over 0·13% of oxygen, when heated during four hours to bright redness in this gas, while spongy iron absorbed at this temperature from 0·30 to 0·48% of oxygen (the latter in one hour, No. 36) and at 417° C. 2·2% of oxygen and 20·3% of carbon in 4·5 hours (No. 28), and in another case 158% of carbon. That the decomposition of carbonic oxide by metallic iron may be a comparatively slow matter is shown by the fact that in four out of five experiments in which Parry heated iron in a measured volume of this gas no diminution of volume could be detected. It is certain that no considerable decomposition of carbonic oxide can have occurred here, for its decomposition is accompanied by contraction of volume whether it take place according to reaction (1), (5), or (6).[a] I have already alluded to Gruner's observation that carbonic oxide deposits hardly any carbon on metallic iron, which implies that it yields it almost no oxygen, for at least an equivalent of carbon must be deposited for each equivalent of oxygen taken by iron from carbonic oxide.[b]

(2) But apart from these reasons we know that carbonic oxide does exist undecomposed in the pores of solid iron, for it has been obtained in small quantities from compact cast-iron, and in considerable amount from blisters of puddled and ingot iron, on boring these metals under water (Nos. 33 to 39, Table 54, p. 106). Clearly it cannot have been generated by boring, nor after the metal had become cold: hence we cannot escape the conclusion that it must have existed as such in the cavities of the iron while still hot.

At the Bethlehem Iron Works it was thought that carbonic oxide was recognized escaping from a fourteen-inch crank pin, made of steel containing 0·09% of carbon, which was being cut in a lathe. The indication (smell) was not conclusive: I mention this to suggest farther observation.[c]

(3) While the fact that carbonic oxide can exist undecomposed for a considerable length of time in the cavities of iron does not prove that it can exist undecomposed in solution (in which the intimacy of contact is immeasurably greater, with probably correspondingly better opportunity to decompose the carbonic oxide), yet it makes it easier to believe. The mere escape of carbonic oxide from molten iron does not in itself prove that this gas had existed as such in the metal, for it may have been formed by reaction between carbon and oxygen or by the decomposition of some oxycarbide at the instant of its escape. It is necessary, then, in each case to consider whether the carbonic oxide could be thus formed.

A. *Troost and Hautefeuille* observed that when iron, long held in tranquil fusion in an atmosphere of carbonic oxide (which, a vacuum to other gases, might be expected to cause the expulsion of all but itself), was suddenly solidified with simultaneous fall of pressure, scattering occurred, "un faible rochage."[d] This certainly strongly suggests that carbonic oxide had been dissolved, but, unfortunately, we do not know that this was the gas which was evolved on solidification.

B. *Parry's Experiment.*—On heating cast-iron in vacuo he extracted from it 0·72% or 47·5 times its own volume of carbonic oxide, together with 0·16% or 146·8 times its own volume of hydrogen when the metal was wrapped in platinum, and 2·04% or 135 times its own volume of carbonic oxide when this precaution was neglected.[e]

Serious reasons for doubting that all the hydrogen which Parry found came from the iron, have been offered in § 176, C. In the case of carbonic oxide these same reasons are reinforced by others. In all but two of his experiments the iron appears to have been in direct contact with the porcelain tube, whose silica could easily generate carbonic oxide by reacting on the carbon of the metal. When this source of error was eliminated by wrapping the metal in platinum, another possibly serious one suggests itself. Could the cast-iron have contained some 0·80% of slag? If so, this slag could generate the 0·72 of carbonic oxide which is found, by reaction on the metal's carbon.

It is uncertain whether cast-iron often contains slag or not. On the one hand, while the conditions under which pig-iron runs into its moulds might permit the occasional admixture of metal and slag, yet, owing to the fluidity of the former and the difference of specific gravity, one would hardly anticipate that slag would be a common constituent of pig-iron. E. Riley, a chemist of most extended experience in this branch of analysis, has never found evidence of the existence of slag in clean solid pig-iron.[f] Their experiments with chlorine left Drown and Shimer in doubt whether the silicon which is not volatilized by chlorine results from the presence of slag or not,[g] and Drown, himself a distinguished authority on the analysis of iron, informs me that he knows of no satisfactory evidence of the presence of slag in cast-iron.

On the other hand, slag is frequently reported in cast-iron. Fresenius found ·665% in spiegeleisen.[h] Percy quotes cast-iron with aluminium, calcium and magnesium which, if they existed as silicates, would imply the presence of about 9% of slag; but he properly questions these numbers.[i] Taking at random the first twenty analyses of cast-iron in my own notes, in which slag is recorded, the proportion of this substance varies from 0·13 to 2.65%, its average proportion being 0·74%. Of these analyses fifteen

[a] That reaction (1) $Fe + xCO = FeO_x + xC$ would cause loss of volume is self-evident. Reaction (5) $FeO_x + yCO = FeO_{x+y} + yC$ can only occur after the iron has been oxidized by (1). Reaction (6) $2CO = C + CO_2$ yields but one volume of carbonic acid for two initial volumes of carbonic oxide.

[b] Watts, Dict. Chem., 2d supp., p. 250, Fr. Comptes Rendus, LXXIII., p. 281.

[c] M. White, Private Communications, Oct. 1 and Nov. 29, 1887.

[d] Comptes Rendus, LXXVI., p. 562, 1873.

[e] 9 and 10, Table 56, p. 108.

[f] E. Riley, Journ. Chem. Soc., XXV., p. 543, 1872. "In dissolving pig-iron in neutral chloride of copper and using a little dilute hydrochloric acid to dissolve any basic iron salt, I have never been able to get any indications of the presence of slag in pig-iron, or have never been able to find satisfactorily aluminium in pig-iron: if the pig contained slag it certainly ought to be present." Idem, p. 542. "I cannot say that, in all my experience, I ever found any evidences of slag in pig-iron when it was perfectly solid, and the pig carefully bored after removing all the outer skin."

[g] Trans. Am. Inst. Mining Engrs., VIII., p. 514.

[h] Kerl, Grundriss der Eisenhüttenkunde, p. 42.

[i] Percy, Iron and Steel, p. 542.

are by Wuth, a trustworthy analyst, and give from ·31 to 1·43 % of slag, or on an average 0·74%.

C. *Bessemer's Experiment.*—Twelve pounds of tranquil molten ingot iron, when exposed by Bessemer in a crucible suitable for holding forty pounds of unmelted iron, to a vacuum of perhaps twelve or thirteen pounds per square inch, boiled so furiously that all but a pound or two overflowed.[a] He found that boiling could always be induced or completely stopped at will by simply lowering or raising the pressure. The gas evolved was sometimes analyzed, and in each case found to be carbonic oxide, by Henry's determination.

This evidence points so strongly[b] to solution that it is well to scrutinize it very carefully. Henry was a most careful analyst: Bessemer's reputation, or better renown, is known to all. It is to be observed, however, that his statements are made in the discussion of another gentleman's paper: that they refer to experiments made some twenty-five years earlier; that it is not clear that they are not made in considerable part or even wholly from memory; that the gas, consisting apparently of carbonic oxide unaccompanied by hydrogen and nitrogen, differs materially from that recovered by Cailletet and Müller from molten iron, and by Stead from iron in the soaking pits, which always contained a considerable proportion of hydrogen and nitrogen.

Still worse, that which Müller obtained from unrecarburized ingot iron (and this appears to be what Bessemer experimented on) contained only from 8·8 to 48% of carbonic oxide, and probably less on an average than that from any other class of molten iron. I think it just to call attention to these points, which certainly detract from the weight of Bessemer's testimony.

Now, if the gas which he obtained were of the composition which Müller found in similar cases, containing perhaps 25% of carbonic oxide and 75% of hydrogen and nitrogen, it is altogether possible that the fall of pressure caused the latter gases to escape from solution, and that the stirring caused by their escape gave carbon and oxygen previously present in the iron, but not united, an opportunity to unite and escape as carbonic oxide, and that the quantity of this gas thus set free might form one quarter of the total escaping gas. I do not say that this would be a probable, but a conceivable explanation.

Were we to reject Bessemer's experiment, then the evidence which has been adduced, together with further evidence to be detailed chiefly in §§ 213, 214 and 218, and consisting chiefly of the resemblance of the behavior of carbonic oxide to that of hydrogen and nitrogen in escaping in iron; of the protracted and deferred escape of carbonic oxide when no reaction forming it is to be expected; of the arrest of the escape of carbonic oxide by chemical additions which would be expected to stimulate it; and of the remarkably close similarity of the blowholes which are probably partly formed by carbonic oxide to those formed by air in ice, as regards their shape and position; these still seem to create a strong probability that carbonic oxide does dissolve, but not to prove it.

[a] Journ. Iron and St. Inst., 1881, p. 197.

[b] It is quite possible that, accepting Bessemer's statement, these may be merely dissociation phenomena. If carbonate of lime is highly heated in a closed vessel it dissociates and evolves carbonic anhydride: the escape of gas may be completely arrested and started again by raising or lowering the pressure of this gas, its gaseous tension. Now in Bessemer's experiments the melted metal may not have contained carbonic oxide as such but some oxycarbide of iron. Lowering the pressure might cause the non-volatile iron-carbon or iron-oxygen compounds to dissociate, and their dissociation would lead to the formation and escape of carbonic oxide; increase of pressure would again check their dissociation and stop the evolution of gas. But by parity of reasoning every case of evolution of gas by a liquid may be regarded as an instance of dissociation by those who regard solution as a form of chemical combination. Indeed, even some of those who class these as radically different processes regard some apparently typical cases of gas solution as chemical unions, believing for instance that carbonic anhydride, CO_2, when dissolved in water forms a true acid H_2CO_3, which is broken up when carbonic anhydride escapes from the liquid. (Watts, Dict. Chem. I., p. 772.)

§ 189. OTHER INSTANCES OF THE EVOLUTION OF CARBONIC OXIDE are condensed in Table 68. In cases 1 to 4 the gas was extracted by heating in vacuo: in 5 and 6 it was collected from molten or solidifying metal: in 7, 8 and 9 it was recovered by boring under water.

The greatest quantity is that obtained by heating in vacuo, 5·29 volumes being found by Graham and 135 by Parry: next comes that evolved from molten and solidifying metal, reaching perhaps about 1 volume: while that obtained by boring cold metal does not exceed 0·011 volumes, expect perhaps in those cases where gas is found in distinct blisters.

TABLE 68.—CARBONIC OXIDE IN COMMERCIAL IRON PREVIOUSLY UNTREATED.

No.	Observer.	Mode of extraction, etc.	Cast-iron. %	Cast-iron. Vol.	Wrought-iron. %	Wrought-iron. Vol.	Steel. %	Steel. Vol.
1.	Graham......	Heating in vacuo.	......	......	·021@ ·080	1·39@ 5·29		
	Troost and H...	" "	·0007	·04	·0095	·187	·0008	·02
2.	Parry	" "	·0005@ 2·04	·046@ 185·00	·0108	·08	·56	87·29
3	Zyromski	" "	......	......	·083	2·18	·0005	·43
4. 5.	Müller (see note)	Evolved from molten or solidifying metal.	·0069 ·0091	·46@ ·69	......	......	·015	1·24 (?)
	Stead (see note)	" "	......	......	......	......	·0028	·19 (?)
6 7.	Müller........	Boring cold metal.	·000015 @ ·00017	·001@ ·011	......	......	·000075	0 @ ·006
8.	Stead	" " "	......	......	......	......	·00008	0 @ ·004

1. Journ. Chem. Soc., XX., p. 285, 1867, and Chem. News, XV., p. 273, 1867. Wrought-iron wire and horse nails, Nos 24 and 27, Table 56. 2. Comptes Rendus, LXX., p. 562, 1873. Iron cylinders weighing 500 grammes were heated at 800° C. in vacuo for 190 hours. Nos. 11, 16 and 30, Table 56. 3. Journ. Iron and St. Inst., 1872, II., p. 240; 1873, I., p. 430; 1874, I., p. 93; and 1881, I., p. 189: these cases are given in detail in Table 56. 4. Stahl und Eisen, 1884, p. 386: Journ. Iron and St. Inst., 1884, II., p. 625. Nos 21 and 22, Table 56. 5. Iron, 1884, p. 188. Müller found from 1 to 1·5 volumes of gas of undetermined composition escaping from Bessemer steel during solidification: and in gas escaping under similar conditions he found in general from 8·8 to 62 % of carbonic oxide: the figures in this line are only very roughly approximate. See Table 55. 6. Stead found 12·5% of carbonic oxide in the gas escaping from solidifying steel. Assuming that, as found by Müller, the steel evolved about 1·5 volumes of gas, we have 0·19 volumes of carbonic oxide thus evolved. This, like the preceding, is simply to give a rough idea of the evolution of this gas. 7. and 8. The solidified metal is bored under water, and the gas thus released caught and measured. See Table 54. Also Iron, 1883, pp. 51, 115: Stahl und Eisen. 1883, p. 466.

§ 190. THE APPARENT ABSORPTION OF CARBONIC OXIDE by iron has been observed by Graham, Troost and Hautefeuille and Parry. Troost and Hautefeuille found that much less carbonic oxide could be extracted from iron on heating in vacuo when in its natural state or after soaking in hydrogen, than when the samples previously exhausted after soaking in hydrogen were later exhausted after heating in carbonic oxide. Clearly if the carbonic oxide evolved arose from oxygen and carbon derived in process of manufacture and initially present, the iron would evolve less of it at each heating in vacuo than at the preceding: therefore when heated in carbonic oxide it must have absorbed either that gas as such, or its dissociated elements: but which we cannot tell, for if the oxygen and carbon had been absorbed separately they might recombine and escape as carbonic oxide when the iron was again heated in vacuo.

Their results are condensed in Table 69 and detailed in Table 57.

Parry, too, in one out of five experiments, No. 66, Table 57, found that wrought-iron, previously heated in vacuo till only traces of gas escaped, when heated in carbonic oxide during 28 hours absorbed by direct measurement 4·5 times its own volume of this gas, of which it

TABLE 69.—INFLUENCE OF PREVIOUS EXPOSURE TO CARBONIC OXIDE ON THE EVOLUTION OF THAT GAS IN VACUO.

Description.	Weight taken.	In natural state. Vol. CO evolved in vacuo. Per 100 of gas evolved.	In natural state. Vol. CO evolved in vacuo. Per vol. iron.	After heating in hydrogen. Vol. CO evolved in vacuo. Per 100 of gas evolved.	After heating in hydrogen. Vol. CO evolved in vacuo. Per vol. iron.	After heating in carbonic oxide. Vol. CO evolved in vacuo. Per 100 of gas evolved.	After heating in carbonic oxide. Vol. CO evolved in vacuo. Per vol. iron.
	Grms.						
Cast-iron, T. & H. … …	500	16·76	0·040	2·86	0·016	66·99	0·211
Cast-steel, T. & H. … .	500	63·65	0·051	11·53	0·013	62·59	0·029
Wrought-iron, "	500	53·88	0·167	4·81	0·009	97·85	0·211
Wrought-iron wire, Graham … … … .	39	67·	5·29	8·	0·040	49·9	4·150

NOTE.—The larger volumes obtained by Graham than by Troost and Hautefeuille are explicable by the fact that he treated small wire, they thick cylinders.

evolved 3·2 volumes when again heated in vacuo without removal from the apparatus.[a] Here too it is uncertain whether any carbonic oxide was taken up as such, or whether the total apparent absorption was due to the dissociation of carbonic oxide: but that carbonic oxide was dissociated to a certain extent is indicated by the fact that the residual gas contained from 4 to 6% of carbonic acid,[b] doubtless arising from reactions (6) or (1) and (4) of § 185.

If it were positively proved that iron does not absorb carbonic oxide when heated in this gas, this would not prove that it could not dissolve it as such under other conditions. We have seen (§§ 172-3) that iron absorbs nitrogen when heated in this gas or in air only with great difficulty, but readily absorbs it when heated in ammonia.

Hydrogen appears to escape from iron on heating in vacuo at a lower temperature than carbonic oxide. Thus Parry[c] found that at and below full redness, say 1,000° C., both cast and wrought-iron evolved nearly and sometimes quite pure hydrogen, while with further rise of temperature the proportion of carbonic oxide increased. This accords with Graham's statement[d] that the proportion of carbonic oxide to hydrogen evolved when horse-nails were heated in vacuo increased as the exposure was prolonged: Troost and Hautefeuille[e] observed that wrought-iron evolved its hydrogen more readily than its carbonic oxide. On the other hand they found that most of the carbonic oxide evolved from cast-iron and steel in vacuo came off in the first few hours, the hydrogen being retained more tenaciously: here their results seem at a variance with those of Graham and Parry.

We may explain in two ways the fact that the expulsion of carbonic oxide requires a higher temperature than that of hydrogen. Regarding the former gas as dissolved in the metal, we may suppose that its solubility diminishes with rising temperature less rapidly than that of hydrogen: or, regarding it as formed at the instant of escape by the oxidation of carbon by oxygen present in the iron, we may believe that the relative affinity of carbon as compared with that of iron for oxygen increases with rising temperature, so that the carbon is only able to remove the oxygen from the iron at a temperature above that which renders the iron porous enough to permit the escape of hydrogen. This accords with the fact that, while carbonic oxide is comparatively rapidly split up by iron and its oxides at about 500° C., this action almost ceases at bright redness. The greater diffusiveness of hydrogen than of carbonic oxide might explain why but little of the latter accompanied the first escaping portions of hydrogen, but hardly the complete absence of carbonic oxide.

§ 191. INFLUENCE OF CARBONIC OXIDE ON THE PHYSICAL PROPERTIES OF IRON.—An eminent authority[f] believes that carbonic oxide acts like phosphorus, and renders iron cold-short. I have vainly applied to him for evidence. Only one consideration which throws light in on this question suggests itself. Whitworth's liquid compression should increase the quantity of gas dissolved by steel, and if carbonic oxide is soluble Whitworth's steel should contain more than others. Its excellent quality certainly opposes the belief that carbonic oxide is injurious. (See § 230.)

CHAPTER XI.

GENERAL PHENOMENA OF THE ABSORPTION AND ESCAPE OF GAS FROM IRON.

§ 200. A classification of the gases present in molten iron according to the time and condition of their escape, already sketched in § 170, is given in Table 70. Figure

Fig. 11, VOLUME OF GASES ESCAPING FROM IRON. (PARTLY CONJECTURAL.)

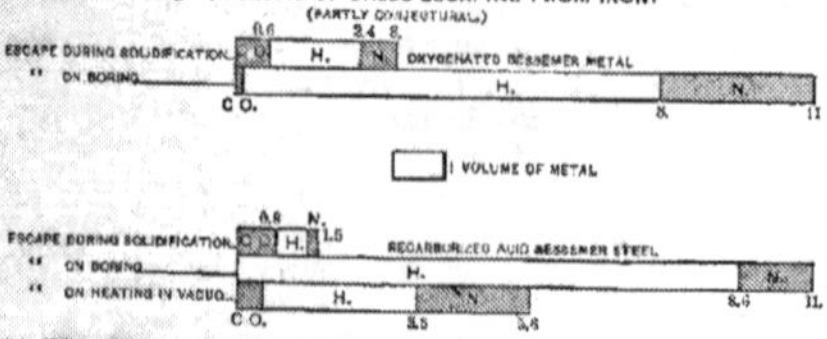

11 illustrates what now appears to be the typical composition and volume of certain of these classes. The numbers here offered must be received cautiously as rough crude generalizations, necessarily partly conjectural, thanks to the scantiness of our data. For instance, I have assumed in Figure 11 that oxygenated Bessemer metal evolves eleven times its own volume of gas when bored. This is a pure guess.

When bored with a sharp drill iron evolves much less gas than this: boring with a dull drill in one case sets free eleven volumes of gas, and possibly still finer comminution might release still more. Again, the gases obtained on heating in vacuo doubtless include at least a part of the gas which would have been set free had the metal being bored before heating in vacuo. Again, the gases escaping during solidification from the already pasty metal are doubtless contaminated with those which escape before solidification from the central portions of the metal, which remain molten longest.

Of two of these classes, A2 which redissolves in the metal,

[a] Journ. Iron and St. Inst., 1873, II., p. 431.
[b] Idem, 1874, I., p. 98.
[c] Journ. Iron and Steel Inst., 1874, I., p. 93: 1873, II., pp. 429-431.
[d] Chem. News, XV., p. 273, 1867.
[e] Comptes Rendus, LXXVI., p. 562, 1873.
[f] Journ. Iron and St. Inst., 1881, I., p. 196.

TABLE 70.—GASES OF STEEL CLASSIFIED ACCORDING TO TIME OF ESCAPE.

Mode of escape, etc.		Effect.	Percentage composition by volume.				Volume of gas per volume of iron.				
			CO.	H.	N.	CO_2	CO.	H.	N.	CO_2	Total.
I. Escape while the metal is so liquid that the passages close.		Scattering	8·6@52·4	2·2@82·5	1·0@48·2	0@8·4	0@1·23	0@1·61	0@0·78	0@·13	0@8·+
II. Remains or is formed after plasticity has set in. A. Held as gas mechanically, or by capillarity, or gasified during plasticity	1. Escapes gradually from blowholes etc., through the walls of the ingot ..	Rising, blowholes, etc...	12·9	20·47@27·21	59·91@66·63						
	2. Redissolves in the metal.										
	3. Remains in pores and blowholes...	....	0@9·2	52·2@92·4	5·9@18·1	....	0@0·006	·06@9·76	0·01@1·73	.. ..	0·66@11·
B. Remains *dissolved* after plasticity has ceased; or is formed by reactions thereafter	1. May be extracted by heating in vacuo.	May affect physical properties, as suggested in § 170......	7·06@66·65	22·72@57·8	11·86@34·7 [6·49]a	2·27 [16·55]a	·02@·48 [37·22]a	·007@8·13 [32·15]a	·002@1·86	·001 [2·15]a	·031@5·48 [70·5]a
	2. Cannot be extracted by heating in vacuo......										

a The numbers in brackets were obtained in Parry's experiments (see § 176, C).
The numbers in this table are derived from those in Tables 54, 55 and 56, pp. 106 to 108.
Those in columns 7 to 10 of line 1 are very rough approximations, inserted merely to give a rough idea of the quantity of each gas escaping. They are arrived at in the following way. Müller found 1 to 1·5 volumes of gas escaping from recarburized steel, and 3 or more volumes from oxygenated metal, during solidification. The minimum for each gas is 0, since in some cases no gas escapes. The maximum for hydrogen is obtained by assuming that in each of the cases in Table 55 in which the composition of the gas from recarburized steel is given 1·5 volumes escapes: and that in the case of oxygenated metal (74, Table 55) 3 volumes escapes. The maxima for the other gases is found in the same way. Thus the maximum for carbonic oxide is derived from Number 86, the maxima for nitrogen and hydrogen from Number 73, and the maximum for carbonic acid from Number 89. The assumption is of course not strictly warranted. We can only say that our present slight knowledge of the subject suggests that these numbers may not be exceeded: they cannot be considered as limits which have actually been reached.
The numbers for Class II., A. 1, give merely the composition of the gas escaping from the ingots in the soaking pits, as determined by Stead, Number 92, Table 55.

and B2 which remains in the solid metal and cannot be extracted even by heating in vacuo, we have little knowledge. §§ 172 and 176 give certain facts which suggest that most and perhaps all of the nitrogen and hydrogen of solid iron can be removed either by heating in vacuo or very fine grinding.

The gases which directly interest the steel-maker are the "mould" gases,[a] those which are evolved during solidification and which cause blowholes. It is the formation of cavities that gives the gas question moment: it is not clear that their sides can ever be so completely welded together, even in small forgings, as to wholly efface their effects. In large forgings it is still more difficult to close them, while in castings their effects may be disastrous. Were we, however to confine our attention solely to the phenomena of this class of gases, we could obtain but a very incomplete notion of the causes of their generation and of the means likely to prevent it: a general study such as we will now attempt may give us a better insight.

I will now detail certain phenomena touching this question, and later seek their explanation and the means of preventing and obliterating gas-formed cavities. The shape and position of the blowholes and pipes is discussed in Chapter XII.

§ 201. CONDITIONS OF THE ESCAPE OF GAS FROM MOLTEN AND SOLIDIFYING METAL.

A. *Scattering and Rising.*—Gas may escape from molten iron so rapidly as to cause violent boiling. In this way the contents of a five-ton ladle may be nearly completely ejected. Commonly a gentle bubbling occurs till the top of the ingot crusts over: after this the gas escaping from the still liquid interior may keep minute passages open, as at J, figure 12, through which it escapes, "scattering" particles of molten metal.

Scattering then is caused by gas which is able to swim to the top of the ingot. Such gas might be evolved either from the still molten interior, or from the already pasty metal, or at their contact, being gasified at the instant of solidification. But when the pasty metal evolves bubbles of gas, whether they form wholly within the already pasty portions as at M, figure 13, or whether they form at the

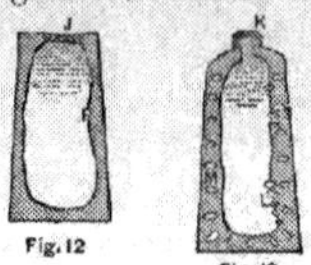

Fig. 12

Fig. 13

contact of the liquid and pasty portions, their spherical ends projecting into the liquid mass as at L, unless they free themselves and swim to the top of the ingot and thus escape, they must occupy room which had been occupied by the metal, and must thus tend to force the still liquid interior upwards, pressing against the ingot top, or even piercing it as at K. This pressure against the top of the ingot causes it to *rise.* This rising is often gradual, the top of the ingot being gradually forced upwards, till, even if the mould was originally but half filled, the top of the ingot may eventually protrude above that of the mould.

The blowholes in ice appear to form like those at L, their ends projecting into the still liquid water. Water passes so suddenly from the liquid to the solid state that, once the blowhole is formed, it does not appear to be subsequently enlarged by fresh secretions of gas from the surrounding ice. Just how the blowholes form in steel is not certain. On the one hand, when the molten interior of partly solidified ingots of rising steel is poured out,[b] the perforations found in the inner side of the shell indicate that the blowholes initially form as at L, figure 13: on the other hand, the gradual rising of the whole top of the ingot suggests that, even after the blowhole is formed and completely inclosed, fresh gas enters it from the adjoining metal, increasing the pressure till it becomes strong enough to elongate the already partly solidified walls of the ingot.

Thus gas which forms within the ingot during solidification will cause frothing, boiling, or "scattering" if it is able to swim to the upper portion of the mass and escape, and "rising" if it is unable to escape.

Thus scattering, when unaccompanied by rising, ap-

a For brevity I frequently refer to the gases evolved from molten and solidifying iron at the atmospheric pressure as "mould gases," to those found on boring the cold solidified metal under water, etc., as "boring gases," and to those extracted on heating it in vacuo as "vacuum gases."

b See figure 82, § 222.

pears to be due to the early escape of gas: while rising is rather connected with its later escape. Clearly the bubbles which cause rising must form blowholes: hence the blowholes are referable to the late escape of gas.[a]

It would not be anticipated that the escape of gas at the instant of solidification would necessarily cause rising and blowholes. If the gas then evolved remains attached by capillarity to the growing walls as at L, or if it be mechanically enclosed by the metal, it will cause blowholes. But it is altogether conceivable that it may not be detained in either of these ways, but that all of it may swim to the surface. As the solid portion gradually encroaches on the liquid interior, the condition and texture of its surface may vary according to the rate of solidification, the composition of the metal, etc.: and some kinds of surfaces may be expected to have a greater tendency to retain gas bubbles by capillarity than others. Again, if the metal passes directly from a highly liquid to a distinctly solid condition, gas set free at the instant of solidification should have a better chance of escaping from the solidifying metal and of swimming upward to the surface, than if the metal passed through an intermediate pasty or gummy state.

So, too, if the metal on solidifying becomes porous, gas which forms will be more likely to work its way out through the ingot's walls and less likely to collect and push the metal aside so as to form blowholes, than if the metal becomes pasty or gummy on solidifying.

According to Müller both grey and white cast-iron evolve gas copiously in setting. White iron often contains blowholes, grey iron rarely does. It is natural to refer this difference to the fact that white iron passes through a pasty condition in solidifying, while grey iron is said to pass more instantaneously from the liquid to the solid state. Indeed, from its behavior in the foundry one would hardly suspect that it evolved gas at all, so tranquil is it, save for the beautiful, kaleidoscopic, shifting play of its surface.

It is probable that the same water may, under different conditions of cooling, yield either very porous, or comparatively compact, or even perfectly solid ice, though it may evolve the same quantity of air in each case. In the first case much of the air is mechanically entangled or retained by capillarity; in the last the conditions of freezing enable it to escape completely. How much more may we expect differences when not only the rate of freezing and the other external conditions differ, but when different varieties of metal differ widely in the order and kind of changes in their physical condition which they themselves undergo in solidifying? With our present imperfect knowledge and with such complex conditions it were idle to seek a full explanation of all the variations in the effects of our escaping gases.

The top of a scattering ingot will evidently be porous, but, if solidification progresses regularly from without inwards and from below upwards, all the gas evolved from the still molten metal and all that is evolved at the instant of solidification may escape through the top crust, or collect beneath it, and the rest of the ingot may be free from blowholes: but it may still contain the central pipe.

If the still molten metal evolves gas so rapidly that it boils violently, and if, as solidification progresses, the escape of gas decreases somewhat, the metal will now sink back. Very soft and especially basic ingot iron may behave in this way to such an extent that it is not practicable to fill the mould at one teeming. With soft basic ingot iron it is often necessary to pour but a little metal at a time, returning perhaps as many as nine times at intervals, and adding a little metal each time as the frothing slackens. This metal often pipes slightly: yet it sometimes develops a sufficient number of blowholes to rise, when, in spite of its previous sinking back, it is strictly speaking a "rising metal." To the superficial observer its rising is masked by the more violent and conspicuous frothing which precedes it. In this case our nomenclature is rather misleading, and calls for a change. Confusion may be lessened by calling such metal "blowhole-forming" rather than "rising."

B. *Piping* is due to the contraction of the interior of the ingot after the exterior has grown cool and rigid. The volume and position of the pipe will be considered in §§ 224–5. Suffice it here to point out that the blowholes, displacing the molten or pasty metal and forcing it inwards and upwards, must diminish and may obliterate the pipe. And in fact, other things being equal, the fewer and smaller the blowholes, the larger is the pipe. But that portion of the blowholes which forms before the ingot-top has frozen across merely raises the level of the ingot-top, and does not lessen the volume of the pipe.

Piping proper is not to be confounded with the sinking back which occurs when metal which has been boiling becomes relatively tranquil, or at least boils less violently: this occurs because the evolution of gas slackens, and it has but little and remote connection with contraction.

§ 202. WHAT CLASSES SCATTER AND RISE?—Irons may be classified into those which

1. Neither scatter nor acquire blowholes. 2. Scatter without acquiring blowholes.	They usually pipe.
3. Acquire blowholes (rise) without scattering. 4. Both scatter and acquire blowholes (rise).	They do not usually pipe.

Classes of iron which scatter much usually acquire blowholes, and those which acquire blowholes abundantly usually scatter.[b]

A. *Influence of Temperature.*—An excessively high casting temperature renders the metal wild,[c] and favors the formation of blowholes, but, according to Walrand,[d] only when the metal is cast in metallic moulds whose walls

[a] Müller's calculation, implying that if the gas found in the cold blowholes had existed in them when the metal was at 1,400° C. its pressure would have been between about 191 and about 348 pounds per square inch, harmonizes with the view that the blowholes are formed by a late rather than an early escape of gas during solidification, and that much gas enters them after they have been completely enclosed by pasty metal. For, unless the metal were decidedly stiff and hence comparatively cool, we should expect that gas at such a pressure and in the considerable quantity in which it exists in the larger blowholes, would push the surrounding metal aside and enlarge its own cavity till its pressure became much diminished, unless indeed the ingot's outer crust had become so strong and rigid as to completely resist the expansive tendency. In arriving at these numbers Müller deducts for the gas which, from boring solid blowhole-less iron, he infers exists in the solid metal between the blowholes. Cf. § 205, B. The pressure which he arrives at appears to me somewhat conjectural. Iron, Jan. 19, 1883, p. 52: Sept. 14, 1883, p. 244.

[b] The statements in this chapter concerning the behavior of the different classes of iron, are in large measure based on Müller's authority, in part on personal observation. My own observations are not sufficiently extended to enable me to speak with perfect confidence on certain points; nor do I feel certain that the published statements of others on these same points are based on sufficiently systematic observation.

[c] Stead, Journ. Iron and St. Inst., 1882, II., p. 526.

[d] Troilius, Van Nostrand's Eng. Mag., XXXIII., p. 364, 1885, from Jernkont. Ann.

have become oxidized. In this case an external zone of innumerable small, narrow, very elongated, closely packed blowholes forms, causing the ingot to crack in forging. In soft basic ingot iron an excessively high temperature produces numerous pear-shaped, subcutaneous blowholes, together with many central ones.[a]

An unduly low casting temperature likewise causes rising and blowholes under many conditions, whose limits are not well known.

B. *Influence of Composition and of Additions.*—In general, the freer the iron from carbon, silicon and manganese, the more does it form blowholes. Thus oxygenated metal scatters violently and forms blowholes.[b] Ingot iron comes next: it occasionally rises so violently as to burst the firmly wedged cover from its mould, causing a violent explosion. If at the same time it be unduly cool it boils all the more violently. Highly carburized steel is normally comparatively tranquil, is nearly or quite free from blowholes, and pipes deeply: the harder *i. e.* more highly carburetted crucible steels pipe more deeply than the softer ones.

There may be exceptions to this rule. Thus in the basic Bessemer process it is found that steel which has not been thoroughly after-blown, and hence has say 0·15% of phosphorus or more, is much wilder than that which is thoroughly dephosphorized: it boils like porridge, with large bubbles and violent spirting.[a]

A bath of oxygenated metal which, if recarburized with large additions reacts violently and yields solid ingots, with smaller additions of spiegeleisen or ferromanganese may give porous ingots,[c] apparently because it then has so much less carbon and manganese.

But, while the addition of silicon usually completely stops both rising and scattering, its mere presence is no guarantee of soundness. Not only does siliciferous grey cast-iron occasionally rise, but even Bessemer steel retaining 0·3, 0·6 or even 1% of the silicon initially in the cast-iron, and obtained by interrupted blowing and hence unrecarburized, often rises so suddenly as to hardly leave time for closing the mould.[d] It appears therefore that it is not the mere presence of silicon but the fact that it has been added shortly before casting that prevents blowholes and rising.

Table 70 A gives the results of several experiments on the influence of recarburizing additions on the evolution of gas, with other matter elsewhere referred to in connection with these experiments.

Here the degree of tranquillity which the recarburizing addition produces is roughly proportional to the quantity of silicon and manganese which the recarburized steel holds, and bears no traceable relation to the quantity of these elements which is oxidized. Thus 1 and 5, which retain about ·66% of manganese but almost no silicon, scatter and rise, and become porous: 2, 6 and 7, retaining more silicon, do not scatter, rise very little and contain

[a] J. Hartshorne, private communication, March 1st, 1888.

[b] As pointed out at the end of § 201, A, oxygenated metal and soft ingot iron often sink back in the mould, so that fresh metal has to be added after teeming: but nevertheless oxygenated metal is strictly speaking a "rising," *i. e.* blowhole-forming metal, and soft ingot iron often is.

[c] Müller, Iron, Feb. 22, 1884, p. 161.

[d] Idem, Jan. 6th, 1883, p. 18. Even 16% ferro-silicon may be full of blowholes.

TABLE 70 A.—RECARBURIZING REACTIONS IN THE BESSEMER PROCESS.

These cases are numbered to correspond with those in Tables 42, 48, and 76, pp. 93-94.

Number and observer.	1 M.			2 M.			3 M.			4 M.		
Condition of the metal before recarburizing. Acid or basic	Basic.			Basic.			Basic.			Basic.		
Previously recarburized a	No.			No.			Yes.			No.		
With	......			......			......			......		
Containing	......			......			......			......		
Description of metal	Oxygenated.			Oxygenated.			Rail steel, 0·25 % carbon.			Oxygenated.		
Details of recarburizing. Recarburized in	Iron moulds.			Iron moulds.			Iron moulds.			Iron moulds.		
Slag present or no	No.			No.			No.			No.		
Recarburized with	Spiegeleisen.			Ferro-silicon.			Spiegeleisen.			Silicide of manganese.		
	C.	Si.	Mn.	C.	Si.	Mn.	C.	Si.	Mn.	C.	Si.	Mn.
Containing	4·22	0·41	8·12	1·64	0·86	2·05	..		..	5·18	6·10	28·35
Present before recarburizing b	·029	·016	·160	·033	·003	·144	....	..	...	·085	·021	·181
Added	·268	·026	·516	·059	·355	·073	...	...	....	·182	·318	1·487
Total	·297	·042	·676	·092	·358	·217	...	....	....	·135	·339	1·668
After recarburizing	·242	·017	·659	·062	·238	·186	...	....	...	·175	·346	1·604
Removed	·055	·025	·017	·030	·120	·031	...	...	...	·092	— ·007	·064
Oxygen corresponding	·078	·043	·005	·040	·205?	·009	...	....	..	·027	— ·012	·019
Degrees of Rising	Moderate.			Rises a little.			Slight.			None.		
Scattering	Scatters.			No scattering.			Slight.			None.		
Solidity	Porous.			A few blowholes.			A few blowholes.			Complete.		
Composition of gas. CO	58·3			32·6			55·2			......		
H	30·9			51·0			37·9			......		
N	6·8			7·5			3·2			......		
CO_2	4·0			5·9			3·7			......		
Time after casting when collected	7 mins. after casting.			7 mins. after casting.			......			......		

Number and observer.	5 M.			6 M.			7 M.			
Condition of the metal before recarburizing. Acid or basic	Basic.			Basic.			Basic.			
Previously recarburized a	Yes.			Yes.			Probably not.			
With	2 % ferro-manganese.			2 % ferro-manganese.						
Containing	73 % Mn. (?).			70 % Mn. (?).						
Description of metal	Non-redshort.			Scattering.						
Details of recarburizing. Recarburized in	Iron moulds.			Iron moulds.			Ladle.			
Slag present or no	No.			No.			Yes.			
Recarburized with	Spiegeleisen.			Ferro-silicon.			Ferro-silicon and ferro-manganese.			
	C.	Si.	Mn.	C.	Si.	Mn.	C.	Si.	Mn.	P.
Containing	4·26	·85	7·94	1·027	10·05	2·057				
Present before recarburizing b	·089	·014	·311	·075	·007	·480	·002	·002	·058	·078
Added	·135	·015	·345	·054	·339	·069	·140	·590	1·210	...
Total	·224	·029	·656	·129	·346	·549	·142	·592	1·268	...
After recarburizing	·205	·018	·667	·127	·314	·585	·115	·162	·944	·097
Removed	·019	·011	— ·011	·002	·032	— ·036	·027	·370	·889	....
Oxygen corresponding	·16	·02	·40	·18	·05	·40	·036	·683	·118	....
Degrees of Rising	Moderate.			None.			Rose.			
Scattering	Scatters.			None.			None.			
Solidity	Porous.			Nearly complete			A zone of blowholes			
Composition of gas. CO	56·4	42·1		38·6	36·6		34·7	30·8		
H	29·6	42·8		45·9	44·5		58·0	65·8		
N	10·6	11·1		7·8	11·9		4·1	1·9		
CO_2	3·4	4·0		6·7	7·9		3·2	1·5		
Time after casting when collected	7 mins.	12 mins.		......			......			

Number and observer.	8 M.			9 M.			11 K.		
Condition of the metal before recarburizing. Acid or basic	Basic.			Acid.			Acid.		
Previously recarburized a	Probably not.								
With									
Containing									
Description of metal									
Details of recarburizing. Recarburized in	Converter.								
Slag present or no	Yes.								
Recarburized with	Ferro-silicon and ferro-manganese.								
	C.	Si.	P.	C.	Si.	Mn.	C.	Si.	Mn.
Containing									
Present before recarburizing b	....	....	·106	·005	·113	·230	·030	·035	·088
Added	....	..	...	·332	·047	·836	·518	·077	2·029
Total	....	....	....	·337	·160	1·066	·548	·112	2·118
After recarburizing	....	·011	·515	·256	·208	·712	·370	·060	1·170
Removed	..	·70+	....	·081	— ·078	·354	·178	·052	·948
Oxygen corresponding	..	....	...	·108	— ·125	·102	·217	·060	·274
Degrees of Rising	Rose.								
Scattering									
Solidity	Contained blowholes.								
Composition of gas. CO	64·6	44·1							
H	18·9	41·6							
N	14·4	10·8							
CO_2	2·1	3·7							
Time after casting when collected	Early mould.	Late mould.							

M = Müller, K = King.

a In certain cases the metal had been partially recarburized before receiving the recarburizing additions whose reaction forms the basis of this table.

b The numbers in this line give the carbon, etc., per 100 of the weight of the metal after recarburizing.

"Oxygen corresponding" is calculated on the assumption that the reactions are $Mn + O = MnO$; $Si + 3FeO = 2Fe + FeSiO_3$; and $C + O = CO$.

1. Spiegeleisen added in the mould to oxygenated basic metal causes very violent brief ebullition, with a flame a yard high. The steel scatters, rises slightly, and yields porous ingots. Stahl und Eisen, IV., p. 72. The manganese removed appears to be incorrectly calculated in the original memoir.

2. Ferro-silicon added in this proportion in the moulds to oxygenated basic metal immediately arrests every visible development of gas. The steel becomes perfectly quiet, does not scatter, always rises a little, contains a few blowholes, mostly sporadic, and is slightly red-short. Idem, p. 73.

3. To basic rail steel of ·25% carbon, which itself develops much gas and scatters actively, melted spiegeleisen is added. No boiling occurs, the development of gas at once diminishes and soon ceases. The steel rises slightly and has scattered blowholes. Idem, p. 72.

4. The addition of a siliciferous ferro-manganese to oxygenated basic metal instantly and completely quiets the metal. Almost no gas escapes: the metal is free from pores. Idem, p. 73.

5. To basic ingot, produced by adding 2 % of ferro-manganese in the converter, 11·56 kg. of spiegeleisen are added, causing rather active boiling and a spiegel flame. The steel scatters with moderate rising, forming a porous ingot of 272 kg. Idem, p. 72.

6. To a basic ingot iron produced with 2 % of ferro-manganese, which scattered, rose slowly, and gave ingots with few scattered blowholes, 9·65 kg. of ferro-silicon is added. This arrested all movement and all visible escape of gas: the ingot, weighing 236 kg., had a zone with a few blow-holes. Idem, p. 73.

7. 5 % of ferro-silicon and 2 % of ferro-manganese of 70 % manganese, both red hot, were added in the ladle, and the metal poured on them from the converter. There was no reaction; the steel was perfectly quiet but rose, and acquired a marginal zone of blowholes. Stahl und Eisen, IV., p. 71, 1884; Iron, 1883, p. 246, 1884, p. 187.

8. 5 % of ferro-silicon and 2·5 % of ferro-manganese were added in a molten state to oxygenated basic metal in the converter. The steel was quiet but rose. Idem, III., pp. 446, 452; Iron, 1883, pp. 244-6.

9. To a charge of blown steel 600 kg. of spiegeleisen was added, probably in a molten state in the converter. The weight of the resulting ingots was 7798 kg. There appear to be certain discrepancies in the numbers which Müller gives concerning this case. Zeit. Vereins. Deutsch. Ing., XXII, p. 385.

11. To a charge of blown steel metal 2880 lbs. of spiegeleisen and 40 lbs. of ferro-manganese are added, the former presumably in a molten state in the converter, the latter probably red hot but not molten. Trans. Am. Inst. Mining Engineers, IX., p. 258.

TABLE 71.—BEHAVIOR OF IRON BEFORE AND DURING SOLIDIFICATION.

No.	Description of iron.	Casting temperature.	Behavior before teeming.	Behavior in moulds. Early.	Behavior in moulds. Late.	Piping.	Blowholes. Quantity.	Blowholes. Position.
	CAST-IRON AND INTERMEDIATE BESSEMER PRODUCTS.							
1...	Grey cast-iron	....	Scintillates very little in running.	Evolves much gas, (a) but few sparks.	Very rarely rises (a)	Pipes	Usually none (a).	
2...	Basic Bessemer cast-iron....	....	....	Evolves less gas than 1 do (a)	....	"	" "	
3...	White cast-iron	....	Scintillates in running: sluggish.	....	....	....	Usually has blowholes (m).	
4...	Spiegeleisen	....	Evolves gas copiously (a)	....	Rarely if ever rises (a).	Pipes	Usually none (a).	
5...	Half blown Bessemer metal...	....	Quiet in the ladle (b)...	Froths much, sparkles (b)...	Scatters; evolves gas actively	....	Is solid (b).	
6...	Oxygenated metal, acid or basic, Bessemer or open hearth.	....	Rather quiet in the converter (c, n) †	Scatters violently (c) (n) †....	Rises (c) (n) †	No pipe (c) ...	Contains blowholes †	Sporadic blowholes, and a zone of pores.†
	ACID BESSEMER METAL.							
7...	Rail and other INGOT STEEL........	Excessively HOT ..	Spiegel reaction violent: much gas evolved in ladle (n).	Rises and sinks (n)	See note (p)	See note (p)....	Innumerable (f) small, elongated.†	Extern'l zone (f)(n)†
8...		Normal........	Spiegel reaction usually moderate (n).	Scatters slightly if at all (n)..	Does not rise (n)†	Pipes †	Few or none	Sporadic (n).
9...		Excessively COOL...	No spiegel reaction; quiet in ladle (n).	Scatters (n)........	Rises (n)........	No pipe (n)†...	Many: metal is spongy (f) (n)	External zone: also many large sporadic ones (f) (n) †.
10...	INGOT IRON	Excessively HOT...	Quiet in converter, evolves gas in ladle (n)	" (n)	" (n)	" " (n)...	Few (n)	Sporadic (n).
11...		Normal........	Quiet in converter, quiet in ladle (n).	" (n)	" (n)........	" " (n)...	A moderate n'mb'r (n)	External zone; also sporadic ones (n).
12...		Excessively COOL...	Very wild (n)†	Boils & scatters violently (n)†	" (n)	" " (n)†..	Very many: metal very spongy (f) (n) †	External zone: also very many sporadic ones.
13...	Bochum, usual hot blows. ..	HOT	Violent spiegel reaction; blaze in ladle (d).	Does not scatter (d)........	Does not rise (d)........	Pipes........	None (d)...	
	BASIC BESSEMER METAL.							
14.	BASIC INGOT IRON, C. 0·08, Si. trace, Mn. 0·20@0·25; recarburized with ferro-manganese in converter and spiegeleisen in ladle.	Excessively HOT..	Ferro reaction (in converter) very quiet (h) (o) Spiegel reaction (in ladle) generally moderate (o)....	Much wilder than 15 & 16 (o).	Rises but little if at all (o)	Usually a moderate pipe: sometimes none (o).....	A moderate number (h) (o), rather large and irregular (o)...	External zone, also central blowholes (o).
15.		Normal		Rises rapidly during teeming and sinks again (o). Scatters and boils much (h)				A zone about midway between shell and centre (o).
16.		Excessively COOL.						Large blowholes scattered through ingot (o).
17...	Basic steel made by interrupted blowing and without recarburizing, holding say ·15% P. If now recarburized it becomes wild.	Quiet in ladle and mould (j).		Scatters but little if at all (j).	Rises but little & slowly (j)	....	Few (j).	
18...	Basic metal partially recarburized with 2% of ferromanganese, so as to hold ·08% C, 0·007% Si, 0·58% Mn.	....		Scatters much (l)........	Rises slowly (l)........	....	Few (l)........	Radial (l).
19...	Basic metal recarburized with ferrosilicon alone, so as to hold about 0·8% of silicon.	Quiet (k)........		Perfectly quiet; does not scatter (k).	Rises a little (k)...	....	A m'derate n'mb'r (k)	Scattered (l).
20...	Oxygenated basic metal recarburized with ferro-silico-manganese, so as to hold ·17% C, ·35% Si, and 1·6% Mn.	Quiet (l)........		Perfectly quiet; does not scatter (l).	Does not rise (l)........	....	None (l)........ ...	Mostly sporadic (k).
	CRUCIBLE STEEL.							
23...	High-carbon crucible steel........		Quiet: very few bubbles.	Quiet: a little shower of sparks.	Does not rise...	Pipes deeply ..	Few or none........	

(a) Müller, Stahl und Eisen, III., p. 418, 1883: Iron, Sept. 14, 1883, p. 245.
(b) Idem, Stahl und Eisen, IV., p. 74: Iron, Feb. 15, 1884, p. 138. "Zu dichten Blöcken erstarrte." I do not think that Müller's statement that the ingots were solid necessarily implies that they were absolutely free from blowholes.
(c) Idem, Stahl und Eisen, III., p. 450: IV., p. 75: Iron, Jan. 5, p. 13, Sept. 14, p. 245, 1883: Feb. 15, p. 138, 1884.
(d) Idem, Stahl und Eis., III., p. 449: Iron, Sept. 14, 1883, p. 245.
(e) Walrand, Trollius, Van Nostrand's Eng. Mag., XXXIII., p. 368, 1885, from Jernkont. Ann.
(f) Idem, p. 364.
(g) Stead, Journal. Iron and St. Inst., 1882, II., p. 526.
(h) Müller, Stahl und Eisen, III., p. 451, 1883. "Ziemlich dicke Blöcke."
(i) Idem, IV., pp. 72-9, 1884. This appears to be the usual behavior of such metal.
(j) Idem, III., pp. 446-452, 1883. The behavior of the blown metal varies greatly; now it is quiet, yielding rather solid ingots, now it scatters and rises much: but according to Müller, if the after blow is limited so that the metal retains some .15% phosphorus, the unrecarburized metal is quiet and rises little. But if spiegel be added the metal becomes wild again.
(k) Idem, IV., p. 72, 1884. This appears to be the result of four experiments. The steel was slightly redshort, though it contained only about 0·07% of sulphur. Number 2, Table 70 A, gives the details of the reaction of one of these four experiments.
(l) Idem, p. 75. The details of the reaction are given in Number 4, Table 70 A. It is not clear that the statements in this line refer to more than a single experiment.
(m) Muller, Iron, Jan. 5th, 1884, p. 17.
(n) R. Forsyth, Private Communication, March 3d, 1883.
(o) J. Hartshorne, Private Communication, March 1st, 1883. Thoroughly afterblown metal is recarburized with 0·5 to 0·8% of ferromanganese containing 80% of manganese, added red hot in the converter, and then with 1% to 1·5% of spiegeleisen containing 10% of manganese, added red hot in the ladle after half of the charge has been poured into the ladle. The ferromanganese usually produces but little flame, but sometimes a large flame, with no traceable difference in the results. The spiegel also produces a reaction which, though usually quiet, is sometimes violent. The steel is poured from a first ladle into a second before teeming: this transfer occasionally causes a reaction. The metal froths so much that the mould is filled only about one third full at first, then, after filling other moulds, successive small additions of steel are made, till the mould is finally filled to within four inches of the top. This is substantially the practice at Teplitz and Kladno.
(p) Opinions differ as to the effects of excessively high casting temperature on acid ingot steel. Some find that it causes rising, others that it does not.
Thus Stead finds that, if Bessemer steel has just the right temperature, it does not rise: if the temperature be higher the steel swells up and flows over the tops of the moulds. (Journ. Iron and St. Inst., 1882, II., p. 526). Müller describes steel made by the direct Bessemer process, which contains 1% of silicon and rises very rapidly. So high a percentage of silicon almost necessarily implies an excessively high temperature. (Iron, Jan. 5th, 1883, p. 18). Walrand states (Van Nostrand's Eng. Mag., XXXIII., p. 361), that, if Bessemer steel be cast at too high a temperature, it yields honeycombed ingots.
On the other hand, a most experienced Bessemer steel-maker, in whose powers of observation I place great confidence, informs me that, in his experience, excessively hot-cast Bessemer rail steel does not rise, but pipes. It is probable that an excessively high temperature leads to rising under certain conditions, but not under others. What those conditions are I do not know.
† The testimony concerning this point is quite harmonious.

very few blowholes: 4, which holds after recarburizing ·346% of silicon and much more manganese than the rest, neither scatters nor rises, and contains no blowholes. No such connection however can be traced between the proportion of silicon and manganese oxidized or the proportion of oxygen removed by the reaction, and the behavior of the metal. Thus, to take those which were under substantially the same conditions before receiving the addition, 2, which is intermediate in behavior between 1 and 4, more tranquil than the former but less than the latter, yet has more oxygen removed by the reaction than either. 1, which becomes less tranquil than 4, yet loses more oxygen: but 5, though it becomes less tranquil than 6, loses less oxygen.

C. *Influence of the Process of Manufacture.*—*In the acid Bessemer process*, according to Müller, if the blowing be cut rather short so that the metal is not fully oxygenated, a weak reaction follows the addition of spiegeleisen, and the resulting steel rises and often scatters (suggesting that acid Bessemer steel is a rising rather than a scattering metal): while, under like conditions, longer blowing would cause a more violent reaction and the steel would neither rise nor scatter.[a] We have just

[a] Müller, Iron, March 30, 1883, p. 267, Feb. 23, 1884, p. 161.

seen that a weak reaction due to adding but little spiegeleisen is also followed by rising.

Oxygenated basic metal, though quiet in the converter, boils in the ladle, and evolves gas copiously in the moulds both before and during setting, and yields porous ingots. According to Müller if recarburized with spiegeleisen it evolves gas violently in the ladle, and boils and scatters in the moulds: yet it may yield comparatively solid ingots: *i. e.* it tends to scatter rather than to rise. (No. 1, 70A.) But if a moderate amount of ferro-silicon be added instead of spiegeleisen, the escape of gas at once ceases, the steel does not scatter, but may rise somewhat[a] (No. 2, idem.) With larger additions of silicon and manganese all escape of gas instantly and permanently ceases, and the metal neither scatters nor rises. (No. 4, idem.)

It is generally stated that the tendency to rise is greatest in Bessemer steel, intermediate in open-hearth steel, and least in crucible steel. But basic Bessemer steel, though it is excessively wild before solidification, is thought by some experienced steel makers to rise less and acquire blowholes less than metal of like composition made by the open hearth or acid Bessemer process

Crucible steel is extremely tranquil in the crucible during teeming, a few small bubbles lazily escaping from its surface, apparently of combustible gas, as the crucible is partly filled with a slowly-curling transparent blue flame. A beautiful shower of sparks escapes from the surface of the steel in the mould: it solidifies tranquilly, piping deeply.

Table 71 indicates the behavior of some of the more important varieties of iron before and during solidification.

Some believe that, if the proportion of carbon, manganese and silicon be allowed to fall so low in the gradual decarburization of the bath in the open-hearth process that the metal becomes oxygenated, a tendency to form blowholes is established which, while it may be greatly lessened by subsequent deoxygenating additions of silicon, etc., can be fully eradicated only with great difficulty, if at all. Others deny this, admitting however that it is important to prevent oxygenation, since, if oxygen be absorbed, it is hard to ascertain how much is present, and how much silicon, etc., must be added to remove it.[b]

D. *Influence of Pressure.*—Bessemer proved that the escape of gas from molten steel was governed by the existing pressure. The gentle ebullition of molten steel was rendered furious by lowering the pressure, and wholly stopped by raising it.[c] Troost and Hautefeuille observed that, after cast-iron had been long held fused in an atmosphere of hydrogen, bubbles of gas escaped if the pressure suddenly fell, though the metal remained perfectly tranquil as long as the pressure was constant.[d]

But falling pressure does not always induce a rapid escape of gas. These observers found that phosphoric cast iron would not boil on fall of pressure unless the previous exposure to hydrogen were greatly prolonged, and after highly silicious cast-iron had been fused in hydrogen they could only induce a visible escape of gas by cooling and solidifying the metal in a complete vacuum: even then it scattered but feebly. They had to resort to the same manœuvre to induce a visible escape of gas from iron long held in fusion in an atmosphere of carbonic oxide.[d] That pressure raises the solubility of gases in hot solid iron also has been abundantly proved by the absorption of hydrogen (and carbonic oxide?) when exposed to the hot metal, and their subsequent expulsion when it was heated in vacuo, observed by these chemists as well as by Graham and Parry. (See §§ 176, 188, 189, 190, pp. 110, 123, 124.)

E. *Influence of Agitation and Solidification.*—Agitation expels gas from molten steel. Thus half-blown acid metal, oxygenated acid metal, and spiegel-recarburized basic ingot iron are comparatively quiet while lying undisturbed in the converter, but boil when poured from converter to ladle or from ladle to mould. In no case, so far as I know, does the opposite hold true. This may be attributed to the agitation due to pouring and enhanced by the rapid circulation of the metal, due to its contact with walls of the freshly entered vessel, necessarily much cooler than the metal: they cool it, locally change its density, and so induce circulation. As the walls grow hotter this effect diminishes. So, too, the bath in the open-hearth furnace is often made to boil by stirring, much as champagne is. Solidification also evidently expels gas from steel. Thus in certain cases acid Bessemer steel is perfectly quiet in the converter and for a few moments after pouring into the moulds: then, as solidification sets in, it begins to rise.[e] It is possible that the boiling which sometimes follows transferring into the ladle is enhanced by temporary solidification of the metal against its cool walls. More conclusive is the fact that while slow solidification, by affording the gases which it expels time to escape, yields comparatively solid ingots, sudden freezing may under otherwise like conditions yield extreme spongy ones. Thus Brustlein found that steel, which when cast in the usual way gave pretty solid ingots,[f] rose very much and formed a veritable sponge[g] when cast in a water-cooled copper mold six inches in diameter. In harmony with this result are the explosions which often occur when a piece of cold iron is dropped into molten steel, a thin coating of steel momentarily solidifying on the surface of the cold lump,[h] and the fact that the less carbon steel contains the more does it tend to boil in the moulds, for the lower the carbon the higher the melting point and the more suddenly does the steel set, *cœteris paribus*. (§ 202 B, p. 128.) But, though in harmony with Brustlein's result, I will not insist that these phenomena are due to the same cause.

That solidification does not always cause an important escape of gas is suggested by the fact that some varieties of iron neither scatter nor rise, and proved by the observations of Troost and Hautefeuille, mentioned in § 202 D, and by the following experiment by Parry. Grey cast-iron was fused in an atmosphere of hydrogen: on solidifying it in vacuo without removal from the apparatus, only a few bubbles of gas were obtained, though on reheating (in vacuo?) it was found to have absorbed much hydrogen.[i]

F. *Protracted Escape.*—Gases, consisting as usual of

[a] Iron, Feb. 15, 1884, pp. 138-9.

[b] Cf. Holley, Metallurgical Review, II., p. 211, 1878.

[c] Jour. Iron and St. Inst., 1881, I., p. 193: cf. § 188, C.

[d] Comptes Rendus, LXXVI., p. 562, 1873. Before the fall of pressure the metal was not simply comparatively but absolutely tranquil. "On n'observe aucune projection, aucune dégagement gazeux."

[e] Müller, Iron, Sept. 14, 1883, p. 244.

[f] Stahl und Eisen, III., p. 251, 1883, No. 5. "Einen ziemlich gesunden Block."

[g] "Glich der so erhaltene Block buchstäblich einem Schwamm."

[h] Ledebur, Handbuch, p. 268.

[i] Journ. Iron and Steel Inst., 1874, I., p. 94.

hydrogen, nitrogen and carbonic oxide, escape from steel cast in the ordinary way, long after solidification is complete. Müller states that combustible gas may be obtained from ingots of compact Bessemer or even crucible steel 45 minutes after teeming, when they are probably completely solidified, if, as I understand, he refers to ingots of usual size cast in iron moulds. For, even within eleven minutes after teeming, Bessemer ingots fourteen inches square are so far solidified that they may safely be stripped, and after four minutes more, or altogether fifteen minutes, they may be lifted with tongs. Even later, after the steel has been withdrawn and placed in soaking pits, it continues to evolve a large quantity of gas. (92, Table 55, p. 107.)

H. W. Lash,[a] casting a large ingot with a thick high sinking head, in a mould surrounded with non-conducting material, enabled gas to escape from it for hours by opening a narrow hole lengthwise through the sinking head while it was soft. This hole of course remained open, permitting the escape of gas, but by its length and narrowness preventing rapid radiation of heat. It enabled him to watch the internal ebullition which continued for $2\frac{1}{2}$ hours, and to remove with a rod any incipient scum which froze on the surface of the liquid mass. This device greatly increased the solidity of the ingot. It is not probable that the gas which thus persistently escaped was formed by the oxidation of the metal's carbon by the small quantity of air which, by diffusion and owing to its greater density, would gradually pass down through such a long narrow hole: for its oxygen was probably wholly absorbed by the incandescent metal through which its path lay. Being rapidly heated and lightened as it entered the hole, the action of gravity probably soon became unimportant, and the descent of the atmospheric oxygen then became dependent on diffusion alone, a slow process.

The protracted escape of gas is discussed in § 214 B.

§ 203. The Extraction of Gas in Vacuo.—Graham found that the rate at which iron evolved gas when heated in vacuo steadily diminished, iron wire becoming apparently nearly exhausted after seven hours heating. Parry, however, found that iron continued to evolve gas even for seven days, and that though the escape of gas gradually ceased when iron was exposed to a red heat, it started up again when the temperature was raised, and this continued up to the highest temperature attainable.[b] A vacuum could be formed and maintained for hours by lowering the temperature to a point below that at which gas was being evolved.[c] § 176, C, p. 111, presents certain reasons for doubting whether the gas which escaped so persistently actually proceeded from the iron.

The absorption of hydrogen and of either carbonic oxide as such or of its dissociated elements has been measured directly and indirectly by several observers, as described in §§ 176 A and 190, pp. 110 and 124.

§ 205. Quantity of Gas Evolved.

A. *From Spiegel Reaction.*—In the reactions of the acid Bessemer process described by Müller and King (Table 70 A, p. 128), from ·08 to ·173% of carbon are removed. Assuming that this escapes as carbonic oxide accompanied, as in 93, Table 55, p. 107, by 20% of other

Table 72.—Influence of Temperature and Length of Exposure on the Volume and Composition of Gas Extracted in Vacuo.

	Case 1. Grey cast-iron.							Case 2. Grey cast-iron.			
Temperature	Red.	Red.	Red.	Red.	Red.	Red.	White.	Red.	White.	White.	White.
Hours	0@7	8@17	18@26	27@36	37@51	52@61	61@76	0@14	14@28	28@46	16@52
Vol. gas p. hr	3·2	2·66	1·4	1·37	1·08	1·37	1·41	0·82	3·98	2·80	3·30
% CO	30·4	36·	43·8	46·2	34·2	38·2	38·1	30·	51·1	53·	64·
% H	66·1	64·1	55·9	52·8	64·3	61·8	61·9	68·2	48·9	47·0	35·5

	3. Grey cast-iron.			4. Grey cast-iron.			5. Grey cast-iron.		
Temperature	Red.	Full red.	Full.	Dull red.	Red.	High.			
Hours	0@12	13@17	18@59	0@9	10@24	25@36	0@3	4@19	20@24
Vol. gas per hour	5·9	10·4	1·66	4·96	1·51	1·88	3·4	0·18	0·17
% CO in gas	19·	20·	33·8	26·	25·8	13·		7·7	
% H " "	78·	80·	66·	74·	74·	86·		91·2	

	6. Cast-iron.		7. Bessemer steel.			8. Wrought-iron.				
Temperature			Bright red.			Red.				
Hours	0@128	128@185	0@24	25@48	48@60	0@2	3	4@5	6	7
Vol. gas per hour			1·4	1·8	0·22	4·5	2·2	0·6	0·2	0·1
% CO in gas	47·	17	67·7	41·8	8·4					
% H " "			29·7	52·5	90·1					

Cases 1 to 4, grey cast-iron, Parry, Jour. Iron and St. Inst., 1874, I., p. 99. 3d and 4th wrapped in platinum. 5th case, grey cast-iron, Idem, p. 98. 6th case, grey cast-iron, Idem, 1881, I., p. 190. 7th case, Bessemer steel, Idem. 8th case, wrought-iron, Graham, Jour. Chem. Soc., 1867, XX., p. 285. These cases are given also in Table 56, Nos. 5 to 19, 20, and 26. In every case the volume of gas per volume of metal is referred to.

gases, from 15 to 33 volumes, measured at the ordinary temperature, would escape. I give these numbers for comparison with the quantity observed to escape from the moulds.

In a spiegel reaction at Joliet, in which molten spiegel was added in the usual manner to blown acid Bessemer steel, only 0·025% of carbon was oxidized, which with the same assumptions implies the escape of about 5 volumes of gas.[d]

B. *In Solidifying.*—An ingot of non-rising acid Bessemer steel gave off between 1 and 1·5 volumes of gas during the first twenty minutes after casting, as measured by Müller with a crude meter at the ordinary temperature. Oxygenated metal evolved gas so rapidly that he was unable to measure it, but he was convinced that it gave off at least thrice its own volume.[e] At 1800° C. these quantities become 7·6, 11·4 and 22·8 volumes.

In five cases Müller calculated that the gas which he extracted on boring existed in the blowholes at a pressure of from 38 to 69 pounds per square inch (2·6 to 5 atmospheres). Hence, if this same quantity had been present as gas when the metal was somewhat below its freezing point, say 1400° C., its pressure would have been from about 191 to about 346 pounds per square inch. That the gas actually existed under considerable pressure in the cold metal is further indicated by his statement that, in some cases, gas escaped from the boring hollow as soon as the point of the drill penetrated the first blowholes.[f] The high pressure which exists within the ingot shortly after teeming occasionally manifests itself by bursting the strongly fastened cover from the mould, and spurting the metal high in the air.

C. *On boring under water*, etc., the more porous the metal and the more finely it is comminuted by the drill, the more gas does it evolve in general. Thus Table 73 shows that the greatest quantity of gas per volume of metal which any specimen of only slightly porous steel evolves is smaller than the least quantity which is evolved by any very porous steel.

a Private communication.
b Journ. Iron and Steel Inst., 1881, I., p. 189.
c Idem, 1873, II., p. 429.
d F. A. Emmerton, private communication, Feb. 4, 1888.
e Iron, Feb. 15, 1884, p. 138.
f Iron, January 19, 1883, p. 52.

TABLE 73.—GASES OBTAINED BY BORING WITH SHARP DRILL.

Material.	Number of cases.	Number free from CO.	Hydrogen. Minimum.	Hydrogen. Maximum.	Hydrogen. Average.	Nitrogen. Minimum.	Nitrogen. Maximum.	Nitrogen. Average.	Carbonic Oxide. Minimum.	Carbonic Oxide. Maximum.	Carbonic Oxide. Average.	Volume of gas per vol. metal. Minimum.	Volume of gas per vol. metal. Maximum.	Volume of gas per vol. metal. Average.
Steel	22	11	62·9	92·4		6·9	48·1		0	2·2		·05	·78	
Very porous steel..	7	2	73·1	90·8	85·96	9·8	20·8	13·42	0	1·65	·59	·25	·78	·50
Slightly porous steel	4	3	54·7	86·4	68·60	12·7	45·8	30·07	0	0·4	·10	·06	·22	·16
Solid steel.........	7	4	52·9	92·4	72·94	5·9	48·1	26·64	0	1·6	·61	·05	·21a	·11a
Cast-iron.........	7	....	52·1	86·5	......	9·2	45·5	......	7	4·3	....	·035	·75	

a Omitting the result (11 volumes) obtained by boring with a dull drill.

0·75 volumes of gas is the largest quantity obtained by boring with a sharp drill; this is decidedly less than escapes during the solidification of molten metal, and very much less than may be extracted by heating in vacuo. With finer comminution six and even eleven volumes of gas per volume of metal have been extracted. The latter is probably far more than escapes during the solidification of most varieties of iron, and is about as much as any observer save Parry has extracted from commercial iron in vacuo.

From one and the same ingot Stead obtained 52 times as much gas on finely comminuting it with a dull drill as when it was cut into comparatively coarse chips with a sharp one: and from cast-iron a dull drill extracted eight times as much as a sharp one. (Nos. 16–17, 40–41, Table 54, p. 106.) Still finer comminution, exposing still more of the minute pores, might set free a still larger volume of gas. It is not clear that the whole of the gas extracted by triturating with a dull drill was released thereby from simple mechanical retention, for this action might well liberate gas held in adhesion. (See § 170, p. 105.)

D. On heating in vacuo Troost and Hautefeuille extracted in no case more than 0·42 volumes of gas, while Graham extracted in one case 12·55 volumes, and Parry 340 volumes: but we have seen reason for doubting his results.

It is not clear why Troost and Hautefeuille obtained so little gas, for they employed a temperature (800° C.) approaching that of Graham's experiments, and they exhausted their specimens during very nearly eight days, while his exposures were but from one to seven hours. Possibly the shape of the pieces treated may have had some influence: Graham employed fine wires, number 23 gauge or about ·025 inch (0·64 mm.) in diameter: Troost and Hautefeuille treated cylinders weighing 500 grammes each, while Parry employed sometimes "clean lumps," sometimes drillings. Possibly, too, part of the gas obtained by Graham came from some source other than the iron.

Clearly the gases which the iron would have released if previously comminuted form a part of those which it gives off when heated in vacuo, and how large a part we cannot now tell.

§ 206. QUANTITY OF GAS ABSORBED.—Graham and Parry both found that previously untreated iron evolved much more hydrogen and carbonic oxide when heated in vacuo than it reabsorbed when heated in these gases.

Thus, Parry extracted as much as 205 volumes of hydrogen and 135 of carbonic oxide from a specimen of cast-iron which only reabsorbed 20 volumes of hydrogen and which absorbed no carbonic oxide:[a] and in no case did he induce iron to absorb more than 22·4 volumes of hydrogen and 4·5 of carbonic oxide. Graham extracted nearly thrice as much gas on exhausting previously untreated iron as he could later obtain from it on twice exhausting it, first after soaking in hydrogen and then after soaking in carbonic oxide.[b]

But, at least in case of hydrogen, it is not certain that in their absorption experiments the metal became saturated with gas: possibly if soaked long enough in hydrogen it might have absorbed as much gas as it previously emitted.

Troost and Hautefeuille obtained results diametrically opposed to these. They extracted from 2·3 to 12·8 times as much hydrogen and from 1·8 to 5·3[c] times as much carbonic oxide from iron which had been soaked in these gases as from the same specimens in their natural state.[d]

The hydrogen which previously exhausted iron absorbs when soaked in this gas, is again and usually fully expelled on heating in vacuo: specimens which absorbed 20 and 14·1 volumes by direct measurement, subsequently emitted 20 and 13·4 volumes of hydrogen.[e] A third specimen absorbed 13 volumes, but when reheated in vacuo evolved only 10·5, and further heating extracted no more gas, perhaps because the temperature at which the iron was exhausted was lower than that at which it soaked in hydrogen.[e] In the sole case in which Parry directly observed the absorption of carbonic oxide by iron, only 71% of the absorbed gas could later be extracted in vacuo: but part or indeed all of the apparent absorption of carbonic oxide may have been due to the absorption of its dissociated elements.

§ 207. THE COMPOSITION OF THE GASES EVOLVED BY IRON is detailed in Tables 54 to 57 and 70 A, and is condensed in Table 70, pp. 106–9, 129.

A. *In general* we may divide the gases into two groups,

I. The carbonic oxide group, comprising carbonic oxide and acid, and

II. The hydrogen group, comprising hydrogen and nitrogen.

Carbonic acid is not found in the boring gases, and it occurs but sparingly in those from the moulds and from heating in vacuo. It may arise from the oxidation of part of the carbonic oxide evolved, and, as the volume of carbonic acid is the same as that of the carbonic oxide from which it is derived, we may consider these gases jointly.

B. *The carbonic oxide group* usually constitutes somewhat more than half of the mould gas from basic Bessemer steel which has been recarburized with spiegeleisen or ferro-manganese or both, but less than half of the mould gases from all other varieties of iron and of the vacuum-extracted gases from all varieties of iron, and is invariably almost completely absent from the boring gases, which consist essentially of the hydrogen group.[f] Spiegel-recarburized basic steel, be it remembered, is distinctly a scattering rather than a rising steel. (§ 202 C, Table 71, p. 129.) For brevity I shall call "spiegel-recarburized" steel both that recarburized with spiegeleisen and that recarburized with

a 10, 46, 60, Tables 56–7, pp. 108–9.

b Numbers 30, 39, 34, 54 and 57, Idem.

c Or from 1·05 to 4·3 times as much, if we include the carbonic acid with the carbonic oxide.

d See numbers 11, 15, 16, 17, 18, 30, 31, 36, 47, 50, 58, 61, 63, 65, Tables 56–7.

e Numbers 12–43, 13–45, 32–52 and 35–66, Tables 56–7.

f It has been attempted to prove that the hydrogen found on boring proceeds not from the pores thus laid bare but from the decomposition of water: this will be discussed in § 218.

ferro-manganese, to distinguish them from that recarburized with ferro-silicon.

C. *In the hydrogen group* hydrogen almost invariably preponderates, and in the great majority of cases greatly preponderates over nitrogen, whether in mould, boring or vacuum extracted cases, with the single exception of the mould-gases from spiegel-recarburized basic Bessemer steel, which usually contain far more nitrogen than hydrogen. In most of the other classes the ratio of hydrogen to nitrogen usually lies between 1·5 : 1 and 6 : 1. But, in the vacuum extracted gases from all classes of cast-iron tested, and in the mould gases from certain classes of cast-iron this ratio is much higher, rising often to 25 : 1 and sometimes to 100 : 1. Indeed nitrogen is sometimes reported as wholly absent.

D. Two varieties of iron, then, differ from the rest in the composition of the gases which they yield, spiegel-recarburized basic Bessemer steel, whose mould gases are usually exceptionally free from hydrogen, and cast-iron, whose vacuum-extracted and mould gases are exceptionally free from nitrogen. All the other classes of iron tested evolve on solidifying and in vacuo gases of one common type of composition, and on boring gases of a second type, differing from the first in lacking carbonic oxide. These normal types and the exceptional ones just described are summed up in Table 75. It is to be understood that these numbers represent not the extreme but the usual limits of composition.

TABLE 75.—DOMINANT TYPES OF COMPOSITION OF GASES EVOLVED BY IRON.

Metal.	Time of escape.	Composition of gases, CO group.	Composition of gases, H group.	Composition of H group, H.	Composition of H group, N.
Spiegel-recarburized basic Bessemer steel	In moulds	55@75%	25@45%	10@60	40@90
Cast-iron	In moulds	87@58	42@68%	75@99	1@25
"	In vacuo	0@58	41@100	93@100	0@8
Normal compositions, all classes except the above	Moulds and vacuo	12@56	50@88	60 90	10@40
	Boring	0@4·8	95·7@100		

But withal the compositions thus referred to a common type differ considerably among themselves, and the relations of their variations to those of the source, history, composition and structure of the mother metal are in general little understood. In many cases the gases emitted under like conditions by similar specimens of the same variety of iron differ as much among themselves as those from different varieties of iron.

E. There are, however, certain strongly marked features in the composition of the gases evolved by cast-iron and by the intermediate and finished products of the Bessemer and open-hearth processes, which characterize the different stages of these processes. I attempt to explain certain of these in § 217. They are illustrated in figure 14. In sketching them I have comparatively few analyses to guide me: further light may wholly change the aspect, and my present sketch is merely provisional.

Considering first, not the gas evolved in the converting operation itself but that which escapes when a given product is removed from the converter and allowed to solidify undisturbed in moulds, we note that the proportion of carbonic oxide diminishes with progressing decarburization, from about 50% in case of cast-iron to about 44% in case of half-blown Bessemer metal; thence to about 27% in case of ingot iron obtained by interrupting the blow and without recarburizing,[a] and thence to about 20% in case of oxygenated Bessemer metal. It is somewhat higher in case of oxygenated open-hearth metal, viz.:—about 47%. (Be it remembered that Snelus[b] and Tamm[c] independently found that the proportion of nitrogen to

INFLUENCE OF STAGE OF MANUFACTURE ON THE PROPORTION OF CARBONIC OXIDE IN THE MOULD AND OTHER GASES. PROVISIONAL SKETCH.

Fig. 14

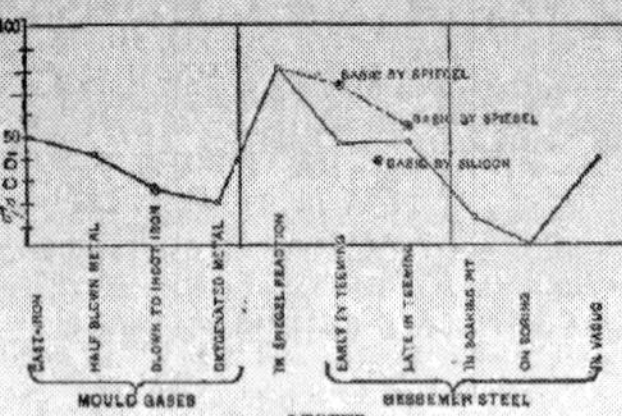

LEGEND.
○ Acid Bessemer Process. ⊙ Basic Bessemer Process.

hydrogen in the gases escaping from the Bessemer converter diminished greatly during the blow, in Snelus' case from 98·4 : 1 to 30·7 : 1 and in Tamm's from ∞ : 1 to 48 : 1, teaching that, at least in Tamm's case, the metal rapidly absorbed hydrogen from the blast during the early part of the blow, perhaps again emitting towards the end of the operation a portion of that absorbed at its beginning).

To our oxygenated metal, which of itself evolves gases containing about 20% of carbonic oxide, we add spiegeleisen, when of course a violent evolution of gas, containing about 80% of carbonic oxide, occurs. As the resulting steel gradually cools, the proportion of carbonic oxide in the escaping gases steadily diminishes from 80% during the spiegel reaction to 72% during early teeming and 60% during solidification in case of spiegel-recarburized basic Bessemer steel; to 46% in the mould gases of acid Bessemer steel (in acid steel the proportion of carbonic oxide remains nearly constant during teeming and solidification), and 32% in those of silicon-recarburized basic steel, (No. 91, Table 55, p. 107; No. 7, Table 70 A, p. 128).[d] Thence it declines to 13% in the soaking-pit gases of the solidified ingot, and finally thence to about 1% in the gases released by boring the completely cooled steel. But when this is again heated in vacuo the proportion of carbonic oxide rises to 25 or even 50%, and the gas found on boring blisters in the cold metal also contains a large proportion of carbonic oxide.

To sum this up, the proportion of carbonic oxide in the mould gases from products taken at different stages of the Bessemer process gradually diminishes, reaching a minimum in oxygenated metal: turning from the mould gases to those of the spiegel reaction we find that carbonic oxide here leaps to a maximum, to again decrease as the recarburized molten metal cools and sets, becoming nil in the boring gases, but again rising when the cold metal is reheated.

a Nos. 88-89, Table 55, p. 107. Carbonic acid is here included.

b Journal of the Iron and Steel Institute, 1871, II., p. 257.

c Ledebur, Handbuch der Eisen-Hüttenkunde, p. 927.

d In No. 90, Table 55 = No. 8, Table 70A, the metal was recarburized with ferro-silicon and ferro-manganese, yet its mould gases held from 44 to 64·6% of carbonic oxide: in this case, however, the recarburizing additions were made in the converter, and the silicon was oxidized by the phosphoric acid of the slag, so that the oxygen of the metal was chiefly removed by carbon. In No. 91, however, the action of the slag was diminished by adding the recarburizers in the ladle, and in this case, as shown in Table 70A, the oxygen of the metal was taken up by silicon and manganese.

F. *The influence of the composition of the metal* on that of its mould gases is not in general easy to trace. We have indeed just noted that those of cast-iron, with its high proportion of carbon, contain comparatively little nitrogen: and the preceding paragraph shows striking changes in the proportion of carbonic oxide, due however rather to the history and treatment of the metal than to its composition. The gases of steel of different compositions, but produced under substantially like conditions, might be expected to exhibit corresponding differences, those of spring differing from those of rail steel, and both from those of ingot iron: but I have not succeeded in tracing such relations confidently, perhaps because we have so few analyses that the influence of the composition of the mother metal is masked by that of other variables.

G. *The influence of the recarburizing additions* on these gases is more conspicuous. We have just noted that if basic Bessemer steel is recarburized with spiegeleisen, its mould gases are rich in carbonic oxide, but not if it is recarburized with ferro-silicon. The influence of silicon is farther illustrated by the fact that if we add ferro-silicon to molten basic ingot iron which, though already partially recarburized with 2% of ferro-manganese, scatters actively and doubtless gives off chiefly carbonic oxide (at least this has always been the chief gas from other specimens under like conditions) the scattering now completely stops, and the mould gases hold only 44% of carbonic oxide plus acid. A few blowholes may still form however.[a]

§ 208. THE COMPOSITION OF THE BORING AND VACUUM-EXTRACTED GASES.—I have succeeded poorly in tracing the relations between the composition of these gases and the source, structure and composition of the mother metal.

A. *The boring gases* from cast-iron contain slightly more carbonic oxide than those from steel, viz.: from 2·5 to 4·3% against 0 to 2·2%. Those from forged steel (9, 10, 12 Table 54, p. 106) contain much less hydrogen and consequently much more nitrogen than those from most of the unforged steels, and, in the sole case in which the blowholes gases have been collected from the same steel both before and after forging, those from the forged piece contained but 73·4% of hydrogen against 92·4% in those before forging. (11 and 12 id.) This may be accidental, or it may mean that the more diffusive hydrogen has more fully escaped during heating and forging.

When the same steel was attacked with both dull and sharp drills, (16, 17, id.) the dull drill released gas considerably richer in hydrogen than the other, viz.: 88·7 vs. 67·1%. This, however, was probably accidental, perhaps due to boring different portions of the ingot: for, a piece of cast-iron evolved gas of almost exactly the same composition when attacked by a dull as when bored by a sharp drill (40, 41, id).

The composition of the gases obtained by boring the blisters which occasionally form on both weld and ingot iron, differs very strikingly from that of the other boring gases, containing 27·2 and 70·42% of carbonic oxide (33 and 34, Table 54).

The vacuum extracted gases from cast-iron have already been shown (Table 75, § 207, D) to hold less nitrogen than those from other classes of metal: but beyond this all is uncertain. Parry indeed repeatedly stated that the higher the temperature the larger the ratio of carbonic oxide to hydrogen in those gases. He states that at dull redness, and in one place that even at full redness pure hydrogen is evolved, and that with further rise of temperature a continually increasing proportion of carbonic oxide escapes from both cast and wrought-iron.[b] In a careful study of his published results, however, I find little support for these assertions. Thus, in Table 72, we note that even at dull redness a large proportion of carbonic oxide escapes, and that in two out of the six cases in which the same piece of iron is successively exposed different temperatures (the higher always following the lower) the proportion of carbonic oxide is lower at the higher temperature. Nor can a more constant relation be traced between the proportion of carbonic oxide and the progress of exhaustion. There are ten sets of cases in this table, each giving the composition of the gas evolved during two successive periods at constant temperature. In four the ratio of carbonic oxide to hydrogen is higher, in five lower and in one the same in the later as in the earlier period. Troost and Hautefeuille moreover found this ratio higher in case of cylinders of cast-iron and steel, and lower in case of a cylinder of wrought-iron, in the early than in the later portion of their exposures to a vacuum: or, as they put it, wrought-iron retains carbonic oxide more tenaciously than hydrogen, while with cast-iron and steel the reverse is true.[c] To generalize from such scanty data would be extremely rash.

§ 210. WHAT CAUSES BLOWHOLES? We have seen that they are gas bubbles mechanically retained by the pasty metal, or held by capillarity to the surface of the solidifying metal. Their formation requires first a metal of the proper consistency to retain them mechanically, or one whose surface in solidifying retains them by capillarity: and second the evolution of gas within it. Why certain classes of metal which evolve gas during or at least just before solidification do not acquire blowholes while others do, we cannot now and perhaps never can tell. Little is recorded even of the changes in consistency which different classes of metal undergo: as to the capillary retention of gas by different classes of iron we are completely in the dark.

Three sources of gas bubbles have been suggested: 1st, the mechanical retention of air drawn down with the stream of metal while teeming: 2d, the formation of carbonic oxide at the instant of its escape by chemical reactions: 3d, the gasification of substances which had existed in some non-gaseous state (solution, chemical union) and which had earlier been formed by reaction or acquired from the atmosphere or the furnace gases. Pourcel would explain all the phenomena by the second cause, while Müller victoriously champions the importance of the third. Indeed, we are indebted to his zeal and eloquence for most of the evidence and reasoning which now render the solution theory well-nigh impregnable if taken in its modified form, as holding solution as an important cause of blowholes. He has really built it up, maintaining it almost single-handed, with vigorous defense and brilliant attack, against his numerous and well equipped opponents.

The discussion which occupies the remainder of this chapter leads to the conclusion that blowholes are chiefly

[a] No. 6, Table 70 A, § 202, p. 128.

[b] Jour. Iron and St. Inst., 1873, II., p. 429, 431: Idem, 1874, I., p. 93.

[c] Comptes Rendus, LXXVI., p. 564, 1873.

due to hydrogen and nitrogen escaping from solution: that carbonic oxide co-operates, probably also escaping at least in part from solution but perhaps partly and possibly wholly from immediately preceding reaction: and that the retention of air mechanically drawn down in teeming contributes but slightly in those cases which have been thoroughly studied and described. Let us first note that, besides the gas escaping from within the metal, carbonic oxide may be formed by superficial action between the metal's carbon and the oxygen of the atmosphere or of the containing vessel.

§ 211. THE MECHANICAL THEORY holds that a large quantity of air is drawn down by the falling stream of metal, just as it is by the falling water in the trompe, and that the metal is so mucilaginous that the air bubbles are imprisoned.[a] Some air may be thus drawn down, and it may under certain conditions contribute, and perhaps largely, to the porosity of the metal.

It is, however, easy to exaggerate the importance of this action. It is the liquidity of the falling stream of water in the trompe that enables it to split up into many fine streams, which collectively offer great surface, and thus by their friction drag down great volumes of air. If the steel is liquid it may indeed drag down much air, but should quickly release it; and that blowhole forming steel often is liquid when teemed is certain. If it is thick and mucilaginous, it will hold in teeming to a single contracting stream with but little surface, and hence will drag but little air with it. There may, however, be intermediate cases in which the steel is highly liquid while falling through the air, and so drags much air with it, yet, becoming mucilaginous shortly after, may retain the air thus dragged down before it has time to escape; or having become mucilaginous it may entangle air bubbles drawn down by later falling portions of highly liquid steel. Under such special conditions it is not improbable that blowholes may be in large part due to mechanical action. But in many important cases this combination of circumstances does not exist, yet blowholes abound.

Quite independently of this, however, six collectively sufficient reasons, which I now detail, demonstrate that air mechanically drawn down is not a chief cause of blowholes in those cases which have been most carefully studied and most fully described.

1. The gases escaping before and during solidification and those found in the blowholes on boring the cold metal consist chiefly of hydrogen: their composition cannot be readily explained by mechanical retention.[b]

II. Air escaping from mechanical entanglement would form spheroidal cavities, while blowholes are usually lenticular or tubular, with horizontal axes perpendicular to the cooling surfaces, and arranged in concentric vertical layers often of decided regularity.

III. It is inconceivable that the addition of silicon, which often instantly and totally stops the escape of gas bubbles, should mechanically prevent the escape of mechanically held air.

IV. Mechanically held air would escape continuously, in gradually and regularly diminishing quantity, while in many cases steel lying perfectly tranquil for a time, only begins to evolve gas after freezing reaches a certain point (§ 202, E.).

V. Increase of pressure completely arrests the evolution of gas from molten metal: it might retard but it certainly could not completely stop the escape of gas which was simply mechanically entangled and insoluble. Conversely, a fall of pressure causes a lively escape of gas from previously perfectly tranquil molten metal, which could not have remained tranquil had it held mechanically suspended gas. (§§ 188, C., p. 124; 202, D).

VI. It is inconceivable that molten steel should hold purely mechanically anything like the quantity of gas which it evolves in solidifying. It is generous to admit that the highly fluid metal could hold mechanically one tenth of its own volume of gas as gas, even for an instant: yet Müller found that even comparatively quiet steel evolved in the moulds between 7·6 and 11·4 times its own volume of gas, measured at 1,800° C., while oxygenated metal evolved about 23 times its own volume. (Cf. § 205, B.) The mechanical theory then breaks down quantitatively as well as qualitatively, and we must call on chemistry or physics or both. Some of the reasons which support the reaction and solution theories further weigh against the mechanical hypothesis.

The fact that the top of the ingot is more porous than the bottom is adduced to support the mechanical theory. But from whatever source gas is evolved, whether from mechanical retention, solution or reaction, that which is not held down mechanically or by capillarity will of course rise to the upper part of the ingot.

Pasty metal would also flow down from the top to feed contraction cavities. In a freezing ice bottle, though the water be absolutely free from bubbles, the ice formed from it is porous, and under certain conditions the pores are much more abundant above than below. Moreover, if the gases evolved by iron escape from solution, the ferrostatic pressure at the bottom of the ingot would tend to retain them in solution.

Let us now turn to the other sources of gas.

---

[a] Proc. U. S. Naval Inst., XII., 3, pp. 379–382; Trans. Am. Inst. Mining Engrs., XIV., p. 123, 1886.

[b] To reconcile the absence of oxygen from the blowhole gases with their supposed atmospheric origin, it has been supposed that the atmospheric oxygen has been consumed in oxidizing the iron: while the atmospheric moisture has been assumed to be the source of their hydrogen. But the ratio of hydrogen to nitrogen in these gases is far greater than in air saturated with moisture. This ratio can only be accounted for by supposing that part of the atmospheric nitrogen has been absorbed by the metal: but the moment this is admitted the theory ceases to be mechanical, and nearly coincides with that of solution, which supposes that the gases evolved during solidification were originally of atmospheric origin.

One cubic metre of air saturated with moisture at 10 C. holds 9·74 grms of aqueous vapor, containing 1·08 grms of hydrogen, which if set free would occupy 12·09 litres. The air would hold about 790 litres of nitrogen or about 65·3 volumes of nitrogen to one of hydrogen. The gas evolved by iron during solidification contains in exceptional cases as much as 58·3% by volume of hydrogen with but 0·5% of nitrogen, or 116·6 : 1. Hence this gas holds 116·6 × 65·3 = 7,614 times as much hydrogen per unit of nitrogen as saturated air does.

But we need not turn to exceptional compositions. The ratio of hydrogen to nitrogen in the gases evolved from iron and steel is usually from 1·5 : 1 to 6 : 1, or from about 100 to 400 times as great as in air saturated with moisture at 10° C. (§ 207, C.) At higher temperatures air can hold more moisture than at 10° C. At 35° C. (95° F.) it can hold about four times as much: but even then its ratio of hydrogen to nitrogen is only from one twenty-fifth to one one-hundredth of that usual in the gases from iron: and, moreover, the air is very rarely saturated with moisture except in the most moist climates.

It is hardly supposable that the hydrogen arises from moisture in or around the moulds, for in many cases these were of iron, and water if present would have been visible: we can hardly believe that Müller would be so grossly careless as to allow his work to be thus completely vitiated.

§ 212. The Reaction and Solution Theories.[a]

Numerous analyses of the gases escaping from iron under a great variety of conditions show that those which form blowholes escape in large part from previous solution.

But quite independently of this a mass of cogent cumulative evidence leads to the same conclusion. Its chief points are that the escape of gas from both molten and solid iron can be stimulated and arrested by purely physical means, and in case of molten iron by independent chemical means, both of which almost certainly act through the metals solvent power: that gas escapes and blowholes form when no gas-forming reaction is probable: and that the phenomena of the escape and absorption of gas in general by iron are very closely analogous to those of its escape and absorption by other substances in which it is undoubtedly in solution, if there be such a thing as solution.

From the fact that only nitrogen and hydrogen are found on boring cold blowhole-holding iron, and from other suggestive facts, it has been inferred that these gases alone cause blowholes: but this inference is not justified. There is good reason to believe that carbonic oxide co-operates in forming blowholes: this granted, it it is uncertain whether it escapes from solution, or reaction, or both.

§§ 213 to 218 chiefly present the evidence and reasoning which show that a part at least of these gases escapes from solution, § 219 the reasons for regarding reaction as a contributory cause.

[a] Many may hold that, in the ultimate analysis of our phenomena, all gases which escape from molten liquids, save the trifling quantity held by capillary attraction, are formed at the instant of escape by chemical reaction of one kind or another: that before their escape they had been held, if partly or even chiefly by physical forces, still at least partly by chemical ones; that in escaping the gas breaks its chemical bonds, which in itself implies a chemical reaction. Indeed, even those who regard chemical union and solution as radically different are sometimes puzzled to draw the line, and some of them class apparently typical cases of solution as instances of chemical union: *e. g.* holding that carbonic anhydride (CO_2) is not absorbed as such by water, but enters it through a chemical reaction, $CO_2 + H_2O = H_2CO_3$, and that it is generated at the instant of its escape from soda water by the reverse reaction. In this view all the gases emitted by molten iron, save the slight proportion mechanically held, are generated by reaction at the instant of escape. Others again may consider that hydrogen and nitrogen are held by purely physical bonds, and hence that no chemical reaction is directly connected with their escape, and that this may be true of a portion of the carbonic oxide evolved, while another may be generated by reaction at the instant of escape. Still others may hold that nitrogen and hydrogen are in typical chemical union with the metal, or alloyed with it, but that carbonic oxide cannot be, and that it may either exist in and escape from a state of purely physical solution, or escape while being formed by reactions.

In the first view the important question is "are blowholes due to hydrogen and nitrogen, or to carbonic oxide?" In the second and third views this question remains, and a second one arises, "If by carbonic oxide, does this gas escape from previous solution, or is it generated at the instant of escape by reaction?" The subject admits different lines of treatment corresponding to these different standpoints; but space forbids this. Practically I believe that the convenience of a plurality of readers will be complied with by assuming that hydrogen and nitrogen, except in so far as they are held mechanically or by capillarity, exist in iron in solution, if at all, and hence if they escape it must be from solution, employing this word purposely in a vague generic sense, including all the non-gaseous states, whether chemical or physical, chemical union, alloying, adhesion: and by admitting that it is quite different with carbonic oxide. It is certain that this gas may escape from immediately preceding reaction: but we must for the present treat it as an open question whether it can also exist in solution. This plan of treatment has its manifest drawbacks, but, with the existing limitations of space and language I see no better.

The most ardent advocate of the solution theory must admit that it is conceivable that carbonic oxide may escape from solution. For if this gas dissolves, still if its formation is continued the metal must eventually become saturated with it, and should more form it must escape as fast as formed.

These questions are of practical importance, for the means of preventing the escape of a previously dissolved gas may naturally be expected to differ from those appropriate for preventing the oxidation of carbon and the new formation of carbonic oxide; and the means for preventing the absorption and evolution of carbonic oxide on the one hand and of hydrogen and nitrogen on the other may be expected to differ.

I must again point out that, though mechanical retention is not an important cause of the presence of blowhole-forming gases in the cases which we will now study, it may be under other conditions.

§ 213. Evidence from the Composition of the Gases.—We have seen in § 207 B, and Tables 55–75, that the hydrogen group always forms a large and usually the chief portion of the mould gases from rising, *i. e.* blowholes forming as well as from most of the classes of non-rising steel, of the soaking pit gases, and of the gases obtained on heating in vacuo; and that it is always practically the sole constituent of the gases found in the blowholes themselves on boring: in brief the gases exhaled before, during, and after the period when blowholes form are largely of this group. The chain of evidence could hardly be more complete. It is next to certain then that hydrogen and nitrogen are an important cause of blowholes; that their proportions cannot be mechanically accounted for;[b] that they come from no reaction in the common sense of the word; and hence that they arise from previous solution in the sense here employed.

But, if more closely studied, some features of the composition of the mould gases suggest that hydrogen and nitrogen play an even more important part in the formation of blowholes than at first appears, and that the carbonic oxide which is often abundantly present in these mould gases is connected rather with the early escape of gas, which causes harmless frothing and scattering, than with the later escape during solidification, which causes rising and blowholes. (§§ 201, A; 207, E.)

I. The proportion of carbonic oxide is very much larger in the early than in the late escaping mould gases, constantly decreasing from say 80% in the spiegel reaction gases to say 13% in those of the soaking pit.

II. Spiegel-recarburized basic Bessemer steel, the only variety of iron whose mould gases are known to be usually rich in carbonic oxide, scatters much but rises little, and is relatively free from blowholes.

Moreover, as the scattering diminishes, so does the proportion of carbonic oxide in the gases evolved. Thus, in numbers 84–5 and 86–7, Table 55, page 107, the proportion of carbonic oxide in the gases evolved by basic steel is much less after solidification than in the gases from the same steel during teeming, which is the scattering period, to wit, 54·1 and 62·0% against 81·7 and 77·9%. If we add ferro-silicon to the scattering, carbonic oxide evolving basic steel, the scattering and the proportion of carbonic oxide per 100 of gas evolved both decrease, while the rising may continue. (§ 202 C.: § 207 E., G.)

Further, there is reason to believe that the very treatment which causes this basic steel to scatter also causes it to evolve gas rich in carbonic oxide. For it is stated that basic ingot iron produced by interrupted blowing and without recarburizing, from which our spiegel-recarburized basic steel may be made, neither scatters nor evolves gas rich in carbonic oxide (Table 71, p. 129). If recarburized with spiegeleisen it does both, if with ferro-silicon it does neither. (§ 202 C, p. 129.)

We will now consider the evidence which, independently of the composition of the gases, shows that they arise in large part from solution.

§ 214. Evidence from Analogy.—The solubility of

[b] See foot note to § 211, p. 135.

gases in solids and liquids rises with the pressure: in solids and most liquids it falls with rising temperature: it is far greater in liquids than in solids: hence most liquids in solidifying expel much of their dissolved gases. Thus water in freezing expels air; silver spits, expelling its oxygen; copper and nickel expel gas, and blowholes

Fig. 15, CONJECTURED GENERAL SHAPE OF CURVE OF SOLUBILITY OF GASES IN IRON.

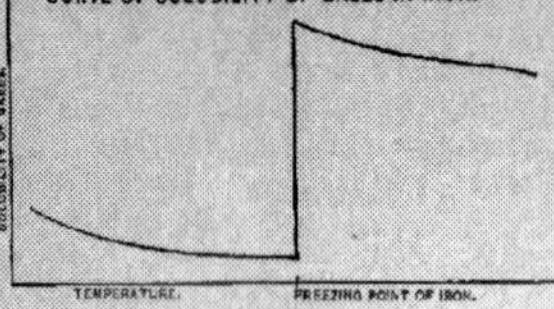

Fig. 15.

form within them. Figure 15 sketches the influence of temperature on solubility, a gentle rise as the temperature falls towards the freezing point, a sudden fall, another gentle rise as the temperature declines still farther. The absorption and expulsion of gases by solids and liquids, at first rapid then gradually slackening, is extremely protracted, probably ceasing asymtotically[a]: agitation hastens the expulsion of gas from liquids. The gas expelled by freezing water forms lenticular blowholes, their longer axes normal to the cooling surfaces, and the blowholes themselves lie in regular layers parallel with those surfaces. This is probably true of other freezing liquids.

Mark now how accurately these phenomena are reproduced by iron. That the solubility of gases in both molten and solid iron rises with the pressure has already been shown, by the ebullition and tranquillity produced by lowering and raising the pressure to which molten metal is exposed (§ 188 C, p. 124, § 202 D), and by the extraction of hydrogen, carbonic oxide and nitrogen from solid iron heated in vacuo, and their reabsorption when the first two gases and ammonia are exposed under pressure to the hot metal (§§ 172, p. 106, 203). We have seen that agitation, as in pouring and stirring, expels gas from molten iron as from other gas-charged liquids (§ 202 E): and by its blowholes, and better by the violent escape of gas on very sudden cooling, that iron like other liquids expels gas in solidifying (Id.). We have noted the protracted escape of gas from hot solid iron in the moulds, in the soaking pit, and in vacuo (§§ 202 F, 203). Finally the shape and position of the cavities in ingot iron and steel, normal to the cooling surface, resembles those of the bubbles in a frozen ice bottle far more closely than we could expect, in view of the very different conditions under which water and iron solidify, and of the differences in their physical properties, thermal conductivity, specific heat, dilatation, viscosity, etc., which might well modify the shape and distribution of the gas bubbles profoundly. (§ 216.)

Three of these phenomena, the expulsion of gas by agitation, the shape and position of blowholes, and the protracted escape, may be harmonized more or less completely with the reaction theory, though to my mind they harmonize decidedly better with that of solution. I will not say that the phenomena of the expulsion and retention of gas by fall and rise of pressure, of its expulsion on solidification, and of its protracted escape, cannot be harmonized with the former theory, yet their accord with it must be forced, harsh and strident, while with the solution theory it is so harmonious, smooth and flowing that, even without the irresistible argument of the composition of the gases, this theory in its restricted sense would almost compel acceptance.

Two points suggest themselves in which the behavior of iron might at first be thought to differ from that of other solvents. Half blown Bessemer metal evolves gas copiously: it therefore seems to be supersaturated: if its solvent power falls on solidification it should still evolve gas and rise: but it is stated that it yields solid ingots.[b] Rising however requires not only the escape of gas during solidification but that the metal shall be of a certain consistency[c] and structure, which it may be inferred are lacking in this case.

Again, the escape of carbonic before and during solidification implies that the metal is supersaturated with this gas: we therefore expect to find it in the blowholes on boring the cold metal. Its absence is referred in § 217 to its reabsorption or decomposition.

A. *Temperature and Solvent Power.*—While freezing lowers the solvent power of iron as of other solvents for gases, there is no conclusive evidence that, at temperatures which do not include the freezing point, its solvent power follows the usual law and rises with fall of temperature: nor on the other hand is there good reason to doubt that it does. This uncertainty is not surprising in view of the complexity of our conditions, of the proximity of molten iron to its freezing point, of the long range of temperature through which freezing may extend, and of our limited experimental data. False inferences from our available evidence may be prevented by pointing out how inconclusive it really is. This I now attempt.

Parry's observation[d] that the evolution of gas from solid iron could always be completely stopped by lowering the temperature from whitness to redness, and always started afresh when the temperature again rose, seems to indicate that the solvent power rises with falling temperature: for the loss of porosity when the temperature falls to redness is not complete enough to arrest the escape of gas totally. Unfortunately, we are in doubt whether the gas obtained at high temperatures came from his metal.[e]

If it be true that the tendency to rise is stronger in cool than in moderately hot-blown Bessemer steel (§ 202 A, p. 127), it would indicate that the former absorbs or retains more gas at the lower temperature of its manufacture than the latter, and hence has more to evolve in setting, which again would support the contention that the solubility falls with rising temperature. But here the phenomena are so complicated by differences of composition accompanying if not causing these differences in temperature, and by the proximity to the freezing point, at which the solubility curve reverses, that we cannot attach great weight to them.

On the other hand, excessively hot-blown steel is said to rise excessively. This is said to be due to a wholly different cause, a reaction between the carbon of the metal

[a] Charcoal continues to absorb oxygen from the air for at least a month, though most of it is absorbed in a few hours or even seconds. Though gas at first escapes violently from aerated water when uncorked, bubbles long continue to attach themselves to the sides of the vessel which contains it,

[b] Table 71, § 202, p. 129.

[c] § 201 A, p. 126.

[d] § 203.

[e] § 176 C, pp. 111, 114.

and the oxidized surfaces of the mould, which the high temperature causes the metal to wet. Carbonic oxide is thus generated, causing rising and external blowholes.

To test this Walrand polished the interior of one cast-iron mould, removing all oxide, and left a second in the usual oxidized condition. A lot of superheated Bessemer metal poured into both yielded a "perfectly sound" ingot in the former but externally honeycombed ones in the latter.[a] We may reasonably question whether Walrand has here hit the true cause. This formation of external blowholes occurs in hot-blown basic ingot iron, even if it hold but 0·07% of carbon, and it is not clear that the little carbon present would be attacked by the oxide of the moulds with sufficient energy to account for these blowholes. It is highly improbable, to say the least, that the oxide of the mould could oxidize enough of the metal's carbon to produce the violent frothing which occurs before solidification, for this probably calls for the oxidation of at least 0·01% of carbon from the whole ingot: as the mould can only attack the outside of the ingot, a much larger local decarburization seems to be implied.

Parry's observation that iron absorbs hydrogen most readily at high temperatures might suggest that the solubility of this gas rises with the temperature. (§ 176 A, p. 110.) But Graham found a comparatively low temperature most favorable, and Parry's observation, even if uncontradicted, would be more reasonably interpreted as meaning that iron, even though its total absorbing power be less, at first absorbs hydrogen more rapidly at a relatively high temperature because more porous.

The fact that Graham and Parry found that iron evolves much more gas in vacuo than it can be made to reabsorb (§ 206) might suggest that at the exalted temperature of its manufacture its power of dissolving gas is greater than at the relatively low temperature of their absorption experiments, *i. e.* that its solvent power rises with the temperature. But their results are directly opposed by those of Troost and Hautefeuille: and, indeed, during manufacture conditions other than temperature (*e. g.* the presence of nascent gases, § 172, 178 B, p. 106,) may have favored the absorption of gas.

The fact that molten iron often evolves gas in the ladle and moulds in spite of its constantly growing cooler, at first suggests that the solubility of the escaping gas is diminishing instead of rising with the falling temperature. When agitation, due to pouring, and local solidification do not suffice to explain this escape of gas it may, I think, be reasonably ascribed to the slowness with which supersaturated metal expels its excess of gas, and occasionally to a slowly terminating reaction between the carbon of the metal and the oxygen of the moulds, of the atmosphere, or of the metal itself. The agitation due to the escape of such nascent carbonic oxide might well liberate the nitrogen and hydrogen which accompany it.

B. *Protracted and Deferred Escape of Gas.*—Were we ignorant of the composition of the gases, we might refer the protracted escape of gas, continuing from the time of the spiegel reaction up to and during solidification, either on the one hand to gradually diminishing solubility, or protracted escape from a supersaturated solution, or on the other to a persistent and slowly perfected reaction between carbon and oxygen. Such a protracted reaction may be due either to imperfect mixing, or to the inability of the carbon and oxygen to unite immediately, so that, though perfectly mixed and brought into contact molecule with molecule, their union is not perfected for hours. It seems very improbable that the phenomena are due to imperfect mixing.[b] The metal is twice poured, from converter to ladle, from ladle to moulds: the ebullition which occurs both before and after teeming should greatly aid mixing. But, passing this by as inconclusive, we have the fact that if a charge of steel, from which this protracted escape of gas would naturally occur, be thoroughly mixed by raising the converter and blowing air through it after the spiegel reaction, the same protracted escape of gas occurs.[c]

There must be a cause other than imperfect mixing to explain protracted escape of gas when mixing is perfect. Is it tardiness in reacting, or slow escape from solution? It may be the former, though no one has pointed out a chemical phenomenon which is known to be strictly analogous. The slow parting of precipitates,[d] the slow growth of crystals, have been suggested: but in both cases purely physical and mechanical reasons suffice to explain the tardiness. The fine precipitate, if instantaneously formed, may be held to part slowly because fine, because its particles are of such form and texture that they adhere to and hook into each other, slowly coalesce, and long remain too small to settle rapidly: friction opposes gravitation. Our protracted gas escape cannot be of this nature, a gradual rising of mechanically suspended gas bubbles, too minute to coalesce and rise rapidly, because their collective volume (from 7 to 23 times that of the containing metal, § 211, VI.) is far greater than could be thus suspended. The crystal grows slowly, probably because gravity and diffusion, but feebly overcoming friction and inertia, can but slowly move the molecules from distant regions across the solution to the crystal's growing apex. In both cases, then, force has to impel matter over considerable distances: in neither do we know that the reaction is not instantaneous. Reaction whose immediate effects are of a nature which renders them visible as soon as produced and without waiting for subsequent motion or coalescing of their products, often appear to be well-nigh instantaneous. Thus when a drop of sulphocyanide is added to a dilute ferric solution, the full intensity of coloring is very quickly reached.[e]

---

[a] Troilius, Van Nostrand's Eng. Mag., XXXIII., p. 365, 1885.

[b] The heterogeneousness of steel ingots is often adduced as evidence of imperfect mixing. There can be little doubt that is in large part the result of segregation during cooling and solidification, though under certain conditions, as when cold additions are made to molten metal, it may be exaggerated by imperfect mixing. Others have pointed to the protracted stirring needed to uniformly mix black and white paint, and to the veins and striæ in imperfect glass as evidence that steel can be rendered homogeneous only by long stirring. But it is manifestly unfair to liken the mixing of seething highly fluid steel, whose fluidity is attested by the sharp outlines of its stream, by the tiny gas bubbles which are able to part it and travel up through it when it effervesces, by the minute and quickly propagated waves which stirring produces,—it is most unfair to liken it to the mixing of different colored paints, which consist of finely divided solids mechanically suspended in an initially viscous liquid: their coloring matter is solid. Mark rather what brief stirring suffices to mix a drop of ink with a tumbler of water so thoroughly that the eye can detect no sign of heterogeneousness. Does glass on the punty seethe and splash and foam? Does the blower's breath pass through in fine bubbles? Shall we gauge the action of water on the hurdy-gurdy, of other in the atomizer, by that of cold molasses? (Journ. Iron and St. Inst., 1881, II., p. 373.)

[c] Müller, Stahl und Eisen, IV., p. 77, 1884; Iron, Feb. 22, 1884, p. 161. In treating a basic charge he "had the converter raised for several seconds after the spiegel reaction, when the steel did not behave differently in the least in the ladle and mould." and mould." A still more striking case is given in § 331 *Killing.*

[d] Ledebur, Iron, Nov. 11th, 1883, p. 462.

[e] This is an elaboration and extension of Müller's argument, Stahl und Eisen, IV., pp. 76 et seq.; Iron, Feb. 22d, 1884, p. 161.

Metal, which has been perfectly quiet after the end of the spiegel reaction, remains still for a time in the mould, neither froths nor scatters; yet it is said that after solidification has reached a certain point it may begin to rise, and, if unopposed, may double its length,[a] owing to the formation of gas within it.

It seems far more probable that the renewed escape of gas is here due to a fall of solvent power owing to solidification, than that reaction, having once totally ceased, recommences during solidification, especially as the fall of temperature should oppose the oxidation of carbon.

C. *That the shape and position of the blowholes* in ice and in iron respectively are governed by similar causes we infer from their remarkable similarity. As the ice bubbles are doubtless due to the escape of gas (in this case air) during solidification, and as they owe their contour and place to the manner in which the ice grows during the emission of this air, so with the blowholes in iron. The fact that the air in ice escapes from solution does not, however, prove that the blowhole-forming gas in iron also escapes from solution. It is clearly gasified under similar outward conditions, but not necessarily from the same previous state. It is conceivable that the very act of solidification might cause previously uncombined carbon and oxygen to unite in such a manner that their escape would closely simulate that of a previously dissolved gas. But it is certainly far more natural to refer the phenomena to an escape from solution.

§ 215. Rationale of the Action of Silicon.—Our study of the analogy between the behavior of iron and that of other solvents towards gases would be most incomplete if it did not embrace the action of silicon on the escape of gas and on the formation of blowholes.

The addition of 0·1% of lead to molten copper and of 0·12 of magnesium to nickel is said to prevent these metals from evolving gas and from acquiring blowholes while solidifying. These additions appear to act by increasing the metal's solvent power, so that it is able to retain in solution while setting the gas which it holds while molten, and which it would have evolved but for these additions. On uncorking a bottle of soda water it evolves gas violently. The escape of gas soon diminishes, but it continues at a much reduced rate for hours: yet the addition of freshly boiled cold water arrests it at once and completely. Now do silicon and manganese, as Müller contends, act through the iron's solvent power; or do they, as Pourcel maintains, simply prevent the formation of carbonic oxide by being preferentially oxidized? I will endeavor to show (I) that the quieting action of additions of silicon harmonizes better with the former than with the latter view: (II), that the effervescence following the removal of silicon accords with either: but (III) that, while the escape of gas from iron rich in silicon is in perfect harmony with the former view, it seems directly opposed to the latter.

A. In many cases the quieting action of silicon appears to harmonize with either view. Doubtless if added to metal in which the oxidation of carbon was actually occurring it might check that action. But I can recall no case in which it is clear that silicon checks the *blowhole-forming* escape of gas, *i. e.* the escape during solidification, by preventing the oxidation of carbon: on the other hand in those important and striking cases which have actually been investigated, silicon certainly seems to act through the solvent power.

Müller found in three cases (numbers 2, 4 and 6, Table 70 A) that, on adding ferro-silicon or ferro-silico-manganese to molten basic oxygenated or ingot iron, contained in iron moulds and with the action of the slag and of the containing vessel thus nearly eliminated, the protracted escape of gas (carbonic oxide, hydrogen and nitrogen) which had been occurring either immediately diminished or stopped, though part of the carbon present simultaneously disappeared. In number 2 the volume of gas was diminished by about 80%[b]: in number 4 gasification stopped so completely that Müller was unable to collect enough gas for analysis, though the 0·02% of carbon which disappeared should generate carbonic oxide equal in volume to twenty times that of the metal. These results are summarized in Table 76.

Table 76.—Recarburizing Additions which Immediately Check the Escape of Gas though Apparently Causing the Oxidation of Carbon.

Number in Table 70 A.	2.			4.			6.		
	C.	Si.	Mn.	C.	Si.	Mn.	C.	Si.	Mn.
Present in the metal before recarburizing	·033	·053	·144	·033	·021	·181	·075	·007	·480
Added in the recarburizer	·059	·355	·073	·102	·818	1·487	·054	·339	·069
Total	·092	·408	·217	·135	·839	1·668	·129	·346	·549
Present in the recarburized steel	·062	·288	·156	·115	·846	1·604	·127	·314	·585
Loss	·030	·120	·061	·020	—·007	·064	·002	·032	—·036

Here the quieting effect of silicon and manganese certainly does not seem to be due to their preventing the formation of carbonic oxide by being oxidized in preference to carbon, 1, because though in some cases part of the carbon added with them appears to be immediately oxidized, or at least disappears, so that more carbonic oxide appears to be present after than before their addition, yet no gas escapes, neither the carbonic oxide thus formed, nor that carbonic oxide, hydrogen and nitrogen which would have continued to escape had the silicon and manganese not been added. Unfortunately, the quantity of carbon which disappears is so small that it is possible to attribute its disappearance to experimental error. 2, Because the escape of gas was wholly arrested when no silicon and but a trifling quantity of manganese (·06%) appeared to be oxidized, and only by being oxidized should these elements prevent the oxidation of carbon. (No. 4.) But this little manganese may suffice to arrest the oxidation of carbon: and, moreover, more manganese and silicon may be oxidized than is recorded: for, should part of their oxides remain suspended or dissolved in the metal, they would appear on analysis as if unoxidized.

3, Because, on a priori grounds, one would hardly expect that carbonic oxide would be formed in this practically carbonless metal, even before the silicon and manganese were added (§ 216).

4, Because, if it were being formed, one would hardly expect, on a priori grounds, that silicon and manganese could thus totally arrest its formation. For at this exalted temperature the affinity of carbon for oxygen probably greatly outweighs that of silicon and manganese: hence, while under especially favorable conditions (*e. g.* in the presence of a basic slag, or when a very large proportion of silicon is added to metal containing very little carbon), silicon might totally arrest the oxidation of carbon, yet one

[a] I have never seen such a case, but Müller states that rising steel may act thus. Iron, Jan. 5th, 1883, p. 17.

[b] Stahl und Eisen, IV., p. 75, 1884.

would not expect it to when, as in the case under consideration, a very considerable proportion of carbon is added along with it. In each of the ten cases in Table 70 A in which the behavior of carbon on recarburizing is recorded, a considerable quantity of it is oxidized, while in certain cases no silicon and but little manganese is. Indeed in number 9, Table 70 A, no less than 0·073% of silicon appears to be reduced from the slag by the recarburizing additions. This reduction of silicon from the slag also occurs in another spiegel reaction, which will appear later.

5th, Because when oxygenated metal receives a recarburizing addition the resulting tranquillity and freedom from blowholes should, on the reaction theory, be proportional to the quantity of oxygen removed by the silicon and manganese (the more they remove the less remains to react on carbon), but, on the solution theory, proportional to the quantity of these elements which remain in the recarburized steel. Yet in the examples in Table 70 A, the latter is in the main true, while the most solid and tranquil steel of all, 4, is the very one from which the least oxygen is removed, the one which on the reaction theory should become the most porous because retaining the most oxygen to react on carbon. It is but fair to say, however, that it may have lost less oxygen in the reaction than the others because, though apparently produced under like conditions, it may have held less initially.

In brief, while it is possible that silicon and manganese act in these cases by arresting the oxidation of carbon, the phenomena harmonize much better with the view that these additions act through the solvent power.

B. Just as the addition of silicon stops the evolution of gas, so there are reasons for believing that its sudden removal induces violent ebullition. This is not so well seen in the Bessemer process, for, owing to the violent agitation caused by the blast, as the removal of silicon lowers the solvent power of the metal a large portion of the excess of gas is expelled almost as fast as it becomes an excess, and the metal does not become greatly supersaturated. Still, both half-blown and fully-blown Bessemer metal froth, scatter and sparkle much.

Washed pig, *i. e.* cast-iron whose silicon has been very rapidly removed by iron oxide in a reverberatory furnace, effervesces very energetically as it runs from the furnace. This may be due to the sudden fall of solvent power through the removal of silicon. It may, however, be due to the retention of suspended particles of iron ore, which would energetically attack the carbon of the washed metal, with evolution of carbonic oxide.

C. Though the addition of a relatively small quantity of silicon and manganese to boiling, oxygenated, blowhole-forming metal completely arrests the escape of gas, yet hot-blown, unrecarburized, oxygenated, acid Bessemer metal may evolve an abundance of gas, chiefly hydrogen and nitrogen, before and during setting, and may rise very rapidly in spite of holding 1% of silicon: molten grey cast-iron, too, may evolve hydrogen and carbonic oxide copiously and sometimes rises in setting, in spite of its high proportion of silicon. I cannot reconcile these facts with the belief that reaction is the sole cause of the escape of gas. For if the addition of 0·318% of silicon and 1·487% of manganese can completely arrest the oxidation of carbon in oxygenated iron, and if that of ·355% of silicon and ·073% of manganese can so far check it that the metal is perfectly quiet and rises but little (2 and 4, Table 70 A); then surely the presence of 1% of silicon should restrain it enough to prevent extremely rapid rising, and far more should the 1 to 3% of silicon in grey iron prevent it at the relatively low temperature at which this variety of iron sets; for the ratio of the affinity of silicon for oxygen to that of carbon appears to be much greater at low than at high temperatures.

But the phenomena readily agree with the solution theory. If silicon raises the solvent power, it should raise it for both solid and molten metal, so that the sudden fall of solvent power in solidifying should remain. Our hot-blown Bessemer metal,* retaining 1% of the silicon initially in the cast-iron, retains with it its high solvent power, and retains or takes up during the blow a correspondingly high proportion of gas. In setting, its solvent power like that of non-silicious metal suddenly falls, it is unable to retain the large quantity of gas within it, it evolves a portion, it rises violently.

So too our grey cast-iron, its solvent power perhaps increased a considerable while before its escape from the blast furnace by the acquisition of silicon, and thereafter exposed to nascent carbonic oxide, hydrogen, and perhaps nitrogen, may be conceived to become well saturated with those gases, a portion of which is subsequently evolved, their escape perhaps facilitated by the release of pressure, and by the agitation due to atmospheric oxidation of carbon. But our oxygenated metal, acid or basic, Bessemer or open-hearth, holds comparatively little gas, that initially present probably escaping during the converting process as, with the removal of silicon, the metal's solvent power diminishes. On solidifying, its solvent power further falls, and gas is evolved, and the more violently because, owing to its high freezing point, our oxygenated metal is the more suddenly solidified by the cold moulds. But the addition of even as little as 0·318% of silicon might well suffice to raise its solvent power enough to permit it to retain while setting the comparatively small quantity of gas which it contains when molten. Be it remembered that the quantity of gas evolved in setting, which according to Müller is something over three volumes in case of wild oxygenated metal, is probably but a small proportion of that which it still retains in solution. 11 volumes have been extracted on boring and 22 volumes of hydrogen have been absorbed by direct measurement. A comparatively small change of solvent power, then, might well determine the retention or expulsion of enough gas to convert a compact into a spongy metal.

In brief, the fact which appears to be general, that though the presence of silicon does not necessarily prevent the escape of gas, its addition temporarily arrests it, harmonizes so completely with the solution theory that it could be deduced from it, but is diametrically opposed to the belief that the oxidation of carbon is the exclusive cause of blowholes.

Does silicon act by reducing iron oxide? In the Mitis process rising, gas-generating, oxygenated metal is rendered perfectly tranquil by the addition of ferro-

* If as Walrand holds the escape of gas from hot-blown Bessemer steel be due to a reaction between its carbon and the oxygen of the coating of iron oxide on the interior of the mould, the bearing of the phenomenon on the rationale of silicon's action remains unchanged. It still opposes the view that, when silicon does prevent the escape of gas, it does so by preventing reaction, for here this reaction occurs in spite of the abundant silicon; and it still harmonizes with the view that silicon acts by raising the solvent power.

aluminium sufficient to introduce 0·06% of aluminium. As the aluminium appears to be wholly oxidized, so that none of it remains in the metal, it can hardly directly raise the solvent power: its direct influence can hardly survive its departure. Nor is it probable that it acts by preventing the oxidation of carbon, for the metal itself is practically carbonless. But may it not be that the presence of oxygen diminishes the solubility of gas in iron, and that the aluminium, by removing this oxygen, indirectly raises the solvent power? Silicon sometimes produces similar effects under like conditions: may it not act in this same indirect way?

Of course in many cases gas is evolved when iron oxide can hardly be present: in others the silicon added is apparently not oxidized: so that this mode of action can hardly be regarded as the prevalent one. It is striking, however, that several important classes of rising metal do contain iron oxide, *e. g.* oxygenated metal and much of the hot-blown rising Bessemer steel, in which the presence of oxygen is indicated even when it retains as much as 0·6 of silicon. (§ 159, p. 94.)

§ 216. Gases Escape and Blowholes Form when Gas-forming Reactions are Improbable.—At the beginning of the after-blow of the basic Bessemer process only about 0·04% of carbon remains in the metal. The enormous quantity of air introduced during the remaining four minutes or so oxidizes this carbon but slowly, and it remains nearly constant at about ·04%: it has nearly reached a minimum. We teem without recarburizing, and our metal evolves thrice its own volume of gas, and becomes more porous than any other variety of iron.[a] Even if ignorant of the composition of the gas now evolved, it would be hard to believe that this was wholly an escape of carbonic oxide from a suddenly invigorated reaction: for the escape of three volumes of carbonic oxide implies the removal of ·02% of carbon, and it certainly seems most improbable that the small proportion of oxygen which molten iron can contain could rapidly remove half of that persistent residuum of carbon which had defied the great excess of air and the basic slags of the afterblow, especially as the falling temperature probably constantly lowers the relative affinity of carbon for oxygen as compared with that of iron.

Turning from oxygenated metal, in which gas-forming reaction is improbable from lack of carbon, to cast-iron in which it is improbable from lack of oxygen, we have seen that rising and blowholes occasionally occur, even when considerable silicon is present, as in grey iron: when silicon is absent, as in white iron, blowholes are common (Table 71). That during solidification a reaction between carbon and oxygen should generate carbonic oxide and thus liberate gas, would imply that this cast-iron, rich in carbon and silicon, contains oxygen which up to the time of solidification remains uncombined with these elements: (if combined with silicon the resulting silica should rise to the surface by gravity). This in itself is improbable. That the carbon and oxygen which have remained uncombined up to the time of solidification should then combine is improbable, because the falling temperature should constantly diminish the relative affinity of carbon for oxygen.

The formation of blowholes when gas-forming reaction is improbable is further discussed in § 214, B and § 215, A.

§ 217. Rationale of Certain Variations in the Composition of the Gases.

The variations which I now attempt to explain are detailed in § 207 E, and illustrated in figure 14, p. 133.

A. We have seen that, when cast-iron and the intermediate and final products of the Bessemer process are isolated and allowed to solidify in iron moulds, the proportion of carbonic oxide in the gases which they then evolve is greater the more highly carburetted they are. For reasons just detailed this opposes the belief that this carbonic oxide is generated at the instant of solidification by reaction between the carbon and oxygen contained within the metal: for, the more carbon the metal holds the more rapidly and completely should any oxygen present be eliminated, and the less should remain to cause a protracted escape of carbonic oxide in the moulds. But, on the solution theory, we may suppose that the changing composition of the metal changes the relative solubility of the different gases, and thus alters the proportion of carbonic oxide to hydrogen evolved in the moulds. The relatively high proportion of carbonic oxide in the mould gases of highly carburetted iron may be partly due to superficial oxidation by the atmosphere, the surfaces of the moulds, etc.

The high proportion of carbonic oxide in the spiegel-reaction gases and its continuous decrease as the metal solidifies and cools accord well, however, with the reaction theory, since the reaction should very rapidly decrease. But it accords at least as well with the solution theory. The more highly supersaturated a solvent, the more violently should it expel the dissolved substance, and the more marked should be the decline in the rate at which it evolves it. A bottle of soda water when first uncorked evolves gas tumultuously: the retardation, at first extremely conspicuous, can later be detected only by systematic observation. Now at the time of the spiegel reaction our metal should be only moderately supersaturated with hydrogen and nitrogen: hence the rate at which these gases escape should decline but slowly. The spiegel reaction, however, evolving nascent carbonic oxide so copiously within the metal, should greatly supersaturate it with this gas. Hence the decline in the rate at which it escapes should be more marked than in case of hydrogen and nitrogen, and hence the proportion of carbonic oxide to these gases should decline; and so it does.

B. The gases from molten metal, from solidifying metal, from the solid metal in the soaking pits, all contain much carbonic oxide: but when the metal has completely cooled and we bore it we find little or no carbonic oxide, nothing but hydrogen and nitrogen.[b] If we reheat it in vacuo carbonic oxide reappears. If we reheat it in a common furnace, and if by accident a blister forms on it, this blister contains much carbonic oxide. The absence of carbonic

[a] Müller, Stahl und Eisen, IV., p. 75, 1884: Iron, Feb. 15, 1884, p. 138.

[b] Müller (Iron, Sept. 14, 1883, p. 244), can find no explanation of the absence of carbonic oxide from the boring gases, but simply likens it to the fact, surprising to him, that silicon does not crystallize out along with graphite when cast-iron solidifies. But these two cases call for radically different explanations. We do not expect silicon to separate during solidification, because molten commercial irons are never saturated with it; solid iron is known to be capable of retaining far more silicon than molten commercial irons actually contain. (§ 63, p. 37.) We do expect carbon to separate out, because we know that molten iron often contains more carbon than solid iron is capable of retaining: and, if we regard carbonic oxide as dissolved in iron, we expect it too to separate on solidification, because its escape from the molten iron shows that the metal is supersaturated with it, and solidification should increase the supersaturation.

oxide from the boring gases may, however, be explained on either the reaction or solution theory.

On the solution theory the fact that the molten metal gives off carbonic oxide implies that it is supersaturated with this gas: as the solvent power should fall on solidification, carbonic oxide should still be given off: and that it is is shown by its presence in the soaking-pit gases. Why then is it not found in the blowholes on boring? We have seen, figure 15, that after solidification is complete the solvent power should rise with further fall of temperature. Now a large part of the gases set free during solidification probably works its way out at a somewhat lower temperature, through the hot porous metal. It is conceivable that the remaining carbonic oxide is reabsorbed by the metal: but that the solvent power for hydrogen and nitrogen does not rise enough with falling temperature to cause their complete reabsorption, so that they are found on boring.

On the reaction theory as well we should at first expect carbonic oxide in the boring gases, since this theory supposes that this gas is given off during solidification and forms the blowholes. The following explanation of its absence, which is here offered in its entirety for the first time so far as I know, applies to both the reaction and the solution theories.

We have seen in § 185 that at from about 300° to about 700° C. carbonic oxide is split up by iron very readily, the iron absorbing carbon and oxygen. At higher temperatures the tendency towards this reaction is very slight, and iron oxide then reacts readily on deposited carbon, regenerating carbonic oxide. Now the carbonic oxide given off by our white hot iron may be present in the soaking-pit gas and in the moulds gases, because the tendency to split it up is relatively slight at the high temperature at which these gases escape. But, as our iron cools our liberated carbonic oxide splits up while we are passing through the range of temperature, say 300° to 700°, favorable to its decomposition, and so none, or next to none, is found in our cold metal.

If, however, by the formation of a large blister our carbonic oxide accumulates and has but a relatively small surface of iron exposed to it while the metal is cooling, it is easy to see that much or most of it might escape decomposition, and be found as such when the cold blister is bored under water.[a] When our metal is again heated in vacuo we may suppose that the oxygen and carbon which had previously been dissociated recombine, and we find carbonic oxide in our vacuum gases. This view harmonizes with the fact stated by Wedding in this connection,[b] that the cavities in puddled balls, at least after long exposure to the air, are free from carbonic oxide, though doubtless formed in large part by that gas. In either view carbonic oxide is gasified during solidification, along with hydrogen and nitrogen, and coöperates with them to form blowholes.

§ 218. SOURCE OF THE HYDROGEN AND NITROGEN OF THE BORING GASES.

Attempts have been made, by two different lines of argument, to show that the hydrogen and nitrogen of which the boring gases consist are not the causes of blowholes. Neither of these bear scrutiny. We will now consider them separately.

1. It has been argued that the boring gases do not proceed from the blowholes, but from the decomposition of the water in which the boring occurs. This superficially attractive theory received powerful but ephemeral support from E. W. Richards' statement[c] that, on attacking a steel ingot with a dull drill, enormous quantities of hydrogen were evolved, "although no steel had been cut away, showing clearly that the hydrogen was obtained by the decomposition of the water." But he appears to have been misinformed, for Müller flatly contradicts him, and states that 1·5 cubic inches of steel were cut away.[d] This contradiction remains unchallenged as far as I know, and destroys the only important support of this theory.[e]

This instance (Number 17, Table 54, p. 106), really points to the metal, not the water as the source of the boring gases. For it shows that when we finely triturate our metal and

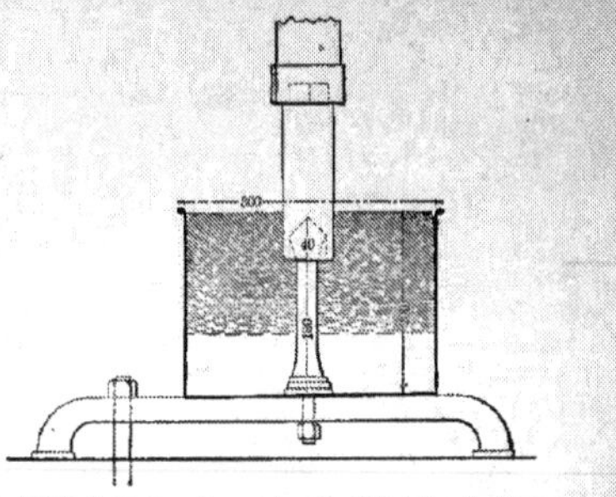

Fig. 16.—Müller's Boring Apparatus, for Obtaining the Gases from the Blowholes, etc., of Cold Metal.

thus lay bare numberless minute pores, we release vastly more gas than when we simply turn comparatively thick shavings, here more than fifty times as much. In this case the dull drill released gas still consisting of hydrogen and nitrogen in normal proportions, though

[a] See reference to numbers 33, 34, Table 54, p. 106.

[b] Stahl und Eisen, III., p. 200, 1883.

[c] Journ. Iron and St. Inst., 1882, II., p. 520.

[d] Iron, 1883, p. 115.

[e] It is true that Walrand (Van Nostrand's Eng. Mag., XXXIII., p. 301, 1885, from Jernkont. Ann.) states that on boring steel under oil and mercury he could not obtain a trace of gas, while on boring under water he always obtained gas, which he found detonated without the addition of air, and he believes that the theory which considers hydrogen as a source of blowholes has no more foundation than the old theory that nitrogen was the essential element of steel.

Such a negative result as his failure to obtain gas on boring under mercury and oil counts for little against the positive determinations which are recorded: it is surprising, but incomparably less so than his brushing aside the great mass of evidence, furnished in large part by most trustworthy observers, which demonstrates the presence of hydrogen in iron and its escape from it, and of which the composition of the boring gases, the only point assailed by him, forms but a single unessential, though indeed valuable, portion.

The *fact* that the gas which he obtained on boring under water would detonate implies that it contained oxygen. The presence of oxygen derived from some source other than the decomposition of the water is readily accounted for. The slightest error in manipulation would admit atmospheric oxygen: had the water in which the boring occurred not been freshly boiled, it might well yield up sufficient oxygen previously dissolved in it to cause detonation. But the complete absence of oxygen from the boring gases of such competent observers as Müller and Stead cannot be harmonized easily if at all with the belief that the hydrogen which they found came from the decomposition of water. Walrand supposes that the drill rotated so rapidly as to become magnetized, thus causing an electric current, which decomposed the water. Müller's drills were actually stationary, the ingot being slowly rotated. Two distinguished physicists inform me that the decomposition of water in this particular way under these conditions is not only extremely improbable but almost inconceivable. Indeed, I am inclined to think that Walrand must mean something quite different from what he says, which is certainly hard to understand.

differing somewhat from those found by the sharp drill, which might easily happen were different portions of the ingot attacked by the two drills. But in another instance a specimen of cast-iron was drilled *A* with a sharp and *B* with a dull drill: though the latter released eight times as much gas per volume of metal as the former, the composition of the gas was alike in the two cases. This would be natural if the gas arose from the metal, but if it arose from the decomposition of the water, the proportion of nitrogen should be less with the dull drill. For, as the nitrogen found must, in this view, have been previously dissolved in the water, and as only a limited amount could be so dissolved, if our drill released it from solution it would be almost pumping against a vacuum, and the proportion of nitrogen should rapidly diminish; actually it increased. It is possible that a little previously dissolved nitrogen might be derived from the water, though it should be very little, as in some of Müller's experiments the water had been freshly boiled. But it is extremely improbable that the volume of nitrogen thus acquired would increase proportionally to the hydrogen. Nor do we lack further evidence that the gas did not come from the water.

A. Steel bored under oil yielded gas similar in composition and quantity to that obtained in boring under water. (No. 2, Table 54.) An ingot bored under mercury yielded gas composed as usual chiefly of hydrogen. The quantity obtained was indeed small: but this is not surprising, for Müller found that the quantity of gas obtained in boring under water was in some cases fifteen times as large as in others.

D. If the gas came from the decomposition of water, solid steel, offering more frictional resistance, should yield more gas per cubic inch cut than porous steel: if from the pores, porous steel should yield the most. Actually it yields on an average nearly four times as much gas as solid steel. (See Table 73, p. 132.)

E. If the gas came from the water, where is the one part of oxygen which it should contain for every two of hydrogen? Where is the atmospheric oxygen which should have dissolved in the water along with the atmospheric nitrogen, and with it should have been released by the drill? In one case only is oxygen found, and then only 0·37% of it. To the suggestion that it has been consumed in oxidizing the iron, suffice it to reply that, in some of Müller's experiments, the metal was cut so slowly that it would not have grown hot enough to assume oxide tints if cut in free air:[a] that in the arrangement employed (Figure 16) ingot and drill were always cooled by contact with water: the supposed decomposition of water would have further lowered the temperature: a fortiori the metal must have been far too cold to take up even the uncombined oxygen of the air: how then could it rapidly decompose previously boiled water? Finally, the first portions of gas evolved would depress the surface of the water below the cutting grinding surfaces, where alone can the decomposition of water be even dreamed of.

F. As elsewhere stated, in certain cases the gas was under such pressure in the metal that it bubbled out from the borehole the moment that the drill reached the first blowholes. This is certainly the behavior of gas previously present in the blowholes and not of that recovered from the water.

G. The gas in the borehole was subjected to pressure above, not below, that of the atmosphere (cf. Figure 16): this would oppose the recovery of gas from the water, and would rather tend to cause the water to absorb the gas evolved by the metal.

The second line of reasoning by which it is attempted to show that hydrogen and nitrogen of the boring gases may not be the chief causes of blowholes, is offered provisionally by Wedding.[b] He suggests that carbonic oxide, formed by reaction in the solidifying metal, causes the blowholes: that it is converted into carbonic acid later on, I suppose by the reaction $2CO = C + CO_2$; that, after the blowholes have been formed, hydrogen and nitrogen enter them: that, on boring, the carbonic acid is absorbed by the water in which the ingot is immersed, so that hydrogen and nitrogen, though perhaps innocent, are alone found. It is sufficient to reply 1st, that though some carbonic oxide might be thus converted into carbonic acid, the reaction would never be complete, but would be arrested as soon as equilibrium was reached.[c d] 2d, that if it were converted into carbonic acid, much of this would be immediately reduced to carbonic oxide by the hot metal.[c e] 3d, that the water in which the ingot is drilled becomes warm, with corresponding decrease in its solvent power for carbonic acid.[f] 4th, that in boring blisters under water plenty of both carbonic oxide and carbonic acid are found, (33 and 34, Table 54) showing that the water by no means necessarily absorbs all our carbonic acid. 5th, that on boring under mercury and oil neither carbonic acid nor oxide is found. 6th, that it would be a gratuitous assumption, which really begs the whole question, to hold that the hydrogen and nitrogen which are evolved before and during solidification along with the carbonic oxide do not coöperate with it to form the blowholes. I know no reason to suspect even faintly that the evolution of hydrogen and nitrogen is temporarily suspended while carbonic oxide is forming the blowholes, to recommence when they have been formed.

§ 219. I have now pointed out that the hydrogen and nitrogen which clearly come from solution, not reaction, constitute a large part of the blowhole-forming gases; that the behavior of gases toward iron is so closely like their behavior towards other solvents as in itself to indicate that they dissolve, and that their blowhole-forming escape is in large part from previous solution: and that in checking the escape of gas silicon acts through the solvent power of the iron.

That blowholes are in large part formed by the escape of hydrogen and nitrogen from previous solution may then be regarded as well established. But carbonic oxide, though not found in the blowholes, probably coöperates with hydrogen and nitrogen in causing them. Though it involves some repetition let us now re-examine the evidence with a view to deciding whether this carbonic oxide, like the hydrogen and nitrogen, escapes from solution or is

[a] Müller, Iron, February 9th, 1883, p. 115.

[b] Stahl und Eisen, III., p. 200, 1883.

[c] See § 182, p. 118.

[d] Bell, Journ. Iron and St. Inst., 1871, I., pp. 140 to 143, 162, 184, Experiments 245, 252, 343, 344, and 254 to 263.

[e] Idem, pp. 109 to 111, Expts. 78-9. Manufacture of Iron and Steel, pp. 185-6.

[f] Müller, Stahl und Eisen, III., p. 445, 1883: Iron, Sept. 14, 1883, p. 244. At 65·6° C. water dissolves only about one fifteenth as much carbonic acid as at 0°. (Storer, Dict. Solubilities.)

formed at the instant of its escape by the oxidation of carbon.

1. While the behavior of gases towards iron resembles their behavior to known solvents so closely as to indicate that they escape in large part from solution, it does not prove that they escape solely from solution. Further study may reveal discrepancies due to the escape of carbonic oxide from reaction.

2. The general resemblance of the behavior of carbonic oxide to that of hydrogen and nitrogen, its escaping simultaneously with these gases which surely come from solution, certainly strongly suggests that it too comes from solution. But while their escape is usually simultaneous, yet the relation between the proportion of carbonic oxide and that of these other gases varies so greatly with varying conditions, as to permit the belief that their escape may be due to different ulterior causes. The ratio of hydrogen to nitrogen in the gases obtained under different conditions indeed varies, but, with few exceptions, within much narrower limits than does the ratio of carbonic oxide to these gases: moreover, it is not shown that the latter variation may not be due to the solubility of the hydrogen group and the non-solubility of carbonic oxide. This consideration does not argue against the solubility of carbonic oxide, but it lessens the force of the argument of analogous behavior.

3. Next we have Bessemer's statement that raising and lowering the pressure completely stopped and accelerated the escape of apparently pure carbonic oxide from molten iron.[a] But there seems to be room for a difference of opinion as to whether the escaping gas was really pure carbonic oxide, and indeed whether more carbonic oxide was present than could be accounted for by the agitation due to the escape of hydrogen and nitrogen from solution.[a]

4. Again, the apparent absorption of carbonic oxide observed by Graham, Parry, and Troost and Hautefeuille[b]: the escape of gas noted by the latter observers when iron was solidified with fall of pressure after long tranquil fusion in an atmosphere of carbonic oxide[c]: and the greatly increased suddenness of escape of gas when iron was suddenly solidified in Brustlein's experiment,[d] all point to the escape of carbonic oxide from solution. But we do not know that it is carbonic oxide and not simply its dissociated elements that is absorbed by hot iron: and we have no analyses of the gas evolved on solidification in the experiments of Troost and Hautefeuille and of Brustlein to tell us that carbonic oxide was among the gases thus expelled.

5. Carbonic oxide escapes from iron in which a gas-forming reaction is improbable, both from oxygenated and hence nearly carbonless iron and from presumably oxygenless cast-iron.

In the latter case it is possible that the carbonic oxide arises from external oxidation.

In the case of afterblown basic metal it would indeed be improbable that all the gas escaping during solidification was carbonic oxide arising from reaction, for probably at least three volumes of gas then escape per volume of metal, which would imply the oxidation of 0·02% of carbon, or half that residue which the enormous excess of air of the afterblow had been powerless to remove.[e] But we do not know that the gas from afterblown basic steel contains any considerable proportion of carbonic oxide, as we have no analysis of it.

The gas from overblown acid Bessemer metal contains about 18% of carbonic oxide.[f]

The escape of three volumes of gas containing this proportion of carbonic oxide calls for the oxidation of 0·004% of carbon. We would hardly expect even this small quantity to be oxidized, especially as the relative affinity of carbon for oxygen probably falls with falling temperature: yet it is far from incredible that it should be.

In short, while the escape of carbonic oxide in these cases certainly suggests that this gas had been dissolved in the metal, it by no means proves it.

6. The fact that the blowholes in ice, clearly formed by gas escaping from solution, so closely resemble those in iron, strongly suggests, but does not prove, that the gases which form the latter also escape from previous solution: and carbonic oxide is probably one of these blowhole-forming gases.[g]

7. Next, the protracted and deferred escape of gas, including carbonic oxide, during solidification is truly far more suggestive of escape from previous solution than of deferred reaction: and indeed when the escape of gas from the molten metal has once ceased but begins again later, the latter source seems decidedly improbable: but, though no exactly similar case has been suggested, even the deferred reaction cannot be called impossible, and the protracted reaction can hardly be called even extremely improbable.[h]

8. Again, we have seen that the addition of silicon and manganese diminishes or even completely stops the evolution of gas, including carbonic oxide, even when but little of these elements is oxidized, and when a portion of the carbon added along with them appears to be oxidized, so that that which appears to stimulate the formation of carbonic oxide stops its escape.[i] Silicon and manganese here undoubtedly arrest the escape of hydrogen and nitrogen by increasing their solubility: but it is possible that they arrest the escape of carbonic oxide by being themselves oxidized and thus stopping its formation. For either silicon or manganese is oxidized to a slight extent in every case, and the proportion of carbon which appears to be oxidized is so minute that its disappearance may be due to experimental error. We have further seen that it is improbable on a priori grounds that silicon and manganese should have the power of preventing the oxidation of carbon under these conditions: but, though improbable, it is far from impossible.

The escape of carbonic oxide from solution and from immediately preceding reaction are, however, far from mutually exclusive.

Be it remembered that, even if we hold that carbonic oxide does dissolve, we must still admit that it may escape from immediately preceding reaction also. In this view the case considered in the last paragraph admits

[a] § 188 C, p. 124.
[b] § 190, p. 124.
[c] § 188 A, p. 123,
[d] § 202 E.
[e] § 210, p. 141.
[f] 73-4, Table 55, p. 107.
[g] § 214, C, p. 139.
[h] § 214, B, p. 138.
[i] § 215, A, p. 139,

another explanation, to wit, that the carbonic oxide which was escaping before the recarburizer was added was being formed as it escaped by the oxidation of carbon, and that the silicon and manganese increased the metal's solvent power so that it was able to retain in solution not only the hydrogen, nitrogen and carbonic oxide which would have continued to escape had the recarburizer not been added, but also that carbonic oxide which is formed by the oxidation of a portion of the carbon of the recarburizer.

In this view the deferred escape of gas from molten metal may be explained comparatively simply. If the escape of carbonic oxide temporarily ceases after the spiegel reaction, we may suppose that, though this gas is constantly being generated by the union of the carbon and oxygen of the metal, yet with falling temperature (Figure 15) its solubility increases at first faster than the gas forms: hence its escape ceases. Later, its solubility perhaps increasing less rapidly, or indeed falling as the freezing point is reached, while its formation continues unabated, the metal again becomes supersaturated, and escape recommences.

Those who hold that the carbonic oxide escaping from iron is always generated by immediately preceding reaction, may go a step farther and claim that reaction is the sole ulterior cause of the escape of gas, both before and during solidification at least in certain cases: that it is the agitation or, if they prefer vagueness, the intermolecular disturbance due to the escape of nascent carbonic oxide that causes the hydrogen and nitrogen to escape; and that the carbonic oxide, the principal, which escapes during plasticity and with its accomplices, hydrogen and nitrogen, forms blowholes, is later decomposed by the hot metal, or reabsorbed, so that the accomplices alone are found on boring. But this does not bear the stamp of probability: indeed it seems almost impossible in many cases, *e. g.* in Bessemer's and Brustlein's experiments, and in the case of oxygenated and almost carbonless basic metal, from which great quantities of hydrogen and nitrogen escape on solidification, though but slight oxidation of carbon can occur, and though the violent agitation of the Bessemer process had failed to expel this hydrogen and nitrogen.

§ 220. RÉSUMÉ.—To sum this discussion up, very numerous analyses of the gases which iron evolves, before, during and after solidification, on boring and on heating in vacuo, prove that these gases usually consist chiefly of hydrogen and nitrogen, which, according to the definitions made in order to render discussion of the points at issue possible, must escape from solution.

But, wholly independently of this conclusive evidence, the behavior of gases towards iron, their absorption and release from both solid and molten metal on rise and fall of pressure, their expulsion on solidification and agitation, their protracted escape, and the shape and position of the cavities which they form, is closely analogous to their behavior towards other solvents. The closeness of this analogy; our inability to reconcile the copious escape of gas from iron rich in silicon with the complete arrest of the escape of gas by slight additions of this element on the reaction theory, and the complete accord of these phenomena with the solution theory; the fact that gases are copiously evolved from both oxygenless and nearly carbonless iron and from other classes in which no gas-forming reaction is to be looked for; and that their escape cannot be accounted for qualitatively or quantitatively by purely mechanical retention of insoluble gas, all point with varying degrees of certainty and, taken collectively, lead irresistibly to the conclusion that gases dissolve in iron, and that at least a very large part of the gases whose escape forms blowholes are dissolved in the metal before that escape.

If successful, the attempt to show that the hydrogen and nitrogen alone found on boring cold iron proceed from the water in which it is bored, not from the iron, would not seriously bear against the remaining evidence and reasoning. But the ratio of nitrogen to hydrogen in these gases and their freedom from oxygen: the fact that the gases obtained in the two instances in which iron has been bored under oil and mercury resembled in composition those obtained on boring under water: the fact that compact yields less gas than porous iron, and the arrangement of the boring apparatus, collectively argue cogently against the aqueous source of the gases. That the absence of carbonic oxide from these gases is not due to its conversion into carbonic acid and subsequent absorption by the boring water, is indicated by the facts that this conversion could not be complete, that neither carbonic oxide or acid is found on boring under oil and mercury, and that in case of blisters both these gases are found even on boring under water.

Further, the changes in the composition of the gases evolved from iron, so far as we have studied them, are quite compatible with the view that they are evolved from solution.

Turning now to carbonic oxide, which accompanies hydrogen and nitrogen in all except the boring gases, there is reason to believe that, in spite of its absence from the blowholes when the metal is cold, it coöperates in forming them while the metal is hot, and is later reabsorbed or decomposed. 1 the general similarity of its behavior to that of hydrogen and nitrogen; 2 its expulsion and absorption with falling and rising pressure; 3 its escape, occurring when no reaction is to be expected, and arrested by silicon when this element appears to act on the solubility and not by being preferentially oxidized: these three collectively very strongly indicate that carbonic oxide dissolves, and that its blowhole-forming escape is usually from previous solution. But it may reasonably be held that they do not prove it. Were carbonic oxide known to dissolve, then in coöperating with hydrogen and nitrogen in the formation of blowholes it would be most natural to suppose that, in the majority of cases, it escaped from solution like its companions.

In a word: it is practically certain that in the many and important classes of cases which have been studied the blowhole-forming gases are chiefly hydrogen and nitrogen escaping from solution: extremely probable that carbonic oxide coöperates: and probable that it too comes in large part from solution. Under other and yet unstudied conditions air mechanically drawn down in teeming may, however, prove to be an important cause of blowholes.

CHAPTER XII.

The Prevention of Blowholes and Pipes.

As a preliminary to the study of the prevention of blowholes and pipes in steel ingots let us next consider their proximate causes, and to that end let us examine their shape and position, and the conditions which exist while they are forming.

§222. Shape and Position of Blowholes.—Blowholes are usually tubular or lenticular cavities. The subcutaneous ones usually lie in zones nearly parallel with the outer surface of the ingot, (Figure 17), and with their axes perpendicular to it. They often form a veritable and decidedly regular honeycomb, composed of egg-ended cylindrical cells, occasionally of nearly uniform diameter and length. In some ingots fourteen inches square I found these cells three inches long and about 0.2 inches in diameter, and in volume perhaps twice as great as the intercellular spandril partitions of steel. But, while these blowholes very constantly lie perpendicularly to the ingot's surface, their length and diameter are often irregular.

The shape and position of those blowholes which lie nearer the center of the ingot are much less regular than those of the subcutaneous ones. In some cases as we pass inwards beyond the zone of subcutaneous blowholes we find a tolerably compact region, while the proportion of blowholes again increases as we approach the center, as shown in Figure 19. This represents a polished bar cut radially from a hammered bloom, the right-hand end having been at the center of the ingot.[a]

Fig. 17, BLOW-HOLES, (MULLER.)

Fig. 18, BLOW-HOLES, (GREENWOOD.)

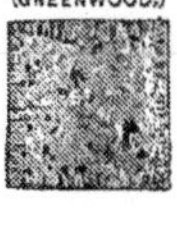

Fig. 19, CENTRAL CAVITIES, (CHERNOFF.)
BAR CUT RADIALLY FROM AN ANNULAR HAMMERED BLOOM.

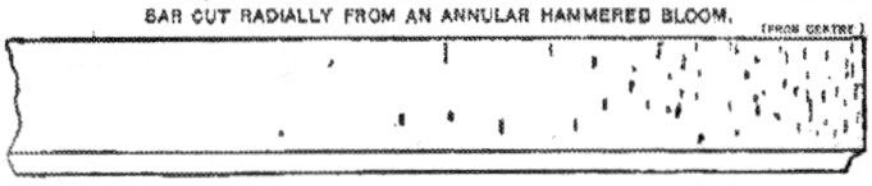

The surface of the blowholes is here smooth, there furrowed lengthwise: now metallic and silvery, now oxidized, now covered with an extremely thin enamel-like coating of a more or less greenish or yellowish gray color, and even brown according to Walrand. I have confirmed Walrand's statement that this coating is instantly removed by hydrochloric acid with evolution of sulphuretted hydrogen, recognized by smell and test-paper. On the whole the surfaces of rather more of the subcutaneous than of the deeper seated blowholes seems to be oxidized: yet the reverse is often true.

In the upper part of the ingot and surrounding its axis is the pipe, its sometimes almost friable sides usually slightly furrowed lengthwise, and dotted with fine crystals (Figures 29 to 31). An enamel-like coating like that in the blowholes often lines the pipe, and in certain cases I have found little yellow or transparent ruby drops and even buttons of what seems to be slag, apparently liquated from the surrounding metal.

Martens finds with the microscope three sets of markings and intrusions in the blowholes.[b]

1st. Stripes, furrows, or foldings, perhaps caused by the compression due to the contraction of the neighboring metal.

2d. Intrusions apparently caused by the entrance of gas from the surrounding metal after the walls of the blowhole have become pasty. They consist chiefly (1) of little knobs, which the gas has forced into the blowhole but has not burst: (2) of pits, the remains of knobs which have burst (Fig. 19 A).

Figs. 19 A to 19 D. Microscopic Intrusions in Blowholes. Martens.

3rd. Intrusions of metal, apparently due not to the escape of gas but to change of volume in the surrounding metal, whether due (A) directly to the necessarily irregular changes in the temperature, which, though generally falling, yet perhaps occasionally rises as in the "after-glow": or (B), as Martens believes, to the solidification of the different components of the mass at different periods, each changing volume as it solidifies: or (C), as we may conjecture, to the successive births of different definite minerals from the mother magma, with decrease or increase of volume as the new-born mineral is denser or less dense than the mass from which it springs. While these intrusions sometimes consist of simple crystals, Figure 19 B, they are more often irregular, Figure 19 C, or of fir-tree shape, Figure 19 D.

Chernoff, too, finds twisted dendritic crystals, like those of Figure 26, on the upper sides of the blowholes.

Figure 20 and the last column of Table 71, § 202 C, indicate the usual positions of blowholes. If the temperature be excessively high, fine, closely packed, elongated, external blowholes form, as A, Figure 20, together with sporadic central ones if the metal be very free from carbon as in I. It is said that if the temperature be normal or low, the blowholes are wider, and tubular or lenticular. With a normal casting temperature they lie, in case of hard steel, chiefly in a zone very near the exterior as at B: in softer steel they lie nearer the center as in C, D and J. If the temperature be rather low, the blowholes lie as in E and F: and if it be excessively low the ingot becomes spongy as at G; while if the metal at the same time be very soft it rises violently, nearly half emptying the mould as at H and K.[c]

Pits.—The fine blowholes which in case of extremely

[a] Chernoff, Revue Universelle, 2d Ser., VII., 1880. The hammering has distorted the cavities, so that their axes are now parallel with that of the bloom.

[b] Stahl und Eisen, VII., p. 341, 1887. I understand that Figures 19 A to D represent actual intrusions.

[c] Van Nostrand's Eng. Mag., XXXIII., p. 362, 1885.

hot-cast steel extend nearly or quite to the ingot's skin (A, figure 20) are thought to be the cause of the pittings with which boiler-plate steel is liable to be covered : at least it is the observation of some open-hearth steel-melters that these pits may be induced by an extremely high casting temperature, and blowholes so close to the ingot's skin seem well-calculated to become filled with iron oxide during heating, the thin skin of metal outside them being comparatively permeable if indeed it is not removed by oxidation, leaving the ends of the blowholes open. The contents of these pits has been found to consist chiefly of iron oxide.

In general, the regular arrangement of the blowholes in a zone parallel with the outer surface, and with the axes of the blowholes normal to that surface, as in E, Figure 20, characterizes rather hard steel : with soft steel the blowholes are less regularly disposed, and a larger proportion is found nearer the center.

The correlation between the shape and position of the blowholes on the one hand, and the conditions of casting and the composition of the metal on the other, does not seem very clearly established.

The shape and position of these blowholes are closely like those of bubbles in ice, which are in general tubular, occasionally lenticular or even spherical. In ice ingots formed by freezing water in glass bottles I find that the axes of the tubules are always perpendicular to the cooling surface, and nearly independent of gravity. The tubules along the sides of the bottle are horizontal : at its shoulder they point downward. In some ice ingots I find the blowholes arranged quite as in ingots of steel : first a row of elongated external tubules, then a quite compact region, then a sharply marked zone of nearly spherical cavities, then another compact zone, and finally a core decidedly porous or even friable. The striking points of resemblance between the blowholes in ice and steel are (1) that they are normal to the cooling surface, (2) that they are arranged in well-marked zones parallel with that surface, (3) that the tubular form is most marked in the subcutaneous blowholes, the deep-seated ones being more nearly spherical, (4) that they are most abundant near the skin and near the center.

The tubular form of the blowholes in ice and iron is readily accounted for. While part of the first-evolved gas may swim to the upper surface, another part attaches itself to the already solidified walls in minute spheres.[a] Into a bubble already formed gas evaporates from a saturated liquid much more readily than if no bubbles are present,[b] as is illustrated by the bumping of many boiling liquids. Hence whatever gas is evolved in the neighborhood of the bubble, by preference passes into it and augments its size. But meanwhile the freezing is progressing, and, as a bubble is a poor conductor of cold (more accurately, of heat), freezing occurs by preference between the bubbles. And so freezing and tubule-growth take place together, the walls expelling gas as they grow, and on this gas the tubules feed. If the evolution of gas increases more rapidly than the freezing, the tubule will increase in diameter as it elongates, and it may reach such a size that gravity overcomes capillarity, and that a bubble detaches itself and swims to the surface.

Chernoff believes that iron solidifies, not in approximately regular parallel layers, but by the growth of pine-tree crystals, whose trunks and branches mechanically imprison the evolved gas and prevent its swimming to the surface. He attributes the twisting of the dendritic crystals (Figure 26) at the top of the blowholes to the partial rise of gas bubbles, which part and even detach the branches of the pine-tree crystals.[c]

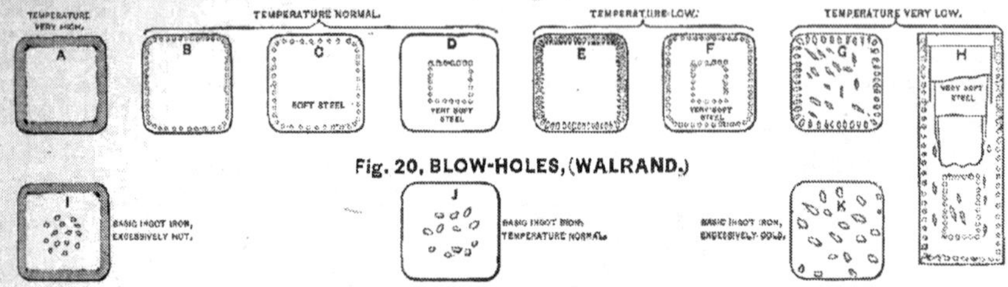

Fig. 20, BLOW-HOLES, (WALRAND.)

A to H, Walrand, Van Nostrand's Engineering Magazine, XXXIII., p. 853. I to K, J. Hartshorne, private communication.

Now, as we shall see in Chapter XIII., the solidification of iron is doubtless a species of crystallization : witness the ingot's columnar structure, most marked near the shell, and in small ingots extending to the center, producing strong radial markings in circular and a maltese cross in square ingots, (Figures 27–28). Indeed, iron occasionally develops beautiful pine-tree crystals, actual instances of which are shown in Figures 25,[d] 29, and 31. One crystal in the former is 2·25 inches wide. Still, it is improbable that the tree-tops usually protrude far enough beyond the solid growth to detain bubbles mechanically. For Müller found,[e] on pouring out the interior of partly frozen ingots at various stages of solidification, and thereby revealing successive stages of the growth of blowholes,

[a] In a freezing water-bottle a persistent rising of minute bubbles occurs simultaneously with the formation of the tubules.

[b] For an admirable elementary explanation of the principles of surface tension see Maxwell, Theory of Heat, pp. 279 et seq.

In a freezing ice bottle in which tubules are forming the spherical ends of the gas bubbles in the tubules appear to project beyond the already frozen walls into the still liquid centre: but this cannot be seen very distinctly. Conversely, when a tubule-holding lump of ice melts in water, the ice may melt quite a distance back from the end of the tubule, leaving a spherical bubble of air, which very clearly projects into the water, but eventually, after the ice has melted back far enough, the bubble detaches itself and rises to the surface.

[c] Revue Universelle, 2d Ser., VII., p. 153, 1880.

[d] Figure 25, from a photograph, represents a bunch of crystals kindly sent me by Mr. John Fulton. It is from the sinking-head cavity of a large steel ingot.

[e] Iron, Jan. 5, 1883, p. 18 ; Sept. 14, 1883, p. 244.

that the inner walls of the hollow ingot were remarkably smooth and even, though perforated with many blow-

Fig. 29.—Crystal from a pipe in steel. Magnified 70 times. Chernoff.

holes in case of rising steel. (Figure 32). Others have observed that the inner walls of "bled" ingots are smooth.

To obtain a little side light on this question I applied the same device to freezing ice-ingots and found their walls very smooth, though perforated with many tubules. With a lens I detected a slight convexity over the mouths of certain blowholes: but apart from this I could detect no excrescences. The mouths of other blowholes were open, showing that the gas bubble probably projected into the still unfrozen water. Yet in the central vugs of one ice-ingot which had cracked and bled, I found large crystals of extraordinary beauty. I often noticed that the first skimming of ice on the upper surface of the water would form through beautiful long needles, which shot across from side to side, as happens in ponds on still nights: yet if the resulting ice-ingots were emptied when partly frozen, the sides of the cavity were invariably smooth and free from excrescences, with perhaps one exception. In one case I found beautiful fig-leaf crystals at the top of an ice-ingot whose interior had been poured out when per-

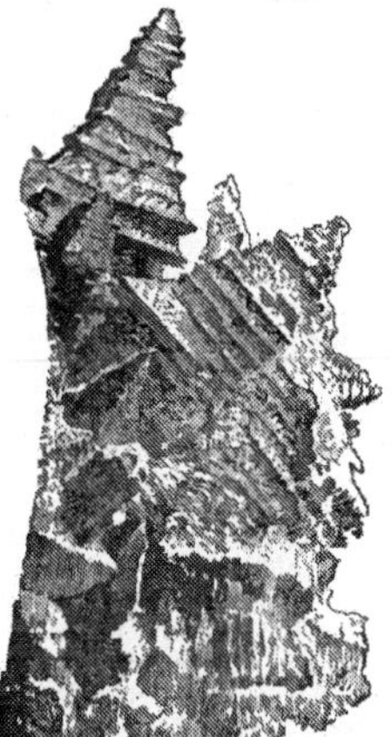

Fig. 25.

Fig. 26.—Dendrite from a blowhole. Chernoff.

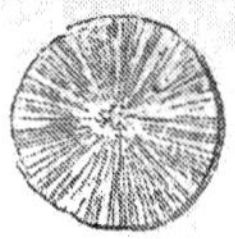

Fig. 27.—Columnar structure of ingots. Chernoff.

Fig. 28.—Columnar structure. Chernoff.

Fig. 30.—Crystals from a pipe in steel. Magnified four times. Chernoff.

Fig. 31. Pine-tree crystal from iron. Knop.

Fig. 32.—Growth of blowholes. Müller.

haps one-sixth of the whole was frozen. From the position of these crystals I fancy that they may have grown in a vug. But, though great pains were taken to pour the water from this ingot so gently that it could not wash off any delicate crystals, the sides of the cavity were extremely smooth, showing at most suggestions of crystalline markings, but perforated with many growing blowholes. In the same way I have often noticed that, on pouring out the interior of a partly solidified block of slag, the sides of the cavity were smooth and free from crystalline markings, although the solidified portion had a strong columnar structure, and although, if allowed to solidify completely, the vugs, even those very near the upper surface which were probably formed early, were usually lined with beautiful and in some cases marvelously beautiful crystals.

This is the result of many hundreds if not thousands of observations: for a long while I had the interior of all pots of slag emptied, leaving a rather thin shell, which it was my custom to examine daily for prills.

In all these cases we find that, in spite of strong columnar structure, and in spite of the strong tendency to form large interlacing crystals in the vugs, solidification appears to take place in smooth parallel layers.

Possibly the crystals are minute at the contact of solid and liquid because growth may occur from numberless points simultaneously, and the growths from neighboring points interrupt each other: while the perfectly smooth surface of contact of liquid and gas offers no points from which new growths may start, and so permits the development of large crystals. It is well known that crystals deposit more readily on rough than on smooth surfaces.

The main axes of growth of ice and iron certainly lie between the blowholes. Whether the position of these main axes initially determines the starting point of the blowholes or vice versa I will not attempt to say: but, once started, the poor conducting power of the tubules and the tendency of solidification to proceed along axes normal to the walls of the mould should both tend to the same result, the tubular shape of the blowholes.

If this be the way in which blowholes form, why are they confined to certain distinct zones? Why does not each individual tubule extend from the shell to the center of the ingot? The explanation is easy. Suppose that our molten iron contains much less gas than it is capable of retaining while molten, yet more than it can retain on solidifying. When the very first layers solidify they become supersaturated with gas and expel the excess: but this may not become gasified, but may simply pass inwards still dissolved, to the adjoining still molten layer. In this way no gas would be evolved as gas till the still liquid layers were actually supersaturated, and the very outer layers might be quite free from blowholes.

But beyond this, during the remainder of the period of solidification many complicated conditions determine whether gas shall or shall not escape at any given moment. Primarily this depends on the solvent power of the metal and on the existing pressure. With gradually falling temperature the curve of solvent power reverses at the freezing point (Figure 15, § 214, p. 137), introducing a first complication, while the factors which govern pressure are simply bewildering. The pressure depends (1) on the temperature, whose curve reverses during the "afterglow," and perhaps at other periods (§ 224, foot note); and (2) on the available space offered to the gas within the ingot, which depends on the ratio of contraction of shell to that of interior. This in turn is governed by two varying quantities, (1) the ratio of cooling of shell to interior, which constantly changes, and (2) the density of the metal, which probably follows a very irregular curve (Figure 34) even with regularly falling temperature. Beyond this, the rupture of internal partitions, owing to contraction or gaseous pressure, and the bending in or out of the shell of the ingot are liable to affect the pressure. With such complexity it is not surprising that the formation of blowholes now ceases, now begins again, only again to cease.

§ 223. Contraction Cavities.—Chernoff believes that it must frequently occur in the solidification of steel that the trunks and branches of adjoining pine-tree crystals completely enclose certain spaces, and prevent all communication between them and the rest of the metal: that as the metal in these spaces cools it must contract, and as its contraction is not fed from without local contraction cavities must arise, and these must be scattered through the ingot. Indeed, in a crystal growing on the sides of the central pipe he finds a cavity which he attributes to contraction (*a*, Figure 29). Where, owing to slow solidification, the pine trees grow slowly, a supply of liquid metal should more easily penetrate to feed these cavities, than where, as at the outside of the ingot, the growth is extremely rapid: on the other hand, when solidification approaches the middle of the ingot we have but a small supply of metal, and of now quite pasty metal at that, to feed these contraction cavities. Hence we should expect the contraction cavities chiefly at the outside and near the center of the ingot: and in this way he accounts for the increased porosity or even friability near the axis of the ingot."[a]

Local contraction may under certain conditions originate cavities near the outside of the ingot: gas would naturally pass into them, first because they are cavities, second because a complete vacuum would initially exist in them: so that we might have two classes of subcutaneous cavities, those originated by gas, and those originated by contraction and then filled with gas. It seems improbable, however, that local contraction often originates subcutaneous cavities. In the first place, the addition of silicon, etc., suppressing the escape of gas, also completely suppresses the subcutaneous blowholes, the central pipe and the porous region about it still remaining: silicon should not prevent local contraction, hence it is not probable that the subcutaneous cavities which it suppresses are true contraction cavities. In the second place the smoothness of the inner surface of ingots and ice bottles which have been partially frozen indicates that the solid growth of the branches and the solidification of the matter between them keep pace with that of the trunks so closely, and that the growth proceeds through trunks so closely adjacent, that none but microscopic cavities would be formed between them. In the third place it is probable that iron actually expands in the very act of solidification, though indeed contracting as the temperature falls still farther: contraction would not occur in any one of these local retreats till the metal in that retreat was distinctly solid[a]: it is very doubtful whether contraction would then actually cause even a microscopic cavity: it would be more likely to temporarily distend the metal.

It is clear that the cavities in the neighborhood of the central pipe are far too large to have been caused by the contraction of matter originally completely enclosed within crystal tree trunks and so shut out from external sources of supply. They are clearly due to the ebbing away of the material which originally existed in the now hollow spaces, and which has later sunk away into the central pipe, as it yawns and widens with the contraction of the already solidified metal between it and the ingot's skin.

§ 224. Piping. *The Position of the Pipe.*—Let us neglect for the moment the evolution of gas during solidification and cooling. Iron like other substances contracts in cooling: but during solidification it appears to expand, so that its volume follows a reversing curve, whose general form may not be wholly unlike that of Figure 34.[b] In a cooling ingot the changes of volume would follow the

Fig. 34

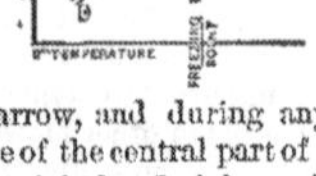

direction of the arrow, and during any given period the changes of volume of the central part of the ingot would lie in this curve to the right hand of those of the outside. During the first moments of solidification, while the outside is

a Revue Universelle, 2d Ser., VII., p. 140, 1880.

a The trunks themselves cannot form till the metal constituting them is at the freezing point, when the metal between them must necessarily be extremely near to that point.

b The curve of volume is probably far more complex than that here shown. In the first place, there is at least one reversal of the direction of change of temperature, that of the "after-glow," when, the temperature having fallen to low redness, suddenly rises again, on the change of hardening to cement carbon. In the second place, Chapter XIII. gives evidence that two or more recrystallizations occur during cooling. These may well cause change of volume (for the density of the new minerals may well differ from that of the old), and may indeed cause the absorption or evolution of heat. But it is not necessary to introduce these complications here.

freezing and the inside passing slowly through A B, the outside tends to expand, the inside to contract: later, while the shell is passing quickly through C D and the inside slowly through A B or even B C, the shell tends to contract more than the inside. As the latter is incompressible, it resists and may tear the outside. Later still, when the shell has grown comparatively cool and hence is contracting slowly, the center is passing through B C while the region intermediate between shell and center is passing comparatively rapidly through C D, and so contracting rather rapidly. Eventually a time t will be reached at which the contraction of the region intermediate between shell and center overtakes and begins to outweigh both the contraction of the now slowly cooling shell and the expansion of the small portion of the center which is passing through B C: when this point is reached a cavity or pipe will tend to form. If the shell of the ingot is still hot enough to be plastic, it may bend in and follow up the contraction of the interior, and this will continue till the time t' when the crust becomes too rigid to bend farther. This bending in clearly takes places much more readily in square than in round ingots, and still more readily in oblong ones: and we consequently find that round ingots are more and oblong ones less subject to serious piping than square ones.[a]

In a spherical ingot through whose walls heat is conducted uniformly in every direction, this cavity would lie at the center (Figure 35) but for gravity.

Fig. 35

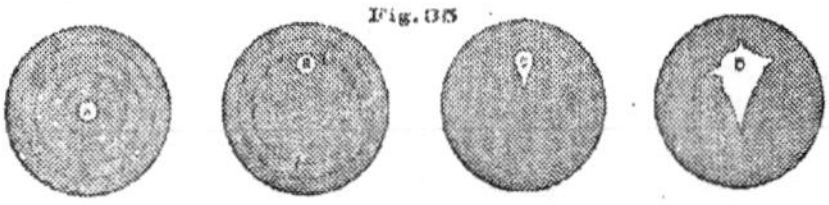

At any instant during cooling we may distinguish a set of isotherms, such as are sketched in broken lines in Figures 35, 36, 37. Solidification follows approximately similar lines. Now the top of the pipe will lie at the top of that layer or isotherm i, (B, Fig. 35), which at the time t' is just too viscid to flow down towards the bottom of the growing cavity. In other words the vacuous bubble will rise through the still liquid layers, and through the slightly viscid ones till it reaches one just too viscid to

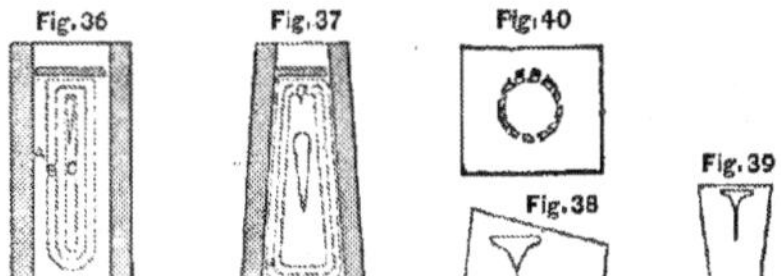

Figures 36-7.—Isotherms and position of pipe in prismatic and pyramidal ingots, the latter exaggerated. Figures 38-9.—Position of pipe in overturned and inverted ingots. Figure 40.—Pipe distributed by rotating ingot during solidification. Figures 38, 39 and 40 from Walrand, Van Nostrand's Eng. Mag., XXXIII., p. 353.

allow it to rise farther. With further solidification and contraction, as the metal draws apart centrifugally, the still fluid portions flow down to fill the bottom of the growing cavity, whose upper surface remains ever at the same point, (though indeed cracks may rise beyond as at D). But during a later stage the metal is too viscid to flow, and as it still contracts it draws apart somewhat as in C. If the metal contracts a great deal while it is mobile enough to draw apart but too viscid to run down from above to fill the lower parts of the cavity, a deep pipe may arise as at D.

In a prismatic ingot the pipe will lie as in Figure 36: if overturned it lies as in Figure 38: if inverted, as in Figure 39: if rolled over and over during solidification it may be broken up into many pipelets as in Figure 40. Figure 38

Fig. 38 A

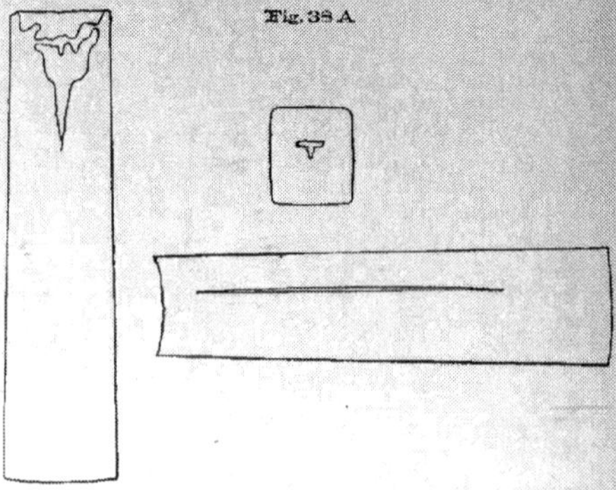

tells one disadvantage of heating ingots on their sides in common reverberatory furnaces, instead of on end, as in soaking-pits and similar furnaces. This point is brought out more plainly and probably more accurately in Figure 38 A, which shows the position of the pipe in ingots recently broken at an American Bessemer works, one of them standing upright, the other lying on its side while solidifying.

In order that the pipe may injure as little as possible of the ingot, it and hence the top of isotherm i should lie as high as possible: in other words solidification should be more rapid in the lower than in the upper part of the ingot, so that the last freezing portion which must hold the pipe may be as near the top of the ingot as possible. Hence the practice of certain American Bessemer works of filling the tops of the rail-ingot moulds above the steel with charcoal or coke dust,[b] and Krupp's plan of keeping the top of the ingot hot,[c] (1) by lining the top of the mould with refractory material, (2) by pouring molten slag upon the molten steel in the mould, and (3) by placing a thick cover of refractory material upon the molten metal or slag: these expedients further serve a special purpose in connection with his mode of compression. Hence too the use of the hot-top sinking head, (§ 227).

To the same end, if the ingot is to be heated or soaked on end, it should be placed in the furnace or pit as soon after teeming as possible, so that as much as possible of its upper part may be molten and so available as a sinking head to flow down and fill the pipe.

The isotherms and through them the pipe are liable to be lowered by strongly tapering moulds and by bottom

[a] Cf. Adamson and Snelus, Journ. Iron and Steel, 1887, I., pp. 148, 156.

[b] This practice involved so much delay that it has recently been abandoned: the manager believes it more profitable to allow the ingot to solidify rapidly, and to crop off a larger proportion of its upper end on account of unsoundness.

[c] F. A. Krupp, British Patent 2,860, June 30th, 1881.

casting. In the latter the first entering portion of metal, which forms the top of the ingot, is cooled much by the initially cool gate and runners: as these become heated by the passing iron they cool the last entering portion less.[a] In strongly tapering moulds as in Fig. 37 the isotherms are crowded together at the top of the ingot, where the metal freezes across early, and hence cannot flow down to fill the cavity which grows beneath: this tends to cause a deep-seated pipe.

Let us now briefly consider the effect of the rate of cooling not on the volume but on the position of the pipe. Quick cooling crowds the isotherms together, and causes them to follow each other inwards rapidly. Up to a certain time, t', the upper part of the axial metal, or sinking-head metal, will be hot enough to flow down and fill the cavity which forms beneath, and to raise it to a relatively harmless position. Now the closer together the isotherms are, the farther will the cooling and contraction of any given layer have proceeded when the time t' is reached, and hence the less will that layer cool and contract after t'. Hence, the more rapid the cooling the more of the cavity will be raised by the sinking-head metal to a harmless position, and the less of this cavity will be formed after the sinking-head metal has frozen.

On the other hand, however, quick cooling drives the isotherms inwards rapidly. In a long ingot an appreciable length of time is needed to enable the sinking-head metal to flow down, and it is quite possible that very rapid solidification may force the isotherms inwards so rapidly that freezing overtakes the sinking-head metal before it has time to flow far down the walls of the cavity, and so may deepen the pipe. Indeed, as the pipe is due to difference in the rate of contraction of shell and interior, and as this difference should be the less the more slowly the ingot cools, slow cooling should lead to a smaller pipe than rapid cooling. When ingots are placed in pits or furnaces while their interior is still molten, and are then rolled without great fall of temperature, it is not clear that any important pipe forms at all. Certainly the pipe which then forms should be very much smaller than when the ingot is allowed to solidify and cool rapidly. As experiments on the size and position of pipes have usually been made on ingots which have cooled comparatively rapidly, they are liable to give a greatly exaggerated idea of the size of pipe which actually arises in practice, in which the ingot cools and contracts not only little but comparatively uniformly.

Taking the above considerations together, we should expect that rapid cooling would raise the greater part of the pipe to a harmless position, while at the same time it may actually cause a thin tail or pipelet to extend deeper than it would were the cooling slower.

The results of such speculation must be received with extreme caution: they are offered simply as speculation, and to stimulate thought and observation.

Rapid solidification is to be looked for *A* in ingots cast too near their freezing point, *B* in those cast in iron instead of sand moulds, and *C* in narrow ingots.

§ 225. The Volume of the Pipe, assuming for the moment that it is not diminished by the formation of blowholes, will equal the excess of the net contraction of the interior over that of the shell during the cooling subsequent to t'. If we know accurately the laws which the thermal conductivity and dilatation of cooling and solidifying steel follow, we could discuss with confidence the effect of variations in the conditions of casting and cooling on this excess: in our comparative ignorance we may conjecture that it will be roughly proportional to the difference between the temperature of the outside and the average temperature of the inside at the time t' when the shell becomes rigid, and that this difference will be the greater the more rapidly heat is conducted away from the metal by the mould: hence the pipe should be greater in ingots cast in iron than in those cast in sand moulds, and greater when cold than when hot iron moulds are employed. Even the iron rail-ingot moulds are now intentionally heated at some American Bessemer works before teeming, to lessen the pipe.

In regard to ingots of large as compared with those of small cross-section the case is less simple. If the power of the mould to abstract heat increased proportionally to the mass of the ingot, then the center of the large ingot should be hotter than that of the small ingot, when the outer shell becomes rigid: being hotter, the subsequent contraction of the center of the larger ingot would be greater, and hence its pipe should be greater than that of the small ingot. But the thermal capacity of the mould of a large ingot relatively to that of the ingot itself, and hence its power of abstracting heat from the ingot, is usually much smaller than in the case of small ingots. Before the shell of the large ingot begins to become rigid its mould has become highly heated; that of the small ingot remains cold up to and past the time t'. The cold mould of the small ingot may well lead to a difference between the average temperature of outside and that of inside at the critical time t' greater than the corresponding difference in case of the large ingot, whose hot mould abstracts heat but slowly from the ingot's shell, which long remains hot and plastic. This would give the small ingot a pipe larger in proportion to its size than that of the large ingot.

Similar reasoning applies to the case of very hot and rather cool-cast ingots.

We have no very satisfactory data as to the total contraction of volume which the particles of steel undergo during solidification and cooling. The shortening effected by Whitworth's fluid compression suggests that the total contraction is not far from 13 or 14% by volume. The enormous pressure which he employs is said to shorten ingots of uniform cross-section by 12·5% (1·5 inches per foot) in addition to the longitudinal contraction of similar uncompressed ingots, which varies from 1 to 2·6%[b] (1–8th to 5–16ths inch per foot); so that we here have a total longitudinal contraction of at least 13.5%. If we knew the transverse contraction and if we knew that Whitworth's compression left no cavities, we could calculate the total contraction. But we do not. During the early part of the compression the ingot probably expands transversely, the enormous pressure as well as the rising temperature dilating the mould, and the ingot spreading laterally and following up this dilatation. Later, after the walls of the ingot have grown so cold that they defy even the action of Whitworth's press, say from dull redness down, a very

[a] Walrand, Van Nostrand's Eng. Mag., XXXIII., p. 356, 1885.

[b] In a case within the writer's knowledge the shrinkage on steel cylinders 2 feet in diameter has been 5-16ths inch per foot, or 2·6 per cent. linearly.

considerable transverse contraction probably occurs. If we assume that this roughly equals the transverse dilatation which occurs earlier, we have a total contraction of 13.5% by volume.

The volume of the pipe in the six-inch steel gun lately cast by the Pittsburgh Steel Casting Company must have been about 6·4% of that of the original molten metal.[a]

If we assume that the external shrinkage here was 0·25 inch per linear foot, or 6·12% by volume, and further assume that the metal was free from blowholes, we have a total contraction, external and internal, of 12·49% by volume, which is not far from that deduced from Whitworth's compression. And the contraction should be substantially the same in both cases, since Whitworth's compression probably does not affect the density of the solid portion of the cold metal.

This total contraction should be composed of the external shrinkage, the volume of the blowholes, and that of the pipe. Changes in the shape, size, etc., of castings, or in other conditions, which increase the external shrinkage diminish the pipe, provided the volume of the blowholes and the density of the cold metal remains unaltered. To put it algebraically,

Let VM, VC, VP, VS and VB = the volumes of the molten metal, the cold metal, the pipe, the external shrinkage and the blowholes respectively, VC of course being the volume occupied by the ultimate particles of the cold metal, excluding all cavities, large and small,

Then $VM = VC + VP + VS + VB$.

If VM, VC and VB be constant, then the larger VS is the smaller will VP be.

The maximum volume of pipe. The smallest linear contraction in case of steel castings is probably about 1%, which implies a contraction of 3% by volume. If, as we have estimated, the total contraction be about 14%, then the maximum volume of pipe, which would of course occur when there were no blowholes, so that $VB = 0$, would be $14 - 3 = 11$% of the volume of the metal when molten, or 11·3% of that of the cold ingot.

The volume of the pipe is usually much less than this. Of 78 rail ingots, each weighing about 3,300 pounds, which were broken at an American Bessemer works, all but two showed decided pipes or masses of honeycombed cavities. In thirty instances their volumes ranged from 6 to 136 cubic inches, the average being 30 inches.[b] The largest of these pipes represents only about 1% of the volume of the molten metal.

§ 226. Surface cracks in steel ingots are chiefly vertical (longitudinal) and horizontal (transverse).

Longitudinal cracks appear to be due chiefly (1) to the ferrostatic pressure of the molten steel against the thin shell, when the mould, expanding, draws away and leaves it unsupported: and (2) to the excess of the early contraction of the shell over that of the interior. In the case of square ingots this excess tends to relieve itself by drawing in the corners of the square and bulging out its sides, so that its section becomes more nearly circular, as in A, Figure 41. Later, when the contraction of the interior overtakes and out-runs that of the outside, the tables are turned, and now the sides of the square tend to bend in and follow up the contraction of the interior. This bulging and approach to a circular section can take place more or less with all sections except one initially circular; hence in cylindrical and conical ingots the excess of contraction of shell over interior can relieve itself only by making the ingot slightly barrel shaped, which must tend to cause longitudinal cracks, such as would arise were the staves of a barrel rectangular instead of curved, and such as are shown in exaggeration by the dotted lines in Figure

Fig. 41. CRACKS, EXTERNAL AND INTERNAL.

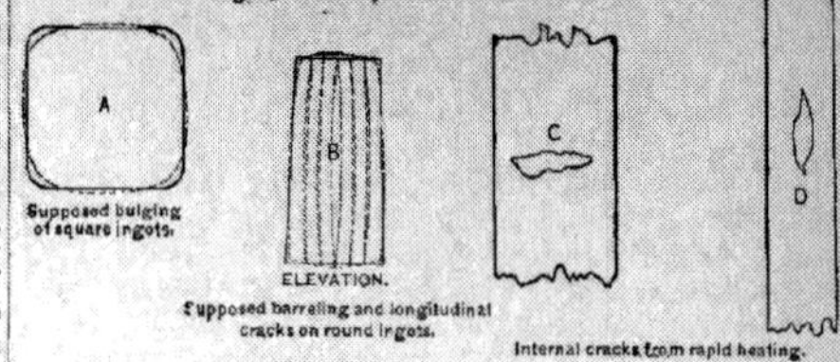

41 B: and hence the very strong tendency of round ingots to acquire longitudinal cracks.

As these cracks are in large part due to difference between the rates of cooling of outside and inside, they are to be especially looked for when this difference is greatest, *e. g.* in ingots cast in cold metallic moulds. The effects of ferrostatic pressure are most severe in tall, in bottom-cast, and in hot-cast ingots, for here the shell of the lower part of the ingot is comparatively thin after the ferrostatic pressure has become severe.

Transverse cracks as well may be due to the more rapid contraction of shell than of interior. They may also arise if the ingot attaches itself to the mould at different levels, for then its contraction is resisted by the mould, which is indeed expanding. They are most likely to occur if the mould be rough, if the casting temperature be excessively high, and if the steel in teeming strike against the sides of the mould. Hence transverse cracks arise less frequently with bottom than with top casting. Tapering moulds also lessen the tendency towards transverse cracking, for in them the longitudinal as well as the transverse contraction of the ingot and expansion of the mould tend to separate mould from ingot. Should a fin of metal connected with the ingot become attached to the top of the mould, (and this often occurs from leakage while the ladle is passing from one mould to the next), as with their changing temperatures the mould elongates and the ingot shortens, this fin tends to suspend the ingot, whose weight may tear its thin skin. These fins should be carefully removed.[c]

Snakes, sinuous markings on steel plates, are probably due to external cracks, which are drawn out into irregular serpentine shapes as the ingot is rolled now longitudinally, now diagonally, now transversely.

Internal Cracks.—Just as the too rapid contraction of the shell in cooling causes surface cracks, so its too rapid expansion in heating causes internal ones. If a cold ingot be placed in a hot furnace, the shell of the ingot expands and may elongate so rapidly that the expansion of the slowly heating interior cannot keep pace with it, when

a This number is reached from data furnished me by Mr. Wm. Hainsworth of the Pittsburgh Steel Casting Company.

b Private communication, F. A. Emmerton, Feb. 4th, 1888.

c Concerning surface cracks, cf. Walrand, loc. cit.

internal cracks form as shown at C, Figure 41, often with a loud report. These cavities on forging become elongated as at D, and may break through to the surface, causing incurable defects, sometimes so serious that the ingot must be cut to pieces. From this cause the proportion of cracked or "second quality" rails is greater when rail ingots are allowed to cool, than when they are charged into the heating furnace while still hot from teeming. Ingots which for any reason are allowed to cool should not be charged into a hot furnace. They should either be charged when the furnace is cool (say on Sunday night or early Monday morning) and be gradually heated with it, or else be preheated to redness in a comparatively cool auxiliary furnace, and then be transferred to the regular white-hot heating furnace.

Thus, in order to guard against cracks both external and internal the ingot should be placed in the heating furnace as soon after casting as possible. Some would teem the steel into moulds standing close to the heating furnace. A more practicable plan is that of the Pittsburgh Steel Casting Company, in which the steel is cast in moulds standing on a car, which is raised by a hydraulic jack immediately after teeming, and drawn by a locomotive to the side of the heating furnace, where the moulds are stripped, and the ingot immediately charged. As the wheels of the car are liable to become clogged with the metal splashed in teeming, it might be better to cast the ingots in a group on a single base plate, which could then be quickly raised by a crane and placed on a car. But these matters may be considered more advantageously elsewhere.

Both for given volume and for given cross-section, the longer the ingot the more liable is it to acquire cracks, both external and internal: in other words, short stumpy ingots are less liable to cracks than long and than thin ones.

Hammering between Flat Dies is liable to cause a central pipe-like crack in round steel bars: hence it is better to employ swedges, or, if possible, grooved rolls.[a] It is said that this same tendency is met in rolling round bars by Simond's rolling machinery,[b] in which the pressure appears to be applied along two lines diametrically opposite, just as in hammering between flat dies.

Let us now consider the means of preventing blowholes and pipes.

§ 227. A SINKING HEAD (rising or feeding head) raises the pipe to a more or less harmless position, but probably does not directly affect its volume. If it affects the volume and position of the blowholes it should be through increasing the ferrostatic pressure within the ingot. Usually the walls of the sinking head are of the same material as the mould, and simply form a continuation of it. In order that the sinking head shall sink and feed efficiently it must not only be so wide that it will not freeze across till the ingot beneath has completely solidified, but its volume must be such that it will preserve molten up to this point enough metal to fill the cavity due to the contraction of the ingot's interior.

If the maximum volume of pipe is as we have estimated 11% of the volume of the hot ingot, and if from one-third

[a] Cf. Metcalf, Trans. Am. Soc. Civ. Engineers, XV., p. 290, 1887.

[b] Described in the Iron Age, XLI., p. 269, 1888, and in Stahl und Eisen, VIII., p. 255, 1888.

TABLE 78.—SINKING HEAD AND CROPPINGS, ETC., FROM TOP OF STEEL INGOTS AND CASTINGS, REJECTED FOR UNSOUNDNESS.

Number.	Description of ingot or casting.				Weight of portion rejected from top of ingot or casting, per 100 of total weight.	Volume of sinking head per 100 of total volume of casting + sinking head.
	American Bessemer rail ingots; Weight of croppings per 100 of weight of ingot.					
	Name of works.	Size of ingot	Bloom cropping.	Crop'ng of upper end of upper rail.		
1..	A.	14″ × 14″	7·5	1·00	8·5	
2..	B.	10″ × 10″	9·0	0·75	9·75	
3..	C.	14″ × 14″	7·84	0·74	8·58	
4..	D.	14·5″ × 14·5″	5·8	0·67	6·47	
5..	E.	14″ × 14″	8·53	0·75	9·28	
6	F.	14″ × 14″	5	0·80	5·80	
	Crucible steel ingots; Weight of upper portion rejected on account of pipe, per 100 of total weight of ingot.					
7..	Saw steel				30·	
8..	Mild steel				10 to 20	
9..	High carbon steel				20 to 35	
10..	Badly melted steel				100	
	Ordnance ingots.					
11..	U. S. Navy, reject at least				30·	
12..	U. S. Army, reject at least				33·3	
13..	*Miscellaneous ingots* (Walrand)				......	16·7
14..	" " (Chernoff)				13·7 to 25	
	Castings proper.					
15..	Terre Noire, 10″ projectiles				......	20 to 25
16.	6″ steel cast gun, Pittsburgh Steel Casting Co.				17·6	25·5
17..	Plain cylindrical castings for rolls, Norway Iron Works, Boston				......	25
18.	Mitis castings, 0·5 to 10 lbs., weight of sprue per 100 of total				25	
19..	Do. do. do. castings weighing 10 to 100 lbs.				10	
20..	Cast-iron guns, U. S. Army				16·7	

1 to 7. Private notes.
8 to 10. Wm. Metcalf, private communication, January, 1888.
11, 12. Capt. D. A. Lyle, U. S. Army, private communication, Feb. 25, 1888. 11. Ingots weighing up to about 21 tons. At least 30% by weight is rejected from the top and at least 5% from the bottom. The lower end is the breech end. 12. At least 33·3% of the total weight of the ingot is rejected from the top end, and at least 6% from the lower end.
13. Walrand, Van Nostrand's Eng. Mag., XXXIII., p. 857, 1885.
14. Chernoff, Revue Univ, 2nd. Ser., VII., p. 145, 1880.
15. Terre Noire solid steel castings for projectiles, mould proper of iron, walls of sinking head of hot sand. Holley, Metallurgical Review, II., p. 379, 1878.
16. 6-inch cast steel gun of the Pittsburgh Steel Casting Co., private communication, Wm. Hainsworth, Jan. 28th, 1888.
Total weight of head when cast, estimated at .... 3,700 lbs.
" " " " when cold, " " .... 2,850 "
Total weight of gun including sinking head, estimated at .... 15,200 "
The composition and properties of the metal of which this gun consists are given in Table 90.
17. G. H. Billings, private communication.
18, 19. P. Ostberg, private communication. These numbers seem to me surprisingly low.
20. Capt. D. A. Lyle.

to one-half the volume of the sinking head is available for feeding, then the greatest needed volume of sinking head should be from about 20 to about 28% of the total volume of the hot ingot or casting including the sinking head itself, or from 25 to 38% of the volume of the casting proper excluding the sinking head. The volume of sinking head actually employed, and the proportion of the ingot or other casting which is rejected on account of unsoundness in certain cases, are given in Table 78. As pipes in rail ingots are partly effaced in the subsequent rolling, while in castings proper (*i. e.* those which are employed without forging) they remain of their full initial size, special pains are taken to avoid them in castings: and we note that the proportion of sinking head by weight is much smaller in rail ingots than in castings proper, varying in the former between the narrow limits of 5·6 and 9·75%, while in the latter it runs from 17·6 to 25%. That portion of the top of the rail ingot which is subsequently cropped off on account of unsoundness is for convenience here classed as a sinking head: and with it may be included the crop end of the rail made from the steel next the top of the ingot. Formerly many works cropped from the bloom only 5% of the weight of the ingot: but this brings the upper end of the upper rail uncomfortably near the porous or piped region of the ingot top: and as the rail receives the hardest usage at its end, the impact of the approaching wheel, it is better to crop off 7·5%: the subsequent rail cropping removes another 1% of the top end.

Since the above was written I learn that at one American Bessemer works 10% of the weight of the ingot is cropped from its upper end, and about 1% more in the upper cropping of the upper rail.

Some Bessemer rail ingots from a well known American works have been cut in two longitudinally, when a very deep and rather narrow pipe was found, somewhat as in Figure 37, § 224. It would be manifestly impossible to remove this by cropping. Indeed, the unsoundness of the crop end of the rail ingot is due probably more to imprisoned gas bubbles which have risen from below, than to the pipe proper. Crucible steel ingots are usually very narrow, and are cast in iron moulds. The large proportion of their weight which is rejected on account of piping harmonizes with the deductions in § 225.

Hot-Top Sinking Head.—When iron moulds are employed, the sinking head will solidify relatively slowly, and so feed the more efficiently, if its walls be of clay or other poorly conducting substance (as in Figure 42), especially if this be previously heated, as in the Terre Noire practice of casting steel projectiles.[a]

Fig. 42

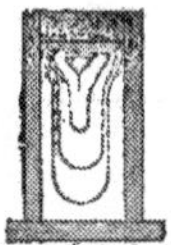

Hot-top sinking head, (Walrand).

The feeding of the sinking head may be assisted in steel as it is in iron castings by working a rod up and down through it, to break through any bridging that may occur either in the sinking head itself or the upper part of the ingot, and so to maintain a passage through which feeding may occur. But this as well as the "hot-top" sinking head rather encourages the late escape of gas, which leads to the formation of blowholes. For if the top of the ingot be allowed to solidify rapidly, or better still if its solidification be hastened by pouring water on it, the upper crust bottles up the gas set free within the ingot, the gaseous pressure within rises and thus tends to prevent the further evolution of gas.

Special Forms of Sinking-Head.—If a series of moulds be placed one above another, with perforated diaphragms of refractory material between, each ingot serves as a sinking-head to the next lower one and the piping may be concentrated in the upper ingot. This arrangement suggests itself most readily for tyre and similar ingots: but recent inventions aim to apply it to common pyramidal ingots as well. This is done by lowering the ingot as soon as its crust has solidified, and casting a second on top of it. They unite in the center, and the second feeds the piping of the first. In the case of small ingots, the cold-shut due to intermittent teeming makes it easy to separate the ingots, which is done while they are still so hot as to be weak: should the cold-shut be insufficient, some special device is employed. The steel is thus cast in continuous notched bars, later broken at the notches. Each ingot should have nearly the same composition as the steel fed to its pipe, as otherwise it will be heterogeneous; this means that successive ingots must have closely similar compositions.

In Boulton's arrangement, which consists essentially of a vertical frame A A, in which four moulds are held in column by spring clamps, a mould with a bottom is first filled, standing in the position occupied by the empty mould D in Figure 42, A. A perforated asbestos diaphragm is now placed upon it, and on this an empty bottomless mould, when both moulds are forced down by appropriate mechanism, the empty mould now occupying the position originally held by the first mould. The second mould having been filled, it receives its asbestos diaphragm, a third mould is placed upon it, all three are pushed down, and so on. After three moulds have been filled, matters stand as in Figure 42 A, a fourth mould being now in position for teeming, and the first having reached the pocket B. The ram C in the hydraulic cylinder E is now forced against the first mould, breaking its ingot away from that in the second mould, as shown. The opposite ram C′ returns the first mould to its former position, the column of moulds and ingots is again forced down, and so on. The asbestos diaphragms which separate the ingots make it easier to break them apart.[b]

Fig. 42 A. BOULTON'S CASTING ARRANGEMENT.

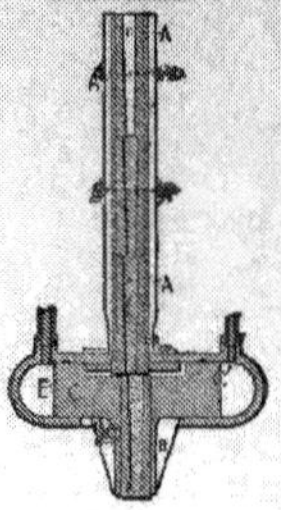

A A, frame of I beams, held together by spiral springs. *B*, pocket, holding the lower mould. *C*, *C′*, rams for breaking lower ingot away from next higher one. *D*, empty mould, ready to receive the next lot of steel. *E*, hydraulic cylinder for moving the ram *C*.

Hinsdale uses a single, stationary, bottomless, water or steam-cooled mould. The ingot is drawn down by mechanism as soon as its crust has solidified, till only its upper end remains in the mould, when a second is cast upon it, uniting with it in the centre and feeding its pipe, yet readily detached later.[c] In order that the top of one ingot may fully close the bottom of the mould while the succeeding ingot is being cast, there must be little or no taper: hence difficulty in drawing the weak tender ingot through the mould, and danger of cracking and bleeding.

[a] Holley, Metallurg. Rev. II., p. 379, 1878.

[b] J. B. D. A. Boulton, U. S. Patent 365,902, July 5th, 1887. Messrs. Spaulding and Jennings, West Bergen, New Jersey, who have one of Boulton's machines, write me (April 25th, 1888) that they regard it as successful. The first cast in it was made on December 20th, 1887.

[c] W. R. Hinsdale, priv. com., April 21-26th, 1888. U. S. Patent Application, 222,371.

§ 228. Agitation during Solidification.—Imagining that the pine-tree crystals, already referred to in § 222, were an important cause of blowholes, their tops protruding so far beyond the completely solidified portion of the ingot and into its still molten center as to mechanically detain rising gas bubbles, imprisoning them in the solidifying mass and thus causing blowholes, Chernoff would wash these crystals off, swashing the molten metal against them, by rotating the solidifying ingot at a constantly altering speed, with occasional reversals.[a] Webb has used this method successfully in casting locomotive driving wheels, the rate of rotation gradually increasing till it reaches some fifty revolutions per minute, then gradually decreasing.[b]

Forsyth[c] would rapidly hammer the sides of the ingot mould, the jarring thus caused interfering with crystallization, and the waves set up washing off the delicate incipient crystalline axes.

On repeatedly applying Chernoff's method to freezing ice bottles I find that the formation of tubules is wholly prevented: many very minute spherical cavities result, whose total volume is much less than that of the tubules usually present. On remelting one lot of ice thus frozen and allowing it to resolidify tranquilly without removal from the bottle, it developed a great mass of tubules, whose volume I estimated as at least ten times as large as that of the spheres formerly present.

Both with ice and steel it is probable that agitation, whether due to rotation or jarring, simply mechanically detaches the gas bubbles which adhere to the solidifying surfaces, and so promotes solidification in continuous layers free from blowholes.

Rotation should greatly diminish the volume of the pipe, by stirring up the molten and even pasty metal, thus rendering its temperature more uniform throughout its cross section. Hot metal from the interior is washed against the frozen shell, the cooling of the former is hastened, that of the latter retarded: thus the difference between the mean temperature of interior and that of shell at all times during freezing, including of course the time t', is greatly dimished, and we have seen that the volume of the pipe should depend on this difference at the time t'. (§ 225.)

Rotation, in that it hastens the cooling of the center of the ingot, should oppose segregation: but if extremely rapid it might possibly favor segregation by forcing the heavier components centrifugally and the lighter components centripetally, somewhat as the rapid rotation of milk hastens the separation of cream.

§ 229. Liquid Compression, or subjecting the steel while still molten to pressure, was described by Bessemer in 1856, and has since been often tried, and abandoned because it did no good commensurate with its cost. It is said to be practiced by Whitworth and at Aboukoff, with what result we will shortly consider.

A. *Whitworth*[d] casts his steel in a flask consisting of a steel cylinder L, Figure 43, supported by steel hoops K. Within this is arranged a lining of unconnected iron rods M, pierced with numerous small holes for the escape of gas as shown, and within this[e] a layer of moulding sand. N. By means of the car C, flask and steel are quickly

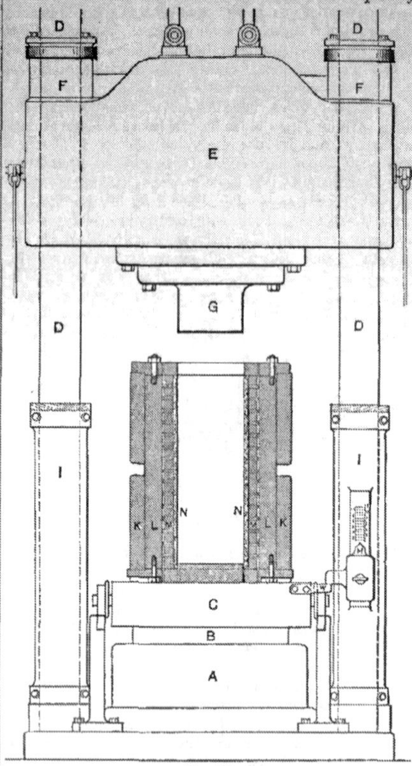

Fig. 43.
Whitworth's Casting Press for Liquid Compression.
(Press in elevation, mould in section.)

A, Main compressing cylinder. *B*, its plunger. *C*, carriage on which the flask rests. *D D*, four hollow pillars guiding and supporting the main cross-head. *E*, the main cross-head, raised and lowered by a hydraulic cylinder above it. *F F*, nuts for locking the main cross-head. *G*, boss against which the steel in the mould is forced. *H*, indicator, showing the rise of the main plunger *B*. *I I*, split stops, fastened to the pillars with bolts and clips, to support the main cross-head when the press is not in use. *K K*, steel jackets for mould. *L L*, the mould. *M M*, perforated cast-iron bagging. *N N*, inner sand lining.

transferred to the top of the vertical plunger B of a powerful hydraulic press. A is the cylinder in which this plunger plays.

A massive crosshead E forming the cap of the press is immediately lowered until a projection G on its lower sur-

[a] Revue universelle, 2nd ser. VII., p. 154, 1880.

[b] F. W. Webb of Crewe, Journ. Iron and St. Inst., 1882, II., p. 522.

[c] Private communication.

[d] Rept. Select Committee of U. S. Senate on Ordnance and War Ships, 1886, p. 23: Proc. U. S. Naval Inst., X., p. 637, Jaques. In British patent 1292, May 31st, 1856, Bessemer shows and describes an ingot mould with a vertical hydraulic ram at the bottom, and a sliding cover, for compressing the ingot when semi-fluid or after solidification. Whitworth, whose earliest patent which I have met relating to the compression of steel is that of Nov. 24th, 1865, No. 3,018 (British), thus seems to be antedated by some nine years: but his name has become so firmly attached to this method of compression that it would be difficult to replace it with Bessemer's, if, indeed, Whitworth's successful development of this process does not justify naming it after him. (Cf. Journ. Iron and Steel Inst., 1881, I., p. 107.) Cf. Greenwood, Liquid Compression. Proc. Inst. Civ. Engrs., XCVIII., Part IV., 1889.

[e] "Steel and Iron," Greenwood, p. 510.

face comes in contact with the upper surface of the liquid steel, completely closing the mould, when the crosshead is locked in position, and the plunger B on which the flask and its carriage rest is raised, forcing the steel upwards against the rigidly fixed crosshead. The device of moving the crosshead hastens matters, since it can be moved much faster than the slowly moving plunger of the hydraulic press: and it moreover enables us to restrict stroke of the latter to the distance by which the ingot is actually compressed longitudinally.

The pressure on the steel is gradually increased, usually till it reaches 6 tons, occasionally till it reaches 20 tons per square inch of the horizontal section of the ingot. The press at Aboukoff exerts a total pressure of 10,000 tons.[a] With a 45 ton ingot the maximum pressure is reached in about 35 minutes.

During this time there is a "continuous and violent" evolution of gas and flame, and the ingot is compressed by one eighth of its length. A pressure of 1,500 lbs. per square inch from an accumulator is now substituted for the direct pressure of the pump, and is maintained until the—"metal is sufficiently cooled to insure no farther contraction in the mould"—(which taken literally means till it is completely cold, so as to follow up the contracting steel and prevent the formation of external contraction cracks, from local adhesion to the sides of the mould or from other cause.

The gas evolved is said to be chiefly carbonic oxide, and its evolution is said to cease towards the end of the compression.

At St. Etienne, at Worcester, Mass., and at Neuberg in Styria somewhat similar methods of compression have been employed. At Neuberg a total pressure of from 400 to 700 tons was applied, and maintained only for from 30 to 60 seconds.[b]

Whitworth attacks the ingot at its strongest point, so that to accomplish given compression he has to expend the maximum of energy. To create even a slight pressure within the soft interior he must actually compress

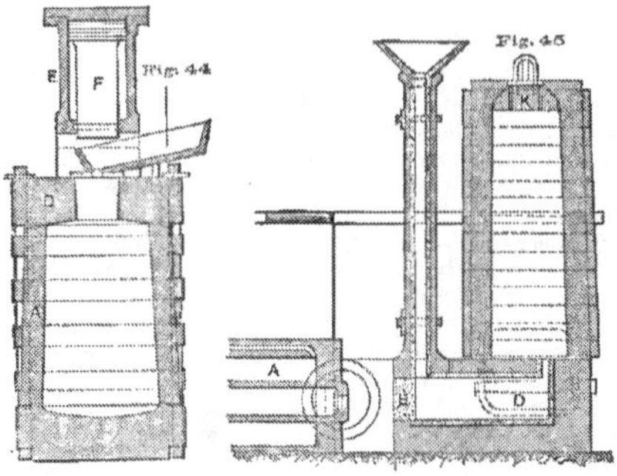

Daelen's Liquid Compression Apparatus.

the most unyielding portion, the early freezing walls, and that too in a direction in which they resist most powerfully. In other methods the ingot is attacked at much weaker points.

a "Steel and Iron," Greenwood, p. 510.
b Engineering, XX., p. 107, 1875.

B. *Daelen* employs a number of expedients for compressing steel, one of which is illustrated in Figure 44. The steel is cast in a powerfully clamped iron mould A A, (which, however, might be lined with sand, with an arrangement like Whitworth's for the escape of gas), filling it to the top of the cover D. The plunger F of a hydraulic cylinder E is then forced down into G, driving the metal into the body of the ingot. With small ingots the steel is bottom-cast in groups (Figure 45) with rather large runners, and the moulds, whose tops are closed, are strongly clamped to the base plate. A horizontal plunger A is forced by hydraulic pressure into one of these runners D, which had been temporarily closed with a brick plug E, forcing the steel thence into the moulds. The gas may escape through small holes in the mould-top, K.[c] Daelen's apparatus is not now in actual use.[d]

C. S. T. Williams[e] employs a mould, one of whose inner faces is concave as shown in Figure 46, which represents the apparatus after the compression has taken place. As

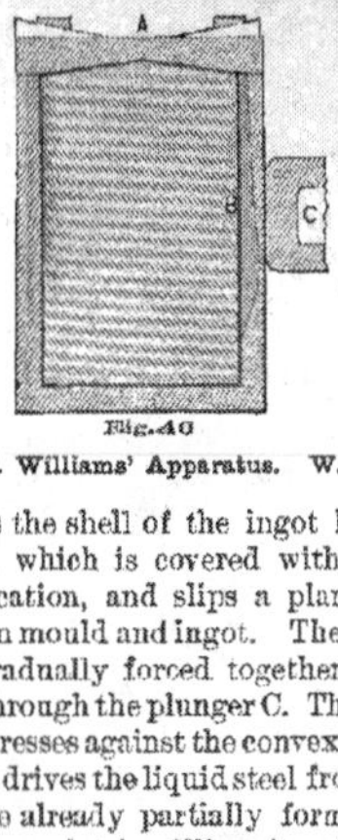

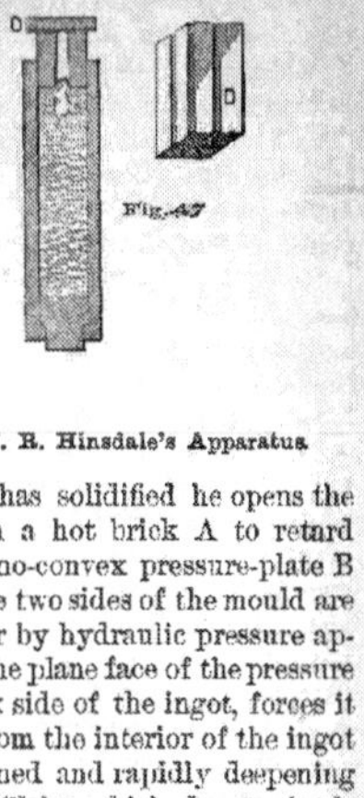

S. T. Williams' Apparatus. W. R. Hinsdale's Apparatus.

soon as the shell of the ingot has solidified he opens the mould, which is covered with a hot brick A to retard solidification, and slips a plano-convex pressure-plate B between mould and ingot. The two sides of the mould are now gradually forced together by hydraulic pressure applied through the plunger C. The plane face of the pressure plate presses against the convex side of the ingot, forces it in, and drives the liquid steel from the interior of the ingot into the already partially formed and rapidly deepening pipe, completely filling it. Slabs which I examined, hammered from these compressed ingots and broken across, showed clearly that the pipe had been filled to overflowing. This process has been in use at Henry Disston & Sons' Tacony Works for over two years, and I am informed that during this time not a saw has split on account of piping. Fifteen presses are now in use, and 12 more are building. Formerly about 30% of the weight of the ingot had to be rejected on account of piping, now only 5%. The cost of remelting the piped end is estimated by Mr. Williams at two cents per pound, if direct firing be used. This seems to me excessive. Another and most competent crucible-steel maker, who fires with gas, estimates it at half a cent a pound. Let us take it at 1·0 cents per pound for direct firing and 0·5 cents for gas firing. At Tacony one man at $2.00 per day compresses one ton of ingots in one hour.[f]

c Engineering, XX., p. 278, 1875; Jeans, Steel, p. 501.
d R. M. Daelen, private communication, Feb. 13, 1888.
e U. S. Patent 331,850, Dec. 8th, 1885.
f S. T. Williams, Superintendent of the Tacony Works, private communication, March 28th, 1888.

From this we may calculate as follows, assuming that each man engaged in compression does eight effective hours work daily. I think it more conservative to assume that the weight to be remelted, when compression is not employed, at 25% than at 30%.

	$ per ton of ingots. Direct firing.	Gas firing.
Saving by diminishing remelting $\frac{(25\% - 5\%)}{100} \times 2240$ Lbs. $\times$ (0·01 and 0·005) $	$4.48	$2.24
Labor of compression $\frac{\$2.00}{8}$	0.25	0.25
Difference per ton of ingots	$4.23	$1.99
" " pound "	0·19 ct.	0·09 cts.

0·19 cent per pound will certainly and 0·09 cent will perhaps more than cover the incidental costs of compression, such as power, depreciation, and the shorter life of the moulds.

In 1883 Mr. William Metcalf believed that compression would cost more than remelting for small crucible steel ingots.[a] This, however, referred to a much more costly and probably much less effective method of compression:[b] moreover, the cost of remelting at his admirably conducted establishment, especially with natural gas, is comparatively low.

While this method is well suited to the flat saw ingots, it remains to be seen whether it can be applied readily to common square pyramidal ingots.

D. *G. W. Billings* employs a common mould, replacing its bottom by a piston, which is forced upwards as soon as teeming is completed, pressing the top of the ingot against a resistance plate which has been slipped in meanwhile.[c]

E. *W. R. Hinsdale* found that an ingot of high-carbon steel, 3·5 inches square, to which a pressure of 12,000 pounds per square inch was applied within five seconds after casting, contained when cold innumerable blowholes. Under a pressure of 60,000 pounds per square inch, applied 30 or 40 seconds after casting, it shortened by about one eighth of its length, to wit, from 25 to 22 inches, and after cooling had a fracture like that of a forged bar; but the pipe remained in the attenuated shape of such a flaw as one finds in a bar forged from the piped end of an ingot. When, however, a pressure of 20,000 pounds per square inch was applied after the same interval through a perforated plunger D, Figure 47, the crust of metal under the perforation broke with a loud report, and a punching, followed by gas and molten metal, shot into the perforation, forming a stud which was the only scrap, as the ingot itself was absolutely solid.[d]

Daelen bulges in the top or bottom, Williams the side of the ingot: both avoid the enormous waste of energy implied in compressing the already frozen walls longitudinally. There appears to be no limit to the pressure which can be obtained by Daelen's system. Were a high pressure applied in Williams' system it would probably burst the top or convex side of the ingot, which would hardly fit the mould as exactly as is shown in the cut. It may be questioned whether it be practicable to arrange his mould so that its different parts shall slide past each other, and still be strong enough and tight enough to prevent the escape of molten metal under heavy pressure.

Hinsdale's modification might well increase the efficiency of Whitworth's system as a means of obliterating the pipe.

[a] Proc. Engineers Soc. West. Penn., 1888, 251.

[b] G. W. Billings' method.

[c] U. S. Patents 298, 661-2, May 13th, 1884.

[d] W. R. Hinsdale, private communication, March 13th, April 26th, 1888, U. S. Patent 332,656, Dec. 15th, 1885.

GASEOUS PRESSURE has been applied to molten steel in several ways. It has an advantage over Whitworth's method, in that the compressed gas attacks the ingot at every point, including the weakest ones. Even if the externally applied gas does not itself enter or compress the metal, it still tends to prevent internally liberated gas from escaping through the ingot's shell, to raise the pressure within the ingot, and thus to check the internal liberation of gas and the formation of blowholes. In this it tends to increase the pipe: but if powerful enough to bend in the sides or top of the ingot by ever so little, it lessens and may obliterate the pipe.

F. *Bessemer* patented in 1869 methods of creating a gaseous pressure in ingot moulds by the combustion of gas yielding substances, and by the vaporization of liquids.

G. *Krupp* employed liquid carbonic acid, and is said to have obtained a pressure of five tons per square inch.[e]

The interior of a massive, tightly closed mould, after it has received the molten steel, is connected with a vessel containing liquid carbonic acid: part of the carbonic acid immediately volatilizes, raising the gaseous pressure, which may be regulated by controlling the temperature of the carbonic acid. This is readily done by raising or lowering the temperature of an oil or water bath in which the vessel containing it is immersed, by circulating steam or cold water.

To prevent the escape of carbonic acid from his mould Krupp tightens the joint between mould and cover by a thin ring of copper or steel, with a channel-, angle-, or T-shaped cross section (A, B, C, Figure 48), which acts like the leather cup-packing of hydraulic cylinders, and becomes tighter the higher the pressure rises. Another expedient is to squeeze a round copper or steel ring in a rectangular recess between cover and mould (D, Figure 48).

Fig. 48.—JOINTS BETWEEN INGOT-MOULD AND COVER (F. A. KRUPP).

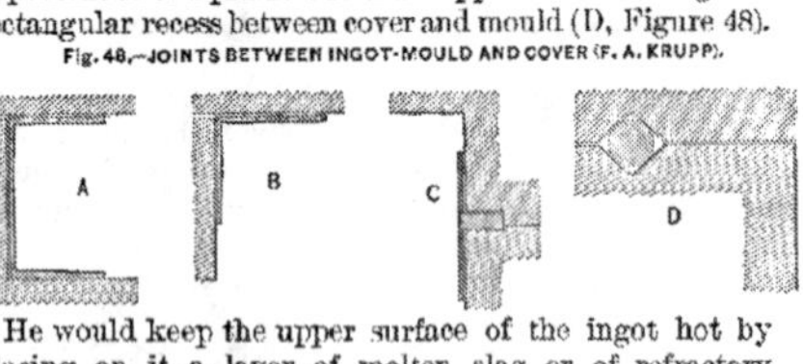

He would keep the upper surface of the ingot hot by placing on it a layer of molten slag or of refractory material, or by lining the mould top with non-conducting material, apparently so that the ingot top, long remaining soft and flexible, may transmit the pressure to the interior of the ingot.

H. The explosion of gunpowder within the firmly closed mould, proposed by Galy-Cazalat,[f] might lend pyrotechnic interest. Ingenious methods of introducing and exploding the powder and of rendering its presence effective are proposed by James Henderson, who also suggests obtaining steam pressure by introducing ice.[g]

I. *W. R. Jones*[h] of Pittsburgh formerly blew steam into the tops of his ingot-moulds, at a pressure of 80 to 150 lbs., immediately after casting. The moulds were tightly closed at the top, while their stools had grooves 5-8th inch

[e] British patent 2,860, June 30, 1881, F. A. Krupp to A. Longsdon. Krupp here describes ingot moulds of many forms for compression, both for top and bottom castings.

[f] U. S. patent 62,118, Galy Cazolat (sic), Feb. 19, 1867. British patent 3,300, Dec. 21st, 1865, Galy-Cazalat.

[g] U. S. patents 315,741, April 14th, 1885, and 316,544, April 28th, 1885.

[h] Journal of the Iron and Steel Institute, 1879, II., p. 476; Jeans, Steel, p. 503.

wide and 1-16th inch deep, for the escape of gas, and communicating with the outer air. It is said that the molten steel considerately does not enter these grooves, but that the gases escape from them with a loud roar, and that the ingot is freer from piping then when cast in the usual way. What appears to be a slight modification of this method is said to have been adopted at Barrow and at the works of Messrs. Bolckow, Vaughan & Co.[a]

Now as the ingot, whose outer crust solidifies almost instantly, cools and contracts, it would be expected to draw away from the sides of the mould, which, being rapidly heated, expands and increases the space between itself and the contracting ingot. The steam blown in at the top of the mould is thus permitted to pass down between the ingot and mould and to escape (together with any gas actually evolved from the ingot) through the holes which have been provided in the stool of the mould. That the steam, with such ample means of escape, should under these conditions exert a pressure on the steel at all commensurate with that which the rapidly cooling exterior of the ingot exerts on the comparatively slowly cooling interior, or that indeed it should exert any pressure worth considering, is improbable. It seems like merely substituting an atmosphere of steam for one of ingot gas. Whatever influence the steam has would naturally be attributed to its cooling the crust of the ingot and thus preventing rising, acting like so much water.

In practice it is difficult to tighten the joints quickly, and, in spite of the many advantages claimed for this procedure, Captain Jones does not now employ it.[b]

J. *The Accumulation of Gaseous Pressure within* the ingot itself is promoted by chilling its top with water, which bottles up the gas evolved during solidification. This of course tends to arrest further evolution of gas, and thus to check the formation of blowholes: but this local cooling must tend to lower the pipe by hindering the steel in the top of the ingot from flowing down to feed it.

§ 230. Effect of Liquid Compression.—Let us first consider what benefits should be expected from liquid compression, and then what have actually been traced to it.

We may divide the compression into two periods, before and after the passage from the liquid to the plastic state, or into "liquid" and "plastic compression."

It is hard to see how liquid compression can have any beneficial effect. Liquids are practically incompressible: that the steel is not enduringly compressed will be shown. If the liquid steel is not giving off gas, applying compression will effect nothing. If it is, compression cannot hasten the escape of the gas-bubbles,[c] which will rise by gravity to the surface with or without compression; but it must tend to retard or even stop the evolution of gas, whose solubility increases with the pressure, and thus to increase the quantity of gas retained by the steel, the supersaturation which occurs at the moment of solidification, the volume of gas then evolved, and the extent to which blowholes form.

Plastic compression, however, may actually squeeze the blowhole-gas out through the crust of the ingot as we squeeze water out of a sponge: it may cause the reabsorption of part or indeed all of the gas contained in the blowholes, and may squeeze and weld the sides of the pipe together: and if gas remain which is neither squeezed out nor reabsorbed, the pressure will diminish the size of the cavities which contain it. The gas which is thus reabsorbed and compressed is not indeed eliminated: and it is possible that it may be re-evolved and may re-expand should plasticity without compression recur: but it could then hardly form in the relatively stiff pasty metal as large cavities as it would have caused at the higher temperature and in the less viscous metal of its first liberation.[d]

In this view it seems desirable to postpone compression as long as possible, so that, before it begins, as much as possible of the gas may voluntarily escape. Indeed, it would be well to hasten its escape from the molten metal by creating a partial vacuum.

Small ingots may solidify so quickly that we cannot in practice discriminate between liquid and plastic compression: but the distinction may be valuable for large ingots.[e]

Nearly two years after the above was written, and shortly before going to press, I receive what seems to be a striking confirmation of the correctness of these inferences. On applying a pressure of 12,000 pounds per square inch to the bottom of some 3·5 inch square ingots soon after teeming, Mr. W. R. Hinsdale found that, if the pressure were applied as soon as possible, the ingot contained innumerable round cavities: while if he waited a little before applying the pressure, blowholes were found only in the upper part of the ingot, and the longer he waited the nearer to the pipe the blowholes were, till at last they disappeared, the pipe remaining.[f] Now the pressure should not retard the upward swimming of bubbles, provided that they remain as bubbles; indeed, in the belief of many, pressure tends to liquefy iron as it does ice. The most simple explanation seems to be that gas bubbles were rising through the steel: (they would naturally be found latest in the top of the ingot, because it is cast latest, and because bubbles rise thither from below): that pressure caused their reabsorption: that this gas was again set free, either on solidification or fall of pressure, causing blowholes. Hence the longer compression was deferred the less gas was present to be temporarily absorbed, and the fewer blowholes formed on its re-emission.

Plastic compression then is sound in principle: the difficulty is in applying it. Whitworth is able to employ an enormous pressure, but at a disadvantage. Daelen's method permits as great a pressure at much better advantage: his method appears much the more reasonable; yet it is not employed.

[a] Journ. Franklin Inst., CX., p. 19, 191, 1880.

[b] In a paper read in December, 1878, Chernoff speaks of casting under a steam pressure of 88 to 147 pounds per sq. inch, the method of la Chaléassière, in France.

[c] The mental fogginess of many prominent metallurgists on this subject is disheartening. We hear them talk of pressure applied to the upper surface of liquid steel forcing gas bubbles to travel downwards. Let them experiment with an ordinary soda-water syphon, which is in precisely the condition of ordinary gas-bearing liquid steel, and endeavor to grasp the A B C of physics. Let them slightly release the pressure by drawing a little water: bubbles will immediately rise: let them immediately increase the pressure again. Will the upward path of these bubbles be reversed by the pressure, and will they now travel downwards? The increased pressure may cause their reabsorption, but it will not alter the direction of their travel, which is determined by gravity alone. The effect of pressure in expelling fluids from pasty solids is clearly shown in the expulsion of cinder from a puddle-ball by squeezing: the direction which the cinder takes in escaping is not directly away from and in the line of the compressing force, but each particle follows its own path of least resistance, which will in general be nearly normal to the nearest surface. A gas would be affected in precisely the same way but it is not so easy to illustrate this experimentally.

[d] Cf. the author, Proc. Soc. Arts, Mass. Inst. Technology, 1886-7, p. 18.

[e] See experiment by H. W. Lash, § 209, F.

[f] W. R. Hinsdale, Private Communication, March 13, 1888.

In the case of small ingots several of the methods which we have considered might be expected to completely prevent both pipes and blowholes.

In the case of large ingots it should be comparatively easy to prevent blowholes in the layers which solidify first: but it is far from clear that any of these methods should be able to prevent central cavities, or that the compression which they effect should even compensate for the increased proportion of gas in the solidifying metal, due to the immediately preceding liquid compression. To make the center of a large ingot compact, the compression must follow up the contraction till the very central portions have cooled far below their freezing point, which means greatly distorting an enormous mass of already solidified and more or less rigid metal.

The pressure required at the cavities themselves in order to close them is probably slight:[a] the difficulty is to transmit any pressure whatever to them through an enormous thickness of outer and resistance metal.

In comparing Whitworth's compression with forging it is to be remembered that, while the former has advantages in acting before blowholes form instead of attempting to efface those already created, and in being applied at a temperature which is higher and hence more favorable to the welding of cavities than is permissible in forging, yet it labors under the disadvantage of having to compress the whole cross-section of the ingot at once, attacking it in the path of greatest resistance. Forging under a powerful hydraulic press has the great advantage of concentrating its pressure on a small portion of the metal, attacking it piecemeal. It is by no means clear a priori that this may not outweigh its disadvantage of working at a lower temperature.

I see no reason to anticipate that liquid compression should benefit the metal otherwise than by preventing the formation of cavities. Indeed one would hardly expect that it could produce the kneading and rubbing together of the particles which forging gives, and which is generally thought to be extremely beneficial, since this implies motion of the particles on each other. It should, however, tend to prevent external cracks

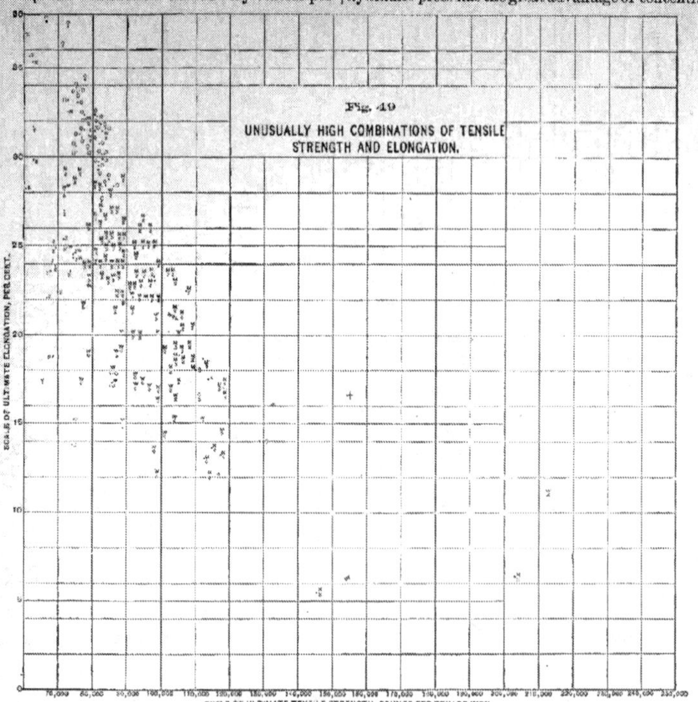

Fig. 49
UNUSUALLY HIGH COMBINATIONS OF TENSILE STRENGTH AND ELONGATION.

The numerals indicate the length in inches in which the percentage of elongation is taken: the letters indicate the origin of the steel, thus: *C* = Cambria, Johnstown, Pa. *M* = Midvale Nicetown, Pa. *O* = Otis, Cleveland, Ohio. *W* = Whitworth. + = Unforged castings. Most of the Cambria, Midvale and Otis cases are from the reports of the Chief of Ordnance, U. S. Army from 1877 to 1886 inclusive.

[a] Walrand states (*Van Nostrand Eng. Mag.*, XXXIII., p. 362, 1885) that he finds that a pressure of from 74 to 88 pounds per square inch always greatly lessens the blowholes; and Chernoff states (Rev. Univ., 2d ser., VII., p. 149, 1880) that but slight pressure suffices to arrest the escape of gas. The extreme violence with which gas escaped from previously tranquil steel in Bessemer's experiment (§ 188 C.) on lowering the pressure by some 12 to 13 pounds per square inch certainly suggests that a small increase of pressure should materially reduce the escape of gas.

Evidence of the Effects of Compression.—The only two methods which have stood the test of experience are those of Whitworth and of Williams. The evidence of the effect of the latter has already been stated; let us now consider the evidence of the effect of Whitworth's method.

It is reported that his compression shortens large ingots by 12·5%, which certainly implies that it greatly diminishes their cavities, but not that it eliminates them completely. It is further stated his compression has been successfully applied only to pieces of simple form, and that even these are subsequently forged.

I know no evidence that his compressed ingots are freer from cavities than steel cast without compression is after it has been forged with suitable apparatus, *i. e.* rolls and hammers for small pieces, hydraulic presses for large ones. I here except the sinking-head portion of uncompressed steel.

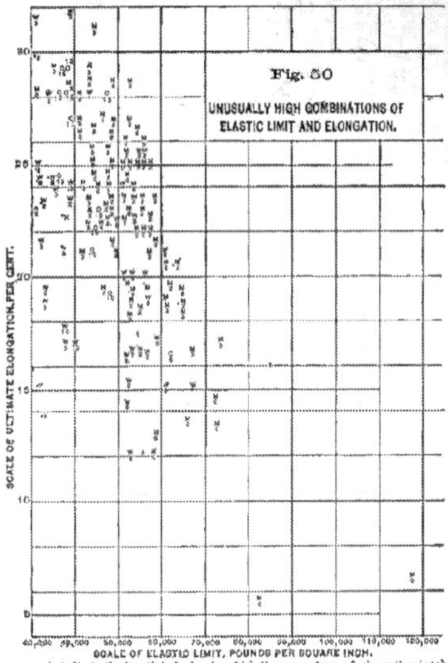

The numerals indicate the length in inches in which the percentage of elongation is taken: the letters indicate the origin of the steel, thus: *C* = Cambria, Johnstown, Pa. *M* = Midvale, Nicetown, Pa. *O* = Otis, Cleveland, O. *W* = Whitworth. + = Unforged castings. Most of the Cambria, Midvale and Otis cases are from the reports of the Chief of Ordnance, U. S. Army, from 1877 to 1886 inclusive.

Liquid compression probably does not increase the density; Percy finds the specific gravity of liquid compressed steel identical with that of similar steel uncompressed.[a]

Greenwood, indeed, finds the specific gravity of compressed steel of 0·54% of carbon 7·8791, while that of the bottom of an ingot of the same steel cast in a chill mould was 7·8542; but this difference of 0·0249 may be due to the sudden cooling caused by the walls of the chill mould, or to minute blowholes. Indeed, the important question is whether forgings, etc., from an uncompressed ingot are lighter than those from a compressed one.

Nor do I find any evidence that Whitworth's compression benefits the properties of steel otherwise than by diminishing cavities. We have plenty of vehement assertions on one side and on the other: but the experienced metallurgist, who to his sorrow knows the difficulty of tracing the causal relation, will receive them cautiously till the nature of their supporting evidence is made clear.

Members of the United States Gun Foundry Board of 1883 saw Whitworth's compressing apparatus in actual use. From the board's report, which commends Whitworth's procedure most highly,[b] one might infer that it meant to indorse liquid compression as such. But his procedure consists of two wholly distinct operations, 1, liquid compression, 2, forging under the hydraulic press after solidification. I questioned a member of the board,[c] whose name carries certainly as much weight as that of any of his associates. From his reply I gather that the board was convinced (1) that Whitworth's steel excelled all others and (2) that the action of the hydraulic forging press was far more beneficial to large masses than that of the hammer: but that it did not intend to indorse liquid compression specially, though impressed by Whitworth's conviction that it was valuable. It is possible that they weighed philoprogenitiveness, the inventor's natural parental bias, too lightly.

Indeed, one could hardly know that the admirable qualities of Whitworth's steel were at all due to liquid compression, without comparing a great number of his hydraulic-forged pieces which had been compressed while molten with others similar but not compressed. If such a comparison has ever been made, its results have not, I believe, been offered to the public, nor, I am very confident, to the board. Judging from its report and from the answers of two of its members to my inquiries, it seems to me pretty clear that the evidence which the board obtained was of such a nature that, while it might suggest, it could not begin to prove that liquid compression benefits large masses which are to be forged afterward under the hydraulic press, otherwise than by diminishing the pipe and preventing external cracks: but we may reasonably doubt whether these advantages would repay the cost of a liquid compression apparatus.

The hold which a long-used brand and a famous name like Whitworth's have on the imagination, and the difficulty of substituting for a familiar material a new one which, though of equal or even greater fitness, differs slightly from it, suffice to explain the frequent belief of gunmakers in the unapproachable quality of Whitworth's steel.[d]

General Benét, commenting on the properties of some steel hoops from Midvale, remarks that they "are fully equal to the highest claimed by Whitworth & Co. for the characteristics of their steel hoops."[e]

Greenwood says of the many compressed ingots cut up at Abouchoff that they "presented either no visible cavity, or only perhaps an axial pipe or porosity into which a pin or wire might be inserted." Hence in designing ingots, while allowance is of course made for loss in forging and turning, none is made for unsoundness at the ingot-top, of which from 5 to 35% is rejected in case of uncompressed ingots. He mentions a liquid-compressed ingot 34·25 inches in diameter and 70·5 inches long, cut lengthwise into three pieces, which showed no sign of honeycomb or blowhole; and he states that two trunnion-pieces for 12-inch breech-loading guns, weighing 118 cwt., as finished forgings, are habitually cut and forged from a liquid-compressed ingot 38 inches in diameter and 48 inches long, weighing 146 cwt., and that five trunnion-pieces for 6-inch guns, weighing as finished forgings 52 cwt., are habitually cut and forged from a liquid-compressed ingot 22 inches in diameter and 66 inches long weighing 65 cwt. The total loss due to cutting, punching and oxidation is about 20% in these cases.[f] This is certainly excellent practice, and Greenwood's important and welcome evidence puts matters in much better light. There is much evidence, however, which is less favorable. Thus Maitland, whom Greenwood quotes, says guardedly of Whitworth's castings that they are very sound as a rule, thus implying exceptions. Greenwood admits that seams and roaks occur, and that there are even exceptional rejections on account of faulty metal.

[a] Journ. Iron and Steel Inst., 1888, I., p. 29.
[b] Proc. U. S. Naval Inst., X., pp. 633, 637, 642; also Rept. U. S. Gun Foundry B'd.
[c] Lt. Col. Henry L. Abbot, Private Communications, Feb. 14th and 29th, 1888.
[d] Hotchkiss, the famous gun-maker, stated in August, 1884, that, though forced by government to try Schneider steel, it is very different from (meaning apparently very inferior to) Whitworth steel. Yet in November, 1885, Hotchkiss & Co. state that they use Schneider steel extensively, and that it possesses the qualities needed for guns. Report of Select Committee on Ordnance and War Ships, p. 443.
[e] Rept. Chief of Ordnance, U. S. Army, 1884, p. 12.
[f] The Treatment of Steel by Hydraulic Pressure, Proc. Inst. Civ. Eng., XCVIII., IV., 1889.

Though his compression is patented, Whitworth has never, I believe, permitted experts to observe it, if we except the distinguished members of the United States Gun Foundry Board: and they do not appear to be experts in metallurgy. Asked by Hewitt if he compressed large gun tubes, he hesitated and finally admitted that he did not.[a] It has seemed to many that Whitworth's attitude has not been one of confidence in the value of his compression.

Gautier states that Whitworth's former superintendent, Annable, exposes the futility of liquid compression in a paper presented to the Iron and Steel Institute but discreetly rejected.[b]

Annable states that he is not confident that a single one of the 1,500 ingots which he compressed was really solid: that the compressed ingot contains a pipe whose volume rises to 244 cubic inches, filled with gas found to be explosive: that to obtain sound metal the upper third of the ingot must be cut off: that compressed steel forges exactly like uncompressed: and that the walls of the mould become glazed, preventing the escape of gas.

Gautier's paper gives the impression that he and Annable are strongly biased; and such bias on Annable's part is easily understood. His bad results, in view of Greenwood's success, seem to teach merely that great care, or special knowledge, or special precautions are needed.

To throw some light on the question whether liquid compression gives a higher combination of either ultimate or elastic tensile strength with ductility than is otherwise attainable, I have endeavored to find the best recorded combinations of these properties both in Whitworth's steel and in that of other makers. The best which I have found are given in Figure 48, and a few of the very best are collected in Table 79.

While the results here brought together show what no one doubted, that Whitworth's steel is admirable, it further shows that, unless I have accidentally met the records of only his poorer steel, it does not excel the best American steel in its combination of ultimate or elastic tensile strength with ultimate elongation. One of Whitworth's steels does, indeed, greatly excel all others: but one swallow makes no summer.

To sum up, in proper hands the liquid compression of large masses, if powerful enough, according to our present evidence, does prevent pipes, blowholes and cracks almost completely, so that we may avoid the expense to which we are put in common practice of remelting from 5 to 35% of the weight of each ingot on account of unsoundness. But it is doubtful whether this is in itself sufficient to repay the cost of the apparatus:[c] and I find no evidence that liquid compression improves the metal. The compression of small ingots has received one satisfactory solution (§ 229, C.)

§ 231. EXHAUSTION, already hinted at in discussing liquid compression, has been proposed.[d] Removing gas from the molten steel leaves so much the less to escape during plasticity and cause blowholes: but of course the exhaustion must cease before solidification sets in even in the exterior of the ingot, or the cure will but aggravate the malady. Except in the very largest castings this condition might be hard to comply with.

[a] Appendix to Report U. S. Commission on Ordnance and War Ships, 1885, p. 27.

[b] Genie Civil, II., p. 385.

[c] The additional cost of equipping a gun-making plant for liquid compression was estimated by the Gun Foundry Board at $175,000 (Report, p. 50; Proc. U. S. Naval Inst., X., p. 851, Jaques), and by Mr. J. Morgan, Jr., Chief-Engineer of the Cambria Iron Company, at $200,000 to $300,000 (Appendix to Rept U. S. Commission on Ordnance and War Ships, appointed under resolution of July 6, 1884, p. 27).

[d] Proposed by L. Nessel, Metallurg. Rev., I., p. 494, from Oest. Zeit., No. 43, 1877.

TABLE 79.—HIGH COMBINATIONS OF STRENGTH AND DUCTILITY.

Number.	Tensile strength, pounds per square inch.	Elastic limit, pounds per square inch.	Elongation, %	Elongation, In.	Contraction of area.
WHITWORTH'S STEEL.					
1	94,720		17·5	6"	47·2
2	100,560	59,000	14·8	6	39·2
3	98,000		18·5	6	44·6
4	92,120	59,000	17·	6	52·2
5	91,300	40,000	17·2	6	32·2
6	75,600	60,000	17·3	6	47·2
7	86,880	37,000	2·1	2	34·6
8	76,680	38,000	19·	3	33·4
9	79,320	39,000	23·3	2	33·5
10	88,400	50,000	22·	3	47·2
11	95,280	55,000	25·5	2	52·2
12	82,540	51,000	21·5	2	49·7
13	84,600	34,000	23·	2	49·7
14	86,640	53,000	24·7	2	47·2
15	89,320	54,000	24·	2	47·2
16	84,000	44,000	20·	3	41·6
17	104,000	60,800	21·	2	44·6
18	98,980	62,900	20·	2	36·4
19	97,000	59,700	17·8	2	36·4
20	100,560	58,000	12·	2	11·8
21	91,600	51,000	20·	2	36·4
22	88,000	56,000	20·		
	@	@	@		
23	112,000	67,200	18·		
24	106,024	......	20·		
25	71,686	42,560	28·		
	@	@	@		
26	86,840	51,520	34·		
27	212,300	......	11·		
28	89,600	......	32·		
29	107,520	......	24·		
30	129,920	......	17·		
31	102,820	......	19·		
32	161,280	......	14·		
STEEL OTHER THAN WHITWORTH'S.					
33	90,000	......	22·	8	
34	140,000	......	12·	4	
35	147,200	......	15·	4	
36	123,800	......	17·	4	
37	132,700	84,863	16·	2	81·07
38	155,000	......	16·6		
39	119,969	......	16·5		
40	102,000	61,400	26		
41	130,000	......	14·	10	
42	134,000	......	17·2		
43	114,000	54,000	17·50	4	
	@	@	@		
44	116,000	57,000	17·2	4	
45	126,000	70,000	17·0		
46	112,000	64,000	18·6		
47	117,410	72,000	14·5	6	45·7
48	117,810	72,000	15·88	6	48·7
49	117,440	73,000	17·00	3	47.2
50	118,000	73,000	17·83	8	43·7
51	112,300	69,500	19·8	3	39·0
52	145,400 / 209,250	88,510 / 118,868	5·5 / 5·2	8 / 8	9·2 / 20·6
53	115,160	46,000	13·67	6	39·2
54	105,200	65,000	19·83	8	52·2
55	109,240	66,000	17·67	8	44·6
56	79,000	35,000	24·	8	30·8
57	82,400	41,000	28·	8	42·0
58	79,120	40,000	26·	8	42·0
59	79,880	45,000	30·7	8	56·3
60	78,480	46,000	32·	8	56·8
61	106,000	60,000	19·	2	

1 to 13, Rept. Chf. Ordnance, U. S. A., 1884, p. 557. **14 to 21,** Maj F. H. Parker, U. S. A., Rept. Select Committee Ordnance and War Ships, p. 334, 1886. **22 to 26,** Proc. U. S. Naval Inst., X, pp. 363-4, Benét, Jaques. **25 and 26,** untempered, the rest tempered. **27,** Hardisty. **28 to 32,** Whitworth, "Guns and Steel," p. 18. These are properties claimed for certain of his steels. **33 to 36,** Norway Iron-Works private communication. **37,** Pittsburgh Steel Casting Co., private communication; also American Manufacturer, March 4th, 1887. **38,** Unforged casting, Chernoff, Revue Universelle, 1877, I., p. 405. **39,** Metcalf, unhardened crucible steel. Metallurg. Rev., I., p. 403. **40,** Pittsburgh Steel Casting Co., Rept. Select. Comm. Ord. and War Ships, p. 356. **41,** Bethlehem, Bessemer steel, private communication. **42,** Crescent, Bessemer steel, Journ. Iron and St. Inst., 1883, II., p. 603. **43-4,** Terre Noire, unforged annealed open-hearth casting. Jeans, Steel, p. 807. **45-6,** two bars prepared by Gruner. Journ. Iron and Steel Inst., 1883, II., p. 811, from Ann. Mines, 1883, I. **47 to 50,** Midvale, Rept. Select Comm. Ord. and War Ships, p. 384. **51-2,** Cambria, Idem, p. 309. **53 to 60,** Midvale, Idem, p. 385: untempered. **61,** Midvale, Proc. U. S. Naval Inst., XIII., p. 25.

§ 232. SLOW COOLING. We have already seen that slow cooling should diminish the volume of the pipe,[e] and it appears that it tends to prevent blowholes as well. Thus Chernoff[f] finds that if moderately hot steel be cast in a mould one side of which is of sand and the other of iron, blowholes form next the iron side of the mould but none along the sand side. (Fig. 51.) In two sets of experiments I thought there were more tubules in rapidly frozen than in slowly frozen ice from the same water: but the indications were not conclusive.

[e] § 225.

[f] Revue Universelle, 2d Ser., VII., p. 135, 1880.

I am not sure that I understand Chernoff's explanation of the greater solidity of the slowly cooled steel. It seems to be as follows. The steel is less prone to wet the sand than the iron side of the mould, because at the sand side both steel and mould are hotter than at the other: as the steel wets the mould less, so bubbles are less likely to be

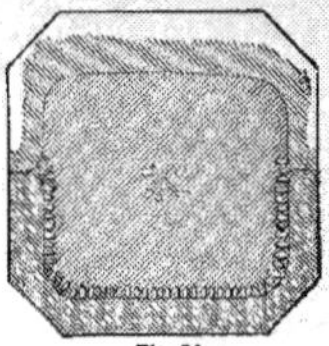

Fig. 51
Influence of rate of cooling on subcutaneous blow-holes. (Chernoff.)

detained. Now this may be true before solidification sets in: but I see no reason to expect that, after the outer shell has frozen, the fact that before freezing it had not wet the mould should now prevent it from retaining gas bubbles.

Wetting the mould can have nothing to do with the greater abundance of blowholes in rapidly than in slowly frozen ice, for here the initial conditions are the same in both cases, and the mould as wet as possible in each. I offer the following as a simpler explanation, but not as the sole nor indeed as necessarily the chief one.

When the first layers solidify, their falling solvent power expels a portion of their gas, which however may not be evolved as gas, but remaining dissolved may pass by diffusion into the adjoining still molten layers, much as the alcohol of freezing cider is forced towards the centre. If, however, the layers adjoining that which is freezing are saturated and hence unable to receive more gas, that expelled from the outer freezing layer will be gasified and may form blowholes. Now diffusion is a slow process, and, if the metal solidifies rapidly, the previously dissolved gas will be driven inwards from the freezing layers into the adjoining ones faster than it can pass by diffusion through these intermediate layers into the central region: the intermediate layers soon become supersaturated, gasification and the formation of blowholes set in.

Again, if it be true that during solidification the tops of pine-tree crystals project beyond the compactly frozen mass into the molten interior, they would appear more likely to entrap and mechanically arrest rising gas bubbles, and to prevent growing bubbles from detaching themselves and rising, if their growth and the shooting out of their branches were rapid than if these processes were slow.

Indeed, whatever be the manner in which the solid portion of the metal grows, rapid growth would seem to offer less opportunity for evolved gas to free itself and swim to the surface than slow growth.

It is much harder to prevent blowholes in small than in large castings, and probably because the former, the ratio of their mass to that of their moulds and to the cooling surface being relatively small, cool and solidify faster.

While slow cooling tends to prevent piping and blowholes, it may lead to segregation, the concentration of the foreign elements in certain portions of the casting. A double injury results: the metal is heterogeneous, and it has not the composition aimed at.

Wellman would cool slowly by lining common prismatic cast-iron ingot-moulds with refractory matter.[a]

§ 233. CHEMICAL ADDITIONS, silicon,[b] manganese, carbon aluminium.[c] The action of the latter is obscure: as that of the former three is probably due to their increasing the solubility of the gases in the metal, they should be and are added immediately before casting. Needless to say that, by checking the escape of gas during solidification and so preventing the formation of blowholes, they favor the formation of pipes.

The proportion of silicon and manganese which are

[a] U. S. Patent, 298,642, May 13th, 1884, S. T. Wellman. The immediate object of the invention is to cool the ingot so slowly and hence uniformly that it may be forged immediately on removal from the mould, without furnacing.

[b] Cf. § 215.

[c] Cf. § 140, B, p. 87.

TABLE 80.—COMPOSITION AND PROPERTIES OF UNFORGED STEEL CASTINGS (CF. TABLE 9, PAGE 19).

Number.	Authority.	Description.	Composition. C.	Si.	M.	P.	S.	Physical properties. Tensile strength, lbs. per sq. in.	Elastic limit, lbs. per sq. in.	Elongation. %	In.	Contraction of area.
1	A.	Terre Noire projectiles	·45@·60	·25@·80	·50@·60							
2	P. N.	Miscellaneous castings: Works Q	·20@·66	·10@·15	·5 @1·0							
3	"	" " " C	·35@·50	·2 @·20±	1·0±							
4	"	Rolls: Works C	·66	·20±	1·±							
5	P.	Cylinders about 6′ × 6′ and 9″ thick	·65	·25@·80	1· @1·3			70,000+		8+		
6	S.	Miscellaneous castings	·11	·40	·61			68,000		12	2″	
7	"	" "	·22	·19	·48			68,000		12	2″	
8	"	" "	·89	·30	·25			55,000		9	2″	
9	"	" "	·27	·33	·39			70,000		6	2″	
10	"	" "	·28	·23	·38			64,000		7·5	2″	
11		Graz castings	·4 @·5	·3 @·4	·45@·60							
12	J. H.	Large sound castings	·25	·25	·3 @·4							
13	"	Small " "	·4	·20	·4 @·6							
14	A. H.	Terre Noire soft steel castings	·18±	·263	·66			72,576	38,080	25·6	4″	43·5
15	"	" " very hard "	·7 @1·2	·5 @·6	·7 @1·6							
16	"	" " " soft "	·18@·20	·10@·25	·40@1·90							
21	W. H.	6 in. cast-steel gun, unannealed	·89	·299	1·01			92,706	51,960	12·5		
22	W. H.	20 foot steel cast cylinder, FORGED	·95	·408	·74			132,700	84,808	16	2″	31·07
23	B.	Rolling mill roll, open-hearth steel; broke in use	·42	·42	·96							
24	B.	" " " " " " " "	1·15	·77	1·30							
25	B.	" " " " " remarkably tough	·45	·11	·65							
26	B.	" " " crucible steel	·57	·29	·42							
27	E.	Hard steel for projectiles. Terre Noire	·635	·55	·95					1·	3·93″	
28	E.	Medium hard steel " "	·425	·215	·75					12·	3·93″	
29	E.	Soft metal " "	·260	·25	·41					22·8	3·93″	

1. Åkerman, Journ. Iron and St. Inst., 1879, II., p. 590.
2 to 4. Private notes.
5. Pourcel, Journ. Iron and St. Inst., 1882, II., p. 509.
6 to 10. Salom, Trans. Am. Inst. Mining Engrs., XIV., p. 126, 1886.
11. Graz, Steel Castings, Engineering, 1882, II., p. 352.
12, 13. Hardisty, Journ. Iron and St. Inst., 1886, I., p. 128.
14. Holley, Priv. Rept. on Terre Noire process, 2d Ser., VII., p. 47.
15, 16. Holley, Priv. Rept., 2d Ser., IX., p. 24.
21. 6 in. cast-steel gun, cast by the Pittsburg Steel Casting Co. Private communication, Wm. Hainsworth. Eight tests made at Washington on pieces from this gun are reported to have given the following average results: Tensile strength, 80,198; elastic limit, 43,395; elongation, 9·5; reduction of area, 11·70.
22. Cylinders 20 feet by 20 feet, by the Pittsburg Steel Casting Co., for a hydraulic forging press. The tests were made by Carnegie, Phipps & Co. on a piece forged from the casting. Private communication March 25, 1887.
23 to 26. G. H. Billings, Norway Iron Works. Private communication, Feb. 10, 1883.
27 to 29. Euverte, Mem. Société des Ingenieurs Civils, 1877, p. 153. Eng. and Mining Jl., 1877, p. 869.

needed to prevent blowholes may be inferred from the examples in Table 80, while the proportion of these elements that should be added in order to produce given composition will be considered in treating of the open-hearth process. Suffice it here to say that, in general, the more carbon is present the less silicon and manganese are required.

Of especial present interest is No. 21 of Table 80, the six-inch steel cast gun lately made by the Pittsburgh Steel Casting Company. The composition and physical properties of many other unforged steel castings are given in Table 9, p. 19.

It is in large part owing to the great advances in preventing blowholes by the use of silicon and manganese that methods of liquid compression have received so little attention of late.

§ 234. Descending Mould-Bottom.—In order to shorten the fall of the metal during teeming, and thus to diminish the quantity of air drawn down by the friction of the falling stream, G. W. Billings places within his vertical prismatic mould a piston moved by a cylinder standing beneath. When teeming begins this piston is raised to near the top of the mould, and is gradually lowered as teeming proceeds, so as to keep the upper surface of the molten metal always near the mould top.[a] As the mould can have little or no taper and as there must therefore be considerable play, one fears that the molten metal may run down past the piston, jam it, and perhaps freeze upon the mechanism beneath; and that the ingot may stick to the mould and refuse to descend with the piston.

§ 235. Dead-melting or killing, *i. e.* holding steel in a molten state before casting, greatly lessens the formation of blowholes. Thus crucible steel which would yield honeycombed ingots if poured as soon as melted, yields solid ones if "killed," *i. e.* simply held molten for say an hour.

As shown in § 361, killing in the crucible process probably acts chiefly through enabling the molten metal to absorb silicon from the walls of the crucible, thus increasing its solvent power for gas, so that it is able to retain during solidification the gas which it contains while molten.

CHAPTER XIII.

Structure and Related Subjects.

§ 236. In general.—The structure of iron may be studied by microscopic examination of polished and of etched surfaces, and through its fracture. The former tells us the true condition of the metal before it is subjected to the strains which cause rupture: while the fracture rather tells us of the planes of weakness in the metal, functions of the structure and of the method of rupture jointly. Each method throws valuable light on the structure.

Passing ever from the simpler to the complex, let us first consider the former. But let it not be thought that because the simpler it is the easier. The difficulties attending the microscopic study of the ultimate structure as revealed by polished sections, due in part to the considerable length of the waves of light when compared with the size of the ultimate crystals of the metal, are so great that the results obtained by one observer only, Sorby, have given us any important insight into the question.

Pushing the etching of polished surfaces a degree further leads to a third method of study, differential solution, or dissolving certain of the components of the metal by appropriate solvents, as in Weyl's method, obtaining the other components as a skeleton which preserves the original structure. By this plan, which promises a rich harvest, Osmond and Werth have already reached valuable results.

After considering the facts reached by these methods, we may in this connection conveniently study segregation (a cause of local variation of structure), as well as the effects of heat treatment, forging, cold-rolling, wire-drawing and punching on the physical properties of the metal as taught by the testing machine.

Part 1st, Microscopic Study of Polished Sections.

§ 237. General Phenomena.—From the microscopic study of polished sections iron appears to be constituted, like granite and similar compound crystalline rocks, of grains of several distinct crystalline minerals, of which seven common ones have already been recognized, through peculiarities of crystalline form and habit, color, lustre, hardness and behavior towards solvents. Their nature, size, shape and orientation, and through these the structure and physical properties of the metal as a whole, seem to depend chiefly:

1. On the ultimate chemical composition of the mass;

2. On the mechanical treatment which it has undergone;

3. On the conditions under which it has been heated and cooled, *i. e.*, its "heat-treatment," which may induce the ultimate components of the mass to regroup themselves in new combinations, thus causing one set of minerals to give place to another.

It is too early to insist that these apparently distinct substances are true minerals, that the general features of their life-history,—*e. g.* the constancy of their composition, crystalline form, hardness, density, color, etc.,—are so far like those of the minerals of nature as to make it expedient to class them permanently in the same division of nature's objects. Some distinct class-name suggesting their resemblance to minerals, such as "metarals," may be found desirable. Meanwhile, the known phenomena can be conveniently presented by classing these substances provisionally as minerals, and by provisionally assigning them mineralogical names.

During the initial crystallization of the mass from a molten or semi-molten state some one dominant mineral,

[a] U. S. Patent, 298,661-2, May 13, 1884. Cf. U. S. Patent, 319,779-80, June 9, 1885, F. Billings and W. R. Hinsdale.

dominant through its abundance, though its higher freezing point, through strong crystallizing tendency or what not, seems to determine the form, size and orientation of its own crystallization: it displaces the other components to a certain extent. A second component mineral crystallizes next, and has the second place in determining the structure. As the dominant mineral has already determined the position of the components of this secondary mineral, the crystallization of the latter can do little more than to determine the size, shape and orientation of its own crystals, and even these may have been already determined to a great extent by the space which the dominant mineral has left the second one to form in. And so on with a third and fourth.

To illustrate. Certain meteoric irons consist chiefly of three minerals, a dominant metallic one, a second metallic one, and a phosphide of iron and nickel, schreibersite. The dominant metallic one appears to crystallize first in strongly marked, regular, thin meshes of the Widmanstätten figuring (figure 52). Between these meshes the second mineral crystallizes, while the schreibersite lies between these two sets of crystals, dislodged, residual from the solidification of its more powerful elder brothers.

Now after this original crystallization has occurred, with change of temperature, affinities changing, the elements present may re-group themselves forming new minerals, or the old minerals may assume new crystalline shapes. But the position and the general outline

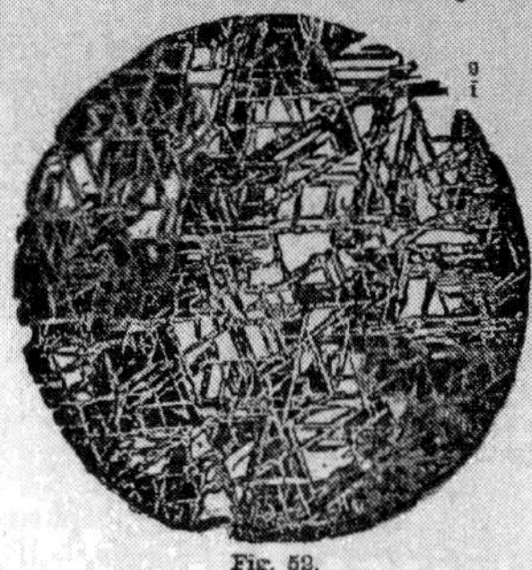

Fig. 52.
Tazewell meteoric iron, Sorby, showing Widmanstätten figuring.

of the crystals of the new species may still be determined by the original crystallization, for this has distributed the elements in certain proportions, and, in recrystallizing

TABLE 31.—MINERALS WHICH COMPOSE IRON.

Number.	Name. Sorby's.	Name. Suggested here.	Probable composition.	Occurrence. An important constituent of	Occurrence. Little or none present in.	Occurrence. Occurs chiefly in.	Color by Direct illumination.	Color by Oblique illumination.	Lustre.	Behavior on heating.	Form, habit, etc.	Hardness.	Relative solubility.
1.	Free iron.	Ferrite.	Nearly pure iron.	Malleable iron, chief component. Open grey cast-iron, especially when annealed. Forms about ⅔ of pearlyte.	....	Malleable iron.	......	....	......	Crystallizes, segregates from thin plates to grains.	Crystals, probably interfering cubes or octahedra, homogeneous, malleable! Nearly or quite equiaxed after hot forging: elongated by cold-work: made equiaxed by reheating. Sometimes as shells surrounding and shooting into crystals of pearlyte: also as parallel plates within and dowelling the crystals together. In grey pig probably as about layer against graphite	Comparatively soft.	More soluble than cementite
2.	Iron combined with carbon in the intensely hard compound.	Cementite	Iron with carbon.	About ⅓ of refined white cast-iron, and ½ of spiegeleisen. About ⅓ of pearlyte	Open grey cast-iron, soft steels, weld- and ingot-iron.	......	Intensely brilliant.	Perfectly black.	......	Changes little, segrating somewhat. Changes to ferrite on losing its carbon.	Usually structure-less, occasionally in flat plates, say, ·00,001@·02 in. thick. In blister-steel as net-work surrounding and occasionally shooting into crystals of pearlyte.	Intensely hard. 6 (Müller)	Less soluble than ferrite.
3.	"The pearly constituent or compound" recrystallized	Pearlyte.	A mixture of about ⅔ ferrite and ⅓ cementite.	Ingot- and weld-steel of all kinds unless hardened. Almost sole component of moderately hard steel (·70 % carbon ?).	Very soft iron.	....	Dark on brilliant metallic ground in refined white pig.	Bright and pearly on black ground in refined white pig.	....	Components combine at a high temperature to form hardenite.	Pearly, fine parallel plates, curved and straight, of ferrite, 1-40,000 in. alternated with cementite 1-80,000 in. thick. In soft ingots in irregular groups, often 1-30 in. diam., independent of ingot-structure. Also in ostrich-feather crystals in white pig iron.		
4.	"The pearly constituent or compound" imperfectly stallized.	Hardenite	Iron and hardening carbon probably in all proportions up to 2 or possibly 3 %.	In Bessemer and probably all other classes of steel when quenched. Arises from union of all minerals present.	Annealed or slowly cooled steel and cast-iron and in very soft iron under all conditions	....	....	....	....	Separates (probably below W) into pearlyte and free ferrite or cementite.	Very minute grains, about 1-20,000 in. diam.	Intensely hard.	More soluble than cementite
5.	Ruby and dark crystals.	Sorbite.	Perhaps silicon or nitride of titanium.	....	Weld iron and good cast-steel.	Cast-iron.	Ruby and deep blue.		....	....	Triangles, rhombs, hexagons, complex crosses, less than 1-1000 in. in diameter.		
6.	Graphite.		Carbon.	Cast-iron.	Steel, ingot and weld iron.	Cast-iron.	Iron black.		Metallic	Changes but little and slowly.	Comparatively large, somewhat irregular plates, often bent, tapering edges, laminar. In grey Scotch pig, uniformly distributed, ·03@·05 in. broad, ·0005@·0010 in. thick. In No. 3 pig partly in irregular radiating groups.	1 to 2.	Insoluble.
7.	Slag.		....	Weld iron and steel.	Ingot iron and ingot steel.	....	Black.		....	....	In hammered blooms is in irregular patches; in bar, plate, etc., iron in fine threads. Very irregularly distributed.		
8.	Undetermined residue.		Probably matrix or residue from formation of substances 1 to 6, and hence of widely varying composition.	Cast-iron.	....	....	... .		Metallic				
9.	More soluble metallic substance.		....	Components of meteoric iron.	....	....	....		... .	... .	A rhombic lattice- or net-work, orientation often uniform over a considerable area.	... .	More soluble than 10.
10.	Less soluble metallic substance.		....		....	....	....		....	....	Often crystallized in relation to the orientation of the inclosing net-work of No. 10.	....	Less soluble than 9.
11.	Schreibersite.		Iron, 55·4@67·2%. Nickel, 4·2@28·1%. Phosphorus, 7·3@14·9%.		. . ..	.. ...	. ...		.....	....	Often a thin skin covering the net-work of No. 10.		

the crystallizing force can move each molecule but a short distance. Thus in certain meteoric irons, while the original Widmanstätten figuring is readily traced by the layer of schreibersite which still exists, the ultimate structure of the material composing the net-work is in no way related to the shape of the net-work itself, but consists "of a mass of interfering granular crystals,"* apparently due to recrystallization. Under other conditions the recrystallizing force may be so great as to efface all

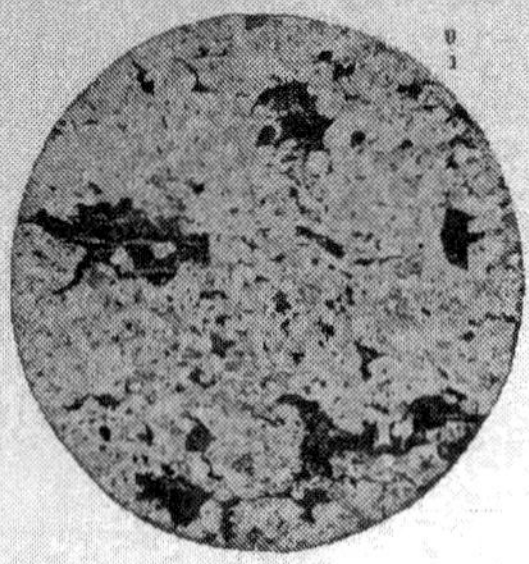

Fig. 53.
Hammered wrought-iron bloom, Sorby, showing large black patches of slag.

pre-existing crystallization. Examples will follow: suffice it here to say that in commercial iron we now find the effects of but a single crystallization, now the superimposed effects of two if not three successive ones. As a mineral is more likely to be the dominant one when abundantly present, so we find that a given mineral,—here forming the bulk, there but a small fraction of the whole,—may here form the nucleus around which the others crys-

Fig. 54.
Longitudinal section of wrought-iron armor-plate, Sorby, showing welds and crystals (of ferrite?)

tallize, may there lie as a residual layer between the crystals of the other minerals.

§ 238. The Components of Iron Described.—Both for brevity and clearness in describing the chief minerals which have been recognized in iron, I venture to substitute mineralogical names for Sorby's cumbrous ones.

It is not improbable that some of our present species may hereafter be subdivided. Their form, composition and other characteristics, like those of many natural minerals, probably vary within rather wide limits. As most of them occur in minute if not microscopic crystals which have not been separated for analysis, we can only arrive at their composition indirectly.

Table 81 describes the properties of these minerals.

A. *Ferrite* is probably nearly pure iron. It occurs in two distinct conditions, I., as a separate constituent, II., as a component of pearlyte.

I. As a separate mineral, ferrite is the chief component of all irons nearly free from combined carbon, to wit soft weld-

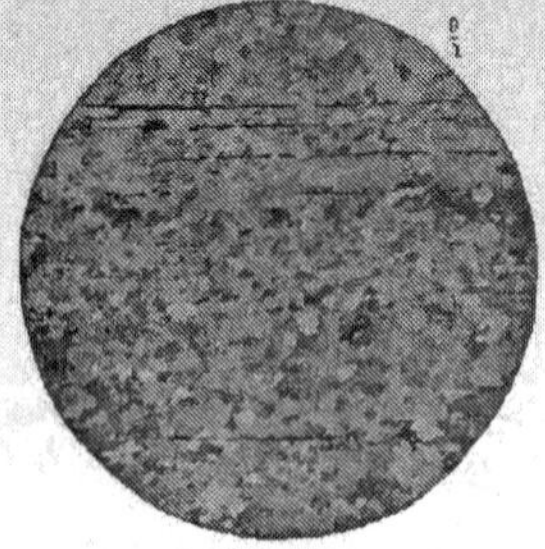

Fig. 55.
Longitudinal section of wrought-iron bar, Sorby, showing rods of slag, and crystals of ferrite.

and ingot-iron and certain very open gray cast-irons, which consist chiefly of iron and graphite, the iron here usually containing considerable silicon. In general the proportion of ferrite decreases as that of combined carbon increases, so that it is nearly or quite absent from hard steels and from all cast-iron except the very gray.

When, as in soft ingot- and weld-iron, it is almost the

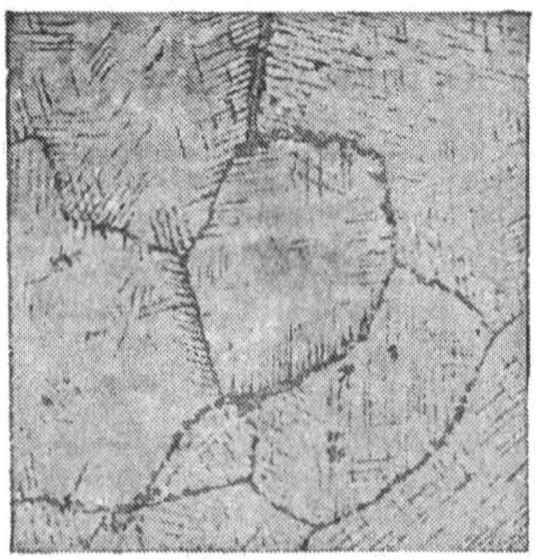

Fig. 56.
Transverse section of Bessemer ingot (0·42% C), Sorby. Polygons are pearlyte, net-work is ferrite.

sole constituent, it occurs in grains which are almost certainly more or less imperfect interfering crystals, cubes, octahedra, pentagonal dodecahedra, and perhaps other forms of the monometric or regular system. (Figures 53, 54 and 55.) Individually malleable grains 0·25 inch in diameter, probably of ferrite, are mentioned in § 246, B. When much slag is present, as in weld-iron, it is drawn out by rolling into fibres: the mass as a whole is fibrous: but even here the metallic or ferrite quasi-fibres usually consist of separate equiaxed grains.

*Sorby, Journ. Iron and Steel Inst., 1887, I., p. 285.

When, as in rather soft steels and in gray cast-iron, ferrite as a separate mineral is present in but small quantity, it is distributed as a net-work or as a series of shells surrounding crystals of the other components. Thus, in

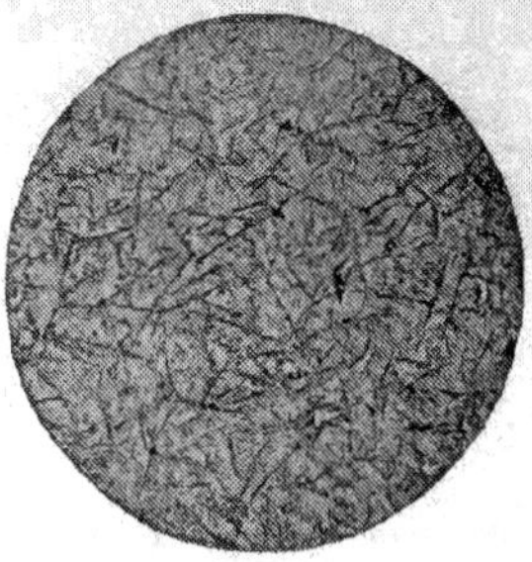

Fig. 57.
Grey cast-iron, Sorby. Prominent plates are graphite: matrix probably ferrite and pearlyte.

an ingot of rather soft steel (figure 56), what appears to be ferrite is indicated by the dark parallel plates and the net-work enclosing irregular grains which consist of pearlyte. The spines which run from the net-work of ferrite appear to dowel the crystals of pearlyte together. Here, too, the ferrite in the thicker strings may be seen to consist of small grains like those in weld-iron.

In some gray cast-iron, on the other hand, what appears to be ferrite exists as stout layers in contact with the crystals of graphite. (Figure 57.)

II. Ferrite as a constituent of pearlyte is described below.

B. *Cementite* (Sorby's "intensely hard compound") occurs I. as a separate mineral, II. as a component of pearlyte. From Sorby's researches it appears to be an intensely hard, brilliant, homogeneous, structureless carbide of iron, containing the whole of the cement carbon. It has not been recognized in and is probably absent from hardened steel, but is abundantly present in that which is unhardened.

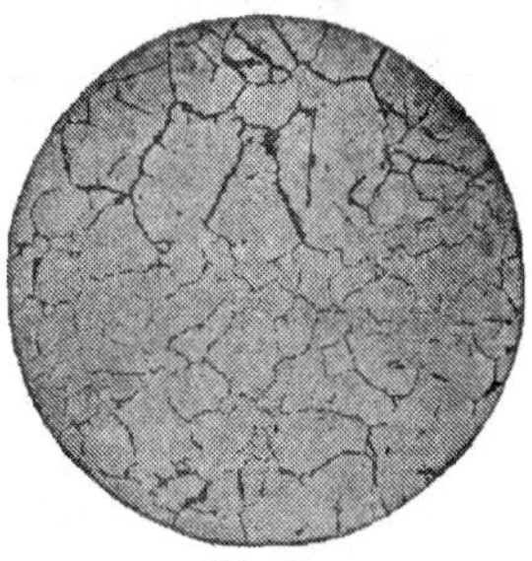

Fig. 58.
Longitudinal section of blister steel, Sorby. Light polygons are pearlyte, black net-work is cementite.

Osmond and Werth thought their cell-shells (§ 239), which were probably cementite enclosing kernels of pearlyte, more hard and rigid than the kernels: and, on etching polished sections of cold-hammered steel, they found that while the kernels (pearlyte?) were elongated, the shells (cementite?) were shattered so as to suggest the schistosity of rocks.[a]

The relation between the proportion of cementite present as a separate mineral and that of combined carbon will be considered in C. In blister steel Sorby found the cementite as a net-work surrounding irregular grains of pearlyte (figure 58), and occasionally shooting into them so as to dowel them together, like but less than the ferrite of soft steel (figure 56). In bar iron which had been partly converted into blister steel by cementation, he found plates of cementite towards the outside, which were visible to the naked eye on etching. In spiegeleisen cementite appears to form the large plates "so conspicuous in fractures," here perhaps containing much manganese.

The carbide-residue[b] obtained by Müller on dissolving unhardened steel in dilute sulphuric acid, probably representing cementite perhaps more or less altered by the solvent, consists of rough-surfaced, silver-lustred, gray, irregular, generally roundish grains, seldom over 0·0004 inch (0·01 mm.) in diameter, apparently of a single substance. They scratch glass and felspar, but not quartz (H = 6), are exceedingly brittle, pyrophoric, attracted

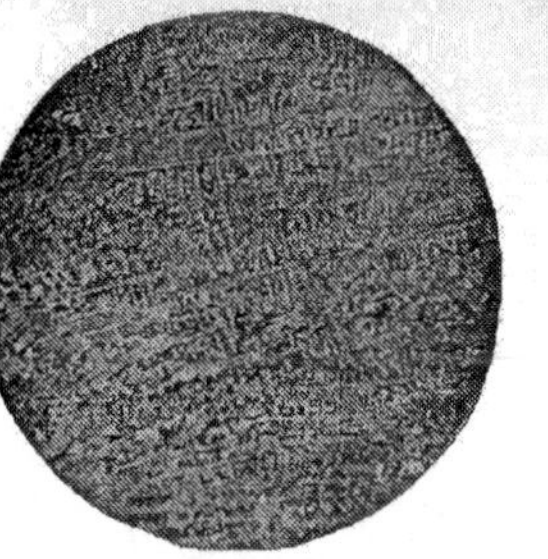

Fig. 59.
Transverse section of white refined cast-iron, Sorby. Feather crystals are pearlyte; the black matrix is cementite.

and permanently magnetized by the magnet, unmelted at redness, insoluble in cold dilute acids, attacked with extreme difficulty by copper-salt solution, but soluble in boiling moderately concentrated hydrochloric and sulphuric acid, leaving a slight residue.[c]

Cementite as a component of pearlyte is described in the next paragraph.

C. *Pearlyte* (Sorby's pearly constituent) is composed of very minute parallel curved or straight plates, often showing very brilliant interference colors, and composed alternately of cementite and ferrite, which form about one-third and two-thirds of the whole respectively. It is, therefore, as its spelling implies, a lithological rather than a mineralogical unit. It is clearly not a mere accidental mixture, nor are its plates due to cleavage, but they are apparently joint paramorphs after a single pre-existing mineral, probably hardenite.

Our present data give no certain information about the composition of pearlyte: but they tend to show that it varies within rather wide limits, some facts suggesting that it contains not over 0·67% of carbon, others that it

[a] Ann. Mines, 8th ser., VIII., pp. 15. 79, 1885.
[b] Cf. § 9, p. 6.
[c] Stahl und Eisen, VIII., p. 291, 1888.

contains not less than 1·5%.[a] Whether the discrepancy is due to variations in the composition or in the relative proportions of its two components, or to errors of observation, is uncertain.

It appears that cementite and ferrite usually unite as far as possible to form pearlyte, so that any free cementite is simply an excess over that which is needed to form pearlyte with the whole of the ferrite, present: so with the ferrite, mutatis mutandis. Thus pearlyte may be accompanied by either ferrite or cementite, but not usually by both together in the same the region. Hence, as the proportion of combined carbon increases in unhardened metal from nil, we have first pure ferrite, then ferrite with a proportion of pearlyte which increases up to 100%, and in turn diminishes as the proportion of combined carbon increases further, being replaced more and more by free cementite.

For example, Sorby finds that the least carburetted iron consists of free ferrite with only a little pearlyte, and apparently no free cementite: that moderately hard steel (with say ·67% of carbon) consits almost solely of pearlyte, with very little of either free cementite or free ferrite: that hard steel (with say 1·08% of carbon) contains pearlyte together with some free cementite: that still harder steel (with perhaps 2% of carbon) contains pearlyte with much cementite: that white cast-iron is composed of about two-thirds pearlyte and one-third cementite: while spiegeleisen, finally, contains about 50% of each.

So, too, he finds that the centre of a bar of soft iron, partly converted into steel by cementation, consists chiefly of grains of ferrite: around this is a ring of almost pure pearlyte: while the outside, the most carburetted part, consists of pearlyte with scattered plates of cementite. After further cementation he found that the cementite now penetrated to the centre of the bar, replacing the ferrite: but the outer part of the bar now contained little or no more cementite than before.

Pearlyte crystallizes most characteristically in ingots of moderately hard steel, of which it is almost the sole component, occurring chiefly in irregular groups of plates radiating at all azimuths from central points distributed with little or no relation to the primary crystals (the conspicuous prismatic or columnar ones, normal to the cooling surface, and seen on fracture, figures 64, 65, 68), and indeed often branching from one into another, dovetailing them together.

In softer and harder steel ingots and in gray cast-iron the radiate grouping of the pearlyte is interfered with by the presence of ferrite, cementite, and graphite respectively, while in forgings less time is usually available for recrystallization than in ingots: small bars indeed do not show the characteristic "structure, but look as if the constituents had been broken up, irregularly mixed, and cooled so rapidly as to prevent the development of definite crystals."[b]

In Sorby's "forge" and "white refined" cast-iron pearlyte forms ostrich-feather crystals, figure 59, in the latter metal within a matrix of cementite.

The crystalline form of the minerals which compose the crystalline rocks varies in a similar way. Thus, among the varieties of a single mineral, amphibole, we have the granular pargasite, the needle-like actinolite, and the fine thread-like asbestus.

Long exposed to a high temperature, as in annealing, pearlyte draws together and separates itself in more perfect crystals from the ferrite or cementite which accompanies it; and, in some cases, part of it is resolved into thicker laminæ or even more solid masses of free cementite and ferrite. If, however, the pearlyte be initially accompanied by graphite, its cementite apparently tends to split up into graphite and ferrite at a moderately high temperature, which suggests that the graphite-forming tendency initially unsatisfied, with favoring temperature, now reasserts itself.

D. *Hardenite* is the characteristic component of hardened steel, a compound of iron and hardening carbon. On quenching a steel, which had consisted of a net-work of ferrite enclosing kernels of pearlyte (figure 56), Sorby could still detect traces of the the original net-work: but the ultimate structure was now so fine that even a power of 400 linear showed little more than that the grains were now about 1-20,000th inch in diameter, and no longer revealed the fine laminations of pearlyte. The abrupt changes in the chemical behavior, hardness, fracture and microscopic structure effected by quenching leave little doubt that the ferrite and cementite of pearlyte unite at a high temperature to form a new compound, which we may term hardenite, in which the carbon exists in the hardening state. All the evidence, from whatever source, indicates that this hardenite is preserved by quenching, but gradually splits up during slow cooling, ultimately yielding ferrite and cementite, and thus forming pearlyte.

The micro-structural changes induced by quenching are not fully understood: the comparative coarseness of the waves of light makes their study very difficult. It is probable that the change from pearlyte to hardenite coincides with the change from cement to hardening carbon, and hence that it occurs at or about a low yellow heat (Brinnell's W): but direct evidence is lacking.

Now the composition of hardenite may be approximately constant, or, like that of obsidian, it may be altogether indefinite. If constant, we may suppose that, when steel

[a] These numbers, arrived at somewhat as in the reconstruction of fossils, must be taken as very rough approximations. In Bessemer steel, apparently of 0·49% of carbon, Sorby finds pearlyte and ferrite, apparently about 10% the latter, which would imply that pearlyte here contains about 0·54% of carbon. A soft steel ingot which was composed almost solely of pearlyte, and whose composition may therefore be taken as approximately that of this mineral, was the softest of three whose average carbon was about 1·25%: the carbon of the ingot of intermediate hardness was 1·08%. This ingot consisted of pearlyte with cementite, and was therefore clearly more highly carburetted than cementite. Hence cementite contains somewhere between 0·49 and 1·08% of carbon. Now the hard ingot of the three, described as "very hard steel" made from Swedish iron by cementation and crucible melting, would not be likely to contain more than 2% of carbon. If it had 2%, then our data imply that the softest of the three had 0·67% of carbon. If the hard ingot held less than 2% of carbon, the soft one must hold more than 0·67%. But the soft ingot is described as of "soft" (crucible) "steel," a term which would hardly be used if more than 0·67% of carbon were present.

If, as Sorby estimates by the eye, pearlyte consists of two parts by volume of ferrite and one of cementite, and if these two minerals have nearly the same density, then the conclusion that pearlyte has about 0·67% of carbon implies that cementite has about 2%.

On the other hand, Sorby finds that spiegeleisen of the kind made twenty years ago consists of about equal parts of cementite and pearlyte. This implies that the free cementite together with that in the pearlyte constitute about 67% of the whole mass. It is not likely that the spiegeleisen contained less than 3% of carbon: hence the cementite should contain not less than 4·5% of carbon, or the pearlyte not less than 1·5%.

If, as is more likely, the spiegeleisen contained 5% of carbon, its cementite should contain 7·5 of carbon. This is almost exactly the composition of the carbide which Abel and Müller isolate on dissolving steel in mild solvents. (Cf. Müller, Stahl und Eisen, VIII., p. 292, 1888.)

Were the spiegeleisen to contain, in addition to pearlyte and cementite, a mineral exceedingly rich in carbon, the discrepancy would disappear,

[b] Sorby, Op. Cit., p. 276.

TABLE 82.—COMPOSITION OF SLAG IN WELD IRON.

No.	1	2	3	4	5	6	7	8	9	10	11	12	13	14	15	16	17	18	19
Silica	12·86	1·55	2·01	8·87	0	4·09	6·49	3·62	9·21	0·44	10·84	2·37	1·39	7·65	9·4	2·86	0	......	......
Phosphoric acid	3·28	·32	......	......	......	......	......	......	......	......	......	......	......	......	......	......	......	......	......
Ferrous oxide	55·71	85·87	......	......	......	......	......	......	......	......	......	......	......	......	......	......	......	......	......
Ferric oxide	25·64	11·50	80·42	66·24	94·20	82·09	81·63	88·71	83·20	87·18	76·21	96·28	94·16	90·74	96·94	96·19	98·95	......	......
Oxide of Manganese	·51	·32	......	......	......	......	......	......	......	0·43	7·07	1·01	......	0·40	0·37	......	......	......	......
Alumina	1·34	......	......	......	......	......	......	......	......	......	......	......	......	......	......	......	......	......	......
Sulphur	·124	·028	......	......	......	......	......	......	......	......	......	......	......	......	......	......	......	......	......
Chromic oxide	......	......	14·90	30·56	3·62	16·76	15·77	12·88	12·08	8·01	5·52	1·61	6·94	......	......	2·62	5·21	......	......
Cuprous oxide	......	......	0	0	0	0	0	0	0	0	tr.	0	0·14	tr.	0	tr.	0	......	......

1. Slag from puddled ball, Bell, Manufacture of Iron and Steel, p. 360.
2. Slag from West Yorkshire boiler-plate, *idem*.
3 to 17. Calculated from data in Rept. of U. S. Bd. on Testing Iron, Steel, etc., 1881, I., p. 223.

is strongly heated, the components of pearlyte alone unite to form hardenite, the initially separate ferrite or cementite remaining separate. If indefinite, and this seems to me far the more probable view, we may suppose that it is formed by the union of the initially separate cementite or ferrite jointly with the two components of pearlyte, yielding a single substance, which is preserved during sudden cooling simply because, like obsidian, it has not time to separate into definite compounds. That such an indiscriminate union occurs when steel melts is altogether probable: but whether it occurs at lower temperatures, say between a dull yellow and whiteness, is uncertain.

The fact that hardened steel usually contains some cement carbon, indicating the presence of cementite, might suggest that hardenite tends toward certain definite compositions, and that, when some one of these is reached (which one would depend on the special conditions of the case), it declines to assimilate the rest of the carbon, which remains as cementite. Thus in hardened steel Abel[a] found some 4·7% of the total carbon insoluble in his solvent, i. e. as cement carbon: by Weyl's method Osmond and Werth[b] found in hardened steel a delicate net-work holding by indirect calculation about 62% of the total carbon. But a far more probable explanation is that, even in their rapid coolings, the interior of the metal passed slowly enough through the range of temperature in which hardenite changes to cementite and ferrite, to permit a considerable formation of these latter minerals. In harmony with this is Müller's finding absolutely no cement carbon in fine shavings of tool steel quenched extremely rapidly. In white cast-iron, however, he found a certain quantity of cement carbon, even after extremely rapid quenching.[c] Further observations are needed.

Again, the apparently constant proportions of cementite and ferrite of which pearlyte consists strongly indicate that it springs from the decomposition of some mineral of tolerably constant composition: this in turn suggests that hardenite has the definite ultimate composition of pearlyte, and that, just as annealed steel consists of pearlyte with either ferrite or cementite, so hardened steel consists of a mixture of one of these two minerals with hardenite. This view is opposed (1) by the homogeneous appearance of hardened steel, in which the highest powers fail to discover a trace of either ferrite or cementite, and (2) by the fact that hardened steel of 2% of carbon is harder than that of say 0·67%, though the latter should be nearly pure hardenite (if, as this view assumes, hardenite has the same ultimate composition as pearlyte), and the former hardenite mixed with much cementite, while the softness of annealed steel indicates that cementite is softer than hardenite.[d]

Yet, by a possible if unwelcomely complex supposition, we may hold that hardenite, obsidian-like, is of indefinite composition—the sole constituent of hardened steel—and yet that pearlyte springs from the decomposition of a mineral of definite composition. For during slow cooling our indefinite hardenite may first split up into (1) a suppositious mineral of definite composition—call it "mother-of-pearlyte"—and (2) separate cementite or ferrite as the case may be. Later the mother-of-pearlyte splits up into the well-known parallel layers of ferrite and cementite, which constitute pearlyte. But without more facts we can hold no theory confidently.[e]

E. *Sorbite* (Sorby's ruby and deep blue crystals) has been detected by Sorby in many cast-irons, but in no other class of iron, as beautiful triangles, rhombs, hexagons and complex crosses, sometimes imbedded in graphite, usually less than 1-1000th inch in diameter, in his opinion modifications of one substance, possibly silicon or nitride of titanium.[f]

F. *Slag*, occurring chiefly in weld metal, initially in irregular patches (figure 53), is drawn out into threads by forging (figure 54), and probably contributes to the fibrousness of the enclosing metal.[g] At a high temperature it probably tends to draw together, for it has been found in almost perfect spheres within half-inch crystals of iron, probably of ferrite, in iron long held in the puddling furnace.[h]

Goedicke reports about 1% of slag in once re-rolled fine-grained puddled iron, and 1·5 to 2% in fibrous puddled iron.[i] 43 specimens of chain-cable weld-iron examined by the United States Board on Testing Iron, etc., contained from ·192 to 2·202 of slag, or 0·904% on an average.[j] The composition of these and other slags from weld iron is given in Table 82, while Table 26, p. 58, gives the composition of slag from the puddling furnace, which is here invariably much richer in silica than that from weld-iron itself. This suggests that during heating and forging the proportion of iron oxide in the slag of weld iron increases, by the oxidation of neighboring metal. As no such oxidation has been observed within ingot iron, which is usually nearly or quite free from slag, this in turn suggests that the presence of slag induces the oxidation of the iron

[a] Cf. p. 6.
[b] Ann. Mines, 8th ser., VIII., p. 20, 1885.
[c] Stahl und Eisen, VIII., p. 294, 1888, May.

[d] It will be remembered that cementite is much richer in carbon than pearlyte, (which is a mixture of cementite with the carbonless ferrite) and hence than hardenite in this view; Sorby found that unhardened soft steel ingots consisted of nearly pure pearlyte, more highly carburetted ones of pearlyte with much cementite.
[e] I believe that this idea is here suggested for the first time.
[f] Cf. § 63, p. 37. Journ. Iron and Steel Inst., 1886, I., p. 144; 1887, I., p. 278, 261.
[g] The fibrousness of weld iron is discussed in § 259.
[h] Sorby, Journ. Iron and Steel Inst., 1877, I., p. 262.
[i] Oest. Zeitschrift, XXXIV., p. 536, 1886.
[j] Rept. Bd. on Testing Iron, Steel and other metals, I., p. 223, 1881: Trans. Am. Inst. Mining Engrs., VI., p. 102.

itself. It is indeed conceivable that the silica of the slag is reduced by the excess of metallic iron surrounding it.

Table 83, calculated from the data of this board's report, shows how little connection can be traced between the proportion of slag and the physical properties of these irons.

Ingot-metal also, especially if poor in manganese, undoubtedly sometimes contains slag, probably springing chiefly from the formation of silica by reactions within the metal.[a] But we have little information concerning this slag. It has been thought to weaken the metal, and even to render it hot-short.

TABLE 83.—ANALYSIS OF THE INFLUENCE OF SLAG ON THE PROPERTIES OF WELD IRON, AND ON ITS PERCENTAGE OF CARBON.

Twelve weld irons numbered according to their tensile strength, etc., (1 highest) and placed in the order of the percentage of slag (highest first).

Number for												
Tensile strength	7	9	18	14	15	5	6	3	15	10	9	1
Reduction of area	14	3	2	16	1	10	8	9	4	5	9	17
Elongation	10	1	4	15	3	8	2	9	6	11	13	16
Welding value	9	4	2	...	8	12	10	6	5	...	13	
Shocks-resisting power	13	7	1	14	4	11	9	6	4	6	12	14
Per cent of carbon	4	5	11	7	8	3	8	9	10	8	9	1
Per cent of slag	1	2	3	4	5	6	7	8	9	10	11	12

This table is derived from data in the Report of the U. S. Board to Test Iron, Steel, etc., 1881, I., p. 224, Table 111.

At Avesta slag was at one time mixed with the Bessemer ingot iron when this was poured into the moulds. (Cf. § 259).

Wedding finds the slag in fibrous iron in the form of thin pods, which completely envelope every fibre of iron.[b] But Sorby, whose authority is of the very highest, and who questions the trustworthiness of Wedding's method of examination,[c] finds the slag in lumps in iron blooms, which, by forging, are drawn out into long thin rods, not pods, (figures 53 and 55).[d] But, even if uncontradicted, we could hardly accept Wedding's statement.

If such continuous surfaces of slag stretch across an iron bar, no matter how zigzag, involved and complex those surfaces may be, so long as they are continuous they must receive and transmit the entire tensile stress to which the bar is subjected: and, as the strength of a chain is that of its weakest link, so the strength of such a bar would be the strength of slag, not iron: of slag protected if you will from transverse stress by iron: of slag so hooked into fibres of iron that the stress is evenly distributed, but still of slag. And, moreover, these involved surfaces of slag which have to finally support the total stress are so attenuated that they often represent only some 1·5% of the weight of the bar. This seems so preposterous that I believe that Dr. Wedding must mean something very different from what he seems to: and certain phrases of his support this belief.

G. *Other substances.* Carbide of titanium, found in cast-iron, has already been described.[e]

H. *The Residual Compound*[f] which occurs in cast-iron is probably of wholly indefinite composition, being the residue left from the crystallization of definite minerals. Thus in a gray cast-iron it appeared to be cementite modified by impurities: in an annealed number 3 cast-iron it appeared to be a mixture of metallic iron with some other metallic substance, and resembled complex ripples.

[a] Cf. 81, p. 43. Journ. Iron and Steel Inst., 1877, I., p. 44.

[b] Journ. Iron and Steel Inst., 1885, I., p. 193. "None of these wires or fibres is directly connected with its neighbors, either in a lateral or longitudinal direction."

[c] Idem, 203.

[d] Idem, 1887, I., p. 262.

[e] § 18, p. 7.

[f] Sorby, op. cit., pp. 261, 277, 280.

§ 239. OTHER EVIDENCE OF THE COMPOSITE STRUCTURE OF IRON.—Osmond and Werth, on attacking with cold dilute nitric acid plates of annealed cast-steel, $\frac{8}{10,000}$ to $\frac{12}{10,000}$ of an inch thick, fastened to glass with Canada balsam, obtained a residual net-work of iron-carbide (cementite?), what they took for iron but what was probably pearlyte having existed as kernels within the meshes of the net-work and having dissolved.[g]

They find the minute cells of this net-work grouped in composite cells of a larger net-work, whose meshes are of a comparatively soluble substance which is free from carbide, but whose composition seems most uncertain. Their description suggests that these two sets of meshes are the fruit of a primary and a secondary crystallization respectively. Indeed the composite cells appear to them to result from dendritic growths, which, developing independently, have limited each other. As the residual net-work of iron-carbide obtained on dissolving steel by Weyl's method, *i. e.* on immersing it as the positive pole in a Bunsen cell, in dilute hydrochloric acid, retains the form and dimensions of the steel, they infer that this net-work is continuous within the metal.

Hardened steel, in which as we have seen Sorby could detect little evidence of structure, they too find much less complex, the rapid cooling having apparently opposed the formation and segregation of definite minerals, as it does in case of obsidian, and as it opposes the devitrification of glass. The simple cells alone are found, and the carbide which surrounds them is now in much smaller proportion than in annealed steel, so that most of the carbon present seems to be uniformly dissolved within the metallic kernels.

On these and other important observations they base their "cellular theory of steel,"[h] which, based on certain known and supposed properties of the metal's constituents, may be regarded as a special case of the more general proposition that the properties of the composite mass depend on those of its components and on their mutual adhesion, a proposition which is self-evident if the composite nature of steel, earlier pointed out by Sorby, be admitted.

Treating copper and zinc ingots separately by Weyl's method with a Bunsen cell (zinc in 5 of concentrated hydrochloric acid to 95 of water, copper in 5 of sulphuric acid to 95% water), they found the same general organization as in steel ingots,—metallic kernels dendritically arranged, their mutually limiting surfaces grouping them in composite cells. The residue from zinc consisted of spangles of an alloy containing about 30% of tin, 56% of lead and 15% of zinc, though the ingot as a whole contained only 0·28% of tin and 1·05% of lead. They justly say that this concentration of the impurities as a skeleton of very thin leaves throughout the mass, goes far towards explaining the wonderful influence of minute quantities of impurities on the properties of the metals in general.[i] For the properties of these leaves, minute as they are, may affect the properties of the whole as markedly as the

[g] Comptes Rendus, C., p. 450, 1885. Ann. Mines, 8th Ser., VIII., p. 9. Journ. Iron and Steel Inst., 1885, I., p. 273.

[h] This, together with its supporting evidence, is set forth at great length in the Annales des Mines, loc. cit. Additional discussion and facts appear in Stahl und Eisen, VI., p. 539, 1886; while Ledebur reviews it on p. 374 of the same volume. For our purposes it is more convenient to consider certain features of it in appropriate places, than to discuss it as a whole.

[i] Stahl und Eisen, VI., p. 541, 1886. Cf. pp. 2, 3, 4 of the present work.

minute flakes of mica in gneiss, or as certain weak links in a powerful chain.

Wedding observed that ingot metal, unless very quickly cooled, consisted of kernels enclosed in a mesh-work, which he names "crystalline" and "homogeneous" iron respectively: and he further noticed that the mesh-work was sometimes harder and sometimes softer than the kernels. But later investigation shows that these provisional names must be discarded, because with changing proportions a given mineral now forms the mesh-work, now the kernels.[a]

Sorby, Osmond and Werth, and Wedding all noticed that the composite structure was most strongly marked in unforged castings, and became less and less pronounced as the sectional area was reduced by forging.

PART 2D, FRACTURE.

§ 240. IN GENERAL.—If iron were perfectly homogeneous and without cleavage or crystallization of any kind, then the path of least resistance would be a short one, and the fracture would be smooth: but it never is. On some cases, *e. g.* in that of the columnar structure at the outside of steel ingots, the fracture follows certain large and well defined planes: it is coarse-crystalline. In others, as in properly hardened tool-steel, it follows very minute or even microscopic planes, and so has a porcelanic look. In general it follows planes, be they large or small The large columnar fracture-planes at the outside of ingots pretty clearly bound individual crystals, but in many cases it is as yet uncertain whether the planes shown on fracture are the boundaries of true crystals—distorted and imperfect, but crystals still—or merely cleavage planes within those crystals.

Now whether we admit that iron is composed of crystals of dissimilar minerals or hold that its different grains are of similar nature, it is clear that these grains may be so shaped and constituted that the cohesion between the particles of the individual crystal may be greater or may be less than the adhesion between adjoining crystals. In the former case (1) rupture passes between the faces of adjoining crystals, in the latter (2), it strikes across their bodies, or, if the difference is slight, follows the general direction of the crystal faces, yet deviating slightly to the right and left, so that some particles of each crystal adhere to the face of its neighbor. Again, large strongly-adhering crystals may be separated by a thin weak mesh-work, through which rupture passes. Or some crystals may be readily detached from their neighbors while others adhere tenaciously, when (3) rupture passes in part between the crystals and in part through their bodies. Strong adhesion may be in large part due to dowelling or branching spines shooting from one crystal into its neighbor. It is natural to refer fractures whose facets are smooth and bright to the first of these cases, those whose facets are dull-faced to the second, and those in part bright in part dull to the third. But till the relations between the fracture and the ultimate structure, as revealed by polished sections, is far more clearly made out, these references must be provisional.

It is not to be expected that, in our present ignorance of these relations and our consequent inability to fully interpret the phenomena of fracture, these phenomena can be reduced to simple laws. Indeed, we have to be thankful that, probably owing to the predominant influence of three of the constituent minerals, Brinnell's researches permit us to reduce an important part of them to even cumbrous laws. We must here recall the changes which heat-treatment induces in the condition of carbon, sketched in Figure 60.[b]

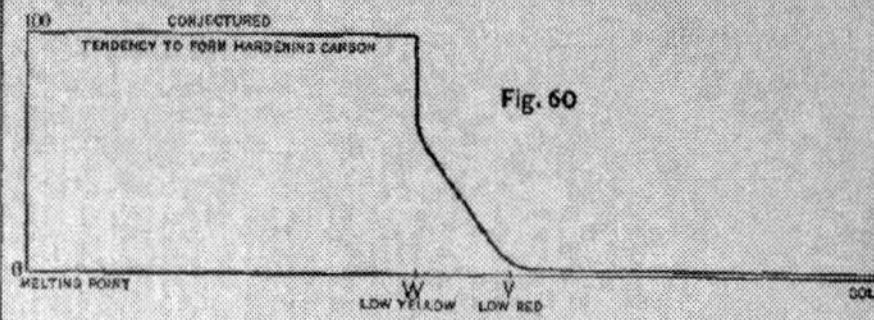

Fig. 60

Above W carbon tends to become wholly hardening, below V to become wholly cement, between W and V to distribute itself between both states according to unknown laws. The change from hardening to cement, always slow, is the slower and the more incomplete the lower the temperature, and cannot occur in the cold. Hence steels (A) slowly cooled and (B) quenched from W or above are (A) soft and (B) hard respectively, because the former's carbon has while the latter's has not had time to change from hardening to cement: tempered steel has intermediate hardness because gentle reheating has permitted partial change.

These views, deduced from wholly independent data, are supported by Brinnell's very important experiments, the results of which are graphically represented in Figure 61.

He finds[c] that when hardened steel is dipped into nitric acid of 1·23 sp. gr. it becomes covered with a black-brown, sooty, amorphous layer of carbon, giving a brown streak on white paper: that unhardened steel under these conditions acquires a coating which inclines to blue, gives a black gray streak, and appears to be crystalline. We may join him in provisionally terming these hardening and cement carbon respectively, remembering that we use these names somewhat generically, to indicate conditions of carbon each of which may be shown later to comprise several distinct varieties.[d] How far these changes of carbon-condition agree with those of hardness will be shown in § 257.

The following paragraphs detail the teaching of Brinnell's experiments, first as to the condition of carbon as inferred from the tests just described, second as to fracture. Many of the inferences are my own: but this matters little, for the evidence in support of each is given, and the reader can satisfy himself as to its validity.

§ 242. BRINNELL'S EXPERIMENTS ON THE CONDITIONS OF CARBON.—*I. That the change from cement to hardening carbon does not occur below* W, *but is sudden and complete at* W, is indicated by the following experiments. In 3, 4, 20 and 21[c] the carbon is initially cement. On

a Journ. Iron and Steel Inst., 1885, I., p. 194.

b Figure 2, which sketched these tendencies, was complicated by the graphite-forming tendency, which may be neglected here. Whether the curve reaches its maximum at W, or whether it continues to rise from W to the melting point, is uncertain. The hardness seems to increase as the quenching-temperature continues to rise beyond W, but this may be because the higher quenching-temperature leads to greater stress from uneven cooling, or to changes in crystallization.

c J. A. Brinnell, Stahl und Eisen, V., p. 611, 1885; from Jernkontoret's Annaler, 1885. Also a much over-condensed unintelligible translation in "Notes on Construction of Ordnance, No. 37," Ordnance Dept., Washington, June 22, 1886. Cf. Coffin, Trans. Am. Soc. Civ. Eng., XV , p. 818. This paper is by far the most important contribution to our knowledge of the fracture of steel since Chernoff's classical work.

d It has been proposed to abandon the name "cement" for "non-hardening." We can adopt Rinman's name "cement" as meaning the carbon of unhardened steel, without thereby committing ourselves to any particular theory as to its composition. These names are only provisional. As "cement" is well established, and as every new name increases confusion, we may as well keep the old till we know enough to frame moderately permanent new ones.

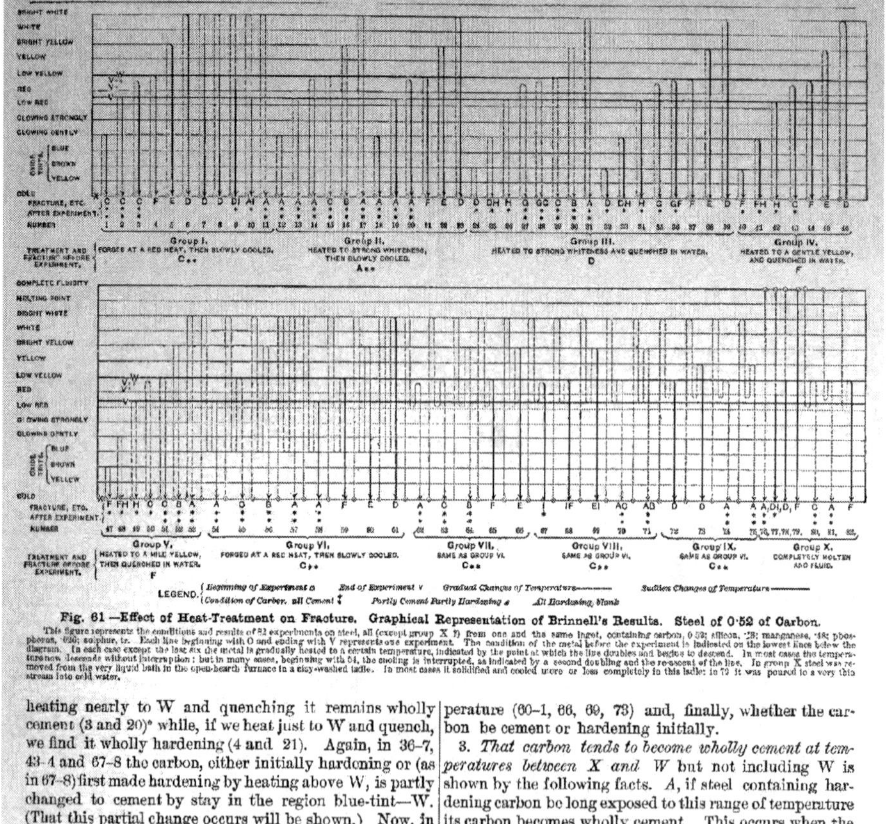

Fig. 61.—Effect of Heat-Treatment on Fracture. Graphical Representation of Brinnell's Results. Steel of 0·52 of Carbon.

This figure represents the conditions and results of 82 experiments on steel, all (except group X ?) from one and the same ingot, containing carbon, 0·52; silicon, ·28; manganese, ·48; phosphorus, ·030; sulphur, tr. Each line beginning with O and ending with V represents one experiment. The condition of the metal before the experiment is indicated on the lowest lines below the diagram. In each case except the last six the metal is gradually heated to a certain temperature, indicated by the point at which the line doubles and begins to descend. In most cases the temperature now descends without interruption: but in many cases, beginning with 54, the cooling is interrupted, as indicated by a second doubling and the re-ascent of the line. In group X steel was removed from the very liquid bath in the open-hearth furnace in a clay-washed ladle. In most cases it solidified and cooled more or less completely in this ladle: in 79 it was poured in a very thin stream into cold water.

heating nearly to W and quenching it remains wholly cement (3 and 20)* while, if we heat just to W and quench, we find it wholly hardening (4 and 21). Again, in 36–7, 43–4 and 67–8 the carbon, either initially hardening or (as in 67–8) first made hardening by heating above W, is partly changed to cement by stay in the region blue-tint—W. (That this partial change occurs will be shown.) Now, in 36, 43 and 67 the steel is quenched after heating nearly but not quite to W, while in 37, 44 and 68 it is quenched after heating just to W. In the former three the carbon remains partly cement, in the latter it is found to be wholly hardening.

2. *That carbon remains in the hardening state at all temperatures above W* is shown by the fact that, whenever steel is quenched from a point above W, and so hurried through the range W X in which it is possible for the carbon to change back from hardening to cement, only hardening carbon is found. This is true whether the quenching be from a yellow heat (73), a bright yellow (5, 7, 22, 38 45, 60, 66, 69), a bright white (6, 23, 39, 46, 61), or from a temperature above the melting point (79): and whether it be preceded by a fall (7, 8 78) or a rise of temperature, and whether this rise be direct from the cold (5 6, 22–3, 38–9, 45 6), or be preceded by oscillations of temperature (60–1, 66, 69, 73) and, finally, whether the carbon be cement or hardening initially.

3. *That carbon tends to become wholly cement at temperatures between X and W* but not including W is shown by the following facts. *A*, if steel containing hardening carbon be long exposed to this range of temperature its carbon becomes wholly cement. This occurs when the steel cools slowly from W to X (11, 15, 29, 30, 31, 51 to 57, 63–4, 70–1, 74–5–6, 80–1); when it is cooled from W to blue, heated to V and quenched (58); and in two out of three cases in which it is slowly heated and cooled between X and V++ (27–8).

B, when the carbon is initially all cement none of it changes to hardening below W, even at temperatures barely below W (3, 14, 20).

C, when it is initially all hardening or is made hardening by heating to W, at least part of it always becomes cement during any subsequent appreciably long exposure to temperatures between a brown tint and W.

These last two facts are true whether the steel be quenched after the exposure (B, 1, 2, 3, 18 to 20; C, 9, 10, 32 to 36, 40 to 43, 67, 77), or slowly cooled (B, 12 to 14; C, 24 to 26, 47 to 49).

4. *That the change from hardening to cement carbon is always slow* is shown by the fact that no cement carbon is formed when steel passes rapidly, as in quenching,

* In this and the succeeding section, unless otherwise stated, numerals refer to the numbers of Brinnell's experiments, Figure 61.

through the range W X, (6 to 8, 21 to 23, 37 to 39, 44 to 46, 59 to 61, 65–6, 68–9, 72–3, 78–9, 82), and that if the carbon be hardening it does not change completely to cement unless the steel be long exposed to temperatures between a blue tint and W. *E. g.* this change is only partial if the steel be heated *from X only to V or some lower point* and slowly cooled (24 to 26, 47 to 49), or from X only to some point below W and quenched, (32 to 36, 40 to 43), or if it be cooled slowly from above W only as far as V and then quenched (9, 10, 77).

5. *That the change from hardening to cement carbon is most rapid at V* is probable, though not readily proved, as Brinnell's test for these two forms of carbon is qualitative only.

We thus have two critical temperatures, W and V. At W and all higher points the carbon becomes hardening instantly; at all points below W, even those very slightly below it, the carbon becomes cement slowly. This latter change appears to occur most rapidly at V.

§ 243. Brinnell's Results Concerning Fracture.—He recognizes nine distinct simple types of fracture, supposed to result from nine corresponding types of structure, set forth at length in Table 85, and more briefly here.

Hardening carbon.			Cement carbon.		Transition from hardening to cement carbon.
Bright porcelanic,[a]		F.	Bright hackly[b] crystalline.	Fine C.	Dull porcelanic[a] H.
Bright granular crystalline.	Fine	E.		Medium B.	Leafy crystalline G.
	Coarse	D.		Coarse A.	Dull coarse crystalline I.

As Table 85 indicates, there is reason to suspect the existence of four more types.

Usually the whole fracture belongs to some one of these types: but in some cases, in which the transition from one type to another is incomplete, different portions of one and the same fracture belong to two quite distinct types: *i. e.* the fracture is composite.

The chief changes of fracture as inferred from our present data are probably as follows.

1. When cold steel is gradually heated the fractures change thus:[c]

Table 84.—General Summary of Fracture Changes.

Fracture of cold steel.	Change at a gentle glow to	Further change at V to	Further change at V + to	Further change at V + + to	Further change at W to	Further change at light yellow to	Further change at bright white to
F	F H	H	C	C (?)	F	E	D
E	E H (?)	H (?)	(?)	(?)	F (?)	E (?)	D (?)
D	D H	H	C	G F	F	E	D
C	C	C	C	C	F	E	D
B	B (?)	B (?)	B (?)	B (?)	F (?)	E (?)	D (?)
A	A	A	A	A	F	E	D

2. The fractures thus set up may be preserved by sudden cooling: but, if cooled slowly instead of suddenly from the temperatures at which they are thus formed, they behave as follows:

F, E, D } Change between W and X to { C, B, A } Coarse follows coarse, fine yields fine.

C (?), B (?), A } Remain unaltered.

These statements will be verified in § 244.

Under the special conditions of Brinnell's experiments changes of temperature appear to affect the fracture thus:

1. Those either rising or falling which change the condition of the carbon, always change the fracture from the hardening-carbon (granular) group toward the cement-carbon (hackly) group, or back, the change of structure-group being simultaneous with and like in direction and rapidity to that of carbon, sudden, direct, and at W from cement to hardening; slow, through intermediate transition fractures, and between W and X from hardening to cement.

2. Those which do not change the condition of carbon,

A. If falling do not change the type of fracture,

B. If rising do not change the existing fracture till they pass the temperature at which it was acquired: beyond this they coarsen it.

3. Exposure to a white or higher heat without subsequent forging always causes coarse crystallization (the higher the coarser), which indeed cannot be originated otherwise.

4. To break up by heat-treatment coarse crystalline structure once acquired, the temperature must be varied so as to change the condition of carbon: heating *to or slightly above W* is probably the only way of effacing it completely.

5. Fine structures F and C once acquired can be materially coarsened only by heating *above W*, the structure remaining moderately fine up to a bright yellow.

Brinnell adopts the usual assumption that sudden cooling (*e. g.* by quenching) does not in itself alter the structure of the metal, but merely preserves that which existed at the instant preceding the quenching. This is neither self-evident nor experimentally proved. It is certainly improbable that quenching should originate, but not that it should modify crystalline structure. Indeed, in the case of pieces of large cross-section, the different layers must cool and contract during quenching at such different rates that interstratal movements must arise which might well alter or destroy pre-existing crystallization. In small bars, however, this motion is probably slight, and here the assumption that quenching fixes the existing structure is hardly improbable: as it greatly facilitates discussion, we may adopt it provisionally.

As it appears to be a general rule that the finer the fracture, other things being equal, the better the condition of the steel, so the means of acquiring and preserving the fine fractures, F of properly hardened steel and C of unhardened steel, are of great importance: not less important are those of avoiding the coarse fractures D and A.

§ 244. Details of Fractures.—We will now consider in more detail the nine fractures and the conditions under which they are acquired and lost. But the true way to obtain a clear notion of them and of their changes is to study them at the forge, a task which I heartily commend to my readers.

The general scheme of the subject, as far as I understand it, is set forth in Table 85.

a. *Group* 1. The lower member, F, bright porcelanic, the characteristic fracture of properly hardened steel, is acquired under two sets of conditions,

1, When molten steel is suddenly solidified and immediately completely cooled (79). In the brief instant afforded, the crystalline force can only assert itself far enough to produce a porcelanic structure.

a Brinnell terms these fractures "amorphous:" as this word signifies absolute freedom from crystalline structure, such as is found in glass, and as these fractures are probably simply extremely fine-grained yet crystalline, "porcelanic" seems to me more accurate.

b "Zackig." Others translate this "pointed crystalline." "Hackly" is well-established, briefer, and I think more expressive.

c Where a letter is followed by (?) direct evidence is lacking.

TABLE 85.—GENERAL SCHEME OF BRINNELL'S FRACTURES. Condition of Carbon: †† all hardening; †* part hardening, part cement; ** all cement.
Read from left to right, and from above downwards.

	GROUP 1. ††	GROUP 2; transition from †† to ** between W and V.	GROUP 3. **	GROUP 4. Transition † to * between 20° Cent. and redness. § 1.	GROUP 4. § 2.
Characteristics of group as a whole.	Bright { Porcelanic, and granular-crystalline. **Acquired.** All the * groups (2, 3, 4) change suddenly to F at W, as * changes to †. F and D acquired on solidification. **Lost.** Change to corresponding members of groups {2; 4} when † changes to * at temperatures {between W and V; between 20° C. and low redness}. Finer members {F; E} change to coarser {E; D} when temperature rises to {bright yellow; bright white}.	Dull crystalline. **Acquired.** Succeeds Group 1 gradually when temperature descends from above W towards V } † beginning to change to *. **Lost.** Changes to Group 3 gradually, when temperature descends from above V to below V. } Change of † to * being complete.	Bright hackly (pointed crystalline). Color of the fracture inclined towards BLUE. **Acquired.** Gradually succeed Groups 1, 2, as temperature descends slowly from W or above to some point below W } † changes to * completely. **Lost.** Change suddenly to F when temperature rises to W. } * changing to †. Do not change below W.	Dull porcelanic. DARK GRAY, fibrous, wholly without crystallization. **Acquired.** Gradually succeed Group 1 as temperature rises from 20° C. to points between a brown tint temperature and V } † beginning to change to *. **Lost.** Change to § 2 as temperature rises still farther, to between V and W. } † changing to * more completely.	{ Fine hackly. { Leafy crystalline. Color of the fracture inclined towards BLUE. **Acquired.** Succeed § 1 as temperature rises to between V and W. } † changing to * more completely. **Lost.** Change to F as temperature rises to W; i. e. crystallization is effaced. } * changing to †.
Characteristics of separate members of each group.	**F.** BRIGHT PORCELANIC, no decided crystallization visible to the naked eye. **Acquired.** 1. On sudden solidification. 2 to 7. Succeeds groups 2, 3, 4 at W, suddenly. } * changing to †. **Lost.** 8. Changes to C when temperature descends from W past V. 9. Changes to H when temperature rises from 20° C. towards V. } † changing to *. 10. Changes to E when temperature rises from W to lighter yellow.	The transition fracture from F towards C has not been described.	**C.** FINE HACKLY. Facets SHINING. Fracture color inclined towards BLUE. **Acquired.** 8. Succeeds F as temperature descends from W to some lower point. Change probably gradual. } † changing to * fully. **Lost.** 3. Changes suddenly to F when temperature rises to W. } * changing to †. Does not change below W.	**H-from-F.**[a] PORCELANIC: dull: fibrous. Wholly without crystallization. DARK GRAY. **Acquired.** 9. Gradually succeeds F as the temperature rises from 20° C. to points between a brown tint temperature and V. } † beginning to change to *. **Lost.** 18 Changes to C when temperature rises still farther to between V and W. } † changing to * further.	**C.**[b] FINE HACKLY. Facets SHINING. Fracture-color inclined towards BLUE. **Acquired.** 18. Succeeds H-from-F as temperature rises to between V and W. } † changing to * further. **Lost.** 6. Changes to F as temperature reaches W. } * changing to †.
	E. FINE GRANULAR-CRYSTALLINE. Facets SILVER-SHINING (Metcalf, fiery). **Acquired.** 10 Replaces F when temperature rises to bright yellow. **Lost.** 11. Changes to B when temperature descends from light yellow past W and V. } † changing to *. 12 Changes to D when temperature rises from bright yellow to bright whiteness.	The transition fracture from E towards B has not been described.	**B.** HACKLY. Facets SHINING. Color of the fracture inclined towards BLUE. **Acquired.** 11. Succeeds E as temperature descends from light yellow to some point below W. Change probably gradual. } † changing to * fully. **Lost.** 4. Probably changes suddenly to F when temperature rises to W. } * changing to †.	The changes from E from 20° centigrade	as the temperature rises have not been investigated.
	D. COARSE GRANULAR-CRYSTALLINE. FACETS SILVER-SHINING (Metcalf, very lustrous). Fracture WHITE (Metcalf, yellowish). **Acquired.** 12. Replaces E when temperature rises to bright whiteness. 13. Acquired on slow solidification. 13-5. Sometimes replaces I-from-D when temperature returns to W.[d] **Lost.** 14. Changes to I when temperature descends from bright whiteness past W and V. 15. Changes to H when temperature rises from 20° C. towards V. } † changing to *.	**I.** COARSE CRYSTALLINE. Facets shine like dull-beaten silver. **Acquired.** 14. Gradually replaces D when temperature descends from a bright white past W toward V. } † beginning to change to *. 16. Replaces A when temperature rises from V to W. } * changing back to †. **Lost.** 17. Changes gradually to A when temperature descends below V. } Change from † to * being completed. 2. I-from-A changes to F when temperature rises to W } * changing to †. 13-5. I-from-D sometimes returns to D when temperature returns to W.[d]	**A.** COARSE HACKLY. Facets SHINING. Color of the fracture inclined towards BLUE. **Acquired.** 17. Gradually succeeds I as temperature descends from a bright white to some point below W. } † changing to * completely. **Lost.** 15. Changes suddenly to F when temperature rises to W. } * changing to †. 16. When freshly formed, changes to I when temperature rises from V towards W. } * changing to †. Does not change below V.	**H from-D**[a] PORCELANIC: dull: fibrous. Wholly without crystallization. DARK GRAY. **Acquired.** 15. Gradually succeeds D when the temperature rises from 20° C. to points between a brown tint temperature and V. } † beginning to change to *. **Lost.** 19. Changes to G when temperature rises still farther to between V and W. } † changing to * more completely.	**G.** LEAFY CRYSTALLINE. FACETS SHINING. Color of the fracture inclined towards BLUE. **Acquired.** 19. Succeeds H-from-D when temperature rises to between V and W. } † changing to * more completely. **Lost.** 7. Changes to F as temperature reaches W. } * changing to †.

2, Whenever cement carbon changes to hardening: this change seems to be so violent that it effaces all pre-existing crystallization, and here too the steel becomes porcelanic. When cold steel is heated to just below W its carbon, if not initially cement, becomes cement: and on reaching W the change to hardening carbon occurs suddenly: hence, whenever cold steel is heated to but not far above W and quenched, a porcelanic fracture is found[a] (4, 21, 37, 44). Simple exposure to W does not in itself destroy pre-existing crystallization and render the steel porcelanic: the change from cement to hardening carbon must occur; otherwise the pre-existing crystallization remains. Thus if steel be heated above W its carbon remains hardening: if we now cool it to W no change of carbon occurs, and the steel if now quenched will not be found porcelanic (8, 78). But, by cooling the steel far enough below W (*e. g.* to below V) to change its carbon to cement, and again heating to W, this cement carbon reverts to the hardening state, and the steel, if now quenched, will be found porcelanic (59, 65, 82).

If the temperature fall from above W to some point so slightly below it that but a part of the hardening carbon changes to cement, and if the temperature be again raised to W, it appears that only those crystals which had changed to cement will now undergo a change of carbon, and they alone will now become porcelanic, F: the rest will preserve the crystallization which they had before, when

[a] This is shown by direct experiment for steel whose fracture is either C, A or G initially. The analogy of C and A leaves little doubt that B would undergo the same change. D and H certainly and E probably change to G when cold steel is heated to V + +, and hence eventually yield F at W. The behavior of I, a transition fracture unlikely to arise in practice, has not been studied, but all analogy indicates that it too would change to F at W.

their temperature was above W, and a composite fracture arises (68).

Easily acquired by quenching from W, F is as easily lost, by exposure to any high temperature either above or below W. Below V it only changes to the dull porcelanic fracture H (41-2, 48-9): between V and W to the fine grained fracture G (43, 50): while above W it changes to the coarser members of its own group, E and D (5-6, 22-3, 38-9, 45-6). In short, below W (carbon changing) it changes only to fine-grained and hence desirable fractures, while above (carbon constant) it like all others grows coarser.

E and D, the upper members of this group, thus acquired, are not removed or rendered finer by simply lowering the temperature again towards W (7-8). E, acquired at a bright yellow, grows coarser and changes to D as the temperature rises to bright whiteness (5, 6, 22-3, 38-9, 45-6, 60-1). In slow cooling *below* W, E and D change gradually with changing carbon in passing through and below the critical range W-V to the cement-carbon hackly B and A respectively, the former medium, the latter coarse (B, 16, 30, 52, 56; A, 17, 31, 53, 57). During this transition D passes through the dull-crystalline fracture I (9, 10, 67), and it is probable that further study would detect similar transitions states following E and F.

D is also acquired during slow cooling from the melting point to W (78).

If D be preserved by sudden cooling, and if the metal be again gently heated, as its carbon gradually changes to cement its fracture first becomes dull porcelanic, H, as V is approached (25-6, 33-4), changing further to flaky crystalline G as the temperature nears W (27-8, 35-6), at W of course changing suddenly to the bright porcelanic F (37). Similar changes probably occur in case of fracture E.

b. *Group 2, Transition Fracture*, I. Our data are too scanty to permit us to speak with certainty concerning this transition fracture, but the following hypothesis appears to fit our present facts. The transition from the granular-crystalline hardening-carbon group (F E D), to the hackly cement-carbon group (C B A), is not sudden like the reverse change, but occurs gradually as the steel cools through the range W V, thus corresponding to the gradual simultaneous change of carbon from hardening to cement. While this change is occurring the faces of the crystals become dull: this suggests that the cohesion between the particles of each individual crystal is no longer in great excess over the adhesion between the faces of adjoining crystals, and hence the surface of fracture penetrates here and there beneath the crystalline faces, and the particles of one crystal adhere to and dull the faces of its neighbor. Though the crystals are thus dulled, we have no evidence that their form is changed This dulling of the facets is apparently the essential feature of the transition fracture I.

Let us now trace this transition, and note the effects of arresting it at different stages, whether by sudden cooling, or by a rise instead of a further fall of temperature.[a]

I. *At V+*. If D be acquired by heating to bright whiteness, and if the steel be now slowly cooled to V+, and if the structure acquired thereby be fixed by quenching (9, 77), we find that part of the crystals have entered the transition stage, are dull-faced, I, suggesting that fracture penetrates beneath their faces. Others remain unchanged, mirror-bright, as D, suggesting that the fracture still follows their faces accurately. Part of the carbon has simultaneously changed from hardening to cement. But in descending from W to V+ the change of crystallization appears to be so slight, so merely incipient that the old crystallization has simply tottered, not fallen; so that if the temperature immediately return to W (72) the old regime, fracture D, is completely restored even in those crystals which at V+ had changed to I.

D thus regained is not further changed by raising the temperature above W (73), but it changes as usual to A (doubtless through I) when the temperature again falls slowly past W and V (74-5), carbon changing to cement.

II. *At V*. If D be acquired by heating to bright whiteness, and if the steel be slowly cooled a little farther than in the case last considered, to wit to V, and if the structure now acquired be fixed by quenching (10), we find that those crystals which at V+ had become dull, I, have now apparently changed to hackly, A, while the rest have become dull, I, preparatory to that change, and we have the composite fracture AI. In verification of his belief that the carbon of some crystals had changed to cement, while that of the others still remained hardening, Brinnell found that on polishing a bar of steel thus treated, shining specks scattered across the surface stood up above the surrounding steel: with a diamond he found them harder than the rest: while etching for twenty-four hours with very dilute nitric acid made one set of crystals stand forth sharply beyond the others, which were far more corroded by the acid. This, however, is not conclusive: the harder crystals may have been cementite, surrounded by the softer pearlyte.

If, after this slow cooling to V, we raise the temperature, the hackly A (cement carbon) crystals change back to F on reaching W, their carbon changing to hardening: but the transition I crystals remain as I, and on now quenching we get a composite fracture IF (68). If, instead of quenching from W, we cool slowly to below V, I and F naturally change to A and C respectively, and the composite fracture AC arises (70). If the reheating from V be carried above W, the transition I crystals still remain unchanged, while F of course changes to E, and we naturally obtain the composite fractures IE and AB on sudden and slow cooling respectively (69, 71).

When the slow cooling was interrupted at V+ and the temperature then raised to W, the I crystals changed back to D: but in our present case (68-9) they remain unchanged at and above W. We may conjecture that this is because the more extended slow cooling in the present case affects the structure more profoundly, so that, on the return to W, the pre-existing crystallization no longer asserts itself as before, the pre-existing great excess of the cohesion of the particles of each individual crystal over the cohesion between adjoining crystals is not so completely restored, fracture does not follow the crystal faces so accurately as before, dull faced crystals, I, persist.

III. *Below V*. If the slow cooling be carried but slightly below V, the transition probably becomes complete. This is indicated indirectly. On immediately reheating steel whose temperature has fallen from bright white-

[a] The transition from D to A has been studied: those from E to B and from F to C have not: but it is not improbable that transition fractures analogous to I may be developed in these latter cases by interrupting the transition.

ness to slightly below V, fractures F and E arise as soon as we reach W and bright yellow respectively (65–6). Now if, on cooling to just below V, the change from granular to hackly were incomplete, then when the temperature rises again to W and a bright yellow we would find composite fractures, as in the cases under II. : while in fact we obtain F and E unmixed. Again, Coffin states[a] that if steel be heated to W, quenched to V and thence slowly cooled, its fracture is perfectly porcelanic. The means at his disposal did not permit close measurements of temperature, and it is probable from analogy that his quenching cooled the steel slightly below instead of just to V. This indicates that F does not change to C at temperatures materially below V, and suggests that the change from F to C, which occurs regularly when steel with fracture F is slowly cooled from W to X, is completed before the temperature has fallen materially below V.

V then appears to be a critical temperature for these changes of fracture.

IV. Finally, if the slow fall of temperature be carried far below V and arrested at a blue oxide-tint, and if the temperature be raised again to W or bright yellow or bright white with subsequent quenching, we still obtain the characteristic fractures of these three temperatures, F, E and D, just as in the last paragraph (59, 60, 61), which naturally change to hackly C, B and A if slow cooling, which changes the carbon to cement, replace this quenching (55, 56, 57).

c. *Group* 3. The eventual change of the granular-crystalline hardening-carbon fractures F, E and D, to the hackly cement-carbon ones C, B and A on slow cooling from the formation-temperatures of the former to below V, is illustrated by experiments 15, 29, and 51; by 16, 30 and 52; and by 11, 17, 31, 53 and 75 respectively. In each case we assume that a granular fracture, F, E or D, existed before the slow cooling, because we find it in a parallel experiment in which sudden is substituted for slow cooling.

The hackly fractures thus acquired do not change unless the carbon changes back to hardening, *i. e.* unless the temperature rises again to W, at which point they are effaced and changed to F. Repeated heating and cooling, swift or slow, between the cold and V, do not affect them.[b]

d. *Group* 4. *Transition from Hardening to Cement Carbon, temperature rising from X toward W.*—If the hardening-carbon granular-crystalline fractures of group 1, F, E, D, are preserved by sudden cooling, they gradually change as, with gradually rising temperature, the carbon changes to cement. At first the change of carbon seems to outrun that of structure, for by the time that a brown tint is reached part of the carbon has changed to cement (24, 32, 40, 47) while no corresponding change of structure has been recognized. With further rise of temperature the dull porcelanic H replaces the fractures of group 1, partially at an incipient glow (25, 33, 41, 48), wholly at V, (26, 31, 42, 49). With still further rise to slightly above V crystallization again sets in, and appears to be the coarser the coarser the pre-existing fracture of group 1 had been, C, fine hackly, replacing F, (43), G, leafy crystalline, succeeding D (35). This suggests that the change of carbon from hardening to cement had not destroyed the pre-existing crystallization of group 1, but had merely masked it by strengthening the inter-crystalline adhesion, so that the fracture obtained at V struck across the crystals themselves, in preference to following their faces: and that the inter-crystalline adhesion again falls on rise of temperature to V +, the effects of the old crystallization are felt again, again fracture tends to follow the faces of the crystals, those which had formerly yielded the coarse D now affording the leafy G, those which had given rise to F now yielding the fine hackly C.

The changes which fracture E undergoes on reheating have yet to be investigated.

§ 245. Certain Features of the Change from Group to Group.—There are three chief changes of carbon-condition, 1, *from cement to hardening* when the temperature rises past W ; *from hardening to cement*, 2, in slow cooling from above W to V, and 3 when the temperature of quenched steel rises from X towards V.

The suddenness of the first, corresponding to the suddenness of the accompanying carbon-change, and the slowness of the second and third, harmonize well with if they do not explain the fact that pre-existing crystallization is completely and permanently effaced by the first, but only modified by the second and temporarily masked by the third.

But though in the experiments of Figure 61, and in those of Coffin on steel containing like Brinnell's 0·50% of carbon, by this first change the pre-existing crystallization seems to be effaced, so that it does not influence the results of subsequent manipulation, yet Coffin found that, when only 0·20% of carbon was present, heating to W and quenching only partly broke up the pre-existing coarse structure, some of whose coarse crystals still remained. A second heating to W, however, induced the expected porcelanic fracture. The first sudden change of carbon from cement to hardening seemed to weaken the crystalline structure, the second to efface it.[c] In his view the destruction of crystallization requires energy : this is supplied by the changing condition of carbon. Little carbon present, means little carbon to change, little energy exerted, little effect on crystallization.

Even in relatively highly carburetted steel it may be necessary to repeat this heating to W if the crystalline structure has been tenaciously fixed, as Metcalf pointed out years ago.[d]

Position of W. According to Chernoff, while the changes in the temperature of *b*(W) are not readily recognized by the inexpert eye, this point rises slightly as the proportion of carbon falls, being at a not-brilliant red for certain steels, while for wrought-iron it lies at a white heat.[f] Metcalf recognizes and employs fifteen different temperatures for refining steel of different percentages of carbon, *i. e.* for rendering them porcelanic by heating to W.[e] Coffin, however, finds that W lies at practically the same temperature for steels whose carbon varies between 0·25 and 1·5%.[g] Exact pyrometic observations are probably needed.

[a] Mechanics, Dec., 1887, p. 318, Proposition 9: Trans. Am. Soc. Mech. Engineers, IX., 1888. Coffin terms this fracture "Perfectly amorphous."

[b] Idem, proposition 5.

[c] J. Coffin: Steel Car Axles, Trans. American Society of Mechanical Engineers, IX., 1888: "Mechanics," 1887, p. 317.

[d] "The Treatment of Steel," p. 25.

[e] Trans. Am. Soc. Civil Engineers, XV., p. 385, 1887. The Treatment of Steel, p. 35.

[f] Rev. Universelle, 2d ser., I., p. 401, 1877. "Le rouge non brillant."

[g] Trans. Am. Soc. Civ. Engineers, XV., p. 326, 1887.

It is possible that W represents a range of temperature, not a point: or that, while the critical point is constant, it is expedient to quench soft steels from slightly above it, hard ones from slightly below.

There are two points, nearly constant for most classes of malleable iron and steel, at which the metal evolves an abnormal quantity of heat during falling temperature. The lower one lies between 660° and 705° C., and very probably corresponds to V. The upper lies according to Pionchon between 1,000° and 1,500° C., according to Osmond between 810° and 900°, and may possibly be W. The position of each is nearly independent of the proportion of carbon present. (Cf. § 257.)

§ 246. Influence of Rate of Cooling on Coarseness of Grain.—There appears to be a maximum degree of coarseness or size of grain for each temperature, varying with the composition of the metal and rising with its sectional area and with the temperature, at least when this is above W. The development of crystallization of course takes time.[a]

A. With small bars the necessarily rather slowly rising temperature appears to afford time for developing approximately the maximum coarseness corresponding to the temperature reached, so that their fracture depends chiefly on the highest temperature to which they have been exposed, and but little on the rate of cooling.[b] Of course, if the metal be forged or fused after the rise of temperature, the crystallization acquired is destroyed again: and so it is if the rise of temperature be to W. In any of these cases the coarseness of fracture must increase with the slowness of cooling. That it does after forging and fusion is well known: and Coffin finds that it does in case of the hackly C, formed during slow cooling from W.[c]

Wedding says unqualifiedly that the size of grain increases with the slowness of cooling, cæteris paribus;[d] but qualification is surely needed.

Coffin concludes from his experiments that, after the maximum coarseness for given temperature has been reached, further exposure merely changes "the relative cohesion between different (crystal) faces, causing cleavage surfaces." I suppose that he means that it increases the ratio of the intercrystalline adhesion to that of the cohesion of the particles of the individual crystal, so that rupture occasionally penetrates into the individual crystals, and follows their cleavage planes.[e]

B. Large masses seem to present rather different conditions. Though Percy reports buttons of iron whose crystals were so large that their cleavage planes extended completely across the fracture,[f] yet it is probably true that crystals tend to a larger size in large masses of iron than in small bars.

Thus the diameter of crystals occurring, not in vugs but in the metal itself, reaches 0·25 inch in slowly cooled, friable ingot iron reported by Bessemer,[g] and 0·5 inch in Chernoff's forged steel shaft,[h] in Percy's long-heated puddled iron,[i] and in a long-used porter-bar described by Thurston.[j] Ordinary heating does not appear to occupy time enough to satisfy the crystallizing capacity of large masses, which therefore tends to assert itself during cooling; and here the rate and duration of cooling probably affect the size of the grain much more than in case of small bars.[k]

Another possible reason why the rate of cooling should affect the structure of large more than small pieces, lies in the fact that, in quenching, the difference between the rates of cooling of outside and inside is greater in the former than in the latter. Hence severe interstratal movements may be expected in large masses, which like forging might be expected to break up already existing crystallization, while when small bars are quenched the different layers cool and contract at more nearly similar rates. Metcalf admits[l] that, while the influence of the rate of cooling is hardly appreciable in case of bars 0·125 inch thick, it is more readily detected in those 0·25 inch thick, and conspicuous in bars 1·5 inches square. The outside of such a bar quenched from a very high temperature consists of coarse crystals: they become rigid so instantaneously that they preserve the form acquired at the high temperature. The interior is flaky, and might even be called fine-grained: it is indeed much finer than if the bar had been slowly cooled.[l] The fracture of such a bar is sketched at the right of figure 62.

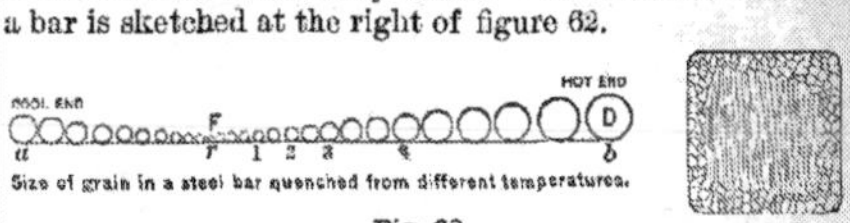

Fig. 62.

§ 247. Forging strongly opposes crystallization, in case of both iron and steel, ingot and weld. Like agitation in the case of salts crystallizing from aqueous solution, it appears to arrest the development of crystalline structure, and to break up more or less completely that which has already been developed. The former action is probably due to its altering the position of the particles with reference to the axes around which they were about to crystallize.

The second (in case of iron) is probably due in part to its increasing the cohesion between adjoining crystals, *i. e.* welding their faces together, so that fracture now follows the shorter path across their bodies: perhaps also in part to its breaking them up into cleavage blocks, like the blocks readily broken from many crystals of galena, or to its destroying the original crystals altogether, new and smaller ones springing up from their ruins: and possibly to its elongating the crystals themselves, and so elongating the path which rupture would have to take were it to follow their faces, and thus the more inclining it to strike

[a] Brinnell indeed states that when the carbon has wholly or mainly changed from hardening to cement, whether with rising or falling temperature, crystallization occurs instantaneously, (*ganz plötzlich*. Stahl und Eisen, V., p. 620, 1885). Coffin, however, states that many experiments of his refute Brinnell's proposition which contains this statement, and thinks that Brinnell's experiments do not verify it (Trans. Am. Soc. Civ. Eng., XV., p. 319). I have not succeeded in reconciling it with Brinnell's experiments, *e. g.* with his 9 and 10, figure 61.

[b] This statement applies to the coarseness, not the kind of fracture. We have seen that rapid cooling from above W preserves the granular, while slow cooling yields the hackly fractures.

[c] Op. cit., p. 325. Table 87, § 250, gives absolute measurements of the increase in size of grain on slow cooling from W to V.

[d] Jour. Iron and Steel Inst., 1885, I., p. 190.

[e] Trans. Am. Soc. Mech. Eng., IX., 1888, propositions 7 and 8.

[f] Iron and Steel, p. 10.

[g] Cf. § 54, p. 33. Cf. Iron Age, XLII., p. 57, 1888.

[h] Rev. Univ., 2d Ser., I., p. 409.

[i] Sorby, Jour. Iron and Steel Inst., 1887, I., p. 262.

[j] Thurston, Mat'ls of Engineering, II., p. 580.

[k] Coffin, op. cit, proposition 6th, states that if steel be heated "above W, its crystallization is in the most part determined by the temperature and occurs while heating:" it is probable that he here generalizes from experiments with small bars, and overlooks the very different conditions which accompany larger masses.

[l] Trans. Am. Soc. Civ. Engs., XV., p. 388, 1887.

TABLE 86.—METCALF'S VIEWS ON THE INFLUENCE OF THE QUENCHING-TEMPERATURE ON THE FRACTURE, ETC.

Number	1.	2.	3.	4.	5.	6.	7.	8.
Quenching-temperature	Scintillating.	White.	Bright yellow.	Orange.	Bright red.	Red.	Low red.	Black.
PROPERTIES OF THE QUENCHED METAL.								
Hardness	Scratches glass.	Extremely hard.			Well hardened.		Hard enough for tap teeth.	Not hardened.
Brittleness	Like glass.	Almost like glass.	Slightly tougher than 2.	Tougher than 3.	Tougher than 4; breaks easily.	Stronger than 8.		
Fracture	Coarse; very lustrous; yellowish.	Coarse; less yellow than 1.	Finer than 2; fiery.	Slightly finer than 3; fiery.	Same size as 8, but fiery. Finer than 4.	Much finer; not fiery; refined.	Edges refined middle coarser.	Coarser than 6 and 7; the original grain.
Specific gravity	7·720		7·748		7·761	7·781	7·804	7·825

across their bodies or to follow the imperfectly developed cleavage planes. But, whatever be the rationale of its action, it is certainly a most powerful means of counteracting the crystallizing tendency, and little crystallization will arise during forging which is sufficiently powerful to make its effect felt to the middle of the mass.

The case of rivets illustrates this forcibly. It is said that when they fail it is always at the head which is not struck during riveting; the riveter's blows against the struck head while it is cooling prevent crystallization and consequent brittleness.[a]

Coffin has observed that, while a bar quenched after its temperature has risen slowly to a light yellow is coarse grained, if it be quenched from this temperature immediately after rolling it is fine grained.[b]

If forging be followed by slow cooling, it is clear that the higher the temperature at which it ceases the coarser will the crystallization become, the worse the steel. Hence the importance of a low finishing-temperature in forging, to which § 250 and § 264 et seq. refer again. Suffice it here to say that the superiority of thin over thick forgings, usually attributed to extra work, is probably due in large part to lower finishing-temperature, especially in case of ingot-metal.

§ 248. THE VIEWS OF OTHERS ON HEAT-TREATMENT AND FRACTURE.—*A. Metcalf* believes that the fracture depends first and apparently foremost on the last maximum temperature, secondly and apparently secondarily on the rate of cooling.[c] He sketches in Figure 62 the influence of the last maximum temperature on the size of the grain in different portions of a steel bar which has been quenched after heating its right-hand end to bright whiteness, the left-hand end being below redness, and the intermediate portions, heated by conduction, being at intermediate temperatures. We note the coarse grain (D) of the white-hot part, the finer grain (E) of the portion which had been at a bright yellow, the extremely fine grain (F) of that which had been at W, and the gradually increasing size as we pass to the left from W. I have interpolated these letters.

I attempt in Table 86 to condense his views on the fracture, etc., of different parts of bars thus treated, set forth fully in the Metallurgical Review, I., p. 245.

He points out that the rate of cooling *from the melting point* influences the size of grain greatly, slow and rapid cooling yielding large and small crystals respectively.

The minor differences between his views and Brinnell's we may reasonably refer to the searchingness of the latter's investigation, bringing out details which in common practice would escape notice.[d]

B. Chernoff in the main anticipated Brinnell's general conclusions regarding structure, besides reaching other important ones which lay outside the field of the latter's researches, yet naturally failing to note important distinctions which the subtle experiments of the Swedish investigator have brought to light. In certain diagrams, which I have rotated 90° in Figure 63 to facilitate comparison with Brinnell's, (Figure 61) he indicates four points which apparently coincide with Brinnell's cold, V, W, and the melting point. His *a* is a dark cherry-red, his *b* a "not brilliant" red. These temperatures are slightly below those of Brinnell's V and W, but not more than may be readily due to the probable difference between the steels which these two observers employed. Chernoff points out that, the higher the carbon, the lower are these points. He employed an ordinary hard steel, which we may suppose had between ·75 and 1·00% of carbon. For very soft steel he puts *b* at a white heat. Brinnell, on the other hand employed a steel with 0·52% of carbon, whose W would stand between the "not brilliant red" and the white of Chernoff's hard steel and very soft steel, or just about where Brinnell places it, at a low yellow.

His chief results are as follows.

1. Steel cannot be hardened below V.

2. Between X and W heating and cooling, fast or slow, affect the structure little if at all.[e] Very protracted exposure to temperatures approaching W, however, probably gradually alters the structure,[f] though he could observe no change on exposing steel bars for about eight hours to temperatures near W.

3. As soon as the temperature reaches W the structure changes rapidly from granular or crystalline to amorphous.[g]

4. With *rising temperature* it remains amorphous up to the melting point.[g]

[a] Metcalf, Iron Age, XXXIX., May 19th, 1887, p. 17.

[b] Private communication, March 28th, 1888.

[c] Trans. Am. Soc. Civ. Eng., XV., pp. 284, 287, 386, 388, 1887. Cf. "Treatment of Steel," pp. 28, 32.

[d] Rejecting the carbon-theory of hardening, he says of Brinnell's fracture-results, "the results given, as far as they can be explained in words, agree with our shop experience, and they indicate clearly what has long been an axiom with us, *i. e.* that a fracture of steel always indicates the highest temperature to which the steel was last subjected, no matter how it may have been cooled, provided it had not been hammered or rolled, or otherwise worked mechanically." Op. cit., p. 385. Mr. Metcalf quotes me (Idem., p. 380) as saying that slow cooling always produces coarse crystals, and quick cooling fine ones. I think he must have quoted from memory, for I do not believe that I have ever written so dogmatically and unqualifiedly on this point. He probably refers to my statements in this journal, pp. 315, 332, April 30th and May 7th, 1887, which, though incomparably less sweeping, I now regard as overstatements. I, like many, was misled by Chernoff.

[e] "Quand la température s'élève de o à b (W) la texture de l'acier est invariable." "L'acier, chauffé en dessous de b ne change pas de structure, qu'il soit refroidi brusquement ou lentement." Rev. Universelle, 2d ser., I., p. 402, 1877.

[f] "Toutefois, cette expression doit être prise sous cette reserve." "En ce que concerne l'état d'un acier chauffé et par suite ramolli, surtout à des températures voisines de B, il est probable que le changement de texture sera plus grande." Loc cit.

[g] "Aussitôt que la temperature a atteint le point B, l'acier passe rapidement de l'état grenu ou crystallin à l'état amorphe, qu'il conserve jusqu'à son point de fusion." Loc. cit.

5. *Falling temperature* between W and the melting point induces crystallization, the more powerfully the higher the temperature, so that, as the descending temperature approaches W, the strength of the tendency to crystallize falls off sharply, as sketched by the abscissæ of the curve in Figure 63. This crystallization makes the metal very tender as long as the temperature remains high.

His remarks suggest that coarse crystallization does not occur at *stationary* high temperature: but I do not find that he states this directly.

6. If steel thus made tender be again cooled completely, the individual crystals, if they have not been parted mechanically at the high temperature, become so strongly coherent that fracture now occurs across their bodies, and not along their faces.

The last two propositions are not distinctly enunciated by Chernoff. They give his views as I understand them, and the reader must allow for refraction

§ 249. Discussion of Chernoff's Views.—The first three propositions accord with the results of Brinnell and of others.

The first agrees with Brinnell's observation that, if previously annealed steel be quenched from V or even from V+, its carbon remains wholly cement and it retains the cement-carbon hackly fracture: and with mine (p. 12), that no readily perceptible increase in hardness is produced by quenching from below dull redness, though as the quenching temperature rises still farther the hardness increases suddenly.[a]

The second agrees exactly with Brinnell's results as regards the cement-carbon fractures A, B, C, and pretty closely as regards the porcelanic F, which changes comparatively little at temperatures below W, but not as regards the coarse-crystalline D, which according to Brinnel becomes dull-amorphous at H. But, as D is only rendered visible by unusual treatment, there is little doubt that the change which it suffers at V escaped Chernoff's observation.

The *third* agrees exactly with Brinnell's and Metcalf's results.

For the *sixth* (pardon the inversion) I find no evidence. I am tempted to ascribe it to heterophasia or to error in translation, for it is certain that the brittleness of overheated steel and its tendency to break with sharp, well-defined crystals does in a measure survive cooling.

The *fourth* and *fifth* contain what I regard as an extremely serious error, to wit, that coarse crystallization does not set in while the temperature is rising. I first offer evidence in rebuttal, and then point out certain possible reasons for Chernoff's statement.

1. In Brinnell's experiments 5, 22, 38 and 45 (Figure 61) the fracture is granular-crystalline, E, and in his 6, 23, 39 and 46 it is coarse granular-crystalline, D, when steel is quenched immediately after slow rise of temperature.

[a] Metcalf indeed states (op. cit., p. 384), that a hardening effect is produced by quenching from 100° C., and that quenching from any temperature above that of the atmosphere produces appreciable hardening.

It is, indeed, by no means improbable that slight changes in hardness proper may occur on quenching from temperatures far below W and V, changes due in turn to slight variations in the crystallization, arrangement, or even composition of the component minerals of steel, to changes of stress or what not. But these trifling changes are comparable to those which occur in other metals under varying treatment, and not to the unparalleled change which occurs in steel when the quenching temperature rises to the critical point W, a change so vastly greater that it differs from them in kind. A theory which explains this change is not to be rejected because it explains these minor independent changes of hardness in a different way.

2. In the following experiments I compared the fractures which followed slowly rising with these which followed slowly falling temperature.

A. A bar of hard open-hearth steel 0·37 inch square was cut into three pieces each two feet long. These were placed in contact with each other, imbedded in pulverized fire clay, and heated at one end to dazzling whiteness, the remainder being heated solely by conduction. The first and second were drawn and quenched after 160 and 320 minutes respectively. The third was cooled extremely slowly by allowing the fire to burn out gradually, while the bar remained undisturbed and still imbedded in the hot clay. Thus the first bar should record the structure at different temperatures during rising temperature, the second when the temperature was nearly stationary, the third the structure induced by slow cooling from these various temperatures.

Fractures made at points 0·5 inch apart formed a series in each bar like that of Metcalf's experiment, Figure 62. The first two had, at about the same points in their length, the characteristic porcelanic or refined fracture F. In the third this was replaced by a fine crystalline fracture, which I take to correspond to Brinnell's C. But the important point is that the highly heated portions of the three bars gave fractures with nearly the same degrees of coarseness.

B. Two pieces of the same steel were heated in white-hot pulverized fire clay in a muffle for 90 minutes: then one was withdrawn and quenched to dull redness, then replaced against the other till, by transfer of heat, their temperatures became apparently identical: both were then quenched. Here the conditions were the same, except that the temperature of one had been rising, that of the other falling, immediately before quenching. According to Chernoff the former should have been porcelanic, the latter crystalline. I could detect no difference in the coarseness of their fractures with a lens, nor could Mr. F. L. Garrison with the microscope.[b] Similar results were obtained in many other experiments.

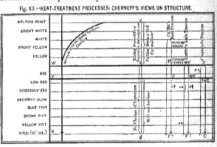

Fig. 63.—HEAT-TREATMENT PROCESSES: CHERNOFF'S VIEWS ON STRUCTURE.

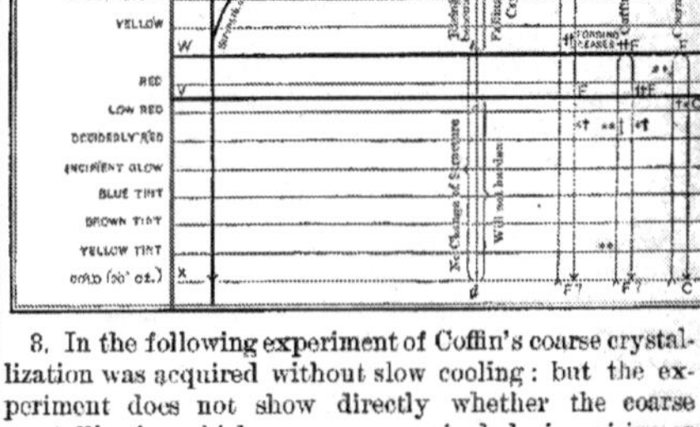

8. In the following experiment of Coffin's coarse crystallization was acquired without slow cooling: but the experiment does not show directly whether the coarse crystallization which arose was acquired during rising or during stationary temperature, or, as is more probable, during both. Two pieces of steel, 1 and 2, containing

[b] I have to thank Mr. Garrison for kindly examining with the microscope some fifty fractures of steel which had been treated with a view to testing the truth of this statement of Chernoff's.

0.4% of carbon, cut from the same bar 1 inch by 4 inches, were both held during 30 hours at temperatures which varied between low whiteness and a point very slightly lower. 1 was then quenched in oil, while 2 was cooled slowly to W and then quenched. The fracture of 1 was but slightly finer than that of 2.[a] Both were coarse crystalline.

Seek we now explanations of Chernoff's statements.

1. The context indicates that they are based in large part on the analogy of the crystallization of certain hydrated salts. As I understand him, there is quite a range of temperature above the melting point of alum, that point at which the crystals dissolve in their own water of crystallization, through which this salt remains liquid while the temperature is rising, but solidifies and crystallizes if the temperature falls, and that too long before it falls to the original melting point.[b] Slow, quiet cooling favors, sudden cooling and agitation oppose the formation of large crystals.

He conceives that the carbon of steel in a roughly similar way "dissolves" the iron itself, *i. e.* renders the whole mass amorphous at temperatures above W, and holds it amorphous as long as the temperature is rising (or stationary): but when the temperature falls, and long before it reaches W again, crystallization sets in, and is the coarser the higher the temperature has been, the slower and more tranquil the cooling. Such analogies only suggest, never prove, often mislead.

2. They seem to be further based on the fact that certain steel ingots, which had been held unnecessarily long at a high temperature, and which had cooled slightly before forging, broke with a strongly developed crystalline fracture at the first blows of the hammer. In one case the ingot was raised to a bright orange: then, while awaiting its turn at the hammer and without removal from the furnace, its temperature was allowed to fall to a bright red. It was then hammered, but broke at the first blow.

In another case when a forging which had been thus treated was turned in a lathe, a cavity, lined with crystals some of which were 0.5 inch in diameter, was found, formed in his opinion by the first blows of the hammer, which separated the weakly united crystals.

As he describes these cases, however, long exposure to a high temperature seems quite as competent as the slow decline of temperature to explain the crystallization and consequent brittleness.

3. The evidence rebutting Chernoff's statements is based on experiments with small bars. In these, as already shown, the interstratal movements which quenching produces and which tend to break up crystallization, should be much less severe than in large masses. As to the effect of quenching on the fracture of large masses I have no evidence. It is possible that in them extremely rapid cooling may completely efface crystallization, thus suggesting fallaciously that slow cooling alone originates the coarse crystallization which it preserves.

4. At the melting point, and perhaps at temperatures between it and bright whiteness, pre-existing crystallization is effaced, and so it is when the temperature, rising from the cold, reaches W. It is possible that, finding steel quenched from these temperatures porcelanic, Chernoff inferred that it would be when quenched from intermediate temperatures.

I have shown at this length the opportunities for error, because the positive and generally accepted statements of this most brilliant metallurgist cannot be dismissed lightly.

To sum up, in most of the points in which Brinnell's statements are opposed by those of others it seems quite clear that he is right.

§ 250. METHODS OF HEAT-TREATMENT.—PRACTICAL APPLICATIONS of the foregoing follow. 1. The more or less complete *restoration of overheated and even of burnt steel*, by reheating to W, repeatedly if need be, followed by forging, by quenching, or by undisturbed slow cooling according to the requirements of the case. (See § 263.)

2. *The annealing of steel castings*, which not only relieves the initial stresses, but effaces the columnar structure, renders the fracture very much finer, and greatly increases strength, elastic limit and ductility.[c] (Cf. Table 9, p. 19.)

On account of the tendency to crystallize above W, and also while the temperature is falling from W to V, Coffin anneals by heating to or slightly above W, cooling rather rapidly to V by opening the furnace doors, then closing them and finishing the cooling very slowly.[d] To hasten cooling, one side and the top of the furnace may be movable and counter-weighted: while, if the piece be large, it may be run in and out on a truck whose top forms the furnace-bottom, and which with its load is run into the open air in cooling to V.

Here, as in annealing in general, while the temperature should reach W, it should rise no further beyond W than is needed to assure us that this point has been reached: and the cooling should not be excessively slow. Ignorance of these cardinal principles has probably been the chief cause of the injury so often done by annealing, and thus of the somewhat widespread distrust of this operation.

3. *Means of accelerating cooling after forging has ceased.*—Power is saved by using a high temperature for forging—the metal being then the softer—but at the risk of excessive crystallization during the subsequent cooling. Hence expedients to hasten this cooling.[e]

Coffin's rail-process (Figure 63) consists in immersing

[a] Private communication, March 28th, 1888.

[b] Of course the melting and freezing points of a substance do not necessarily coincide.

[c] The almost complete lack of ductility of many unannealed steel castings which on annealing become very ductile, shows the accuracy of the definition of steel "an alloy of iron which is cast while in a fluid state into a malleable ingot." The ingot is usually not malleable, and does not become so till reheated. (Cf., p. 1.)

[d] Trans. Am. Soc. Civ. Eng., XV., p. 325, 1887.

[e] While the undisturbed slow cooling from an excessively high temperature to which rails rolled unduly hot are exposed, doubtless tends to induce a coarse crystalline structure and consequent brittleness, especially in case of phosphoric iron, this tendency has unfortunately been most grossly exaggerated. So well conducted a journal as the "Railroad Gazette" (1886, p. 316), gravely stated that a prick punch could be driven by a moderate blow nearly up to the hilt into a rail which had been finished unduly hot, and that the best steel can "be so softened by heating and annealing as to be almost as soft as lead, and equally unable to resist impact and abrasion." From this nonsense and from positive and absurdly untrue statements which follow as to the existing method of rolling, the editor appears to have been the victim of a hoax. It is doubtful, indeed, whether one could readily detect the difference between the *hardness* proper of two rails, one of which had been finished at a light yellow and the other at a cherry-red, though the difference in *structure* would indeed be readily seen. What is surprising and depressing is that such a person could be made to believe such rubbish. (Cf. Engineering and Mining Journal, XLI., p. 390, 1886.)

R. W. Hunt reports rails which, under apparently identical conditions, greatly outlasted others apparently similar in all respects including section, except that the latter had much thicker (deeper) heads than the former, and hence for given quality of metal should have lasted much the longer. The inferiority of the thick-headed rails is reasonably referred to their higher finishing temperature and slower cooling. ("Steel Rails," a paper read before the Am. Inst. Mining Engineers, Oct. 5th, 1888, to appear in Transactions, Vol. XVII., 1889.)

the rail in water immediately after leaving the rolls, till its temperature falls to V, then allowing it to cool slowly in the air. To equalize the cooling, submerged jets of water play on the thick rail-head. The rapid cooling to V removes the opportunity for crystallization: the slow cooling from V down allows most of the carbon to pass to the cement state, and avoids the stresses of unequal contraction which would arise were the sudden cooling more complete. Toughness is promoted in both ways.[a]

To further equalize the cooling, I suggest holding the rail by a guard, which incloses web and flange so as to restrict the circulation of water about these thinner parts, as is successfully done in hardening mowing-machine knives.

4. *Lowering the finishing-temperature*, whether by rolling slowly, by rolling double or quadruple lengths—this has been found to improve the quality of wrought-iron greatly,—by employing thicker piles or ingots, or by throwing a jet of water, steam or air on the metal during the last part of the rolling so as to cool it nearly or quite to V, as is done in tyre-rolling. In case of rails the thick, slowly cooling head may be advantageously cooled thus during the late passes.

Three uniformly heated steel bars cut from a single billet were rolled by a competent American metallurgist, one very fast, one normally, one very slowly: their merit was inversely as their finishing temperature.

The tyre-roller's aim in lowering the finishing temperature is that scale may not form after rolling ceases, and thus that the tyre's surface may be smooth: doubtless he is sometimes ignorant of the incidental great structural benefit to his metal. Eye-bar makers, however, formerly ignorant of the structural injury due to hot finishing, have lately been forced by the repeated failures and rejection of hot-finished eye-bars when tested whole, to lower their finishing temperature expressly to benefit the metal structurally. They hold the bars before the last passes, till they have cooled properly.

Thermo-tension,[b] or subjecting the red-hot metal to high tensile stress which is maintained during cooling, may perhaps come under this head. If, owing to the tension, the piece elongates, or does not shorten in conformity to the cooling, its diameter must decrease more than conformably to the cooling, which implies a movement of the particles among themselves: this, like forging, may so long as it lasts suffice to prevent crystallization. It is possible that this destruction of previous crystallization occurs chiefly or even wholly as the metal cools past the temperature of weakness at or near V, which will be described in § 256, D.

5. *Clémandot*[c] subjects bars of cherry-red-hot high-carbon steel to a pressure of say 14,000 to 43,000 pounds per square inch, exerted preferably by the smooth, cold faces of a hydraulic press. The steel is said to be fine-grained, harder and stronger than unhardened steel, yet practically as ductile, and specially suitable for magnets. The scanty statements about it are not over-convincing. The rationale is not known. It may be that the distortion due to the pressure rapidly breaks up any crystallization acquired during rising temperature, while the cold press-faces cool the steel so fast as to prevent further crystallization and to hinder the change of carbon from the hardening to the cement state. Indeed, Lan finds that, under identical conditions, a decidedly larger proportion of the total carbon is in the hardening state in steel treated by Clémandot's process than in that cooled in the usual way. The mean of five pairs of concordant analyses showed that a steel containing 0·70% of carbon had 0·585% of hardening carbon when thus compressed, but only 0·49% when uncompressed.

This process is probably inapplicable to large pieces, as the removal of heat from them would necessarily be slow. It is said to be applied to magnets successfully[d] and with surprising results, imparting to them a coercive force, less intense indeed than that due to quenching-hardening, but apparently more enduring. For, while the coercive force of quenching-hardened steel falls greatly on tempering, Carnot states that that of compression-hardened steel is not lessened even by reheating and forging.[e] Compression-hardening has further advantages over quenching-hardening in that it neither cracks even the hardest steels, nor makes them untoolably hard. Unlike quenching- and hammer-hardening it apparently does not lower the density. The results in Table 86 A are reported.[e]

I suggest hastening the cooling by pressing with thick copper blocks, iced before or during compression.

6. *In Chernoff's process* the cooled forging or casting is heated to W, so as to acquire a porcelanic structure, then slowly cooled. As it is impracticable to heat exactly to W, and as the porcelanic structure is not acquired till W is reached, he recommended heating slightly above W; and, on account of the tendency to crystallize in cooling from above W, to quench till the temperature fell to

[a] U. S. Patents 368,132 and 378,082, August 9th, 1887, and February 21st 1888. After leaving the rolls the rail has its crop-ends sawn off at once as usual, and thence passes between feed-rollers, of which several pairs grasp it firmly, and which lie above a water-bosh. When the rail has arrived above this bosh the rollers are stopped, and the bosh raised by bell-crank levers, submerging the rail, while sprays of water play on its head to equalize the cooling, the thick head naturally tending to cool more slowly than the web and flange. When the rail has cooled so far that its remaining heat would suffice when evenly distributed to bring its temperature to V (a low red), the bosh is lowered, and the rail thenceforth allowed to cool slowly.

[b] Thurston, Matls. of Engineering, I., p. 526: Metallurg. Rev., I., p. 10. Also Jarolinek, Journ. Iron and Steel Inst., 1885, II., p. 942, from Dingler's Pol. Journ., CCLV., pp. 1-9, 56-60.

[c] "Trempe par compression," Le Genie Civil, V., p. 217, 1884; Comptes Rendus XCIV., p. 959, April 3d, 1882: Journ. Iron and St. Inst., 1882, I., pp. 335, 382. Cf. Percy, idem, 1885, I., p. 31, who incorrectly thinks that the principle is covered by Whitworth's method of compression: the rate of cooling forms an essential difference.

[d] L. Clémandot, Private Communication, Sept. 21, 1888.

[e] A. Carnot, Rept. Committee on Chemical Arts, of la Société d'Encouragement, Reprint "La Trempe par Compression," Paris, Steinheil, 1886.

Table 86 A.—Influence of Clémandot's Process of Compression-hardening (Carnot, op. cit.).

	Composition.						Properties under tensile test.						Specific gravity.		
							Uncompressed.			Compressed.					
	Carbon.	Silicon.	Manganese.	Phosphorus.	Sulphur.	Tungsten.	Tensile strength, lbs. per sq. in.	Elastic limit, lbs. per sq. in.	Elongation, % in 3 in.	Tensile strength, lbs. per sq. in.	Elastic limit, lbs. per sq. in.	Elongation, % in 3 in.	Natural.	Hardened.	Compressed.
1	·10	·06	·84	·02	·08	....	57,600	34,180	42	65,100	46,900	37	....	....	....
2	·25	·07	·12	·03	·08	....	60,800	32,300	32	73,600	49,100	30	....	....	....
3	....	....	....	....	....	....	83,200	41,200	25	108,800	81,700	24	....	....	....
4	·51	·11	·34	·63	·02	....	89,600	44,800	24	109,500	72,500	20	....	....	....
5	·62	·16	·22	[illegible]	·08	3·02	....	....	....	....	....	....	7·888	7·882	7·888
6	·81	·19	[illegible]	·68	·06	....	113,100	59,750	10	104,158	113,906	10	7·709	7·720	7·777

or below W, then to cool slowly so as to avoid the stresses which quenching to the cold would cause.[a]

7. *Coffin's axle-process*, in use at the Cambria Iron Works, goes a distinct step beyond Chernoff's. Recognizing the tendency to crystallize during slow cooling from W to V, Coffin heats to slightly above W, quenches to V, then cools slowly.

Six axles tested within a month of adopting this process showed the following admirable properties.

	Tensile strength, pounds per square inch.		Elongation in 8 inches.	Contraction of area.
	Elastic.	Ultimate.		
Maximum	46,340	95,600	20	42
Minimum	39,120	80,900	13·1	16·5
Average	42,420	87,830	16·5	30·9

Two halves of an axle, one treated by this process, the other untreated, gave the following results.[b]

	Tensile strength, pounds per square inch.		Elongation in 4 inches.	Contraction of area.
	Elastic.	Ultimate.		
Untreated	36,000	71,520	24·5%	51·5%
Treated	44,000	72,020	24·07%	57·2%

Chernoff obtained the following results. Of three samples broken from the same bar of steel, A was simply cooled slowly after forging: B was reheated to W[c] and slowly cooled: C was reheated to W,[d] quenched in water to a reddish brown, then slowly cooled. The size of grain was as follows:

TABLE 87.—EFFECT OF COFFIN'S PROCESS ON SIZE OF GRAIN.

	Mean diameter of central grains.	
	Inches.	Mm.
A, slowly cooled after forging	0·1414	3·675
B, reheated to W, then slowly cooled	0·0048	0·122
C, reheated a little higher than B, quenched to V, then slowly cooled	0·0004	0·010

A broke under a single hand-hammer blow, B required five such blows, C could be broken only by a steam-hammer. Of a similar series from a railway-tyre, A broke under one blow of a 5-ton hammer, B under four blows, and C under five heavy blows.

In thus quenching nearly to V instead of barely below W as he himself thought sufficient, Chernoff practically used Coffin's process in these cases, but apparently blindly, and without recognizing its nature or advantages, for clearly he believed that no important crystallization occurs below W. Hence in practicing his own process, he and others might often or even habitually cool to but slightly below W instead of to V.

The rail-process seems specially adapted to rolled, the axle- to hammered pieces: for the time offered for crystallization in one part of a hammered piece after it has been hammered, and while the remainder of the piece is hammering, may permit much crystallization, which simple quenching would not remove, but which is removed when the temperature is later raised to W. Beyond this the more expensive axle-process should give a finer fracture and hence better quality than the rail-process.

These methods differ from Jarolimek's interrupted cooling (p. 24), in that, while retaining a fine-grained structure, they aim to avoid hardening. Lead-hardening[e]—quenching in molten lead, said to be used in France for armor-plates—should give an intermediate result, retaining part of the carbon in the hardening state, while setting up far less severe stresses than those due to oil-quenching. The severity of these has led many eminent engineers—among them Adamson, Bramwell, Maitland and J. Riley,—to question the advisability of oil-hardening.[f] It seems probable that hardening must in many cases, *e. g.* those of guns, projectiles and armor-plates, be made less severe than at present, retaining much of the carbon in the hardening state, but avoiding great intensity of stress, whether by less violent cooling, (as with molten lead): or by interrupting or retarding the cooling after it has passed a certain point, (as by dipping momentarily in oil, then in lead, or vice versa, according to the conditions of the case): or by tempering after hardening.

To Find the Temperatures W and V.—A cold steel bar, preferably but not necessarily of like composition with the steel to be treated, and about ¾" square by four feet long, is placed in a hot furnace, its ends resting on two bricks. When its temperature reaches W it will bend down suddenly. Remove and support it at its ends in the open air: when its temperature falling reaches V it will again bend suddenly. Da capo, quantum libet. (Cf. § 254, B, 3, and § 256, D).

Or heat such a bar to redness, nick all around at nine points half an inch apart, the first next to one end; cool gently; heat this end to dazzling whiteness, the heat running back by conduction till the last nick is nearly red; note the temperature at each nick; quench; wipe; break at the nicks. That which has the finest grain was near W when quenched. Here the color produced by spotting with nitric acid of 1·23 sp. gr., the hardness, and probably the coercive force change abruptly.

V may be recognized by the sudden loss and the sudden recovery of magnetism as the temperature rises and falls past it.

Enormous advantages may be anticipated from the systematic study of heat-treatment, of which we now know but little. In treating important pieces the temperature should be controlled by pyrometer, not the eye.

CHANGES OF CRYSTALLIZATION, ETC.

THE SALIENT FEATURES OF CRYSTALLIZATION can now be considered in a more general way.

§ 251. *Governing Crystallization.* The following cases, though insufficient to establish, go to show that in the struggle for dominance between the component minerals of steel, those (1) which separate earliest and (2) those most abundantly present are best equipped: one of these will usually determine the general structure of the mass, and distribute the others, often as a meshwork between its own crystals.

Sorby finds that, in those parts of wrought-iron which have but little pearlyte, this mineral is distributed as a meshwork between the crystals of ferrite: in adjoining regions, where pearlyte is in relatively large proportion, it

[a] Revue Universelle, 2d Ser., VII., p. 415, 1877.

[b] Trans. Am. Soc. Mechan. Engineers, IX., p. 142: Mechanics, Dec., 1887, p. 317.

[c] "Un peu au-dessus du rouge clair non brillant."

[d] "Au rouge clair." Thus the second piece may have been raised to a little higher temperature than the third: yet hardly enough to account for the great difference in the size of their grains.

[e] Gautier, Jour. Iron and St. Inst., 1888, I., p. 159.

[f] Maitland, "The Treatment of Gun Steel," excerpt Proc. Inst. Civ. Eng., LXXXIX., pp. 21, 48, 58, 77, 129; 1887. It appears to be no uncommon thing for hardened steel projectiles to crack or even burst. Bramwell states that a visitor to a projectile-factory was warned lately that "those things are going off at all times, and occasionally they fly with very considerable violence," (Prince Rupert's drops one would say) and that a steel gun-tube has broken to pieces in the lathe.

apparently has crystallized first and distributed the ferrite between its crystals. So, too, in cast-iron: in grey iron, rich in graphite, the graphite appears to have crystallized first and determined the structure of the whole: in No. 3 pig-iron Sorby finds that, in those regions which contain the most graphite, this mineral appears to govern the crystallization, and we may surmise that this happens because, though the total quantity of graphite is small, yet, owing to its high melting point, it tends to crystallize very early. In the less graphitic portions of the same pig the pearlyte appears to govern the crystallization of the whole, and so it does throughout the still less graphitic forge pig.

Again, in refined white cast-iron, in which there is about twice as much pearlyte as cementite, the pearlyte seems to govern: in spiegeleisen these two minerals are in about equal proportions, and here cementite seems to govern.

§252. Recrystallization.—We can readily understand that the minerals thus distributed as a meshwork between the crystals of their more powerful elder brothers should be in unstable equilibrium, and that, when opportunity offers, they should seek to acquire their normal crystalline polarity, to break their bonds, to crystallize anew. So, too, crystals which have been distorted by forging or by the interstratal motion due to quenching, and crystals of minerals new-created by change of affinities due to change of temperature as at V and W, should seek, the former to recover, the latter to attain their normal polarity. Those whose growth has been dwarfed by short or feeble heating may, when softening high temperature again permits, remarshal their squads into platoons, companies, regiments, the aggregating crystalline tendency asserting itself and forming larger and larger crystals. Each crystal in growing must feed on its neighbors, drawing a little perhaps from the mesh-work which surrounds it. Hence, if the average size of the crystals is to increase, some must cease to exist, must merge in their neighbors. If, be it from more robust individuality, be it because separated by a greater thickness of mesh-work, the neighbor on one side resist assimilation more stubbornly than that on the other, growth will be uneven: while under extremely favorable conditions, *e. g.* during very long strong heating, these asymmetrical grains may give and take till symmetrical cubes or octahedra result. And such is the case.

The structure of many minerals, *e. g.* magnetite, reminds us in one respect of that of iron. We find the grains usually of most irregular shape, approaching by insensible gradations, as conditions are more and more favorable, to the almost absolute perfection of crystalline form which individual magnetite crystals occasionally show. So too in granular iron, the grains, usually irregular, under favoring circumstances are occasionally extremely well developed crystals; and between the two extremes the gradations appear as insensible as in case of magnetite.

Hence we may regard the uneven, asymmetrical but often smooth-faced grains as very imperfect crystals, or at least as fragments of crystals broken through their cleavage planes.[a]

[a] Thurston indeed thinks that granular structure is confounded with real crystallization; and that granular fracture and crystalline structure are apparently distinct in nature (Mat'ls of Engineering, II., pp. 579-82). Most of us, however, would accept the dictum "All granular and fibrous (inorganic) bodies"—"must be regarded as collections of imperfectly formed crystals," at least for cases like the present. (Watts, Dictionary of Chemistry, II., p. 115).

Finally, special conditions may force a certain mode of growth, to which the metal is not naturally inclined: on heating after these conditions have ceased to exist, these quasi abnormal crystals may readily give way to more normal ones. Such are the columnar crystals forced on solidifying steel ingots by the rapid removal of heat by the mould, and removed by simple reheating.

Our fracture studies tell us little of the nature of the crystalline changes which they record: but of this nature something has been learnt from polished sections. We will now consider certain prominent cases of recrystallization, and incidentally certain features of the initial crystallization.

§ 253. Recrystallization on Slow Cooling from the Melting Point.—In an ingot of hard cast steel there are, to judge from Sorby's description, the records of three successive crystallizations. First we have the large

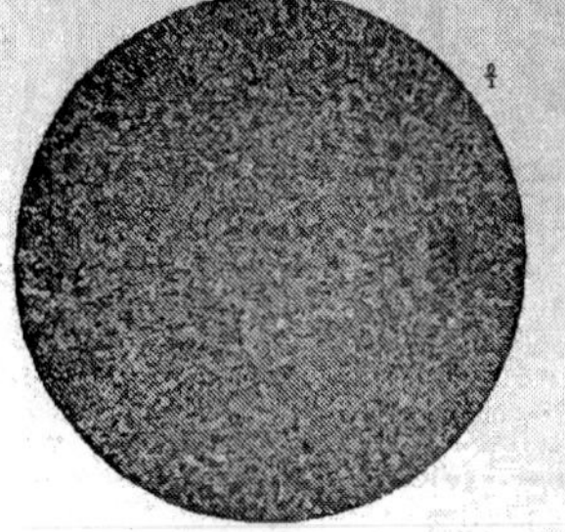

Fig. 63A.

Transverse section of cast-steel ingot, Sorby. Nearly wholly pearlyte.

prismatic columnar crystals, normal to the cooling surface, and conspicuous on fracture (Figures 64, 65 and 68). They apparently represent the first crystallization, be it of hardenite, be it of the hypothetical mother-of-pearlyte, which in this case has expelled the excess of cementite present, distributing it as an elongated mesh-work between the crystals. Secondly, these columnar crystals are chiefly composed of groups of pearlyte, disposed with little or no relation to the columnar structure, indeed shooting from one column into another, and apparently formed from the substance of the primary crystals by a second crystallization. Finally, by a third crystallization, each of the individual members of the radial groups of pearlyte has split into parallel layers of cementite and ferrite, which apparently occupy the space previously occupied by a simple undivided crystal.

The composite ingot-structure, recognized in large part by color-differences and by the use of high powers, is shown very imperfectly by photography, Figure 63 A.

So Osmond and Werth, on etching the polished section of an ingot containing 0·50% of carbon, find that it is composed of (a) simple cells in (b) dendritic, mutually limiting groups, and these again may form (c) complex coverless agglomerations.[b]

In connection with these evidences of repeated recrystallization, it is interesting to recall the repeated evolutions of heat during the slow cooling of iron, which

[b] Annales des Mines, 8th ser., VIII., p. 13, 1885.

manifest themselves by retarding or even reversing the fall of temperature (§§ 254–7).

This columnar ingot-structure is the less marked the freer the steel from carbon, perhaps because the soft steels pass less directly from the liquid to the solid state than the harder ones, the pasty condition which characterizes their solidification being opposed to the formation of crystals.[a] In small ingots, say three inches in diameter, the columns may extend to the centre (Figures 27–8, § 222, p. 148): in larger ones they form an external layer, which often ends quite abruptly, and is succeeded by a region with a granular or polyhedral structure. The columnar crystals

Fig. 64. Fig. 65.

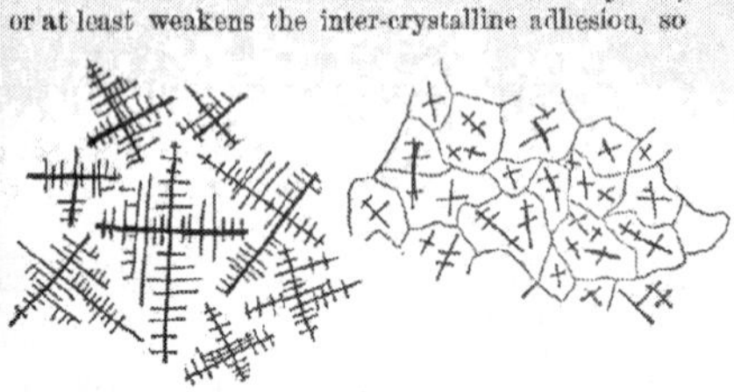

Longitudinal sections of steel ingots, transverse to main axes of the columnar crystals. (Chernoff.)

Fig. 66. Supposed lateral axes of the columnar crystals.

Fig. 67. Resulting irregular cross-section of the columnar crystals.

adhere to each other comparatively feebly: this favors external cracking, both in cooling and in the early passes in the blooming mill. These cracks usually pass between the columnar crystals, revealing their surfaces, rather than across them. Figures 64–5 show bunches of these crystals in my collection, from the outside of a "cobble" or ingot which cracked so badly that it had to be cut up. In Figure 64 the columns have been twisted by the rolls: the granular structure is also seen. Figure 68 shows the columnar structure, and its abrupt change to the granular.

The asymmetry of these columns may be referred to three facts.

1. The distance between the main axis of adjoining columns varies irregularly. 2. The directions of the lateral axes of neighboring crystals bear little relation to each other. For both these reasons the lateral growth of a given column is likely to be interrupted by that of its neighbors at different distances from its main axis on its different sides. 3. That the different lateral axes of a given column appear to grow at different rates.[b] These lateral axes are sketched in Figure 66, and the boundaries of the columns in Figure 67.

The exterior columnar structure is clearly due to the rapid escape of heat from the shell of the ingot into the mould. We may suppose that the metal naturally tends to crystallize in equiaxed grains: that there is a struggle between this tendency and the tendency to crystallize in indefinitely long prisms which the rapid outward cooling sets up. As the walls thicken and the flow of heat outwards slackens, the prismatic tendency weakens: the sudden transition from the prismatic to the equiaxed formation suggests that no resultant, no compromise is possible, so that from the moment when the equiaxial tendency outweighs the prismatic it reigns alone, as if its rival were not.

Chernoff[c] pointed out that, in large ingots, this granular region is succeeded by an inner more compact one. He refers the granular region to the interstratal movements which must occur during even slow cooling, and which must be especially great in large ingots, and more marked near the outside than in the centre, because much of this motion must have ended before the centre has solidified. We may conceive that this motion, occurring while the region which we find granular is at a certain critical temperature of inter-crystalline weakness, breaks or weakens the mesh-work which surrounds the crystals, or at least weakens the inter-crystalline adhesion, so

Fig. 68.

Cross section of steel ingot, natural size, showing columnar and granular structures, and blowholes. (Martens.)

that when rupture subsequently occurs it passes between the crystals: while in the central portion, the inter-crystalline adhesion being unimpaired, rupture strikes more or less into the bodies of the crystals, the fracture is more compact.

[a] Chernoff, Rev. Universelle, 2d ser., VII., p. 130, 1880.

[b] Idem, p. 141.

[c] Idem, pp. 131, 143. I have carried these speculations a step beyond his.

Osmond and Werth[a] explain the granular region by supposing that it begins at the moment when the interior as a whole has reached the freezing point: from this time on solidification occurs from internal centres of organization growing in all directions. But is there such a moment? Will not each successive layer reach this point after the one outside it?

§ 254. RECRYSTALLIZATION ON REHEATING SLOWLY COOLED METAL.—*A. On simple prolonged exposure to a high temperature*, to judge from Sorby's microscopic studies, it seems that, even when no chemical change is apparent, each of the several minerals draws together and separates more distinctly from the others. Thus the pearlyte and free ferrite separate from each other as more distinct crystals when wrought-iron is annealed, and some of the combined cementite separates from the pearlyte: when steel of 0·49% of carbon is annealed, the free ferrite, originally distributed as mesh-work plates within and between the dominant crystals of pearlyte (Figure 56), draws together into grains.[b]

B, at V.—During the gradual heating of iron several marked phenomena occur at or near V. The rise of temperature is retarded or perhaps even reversed[d]: the expansion is checked and reversed, so that the metal contracts momentarily, and then re-expands[c]: a dry crackling sound is heard[c]: the thermo-electric deportment becomes anomalous[e]: the coercive force[fgh] and the power of being rendered a *temporary* magnet[g] (whether by electric current or by another magnet) and hence of being attracted by the magnet,[f] almost disappear, the latter at least through a series of distinct and separate diminutions[g]: and the specific heat (as inferred from the quantity of heat given out by the metal when immersed in a calorimeter) suddenly increases, remaining astonishingly high from 660° to 720° C., when it again descends somewhat, but remains about twice as great as at the ordinary temperature.[i] The changes in attraction by the magnet and in specific heat have been directly proved to be simultaneous[j]: the other changes, too, as far as we can tell without precise measurements, occur simultaneously with these.

Nickel and cobalt lose their power of being attracted by the magnet, and undergo like simultaneous changes in specific heat,[j] nickel between 220° and 400° C., cobalt at about 900° C. The thermo-electric power of nickel, also, behaves anomalously at the critical point of this metal.[e] Of these phenomena, the loss of magnetism, the thermo-electric change, the change of specific heat and the retardation of rise of temperature have been noted in almost and in some cases quite carbonless iron: the momentary contraction, however, readily detected in hard iron and especially in steel, could not be detected in very soft iron, at least in certain specimens.

If the quenching-temperature of steel be gradually raised, the coercive force of the quenched metal remains nearly constant till some temperature reported to be 875° C., or between V and W, is reached: with further rise of temperature, at least to above 1,075° C., the coercive force increases rapidly.

C, at W. To the sudden porcelanization of fracture which occurs when steel is heated to W, correspond not only the apparently simultaneous sudden change from cement to hardening carbon and sudden increase of hardening power, but also the appearance of polished sections, and certain very marked thermal and other phenomena.

1. Polished Sections: By their study Sorby finds that when a steel ingot of 0·49% of carbon is quenched from redness, the composite structure with its marks of successive crystallizations is no more. Traces of the original net-work can be seen: "but on the whole the grain is so fine and uniform that even a power of 400 linear fails to reveal the ultimate constitution, and shows little more than that the grains are somewhere about $\frac{1}{20000}$ inch in diameter."[k] Just as our fracture studies show that the crystalline force exerted when cement changes to hardening carbon at W is so great as to completely eradicate all previous crystallization, so the microscope teaches that this force here reunites the comparatively widely scattered particles of the different minerals, forming a single new compound, hardenite, though to do this it probably has to move some of them considerable distances. Osmond and Werth too cannot find their composite cells in etched polished sections of hardened steel; and its structure as revealed by Weyl's method differs greatly from that of unhardened steel.[l] While the temperature at which these changes in the appearance of polished sections occurs has not been determined directly, we infer that it probably is W, from the fact that the fracture and the condition of carbon change at this point, and that the hardening power is acquired here.

2. *Coffin's Weld.*[m]—If a bar of tool steel, say $\frac{3}{8}$ inch square, be broken, and the fresh fractures placed in apposition; or if two of its surfaces be accurately planed by grinding and put together: and if the pieces thus in close contact be inclosed in platinum foil to exclude the air, and heated to W in the flame of a Bunsen burner or otherwise, they will unite more or less completely. This does not seem to be like the cold welding of lead, for it does not appear to occur below W. It is here interesting to note Chernoff's remark that the intimate contact of two

[a] Annales des Mines, 8th ser., VIII., p. 69, 1885. The resemblance which they note between the granular region and lead bullets powerfully pressed together in a mould does not imply that the former grows under pressure, for the granulation occurs in central regions which are not likely to be in compression during or after freezing. The hexagonal structure of the bee's honey-comb does not imply pressure, unless indeed of circumstances.

[b] Jour. Iron and Steel Inst., 1887, I., pp. 269, 272.

[c] Barrett, Phil. Mag. XLVI., p. 473, 1873.

[d] Osmond, Transformations du Fer et du Carbone, 1888.

[e] Tait, Trans. Roy. Soc. Edinbgh., XXVII., p. 125, 1873: Proc. Roy. Soc. Edinbgh., VIII., p. 33, 1873.

[f] Gilbert.

[g] Gore, Phil. Mag., XL., p. 170, 1870.

[h] Coercive force, or retentiveness, the power of becoming and of remaining a *permanent* magnet.

[i] Pionchon, Comptes Rendus, CII., p. 1455, 1886. Pionchon obtained the following expressions for the specific heat of iron:

From 0° to 660° $q_0^t = 0{\cdot}11012t + 0{\cdot}000025{,}333{,}33t^2 + 0{\cdot}000{,}000{,}054{,}66664t^3$.

From 660° to 720° $q_0^t = 0{\cdot}57803t - 0{\cdot}001{,}435{,}987t^2 + 0{\cdot}000{,}001{,}195t^3$.

From 720° to 1,000°, $q_0^t = 0{\cdot}218t - 39$.

From 1050° to 1200°, $q_0^t = 0{\cdot}198{,}87t - 23\ 44$.

Comptes Rendus, CII., pp. 675, 1454: CIII., p. 1122.

From this it appears that during the cooling of iron two abnormal evolutions of heat occur; a lower one between 660° and 720° C., a r 1, absorbing 5·8 calories, and a higher one at about 1050°.

[j] Idem., CIII., p. 1124, 1886.

[k] Jour. Iron and Steel Inst., 1887, I., p. 276.

[l] Annales des Mines, 8th Ser., VIII., pp. 14, 8.

[m] Trans. Am. Soc. Mech. Eng., IX., to appear. Mr. Coffin performed this experiment successfully at the Philadelphia meeting of this society, using a Bunsen burner: and I have pieces which he has welded, which by their sharpness, color and freedom from scale show beyond question that they were united either at a temperature very far below the usual welding point of steel, or else with almost perfect exclusion of oxygen.

surfaces of iron of the same nature heated to a temperature above B (*i. e.* W ?) suffices to unite them.[a]

Mr. Coffin reasonably ascribes the union to the sudden and violent change of crystallization which occurs at W. The elements rearrange themselves, seeking new alliances with such energy that neighboring molecules, not only in different crystals but actually in different bars, unite.

3. *Coffin's Bend.*—A steel bar A was heated to above W and then, without removing it from the furnace, supports were placed beneath its ends, and the temperature held constant for thirty minutes, during which no perceptible deflection occurred. It was withdrawn, cooled, and replaced on supports in the hot furnace. When its temperature had again risen to about W the bar began to deflect.[b]

In a similar experiment tried in my presence, two straight steel bars, 2 and 3, containing 0·67% of carbon, ⅝ inch square and 4 feet long, were heated near each other in a reverberatory furnace. 3 was supported at its ends only, 2 lay on the level hearth. 150 seconds after entering the furnace and while at a low yellow 3 began to bend, and bent about one inch in the next 120 seconds. It then appeared to cease bending. Removed from the furnace 5·5 minutes later and slowly cooled, its total deflection was found to be 1·06 inches, showing that practically all the bending had occurred during two minutes while it was passing a certain critical range, above which it ceased to bend. 2, now apparently hotter than 3 had been when bending, was supported at its ends: no deflection could be detected.

Clearly the bending here is not due to the temperature as such, but to something which happens while the temperature is passing W, and apparently during the change from the cement- to the hardening-carbon crystallization. Like instances of the temporary weakening of steel during other changes of crystallization will be described in §§ 255 and 256 D.

4. *Thermal Phenomena.*—The apparent specific heat, at least of pure iron, rises suddenly at about 1,050° C.

§ 255. Recrystallization on Reheating Quenched Steel.—In line with Brinnell's experiment showing that, though the cement-carbon hackly fractures of annealed steel do not change on reheating to below W, the hardening-carbon granular fractures do; with the heat evolution and with the change of carbon from hardening to cement which occur when hardened steel is reheated to 210° C. (410° F., a pale straw color), is the following experiment of Coffin's, showing that hardened steel becomes more flexible on slight rise of temperature than tempered, *i. e.* partly annealed steel does.

Two exactly similar half-inch square steel bars, five inches long, A and B, Figure 69, were hardened. A was

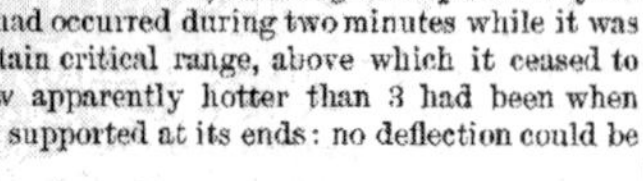

Fig. 69.

then heated to a blue tint, part of its carbon presumably becoming cement. They were then clamped together at the ends, wedged apart slightly in the middle, heated slowly and uniformly to a light straw color, and slowly cooled. A, in which no change of carbon should have occurred, retained its previous shape, while B, whose carbon should have changed in part to cement during heating, became slightly concave towards its mate.[c]

The flexibility of steel under these conditions seems to be known and taken advantage of by makers of steel tools, who correct the shape of the hardened tools slightly, by pressure applied on reheating them to but not above a very light straw tint.[d]

§ 256. Recrystallization During Slow Cooling from W.—Here a remarkable evolution of heat, known as the "after-glow," "recalescence" or "Gore's phenomenon," manifested by marked rise of temperature and re-expansion, and accompanied by great temporary increase of flexibility, occurs, beginning apparently as the temperature approaches V, which as we have seen appears to be a critical point for the change of carbon from hardening to cement, and of fracture from granular to hackly. Its intensity increases with the proportion of carbon present. Barrett failed to detect it in case of manganese steel,[e] nor could I detect it by the eye in case of the tungsten steels Nos. 5 and 6 of Table 34. But I found it well marked in case of chrome steel.

Other but less marked liberations of heat during cooling, and also during rise of temperature, will be considered in § 257.

A. *The rise of temperature*, so marked as to force itself on the attention of several observers independently, is readily detected by watching in a dark place the gradual cooling of a flat high-carbon steel bar, which has been highly heated at one end. The color does not die out gradually, as in the case of a bar of platinum, copper or wrought-iron (7 to 10, Figure 70), but we get the remarkable phenomena observed by Brinnell and shown in 1 to 5, Figure 70. A bright band suddenly appears near the boundary between the yet-glowing and the non-glowing portions of the bar, and gradually spreads over the whole surface of the glowing region. This indicates that as the temperature of each point falls to a certain critical degree, probably V, it again rises. After this the color dies out normally, as in 7 to 10. The after-glow may also be detected by comparing in a dark place the appearance during cooling of a wrought-iron and of a high-carbon steel bar, initially at the same temperature. The cooling of the steel first outstrips that of the wrought-iron: but soon the wrought-iron overtakes the steel, which indeed brightens visibly.

Barrett has proved that there is an actual increase of thermal as well as of luminous radiation[f] at the critical point in case of cooling steel.

C. *The actual expansion* which accompanies the after-glow has been detected by Gore,[g] Barrett,[h] and Coffin,[i] and has set hundreds or thousands of mill-men puzzling over the numerous reversals of curvature of rails on the hot-bed.[j] Coffin found that the retardation of contraction increased greatly with the proportion of carbon. A four-

[a] Revue Universelle, 1877, I.

[b] Trans. Am. Soc. Civ. Eng., XV., p. 324, 1887.

[c] Trans. Am. Soc. Civ. Eng., XV., p. 324, 1887.

[d] T. R. Almond, Trans. Am. Soc. Mech. Eng., IX., p. 151, 1888.

[e] Discussion of a paper on manganese steel, excerpt Proc. Inst. Civ. Eng., XCIII., p. 116, 1887-8.

[f] Phil. Mag., XLVI., p. 476, 1873.

[g] Phil. Mag., XXXVIII., p. 59, 1869.

[h] Idem, XLVI., p. 472, 1873.

[i] American Machinist, Jan. 15th, 1887, p. 4.

[j] Sweet, Trans. Am. Soc. Mech. Eng., VII., p. 154, 1886.

foot bar, with 0·90% of carbon, in cooling from an orange heat contracted $\frac{1}{8}$″, re-expanded $\frac{1}{32}$″, then again contracted $\frac{9}{16}$″: a similar bar with 0·17% of carbon contracted pretty regularly during 45 seconds, then ceased to contract measurably for 20 seconds, then again contracted. A bar with 0·07% of carbon contracted continuously but not quite regularly. Barrett, too, though unable to detect this expansion in some very soft wrought-iron, found it very marked in hard wrought-iron, and especially so in steel.

The after-glow has been referred to an evolution of heat due to the pressure of the more rapidly cooling outside on the interior. In thick bars, whose outside is appreci-

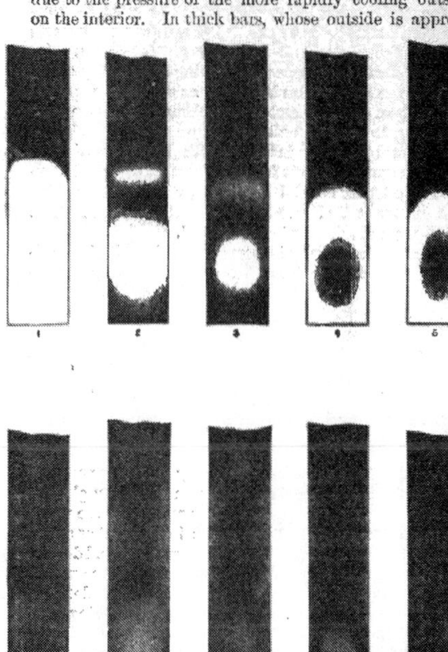

Fig. 70.

Appearance during slow cooling of a bar of tool steel heated at one end. Brinnell.

ably cooler than the inside during cooling, the after-glow occurs somewhat gradually, and might possibly be referred to such a cause. Were this the true cause, however, when we come to small wires, whose outside and inside cool at nearly identical rates, the after-glow should become very faint. But it is precisely in these that it is remarkable. Not only are heat and light evolved, but the wire expands with a sudden *jerk* when the cooling reaches a certain point. Barrett, using a multiplying index to follow the movement of the wire, which was heated by an electric current, reports among other tests "wire bright red: contact broken, index fell from 32 to 20, jerked forward to 24·5, then fell to 4: wire cold." The suddenness of the phenomena, the actual expansion and other features seem to show conclusively that some molecular change occurs within the metal, and that the recalescence is not simply due to the pressure of shell on core.

D. *Coffin's Bend.*—Coffin finds that the change from hardening to cement carbon in slow cooling past V, like the same change on heating to a straw tint, and like the change from cement to hardening carbon in heating past W, is accompanied by a great depression of the transverse elastic limit. In an experiment which he carried out with my assistance, a steel bar four feet long and $\frac{5}{8}$ inch square, with 0·67% of carbon, was heated on the level hearth of a reverberatory furnace to a low yellow, say W, then removed, supported at its ends in the outer air, and loaded in the middle with 7·5 pounds. During the first 90 seconds after removal it did not bend perceptibly: in the next 35 it bent 1·5 inches, and then stopped bending altogether. The bending began and ended gradually. In several other experiments we found that the deflection was proportional to the theoretical deflecting power of the loads. In one case a $\frac{5}{8}$ inch steel bar, four feet long, with a load of 7·5 pounds in the middle, began bending 135 seconds after leaving the furnace, and bent 0·3 inch between the 135th and the 250th second: a load of about 150 pounds applied 30 seconds later produced no further deflection that we could detect with our rough appliances.[a]

Finally, the total deflection under given load appears to be the same whether the temperature descend rather rapidly or extremely slowly past the critical range.

In straightening railway axles Coffin takes advantage of this temporary increase of flexibility, by applying to the axle's convex side, while the temperature is *falling* past V, a very gentle pressure, one which would not bend the axle if after cooling it were *reheated to* V.

E. The magnetic and thermo-electric properties undergo changes opposite in sign to those which occur in heating past V. A cooling iron wire in contact with a magnet and surrounded by a coil of copper wire induces an electric current in this wire as its temperature passes some point which is at or near V.[b]

It is noteworthy that neither this last phenomenon nor the expansion, the evolution of heat nor the momentary depression of the elastic limit occur in cooling past V, unless the temperature has previously been far above V, presumably at W[c]: nor do the carbon-condition, the fracture and the hardening power change in cooling past V, unless the temperature has just before reached W.

Moreover, some at least of these phenomena which occur at V are much more intense in cooling than in heating. Thus, the increase of magnetizability in cooling, though indeed composed of three successive steps, has one which is much more sudden and violent than any which occurs during heating[d]: the expansion at V during cooling is much greater than the contraction during heating. Gore, indeed, could detect no contraction[e]: in two experiments of Barrett's the expansion in cooling seems to have been about thrice as large as the contraction on heating.[f] This accords with the fact that marked changes in the hardening power, the fracture, and the condition

[a] These experiments will be described in the Technology Quarterly, Volume II.
[b] Phil. Mag., XXXVIII., p. 66.
[c] Idem, XLVI., p. 475.
[d] Gore, Phil. Mag., XL., p. 174.
[e] Idem, XXXVIII., p. 69.
[f] Idem, XLVI., p. 474.

TABLE 87 A.—RETARDATIONS IN THE HEATING AND COOLING CURVES OF IRON. OSMOND AND PIONCHON (FIG. 71).

Number.	Description of metal.	No. of curve in fig. 71.		C.	Si.	Mn.	P.	S.	a_3 Limit.	a_3 Max.	a_3 Limit.	a_3 Size.	a_2 Limit.	a_2 Max.	a_2 Limit.	a_2 Size.	a_1 Limit.	a_1 Max.	a_1 Limit.	a_1 Size.
	Unhardened metal.								°C	°C	°C		°C	°C	°C		°C	°C	°C	
A.	Iron by hydrogen, Pionchon.		*Heating*						**1,050**		**1,000**						**720**		**660**	
C.	Phosphide iron	1	Cooling	·05	·0[illegible]	tr.	·38	·02		[illegible]		Small		[illegible]		Small		660		Very slight.
D.	Electrolytic iron	2	Cooling	·08					[illegible]	[illegible]	[illegible]	Sudden, high, brief	750	73[illegible]	720			66[illegible]		Very slight.
E.	" "	3	*Heating*						**900**	**867**	**840**	*Slight*	**730**	**720**	**710**	*Slight, very flat*				*Missing.*
F.	Extra soft steel, basic open-hearth	4	Cooling	·16	·01	·11	·0[illegible]	·02	845	822	800	Moderate	725	73[illegible]	710	Small	680	65[illegible]	645	Small.
G.	The same	5	*Heating*						**920**	**900**	**835**	*Slight*	**755**	**725**		*Slight*		**690?**		*Very obscure.*
H.	Soft steel, basic Bessemer	6	Cooling	·29	·06	·27	·05	·06		[illegible]		Very slight	780	721	690	Strong	680	66[illegible]	640	Of good size.
I.	Half-hard steel, acid open-hearth	7	Cooling	·57	·0[illegible]	·2[illegible]	·05	·02		[illegible]		Very slight	720	695				66[illegible]	64[illegible]	Very strong
J.	The same		*Heating*						*Not examined.*								**720**	**705**	**690**	
K.	Hard steel, crucible	11	Cooling	1·25	·19	·19	·02	·02		[illegible]						Absent	7[illegible]	67[illegible]	645	Extremely strong.
L.	The same	15	*Heating*														**720**[a]	**705**[a]	**698**[a]	*Hardened steel.*
M.	White cast iron, Swedish	13	Cooling	4·10	·22	·12	·02	·04				Probably absent					710	685	660	Very strong.
N.	Basic Bessemer steel, % of manganese varying		"	·32	·0[illegible]	·50	·05	·0[illegible]		[illegible]		Very slight	740	705	660	Moderate	660	640	620	Strong.
O.			"	·42	·08	1·0[illegible]	·0[illegible]	·0[illegible]		[illegible]		" "		66[illegible]		Slight		625	600	Very strong.
P.			"	·46	·07	1·[illegible]	·07	·0[illegible]		[illegible]		Extremely slight		65[illegible]				620	[illegible]	" "
Q.	Tungsten steel, tungsten 3·47%	8-9	Cooling	·71	·11	·73	·01	·04				Probably absent		700 / [illegible]		Small / Extremely slight		[illegible] / 515		Strong. / Enormous.
R.	Chrome steel	10	"	·33				Cr. 1·0[illegible]		872		Extremely slight	770	727		Strong		660		Moderate.
S.	" "		"	[illegible]				2·00										6[illegible]6		Temperature rises to [illegible]° and 710°.
T.	" "		"	2·00				10. @ 12·										[illegible]4		
U.	Rohlsbort (sulphurous) basic Bessemer steel		Cooling	·45	·08	·51	·16	S. ·28		810		Very slight	780	735		Moderate		671	645	Strong.
	Accelerations in heating (tempering) curves of hardened steel.								d_4				d_2				d_1			
V.	Half-hard steel (same as number I)		*Heating*											**345**		*Slight*				
W.	Hard steel (same as number K)	15	"							**680**		*Moderate*		**353**		*Strong*		**210**		*Slight*

a Hardened steel.
Italics and heavy-faced type refer to heating, *i. e.* to rising temperature: the others to falling temperature.

of carbon have been detected at V in cooling (from W), but not in heating.

§ 257. THERMAL PHENOMENA DURING HEATING AND COOLING; α AND β IRON.[a]—Digressing, let us consider the interesting theories of Osmond and Werth, and, to that end, note the thermal phenomena which occur when iron is heated and cooled. These are represented graphically in Figure 71. If a bar of unhardened steel be heated say to 500° C., and be then allowed to cool gradually, losing heat by radiation, and if we plot successive degrees of temperature as abscissæ and the intervals of time occupied in cooling from each degree to the next lower as ordinates, we obtain smooth curves, rising regularly as, with nearer approach to the temperature of the atmosphere, radiation becomes slower. But like curves plotted for cooling from higher temperatures are extremely irregular, showing that at certain temperatures either the specific heat changes abruptly, or, as seems more probable, some change occurs within the metal, accompanied by absorption or emission of heat. Like irregularities occur during gradual heating.

Heat liberated { retards cooling, raising the cooling curve locally. / hastens heating, lowering the heating curve locally.

Heat absorbed { hastens cooling, lowering the cooling curve locally. / retards heating, raising the heating curve locally.

Osmond recognizes three chief irregularities in these curves. Those which occur during heating he terms a_c, those during cooling a_r: those which occur at the lowest temperature he names a_{c1} and a_{r1}: those at the intermediate and highest temperatures he names a_{c2}, a_{c3}, a_{r2} and a_{r3} respectively. When he thinks that two or all of these irregularities coalesce, he gives them such names as a_{c21} and a_{r321}.

a Ann. Mines, 8th Ser., VIII., p. 5, 1885. "Transformations du Fer et du Carbone dans les Fers, les Aciers, et les Fontes Blanches," Osmond, Paris, 1888, Stahl und Eisen VI., pp. 374, 820, 1886: Idem, VII., p. 447, 1887: Idem, VIII., p. 364, 1888. Comptes Rendus, CIII., pp. 743, 1135: Idem, CIV., p. 985. Cf. Müller, Stahl und Eisen, VIII., p. 291, 1888.

Under favorable conditions H. Tomlinson detects as many as seven recalescences during the cooling of iron from whiteness: two decided ones are generally noticed, one between 500° and 1,000° C., the other below 500°.[b]

In the series of irons experimented on by Osmond, detailed

CURVE OF TEMPERING HARDENED STEEL, OSMOND.

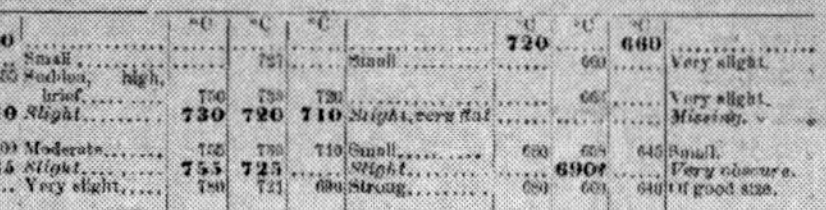

Fig. 71

in Table 87 A, we find that the position of two of these elevations, a_{r1} and a_{r3}, is tolerably constant for given conditions of heating and cooling, and nearly independent of chemical composition. a_{r1} is raised only 14° C. by increase of carbon from 0·05 to 1·25%; but it is lowered about 40° by an increase of manganese from 0·27 to 1·08%. The higher the temperature which precedes cooling and the more rapid the cooling, the lower is a_{r1} for steels with 0·57 and 1·25% of carbon.

The statement that the position of a_{r3} is nearly independent of composition is on my own authority, and directly opposed to Osmond's view. According to him a_{r3} descends rapidly with increasing carbon, merging in a_{r2} when the carbon reaches 0·20%. Here, however, he appears to strain the facts to fit his theory. The reader can verify from Figure 71 the existence, in eight out of the nine cooling curves, of a slight rise whose crest lies within the narrow limits 815° and 872° C.

The height of a_{r1} and perhaps also that of a_{r2} varies greatly with the composition. a_{r1}, insignificant in iron with ·05 or ·08% of carbon, increases constantly and very greatly with rising carbon till this reaches 1·25%: with further increase to 4·1% it again decreases. Increasing

b Jour. Iron and Steel Inst., 1888, I., p. 355, from Trans. Proc. Phys. Soc., London, IX., pp. 107-123

chromium probably heightens it, as does tungsten (3·5%, ±) in one case: in another case tungsten shortens it, while neither manganese (changing from 0 to 1·08%) sulphur, phosphorus nor silicon seems to affect it. 20% of manganese, however, effaces it, and 6·3% of tungsten probably greatly shortens it. The temperature assigned by Osmond to a_{r1} agrees well with Pionchon's observation that the specific heat of iron was much higher in the range 660° to 720° C. than at lower or at immediately higher temperatures.

I trace no simple relation between the percentage of carbon and the height of a_{r3}. Neither chromium, silicon, sulphur, silicon, nor phosphorus nor a little manganese

Fig. 71. CURVES OF COOLING AND HEATING: OSMOND.

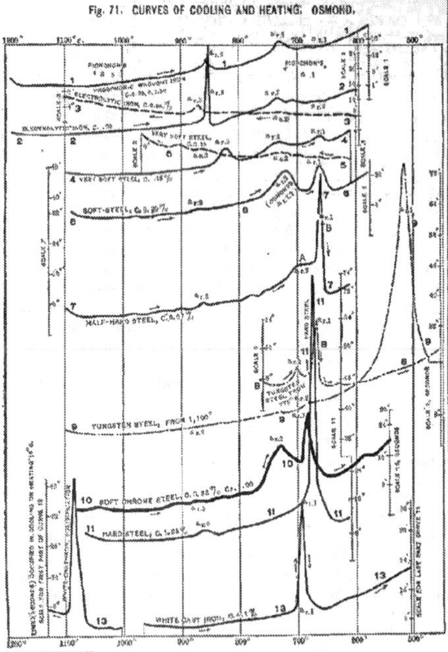

(1·08%) seems to affect it, but it is missing in ferro-manganese, in white cast-iron, and in tungsten steel.

In one case only, that of electrolytic iron, curve 2, does a_{r3} reach a considerable height, and here its height may be due not to the relative freedom from carbon, but to some individual peculiarity of the specimen tested, for a_{c3} in this same specimen is very short: further, a_{r3} is short in phosphoric iron, number 1, which has still less carbon. Pionchon noticed no absorption of heat in this range, but he found one at a much higher temperature, about 1050° C., both in very pure commercial iron and in iron reduced by pure hydrogen from pure ferric oxide.

While a_{r1} and a_{r3} seem to be distinct entities, as much cannot be said confidently of a_{r2}. Those retardations which are called a_{r2} vary so much in position and height in different steels as to suggest that they are not due to the same cause. Grouping them provisionally as a_{r2}, we note that, with rising carbon, the temperature of this retardation falls continuously, from 727° with 0·05% of carbon to 695° with carbon 0·57%, now nearly merging in a_{r1}, which seems to swallow it completely when 1·25 or 4·1% of carbon is present. As manganese rises from 0·27 to 1·08%, a_{r2} falls some 69° C., of which 35° may be due to the simultaneous rise of carbon. With 20% of manganese it is no longer visible. Rising tungsten in one case raises, in another almost effaces it: sulphur perhaps raises it: but neither chromium, phosphorus nor silicon changes its position.

Its height seems on the whole to increase with rising carbon, but not constantly, and perhaps with rising chromium; but it is lessened by tungsten, while rising manganese lessens and finally effaces it. Silicon, sulphur and phosphorus do not seem to affect its height.

a_c has been studied much less than a_r. Only two elevations can in general be traced, and these seem much less marked than those with falling temperature. The upper one is slightly above a_{r3}, and probably corresponds to it: and hence may be called a_{c3} provisionally. The second lies between a_{r1} and a_{r2}: Osmond calls it a_{c1} in some cases, a_{c2} in others, implying that it corresponds to a_{r1} in the former and to a_{r2} in the latter: but this correspondence seems to be very doubtful except in the case of steel with 1·25% of carbon, with which a very strongly marked elevation occurs at 705° C., 31° higher than a_{r1}: this may well be called a_{c1}.

When hardened steel is reheated, three if not four depressions occur between the common temperature and 680° C. (V). We may name the lowest of these d_1, the others d_2, d_3, etc.

§ 257A. Discussion. Of these flexures, two only, a_{r3} and a_{r1}, seem to have definite positions. a_{r2} indeed seems to vary with some regularity: but beyond these we find two, three or even more flexures. In the cooling-curve of electrolytic iron eight distinct flexures exist. Osmond often classes two distinct elevations as one, *e. g.* that marked a_{r2} and the one at its right in the cooling curve of electrolytic iron (3): in other cases he asssumes that one elevation really consists of two or even three, *e. g.* the great elevation in the cooling-curve (11) of steel with 1·25% of carbon, which he terms a_{r123}. For the assumptions, apparently deemed essential to his theory, I see little warrant.

a_{r1} is probably a phenomenon of the after-glow, of the rapid change from hardening to cement carbon (this Osmond admits) and from hard to soft steel. This is indicated by its absolute position, 700° C., (1,300° F., a dull red), and by the fact that its height is roughly proportional to the intensity of these changes. Let H = the ratio of the hardness in the quenched to that of the slowly cooled state, or the intensity of the hardness-change, I = the intensity of the after-glow, and J = the height of a_{r1}.

As carbon increases from 0·05% to 1·25%, H, I and J increase apparently continuously and roughly proportionally, from insignificant to most striking phenomena: before the carbon rises high enough to form white cast-iron, however, both H and J have diminished somewhat. A moderate quantity, say 1% of manganese apparently affects neither H, I nor J seriously, and the same may be true of a little chromium:[b] a large proportion of manganese, as in ferro-manganese and Hadfield's steel, greatly diminishes or effaces all three.[a] In regard to tungsten alone have we even an apparent anomaly. A large proportion, say 6%, of tungsten greatly diminishes if it does not efface H and I: while in curves 8 and 9 3·47% in one case lessens, in another enormously increases a_{r1}. Our data are too scanty for analysis: but it may be doubted whether this small proportion of tungsten would greatly diminish H and I; and, further, the great retardation in curve 9 lies so much below the temperature of a_{r1} in all the other curves, that we may reasonably doubt whether it really is a_{r1}: it may well represent some other change within the metal.

As sudden cooling prevents the heat-yielding change from hardening to cement carbon, it is natural that when hardened steel is reheated, and while its carbon is gradually changing to cement, heat should be evolved, causing the depressions d_1, etc., in the heating-curve number 15 of Figure 71.

d_1 seems to occur at the same temperature as the temporary weakening of hardened steel noted in § 255. It will be interesting to see whether a second weakening occurs at 353°, corresponding to d_3.

The meaning of a_{r2} and a_{r3} is not clear. The constant position of a_{r3} suggests that this point is the W of Brinnell and the b of Chernoff: but the temperature, 810° to 900° C., which Osmond assigns it, seems rather lower than that of W and b, while the range of temperature 1,000 to 1,050°, in which Pionchon found his second absorption of heat, and which we may call Pionchon's a_3, seems very near W and b.

The reason why raising the initial temperature and increasing the rapidity of cooling cause a_{r1} to occur at a lower temperature, may be that at the higher temperature the crystalline form becomes more firmly fixed, as in the burning of iron, § 263, and so resists more strongly the tendency to change on cooling past the critical point: and that, as we have already seen, the change from hardening to cement carbon is always a slow one.

We have so few facts concerning a_c that speculation were premature. One naturally asks whether retardations of heating, corresponding to and a little higher than a_{r1}, a_{r2} and a_{r3} respectively, exist, indicating that the changes which occur in cooling are each reversed at a little higher[c] temperature in heating. In few if any cases is such a correspondence clear. Indeed, it seems evident that the lower elevation in heating, which we call a_{c1}, is not due to a change the reverse of that which causes a_{r1}.

Thus, while a_{r1} seems directly connected with the change of carbon from hardening to cement, a_{c1} does not seem to represent the reverse change: for it appears to be well marked in Pionchon's carbonless iron. Moreover, a_{c1} occurs between 600° and 705° C.: while the chief change of carbon from cement to hardening, and of steel from soft to hard, occurs only at a much higher temperature, a low yellow, say 1000 to 1100°. Whether its intensity, like that of a_{r1}, is proportional to the percentage of carbon is uncertain. No increase can be traced confidently with carbon rising from 0·05 to 0·16%, in *unhardened* steel. In hardened steel of 1·25% of carbon a_{c1} is very strong, but whether because of the high carbon or of the hardening is not clear. If of the hardening, a_{c1} might correspond to the change of fracture from F and D to H at about 700° C., which has no analogue in case of unhardened steel. We do not refer it to change from hardening to cement carbon, which probably continues to take place at 700°, as this should liberate heat and depress the heating curve, while a_{c1} is in this case a sharp elevation.

The study of fracture and of polished sections shows that changes of crystallization and of mineral species occur during heating and cooling. Some of these have been definitely located at V, and W. Others seem to occur progressively, but not necessarily at constant rate, when hardened steel is heated from the cold towards W. The position of others, *e. g.* that from F to E and from E to D, the formation of ferrite, cementite and pearlyte from the probably obsidian-like hardenite, is yet only roughly known. To these known and apparently sufficient causes it seems not unnatural to ascribe the flexures other than a_{r1} and a_{r3}. Indeed, in case of ferro-manganese, Osmond does refer the series of perturbations which occurs between 900° and the melting point, to such changes, or, as he puts it, to liquation.

These evolutions of heat are not confined to iron. Person found that the alloy, bismuth 8 parts, lead 5, and tin 3, after solidifying at 96 to 94° C., cooled regularly till it reached 57°: its temperature then rose one or two degrees, with marked expansion. If the molten alloy be quenched, so as to prevent the molecular change which evolves heat, after removal from the water it grows so hot as to burn the fingers, evidently because the heat-yielding change which was prevented by quenching now occurs.[d]

Osmond's Theory.[e]—The resemblance between the effects of quenching and of cold-working on iron and steel appears to Osmond so close as to indicate that these operations act through causing a common chemical change. As cold-working does not change the condition of carbon, an allotropic change in the iron itself is invoked. He imagines two allotropic modifications,

α iron, which predominates in annealed metal, soft and malleable, and

β iron, hard, strong, and brittle, which characterizes quenched and cold-worked iron, in which it is mixed with more or less α iron, according to the intensity of the causes which have formed it.

α iron is changed to β, I, by cold-working, II, by raising the temperature past a certain critical point or range. β iron changes to α at temperatures which, though high, are

[a] "Manganese," R. A. Hadfield, p. 77; Excerpt Min. Proc. Inst. Civ. Eng., XCIII., 1887-8.

[b] I find a surprising if accidental correspondence between my observations and Osmond's. When I first tried chrome steels I failed to note the after-glow; on repeating the experiment I found to my surprise a very marked after-glow. I attributed my failure to notice it the first time to malobservation: but I now find from Osmond's experiments that, if the initial temperature is low, say 800° C., chrome steel shows but an arrest of cooling at a_{r1}: while, if slowly cooled from 1100° C., a very marked rise of temperature occurs at a_{r1}: thus my failure was probably due to not heating high enough initially.

[c] At a slightly higher point, because, if crystalline tendency or chemical affinity changes at a certain point, we may suppose that at that point itself equilibrium between the two crystalline tendencies or between the two chemical affinities exists. In heating or cooling we must pass an appreciable distance beyond that point before departing far enough from exact equilibrium to overcome chemical inertia.

[d] Comptes Rendus, XXV., p. 444: also Ledebur, Stahl und Eisen, VII., p. 450, 1887.

[e] Osmond, op. cit.: also Ann. Mines, 8th ser., VIII., pp. 42, 65; Comptes Rendus, CIII., pp. 743, 1135; CIV., p. 985. Cf. Ledebur, Stahl und Eisen, VI., p. 371, 1886; VII., p. 447, 1887; VIII., p. 364, 1888; also Müller, idem., VIII., p. 29', 1888.

below this critical point, freely if carbon be absent, slowly if it be present, carbon acting as a brake. Hence both cold-worked iron and steel and hardened steel are softened by reheating, β changing to α. High-carbon steel is hard after quenching, because its carbon has impeded the change from β to α iron, soft after slow cooling because change from β to α has had time to occur in spite of the retarding effect of the carbon. Carbonless iron is not hardened by quenching, because this change has not been checked; while with intermediate percentages of carbon quenching produces intermediate degrees of hardness by impeding this change more or less.

Discussion.—Osmond's theory implies three distinct propositions, (1) that the wonderful difference in hardness, ductility, coercive force, etc., between suddenly and slowly cooled steel is a feature of an allotropic change, call it the $\alpha\ \beta$ change, which occurs spontaneously with certain changes of temperature: (2) that the $\alpha\ \beta$ change is distinct from though influenced by the change in carbon-condition: (3) that distortion in the cold (as in cold-rolling) produces the $\alpha\beta$ change. Here we have three known changes, that in hardness, strength, ductility, coercive force, etc., which we may call the *hardness-change:* that in carbon-condition, the *carbon-change:* and that due to cold-working, the *cold-work* change: and one hypothetical change, the $\alpha\ \beta$ change. Experiments which I will describe later go to show that the only direct evidence of the existence of a separate $\alpha\ \beta$ change during heating and cooling is untrustworthy.

In a later section, treating of cold-working, finding that the ulterior and tangible effects of cold-working iron and steel resemble those of cold-working the other metals as much if not more than those of heating and quenching steel, I infer that the proximate effects of cold-working iron are classed more reasonably as like in nature to those of the like process of cold-working the other metals (which hardly creates β brass, bronze, German silver, etc.), than as like in nature to those of the unlike process of quenching. If I am right here, Osmond's theory is superfluous.

Turning now to the first two propositions, as suddenly and slowly cooled steel are so unlike that one would hardly suspect from mere physical examination that they were different forms of the same material, we would not quarrel with Osmond for terming the change from one to the other allotropic. The word may be applied legitimately to less striking changes.

Next, if we divide the phenomena which occur during rising temperature provisionally into those noted at V (a sudden absorption of heat, a sudden loss of magnetism, a sudden change in thermo-electric power), and those observed at W (the change in carbon-condition, in fracture and probably in appearance of polished sections, the sudden accession of the hardening power, the momentary loss of elastic limit, the surprising welding noted by Coffin), or into the V and the W groups, we may admit that the V group is distinct from the carbon change, for two reasons. First, the carbon change as shown by nitric acid spotting does not occur till the temperature rises above V, nearly or quite to W; the force of this is lessened by the fact that we are not absolutely certain that the nitric acid test gives sure indications of the carbon-condition. Second, because at least one member of the V group has been detected by Pionchon in wholly carbonless iron, reduced by hydrogen from pure ferric oxide. In this a sudden absorption of heat was indicated in the following way. The iron was heated and at once cooled suddenly in a calorimeter, and the operation was repeated at a gradually rising series of temperatures. The total heat of cooling increased regularly up to about 660° C.; but between this point and 720° C. it increased suddenly and greatly, showing that in cooling from this range, which includes V, some change occurs which evolves heat, and which does not occur in cooling from below V. This indicates that a corresponding absorption of heat occurs in heating past V.[a]

Further, he detected the loss of the magnetic properties simultaneously with the absorption of heat, apparently either in this same iron, or in another containing only traces of carbon and silicon, in which the absorption of heat was practically identical with that in the absolutely carbonless iron.[b]

But the fact that the V group is distinct from the carbon change does not help Osmond's theory, for the carbon change and the hardness change are both members of the W group.

The question then arises, are the members of the W group simultaneous effects of a single change, or have we here two or more essentially distinct changes, one of carbon-condition, the other from soft to hard steel? During cooling the changes of this group, while probably most marked at V, seem to be spread out over a greater range of temperature than during heating: and if the group really consists of two distinct changes we might expect them to occur at different periods during cooling if anywhere.

We have seen that the position and intensity of a_{r1} indicate that it represents the carbon-change. Can we go further and identify the other retardations, saying that a_{r1} represents only the carbon change, the other changes of the W group being represented by this other retardation, the V group by that? Osmond attempts this, but I think that one cannot do it confidently without either more data or a more searching and much more impartial analysis of our present data than he gives us. In fact, I see no strong evidence that these retardations do not represent simply successive similar steps of one great change, including both the V and the W groups, a_{r1} being a vast stride, a_{r2} and a_{r3} timid fumblings.

Admitting that a_{r1} represents the carbon change, he holds that a_{r2} and a_{r3} represent the hypothetical $\alpha\ \beta$ change. Were this true, then since the intensity of the hardness-change seems roughly proportional to the size of a_{r1} (§ 258), but without clear relation to that of a_{r2} and a_{r3}, one would still regard the hardness-change as a feature of the carbon-change and not of the $\alpha\ \beta$ change.

Thus a_{r3} is slight in the non-hardening iron with 0·05% of carbon and in the intensely hardening high-carbon steel, while extremely high in the non-hardening electrolytic iron (curves 1, 11 and 3).

---

[a] Pionchon proved that this absorption of heat was not due to experimental error, by showing that it did not occur with other metals.

[b] A striking feature of this V group is that it does not seem to include a sudden change of tensile strength, elastic limit or ductility: these properties seem to change gradually as V is passed, though it is possible that a *momentary* weakening in passing V may be detected hereafter, like that in *rising* past W and in *falling* past V. This reminds us that, tremendous as are the changes caused by sudden cooling, this operation does not affect the modulus of elasticity greatly. Whether we regard the hardening changes as the result of mechanical, physical, crystalline or chemical changes, the relative constancy of this property while the others are revolutionized is at first sight most surprising.

The *position* of a_{r2} indeed bears some relation to the intensity of the hardness-change, for the temperature at which it occurs descends as the carbon rises. Its *intensity*, however, not its position, should be but is not proportional to that of the hardness-change. Most marked in the but slightly hardening steel with ·20% of carbon, and in the well hardening chrome steel, it is slight or absent in the slightly hardening steel with 0·16% of carbon, in the non-hardening ferro-manganese, and in the intensely hardening high-carbon steel. In the latter indeed it is perhaps swallowed up in a_{r1}. It is more marked with 0·05 and 0·08% than with 0·16% of carbon, more marked with ·20% than with ·57% of carbon if we may judge by its steepness in the curve for the latter.

The crucial test, however, is to quench at some point below a_{r3} and a_{r2} but above a_{r1}: when, on Osmond's theory, the steel should be soft while the carbon is hardening: on the carbon theory, which regards a_{r1} as identical with Brinnell's V, and a_{r3} as probably identical with his W, the metal should be partly softened and should have part of its carbon in the hardening, part in the cement state. From this test neither Osmond nor I have shrunk. He reports that when steel of 0·57 of carbon is quenched from A, curve 7, it is hard and the carbon hardening: while if quenched from B it is soft, the carbon still being hardening.[a] This is, I believe, the only direct evidence of the existence of a distinct α β change; it therefore merits attention.

In view of what follows, it is perhaps superfluous to point out that these results agree poorly with his theory. Steel quenched from the crest of a_{r2}, should be already partly softened, having passed all of a_{r3} and half of a_{r2}: yet he reports it as hardened unqualifiedly. Steel quenched from B, on the cooler slope of a_{r1}, should have part if not most of its carbon in the cement state, yet he reports "hardening carbon" without qualification.

Lacking time for an elaborate investigation, I have made the following tests, which indicate either that the steel on which Osmond experimented differed strangely from all those which I have tested, or, as seems more probable, that he is simply mistaken. The right-hand end of a copper box, Figure 72, 12″ × 0·44″ × 0·88″ inside, with walls 0·44″ thick, was placed within a muffle furnace heated to a light yellow, the left-hand end projecting into the outer air. Thanks to the high thermal conductivity of copper, the temperature descended very slowly and regularly in passing from right to left. Within this after it was thoroughly heated I placed two bars of steel cut from the same piece, containing about 0·50% of carbon, 0·375 inch square, previously nicked hot on one side at points .05 inch apart, and polished on the opposite face. After 1½ minutes I began drawing bar I back, a little at a time, till after 25 minutes more I had drawn it back 3·5 inch, in 18 small movements of about 0·2 inch. each I then drew and quenched each bar. Bar I was re-polished, its carbon condition determined by nitric acid spotting, its hardness by drawing the same edge of the same file, at as nearly constant speed and pressure as I could, across its edge twenty times at each of many points, care being taken to choose the order of these points so that the gradual dulling of the file's edge might not mislead me: the depth of the file mark gave a rough measure of hardness. The carbon condition and the hardness of bar I and the hardness of bar II were noted independently.

We have in bar I a series of points each of which before quenching had cooled from above W to a little lower point than its neighbor. While we have no absolute measure of these temperatures, we here have evidence of the relative positions of the carbon-change and the hardness change during cooling. Instead of finding, as Osmond's statements imply, a sudden change in hardness at one point, and then a sudden change of carbon-condition at a point which had been cooler, I found, as Brinnell's results confirmed by Coffin would lead us to expect, that these changes cover a long region and are apparently simultaneous. The carbon-change could indeed be traced over a longer space than the hardness-change, probably because slight carbon-changes are recognized by the eye more easily than equally slight hardness-changes are by the file. I have repeated this experiment many times with Bessemer rail-steel of about 0·40% of carbon, Bessemer steel of about 0 50% of carbon, and crucible tool steel of several grades, always with the same result.[b]

Fig. 72 a.

SECTIONAL PLAN.

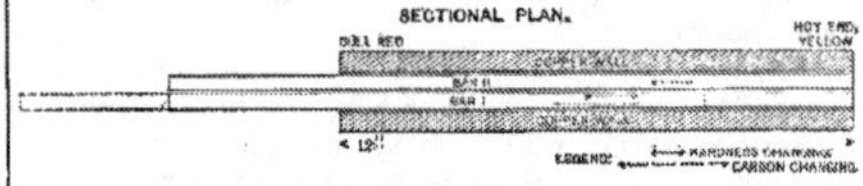

Fig. 72 b.

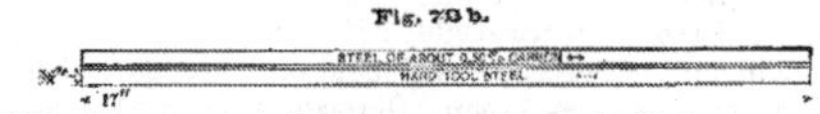

Thus there seems to be no reason to doubt, but every reason to believe, that the hardness-change is simul-

[a] "19e chauffage (rapide) à 770·8; refroidissement à l'air jusqu' à 697·8; trempé à 697·8; métal trempé; carbone de trempe. 20e chauffage (rapide) à 784·1; refroidissement à l'air jusqu' à 658; trempé à 658; métal doux; carbone de trempe." Trans. du Fer, etc., p. 87 "Essayons enfin les échantillons ainsi préparés, à la lime, pour juger de leur dureté et à la touche par l'acide azotique, pour vérifier l'état du carbone." Idem, p. 38. However untrustworthy these methods may be, they may properly be used in rebuttal of Osmond's representations of what they themselves show: and in this way I use them in the experiments which I am about to describe.

[b] It will be noticed that the change from hard to soft in bar I which was gradually cooling when quenched appears to occur at a somewhat lower temperature and to extend over a longer space than in the reverse change from soft to hard, in both respects agreeing fairly with Brinnell's results showing that the change from hardening to cement carbon occurs gradually in the range W-V while the reverse change occurs rapidly at W. In this particular case the difference between the length and position of change from hard to soft was much less marked than in most of my other experiments, and I am inclined to think that in drawing back bar I the temperature of bar II must have been temporarily raised and then again lowered: for in another experiment (Figure 72 b) in which both bars were drawn and quenched immediately after heating for 16 minutes in this box, the change of hardness covered a length of only 0·25 inch. In this case one bar was from the same piece as those shown in Figure 72, the other of hard crucible tool steel: yet the range covered by the change from soft to hard had almost exactly the same position in both bars. The slight difference was probably due wholly to experimental error, since the change occurred if anything at a lower temperature in the low than in the high-carbon steel. The agreement is as close as could be expected with such rough tests: it tends to confirm Coffin's belief that the position of W is independent of the proportion of carbon (§ 245, p. 175).

In all these experiments I found that the change from soft to hard steel and back occurred simultaneously with the change of carbon as shown by nitric acid spotting, though naturally their limits did not coincide exactly, as is inevitable with two such rough tests. Further, the change from soft to hard coincided with the change from coarse fracture (Brinnell's B) to fine (Brinnell's F). While the change from soft to hard was always more sudden than the reverse change, the difference between the suddenness of these two changes seemed to me less marked than one would infer from Brinnell's results. I hope to present in an appendix more trustworthy results as to the change in hardness, obtained by scratching with the diamond or by indentation. These methods may not, indeed, give like results, one telling the hardness of the very skin, the other that of skin and relatively deep subcutaneous layers, whose hardness may vary at a different rate from that of the skin.

taneous during both heating and cooling with the carbon-change, and is a direct result of it. This admitted, it becomes relatively unimportant whether any phenomena of the W group be independent of the carbon-change and liable to occur separately from it. We may note, however, that Pionchon found indications of a change at W in perfectly carbonless iron, whose specific heat seemed to change at this point. This change may be wholly independent of the carbon-change, occurring whether carbon be present or not; it may precipitate the carbon-change, which in turn introduces practically wholly new phenomena, the hardness-change, of which not more than the germ (if even that) occurs in carbonless iron.

A possible simple explanation of the discrepancy between Osmond's results and mine is that he judged the hardness in the usual way, simply by the feeling of the file, and not by the depth of the indentation produced by a fixed number of like strokes. The feeling readily detects the slight difference between that degree of hardness which just forbids and that which permits the file to bite, but not slight differences between this and slightly lower degrees of hardness. It exaggerates greatly the first slight decline in hardness. Judging from my results, in the steel which he pronounced soft though with hardening carbon both carbon and hardness had begun to change. When compared with that of a fully annealed piece the carbon-tint indeed seems wholly hardening: while judged simply by the feeling the steel seems soft: blacksmiths to whom I have submitted steel in this condition have always pronounced it soft. Yet careful comparison of carbon-tint and depth of indentation with those of like steel quenched from slightly higher and slightly lower temperatures seems to show clearly that both hardness and carbon-tint have changed, and apparently in not unlike degree.

Let us now consider Osmond's allotropic theory as applied to the phenomena of tempering, turning to curve 15. He holds that d_1 and d_4 represent the change from hardening to cement, and hence that d_4 can only represent that from β to α iron, because he found by Weyl's method that the carbon was cement in steel which had been held for thirty minutes in molten lead at about 400° C.

But Weyl's method could hardly give trustworthy information as to the completeness of the change from hardening to cement, as Osmond admits[a]: but, accepting it, it does not justify his inference, for in curve 15 only two minutes and a few seconds were occupied in passing from 98° to 620° C., or far past d_1 and d_2. That these two depressions do not represent the whole change from hardening to cement, and hence that d_4 may be regarded as due to the continuation of that change, is shown by Abel's discovery that less than half the carbon of hardened steel became cement during six hours exposure to say a blue heat, say 300° C.,[b] and that this change occurred gradually at both a blue and a straw heat; and is further indicated by the results of Barus and Strouhal,[c] who found that the thermo-electric power of hardened steel increased continuously with rising tempering-temperature, and was far from reaching a maximum at 330° C.

Again, Coffin finds that the proportion of the carbon which is in the hardening state (as indicated by nitric acid spotting) diminishes continuously, as the temperature at which hardened steel is subsequently tempered is raised from the cold up to redness, say 900° C.[d] As the hardness diminishes continuously and gradually, we more naturally attribute its change to the change of carbon known to be simultaneous, gradual and continuous, rather than to two distinct causes operating jerkily, change of carbon falsely supposed to be confined to lower temperatures, imagined allotropic change of iron unwarrantably supposed to occur at d_4.

Finally, undaunted by the fact that hardened steel is actually softened by heating past d_1, and still more if heated to d_2, though his theory holds that β changes to α only when the temperature reaches d_4, Osmond explains that this softening is not due to the simultaneous change from hardening to cement carbon, but to the fact that this change causes some of the iron to leave the β state in order to form a carbide (cementite) with the now-forming cement carbon. Unfortunately, Müller has proved that this cementite is extremely hard and brittle, scratching glass: Sorby was convinced that it was extremely hard. Now the change from brittle β iron to a mixture of part β iron and part glass-hard carbide, does not explain the softening and toughening which occurs when hardened steel is tempered: while the carbon-theory, holding that in tempering a harder compound of all the iron with hardening carbon (hardenite) is gradually and progressively changed to a mixture of uncombined soft iron and hard carbide, ferrite and cementite, explains the softening clearly and in accordance with the known facts.

To sum up, Osmond's theory accords neither with our old nor his new facts: while the latter like the former harmonize well with the carbon-theory. The carbon-change being a fact, the $\alpha\beta$ allotropic change of iron as yet wholly unproved, the balance of present probability is readily seen.

§ 253. Recrystallization at High Temperatures after Forging.—The microscope shows, as we should expect, that cold-working distorts the crystals which compose iron; and further, as we might not expect, that this distortion is effaced when the metal is reheated; and that the distortion of the grains which doubtless occurs during hot working is effaced before the metal grows cold, the ultimate grains in both cases becoming nearly or quite equiaxed. If this occurred through each crystal's drawing together and resuming its initial shape while retaining all its original particles, the bar as a whole would regain its initial shape, like a stretched bar of India-rubber. A cold rolled bar, however, changes shape so little on reheating as to show that a rearrangement of particles occurs, and that practically new crystals arise.

a Ann. Mines, 8th ser., VIII., p. 90, 1885.

b Table 2, p. 12.

c Bulletin 14, U. S. Geological Survey, pp. 54-5, 1885.

d Trans. Am. Soc. Civ. Engineers, XV., p. 829, 1887. Twelve pieces from the same bar of tool steel were similarly hardened, numbered, tempered at temperatures rising gradually from the cold to full redness, repolished, touched with nitric acid on the unnumbered side for 45 seconds, washed, and arranged in the order of their color, numbered side down. Turning the numbered sides up, their order was found to agree exactly with their numbering, and hence with their tempering temperature. The differences between the two coolest (untempered and very faint straw-tempered) and between the three hottest (ash-grey to full red) was recognized with difficulty. We have, indeed, no conclusive evidence that these changes of color are due to increasing proportion of cement carbon though this is extremely probable: but their progressive change indicates that they are due to some change which goes on continuously in tempering, from the cold to redness. Tempering a hardened steel bar in the copper box already described, the tempering-temperature rising so gradually that the change from a grey tint to purple occupied twelve inches, I found that the hardness measured by abrasion decreased gradually and continuously, and not by jerks.

A. *Distortion in Cold Working.*—*Sorby*[a] drew out a bar of weld-iron, 1·8 inches square, to about 2·25 times its original length by cold-forging: the microscope showed that the grains were broken down, and twice or thrice as long in the line of the length of the bar as transversely. On exposure to redness during 80 hours, crystals again became equiaxed.

Martens[b] hammered cubes of rail-steel on one face, till they began to crack, then nicked and split them. Their fractures, Figures 73–4, indicate that the grains were flattened into sheets parallel with the hammered face.

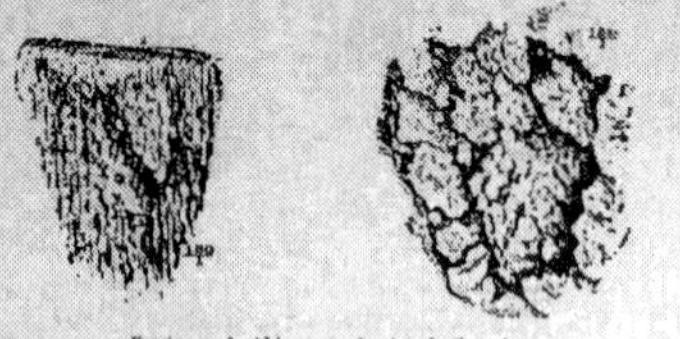

Fractures of cold-hammered cube of rail-steel.
Figure 73, Fracture on section perpendicular to hammered face. Figure 74, Fracture on section parallel to hammered face.

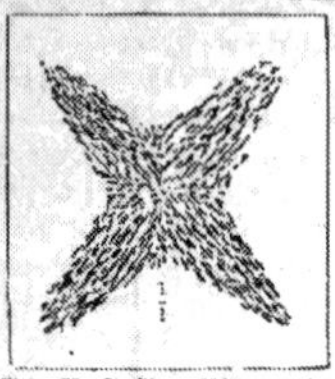

Figure 75.—Steel bar cold-hammered on all four faces. Etched section.

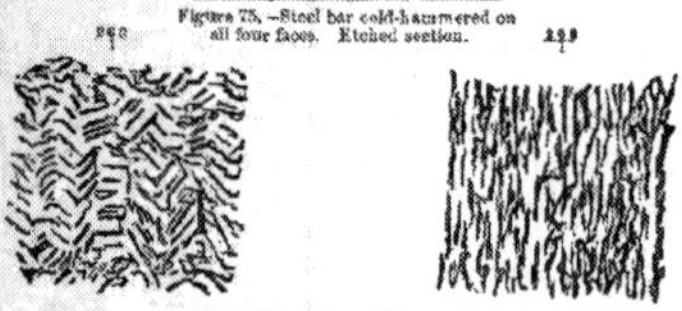

Schistosity of Bent Wrought-Iron. (Sorby.)
Figure 76, Somewhat bent. Figure 77, Much bent.

Osmond and Werth,[c] etching (with nitric acid, 36°B.) steel which had been hammered cold on all four sides, find a St. Andrew's-cross, Figure 75, coinciding with Tresca's zones of transmission of force. In the most fatigued parts the simple cells (pearlyte?) are lengthened along the planes of movement, in which their relatively brittle shells (cementite?) are shattered, in such a way as to recall the schistosity of rocks.

B. *The Distortion in Hot Forging* which evidently must occur, is illustrated by Figures 55, (p. 165), 76 and 77, the first showing the rodlike or fibrous arrangement of the slag in rolled bars, the second arrangement of the slag and metal at the concave side of a wrought-iron bar bent somewhat at redness, the third that in such a bar bent so much as to cause great squeezing, the structure-lines being here normal to the surface of the bar. This structure shows why, when a bar thus bent is again opened, rupture readily occurs in planes perpendicular to the surface.[d]

[a] Journ. Iron and Steel Inst., 1887, I., p. 263.
[b] Stahl und Eisen, VII., p. 239, 1887.
[c] Comptes Rendus, C., p. 452, 1885; Ann. Mines, 8th Ser., VIII., p. 15, 1885.
[d] Figures 76–7, originally intended to illustrate the schistosity of rocks, show the structure of hot-bent wrought-iron almost exactly, according to Sorby. (Journ. Iron and St. Inst., 1887, I., p. 260.)

The Grain of Hot-Forged Iron Equiaxed.—Sorby found that the ultimate crystals of ferrite, cementite and pearlyte in bars of ingot-steel and of weld-iron, the former drawn out to 6·25 times its initial length by hot forging, were but little if at all longer in the direction of the length of the bar than transversely. A bar about one-inch square, forged from a Bessemer ingot, showed traces of the original ferrite network, disturbed and drawn out: apart from this network, some only of the crystals of ferrite and pearlyte remained distorted by the elongation; and even these probably owed their distortion to forging prolonged till the metal was too cold to recrystallize fully.

The large patches in Figure 54, p. 165, some light, some dark, may be the traces of large crystals distorted by forging, surviving the recrystallization which has given rise to the small nearly equiaxed grains which now compose them.

The slag of weld-iron remains for the most part drawn out into long fibres. A moderate quantity of slag does not prevent the neighboring metallic grains from recrystallizing equiaxially. Figure 55 contrasts the fibre of the slag with the equiaxed grains of the metal itself. But when the proportion of slag is excessive, the iron itself "might be said to have a sort of fibre,"[e] even after hot forging. I understand that this "sort of fibre" is more apparent than real, the grains themselves being equiaxed, yet separated into quasi fibres by layers of slag, like a mass of minute cubes of iron very highly magnetized, divided up into rows by thin strips of glass, the strength and ductility of the whole being due to the magnetization of the iron cubes, and being merely lessened by the glass. Such iron may be likened to a gneiss, the crystals of felspar and quartz with their axes in all azimuths, the plates of mica lying parallel and causing cleavage. In this view wrought-iron may indeed be said to have fibre: but the fibre as such should weaken, not toughen.

The grains of hot-worked ingot-iron and steel examined by Wedding[f] and by Osmond and Werth also appear to be equiaxed.

Slag, though retaining the shape acquired in forging much more tenaciously than metal, under favorable conditions seems to draw together. Sorby finds it in almost perfect spheres within crystals of wrought-iron, very long heated.[g]

D. *Lengthwise vs. Crosswise Properties.*—Table 88 shows that, as we should expect, the strength and ductility of wrought-iron are much higher along than across the direction of rolling, the difference being probably due to the presence of longitudinal threads, sheets, etc., of slag. There is a general belief that a like but less marked difference exists in case of ingot-metal. The data in Table 88 indicate that this difference, if it exists at all, is very slight; but those on which Table 88A is based have been thought to indicate that it is very great even in case of ingot-metal.

The value of the evidence in Table 88 is somewhat lessened by the fact that, in most cases, we are not perfectly sure that the rolling has been chiefly lengthwise of the plate. But, in a great group of cases given by Riley,

[e] Idem, p. 263.
[f] Idem, 1885, I., p. Plate III.
[g] Idem., 1887, I., p. 262.

TABLE 88.—INFLUENCE OF THE DIRECTION OF ROLLING.

The properties of test pieces cut from plates of weld iron, ingot iron and ingot steel parallel with the length of the plate, compared with those of similar test pieces cut perpendicularly to it.

Number.	Observer.	General description.	Thickness, Inches.	Number of groups in which the maximum crosswise tensile strength exceeds or equals minimum lengthwise tensile strength.	Total number of groups or cases.		Number of groups in which the average crosswise properties are less than the lengthwise.				Deficit (−) or excess (+) of the crosswise over the lengthwise properties, measured in percentages of the lengthwise properties.			
					Groups.	Cases.	Tensile strength	Elastic limit.	Final elongation.	Reduction of area.	Tensile strength	Elastic limit.	Final elongation.	Final reduction of area.
											%.	%.	%.	%.
1	Kirkaldy	Crucible-steel plates	·187@·375	4	4	40	1	......	2	1	−0·32	......	+1·5	+26·4
2	J. Riley	Ingot-iron plates	·25@1·00	......	56	432	29	......	46	50	+0·1	......	−6·06	−16·97
2A	"	The 1 inch thick plates of Number 2	1·00	......	20	...	11	......	15	18	+0·1	......	−7·9	−12·06
2B	"	" ½ " " " " "	·50	......	16	...	8	......	13	14	−0·45	......	−7·77	−17·11
2C	"	" ¼ " " " " "	·25	......	20	...	10	......	13	15	0·	......	−7·82	−16·68
3	Gatewood	Ingot-iron plates	·50	2	2	8	2	......	2	1	−0·76	......	−12·4	−4·27
4	Barba	" " "	......	......	3	23	......	......	......	......	+0·2	......	−3·6	
5	A. E. Hunt	" " "	·21@·63	......	..	17	......	......	......	......	−7·19	......	+14·6	−1·27
6	Kirkaldy	" " "	·25@1·0	......	..	48	......	......	......	......	−0·3	0		
7	"	The 1 inch plates of Number 5	1·00	......	......	......	......	......	......	......	0	−0·7		
8	"	" ¾ " " " "	·75	......	......	......	......	......	......	......	−1·4	−1·3		
9	"	" ½ " " " "	·50	......	......	......	......	......	......	......	−1·0	−0·6		
10	"	" ¼ " " " "	·25	......	......	......	......	......	......	......	+1·3	+0·5		
11	"	Puddled steel plates	·12@·81	8	8	37	5		6	5	−14·91	......	−35·08	−38·14
12	"	Wrought-iron plates	·19@·94	21	26	325	25		25	25	−5·92	......	−41·42	−42·01

1. Kirkaldy, Expts. on Wrought-iron and Steel, 1866, p. 145, table II. Of the 40 tests 22 are lengthwise, 18 crosswise.
2. J. Riley, Journ. Iron and St. Inst., 1887, I., p. 144, sheet III., abstract I. All from 12 ingots from a single charge of steel, probably open-hearth.
3. Assistant Naval Constructor R. Gatewood, U. S. N., Rept. U. S. Naval Advisory Bd. on mild steel, 1886, p. 124, table XXIV. The pieces were all cut from the same plate, apparently of open-hearth steel of 0·16% carbon, made at the Chester Rolling Mills.
4. Use of Steel, Barba, Holley, pp. 28, 29, tables V., VII. The elongation is given in only two cases, each of which appears to be the average of an unknown number of tests. Twenty-eight results for tensile strength are given, of which two at least represent more than one test. The remaining 26 results are obtained from punched plates.
5. A. E. Hunt, Trans. Am. Inst. Mining Engrs., XII., p. 810, 1884. The tests were all made on steel from a single open-hearth charge containing 0·13% of carbon. Of the 17 tests, 13 were made parallel with and 4 across the direction of rolling.
6 to 10. Kirkaldy, Gatewood, Rept. U. S. Naval Advisory Bd. on mild steel, 1886, p. 133, from Parliamentary Paper, C, 2897, London, 1881.
11. Kirkaldy, Expts. on Wrought-iron and Steel, p. 145. Of the 37 tests, 20 were made lengthwise, 17 crosswise.
12. Idem, p. 150. Of the 325 tests, 163 are lengthwise, 162 crosswise.

and included in Number 2 of Table 88, all the rolling was lengthwise of the plate, and here the lengthwise and crosswise properties are practically identical.

From a study of the first nine lines of Table 88A, which all refer to the same material, we cannot say confidently that the forging has improved the properties of test-pieces taken lengthwise more than those of test-pieces taken transversely. In seven cases the ratio of the lengthwise to the transverse properties is greater, in five it is less, after than before forging. From such contradictory data no safe conclusion can be drawn.

The last nine lines at first seem to indicate that forging benefits the metal more along than across the direction of forging; for in every case the ratio of the lengthwise to the transverse properties is greater after than before forging. But two facts raise our suspicion, and tempt us to look beneath the surface. First, if this action is due to setting up a sort of fibre parallel with the direction of forging, how comes it to be as strong in the oil-hardened as in the unhardened test-pieces?

If the metal was reheated for oil-hardening after forging ceased, the reheating should according to Sorby at least tend to efface the grain, and so to equalize the lengthwise and crosswise properties. Again, how is it that the crosswise properties of the original ingot are so much better than the lengthwise? Does not this suggest another explanation, also competent to explain the slight excess of the lengthwise over the transverse properties in case of ingot-metal, shown in Table 88?[a] In our ingot the blowholes, even the minute ones which might escape notice in the test-piece, lie radially, presenting their *ends* to transverse, their *sides* to longitudinal stress. This should make the transverse test-pieces cut from the unforged metal stronger than the longitudinal ones; and so we find them in lines 13 to 15 of Table 88A. Flattening the ingot cheese-wise should exaggerate this excess of the radial over the axial properties, and so it does in lines 16 to 18. But drawing the ingot out lengthwise should draw the blowholes and similar cavities out lengthwise of the ingot, so that they will present their ends to longitudinal and their sides to transverse stress, and the longitudinal test-pieces should be somewhat stronger than the transverse, and so they are in lines 19 to 21 of Table 88A, and so they may be to a slight extent in Table 88 taken as a whole.

[a] Cf. J. Head, Journ. Iron and Steel Inst., 1886, I., p. 100.

Three facts go to show that any excess of the longitudinal over the transverse properties is not due directly to the formation of fibre parallel with the length of the plate, owing to rolling at so low a temperature during the last passes that the elongated grains cannot thereafter become equiaxed. 1, The excess in question is as great in annealed as in unannealed ingot-metal, while annealing removes the effects of cold-working nearly or quite completely, including the distortion of the grains. 2, The excess is nearly and perhaps quite as great in thick as in thin and hence cooler finished plates. 3, Cold-rolling seems to increase the strength as much in one direction as in another.

To sum up, the properties of ingot-metal are probably in general nearly independent of the direction of rolling or hammering as such: any slight difference between the lengthwise and the transverse properties may be due in part, and perhaps wholly, not to the existence of a definite direction of grain or fibre such as exists in wood, but to the longitudinal drawing-out of cavities, often minute or even microscopic.

§ 259. CHANGE OF CRYSTALLIZATION IN THE COLD.—Do shock, vibration, flexure, etc., change the crystallization of iron at the ordinary temperature? Do they make tough fibrous iron brittle and crystalline? Iron is sold me as tough and fibrous: after long vibration it breaks with a crystalline fracture: have I a prima facie case against the seller? May the properties and crystallization of the metal while at rest change in the cold? Before answering, let us consider the nature of crystalline and fibrous iron.

Fibre in Iron and Steel.—Whether the metal yields a fibrous, a silky, or a crystalline fracture depends (1) on the properties of the metal itself, and (2) on the mode of rupture. Certain tough irons yield a fibrous fracture under favorable conditions, *e. g.* when nicked on one side and bent slowly away from the nick, but a crystalline one under others, *e. g.* when nicked all around and broken

TABLE 88 A.—INFLUENCE OF DIRECTION OF FORGING, FROM MAITLAND'S DATA. (EXCESSES +, DEFICITS —.)

No.	Description.	Test pieces taken.	Tensile strength, lbs. per sq. in. Unhardened.	Tensile strength, Oil hardened.	Elastic limit, lbs. per sq. in. Unhardened.	Elastic limit, Oil hardened.	Elongation, % in 2 inches. Unhardened.	Elongation, Oil hardened.	Work of rupture, inch-tons per cubic inch. Unhardened.	Work of rupture, Oil hardened.
1...	Unforged, heated once.	Lengthwise........	72,800	99,126	35,892	....	21·5	7·25	5·15	....
2...		Crosswise........	70,504	100,240	34,884	....	14·875	7·875	8·90	....
3...		% deficit of No. 2........	—3·25	+1·18	—2·80	....	—30·77	+8·54	—82·17	....
4...	Heated twice, forged once........	Lengthwise........	71,008	99,904	32,256	....	27·9	16·75	6·87	....
5...		Crosswise........	69,328	90,598	31,752	54,432	20·25	10·875	5·12	....
6...		% deficit of No. 5........	—2·35	—9·02	—1·56	....	—25·9	—35·07	—25·54	....
7...	Heated four times, forged thrice........	Lengthwise........	74,816	92,512	54,536	39,248	30·5	24·75	9·87	9·06
8...		Crosswise........	70,448	98,072	48,456	55,464	25·5	19·75	6·12	5·25
9...		% deficit of No. 8........	—5·84	+0·65	—16·85	—1·88	—12·9	—20·20	—82·58	—40·54
13...	Round ingot, unforged.	Axially........	64,908	77,728	....	....	9·25	9·25	....	....
14...		Radially........	69,216	75,482	....	....	15·55	11·5	....	....
15...		% deficit of No. 14........	+10·55	—2·88	....	....	+68·11	+24·32	....	....
16...	Round ingot, flattened.	Radially........	78,624	97,216	33,376	56,000	26·0	18·75	6·94	7·88
17...		Axially........	41,152	91,392	30,464	....	8·25	6·75	1·97	....
18...		% deficit of No. 17........	—16·28	—5·99	—9·73	....	—68·27	—64·00	—78·85	....
19...	Round ingot, lengthened	Axially........	74,368	87,396	32,200	56,448	28·0	24·25	9·10	9·50
20...		Radially........	66,080	74,256	30,688	....	17·75	11·9	3·50	6·26
21...		% deficit of No. 20........	—11·15	—15·33	—21·72	....	—38·72	—54·64	—62·0	—18·92

1 to **9**, two pieces were cut from the same ingot "so as to be of equal quality." One was forged successively from the section 10" × 10" to 7" × 7", to 5" × 5" and to 5" × 2·5", each reduction occurring at one heating. The other piece was heated together with the first, but not forged. **1** to **3** gives the properties of the second piece heated once but not forged; **4** to **6** those of the first piece heated twice and forged once, from 10" × 10" to 7" × 7"; **7** to **9** those of the first piece heated four times and forged thrice, the total reduction being from 10" × 10" to 5" × 2·5".
13 to **21**. From the upper part of a circular ingot longitudinal and transverse test pieces were cut, numbers **13** to **15**. A part of the same ingot was then flattened down into a cheese, and test pieces were taken transversely and axially, **16** to **18**. A third piece was drawn out parallel with the length of the ingot, **19** to **21**.
Maitland, "The Treatment of Gun-Steel," excerpt Proc. Inst. Civ. Eng., lxxxix, 1887.

with a sharp blow.[a][b] Again, good fibrous wrought-iron armor-plates struck by shot shatter like glass, and with a crystalline fracture.[a] The usual explanation is that during slow rupture the individual grains are drawn out into fibres, while in sudden rupture there is not time for this elongation, and accordingly rupture strikes across the piece, between the crystal faces: perhaps rather a re-statement than an explanation.

Thick pieces of soft steel which fail in the bending test usually show a crystalline fracture, though tensile rupture produces in them a silky one.[c] Again, not only do guns, whether cast-iron, wrought-iron or steel, whether of brittle or ductile material, on bursting invariably show a short granular fracture, but Maitland has found that this same fracture invariably arises when steel *tubes* are burst by pressure from within, whether this pressure be suddenly or gradually applied, whether the metal elongates much or little. On the other hand, *rods* torn in two tensilely by explosion of gun-powder or even gun-cotton invariably yield a silky fibrous fracture.[d] In explanation it is pointed out that, under tensile test of a rod or common test-piece, the rupturing stress is in a single direction, and tends to elongate the metal's crystals: that when a tube is burst these crystals are exposed to forces acting simultaneously at right angles, a longitudinal and a tangential stress[e]: the crystal cannot so readily elongate in two directions at once, the tangential stress opposes the tendency of each crystal to elongate lengthwise of the tube, and vice-versa: hence, although the tube as a whole may elongate greatly, its individual crystals elongate but little. Do they then slide past each other?

Further, a punched steel bar yields a crystalline fracture: ream but a knife-blade thickness from the sides of the punch-hole and it yields a silky fracture, rupture in one case apparently starting at the hole's edge and ripping thence—as a ton-strong canvass-roll once notched is ripped by a boy—in the other all parts of the section pull jointly. The change, in the regions apart from the hole, is probably due to changed approach of stress rather than changed condition before stress.

Though the effect of a crack in steel is like in kind to that of a notch in cloth or India-rubber, it is much less in degree, as the following experiments show. Fine saw-cuts were made sometimes on one, sometimes on both edges of steel and of wrought-iron test-pieces: they were then closed at a heat which though high was below the welding heat, thus practically making artificial cracks. These reduced the tensile strength of the remaining section as follows:

TABLE 88 AA.—EFFECT OF CRACKS ON THE TENSILE STRENGTH OF THE REMAINING SECTION. BAKER'S DATA.[a]

	Wrought-iron.		Steel.	
	Tensile strength, lbs. per sq. in.	Loss %.	Tensile strength, lbs. per sq. in.	Loss %.
Strength of solid piece....................	52,610	....	72,800	....
Piece cracked on one edge....................	....	....	55,828;[a] 67,556[b]	24·[a] 48[b]
" " on both edges....................	50,406	4·2	70,336	2·6

[a] "The Working of Steel," Proc. Inst. Civ. Eng., LXXXIV., p. 164, 1886. [a] When held in the usual way. [b] When held by a pin.

A fine knife-cut on each edge of a strip of India-rubber reduced the strength of the remaining section by from 60 to 70 per cent.

To arrest the development of cracks, Metcalf recommends drilling holes at their ends.[f] A rounded notch or a drilled hole increases the strength of a common test-piece per unit of remaining section, at the expense of the elongation.

A fibrous fracture is most readily developed

A, in tough irons, hence those with little carbon, phosphorus, etc.: and probably those which, by proper heat-treatment, have acquired a fine crystalline structure (*e. g.* those which, since last exposed to an excessively high temperature, have been forged, or reheated to about W): those in which the stress due to quenching to below V has been avoided, etc.

It is natural that the grains of tough iron should, during rupture, be drawn out into fibres more readily than those of brittle iron.

B, in slag-bearing, *i. e.* weld-iron; and, so it is said, more readily in weld-iron with much than in that with little slag, and in rolled than in hammered weld-iron, as the rolling draws the slag more into longitudinal rods and strips. We can understand that longitudinal threads or blades of slag between the equiaxed grains of metal, (Figure 55) like blades of mica among highly magnetized cubes of iron, should tend to promote fibrousness of frac-

[a] Percy, Iron and Steel, pp. 10, 11. I have verified this. Thurston vouches for this effect on armor-plate. Matls. of Engineering, II., p. 593.
[b] Cf. Bayles, Trans. Am. Soc. Mech. Eng., VII., p. 270.
[c] J. Riley: paper 2236, "The Treatment of Gun-Steel," Proc. Inst. Civ. Eng., LXXXIX., p. 187, 1887.
[d] Maitland, do., p. 120–1.
[e] Barlow, idem., p. 203. I would point out that in the bending test we have these same conditions, tangential and radial stress acting simultaneously. A fragment of the Pittsburgh six-inch steel cast gun which I have shows this short granular fracture

[f] Trans. Eng. Club, W. Penn., 1887, p. 133. Jour. Iron and Steel Inst., 1887, II., p. 352.

ture, though the metal before rupture may have no true fibre in itself.

To this action of the blades of slag may be ascribed the phenomena of "barking,"[a] shown by tough, much-worked wrought-iron. When a nicked bar is broken by bending under impact, the skin at the convex side soon separates, like the bark and outer fibres of a bough thus broken, from the main body of the piece, which bends much farther before breaking.[a]

Though toughness may produce fibre during strain and rupture, we do not know that fibre existing before strain produces toughness. Indeed, we have seen that the grains of cold-worked and hence brittle iron are fibrous, or at least elongated, while those of tough hot-worked iron are equiaxed. Moreover, it is not clear that the fact that the former are not equiaxed has any important direct effect on the properties of the metal, for the strength of cold-worked iron seems as high across as along the grain.

Again because toughness and slag both produce fibre, some befogged ones infer that slag produces toughness. Health, rouge and intemperance redden the cheeks: do rouge and rum give health?

These fallacies pricked, let us examine (I.) the reasons to expect that slag should toughen iron, and (II.) the evidence that it does.

I. Slag may affect iron (a) chemically and (b) mechanically. Chemically, the slag of weld-iron may toughen the metal by oxidizing carbon and silicon, for the basic iron silicates of which it consists are energetic carriers of oxygen. In ingot-metal this action is less important, since the carbon and silicon are better removed otherwise, and since, at least in acid ingot-metal, the acid slag has little oxidizing power.

No relation between the percentage of slag and that of carbon in weld metal can, however, be traced in the results of the United States Board, Table 83, p. 169.

Mechanically, slag (a) breaks up continuity, (b) brings the metal a step towards the condition of a wire rope or the leaves of a book, and (c) hinders rupture from striking straight across the piece

The first action weakens and makes brittle.

The second may promote flexibility, but hardly toughness as measured by final elongation under tensile stress: I do not know that a wire rope excels in elongation a solid bar of equal net sectional area. Moreover, it must lower the transverse strength and ductility as much if not more than it increases the longitudinal flexibility.. The transverse strength of a wire rope is practically nil. And that it does lower the transverse properties we learn from Table 88, which, representing nearly 900 cases, shows that the tensile strength of weld-iron plates is decidedly and its ductility very much (about 40%) less crosswise than lengthwise, while the properties of ingot-metal are nearly independent of the direction of rolling.

The third might be important were the toughness of slag comparable to that of iron: hair toughens mortar. But we cannot confidently expect the brittle feeble rods of slag to obstruct the path of rupture materially.

That they do not is indicated by Baker's experiment in Table 87 A, in which an artificial crack weakens wrought-iron as much as steel. But, on the other hand, the behavior of tough wrought-iron when broken by nicking and bending seems to indicate that, under these conditions, rupture is prevented from striking across the piece, but probably less by the resistance of the slag itself than by the lack of continuity due to the presence of slag. In this view slag-bearing iron, like wire-rope, should excel in flexibility rather than ductility as measured by elongation and contraction under tensile rupture.

II. For evidence of the toughening effect of slag we have (*a*) the toughness of certain Swedish and other weld-iron. Surprisingly tough they certainly are: but it does not yet seem clearly shown that ingot-iron as free from carbon, silicon, manganese and especially from unoxidized phosphorus is less tough.

(*b*). The toughness and fibrousness of Avesta Bessemer ingot-iron, into which slag was said to be poured intentionally. But the trifling quantity of probably irregularly distributed slag in Avesta metal, reported to be as low at times as 0·05%, seems a wholly inadequate cause. Indeed, after this practice, probably as useless as it seemed senseless, was abandoned, the fibrousness and toughness of the metal remained unimpaired. A cynic might regard the claim that the Avesta metal excelled because it contained slag, as an attempt to make a virtue of necessity, on the part of steel-makers whose crude plant permitted slag to run into the ingot-moulds nolens volens. It would, indeed, seem about as easy to mix slag and steel effectively, as corks and water.[b]

The scanty data of the United States test board, Table 83, while suggesting that slag weakens wrought-iron tensilely, give no weighty indications as to its effect on toughness.

The Terre Noire engineers believed that a minute quantity of slag made ingot metal weak and even red-short.[c]

In brief, while we see no strong reason why slag should benefit iron in any way, and while we have no strong evidence that it does, yet our knowledge of the rôle which it plays in wrought-iron is too crude to warrant our holding confidently that it does not toughen the metal in certain ill-defined ways.

The prevalent belief that wrought-iron is tougher than ingot-iron of like composition certainly implies that, under certain conditions, slag does toughen iron. The foundations of this belief, however, do not seem to be of the firmest.

As fibre appears to be due to the drawing out of the previously equiaxed grains of iron by favorable mode of rupture, we may define $\left\{\begin{matrix}\text{fibrous}\\ \text{crystalline}\end{matrix}\right\}$ iron as that whose grains $\left\{\begin{matrix}\text{are}\\ \text{are not}\end{matrix}\right\}$ readily drawn out into fibres during rupture, or that which $\left\{\begin{matrix}\text{can}\\ \text{can not}\end{matrix}\right\}$ be readily made to yield a fibrous fracture.

§ 260. Influence of Vibration, etc.—The question left now resolves itself into two: (1) Do vibration, etc., induce coarser crystallization; and (2) do they, without altering the shape or size of the crystals, increase the tendency to yield a crystalline fracture?

[a] This is admirably illustrated in Rept. U. S. B'd. on testing iron, steel, etc., I., p. 125.

[b] Fischer, Oest. Zeitschrift, XXXIV., p. 244, 1886. Goodicke, Idem, p. 536. Drown, Proc. Soc. Arts, Mass. Inst. Technology, 1885-6, p. 150. Raymond, Howe, Eng. and Mining Jl., XLII., pp. 181, 219: 1886.

[c] Gautier, Journ. Iron and Steel Inst., 1877, I., pp. 43-4. Also Holley, Metallurg. Review, II., p. 210, "The interposed slag must necessarily decrease (its) strength and ductility."

1. Regarding iron as a viscous liquid, it is not intrinsically improbable that the size of its crystals should change at the ordinary temperature, eminent but dogmatic engineers to the contrary notwithstanding. The crystals of native silver and of "moss copper" are credibly reported as changing their shape somewhat rapidly in mineralogical cabinets.[a] Given such a tendency, vibration might well increase it. Agitation precipitates the crystallization of water tranquilly cooled below 0° C. Instances of important changes in iron at relatively low temperatures are that of density at 100° C. observed by Langley, of stress at 60° by Barus and Strouhal, of carbon at a brown tint by Brinnell, of flexibility by Coffin at a straw tint.

2. It is, however, easier, and for most purposes enough, to answer the second question. We can readily understand that vibration should increase the tendency to break with a crystalline fracture. First, every variation of stress alters the shape of the metal: and all vibration and shock must cause variation of stress. Now, if the metal is a composite mass of crystals of different minerals, say kernels of pearlyte imbedded in a meshwork of ferrite, Figure 56, p. 165, when it is deformed these minerals, both on account of their different moduli of elasticity and of their different shapes, may receive stress and resist deformation unequally: the thin meshes of ferrite may be strained far more than the kernels of pearlyte, or vice versa. Differently deformed, the harder may gradually wear into the softer, the more brittle be gradually disintegrated by excessive stress on its most burdened saliences. Again, repeated deformation may weaken the cement between the large crystals of the first order more than that between the smaller secondary crystals (Figure 54). These are not offered as the true condition of affairs, but as instances of the numberless ways in which indefinitely repeated deformation may gradually alter the strength of the metal, the path of least resistance and of rupture, so that rupture may develop a crystalline where it would once have yielded a fibrous fracture. A given degree of deformation may thus have little effect, a but slightly greater one profound influence. Vibration may be harmless if longitudinal, injurious if transverse and so flexure-causing; the flexure the immediate, the vibration an indirect cause. That which would eventually destroy a mass composed of a given group of minerals might be impotent were the proportions, shape, size or mode of arrangement of the minerals altered. Reheated, the disintegrated minerals may reunite. In this view, cases in which prolonged vibration or repeated shock or flexure are known to change the fracture from fibrous to crystalline, show the existence of already reasonably suspected tendencies: those in which no such change occurs merely argue relative power to resist these tendencies.[b]

Again, if stress be applied to iron by some vibrating body whose vibrations are synchronous with the natural vibration of the metal itself, then each vibration of that body creates a stress which tends to increase the amplitude of the metal's vibration, and we can conceive that this might go on till we reached an amplitude so great as to cause rupture, as in the fabled attempt to fiddle a bridge down. As an only slightly different rate of vibration, even if more rapid, would not act in this special way, numberless cases in which iron resists vibration successfully would merely show that the liability to failure in this way was small, not that it did not exist.

The path of least resistance in this type of rupture might well differ greatly from that under static stress, yielding a granular fracture in metal which would usually show a fibrous fracture.

A difficulty in the way of this explanation of failures under vibration is that, if the piece has approximately uniform sectional area for a considerable distance, we would expect that it would undergo a great permanent elongation long before the amplitude of vibration became so great as to cause rupture, and that this very elongation would change the metal's natural rate of vibration, and so remove the cause of danger.

Vibration is said to change the structure of some alloys greatly, making them extraordinarily brittle.[c]

Here are a few of the many instances in which long exposure to vibration has produced no noticeable injury. Thurston vouches for a great and unmistakable improvement in the quality of wrought-iron rails, originally brittle, during prolonged use in the track.[d] Bauschinger reports two cases in which he could detect no loss of strength or change of structure after prolonged exposure to vibration. The first is that of iron in use in a chain bridge during 49 years, and compared with a reserve chain made by the same firm and at the same place, and carefully kept for comparison. In the second case he applied to bolts from another bridge, tests to which they had been subjected twenty-five years before.[e]

Long searching, Percy failed to find conclusive evidence that vibration makes iron crystalline. R. Stephenson tells of the beam of a Corliss engine, apparently uninjured after receiving a shock equal to about 50 tons 8 or 10 times a minute for 20 years, and of a locomotive connecting-rod, which showed no change after receiving 25,000,000 blows, at the rate of eight per second.[f]

The fracture of a wrought-iron bolt, thought to be of Ulster iron, which had held down the anvil of a trip-hammer for twenty years, was highly fibrous, and like that of unused Ulster iron. So, too, with a hammer-head.[g]

Kennedy reports many pieces of wrought-iron and steel, all long used, some broken in use; in none of them did he find distinct indications of fatigue. Baker finds that, when flat bars of soft steel and wrought-iron are bent laterally repeatedly Wöhler-wise till they break off short, their broken halves, even at points where they had been subjected to 90% of the stress which existed at the rup-

[a] Not only do long delicate filaments of silver, evidently not due to mechanical pressure, form below the melting point of this metal when finely divided silver sulphide is heated in hydrogen (Percy, Metallurgy, I., p. 359), and growths of this metal sprout from silver sulphide below 228°C., 440°F., (Liversidge, Chem. News, XXXV., p. 68, 1877); but moss copper has formed visibly within a few minutes on fresh surfaces of copper matte cool enough to be held in the hand, (W. H. Hutchings, Idem, p. 117), and very considerable growth of moss copper and silver in the cold, in one case within a few weeks, in others in periods of about a year, are quite credibly reported by T. A. Readwin and J. H. Collins, (Idem, pp. 144, 154).

[b] Cf. Percy, Jour. Iron and Steel Inst., 1885, I., p. 17; Metcalf, Trans. Am. Inst. Civ. Eng., XV., p. 290, 1887; Hill, Mechanics, 1882.

[c] Percy, Iron and Steel, p. 11. Also "Metallurgy," Vol. I., p. 621. "Some kinds of brass wire become extremely brittle in the course of time, especially if subjected to vibration. I have seen thick brass wire become almost as brittle as glass in the course of a few weeks, after having been kept extended and subjected to vibration."

[d] Mat'ls of Engineering, II., p. 577.

[e] Journ. Franklin Inst., CIX., p. 417; Journ. Iron and Steel Inst., 1880, I., p. 347, fr. Dingler's Polytechnisches Journal.

[f] Treatise on the Resistance of Matls., Wood, p. 212.

[g] G. E. Whitehead, Sup't Rhode Island Tool Co., Providence, R. I., private communication, Aug. 8th, 1888.

tured section, can invariably be bent double without rupture.[a]

The wrought-iron side and main driving rods of locomotive engines have been found fibrous and tough after prolonged use. Some examples follow.

	Condition of service.				Results of tensile tests.					
	Length of service.			Mileage.	Tensile strength.	Elastic limit.	Elongation %.	In.	Contraction of area, %.	
	Passen.	Freight.	Total.							
Side rod..	12 yr.	6	12 yr.	....	43,410	24,450	19·	5"	......	Fibrous.
" " ..	12 "	6	12 "	....	56,880	......	21·	1"	14·2	"
" "	Yr. Mo. 28 5	1 yr. gen. service	Yr. Mo 29 8	910,080	47,820	......	30·	5"	39·	Fibrous and granular.
Main rod..	5 yr.	32 yr. 8 mo	37 8	860,000 est	41,180	20,200	33·	1"	36·5	Fibrous, spongy.

Rept. Tests Metals, Watertown Arsenal, 1885, p. 1,044, 1888.

But, though the fragments of Wöhler-broken bars show no fatigue, some change has occurred in them, for a comparatively few repetitions of stress would now break them. Does this change increase the tendency to break with a crystalline fracture? Our evidence does not permit a certain answer. Whole bars tested after Wöhler-treatment which has not been carried to rupture show a tremendous loss of tensile strength and elongation, but probably because cracks which would eventually lead to rupture have already formed. For instance, 18,140 bendings reduced the tensile strength and elongation of a bar, whose companion had broken under this number of bendings, from 70,000 to 48,000 pounds per square inch and from 20 to 2·6%. Bauschinger, indeed, finds that the strength of Wöhler-treated bars, when subsequently tested with quiescent load, is not lower than initially, but rather higher.[b]

Railway axles and bars broken by Coffin and others by prolonged rotation while slightly bent, seem to fail by the gradual creeping inwards of a thin crack. After this has penetrated a certain distance, the remaining metal gives way suddenly. The fracture of this last broken part does not differ strikingly from that of similar material broken in the natural state. In the case of railway axles, while often fibrous,[c] it seems on the whole more inclined to break with a crystalline fracture, and this inclination is perhaps stronger than in case of unused axles: but of this we cannot be sure.

W. Parker, Chief Engineer-Surveyor of Lloyd's Register, after prolonged consideration of the breakages of marine shafts, finds no reason to believe that the vibration to which they are exposed makes wrought-iron shafts crystalline, or steel shafts more coarsely crystalline.[d]

On the other hand, passing by Fairbairn's famous assertion that "we know that in some cases wrought-iron subjected to continuous vibration assumes a crystalline structure," we have the following experiment by Sorby.[e] He attached a bar of iron to a tilt-hammer so that it vibrated up and down continuously: after fifteen hours it broke with a crystalline fracture. An examination of a longitudinal section of the broken end showed that the *ultimate* structure was no more crystalline than that of similar iron in its natural state: yet some of the crystals appeared to be slightly separated from each other, instead of being as usual in exact apposition.

Again, Martens invariably finds that the fracture of the tension side of a bar broken by oft-repeated slight flexure, as in Wöhler's experiments, is much finer than that of the compression side: the change is very abrupt, occurring along a line which, in round bars, is nearly straight and perpendicular to the line of bending, but is curved and sometimes nearly a half-oval in square bars.[f] On the polished section he could find no trace of this line with the microscope: the ultimate structure seemed uniform throughout the region where this line occurs. The change then appears to be, not in the size or arrangement of the crystals, but in their adhesion or in the path of rupture.

These changes in the path of least resistance are probably due, not to the last application of stress, but to the accumulated effect of repeated stresses. Here then stresses long antecedent to rupture appear to affect the fracture. But Bauschinger finds that, while rupture by repeated stress produces these markings in the fracture, if a fragment of a Wöhler-broken bar be again broken in the normal way, the fracture now obtained is exactly like that of similar bars which have not been subjected to Wöhler-treatment. So with bars which have been long subjected to Wöhler-treatment without actual rupture. Hence he concludes that stress applied to iron and steel millions of times does not affect the structure.[h]

Again, it is the conviction of the users of trip-hammers and of rock-drills that the head-bolts of the former and certain parts, *e. g.* the rocker-pins, of the latter become crystalline, *i. e.* that metal which before use would yield a fibrous after use shows a crystalline fracture.[g]

The fracture of a 40-year-old five-inch connecting-bar of the 300-ton Washington Navy Yard testing machine, which broke under a load of about 100 tons (its original strength should have been some 400 tons) was for most part distinctly crystalline, with some large well-defined

[a] Trans. Am. Soc. Mech. Eng., VIII., p. 163, 1887. Baker's statement has been incorrectly interpreted as meaning that a bar, subjected repeatedly to 90% of the stress *a single application* of which would suffice to break it, may show no sign of change: he means that it may show no injury when bent a certain number of times under 90% of that stress which applied *the same number of times* would break it: (Idem, p. 174). This is true, the other absurd. The court may be assumed to know some law.

[b] Mittheil aus dem Mech-Tech. Lab. in München, XV., p. 42, 1886.

[c] Cf. Rankine, Civil Engineering, 1870, p. 506. On the Pennsylvania Railroad the fracture of wrought-iron axles is usually more or less fibrous, that of steel axles granular; but as a whole there seems to be a tendency, stronger in steel than in wrought-iron, towards a crystalline fracture (Dr. C. B. Dudley, private communications, May 9th, Sept. 18th, 1888).

Railway axles and the bars experimented on by Coffin and others break "in detail" as it is called. The fracture shows two very sharply separated parts: an inner, slightly excentric, sub-circular region, occupying perhaps one quarter of the total area, with a fresh fracture, much like that of a bar broken in the usual way, *e. g.* by nicking and bending. The remainder of the bar has a nearly smooth fracture, not unlike that of Etruscan gold, and suggesting that it has been long broken, and that the opposite faces have worn each other smooth. The abruptness of the transition is not very readily understood. Railway crank-axles are sometime run till an incipient crack appears, then hooped: marine shafts are used for a further definite time after a flaw first appears. (Baker, Trans. Am. Soc. Mech. Eng., VIII., p. 163, 1887.)

Baker states that, though the crank and straight driving axles of locomotives bend but $\frac{1}{32}$ and $\frac{1}{16}$ inch respectively under the heaviest stress to which they are subject, yet in 1883 one iron axle in fifty broke in running, and one in fifteen was renewed on account of defects: further, that during the preceding three years (1882–4) no less than 228 ocean steamers were disabled by broken shafts, whose average safe life is put at about three or four years. (Rept. British Ass., 1885, pp. 1185-6.)

[d] Private communication, Feb. 5th, 1889.

[e] Jour. Iron and Steel Inst., 1887, I., p. 265.

[f] Stahl und Eisen, VII., 238, 1887. He speaks of these lines as ellipses, but, judging from his illustrations it is improbable that they are parts of true ellipses. He describes them, certain rays normal to and crossing them, and attendant phenomena, minutely.

[g] G. R. Stetson, Trans. Am. Soc. Mech. Eng., VII., p. 267, 1886: Rand Drill Company, private communications, Aug. 2d, 1888. Cf. Wood, "Treatise on Resistance of Mat'ls," p. 214.

[h] Loc. cit.

crystals "bright as mica," whose diameter must have reached 0·5 inch to judge from Thurston's illustration. Purposely broken about one foot from the original break, it showed the same fracture. As it was carefully made from excellent material, Beardslee regards it as an "unmistakable instance of crystallization, which was probably produced by alternations of severe stress, sudden strains, recoils, and rest."[a]

A 20-foot porter-bar at the Morgan Iron Works broke under the jar of the hammer, at a point where its diameter was about 15 inches, and where it was unstrained by the load, with a fracture in large part crystalline, one crystal having faces 0·5 inch square.[b] We are not informed whether its temperature may not often have been high enough to greatly promote crystallization; *i. e.* whether the crystallization was due to jar in the cold, or to heat jointly with jar.

Now I find nothing here which indicates strongly that any change in crystallization occurs under vibration or shock. The cases of the Washington testing machine and of the Morgan Iron Works porter bar may well be due to over-heating during manufacture. Finding the users of trip-hammers very positive in their assurances that their bolts became crystalline, I made some bolts for certain trip-hammers, using for one hammer an iron like, if not *the same as that* habitually used for its bolts, and reserving part of the iron for comparison. The most striking result, unfortunately a psychological not a metallurgical one, was that the bolts actually lasted not merely longer, but incomparably longer than I was, at least in one case, assured that they could. They have already run over four months, and only one has failed. The fracture, is closely like that of bars broken "in detail," Wöhler-wise, by prolonged rotation while slightly bent, already described. The sub-circular, somewhat eccentric part last broken resembled closely the fracture of the reserved part of the same bar broken by nicking and bending. I could find no suggestion of granulation in the fracture, either where the bolt had broken in use in the trip-hammer, or where subsequently nicked and broken with a sledge, or where pulled apart in the testing machine. The properties of the bolt broken in use were practically identical with those of the iron reserved for comparison.

	Tensile strength, Lbs. per sq. in.	Breaking load, Lbs. per sq. in.	Elongation % in ½ in.	Contraction of area %.	Fracture.
Bolt broken in use	51,867	49,845	48·4	45·6	100% fibrous.
Piece reserved for comparison	57,168	50,461	42·4	47·8	100% fibrous

Nor in Bessemer steel trip-hammer bolts broken in use do I find any indication of granulation. Nearly the whole fracture is of the fine, apparently smooth-worn type, the sub-central crystalline part being very small. Nicking and breaking the fragments with a sledge, we get a perfectly normal fracture.

To sum up, while vibration and shock often cause rupture under light stress, and while it is proverbially difficult to prove a negative, we have, I think, every reason to believe that the granulation and crystallization of iron under vibration and shock is a myth.

Touching the relative power of low- and of high-carbon steel to resist vibration and shock we have the following evidence.

Metcalf found that steam-hammer piston-rods made from steel with 0·60% of carbon lasted over two years, while under like conditions those of mild steel lasted but six and those of wrought-iron but three months; and that the endurance of rapidly reciprocating pitmans increased with their percentage of carbon, at least till this reached 0·84%.[c] The feed-rollers in blooming mills receive extremely severe blows from the bloom, which often butts against them like a tremendous battering-ram. At first these rollers were made of soft steel, in the belief that a tough material was needed to resist these shocks: but experience shows that they endure much longer when made of hard steel.

From such facts it has been inferred that hard steel is better fitted to resist shock and vibration than soft steel; the inference is hardly justified. Here pieces of soft steel are compared with enormously stronger ones of hard steel, which endured longer probably simply because the bending which they underwent was so much farther below that corresponding to their elastic limit. The hammer-rods, pitmans and rollers of soft steel might well have outlasted those of hard, if so proportioned as to have as great transverse elastic limit.[d]

In harmony with this view are Baker's results given in Table 88 B. Here hard steel indeed endures repeated bending under given absolute stress better than wrought-iron and soft steel, yet excels these classes in this form of endurance much less than in tensile and compressive strength and elastic limit.

Comparing cases in which the stress on each variety is a given percentage of its ultimate tensile strength under single load, hard steel breaks down much the earliest.

TABLE 88 B.—PATIENCE OF IRON UNDER REPEATED BENDING. BAKER.

Factor A.	Hard Steel.		Soft Steel.		Wrought-iron.	
	Thousands of revs.	Stress, lbs. per sq. in.	Thousands of revs.	Stress, lbs. per sq. in.	Thousands of revs.	Stress, lbs. per sq. in.
1·66@1·75	....	....	40·5@60·2	36,000	108@142	34@36,000
1·75@1·90	5·8	67,000	65·4@155	34,000	39@121	32,000
1·93@2·0	7·6	65,000	....	....	40@481	31@33,000
2·06@2·42	11·6@32·4	58,500@51,000	14,876	26,000	....	....
2·48@2·72	26·1	46,500	....	....	....	....
3·06	151·8	40,500	....	....	....	....
3·70	472·5	34,000	....	....	....	....

Rotating spindles, usually 1 inch diameter, and projecting 16 inches from the shaft in which they are fixed, revolve day and night, weighted at the unsupported end, so that each fibre is alternately in tension and compression. "Thousands of revolutions" refers to the number of revolutions endured before rupture. Factor A is the ratio of the ultimate tensile strength to the calculated tensile stress on the outer fibres due to the weight.

The hard steel is an excellent drift-steel, tensile strength about 120,000 lbs., elongation about 14% in 8 inches. Soft steel is fine rivet-steel, tensile strength about 60,000 lbs., elongation 28%. Wrought-iron is the best rivet-iron, tensile strength about 60,000 lbs., elongation 28% in 8". Trans. Am. Soc. Mech. Eng., VIII., p. 160, 1887.

§ 261. CHANGE OF CRYSTALLIZATION AND OF PROPERTIES IN THE COLD WHILE AT REST.—There is a common belief that iron of various classes (wrought-iron, steel tools, etc.), is improved by long rest and exposure to the weather.[e] Ledebur shows that the latter may lead to serious injury through absorption of nascent hydrogen.[f] We shall see in § 269 that the tensile strength and elastic limit of iron which has been distorted beyond its elastic limit do increase for a long time, probably for many years, at an ever retarded rate. Further, internal stress induced by irregular cooling or by cold-working may be gradually relieved during rest, to the benefit of the metal, especially

[a] Rept. U. S. Bd., to test iron, etc., I., p. 126; Thurston, Mat'ls of Engineering, II., p. 578.

[b] Thurston, Mat'ls of Engineering, II., p. 580.

[c] Metallurgical Review, I., p. 400. Cf. Kent. Trans. Am. Inst. Mining Engineers, VIII., p. 76, 1880.

[d] Cf. Lindenthal, Trans. Am. Soc. Civ. Engrs., XV., p. 376–7, 1887.

[e] Thurston, Mat'ls. of Engineering, II., p. 576: W. Hewitt, Trans. Am. Soc. Mech. Eng., IX., p. 47, 1888.

[f] Cf. § 178, p. 114.

if the temperature be raised. Here then we have two reasonable explanations of this belief.

We have seen that the thermo-electric power, thought to be a true index of stress, changes rapidly when steel is heated to 66° C. (151° F.)[a]: iron might easily reach this temperature in our climate when exposed to the summer sun: tools left in boilers are of course continuously exposed to far higher temperatures, and they are especially prized.

An improvement so great that we hesitate to ascribe it to differences in the conditions of manufacture or of trial, is reported in Rodman cast-iron guns during rest: it is as follows.

TABLE 90.—EFFECT OF REST ON CAST-IRON GUNS.[a]

	Tensile strength.	Endurance.
Cast in 1851 and tested soon after	37,811 lbs.	72 fires.
Cast in 1846 and tested in 1852	29,424 "	2,582 "
Cast in 1846 and tested in 1859	22,969 "	836 "

a Thurston, Matls. of Engineering, II., p. 389, fr. Rodman. Rept. Expts. on Strength and Other Properties of Metal for Cannon, Rand, p. 217, 1856.

But Mr. Wm. P. Hunt informs me that, in the case of discs cut from the muzzles of Rodman cast-iron guns, the initial stress due to casting around a water cooled core did not diminish materially during some ten years' rest.[b]

Both the galvanized and the ungalvanized wire supplied for the East River Bridge often gained strength by simple rest, the ungalvanized often gaining five per cent. in a week or two.[c]

Examining 12 groups of specimens from 102 heats of structural open-hearth steel, under uniform conditions of working and testing, and collectively embracing 446 tests, E. C. Felton found those tested more than twenty-four hours after rolling slightly but fairly constantly stronger and more ductile than those tested within twenty-four hours. The elastic limit was less constantly affected. In eight out of the twelve groups it was lower; in the four others it was greater in the late than in the early tested pieces. In other words, the repose appeared to increase the tensile strength and ductility slightly, but to have no constant effect on the elastic limit.[d] His results are condensed in Table 91.

TABLE 91.—EFFECT OF REPOSE ON THE PROPERTIES OF 12 GROUPS OF STEEL SPECIMENS. FELTON.

Increase (+) or Decrease (—).	Tensile strength.	Elastic limit.	Elongation.	Reduction of area.
Hand rounds (finished colder)	+0·15%	—0·5%	+2·4	+6·3
Guide rounds (finished hotter)	+0·07%	—0·6%	+1·4	+2·1
Number of groups in which an increase appeared to occur during rest	11	4	10	12

From the foregoing we see that the strength of iron in certain cases increases with rest immediately after stress, and after forging.

§ 261A. PERSISTENCE OF CRYSTALLINE FORM after the mineral which caused it has ceased to exist, is illustrated, 1st by hardened Bessemer steel (apparently of 0·49% of carbon), which, though apparently wholly converted into hardenite, yet shows traces of the network structure which had initially existed between the primary prismatic crystals, conspicuous on fracture: 2nd by malleable castings, whose interior shows the laminar structure of pearlyte, though analysis indicates that it has not enough carbon to form pearlyte.

One would expect the ferrite, of which these castings probably consist, to crystallize as usual in its characteristic interfering grains: but it seems to remain as a pseudomorph after pearlyte, in unexpected crystalline equilibrium.[e]

H. Stein found that the Maltese cross[f] of comparatively soft material (pearlyte?) and the diagonals of harder material (cementite?) which etching developed in square ingots of drill steel, persisted when these ingots were forged into rectangles, squares, and octagons successively, and could be developed by etching in the round drill-rods. If the drill-bit came wholly within the Maltese cross, all was well; but if it crossed into the parting diagonals (or St. Andrew's cross) the different parts could not be hardened alike, the diagonals becoming harder than the cross. On using round instead of square ingots the trouble ceased.[g] Here we may surmise that the cementite which, according to Sorby, the primary pearlyte crystals expel, and which is distributed as a network between them, is by the same action concentrated in these diagonals to such a degree that quenching and repeated forging fail to redistribute it. I have often seen this cross in the fracture of ⅝-inch square bars forged from two-inch-square test-ingots of Bessemer rail-steel.

§ 262. OVERHEATING AND BURNING.—A. *Phenomena.* The burning of iron and steel is probably another instance of persistence of crystalline form.[h]

We have seen that the coarse crystalline structure A and D of iron[i] which has been exposed to a very high temperature may be removed by reheating, preferably to W, and also by careful forging. The accompanying brittleness and weakness are simultaneously greatly diminished, but it is doubtful if they can ever be completely effaced.[j] Such iron is said to have been *overheated.* By excessively long or strong overheating the iron may become *burnt,* and the coarseness and brittleness due to burning are removed with greater difficulty and much less completely than those due to overheating, yet in quite the same manner and by the same expedients.

Burnt iron is cold-short and brittle, can be forged and

a Barus and Strouhal, Bull. U. S. Geol. Survey, 14, pp. 54-5: Cf. §§ 53-4, this work.

b Private communication, April 12th, 1888. Wm. P. Hunt, President of the South Boston Iron Company. Discs one inch or more in thickness were cut from the muzzles of the Rodman guns cast at the South Boston Iron Works, and the initial stress was roughly determined by cutting a slot (AA Fig. 78) across them in a planing machine. When this slot had been cut to within about a quarter of an inch of the bottom the stress would tear the remaining metal apart, and the thickness of this metal indicated the amount of stress. Mr. Hunt found that the stress thus determined was substantially the same in two discs cut from the same gun, one tested at the time of casting, the other some ten years later.

Fig. 78

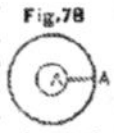

c Collingwood, Trans. Am. Soc. Civ. Eng., IX., p. 171, 1880. He refers the gain to "the accommodation of strain induced by the drawing."

d Trans. Am. Soc. Mech. Engineers, IX., 1888. It is true that, as Mr. Felton says, on an average the elastic limit is lowered by the repose. But the number of cases in which the reverse is true is so great that this result should, I think, carry little weight. So too Mr. Felton endeavors to explain the fact that the repose affects the ductility and elasticity of the hands round more but their tensile strength less on an average than those of the comparatively hot-rolled guide rounds. Here, too, the exceptions are so very numerous as to suggest that this fact represents no general law except, perhaps, as regards tensile strength, but is simply such an accidental result as may always be looked for. Averages of the heights of 20 blue and 20 brown-eyed men would give one set, say the brown-eyed, as slightly taller than the other: from which no one would deduce a relation between eye-color and height.

e Sorby, Journ. Iron and Steel Inst., 1887, I., p. 282.

f Such a Maltese cross is represented by the shaded portion of Figure 28, § 222, the light portions representing the diagonal, probably of cementite.

g Iron Age, June 30th, 1887, p. 15.

h As far as my observation goes, "burnt" as applied to iron is used far more frequently to indicate the possession of the peculiar properties shortly to be pointed out, than to indicate that it is oxidized. As it is not desirable that a class-name should be based on the possession of either of two different and apparently independent properties, we should select the former as the better established, regretting that this word "burnt," whose usual meaning is so nearly synonymous with "oxidized," should here have a confusingly different meaning.

i In this section I use the word generically to include all malleable iron and steel.

j "For 'burned steel,' which is oxidized steel, there is only one way of restoration, and that is through the knobbling fire or the blast furnace. "Overheating" "is always injurious." Metcalf, Treatment of Steel, p. 50.

welded only with care, and has low tensile strength. Its fracture, which is illustrated in Figure 79, is coarse and even flaky crystalline, with brilliant and, according to M. W. Williams,[a] rounded or conchoidal facets. But, under a strong lens, its facets appear to me quite plane. Ingot-metal is thought to burn more readily than the corresponding varieties of weld-metal. The presence of phosphorus and carbon increase the tendency to burn, that of manganese is thought to oppose it.

The degree to which burning occurs during high heating, while mainly dependent on the length and strength of the

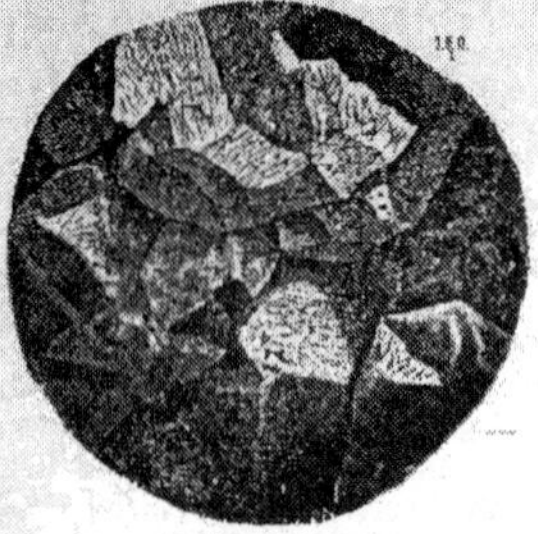

Fig. 79.
Fracture of Burnt Steel. Martens.

heating, may further depend on conditions as yet unknown. W. Garrett describes a case in which ingot-steel of 0·74% of carbon was heated so highly that it became badly deformed, and could hardly be introduced into the rolls: yet it rolled well, and behaved normally under physical tests. This and similar cases led him to assert that neither open-hearth nor Bessemer steel is made brittle by overheating.[b] A more accurate statement would be that they are not *always* made *seriously* brittle. There is little doubt that such exposure is very likely to injure steel, though the injury might not be noticed in rough testing, especially as forging tends to efface it. The belief that steel cannot be burnt has no doubt gained ground from the fact that prolonged overheating and even burning do not necessarily remove any of the carbon. The carbon remained constant in the above and another instance described by Garrett; in the reported experiments of Leeds; and in three out of Ledebur's five experiments on burning, recorded in Table 92. If, however, burning be simply a structural change, there is no reason why it should expel carbon.

TABLE 92.—BURNING AND OXIDATION. (LEDEBUR.)

		Composition.							Excess (+) or deficit (—) of oxygen in the burnt over that in the unburnt steel.
		Carbon.	Silicon.	Manganese.	Phosphorus.	Sulphur.	Copper, nickel, cobalt.	Oxygen.	
Weld steel.									
Bloomary steel......	Sound.	0·807	[illegible]	0·101	0·010	0·008	0·045	0·058	— 0·019
	Burnt.	0·726	0·024	0·098	0·024	0·003	0·028	0·089	
Puddled steel......	Sound.	0·882	0·118	0·187	0·081	0·007	0·046	0·060	— 0·006
	Burnt.	0·868	0·093	0·126	[illegible]	0·004	0·024	0·054	
Shear (garb.) steel......	Sound.	0·827	0·083	0·010	0·027	0·034	0·058	0·037	+ 0·006
	Burnt.	0·798	0·036	0·010	tr.	0·005	0·053	0·043	
Ingot steel.									
Bessemer steel......	Sound.	0·673	0·297	0·473	0·036	0·010	0·045	0·007	+ 0·017
	Burnt.	0·681	0·400	0·178	0·070	[illegible]	0·084	0·124	
Crucible steel......	Sound.	0·917	0·098	0·125	0·025	0·005	0·107	0·046	+ 0·016
	Burnt.	0·916	0·093	0·150	0·025	[illegible]	0·136	0·063	

One end of a bar of each kind of steel, about 16 inches (48 cm.) long, was heated to incipient fusion for about four minutes, in a charcoal fire: on removal all showed the characteristic scintillations of burnt steel. After filing off the outer skin samples were taken from the burnt and unburnt ends, by means of sharp files previously cleaned with ether and alcohol. Ledebur, Jahrbuch für Berg- und Hüttenwesen im Königreich Sachsen, 1883, p. 25.

B. *The Rationale of Burning.* Is burning due to oxidation, or is it solely a structural change, an exaggeration of the effects of overheating, consisting essentially in the formation of coarse, feebly adhering crystals, an exaggeration often accompanied by oxidation, but independent of it?[c]

It is natural to attribute burning to oxidation, 1st, because if the exposure be sufficiently prolonged, for months for instance, the metal evidently becomes oxidized: 2d, because iron is often exposed to oxidizing conditions while burning: 3d, because the burning of most substances is known to be oxidation; hence, by a shallow fallacy, the burning of iron is assumed to be oxidation: 4th, because oxygen has long been the common scapegoat for most of the mischief which the iron-worker can lay to no other culprit.

Of late this belief has received seeming confirmation from the supposed experiments of Leeds, who according to rumor found that, during intentional burning, steel lost no carbon but took up much oxygen: that if the oxygen thus taken up was removed the steel was completely restored: and that, if enclosed in a tightly luted box, steel can be heated and cooled indefinitely without injury. These statements seemed to me in some respects improbable and unlike Professor Leeds' usual utterances. That steel should take up much oxygen at the high temperature at which burning occurs, without losing any of its carbon, is opposed to all experience. On asking Professor Leeds to describe the conditions of his experiments,

[a] Jour. Chem. Soc., New Ser., IX., Part II., p. 790, 1871.

[b] Trans. Am. Inst. Mining Engineers, XIV., p. 798, 1886.

[c] We have seen that, during long exposure to a high temperature, as when an ingot of steel cools slowly, the dominant minerals tend to form large crystals, expelling the other minerals, which form a network between the dominant crystals. When steel is re-heated to W the secondary minerals appear to recombine with the dominant ones to form a nearly homogeneous whole: at least when steel is quenched after heating to W only extremely minute and apparently uniform crystals can be seen. This suggests to me two possible explanations of the phenomena of burning.

1. In ordinary overheating moderately large crystals of the dominant minerals form. The secondary minerals are distributed in relatively thick layers between the faces of the dominant ones, forming planes of weakness. Now the longer the over-heating the larger should these dominant crystals become, and the farther apart should be the meshes which the secondary minerals form. Overheated steel can be restored, because the meshes of the secondary minerals are still so near together that the recrystallization which occurs at W is able to cause their re-absorption and incorporation with the materials of the dominant minerals: burnt steel cannot, because the meshes have become so far separated that their material cannot be completely redistributed on recrystallization, but remains, forming a meshwork of weakness.

Two objections, neither of them conclusive, suggest themselves. (A) If it is simply a question of long exposure to a high temperature, how is it that a slowly cooled ingot, necessarily exposed during and immediately after solidification to a very high temperature, is easily restored, while a forged bar when exposed to a necessarily lower temperature becomes permanently injured? In the first place this objection weighs as heavily against the oxidation as against the crystallization theory. In the second place the crystalline changes which occur with falling temperature, as in the case of the ingot, should differ from those induced by rising temperature, as in the bar which is burning.

B. If burning is due to a separation of the secondary minerals, how is it that pure iron, which consists wholly of ferrite with no secondary minerals, burns? We do not know that such iron would burn. But it is true that the less carbon iron contains, *i. e.* the less of the common secondary minerals, cementite, pearlyte, etc., it contains, the less liable it is to burn.

(2). A slightly different view is that in burnt steel the coarse crystalline structure has become so firmly fixed and persistent through the long exposure to high temperature, its polarity has become so powerful, that it defies the tendency to recrystallization which arises when the temperature rises to W, but that in merely overheated steel this polarity has not become so powerful.

I learned that these statements either are a hoax, or else have been attributed to the wrong person.[a]

In contrast with these inconclusive reasons, witness the following.

I. *Burning may Occur without Oxidation.*—In two out of the five cases in Table 92 the burnt ends of the bars have less oxygen than the unburnt ends: in the three other cases the gain of oxygen is too slight to indicate that it is connected with the change in the metal's properties.

Nor is the loss of carbon, silicon or manganese sufficiently constant here to indicate that it is a real characteristic of burning. M. W. Williams indeed found that, after long exposure, burnt wrought-iron always contained iron oxide, but that burnt steel did not: the burning in case of steel was always accompanied by loss of carbon, which is hardly surprising, as his exposures lasted from a few hours to four days.[b]

II. *Oxidation may Occur without Burning.*—Ledebur describes three specimens of after-blown basic metal (numbers 1 to 3 of Table 43) which contained from 0·171 to 0·244% of oxygen, or from 2·7 to 3·9 times as much as the most highly oxygenated of the burnt steels of Table 92, and which had much finer structure than the burnt weld-iron with which he compared it, and lacked the characteristic brilliant fracture.[c] However much we may distrust our methods for determining oxygen, we can hardly doubt that after-blown basic metal is well saturated with this element.

While overblown Bessemer metal and burnt iron are alike in being difficultly forgeable, yet the overblown and the burnt iron which I have examined seem, on careful comparison, very unlike. Overblown metal I find lacks the brilliant fracture of burnt iron, and is fairly tough when cold: where solid, thin pieces can be bent double, and the bend hammered flat without cracking. The metal can be forged with care at and above a light yellow, but is extremely yellow-short and red-short. I do not find that it is greatly improved by forging: a piece which I forged with great difficulty into a bar about ¼" square broke on bending cold about 30°: it was here very unsound, and rupture was doubtless hastened by the cracks due to red-shortness. Allowing for this, however, and making many bends on many different small and large pieces, I could not assure myself that forging increased the cold-ductility.

Taking now some ⅜" round wrought-iron, which bent 170° to a radius of about ⅛" before rupture, and "barked"[d] like other tough wrought-irons, with a very fibrous fracture, I burnt and then slowly cooled it. It now broke short without appreciable bending, showing the characteristic brilliant fracture. Heated to gentle whiteness and bent slightly, it began to crumble. Forged with care and gently upset it bent to about 120° at very dull redness (a most trying heat) before rupture. Cooled, a piece about ¼" square bent 45° before rupture, yielding an only moderately bright fracture, partly silky, partly crystalline with facets of moderate size.

In short, these pieces of overblown iron differ from those of burnt iron with which they were compared, in fracture, in being initially only yellow and red-short instead of generally hot-short: in being fairly malleable when cold instead of extremely cold-short: in being benefited slightly instead of very greatly by forging. No certain inference can be drawn from such isolated cases: but, indicating that oxygenated metal is unlike burnt iron, they certainly tally with the rest of our evidence.

Over-blown acid Bessemer steel was cast in a wrought-iron box, and rolled to a round bar 1·12 inches in diameter. The skin of wrought-iron was turned off in a lathe. After nicking and breaking I found the fracture extremely silky. At bright whiteness the metal forged well with but slight care, but became brittle at a moderate yellow heat. I could see no strong resemblance to burnt iron in its behavior or fracture.

III. *Burning is Apparently Cured without Removal of Oxygen.*—The characteristics of burnt iron can be removed in very great part by careful forging, which certainly appears to act here directly on the structure, physically, as it does in case of overheated iron, and not by expelling oxygen. By careful hammering, burnt wrought-iron with a galena-like, flaky, crystalline fracture, may be made to yield a thoroughly fibrous one.[e]

In a bar of burnt steel Boker found that part of the silicon existed as such, and part as silica. He reheated one end of the bar in a reducing fire and forged it lightly, so as to restore it; the proportion of silica was still the same as in the unrestored part.[f] The value of his evidence is lessened by the fact that the two parts of his bar which these analyses represent had not initially undergone the same amount of burning, and hence may not have had the same proportion of silica initially.

TABLE 93.—SILICON AND SILICA IN DIFFERENT PARTS OF A BURNT CRUCIBLE-STEEL BAR (BÖKER).

	In the burnt bar without farther treatment.	After restoring.	On further burning under oxidizing conditions.
Silicon as such (difference)	0·138%	0·184%	0·024%
Silicon as silica	0·063%	0·067%	0·177%

V. Finally carbon and phosphorus, which should protect iron from oxidation, greatly increase the tendency to burn: for the more highly carburetted and the more highly phosphoretted the iron the more readily does it burn.

This cumulative evidence strongly indicates that burning is not oxidation, but the result of a structural change not dependent on oxidation, though possibly favored by it. For positive proof, heating with complete exclusion of oxygen seems necessary.

SEGREGATION.[g]

§264. That cast-iron is sometimes heterogeneous has long been known. Abel found the last-solidifying part of phosphoric cast-iron abnormally rich in phosphorus:[h] and,

[a] Jour. Iron and Steel Inst., 1880, II., p. 717: "Prof. Albert R. Leeds, of Stevens Institute," is distinctly credited with these statements. Ledebur, Jahrbuch für das Berg- und Hüttenwesen im Königreich Sachsen, 1883, refers to him as "Prof. Leeds" simply. The Oesterreichische Zeitschrift für Berg- und Hüttenwesen, XXIX., p. 275, 1881, credits "Professor A. R. Leeds" with these experiments. The Berg-und Hüttenmannisches Zeitung, XL., p. 122, 1881, credits them to "Leeds." Here my patience failed. Professor Albert R. Leeds, of Stevens Institute, Hoboken, New Jersey, writes me on receipt of the abstract of his paper from the Journal of the Iron and Steel Institute, "I never tried such experiments as I am credited with," "and the slip you send me is the first time I have seen myself alluded to in connection with the subject" (Private Communications, March 30th and April 3d, 1888).

[b] Van Nostrand's Eng. Mag., V., p. 51, 1871: Journ. Chem. Soc., New Ser., IX., part II., p. 790, 1871.

[c] Op. cit., p. 22.

[d] Cf. Rept. U. S. Bd. on Testing Iron, etc., I., p. 125, 1881.

[e] Percy, Iron and Steel, p. 7.

[f] Stahl und Eisen, VI., p. 634, 1886. Wedding here describes the microscopic appearance of burnt and of restored steel.

[g] Segregation in steel ingots, cf. Stahl und Eisen, IV., p. 646, VI., p. 143: Journ. Iron and St. Inst., 1881, pp. 199, 379. In cast-iron, cf. Stahl und Eisen, IV., p. 634, VI., pp. 143, 244: VII., p. 170: VIII., p. 22.

[h] Percy, Iron and Steel, p. 664, A. D. 1864.

more than thirty-three years ago, he found wart-like excrescences of nearly pure sulphide of iron on the surface of spherical shot made from very sulphurous cast-iron.[a] These phenomena were properly ascribed to segregation and liquation[b] during solidification: and Lawrow and Kalakoutsky seem to have noted segregation in steel ingots as early as 1867.[c] Nevertheless, much as segregation in cast-iron and in very many of the well-known allows, *e. g.* those of copper-tin (bronzes) and of copper-lead, should lead us to expect it, segregation in steel ingots seems to have been generally overlooked until comparatively lately.

It was observed by Forsyth[d] in 1879 and described in 1881 by Stubbs[e] and (later) by Snelus.[f] Hard spots had indeed been noted in steel, but had been ascribed apparently with perfect confidence to imperfect mixing of the recarburizing additions with the mass of the metal.[g] Indeed, even so broad-minded and intelligent a man as Snelus received Stubbs' announcement of segregation in steel ingots most incredulously: "he could not conceive that there could be" such "interchange of elements" "in the time allowed for it."

It is doubtless possible to introduce a quantity of cold recarburizing metal just before teeming in such a way that part of it may not melt in time to become thoroughly diffused: but such evidence as I can find goes to show that the hard centres and other irregularities now so well known are in the main due to segregation.

First, we find that some molten metals diffuse in others with extraordinary rapidity. Thus Roberts found that the diffusion-rate of silver and of gold in lead was about one foot in five minutes, or not much less than that of oxygen in hydrogen, or than the rate of transmission of heat through iron. The result reached in forty minutes with gold and lead would require at least twenty years were these metals replaced by salt and water. In other cases, however, such as copper-antimony, diffusion is comparatively slow.[h] But, clearly, it is not intrinsically improbable that the recarburizer should become uniformly distributed, especially when we remember how the mobile metal is mixed as it pours from converter or furnace to ladle, and from ladle to mould.

Next, manganese, so abundant in the recarburizer but almost wholly absent from the unrecarburized metal, is probably on the whole much more uniformly distributed that any other of the non-ferrous[i] substances present.

Next, if heterogeneousness were chiefly due to imperfect mixing, we would expect differences between different ingots of a single heat at least as marked as between different parts of a single ingot: but so far as my observation goes the composition of the different ingots of a heat is remarkably constant. Witness the case in Table 94.

TABLE 94.—SIMILARITY OF COMPOSITION OF DIFFERENT PARTS OF A HEAT OF STEEL.

	C.	Si.	Mn.	P.	S.
First test-ladleful	·10	·005	·87	·022	·085
Second " "	·10	·005	·87	·022	·083
Third " "	·10	·005	·86	·023	·081
Fourth " "	·10	·005	·86	·023	·083

Cold ferromanganese was added to an open-hearth charge three or four minutes before tapping. Four test-ladlefuls were taken from the beginning, middle and end of the cast during teeming. E. C. Acker, private communication, Oct. 28, 1888.

At an American Bessemer works crop ends from each of the three ingots of each of about fifteen heats were analyzed for manganese: the variation was within the limits of analytical error. These heats were recarburized by adding red-hot crushed ferromanganese in the ladle.[j]

Two tests from each of twelve ingots of one open-hearth steel heat, and two from each of seven ingots of another were pulled. The tensile strength and elongation lay between the following limits.

TABLE 95.—UNIFORMITY IN OPEN-HEARTH STEEL. H. H. CAMPBELL.

Heat.	Number of ingots tested.	Tensile strength. Lbs. per sq. in.			% C. corresponding to this variation.	Elongation, % in 8″.		
		Maximum.	Minimum.	Variation.		Maximum.	Minimum.	Variation.
4533	10	84,640	80,800	3,840	·059	25·7	25	8·7
4534	7	76,050	74,180	4,870	·075	21	23·9	8·1

If we assume that the variation in tensile strength was here due wholly to varying carbon-content, the tensile strength varying at the rate of 65,000 pounds per 1% variation of carbon, we have a variation of 0·059% of carbon between the strongest and weakest test-piece of the first heat, and of 0·075% between those of the other.

Two test-ingots were taken, one during the first and one during the last third of the teeming, from each of twelve open-hearth steel heats. The greatest difference in tensile strength between the two tests of any one heat was 2,960 pounds per square inch, implying on the assumptions just made a variation of carbon of 0·045%. The greatest variation in elongation was from 21·5 to 25% in eight inches.[k]

Finally, the shape and position of the parts which have abnormal composition is far more readily referred to segregation than to imperfect mixing. The segregation usually occurs near the top of the ingot. Figure 80 shows how the carbon gradually concentrates in a pear-shaped mass near the ingot-top. In broken rail-ingots I have seen what appeared to be this pear-shaped mass very strongly marked by a peculiar structure. Figure 81 shows a relatively slight concentration of several elements in the upper part of a very large ingot. Figure 82 probably indi-

[a] Journ. Iron and Steel Inst., 1881, II., p. 392.

[b] For convenience I use segregation to designate a concentration inwards, and liquation to designate an expulsion of matter outwards from the exterior of the mass, but without insisting on the propriety of this terminology. The metal other than the segregation is known as the "mother metal:" it is not closely analogous to "mother-liquor," for it is in general the first-crystallized and purer substance, the segregation being the residue left from its crystallization: while mother-liquor is the impure residue left by the early-formed relatively pure crystals.

[c] Chernoff, Rev. Univ., 2d Ser., VII., p. 140, in a paper read in 1878, states that these gentlemen remarked and proved liquation in steel ingots, referring to the "Journal d'artillerie de 1866 et 1867." I have been unable to find any further reference to them or to their discovery in the metallurgical and chemical publications of that period.

[d] In February, 1879, Forsyth found a hard spot in the head of a broken Bessemer steel rail, near the junction of head and web. Analyzing it, he found very marked segregation. He then examined many others, with results given in Table 96. Many of these examinations were made for the Chicago, Burlington & Quincy Railroad, and I have to thank Mr. Stone of that road, as well as Mr. Forsyth, for permission to publish these results.

[e] Journ. Iron and St. Inst., 1881, I., p. 199.

[f] Idem., II., p. 379.

[g] Bessemer (Journ. Iron and St. Inst., 1881, II., p. 395), admits finding, in the early days of the Bessemer process (*i. e.* sometime after 1854), a vein in a Bessemer steel hydraulic cylinder so hard that the tool would not cut it: but he apparently attributes it to imperfect mixing. In his famous Cheltenham paper he says: "To persons conversant with the manufacture of iron, it will be at once apparent that the ingots of malleable metal which I have described will have no hard or steely parts, such as is found in puddled iron," etc. (Jeans, Steel, p. 51.)

Dudley (Trans. Am. Inst. Min. Eng., IX., p. 588, 1881), says, "Come where steel is being cut and shaped, and I will show you that it is often necessary to stop the lathe or planer and take a cold-chisel to cut out a hard spot"—which—"is simply a part of the spiegel which was not thoroughly mixed with the mass."

[h] Rept. British Ass., 1883, p. 464: Engineering, XXXVI., p. 308, 1883. W. Chandler Roberts, Sir William Thomson.

[i] It is customary to speak of the segregated substances as "metalloids": but this leaves out manganese, to say nothing of copper, slag, arsenic and antimony.

[j] E. F. Wood, private communication, Jan. 26th, 1889.

[k] H. H. Campbell, Trans. Am. Inst. Mining Eng., XIV., p. 358, 1886. The open-hearth furnace was stationary.

cates the true nature of the concentration, and suggests that it should be studied by analyzing small borings taken discriminatingly from etched polished sections.

F. A. Emmerton finds that if an ingot be overturned when partly solidified, the segregation will now be found at the point indicated in Figure 84.[a] This shows that the position of the segregation is due at least in part to gravitation.

It is stated that the segregation occurs at a lower point in bottom- than in top-poured ingots, which would indicate that it tends to move to the last-freezing point.

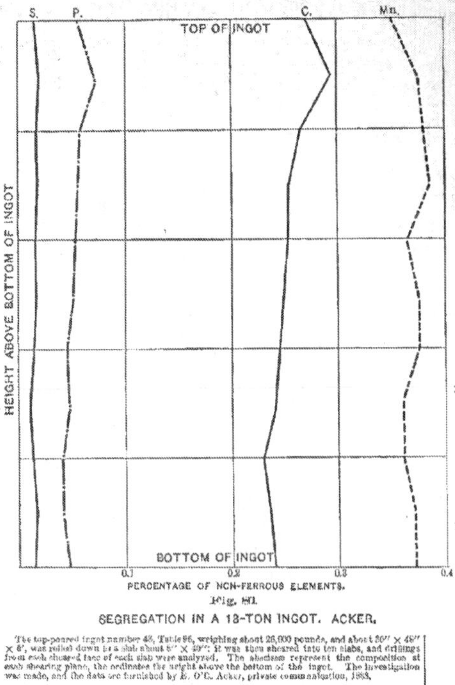

Fig. 81.

SEGREGATION IN A 13-TON INGOT. ACKER.

The top-poured ingot number 48, Table 96, weighing about 26,000 pounds, and about 30″ × 48″ × 8′, was rolled down to a slab about 8″ × 40″; it was then sheared into ten slabs, and drillings from each sheared face of each slab were analyzed. The abscissæ represent the composition at each shearing plane, the ordinates the height above the bottom of the ingot. The investigation was made, and the data are furnished by E. O'C. Acker, private communication, 1888.

The results given in Table 96, most of them here published for the first time, show how serious the irregularity of composition may be. W. Richards[b] states that, with carefully checked analyses, the carbon in his large ingots varies by from 0·10 to 0·15%: while J. Riley[c] states that the variation of carbon is not infrequently nearly 0·50% in one and the same ingot.

While segregation may occasionally be harmless or even beneficial, *e. g.* by concentrating the impurities in the neutral axis of the piece where little or no strength is needed, or by concentrating them in the ingot-top, which is subsequently cut off as in case of gun-ingots, it is doubtless usually injurious. Heterogeneous composition usually implies heterogeneous strength and ductility: and the strength of a heterogeneous substance is usually nearer the strength of the weakest component or part than the average of all the parts: the piece tends to break down piecemeal. So with ductility.

§ 265. The Causes of Segregation in Steel Ingots. —The same forces which lead to the differentiation of cooling steel into the minerals already described (§ 237, p. 163) and of solidifying rock-magmas into the complex crystalline granite, doleryte, etc., are probably the cause of the segregation in cast-iron, in steel, and in alloys in

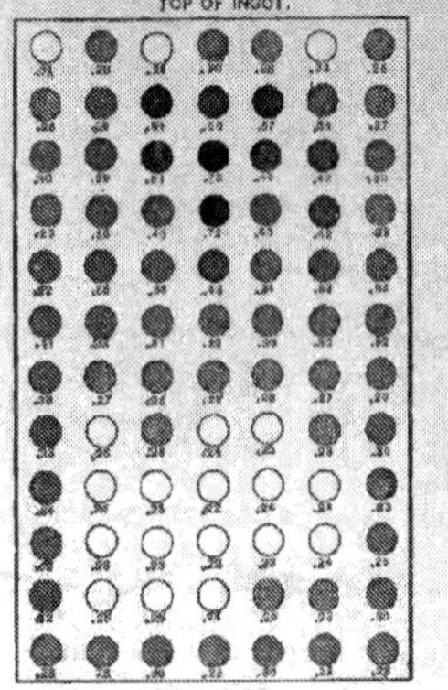

Figure 80.

Percentage of carbon at different points in the vertical section of a large ingot. Maitland, the Treatment of Gun-Steel, Excerpt Proc. Inst. Civ. Eng., LXXXIX., p. 12, 1887. The depth of shading of the spots is roughly proportional to the proportion of carbon.

Fig. 83.

No. 92, Table 96. Segregation in Sheffield steel, developed by etching. H. Eccles, Journ. Iron and St. Inst., 1888, I., p. 79.

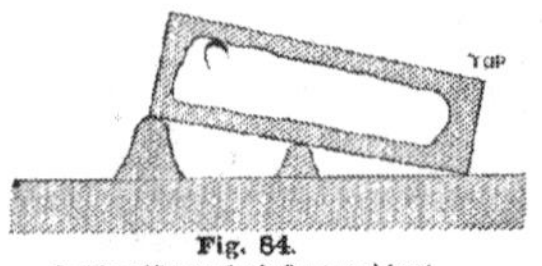

Fig. 84.

Position of Segregation in Overturned Ingot.

general. There is the struggle between crystalline force and surface tension aided by gravity, on the one hand, tending towards differentiation, and of diffusion on the other, tending towards uniformity.

As the temperature sinks towards the freezing-point, surface tension probably increases, the different components tend less powerfully to diffuse among each other and more to draw apart in drops, as oil separates from water, the lighter to rise, the denser to sink. Further, as the complex molten mass cools past the freezing-point of a certain potentially present compound, into which certain elements might group themselves, this compound tends to form, to solidify, to crystallize, to expel the more fusible residue, as a salt crystallizing from an aqueous solution

a Private communication, January, 1886.
b Journ. Iron and Steel Inst., 1886, I., pp. 113-114.

expels the mother liquor, which is gradually driven inwards towards the last-freezing region.

Now *time* is required to effect a considerable separation and segregation in either of these ways: whether to enable the lighter separated bodies to coalesce into masses of such size that they may rise readily by gravity, or to enable the first-freezing compounds to select and reject the more fusible ones, and to push them thus into the still molten interior: hence we infer that here, as in the solidification of other alloys, and in the crystallization of salts from aqueous solutions, slow cooling favors separation.

The masses which separate or segregate should be 1, compounds which differ much in fusibility from the rest, of the mass: 2, compounds whose components have a strong affinity for each other, and which hence tend strongly to form during cooling: 3, compounds which differ greatly in density from the rest of the mass. Now slight differences in the composition or rate of cooling or of pressure may greatly change the resultant of the separating forces. Here one set of substances tends to form, and of this set one is light, fusible, and highly phosphoric; phosphorus segregrates markedly: there, the proportion of phosphorus remaining the same and that of some other element, say manganese, changing; or, the composition being constant, some change in crystallizing conditions tending to establish a different set of compounds, our light, fusible, phosphoric compound no longer forms, no segregation of phosphorus occurs. (Cf. p. 2, 2nd col.) Hence, while we confidently anticipate that a given element, say phosphorus, will tend most strongly to segregate when abundantly present, we may expect perplexing exceptions and contradictions.

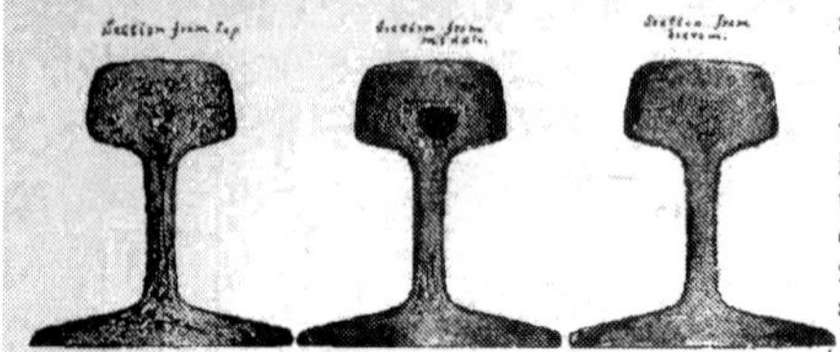

Fig. 82.

Segregation in a Rail Ingot.

The rails made from a single ingot are planed at points corresponding to the bottom, middle and top of the ingot; these sections are etched with acid, and nature-prints obtained. F. A. Emmerton, private communication, January, 1886.

The strong affinity of carbon, phosphorus and sulphur, as compared with that of manganese, for iron, and the greater fusibility and lower density of carbides, phosphides and sulphides than of manganese-iron alloys, should favor the segregation of carbon, phosphorus and sulphur as compared with manganese, and compensate more or less for the fact that the often much larger percentage of manganese than of these metalloids should favor the segregation of this metal.

With our present scanty information it were quackery to attempt a complete explanation of the instances of segregation at hand. A glance at Figure 82 shows that borings taken from immediately adjoining points might give widely different compositions. As borings have almost necessarily been taken very blindly, we have here still another reason to anticipate very discordant results. In Figure 82 at least two different compounds seem to have segregated. Now, should one of these be highly phosphoric and the other not, our borings, should they penetrate only the non-phosphoric bunches, might falsely say that there was no segregation of phosphorus, nay, even that this element was chiefly concentrated in the mother-metal.

Again, while phosphorus increases the fusibility of iron greatly, it does not at all follow that when the mass splits up into a more and a less fusible part, the more fusible will always hold more phosphorus than the other. The elements group themselves in accordance with their chemical affinities, and it may often happen that the more phosphoric of two compounds may be the less fusible, the influence of its excess of phosphorus being outweighed by that of its deficit, say, of carbon. So with the other elements.

But, though our results are as discordant as we could well expect, certain of their features deserve notice.

§ 266. What Elements Segregate Most?—Of cast-iron we have hardly enough cases to justify generalization: let us therefore confine our attention to the steels, Table 96.

Phosphorus segregates in a greater proportion of cases than any other element, and, sparingly as it is present, it segregates on an algebraic average to a greater extent than any other element except carbon. As the influence of a given absolute quantity of phosphorus is so much greater than that of the other elements, so is its segregation much more important than theirs. Still, in no less than 13 out of the 59 cases the segregation contains less phosphorus than the mother metal, but in no case very decidedly less, its greatest deficit being less than 0·02%. In each of the four cases in which the phosphorus in the segregation exceeds that in the mother-metal by more than 0·11% there is also a very heavy segregation of carbon, in two of them a heavy segregation of manganese and in two a heavy segregation of sulphur. The segregation-excess of phosphorus amounts to 0·05% or more in 17 out of the 59 cases given.

Sulphur.—The segregation of sulphur probably comes next in importance, though the greatest excess, 0·192%, is much less important than the maximum phosphorus excess, 0·277%. Out of the ten cases in which the segregation-excess of sulphur is 0·05% or more, there is a very considerable segregation of phosphorus in 7, of carbon in 5, of manganese in only one. This suggests that sulphur and phosphorus tend to segregate together. We may not infer, however, that this is untrue of sulphur and manganese. In nearly every case in which manganese segregates, a larger and usually a very much larger proportion of the sulphur present segregates along with it: and in very many cases the segregation-excess[a] of sulphur is larger absolutely than that of manganese, in spite of the relatively small proportion of sulphur present. As far as this goes, it harmonizes with the evidence in § 81, p. 43, showing that manganese tends to drag sulphur off.

Carbon.—The average segregation-excess of carbon is greater than that of any other element, and in five cases it exceeds 0·44%. The segregation of carbon when severe is usually accompanied by a severe segregation of some other element; but of now one, now another, without

[a] By the "segregation-excess" of a given element, I mean the excess of the percentage of that element in the segregation over that in the mother-metal. So with "segregation-deficit."

TABLE 95.—SEGREGATION IN STEEL AND CAST-IRON.

Number.	Description.	Carbon. A. Mother-metal.	Carbon. B. Segregation.	Carbon. B − A.	Silicon. A. Mother-metal.	Silicon. B. Segregation.	Silicon. B − A.	Manganese. A. Mother-metal.	Manganese. B. Segregation.	Manganese. B − A.	Phosphorus. A. Mother-metal.	Phosphorus. B. Segregation.	Phosphorus. B − A.	Sulphur. A. Mother-metal.	Sulphur. B. Segregation.	Sulphur. B − A.	Copper. A. Mother-metal.	Copper. B. Segregation.	Copper. B − A.	Slag. A. Mother-metal.	Slag. B. Segregation.	Slag. B − A.
	STEEL.																					
1.	R. Forsyth's Bessemer-steel rails. Bad rail	·495	·495	0	·094	·126	+ ·032	1·744	1·643	− **·101**	·121	·130	+ ·009	·066	·075	+ ·009	·014	·017	+ ·003	·030	·138	+ **·108**
2.		·478	·465	− ·008	·187	·128	− ·009	1·329	1·311	− ·018	·146	·161	+ ·015	·048	·045	− ·003	·077	·083	+ ·007	·004	·034	− ·020
3.	Good rail—wore well	·686	·865	+ **·179**	·041	·041	·000	·910	·915	+ ·005	·088	·124	+ ·036	·146	·217	+ **·071**	·075	·077	+ ·002	·022	·040	+ ·018
4.		·472	·409	− ·063	·086	·307	+ **·221**	1·034	1·185	+ ·071	·128	·120	− ·008	·126	·111	− ·015	·008	·007	− ·001			
5.		·476	·411	− ·065	·086	·084	− ·002	1·355	1·336	− ·019	·128	·117	− ·011	·119	·116	− ·003	·008	·007	− ·001			
6.		·475	·460	− ·015	·080	·087	+ ·007	1·348	1·018	− ·030	·128	·121	− ·007	·126	·116	− ·010	·002	·021	+ **·019**			
7.	Good rail—wore well	·672	·737	+ ·065	·041	·043	+ ·002	·816	·831	+ ·015	·083	·099	+ ·016	·182	·173	+ ·041	·074	·073	− ·001	·022	·024	+ ·002
8.	Bad rail	·380	·425	+ ·045	·026	·020	− ·006	1·085	1·080	− ·005	·144	·202	+ **·058**	·054	·084	+ ·030	·008	·011	+ ·003	·026	·056	+ ·030
9.		·390	·518	+ **·128**	·026	·023	− ·003	1·056	1·131	+ ·075	·130	·207	+ **·077**	·059	·119	+ **·060**	·016	·014	− ·002	·024	·028	+ ·004
10.		·367	·306	− ·061	·026	·032	+ ·006	·833	·816	− ·017	·090	·074	− ·016	·045	·034	− ·011	·244	·239	− ·005	·052	·076	+ ·024
11.		·395	·387	− ·008	·086	·087	+ ·001	·856	·881	+ ·025	·106	·100	− ·006	·054	·049	− ·005	·005	·005	·000			
12.	Broke in testing	·290	·740	+ **·450**	…	…	…	·970	1·220	+ **·250**	·0728	·350	+ **·277**									
13.		·332	·333	+ ·001	·023	·022	− ·001	·793	·778	− ·015	·084	·093	+ ·009	·044	·051	+ ·007	·133	·133	0	·032	·032	0
14.	Good rail—wore well	·366	·374	+ ·008	·107	·099	− ·008	·813	·768	− ·045	·147	·147	·000	·090	·087	− ·003	·053	·054	+ ·001	·016	·024	+ ·008
15.		·314	·311	− ·003	·050	·114	+ **·064**	·801	·883	+ ·082	·107	·103	− ·004	·054	·050	− ·004	·031	·029	− ·002	·044	·032	− ·012
16.		·323	·278	− ·045	·029	·048	+ ·019	·791	·739	− ·092	·066	·078	− ·013	·039	·029	− ·010	·041	·021	− **·010**	·028	·050	+ ·022
17.		·304	·276	− ·028	·035	·042	+ ·007	·795	·804	+ ·009	·143	·136	− ·007	·088	·073	− ·010	·010	…	…	·040	·034	− ·006
18.		·333	·445	+ **·112**	·028	·028	·000	·755	·892	+ **·137**	·081	·126	+ ·045	·029	·060	+ ·031	·005	·007	+ ·002			
19.		·318	·319	+ ·001	·059	·063	+ ·005	·761	·758	− ·003	·102	·098	− ·004	·056	·055	− ·001	·042	·035	− ·007	·062	·068	+ ·006
20.	Bad rail	·236	·305	+ ·069	·049	·126	+ **·077**	·795	·832	+ ·037	·094	·159	+ **·065**	·043	·104	+ **·061**	·018	·014	+ ·003	·020	·162	+ **·142**
21.		·258	·315	− ·028	·085	·086	+ ·001	·672	·657	− ·015	·107	·098	− ·009	·018	·047	− ·001	·006	·006	0			
22.	Bad rail	·301	·393	+ ·092	·084	·031	− ·053	·710	·853	+ **·143**	·145	·231	+ **·086**	·038	·079	+ ·041	·106	·105	− ·001	·022	·034	+ ·012
23.		·284	·268	− ·016	·062	·048	− ·014	·717	·744	+ ·027	·101	·101	·000	·051	·054	+ ·003	·037	·036	− ·001	·030	·032	+ ·002
24.	Broke in testing	·200	·300	+ ·100	…	…	…	·720	·950	+ **·230**	·075	·160	+ **·085**									
25.	Good rail—wore well	·471	·462	− ·009	·475	·455	− ·020	·411	·413	+ ·002	·050	·068	+ ·008	·043	·047	+ ·004	·065	·056	− ·009	·060	·060	0
26.		·248	·274	+ ·026	·019	·019	·000	·620	·646	+ ·026	·066	·109	+ ·043	·046	·060	+ ·014	·172	·186	+ **·014**	·031	·036	+ ·005
27.	Bad rail	·252	·303	+ ·051	·008	·009	+ ·001	·604	·587	− ·017	·194	·240	+ ·046	·107	·143	+ ·036	·011	·013	+ ·002	·020	·020	0
28.		·265	·268	+ ·003	·022	·029	+ ·007	·580	·682	+ ·092	·125	·135	+ ·010	·057	·080	+ ·023	·819	·843	+ **·024**	·028	·050	+ ·022
29.	Bad rail	·233	·315	+ ·068	·016	·012	− ·004	·575	·553	+ ·008	·089	·135	+ ·046	·050	·101	+ **·051**	·049	·049	0	·074	·032	− ·042
30.		·204	·183	− ·021	·010	·018	+ ·008	·570	·567	− ·008	·158	·180	− ·019	·063	·063	− ·002	·036	·014	− **·022**	·028	·044	− ·016
31.	Failed in track	·310	·600	+ **·290**	·089	·089	·000	·684	·792	+ **·108**	·1092	·2856	+ **·1764**									
32.		·208	·175	− ·023	·025	·037	+ ·012	·492	·530	+ ·038	·122	·109	− ·013	·078	·072	− ·006	·011	·028	+ **·017**	·044	·044	0
33.		…	…	…	…	…	…	·360	·580	+ **·220**	·092	·193	+ **·101**									
34.		…	…	…	…	…	…	·860	·830	− ·030	·115	·165	+ **·050**									
35.		…	…	…	…	…	…	…	…	…	·126	·187	+ **·061**									
36.	Bessemer ingot	·090	·100	+ ·010	·013	·015	+ ·002	…	…	…	·086	·197	+ **·111**	·023	·078	+ **·055**						
37.	Tyre steel	·520	·600	+ ·070	·020	·070	+ **·050**	·600	·470	− **·130**	·089	·110	+ ·030									
38.	R. O'C. Acker. Boiler plate	·110	…	…	…	…	…	·390	·410	+ ·020	·017	·024	+ ·007	·021	·031	+ ·010						
39.	Boiler plate	…	…	…	…	…	…	…	…	…	·051	·072	+ ·021	·027	·052	+ ·025						
41.	18-ton ingot	·150	·180	+ ·030	…	…	…	·660	·720	+ ·060	·054	·087	+ ·033	·020	·039	+ ·019						
42.	Ingot	…	…	…	…	…	…	…	…	…	·016	·026	+ ·010	·014	·040	+ ·026						
43.	Ingot	·190	·300	+ **·110**	…	…	…	…	…	…	·048	·074	+ ·026									
45.	Steel rail	·270	·410	+ **·140**	·015	…	…	·860	…	…	·091	·283	+ **·192**	·078	·270	+ **·192**						
46.	Ingot, 66″ long	·370	·920	+ **·550**	·006	·043	+ ·037	·498	·585	+ ·087	·096	·261	+ **·165**	·025	·161	+ **·136**						
47.	Ingot, 7′ long	·440	·770	+ **·330**	a.	…	…	·514	·558	+ ·044	·052	·142	+ **·090**	·040	·187	+ **·147**						
48.	" "	·190	·210	+ ·020	0	0	0	·860	·842	− ·018	·050	·068	+ ·018	·044	·056	+ ·012						
49.	" "	·420	·420	·000	tr	tr	0	·738	·755	+ ·017	·044	·056	+ ·012	·039	·046	+ ·007						
50.	83″ steel rail	·380	1·200	+ **·520**	·410	·410	0	·690	·840	+ **·150**	·074	·100	+ ·026									
51.	Steel plates, Eccles	·118	·160	+ ·046	tr	tr	0	·576	·590	+ ·014	·038	·112	+ **·074**	·030	·073	+ ·043						
52.		·105	·125	+ ·050	tr	tr	0	·576	·625	+ ·079	·087	·106	+ ·019	·105	·239	+ **·134**						
53.		·115	·135	+ ·020	tr	tr	0	·018	·018	0	·044	·051	+ ·007	·041	·072	+ ·031						
54.		·150	·240	+ ·090	·010	·010	·000	·648	·614	− ·034	·060	·127	+ **·067**	·054	·155	+ **·101**						
55.	19″ shaft	·452	·898	+ **·446**	·106	·123	+ ·017	·690	·818	+ **·128**	·059	·139	+ **·080**	·014	·031	+ ·017						
56.	Bessemer steel tyres	·296	·241	− ·045	·864	·944	+ **·080**	1·100	1·218	+ **·118**	·063	·068	+ ·005									
57.		·205	·205	·000	·305	·321	+ ·016	·594	·613	+ ·019	·103	·104	+ ·001									
58.		·294	·252	− ·042	·252	·240	− ·012	·545	·509	− ·036	·050	·073	+ ·023									
59.	Ingot	·775	·725	− ·050	·078	·023	− **·055**	·425	·306	− **·119**	·032	·014	− ·018	·027	·023	− ·004						
60.	Bar of Krupp steel	·852	1·020	+ **·168**	·130	·195	+ **·065**	·443	·420	− ·023	·044	·050	+ ·006	0	·005	+ ·005	·234	·224	− ·010			
61.		·30 ±	·780	+ **·480**																		
62.	Lividia boilers	·095	·200	+ **·105**	…	…	…	·831	·871	+ ·040	·039	·095	+ ·006	·036	·177	+ ·141						
	SUMMARY OF SEGREGATIONS IN STEEL.																					
	No. of + cases	…	…	34	…	…	23	…	…	32	…	…	44	…	…	32	…	…	12	…	…	15
	" − "	…	…	17	…	…	12	…	…	20	…	…	18	…	…	15	…	…	18	…	…	4
	" 0 "	…	…	8	…	…	11	…	…	1	…	…	2	…	…	0	…	…	4	…	…	4
	Maximum + case	…	…	+ ·550	…	…	+ ·221	…	…	+ ·250	…	…	+ ·2772	…	…	+ ·192	…	…	+ ·024	…	…	+ ·142
	Maximum − case	…	…	− ·065	…	…	− ·055	…	…	− ·130	…	…	− ·019	…	…	− ·015	…	…	− ·022	…	…	− ·042
	Algebraic av'ge	…	…	+ ·080	…	…	+ ·013	…	…	+ ·029	…	…	+ ·033	…	…	+ ·032	…	…	+ ·0009	…	…	+ ·016
	Arithmetr. av'ge	…	…	·100	…	…	·019	…	…	·055	…	…	·043	…	…	·036	…	…	·0068	…	…	·023
	CAST-IRON.																					
101.	Gruson armor	3·310	3·030	− **·280**	·260	·700	+ **·440**	1·030	1·080	+ ·050												
102.	Chilled	3·270	3·060	− ·210	·913	1·019	+ ·106	1·640	1·010	− **·630**												
103.	Grey-iron	3·975	3·409	− **·566**	3·653	3·678	+ ·025	1·080	1·320	− **·260**	·018	·005	− ·013	·027	·019	− ·008	·037	·027	− ·010	Arsenic.		
104.		2·764	2·864	− **·900**	3·140	3·158	+ ·018	·852	·931	+ ·079	·885	·826	− ·059	·010	·018	+ ·008	·058	·051	− ·007	·0640	·134	+ **·070**
105.	Cleveland iron	3·000	1·750	− **1·250**	1·630	·790	− **·840**	·355	·288	− ·067	1·530	6·840	+ **5·310**	·120	·060	− ·060						
106.	Spiegeleisen	4·391	4·808	+ ·417	·390	·200	− **·135**	6·120	6·570	+ **·450**	·525	·171	− **·354**									
107.		4·676	4·768	+ ·092	·521	·229	− **·292**	6·008	6·970	+ **·962**	·591	·378	− **·213**									
108.		4·283	4·027	+ ·344	·313	·101	− **·212**	5·872	6·380	+ **·508**	·561	·272	− **·289**							Slag.		
109.	6-ton block	3·202			·640						1·318			·193						1·460		
110.		2·930	2·940	+ ·010		·760	+ **·120**	…	…	…		1·340	+ ·028		·067	− ·192	…	…	…		·920	− ·540
	No. of + cases	…	…	3	…	…	5	…	…	5	…	…	2			1	…	…	0	…	…	1
	" − "	…	…	6	…	…	4	…	…	3	…	…	5	…	…		…	…	2	…	…	1
	Maximum + case	…	…	+ ·417	…	…	+ ·440	…	…	+ ·962	…	…	+ 5·310	…	…	+ ·008	…	…	…	…	…	+ ·070
	Maximum − case	…	…	− 1·250	…	…	− ·840	…	…	− ·630	…	…	− ·354	…	…	− ·192	…	…	− ·010	…	…	− ·540
	Liquations.																					
115.		3·411	3·069	− **·347**	2·044	1·635	− ·409	0·430	0·420	− ·010	0·440	1·984	+ 1·544	0·086	0·052	− ·034	0·028	0·012	− ·016			
116.	Siegen cast-iron	…	…	…	…	…	…	…	…	…	·823	2·466	+ 1·643									
117.		3·463	3·818	+ **·355**	2·186	1·965	− ·221	2·620	5·188	+ **2·568**	…	…	…	·056	·223	+ ·167						
118.		3·590	4·020	+ **·430**	1·790	3·150	+ **1·36**	·630	·870	+ **·240**	·680	2·190	+ **1.510**	·050	·050	0						

1 to **35.** R. Forsyth, private communication, Jan. 27th, 1886.

36. B. W. Cheever, Trans. Am. Inst. Min. Eng., XIII., p. 167. Bessemer-steel ingot 18″ × 18″ × 4′ 6″. Mother-metal = point at outside; segregation = axis 2′ 6″ from bottom.

37. Borings from metal originally at the outside (mother-metal) and originally at the center (segregation) of a 550 lb. open-hearth steel tyre-ingot. Zeitschr., Stahl und Eisen, IV., p. 646, 1884. Also Jour. Iron and Steel Inst., 1884, II., p. 672.

38 to **43.** R. O'C. Acker, private communication, 1886.

38. ⅜-inch boiler-plate rolled from 10″ × 18″ ingot: mother-metal = bottom-end of plate, segregation = middle. **39.** Bottom-end and middle of another boiler-plate. **40.** Test-ingot of heat, and point near top of a boiler plate ingot 10″ × 18″ × 8″.

42. Open hearth ingot, 10″ × 18″ × 8″ top end: mother-metal points at outside: segregation = 4″ from top, in axis of ingot.

43. 26,000-lb. ingot, cf. Figure 81. Mother-metal [illegible] ingot of [illegible]: segregation = a point in the axis near the top of the ingot.

46. F. Stubbs, Journ. Iron and St. Inst., 1884, I., p. 199. Ingot 7′ 6″ long: mother-metal [illegible] 2′ 6″ from bottom; segregation = 1′ 11″ from top.

47. Snelus, Journ. Iron and St. Inst., 1881, II., p. 879. After recarburizing with spiegeleisen the Bessemer converter was turned up and the blast sent through the metal for nearly a min-

apparent rule. In 63% of the cases there is a greater or less segregation-excess of carbon: and in only 4 out of 54 is there a segregation-deficit of as much as 0·05%. When we turn to the cast-irons, however, the segregation-deficit of carbon is usually very severe. There is a segregation-deficit in every case except 106 to 108, and here we have reason to believe that what appears to be a segregation is really the first-solidified part, spanning subsequently-formed vugs.

Ledebur suggests plausibly that the segregation-deficit of carbon in case of cast-iron may arise because an increase of carbon beyond a certain point, say 3%, actually decreases fusibility: so that here the less carburetted compound is the more fusible, and hence segregates.

Manganese and Silicon.—In the cases here presented the segregation of manganese and of silicon is in general much less important than that of carbon, phosphorus and sulphur, in the case of silicon perhaps because little silicon is usually present, and in case of manganese for the reasons already given. Still, the segregation-excess of manganese reaches 0·128% in eight cases and 0·22% in three. We have only one very severe segregration-excess of silicon, 0·221% in Number 4.

Perhaps the worst cases are Numbers 12, the end of a rail rolled at Chicago in 1879, broken in testing, and showing a hard spot on head and web, with segregation-excess of 0·45% of carbon, 0·25% of manganese, and 0·277% of phosphorus: Number 46, a very large ingot reported by Stubbs, with a segregation-excess of 0·55% of carbon: and Number 50, a 33-inch steel roll with a segregation excess of 0·52% of carbon.

§ 267. SPECIAL FEATURES OF SEGREGATION.—By applying severe pressure to partly solidified cast-iron, Stead caused the molten interior, into which much phosphorus had already segregated, to burst the still tender walls and gush out.[a] The ejected matter contained 6·84% of phosphorus, while the cast-iron treated held but 1·53% (No. 105, Table 94). Now in a like way the pressure which the rapidly cooling and contracting walls exert on the interior during the early part of the solidification may squeeze drops of the still molten metal through the walls, as mercury is squeezed through chamois. Riley's pea-like drops, containing over 4% of phosphorus, occurring on phosphoric cast-iron,[b] are doubtless instances of this action; others are given in Numbers 115 to 118 of Table 96.

The excess of contraction of the interior over that of the exterior after the period when the shell has become rigid, causes internal cavities; and in and around these cavities we may expect to find the last-freezing part of the metal, and the segregation if any there be. Occasionally it shoots out in little pine-tree crystals into these vugs.

But we may find in the vugs not the last- but the first-freezing part of the metal. Thus, if in a narrow casting, such as a pig of spiegeleisen, early forming crystals shoot completely across the mass, these crystals may be found stretching across the vug which forms by contraction later. Of this we seem to have an example in Numbers 106-108 of Table 96, for the composition of the vug-crystals indicates that they are less fusible than the mother-metal.

In exceptional cases the segregated matter is found as a kidney-shaped mass within the central vugs, as in Number 104, Table 96, sometimes wholly detached, in other cases attached to the mother-metal at few points. Ledebur plausibly supposes that the segregation separates from the mother-metal because its coefficient of expansion is higher, *i. e.* it shrinks away from surrounding metal. Possibly, however, the segregation while molten refuses to wet the mother-metal, lying like mercury on glass, or oil in water: later, when the excess of contraction of interior over shell causes a vug to form, parting occurs more readily at the junction of the mutually repellent segregation and mother-metal, than through the mother-metal proper, *i. e.* the mother-metal shrinks away from the segregation.

The microscope tells us that iron and unhardened steel are never homogeneous, microscopically speaking: we may regard the microscopic minerals described in §§ 237-8, pp. 163 et seq., as microscopic segregations. But it is probable that much iron and steel contains segregations intermediate between these microscopic ones and the very serious ones shown in Figure 82. It may well happen that the comparatively large quantities of metal which we take in common sampling may include several small segregations and several small lots of mother-metal, and that these may balance each other so that borings in different spots may have like *average* compositions. But T. T. Morrell finds that when very small borings are made, say of 50 mg each, the quantity of carbon at

[a] In 1883 I proposed concentrating the phosphorus of phosphoric cast-iron by casting the metal in large blocks as it ran from the blast-furnace, and bleeding them when partly solidified, thus obtaining relatively pure shells.

[b] E. Riley, Journ. Iron and St. Inst., 1881, II., p. 393.

etc. Cooled very slowly in moulding sand, so that though cast on Saturday it was not solid on Monday. Ingot 7' × 19'' × 19''. Mother-metal = average composition at outside. Segregation = centre of a slice cut 21'' from the top. (Manganese from slices near bottom and near top.)

48. Idem. Open-hearth steel ingot 3' 6'' × 21'' × 17''. Mother-metal = slice 4'' from bottom: segregation = slice 10'' from top.

49. Idem. Bessemer rail ingot, 4' × 13'' × 18'' at bottom. Mother-metal = slice 3½'' from bottom, segregation = slice 12'' from top.

50. A broken steel roll, 33'' in diameter. Mother-metal = chippings from exterior, segregation = chippings from centre. Source withheld.

51 to 54. H. Eccles, Journ. Iron and St. Inst., 1888, I., p. 73. Steel plates. Mother-metal = planings from outside of plate: segregation = cuttings from inside of plate.

55. Forged steel shaft, about 19 in diameter. Mother-metal = large end of shaft, segregation = small end. Source withheld.

56 to 58. Bessemer steel tyres, Ledebur, Stahl und Eisen, VI., p. 141, 1883. Borings, obtained with a slowly moving dull drill, were sifted through a very fine sieve. For comparison with the other results here collected, the coarser borings, representing the tougher material, are here classed as mother-metal, the finer and more brittle ones as segregation, though they hardly come within the legitimate use of these words.

59. An ingot weighing several tons was drilled at top and bottom. Mother-metal = bottom. Segregation = top. W. Metcalf, Trans Am Soc. Civ. Eng., XV., p. 286, 1887.

60. A large bar of steel made for rolls by Krupp. Mother-metal = outer turnings: segregation = inner borings. Idem.

61. A sound ingot. Mother-metal = approximate average composition of outside, segregation = spot near the top containing the maximum of carbon. Maitland, The Treatment of Gun-Steel, Excerpt. Proc. Inst Civ. Eng., LXXXIX., p. 12. 1887.

62. Fourteen layers, each 1-16th inch thick, were planed from one of the Lividia's boiler-plates. Mother-metal is the average of the two outer layers: segregation is the layer richest in carbon, phosphorus and sulphur. The manganese varied only between the limits 0·237 to 0·410%. W. Parker, Trans. Inst Nav. Arch., XXII., p. 20, 1881.

101. Crust and inner part of Gruson chilled cast iron armor. Ledebur, Stahl und Eisen, IV., p. 635, 1881.

102. Ditto, ditto, for a chilled cast iron tread-wheel. Idem.

103. Very slowly cooled dark-gray Bilbao cast iron. Idem.

104. Mother metal, dark gray, coarse-grained pig iron: segregation, light grey, fine-grained, kidney-shaped mass contained in a vug, and in some cases wholly detached from the walls. Idem.

105. About 100 lbs. of Cleveland cast-iron was cast in a mould, and when it had become pasty was subjected to severe pressure: the still molten internal part gushed out: it is here given as segregation. Mother-metal = the composition of the cast-iron used. A second experiment gave like results. J. E. Stead, Dingler's Polytech Journ. CCXXX., p. 276, 1878. From Iron, X., pp. 508, 586, 631, 1877.

106 to 108. Mother-metal = a fine-grained spiegeleisen, yielding when attacked by acids a brown residue of carbon, silica and iron. Segregation = smooth, mirror-like, parallel or acutely crossing, leafy crystals stretching across the vugs: perhaps 0·004'' (0·1 mm.) thick in their middle, thicker where attached to the walls of the vugs: quickly acquiring in the air a thin, deep-blue, oxide tint; leaving a residue of pure silica when attacked by acids. B. Platz, Stahl und Eisen, VI., p. 244, 1886.

109. Five or six tons of white cast-iron were very slowly cooled in a previously warmed mould, covered with sand. Mother metal, upper figures = composition of original cast-iron: lower figures = average of composition at four points at the outside of the cooled block. Segregation = a point near the center. Bell. Journ. Iron and St. Inst., 1871, II., p. 293.

115. Mother-metal, gray easily worked iron: liquation, brittle drops and thin sheets on the outside of the metal pulverizable in a mortar. Ledebur, Stahl und Eisen, IV., p. 637, 1884.

116. In Siegen cast iron (mother-metal) were found pea-sized globular liquations. O. Lentz, Stahl und Eisen. VI., p. 443, 1886.

117. Specks floating on the surface of molten cast-iron, and the cast iron itself. Ledebur, Handbuch der Eisenhüttenkunde., p. 257.

118. Molten cast-iron, and matter separated from its surface by Schneider's separator. Ledebur, Stahl und Eisen, VII., p. 171. 1887.

neighboring points in the same piece of steel usually varies through a range of about 0·06 or 0·07%.[a]

In this view such admirable uniformity of composition as is indicated in Table 97 may be more apparent than real.

TABLE 97.—COMPOSITION OF PENNSYLVANIA STEEL RAIL.

	C.	Si.	Mn.	P.	S.
Head	0·39	0·01	0·51	0·099	0·09
Web	0·39	0·01	0·51	0·100	0·08
Flange	0·39	0·01	0·51	0·098	0·04

A rail rolled at the Pennsylvania Steel Works in 1869, and in use on the Pennsylvania Railroad until 1887. F. W. Wood, private communication, June 29th, 1888.

A separation, which however appears in some cases to be rather a stratification than a segregation, may occur while the metal is molten. Beside the drop-like particles which occasionally swim on the surface of molten iron, we have the observations given in Table 98. Here the top of pigs of basic cast-iron has more phosphorus in 17 out of 20 cases and more manganese in 12 out of 15 cases than the centre. Further, comparing the middle pigs of each of ten beds from the same casting of basic cast-iron, the proportion of manganese increased continuously from the first to the last bed (except that it was alike in the 8th and 9th beds), but here the behavior of phosphorus is very irregular. These observations suggest that manganese tends to rise by gravity in the molten mass:

TABLE 98.—STRATIFICATION OF PHOSPHORUS AND MANGANESE, (Reinhardt).[b]

	Phosphorus %		Manganese %	
Average of top	2·6575	20 basic pigs.	2·618	15 basic pigs.
" bottom	2·3676		2·714	
Difference	+ ·2899		+ ·098	
Middle pigs of last five beds	2·806		2·971	
Middle pigs of first five beds	2·840		2·588	
Difference	− 0·034		+ ·383	

The difference between the composition of the early and late beds clearly cannot be referred to segregation during solidification. Nor is it probable that the difference between the top and centre of the individual pigs is chiefly due to segregation: for two of these pigs were examined at several different points, and, excluding the top, phosphorus and manganese seem to be rather higher in the middle than at the outside.

So, too, J. W. Thomas found that the proportion of silicon in the pigs of two casts fell greatly between the first and third beds, but thereafter remained nearly constant.[c] His results follow:

Bed.	1.	3.	5.	7.	9.	11.	13.
1st set % Si	3·228	2·058	1·890	1·800	1·831	1·884	
2d set % Si	2·021	1·732	1·741	1·765	1·722	1·783	1·858

The crusts which occasionally form on pig-iron may be due in part to the liquation of oxidizable elements, in part as Ledebur suggests to the volatilization of sulphides and cyanides, which are oxidized by the moisture in the casting-house sand, and condensed on the sides of the pig: in this view they are condensed fume. Examples are given in Table 99.

TABLE 99.—CRUSTS, ETC., ON CAST-IRON.

	Crusts.										
	Graphite.	SiO_2.	TiO_2.	Al_2O_3.	FeO.	Fe_2O_3.	MnO_2.	CaO.	MgO.	K_2O.	Sb_2O
1	4·55	75·95	1·12	4·90	8·56	......	5·75	·92	·40	1·60	·06
2	......	40·66	3·29	3·36	......	58·41	4·97	1·67	·55	......	......
3	......	50·86	5·77	......	......	82·11	9·96	0·10	0	......	......
4	......	22·84	4·45	9	......	67·06	3·80	0·04	0	......	......
5	......	94·87	·95	......	·93		·25	0	0	......	......

	Crusts.				Cast-Iron Accompanying.				
	P_2O_5.	S.	V_2O_5	Cr_2O_3	Carbon.	Si.	Mn.	P.	S.
1	tr.	·95	......	......	3·310	3·27	·44	1·182	·018
2	·06	......	1·32	......	......	0·51 @ 0·34	·375	·503 @ ·81	·035
3	·12	......	1·15	......	......	......	......	......	......
4	......	......	......	6·15	......	......	......	......	......
5	......	......	......	......	......	1·4	......	......	......

1. A yellowish white, readily detached, moss-like mass of threads or stemlets, filling cavities on the exterior of dark-grey, coarse-grained pig-iron, which were deep, irregular, and clearly formed by the escape of gas during solidification. The iron which contained this substance always smoked much in casting. The alumina may have come from the casting-beds. Ledebur, Stahl und Eisen, IV., p. 635, 1884.

2. Crust on pig-iron made at Pequest, N. J.; the vanadic acid is from a second specimen examined by Drown. Robertson and Firmstone, Trans. Am. Inst. Min. Eng., XII., p. 641.

3. Like crusts from Glendon, Pa., Idem.

4. Crusts similar to No. 2, from Pequest; G. Auchy, Idem, p. 644.

5. Crusts from pig-iron made at Riegelsville, Pa. B. F. Fackenthal, Jr., private communication, June 11 1886.

Figures 80 and 81 show that the proportion of carbon in the very shell of the ingot is higher than at points slightly nearer the centre. In Figure 81 this is shown by the deflection of the carbon-line to the left. It is readily understood. The very skin freezes too fast to permit segregation, and hence has approximately the average composition of the molten mass. In the more slowly cooling parts slightly within the skin time is afforded for segregation and the centripetal expulsion of fusible, highly carburetted compounds.

§268. To PREVENT HETEROGENEOUSNESS, in so far as it is due to segregation, the natural steps are to hasten cooling, by keeping the thickness of the ingots within bounds, and by using iron moulds as far as practicable, or, in case sand moulds must be used, by breaking up the mould soon after the outside of the mass has set, so as to hasten the solidification of the interior. But as we have already seen, rapid cooling should tend to increase the volume of the pipe, and the formation of both blowholes and cracks. (Cf. pp. 151, 152, 161.) We should therefore cast in ingots of moderate size, and cool at a moderate rate. An excessive casting temperature promotes slow cooling, while increasing the tendency to form cracks and blowholes, and should thus on every account be avoided. It is the actual experience at some American Bessemer works that stickers (ingots which do not leave the mould readily, usually because cast too hot), show excessive segregation.

To make the metal quite homogeneous before teeming, in the crucible process we have to mix the contents of the several crucibles, in the Bessemer and open-hearth processes to mix the recarburizer with the rest of the metal thoroughly. The mixing may be done in the casting ladle (in the crucible process, the different crucible-fuls may to that end be run into a common ladle), *e. g.* by means of Allen's agitator, Figure 85, or by poling, *i. e.* inserting a pole of green wood into the ladle, when steam and hydrocarbons distill, stirring the mass: or by pouring from one ladle to another, as is done in Britain.

In the Bessemer process we may turn the converter up for a few seconds after adding the recarburizer. In the open-hearth furnace the recarburized bath may be vigorously stirred or poled: or mixed by rotating the hearth, as in the Pernot furnace. Indeed, greater uniformity of product is claimed as an important advantage of this furnace: but the results given in Tables 94 and 95, and immediately after, obtained in a stationary open-hearth furnace, go to show that uniformity may be attained without resorting to the Pernot furnace.

Allen's agitator has been tried at several American works, but generally abandoned. Its use, by postponing teeming, delays the pit-men, a very costly gang, and cools the metal, often undesirably, without fully compensating advantage as regards increased solidity or homogeneousness. In some American Bessemer works poling is still

[a] T. T. Morrell, private communication, June, 1888.
[b] C. Reinhardt, Stahl und Eisen, VIII., p. 22, 1888.
[c] Jour. Iron and Steel Inst., 1888, II., p. 241, from Jour. Anal. Chem., II., p. 148.

resorted to: a pole is held in the casting ladle, while the steel is pouring into it from the converter.

Now that it is known that the hard spots in steel are usually due to segregation rather than to imperfect mixing, mechanical agitation receives less attention than formerly. But segregation may be favored by imperfect mixing: for, since the tendency of a given element, say carbon, to segregate appears to increase as the proportion of that element present increases, so in a high-carbon streak in the molten metal due to imperfect mixing, the tendency towards the segregation of high-carbon fusible compounds may be exceptionally strong. In this way we may explain W. Richards' statement[a] that, after trying Allen's agitator, poling, and long repose in the converter to overcome the irregularity in carbon in his large ingots, he obtained almost complete uniformity as regards carbon by pouring from one ladle to another.

But this transfer may have hindered segregation simply by cooling the metal, so that it solidified more rapidly.

How much segregation is usual? From the foregoing we see that this question cannot be answered with confidence till we have the results of a great number of carefully studied cases: for the examination of a few spots at random may fail to detect the segregation. . . The cases in Table 96 are as a whole much worse than the average, for clearly the bad cases attract most attention: yet in 22 out of its 54 cases the segregation of carbon is not over 0·03% arithmetically. I can only say that, while we know that segregation is liable to be very serious, we believe that with reasonable care it may be kept within harmless limits in ingots of moderate thickness.

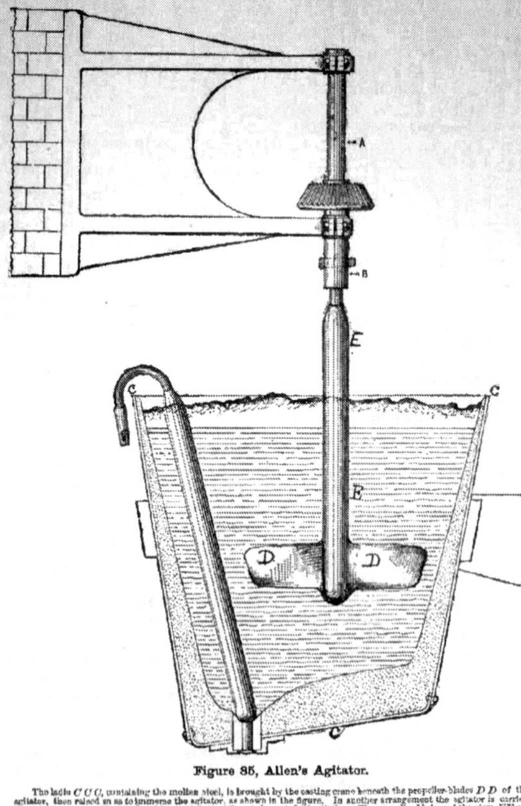

Figure 85, Allen's Agitator.

The ladle *C C C*, containing the molten steel, is brought by the casting crane beneath the propeller-blades *D D* of the agitator, then raised so as to immerse the agitator, as shown in the figure. In another arrangement the agitator is carried by a small crane, and is raised and lowered during the whole period of agitation. The propeller-blade and the stem *EE* are coated with clay.

[a] Journ. Iron and St. Inst., 1886, I., p. 113.

CHAPTER XIV.

COLD WORKING, HOT WORKING, WELDING.

§ 269. **COLD-WORKING IN GENERAL.**—It is probable that all forms of moderate permanent distortion of iron and steel in the cold, whether by stretching, compressing, or twisting, by cold-rolling, cold-hammering, wire-drawing, or otherwise, increase the tensile strength and hardness and still more the elastic limit,[a] while lower-

[a] The proportionality limit is indeed temporarily lowered by stretching, but quickly rises again. Cf. § 270.

TABLE 109.—INFLUENCE OF COLD WORKING ON THE PROPERTIES OF IRON.

Number.	Authority	Description	Size. Initial, inches.	Size. Final. B. W. G.	Size. Final. Inches.	Tensile strength, pounds per square inch. Initial bar.	Hard drawn.	Annealed.	Elastic limit, pounds per square inch. Initial bar.	Hard drawn.	Annealed.	Elongation. Percentage. Initial bar.	Hard drawn.	Annealed.	Length, inches, in which elongation is measured.	Reduction of area, Per cent. Initial bar.	Hard drawn.	Annealed.	Increase of tensile strength, etc., by cold working, per 100 of the tensile strength, etc., before cold working. Tensile strength.	Elastic limit.	Elongation.	Contraction of area.
		A. WIRE DRAWING.																				
1	C	Wire obtainable in quantity	......	7 and 8	·187,165	70@75,000	160,000	......	40,000	80,000+	......	15	4	......	12	......	......	......	+121	+100	−73	
2	B	Charcoal iron wire, Bigby	......	14	·083	......	102,884	......	......	......	......	......	0·80	......	15·74							
3	"	Ingot-iron wire, Firminy	......	"	"	......	127,950	......	......	......	......	......	0·87	......	"							
4	"	" steel " "	......	"	"	......	191,070	......	......	......	......	......	0·91	......	"							
5	"	" " " "	......	"	"	......	227,552	......	......	......	......	......	0·75	......	"							
6	"	" iron " "	......	"	"	52,614	91,008	66,847	......	......	......	8·45	0·74	22·00	"	......	......	......	+73	......	−32	
7	"	" " " "	......	"	"	58,250	89,560	61,158	......	......	......	7·46	0·62	22·00	"	......	......	......	+61	......	−32	
8	"	" " " "	......	"	"	54,066	85,820	60,692	......	......	......	16·79	0·31	20·52	12·2±	......	......	......	+56	......	−98	
9	"	" " " "	......	"	"	52,614	85,820	60,692	......	......	......	16·25	0·50	20·60	"	......	......	......	+62	......	−97	
10	"	Ingot steel wire, Firminy. A wire-rod, B hardened wire C finished, D annealed wire	......	"	"	A121,980	B180,594 C231,760	D119,472	......	......	......	A6·62	B3·41 C1·75	D8·00	14± "	......	......	......	+41 B +91 C	......	−48 B −74 C	
11	"	A wire-rod, B hardened wire C finished, D annealed wire	......	"	"	A142,900	B191,970 C220,410	D126,583	......	......	......	A7·00	B2·05 C1·47	D6·83	" "	......	......	......	+35 B +55 C	......	−58 B −79 C	
12	"	A wire-rod, B hardened wire C finished wire	......	"	"	A136,420	B200,802 C234,690	......	......	......	......	A6·54	B4·70 C1·18	......	15·74 15·74	......	......	......	+28 B +50 C	......	−28 B −82 C	
13	"	A wire-rod, B hardened wire C finished wire	......	"	"	A139,356	B216,144 C231,796	......	......	......	......	A6·17	B5·67 C1·36	......	" "	......	......	......	+55 B +66 C	......	−8 B −78 C	
14	M	Open-hearth steel wire billets and square wire from them, drawn in 10 straight draughts	2 2	......	0·15 sq. "	E70,000 F86,790	171,760 @ 178,880	......	......	100,000±	......	E30·00 F37·45	1·4 @ 2·6	......	10	E 50 F 61·80	9·2 @ 21·8	......	+145±	......	−90±	
15	"	The same annealed after the 6th draught	2	......	"	"	181,020	......	......	......	......	......	1·39	......	......	......	85·0	......	+51			
16	T	Usual properties of wrought-iron wire	1 " "	10 15 20	......	60,000 " "	90,000 100,000 111,000	......	......	......	......	......	......	......	......	......	......	......	+50 +67 +85			
17	A	Steel wire hard-drawn, apparently h'd'nd, and same slightly ann'l'd																				
			......	......	0·2	......	......	......	......	56,000	78,400	......	......	......	......	......	......	......	......			
18	A′	Mild steel wire-rods, hard-drawn wire, and annealed wire, all from the same billet	·3	3	·259	67,939	109,854	60,726	47,846	61,533	......	22·8	1·9	15·2	8	60·42	19·32	69·63	+60·62	+28·61	−91·67	−67·49
19	A′	"	·284	4	·238	64,489	98,762	62,138	45,629	67,469	44,581	19·3	3·2	17·5	8	64·78	34·21	64·32	+53·14	+47·86	−83·84	−47·19
20	A′	"	·238	6	·203	67,782	107,722	63,750	49,078	90,070	48,762	21·7	3·8	23·6	8	66·46	45·55	66·43	+58·92	+83·52	−83·87	−31·36
21	A′	"	·23	8	·165	66,170	126,246	59,000	46,868	105,997	42,224	21·6	1·0	21·2	8	68·11	37·88	70·14	+90·69	+126·08	−95·37	−44·38
22	A′	"	·22	10	·134	66,170	122,035	67,837	46,883	85,725	49,238	21·6	0·87	22·4	8	68·11	22·05	66·17	+84·43	+82·85	−96·20	−67·63
		B. COLD ROLLING, ETC.																				
24	Wo	......	......	......	......	71,580	86,540	......	40,744	78,940	......	30	14	......	2	......	......	......	+21	+94	−56	
25	B	Pieces cut from Creusot steel, and hammered cold till they were lengthened by about 7·5%	......	......	......	65,184	76,984	......	......	......	......	21·5	9·7	......	......	......	......	......	+20	......	−60	
26	B	"	......	......	......	62,882	71,068	......	......	......	......	28·5	6	......	......	......	......	......	+13	......	−74	
27	B	"	......	......	......	56,000	67,200	......	......	......	......	35	10	......	......	......	......	......	+20	......	−71	
28		Norway Steel and Iron Co., compressed steel (G. H. Billings' patents)	......	......	......	58,000	70,000	......	27,000	61,000	......	......	......	......	......	......	......	......	+21	+126		
29		"	2·09	......	1·986	55,400	70,420	......	26,540	61,100	......	84·6	15·6	......	5	42·9	33·5	......	+27	+130	−55	
30		"	2·03	......	1·808	55,400	61,890	......	......	......	......	......	0·75	......	20	42·8	16·7	......	+18	+178		
31		"	·94	......	·75	64,076	99,445	......	35,950	94,554	......	88	6	......	......	58	30	......	+55	......	−82	
32	M	Jones & Laughlin's cold-rol'd iron	......	......	......	57,250	92,623	......	......	......	......	......	......	......	......	......	......	......	+61			
33	M	" " " " "	......	......	......	49,510	66,862	......	......	......	......	......	......	......	......	......	......	......	+35			
34	Wa	Puddled iron	......	......	·75	53,760	88,156	......	37,250	66,427	......	......	......	......	......	......	......	......	+49	+84		
35	Wa	Charcoal bloom iron	......	......	·75	50,227	99,298	......	42,480	87,296	......	......	......	......	10	......	......	......	+95	+106		
36	F	......	1·07	......	1·00	58,627	88,229	......	......	......	......	20·0	7·9	......	10	......	......	......	+50	......	−60	
37	T	Cold-rolled iron, Jones & Laughlin's, Lauth's patent	......	......	......	52,500	69,006	51,000	30,000	59,000	33,000	24·58	10·42	25·00	10	......	......	......	+31	+97	−58	
38	"	"	2·56	......	2·44	46,738	66,100	46,300	28,600	60,300	31,400	26·25	2·75	14·25	10	......	......	......	+41	+111	−90	
39	"	The same	2·06	......	2	48,530	66,983	48,600	28,200	57,500	31,800	24·00	......	12·50	10	......	......	......	+38	+104		
40	"	" "	1·37	......	1·31	50,800	67,888	49,500	24,800	57,467	31,600	......	6·00	9·50	10	......	......	......	+35	+130		
41	"	" "	1·06	......	1	47,400	68,167	50,900	27,700	60,367	32,700	......	8·05	12·05	10	......	......	......	+44	+118		
42	"	" "	·67	......	·68	48,167	73,833	48,700	29,200	63,833	33,800	19·35	4·53	15·80	10	......	......	......	+53	+119	−77	
43	"	Cold-swaged steel	......	......	2·40	......	96,870	......	......	......	......	......	16·4	......	5	......	87					

1. Wire of this quality was found to be procurable in large lots for the East River Bridge. The elastic limit was always more than half the ultimate tensile strength. The "initial" bar here refer to pieces of cross-section fitted for common bridge members. F. Collingwood, Trans. Am. Soc. Civ. Eng., IX., p. 170, 1880.

2 to 13. A. Bonneau, Rev. Univ. 2d Ser., IX., p. 323, 1881. 10 to 13 give the properties **A** of the wire rod, **B** of the hardened, *i. e.* quenched, wire (fil trempé et revenu), **C** of the finished wire, which has apparently undergone additional drawing after hardening; and **D** of the finished wire annealed.

14. Open-hearth steel wire billets, 2 inches square, made by the Otis Iron and Steel Company. **E** the properties specified by contract, **F** the maximum of each of the properties in the billets tested. Rept. Chf. Ordnance, U. S. Army, 1884, p. 440. The billets were rolled into rods 0·5 inches square, annealed during 45 hours (temperature rising to about 983° C., 1800° F., during 7 to 8 hours, then slowly cooling to about 343° C., 650° F., during about 40 hours). They were then drawn in 10 draughts without further annealing to 0·15 inches square. Idem, 1885, p. 473, Lieut. W. M. Metcalfe. The details of the operations are given at great length.

15. One coil of the wire of No. 14 was lightly annealed between the 5th and 6th draughts, which reduced the tensile strength greatly, and greatly increased the reduction of area, but without increasing the elongation.

16. Usual properties of wrought-iron wire, Thurston, Matls of Engineering, II., p. 201.

17. Slight annealing greatly raises the elastic limit of thick and apparently hardened (quenched) wire. Sir W. Armstrong, Journ. Iron and Steel Inst., 1882, II., p. 701, from paper read before Sect. G, British Ass. Aug., 1882. Thinner wire is simply softened without increase of elastic limit by annealing.

18 to 20. A two-inch billet of mild steel, carbon 0·115, silicon 0·009, phosphorus 0·079, were rolled hot to Numbers 1, 2, 4, and 5 B. W. respectively, and the resulting rods were drawn at a single draught to Numbers 3, 4, 6, and 8 B. W. G. The Number 8 wire was further drawn to Number 10 B. W. G. without annealing, and apparently in two additional draughts. The reduction of sectional area by wire drawing was thus 37·5, 24·7, 32·5 46 and 56%. Horace Allen, Excerpt, Proc. Inst. Civ. Eng., XCIV, p. 1888. The density of these materials is given in Table 105.

21. Thoroughly annealed steel had the properties given under "initial": after cold-hammering on only one pair of faces it had those given under "hard drawn." Woodbridge, Birnie, Proc. U. S. Naval Inst. XIII., p. 66, 1887, from Notes on Construction of Ordnance, No. 3, Washington, July 20th, 1882.

25 to 27. Treatment of steel, Barba, Holley, pp. 50 to 54. Soft steel was hammered out cold, till its length was increased by about 7·5%. The hard-drawn results in number 25 represent the mean obtained with six bars, and their properties are compared with the mean of similar but untreated pieces. For 26-7 it is probable but not certain that the initial and hard-drawn results are from material originally of the same piece.

28. Circular of the Norway Steel and Iron Company. The steel contains about 0·14% of carbon, 0·40% of manganese, and 0·01 of silicon.

29-30. Eng. and Mining Jl., XXXV., p. 222, 1883. From tests on the Watertown testing machine. A single bar of hot-rolled steel was cut into three pieces. The first was tested without further treatment (here given as the "initial" bar); the second after a single draught, which reduced its diameter from 2·03 to 1·986 inches; the third also after a single but more severe draught, which reduced its diameter from 2·03 to 1·808 inches. The modulus of elasticity of the uncompressed bar was 29,000,000: that of the first of the two compressed (hard-drawn) bars was 31,000,000. In compressive tests, the permanent set and the compression was almost exactly the same in the compressed as in the uncompressed steel.

31. G. H. Billings, private communication, May 9th, 1888. The initial and the hard-drawn pieces are from the same bar. The initial was turned down to ¾-inch diameter in a lathe before testing. Modulus of elasticity of the uncompressed (initial) bar 29,400,000; of the compressed (hard-drawn) 36,400,000.

32-33. Tests by Merrick & Sons, Southwark Fdry, Thurston, Rept. on Cold-rolled Iron, 1887, p. 12.

34-35. W. Wade, 1860: Idem, p. 10.

36. Wm. Fairbairn, : Rankine, Civil Engineering, 1876, p. XVI. Also Thurston, Op. Cit., p. 7.

37-42. Thurston, Op. Cit., pp. 62-3, 100. In Nos. 38 to 42 the "initial" and the "cold-rolled" results each represent three bars. The cold-rolled pieces were from the same bars as the "initial" or hot-rolled ones. All were tested as they came from the rolls, without subsequent reduction in the lathe.

43. Midvale steel, cold-swaged at Washington Navy Yard. The elongation was 8% on 30 inches, and 16·4% on the 5 inches where rupture occurred. Rept Tests on Strength of Struct. Matl. Watertown Arsenal, 1883, p. 173.

TABLE 101.—INFLUENCE OF STRETCHING BEYOND THE ELASTIC LIMIT ON THE MODULUS OF ELASTICITY, ELASTIC LIMIT, ETC.; AND MODIFICATIONS OF THIS INFLUENCE BY REST AND FURTHER TREATMENT. BAUSCHINGER.

	Treatment prior to pulling, and subsequent to last preceding pulling.	I. Wrought-iron. (938a) Interval of rest.	I. Max. load.	I. Modulus of elasticity, thousands.	I. Proportion limit.	I. Stretching point.	II. Wrought-iron. (938b) Interval of rest.	II. Max. load.	II. Modulus of elasticity, thousands.	II. Proportionality limit.	II. Stretching point.
1	Previously untreated	.....	31,575	29,187	20,054	27,608	.....	31,575	28,872	20,004	28,730
2	Brief rest	20'	40,251	27,738	14,863	31,575	19h	40,585	28,864	28,015	34,704
3	"	20'	47,646	27,592	14,934	41,744	27h	47,262	28,161	35,418	44,375
4	"	20'	49,489	27,439	15,566	49,493	24h	45,073	28,161	39,894	> 48,073
5											
6	Long rest	3y 81d	55,184	30,295	52,198	> 55,185	3y 28d	54,381	30,436	49,780	> 54,381
7											
8	Cold-working (hammering)	3d	51,344	30,329	20,623	51,344	17h	52,656	30,579	24,463	50,491
9	Rest	2y 39d	61,727	29,019	6,827	60,020	2y 62d	61,869	28,019	30,864	66,169
10	Heated to 250° C.	.....	.....	.....	.....	.....	.....	.....	.....	.....	.....
11	Heated to 400° C.	.....	.....	.....	.....	.....	.....	.....	.....	.....	.....
12	" 400° C.			cooled	slowly				cooled	quickly.	
13	" 500° C.	2d	56,814	23,161	47,981	58,991	0	45,793	37,877	19,485	43,518
14	Rest	.....	.....	.....	.....	.....	.....	.....	.....	.....	.....
15											
16	Heated to 500° C.	.....	.....	.....	.....	.....	.....	.....	.....	.....	.....
17	Heated to cherry redness	19d	48,824	quen-	ched.	37,975	.....	.....	.....	.....	.....
18	Long rest, after stress of 51771 lb. per sq. inch.	.....	.....	.....	.....	.....	.....	.....	.....	.....	.....

	Treatment	III. Wrought-iron. (938c) Interval of rest.	III. Max. load.	III. Modulus of elasticity, thousands.	III. Proportionality limit.	III. Stretching point.	IV. Wrought-iron. (938d) Interval of rest.	IV. Max. load.	IV. Modulus of elasticity, thousands.	IV. Proportionality limit.	IV. Stretching point.
1	Previously untreated	.....	31,651	29,086	28,183	29,015	.....	31,432	29,137	29,399	30,010
2	Brief rest	51h	40,585	28,308	28,563	34,704	86h	40,035	28,780	31,801	34,704
3	"	41h	45,073	28,305	30,113	45,086	68h	41,078	28,181	35,273	44,288
4	"	45h	48,642	28,019	45,513	> 48,642	64h	45,500	28,588	43,948	> 43,300
5											
6	Long rest	3y 21d	54,758	30,436	38,336	> 54,758	3y 31d	54,616	31,006	51,029	> 49,466
7											
8	Cold-working (hammering)	.....	.....	.....	.....	.....	.....	.....	.....	.....	.....
9	Rest	.....	.....	.....	.....	.....	.....	.....	.....	.....	.....
10	Heated to 250° C.			cooled	slowly				cooled	quickly.	
11	Heated to 400° C.	1d	43,358	30,779	42,688	> 43,358	24h	38,411	30,678	27,436	> 38,411
12	" 400° C.	0	28,285	33,138	27,400	> 38,268			cooled	slowly	
13	" 500° C.	.....	.....	.....	.....	.....	48h	38,411	30,864	30,285	> 38,411
14	Rest	12h	42,668	30,432	36,268	> 42,668	.....	.....	.....	.....	.....
15				cooled	quickly.				cooled	quickly.	
16	Heated to 500° C.	2d	24,821	33,152	6,116	> 24,821	6h	24,179	.....	.....	> 24,179
17	Heated to cherry redness	.....	.....	.....	.....	.....	.....	.....	.....	.....	.....
18	Long rest, after stress of 51771 lb. per sq. inch.	2y 62d	55,185	28,446	49,069	53,620					

	Treatment	V. (938d) Interval of rest.	V. Max. load.	V. Modulus of elasticity, thousands.	V. Proportionality limit.	V. Stretching point.	VI. (1850f) Interval of rest.	VI. Max. load.	VI. Modulus of elasticity, thousands.	VI. Proportionality limit.	VI. Stretching point.
1	Previously untreated	.....	46,153	29,726	26,028	46,309	.....	43,299	31,148	35,344	36,496
2	Brief rest	69h	54,735	29,299	48,237	51,918	30'	52,777	30,321	18,227	46,935
3	"	4h	70,119	28,872	8,818	55,489	30'	59,878	31,261	8,960	53,994
4	"	46h	71,825	30,010	14,934	> 71,825	30'	61,585	30,366	[illegible]	[illegible]
5											
6	Long rest	3y 27d	72,116	32,499	> 72,110	> 72,110	3y 30d	61,585	33,231	> 61,585	> 61,585
7											
8	Cold-working (hammering)	2d	49,556	32,061	27,023	49,520					
9	Rest										
10	Heated to 250° C.	.....	.....	.....	.....	.....	.....	.....	.....	.....	.....
11	Heated to 400° C.	.....	.....	Heated	to 250° C.	and	cooled	slowly	ten	times, a	.....
12	" 400° C.	.....	.....	.....	.....	.....	.....	.....	cooled	quickly.	.....
13	" 500° C.	.....	.....	.....	.....	.....	21h	24,463	33,281	16,926	> 24,463
14	Rest	.....	.....	.....	.....	.....	41h	38,820	32,997	27,725	> 38,820
15											
16	Heated to 500° C.			cooled	quickly.	.....	.....	.....	.....	.....	.....
17	Heated to cherry redness	2y 79d	54,618	.....	.....	53,051					
18	Long rest, after stress of 51771 lb. per sq. inch.										

	Treatment	VII. (1850e) Interval of rest.	VII. Max. load.	VII. Modulus of elasticity, thousands.	VII. Proportionality limit.	VII. Stretching point.
1	Previously untreated	.....	42,242	31,717	33,180	36,328
2	Brief rest	2h	51,771	31,851	11,281	48,095
3	"	15h	59,167	31,717	17,779	58,193
4	"	7h	61,016	32,286	15,218	61,016
5						
6	Long rest	3y 29d	61,016	33,189	> 61,016	> 61,016
7						
8	Cold-working (hammering)					
9	Rest					
10	Heated to 250° C.	33 8h	61,016	33,566	> 61,016	> 61,016
11	Heated to 400° C.	5d	61,016	33,424	> 61,016	> 61,016
12	" 400° C.					
13	" 500° C.					
14	Rest	2y 79d	69,407	31,296	61,869	67,985
15				cooled	quickly.	
16	Heated to 500° C.	2d	55,886	31,096	36,256	54,990
17	Heated to cherry redness					
18	Long rest, after stress of 51771 lb. per sq. inch.					

	Treatment prior to pulling, and subsequent to last preceding pulling.	IX. (1850c) Rate of cooling.	IX. Interval of rest.	IX. Max. load.	IX. Modulus of elasticity, thousands.	IX. Proportionality limit.	IX. Stretching point.	X. (1850d) Rate of cooling.	X. Interval of rest.	X. Max. load.	X. Modulus of elasticity, thousands.	X. Proportionality limit.	X. Stretching point.	XI. (1850b) Rate of cooling.	XI. Interval of rest.	XI. Max. load.	XI. Modulus of elasticity, thousands.	XI. Proportionality limit.	XI. Stretching point.
19	Previously untreated	.....	.....	44,944	32,286	37,588	42,130	.....	.....	42,284	32,428	33,986	39,689	.....	.....	42,526	32,857	36,259	39,662
20	Cold hammering	.....	20'	51,918	31,575	5,881	46,158	.....	24h	52,798	32,144	11,302	48,451	.....	51h	50,624	31,575	48,906	49,538
21	" "	.....	25'	55,886	29,868	14,721	53,051	.....	13½h	56,898	32,144	11,805	53,051	.....	47h	56,688	31,576	41,246	55,896
22	" "	.....	25'	60,550	25,590	15,219	60,589	.....	0½h	60,447	31,006	12,089	60,447	.....	46h	60,589	31,432	44,802	> 60,589
23	Long rest	.....	3y 56d	60,589	33,708	> 60,589	> 60,589	.....	3y 53d	60,731	33,566	> 60,731	> 60,731	.....	8y 50d	60,589	33,139	> 60,589	> 60,589
24	Heated to 200° C., and cooled quickly	.....	.....	.....	.....	.....	.....	.....	.....	.....	.....	.....	.....	cooled quickly.	1d	60,589	33,139	> 60,589	> 60,589
25	" " ten times and cooled quickly	.....	.....	.....	.....	.....	.....	.....	.....	.....	.....	.....	.....		2d	60,589	33,139	> 60,589	> 60,589
26	" 250° C., and cooled quickly	.....	.....	.....	.....	.....	.....	.....	.....	.....	.....	.....	.....		18 1h	60,589	33,139	> 60,589	> 60,589
27	" " ten times and cooled quickly	.....	.....	.....	.....	.....	.....	.....	.....	.....	.....	.....	.....		4d	60,589	33,139	> 60,589	> 60,589
28	" 300° C.	Cooled slowly.	.....	.....	.....	.....	.....	cooled slowly.	9d 5h	60,731	33,566	> 60,731	> 60,731		2d	60,588	33,139	> 60,589	> 60,589
29	" 350° C.		.....	.....	.....	.....	.....		brief	60,731	33,424	> 60,731	> 60,731		21h	60,588	33,281	54,816	> 60,589
30	" 400° C.		.....	.....	.....	.....	.....		brief	60,731	33,708	> 60,731	> 60,731		1d	57,602	33,281	51,620	57,602
31	" 400° C., again		.....	.....	.....	.....	.....		.....	.....	.....	.....	.....		1d	> 60,589	33,281	> 60,589	> 60,589
	" 450° C.		.....	.....	.....	.....	.....		brief	60,731	33,281	57,745	> 60,731		17h	57,602	34,139	51,889	> 57,602
32	" " C.		.....	.....	.....	.....	.....		brief	60,731	33,424	59,589	> 60,731		.....	.....	.....	.....	.....
33	" 300° C.		1d ±	60,589	33,566	57,802	> 60,589		brief	60,731	33,286	56,180	60,731		1d	60,389	33,281	27,306	45,513
34	Long rest	.....	.....	.....	.....	.....	.....		.....	.....	.....	.....	.....		2y 73d	64,429	31,148	62,582	64,129
35	Heated to 300° C.		1d ±	60,589	33,281	> 60,589	> 60,589		.....	.....	.....	.....	.....	.....	0	58,891	31,006	42,956	53,183
36	" 350° C.	.....	.....	.....	.....	.....	.....		27h	60,731	33,424	51,689	52,460						
37	" 400° C.	cooled quickly.	1d ±	48,500	33,128	32,378	> 48,500		2d	46,927	34,566	50,524	> 46,927						
38	Long rest, then loaded with 61,286 lbs. per sq. inch, then tested	.....	.....	.....	.....	.....	.....		2y 71d	65,425	30,579	26,455	62,489						
39	Brief rest	.....	.....	.....	.....	.....	.....		3d	68,554	31,006	28,455	63,425						
40	Heated to 500° C.	.....	.....	.....	.....	.....	.....		brief	68,554	31,290	60,425	65,425						
41	" cherry redness	.....	.....	.....	.....	.....	.....	quickly.	17d	54,047	31,858	9,387	51,028						

A given test-piece is subjected to tensile stress (pull) many times in succession, the stress usually being greater than the existing stretching-point but less than the existing ultimate tensile strength. The modulus of elasticity, proportionality-limit and stretching-point (common elastic-limit) are determined after each pull and given in successive lines. Between successive pulls the piece usually undergoes some treatment, or is allowed to rest, as indicated in the second column. All the results in a given set of columns (e. g., I., II., etc.) are the successive results for a single test-piece. The only exceptions are in line 38, in which the piece is subjected to a pull of 61,286 lbs. per sq. in. after receiving the pull in line 37 and before receiving that in line 38: and a similar case in line 18. When a line is blank in a given group of columns, the treatment given in column headed "Treatment prior," etc., has been omitted.

The difference between the properties in any given line, say line N, and those in the preceding line, say N-1, line N and those in line N-1 is due to the treatment or rest described in column 2, (Treatment prior, etc.) jointly with the pull given in line N-1, and in many cases with the preceding previous pulls and treatments.

Each number in the columns maximum load gives the maximum load to which the piece was subjected during the experiment represented by the line in which it occurs.

Bauschinger, Mittheil. aus dem Mechanisch-Technischen Lab. der K. Hochschule in München, XV., 1886.

I. to **IV.**, four bars of (apparently the same) wrought-iron, 0.98 inches in diameter, I. and II. 13.6 inches long, III. and IV. 9.84 inches long. Original numbers, 938 a, b, c and d.

V. a bar of Bessemer steel; original number 938.

VI. to **XI.**, five like round bars of Bessemer steel, turned from the same piece. Original numbers, 1850 f, e, c, d, b.

Where the interval is given as 0, the experiments followed each other immediately; of course an appreciable but minute time must have elapsed. When it is given as brief, a few hours intervened.

After cold-hammering the piece was in each case dressed in a lathe before testing.

"Cooled slowly," "cooled quickly" and "quenched" in lines 1 to 18 refer to numbers lying immediately beneath.

In the intervals of rest, ' = minutes, d = days, y = years.

This refers to set VII. in line 11.

ing the density: and that the changes which distortion induces, at least in the case of tensile strength and elastic limit, continue at an ever decreasing rate for years after the distortion has ceased, and are accelerated and perhaps exaggerated by gentle heating, but are lessened or even wholly removed by heating to redness. I do not here refer to Wöhler-like indefinitely repeated stresses, which, even if below the initial elastic limit, may eventually destroy the piece.[a]

TABLE 102.—INFLUENCE OF TWISTING ON TENSILE STRENGTH OF WROUGHT-IRON AND SOFT STEEL.—Gilmore.

Number.	Description of test piece.				Tensile strength, pounds per sq. in.
	Material.	Round or square.	Thickness, inches.	Length, inches.	Before twisting.
1.	Wrought-iron.	Round.	3/4	8	54,180
2.	"	Square.	3/4	8	55,325
3.	Steel.	Round.	3/4	12	57,360
4.	Wrought-iron.	Square.	·75	12	52,545

Number.	Tensile strength, pounds per square inch. After twisting.												
	¼ turn.	½ turn.	¾ turn.	1 turn.	1½ turns.	2 turns.	2½ turns.	3 turns.	4½ turns.	5½ turns.	7 turns.	11 turns.	18 turns.
1.	......	......	59,020	68,400	......	64,750	55,000	......	broken	broken			
2.	......	57,265	58,050	64,665	65,255	......	broken	broken					
3.	57,746	54,765	58,805	......	......	......	......	......	......	......	......	......	broke.
4.	58,930	63,410	56,265										

Lieut. F. P. Gilmore, U. S. Navy, Trans. Tech. Soc. Pacific Coast, V., p. 108, 1888.

TABLE 103.—EFFECTS OF COLD BENDING (RADIUS 8.5″) AND ANNEALING. PARKER.

No.	Tensile strength, pounds per square inch.	Elastic limit, pounds per square inch.a	Elongation % in 10 inches.	Contraction of area, %.	Treatment before testing.
1.	65,998	35,376	27·8	53·6	Untreated.
2.	68,160	32,480	25·1	52·6	Bent and straightened cold.
3.	69,898	26,120	20·7	51·5	Bent and straightened at a blue heat.
4.	78,248	38,160	17·6	32·0	Quenched.
5.	60,704	34,272	29·2	53·5	Bent and straightened cold four times: then annealed.

1. A plain piece of steel 1·5″ × 0·76″. 2. A similar piece of the same material bent cold with a radius of 8·5 inches, and then straightened. 3. The same as 2, but bent at a blue heat. 4. A similar piece heated and quenched in cold water. 5. Bent in the same way as 2, but four times instead of once: then heated to redness and allowed to cool. Parker, Journ. Iron and Steel Inst., 1887, I., p. 136.

a This is probably the "proportionality limit."

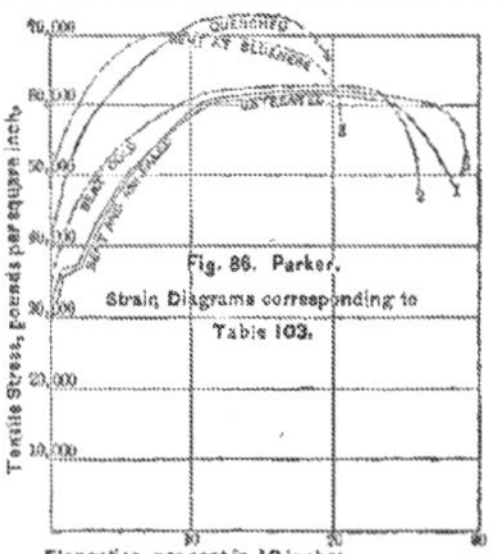

Fig. 86. Parker. Strain Diagrams corresponding to Table 103.

The jog shown in lines 1 and 5 is very common in the strain-diagrams of wrought-iron and steel when neither hardened nor cold-worked, but not in those of other metals. A not wholly dissimilar jog also occurs in the torsional strain-diagrams of locust and hickory wood.

The effect on the modulus of elasticity is relatively slight (usually less than 5%, sometimes less than 1%), and less constant. The modulus is usually lowered slightly but is sometimes raised by cold-stretching and cold-hammering: (*e. g.*, table 101, VI., 3; VII., 2; I., 8; and II., 5). During rest after stretching in Bauschinger's experiments it seems usually to undergo a change opposite in sign to that noted immediately or shortly after stretching or cold-hammering, and greater in amount, and so returns past and to a point slightly above or slightly below its original value as the case may be (*e. g.*, table 101, line 6, cases I., II., III., IV., VI.; line 23, cases IX., X., XI.; line 9, cases I., II.; exceptions, line 6, cases V., VII). But this can hardly be put forth confidently.

Similar changes occur in other malleable metals, and, like those in iron and steel, increase during rest after distortion. Thus Bauschinger noted that if a piece of zinc were subjected to a stress S beyond its proportionality limit, and again tested within a few minutes, the proportionality limit had now risen to S: but on allowing the same piece of zinc to rest for about a day after the application of the stress S, the proportionality limit was now found to have risen from S, which was 1,393 pounds, to 1,508 pounds per square inch.[b]

Local Cold-Working, however, though its immediate effect may be to strengthen the part worked, may greatly weaken the piece as a whole. For instance, suppose that we hammer the side A of the piece shown in Figure 87,

Fig. 87

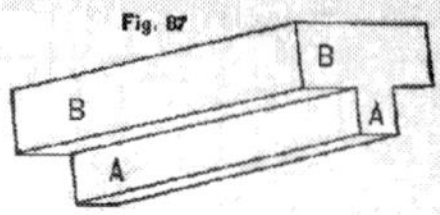

and thus strengthen it and raise its elastic limit without changing the properties of the side B, striking A first crosswise then lengthwise so as to avoid distorting the piece. If we now stretch the piece as a whole in tensile test, all will go on normally till the stress per square inch reaches the initial elastic limit of the material.[c] But after we pass this point B stretches more under given increment of stress than A. A, standing up to its work, bears an undue share of the stress. The stress on A, whose power of elongation is less than that of B, reaches the ultimate tensile strength, and A parts while the stress on B, which has all the time been stretching instead of resisting, is still relatively small.

Once A is broken, B has now to bear the whole stress: indeed, as A breaks it may start a crack which will quickly rip across the piece.

This ultimate weakening effect of a local strengthening is clearly due to heterogeneousness of elastic limit and of power of elongation.

But such local cold-working need not necessarily weaken the piece. If, for instance, it were the side B instead of A that had been cold-worked, the cold-worked and the strengthened portion being thus the greater not the smaller of the two, its strength alone might be decidedly greater than the initial strength of the whole piece before cold-working: so that even if B had to bear the whole stress and received no assistance from A, the piece as a whole would be stronger than before receiving the local cold-working. Hence local cold-working may strengthen or weaken the piece according to the special conditions of

a B. Baker, Trans. Am. Soc. Mech. Eng., VIII., p. 162, 1884, gives an instance in which a rotating spindle, weighted at its free end so as to cause alternate tension and compression in any given fibre, broke after 472,500 revolutions, the actual stress being only one third of the stress at transverse elastic limit. On the other hand Bauschinger concludes that 5 to 15 million repetitions of tensile stress, whose lower limit is zero and whose upper limit is near the original proportionality limit, do not cause rupture. (Mittheil aus Mech.-Tech. Lab. in München, XV., p. 37, 1886.)

b Op. Cit., p. 3.

c For simplicity I here ignore the usual slight depression of the modulus of elasticity due to cold-distortion. Lowering the modulus of A would increase, raising it would diminish these effects.

the case, such as the proportion of the whole which is worked cold, the shape and position of the part worked cold, the intensity of the cold-working, etc.

Moreover, cold-working in general and local cold-working in particular should set up severe stress: this may tend to weaken the metal. While it is in general outweighed by the direct strengthening effect of cold-working, it may under many conditions outweigh the direct strengthening effect. Local cold-working may, further, directly cause local incipient rupture.

Thus it is not surprising that local or excessive or ill-advised cold-working weakens the metal.

Apparent instances of the disastrous effect of heterogeneousness of strength due to local strengthening are the breakage of steel rails through their punched bolt-holes, the usual weakness of punched steel plates, and possibly Sweet's rail-breaking method, in which a single blow from a sledge usually suffices to break a nicked rail.[a] A steel rail which untreated would endure the blow of a 2,000 pound ram falling fifteen feet, will sometimes if punched break with a fall of one foot.[b]

Steel rails are reported as breaking in the track soon after being struck by a derailed engine; and, when they are broken in normal use, rupture is said to occur usually where the rail has been pressed by the gag which is used in cold-straightening, and which should not be allowed to touch the flange of the rail, thinner, less supported and more liable to severe deformation than the head.[c] The breakage of steel plates, angles, etc., which gave serious alarm during the early employment of steel for structural purposes, was in many cases attributed to too abrupt cold-bending. From the foregoing we see the importance of bending to curves of long radius, of striking with copper-faced or even wooden mallets rather than iron sledges, or applying bending-pressure through wooden blocks, etc., to make the bends less abrupt

§ 270. THE SEVERAL PROPERTIES IN DETAIL.—*The Elastic Limit.*[d] Stretching lowers the proportionality limit.[d] often to zero, so that that if the piece be re-tested immediately after stretching, either no proportionality limit or only a very low one is found. (Table 101, I., 2, 3, 4; V., 3; VI., 2, 3; VII., 2, 4). But after brief rest it is found to have risen beyond the original (idem, II., 2). Cold-hammering also lowers it, and sometimes it does not fully recover even after years of rest (idem).

In the case of tensional stretching the stretching point, if determined immediately after stretching has ceased, has become equal to the tension which produced the stretching: so that if, while pulling the test-piece in the testing machine, we interrupt the stress for a moment and immediately reapply it, we obtain diagrams like curve 3 of Figure 88. The diagram CB is practically that of a new metal, with a new and much higher stretching point than that of the original diagram OA.

If, however, the stress be reapplied not immediately but after a considerable interval, the new stretching point is in many cases found much higher than the preceding maximum stress, and our new diagram is like G H I in curve 2. Like results are obtained if, instead of wholly removing the stress, we hold it constant, as in curve 4. Indeed, at least in certain cases, we get approximately the same diagram whether the stress be wholly removed or simply held constant. Mr. G. W. Bissell informs me that he has found this true of a specimen of brass.[e]

In short, simple momentary interruption of stress produces simply a crevice like A C E (curve 3) in our diagram, whose shape but for this is hardly altered: so that the interruption simply reveals the elevation of the stretching point which the stretching has caused, but does not in itself change the stretching point, does not materially change the shape of the diagram beyond the point E, leads to no gain in tensile strength. But, during a considerable time after the stretching, the stretching point goes on rising, and with it the tensile strength, for the line HI in curve 2 will lead to a higher ultimate tensile strength than the line LF or the line MN.

It is altogether probable that closer examination will find a similar state of things in case of other forms of cold-distortion. This strengthening during rest was, according to Bauschinger, discovered by Wöhler[f]; Styffe certainly knew it by 1869[g]; Thurston and Beardsley rediscovered

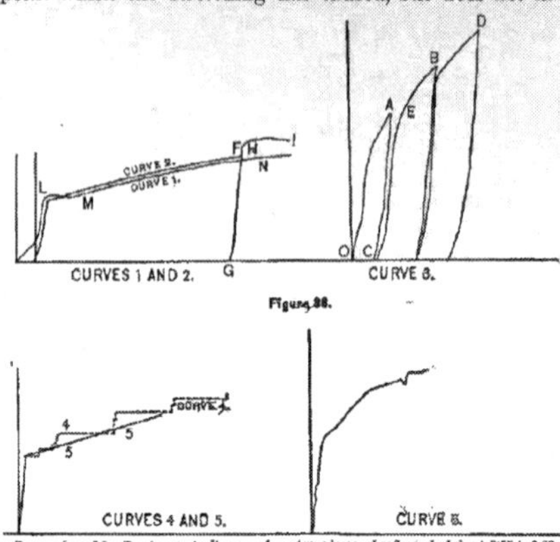

Figure 88.

Curves 1 and 2. Torsion-strain diagrams from two pieces of soft steel of about 0·15 to 0·20 % of carbon, cut from adjacent parts of the same bar. In 1 the stress was continuous, in 2 interrupted. G. W. Bissell, Private Communication, Jan. 15th, 1889.

Curve 3, Torsion-strain diagram of very hard steel (Jessop's) used for tack plates. At A stress was removed for two days; at B the piece was left under stress for one day. Stress was then interrupted momentarily, immediately reapplied, and carried to D. Here the stretching point fails to rise above the last previous maximum stress. Idem. This investigation was kindly made by Mr. Bissell for this work.

Curves 4 and 5. Transverse-strain diagrams of common wrought-iron, weighted with a dead load. In 4 the load was increased intermittently, in 5 it was increased steadily so as to give as little time for elevation of the elastic limit as possible. Thurston, Matls. of Engineering, II., p. 598.

Curve 6. Interrupted-strain diagram of tool steel. Idem, p. 611.

[a] Trans. Am. Inst. Mining Engineers, III., p. 92.

[b] J. Fritz, Trans. Am. Inst. Mining Engineers, III., p. 91, 1875.

[c] Holley, Trans. Am. Inst. Mining Engineers, VIII., p. 404, 1880.

[d] 'Twere foreign to the purpose of this work to discuss the several different points selected by different writers for the elastic limit. We may, however, note two, "the proportionality limit," or point at which Hooke's law "ut tensio sic vis" ceases to be true, and the "stretching point" or "breaking down point," "Streckgrenze," at which the increase of extension becomes altogether disproportionate to the increase of stress, and at which in common continuous testing the beam of the testing-machine drops, and the scale on the surface of the metal cracks. The second may not be so definite a point as the first, but it certainly seems a point of much greater importance for constructional purposes. And after all the fact that a point can be accurately defined and measured is in general of relatively little importance: the chief thing is that it should represent some property important as regards the chief uses of the material, and this the stretching point does.

[e] Private communication, Dec. 24th, 1888.

[f] Mittheil. ante. cit. p. 3. From Erbkam, Ztsch't für Bauwesen, 1863, pp. 245—6. Cf. Bauschinger, Dingler, CCXXIV., p. 1, 1877: Uchatius, Dingler, CCXXIII., p. 242, 1877.

[g] "Sometimes we have even found that the limit of elasticity in stretched bars has been perceptibly raised by merely allowing the bar to remain at rest for several days after stretching." Iron and Steel, Styffe, Sandberg, p. 100, 1869.

it independently in 1873.[a] Some of Beardslee's results are here given:

TABLE 104.—INCREASE OF TENSILE STRENGTH BY REST.—Beardslee.

Length of rest	1 to 3 min.	1 to 8 hrs.	1 day.	3 days.	5 days.	5 to 42 days.	6 mos.
Increase of tensile strength	1.4%	3.3	3.2	10.2	17.3	15.3	17.9
Number of tests	5	3	5	10	2	5	12

It is not clear just what conditions cause this increase in tensile strength and elastic limit after distortion has ceased. The U. S. Test Board could obtain no positive evidence that it occurred at all in case of weld-steel. In some wrought-irons it occurs much more quickly than in others. It is probable that it is less marked in ingot- than in weld-metal, and less marked in high- than in low-carbon ingot-metal. There seems to be little doubt that it sometimes occurs in ingot-metal.

It is shown in Curves 3 and 6 of Figure 88, which are interrupted-strain diagrams, the former of Bessemer steel of 0·15 to 0·20% of carbon, the latter of tool-steel. Steel with even as much as 1% of carbon undergoes a very great elevation of the elastic limit when stretched at about 400° F. (205° C.) cooled to 70° F., and further tested.[b]

Heating to 500° C. (932° F., see Table 101) diminishes and if more intense may wholly remove these effects of cold-distortion (see Table 100). But heating to a lower temperature, say 200° to 300° C. (392° to 572° F.) has the surprising effect of intensifying them, as rest does. Apparently the distortion starts a strengthening change in the metal: this change once started goes on and gradually approaches a maximum even at the ordinary temperature, and is accelerated by moderate heating, say to 300°: but it is counteracted more or less completely and even effaced by some other change, be it crystalline, molecular, allotropic, or whatever, which becomes marked at 500° C. and very marked at redness. It is of course possible that the gentle heating acts by relieving stress.

W. H. Paine found, between 1856 and 1861, that drawing cold-rolled steel tape through a bath of molten tin, zinc or lead raised its transverse elastic limit, and this method was used for the wire of the East River bridge, which was thereby increased both in tensile strength and elastic limit. But he found that, when a bath of molten zinc was used, it was necessary to pass the tape through very rapidly, lest its elastic limit be lowered instead of being raised.[c]

That the density is diminished by stretching was shown by Styffe for puddled iron and for weld- and ingot-steel.[d] Deering found that the specific gravity of steel wire fell from 7·8142 before stress to 7·8082 after rupture.[e] H. Allen found the specific gravity at the fractured end of a tensile test piece of unhardened soft steel (carbon 0·115%) only 7·819 against 7·826 for the unstrained end.[f] Major Wade found in 1860 that cold-rolled iron was lighter than the same iron rolled hot.[g] The specific gravity has been found to fall from 7·828 to 7·817 and then to 7·780 on repeated cold-hammering[h]; from about 7·82 in wrought-iron to 7·78 in a punching[i] from it; and from 7·839 to to 7.836 and later to 7·791 in wire drawing.[j] H. Allen, finally, reports the changes of density given in Table 105: while hot rolling here seems to increase the density, so that annealing again lowers it, wire-drawing lowers it greatly, annealing now increasing it, and in one case bringing it back nearly to that of the annealed wire-rod.[k]

TABLE 105.—DECREASE OF DENSITY ON WIRE DRAWING. (ALLEN.)

	Diameter, inches.	Sp. gr. Unannealed.	Sp. gr. Annealed.
Billet (hot rolled)	2" sq.	7·826	....
Wire rods } Hot rolled }	0·30	7·832	7·820
	0·284	7·838	7·825
Wire drawn from rod 0·3" in diameter	0·259	7·835	7·847
" " 0·22" "	0·134	7·815	7·821

Resilience and Stiffness.—As cold-working affects the modulus of elasticity relatively little (note the parallelism of the elasticity lines in Figures 88, 89: note that, till we approach the elastic limit, the strain diagrams of hot- and cold-rolled irons coincide) while often doubling the elastic limit, it increases the elastic resilience enormously, tripling or even quadrupling it. It clearly increases the stiffness as measured by the total amount of pressure which the piece can undergo without permanent set: and it is generally but probably falsely thought to increase the stiffness as measured by the temporary deflection produced by a stress within the elastic limit. This, surely, should be an error, for this deflection should be proportional to the modulus of elasticity. So with high- and low-carbon steel: the former is generally thought stiffer than the latter. Some of our most intelligent engineers who have given the subject most thought habitually employ high-carbon steel where unusual stiffness and rigidity are needed, admitting that its modulus is nearly

[a] Rept. U. S. Bd. on Testing Iron, Steel, etc., I., p. 107: Thurston, Mat'ls of Engineering, II., p. 600.

This growth of the tensile strength and elastic limit after stretching should tend to produce higher ultimate tensile strength during slow than during fast pulling. But other factors may modify this effect, notably the greater opportunity for flow and consequent local reduction of area during slow pulling, and, in case the pulling is extremely rapid, the effect of vis viva. Hence we may expect that a certain rate of pulling, varying with the composition, shape and condition of the test-piece, will give the maximum tensile strength. Thus Gatewood and Denny obtain higher, but Marshall, Thurston, and I believe Kirkaldy, lower tensile strength with fast than with slow pulling. (Gatewood, Rept. U. S. Nav. Advisory B'd on Mild Steel, 1886, p. 124: Denny, Proc. Inst. Nav. Arch., 1880: Marshall, Trans. Am. Inst. Mining Engineers, XIII., p. 149. Thurston, Mat'ls of Engineering, II., p. 392.)

The vastly greater elongation under violently than under gradually applied tensile stress is probably due to the fact that in gradual pulling the failure of the piece at a single weak spot prevents the stress over the rest of the bar from reaching the point at which rapid stretching sets in. When a bar is torn explosively its whole length reaches this stress and stretches under it, though momentarily: indeed, Maitland sometimes found that the test-piece broke in two places simultaneously. He found that steel which gave 27% elongation in 2 inches under static stress, when torn explosively, *e. g.* with gun-cotton, gave from 47 to 62% elongation. ("The Treatment of Gun-Steel," Excerpt Proc. Inst. Civ. Eng., LXXXIX., p. 9, 1887.) The enormous stretching power of wrought-iron under shock was (according to B. Baker) pointed out by Robins in 1742: a musket-barrel "ballooned" to nearly double its original diameter.

[b] J. E. Howard, Watertown Arsenal, priv. commun., Feb. 8th, 1889.

[c] Zinc melts at about 412° C. (774° F.). Testimony of W. H. Paine in suit of Alanson Cary et al. vs. Lowell Mfg. Co., Lit., U. S. Circuit C't Western Dist. of Penn.: Deposition Oct. 21, 1885.

Paradoxically the gentle heating not only thus stiffened the tape where too soft, but toughened it where too brittle, in the latter case, we may surmise, by relieving internal stress induced by locally excessive cold-working. Styffe noted that a gentle heat, say 150° C. (300° F.), raised the elastic limit of previously cold-worked iron (Iron and Steel, p. 37, 108). Jarolimek has lately rediscovered this, and published experiments. (Dingler, CCLV., p. 1, 1885; also Journ. Iron and St. Inst., 1885, II., p. 641.) Armstrong noted that the elastic limit of hard-drawn steel wire was raised by gentle annealing. (No. 17, Table 100. Cf. Rept. British Ass., 1882, p. 403.)

[d] Iron and Steel, Styffe, Sandberg, pp. 66, 130, 1869.

[e] Percy, Jour. Iron and Steel Inst., 1886, I., p. 63.

[f] "The Effect of Rolling and of Wire-drawing upon Mild Steel." Excerpt Proc. Inst. Civ. Eng., XCIV., p. 10, 1888.

[g] W. Metcalf, Private communication. Exact and scrupulously conscientious as his work always was, this result surprised Major Wade so much that he would not accept it till it had been verified by his then assistant, Mr. Metcalf, who was, meanwhile, ignorant of its nature. Cf. also "Rept. on Cold Rolled-Iron," R. H. Thurston, private print, p. 12

[h] Langley, "The Treatment of Steel," Miller, Metcalf and Parkin, p. 42.

[i] Cf. § 285. Journ. Franklin Inst., CV., p. 145, 1878.

[j] Osmond and Werth, Annales des Mines, 8th Ser., VIII., p. 44, 1885.

[k] Excerpt Proc. Inst. Civ. Eng., XCIV., 1888. The properties of this billet and of these rods and wires are given in tables 100 and 105. The rods and wires are made from the billet here given.

the same as that of low-carbon steel, and admitting the anomaly. It should be more *resilient* than low-carbon steel, but not *stiffer* within the elastic limit.[a]

§ 271. Different Forms of Cold-Working.—Some of the individual effects of cold-working have been long and widely known, but they have in general been referred to this or that special form of cold-distortion, and relatively few have suspected that it is the cold-distortion itself, and not simply its special form which produces these effects. Few have suspected the general law that all forms of cold-distortion produce them. All know the effects of wire-drawing and cold rolling: many who are well informed have even lately been surprised to find that twisting and bending produce these effects, and have even then failed to note the resemblance.[b]

A. The effect of simple *stretching*, as in tensile testing, is shown in lines 1 to 6 of Table 101, chiefly as an elevation of the elastic limit (stretching point). Bauschinger, pulling the same bar of common wrought-iron asunder repeatedly, reducing its section with a round file each time at the point tested, found that, when weeks and months elapsed between successive pullings, the tensile strength rose at each experiment, from 45,513 pounds per square inch at the first to 62,580 at the seventh. When only a few minutes elapsed between successive pullings the gain was much less, but still marked, successive determinations giving 41,246; 44,091; 46,935; 48,358; 47,646: and 49,069 pounds per square inch.[c]

The effect of *cold bending* is shown in Table 103 and Figure 86. The tensile strength is slightly raised, and the ductility lowered. A comparison of curves 1 and 5 shows how completely annealing removes the effects of cold-bending. The elastic limit here given is probably the proportionality limit.

The strengthening effect of *cold-twisting* is shown in Table 102.

B. *Cold-rolling, cold-drawing and wire-drawing* increase the ultimate tensile strength greatly, the elastic limit still more (cold-rolling and drawing usually double it at least), but usually with a loss of ductility in intermediate proportion. The density is lowered slightly.

Thus in the last four columns of Table 100 the percentage of increase of elastic limit due to cold-working is with few exceptions greater than that of tensile strength, and in the great majority of cases over thrice as large: the difference is especially noticeable in case of cold-drawing, Numbers 28 to 31. For cold-drawing and cold-rolling the percentage of loss of elongation is invariably intermediate, greater than that of increase of tensile strength and less than that of elastic limit. In wire-drawing the loss of ductility, while often very severe, rising even to 98%, is occasionally much less for given increase of tensile strength than any here recorded in case of cold-rolling or cold-drawing: thus in Number 12 B the loss of elongation just equals and in Number 13 B is but one seventh of the gain in tensile strength.

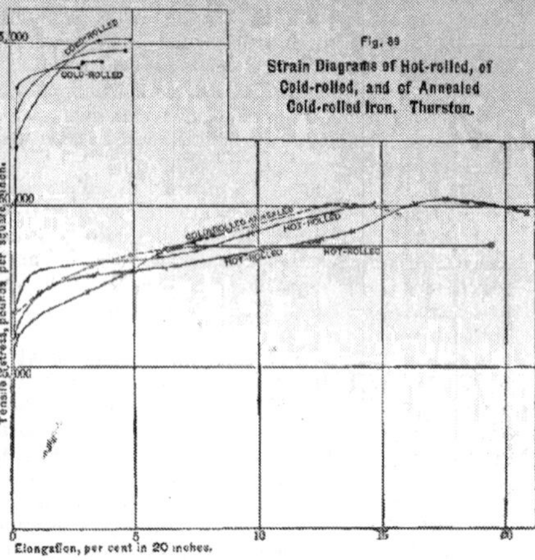

Fig. 89
Strain Diagrams of Hot-rolled, of Cold-rolled, and of Annealed Cold-rolled Iron. Thurston.

Further, while the six or seven draughts of each set in Table 106 increase the tensile strength by about half, the loss in elongation is much less, and in two cases nil. The comparative flatness of some of the broken (wire-drawing) lines in Figure 90 illustrate the small loss of ductility in wire-drawing.

But in these cases the initial elongation is small: when initially high the elongation falls as much in wire-drawing as in cold-rolling or cold drawing. Hence I attribute the cases of small loss in wire-drawing not to any special advantage in this process, but to a supposed general principle that the smaller the percentage of elongation the smaller the percentage of that percentage removed for given percentage of increase of tensile strength, whether by increase of carbon or by mechanical treatment. In other words, to pass from great to greater toughness implies heavy loss of strength: to pass from great strength to greater does not mean severe sacrifice of toughness. We note in figure 90, as in Table 6 A and as seen by comparing figures 3 and 5 (pp. 14, 16, 17), that as tensile strength increases elongation at first falls off very rapidly, from say 25 % to 5 %, but thenceforth slowly, remaining between 1 and 2 %, even though the tensile strength rises above 400,000 pounds per square inch.

As the cold-working in wire-drawing is probably somewhat localized, being more intense on the outside than in the interior, so, as we should anticipate, it does not always strengthen the wire as a whole, the local strengthening being outweighed probably by the heterogeneousness of strength, or by initial stress, or both; incipient cracks, too, later drawn out, perhaps weakening the wire. Thus,

[a] Cf. Styffe, Iron and Steel, p. 69; also the author, Eng. and Mining Jr., XX., 1875.

[b] T. Andrews finds that, when wrought-iron axles are subjected to severe blows, as in drop-testing, and rotated 180° after each, the later blows cause less deflection than the early ones, *i. e.*, the axle's elastic limit rises. The progressive decrease of deflection was very marked at 212° F. (100° C.) and at 120° and 100° F. (49° and 38° C.), but it could not be traced when the axles were at 7° to 10° F. (Excerpt Proc. Inst. Civ. Engineers, LXXXVII., 1886-7.) Barba noticed that steel angle-bars became stiffer and harder to bend after they had been partly bent; on bending less abruptly this effect diminished. This effect was less marked when, by the use of blocks, bends of longer radius were made. (The Use of Steel, p. 74.) Indeed, I find in conversation that many blacksmiths and other iron workers and users realize that, in bending cold iron, the resistance increases for a time, and that somewhat heavier blows are needed to straighten it after cold bending than sufficed to bend it. In one case the men reported to their foreman that certain crow-bars were not stiff enough; he said, "straighten them when they bend, and they will soon be stiff enough."

[c] Dingler's Polytechnisches Journal, CCXXIV., p. 1, 1877.

in Figure 100, the strength of the tempered wire of Test II falls at the fourth draught: the same thing occurred at the fourth draught of Test III of Table 106. On my communicating these results to Mr. Spilsbury, he repeated the tests, thinking the irregularity accidental: but in a fourth and fifth test the same weakening recurred at the fourth draught. The cause is not yet known.

TABLE 106.—THE EFFECTS OF SUCCESSIVE DRAUGHTS IN WIRE DRAWING. (SPILSBURY'S DATA. SEE FIGURE 100.)

Test No.	Draught No.	Diameter. Inches.	Diameter. B. W. G.	Reduction. Ratio a	Reduction. % reduction of diameter.	Tensile strength. Lbs. per sq. in.	Tensile strength. Increase over preceding, %	Elongation, % in 6"	Number of twists in 6" before rupture.	Number of 180° bends before rupture
1 tempered.	1	·158	8·71	......	......	152,000	......	8·12	10	8
	2	·129	10·36	·84	16	160,750	5·7	4·17	7	8
	3	·110	11·91	·85	15	172,600	7·4	2·08	8	7
	4	·093	13·17	·85	15	194,800	12·6	8·12	13	7
	5	·075	14·73	·81	19	215,000	10·7	2·08	14	4
	6	·060	16·71	·80	20	235,200	9·4	1·56	18	5
1 not tempered.	1	·158	8·71	......	......	105,800	......	4·17	27	9
	2	·129	10·36	·84	16	120,900	14·8	8·12	13	8
	3	·110	11·91	·85	15	126,800	4·5	2·08	9	10
	4	·093	13·17	·85	15	147,200	16·5	5·12	7	7
	5	·074	14·82	·80	20	167,400	13·7	4·17	16	8
	6	·060	16·71	·81	19	178,300	6·5	8·12	18	7
2 tempered.	1	·137	9·79	......	......	143,400	......	8·12	16	6
	2	·118	11·13	·86	14	156,300	9·0	8·12	20	6
	3	·099	12·71	·84	16	159,000	20·5	2·08	9	6
	4	·080	14·27	·81	19	157,000	−1·1	2·86	10	4
	5	·065	16·0	·81	19	212,500	13·6	2·08	19	6
	6	·053	17·56	·82	18	231,200	8·8	2·08	21	7
2 not tempered.	1	·137	9·79	......	......	116,000	......	8·12	27	8
	2	·118	11·18	·86	14	134,000	15·5	2·08	12	8
	3	·098	12·78	·83	17	137,000	2·2	3·12	8	9
	4	·078	14·36	·81	19	152,000	10·2	8·12	12	9
	5	·063	16·0	·82	18	171,800	13·0	2·08	9	6
	6	·053	17·56	·82	18	174,500	1·6	2·08	7	8
3 tempered.	1	·170	7·67	......	......	163,000	......	8·12	19	6
	2	·148	9·0	·87	13	169,400	3·9	2·08	14	6
	3	·126	10·37	·85	15	198,500	17·2	8·12	14	7
	4	·110	11·91	·87	13	197,300	−0·6	6·12	17	6
	5	·085	13·63	·77	23	222,900	13·0	2·08	21	7
	6	·078	14·45	·92	8	235,400	5·6	3·12	18	9
	7	·063	16·29	·81	19	263,000	11·7	3·12	21	8
3 not tempered.	1	·170	7·67	......	......	148,700	......	3·12	26	6
	2	·149	8·94	·88	12	113,800	−23·5	2·08	24	9
	3	·127	10·30	·85	15	123,500	8·5	3·12	16	10
	4	·110	11·91	·87	13	156,300	26·6	3·12	16	8
	5	·085	13·83	·77	23	174,500	11·6	3·12	20	6
	6	·078	14·45	·92	8	167,400	−4·1	6·12	19	10
	7	·063	15·29	·81	19	192,500	15·0	3·12	11	9

a This is the ratio of the diameter after the draught to that before it.

One might suppose the effect of cold-rolling much more

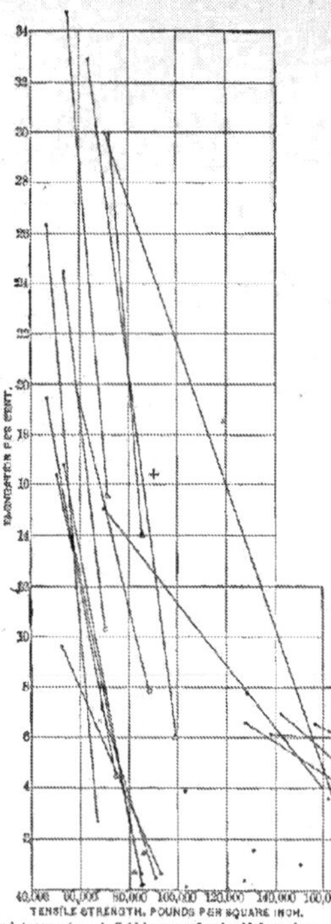
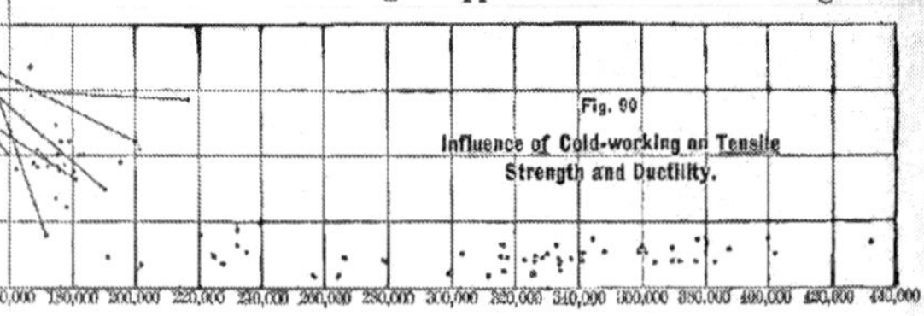

Hard-drawn wire. Δ Cold-hammered and cold-drawn bars, etc. O Cold-rolled bars, etc. When two points are connected by a line, the upper represents the properties of the metal before cold-working, the lower after cold-working, the length and direction of the connecting line indicating the degree and nature of the change effected by the cold-working.

Most of the data are from Table 100, § 209; Engineering, Feb. 16, 1877, p. 135 (wire for Brooklyn Bridge); Journ. Iron and St. Inst., 1886, I., pp. 68, et seq., Percy, Maitland; and Rept. Tests of Metals at Watertown U. S. Arsenal, 1885, pp. 657 to 663 (wires for wire-wound guns).

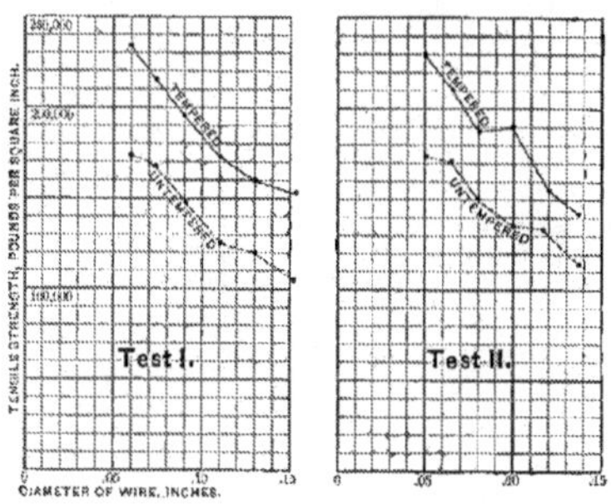

Fig. 100.—Tensile strength of wire after successive draughts. Spilsbury data.

These curves represent the tensile strength of unannealed wire after each of several successive draughts. E. G. Spilsbury, private communication, June, 1888.

severe on the skin than on the interior of the bar: but the results in Table 107 do not indicate any marked localization: the strength per square inch of the centre of the bar is very nearly as great as that of the whole bar.

TABLE 107.—ILLUSTRATING THE DEPTH TO WHICH THE EFFECT OF COLD-ROLLING EXTENDS. (Thurston)

Diameter, inches.	Cold rolled iron. Tensile strength, lbs. per sq. in.	Cold rolled iron. Elastic limit, lbs. per sq. in.	Cold rolled iron. Elongation.	Cold rolled iron. Reduction of area.	Untreated iron. Tensile strength, lbs. per sq. in.	Untreated iron. Elastic limit, lbs. per sq. in.	Untreated iron. Elongation.	Untreated iron. Reduction of area.
2	66,933	57,500	.....	24·83				
1¾	66,900	63,200	6·00	29·44	48,700	30,300	30·00	41·38
1½	68,500	56,600	7·86	26·30	48,500	30,500	25·70	40·18
1	60,600	56,700	6·55	31·12	47,900	26,000	21·30	39·14
[illegible]	65,850	54,900	11·07	31·85	58,450	25,300	26·36	34·13
[illegible]	65,650	56,600	9·00	29·66	49,380	23,300	21·57	37·85
[illegible]	66,650	53,400	6·22	29·47	50,520	24,100	24·57	43·24
[illegible]	60,200	56,600	3·14	27·70	60,180	23,900	19·57	40·42
[illegible]	63,400	54,200	7·29	28·80	52,540	31,800	20·57	46·24
[illegible]	64,660	50,500	3·48	28·60	42,980	32,100	18·98	47·28

a Two-inch wrought-iron bars, some cold-rolled, some untreated, had their diameters reduced by turning in a lathe to the sizes indicated in the first column, and were then subjected to tensile test, with the results given in the remaining columns. R. H. Thurston, Report on Cold-Rolled Iron, 1878.

The gain in elastic limit seems on the whole higher in

cold-drawing than in cold-rolling, and—in the sole case in which the loss of elongation is also given—with less than corresponding loss of ductility: from which single case no inference should be drawn. The greater increase in elastic limit I incline to attribute to greater reduction in drawing than in rolling, and to believe that, with heavier reduction, an equal increase could be obtained in cold-rolling.

The modulus of elasticity is affected relatively little. Here it seems to be lowered[a] slightly, there to be slightly raised. As the elastic limit is usually at least doubled, the elastic resilience is enormously increased, according to Thurston by from 300 to 400%.

The transverse strength and elastic limit seem to be increased by cold-rolling in about the same proportion as the tensile, the transverse like the tensile modulus of elasticity now rising now falling on cold-rolling.

Torsionally, the elastic limit is about doubled by cold-rolling, like the tensile and transverse elastic limits, while the ultimate strength is raised but little, and the modulus of elasticity apparently lowered.

Thus most of the effects seem to be alike in all directions, and independent of the longitudinal fibre set up by cold-rolling (Cf. § 258, A., p. 193).

Annealing probably completely removes the effects of these as of other forms of cold-working. In Table 100 the tensile strength and ductility of the annealed wire are now somewhat higher, now somewhat lower than those of the wire-rod. So with cold-rolled and annealed bars in the same table. The strain diagrams of cold-rolled and annealed iron, as in Figure 89, sometimes coincide with those of the same metal hot rolled. In other cases the annealing fails to depress the elastic limit to its original position, probably because incomplete.

Some who should know better have said that the tensile strength elongation, etc., of cold-rolled or wire-drawn iron differed from those of the untreated metal simply because we now reckon these properties on the section reduced by cold-rolling or wire-drawing, and on the length thus increased: and that, if reckoned on the dimensions of the metal before cold-rolling, they would be the same as those of the untreated metal. This, however, is manifestly untrue. For example, in number 38 of Table 100, the cold-rolling reduces one inch of cross-section of metal to 0·9044 square inches: the absolute tensile strength and elastic limit of the original one square inch were 46,733 and 28,600 pounds respectively: those (not per square inch but absolute) of the 0·9044 square inches left from this original one square inch are 59,780 and 54,530 pounds respectively: the absolute elastic limit of the bar as a whole is nearly doubled. So, too, one running inch of the original bar is in the same case drawn out in tensile testing to 1·2625 inches. In cold-rolling this one inch is drawn out to 1·106 inches, and when this elongated bar is then tested tensilely this 1·106 inches is further drawn out to only 1·135 inches before rupture. Thus the total elongation in cold-rolling plus tensile testing of the cold-rolled bar is only 13·5%, while the elongation of the same metal tensilely tested before cold-rolling was 26·25%. Thus the change induced by cold-rolling is not simply an apparent but a real one. Indeed, a glance at curves 2, 4 and 6, Figure 88, should show one how real the change due to rest after cold-stretching is.

§ 272. THE RATIONALE OF THE EFFECTS OF COLD WORKING is uncertain. It evidently produces in the metal some change or changes, which once started apparently continue long after the cold-working has ceased. But the nature of this change seems to me very obscure I offer no theory, but consider two which have been proposed and seem incompetent.

As has been already pointed out, Osmond, apparently struck by the certainly remarkable resemblance between the ulterior effects of quenching and those of cold-working on the tensile strength and elastic limit of steel, believes that the immediate effects of these two operations are like in kind, an allotropic change from to β iron.

We have seen that the phenomena of quenching-hardening can be explained without calling in the α β change, by other and known causes: and we failed to find any marked indication that this supposed α β change had any marked effect, or that it even existed in the case of heating and quenching.

Now, quenching and cold-working are utterly unlike not only in their procedure but in those of their immediate chemical and structural effects which are known. The former changes the chemical condition of carbon and the mineralogical constitution of the metal completely: the latter does neither, apparently simply mechanically distorting the individual crystals.[b]

Yet Osmond would persuade us that these operations act chiefly through a common hypothetical immediate effect, the α β change; and that the known tremendous immediate effects of quenching are relatively unimportant.

Clearly, he must show that the resemblance between the ultimate effects of these two apparently unlike operations is too close to be accidental, so close as to imply a common immediate effect. But here we are confronted with a new difficulty.

Cold-working affects the other malleable metals much as it does iron. It will hardly be claimed that it does so by creating a β copper, silver, brass, bronze, etc. It is then most natural to infer that the like operations of cold-working iron and steel on the one hand and cold-working the other metals on the other, act by producing the same kind of change: and we would abandon this inference and hold with Osmond that cold-working produces one kind of change in the other metals and a second kind in iron and steel, and that this second kind is the same as that produced by the unlike operation of quenching, only in case we find that the effects of cold working iron and steel resemble those of quenching steel much

[a] Thurston (Rept. on Cold-Rolled Iron and Steel, 1878, private print, pp. 80, 98; also Mat'ls of Engineering, II., p. 617) found that cold-rolling raised the modulus from about 25,000,000 to about 26,000,000 pounds per square inch on an average. In many of his experiments, however, it actually lowered the modulus. Hence it seems probable that as Styffe believed (Iron and Steel, p. 69), the modulus is lowered temporarily by cold-rolling, rising during rest as in Bauschinger's stretching tests, Table 101, to or beyond its initial value. It may well be that the bars whose modulus Thurston found lowered by cold-rolling had been rolled shortly before testing, and that later the modulus would have been found higher.

[b] Cf. § 57, p. 35. In addition to Abel's testimony that cold-working does not change the condition of carbon, we have that of Osmond and Werth, who obtain the following proportions of carbon in the same steel after different treatment.

	Eggertz method.	Boussingault method.
Untreated	·50	·49
Hardened by quenching	·32	·52
Hardened by quenching, then annealed	·48	·53
Cold-worked	·52	..

Ann. Mines, 8th Ser., VIII., p. 26.

The quantity of carbon found by Eggertz's method, while lessened by quenching-hardening and increased again by annealing, is not affected by cold-working.

more closely than they resemble those of cold-working the other metals.

Let us now examine these resemblances in some detail.

§ 273. Resemblance Between the Effects of Quenching and of Cold-Working.—Osmond claims[a] that when steel undergoes either operation

1, it absorbs heat:

2, its malleableness,
3, its density,
4, its thermo-electric constants, and
5, its electric conductivity
} diminish:

6, its coefficient of dilatation increases: and,

7, its chemical reactions become more energetic. To these we may add,

8, its hardness, strength and elastic limit increase. He further states that,

9, the strain-diagrams of brass and bronze are smooth: those of soft iron and steel consist of two smooth curves, united by an abrupt jog at the stretching point, shown in curves 1 and 2 of Figure 88. He might add that this jog is absent, usually at least, from the diagrams of cold-worked and hardened iron and steel. This suggests to him that these two curves represent two different metals, α iron up to the elastic limit, β iron above it, the distortion which occurs at this point, like that of cold-working, determining the change from the former to the latter.[b]

Taking these up in order, 1, that the change from the annealed to the hardened state is accompanied by absorption of heat, the phenomena of the after-glow and the retardations of both rising and falling temperature show. That cold-working causes a similar absorption of heat Osmond and Werth infer from their calorimetric studies, in which they find that cold-forged like quenched steel when dissolved in double chloride of copper and ammonium gives out more heat than annealed steel: the difference in different steels was far from proportional to the percentage of carbon present. They appear to have reached closely agreeing duplicate results, whose mean is given in § 14, p. 7.

Cold-worked copper, on the other hand, gave out the same quantity of heat as annealed copper. The difference in rise of temperature between annealed and cold-worked steel was, however, only about 0·1° C., while between duplicate results from similar samples the difference was in one case one third as large as this. The difference, moreover, is probably not proportional to the other effects of the cold-working, being almost as great in case of steel with 0·16% of carbon as in that with 1·17%, while it is probable that cold-working affects the properties of high- more than those of low-carbon steel. Such minute differences in heat-evolution seem less naturally ascribed to allotropism than to unnoted differences in conditions, *e. g.*, initial dissimiliarity of composition, due say to segregation; or possibly to some effect of the hydrogen in which the powder of the annealed metal was annealed.[c] Osmond calls in a giant to do a boy's work.

If, however, we admit that cold-working increases the evolution of heat on subsequent solution, this merely implies that it stores energy in some way, which is not necessarily through the α β change. The shattering, stretching or crumpling of resilient crystals, the creation of stress, macro- or micro-, are possible causes. Further, there is so much obscurity about the thermal relations of the compounds of iron and carbon that we can draw no safe inferences from such scanty data. Indeed, while Osmond and Werth find that heat is *set free* when carbon and iron combine, and while the fact that gray cast-iron, though melting at a higher temperature than white cast-iron yet according to Gruner has less latent heat of fusion, points in the same direction,[d] yet such eminent observers as Troost and Hautefeuille found that the combination of iron and carbon was attended with *absorption* of heat.

2. Both operations diminish malleableness.

3 The loss of density due to quenching is readily referred, if not to the stress born of uneven contraction, at least to the chemical and mineralogical changes which heating and quenching cause. It cannot be regarded as a proof of allotropic change from α to β iron, because when soft wrought-iron is quenched its specific gravity is lowered, like that of steel:[e] yet on Osmond's theory its iron is α even after quenching.

4–5. I do not see that they offer any evidence that quenching and cold-working affect these properties alike. Indeed Barus and Strouhal, to whom they refer, state that the specific resistance is smaller in hard-drawn and greater in quenched wire than in soft wire.[f]

6. As regards the coefficient of dilatation, my knowledge is so fragmentary that I can reach no safe conclusion. If we confine ourselves to comparing results obtained by the same observers, it seems that cold-working and quenching, while both increasing the coefficient, do so in a ratio so disproportionate to that of their effects on the other properties as to form a serious discrepancy. Thus the data of Lavoisier and Laplace indicate that quenching increases the coefficient thirty times as much as wire-drawing. On the other hand, Troughton assigns to the coefficient of iron wire a value which, compared with the results given below would indicate that the effect of cold-working exceeded that of quenching.

Table 109.—Dilatation. Length at 100° C. of a rod whose length at 0° C. is 1.

	Hard	Soft.	Difference
Steel, hard vs. annealed, Fizeau	1·001,329	1·001,101	(0·000)234
Steel, yellow-tempered vs. untempered, Lavoisier and Laplace	1,001,377	1,001,079	298
Iron, wire-drawn vs. soft. Idem	1,001,235	1,001,220	15
Iron, wire, Troughton 1,001,440	....	....	....

7. Osmond and Werth find that cold-working increases the rapidity of corrosion of steel in dilute hydrochloric, nitric, sulphuric and acetic acids.[g] Quenching, however, probably produces the opposite effect. Barus and Strouhal found that as hardened steel was tempered at successively higher temperatures, the rate at which it dissolved in hydrochloric acid continually increased, and that hardened steel was electro-negative to the same steel

[a] Annales des Mines, 8th Ser., VIII., p. 48, 1885.

[b] Stahl und Eisen, VI., p. 540, 1886.

[c] The cold-working consisted in hammering bars 0·7888 inches square down to 0·197 inches square. Fearing that the action of the file used in removing material for analysis from the annealed bars would be equivalent to slight cold-working, the powder filed from the annealed pieces was reheated and cooled in hydrogen. Now hydrogen appears to have some obscure effect on the condition of carbon. Steel which in its natural state showed 0·91% of carbon by Eggertz's test, after heating in hydrogen showed only 0·45%; while on heating in vacuo no such change occurred. The hydrogen appears to have caused some change. It probably did not expel carbon, for the loss of weight on heating in hydrogen was found to be only 0·007%.

[d] Jüptner, Jour. Iron and St. Inst., 1887, II., p. 332, fr. Oest. Zeit., XXXV., pp. 12—461—4.

[e] Wrightson, Journ. Iron and St., Inst., 1879, II., p. 424, found the sp. gr. of wrought-iron reduced from 7·64 to 7·562, a loss of 1·02%, by fifty quenchings.

[f] Bull. 14, U. S. Geological Survey, p. 220.

[g] Ann. Mines, 8th Ser., VIII., p. 46, 1885.

annealed, both in distilled water and in zinc sulphate.[a] Further, Monroe found the hardened points of two cold-chisels long immersed in sea-water wholly uncorroded, their unhardened bodies being deeply pitted; and he learns of a similar phenomena in case of a hammer.[b]

Osmond and Werth, however, believe that hardening like cold-working increases the solubility, but apparently on quite insufficient ground. They rely on Gruner's finding in one case that hardened steel dissolved more rapidly in acidulated water than annealed steel, and on analogous results of their own experiments. It is probable that Gruner's result to which they refer is Number 40–1 of Table 44, p. 94, in which, unfortunately, *manganese steel was tried.*

Its behavior, of course, throws no light on that of carbon steel, since manganese steel does not undergo the very change in question, the change of hardness when quenched from a high temperature. Osmond and Werth do not give us their own results. Actually, Gruner's evidence appears to agree with that of Barus and Strouhal and that of Monroe: in sea-water Gruner found that hardened steel corroded less than the same steels annealed.

8. Both quenching and cold-working harden and strengthen steel, at the same time raising its elastic limit and making it brittle, usually without greatly affecting the modulus of elasticity. But the ratio of gain of one property to that of another on quenching is widely different from that on cold-working. Thus quenching increases the hardness enormously, the tensile strength relatively little: indeed it occasionally lowers the latter. Cold working even when doubling the tensile strength increases the hardness but little. A quenching which makes previously soft steel utterly unfileable may raise its tensile strength by less than 25%: while the unskilled hand can hardly detect with the file the hardening effect of a cold-working which may nearly double the tensile strength. As regards the ratio of increase of tensile strength to that of elastic limit the case is better, but there is still quite a discrepancy. In forty-nine cases in Tables 8, 9 and 10, pp. 18 to 20, the average increase of tensile strength on quenching is only about half as great as that of elastic limit: in 12 cases in Table 100 the average increase of tensile strength is nearly one third as great as that of elastic limit. These discrepancies may be explained away later: indeed, I think it likely that the former discrepancy is in large part due to difference in the intensity and distribution of internal stress.[a] While then, the effects of quenching and of cold-working on these properties are not so hopelessly unlike as to disprove Osmond's theory, certainly they are not yet shown to be so like as to give it important support.

We have seen that the elevation of the elastic limit due to cold-working is increased by gentle heating (to 200° or 300°, § 270). Jarolimek, applying to steel springs hardened by quenching the same gentle heating which he had found to raise the elastic limit of like springs which had been distorted, *i. e.* cold-worked, found that it did not increase their elastic limit.[c] Indeed, the general phenomena of tempering hardened steel would lead us to expect that reheating to 300° C. (572° F., a blue oxide tint) would lower the elastic limit (Table II., p. 22). Should further investigation confirm Jarolimek's results, this would constitute a serious difference between the effects of quenching and those of cold working.

Further, the effect of quenching on tensile strength seems instantaneous: while cold-working, at least cold-stretching, does not seem to affect tensile strength at all immediately, the growth of tensile strength occurring gradually after the stretching has occurred.

The ninth point may be dismissed summarily. Not only are the strain diagrams of soft iron often without jog, but we cannot even regard greater sharpness of bend at the elastic limit as a constant characteristic of non-cold-worked iron, distinguishing it from other materials, nor hence as an indication of allotropic change due to cold-working at the elastic limit. Doubtless on an average the bend is sharper for hot-rolled weld iron than for cold-worked iron and other metals: but the reverse is probably often true. Thus Thurston gives cases in which the bend is apparently sharper in cold-rolled than in similar but hot-rolled iron.[d] Again, we find many strain-diagrams for steel of carbon varying from 0·15 to 1·32% which are smooth at the elastic limit, together with strain-diagrams for copper with a sharp bend.

Osmond and Werth would distinguish highly carburetted steel from ingot-iron by the smoothness of its strain diagram. Yet it is of the two probably the more influenced by cold-distortion, including that at the elastic limit, and should,—if this distortion acts through allotropic change, and if the jog results from this change,—show the greater jog.[e]

We have seen that this jog characterizes locust and hickory wood.[f]

§ 274. Resemblance Between the Effects of Cold-working Iron and those of Cold-working other Metals.—Time fails me for an exhaustive study: I can merely turn to the readily accessible data.

Under cold-work the other metals, like iron, become harder, stronger, more elastic and resilient, more brittle: their strain-diagrams undergo changes like those of iron: their modulus of elasticity, like that of iron, seems to be increased but little, judging from the elasticity-lines of interrupted-strain diagrams. Like that of iron the electric conductivity of some (*e. g.* platinum and German silver) is increased by cold-working, while that of others is less-

[a] Am. Journ. Sci., 3d Ser., XXXII., p. 276, 1886. "The rate at which solution takes place increases as temper continually decreases." "As hardness increases the hydro-electric position of steel moves continually in an electro-negative direction."

[b] Journ. Franklin Inst., LXXXV., p. 300, 1883, Prof. C. E. Munroe, U. S. Naval Academy. In case of the chisels the corrosion was most marked at the junction of the hardened and unhardened parts; and the same was true in the experiments of Barus and Strouhal. In the case of the hammer it is possible that the difference in corrosion may have been due to the face being initially of a harder steel welded to softer metal.

[c] Dinglers' Polytechnisches Journal, CCLV., p. 3, 1885.

[d] Rept. on cold-rolled iron, private print, Plate VII., numbers 1104 A and 1105 A; Plate XVI., numbers 1,203 A, 1,204 A and 1,218.

[e] Osmond and Werth state that this jog occurs in the strain-diagrams of absolutely all classes of weld and ingot-iron as distinguished from hard and hardened sorts, and they give us to understand that this is an essential characteristic of soft iron as distinguished from other materials in general. They seem to be wholly in error. Not to multiply cases needlessly, jog-less diagrams of ingot-iron sometimes quite soft, are given by the U. S. Test Board (Nos. 1091 B., 1060 D, and 1583, the former two with 0·23 and 0·24 of carbon, the latter with still less, judging from its tensile strength 54,760 lbs.); by Kirkaldy (Expts. on Fagersta steel, Series D., pl. I., No. 1054, with 0·15 of carbon), and by Gatewood (Rept. of U. S. Naval Advisory Board on Mild Steel, pl. XVIII., with 0·16 of carbon). Further, jogged diagrams of hard steel are given by the U. S. Test Board (Nos. 1053 A. and C., 1056 A., B. and C., and 1058 A. B. and C. with ·973, ·994 and ·905% of carbon respectively. Further, many of the torsion diagrams of tool-steel here show decided jogs.

[f] Matls. of Engineering, II., p. 531. Thurston regards the jog as a sign of heterogeneousness.

ened (*e. g.* gold, copper, silver, zinc): probably like that of iron the coefficient of dilation increases very slightly.[a]

Cold-working condenses the metal by closing cavities, lightens it by some other immodiate effect. In case of iron the lightening outweighs the condensation. To judge from published tables the reverse is in general true of the other metals. But the case is simpler if we consider the effect of annealing on the density of cold-worked metals, for here the closing of cavities is eliminated. The density of cold-worked iron is apparently increased by annealing: that of cold-drawn copper and brass seems to be very slightly increased, judging from the following results obtained for me in Drown's laboratory.

	Copper.	Brass.
Sp. gr. when annealed	8·908	8·503
Sp. gr. when unannealed	8·905	8·499
Difference	+ 0·003	+ 0·004

In the case of cold-rolled coin-silver my assistant obtained the following results, indicating that this alloy too is lightened by cold-rolling.

Sp. gr. when annealed	10·1716	
Sp. gr. when unannealed	10·1674	(10·1676, 10·1672)
	+ ·0042	

In three series of experiments O'Neill[b] found that the cold-hammering lowered the density of copper. I here condense his results. The numbers in each of the first sets are the mean of ten results:

Uncompressed	8·879	8·809	8·835
The same pieces compressed	8·855	8·878	8·667
" " annealed	8·884a	8·896b	
Gain	+0·029	+0·018	

a Annealed in red-hot sand and again cleaned.
b Five of the same pieces annealed in a charcoal fire.

It is true that Baudrimont found that the density of wires of iron, silver, copper and other metals was diminished by annealing: and that cold-rolling increased the density of the annealed copper and iron wires enormously, *e. g.* from 7·5361 to 7·7334.[c] I can hardly credit his results. They indeed agree with the others here presented, in showing that the effect of cold working on iron is like in sign to its effect on other metals.

The points of similarity between the effects of cold-working iron on the one hand, and of hardening it and of cold-working the other metals on the other, are here summed up.

TABLE 110.—EFFECTS, ETC., OF COLD-WORKING IRON COMPARED WITH THOSE OF HARDENING IT AND OF COLD-WORKING OTHER METALS.

		Hardening iron, like or unlike cold-working iron.	Cold-working other metals, like or unlike cold-working iron.
Effect on	Malleableness	Roughly like in kind, but very different in proportion among themselves.	Like in kind: not known how like in proportion.
	Tensile strength		
	Elastic limit		
	Modulus of elasticity		
	Hardness		
	Evolution of heat during solution	Like (?)	Unlike for copper
	Electric conductivity	Opposite	Like for some metals
	Heat-expansion	Doubtful	Like
	Chemical activity	Probably opposite	
	Density	Like	Like
	Condition of carbon	Unlike	
	Structural condition	"	Probably like
Removal of effects by heating		Like in part	Like
Apparent nature of processes		Unlike	Identical
Intensity of stress		Unlike	Probably like

Let each judge for himself the closeness of these resemblances. To me it seems that, while the resemblance between the effects of cold-working and those of quenching steel is striking at first sight, on examination it seems more apparent than real, and not so close that it may not well be accidental. On the whole it seems less complete than the resemblance between the effects of cold-working iron and those of cold-working the other metals, though unfortunately our data here are scanty. The former resemblance is at a disadvantage as regards electric conductivity; probably as regards the proportion between the gain of tensile strength, etc., and that of hardness; and probably as regards the progressive nature of the change in tensile strength and elastic limit.

In short, the probabilities seem strongly against Osmond's theory, and in favor of the belief that cold-working produces a special kind of change, the *cold-work change*, roughly alike in the different malleable metals.

What the nature of this change is I will not attempt to say, beyond surmising that it is essentially physical. It has been thought to consist essentially in stress: but this seems wholly improbable, for two chief and two minor reasons.

1st, While there is certainly stress in much cold-worked iron,[d] Thurston's results in Table 107 indicate that it is very mild.

Here the tensile strength and elastic limit of cylinders of progressively decreasing diameter, turned from cold-rolled wrought-iron bars two inches in diameter, decrease but slightly with the diameter, indeed hardly more than in case of like but hot-rolled bars. In § 54 B., p. 32, I showed that the tensile strength of a hardened steel bar differed greatly from that of small cylinders turned from it. The difference clearly was not due to the slower cooling of the centre, for this was stronger than the average of the whole bar, but probably to stress.

2d, Cold-working in one direction seems to affect the properties of the metal alike in all directions: *e. g.* longitudinal extension, as in cold-rolling, seeming to increase the transverse and torsional as much as the longitudinal and elastic limit. The stress caused by cold-rolling should not be uniform in all directions.

3d, It is not easy to understand how stress, as such, should materially increase the hardness proper, the resistance to abrasion and indentation.

4th, Gentle heating, which should relieve stress, intensifies the effect of cold-working.

WIRE-DRAWING.

§ 275. IN WIRE-DRAWING the cold wire, coated with a lubricant, is drawn through a succession of conical gently tapering holes in extremely hard steel or cast-iron dies or "draw-plates," each hole a little smaller than the preceding and each slightly diminishing the diameter of the wire. The metal gradually becomes hard and brittle, and must be annealed from time to time, and then, to remove the

a The excess of the linear expansion between 0° and 100° C. for the harder over that for the softer state is as follows:

Iron, wire-drawn vs. soft Lavois. and Laplace	0·000,01400
Gold, standard, unannealed vs. annealed, idem	3794
Brass wire vs. cast, Smeaton	5300
Zinc, hammered vs. unstated, Smeaton	6600

It is not clear that the coefficients for the two states of brass are comparable, as the composition of this alloy varies widely.

b Manchester Phil Soc., II., p. 56, March 5th, 1861. Also Percy, Fuel, p. 287, 1861.

c Ann. Chim. Phys., 2d Ser., LX., p. 78, 1835.

d To prove the existence of stress in cold-worked bars, I slit a round steel bar, whose diameter had been reduced from 0·8 to 0·7467 inches by a single cold-draught through a die, for a distance of 4·25 inches from one end, making a crude tuning fork of it. When released, the ends of the tynes sprang *apart* by 0·0413 inches: had the bar been quenched instead of cold-drawn its tynes would have sprung *towards* each other.

Since then I learn that Baker has shown the presence of stress in cold-bent iron in two experiments. 1. On planing off the outside of a cold-bent steel boiler plate, the radius of curvature changed. 2d. An initially crooked steel bar 11 inches wide and 12 feet long was straightened, and sawed lengthwise through the middle: it immediately bent to the theoretically calculated curvature. ("The Use and Testing of Open-Hearth Steel for Boiler-Making," Excerpt, Proc. Inst. Civ. Eng., XCII., pp. 40-7, 1888.)

coat of oxide produced in annealing, it must be pickled before further drawing, and then washed to remove the pickling acid. The whole procedure may indeed be regarded as made up of one or more similar series of operations, each series consisting of pickling, washing, lubricating, several draughts and an annealing. We will now consider these several operations separately.

§ 276. POINTING AND PICKLING.—The coiled *wire-rod*, (*i. e.* the wire as it leaves the rolling mill and before drawing, covered with a scale due to the high temperature of rolling), first has one end pointed so that it may enter the draw-plate readily. To remove the scale which if left on would greatly increase the resistance and rapidly wear out the die, the wire is next pickled either in dilute sulphuric acid, say of from 1 to 3 parts of 60° B acid to 100 of water, and at say 101° F. (38° C.), the immersion lasting say 35 to 50 minutes, or in hydrochloric acid. It is then washed, preferably with a hose.

The later picklings, which follow the annealing of the partly drawn wire, are like that of the wire-rod: the finer the wire the more thoroughly must it be washed to remove the acid. Wire finer than No. 14 B. W. G. is usually "batted" while washing, *i. e.* beaten vigorously by two workmen with long wooden sticks, say $6' \times 1\frac{1}{2}'' \times 2''$, while a hose plays on it.

The consumption of acid per ton of wire is estimated by Bädeker[a] for certain conditions at 47·6 to 54 pounds, by Wedding[b] at 54 to 65 pounds, of which 14 pounds are used in pickling drawn wire. At an American wire mill 18·3 pounds of acid were used per ton of wire rods on the first pickling, on a test trial.

When its acid has been so far neutralized that it is no longer efficient, the pickling liquor is in some mills run to waste: in others its ferrous sulphate is crystallized out as copperas, the mother-liquors are evaporated to dryness, and the residue roasted, yielding Venetian red (ferric-oxide, colcothar). In this country the sulphuric acid driven off in roasting the residue is wholly lost: but it might be condensed as Nordhausen acid.[c]

§ 277. LUBRICATION.—Any common lubricant would be squeezed out by the pressure between wire and die, which would then abrade each other. Certain coatings, such as lime, flour, hydrated iron-oxide, and salt, strangely enough adhere to the wire tenaciously and, instead of being scraped off by the die, seem to elongate as an extremely thin apparently continuous sheath, so that wire and draw-plate do not touch each other.

According to the mode of coating the wire with lubricant, wire-drawing is divided into dry drawing and wet drawing. In both cases the coating is applied by immersing the hank of wire into a solution containing the lubricating substance. In dry drawing the hank is removed from the liquor and dried or baked before drawing; in wet drawing it is drawn directly from the solution, in which it stands immersed, wound upon a reel. In dry drawing several draughts are given between successive lubricatings, the lubricant being applied say after each annealing and pickling. In wet drawing the wire is lubricated before each draught, the hank of wire as soon as it has passed completely through the die being returned to the tub which contains the coating solution, and at once undergoing a fresh draught. In dry drawing the wire must be well smeared with tallow outside the dry coat of lubricant: to this end a lump of tallow is placed against the entering side of the die C, Figure 101, and through it the wire draws. In wet drawing no grease is used.

Coarse wire is almost always drawn dry, while in case of fine wire the earlier draughts are dry, the later wet, the change from dry to wet usually occurring not earlier than number 14 and not later than number 18 wire-gauge.

In many cases the wire is drawn dry until the last pickling, which usually comes immediately after the last annealing, say at 14 gauge for wire which is to be drawn to 20 gauge, or at 19 gauge for wire which is to be drawn finer. The grease of the dry drawing is charred in annealing and removed in pickling: thereafter the wire is drawn wet. In other works the change from dry to wet occurs at 14 gauge, while the last annealing occurs at 19 gauge: but wire is rarely drawn dry after the last pickling.

The more common dry coatings are lime, flour, and the "water-coating." The former two are applied by simply dipping the coil of wire in thin lime-water or flour paste, and then baking it in a large oven, whose temperature is in some cases so low that one may walk into it (say 150° F., 66° C.), in other cases as high as 650° F. (344° C.). It is said that unless thus rapidly dried the lime or flour coating does not adhere well: but the baking probably fulfills another very important office, to wit, hastening the expulsion of hydrogen which is absorbed during pickling, and which makes the wire brittle and liable to break in drawing.[d]

A water coating, confusingly enough, is a dry coating. It apparently consists of hydrated iron-oxide, and is produced by exposing the pickled and washed hank of wire to the air, sprinkling it from time to time to hasten rusting. The care required in producing this coating makes it more expensive than the lime coating, but it is more a efficient and more persistent lubricant. In some cases water-coated wire is subsequently lime-coated before drawing.

A coating of salt, according to Morgan,[e] adheres to wire much more tenaciously than either flour or lime, and is therefore well fitted to resist the heavy pressure in drawing steel wire, especially in the early draughts in which the reduction is severe. So salt was extensively used for a time in dry wire-drawing, sometimes mixed with lime: but it induces rusting so much that its use has been generally if not wholly abandoned.

Its behavior in wire-drawing is instructive as illustrating that of dry coatings in general. Thompson[f] found that it persisted through seven draughts, the proportion of salt per square inch of surface diminishing rapidly during the first two draughts, suggesting that part of it was scraped off, but thenceforth slowly. After the first draught the salt was invisible, though readily tasted. Exposed to a pressure of 192,000 pounds per square inch

[a] Stahl und Eisen, VI., p. 182, 1886. Iron Age Apl. I., 1886, p. 25.

[b] Stahl und Eisen, VI., p. 14, 1886.

[c] Concerning the manufacture of Nordhausen or fuming sulphuric acid from copperas-slate Cf. Lange, Sulphuric Acid and Alkali, I., p. 631, 1879, Fr. Wagner's Jahresbericht, 1873, p. 220, also Traité de Chimie Technologique et Industrielle, Knapp, Mérijot et Debize, II., p. 403.

[d] Cf., § 178 B, pp. 114, et seq., especially p. 117.

[e] C. H. Morgan, Trans. Am. Inst. Mining Engineers, IX., p. 672. He appears to have originated the use of salt in wire-drawing in 1878.

[f] Idem., p. 300-1.

between plane surfaces, salt was converted into a thin transparent wafer. Some of Thompson's results follow.

TABLE 111.—PERSISTENCE OF THE SALT-COATING IN WIRE DRAWING (THOMPSON).

	Diameter. Inches.	Salt per square inch. Grammes.		Total salt per running foot. Grammes.	
		Wire B.	Wire C.	Wire A.	Wire C.
Initial	0·192	....	0·01390	....	0·0948
After 1st draught	0·154	0·00110	0·00127	0·0044	0·0072
" 2d "	0·131	0·00060	0·00050	0·0030	0·0025
" 3d "	0·113	0·00044	0·00043	0·0019	0·0014
" 4th "	0·102	0·00040	0·00036	0·0016	0·0015
" 5th "	0·092	0·00039	0·00039	0·0013	0·0013
" 6th "	0·075	0·00032	0·00027	0·0011	0·0008
" 7th "	0·067	Broke	0·00027	Broke	0·0008
" 8th "	......	....	Broke	....	Broke

The most common wet coating is that known as "lees" coating. Examples of its preparation follow:

1. Rye-flour "lees" are made by stirring two or three pounds of flour in a barrel of water.

2. Two parts "lees" liquor are mixed with one of milk of lime.[a]

3. 16·5 pounds of wheat-flour are boiled with 9 gallons of water, a little yeast is added and fermentation follows.[b]

Lacquer. Before wire is drawn wet it is often lacquered, *i. e.*, coated with copper by immersion in a slightly acidulated copper-sulphate solution, usually for a few seconds only, exceptionally for even half an hour. It is then immersed in the "lees" liquor and drawn. Should it be badly scratched in drawing it may be lacquered again after one or more draughts: otherwise the lacquering is not repeated, one wet draught following another immediately. At some works a little copper-sulphate is often added to the "lees" liquor to cause a slight deposit of copper on the wire: those who do not follow this custom of course denounce it as useless.

The copper greatly assists lubrication: but as its color persists through two or three draughts, wire which is to have a bright finish should not be lacquered within say three draughts of the last.

The preparation of the wet coating is in the hands of the individual wire-drawer himself, and he guards it jealously: even the superintendent professes ignorance of its composition. But the management exercises a certain control: *e. g.* it will not permit the use of more than a certain quantity of copper-sulphate.

Dry vs. Wet Drawing. Let us consider the relative advantages of these methods of drawing, especially seeking the reason why dry drawing is confined to coarse, wet to fine wire.

1. Wire-drawers say that in dry drawing the die cuts less under a heavy than under a light draught or reduction.

The following advantages are claimed for dry over wet drawing:

2. The wire tends less to rust, thanks to the grease coating.

It is cheaper than wet drawing:—

3. Because, as the dry coating is a better lubricant, the draughts may be heavier than in wet drawing.

4. Because it requires a less thorough washing after pickling, the lime partly neutralizing the acid if any remains.

5. Because it requires slightly less floor-room, the tubs needed for wet drawing necessarily occupying more room than the simple reels of dry drawing.

[a] Metcalfe, Rep. Chf. Ordnance U. S. A., 1885, p. 476.
[b] Fréson, Revue Universelle, 2d Ser., XVIII., p. 145. 1885.

Dry drawing is said to labor under the following disadvantages:

6. It lubricates less certainly than wet drawing. For if the drawer be inattentive (and each drawer has several lots of wire drawing under his charge simultaneously), some of the wire may fail to be coated with tallow: while the wet coating is necessarily continuous.

7. Its grease dulls the wire, and persists through many draughts.

8. The dry coating cuts the die more than the wet coating does.

The third and eighth propositions at first seem to harmonize poorly. Their discordance appears to be resolved by the first proposition: the probable explanation is that the dry coating lubricates best for heavy, the wet for light reductions.

Of these considerations, the first commends dry drawing for coarse rather than for fine wire, the third gives it a greater advantage for coarse than for fine wire, which, owing to its small sectional area, would break if too heavy a reduction were attempted

The sixth, seventh and eighth tend to confine dry drawing to coarse sizes, weighing lightly against the dry drawing of coarse but heavily against that of fine wire. The sixth for this reason:—annealing is especially undesirable in case of fine wire, for, thanks to its greater surface, more oxidation occurs in annealing, and the pickling needed to remove the oxide formed in annealing obviously must consume more of both acid and wire than in case of coarse wire: washing the acid from the pickled fine wire is also difficult and costly. Hence with fine wire annealing must be dispensed with as far as possible: *i. e.* fine wire must undergo many draughts without annealing. Because it is made brittle by these repeated draughts without annealing as well as because of its small sectional area, the tendency of fine wire to break in drawing is relatively great: hence, finally, for fine wire, because of its greater liability to break, the more certain lubrication of wet drawing is needed. The seventh because the bright finish which wet drawing alone can give is much oftener needed in case of fine than of coarse wire: this tends to establish wet drawing as the normal procedure for fine wire.

The eighth because the enlargement of the die must be more carefully guarded against in case of fine than of coarse wire. (a) Because the coils of fine wire are so much longer than those of coarse, and owing to the infrequency of annealing, the fine wire is as a whole harder than coarse wire: hence the *absolute* wear of the die during the passage of a single coil and the absolute difference in diameter between the ends of the coil are greater under like conditions for fine than for coarse wire. (b) Because the finer the wire the more objectionable is a given absolute variation in diameter.

Thus we see that a variety of considerations all tend to the same result, some by giving dry drawing special advantages in case of coarse wire, others by giving it special disadvantages in case of fine.

Wet drawing was unsuccessful in case of the coarse square wire for the Woodbridge gun, and was abandoned in favor of dry drawing.

§ 278. DRAWING.—The hank of wire is coiled on a reel D, Figure 101. Its previously tapered end is then passed through the draw-plate C, grasped by grippers, and a

TABLE 112.—BIRMINGHAM WIRE GAUGE (B. W. G.).

No. B. W. G.	0000	000	00	0	1	2	3	4	5	6	7	8	9	10	11	12	13	14	15	16
Diameter, inches	·454	·425	·38	·34	·30	·284	·259	·238	·220	·203	·180	·165	·148	·134	·120	·109	·095	·083	·072	·065
Difference in diam., inches	·029	·043	·040	·046	·016	·025	·021	·018	·017	·023	·015	·017	·014	·014	·011	·014	·012	·011	·007	·007
No. B. W. G.	17	18	19	20	21	22	23	24	25	26	27	28	29	30	31	32	33	34	35	36
Diameter, inches	·058	·049	·042	·035	·032	·028	·025	·022	·020	·018	·016	·014	·013	·012	·010	·009	·008	·007	·005	·004
Difference in diam., inches	·009	·007	·007	·003	·004	·003	·003	·002	·002	·002	·002	·001	·001	·002	·001	·001	·001	·002	·001	

little of the wire is drawn through. It is then fastened to the drum or "block" A, which is now rotated by gearing, gradually drawing the wire completely through the draw-plate. In wet drawing the reel stands in a wooden tub which holds the lees liquor.

The tendency of modern practice is towards heavier draughts. Thus while some mills reduce from 6 (rod) to 12 gauge in six draughts, the more advanced use but three or at most four draughts. The reduction may be heavier in the draught immediately following an annealing than in later ones. After wire has been reduced to about 18 or 20 gauge, further reduction is usually at the rate of one gauge number per draught.

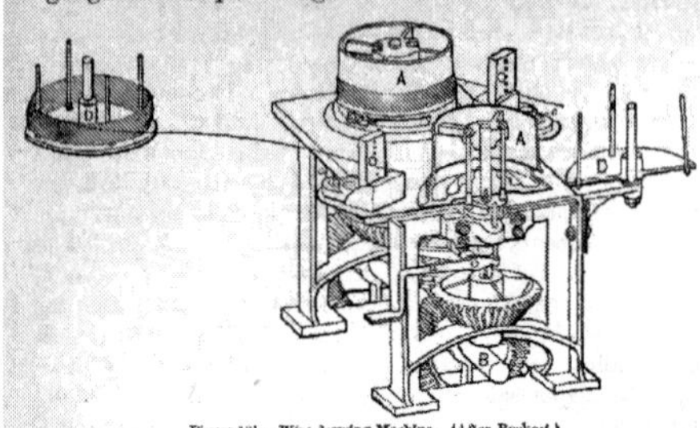

Figure 101.—Wire-drawing Machine. (After Beckert.)

A The power-driven drum or "block" which draws the wire through the draw-plate, and on which the drawn wire coils.
B The shaft which drives **A**.
C The die or draw-plate through which the wire is drawn.
D The reel on which the wire to be drawn is coiled.
The wire passes from **D** through **C** to **A**.

The resistance which the wire offers to drawing depends on its hardness, on the reduction, and on the taper of the hole. In the following table the resistance offered by hard steel wire (No. III.) is over thrice that offered by soft Swedish iron wire (No. I) under like conditions.

TABLE 113.—RESISTANCE OF WIRE TO DRAWING (MORGAN, LOC. CIT).

	I. Soft Swedish iron wire.		II. Half-hard Bessemer steel wire.		III. Hard crucible steel wire.	
Diameter before drawing	0·224″	5 gauge	0·226″	5 gauge	0·224″	5 gauge
" after "	0·191	6½ gauge	0·197	6½ gauge	0·193	6½ gauge
Reduction of area, per cent.	27·3	....	24·9	....	26·6	
Length of taper of wire in die	0·28	....	0·29	....	0·84	
Resistance, pounds	1,060	....	3,064	....	3,450	
Carbon, per cent.	....	....	0·45	....	0·86	
Silicon	·031	....	·068	....	·209	
Manganese	·399	....	1·04	....	0·461	
Sulphur	·006	....	·052	....	·025	
Phosphorus	·064	....	·144	....	·114	

H. ALLEN (PROC. INST. CIV. ENG., XCIV., 1888).

	IV. Mild steel.	V. Mild steel.	VI. Mild steel.
Diameter before drawing	·265	·221	·205
" after "	·220	·183	·165
Resistance, pounds	2,200	1,850	1,600
Carbon, per cent.		0·115	
Silicon		0·009	
Manganese		0·410	
Sulphur		0·068	
Phosphorus		0·072	

I. to III., Morgan, Trans. Am. Inst. Min. Eng., IX., p. 612.
IV. to VI., H. Allen, excerpt Proc. Inst. Civ. Eng., XCIV., 1888.
The resistance in pounds is given by Morgan as 1·060, 3·064 and 3·450, but the decimal point is apparently here given by typographical error for a comma.

In Vávra's experiments on drawing Bohemian iron wire, the speed of the drawn wire varied from 120 feet per minute for 0·24″ diameter (4 gauge) to 199 feet for 0·7″ diameter (15 gauge).[a] Bädeker gives the usual speed as from 148 to 180 feet per minute.[b]

The finer, *i. e.*, more flexible, the wire the smaller is the diameter of the block employed. The diameter and speed of block and the usual reduction per draught at a well-known American wire-mill are given in Table 114.

TABLE 114.—SOME DETAILS OF WIRE-DRAWING IN AN AMERICAN MILL.

Block: Designation.	Block: Diameter, inches.	Block: Revs per minute.	Block: Circumferential velocity, feet per minute.	Reduction: Size, Initial, B. W. G.	Reduction: Size, Initial, Inches. A.	Reduction: Size, Final, B. W. G.	Reduction: Size, Final, Inches. B.	Ratio of final diam. to initial.
Rippers	26	45	306·8	5	·22	6½	·19	·86
				6½	·19	7½	·18	·95
8 size	22	45	....	7½	·160	9	·148	·87
	22	45	....	9	·148	10½	·134	·90
12 size	22	60	345·6	10½	·134	12	·12	·89
14 size	22	....	....	12	·109	13	·095	·87
	22	....	....	13	·095	14	·083	·87
	22	78	432	14	·083	15	·072	·87
	22	....	....	15	·072	16	·065	·99
16-inch blocks	16	90	377	16	·065	17	·058	·89
	16	90	377	17	·058	18	·049	·84
	16	....	....	18	·049	19	·042	·86
	16	....	....	19	·042	20	·035	·83
8-inch blocks	8	56	117·3	20	·035	21	·032	·91
	8	56	117·3	21	·032	22	·028	·87
	8	56	117·3	22	·028	23	·025	·89
	8	56	117·3	23	·025	24	·022	·88
	8	56	117·3	24	·022	25	·02	·91

Where great strength is sought the reduction may be twice or even two and a half times as great as this.

Draw-Plates, Figure 102, examples of whose composition are given in Table 115, are usually made of intensely hard steel, sometimes it is said of chrome or tungsten steel. For comparison examples of the composition of mint dies are given:

TABLE 115.—COMPOSITION OF WIRE AND MINT DIES.

No.	Authority.	Description.	Carbon.	Silicon.	Manganese.	Phosphorus.	Sulphur.	Tungsten.
1..	Metcalf.	Wire dies too soft	1·37	......	......	......	......	0·78
2..	"	" "	1·70	0·20	0·287	0·02	0·093	
3..	"	" best European	2·80	0·14	0·26	0·09	0·083	
4..	"	" " American, as good as No. 3	2·37	0·20	0·18	0·08	0·093	
5..	"	" very good	1·97	0·013	0·306	0·014	0·009	
6..	"	" "	1·09	0·119	0·356	0·019	tr.	
8..	Roberts.	Best mint dies	0·83	0·05	0·10	......	tr.	
9..	"	" "	1·07	0·06	0·13	tr.	tr.	
10..	"	Mint dies, apt to crack in hardening	0·79	0·18	0·24	0·01	0·01	Cu. 0·02
11..	"	" " "	1·19	0·29	0·15	tr.	tr.	
12..	....	Best American mint-dies, Foster's steel	1·20	0·17	0·28	0·004	0·029	

1 to 4, Trans. Am. Inst. Min. Engrs. IX., p. 549, 1881. Number 3 appears to approach the composition of Wootz, which, according to Chernoff, contains 2% of carbon, yet is malleable. Rev. Univ. 1877, I., p. 466. **5, 6.** Unusually good dies: good malleable cast-steel. The diameter of a coil of wire 1,160 feet long of 1% of carbon, drawn through such a die from .105″ to .092″, did not vary by 0·00025″. Trans. Am. Soc. Civil Engrs., XV., p. 203, 1887. **8 to 11,** W. C. Roberts, Chem. News, XLIII., p. 239, 1881; Jour. Iron and Steel Inst., 1881, II., p. 907. From number 8 200,000 florins were struck, while the normal output per die is 50,000. From 9 the average output is 54,000 pieces. **10** and **11** are apt to crack in hardening. Mint die steel is so soft as to take the impression from a bronze piece. I have a bronze coin struck from a die so prepared. Under a strong lens it is seen to be less sharp than common coins, but under casual observation it would probably pass unnoticed.

12. Mint die steel made by Alex. Foster & Co., Philadelphia. C. E. Barber (Engraver U. S. Mint at Philadelphia, private communications May 21st, July 31st, 1888), states that, after employing Jessop's steel, he introduced the use of Foster's steel in 1876. "It has proved superior to any other, giving us a far greater average per pair of dies than any steel ever used in this mint, and, so far as I am able to learn, our average is better than any of the mints in Europe." The composition here given was kindly determined by Messrs. Hunt and Clapp, of Pittsburg, for this work. The average output per silver-dollar die in 1887 was 312,307 pieces; 536,148 has been reached for an average in making bronze one cent pieces.

The wire-drawer himself makes the holes in his die, punching or "pricking" them: this is said to demand great skill, the least inaccuracy breaking the punch in the hole. As the die wears it is closed from time to time, say every few hours, by hammering the metal together around the small end of the hole.

[a] Jour. Iron and St. Inst., 1884, I., p. 227. Oest. Zeit. XXXII., p. 199.
[b] Stahl und Eisen VI., p. 182, 1886; Iron Age, April 1, 1886, p. 25.

Hard white cast-iron dies also are used for the coarser sizes of wire, say Number 9 B. W. G. and coarser. It might indeed be difficult to make holes in this material small enough for the very fine sizes of wire: the punching or pricking used in case of steel dies is hardly applicable to the white cast-iron. When the hole in a cast-iron die wears unduly large, it can be reamed out and used for the next larger size of wire.

The relative merit of cast-iron and steel dies for the coarser sizes is in dispute; each is used in important and intelligently conducted American mills.

When extreme accuracy is sought a sectional steel die may be used, the play between its sections being initially too small to cause a fin on the wire, yet such that, by gradually taking it up, the drawer can compensate for the wear which occurs in drawing a single long coil. Gems too may be used for accurate drawing. Their use is rare in this country, but much more common I am told in Britain.

The draw-plate is in some cases canted slightly to the rear, say by from 2° to 8°, to "kill" the wire, *i. e.* to prevent the tendency to spring out into an unmanageably large coil on removal from the drum: experiments in drawing wire for the Woodbridge gun tended to show that this was not strictly necessary.

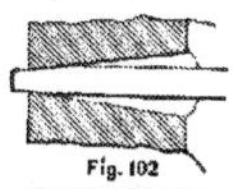

Fig. 102
Drawplate (Morgan).

§ 279. ANNEALING.—The coarser sizes of wire and any wire-rods which may have been rolled at so low a temperature as to render annealing desirable, are often annealed in muffles:[a] the finer sizes are annealed in pots (figure 103), which permit less oxidation. They are usually of cast-iron, sometimes of boiler-plate. The covers are often double, to exclude the air more completely. The annealing temperature may be about 700° to 800° C. (1292° to 1472° F.), and sometimes as high as 982° C. (1800° F.). In certain cases, *e. g.* immediately before galvanizing, wire may be annealed by passing through pipes, or between iron plates, each externally heated. (Figure 105).

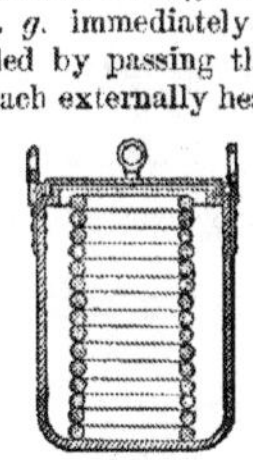

Fig. 103
Annealing Pot.

I have already pointed out that fine wire cannot well be annealed, its enormous proportion of surface leading to excessive oxidation in annealing and excessive corrosion and consumption of acid in pickling, its fineness making it hard to wash. In practice it is rare to anneal wire finer than 19 gauge, and in some mills none finer than 14 gauge is annealed (save of course the final annealing after the last draught in case of wire which is to be sold as annealed). Thus No. 33 wire must usually undergo 14 and sometimes 19 passes without annealing:[b] this is so trying that only the best, *i. e.* costliest, metal can be drawn to the finer sizes, and even then the loss by breakage is serious.

Even with coarser wire the loss of iron by corrosion, the consumption of acid for pickling, and the pollution of streams with the pickling liquor, are serious matters; the tendency of modern practice is towards less frequent annealing. In drawing from wire-rod to fine wire there were formerly as many as four annealings, to-day only two in the best mills. Wire-rods can now be rolled hot to 6 gauge in repeating mills such as Garrett's, and at least to 8 gauge in continuous (Bedson) mills: from the former size the wire can be drawn to 12 or even 13 gauge, from the latter to 14 gauge, without annealing.

The bad consequences of annealing just noticed are due to the oxidation which it entails: a non-oxidizing annealing is urgently needed not only that we may avoid them, but also for making wire which is to be at once bright and very tough: for many purposes a "bright annealed" wire is in demand. Hence the many devices for rendering annealing non-oxidizing, and for removing the oxide coating without pickling. Some of the former have at least succeeded in diminishing oxidation so far that a much less concentrated acid is needed for pickling, lessening the consumption of acid and loss of iron. Indeed, Bädeker[c] states that, when using new double-covered pots, many wire-drawers avoid pickling middle-sized wire (9 to 15 gauge?), the fine wire drawn from it being as bright as that from pickled wire. Of these devices we may note the following.

1. Mechanical devices for removing the scale.[d] In some of these the wire is bent back and forth *e. g.* as in Adt's apparatus, Figure 104, by passing between a series of rolls with parallel axes placed staggeringly, the wire being bent first vertically then horizontally. In others the wire is stretched up to its elastic limit, when much of the scale falls off. Employing a set of rolls for bending the wire Bädeker[e] uses only 6·5 pounds of 60° B. sulphuric acid per ton of wire.

2. Devices for diminishing the quantity of void in the annealing pots, *e. g.* by placing the coils of wire in annular spaces, by filling the voids with sand or infusorial earth, etc.

3. Filling the pots with non-oxidizing gases, carbonic oxide, producer gas, gas distilled from coal, horn, wood, etc., gas-yielding substances being sometimes enclosed in the pots, out of contact of the wire.

[a] Ovens heated from without, so that the charge within them is not exposed to the fuel nor to the products of its combustion.

[b] Though coarse wire is raised in some cases to above 230° C. (446° F., the melting point of tin) by the friction in the draw plate, yet fine wire remains so cool that it may be grasped in the fingers as it issues from the draw-plate: its highest temperature in drawing may not be above 180° F. (82° C.), at which no important annealing probably occurs. It is most improbable that the wire is materially hotter even at the instant when it is in the draw-plate, for we see no path through which heat can escape rapidly enough to account for a rapid fall of temperature after the wire has left the plate. Nor do we notice a very rapid rise of temperature as we slide our fingers along the departing wire towards the draw-plate.

[c] Bädeker, loc. cit. He exhibited coils of No. 21 wire (0·032″, 0·8mm.) which had never been pickled, even after leaving the rolling-mill, the rolling-mill scale probably having been removed mechanically, and serious oxidation having been avoided in the subsequent annealing.

[d] Wedding describes and illustrates many of these devices in Stahl und Eisen, VI., p. 14, 1886, No. 1.

[e] Idem, p. 182; Iron Age, April 1st, 1886, p. 25.

Nitrogen should be perfectly harmless and efficient:[a] hydrogen and hydrogen-bearing gases might be injurious.[b] Carbonic acid would oxidize the iron; and even carbonic

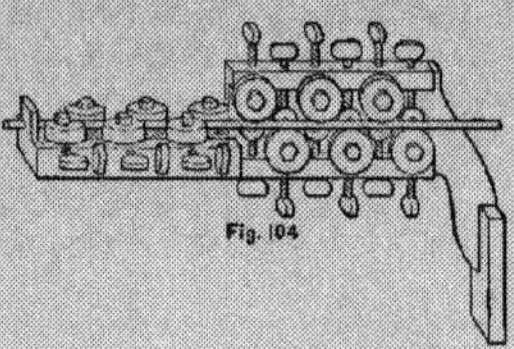

Adt's Apparatus for Removing Scale from Wire.

oxide would oxidize it slightly,[c] but perhaps so slightly that its effects would be wholly removed in drawing: it might be generated in the pots by enclosing charcoal in them, but this would have to be kept out of contact of the wire lest carburization occur. It has been proposed to generate carbonic oxide in the pots by placing calcite and coke or charcoal within them. So too the hot pipes used for annealing wire may be filled with non-oxidizing gases: but the wire will still oxidize in cooling unless protected, *e. g.* by passing at once into water.

4. Similar to the last is the plan of placing iron filings within the pots to consume the oxygen present, leaving an atmosphere of nitrogen. It is said to have given good results.[d] I suggest the use of iron sponge as a much more energetic and probably cheaper absorbent.

5. *Wrought-iron* or *steel* instead of cast-iron pots,[e] preferably enclosed in cast-iron ones to avoid injury by the flames.

6. By annealing in a bath of lead, which melts at 335° C. (635° F.) Wedding[f] would avoid oxidation. Bädeker[g] assails the project vigorously, holding that the wire would not grow hot enough to be annealed if passed through a lead bath of reasonable size at the speed employed in drawing: this may be true of wire-rod, but I doubt if it is of wire of moderate size. Apart from this, the lead would probably adhere to the wire in spots: this would be disastrous except when the wire was to be galvanized. Further, as iron acquires an oxide tint at 220° C. and becomes dark blue at about 316° C., more or less oxidation would certainly occur in cooling, unless the wire were specially protected after leaving the lead.

In certain cases where extraordinary strength is needed steel wire is hardened by quenching before receiving the final passes, but this causes a great loss of ductility. Hence for extreme strength combined with a moderate amount of ductility wire is better hardened after it has received its last draught. Armstrong[h] states that the elastic limit of wire is raised by careful annealing, though the tensile strength simultaneously falls, as in No. 17, Table 100, p. 210.

§ 280. Examples of Wire-Drawing.—Table 116 summarizes the general procedure in certain cases.

The practice in examples 6 to 9 is much better than that in the first five examples, while that in Number 10 is better still.

In drawing the wire for the Woodbridge wire-wound gun, annealed half-inch square open hearth rods of 0·31

a § 172, p. 106.
b § 178, A, p. 114.
c § 182, p. 118.
d Ichland, Stahl und Eisen, VI., p. 23, 1886.
e U. S. patent, 377,000, Jan. 24th, 1888, J. Withington: Iron Age, XLI., p. 274, 1888: Beckert, Leitfaden zur Eisenhüttenkunde, p. 404, 1885.
f Stahl und Eisen, VI., pp. 14, 183, 1886.
g Idem, pp. 181, 276. Iron Age, Apl. 1, 1886, p. 25.
h Rept. British Ass., 1882, p. 403. Cf. § 270, p. 214.

Table 116.—Examples of General Procedure in Wire-Drawing.

	Example 1.	Example 2.	Example 3.	Example 4.	Example 5.
Description of iron.	Bessemer steel of 0·45% carbon, for pins.	Bessemer steel of 0·15% carbon, for fencing.	Bessemer steel of 0·50% carbon, for coppering.	Charcoal iron for telephone wire.	Swedish iron for fine wire.
Initial size.	No. 6 rod.	No. 6 rod.	No. 5½ rod.	No. 6 rod.	No. 4. rod.
Procedure before first draught.	Pickle, wash, dip in flour-water, dry.	Pickle, wash, dip in salt, dry.	Pickle, wash, lacquer, coat, dry.	Pickle (?), wash (?), dip in flour-water (?).	Pickle, wash, dip in hot water, then in lust soin.
First set of draughts, Nos. B. W. G.	8, 9½ (drawn dry).	8½, 10½, 11½, 12½ (drawn dry).	8½, 9½ (drawn dry)	8½, 10, 11, 12 (drawn dry).?	6½, 8½ (drawn dry).
Procedure between first and second sets of draughts.	Anneal, pickle (?), wash (?), dip in flour-water, dry.	Coat with oil or zinc.	Pickle, wash, lacquer, coat, dry.	Anneal, pickle, wash, coat with flour.	Anneal, pickle, wash, dip in flour and lime-water, drain, dry.
Second sets of draughts, Nos. B. W. G	11½, 12½ (drawn dry).	....	10½ (drawn dry).	13, 14 (drawn dry ?).	10½, 11½, 12½ (drawn dry).
Procedure between second and third sets of draughts.	Anneal, pickle (?), wash (?), dip in flour-water, dry.	....	Lacquer.	....	Anneal, pickle, wash, dip in flour- and lime water, drain, dry.
Third set of draughts, Nos B. W. G	14, 15½ (drawn dry).	....	11 (drawn wet).	....	14, 15½ (drawn dry).
Procedure between third and fourth sets of draughts.	Anneal (?), pickle, wash (?), lacquer.	....	....	....	Anneal, pickle (?), wash, lacquer.
Fourth set of draughts, Nos. B. W. G	15½, 16½ (drawn wet).	....	....	....	16½, 17½, 18½, 19½ (drawn wet).
Procedure between fourth and fifth sets of draughts.	Anneal, pickle, wash, bat, lacquer.	....	....	....	Anneal, pickle, wash, bat, lacquer.
Fifth set of draughts, Nos. B. W. G.	17½, 18½, 19, 19½, 20, 21 (drawn wet).	....	....	....	20½, 21½, 23½, 24½, 27, 28, 31, 33, 34, 35, 36 (drawn wet).

		Example 6.	Example 7.	Example 8.	Example 9.	Example 10.
Description of iron.		Swedish iron for Western Union telegraph wire.	Bessemer steel of 0·10% carbon, for fencing.	Bessemer steel of 0·15% carbon, for fencing.	Bessemer steel of 0·10% carbon, for harvester wire.	Swedish iron for fine wire.
Initial size.		No. 4½ rod.	No. 5 rod.	No. 5 rod.	No. 5 rod.	No. 6 rod.
Procedure before first draught.		Pickle, wash, lime-coat, bake.	Pickle, wash, lime-coat, bake	Pickle, wash, lime-coat twice, bake.	Pickle, wash, lime-coat, bake.	Pickle, wash, lime-coat, bake.
First set of draughts	Nos. B. W. G.	5, 6 (drawn dry).	6½, 7½, 9 (drawn dry).	6½, 8, 9½, 10½, 12 (dry)	6½, 7½, 9 (drawn dry).	In 3 or 4 draughts to No. 12 (drawn dry).
	Reduction %	4, 8.	13, 12, 13.	....	18, 12, 13.	....
Procedure between first and second sets of draughts.		Anneal, pickle, wash, lime-coat, bake.	Muffle, pickle, wash, lime-coat, bake.	....	Muffle, pickle, wash, lime-coat, bake.	Anneal, pickle, wash, lime coat, bake.
Second set of draughts	Nos. B. W. G	7, 8 (drawn dry).	10½, 12 (drawn dry).	....	10½, 12, 13, 14 (drawn dry).	In 6 draughts to No. 18 (2 draughts dry, then lacquer and draw wet.
	Reduction %	1, 8.	14, 14.	....	14, 14, 13, 13.	
Procedure between second and third sets of draughts.		Anneal, pickle, wash, lime-coat, stand for 1 to 7 days, bake, galvanize.	....	....	Anneal, pickle, wash, bat, stand in water, immerse in "lees."	Anneal, pickle, wash, bat.
Third set of draughts	Nos. B. W. G.	....	....	....	15, 16, 17, 18, 19, 20 (drawn wet).	20, 21, 22, 23, 24, 25, 26, 27, 28, 29, 30, 31, 32, 33 (drawn wet).
	Reduction %.	....	....	....	13, 13, 11, 10, 11, 17.	9 - 11—9—11—7—17

Each column represents the procedure in some one case. The numbers in each horizontal line in a given column represent the size of the wire (gauge number) on emerging from passes which succeed each other without intervening treatment: the text indicates the operations between the last pass of the preceding and the first of the following line. Examples 1 to 5 from Freson, Rev. Univ. 2d Ser., XVIII., p. 1[illegible], 1885, "Les Tréfileries Américaines." Examples 6 to 10 from the author's notes.

to 0·32% of carbon were reduced to 0·15″ square wire in ten draughts *without annealing*, the corners of the wire being slightly rounded. The wire was coated with lime-flour paste and dried before each draught: after the second draught (and apparently after all subsequent ones) the wire was lacquered before the lime-flour coating was applied. The speed of drawing varied from fifteen feet per minute for the first to twenty-seven for the last draught. The ratios of reduction and the absolute reductions were as follows:

TABLE 117.—REDUCTION IN DRAWING GUN-WIRE (METCALFE).

No. of draught.	Initial size.	1.	2.	3.	4.	5.	6.	7.	8.	9.	10.
Assigned size, inches	0·5	0·445	0·394	0·349	0·310	0·274	0·243	0·215	0·191	0·169	0·150
Reduction, per side, inches	......	0·055	0·051	0·045	0·039	0·036	0·031	0·028	0·024	0·022	0·019
Reduction, ratio	......	·89	·885	·886	·888	·884	·887	·885	·884	·883	·888

The dies were 1·75 inches thick: the holes were tapered, about 1 in 5, at the outside face, but square and straight through the inner half of the plates thickness.

Though the wire was of admirable material, there were so many breakages that the scrap and defective wire were estimated at fully ten per cent. of the total weight: hence the conclusion that this is about as severe treatment as iron can successfully endure. (The scrap appears to have been chiefly pieces weighing less than twenty pounds).[a]

§ 281. PROTECTIVE COATINGS.—*A copper coating* is given by dipping the coiled wire in acid, washing this off in water, then immersing the wire for a few seconds in a copper-sulphate solution acidulated with sulphuric acid, when copper precipitates on the iron. The wire is then drawn to brighten it. It is then sometimes again copper-coated and further drawn.

For galvanizing the wire is usually first annealed, *e. g.*, by passing through an iron muffle as at A, in Figure 105.

It passes thence immediately into a bath B of say hydrochloric acid, and thence through a bath of molten zinc in an iron kettle[b] D, thence through a notch in a pair of pincers E (Figure 105 and Figure 106) in which the excess of zinc is scraped off: thence finally to a power-driven drum F, on which it is coiled. The scraping pincers may readily be opened, to allow the joint between successive coils of wire to pass. In practice several wires side by side, each guided by its own set of sheaves, G, H, and coiling on its own drum F, pass through these baths simultaneously.

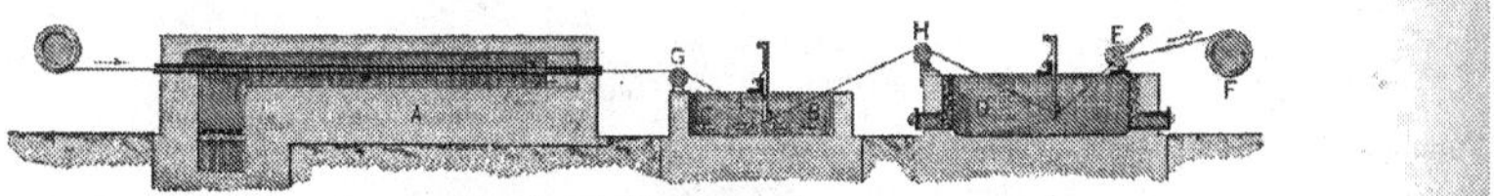

Figure 105.—Galvanizing Plant (Bockert).

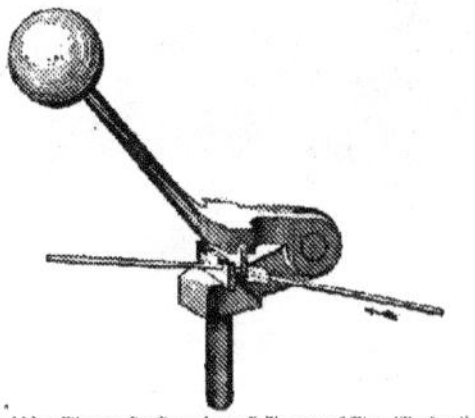

Fig. 106.—Pincers for Scraping off Excess of Zinc (Beckert).

Tinning is usually applied to finer wire which does not need annealing: otherwise the procedure is much the same as in galvanizing. The wire is passed through a bath of acid, thence directly into one of molten tin, thence through pincers which scrape off the excess of tin, thence through a bath of castile-soap water, thence to the drum on which it is coiled. The soap coating is to prevent the wire from turning black. The wire is often further drawn after tinning, to give it a bright coat.

§ 282. TESTS FOR WIRE.—Besides the usual tensile tests, wire for rope and many other purposes is tested for flexibility. This property is usually gauged by the number of times the wire can be kinked, as in Figure 107, and straightened. This very crude test evidently offers great temptation for trickery, and must give way to more trustworthy methods, such as that of bending back and forth 180° between round-cornered iron cheek-pieces (Figure 108) which grasp the wire firmly, so that successive bendings

Fig. 107.—Kink-test for Wire

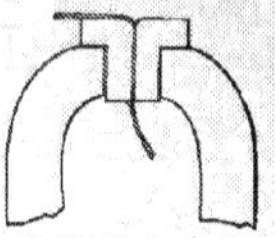

Fig. 108.—Bending test for Wire.

must occur at the same spot. The free end of the wire is held in pincers, so that rotation of the wire around its own axis may be prevented. Table 118 gives the number of bends required by the German government in case of rope wire.

TABLE 118.—BENDINGS (FIGURE 108) REQUIRED BY THE GERMAN GOVERNMENT FOR ROPE WIRE.*

Diameter of wire, inches	·122	·11	·098	·076	·070	·062	·055	·049
Size of wire, B. W. G. #	11	12	13½	14½	15½	16½	17½	19½
Number of bends required, for hard steel	6@7	7@8	8@9	12@14	14@15	15@16	16@17	17@18
Number of bends required, for ingot- and weld-iron	4@6	5@7	5@7	7@8	7@8	8@9	10@12	12@14

* Communicated by Mr. E. Gibbon Spilsbury, Managing Director of the Trenton Iron Company.

COLD-ROLLING AND COLD-DRAWING.

§ 283. IN COLD-ROLLING[c] the previously pickled bar is passed repeatedly between highly polished chilled cast-iron rollers, the reduction being controlled by frequent calipering. The general disposition of the roll-train is the same as for hot-rolling, but permits unusually accurate adjustment of the rolls. Round bars are rolled over and over in the same groove, and rotated slightly between passes, for of course only a short arc at the top and bottom of the groove can conform accurately to the sec-

[a] Metcalfe, Rept. Chief Ordnance, 1885, pp. 436, 473.

[b] Concerning the zinc-iron alloy which collects in this kettle C F, § 145, p. 84. As the alloy collects at the bottom, the kettle is heated on its sides but not from beneath.

[c] Bernard Lauth, U. S. patent 31,546, Feb. 26th, 1861.

tion aimed at. Thus, at one mill, round bars receive on an average from 30 to 40 passes each, with a total reduction in diameter of about $\frac{1}{32}$ inch when less than three inches in diameter, and about $\frac{1}{16}$ inch when larger.[a] The output from each stand is evidently chiefly dependent on the circumferential velocity of the rolls, and on the accuracy of section aimed at, for great accuracy demands not only very careful calipering but very many passes, with very slight rotation between each pass and the following. In practice extreme accuracy is generally needed, for the round bar must generally be in "wring fit," *i. e.*, it must fit the coupling or other piece which is to receive it so closely that, while it cannot be readily slid or pushed on, it can be wrung on. With section accurate to within $\frac{1}{1000}$ inch, this mill turns out about 1000 running feet, or say 50 bars, per train of rolls per shift.

Freson[b] gives the following details of practice at an American mill. After pickling in liquor composed of ten parts of water and one of sulphuric acid of 60° B, the bars are dipped in lime-water, dried, and rolled repeatedly through a single groove, with reductions of from $\frac{1}{350}''$ to $\frac{1}{150}''$ at a pass There are three roll-trains of the following dimensions:

TABLE 119.—TRAINS FOR COLD-ROLLING AT AN AMERICAN MILL.

	Number of stands.	Distance between centres, inches.	Revolutions per minute.	Circumferential velocity, feet per minute.	Product.
1st train.......	4 stands + 1 polishing stand	18″	40 @ 45	188′ @ 212′	Rounds, 1½″ @ 4½″ diameter.
2d train.......	2	12″	40 @ 45	126′ @ 141′	Rounds, ¾″ @ 1½″ diameter.e
3d train.......	1	10″	60 @ 60	131′ @ 157′	Rounds, ¼″ @ ¾″ diameter.
	1	12″	50 @ 60	157′ @ 188′	Flats and squares.

e Given as 5·4″ @ 1½″ in the original, but probably by typographical error.

Some of the details of rolling are as follows:

TABLE 120.—COLD-ROLLING AT AN AMERICAN MILL, CONCLUDED.

Diameter of bar, initial, inches	2·56	1·5	0·75
Diameter of bar, final	2·36	1·38	0·63
Reduction of diameter, %	8%	8%	16%
Number of passes	42	30	31
Time occupied, minutes	28	13	15
Men employed	3	3	1, + 1 boy
(Freson's data end here)			
Men × minutes	84	39	22·5

Average men × minutes = 48·5 or 24 25 cents per bar, assuming that eight effective hours work cost $2.40.

The degree to which cold-rolling may be carried is indicated by the results of the following experiments.[c] Thoroughly annealed open-hearth steel bars, apparently containing 0·31 to 0·32% of carbon[d] and 4·5 inches square, were to be reduced to 3·43 inches square in the fewest possible passes. Rolls 22 inches in diameter and 18 inches long were employed. The first pair of rolls tried had a single groove 2·42″ deep (the semi-diagonal of 3·43″) in each roll, with an angle of 91°, and closed with a fillet of 0·17″ radius. The lower roll broke through the bottom of the groove after 24 passes on a 12 foot bar, reducing at the rate of 82 passes per inch (*i. e.* such that 82 passes would reduce the side of the square by 1″) and 6 passes at the rate of 120 per inch. The failure was attributed chiefly to the sharpness of the corners of the bar, which cut into the roll, and this sharpness in turn (A) to the depth of groove, which increased the drag of the bar on the bottom of the groove, (B) to the short radius of the fillet, and (C) to the small angle (91°) of the groove.

The second pair of rolls had two grooves 1·9″ deep, with an angle of 93°, and a fillet of 0·3″ radius. After rolling five 24-foot bars with a reduction of 109 per inch, the upper roll cracked in two through the bottom of the groove with very little warning, showing a chill 5″ to 6″ deep: the failure was attributed to excessive depth of chill. A third set of rolls, apparently like the second, but with a guaranteed chill of two inches, rolled seven 24-foot bars without mishap or apparent injury, reducing at the rate of from 132 to 140 passes to the inch. These results are here condensed.

TABLE 121.—EXPERIMENTS IN COLD-ROLLING 4½″ STEEL BARS.

Expt. No.	Description of rolls. Grooves. No.	Depth.	Angle.	Fillet radius.	Depth of Chill.	Performance.	Passes per 1″ reduction.	Result.
1.	1.	2·42″	91°	0·17″	....	1 bar { 24 passes, + 6 " }	82 / 120	Roll broke.
2.	2.	1·36″	93°	0·30″	5″ @ 6″	5 24′ bars.	109	Roll broke.
3.	2.(?)	1·5″	96°(?)	0·30″(?)	2″ estimate.	7 24′ bars.	132 @ 140	No accident: roll intact.

§ 284. COLD-DRAWING.—Previously pickled steel and iron bars, round, square, hexagonal, etc., are drawn cold through a die to strengthen them, raise their elastic limit, polish them, and give them accurately uniform section. The bar in emerging from the die tends strongly to warp, and to lessen this tendency Billings' self-centring apparatus[e] is devised. As this is the best-known apparatus, let it suffice as an example of the general procedure.

The end of the rod R, having been hammered down so that it may pass through the die S, is grasped by the clutch *a*, which is shown in transverse section in Figure 110, and is practically a pair of wedges like those of common iron-testing machines, with semi-cylindrical toothed recesses for grasping the rod. The draw-bar E, moved by a hydraulic cylinder, then pulls the clutch to the right, drawing the bar through the die. In the device shown the die-seat *f* rests on four rollers *c*, and is tipped so as to centre the die by four set-screws *m m*, of which only two are here shown. In another arrangement the die-seat is hung in gimbals on knife-edges, and in still another the spherical-ended die-seat rests in a spherical recess in the draw-bench, forming a ball-joint. In both cases the die may be centered by set-screws as in Figure 109, or may be allowed to centre itself.

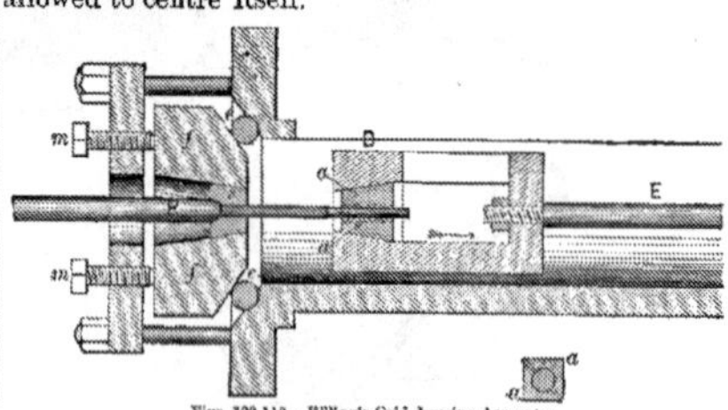

Figs. 109-110.—Billing's Cold-drawing Apparatus.

In spite of these expedients the bar usually becomes slightly bent in drawing, the camber in many bars which I have seen varying from nothing to 1·5 inches in 20 feet, estimated by the eye. The bar is next straightened by passing it between three horizontal rollers.

a Private communication from the management, June 27th, 1888.
b Revue Universelle, 2d ser., XVIII., p. 338, 1885.
c Medcalfe, Rept. Chf. Ordnance, U. S. Army, 1885, p. 469.
d Idem, 1884, pp. 432-3.
e U. S. patents 130,465, G. H. Billings, Feb. 26th, 1872: 295,898, C. C. Billings, April 1st, 1884. Engineering and Mining Jl., XXXV., p. 222, 1883. Revue Universelle, 2nd ser., XVIII., p. 351, 1885; Stahl und Eisen, VI, p. 177, 1886.

On an output of six tons about ten men are employed: this includes

Two at each drawing press	
Two straighteners	2
Machinist	1
Pickling	2
Other	1
Total	10

Details.—At an American mill bars from ⅜ to 3 inches in diameter are thus drawn, of round, square, and other simple sections. The usual reduction is about 1-16 inch, but occasionally as much as 3-16 inch per draught. The total reduction is usually effected in one, but occasionally in two draughts. There are two drawing benches, with hydraulic cylinders 15 inches and 8 inches in diameter respectively, with a stroke of about 23 feet, and with hydraulic pressure of about 600 pounds per square inch. Their capacity, which greatly exceeds that of the rest of the department, is estimated roughly at 20 tons per shift, or rather more if running chiefly on the larger sizes. The engine which furnishes the power is so small that about 2 min. 30 sec. are required to draw bars of the larger sizes, and the return stroke takes 1 min. 30 sec.: add 20 sec. for attaching the clutch, and we have a total of 4 min. 20 sec. Mr. Billings assures me, however, that there is no difficulty in drawing at the rate of 1 min. or even less per draught. The dies are made of hard carbon-steel, which has proved more suitable than Mushet's. In drawing about 2,000 running feet, or 100 bars, the diameter of the die becomes enlarged by about 0·001 inch. It is then slightly closed by heating and hammering, and dressed on a conical emery wheel to the exact size desired. The cost of hammering and dressing each die is estimated at ten cents, or at 0·1 cent per bar drawn.

Cold-Rolling and Cold-Drawing Compared.—The following very rough calculation, necessarily based in large part on estimate, aims solely to compare these two processes, and does not take into account items of cost which are substantially the same in each, such as pickling, straightening, and cutting to length.

I have no direct means of comparing the cost for power, repairs and interest, but from general knowledge of the two processes I believe that it is much higher for rolling than for drawing. Still, let us assume that they are equal, and further let us take the actual time of drawing with the present somewhat tentatively constructed plant and with insufficient power, assuming, however, that operations are on a large scale, so that the time of the men who hammer down the ends of the bars and cut off the ends in lathes is fully employed.

The waste is greater in cold-drawing than in rolling, because the end which is hammered down to enable it to enter the die must be cut off at any rate. Taking this excess at 1·5 pounds per bar, and charging 1¼ cents per pound for the difference between the value of scrap and of the bar ready for drawing, we arrive at 1·87 cents per bar as the amount chargeable to cold-drawing.

	Min.	Cents.
Debit of cold-drawing, per bar.		
Excess of waste		1·87
Hammering down the end of the bar, 1 man 2 minutes	2	
Drawing, 2 men 4·5 minutes	9	
Cutting off the end of the bar, 1 man 2 minutes	2	
Total, minutes	13	
13 minutes at $2.40 per 8 effective hours work = 0·5 cts. per minute		6·50
Cost of dressing die, 10 ÷ 100		0·10
Total debit		8·47
Credit, outlay of labor in cold-rolling 48·5 minutes, at 0·5 cts.		24·25
Balance to credit of cold-drawing, cents per bar		15·78

So heavy a balance as this can hardly be outweighed by other unknown differences. Indeed, leaving all estimates aside, it is hard to believe that, with equally careful management, the cost of a single draught can equal that of many passes through rolls, increased by the necessity of frequently calipering the bar. Freson seems to think cold-drawing more expensive than cold-rolling[a]: I think he is mistaken.

PUNCHING AND SHEARING.

§ 285. PUNCHING produces in iron a veritable flow, the particles of metal moving away from the approaching punch in their paths of least resistance. The upper surface is drawn down somewhat like the surface of water over a submerged outlet, as shown in Figure 111. Of the metal initially in the path of the punch a part, whose proportion to the whole seems to vary directly as the thickness of the bar and inversely as the diameter of the hole, and which sometimes amounts to 60% of the whole, is forced laterally, bulging the piece, while the rest is driven directly before the face of the punch as a core. The flow and the small proportion which the rejected core bears to the volume of the hole are illustrated in Figure 112. The natural supposition that the pressure gives the ejected core a density greater than that of the mother-block is incorrect. Indeed, D. Townsend found the density of core and block 7·78 and 7·82 respectively, a difference far beyond the limits of experimental error in careful work.[b]

Figure 111.—Flow of Metal in Punching.

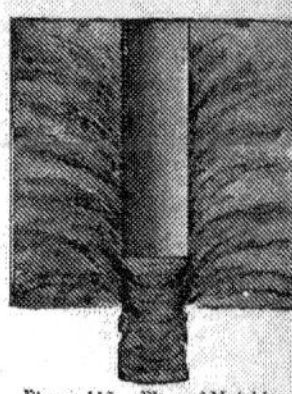

Figure 112.—Flow of Metal in Punching.

Punching usually lowers the strength and ductility of the mother-metal, the loss, at least in case of tensile strength, increasing

1, with the distance of the hole from the edge of the piece, at least in case of soft steel;

2, probably with the proportion of carbon;

3, probably also with the initial hardness of the piece, however caused;

4, with the thickness of the piece; and,

5, as the clearance between punch and die decreases.

The influence of clearance-size seems to decrease with the ratio of width to thickness of bar.

Supporting evidence will be offered shortly.

We can usually remove these effects completely either by heating (whether with fast[c] or slow cooling), or by reaming or countersinking the hole: and perhaps partially, at least in case of thin plates, by hot-riveting, the heat of the rivet causing a partial annealing. But rivet-

[a] Op. Cit., p. 353. "Les Chiffres de la main-d'oeuvre et de l'entretien ont une part plus considérable dans le prix de revient," in cold-drawing than in cold-rolling.

[b] Journal Franklin Inst., CV., p. 145, 1878.

[c] Needless to say, fast cooling sets up new conditions, which, however, are nearly if not quite independent of the previous punching, whose effects are effaced in beating.

TABLE 121 A.—PUNCHING: ITS EFFECTS AND THEIR REMOVAL BY REAMING AND BY ANNEALING.

Number.	Authority.	I. Width (inches)	I. Thickness (inches)	I. Carbon %	Material	Punching: Punch, diam.	Punching: Clearance.	II. Tensile strength, pounds per square inch.	II. Elongation %	II. Elongation inch's	III. Diameter of drilled hole, in.	III. Drilled test-piece Width	III. Drilled test-piece Thickness.	III. Tensile strength pounds per square inch.	III. Elongation %.	III. Percentage of gain of tensile strength by drilling.
1	Ba.	1·95			Ingot-iron and steel.	·66	·02									
2	"	2·34	0·31			·63					·70	2·34	0·31	69,933		
3	"	1·75	0·46			0·66					·66	1·75	·46	77,016		
4	"	2·24				·66					·66			99,770		
5	"	1·95												67,229		
6	"	2·34												61,802		
7	"	2·34				·66					·65			77,190		
8	K.		·129	·15		·77		74,915	10·8	10	·77			81,050	5·7	8·2
9	"		·250	·15		·77		60,480	28·2	10	·77			66,950	14·1	10·7
10	"		·380	·15		·77		51,430	30·1	10	·77			57,250	17·2	11·3
11	"		·495	·15		·77		55,938	36·4	10	·77			63,120	18·7	18·1
12	"		·625	·10		·77		52,924	37·2	10	·77			59,030	19·0	11 5
13	G.	2·00	·510	,12		·69		64,200	25·15	8						
15	Be.					·75					·75					+ 6·8
16	B.	8·	·812			1·09		62,720			1·09	8·	·812	60,216		10·4
17	BG.	1·1	·5&	,12		·5		65,368	24·38	8	·5	1·	·5 &	61,370	5·19	− 8·05
18	"	1·1	·625	·36@·5		·5		121,856	13·56	8	·5	1·	·625	98,896	0·76	− 18·84
20	W.		·36			·75		59,300	22·	8						
21	"		·26			·62		12,128	20·5	8						
22	"					·875		66,528	23·5	8						
23	P.		·7 ±			1·12	·08	60,592			1·12		,675	64,835		
24	"		·7			1·1	·12	62,474								
25	"		·7			1·	·17	62,474								
27	"		·75			1·09 / 1·08	·04 / ·08	59,136								
30	Ba.	2·34			Wrought iron.	·74					·74			37,946		
31	Be.					·75		54,970			·75			50,582		+ 2·0
32	T.					·31		50,820			·31			59,240		+ 2·0
33	"					·47		60,830			·47			65,020		+ 6·6
34	"					·63		61,550			·63			69,070		+ 11·9
35	"					·78		60,690			·78			67,680		+ 9·8
36																+ 6·2
37	P.		·70 ±			1·08	·05 / ·08	44,021			1·14			42,806		− 4·0
38	"		·74			1·1	·08 / ·11	52,237			1·16		,74	50,557		− 8·

Number.	IV. Tensile strength pounds per square inch.	IV. Elongation %.	IV. Percent'ge of gain (+) or loss (−) of tensile strength relative to Solid metal.	IV. Drilled metal.	V. Thickness of reaming, inches.	V. Tensile strength pounds per square inch.	V. Elongation %.	V. Percent'ge of gain (+) or loss (−) of tensile strength relative to Solid metal.	V. Drilled metal.	V. Diameter of reamed hole inches.	VI. Tensile strength pounds per square inch.	VI. Elongation %.	VI. % of gain (+) or loss (−) of tensile strength relative to solid metal.
1	57,924				·089	73,195				·738			
2					·085	67,648			− 3·97	0·70			
3	62,227			− 19·34	·04	76,205			− 1·82	0·66			
4											96,928 hard'n'd		
5	54,858			− 18·39							66,080		
6	49,024			− 20·66									
7											74,794 hard'n'd		
8	12,470	8·2	− 8·39	− 10·39							65,710	10·8	− 5·09
9	59,870	9·6	− 1·01	− 10·58							58,450	14·6	− 2·00
10	51,480	13·5	**+0·40**	− 9·79							50,470	18·1	− 1·18
11	41,250	3·2	− 20·15	− 29·95							51,840	19·3	**+0·98**
12	38,370	1·9	− 26·33	− 33·98							60,040	20·7	− 0·79
13	55,000		− 14·33		·089 ·18	65,560		**+2·12**					
15			− 6·5		·06			**+5·9**		·75			
16	47,376		− 24·47	− 21·55							66,080		
17	51,360	2·38	− 17·24	− 9·47	·08	63,250	4·38	**+1·4**	**+ 4·6**		65,511	4·95	
18	72,210	0·22	− 40·79	− 26·95	·06	105,511	0·44	−13·36	**+ 6·8**		107,811	0·58	
20	61,600	3			·10	72,800	4·				64,900	6·	
21	61,600	1·									75,712	5·	
22	58,240	2·			·12	72,240	4·				71,980	4·	
23	51,841		− 17·8		·12	64,894				1·12	64,915		
24	54,791		− 12·3		·14	57,546		− 1·9		1·15			
25	47,190		− 24·5										
27	44,800 / 41,866		−24·2 / −28·7		·12	68,168		+ 5·8		1·12	71,080		
30	33,261			− 12·31	·04 / ·08	35,526 / 38,528			**+1·50**	·74 / ·74			
31	43,747		−20·5	− 22·09	·06	50,627		**+3.**	**+0·10**	·75			
32	48,120		−19·6		·04	58,380		−3·8		·35	67,930		− 8·4
33	51,308		−15·7		·04	61,999		+2·1		·51	61,130		+ 0·5
34	52,890		−14·1		·04	64,740		+7·4		·67	66,730		+ 8·5
35	54,480		−11·4		·04	65,170		+8·1		·83	61,440		+ 6·2
36			−15·2										+ 1·7
37	35,616 / 34,922		−20 / −22							1·16	42,851		− 4.
38	40,746 / 42,403		−18·8 / − 8·3		·13	47,421		−9·2					

1 to 7, Barba, Holley, Use of Steel; 1 to 5, Terre Noire Bessemer steel plates; 6 and 7, La Creusot open-hearth steel plates.
8 to 12, Kirkaldy, Experiments on Fagersta Steel, Series 2. Bar 12·5 inches wide had three rows of five 0·77-inch holes punched across them, thus removing 36·96 of the width of the piece.
a The percentage of loss for column VI. is obtained by comparing the punched-annealed with the solid annealed metal, because the metal, which was unannealed when punched, is weakened greatly by annealing.
To avoid complicating the Table, I omit the properties of the drilled-annealed metal.
13, Gatewood, Rept. U. S. Naval Advisory Bd. on Mild Steel, 1886, p. 170. The results under punched metal reamed refer to punched metal countersunk through. When the countersinking was stopped.
15, P. D. Bennett, Journ. Iron and St. Inst., 1886, I., p. 378, from Proc. Inst. Mech. Eng., 1886, pp. 44-61.
16, Boyd, Jeans "Steel," from Proc. Inst. Mech. Eng., 1878.
17, 18, Beck-Guerhard "On the Influence of Punching Holes in Soft Steel," 1884 Russian Mining Jl. My statements are based on a translation sent Mr. T. Cooper by the author. Journ. Iron and Steel Inst., 1884, I., p. 290, has an abstract, with many incorrect numbers. No. 17 is the mean of six sets of results, No. 18 of two sets.
20 to 22, Basic Bessemer steel: White, "On some Recent Experiments with Basic Steel," Excerpt Trans. Inst. Nav. Arch., 1887, p. 15.
23 to 27, Parker, Trans. Inst. Nav. Arch., XXVII., p. 418, 1886. From Rept. for Lloyds Register, March 28th, 1878. 23-5, Cammell's Steel; 27 Bolton Steel:
30, Barba, Op. Cit., p. 45. Wrought-iron Plates.
31, Bennett, Loc. Cit., Wrought-iron.
32-5, Lowmoor Wrought-iron Plates, Tetmajer, Stahl und Eisen, VI., p. 173, 1886. All except the drilled specimens were cut from the same plate. The gain of tensile strength due to drilling is obtained by comparing the drilled pieces with untreated pieces from the same plate, whose properties I do not give.
37, 38, Parker, Loc. Cit., 37, Seaward's best best iron boiler-plates; 38, Cammell's best best iron plates.

TABLE 122.—EFFECTS OF PUNCHING.

No.	Material	Dimensions of test-pieces, etc. Width, inches.	Thickness, inches.	Conditions of punching. Diameter, inches Of punch.	Of die. Conical.	Of die. Cylindric'l	Tensile strength, pounds per square inch. Of untreated metal.	Of drilled test-piece.	Of punched test-piece. Conical punching.	Of punched test-piece. Cylindrical punching.	% loss of tensile strength on punching relative to Solid piece. Conical punching	Solid piece. Cylindrical punching.	Drilled piece. Conical punching.	Drilled piece. Cylindrical punching.
1..	Ingot-iron and steel.	1·24	0·27	0·66	0·82	0·76	62,440 estimated		71,075	60,490	+ 2·4	− 12·9		
2..		1·80			0·82	0·76			63,285	57,994	− 8·9	− 16·48		
3..		2·65			0·82	0·76			58,845	56,560	− 15·8	− 18·55		
4..		3·35			0·82	0·76			49,974	56,786	− 28·0	− 26·94		
5..		4·05			0·82	0·76			51,316	54 275	− 26·1	− 21·84		
6..		4·75			0·82	0·76			53,155	51,722	− 23·4	− 25·52		
7..		5·24	·26	·69	·74		71,837		66,035		8·1			
8..			·375	·84	·94		66,292		58,824		15 7			
9..			·47 ±	·97	1·11		64,910		47,891		26 2			
10..			·503	·96	1·1		66,192		48,837		33·8			
11..			0·5	0·89	0·87	0·75			72,867	58,240				
12..			·69	1·12				61,875	49,544				− 33·94	
13..		1	·39	·59		·70		67,209	56,082				− 10·67	
14..		1·2	·28	·39		·70		67,494	59,860				− 11·96	
15..			·45	·875			62,922		63,215					
16..	Wrought-iron.	1·24		0·66	0·81		39,715		37,654		− 5·2			
17..		1·95					"		37,886		− 5·9			
18..		2·62					"		33,824		− 14·8			
19..		3·35					"		32,973		− 17·0			
20..		4·05					"		33,180		− 16·8			
21..		5·26	1·16 ±	1·12	1·37	1·25	41,620 ±	41,620	37,878	34,956	− 9· ±	− 16·0 ±	− 8	− 16·0
22..		1·27	·875	·52		·52		97,76·	111·800				+ 14·40	
23..		1·02	·625	·32		·32		57 020	60,190				+ 5·60	
24..		·89	·625	·52		·52		57,650	64,100				+ 11·20	
25..		·77	·625	·32		·52		62,580	71,990				+ 15·50	

1 to 6, Barba, Holley, Use of Steel, p. 29. Terre Noire Bessemer steel plates.
7 to 10, Parker, Trans. Inst. Nav. Arch., XXVII., p. 421, 1886, from Report to Lloyd's Register, 1878. John Brown's steel.
11, Sharp, idem, 1868, p. 10.
12, Boyd, Jeans, Steel, p. 185, from Proc. Inst. Mech. Engineers, 1878.
13, 14, Jeans, Steel, p. 840. Steel plates from the John Cockerill Works, Seraing. 20, unannealed plates: 21, annealed plates. Each result is the mean of two.
15, Parker, op. cit. Steel from Motala Works, Sweden.
16 to 20, Barba, op. cit., p. 44. Wrought-iron plates.
25, Kirk, Trans. Inst. Nav. Arch., 1877, p. 303, wrought-iron plates.
22 to 25, Hoopes and Townsend, private print, p. 66. This series differs from series 1-6 and 20 to 24, in that the bars were of uniform width, 1·375 inches, when punched, their width being reduced after punching: while in the other series the bar was cut to the width stated before punching. The results are surprising, the more so as the punch fitted the die accurately, a condition which in other cases produces the greatest injury. Messrs. Hoopes and Townsend are makers of cold-pressed nuts, and offer these results as evidence that cold punching does not injure but improves iron. Each result is the mean of two.

ing may be expected in some cases to increase rather than lessen the effects of punching (§ 288). The results of many experiments are summarized in Tables 121A to 123.

TABLE 123.—EFFECT OF PUNCHING AND SUBSEQUENT REAMING ON SOFT INGOT-STEEL. HILL.

Carbon, %.	Size of test piece, inches. Width.	Thickness.	Unpunched. Tensile strength.	Unpunched. Elongation.	Unreamed. Tensile strength.	Unreamed. Elongation.	·02" radius reamed. Tensile strength.	·02" radius reamed. Elongation.	·03" radius reamed. Tensile strength.	·03" radius reamed. Elongation.	·04" radius reamed. Tensile strength.	·04" radius reamed. Elongation.	·06" radius reamed. Tensile strength.	·06" radius reamed. Elongation.
			Tensile strength in pounds per square inch, and % of elongation in 18 inches.		With a hole 0·75 in. in diameter punched, or punched and reamed.									
·30	2 in.	·25	78,200	20·2	62,400	5·6	86,806	19·0						
"	"	·37	88,300	19·6	60,800	5·0	85,900	17·9						
"	"	·50	88,400	17·3	59,100	4·7	83,200	11·2	88,300	16·0				
·40	"	·25	82,900	18·5	66,100	5·1	84,100	18·6						
"	"	·37	86,300	15·9	64,800	4·9	79,300	11·8	87,200	13·0				
"	"	·50	89,800	18·0	61,800	4·8	83,100	4·3	77,400	6·6	90,300	11·7		
·50	"	·25	86,700	14·7	74,900	5·4	76,100	5·0	83,900	13·9				
"	"	·37	88,500	16·1	71,200	8·6	74,100	4·1	79,900	8·7	88,800	11·9		
"	"	·50	91,800	11·4	69,300	2·5	70,900	2·0	78,700	8·0	81,400	4·7	92,900	10·0

Trans. Am. Inst. Mining Engineers, XI., p. 259, 1883.

From around the holes in steel plates, some punched, some drilled, Barba cut rings about 0·19 inches thick, Figure 113. Those from drilled holes A, B, C, could be completely flattened without cracking, and only cracked when partly reopened. They were no harder than the mother-metal. Those from punched holes cracked and broke when bent, as shown at D and E respectively, were harder under the file, and scratched their mother-metal. But if the punched hole first had 0·039 inches reamed from its sides, the ring now obtained could be completely flattened and brought back to the shape of Figure G before cracking. Again, rings cut from unreamed punched holes could, after annealing, be flattened and brought back to the shape of figure I before cracking; in other cases they were cut on a generating line, completely developed, and bent back as in Figure J so as to extend the original interior, without perceptible crack, though with further deformation cracks appeared.

But punching may be harmless or even beneficial. Thus Guerhard found that, under given transverse load, fourteen punched soft-steel fish-plates deflected 2·8% less temporarily and 3·1% less permanently than fourteen similar

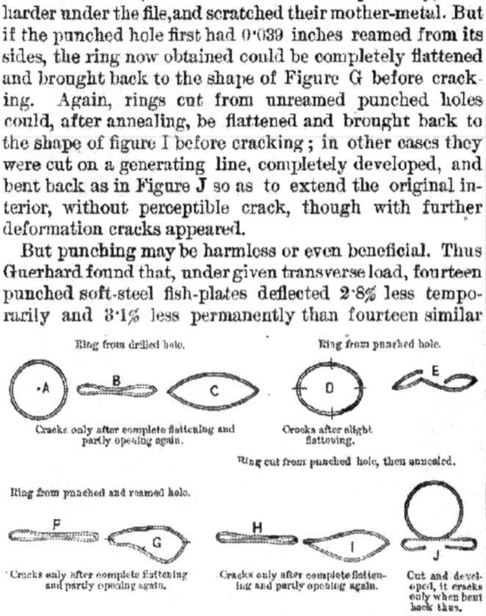

Figure 113.—Malleableness of Rings Cut from Around Punched, Drilled, and Reamed Holes. Barba. Three-fourths natural size.

drilled plates. Thurston found the stripping and bursting strength of many cold-punched wrought-iron nuts much greater than those of similar but hot-pressed nuts, the former excelling the latter in bursting strength on an average by 44% when blank and by 22% when tapped.[a] In Table 122, numbers 22 to 25 are reported to gain strength on punching.[b] Cooper found that the punched holes in soft steel and wrought-iron plates endured as much distortion by drifting as similar punched and reamed holes. As reaming removes the effects of punching one might infer that punching had not lessened the ductility of the metal around the holes. But a quite different explanation is offered in § 288. His results follow.

TABLE 124.—PERCENTAGE OF ELONGATION OF HOLES WHEN DRIFTED TILL THE METAL BEGINS TO CRACK.—(COOPER).

	⅝" steel plates. Max.	⅝" steel plates. Min.	⅝" steel plates. Avge.	⅝" iron plates. Max.	⅝" iron plates. Min.	⅝" iron plates. Avge.	⅝" steel angles. Max.	⅝" steel angles. Min.	⅝" steel angles. Avge.	⅝" iron angles. Max.	⅝" iron angles. Min.	⅝" iron angles. Avge.
Punched....	123	54	97	54	54	54	115	22	100	36	36	36
Punched and reamed....	100	33	106	46	45	46	106	33	73	24	24	24

The steel was very soft, its tensile strength being 56,000 lbs. per sq. in. The holes were enlarged by forcing a long tapered drift into them by sledging. Theodore Cooper, private communication, Sept. 7th, 1888.

Thousands of punched steel boiler-plates have been long in use, with relatively few mishaps. The boiler-plates of the United States vessels Boston, Atlanta and Dolphin were punched, those of the Chicago drilled: up to September 1st, 1884, only seven failures had occurred among the first three collectively, against eight among the last.[c]

§ 286. SHEARING produces effects similar to those of punching, and doubtless acts in similar way. Barba[d] found that soft steel strips, with one edge punched, the other sheared, when bent cracked at both edges under the same degree of distortion. The tendency to crack on the sheared as well as on the punched edge was removed by heating, whether with slow or quick cooling. Goodall found the metal lying within 0·03 inches ($\frac{1}{32}$") of the sheared edge of a steel plate as malleable as that of the unsheared plate; thus the effects of shearing, like those of punching, are restricted to a very thin shell.[e]

The effects of shearing and their removal are illustrated in Tables 16, p. 27, and 125.

TABLE 125.—EFFECT OF SHEARING AND COLD-HAMMERING AND OF SUBSEQUENT ANNEALING ON SOFT INGOT-STEEL. HILL.

Preparation of test piece. (All pieces ⅝" × 2" × 18".)	Tensile strength, pounds per square inch. ·3% C.	Tensile strength ·4% C.	Tensile strength ·5% C.	Elastic limit, pounds per square inch. ·3% C.	Elastic limit ·4% C.	Elastic limit ·5% C.	Elongation % in 13 inches ·3% C.	Elongation ·4% C.	Elongation ·5% C.
Cut in planer....	88,720	89,880	[illegible]	45,170	53,640	69,070	19·1	16·4	11·4
Sheared out....	69,375	75,400	82,930	31,280	41,250	49,960	11·3	8·3	5·2
Sheared, then annealed....	84,950	86,820	92,560	44,880	51,470	59,890	20·2	16·1	12·0
Hammered cold....	85,380	87,560	91,810	63,730	61,180	71,080	5·4	2·5	·7
Hammered cold, then annealed..	82,970	85,890	90,820	46,800	51,710	60,120	16·8	14·1	8·1

Trans. Am. Inst. Mining Engineers, XI., p. 259, 1883.

§ 287. DISCUSSION.—Now for evidence of the influence of the five variables noted at the beginning of § 285.

That of the first is shown in numbers 1 to 6 and 16 to 20 of Table 122. In each of these sets, width alone varying, the loss of strength on punching increases with it. Barba found this true not only of steel but of wrought-iron: of the latter Barnaby[f] found the reverse true, while agreeing with the other observers as regards steel.

That of the second is shown by the smaller percentage of loss in case of wrought-iron than of ingot-metal. But

[a] Hoopes and Townsend, private print.

[b] I deem it proper to state that these results are published by interested persons, and that the tests are not described so fully as to indicate whether full precautions were taken to make them comparable. Personally I believe that they are true.

[c] Gatewood, Rept. U. S. Naval Adv. Bd. Mild Steel, 1886., pp. 77-8.

[d] Op. cit., pp. 36-8.

[e] H. Goodall: Excerpt Proc. Inst. Civ. Eng., XCII., p. 13, 1888. Also Iron Age, XLI., p. 190, 1888. The malleableness was estimated by the distance through which a given drift-pin could be driven at fixed speed through washers cut from the steel plates, before splitting them.

[f] Jour. Iron and Steel Inst., 1870, I., p. 49.

in case of ingot metal of different percentages of carbon, though the results of general experience seem to support my statement, it is not readily verified from the evidence I offer. Of numbers 17 and 18 in Table 121A, the latter, the richer in carbon, is also the more injured: but in Table 123 the reverse is true. It is uncertain whether this is due to some unnoted variable (different proportions of manganese, silicon, phosphorus, different previous heat-treatment, or what not), or whether the injury, increasing as the carbon rises from ·10 to ·30% decreases with further rise of carbon from ·30 to ·50%. While further investigation alone can decide, I incline to the former as the more probable explanation.

The third is offered as a matter of general experience, not supported by direct experimental evidence. Indeed, number 20 of Table 122 suffers slightly more than number 19, from which it seems to differ only in being annealed before punching.

That of the fourth is shown by numbers 8 to 12 of Table 121A, among which the injury increases with the thickness, which is the only variable. Parker, too, found that, as the thickness of the plates rose from ·375 to ·5 and ·625 inches (⅜", ½" and ⅝" respectively), the loss of tensile strength on punching rose from 18% to 26 and 33%.[a]

That of the fifth is shown by numbers 1 to 6, 11 and 21 of Table 122. In each of these cases we have two experiments, differing only on the width of die or bolster: in all but two cases the wider die gives the smaller loss.

The influence of the greater clearance diminishes in numbers 1 to 6 with ratio of thickness to width, apparently disappearing when a width of 3·35 inches is reached. In number 21 this influence is again seen, though the bar is 5·26 inches wide, the greater thickness here apparently compensating for the increased width.

Turning now to the removal of the effects of punching, first note that in numbers 8 to 12, 15, 16, 31, and 32 to 5 of Table 121A the drilled piece is stronger than the untreated metal. This seems to fall under the general law that, for given section, the tensile strength of very short and especially of grooved pieces exceeds that of long ones,[b] in turn due to the more favorable disposition of the material in the grooved piece with regard to the lines of stress, rather than to the smaller chance of flaws existing in the short piece, for after the length increases beyond a certain point the decrease of tensile strength is less marked. Hence, in weighing the relative advantages of punching and drilling for most purposes, the properties of punched should be compared with those of drilled rather than of solid metal. Why the drilled is weaker than the solid metal in number 17 18, 37 and 38 of Table 121A is not clear.

The Influence of Heating is shown in column VI. of Table 121A. In every case in this column the punched metal, after heating, nearly or quite (as in 17 and 18) equals the drilled. In numbers 8 to 12 the properties of the annealed punched metal are compared with those of drilled and annealed metal, for the annealing itself greatly lowers these as well as those of the solid metal. In 4 and 7 the metal is quenched, in the other cases slowly cooled. Clearly it is the heating, not the rate of cooling, that restores the lost strength.

After Reaming (Col. V., Table 121A) the strength of the punched piece usually nearly equals or even excels that of both solid and drilled metal. Even when, as in numbers 2 and 32 to 35 only 0·03 to 0·04 inches is reamed from the sides of the punched holes, the restoration is nearly or even quite complete. But in Table 123 it appears that the thickness which must be reamed to remove the injury increases with the proportion of carbon and with the thickness of the plate, so that while a ¼-inch plate containing 0·30% of carbon is completely restored by reaming ·02 inches, to restore a ½-inch plate containing 0·50% of carbon ·05 inches must be removed. Gatewood found that countersinking, even if carried through only three-quarters of the thickness of the plates, removed about three-quarters of the injury due to punching.

In harmony with the effect of reaming punched plates is that of tapping cold-punched nuts, which removes about half the effect of the punching. (§ 287.)

The local nature of the injury is also shown by experiments by Barba[c] and by Beck-Guerhard,[d] in which they punched holes in steel plates, and then cut and tested strips from these plates, some in close proximity to the punched holes, others farther away: both found the metal's tensile strength and elongation as great near the hole as far from it. Indeed, certain features of Guerhard's results suggest that the metal around the hole was somewhat strengthened.

TABLE 126.—PROPERTIES OF STRIPS FROM PREVIOUSLY PUNCHED STEEL PLATES, THE STRIPS CUT AT VARIOUS DISTANCES FROM THE PUNCHED HOLE.

B = Barba, G = Guerhard.

Position regarding hole.		Farthest.	Nearer.	Nearer.	Close to.	Near.	Further.	Farther.	Farthest.
Tensile strength, pounds per square inch	B...	69,064	70,582	68,768	68,970				
	G...	60,135	57,680	60,028	61,448	61,958	61,981	57,484	63,213
Elongation, %	B...	21	21·5	21	21				
	G...	22·7	19·0	19·0	23·0	20·1	26·8	19·54	19·00

In Barba's experiments, one edge of the strip nearest the hole lay only 0·09 inches from the edge of the hole.

Doubtless, a certain flow occurs at considerable distances from the hole. On the surface of plates highly polished before punching, Guerhard noticed gently curving, eyelash-like lines, convex, felt by the fingers, running outwards for nearly two inches from the edge of the hole, making an angle of 45° with tangents drawn through their points of departure, and readily removed by acid. Cooper had previously described similar lines in the scale surrounding holes punched in iron.[e] Again, punching bulges the neighboring edges of plates, etc, though they lie at some distance from the edge of the punched hole. But the evidence already given shows that the action which causes this far-reaching flow does no considerable injury beyond a narrow ring.

Riveting, in Parker's experiments, increased the strength of punched steel plates 7/16-inch thick by about 4000 pounds per square inch, or say 6%, but it did not improve punched ¾-inch plates

In Bennett's experiments, parallel with numbers 15 and 31 of Table 311, riveting reduced the loss of strength due to punching from 20% to 10% in case of wrought-iron, but did not benefit steel.

In Snelus' experiments, punched unannealed riveted

[a] Proc. Inst. Naval Architects, 1878. Also Jeans, "Steel," p. 734.
[b] Compare Rept. U. S. Board on testing iron, steel, etc., I., p. 91 et seq.

[c] Op. cit. in note to No. 17, Table 121.
[d] Op. cit.
[e] Trans. Am. Soc. Civ. Eng., VII., p. 174, 1878.

joints were much weaker than the punched and annealed and than the drilled joints.[a]

The following experiment of Baker's[b] shows so serious a loss of strength in riveted punched plates that, though the strength of the unriveted punched plate is not given, it is probable that riveting annealed but slightly.

TABLE 127.—RESTORATION BY RIVETING. BAKER.[c]

Description of piece.	Solid.	Punched and riveted.	Drilled and riveted.	Punched and annealed.
Tensile strength............	78,108	67,608@66,633	77,218	79,223
Elongation in 8 in........ ...	23	3·1@2·2	8·2	6·2

J. Ward reports the following results:[c]

	Tensile strength, Pounds per sq. in.	Elongation, Inches.
Untreated plate........	66,301	0·15
Drilled plate........	71,393	0·24
Punched plate........	62,780	0·15
Punched and riveted plate........	60,440	0·10
Punched and galvanized plate........	62,948	0·09
Punched, galvanized and riveted plate........	65,620	0·11

These results, collectively, give little reason to believe that riveting removes materially the effects of punching.

Clearly, the available heat offered by the rivet, both heads included, bears a higher ratio to the volume of the ring to be annealed in thin than in thick plates.

§ 288. RATIONALE OF THE EFFECTS OF PUNCHING AND OF THEIR REMOVAL.—The complete restoration of punched plates by annealing, and the extreme endurance of distortion and the malleableness conferred by annealing on the initially brittle rings cut from around punched holes, show that punching does not usually act chiefly through causing incipient cracks. The restoration by reaming and other evidence indicates that the serious direct injury is confined to a very small ring. Evidently the metal in this ring is distorted and subjected to great pressure in punching: these are the essential conditions of cold-working: after punching it shows the usual characteristics of cold-worked iron, hardness, extreme brittleness, and, if we may judge from the lightness of the punched core, lower density than the hot-worked metal. That the tensile strength of this ring is also very high, like that of other cold-worked iron we infer from the much greater stripping and bursting strength of cold-punched than of hot-pressed nuts, the stress in both stripping and bursting falling in undue proportion on the metal within this ring: and further from the fact that the excess of bursting strength of the cold-punched over the hot-pressed nuts is far greater when they are blank than when tapped, the tapping removing a part of this strong ring.

We may thus conjecture that punching acts directly through cold-working this narrow ring, giving it much higher tensile strength and elastic limit but much lower ductility than the surrounding metal, which is probably affected in the same way but to a much lower degree. Punching in this view increases the average strength of the different layers taken individually, giving, however, a heterogeneousness of strength, elastic limit and ductility, which may be a source of strength or weakness, according to the conditions of stress, as pointed out in § 269.

In complete harmony with this view are the following observations of J. Ward.[d] In each of fourteen pairs of tests, apparently representing seven mild steel plates, (tensile strength about 65,000 lbs., elongation about 25% in 8″) the elongation of the test-piece cut from between rows of punched holes as in Figure 114 fell below that of similar test-pieces from untreated parts of the same plates, by from 1 to 8% of the initial length (eight inches), the average difference being 3·2%. But in only six out of the fourteen pairs was tensile strength of the test-piece from between holes greater than that of the untreated metal. In three out of four cases like test-pieces cut from between drilled holes, had less elongation than those from the untreated metal: this, however, seems to be an accidental variation.

In short, the strips cut from between punched holes had the same strength as the untreated metal, but stretched less.

Now, a glance at Figure 114 makes this clear. The metal near where the punched holes have been stretches less than the rest, presumably because its elastic limit has been raised by the cold-distortion during punching. Thus the elongation of the test-piece as a whole is lessened: but its tensile strength is not affected: for the tensile strength of the test-piece is that of its weakest section, to wit, the non-cold-worked parts A, B and C.

Fig. 114

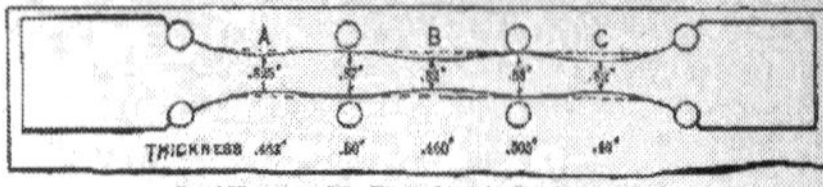

Local Elevation of the Elastic Limit by Punching. Ward.

Further corroborative of this view are the results of experiments of Barba's in which steel strips 0·46″ thick, Figure 114 A, were punched *partly* through at A, the punch being arrested when it had penetrated 0·39″, and so that 0·07 inches thickness remained. "No hole was completely taken out." The strips "dressed on their whole surface" when pulled yielded least in the region partly punched, rupture occurring at B where the punch had not acted.[e] Here the strengthening effect of the cold-working outweighs the weakening effect of heterogeneousness.

Fig. 114 A

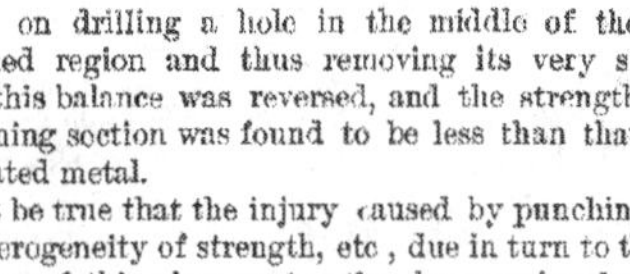

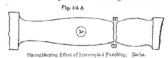

Strengthening Effect of Interrupted Punching. Barba.

But on drilling a hole in the middle of the partly punched region and thus removing its very strongest part, this balance was reversed, and the strength of the remaining section was found to be less than that of the untreated metal.

If it be true that the injury caused by punching is due to heterogeneity of strength, etc., due in turn to the cold-working of this ring, restoration by reaming becomes a matter of course, and by annealing a natural consequence, since annealing, if thorough, removes the effects of all forms of cold-working, solution of continuity of course excepted.

Regarding iron as a viscous liquid, the normal pressure EF of the punch is communicated in all directions, but more and more feebly as the direction departs from that of EF. In conical punching the direction of the pressure which

[a] Kirkaldy, Snelus, Journ. Iron and Steel Inst. 1879. II., pp. 642–3.

[b] The Use and Testing of Open-hearth Steel, etc., Excerpt Proc. Inst. Civ. Eng. XCII., p. 47. 1888.

[c] Trans. Inst. Nav. Arch. XXVII., 1886, p. 121. Each number is the mean of six results.

[d] J. Ward, Trans. Inst. Nav. Arch., XXVII., pp. 106–114, 1886.

[e] The Use of Steel, Barba, Holley, p. 55. I understand that this dressing on the whole surface was carried so far as to remove all visible distortion, whether depression, spreading, or otherwise, due to the punching, leaving the test piece of uniform cross-section. Holley's translation to which alone have I had access, states that the strips were 0·46″ *wide*, and the punch 0·74″ in diameter: but judging from the figure and description, it must mean 0·46″ thick.

falls on AB and CD is farther removed from that of EF than in cylindrical punching: clearly the tendency to force the metal from the block ABCD into the surrounding metal, and hence the pressure against AB and CD are less in Figure 116 than in Figure 115. In a thick plate the

FIGURE 115.

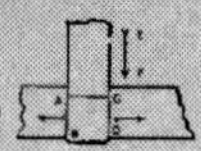

FIGURE 116.

total pressure on AC, and hence the resulting pressure on AB and CD, must be greater than in a thin plate. In a narrow plate the horizontal component of the pressure is readily relieved by the horizontal bulging of the strip as a whole, and the pressure on AB and CD thus lessened. Hence the greater injury in cylindrical than in conical punching, to thick than to thin, and to wide than to narrow plates. For the latter a further reason: as pointed out in § 269, p. 212, the strengthening of the cold-worked part should weigh the more heavily against the weakening due to heterogeneousness of strength, the larger the proportion of the whole sectional area which is cold-worked.

There is general and natural surprise that, in spite of the well-known injury which it does the testing-machine properties punching without reaming or annealing is habitually, successfully, and apparently safely used for both steel and iron boilers and many other important purposes. Not less surprising are Cooper's results, showing how greatly punched holes may be elongated by drifting before the metal cracks. The explanation of this last fact I know not: possibly the first blows on the drift set up a condition closely like that induced by punching, cold-working the ring immediately around the hole, and so quickly remove the initial advantage which the drilled holes had over the punched ones.

Of the apparent practical harmlessness of punching various explanations are offered, none of which seem wholly satisfactory.

The explanation that the structural and boiler plate steel now used is more ductile than that formerly made is beside the point: it will hardly be claimed that it is habitually more ductile than the most ductile steels of Tables 121A and 122, and it is in these that the injury to the testing-machine properties has been abundantly shown. Note the ductility of numbers 8 to 13 and 17 in Table 121. Numbers 8 to 13 in the latter table are from material which when unannealed gave 44·7 % of elongation in 4·5 inches, 61·7 % contraction of area, with 52,475 pound stensile strength and 28,300 pounds elastic limit.

The annealing effect of the heat imparted to the ring around the punched hole by the rivet is a possible but not a satisfactory explanation. In the first place, in the experiments recorded riveting does not seem to benefit thick pieces appreciably, and it is precisely these whose testing-machine properties are most injured by punching and which, therefore, we should expect to be especially treacherous in use. In the second place, we have seen in § 270, p. 214, that gentle heating, say to 300° C. (572° F., a blue oxide-tint), increases or at least accelerates the effects of cold-working, and should, if my explanation is true, still farther raise the elastic limit of the cold-worked ring around the punched hole, the heterogeneousness of elastic limit, and the bad effects of punching: and it may be doubted if any important part of the metal around the punched hole rises above this temperature in riveting. Baker found that the heat imparted by the rivet did not suffice to melt lead, nor even to evaporate water, in some small holes in a plate near the edge of the rivet-hole.[a]

Were we to contend that certain parts of certain plates in our boilers occasionally reach an annealing temperature, the apparent safety of the other plates not exposed to the heat and of punched structures (bridges, ships), etc., which never grow warm, would still confront us. Further explanations, neither of them satisfactory, are the excessive factor of safety (actually of ignorance) used, and that the properties which the metal is actually called on in practice to display are less injured by punching than the testing-machine properties.

Special Forms of Punch.—That the punch may attack the metal gradually, its face, instead of being plane, is sometimes made in steps, is sometimes helical (Kennedy's and others) and sometimes concave-cylindrical, formed by the intersection of a cylinder of large radius with axis perpendicular to that of the punch. Adopted primarily to lessen the stress on the punching machine, these expedients doubtless favor the metal as well. Webb reported the average strength of certain steel plates as 58,579 pounds per square inch when punched with common punches, but as 63,929 pounds when punched with Kennedy's, a difference of eight per cent. in favor of the latter.[b] The step punch, employed for many years in punching steel rails at the Troy Bessemer Works, gave surprisingly good results, but was abandoned years ago in favor of drilling.[c]

Smith's Dynamometer Punch, recording the pressure required in punching, aims to determine quickly and cheaply the hardness of the metal, and thus its fitness for its intended use. It has not come into use.[d]

§ 288A. PRACTICE AS TO PUNCHING.—*A. Structural Work.*—Many of our best bridge-engineers require all punched work to be reamed, say $\frac{1}{16}$ inch all around. Others permit punching without subsequent treatment for riveted work, provided that the punched hole can be increased 25% by drifting, without cracking either the hole or the sheared edge of the plate. But this practice may be regarded as the exception.

The Russian ministry of roads in 1885 forbad both punching and shearing.[e]

At the Forth bridge all work is drilled, and all sheared edges are planed.[f]

I am informed that the best German engineers rarely permit steel for bridges and other important structures to be punched without reaming or annealing, but do not require reaming or annealing in case of punched wrought-iron.[g]

B. *Land-boiler Plates* are generally punched without reaming or annealing. On the Pennsylvania Railroad locomotive boiler-plates less than ¾″ thick are thus treated:

[a] Discussion on "The Use and Testing of Open-hearth Steel," etc. Excerpt Proc. Inst. Civ. Eng., XCII., p. 47, 1888.

[b] Journ. Iron and Steel Inst., 1878, I., p. 143.

[c] R. W. Hunt, School of Mines Quarterly, IV., p. 228, 1883, Private Communication, Oct. 1st, 1888.

[d] Trans. Am. Inst. Mining Engineers, IX., pp. 204, 596.

[e] Eng. and Min. Jl., XLII., p. 93, 1886.

[f] B. Baker, Private Communication, Nov. 24, 1888.

[g] A. Martens, Private Communication, Nov. 1888.

thicker plates are drilled. In England drilling seems to be very much more common than here, in fact to be the rule while here it is the exception.

C. *Marine-boiler Plates*, being much thicker than those of land boilers, are usually drilled, and in the best works are drilled and countersunk in place. The drilling machinery is so excellent that in Britain it is not thought materially more expensive, in view of the greater accuracy of fit, to drill than to punch. Indeed Adamson came to this conclusion soon after 1862.[a] Most American boiler-makers, however, receive this statement with derision. The difference may be due to the more extensive use of gang-drills in Britain than here.

No punching without subsequent reaming or annealing is permitted in case of boilers for the United States navy.[b]

D. *Ship-work* is usually punched. The outer shell-plates are necessarily countersunk, which removes much of the injury due to punching, and some of the best builders ream or anneal the more important members. Yet some ship-builders of the highest standing in Britain and most of those in this country always punch without further treatment (except the countersinking just referred to). In France, too, the mother of drilling, only exceptional pieces are drilled.[c]

For the United States navy steel shell-plates are punched and countersunk: important steel pieces of hull-work are drilled: but many less important steel pieces are punched without subsequent treatment. No wrought-iron plates are used for the hulls, except for monitor-turrets, and these are punched without further treatment. Important wrought-iron pieces (not plates) for the hulls are usually punched without further treatment.[b]

E. Steel rails are always drilled in this country, and, so far as I know, in others

§ 289. Other Forms of Cold-Work.—*Frigo-Tension*, used by bell-hangers to give wire higher elastic limit, consists in subjecting the metal to intermittent stress somewhat above its elastic limit. On the first application the weakest parts stretch; during rest their elastic limit rises; on the next application the next weakest points stretch, gain in elastic limit during the second rest, and so on. The whole piece having been thus affected, on further treatment this succession of effects recurs, raising the elastic limit till it finally coincides with the ultimate tensile strength. Carry the treatment farther and rupture ensues.[d]

When great accuracy of pitch is needed, soft iron chains are treated by this process, being stretched exactly to the pitch sought, and under a stress greater than the expected working stress. The ultimate strength is simultaneously raised.[e]

Cold-hammering acts much like cold-rolling. Steel rods are reduced to wires (*e. g.* Stubs' wire) by rapidly repeated blows of light hammers striking over the whole circumference. The rod is reduced a little, say by $\frac{1}{16}''$ at each operation, and it is said that the whole reduction may be from $1\frac{1}{4}''$ to $\frac{1}{6}''$.[f] The thin shanks of sewing machine needles are in like manner swaged down from a wire by rapid hammering.

It is said that a given weight of wire yields by this method thrice as many needles as by the old method of reducing the diameter of the thinner part of the needle by grinding.[g] Cold-hammering polishes the metal highly, reduces it accurately and uniformly to the section sought, and doubtless raises its elastic limit.

Hammer-hardening.—According to Overman, surgeons' and engravers' instruments acquire, by hammering with a very small polished hammer, great hardness, a finer edge, and greater elasticity than can be given otherwise.[h] Whether this operation is actually practiced for these purposes I know not: but makers of these instruments whom I have asked have never heard of such a procedure, believe that it would not be effective, and actually harden their instruments in oil after heating to redness in a gas-jet, as I know by observation.

Dean's Process[i] of hardening and strengthening the bore of guns, etc., by forcing through them one or a succession of steel cylinders or olives, each slightly (say 0·05 inches) wider than the preceding, successfully used by him and by Uchatius for bronze guns, is said to be applied now in Belgium to steel gun-tubes, and by the Credenda Steel Tube Company to small steel tubes. It does not, however, appear to diminish erosion in case of steel guns.[j]

BLUE-SHORTNESS.

§ 290. Blue-Shortness.[k]—Not only are wrought-iron and steel much more brittle at a blue heat than in the cold or at redness, but, while they are probably not seriously affected by simple exposure to blueness, even if prolonged, yet if they be worked in this range of temperature they remain extremely brittle after cooling, and may indeed be more brittle then than while at blueness (2 and 3, Table 130): this last point however is not certain..

The loss of ductility as measured by endurance of bending and drifting is enormous: that this is not due to incipient cracks is shown by the simultaneous increase of tensile strength, and by the restoration of ductility by annealing. The effect of blue-working on ductility as measured by elongation (on rupture by static tensile stress) is very irregular, and apparently anomalous: in five out of the eight cases in Table 129 the elongation is greater after than before blue-working. Heating to redness may completely remove the effects of blue-working (4, 5, Table 130).

There is thus a general resemblance between the effects of cold- and those of blue-working, and we may suspect that the immediate effect of these two operations is identical in nature. It is true that the gain in elastic limit does

[a] "Open-Hearth Steel for Boiler Making:" Excerpt Proc. Inst. Civ. Eng., XCII., p. 58, 1888.

[b] Asst. Nav. Constructor R. Gatewood, Private Communication, Nov. 25, 1888.

[c] L'Emploi de l'Acier, Périssé, p. 25, 1884. The foregoing statements about punching-practice are based on extensive inquiries which I have made both here and in Britain.

[d] Thurston, Metallurg. Rev., I., p. 126: Matls. of Engineering, III., p. 540.

[e] H. R. Towne, Yale & Towne Mfg. Co., Trans. Am. Soc. Mech. Eng., VIII., p. 180, 1887.

[f] Sweet, Trans. Am. Soc. Mech. Eng., VII., p. 263, 1886.

[g] W. F. Durfee, Idem, Priv. Commun., Feb. 5th, 8th, 1889.

[h] F. Overman, The Manufacture of Steel, p. 61, 1851.

[i] Thurston, Mat'ls of Engineering, III., p. 530; Metallurg. Rev., I., p. 123; Rept. U. S. Commissioners Vienna Exhibition of 1873, III., p. 324; U. S. Patent No. 90,244, May 18, 1869, S. B. Dean.

[j] Maitland, "The Treatment of Gun Steel," Excerpt Proc. Inst. Civ. Eng., LXXXIX., p. 127, 1887.

[k] "The Working of Steel," Stromeyer, Excerpt Proc. Inst. Civ. Eng., LXXXIV., 1886, with a very important discussion. Also U. S. Naval Prof. Papers, No. 21, 1887. A blue heat is here used generically to include straw and blue oxide-tint temperatures, say 220° to 320° C., 430 to 600° F. Brass is said to have a critical temperature of brittleness like that of iron, and some varieties of aluminium bronze appear to have one.

not seem to excel that in tensile strength as markedly in case of blue- as in case of cold-working, nor is it clear that the tensile strength and elastic limit increase during rest after blue- as they do after cold-working. But this is natural: for we saw reason to believe that heating cold-worked iron to blueness greatly accelerated the changes which cold-working starts: so that, when this change is started by distortion at blueness instead of in the cold, it may occur so rapidly and so nearly reach its full growth before the metal grows cold that no considerable further change occurs thereafter. The effects of blue-working are more intense and more injurious than those of cold-working. While the blue-worked iron in tables 128 to 130 is usually somewhat stronger and in one case (very soft steel, 14, Table 129) 8,000 pounds stronger than the corresponding cold-worked iron, the loss of flexibility and drifting power on blue-working is on the whole very much heavier than on similar cold-working. Out of 16 comparable cases in Table 128, the previously blue-worked pieces endures in 14 less than 50% and in 11 less than 25% of the bending endured by the corresponding cold-worked piece.

Adamson,[a] who, after Valton,[b] early called attention to blue-shortness, thinks that it is the more severe the greater the number and aggregate percentage of non-ferrous elements present.[c] No such relation can be traced, however, among the results in tables 128 to 130. Thus the half-hard steel of tables 128 and 129, with 1·17% of non-ferrous elements, cannot be confidently held to suffer more either in flexibility or tensile properties, and whether tested at blueness or after cooling, than the Lowmoor iron with only 0·36% of these elements. Nor is it clear that the wrought-iron, 4 and 5 of Table 129, suffered less than the corresponding steel. Indeed, there is no certainly known connection between composition and blue-shortness.

According to Stromeyer the fracture at blueness is silky, though the steel is fairly rotten: but blue-worked pieces broken cold yield a crystalline fracture.

[a] Journ. Iron and St. Inst., 1878, II., p. 396.

[b] Valton, Metallurg. Rev., I., p. 170, October, 1877.

[c] Jour. Iron and Steel Inst., 1887, I., p. 9. T. Gillott, Jeremiah Head and Isherwood state that steel is injured more than wrought-iron by blue-working. Others hold the opposite view. "The Working of Steel," Stromeyer, pp. 89, 57, 86, 67.

TABLE 128.—EFFECT OF PREVIOUS COLD AND BLUE-HEAT TREATMENT ON FLEXIBILITY (ENDURANCE OF REPEATED BENDING), STROMEYER.

The bendings of last four columns for line 2 were done at blueness, all others were done in the cold.

	Preliminary treatment.	Number of 40° bendings (after preliminary treatment) endured before rupture. I. Lowmoor iron C = 0·02 %.	II. Very soft steel C = 0·05 %.	III. Soft steel C = 0·16 %.	IV. Half-hard steel C = 0·28 %.
1	Unprepared	21	27	6	15
2	Unprepared	8 @ 7 blue.	2·5 @ 7 blue.	1·5 blue.	2·5 blue.
3	Annealed at blueness	14 @ 19	18 @ 27	7 @ 9	3 @ 5
4	Quenched at blueness	17	10 @ 11	6 @ 10	1
5	Annealed at redness	19	25	12·5	21
6	Annealed at redness, then at blueness	......	......	7	22·5
7	Quenched at redness	29	19a at 28	10a	1 @ 24
8	Quenched at redness, then at blueness	......	......	9 @ 12·25	17 @ 26
9	Hammered cold	9	21	......	......
10	Hammered at blueness	6 @ 7	0	......	......
11	Quenched from redness, twisted cold b	23	15	11a	22a
12	Quenched from blueness, twisted cold b	15	13	11a	0·5a
13	Twisted blue b	7	1	9	21

	Length of rest, days, between preliminary treatment and bending.	I. 1	I. 7	I. 35	II. 1	II. 7	II. 35	III. 1	III. 7	III. 35	IV. 1	IV. 7	IV. 35
		Number of 40° bendings endured before rupture.											
14	Bent cold once; then rest	..	......	..	..	......	..	..	10	9	......	20	20
15	Bent cold twice; then rest	..	......	..	..	......	..	9	9	4·5	18·5	21	20
16	Bent once at blueness; then rest	..	16 @ 16	..	..	4 @ 14	..	1	1	1·5	5·5	2	1·5
17	Bent twice at blueness; then rest	..	6 @ 12·5	..	..	0 @ 2	..	0	0	0	1	0	1

a Annealed instead of being quenched.

b In lines 11 to 13 the preliminary treatment for Lowmoor iron and very soft steel was to twist the piece 90° four times in a length of 6 inches, apparently 90° and back twice. In case of soft and half-hard steel it was to twist the piece 45° in a length of 6 inches, one way and back. Each piece of the half-hard and of the soft steel was first baked for two nights in a moulders' core-oven. The bendings of the last four columns were each of about 40° to a radius of 1·75 inches, the piece being bent 40°, straightened, bent 40° in the opposite direction, and so forth. "Blueness" is used generically to include straw and blue oxide-tint temperatures, or say 230° to 316° C. (446° to 600° F.).

In every case except line 2 the numbers in columns I. to IV. are the numbers of bendings in the cold through 40° which the piece, after receiving the treatment specified in the column "preliminary treatment," endured before rupture. In line 2 the numbers indicate the number of 40° bendings at blueness which the piece without previous treatment endured at a blue heat before rupture.

TABLE 130.—EFFECT OF BLUE AND COLD WORK ON DUCTILITY AS INFERRED FROM DRIFTING. STROMEYER.

	Treatment before drifting test.		Drifting temperature.	Endurance of drifting. Diameter, inches, at rupture.
1.	Unprepared		Cold.	1·94 @ 2·06.
2.	"		Blue.	1·91.
3.	Drifted at blueness to 1·5", then	{ Cooled slowly	Cold	1·92 @ 1·91.
4.		Heated to redness and quenched	Cold.	2·2.
5.		" " and cooled slowly	Cold.	2.06 @ 2·5.

Pieces of open-hearth steel frame-plate ½" thick, cut in a planer to about 8" square, had a hole 1" in diameter drilled with its centre 3·5" from each edge. These holes were then treated as indicated, and then drifted with drifts having a taper of 5 per 100 of length, till they split. In certain cases the rupture crack was from 0·85 to 0·12 inches open. (Discussion of Stromeyer's Paper, p. 65.) In each case the test-piece first underwent the treatment given in the second column: was then drifted at the temperature indicated in the third column, till it split, when the hole had been drifted out to the diameter indicated in the third column.

TABLE 129.—EFFECT OF COLD AND BLUE-HEAT TREATMENT ON TENSILE PROPERTIES (STROMEYER).

Preliminary treatment.	Wrought-iron. I. Tensile strength, lbs. per sq. in.	Wrought-iron. I. Elastic lim., lbs. per sq. in.	Wrought-iron. I. Elongation.	Very soft steel. II. Tensile strength, lbs. per sq. in.	Very soft steel. II. Elastic lim., lbs. per sq. in.	Very soft steel. II. Elongation.	Tensile strength, lbs. per sq. in.	Elastic lim., lbs. per sq. in.	Elongation.	Tensile strength, lbs. per sq. in.	Elastic lim., lbs. per sq. in.	Elongation.
{1. Annealed	......	......	......	66,538	43,232	20·1						
{2. Flattened cold	......	......	......	71,080	45,320	12·9						
{3. " blue	......	......	......	81,312	56,000	9·5						
{4. Unprepared	50,621	......	20·5 @ 24	64,514	......	23						
{5. Tested blue	61,424	......	19 @ 16·5	89,192	......	15·2						
{6. Unprepared	......	......	......	64,320	......	44·7						
{7. Bent cold	......	......	......	73,920	......	9						
{8. " blue	......	......	......	72,128	......	3						

Preliminary treatment.	Lowmoor wrought-iron. III. C = 0·02 %. Tensile strength	Elastic lim.	Elongation	Very soft steel. IV. C = 0·05 %. Tensile strength	Elastic lim.	Elongation	Soft steel. V. C = 0·16 %. Tensile strength	Elastic lim.	Elongation	Half-hard steel. VI. C = 0·29 %. Tensile strength	Elastic lim.	Elongation
{9. Unprepared	49,600	28,066	6·7	61,060	40,992	24·8	59,400	36,064	34·7	72,900	43,981	31·5
{10. Blue-annealed	49,960	31,583	14·2	60,560	45,024	10·4 @ 20·6						
{11. Bent cold	52,100	31,584	18·8	63,060	41,411	18·0	65,900	34,244	24·3	71,000	40,992	7·2
{12. " blue	52,960	28,600	7·1	66,000	41,072	20·4	67,000	40,962	20·2	78,000	43,901	15·7
{13. Twisted cold	52,080	31,048	8·5	63,100	38,083	18·3	66,100		16·8			
{14. " blue	55,960	36,512	15·3	71,000	53,184	27·9	67,900	47,158	22·4			

In every case, except line 5, the numbers in columns I. to VI. are the results of tests in the cold made on test-pieces which had endured the treatment specified in the column "preliminary treatment."

In line 5 the previously untreated piece was ruptured tensilely at a blue heat.

The treatment is supposed to be identical for the several columns of each line, except for those of line 9.

The lines braced together are supposed to represent tests of the same material or materials.

All tests were made cold except Number 5, which was tested while blue-hot.

2 and 3, flattened cold on a smith's anvil, and thus thinned apparently by 1·5%.

7 and 8. W. Stroudley, discussion of Stromeyer's paper, p. 84. They were bent once 45°, and straightened by hammering.

9 to 14. The *unprepared* (9) soft and half-hard steel had been annealed from redness.

The *blue-annealed* (10) pieces were kept at blueness during four nights.

The *bent* pieces (11, 12) were bent to a radius of 1½" and flattened: I think this means that they were bent double, and the bend flattened close, and not reopened: but the wording is obscure.

The *twisting* (13, 14) was through an angle of 90° and back, in 12".

Stromeyer, The Working of Steel, except Proc. Inst., Civ. Eng., LXXXIV., 1886.

The strengthening effect of blue-working is well illustrated by bending a common tensile test-piece in the middle while blue-hot, straightening, cooling and pulling it, when it breaks as in Figure 117, the unstrengthened ends contracting and yielding.[a] Extreme blue-shortness is

Fig. 117

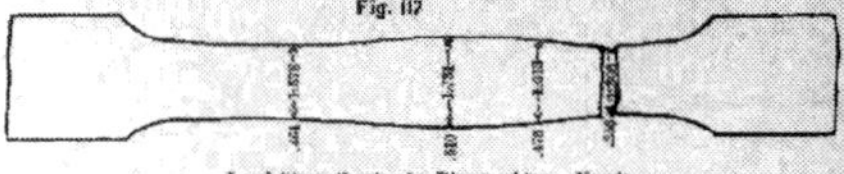

Local Strengthening by Blue-working. Unwin.

reported in the case of a soft-steel gun-coil,[b] which, cooled to blueness owing to delay at the hammer, shattered when struck: and in that of a steel plate[c] which, though very malleable at whiteness and when cold, went to pieces while rolling, as it cooled to below redness.

Valton found that his workmen had long recognized blue-shortness, and avoided hammering at blueness: it is said to have been known in the Yorkshire iron works for more than fifty years, and some steel-makers[d] have long urged their customers to avoid blue-work: yet the discussion on Stromeyer's paper in 1886 showed that many experienced iron-workers then disbelieved in or were ignorant of blue-shortness, and I have found this true of very many American iron-workers.

But while blue-working even in moderation certainly lessens ductility, at least in the great majority of cases, yet the injury is not necessarily fatal. Thus Stromeyer found that two twists of 45° in a length of six inches did not diminish the bending-endurance of very soft steel and Lowmoor iron materially, though four twists of 90° injured them greatly (13, Table 128). Steel plates $\frac{5}{16}''$ thick have been bent to a nearly closed circle 19″ in diameter, flattened again, and again bent the reverse way to the same circle, all at blueness, without sign of rupture.[e]

Two plates, one heated to blueness, the other forged while its temperature fell from bright redness to blueness, were bent double, flattened under a steam-hammer, and again broken open while blue-hot: no crack could be detected at the outside of the bend.[f] Their fractures exactly resembled those of a similar piece bent double and opened similarly but cold. Again, though many recognize that machine-riveting has a great advantage over hand-riveting, in that its work ceases before the rivet cools to blueness, while the hand-riveter usually continues hammering while the rivet is passing blueness[g]: yet relatively few hand-worked rivets fail in use, and the difficulty in getting riveted work apart does not point to serious injury. Millions of car axles, blue from "hot boxes," are chilled with snow and jarred under heavy load at loose rail-joints, yet are apparently unharmed. Among the many thousand steel boilers, tens of thousands of plates must have been worked more or less at blueness: yet failures are rare. Finally, much crucible steel, in the form of bars, plates, etc., is habitually rolled or hammered till its temperature has fallen below visible redness. The lesson thus seems to be, avoid blue-working wholly if you can: if not, then use it cautiously and very moderately, unless you anneal later.

By heating in their bearings marine and other shafts, railway axles, etc., are liable to reach blueness, as are guns through rapid firing, when accidents may readily occur. In practice many of the best American bridge engineers do, others do not positively forbid blue-working. The Russian Ministry of Roads in 1885 ordered that all bending should be hot, apparently at redness.[h]

Blue-working without subsequent annealing is rarely permitted for the steel of the Forth Bridge, though the rivets and small angles and tees are liable to be worked to blueness, and are not subsequently annealed.[i] I am informed that good German bridge engineers permit blue-working occasionally in case of steel, and usually in case of wrought-iron.

It is said that some boiler-makers allow no blue-working, stopping work when the metal becomes so cool that it no longer glows when rubbed with wood: others stop while the metal is still visibly red. Others insist that it is necessary to adjust some work, *e. g.*, marine boiler-fronts, at blueness: that, despite the most careful hot-working, adjustment is needed after the distortion due to cooling, especially as, owing to the endless variety of patterns, flanging in the press at a single heat is not practicable: that adjusting cold would lead to excessive waste of time, as iron is bent more quickly at blueness than when cold: hence these pieces are warmed locally to blueness by applying hot irons. To anneal afterwards would be useless, as fresh adjustment would be needed after cooling. Certain it is that most American, and at least many foreign boiler-makers, habitually adjust at blueness. Blue-working without subsequent annealing is forbidden for boilers for the United States navy, but not for the hull-work.[j]

THE TREACHERY OF STEEL.

§ 291. The Treachery of Steel.—We may arbitrarily divide the failures in steel and wrought-iron into the normal ones which occur because the known proper conditions of manufacture or use are violated, and the really mysterious ones. Of course, many failures placed in the first class might on further examination be found to belong to the second.

The evidence seems to show that of a given number of pieces, say 100,000 of wrought- and 100,000 of ingot-iron, more of the former than of the latter fail in manufacture, assembling and use: ingot-iron is on the whole more trustworthy than puddled iron. But though the failures are fewer among the 100,000 ingot-iron pieces, yet the number of mysterious, *i. e.*, as yet wholly inexplicable failures, is greater among them than among the wrought-iron pieces. To this evidence I will return.

In the early use of Bessemer and open-hearth steel many then unexplained and hence then mysterious failures occurred. With our present knowledge an easy ex-

[a] This result is reported by three observers independently, Unwin, B. Baker and F. W. Webb, (op. cit. pp. 44, 54, 96).

[b] Bramwell and [c] Bessemer, op. cit., pp. 83, 87.

[d] *E. g.*, the Steel Company of Scotland.

[e] W. Parker, [f] W. Anderson, Idem, pp. 39, 61, 41. I use Mr. Anderson's words, as I am not quite certain of their meaning.

[g] In riveting ships' plates the rivet is usually left while hot, and again tightened up when cold, while in boiler-riveting the rivet is worked continuously, and, of course, through the blue heat. This is because the flat counter-sunk head of the former is quickly finished, so that, if it is to be tightened cold, a considerable interruption naturally occurs at blueness: while so much more work is needed in making the conical head of the boiler-rivet that, though worked continuously, it grows nearly cold before it is finished.

[h] Eng. and Mining Jl., XLII., p. 93, 1886.

[i] Private communication, B. Baker, Nov. 2d, 1888.

[j] R. Gatewood, private communication, Nov. 25th, 1888.

planation of most of them would probably have been seen. But even to-day certain unexplained and apparently inexplicable failures occur in steel, inexplicable in spite of full and intelligent investigation. They are extremely rare, but I do not think that they can be ignored or ridiculed. The mystery in some of them may be due to overlooking or purposely suppressing conditions which would readily explain them: but I believe that the true explanation of others lies beyond our present knowledge.

I learn of a few truly mysterious accidents to wrought-iron: they have not attained the publicity that has befallen the mysterious failures of steel, thanks partly to many motives, mostly honorable, and partly to the very nature of the case: the newer metal, on probation, has deserved the closer scrutiny.

But the mysterious accidents reported in case of steel exceed those in case of wrought iron to a greater extent than can be readily accounted for in this way. One additional explanation is that, owing to the very nature of the processes by which steel and wrought-iron are made, carelessness and ignorance, whether in selecting materials, in conducting the processes, or examining the product, is more likely to lead to the making and selling of treacherous steel, treacherous simply because unsuited to the purpose for which it is sold, *i. e.*, too highly carburetted; or positively bad, bad owing to a combination of high phosphorus with high carbon, to serious segregation, to serious pipes, internal cracks, etc. The very pliancy of the steel-making processes, the ease for instance with which the carbon-content of a Bessemer or an open-hearth charge may be raised at the shortest notice from 0·05 to 1%, demands increased watchfulness to prevent and detect unsought variation: invaluable to the watchful and the intelligent, it is a stumbling block to the ignorant and the heedless.

Further, it is conceivable that the presence of slag in wrought-iron, while a source of weakness, may in some obscure way lend a certain security against the mysterious failures whose very nature is obscure.

Let the mysterious class of failures be illustrated by two famous cases, one in which steel plates, which had passed an examination, seemed to become extremely brittle after rolling and testing but before the boilers made from them were tested, a case which caused widespread dismay; and another in which steel, certainly initially good enough to endure the trying conditions of boiler-construction, became astonishingly brittle during two and a half years' service.

§ 292. Two Mysterious Cases.—*The Lividia Case.*[a] Some ¾-inch steel boiler-plates, containing about 0·1 % of carbon, rolled from 22-inch ingots, had passed tensile, and quenching and bending tests well (nearly all the latter being satisfactorily passed by rough sheared unplaned pieces), had been punched, heated slightly, and bent to the proper curvature, and the rivet holes had been reamed out about $\frac{1}{16}$-inch to size in place, when an accidental concussion caused the steel to crack between some rivet holes not in the immediate neighborhood of the spot directly injured. The plates, thought to be injured by punching, were now annealed, but in such a way that some of them may have been much overheated. The boilers were now riveted apparently safely: but one tore asunder in three pieces in hydraulic testing, before reaching 140 pounds pressure, while another was found cracked behind the rivet holes before the testing water was introduced. The metal was now carefully studied. Large pieces could be broken from the plates with a single blow of a hammer: the metal still showed normal tensile strength and elongation, but an abnormal fracture, in part with brilliant facets from one eighth to one quarter-inch wide. Under bending tests, strips cut close to the rivet-holes and others purposely punched were extraordinarily brittle, while others cut at a distance from the rivet-holes behaved normally. Strips containing the original rivet-holes became tough on annealing: others purposely punched were made tough by either reaming or annealing. Examination of one plate showed marked but not extraordinary segregation (No. 62, Table 96). When the plates were rolled to ⅜, or half the original thickness, the fracture and properties in general became normal.

I offer the following explanation: it may not be the true one, but it seems to cover the ground. The plates were bad initially, possibly owing to excessively high casting temperature. Witness the undue brittleness caused by punching and the segregation: but not so bad that they could not pass a somewhat perfunctory examination. If properly annealed they would probably never have been heard from. In annealing they were burnt: witness the brilliant ultra-coarse fracture. The burning was naturally most severe along the edges which would be the hottest part: hence the much greater brittleness near the punched holes than away from them. The burnt steel was naturally made extremely brittle by punching.

The effects of burning were modified to a certain extent by annealing, but not completely removed. The brittleness directly due to burning was greatly lessened: hence the annealed strips bend fairly. But the tendency to become brittle when punched is not removed, or not removed so completely: hence the metal, even when annealed, is again made brittle by punching. But while the annealing applied *before* punching does not remove this liability to be made brittle by punching, applied *after* punching it removes the effect of this operation: hence the fair bends obtained with the metal annealed after punching. Remember, all this is hypothesis: we do not know that the effects of burning persist in this specific way.

The Maginnis Case.[b]—Each of two British steamers, 1 and 2, in the transatlantic and colonial trades, had three boilers built by Jack, from steel made by the Weardale Coal and Iron Company, in two-and-a-half-ton acid Bessemer converters, cast in ingots about nine inches thick, and reduced to plates from ·41 to ·74 inch thick, and containing (at least in case of some cracked combustion chamber plates):

Carbon,	Silicon,	Manganese,	Phosphorus,	Sulphur,
·12@·17	·005@·018	·32@·53	·06@·068	·046@·051

The tensile properties follow.

		Tensile strength, pounds per sq. in.		Elongation, in 10″.
40 tests before leaving the works		58,832@68,095		19·75@27
Tests from cracked combustion chamber plates, steamer 1, 4 tests, fractures fine-crystalline	from	104,026	with	15
	and	106,408	"	7·35
	to	94,720	"	13
Do. do., steamer 2, 7 tests, fractures "fibrous, silky, fine"	from	54,293	"	24·5
	and	56,851	"	8
	to	61,122	"	26

The steel actually used passed an inspection by Lloyds'

[a] W. Parker, Chief Eng., Surveyor to Lloyd's Register, Trans. Inst. Nav. Arch. XXII., p. 19, 1881.

[b] A. Maginnis, "The Engineer," LX., p. 447, 1885. Also W. Kent, Trans. Am. Inst. Min. Eng., XIV., p. 812, 1886.

and the Board of Trade, but forty per cent of that supplied failed to pass, and was replaced. The accepted material endured the usual boiler-shop work, welding included, without mishap. The furnaces were annealed after welding.

With careful scaling and the usual precautions, the boilers behaved normally in service for two-and-a-half years, when they failed in the following remarkable way.

Steamer 1.—Three weeks after blowing down, and while no work beyond the usual scaling was going on, a crack about thirty inches long, open one-eighth inch at bottom and one-sixteenth at top,[a] formed spontaneously in a combustion-chamber plate. About three months later, and a few days after shutting off steam, a circumferential crack over two feet long formed with an alarming report, in a wing furnace from which workmen were removing the scale.

Steamer 2.—At the same period of work as in case of steamer 1, and thirteen days after letting down steam, a crack twenty-seven inches long formed in a combustion-chamber plate with a report which nearly deafened even a boiler-maker. Three months later a further crack formed.

Parts of the plates now being extraordinarily brittle, the boilers were broken up, with startling results. In unriveting the pipes connecting boiler and steam chest, after a few blows they were found cracking in all directions, so much so that none of the nine of steamer 2 came off whole. Next a butt-strap cracked almost across between rivet-holes. Later "a general smash was experienced, the front-plates cracking and starring, and the flanges breaking off. The furnaces at the same time acted in just the same manner, the cracks going through the rivet-holes to such an extent as to allow the ends to come off whole, and so form hoops for the lads to play with in the meal-hour."

I see no easy explanation. Internal strains and deterioration, homogeneousness, crystallization, excessive dimensions of plates, and untrustworthiness of Bessemer steel in general, are justly pointed out by Kent to be improbable causes: innumerable plates appear to be subjected to conditions favoring failure from these causes as much as these plates were. Yet they do not fail, while not one or two, but very many of these plates fail astonishingly. His own explanation, heterogeneousness, owing to imperfectly mixing the recarburizer with the blown metal, hoists with his own petard, because we know that plates, rails, etc., are often if not usually markedly heterogeneous, yet they fail not. Neither is it probable that a degree of heterogeneousness sufficiently unusual to induce such unusual results would have happened to fall on all these plates, representing many different Bessemer blows, especially as good boiler-plate steel had been made for years in these same converters, and, according to the steel-maker, under exactly the same conditions, with one exception—that these plates were thicker than those previously made. Herein lies a possible explanation. Clearly, if the temperature to which the ingot is raised for rolling, the rapidity of rolling, and the reduction per pass be the same, the metal's temperature will be much higher if rolled to a thick than if farther reduced to a thin plate: so that these thick plates, made from thin ingots, may have left the rolls at so high a temperature that serious crystallization occurred during the subsequent slow undisturbed cooling. But this is not wholly satisfying, first, because other pieces of steel, and notably rails, are often finished unduly hot without disaster: and, second, because, so far as I know, an unduly high finishing temperature does not produce this specific effect of yielding a metal which, only moderately bad at first, undergoes extraordinary deterioration under the indefinitely repeated expansion and contraction, vibration, etc., incident to use. This objection, indeed, applies with equal force to all other theories but one, to wit, that the boiler underwent some extraordinary treatment during service, such as being highly heated and then quenched with water. But it is improbable that this would happen to all six of these sister-boilers in two different vessels at the same period of service.

Careless inspection, permitting some plates or heats to pass untested, might account for the difference between the original tensile properties and those found in strips cut from the broken pieces, but not for the extraordinary brittleness after service of plates which before service must all have been at least moderately tough, for they endured the trying ordeal of boiler-making. We can hardly doubt that the metal deteriorated greatly after the boilers were made, though the tendency or liability to deterioration was probably incurred in the steel works or the boiler-shop, or in both: but how incurred we know not.

One striking feature must not be overlooked: the failures occurred when the boilers were not under steam. This may give the future investigator a clue. I am informed that, on the Pennsylvania Railroad, there have been within the last ten years perhaps twenty cases in which the boiler-plates of locomotive engines have snapped when either cold or under half steam. My informant is not sure that a single such case has happened under full steam.[b]

§ 293. CASES THOUGHT TO BE NORMAL, AND OTHERS.—Of the other class of failures which I have termed normal, those which are supposed due to violation of known canons of manufacture or treatment, we find a large part attributed to blue-working:[c] internal stress due to local heating, and heterogeneousness of strength and of elastic limit due to cold-working come in for their share also. In 1881 Parker reported that, in the construction of 1,100 steel boilers, representing 17,000 tons of material, none of Lloyd's surveyors had met a single brittle plate. They had investigated many of the supposed mysterious failures of steel plates which had stood all the required tests, had been riveted into place, and then had been reported to crack without being touched; and they had traced them all clearly to improper manipulation, the metal in the neighborhood of the crack being found ductile as soon as rupture had relieved the internal stress.[d] He gives the following as an example: A 10-foot boiler was nearly completely riveted, when, on returning from dinner, the

[a] These numbers are as given by Maginnis. Others have quoted him incorrectly

[b] Dr. C. B. Dudley, private communication, Nov. 26, 1888.

[c] J. Riley states that in every or nearly every case of mysterious failure of ingot iron that has come before us (the steel makers) we have concluded that it was due to working at blueness. Trans. Inst. Nav. Arch., XXVII., p. 131, 1886.

[d] Trans. Inst. Nav. Arch., XXII., p. 12, 1881.

riveters found that the plate which they had lately been working had torn for a distance of eighteen inches. By accident the bolts that had been holding the furnace up to the front plate had not been taken out. On removing them, the rivet-holes, though originally drilled true in place, were found quite ⅛th inch blind, showing that the furnace had been smaller than the circular part of the plate to which it had to be riveted, had been stretched in riveting, stress being thrown on the metal which eventually sufficed to tear it.[a]

It is surprising that the workmen could put enough stress upon the plate to tear it at all, were it free from initial flaw or weakness: further, as the flue was nine feet in circumference, and as the metal shows 26% elongation in tensile testing, uniform stretch should enlarge the flue by more than two feet before causing rupture, while only ¼ of an inch displacement or 0·12% is actually proved.[b] Thus this explanation is not exactly convincing on its face: yet it may be the true one: for we have seen in § 269 and especially at the end of § 271, B, p. 217, that the total elongation may be greatly lessened by cold-working, and that the effects of cold-working go on increasing long after the cold-working itself has ceased: and so may the capacity for elongation have been here greatly lessened by the peculiar, oft-interrupted, jerky stretching which the material underwent as it was drifted and stretched. Further, it is possible that the stretching, far from being uniformly distributed, may really have been gradually concentrated by successive rivets, so that a continually and at last rapidly increasing proportion fell on successive parts of the plate. Thus we should not scout Mr. Parker's statement,—he voices the opinions of many intelligent engineers—yet it seems to me probable that many failures which are referred to brutal treatment from the boiler-maker may be due to other causes, such as a line of brittleness in an otherwise tough plate, and that a considerable proportion of the failures is still imperfectly explained. We instinctively seek explanations, and, failing a satisfactory one, gull ourselves, and hatch our porcelain nest-eggs.

Many of these surprising cracks in ingot-iron plates occur without reduction of the metal's area at the cracked edge,[c] while under common tensile stress the area would usually be reduced by more than 40 and sometimes by more than 60 per cent. In some of these cases the metal at the very edge of the crack seems tough. Again, sometimes the cracks can be readily extended, or even extend themselves, for a certain distance, while beyond they obstinately refuse to go. Here are a few examples.

In the Maginnis case, some cracks which were started by hammering began by showing a peculiar black shade about half an inch wide, and after another blow a faint hair-like score became visible, which without further blows gradually opened and extended automatically, till fully developed: other cracks formed almost simultaneously with the blow of the hammer. In two cases Maginnis had the metal on one side of the crack held firmly, while that on the other was struck in order to extend the crack, as shown in Figure 118. In one, the crack extended about four inches at the first blow, leaving only 2·5 inches of solid plate. The remaining part was hammered flat and re-straightened without extending the crack. The other was hammered flat in the line of the crack, straightened, and hammered flat in the opposite way without lengthening the crack.

Fig. 118

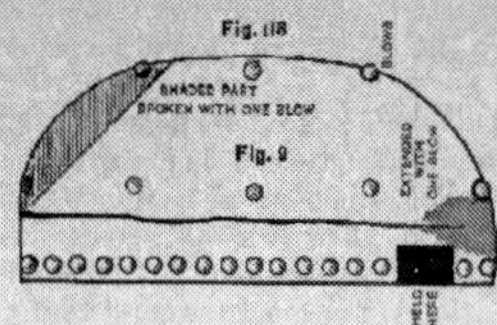

Spontaneous Cracks which cannot be Extended. Maginnis.

In another case a crack with bright crystallized sides, in an open-hearth steel plate, could not be extended by wedging, apparently having gone its full length automatically, and then refusing to go further. Tensile and bending tests from its very sides were normal.[c]

In removing a long-used steel locomotive fire-box to repair its cracked crown-sheet, two opposite side sheets cracked, one of which, containing 0·17% of carbon, was examined at the Watertown arsenal.[d] The crack extended into five stay-bolt holes, stopping 3·5 inches short of the sheet's edge, and was formed with no apparent contraction of the plate's sectional area: its surfaces were granular with a marked radiant appearance. Yet the metal was fairly ductile around and even at the very edge of the crack: for a strip, cut parallel with and including one edge of the crack, was bent 180° and nearly closed down without rupture, and tensile test-pieces cut from near the crack had the following properties:

	Tensile strength lbs. per sq. in.		Elastic limit, lbs. per sq. in.	Elongation, % in 10",		Contraction of area %.
From	64,000	with	41,530	15·2	and	48·4
To	65,918	"	44,240	19·5	"	51·7

C. L. Houston[e] reports that a ⅜-inch steel plate was flanged into a locomotive throat-sheet: the next morning a crack appeared at the opposite, unheated, untreated, planed end, and grew for about a week, finally reaching across the plate to the part which had been heated. The tensile strength of a test-piece which had the crystalline face of the crack for one edge was 68,580 pounds per square inch, its reduction of area 42%, and its fracture fibrous.

The stress induced by sudden cooling is doubtless the cause of the treachery of hardened steel, of which a case has been noted in a foot-note on page 181, and which is farther illustrated by the failure of some steel punches and dies which, after hardening without tempering, were ground 0·001 inch five times alternately on each side, reducing their total thickness by 0·01 inch. A few hours after grinding they began to crack and nearly all were thus ruined.[f] Grinding still more lightly, so that only 0·001 inch was removed in ten grindings (approximately of 0·0001 inch each), the same results followed.[g]

But sudden cooling cannot account for these accidents

[a] W. Parker, discussion of Stromeyer's paper on the Working of Steel, Excerpt Proc. Inst. Civ. Eng., LXXXIV., p. 35, 1886.

[b] Cf. Unwin, Idem. p. 43

[c] A. C. Kirk, Trans. Inst. Nav. Arch., XXVI., p. 263, 1885.

[d] Rept. Tests of Metals at Watertown Arsenal, year 1885, p. 1,053, 1888. This interesting case is here admirably illustrated.

[e] Trans. Am. Soc. Mech. Eng., X., 1889, to appear.

[f] L. K. Fuller, Trans. Am. Soc. Mech. Eng., X., 1889, to appear.

[g] Idem, Private Communication, Dec. 12th, 1888. I have one of these interesting dies in my collection.

to boiler plate steel, for the metal itself is tough as soon as the stress has been relieved by cracking.

The cause of such cracks as these is certainly obscure. They may be due to defects in the ingot, such as a pipe, or heterogeneousness due to segregation or to imperfect mixing. If to a pipe, it is not easy to see why its sides are not welded at least so well that a certain amount of reduction of area occurs on rupture. They may be due to the splitting apart of the coarse crystals which form at a high temperature: but if so it is surprising that these crystals are not broken up during rolling. They may be due to an unduly high finishing temperature: but if so, why does the crack stop so abruptly? They may be due to severe highly localized stress, due in turn to local heating. Such stress combined with unduly high finishing temperature and with heterogeneousness, seems a possible cause. In the first place the very rarity of such failures suggests that they are due, not to a single condition, but to an unusual combination of conditions. Next, heterogeneousness and high finishing temperature help to account for the brilliant coarse crystallization. Heterogeneousness helps to account for the fact that, when these failures occur at all, it is usually in bad steel; because bad steel, whether bad because cast too hot, because too phosphoric, or because so cold that the recarburizer does not melt and diffuse thoroughly, is especially liable to heterogeneousness, high casting temperature clearly favoring segregation, high phosphorus favoring the segregation of phosphoric, brittle, coarsely crystalline bodies. Heterogeneousness and local heating help to account for the extreme localization of the weakness. Suppose a thin streak of some segregated, say phosphoric compound, or of an unmelted lump of recarburizer, existing in the plate: suppose that this compound tends strongly to crystallize coarsely: suppose that, thanks to this and to its different rate of dilatation, our line of weakness is intensified during heating and cooling: that a high finishing temperature further favors coarse crystallization: that, during the cooling which follows some local heating, and while the temperature is sinking past some point of critical weakness, say a blue-heat, irregular contraction induces a stress perpendicular to our streak, sufficient to weaken the adhesion between the dissimilar coarse crystals which constitute it, perhaps sufficient even to part some of them, or at least to break off the dowels which bind them together. The weakness of our streak is now greatly exaggerated, and a relatively slight stress arising in service may suffice to cause rupture. Now if we lacked heterogeneousness, or if the stress due to local heating had such a direction and intensity that it just failed to part our crystals at blueness, or if our segregated body had not been made coarsely crystalline by high finishing temperature, our weak streak might still be but little weaker than the rest of the metal: for while a stress which just fell short of causing incipient rupture at a temperature of critical weakness might do little harm, a slightly greater stress might be disastrous.

The above is not offered as the true explanation: indeed, it seems to me forced: but merely as an example of the kind of rare combination of circumstances which may lead to mysterious failure.

Here are a few other cases.

1. In testing a cylindrical steel boiler 13 feet in diameter, properly designed for 150 pounds pressure, when the pressure reached 240 pounds a plate $1\frac{1}{4}$ inches thick, weighing nearly three tons, tore completely across. The tensile strength of a strip from this plate was 66,304 pounds per square inch, and its elongation 20% in 8 inches: other strips bent nearly double cold, yet the plate now failed under less than a quarter of this stress, and without appreciable elongation or reduction of area. Its failure is attributed to its high proportion of carbon, about 0·30%, unfitting it for the rough treatment of the boiler-shop: and to its thickness, which probably led to finishing at an unduly high temperature and to unduly slow cooling, both leading to coarse crystallization. Admitting these, the low ductility and tensile strength of material which had behaved so well under test is still surprising.[a]

2. A ship's steel stringer plate, worked into place satisfactorily, cracked during the next night not through the rivet-holes or any point of weakness, but through its solid body.[b]

§ 294. THE TRUSTWORTHINESS OF STEEL, both absolute and relative to that of wrought-iron is here evidenced.

First, we have the simple statements of eminent engineers, such as B. Baker,[c] who has had more cases of mysterious fracture with the few tons of wrought-iron than with the 24,000 tons of steel used at the Forth Bridge, where the work is pressed forward night and day with no precautions which would not be needed equally in case the best Lowmoor wrought-iron were used: Sir E. J. Reed,[d] who states that officers and men in the Admiralty dockyards are perfectly enamored of steel, finding it much more trustworthy in every way than wrought-iron: and A. C. Kirk,[e] who, far from having to treat steel more carefully than wrought-iron, habitually and successfully subjects it to treatment which would be fatal to wrought iron.

Then we have such remarkable numerical results as the following. Adamson[f] has lost but one plate among 3,500 received from a certain steel-maker: in welding 600 to 700 feet of steel plates weekly he loses perhaps one plate or so in three months, while with wrought-iron the failures amounted to 12·5%: and not an accident has happened to any of the 3,000 steel boilers which he has built.

Krupp,[g] whose guns are of crucible steel, states that not a single gun made by him during the last seventeen years has burst.

J. Ward[h] of the famous shipbuilding firm of Wm. Denny

[a] W. Parker, "Experience in the Use of Thick Steel Boiler-Plates." Excerpt Proc. Inst. Nav. Arch., XXVI., 1886.

[b] Sir E. J. Reed, discussion of Stromeyer's paper on "The Working of Steel." Excerpt Proc. Inst. Civ. Eng., LXXXIV., p. 73, 1886: Also U. S. Naval Prof. Papers, No. 21, p. 64, 1887.

[c] Engineer in charge of the construction of the Forth Bridge. Trans. Am. Soc Mech. Eng., VIII., p. 168, 1887. It is but fair to state, however, that Mr. Baker permits no punching, requires all sheared edges to be planed, and rarely permits blue-working. (§ 288, A, § 290.) These precautions are doubtless desirable even in case of the best Lowmoor iron, but opinions may differ as to their being necessary.

[d] Discussion on Stromeyer's paper on Mild Steel the Working of Steel. Excerpt Proc. Inst. Civ. Eng., LXXXIV., p. 73, 1886.

[e] Of the great ship-building firm of R. Napier & Sons, Glasgow. Trans. Inst Nav. Arch., XXVII., p. 124, 1886. "With steel, we go round a heavy flang eleven inches deep, as I have done often enough, knocking it down with a steam hammer. I have not had a case of failure. If it had been a piece of (wrought-iron plate I dare not have done such a thing at all, the first blow would have broken it right through. Again, to flange a steel plate for a furnace mouth we push a die right through at one heat which we dare not do in iron."

[f] Discussion on Goodall's paper on "Open-Hearth Steel for Boiler-Making," excerpt. Proc. Inst. Civ. Eng., XCII., p. 63, 1888.

[g] Stahl und Eisen, VIII., p. 52, 1888.

[h] Trans. Inst. Nav. Arch., XXVII., p. 65, 1886.

and Brothers, (which goes on the principle that if steel cannot stand the rough usage of shipyard in punching, shearing and hammering, the sooner it fails the better), in building eighty steel vessels used, up to the year 1880, 7,000 tons or 58,000 pieces of steel, losing six plates and one angle-piece, or about 0·01%; and from 1880 to 1886 48,000 tons of steel or 350,000 pieces, losing 12 pieces, or 0·003%. They have often lost more than four times this amount in a single wrought-iron vessel.

B. Martell,[a] Chief Surveyor of Lloyd's Register, reports that up to and including the year 1885, 444 steel vessels were built, and classed by his company. Among these he learns of seven total losses, which he thinks remarkably few: one was by stranding, two vessels foundered in gales, one was sunk by an iceberg, one by a sailing vessel, two were lost by means not stated. In an investigation by Lloyds' surveyors into the durability of steel vessels, sixty cases were specially reported on: in five out of the eight typical cases which Martell reports, the steel vessel safely endured grounding or collision which would have sunk a wrought-iron one.

At John Brown and Company's Works[b] more than four thousand very large steel boiler-front-plates were made in the five years ending in 1887, being "flanged at one heat all the way round, and without a single failure."

H. Goodall[c] states that, of 4,464 wrought-iron plates which he has used for boiler-making since the introduction of steel for boilers in 1875, 2·68% were defective and 0·2% spoilt in working, or together 2·88%: while of 4,236 steel plates which he used in the same time 1·04% were defective and 0·68% spoilt in working, or together 1·72%: and of this a considerable proportion seems justly chargeable to his workmen's lack of experience with the new material.

W. Parker[d] states that not an accident has occurred under steam among the upwards of 4,000 steel marine boilers built, which represent over 160,000 tons of steel. The Maginnis case, however, suggests that boiler explosions may account for some of the cases in which steamers have been lost without tidings.

Next, it is probable that wrought-iron sometimes fails in the same mysterious way as steel, though strikingly few mysterious failures are reported in case of the former metal. Stromeyer reports two cases, one in which on examining a wrought-iron boiler which had been out of use for about three months, he found a crack twenty-three inches long, extending from one plate into the next, and doubtless, he says, formed within twelve hours previous to his survey: the iron seemed soft in chipping. In the second a plate cracked quite across with a loud report during the dinner-hour, and about two weeks after the boiler was blown down.[e]

It is reported that, about the year 1848, the wrought-iron boiler-furnaces of the British-built steamer Leipzig cracked down the sides after several trips to Hamburg and back, just as in the Maginnis case.[f]

[a] Idem, p. 50.

[b] J. D. Ellis, discussion of Goodall's paper on "Open-hearth Steel for Boiler-making," excerpt Proc. Inst. Civ. Eng., XCII., p. 40, 1888.

[c] Idem, p. 25.

[d] Discussion of Stromeyer's paper on "the Working of Steel," Excerpt Proc. Inst. Civ. Eng., LXXXIV., p. 40, 1886.

[e] Idem, p. 76.

[f] J. Harrison, letter to "The Engineer," LX., p. 504, 1885. I have, unfortunately, little ground for judging how accurately the circumstances of this failure have survived the thirty-five years which elapsed before Mr. Harrison's brief notice of it appeared.

Several inquiries, which I have addressed to engineers whose prolonged experience has been of such a nature as to give them unusual opportunities for observation, have failed to bring to light other failures of wrought-iron boilers which could reasonably be classed as mysterious.

The liability to injury through cold- and blue-working, through local heating, overheating, unduly high finishing temperature, etc., probably increases rapidly both as the percentage of carbon and as that of phosphorus increase. Moreover, the liability to injury by improper heat treatment is probably greater in ingot- than in wrought-iron. Further, heterogeneousness, whether from segregation or imperfect mixing, probably increases the liability to injury. Finally, injury actually received from certain of these causes seems to increase greatly the liability to injury through certain others: overheating and too high finishing temperature to increase the liability to injury through local heating and cold-working, though on this point one may not speak too positively.

In view of these facts, ignoring our natural dread of the untried, we can see three simple reasons why the treachery of steel, once so serious a thing, is now almost of the past.

First, the steel-maker has learnt by experience. He knows to-day far better the effects of a high percentage of carbon or of phosphorus, of cracks, pipes and blowholes, of segregation and imperfect mixing, of over heating, of finishing too hot and too cold. Knowing, he guards against them more effectually, and keeps at home much steel that he would formerly have sent into the market. Those who would not or could not learn and do, have been driven out of the business: the conditions necessary for producing good sound steel by the acid Bessemer and open-hearth processes have been mastered. By and by the basic process came along, with new conditions, new liabilities to unsoundness, a great hue and cry about mysterious fractures followed, and Lloyd's Register provisionally forbade the use of basic steel.[g] Much basic steel was irregular, much brittle throughout: too much carbon, too much phosphorus, too cold teeming, imperfect mixing. Still there was little doubt that, with further experience, these difficulties of the basic process would be mastered as those of the acid process had been. Later still, coming to the present time, these difficulties yield more and more.

A second reason is that steel-users have learnt better what steel will and what it will not endure. It is difficult to estimate the importance of this. On the one hand eminent steel-users[h] insist that they treat steel exactly like wrought-iron, or even more severely, yet with perfect impunity. Many excellent American boiler-makers are absolutely ignorant of the injury caused by blue-working

[g] This occurred on December 17th, 1885, and from then at least till July 27th, 1887, no basic steel was used in vessels classed at Lloyd's. (Martell, "On the Present Position Occupied by Basic Steel." Excerpt, Proc. Inst. Nav. Arch., XXVIII., 1887.) On the day last mentioned, however, W. H. White reported that a small trial lot of basic steel ordered by the Admiralty for the less important parts of vessels, though in part severely tested in working, behaved so well as to show that basic steel could be used confidently for such purposes. ("On Some Recent Experiments with Basic Steel," idem.)

Lloyd's Register now permits the use of basic steel for ship and marine boiler-work, provided that it be made at works inspected and approved, and that it passes the specified tests. (Wm. Parker, Chief Engineer-Surveyor to Lloyd's. Private communication, Feb. 5th, 1889.)

[h] J. Ward, Trans. Inst. Nav. Arch., XXVII., p. 66, 1886, speaking of the remarkable success of his firm in steel ship-building, states not only that in his yard steel receives the same treatment as wrought-iron (save the annealing of certain straps) but that "no amount of instruction would ever gain it better or different treatment at the hands of the workmen than (wrought-) iron has always had." H. H. West echoes these statements (idem, p. 127).

by punching, etc.: full well I know that look, sometimes puzzled, oftener pitying, which a question as to the advisability of avoiding a blue heat, of drilling or reaming, of annealing after severe abuse, calls forth.

Now it seems clear that steel endures certain kinds of abuse much better than wrought-iron, and here it is probably treated as badly and perhaps worse than wrought-iron. But it is probable that other forms of abuse, such as local heating and over-heating, injure it more than wrought-iron. And it seems to me very probable that it is partly because we know and avoid these that we have fewer accidents with ingot-iron to-day than formerly. Several skilled American ship-builders assure me that they still have as many if not more accidents with ingot- than with wrought-iron: and this seems readily explained by supposing that their foremen and workmen do not yet understand the metal's weaknesses fully, for I know that they use admirable metal.

Again, a ship-builder's statement, that in his yard steel is treated exactly like wrought-iron, must be received very cautiously: for differences, apparently slight but really important, arise insensibly, imperfectly realized by ship-builder, foreman or even workmen. Owners of iron-working establishments have assured me, and I believe honestly, that ingot- and wrought-iron were treated exactly alike by their men: within five minutes their blacksmiths have assured me that they dared not heat ingot-iron as highly as wrought-iron, though they were not sure that if they did the ingot-iron would be injured. Ignore not the personal equation: your admirer will e'er minimize, your distruster exaggerate your faults.

THE EFFECT OF WORK.

§ 295. The almost self-evident proposition that wrought-iron,—consisting originally of but slightly adherent particles, and, after fagotting, of wholly inadherent bars,—should be greatly strengthened and toughened by work, abundantly proved by experience, led naturally to the belief that ingot-metal would be similarly improved. We will first consider the actual improvement due to work, and then its rationale.

TABLE 181.—RELATION BETWEEN THICKNESS AND PHYSICAL PROPERTIES OF IRON AND STEEL BARS, PLATES, ETC.
The composition and treatment of the members of each group are believed to be nearly alike, the thickness alone varying considerably.

	Authority.	DESCRIPTION.	Thickness, etc. Absolute, inches.	Thickness, etc. In percentage of thickness, etc., of thickest member of group.	Percentage of excess of tensile strength, etc., over that of thickest member of group. Tensile strength.	Elastic limit.	Elongation.	Reduction of area.	Tensile strength, pounds per square inch.	Elastic limit, pounds per square inch.	Elongation. %.	In.	Contraction of area, %.
			A.	B.	C.	D.	E.	F.	G.	H.	I.		J.
1.	D.	Terre Noire soft ingot-steel, natural state	0·87	100					62,740	39,600	20·68	7·87"	29·02
	"		0·48	49	+ 8·76	+ 8·23	+ 8·14	+ 68·23	65,100	40,890	22·80	"	49·62
	"		0·20	23	+ 5·17	+ 0·54	− 4·46	+ 43·85	65,930	39,824	18·70	"	42·00
	"		0·10	12	+ 26·70	+ 49·01	− 61·29	− 6·46	79,400	59,010	8·00	"	27·70
2.	"	Terre Noire soft ingot-steel, annealed	0·87	100					58,214	30,990	23·60	"	43·49
	"		0·48	49	− 1·05	− 12·59	− 9·22	+ 6·57	57,690	27,028	21·26	"	46·25
	"		0·20	23	+ 3·05	− 18·97	− 8·05	− 9·90	60,080	24,740	21·70	"	39·30
	"		0·10	12	+ 1·71	− 4·70	− 29·66	− 21·19	59,300	29,440	16·60	"	31·60
3.	"	Terre Noire soft ingot-steel, quenched in water of 28° C. from a rather dark red	0·87	100					86,840	41,020	15·30	"	32·35
	"		0·48	49	− 3·83	− 10·23	− 12·42	− 13·07	83,470	36,830	13·40	"	28·12
	"		0·29	23	+ 4·78	− 11·61	− 42·02	− 35·00	90,470	36,260	8·87	"	21·00
	"		0·10	12	+ 5·40	− 16·81	− 51·68	− 6·12	91,026	34,134	7·48	"	30·37
4.	R.	482 tests of 54 plates rolled from 12 ingots from a single heat of open-hearth steel, Unannealed.	1·00	100					61,940	......	22·52	....	33·47
	"		0·50	50	+ 3·67	....	+ 4·60	+ 24·80	64,380	......	28·87	....	41·60
	"		0·25	25	+ 12·30	....	− 5·79	+ 19·15	69,550	......	21·50	....	39·88
	"	482 tests of 54 plates rolled from 12 ingots from a single heat of open-hearth steel, Annealed.	1·00	100					59,160	......	27·02	....	44·42
	"		0·50	50	+ 3·10	....	− 0·70	+ 6·82	61,040	......	26·83	....	47·45
	"		0·25	25	+ 6·17	....	− 13·47	+ 1·36	62,880	......	23·38	....	45·025
5.	B.	....	......	100					63,400	......	21·75	....	43·5
	"	....	......	42·87	+ 6·03	....	− 4·60	+ 8·76	72,520	......	20·75	....	44·1
	"	....	......	28·58	+ 8·11	....	− 10·35	− 1·18	73,940	......	19·5	....	42·0
	"	....	......	14·29	+ 15·30	....	− 17·24	− 4·00	79,060	......	18·0	....	40·3
6.	"	....	......	100·00					66,980	......	22·8	....	47·0
	"	....	......	42·87	+ 3·18	....	− 23·77	+ 4·26	69,110	......	17·9	....	49·0
	"	....	......	28·58	+ 6·29	....	− 10·81	− 13·82	72,520	......	20·0	....	40·6
	"	....	......	14·29	+ 8·92	....	− 1·34	+ 2·34	72,950	......	22·0	....	48·1
7.	"	....	......	100					71,950	......	22·7	....	42·7
	"	....	......	50	+ 7·51	....	− 15·42	+ 0·70	77,360	......	19·2	....	43·0
	"	....	......	25	+ 11·86	....	− 29·52	− 1·64	80,490	......	16·0	....	42·0
8.	"	....	......	100					71,530	......	23·7	....	53·6
	"	....	......	50	− 0·60	....	− 17·72	− 2·80	71,100	......	19·5	....	52·1
	"	....	......	25	+ 5·96	....	− 40·98	− 11·57	75,790	......	14·0	....	47·4
9.	L.	Averages of many (about 500) tests of steel boiler plates made for an American engineer; all made and tested at the same mill	0·75	100					63,000	32,000	25	15"	
	"		0·56	75	− 4·76	+ 15·62	....	....	60,000	37,000	25	"	
	"		0·50	67	− 6·35	+ 25·00	....	....	59,000	40,000	25	"	
	"		0·44	58	− 6·35	+ 25·00	− 4·00	....	59,000	40,000	24	"	
	"		0·37	49	− 7·94	+ 28·12	− 4·00	....	58,000	41,000	24	"	
10.	G.	Bars 2¼" × ⅜"	0·617	100					61,272	......	26·05	8	
	G.	Angles rolled from them	0·380	62	+ 8·85	....	....	....	68,681	......	26·05	"	
12.	W.	Swedish Bessemer billet, 1·5" square, carbon 1·13%	1·5	100					88,390	......	0·10	10	
	"	The same annealed	1·5	100	− 41·82	....	+ 1·50		51,398	......	0·25	10	
	"	" " rolled down to ¾" square	0·75	58	+ 20·48	....	+ 1900·00		106,667	......	2·00	10	
14.	.....	Mean of 48 sets of tests by Kirkaldy on open-hearth steel plates	1	100					60,880	42,670			
	.....		0·75	75	− 7·65	− 17·82	....	....	64,895	35,260			
	.....		0·50	50	− 5·06	− 17·89	....	....	63,130	35,155			
	.....		0·25	25	− 10·24	− 22·05	....	....	62,720	33,262			
15.	.....	Parker. 1¼" boiler-plate	1·25	100					67,290@76,180	......	21·8@28·1	8	
	.....	½" plate of similar metal	·50	40	+ 19·58	....	− 8·91		78,400@91,840		21 @24	8	
16.	.....	H. Allen. Billet, and wire rods rolled from it. Soft steel	2" sq.	100					62,390	38,170	28·1	....	58·95
	.....		0·30	15	+ 8·01	+ 25·85	− 18·86	+ 10·14	67,390	47,846	22·8	....	59·42
	.....		0·284	14	+ 2·53	+ 19·54	− 29·54	+ 20·07	64,480	45,629	19·8	....	64·78
	.....		0·238	12	+ 7·76	+ 28·29	− 27·78	+ 23·03	67,152	49,078	21·7	....	66·49
	.....		0·220	11	+ 5·20	+ 22·03	− 23·13	+ 26·95	66,170	46,853	21·6	....	63·11

1 to 3. From the same cast of soft steel, one ingot 13·8 inches × 8·7 inches was rolled to a plate 0·87 inches thick, which was cut in two, one half tested, the other rolled down to 0·10 inches. A second ingot, 8·7 inches square was rolled to 0·48 inches, cut in two, one half yielding the test-piece, the other being rolled to 0·1. Y. Deshayes, Ann. Mines, 7th series, XV., p. 345.

4. J. Riley, Journ. Iron and Steel Inst., 1887, I., p. 121.

5 to 8. Brauns, Ledebur, Handbuch, p. 935, from Stahl und Eisen, 1883, p. 4.

9. 36 to 40 private notes.

10. Gatewood, Rep't. U. S. Naval Advisory B'd on Mild Steel, 1886, pp. 67-8. From each of 19 heats of Cambria open-hearth steel, pieces from flats 2¼" × ⅜" were tested, and also pieces from angle-irons rolled from these flats, in all 95 tests. In every case the tensile strength of the angle-iron exceeded that of the flat. The angle-irons, however, were not tested on the same machine as the flats.

12. M. White, private communication.

14. Rept. U. S. Naval Advisory B'd on Mild Steel, 1886-1885, p. 138, from British Parliamentary paper, C 9897, London, 1881.

15. W. Parker, "Experience in the Use of Thick Steel Boiler-plates," Inst. Naval Architects, 1885.

16. Pieces from a 2 inch square soft steel billet, carbon 0·11%, silicon 0·03%, phosphorus 0·072, are rolled hot to wire-rods of the diameters given. The wire-rods were annealed before testing, the billet apparently was not. The properties of the unannealed wire-rods are also given in the original, but they do not differ greatly from those here given. H. Allen, excerpt Proc. Inst. Civ. Eng., XCIV., 1888. The density of these specimens is given in Table 431.

§ 296. RELATION BETWEEN THICKNESS OF PIECE AND TESTING-MACHINE PROPERTIES.

A. *Ingot-iron.*—Let us first study the effect of varying thickness with one inch as a maximum, and then for greater thicknesses.

1. *Pieces 1'' thick and less.*—Numbers 4, 9 and 10 of Table 131, collectively representing more than 1,000 tests for each property, indicate that thin plates do not excel thick ones in ductility, at least not in elongation: while as to tensile strength their teaching is contradictory, the thin plates excelling the thick in 4 and 10, but being excelled by them in 9. It is not improbable that this discrepancy is due to differences in the conditions of rolling: possibly the plates of Number 4 were finished so cold as to increase their tensile strength: for we find that in the case of the annealed plates of Number 4 the thin are but little stronger than the thick. So with Numbers 1 and 2 of table 131, and so with the half-inch pieces (Nos. 5 and 11) in table 134, which when annealed are not markedly stronger than the inch pieces. The elastic limit in Number 9, table 131, increases as the thickness decreases, though the tensile strength at the same time diminishes.

The indications, then, seem to be that thinner pieces of soft steel may, but do not necessarily, excel similar ones one inch thick in tensile strength and elastic limit: that they are likely to be less ductile than the one-inch pieces: and that, if heated (*e. g.* for annealing) they are likely to lose much of their excess (if any there be) of tensile strength and elastic limit, while recovering their deficit of elongation.

2. But when we come to pieces as thick or thicker than one inch, the case is different. Of these Kirkaldy

TABLE 133. INFLUENCE OF THE EARLY VS. THE LATE REDUCTIONS ON THE PHYSICAL PROPERTIES OF INGOT-IRON. (KIRKALDY, FAGERSTA STEEL, SERIES C8, 0 15% CARBON.)

		Percentage of increase of properties in reducing from 3'' × 3'' to 1'' × 1''. EARLY REDUCTIONS.				Percentage of increase of properties in reducing from 1'' × 1'' to ½'' × ½''. LATE REDUCTIONS.			
		Tensile strength.	Elastic limit.	Elongation.	Reduction of area.	Tensile strength.	Elastic limit.	Elongation.	Reduction of area.
Unannealed	Hammered	15·3	11·1	—66·9	50·5	10·6	18·8	—84·4	—8·24
	Rolled	8	36·2	—10·6	20·6	11·4	8·8	—20·1	8·8
Annealed	Hammered	6·2	21·5	—42·2	38·3	2·8	6·7	—16·0	7·6
	Rolled	0·9	28·2	— 5·8	14·3	—1·1	4·1	—23	6·4

TABLE 133.—INFLUENCE OF WORK ON REDUCTION ON THE PROPERTIES OF IRON.

Percentage of increase of tensile strength, etc., due to each 1% of diminution of sectional area by hammering.

Number.	Diminution of cross-section. Size of piece, inches. Initial.	Final.	Diminution per 100 of original.	Prop'n of carbon	Gain in tensile strength, %. B1. 0·8%.	B2. 0·6%.	B3. 0·4%.	B4. 0·2.	Average.	Gain in elastic limit, %. B1. 0·8%	B2. 0·6%.	B3. 0·4%.	B4. 0·2	Average.	Gain in elongation, %. B1. 0·8%.	B2. 0·6%	B3. 0·4%.	B4. 0·2	Average.	Gain in contraction of area, %. B1. 0·8%.	B2. 0·6%.	B3. 0·4%	B4. 0·2	Average.
	UNANNEALED STEEL.																							
1	6 × 6	5 × 5	30·6	....	·02	—·21	·39	·18	·11	·18	·05	·18	·48	·20	0·80	—0·38	1·87	2·28	1·00	0·65	—0·32	1·25	0·28	0·34
2	5 × 5	4 × 4	36·0	....	·36	·33	·47	·12	·35	·38	·29	·23	·55	·85	0·00	2·78	4·19	1·08	2·18	0·62	4·37	6·15	2·92	3·50
3	4 × 4	3 × 3	43·7	....	·24	·33	·04	·05	·17	·12	·18	·25	·20	·20	0·27	1·96	0·48	—0·10	·65	0·10	2·09	3·15	0·54	1·42
4	3 × 3	2 × 2	55·6	....	·31	·17	·03	·02	·18	·20	·07	·17	·08	·14	0·28	1·72	0·13	—0·24	·48	0·70	4·01	0·42	0·03	1·29
5	Average of 1 to 4		....	....	·26	·23	·23	·09	·20	·21	·14	·21	·33	·22	0·51	1·87	1·67	0·74	1·07	0·52	2·88	2·74	0·22	1·64
6	6 × 6	2 × 2	88·9	....	·53	·49	·40	·15	·39	·44	·27	·43	·66	·43	1·12	4·81	4·63	1.06	2·85	1·23	11·66	12·94	4·67	7·64
	ANNEALED STEEL.																							
7	6 × 6	5 × 5	30·6	....	·34	—·61	·48	·02	—·02	·04	·09	·27	·41	·21	0·19	—2·27	1·71	∞	......	2·08	—2·60	1·01	0·69	0·74
8	5 × 5	4 × 4	36·0	....	·36	·72	·40	·20	·42	·21	·15	·12	·61	·31	1·85	2·01	0·21	0·38	2·61	1·27	2·83	9·17	1·56	3·57
9	4 × 4	3 × 3	43·7	....	·08	·37	—·03	—·07	·09	·15	·11	·14	·22	·16	0·61	4·18	—0·19	1·02	1·40	1·11	9·10	1·27	0·02	3·00
10	3 × 3	2 × 2	55·6	....	·20	·12	·06	·04	·10	·09	·18	·25	·12	·16	0·81	0·14	0·01	—0·46	0·12	1·60	1·12	0·06	0·05	0·56
11	Average of 7 to 10		....	....	·17	·15	·23	·05	·15	·12	·13	·21	·30	·21	0·86	1·31	1·94	......	......	1·29	2·40	3·10	0·62	1·97
12	6 × 6	2 × 2	88·9	....	·40	·27	·38	·08	·28	·25	·23	·40	·72	·42	2·51	0·56	3·99	0·25	1·90	3·03	2·32	11·84	1·08	4·55

This table is calculated from Kirkaldy's data, "Experimental Enquiry into the Mechanical Properties of Fagersta Steel, 1873." It gives the increase of tensile strength, etc., due to a unit of diminution of sectional area by forging. This increase for each particular reduction (*e. g.* from 4 × 4 to 3 × 3) is measured in percentages of the tensile strength, etc., which the metal has when of the initial area, in this case 4 × 4. The unit of diminution of area is one per cent. of said initial area, in this case $\frac{4 \times 4}{100}$ = 0·16 square inches. *Example.* To find the gain in tensile strength of unannealed steel B3, due to a unit of diminution of area, while being hammered from 4 × 4 to 3 × 3. Tensile strength of the 4 × 4 piece, 72,260 pounds per square inch: of the 3 × 3 piece, 73,580. Gain = 1,320 lbs. = $\frac{1,320 \times 100}{72,260}$ % = 1·827%. Diminution of area = $\frac{(4 \times 4) - (3 \times 3)}{4 \times 4} \times 100\%$ = 43·75%. Gain per 1% diminution of area = $\frac{1·827}{43·75}$ = 0·04%. The results for the other properties are obtained mutatis mutandis.

TABLE 134.—INFLUENCE OF WORK ON REDUCTION ON THE PROPERTIES OF IRON. (ROLLING. KIRKALDY'S DATA).

I. Percentage of excess (+) or deficit (—) of the tensile strength of smaller steel bars over the tensile strength, etc., of similar 3'' square bars.

Number.	Size of piece. Absolute, inches.	In percentage of sectional area of 3 × 3 bar.	Tensile strength. C1 1%	C2 0·5%	C3 0·15%	Elastic limit. C1 1%	C2 0·5%	C3 0·15%	Elongation. C1 1%	C2 0·5%	C3 0·15%	Contraction of area. C1 1%	C2 0·5%	C3 0·15%
	Unannealed Ingot-Steel and Ingot-Iron.													
1	2¼ × 2¼	60·44	+ 11	+ 16	+ 8	+ 7	+ 20	+ 10	+ 83	+ 229	— 35	+ 80	+ 184	— 46
2	2 × 2	44·44	+ 34	+ 35	+ 8	+ 9	+ 26	+ 20	+ 167	+ 556	— 8	+ 2009	+ 373	— 10
3	1½ × 1½	25·00	+ 47	+ 27	+ 4	+ 11	+ 83	+ 28	+ 317	+ 963	— 12	+ 820	+ 320	— 3
4	1 × 1	11·11	+ 71	+ 41	+ 3	+ 20	+ 42	+ 86	+ 916	+ 849	— 11	+ 2300	+ 566	+ 21
5	½ × ½	2·78	+ 55	+ 45	+ 10	+ 81	+ 54	+ 48	+ 1116	+ 540	— 29	+ 3900	+ 877	+ 25
	Annealed Ingot-Steel and Ingot-Iron.													
7	2¼ × 2¼	60·44	+ 11	+ 19	+ 0	— 5	+ 18	+ 14	+ 90	+ 268	— 15	+ 104	+ 587	— 6
8	2 × 2	44·44	+ 25	+ 83	+ 11	+ 5	+ 31	+ 33	+ 180	+ 849	— 23	+ 96	+ 620	— 3
9	1½ × 1½	25·00	+ 49	+ 37	+ 8	+ 21	+ 37	+ 23	+ 185	+ 390	— 31	+ 182	+ 617	6
10	1 × 1	11·11	+ 88	+ 30	+ 5	+ 58	+ 45	+ 21	+ 200	+ 197	— 6	+ 643	+ 635	+ 14
11	½ × ½	2·78	+ 76	+ 33	+ 5	+ 40	+ 49	+ 33	+ 325	+ 158	— 29	+ 971	+ 844	+ 21
	II. Percentage of increase of tensile strength, etc., due to each 1% of diminution of sectional area by rolling, from 3 × 3 to ½ × ½.													
	Unannealed Ingot-Steel and Ingot-Iron.													
13	½ × ½	2·78	+ 0·67	+ 0·46	+ 0·15	+ 31·46	+ 5·55	— 0·20	+ 11·48	+ 5·56	— 0·30			
	Annealed Ingot-Steel and Ingot-Iron.													
14	½ × ½	2·78	+ 0·78	+ 0·64	+ 0·65	......	......	......	+ 8·84	+ 1·68	— 0·30			
	III. Percentage of increase of tensile strength due to 1% of diminution of sectional area by rolling from 1 × 1 to ½ × ½.													
	Unannealed.													
15	....	....	+ ·11	+ ·05	+ ·15	+ ·12	+ ·11	+ ·11	......	......	......	+ ·59	+ ·02	+ ·04
	Annealed.													
16	....	....	+ ·10	......	......	+ ·08	+ ·01	+ ·05	......	......	......	+ ·68	+ ·88	+ ·09

TABLE 135.—INFLUENCE OF THE PROPORTION OF CARBON ON THE INCREASE OF TENSILE STRENGTH, ETC., DUE TO FORGING, ETC. (Kirkaldy.)

			Unannealed steel.					Annealed steel.				
			B1 0·80% C.	B2 0·60% C.	B3 0·40% C.	B4 0·20% C.	Mean.	B1 0·80% C.	B2 0·60% C.	B3 0·40% C.	B4 0·20% C.	Mean
Reduction from 6 × 6 inch ingots to 2 × 2 inch bars by hammering	Tensile strength increased by, %		46·8	48·5	35·8	18·9	36·1	36·5	24·0	33·6	6·7	25·3
	Elastic limit increased by, %		39·1	23·7	38·5	58·5	38·0	22·3	24·6	39·5	64·3	33·8
	Contraction of area increased by, %		113·	1936·	1150·	413·	626·	290·	209·	1968·	136	288·
			C1 1% C.	C2 0·5% C.	C3 0·15% C.			C1 1% C.	C2 0·5% C.	C3 0·15% C.		
Reduction from 3 × 3 bars to ½ × ½ inch bars	Tensile strength increased by, %	Hammered	93·2	36·9	27·4	....	54·2	73·1	17·9	10·2	....	36·2
		Rolled	85·1	45·4	14·8	....	52·6	75·5	38·3	4·3	....	42·3
	Elastic limit " "	Hammered	53·2	131·8	102·5	....	78·7	49·8	60·4	29·7	....	47·8
		Rolled	30·6	58·9	47·5	....	40·8	46·3	49·3	38·5	....	44·3
	Elongation " "	Hammered										
		Rolled	1116·	540·	26·	....	....	825·	158·	— 29·		
	Contraction of area " "	Hammered	4800·	968·	41·	....	160·	1462·	555·	43·	....	148·6
		Rolled	3930·	877·	24·6	....	115·	971·	844	21·	....	120

Calculated from Kirkaldy. "Experimental Enquiry into the Mechanical Properties of Fagersta Steel." The numbers in this table give the increase of tensile strength, etc., due to forging, measured in percentage of the tensile strength, etc., of the 6″ ingots in the first three lines, and measured in percentage of the tensile strength, etc., of the 3″ bars in the last eight lines.

gives twenty-four comparable pairs of cases of soft steel, in which the thinner differs from the thicker in size only: here the thin excels the thick in elastic limit in 22 cases, or 91·7% of the whole, in contraction of area in 21 cases, and in tensile strength in 18 cases, or 75% of the whole (columns B4 in table 133 and C3 in table 134).[a]

Table 132 indicates that the reduction from 3″ to 1″ square increases the elastic limit and contraction of area for soft steel much more than that from 1″ to ½″, without corresponding difference in case of tensile strength.

B. *Ingot-Steel.*—In the cases before us the tensile strength and ductility of ingot-steel are increased very much more than those of ingot-iron by reduction of thickness: but as regards the gain in elastic limit, ingot-iron and steel stand more nearly on a par, that of ingot-iron being greater than that of ingot-steel in Table 133, while in Table 134 neither class has a decided advantage.

Out of 64 pairs of comparable cases of ingot-steel in Kirkaldy's work, the tensile strength, elastic limit, and contraction of area of the thinner excel those of the thicker pieces in 56, 61 and 58 cases respectively, or in 87·5, 95·3, and 90·6% of the total number of cases.

Taking all of Kirkaldy's Fagersta cases together, I can trace no simple relation between the proportion of carbon and the effect of reduction on the elastic limit, whether for annealed or unannealed metal, nor on the ductility for annealed metal: but, within the limits carbon 0·60% and 0·15%, for given diminution of area by hot work, the *higher the carbon the greater the gain in tensile strength for both annealed and unannealed metal,* and in ductility for unannealed metal (Table 135).[b]

2. *Annealed vs. Unannealed.*—If E = the percentage of excess (due to hot working) of any given property in an unannealed bar over that of the unannealed bar or ingot from which it is made, and if E′ = the corresponding excess for annealed steel: then we learn from Tables 133 to 135 that, in case of 2″ bars from 6″ ingots and of ½″ bars from 3″ bars, E for tensile strength is almost always and E for elongation usually greater than E′, but not for elastic limit or contraction of area. Nor does E appear on the whole to be greater than E′ for any of these properties in case of bars of intermediate size made from 6″ ingots and from 3″ bars. In other words, in Kirkaldy's experiments, hot-working appears to increase the elastic limit and contraction of area belonging to the annealed state probably about as much on the whole as those belonging to the unannealed state; and the tensile strength and elongation belonging to the annealed state in very many cases as much as those belonging to the unannealed state.

But in numbers 1, 2 and 4 of Table 131 E is greater than E′ for elastic limit and tensile strength.

This indicates that the improvement differs from that induced by cold-working, which is lessened by annealing. (Cf. § 271, p. 217).

3. *Early vs. Late Reduction.*—If i = the percentage of increase of any property following an amount of hot working which diminishes the sectional area of the piece by 1%, then we find in Table 133 that, for each of the four properties, i is greater when the size is reduced from 5 in. × 5 in. to 4 in. × 4 in. than for either earlier or later reductions. This is true in 83 out of the 96 cases in which i for other reductions is compared with i for reductions from 5 × 5 to 4 × 4. In other words, under these conditions a given percentage of diminution of area between 5 in. × 5 in. and 4 in. × 4 in. does more good than either earlier or later diminutions. Further, i is greater here for reduction from 5 in. to 4 in. than from 4 in. to 3 in. in 28 out of 32 cases; and for 4 in. to 3 in. than for 3 in. to 2 in. in 21 out of 32 cases. Whether this is due to the special conditions of these cases or not, further investigation must

TABLE 136.—IMPROVEMENT OF WROUGHT-IRON F WITH DIMINISHING SIZE.
U. S. Board on Testing Iron, etc., I., p. 88, 1881.

Size of bar. Inches.	Sectional area of pile. Inches.	Sectional area of bar in per cent of area of pile.	Tensile strength, pounds per square inch.		Elastic limit, pounds per square inch.	
			Entire bar.	Core.	Entire bar.	Core.
4	80	15·70	......	46,522	......	28,430
3½	60	13·80	......	46,667	......	26,686
3⅜	80	12·66	......	47,000	......	24,951
3¼	80	10·37	......	47,014	......	24,501
3	80	8·83	......	47,761	......	26,887
2⅞	60	7·42	......	46,166	......	26,823
2¾	80	6·13	47,844	47,423	29,758	28,941
2⅝	72	5·52	48,505	49,200	31,287	32,163
2	72	4·36	47,872	48,280	35,864	31,802
[illegible]	86	7·67	49,744	49,870	35,610	37,042
1⅞	64	6·63	50,547	48,792	35,854	38,492
1¾	86	5·76	50,529	49,144	35,804	34,206
1⅝	86	4·90	50,820	51,538	35,087	36,467
1½	86	4·12	52,880	48,819	39,108	......
1⅜	86	3·41	52,720	49,901	30,609	40,584
1¼	25	8·96	50,149	60,530	35,498	37,771
1⅛	25	3·14	51,921	51,128	39,066	38,066
1	12¼	4·91	50,716	50,874	33,081	33,204
⅞	12¼	3·60	50,678	50,476	33,933	35,958
¾	12¼	2·50	52,297	51,481	34,450	34,545
⅝	9	2·17	52,275	52,770	33,445	39,126
½	9	3·68	54,098	54,108	38,475	40,918
⅜	8	1·60	57,000	56,585	Lost.	Lost.

NOTE.—The number 0·68 in the third column for the ¾″ bar is given thus in the original. Apparently it should be 1·22.

[a] The elongation of the different sizes in Kirkaldy's experiments is not comparable, because the different test-pieces had unlike diameters.

[b] For the effect of annealing as influenced by the proportion of carbon, see § 46, p. 4. Mr. C. A. Marshall announces it as a law that the effect of work is greater and that of heat-treatment less on the physical properties of low- than of high-carbon steel. Doubtless true as regards certain forms of heat-treatment, *e. g.* quenching, this harmonizes poorly with our inferences from Kirkaldy's data as regards work: and in this respect it is also opposed to Metcalf's judgment and experience. Trans. Am. Soc. Civ. Eng., XV., pp. 349, 351, 1887.

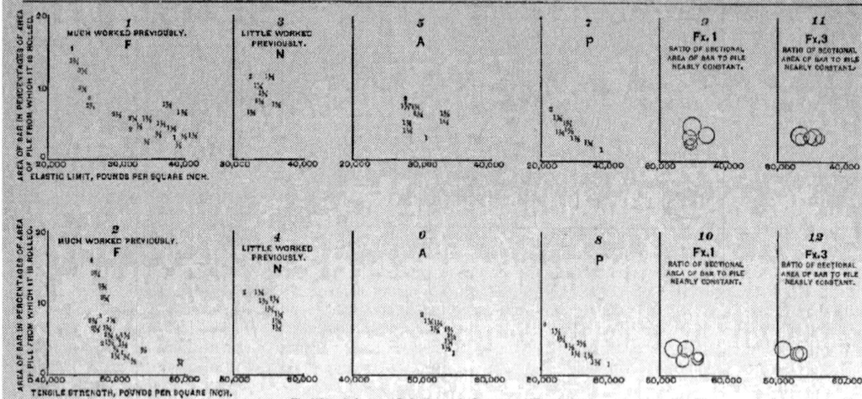

Fig. 118A.—Influence of Reduction on the Properties of Wrought-iron.

The diagrams are to be taken in pairs, 1 with 2, 3 with 4, etc. The tensile strength (even-numbered diagrams) and elastic limit (odd-numbered diagrams) of wrought-iron bars were determined, and the results here plotted. Each pair of diagrams represents results obtained with many bars of the same kind of wrought-iron, but of different thicknesses and produced with different amounts of reduction from the pile from which they were made. The numerals in diagrams 1 to 8 inclusive represent the thickness of the bars tested, in inches. In diagrams 9 to 12 inclusive the results fall so closely together that numerals would have obscured each other; the thickness of the bar is therefore represented in these diagrams by the size of the circles. The results are those of the United States Test Board, Rept. 1881.

decide: but, taken collectively, the evidence here presented seems to indicate pretty strongly that the improvement is on the whole more marked and constant for reductions between large sizes than for those between small sizes, especially when the small sizes are materially below one inch.

Quantitative Effect of Work.—Table 133 indicates that, under the conditions here existing, if the sectional area of the piece be reduced by from 30 to 45% by hot-working, then on an average each 1% of diminution of area increases the tensile strength and elastic limit by about 0·2% and the elongation and contraction of area by about 1·5%

To sum up, diminution in the thickness of ingot-metal is usually but not necessarily accompanied by an increase in tensile strength, elastic limit and ductility: the exceptions are more numerous in case of ductility than of the two other properties, and in case of thin ingot-iron than in other cases. The increase of tensile strength and contraction of area, but apparently not that of elastic limit, usually increases with the proportion of carbon, at least till this reaches 0·6%. The increase is on the whole greater for the early than for the late reductions, and, while often as great in case of annealed as in that of unannealed metal, the latter class in many and perhaps most cases gains most. To verify these inferences, which are only provisional, the study of a much larger number of cases is necessary.

C. *Weld-Iron.*—The results of the United States Test Board, represented graphically in Figure 118A, diagrams 1 to 8, indicate that the tensile strength and elastic limit of weld- like those of ingot-metal increase as the thickness diminishes.[a] In Table 136, the improvement, though halting, continues down to the smallest size reached, 1/4″. From 1 1/4″ to 3/4″ there is little change: from 3/4″ to 1/4″ the improvement is marked.

§ 297. INFLUENCE OF THE THICKNESS OF THE INGOT OR PILE ON THE PROPERTIES OF THE RESULTING BARS, ETC. —The examples in Tables 137–8 seem to indicate that the properties of ingot-iron plates are independent of the size of the ingot from which they are made. Table 137 gives a case in which pieces of various thicknesses were cut from an ingot and rolled down to plates 1/2″ and 1/4″ thick. Pieces 1/2″ and 1/4″ thick were also cut directly from the ingot.

TABLE 137.—INFLUENCE OF THE INITIAL THICKNESS OF THE INGOT FROM WHICH THEY WERE ROLLED ON THE PROPERTIES OF STEEL PLATES. (PARKER).

		Tensile strength, pounds per square inch.	Elongation in 8 inches.
These pieces were all cut from one and the same ingot.	Piece 15 inches thick drawn down to 1/2 inch........	58,016	27·0
	" 12 1/2 " " "	59,186	27·0
	" 10 " " "	59,369	26·0
	" 7 1/2 " " "	58,683	24·0
	" 6 " " "	56,912	22·0
	" 5 " " "	58,464	24·0
	" 3 " " "	58,894	25.5
	" 2 " " "	58,249	26·0
	" 1 " " "	58,240	27·0
	" cut direct from the ingot, 1/2-inch thick........	49,280	9·0
	" 15 inches thick drawn down to 1/4 inch........	68,168	24 5
	" 12 1/2 " " "	65,184	22·5
	" 10 " " "	68,168	22·0
	" 7 1/2 " " "	66,528	16·0
	Piece cut direct from the ingot....................	[illegible]	10·
	The same piece after testing, hammered to 1/2 in. sq..	71,994	11·
	Common plates from the same charge..............	60,928	25·
		59,584	27·
	Pieces 1 1/4 cut from ingot and rolled to 3/4 inch round ..	68,544	28·

Journ. Iron and Steel Inst., 1887, I., pp. 183-4; also 1883, I., p. 106.

TABLE 138.—INFLUENCE OF THICKNESS OF INGOT ON PROPERTIES OF STEEL PLATES

	Size of ingot.	Thickness of plate.	Number of tests.	Tensile strength pounds per sq. in.	Elongation in 8 inches.	Contraction of area.
1	12″ × 6″	0·25″	16	65,500	21·8	38·2
2	24″ × 15″	0·25″	32	64,000	20·9	44·2
3	Thickness 7″	0·25 ±	11 to 15	55,920	29·6	60·2
4	" 12″	0·24	2	52,230	32·5	57·25
5	" 18″	0·238	2	60,115	33	57·75

1 and **2.** From two ingots 24″ × 15″ four slabs 8 inches thick were forged, and from two ingots 12″ × 6″ from the same cast two slabs 4 inches thick. These six slabs were rolled to plates 1/4 inch thick, and from each plate eight tensile tests were made. The results are calculated from J. Riley's data, Journ. Iron and Steel Inst., 1887, I., p. 122, Table I., and Abstract IV. Cf. J. Riley. Idem, 1889, I., p. 77.

3, 4 and **5.** A. E. Hunt, Trans. Am. Inst. Mining Engrs., XII., p. 815. From ingots 7″, 12″ and 18″ thick, all from the same heat of open-hearth steel, of carbon 0·16% plates about 0·25″ thick were rolled. Those from the 7″ ingots were rolled direct from the ingot apparently; those from the 12″ and 18″ ingots were rolled from slabs 5″ thick, hammered from the ingots.

[a] The formulæ $T = \frac{60,000}{\sqrt[4]{d}}$ and $T = 58,000 - \frac{7,000\ A}{B}$, in which d = the diameter, A = the area and B = the periphery of the section, all in inches, and T = the tensile strength in pounds per square inch, are proposed by Thurston and the Edgemoor Iron Co. respectively. Thurston, Matls. of Engineering, II., p. 407, 1885.

While these latter pieces were weak and brittle, the strength and ductility of the rolled plate pieces seem quite independent of the thickness of the piece from which they were rolled.[a]

The examples in Table 139 similarly indicate that the tensile strength and elastic limit of wrought-iron bars of given size is, within the limits here given, independent of the sectional area of the pile from which they are rolled. At least the influence of the size of the pile is here so slight as to be wholly masked by that of other variables.

TABLE 139.—INFLUENCE OF THE INITIAL THICKNESS OF THE PILE FROM WHICH THEY WERE ROLLED ON THE PROPERTIES OF WROUGHT-IRON BARS,

From Data of U. S. Board on Testing Iron, Steel, etc., 1881, pp. I., 88 to 44.

2-inch square bars							1⅝″ square bars.						
		Pile.		Bar.					Pile.		Bar.		
Number.	Name.	Size, inches.	Area, inches.	Area, % of area of pile.	Tensile strength, lbs. per sq. in.	Elastic limit, lbs. per sq. in.	Number.	Name.	Size, inches.	Area, inches.	Area, % of area of pile.	Tensile strength, lbs. per sq. in.	Elastic limit, lbs. per sq. in.
1..	N.	6 × 4½ × 26	27	11·63	51,848	32,461	1	N.	4 × 8¾ × 17	15	5·19	56,478	38,251
2..	A.	....	36	8·72	50,171	27,600	2	A.	....	25	4·90	53,579	27,800
3..	P.	....	45	6·96	50,834	31,878	3	Px.	....	31·5	3·80	56,334	33,921
4..	Fx.	....	49·5	6·35	52,599	31,198	4	F.	....	36	3·41	49,801	40,584
5..	F.	....	72	4·36	48,250	31,892	5	Fx. 3	6 × 6	36	3·41	53,248	33,520
6..	Fx. 1	8 × 10	80	3·93	52,011	34,702	6	P.	....	45	2·72	56,871	36,866
7..	Fx. 3	8 × 10	80	3·93	50,168	33,258	7	Fx. 1	6 × 8	48	2·55	55,307	34,764

§ 208. RATIONALE OF THE EFFECT OF WORK.—We can conceive six ways in which hot-working may influence the properties of iron and steel:

Mechanically
- 1, by expelling slag and by changing its distribution.
- 2, by welding together separate particles or pieces which were initially more or less detached. These two apply chiefly to weld-iron.
- 3, by closing blow-holes and pipes.

Structurally, 4, by preventing or obliterating crystallization.

Specially
- 5, by pressure as such.
- 6, by kneading as such.

Care is needed, especially in case of thin and hence cool-finished pieces, to distinguish the results of hot- from those of cold-working: the latter are probably more thoroughly removed by annealing than the former. Again, the increase of elastic limit probably bears a higher ratio to that of tensile strength in case of cold- than of hot-working. Further, while hot-working toughens, cold-working makes brittle: whence we infer that the cold-working range of temperature has been reached in the following case.

TABLE 139A.—NORMAL AND COOL WORK. BRYAN.

Rolled at	Tensile strength, lbs. per sq. in.				Elongation.			
Bright redness........	70,845	69,942	68,135	59,190	26·9	24·8	24·9	28·3
Dull "	70,513	71,954	64,060	61,590	22·4	22·6	23·8	24·5

Rept. Naval Advisory Bd. on Mild Steel, Gatewood, p. 92, 1886. Part of each of four heats of Cambria "cruiser" steel was rolled at bright redness, part at dull redness. The finishing-temperature is not given.

Of the above six ways, the first three are mechanical. That work may benefit thus is self-evident. The expulsion of slag must occur chiefly during the early part of each rolling or hammering, while the slag is liquid and the metal soft and open. Table 140 tends to show that little is removed in reducing wrought-iron from 2 in. to ½ in.

TABLE 140.—INFLUENCE OF WORK ON THE PROPORTION OF SLAG IN WELD IRON.

		Slag in chain-cable iron of various cross sections										
Diameter of piece, inches.		½.	¾.	1.	1⅛.	1¼.	1⅜ and 1 7-16.	1½.	1⅝ and 1 11-16.	1¾.	1 13-16	2.
Percentage of slag.	Maximum	......	......	1·168	......	1·006	1·738	1·724	1·826	1·280	......	2·262
	Minimum	......	......	0·570	......	0·450	0·192	0·329	0·308	0·334	......	0·548
	Average	·668	·885	·862	1·268	·873	1·058	0·930	·658	·948	0·878	1·228
Number of pieces....		1	1	3	1	2	6	5	5	4	1	4

This table is calculated from data furnished by the U. S. Board on testing iron, steel, etc., Rep., 1881, Vol. I., p. 228, Trans. Am. Inst. Mining Engineers, VI., p. 103, 1879.

The fourth is structural. Here the influence of work is of the same nature as that of heat-treatment.

The fifth and sixth may be called the special effects of work, which cannot be produced otherwise. By chemical additions and by compression in casting we can prevent mechanical defects: by heat-treatment we can in great measure govern the structure. But it is generally believed that work has a further influence: that its pressure and kneading as such work some lasting benefit which is not simply mechanical, which is not the same as that of heat-treatment, but which is comparable to the effect of kneading on clay, on dough, on putty. Let us term this the "special effect" of work.

Now it is a question, and a very important one, whether this special effect exists at all, whether "we want a forging machine at all," whether "the steel can be made to forge itself by static pressure and by heat"[b] with as good results as when forging is added to static pressure and heat: whether "it is possible" (and profitable) "to make a steel in its cast state just as strong as if it had been hammered"[c]: whether the superiority of thin over thick pieces even of mechanically sound ingot-metal (here excluding that improvement due to cold-working and removable by annealing) is due to increased reduction as such, or to the lower temperature at which the thinner piece is habitually finished, and thence to the smaller opportunity for crystallization.

The question may be resolved into two: (1), is there a special effect of work differing in nature from that of heat-treatment? (2), If not, and if their effects are of the same nature, may not these effects often be produced in a higher degree by work than by heat-treatment?

If this special effect exists and is important, then quality will be benefited by casting very thick ingots and giving abundant reduction: if not, we should cast the metal (1) in ingots as thin, *i. e.* as near the shape of the finished piece as we can without causing excessive casting-defects, (external cracks, pipes, blowholes,) weighing the increased cost of reducing thicker ingots to the finished shape and their greater proportion of crop ends against their greater soundness and cheapness; (2) in ingots of a weight convenient for casting and working, remembering that heavy ingots, demanding powerful cranes and roll-trains, etc., mean costly installation, danger of segregation, difficulty with heating-furnace bottoms (Aiken's crane promises to obviate this); light ingots mean excessive cost per ton for handling in casting-pit, furnace and mill. If the use of high working-temperature,—adopted to save power and to close blowholes effectively,—and of thin ingots, lead to finishing the metal so hot that hurtful crystallization during cooling is feared, cool quickly to V: or, if the best quality is needed, reheat to W (Cf. § 250, p. 179).

[a] The ⅜″ plates rolled from the 7½″ piece has low ductility, but this can hardly be attributed to its being rolled from a thin piece, as ⅜″ pieces rolled from 5″, 3″, 2″ and 1″ pieces had shown high ductility.

[b] Metcalf, Trans. Am. Soc. Civ. Eng., XV., p. 306, 1887.

[c] Holley, Metallurg. Rev., II., p. 381, 1878.

Again, if this special effect of work does not exist, or is unimportant, the prospective value and use of steel casting is enormous, enormous the prospective cheapening of steel pieces of castable shape: the gun- the armor-plate- the marine-shaft-question assume a different phase.

While it is conceivable that work should have a special lasting influence, it is not easy to understand what its nature is, that it can survive the complete metamorphoses, not only of crystalline form but actually of mineral species, which heat-treatment causes. It is hard to believe that, when the whole structure of steel has been completely revolutionized by heating to W., it should make any difference whether the supposed special effect had previously been induced or not.

The effect of work surely ceases when the metal melts: I for one find it hard to conceive or believe that the special direct effect of kneading and pressure survives heating to temperatures approaching the melting point. In this view, if this supposed effect exists at all, so that larger ingots yield better finished pieces than smaller sound ingots do, the benefit of each working is still likely to be effaced when the metal is heated again.

Our first question, is the superiority of thin pieces due to lower finishing-temperature or to greater reduction or both, and if to both in what proportion to each, is not easily answered, since the finishing temperature usually sinks as reduction increases. That is to say, if we start with ingot or pile of given size, then the greater the total reduction the lower also will be the finishing temperature. Hence we should expect common practice to answer equivocally, and should look to special cases, in which these two variables do not vary alike, for light. Nor do we look vainly.

To make this question of the finishing-temperature clear, let ordinates in Figure 118 B represent temperature and abscissæ coarseness of grain. Now, the line AW may be taken as representing roughly the size of grain which steel of given composition tends to assume with varying temperature, or the line of maximum coarseness of grain (Cf. Figure 63, p. 178). If the grain be smaller than the maximum for existing temperature it always tends to grow and to approach that maximum. If it be coarser than that maximum it does not tend to shrink back towards the maximum, except when the temperature is *rising* past W. Let us suppose that we cease rolling a piece of steel while its temperature is at L, the mechanical work of the rolls having broken the grain down, and reduced its size to B. During subsequent cooling the grain will grow, somewhat as sketched in the line BCE. If, however, we resume rolling when the grain had reached C, we will again break down the grain, and drive it back to D. And so, keeping on, between passes the grain grows and the temperature simultaneously falls, while at each pass the squeeze which we give the metal breaks up the grain, and the curve of grain and temperature follows the zigzag line BCDG.

If we cease rolling when the temperature has fallen to G, then the grain will grow as the metal cools till the line of the actual size of grain intersects that of the maximum size, the line AW: with further cooling no further growth ensues, and the final size of grain is OP. If we had quenched the metal while at G, the final size of grain would have been OH. If we had ceased rolling when the temperature was at L, the final size of grain in the cooled steel would have been OE. Needless to say, far from pretending that these curves are drawn to scale, I cannot

Fig. 118 B.

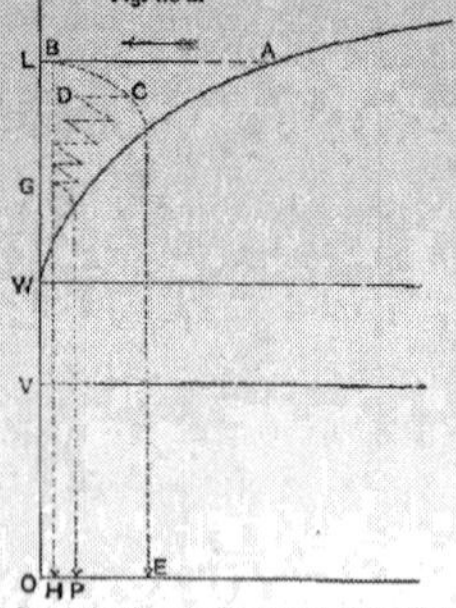

The Influence of the Finishing Temperature on the Size of Grain.

even insist that their general teaching is true: but it certainly seems to harmonize with our phenomena.

If these ideas be true, then the temperature at which rolling or hammering ceases has a most important effect on the size of the grain, and through this on the properties of the metal.

Let us now consider certain cases which throw light on the question as to whether it is the total quantity of reduction which the metal undergoes, or the temperature at which that reduction ceases, *i. e.* the finishing temperature, which chiefly causes the superiority of thin over thick pieces of steel and wrought-iron.

1. If the superiority in question were due to lowered finishing-temperature, and not to increased work, then, since the tendency to crystallize diminishes rapidly with the falling temperature and becomes very faint when V is reached (Figure 61, p. 171), the improvement for given fall of finishing-temperature should diminish as the region covered by this fall is lowered; *i. e.*, the lower the finishing temperature the less should the metal be benefited by lowering it further. If the finishing temperature be already at V, it profits not as regards crystallization to lower it further. Lowering it beyond a certain now-unknown point in turn produces a new different effect, that of cold-working. Now we have seen (§ 296) that the lower the finishing-thickness (and hence the finishing-temperature) the less do thin excel thick pieces, the reduction from 1" or at least from $\frac{3}{4}$" downward often causing no improvement. We reasonably infer that this is because the $\frac{3}{4}$" plate was finished at a safe temperature in these cases; the still thinner pieces are no better though they have received more work, simply because their still lower finishing-temperature is of no material advantage. It may indeed be found that the supposed "special effect" diminishes thus with falling temperature: but one would hardly anticipate it, rather expecting exaggerated effects due to cold-working. Nor can the matter be referred to greater closing of blowholes in the early welding-hot passes, for Table 133 indicates that the very earliest reduction, from 6" to 5", profits the annealed metal but little: so with the unannealed: whence we suppose that the 5" piece is finished so hot that it crystallizes

nearly as much as the 6″, while the 4″ piece is finished materially cooler.

2. In case of wrought-iron the improvement continues down to 1″. In Table 136 the only series which runs below 1″, we saw little change between 1¼″ and ¾″, then a marked increase between ¾″ and ½″. A single series gives no safe guidance. The lack of improvement between 1¼″ and ¾″ may be accidental or normal. If normal, it may be that the 1¼″ is finished at a safe temperature, so that the lower finishing temperatures of the 1⅛″, 1″, ⅞″ and ¾″ bars does not profit them. At ⅝″ cold-working may set in, raising the tensile strength and elastic limit of the ⅝″, ½″, ⅜″ and ¼″ bars. If accidental (perhaps through individual peculiarities, though fortuitous variations in finishing temperature, etc.), it may be that the improvement in wrought-iron continues down to a smaller thickness than in case of ingot-metal, because the working- and hence the finishing-temperature for the former is higher than for the latter, so that a safe finishing-temperature is reached only with thinner bars of the former than of the latter.

3. Further, while in Table 136 the bar-diameter diminishes regularly, the pile-area diminishes only occasionally and by great jumps. Each jump, counteracting the decrease of bar-diameter, should tend to raise the finishing temperature; and, in case of small bars, these jumps actually diminish the improvement which the smaller bar-diameter should give, nay usually turn it into a loss, and this even when the percentage of reduction in the rolls increases.

4. If the superiority of thin pieces were due to the supposed "special effect," one would anticipate that iron previously little worked would receive this special effect more, and be improved more, by reduction than iron previously much worked and in so far saturated with it. If due to finishing temperature, it should be independent of previous work; and in diagrams 1 to 4 of Figure 118A it seems to be: the improvement seems on the whole as great—indeed in elastic limit it is greater—in iron previously much worked as in that previously little worked.

5. In Diagrams 9 to 12, in Figure 118A, the metal on the whole improves slightly as the diameter decreases: the size of pile diminishing almost proportionally to that of bar, the special effect should increase very slightly, and the finishing-temperature decline but little more. These cases give no clear indication as to whether the slight improvement is due to reduction or to finishing-temperature.

6. The United States Test Board believed that the tensile strength and elastic limit of wrought-iron bars tested whole exceeded that of cylinders turned from their middle in a proportion that diminished with the diameter of the bar. This, too, points neither way: for in a thin bar the difference between core and shell, both as to finishing-temperature and amount of work, should be less than in a thick one.

7. What we may provisionally regard as approximately the greatest attainable excellence, since it is, I believe, as yet unsurpassed, has been reached by heat-treatment without forging. Such had Chernoff's famous steel, plotted thus + in Figure 49, page 159.

He cut a coarse-grained, sound, steel ingot into four pieces. One was tested without treatment of any kind: a second was heated to a bright red and hammered till its temperature fell to about W, and then allowed to cool undisturbed: a third was heated to *about*[a] the temperature at which the hammering of the second stopped, and cooled slowly. Their properties are given in Table 141. He says that he has verified his belief that the effects of forging can be produced by heat-treatment, by a whole series of experiments.

TABLE 141.—ANNEALED vs. FORGED STEEL.

		Tensile strength, pounds per square inch.	Elastic limit, pounds per square inch.	Elongation, %.	Reduction of area, %.	Increase of tensile strength, etc., per 100 of that of the ingot, due to treatment: Tensile strength, increase, %.	Elastic limit, increase, %.	Elongation, increase, %.	Reduction of area, increase, %.
Chernoff.	Untreated, direct from ingot..	139,400	....	2·8					
	Forged..................	166,400	....	5·3	......	19·4	.....	130	
	Reheated, without forging ...	155,000	....	16·6	......	11·2	.....	632	
Marshall.	Untreated, direct from casting.	82,400	39,300	4·8	6·6				
	Forged and treated..........	107,240	55,000	13·1	28·1	30·1	100	167	245
	Reheated without forging.....	100,560	46,000	12·1	15·0	22	29	147	127
Tunner.	Untreated, direct from ingot..	47,070	....	0·269	0·1				
	Reheated and forged..........	110,800	58,750	3·46	6·8	135	.....	1136	6300
	Reheated without forging.....	78,800	50,350	0·88	3·2	57	.....	227	3100

Chernoff, Revue Universelle, 2d Ser., I., p. 406, 1877.
Marshall, Trans. Am. Soc. Civ. Eng., XV., p. 345, 1887.
Tunner, Jeans, "Steel," p. 662, 1880, from Oest. Zeitschrift. Steel containing 0·8% of carbon, and free from blowholes, was cut into four pieces of like section. One was tested without treatment. Two others were heated in an annealing furnace for fifteen minutes. Of these one was cooled slowly, the other after reaching dull redness was forged till its section was reduced to one twenty-fifth of its original size.

Holley gives an almost equally remarkable instance, an unforged heat-treated cast gun-tube, whose properties are given in Table 142.

TABLE 142.—PROPERTIES OF AN UNFORGED, HEAT-TREATED STEEL GUN TUBE (Maillard, Holley, Metallurg. Rev., II., p. 382).

		1.	2.	3.	4.
Tensile strength..............	Lbs. per sq. in.	101,920	88,704	85,344	86,240
Elastic limit..............	Lbs. per sq. in.	49,280	49,728	59,400	50,840
Elongation..............		11·1	8·7	18·1	15·8

It will be found that these compare favorably with the very best examples in Figures 49 and 50.

We cannot assert confidently that these castings would have been bettered by work, for their properties equal those of the best heat-treated forgings. But we can claim that Marshall's and Tunner's heat-treated castings (Table 141) could have been made much more nearly equal to their forgings by better heat-treatment, in view of their inferiority to Chernoff's and Maillard's.

8. Finally, if bars and plates of given section and thickness made from large ingots or piles were better than those from smaller ones, we could refer their superiority to more effective mechanical action (the first three of our six modes), and little light would be thrown on our present question. But we find these properties independent of ingot- or pile-area. (Tables 137–8.) This argues directly against the existence of the supposed "special effect," and (admitting that the finishing-temperature is approximately constant for given finishing-thickness) in favor of finishing-temperature as the cause of the superiority of thin pieces. Indeed, one would expect the thicker ingot or pile to lead to somewhat lower finishing-temperature, unless this were purposely regulated, and hence to better quality: but this effect we can hardly trace.

To sum up, most of the facts here presented agree well with either view. All agree with the view that the superiority of thin pieces is due to lower-finishing temperature and not to greater reduction: those under 1, 3 and 4 I think agree rather better, and those under 7 decidedly

[a] Chernoff is incorrectly quoted as saying that the third piece was heated to the temperature at which the forging of the second stopped. He merely says that it was heated to "about" that temperature.

better, with this than with the opposite view, to which those under 8 are directly opposed. Cumulatively, then the evidence raises a presumption in favor of the view that the supposed "special effect" of kneading and pressure as such does not exist, or is relatively unimportant, and that hot-working acts chiefly like heat-treatment in preventing or removing crystallization. But the evidence under 8 is too scanty to be conclusive: and, without an investigation directly aimed to test this theory, we cannot hold it confidently.

Those of us who have held for years as almost an axiom that work directly benefited steel, will not give up their belief readily: I think they will find in the foregoing food for reflection, and reason to doubt but hardly to deny their old faith.

Admitting provisionally that the supposed special effect of work is a myth, and turning to our second question, it seems probable that, to pieces of moderate thickness once freed from cracks and cavities and shaped, we shall learn some day, and indeed soon, to confer a given degree of structural excellence more cheaply by heat-treatment alone than by hot-working alone or jointly by heat-treatment.

But, to give the best results by heat-treatment it now seems necessary to cool quickly to V: this is impossible for the middle of thick solid pieces, so that here heat-treatment alone cannot prevent hurtful crystallization; but for that matter it is hard to see how forging, even hydraulic forging, can either; for the colder outside must to a great extent cut the interior off from foreign pressure before it cools to V. For thick pieces, then, we cannot answer this question as yet.

§ 299. HAMMERING VS. ROLLING.—Clearly these two operations do not act in exactly the same way: the former rather pushes, the latter rather pulls the metal's particles into the desired position.

TABLE 143.—INCREASE OF TENSILE STRENGTH, ETC., ON FORGING AND ROLLING FAGERSTA STEEL FROM 3 × 3 TO ½ × ½ INCH, MEASURED IN PERCENTAGES OF THE TENSILE STRENGTH, ETC., OF THE 3 × 3 BAR. (FROM KIRKALDY'S DATA.)

	By hammering.		By rolling.		Ratio of increase by hammering to increase by rolling.	
	Unannealed steel.	Annealed steel.	Unannealed.	Annealed.	Unannealed.	Annealed.
Tensile strength..	54·2%	36·2%	52·8%	42·8%	1·03 : 1	0·85 : 1
Elastic limit......	78·7	47·8	40·3	44·3	1·95 : 1	1·08 : 1
Contraction of area	169·	148·6	115·	120·	1·46 : 1	1·23 : 1

TABLE 144.—ABSOLUTE EXCESS (OR DEFICIT, —) OF THE TENSILE STRENGTH, ETC., OF HAMMERED BESSEMER STEEL BARS OVER THAT OF SIMILAR BUT ROLLED BARS. (Kirkaldy's Fagersta data).

Size, inches square.	Tensile strength, pounds per square inch.			Elastic limit, pounds per square inch.			Elongation, % in 10 inches.			Reduction of area, %.		
	1% C.	0·50% C.	0·15% C.	1% C.	0·50% C.	0·15% C.	1% C.	0·50% C.	0·15% C.	1% C.	0·50% C.	0·15% C.
	Unannealed Bars.											
½	— 4,290	5,290	11,360	15,600	31,500	23,700	— 1·6	— 9·1	—12·1	0	4·0	—15·0
1	— 6,220	— 4,040	10,660	3,300	6,700	17,400	— 0·8	— ·2	—12·4	— 1·5	15·4	— 5·4
1½	— 7,610	— 1,560	150	8,500	6,200	10,260	— 0·5	2·4	—14·3	— 0·8	23·0	2·8
2	—10,460	— 3,153	— 1,900	3,100	6,500	8,700	— 0·8	8·8	1·2	— 0·1	14·7	6·7
2½	— 5,470	6,250	— 525	1,100	— 1,900	8,400	— 0·1	13·2	6·2	— 0·1	15·9	17·4
3	— 5,843	7,667	3,061	1,300	5,400	5,500	— 0·2	— 0·2	— 5·9	— 0·1	0·0	—15·9
	Annealed Bars.											
½	— 5,320	1,910	4,290	4,900	6,600	4,000	— 0·2	— 2·1	—10·5	— 5·6	4·0	— 8·0
1	— 980	— 5,070	1,680	5,800	700	3,100	1·4	3·0	—15·5	— 6·6	14·3	— 3·6
1½	— 6,580	— 4,970	— 1,510	4,900	4,300	2,200	0·1	— 1·5	— 3·6	— 0·3	9·0	1·1
2	— 9,689	— 1,487	— 1,806	4,300	5,200	2,000	— 0·2	0·9	3·5	— 0·0	2·3	5·1
2½	— 2,970	— 5,490	— 810	1,000	— 1,400	4,700	— 0·5	0·0	— 2·2	— 1·1	9·9	7·8
3	— 1,987	9,447	1,000	2,400	2,250	8,790	— 0·3	3·9	— 6·7	— 1·2	3·0	—11·9

Kirkaldy's Fagersta data as condensed in Table 143, at first seem to show that hammering from 3″ × 3″ to ½″ × ½″ raises the elastic limit much more and the contraction of area somewhat more than rolling. But, looking more closely, we note in Table 144 that the advantage which hammering offers is confined chiefly to the reduction from 1″ to ½″, the rolled bars which are from 1″ to 3″ square being as a whole about as good as the hammered if we take into account tensile strength as well as elastic limit: further, that the difference between the rolled and hammered ½″ bars is greatly lessened by annealing. This suggests strongly that the superiority of the hammered bars is due, not to any occult superiority in the action of the hammer, but simply to the fact that the hammer finishes the thin bar at a much lower temperature than the rolls.

In 240 tests on thirty soft steel plates (carbon 0·18%) 1″, ¾″ and ½″ thick, fifteen from slabs hammered and fifteen from similar slabs rolled from the same ingots, J. Riley found that the plates from the hammered slabs were practically identical in quality with those from the rolled ones, excelling them in tensile strength on average by only 2·4%, while in many cases the results were in favor of rolling. They follow:

TABLE 145.—PROPERTIES OF STEEL PLATES FROM ROLLED AND FROM HAMMERED SLABS, J. Riley. (240 tests.)

	Tensile strength, pounds per square inch.	Elongation in 8 inches, %.	Reduction of area %.
Hammered....	63,280	24·35	42·2
Rolled.........	61,824	24·5	42·5

Journ. Iron and Steel Inst., 1887, I., p. 124 and Sheet 111.

In point of fact, it is very doubtful whether, on the whole, hammering in general practice yields a materially different quality from rolling, which is readily understood if the effect of both is chiefly to prevent or obliterate crystallization: their efficiency in this respect depending in large part on finishing-temperature, here the hammer, there the rolls may finish the piece at the better temperature.

Be this as it may, the considerations which in general practice determine the choice between hammer and rolls for ingot-metal are for the most part those of cheapness and ease of working, and not of quality of product, hammering being employed chiefly for pieces which cannot readily be rolled, *e. g.*, those of varying cross-section, such as axles, or of irregular shape, such as crank-shafts: those which are so large or of which so few of given dimensions are demanded that the preparation of special rolls would not be justified: and bars of tool-steel, these perhaps because the finishing-temperature is more readily controlled in hammering than in rolling. For working red-short or mechanically unsound metal the hammer offers a certain advantage, in that it permits coaxing the material with well-weighted blows, while the reduction in the rolls is usually invariable; and in that unsound spots are easily chipped out by the blows of the hammer itself, while in rolling any needed chipping must be done by hand. In case of weld-metal the sharp blow of the hammer may expel slag more effectually than the more gradual squeeze of the rolls, especially if the piece be rolled alternately in opposite directions (as in reversing and in 3-high mills) since here the slag, instead of being moved ever in the same direction, is squeezed first back, then forth. But these considerations usually count for nothing against the much greater cheapness and rapidity of rolling, and the more accurate section of rolled than of hammered pieces. This is important even in case of intermediate products (blooms): if of accurate section they can be cut more accurately to weight, and less loss in cropping follows.[a]

§ 300. WELDING.—*Its essential conditions* are adhesiveness and contact, and for both plasticity is usually essential, though under the peculiar conditions of Coffin's weld, § 254, p. 184, it is not. Hence the need of a very high temperature, and in fact one near the melting point is used. As under usual conditions the surfaces inevitably become coated with oxide, to ensure contact this oxide must be made so fluid that it readily squeezes out: hence another need of a high temperature to melt the scale; or if a scale-melting heat cannot be used, of some flux to make with the scale a relatively fusible compound.

But an excessive temperature must be avoided. Why? According to current belief because it entails excessive oxidation. In favor of this view it is pointed out that steel scrap, heated "in a box composed of wrought-iron side and end pieces laid together," is r lled on a commercial scale into well-welded bars.[b] As far as contact is concerned an excessive temperature should be harmless, for a thick layer of scale should be as easily expelled as a thin one: and the higher the temperature the more fluid the scale.

I think that the reason why we must avoid an excessive temperature is that it causes the structural deterioration known as burning: but here we are thrown back on the question "is burning essentially oxidation or structural change," already discussed (§ 263). In this view the wrought-iron box facilitates welding steel scrap not by excluding oxygen (enough will surely enter to coat the steel scrap): but by holding together the scrap (crystalline and friable, or even mushy if very hot), so that it may undergo the squeeze of the rolls, which breaks up the coarse crystallization induced by the excessive temperature. But for this the coarsely crystallized steel would crumble at the first pass.[c]

§ 301. WELDING POWER OF DIFFERENT CLASSES OF IRON.

A. *Ingot- vs. Weld-Iron.*—Apparently competent judges insist that ingot iron welds as well, as easily, and even under precisely the same conditions as wrought-iron: all of which is as positively denied by others apparently equally competent A comparison of their printed and of many oral statements indicate:—1, That the conditions most favorable to welding are not the same for these two classes of iron. 2, That the range of conditions which permit excellent welding is narrower in case of ingot- than in that of wrought-iron, so that, 3, in careless hands the latter yields on an average better welds than the former. 4, that this difference diminishes as care and skill increase, so that, under the most favorable conditions and with the greatest skill, each welds practical y perfectly, the strength and ductility at the weld practically equalling that of the rest of he piece. 5, That it is practicable to weld ingot-iron on a commercial scale more perfectly than wrought-iron is usually welded. 6, Finally, as the case and thoroughness of welding of course differ among different varieties of each class, so some varieties of ingot- excel some of wrought-iron in welding power. Some of the evidence follows.[e]

On the one hand several boiler- and ship-builders have assured me that ingot-iron does not weld as well or as easily as wrought-iron: experienced foreign boiler makers and others in some cases hold this view.[d] Results obtained at Berlin appear to be unfavorable to ingot-metal. W. R. Hodge, a boiler-maker for nearly forty years, states that there is still difficulty in wel ing open-hearth steel. Petersen, of Eschweiler, holds that ingot- cannot compare with wrought-iron in welding-power. (Van Nost. Eng. Mag. XXIII., p. 346, 1880.)[e]

On the other hand, we have many assertions not only that ingot-iron welds well and easily, but even that it welds as well or even better than wrought-iron.

Among the former we have Holley's statement that the Terre Noire steel castings weld readily:[f] Tunner's that ingot-iron welds as well and almost as easily as puddled iron:[g] Martell's that it welds as easily and satisfactorily as wrought-iron:[h] and the description by G. Ratliffe[i] and by A. H. Hill,[j] of excellent welds in steel, which endured trying tests successfully. Among the latter we find that, welding some 8,000 feet of ingot-iron plates every quarter-year, Adamson[k] loses only one plate or so: that Zyromski,[l] Cramps and W. E. Koch[m] state that ingot-iron welds as well, and T. J. Bray[n] that it welds better than wrought-iron: with the last, Tetmajer's results seem to agree.[o] A. Thielen[p] says that about half of his basic open-hearth steel is sold as wrought-iron.

Finally, the results in 3, 4 and 5 of Table 146 prove that ingot-iron may be welded with a surprising perfection, much greater than is usual in case of wrought-iron.

In comparing the strength of welded and unwelded pieces we must remember that imperfect welding is not the sole cause of the inferiority of the welded pieces. The high temperature employed in welding tends to cause coarse crystallization.

[a] Mr. J. B. Pearse advocated the use of hammers for blooming rail-ingots on the ground that rolled steel was more graphitic than hammered, quoting a hammered steel with 1·03% of carbon of which 0·65% was graphitic, against a hammered steel with 0·234% carbon all combined. Even if the former very improbable composition be correct, the two steels are not comparable, nor could we attribute the graphite of the former to hammering much more safely than to its being made on, say, Wednesday, or in proximity to, say, potatoes. To-day we know that rolled rail-steel is not graphitic. (Trans. Am. Inst. Mining Engineers, I., pp. 162, 203).

[b] Holley, Trans. Am. Inst. Mining Engineers, VI., p. 112, 1879.

[c] We need not discuss Weddings' explanation (indeed, it is a definition, not an explanation) that welding represents the change from adhesion to cohesion. It is probably a mixture of both, such as we find in granite. I see no practical importance in the question, for adhesion is now weaker, now stronger than cohesion. Witness the splitting of a bank-bill well glued to two flat surfaces which are then forced apart, the cohesion between the bill's particles being weaker than the adhesion of bill to glue. (Journ. Iron and St. Inst., 1885, I., p. 196.)

[d] Discussion of Stromeyer's paper on "The Working of Steel," Excerpt Proc. Inst. Civ. Eng., LXXXIV., p. 67, 1886.

[e] Metcalf would discriminate between the "interlacing" welding of wrought-iron and the "sticking" welding of ingot-iron, holding that, though ingot-iron may be "stuck" with "wonderful success," when a weld in ingot-iron is parted its surfaces are smoother and with less sign of interlacing than in case of wrought-iron, (Trans. Eng. Soc, W. Penn., 1888, p. 30). Apparently in this view he believes (Trans. Am. Soc. Civ. Eng., XV., p. 301, 1887,) that "steel cannot be welded," while in the wider sense he admits that even tool-steel welds well. (The Treatment of Steel, p. 14, 1884.) The distinction may be fair, but for our present purpose we ask how strong the weld is, rather than how its parted surfaces look.

[f] Priv. Rept. 2d ser., VII., p. 45, 1877.

[g] Journ. Iron and St. Inst., 1880, I., pp. 295-7.

[h] Engineering 1878, p. 414, fr. Trans. Inst. Nav. Arch.

[i] Idem, 1879, II., p. 460.

[j] Trans. Am. Inst. Mining Eng., XI., p. 252, 1883.

[k] Discussion of H. Goodall's paper on "Open-hearth Steel for Boiler-making," excerpt Proc. Inst. Civ. Eng., XCII., p. 64, 1888.

[l] Stahl und Eisen, IV., p. 535, 1884.

[m] Trans. Eng. Soc. W. Penn., 1888, pp. 31, 49.

[n] Idem, p. 9.

[o] Iron Age, XXXVI., Nov. 5, p. 5, 1885. This is the inference I draw from his statement that 16·6% of the steel was poorly welded against 23·3% of the wrought-iron.

[p] Jour. Iron and Steel Inst., 1887, II., p. 132.

Of the results in Table 146, those under numbers 1 and 5 deserve especial confidence. Number 4 is given as indicating results obtained in commercial work.

TABLE 146.—STRENGTH OF WELDED SECTION IN PERCENTAGE OF THAT OF THE UNWELDED METAL.

	Wrought-iron, %.	Ingot-iron, %.
1. Chain cables a: among 210 lots		
1 had	85+	
21 "	75— 82 85+	
14 "	70— 65 75+	
107 "	56 @ 70	
67 " less than	56	
2. A German commission found for wrought-iron	81	
" soft ingot-iron (0·10% C.)		71
" harder " (0·38% C.)		58
3. Tests reported by Hupfeld; (8 not over ·12%) Average		98·7
Minimum		92
4. Experience of J. N. Paxman, maximum		92·45
minimum		87·69
5. Bauschinger	91·3	88

1. a Rept. U. S. Bd. on Testing Iron, Steel, etc., I., p. 203. These results are not very closely comparable with the others. In the records of 210 lots of sections of welded wrought-iron chain cables, the strength of the cable is compared with that of the bars from which it was made. Were the weld perfect, the cable should be about twice as strong as the bar. If we assume that the unwelded portion of the weakest link exerts the full resistance of the bar, then when as in the first line of table the strength of the cable is 1·85 times that of the bar, the strength of the weld may be taken as about 85% of that of the bar. This assumption does not seem strictly accurate: but perhaps accurate enough to afford a rough basis for comparison.

2. Ledebur, Handbuch der Eisenhüttenkunde, p. 641, 1884. Results obtained by a commission of the Verein zur Beförderung des Gewerbfleisses. These are numbers 13 and 14, Table 147.

3. Hupfeld, of Prevali, Mittheil aus dem Mech-Tech. Lab. in München, XIV., p. 82, 1886; Van. Nost. Eng. Mag., XXXI., p. 88, 1884. 22 unwelded and 27 welded bars of common Bessemer ingot-iron were tested tensilely.

4. Discussion of H. Goodall's paper on Open-hearth Steel for Boiler-making, excerpt, Proc. Inst. Civ. Eng., XCII., p. 56, 1888.

5. From (apparently) 12 bars of 12 different sizes or shapes, of best-welding Peine (probably) basic ingot-iron, 12 unwelded and 22 welded pieces were tested tensilely. From (apparently) 7 bars of best Nassau wrought-iron, 7 unwelded and 8 welded pieces of 6 different sizes or shapes were tested tensilely. The welded pieces were in general cut from the same bars as the unwelded ones. The results here given are the averages for each class. Six of the welded ingot-iron bars were stronger than the corresponding unwelded pieces. Bauschinger, Mittheil aus Mech.-Tech. Lab. in München, XIV., p. 81, 1886.

Thus in an experiment of Armstrong's a welded coil, though it did not break through the weld, showed lower tensile strength and elastic limit, and much lower elongation than the untreated metal[a]: and Bauschinger appears to have reached similar results for both ingot and wrought-iron.[b]

Before 1864 E. Riley reported that Bessemer ingot-iron welded, though not very well:[c] before 1866 Galloway welded Bessemer steel shavings.[d] Steel boiler-tubes have been successfully welded for many years, though until lately from carefully selected, costly material: now the welding of pipes of common ingot-iron is carried out on a large scale and successfully. H. J. Bray reports that of this pipe, when butt-welded, the proportion which fails on testing with three hundred pounds hydrostatic pressure is less than 0·5%.[e] Two-foot lengths of two-inch pipe, some of ingot- some of wrought-iron, filled with water and firmly closed at their ends, were exposed to the cold. The iron pipes all burst, the steel ones had their diameter increased one-eighth of an inch, but were otherwise uninjured. Hundreds of furnaces and combustion-chambers for marine boilers have been welded successfully.

The readier welding of wrought-iron is usually and reasonably attributed to the slag which it contains. If but a little of this is squeezed out into the weld during welding, that little, uniting with the oxide of iron formed during heating on the faces to be welded, makes it more fluid, more easily expelled.

B. *Effect of Composition on Welding Power.*—Carbon and sulphur certainly lessen the welding power: the effect of silicon is uncertain: the other elements probably lessen it, but I do not know that we have definite proofs that such quantities of them as are commonly met in a carbon steel are seriously hurtful. Arsenic, antimony and copper are said to oppose welding.

Adamson believes it established that, to ensure good welding, the carbon must be low, the manganese four times as much as the carbon, and the silicon, phosphorus, and sulphur collectively not over 0·10%.[f] While adherence to this formula may favor, I doubt very much if it is essential to thorough welding: note how widely the compositions of many steels in Table 147, reported to weld well, differ from it.

TABLE 147.—COMPOSITION OF WELDING AND OF NON-WELDING STEELS.

		Welding power.		Composition. C.	Si.	Mn.	P.	S.
1	H.	Excellent	Pipes	·05	·03	·38	·105	·06
2	K.			·15	tr.	·22	·04	·02
3	"			·14	"	·25	·07	·05
4	"			·14	"	·36	·04	·05
5	"			·18	·08	·58	·04	·02
6	"			·16	·04	·29	·03	·03
7	"			·17	·02	·38	·04	·02
8	"			·14	·08	·72	·06	·04
9	"			·16	·01	·83	·10	·08
10	"	"Not very weldable"		·12	......	·34	·07	·12
11	"		Boiler fronts	·15	·06	·50	·05	·06
12	"			·14	......	·60	·06	·07
13	L.	Fair		·20	......	·20@·30		
14	"	Good		·10	......	·20		
15	"	Wholly unweldable		·12	·0	·12	·12	·06
16	B.	Excellent		·036	·035	......	·106	·048
17	"	Poor		·101	·012	......	·129	·049
18	"	Very bad		·057	·016	......	·077	·061
19	..	Bad		·21	·017	·38	·112	
20	..	Fair		·11	·023	·30	·098	
21	..	"		·12	·019	·24	·132	

1, Admirably welding Bessemer steel for pipes, A. E. Hunt, discussion of T. J. Bray's paper on "Welding Steel Tubes," Trans. Eng. Soc., W. Penn, p. 82, 1888.
2 to 12, Steel welded in large quantities, by W. A. Koch, Idem., p. 52.
13–15, Ledebur, Handbuch der Eisenhüttenkunde, p. 639-41. 13, Strength after welding 57·91% of the unwelded metal. 14, Do. do. 70·92% of that of the unwelded metal. 15, Wholly unweldable Bessemer ingot-iron. Cause of lack of welding power unknown.
16–18, Bauschinger, Mittheil. aus Mech.-Tech. Lab. in Munchen, XIV., p. 81, 1886. They are included in number 5 of Table 146.
19–21, Hard and soft open-hearth ingot-irons, tested by the Berlin Commission. They are included in number 2, Table 146. Bauschinger, loc. cit., from Verhand, Vereins Beförderung des Gewerbfleisses, 1883, p. 144.

Sulphur.—Though Adamson cannot weld ingot-iron uniformly when it contains more than 0·02% of sulphur, the data in Table 147 indicate that even as much as ·06 or ·07% permits the successful welding of pipes. Steel with ·12% of sulphur is reported as not very weldable, and with 0·15% as quite unweldable.

Carbon.—It was formerly thought that the presence of a little carbon was indispensable or at least very favorable to welding: but this, I think is no longer believed. Certain it is that in general the difficulty of welding increases with the proportion of carbon, and the welding power probably practically disappears when the carbon rises above 1·3%. The larger the proportion of other elements present, probably the lower, in general, is the welding power for given percentage of carbon. Thus the welding of apparently common Bessemer steel is said to be hardly possible with 0·20 to 0·35% of carbon, and impracticable with 0·35 to 0·50%:[g] while to the practiced worker the welding of the relatively pure crucible steel is said to be easy with 0·87%, and possible, using the greatest care, with 1·25% of carbon.[h] Though the difference is probably much less than this rather loose wording implies, and though there are welds and welds, it appears to be very marked.

A reason why rising carbon lowers the welding power, is that it lowers the point to which we can heat the metal without danger of burning, but does not lower correspondingly the temperature at which plasticity sets in: indeed, it seems to diminish the plasticity and adhesiveness for given temperature.

Silicon is said by some to injure,[i] by others to improve[j]

[a] Repts. British Assn., 1882, p. 398.
[b] Iron Age, Jan. 7, 1886, p. 13, from Mittheilungen Mech. Tech. Lab., in München, 1885, 12, p. 81.
[c] Percy, "Iron and Steel," p. 7.
[d] Jeans, "Steel," p. 663.
[e] Trans. Eng. Soc. W. Penn., 1888, p. 27-8.

[f] Presidential Address, Jour. Iron and St. Inst., 1887, I., p. 19.
[g] J. Cockerill, Soc., Jour. Iron and St. Inst., 1880, I., p. 318.
[h] H. Leebohm, Sheffield, idem, 1884, II., p. 388. Ledebur, too, puts the welding limit at slightly above 1·2% C.
[i] Ledebur, Handbuch der Eisenhuttenkunde, p. 638. "Silicon doubtless lessens the welding power." Also Peterson, of Eschweiler, Van Nost. Eng. Mag., XXIII., p. 346, 1880.
[j] Koehler, of Bonn, idem: Holley, Priv. Rept., 2d Ser., VII., p. 45: Bohme Jour. Iron and St. Inst., 1884, II., p. 656, from Chem Centralblatt, XV., p. 462, Cf. this work, p. 41.

the welding power; but I doubt if we have any trustworthy evidence. The good welding power of crucible steel, usually rich in silicon, goes to show that silicon is not especially injurious in this respect.

Those who think it beneficial believe that, oxidizing to silica during welding, it yields a flux for the iron-oxide which forms on the surfaces to be welded. It seems to me, however, improbable that the small differences in the silicon content of different steels should have an important direct effect of this kind.

If steel A has 0·50% more silicon than steel B, and if the oxidation of silicon is confined to that layer of metal which is itself oxidized, and if, to fix our ideas, we suppose the iron of that layer to be oxidized to scale-oxide, Fe_3O_4, then the scale which forms on steel A would have only about 0·8% more silica than that formed on steel B, a difference from which one would expect no very important result, either directly or through its causing a corresponding minute quantity of scale-oxide to change to magnetic or even ferrous-oxide. Nor would one expect that the silicon contained in layers of steel beneath those which are themselves oxidized, would be oxidized rapidly, nor, if oxidized, that the infusible microscopic particles of silica would be able to ooze out of the welding surface, and so flux the scale-oxide.

The slag of wrought-iron stands in quite a different position, being, first, fusible and fluid, and second, in relatively large and more or less continuous threads, so that comparatively large quantities of it might be squeezed to the welding surfaces, even from points say half an inch or even an inch back. If the silicon in ingot-metal does favor welding, it may possibly act through difference of potential, or through increasing the metal's plasticity, or changing the composition and hence fusibility of the scale. Manganese is now said to injure,[a] now not to affect the welding power, at least when it does not exceed 1%.[b] The injury attributed to manganese may be due to the carbon, which usually increases with manganese.

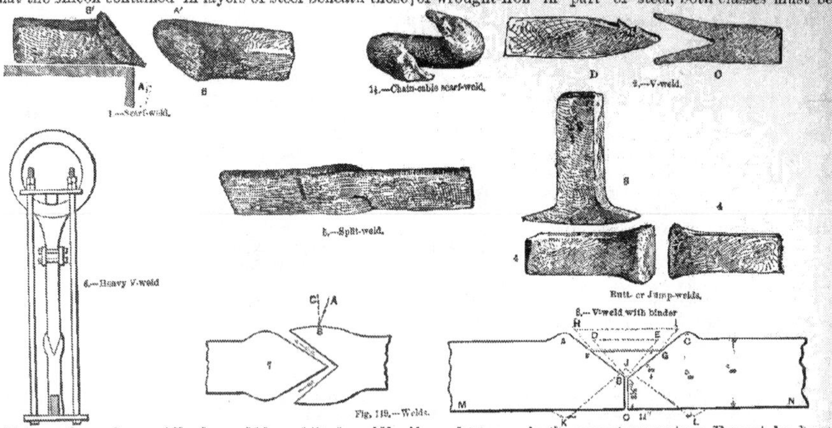

Fig. 119.—Welds.

[a] Ledebur, Handbuch der Eisenhuttenkunde, p. 636. "Silicon doubtless lessens the welding power." Also Peterson, of Eschweiler, Van Nost. Eng. Mag., XXIII., p. 346, 1880.

[b] W. E. Koch, Trans. Eng. Soc. W. Penn., p. 53, 1888. He states, Idem, p. 52, that he has welded steel with from 0·02 to 1·25 of manganese.

Welding unlike irons.—There is a belief that like irons and like steels weld more easily than unlike.[c] Without denying this, my own observations lead me to think it a misleading half-truth. Doubtless wrought-iron welds far more easily to itself than to steel: but it has seemed to me, and many smiths have assured me, that less care and skill are needed to weld steel to wrought-iron than to steel. In welding two classes of iron, A the more, B the less highly carburetted, if they can conveniently be heated separately, either in different furnaces or fires, or in different parts of the same one, each may be (and in practice is) brought to its own welding point, and B being now more plastic and adhesive than A, the conditions seem to favor welding much more than if the hot plastic B were replaced by another piece of relatively cool rigid A. It should be easier to unite a more sticky to a less sticky substance than to unite two less sticky ones.

When, as in case of rail and beam piles, made in part of wrought-iron in part of steel, both classes must be brought to nearly the same temperature, B must be kept down nearly or quite to the low welding heat of A: but even here, since for given temperature B is probably more plastic and adhesive than A, union should be easier than if B were replaced by another piece of A.

In harmony with this view is the not uncommon practice, in welding two pieces of steel, or even in welding steel to the softest basic ingot-iron, of welding a thin piece of wrought-iron between them. The wrought-iron, even at the low welding heat of the steel, is or is thought so much the more adhesive that this double weld seems easier and more thorough than the single weld of steel to steel. In rolling steel-headed, wrought-iron bodied rails, the steel probably welded better to the wrought-iron than it could have to a steel body. But, as it could not weld as well as wrought-iron to wrought-iron, and as the welding was the weak point of wrought-iron rails, there was little reason to expect good results from the steel head.

[c] Holley seemed to hold this view. (Trans. Am. Inst. Min. Eng.) VI., p. 112.

§ 302. MANNER OF WELDING.—The more common welds are illustrated in Figure 119.

The Scarf-Weld, 1, is perhaps the most common of all for steel, especially for small pieces. In some cases the scarfed faces are riveted together with a single rivet, before welding, to aid alignment during welding. The points A A' are made narrower than the body of the piece, apparently to lessen the danger of burning and the degree to which the point cools: and also that the point may be the more deeply imbedded into the opposite face B B' at the first blow, and that the pieces may thus be quickly attached. To compensate for the narrowness of A A', and also to allow for reduction of section in hammering together, the obtuse parts B B' must be made considerably wider than the body of the piece.

In making this weld the piece is so held that the thin point A does not at first come in contact with the anvil, which would cool it below the welding heat. The other point A' is welded to B' with a few light blows: the piece is then rotated 180°, A is in like manner welded to B, and the whole weld is then hammered together.

The scarf-weld as applied to chain-cables is shown at 1½.

The V-weld 2, 6, is applied oftener to heavy pieces. They are more readily aligned and held in place with this than with the scarf-weld during the welding operation. This weld is sometimes started while the pieces to be welded are in the fire, the male piece being pressed into the female, be it by hand, be it (in case of very heavy pieces) by heavy blows from a sledge or even a battering-ram against one end of one piece: be it by drawing the pieces together with bolts as at 6, Figure 119. But we should regard the adhesion thus given chiefly as an aid to alignment, relying on the subsequent hammering for the strength of the weld.

The scarfing angle, both in the scarf- and V-welds, should be rather acute, as shown at 6, so that the component AB of the welding pressure CB which is at right angles to the welding faces may be great, the pressure thus acting chiefly to force these against and less to slide them past each other.

In welding hard steel to wrought-iron by the V-weld, the steel is always used for the male, the wrought-iron for the female piece, as the latter is exposed to the higher temperature. One face of the male piece is generally notched; the female piece is then heated, the male piece placed within it, and the two hammered lightly together. The sharp edges of the notching on the male piece dig into the hot, soft, female piece, and the two are thus readily held in line: thus lightly adhering, they are now heated to a welding heat and hammered firmly together.

The extreme end of the male piece has a fish-tail shape as shown, so that, when it is driven well home, it may fill the extreme crotch of the female piece at its outer surfaces.

The weld shown at 8 is also known as a V-weld. In this particular case a steel forging eight inches square was welded. It was first shaped according to the solid lines, A, B, O, B, C, and bound together with tie-rods, somewhat as shown at 6. It was then heated to a welding heat, and the V-piece D, E, B, was welded in, being reduced to the shape F, G, B, in welding. Then the "binder" H, F, G, I, was welded in and the points A and C hammered down, the upper surface thus being levelled. The other side was then cut past the point of the first weld and shaped as at K, J, L, and a V-piece and a binder were welded in as on the first side.

The jump- or butt-weld, 3, 4, is used oftener for wrought-iron than for steel.

The split-weld, 5, is a good weld for flat thin pieces of steel, such as carriage springs and carriage tyres, to which, clearly, the V-weld is inapplicable, while the pieces are more readily held in place and aligned with the split than with the scarf-weld.

In general the welding faces, as at 4, should not fit accurately, both that there may be a ready path for the escape of the molten scale, and that only a little surface may be brought together at a time, the force of each blow being thus concentrated on a relatively small extent of welding surface. Thus in the V weld the male piece may be more acute than the female, as indicated at 7, though this makes alignment less easy. For like reason machined faces usually weld less thoroughly than rough-forged ones.

So too the hammering should aim to squeeze the slag out as fully as possible: thus in the V-weld the first blows may be struck opposite the crotch of the female piece, say at B, 7, moving thence to the left, so as to squeeze out the slag in the direction of the arrows.

The pieces to be welded should be so shaped that their thickness across the weld is much greater than that of the finished piece is to be, to allow for reduction in hammering the weld together. The hammering and consequent reduction would have to be considerable, even if the welding itself did not require it, and should be kept up till the temperature has sunk much, so as to prevent the coarse crystallization which sets in during undisturbed exposure to a high temperature. For like reason quick fire and work are recommended, to shorten the exposure to the high temperature: and, because of the metal's tenderness, rather gentle blows should be used, the first ones being mere taps, increasing rapidly in force as the coarse, feebly adhering crystals formed during heating are broken up and their successors hammered into firmer union.

The temperature most suitable for welding is a white heat for wrought-iron; a lower white or a bright yellow for soft ingot-iron; a bright yellow for half-hard and for common tool steels; a moderate yellow for the hardest weldable steels. Unfortunately these terms convey no very accurate idea: and what one calls white, another terms light yellow, etc.

Fluxes.—In all usual cases the welding surfaces inevitably become oxidized during heating: to produce actual contact of metal with metal the oxide thus formed must be removed. To remove it mechanically would be useless, for new oxide would form instantly. It therefore must be made so fluid that it will squeeze out as the plastic surfaces are forced together during welding, contact of metal and metal following that of metal and slag immediately, air being wholly excluded.

Wrought- and soft ingot-iron may be safely heated to a temperature at which the iron oxide itself is fluid: this is true even with rail steel of say 0·35 to 0·45% of carbon. Here flux is not usually necessary, though it may facilitate welding. Thus ingot-iron pipes, though demanding a very thorough weld, are welded without flux. If anything, sand is used.

Steel with a higher percentage of carbon cannot be heated to a point at which the oxide itself becomes fluid, without danger of burning: hence a flux must be added to form with the oxide a more fusible compound. The higher the carbon, and the lower consequently the temperature to which the steel can be safely heated, the more fusible must this compound be. Hence, while sand, forming the moderately fusible iron silicates, does well with moderately hard steels; for harder ones, such as tool-steel, borax, which yields the very fusible iron-sodium borate, is used, preferably first melted to expel its water and thus to prevent frothing, and then pulverized. For soft steels, too, borax is sometimes mixed with sand. Ferrocyanide of potassium (yellow prussiate) is liked by some, and is thought to counteract the tendency of the steel to lose carbon during heating.

Beyond these, pulverized clay is used for soft, and numberless nostrums for harder steels. They are mostly alkaline salts, sodium chloride or carbonate, sal ammoniac, etc., and a legion of mixtures, for which the usual ridiculous claims are made. Remembering that the flux cannot benefit the steel itself, and that fluidity and cheapness are probably its sole important qualities, borax and sand leave so little to be desired that they are not likely to be supplanted. Unfortunately, such warnings as these can rarely reach those who need them.

Condensed Instructions.—For tool steel Metcalf[a] recommends a bright yellow heat; and melted and pulverized borax as flux. For ingot-iron Bauschinger advises fluxing with sand; a temperature between redness and whiteness; a quick fire, and quick work:[b] the steam hammer gave much better welds than the hand-hammer. The Steel Company of Scotland recommend a bright yellow heat; if any flux, three parts of sand to one of common salt, moisened; a V-weld, which, with the neighboring parts, is to be lightly hammered during and after welding; and sulphurless coal.[c]

§ 303. ELECTRIC WELDING.[d]—A. IN THOMSON'S PROCESS the pieces to be joined firmly held end to end, aligned, and strongly pressed together by copper clasps, are raised to the welding point by an enormous current of very low potential, which is transmitted to the pieces to be welded by the clamps which hold them, and thus passes through and heats but little of the metal on either side of the joint.

The metal is heated by the resistance which it offers to the passage of the current, quite as a common incandescent burner is, and as the current-strength is under close control and quickly varied, so is the temperature of the metal.

The ends to be united are usually made convex, and, as they soften under the intense heat, the pieces are forced together, and indeed slightly upset. A little borax is added at the joint to liquefy the iron-oxide formed. Sand would be used in welding wrought- or ingot-iron on a large scale.

As the heat developed is proportional to the square of the current strength, *i. e.*, to the ampères—and not proportional to the tension of the current, *i. e.*, to the voltage, very low potential is used, from 0·125 to 6 volts. In

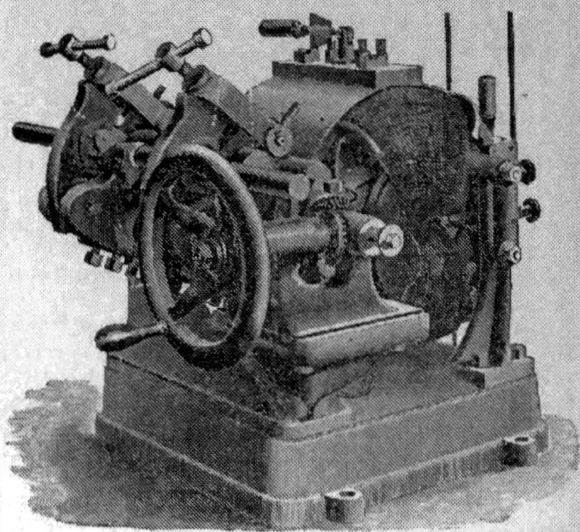

Fig. 121.—Elihu Thomson's Electric-welding Machine.

general the smaller the sectional area of the piece the higher the volts used. Electricity of this low potential is, of course, perfectly harmless to the human body: indeed but a trifling current at such potential would pass through so poor a conductor.

The current (ampères) needed increases with the sectional area of the piece to be welded. As we proceed from very small wires the current needed at first increases a little more rapidly than the sectional area, say with the $2^{\cdot 8}$th power of the diameter. But as the sectional area increases the rate of increase of needed current diminishes, so that in passing from 1″ to 2″ bars the current needed apparently increases less rapidly than the sectional area.

The horse power needed is roughly proportional to the current, and of course increases not only with the sectional area but with the rapidity of heating desired. Thus it is estimated that a 1″ round bar can be welded with 12 horse power, but slowly: to weld it in from 25 to 30 seconds 18 to 20 H. P. should be provided. To weld a 2″ round bar in one minute about 40 H. P. are needed, and say 20 000 ampères.

The preceding data must be taken as very rough approximations to the truth, in view of the paucity of experimental data available and of the many variables.

For given sectional area iron needs much less current to reach given temperature than copper, owing to its lower conductivity both for electricity and heat, its low thermal conductivity preventing the rapid conduction of heat from the intentionally heated parts.

As the resistance increases with the temperature, so while the joint is forming its several parts tend ever to uniform temperature; for, if the temperature be uneven, an undue share of the current passes through the cooler and less resisting parts, and thus their heating is hastened while that of the hotter parts is retarded.

Though it is only within a few months that the process has actually reached a commercial stage, some fifteen or

[a] The Treatment of Steel, p. 14, 1884.

[b] Mittheil. aus Mech.-Tech. Lab. in München, XIV., pp. 34-5, 1885; also Iron Age, Jan. 7, p. 13, 1886.

[c] Journ. Iron and St. Inst., 1881, I., p. 229.

[d] H. D. Hibbard, Trans. Eng. Soc. W. Penn., p. 25, 1889; C. J. H. Woodbury, Trans. Am. Soc. Mech. Eng., X., 1889, to appear: Eng. Min. Jl., XLVII, p. 136, 1889; Engineering, XLVII., p. 571, 1889. Proc. Soc. Arts, Mass. Inst. Technology, p. 35, 1886-7: Journ. Franklin Inst., XCIII., p. 357, 1887. This section is based chiefly on information given me by the Thomson Electric Welding Company, April 3d, 1889.

twenty electric welding machines have already been sent to licensees, for regular use in manufacturing and similar establishments.

The largest sectional area yet welded is that of 2·5″ iron bars, but a larger machine is now building for welding the four-inch-square irons of locomotive frames.

Among the more important uses so far developed are the welding of telegraph wires end to end, especially in installing lines, a portable storage battery being used: welding lead pipes end to end: welding iron-pipes end to end, and so making very tight joints (welding the *seams* of pipes is not yet done); welding brass to iron in pump piston-rods: welding and assembling the drop-forgings, etc., of carriage work. I understand that all these operations are now carried out on a commercial scale.

The links of chains are also welded with success, but not yet commercially, as the chain making machine is not perfected. The links are welded by preference with double welds, one in each of the long sides of the link: links thus welded do not break through the weld, but through the shoulder. The faces to be welded are in this case plane, instead of convex, as in most other cases.

Links can also be welded with a single weld, just as in common chain-welding practice. It might at first be thought that the electricity would pass chiefly through the solid body of the link, as offering the largest sectional area, rather than through the smaller section of the contact between the faces to be welded. But these faces are made flat, and so give broad contact, and moreover the electricity is purposely introduced very close to the faces to be welded, so that the path through them is very much shorter than that around through the solid part of the link: and it actually happens that most of the heat is localized closely at the weld. So in welding locomotive-frames.

Of the many other uses of this interesting process, I need only mention the welding of wire-ropes; an application for a patent for this is now pending.

The strength of the welds, as indicated by the data in Table 148, compares well with that of hand-welds as given in Table 146. In the latter Bauschinger, whose results command implicit confidence, found that wrought-iron lost less than 10% in hand welding, and that ingot-iron lost 12%. With wrought-iron and soft-steel, numbers I., II., IV., V. and VI. of Table 148, the strength of the welded bars is in general very high: in number II., however, there is a very heavy loss of strength in welding. Moreover, in other tests applied to the material used in I., the sectional area at the weld was much greater than in the rest of the bar: nevertheless the bar broke at the weld.

The hard steel, III., lost strength very heavily in welding.

The inference seems to be that admirable welds, equalling if not excelling hand-welds, can be obtained by this process: but that with the degree of skill as represented by the results in Table 148 (especially if we assume that these were obtained from picked welds), the welding is much less certain than hand-welding. As the conditions seem under closer control, one expects that, with experience, as good and more certain welding will be made with this process than by hand.

TABLE 148.—STRENGTH OF ELECTRICALLY WELDED JOINTS.

No.	Material.	Sectional area. At weld sq. in.	Sectional area. Of bar sq. in.	Position of fracture of welded bar.	Tensile strength. Average of unwelded bar, lbs. per sq. in.	Of welded bar in percentage of that of unwelded bar. Maximum.	Minimum.	Average.
I.	Wrought-iron, not welded	......	·408	......	54,363	......	......	......
	The same, welded	·408	·408	At weld	......	94·71	90·60	92·69
II.	Wrought-iron, not welded	......	·196	......	58,165	......	......	......
	The same, welded	·198±	·196	At weld	......	87·56	67·45	77·50
III.	Octagonal steel, not welded	......	·860	......	127,040	......	......	......
	The same, welded	·856±	·860	At weld	......	68·18	50·07	58·16
IV.	Steel, not welded	......	·198	......	75,430	......	......	......
	Steel, welded	·198±	·197±	At or near weld	......	101·63	99·17	100·50
V.	Steel, not welded	......	·308	......	64,900	......	......	......
	Steel, welded	·308	·312	At weld	......	......	......	97·00
VI.	Wrought-iron, not welded	......	·313	......	52,440	......	......	......
	Wrought-iron, welded	·312	·312	At or near weld	......	99·60	98·76	99·13

These results were obtained with the United States testing-machine at Watertown, Mass., in charge of Mr. J. E. Howard. I here give only the results obtained with pieces in which the sectional area at the weld was the same as in the rest of the bar: other cases are less readily comparable.

Electric welding is at a disadvantage in that the metal is exposed to a very high temperature without receiving the work as it cools which it undergoes in hand-welding, and which removes much of the coarse crystallization which arises at the high temperature. In Thomson's process the welded piece is not forged: but it seems to me that it would be very desirable, at least in case of important pieces, to hammer the weld. This would increase the expense considerably, but without it the coarse crystallization set up around the weld will remain a source of weakness, or at least of brittleness.

The advantages claimed for the process are that the alignment is easy and accurate: the welding is extremely rapid: the parts to be welded are visible during heating and their temperature is thus under better control, so that less skillful and hence less costly labor may be used than in hand-welding: and the heat is closely localized, so that less energy is needed and that there is less oxidation and loss of iron than in hand-welding. One might add that the power for generating the electricity may be obtained by burning sulphurous and hence often much cheaper fuel than can be used in hand-welding.

Clearly, as different classes of machines, different current and potential, are needed for different conditions, the process is not applicable to the work of the common jobbing smith, nor to the forges of most establishments, where all kinds of welds are to be made on pieces of all sizes and shapes. But I am confident that the process will find very valuable and somewhat varied fields in establishments in which there is an abundance of work of certain tolerably uniform kinds, so that the welding plant and skilled workmen may be kept occupied. Central jobbing establishments in large manufacturing centres, too, should eventually be profitable.

Important uses in welding cast-iron, and in heating, welding and brazing the other metals, lie beyond the field of this treatise.

B. *In Bernardos' process*[a] an electric arc melts, between

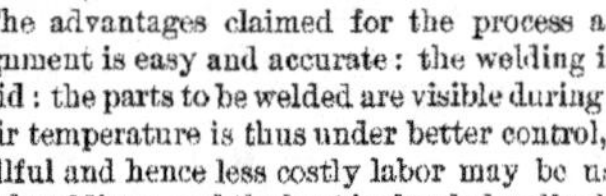

Fig. 121A.

the pieces to be united, chips, etc., of the material of which these pieces are composed. It is therefore a soldering:

[a] Engineering, XLV., p. 173, 1888. Zeit. Vereins. Deut. Ing., XXXI., p. 803, 1887. Scientific Am. Supp., No. 635, p. 10,144, Mch. 3, 1888.

but this is not, as some would persuade us, a fault. The pieces to be welded are made the negative pole, the positive pole being a carbon pencil. Were this arrangement reversed the metal would be oxidized rapidly. As it is, the carbon wastes rapidly, but is of course readily replaced. It is held in a scissor-like tool as shown in Figure 121 A, with a wooden handle through which the flexible electric cable passes, and a screen to further protect the workman's already stoutly gloved hand, his eyes and face being guarded by a dark glass.

In joining plates the edges may be feathered as shown and the furrow filled with iron turnings, which are melted by the arc, fresh turnings being then supplied till the furrow is filled. In joining bars end to end one is centred in a lathe which is connected with the negative pole: the other is pressed against the first and stuck lightly to it with a few touches of the carbon: the lathe then revolves slowly, and iron is added to the joint little by little. Wires are joined by slipping a ring over their hooked ends, and melting the whole to a button.

As compared with Thomson's this process is at a very serious disadvantage in lacking ready control over the temperature, and in the much higher temperature developed, with consequent greater tendency to crystallization in cooling, liability to burn and blister adjacent parts, etc. It is stated that the results of tests furnished by Bernardos indicate a serious loss of tensile strength: the loss of ductility, especially under shock, should be still greater. Subsequent forging may remedy this in certain cases.

It seems less fitted than Thomson's for joining bars and pipes end to end: and, at least at first sight, less fitted for joining wires than Thomson's: in short less desirable than Thomson's where the sectional area to be joined is small. But for joining the edges of large thick plates, for patching thick plates, etc., in short where the sectional area is so very large that it would be extremely difficult to heat it all simultaneously, Bernardos' system seems at first sight to have an advantage. But unless, as here seems improbable, the crystallizing at the weld can be overcome, it will be better to rivet the edges of plates than to weld them by this system. Its future seems less promising than that of Thomson's process, though it is still too early to pronounce judgment with complete confidence.

Bernardos' process is said to have been adopted at the works of Messrs. Struve in Russia: it has not, I believe, been introduced into this country.

§ 304.—The Density of Steel,[a] so far as my observation goes, lies with rare exceptions between the limits sp. gr. 7·6 and 8, that of annealed steel usually lying between 7·82 and 7·87 sp. gr. The sp. gr. of wrought-iron is reported in certain cases as only 7·52. The density is lowered by quenching and by cold-working, but returns almost or quite completely to its initial value when the cold-worked or quenched steel is heated to redness and cooled slowly. Hot-working when above W probably does not affect it, when slightly below W probably raises

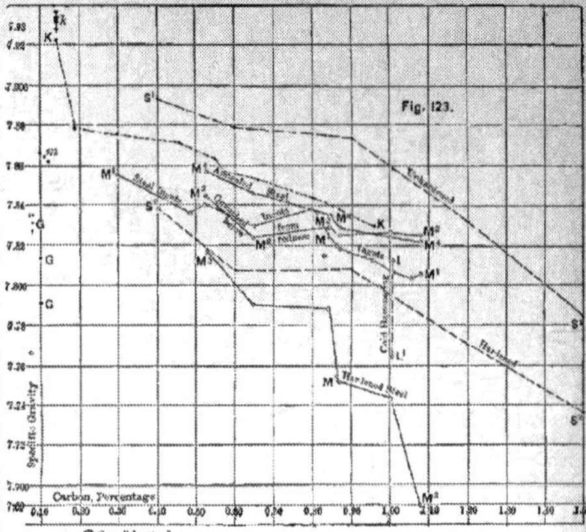

⊙ Crucible steel.
• Bessemer steel and unknown.
v Open-hearth steel.

LL₁, steel of about 1% of carbon. L annealed and L¹ hammered cold. Langley, Metcalf, The Treatment of Steel, p. 37 et seq., 1884. M, of twelve crucible steel ingots, M1, six were hammered and rolled to bars 0·625″ in diameter. One end of each was heated to whiteness, the temperature decreasing gradually towards the other end. They were then quenched in water. M2 gives the density of the part which was slightly below visible redness when quenched, M3 that of the part which was at white-hot when quenched, and M4 that of this last after subsequent slow cooling from a high yellow heat. Idem.

K, Kuppmeyer, forged Bessemer steel, Dingler's Journal, CCXI., p. 22.

S¹, S² Sandviken Bessemer steel. "Metallurgy," Crookes and Röhrig, II., p. 13.

k, W. Kent, Trans. Am. Inst. Mining Engineers, XIV., p. 585, 1886.

M, G. S. Miller, Idem, p. 588, Bessemer steel.

G, F. L. Garrison, Idem, XV., p. 96, 1887, Bessemer steel.

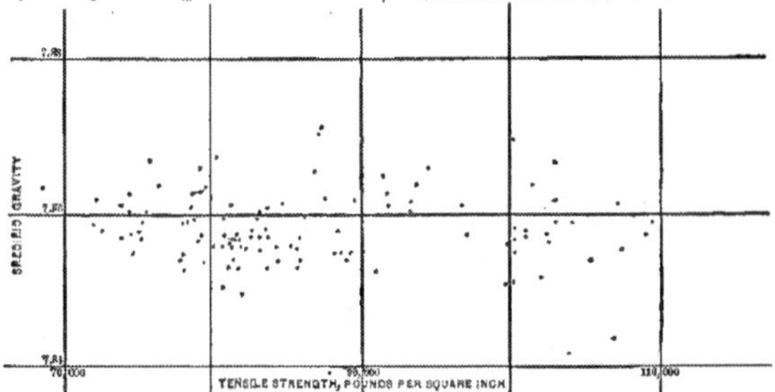

Fig. 124

it. With increasing carbon-content the density probably decreases slightly.

[a] Pure iron, 7·85-7·88: steel, 7·60 to 7·80, Landolt und Börnstein, Phys.-Chem. Tabellen, 1883, p. 78.

Clark's "Constants of Nature," I., p. 13, 1873, gives the sp. gr. of iron as from 6·03 (iron by hydrogen, Stahlschmidt) and 7·130 (reduced by carbon, Playfair and Joule), to 8·007, and 8·1393 (the last electrolytic).

TABLE 149. SPECIFIC GRAVITY OF STEEL.

No.	Authority.	Description.	Sp. Gr.
1	....	Usual limits, unhardened steel	7·85 to 7·87
2	....	Extreme "	7·6 to 8·
3	Hinman.	Unhardened blister steel, 2 pieces........................	7·751 and 7·901
4	"	same pieces hardened	7·558 and 7·708
5	Caron.	Unhardened steel........................	7·817
6	"	the same hardened 30 times........................	7·743
10	Elsner.	Cast steel........................	8·0923
11	"	the same hardened........................	7·764?
14	Wrightson.	Wrought iron........................	7·6100
15	"	the same quenched 50 times........................	7·5520
16	"	" " " 100 "	7·5200
17	"	" " " 125 "	7·5260
18	Kent.	Soft ingot-iron, carbon 0·14	7·9275 to 7·9456
19	Miller.	" " " " 0·10 to 0·12........................	7·800 to 7·866
20	Garrison.	" " " " 0·08 to 0·10........................	7·758 to 7·888
21	Holley.	Annealed casting........................	7·900
22	Kohlman	Bessemer steel ingot........................	7·800
23	"	bloom from 22........................	7·760
24	"	rail from 23........................	7·710
25	Henry.	Wootz........................	7·727
26	Pearson.	"	7·184 @ 7·647
27	"	" hardened	7·165

3 to 4, Percy, Iron and Steel, p. 849, fr. Geschichte des Eisens, 1785, p. 134.
5 to 6, Comptes Rendus, LVI, p. 211, 1863.
7 to 9, Cf. Note to Figure 123.
10, 11, Idem, fr. Jou'n für Prakt. Chem., 1840, XX., p. 110.
14 to 17, T. Wrightson, Journ. Iron and St. Inst., 1879, II., p. 425.
18 to 20, Cf. Note to Figure 123.
21, Holley, Priv. Rept., 2d. Ser., VII., p. 41, 1877. Annealed Terre Noire steel castings
22 to 24, Kohlman, Engineering, 1881, p. 125.
25 to 27, Percy, Iron and Steel, pp. 775–6, 1864.

The effect of cold-working is shown by line LL in Figure 123, where repeated cold-hammering lowers the specific gravity by 0·047: we have seen in § 270 a loss of 0·040 on punching and 0·047 on wire-drawing.

The lightening effect of quenching increases with the suddenness of the cooling, the quenching-temperature, and the proportion of carbon in the steel: thus Langley found that, under like conditions, quenching from whiteness lowered the specific gravity of steel with 0·529% of carbon by 0·026, that of steel with 1·079% of carbon by 0·135.

Quenching from even as low a temperature as 212° F. appears to lower the density slightly: in four cases Langley found that the specific gravity fell by from 0·011 to 0·027.

Repeated quenchings lower the density cumulatively, but at a gradually diminishing rate. Thus Wrightson found that on fifty heatings and quenchings the specific gravity of wrought-iron fell from 7·61 to 7·552: after fifty more heatings and quenchings it had fallen still farther to 7·52, the total loss being 0·120. But after twenty-five additional quenchings it had risen slightly, by 0·006 (to 7·526).

Caron found that thirty quenchings reduced the density of steel by ·074. Much greater losses are reported, so great indeed that one hesitates to accept them. Such are 3 and 4 of Table 149.

The rapid divergence of lines $M^1 M^1$ and $M^2 M^2$ from line $M^3 M^3$ in Figure 12, the first representing steel ingots, the second bars forged from them and quenched from below redness, the last like bars quenched from scintillating whiteness, indicates that the effect of quenching is much greater in high- than in low-carbon steel: but this relation is not well marked in lines $S^1 S^1$ and $S^2 S^2$ of which the first represents unhardened, the second hardened Bessemer steel. But though the difference between the density of high- and that of low-carbon steel depends greatly upon the conditions of cooling, it is probable, to judge from the general direction of lines $M^4 M^4$ and $S^1 S^1$ and K K in Figure 123, that even in well annealed metal the density decreases slightly with rising carbon-content, probably at about the rate of 0·06 per 1% increase of carbon-content. This indicates that cementite is lighter than ferrite.

That hot-forging above W does not materially increase the density we infer from the fact that slowly cooled bars do not appear to be materially denser than the ingots from which they are forged. Indeed, the density of unforged castings is surprisingly high. Thus, Holley reported the specific gravities of annealed Terre Noire castings as 7·9, a point rarely reached by forged steel: Mr. T. T. Morrell found the specific gravity of a rail ingot 7·8464.[a] Figure 124, representing many commercial steels examined by the United States Board on testing iron, steel, etc., shows that the sp. gr. usually lies between 7·85 and 7·87. In Figure 123 a comparison of lines $M^1 M^1$ and $M^4 M^4$ shows that the steel ingots here represented are nearly as dense as the bars forged from them and slowly cooled from a light yellow heat, after previous quenching from whiteness. Broling found that the specific gravity of a button made by melting bar-iron was 7·8439: Percy found that of a button from iron wire to be 7·8707: hammering and cold-rolling reduced it to 7·865.[b]

Chernoff reported that hot-working at a temperature below W increased the density, sometimes to 8. The rolling of rails made from reheated blooms ceases while they are at about W, a low yellow heat: that of rails rolled direct from the ingot without reheating, at a little above V, say a dull red. The density of the latter is said to be about 1 to 1·5% higher than that of the former, which would make their specific gravity from about ·0785 to ·117 higher, or about 7·93. This is inferred from the apparently excessive weight of direct-rolled rails of given section: but I know of no direct determinations.

§ 305. DILATATION. THE FLOATING OF COLD IRON.—It were beyond the scope of this treatise to consider the dilatation of iron exhaustively. (See Table 109, § 273, p. 218.) I will confine myself to two points. First, late investigations at the Watertown Arsenal show that the coefficient of dilatation in like steels diminishes as the proportion of carbon increases.[c] This raises a new difficulty in the way of the tension or stress theory of the hardening of steel, since the high-carbon steel which hardens intensely contracts less on quenching than non-hardening low-carbon material. Quenching from bright redness increased the coefficient of expansion greatly, especially in case of highly carburetted steels.

The floating of solid on molten iron is clearly due to the simplest of possible reasons, to wit, that the solid iron is lighter than the molten iron. Wrightson[d] has shown this in two ways. First by means of his autographic "oncosimeter," he measured the force with which balls of cast-iron immersed in molten cast iron sought to rise or fall, obtaining diagrams like that in Figure 125. He found that, when first immersed, the tendency of the ball was downward: this downward tendency quickly gave way to an upward tendency, which, as the ball grew hotter, gradually reached a maximum, then declined slightly till, at the point of fusion, it suddenly fell to zero.

Reversing, he measured the diameter of a 15·28″ cast-iron ball during cooling, beginning two minutes after casting it in a sand mould. During the first 24 minutes

[a] Private communication, Feb. 20, 1880.
[b] Percy, Iron and Steel, p. 1.
[c] Jas. E. Howard, private communications, Feb. 8th, 20th, 1889.
[d] Journ. Iron and Steel Inst., 1879, II., p. 418: 1880, I., p. 11.

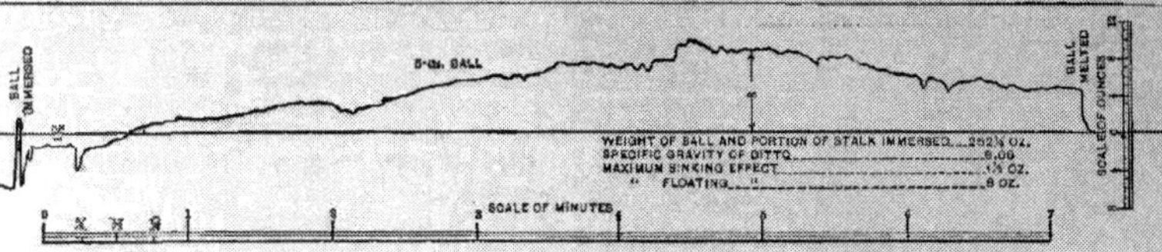

Fig. 125.—Oncosimeter Diagram of the Effort of a Gradually Heating Cast-iron Ball to Sink and Rise in Molten Cast-iron. Wrightson.

the ball expanded 0·078″ in diameter, then remained stationary for 3 h. 13 m., then contracted for more than 4 h. 30 m., the total contraction from the maximum diameter being 0·18″.

Thus in both cases the maximum volume (or minimum density) occurs decidedly below the melting point, so that both solid iron in melting, and molten iron in solidifying and further cooling, first expand to a maximum volume, then again contract.

Moreover, while the cold iron is denser than the molten,

TABLE 150.—COMPOSITION OF STEEL.

SEE FURTHER pp. 18 to 20: 38, guns and rails: 40, silicon steel; 48, manganese steel; 58-4, rail steel; 69, phosphoric steel; 71, phosphoric steel; 74, 78, chrome steel; 81, Tungsten steel; 83, cupriferous steels: 92, oxygen: 162, castings.

	C.	Si.	Mn.	P.	S.
Anchors, cast	·56	·186	·05	·06	·06
Armor-plate, face	·75	·50	1·45	·06	·05
" " protective deck	·28	·02	·48	·07	·05
Augur bit	·65	....	·72		
Axe "overcoat"	·95	·031	·08	·023	·018
" "	1·06	·096	·38	·046	·032
Axles, carriage	·10 to ·25				
" crank	1·05				
" light	·16		·75–·80	·10	
	·15	< ·015	·75–·80	·105	
	·16		·78–·80	·102	
" railway	·46–·52	....	1·11 to ·83	....	·04 or ·10
" "	·15	·012	·60	·07	·046
Beams, tees, angles	·18 to ·21	....	·60 to ·80	as high as ·07	as high as ·06
Boiler-plate	·14	·035	·47	·047	·061
"	·09	·02 to ·08	·2	·07	
"	·16	....	·25	·060	
	·16	....	·75	·066	
"	·16	·014	·52	·047	·05
	....	·03 to ·05	·30 to ·40		
"	·09	·02 to ·05	·80	·07	
	·15		·03	·05	·06
Boulat	3				
Chisels	1·00				
" chipping	·75				
" "	·75	....	·39		
Cutlery, Bessemer	·5 to ·6	....	·1 to 1·1	·05	·06
Die for iron pipes	1·09	1·88	·86		
Drill, rock	·08	....	·21		
" "	1·06	....	·29		
Drop-forgings, complex, {Pistol-stocks, Wrenches}	·09 to ·14	·005, ·015 rare, ·02	·35 to ·65	·04	·04
" " less complex, e. g. pistol-barrels	·14 to ·18	·02±	·5 to ·6	·04	·06
Eye-bars	·13 to ·16	....	....	·03 to ·06	
" "	0·32	0·02	·60	·084	·045
File, saw	1·87	....			
" " mill	1·15	·25	·20	·05	·025
" " 11″ round	1·42	·251	·59	·088	·009
" " 10″ square	1·48	·186	·17	·082	·018
" " 12″ half round	1·43	·270	·22	·002	·014
Fish-plates	·14	·014	·54	·11	·09
Forgings	not over ·30				
" heavy	·3 to ·8	....	....	·04 to ·09	
Guns {English	·25 to ·5	....	·3 to ·08		
Guns {French	more C.				
Guns {Spanish	·23 to ·33	·05 to ·06	·32 to ·38	·005 to ·007	tr.
" barrels	·25	·234	·086	·022	tr.
" " Swedish	·35 to ·45	·25 to ·40	·40 to ·60	·06 or less	
" Krupp	1·18	·83	tr.	·02	0
	·50	·11	·16	·04	·08
" tubes, Woolwich	·335	....	·075		
	·40	....	·126		
	·300	....	·312		
	·417	....	·240		
" " "	·240	....	·216		
	·272	....	·225		
	·143	....	·341		
" " "	·194	....	·248		
Harrow-disc, rail-stock	·85				
Knife-section	·95 to ·108	....	·20		
Lawn-mower knife	·88	....	·32		
Machinery steel, common	·28	·02	·60	·10	
Mower-knife	·98 to 1·24	·826	·18	·051	·063
Nails	·08 to ·12	·01	·4	·08 to ·09	·06 to ·076
"	·10 ·15	·02	·14	·027	
Nail-plate	·10 to ·12	·01 or less	·40	·10±	below ·10
"	·06 to ·10	·009 to ·01	·25 to ·40	·10 to ·12	·045 to ·065
"	·07	·016	·46	·08	·12
Piston-rods, heavy	·15	....	·8	·05	·05
" steam-hammer	·12 to ·15				
Plough-beam	·8 to ·85				
Projectiles, Terre Noire	·45 to ·60	·23 to ·30	·50 to ·60		
" Whitworth *a*	·50	·06	·43		
Projectiles, Krupp	·55	·235	·321	·027	·008
" Hotchkiss	·55	·058	·019 ·054	·054	·035
Punch for fish-plates *h*	1·04	....			
Rails, excellent	....	·11	1·20	·10	
" Dudley's formula	·25 to ·35	not over ·04	·30 to ·40	not over ·10	
" Bethlehem have sometimes been held below	....	....	....	·06	
" some late best American, special order	·50 to ·55	·125	·100 to ·115	·073 to ·080	·07
" now have up to	·60	....			
" cupriferous	·33 to ·48	·03 to ·08	1·05 to 1·25	Cu ·51 to ·66 P	·08 to ·10
" Bethlehem	·40	·10	·80 to ·90	·07	·05 to ·08
" bad U. S. *e*	·34 to ·49	·02 to ·07	1·11 to 1·63	·105 to ·147	·02 to ·107
" welsh steel rails, bad *f*	·20	·10 (?)	·347	·20 to ·26	·075
" average of one month at an American mill	....	....	....	·105	
Razors	1·5				
Rifle, barrels	·22	....	·35 to ·45*d*		
" and shot-gun barrels	·20 to ·24	·01 to ·02	·6 to ·7	·04 to ·06	·05
Rolls	·69	·20±			
" Krupp's	·852	·15	·448	·04	0
	1·020	·195	·425	·05	·038
" 10″ roughing	·40	·02	·60	·10	·06
Saws, good U. S.	·93	·29	·31	·026	
" Jessop's best	·90 to 1·16	·194 to ·86	·14 to ·45	·024 to ·030	
" U. S., very good	1·23	·26	·13	·033	
Screw-wire	·10 to ·12	....	·40	·11 to ·12*g*	·09 to ·12
Screen-plate for stamp-mill	1·11	·293	·17	·009	
Screw-driver	·88	....	·72		
Sett	·87				
Shafts, marine	·30	·13	·57	·068	·042
" " cast	·16	·08	·852	·05	·05
" heavy, forged, Bessemer	·20 to ·30				
Shafting (small)	·17 to ·29	·02±	·5 to ·8	·09	·07
Ship-plate, *b* British	·17	·04	·70 to ·80	·06	·08
Shovel	·08 to ·80				
"	·43				
Spectacle bows	1·64	....	·41		
Springs, Bessemer steel, one mill	·45 to 1·00	0·12	1 to 1·20±	·04 to ·05	·04 to ·06
Springs, bed	·58	....	·72		
" furniture	·40	·12	·93	·09	·10
" British	·55	·05	·5	·06	·06
" clock	·87	....	·94		
" open-hearth	·8	·08	·60	·075	·05
" truck	·60	....	·40		
" washing-machine	1·05	·148	·28	·097	·014
Structural steel	·25	·06	·50		
Upper limit of phosphorus for bridge-members. {Usual	....	....	....	< ·08	
Upper limit of phosphorus for bridge-members. {The most prudent engineers specify	....	....	....	< ·05	
Taps for nuts *i*	1·08				
Taps and dies	1·12				
Tin-plate	·10 to ·15	....	·215 to ·30	·04	·04
Tool-steel, Fagersta	·7	·03	·20	·025	
" " Midvale	1·09	·10	·27	·027	
" " French	1·00	·06	·08	·02	·015
Tool, German	·92	·09	·12	·02	·005
" mason's	·60				
Tyres, carriage	·85				
" Krupp	1·09	·26	·52	·11	·05
" locomotive	0·55				
" R. R.	·22 to ·60	....	·72	·05	·05
" R. R. American *c*	·62 to ·78	....	·80 to 1·00	< ·055	
" " British	·35 to ·55				
" "	·82	·04	0·8	·05	·068
Welding steel	·07	·01 or less	·15 to ·30		
Wire—Bessemer	·04 to ·12	·04	·50	·096	·04 to ·06
" soft Swedish	....	·061	0·899	·034	·008
" occasionally up to	....	....	....	....	·15
"	·13	under ·015	·65 to ·70	·10	
" very strong	·828	·148	·587	0	·039
" fencing	·12 to ·18	·02±	·50 to ·80	·09	·10
" telegraph	·12 to ·15	....	not over ·40	·04	·04
Wootz (Henry)	1·64	·045	....	....	·131

a A famous shot of Whitworth's: the metal had 213,000 pounds tensile strength per square inch, and an elongation of 11%, probably in two inches.
b Ship-plate is usually much like boiler-plate in composition, but with rather more phosphorus
c American tyres are harder than British, probably chiefly because the brake-service is more trying, the weight of cars per wheel heavier, and the track rougher here than in Britain.
d It was necessary to keep the manganese below 0·45%. With higher manganese the turnings were so tough as to deflect the turning tool; with 0·35 to 0·4% of manganese the turnings broke off short.
e Rails habitually made at an American mill using cast-iron direct from the blast-furnace without remelting in cupolas.
f Open-hearth steel rail formerly made in South Wales from old iron rails. Bell, Principles of Manuf. of Iron and Steel, p. 427, 1884.
g The phosphorus is intentionally high, in order that the turnings may break off short, and not clog the cutting tools.
h Punched 27,000 fish-plates.
i Tapped 90,000 nuts.

the difference is slight, less than one fifth as great as the difference between the density of the molten metal and the minimum density which occurs slightly below the melting point.

He deduced the following values.

Specific gravity of solid Cleveland gray cast-iron	6·95
" " " plastic " " "	6·50
" " " molten " " "	6·88

This explanation of the invariable floating of cool on molten iron is so simple and natural to one who has seen ice float on water, that we wonder as much as we regret that energy should have been diverted from our pressing needs to unpromising, far-fetched, if ingenious attempts to attribute it to remote causes, which could hardly operate constantly.

CHAPTER XV

DIRECT PROCESSES.[a]

Wrought-iron and steel are usually made by the indirect method of first making cast-iron in the blast-furnace and then decarburizing it. Direct processes are those in which wrought-iron or spongy iron is made directly from the ore, and either used as such, or converted into steel, usually by melting it with cast-iron, more rarely by cementing it with carbonaceous matter: or in which weld- or even ingot-steel is made directly from the ore.

§ 310. POSSIBILITIES OF THE DIRECT PROCESS.—Before confusing ourselves with the details of the numberless direct processes, let us in a general survey see what are the possibilities, not of this or that particular process, but of the direct process in general, what the advantages which we can conceive and may hence seek, what the necessary obstacles.

The fields for the direct process are the production of weld-metal (wrought-iron weld-steel) to be used as such, and of raw material for the open-hearth and crucible processes.

The former field I think holds out little promise, for weld-metal made by direct process is not only liable to red-shortness and slag-shortness, but also usually varies capriciously in its carbon-content and is markedly heterogeneous.

In the latter field direct-process metal must compete with scrap iron,[b] with cast-iron, and with puddled and charcoal-hearth iron. But if it can compete with the product of the blast-furnace alone (cast-iron), it can surely compete with puddled and charcoal-hearth iron, which have each undergone an additional very costly operation after passing through the blast-furnace; hence we may narrow the discussion and ask, "Can direct-process metal compete with scrap iron?" and "Can it compete with cast-iron?"

Competition with scrap iron. As a material for the crucible and acid open-hearth processes, I do not think that we can forecast the future of direct-process metal with complete confidence.

As a material for the crucible process, direct-process metal made from ores relatively free from phosphorus has a great advantage over most of the scrap iron in the market, in that its phosphorus-content may be known and guaranteed. For this purpose old steel rails are of course quite out of the race. But boiler-plate shearings of known composition are made in great quantities: and with more perfect organization the composition of the plates of worn-out boilers may be known and guaranteed. It is true that most if not all of even the best boiler-plate steel has more phosphorus than is desirable for the crucible process, which, I believe, will be ever more and more restricted to the production of the very best, *i. e.* the least phosphoric, classes of steel. But on the other hand, with the basic open-hearth process looming up, those interested in the future of direct processes should bear in mind that ere long boiler-plate containing even less than 0·02% of phosphorus may be made of enormous quantities. Much the same may be said of direct-process metal considered as competing with scrap iron as a material for the acid open-hearth process.

This process, however, should it continue to flourish, would demand much more scrap iron of guaranteed composition than is likely to be offered. Here, too, old rails are so heavily handicapped by their high phosphorus-content as to be out of the race, at least for the production of those classes of steel for which the open-hearth seems suited.

But it is as a material for the basic open-hearth that the future of direct-process metal seems brightest. We have in this country very extensive deposits of readily mined ore, too phosphoric for either the acid Bessemer or the acid open-hearth processes, but not sufficiently phosphoric to yield cast-iron desirable for the basic Bessemer process. Some of them are situated where fuel suitable for the direct and for the open-hearth processes is very cheap relatively to that suitable for the blast-furnace; the conditions here seem especially favorable to the combination of direct process with basic open-hearth, for the latter readily takes metal of any phosphorus-content whatsoever, high, low or moderate.

Now the extensive development of the basic open-hearth process which may be looked for in these fields, should it itself create a demand for scrap iron. How this demand is to be met one hardly sees.

It hardly seems probable that a great quantity of old rails will be offered. According to Poor's Manual there were about 82,000 miles of iron rails in this country in 1880, of which more than one-quarter had been taken up before 1888, so that on an average somewhere about 300,000 tons of old iron rails have been taken up per annum and sold. This is about the present production of open-hearth steel in this country, and about one-tenth of that of Bessemer steel.

Now no very large proportion of these old rails, so far as I can learn, goes into the open-hearth furnace. They are re-rolled, slit into bars of many kinds, etc. Nor does it seem probable, judging from the statements of railway engineers whom I have consulted, that the supply of old steel rails will increase rapidly. As the old iron rails are taken up, in many cases, *e. g.* where they have stood on sidings, on branches but little used, etc., they are replaced with nearly worn-out steel rails. It seems probable that as the supply of old iron rails ceases, it will be about made good by that of worn-out steel rails, of which a considerable quantity is now sold every year. In the basic open-hearth process, then, we have a great prospective demand for direct-process metal and scrap

[a] See an article by Ledebur, Stahl und Eisen, VI., p. 576, 1886.

[b] In this discussion I use "scrap iron" generically, to include scrap wrought-iron and scrap ingot-metal.

iron, a demand which is likely to outstrip any probable increase in the supply of scrap iron for sale, so that as a remainder we are likely to have a large demand which direct-process metal can fill.

§ 313. Competition with the Blast-Furnace.—In studying this question I consider the relative cost of making metallic iron, whether sponge, blooms or balls, by the direct process, and of making cast-iron in the blast-furnace. I assume that the two competing materials are, 1st, direct-process iron to be used in the open-hearth furnace with a little cast-iron (in a process parallel with the pig-and-scrap process); and, 2d, cast-iron to be used in the open-hearth furnace with ore, in the pig-and-ore process: and this without discussing the relative merits of the pig-and-scrap and the pig-and-ore processes.

If direct process iron can be made as cheaply or nearly as cheaply as cast-iron, it will of course be a much better material for the open-hearth process.

The cost of the combination, blast-furnace plus puddling, as preparatory to the open-hearth process, must ever remain so high that it will be chiefly confined to the production of steel of exceptional purity. Indeed, the basic open-hearth process threatens to extinguish the combination altogether as preparatory to the open-hearth process.

For making steel by the open-hearth and crucible processes we seek metallic iron without much carbon or silicon. In the blast-furnace we not only bring our iron to the metallic state, which can be done at a low temperature, but raise our deoxidized iron to a very much higher temperature, at vast outlay of fuel; this excess of fuel causes such energetic deoxidation that all the phosphorus of the ore is deoxidized and unites with the iron, as does much carbon and silicon, which must later be removed. This does not at first seem the straightest way, but it has enormous incidental advantages, in that the carbon and silicon absorbed prevent the metallic iron from reoxidizing; in that we obtain all the products in a molten condition, in which they can be very cheaply handled; in that we can convert the gangue into a sulphur-devouring basic lime-silicate and can melt this silicate, thus at once removing from the iron the gangue with which it is associated in nature, and the sulphur of the mineral fuel used for smelting.

This procedure, making steel by carburizing iron in the blast-furnace and again decarburizing it, has been long ridiculed as indirect and illogical. But the objection is rather of sentimental than practical importance, unless the indirect and illogical process necessarily costs more than the direct and logical one: metallurgy lives by profit, not logic. Indeed, the cheapest possible process for given results, quality and certainty included, no matter how indirect is logical when all factors are considered: it seems illogical only to the shallow logician who ignores certain premises.

A. *Advantages and Disadvantages of the Direct Process.*—For all ores the direct process has an advantage over the blast-furnace,

1, In yielding iron relatively free from carbon and thus fitter for the open-hearth and crucible processes.

2, In that its gentle deoxidizing conditions may permit dephosphorization—at the cost of heavy loss of iron. The loss of iron may, however, be avoided if dephosphorization be not sought by strengthening the deoxidizing tendencies (Cf. § 315, B I.).

3, In that it can use fuels (producer-gas, water-gas, natural gas) which are often much cheaper than the anthracite, coke and charcoal to which the blast-furnace is apparently hopelessly restricted.

It is at a disadvantage.

4, In leading to greater absorption of sulphur if sulphurous (solid mineral) fuel is used, since at the usual low temperature of the direct processes we cannot melt and hence cannot use the desulphurizing lime slags.

5, In its greater outlay for labor, greater because operations are more scattered, and because the product is usually solid and less easily handled than the molten product of the blast-furnace.

6, In its probably necessarily greater loss of iron.

For rich ores it has a further advantage.

7, In requiring less fuel, thanks chiefly to its lower temperature.

8, In case of lean ores the fuel-consumption of the direct process may be brought below that of the blast-furnace, but only at the cost of heavy loss of iron, which however at the same time causes dephosphorization. The leaner the ore, the heavier the loss of iron to which we must submit in order to obtain the fuel-economy which the direct process permits.

B, *Applicability.* Hence the direct process is especially applicable,

1, To rich ores;

2, To cheap ores, especially if dephosphorization be needed;

3, Where fuel is dear;

4, Where fuels which, though nearly or quite sulphurless, cannot be used in the blast-furnace, are much cheaper per unit of calorific and reducing power than those fuels which are suited for the blast-furnace.

I believe that these are not simple accidents of the direct processes now proposed, but essential conditions of the problem.

§ 314. Discussion.—Let us now consider in some detail the conditions which give rise to these advantages and disadvantages, first noting that, as a material for the open-hearth process, it is not imperative that the product of the direct process should be completely deoxidized. Any small quantity of iron-oxide in the balls of spongy iron, if these were sufficiently dense to sink quickly beneath the slag of the open-hearth furnace, would probably be almost wholly deoxidized by the carbon (and silicon) of the bath during the early part of the process, especially if this were carried out on a basic lining. But towards the end of the operation, when the bath contains but little carbon, any oxidized iron in the sponge-balls would probably escape reduction and would be lost in the slag.

Fuel. To bring 100 parts of iron from the condition of iron ore to that of metallic iron the essential requisites are, enough chemical energy to deoxidize the iron, and enough heat energy to raise the ore to a temperature at which deoxidation can occur.

To deoxidize 100 of iron from magnetic oxide takes $100 \times 1582 = 158,200$ calories.

To develop this quantity of heat needs 19·5 parts of carbon burning to carbonic acid, while to satisfy the equation $Fe_3O_4 + 2C = 3Fe + 2CO_2$ needs only 14·3 parts of carbon. It is conceivable that during the subsequent cooling of the metallic iron and carbonic acid we can almost completely recover the heat expended in raising the iron oxide and carbon to the temperature of deoxidation: so that in one sense a consumption of 19·5 parts of carbon per 100 of iron may be taken as the limit towards which we work, and which in the nature of things we can never quite reach. But even if we admit that half of the heat used in heating the iron oxide and carbon must practically be thrown away, the carbon-requirement rises but little. Some forms of iron oxide begin to deoxidize at temperatures even below 450° C.: but here deoxidation is very slow and probably necessarily very incomplete. Probably it will always be expedient to heat the oxide at least to 800° C. (1472° F.). To do this requires

$$\left(\overset{Fe_3O_4.}{100 \times \frac{100}{72 \cdot 4}} \times \overset{S.H.}{0 \cdot 17} + \overset{C.}{19 \cdot 5} \times \overset{S.H.}{0 \cdot 30}\right)(800° - 20°) = 22{,}877 \text{ calories.}$$

Now, supposing that half of this heat is utilized when the products cool, to supply the other half requires 1·42 parts of carbon, which raises our total carbon-requirement to 21 parts per 100 of iron. In case of ferric oxide the requirement would rise to about 24 parts of carbon per 100 of iron.

As the necessary carbon-requirement is an extremely important factor in any forecast of the probable future of the direct process, let us seek it again in a wholly independent way.

For the deoxidation alone of ferric oxide by carbon, supposing that all the carbon were burnt to carbonic acid by means of oxygen yielded to it by the ore, by the reaction :—

$2Fe_2O_3 + 3C = 4Fe + 3CO_2$,

$4 \times 56 = 224$ of iron needs $3 \times 12 = 36$ of carbon, or 100 kg. of iron needs 16 kg. of carbon, which would develop $16 \times 8{,}080 = 129{,}280$ calories.

But to deoxidize 100 of iron by the above reaction demands $100 \times 1887 = 188{,}700$ calories, or 59,420 calories more than is developed by our carbon: and to develop this excess we must burn $59{,}420 \div 8{,}080 = 7{,}354$ kg. of carbon: so that altogether we need

Reducing carbon	16 kg.
Heating carbon	7·4 "
Total carbon	23·4 kg.,

or 26 parts of a fuel containing 90% of carbon.

But here we assume that all the heat developed in the apparatus and by the reactions is utilized with 100% efficiency, a condition manifestly unattainable: no less unwarrantable is our assumption that all the carbon is oxidized to carbonic acid by the oxygen of the ore. But I think it within the bounds of possibility that a direct process should be devised in which the carbon would be oxidized by the ore so fully that the ratio $\frac{CO_2}{CO}$ in the escaping gases would be 1·34 by weight:[a] in which the reduction could be practically completed without raising the temperature above 800° C.: in which 90% of the heat given out by the spongy iron in cooling from this temperature to 250° C. could be utilized,[b] admitting that all the heat given out as the products cool from 250° down is lost: in which the heat evolved by the combustion of the carbon to $\frac{CO_2}{CO} = 1 \cdot 34$ could be practically completely utilized in heating and reducing the ore: and in which 75% of the heat evolved by the further combustion of the escaping gases could be utilized. But the heat developed by reducing fuel and the escaping gases would not suffice for reducing and heating the ore: additional fuel must be supplied: and we may assume that it is within the bounds of possibility that 75% of the heat evolved in burning this fuel would be utilized. Under these assumptions and neglecting the moisture in the blast, we may calculate the fuel requirement as follows for an ore with 10% of gangue, 90% of ferric oxide, or 63% of iron:

[a] The gases from the Björnbyttan charcoal blast-furnace are reported to have this composition: Bell, Princ. Manuf. Iron and Steel, pp. 276-9, from Åkerman.

[b] The temperature of the gases escaping from the Consett No. 4 and the North Chicago No. 7 furnaces is reported as 248° and 249° C. respectively. Gordon, Journ. Iron and Steel Inst., 1886, II., p. 784.

Composition of the Gases.—The ratio $\frac{CO_2}{CO}$ being 1·34, we would have of carbon burning to carbonic acid $\frac{1 \cdot 34 \times 12}{32 + 12} = \cdot 366$, and to carbonic oxide $\frac{1 \times 12}{16 + 12} = \cdot 4285$: or $\frac{\cdot 366 \times 100}{\cdot 366 + \cdot 4285} = 46 \cdot 04\%$ of the carbon burns to carbonic acid, and 53·96% to carbonic oxide: so that each equivalent of carbon takes up 1·46 of oxygen. Hence to deoxidize 100 kg. iron we need

$16 \times \frac{2}{1 \cdot 46} = 21 \cdot 92$ instead of 16 kg. of carbon: of which

$21 \cdot 92 \times \cdot 4604 = 10 \cdot 09$ kg. burn to carbonic acid, and
$21 \cdot 92 \times \cdot 5396 = 11 \cdot 83$ burn to carbonic oxide.
$\overline{21 \cdot 92}$

The waste gases from the reducing apparatus then will contain, per 100 kg. of iron,

$10 \cdot 09 \times \frac{32}{12} = 26 \cdot 84$ of oxygen, or 36·93 kg. of carbonic acid:

$11 \cdot 83 \times \frac{16}{12} = 15 \cdot 73$ of oxygen, or 27·56 kg. of carbonic oxide.
$\overline{42 \cdot 57}$

As the carbon is supposed to be oxidized by the oxygen of the ore, the waste gases escaping from the ore-reducing chamber may be supposed to be free from nitrogen.

Heat Requirements.—Heating the following substances from 20 to 800° C., a range of 780°.

	Kg.		SH.			Calories.
100 of iron[c]	100	×	·169	=	16·9	
$100 \times \frac{10}{63} = 15 \cdot 87$ of gangue	15·87	×	·22	=	3·5	
36·93 carbonic acid	36·93	×	·2164	=	7·992	
27·56 " oxide	27·56	×	·2479	=	6·832	
Total W. × SH.					35·224	
780 × 35·224						27,475
Reduction of 100 of iron, 100 × 1,887 =						188,700
						216,175

Heat Development.—

10·09 kg. of carbon burn to carbonic acid 10·09 × 8,080	81,530
11·83 kg. burn to carbonic oxide 11·83 × 2,473	29,250
90% of the heat given out by gas, sponge and gangue, in cooling from 800° to 250°, W. × SH. × 550 × ·90 = 35,224 × 550 × ·90 =	17,435
75% of the heat evolved in the further combustion of 27·56 kg. of carbonic oxide to carbonic acid, 27·56 × 2,403 × ·75	49,670
In order to bring the sum up to the heat requirement we must burn 6·32 kg. of carbon, which by assumption would contribute of available heat 8,080 × ·75 × 6·32 =	38,290
	216,175

Reducing carbon needed	21·92 kg. per 100 kg. of iron.
Heating carbon needed	6·32
Total	28·24 or, say 30 kg.

To sum this up, under the several sets of assumptions the carbon requirement for 100 of iron is as follows:—

	For deoxidation.	For heating.	Total.
Pure magnetite	19·5	1·42	21
Pure ferric oxide, 1st calculation	....	....	24
" " 2d "	16·00	7·40	23·4
90% ferric oxide, 10% gangue	21·92	6·32	28·24

I repeat, these are limits towards which we may work.

[c] This is not strictly accurate, because during the first part of the operation we are heating oxide of iron and carbon instead of iron and oxide of carbon. But the error thus introduced is not sufficient to affect our results materially.

Now we find that the modern blast-furnace, wonderfully efficient[a] thermo-chemical engine that it is, almost always uses more than twice and usually more than thrice the largest quantity of fuel above calculated. The following are among the best results thus far published.

	Pounds of carbon per 100 pounds of pig-iron.
Consett furnace	73·9 b
North Chicago Coke Furnace, probably 1885	57·95 c
Martel Charcoal Furnace	54·90 d

While part of the difference is due to our assuming a higher efficiency for the direct process, smaller losses of heat by radiation, etc., than are actually attained in the blast furnace, yet the greater part is clearly due to the fact that the blast furnace does much work which the direct process may avoid.

To compare the requirements of the direct process with those of the blast-furnace, I give in the following table the heat requirements of the latter when smelting Cleveland ore, according to Bell, and those of a direct process in which I assume that the charge is heated to 800° C, that no limestone is used, that neither phosphoric nor silicic acid is deoxidized, and that the loss by radiation, tuyere-water, expansion of blast, etc., is but little more than half as great as in the blast-furnace.

TABLE 152.—HEAT REQUIRED FOR MAKING 20 KG. OF PIG-IRON, AND SPONGE CONTAINING THE SAME QUANTITY (18·6 KG.) OF IRON, FROM CLEVELAND ORE.

	Pig-iron.a			Sponge.		
	Kg.	Cal.	Cal.	Kg.	Cal.	Cal.
Evaporation of the water in the coke.	·58 ×	540 =	313	·30 ×	540 =	168
Reduction of 18·60 kg. of iron from ferric oxide	18·60 ×	1,780 =	33,106	18·60 ×	1,780 =	33,108
Carbon impregnation	·60 ×	2,400 =	1,440			
Expulsion of carbonic acid from limestone	11·66 $CaCO_3$	350 =	4,070			
Decomposition of carbonic acid from limestone	1·32 C	3,200 =	4,224			
Decomposition of water in blast	·05 H	34,000 =	1,700	....	....	900
Reduction of phosphoric, sulphuric and silicic acids	....	....	8,500			
Fusion of cast-iron	20·00 ×	330 =	6,600			
Fusion of slag	27·92 ×	550 =	15,856			
Heating iron: Kg. S. H. To 800° C., 18·6 × ·169 × 800	....	....	....	....	....	2,518
Heating gangue: Kg. S. H. to 800° C., 22·3 × ·22 × 800	....	....	....	....	....	3,907
Radiation, tuyere-water, expansion of blast, etc.	....	....	8,780	....	....	4,500
Carried off in escaping gas	....	....	7,000	....	....	4,000
			87,000			49,085

a Bell, Princ. Manuf. Iron and Steel, p. 95, 1884.

These numbers indicate that, with approximately like efficiency, the direct process may be carried on with a little over half the fuel-consumption of the blast-furnace: and I fancy that this is not very far from the point which it may some day reach.

As already hinted, the chief reason for the greater fuel-consumption in the blast-furnace is that the material is heated, not merely to the temperature of rapid deoxidation, say 800° C., but to a vastly higher temperature, so as to completely liquefy the product. When mineral fuel is used the sulphur which it contains would, unless special precautions were taken, contaminate the iron. To prevent this it is necessary that the slag should contain much lime, so that the sulphur may enter the slag as sulphide of calcium, instead of combining with the iron.

But these highly calcareous slags are exceedingly infusible. In order to liquefy them completely the temperature is raised not simply to the melting point of cast-iron, say 1,050° C. for white iron and 1,200° C. for gray, but probably at least to 1,600° C., and much higher when the open gray iron needed for the Bessemer process is made.[e] This high temperature plays another important part in making iron for the Bessemer process: it affords the strongly carburizing and deoxidizing conditions which give the iron a high proportion of carbon and silicon, but which have a compensating disadvantage in deoxidizing the phosphorus of the burden, and thus causing it to enter the iron.

Beyond this, in using lime we increase the fuel requirement not only by increasing the quantity of material to be heated and melted, but because the decomposition of the limestone absorbs heat, and because the carbonic acid driven off from it attacks the carbon of the fuel, by the reaction

$$CO_2 + C = 2CO,$$

both consuming fuel and absorbing heat.

Again, the deoxidation of phosphoric, sulphuric and silicic acids, and the absorption of carbon by the iron, demand heat and fuel.

In an example given by Bell the items calculated in the last two paragraphs consume 0·48 times as much, the sensible heat carried out by the molten products is 0·70 times as great, and that carried out by radiation, by the tuyere-water and by the escaping gases 0·40 times as great, as the heat needed for deoxidation proper,[f] which is thus but about one-third of the total heat-requirement.

Finally, the high temperature of the blast-furnace greatly increases the loss of heat by radiation and by the tuyere-water: but this is partly offset by its great compactness and concentration. In short, it is clear that, as far as fuel-requirement is concerned, the uncarburetted and hence more valuable product of the direct process should be more cheaply produced than cast-iron.

But, as we shall see, this advantage may, except in case of rich ores, be more apparent than real, since the further treatment of the direct-process metal in the open-hearth or crucible process may necessitate reheating the gangue of the ore to a temperature which is very much higher, and with a heating-efficiency which is very much lower, than those of the blast-furnace: a reheating wholly dispensed with in case the ore is treated by the blast-furnace instead of by direct process.

Cost of Installation. It is generally believed that the output of the direct process from plant of given cost is and must be much less than that of the blast-furnace: but I doubt if this is true. To give a rough idea of the relative cost of installation for the direct and for the blast-furnace process, I here estimate the annual output of iron from $40,000 worth of plant, *i. e.*, the annual output for each $40,000 of cost of installation.

American Bloomary. Assuming that each fire turns out 300 tons a year: furnace assumed at $600, ⅓ of a hammer assumed at $234, other items, excluding buildings, at

a Gruner estimated that in large blast-furnaces from 70 to 88% of the heat generated was utilized. In an example given by Bell 81% of the heat developed is usefully applied. In another case 74% of the total calorific power of the fuel is utilized. (Princ. Manuf. Iron and Steel, p. 144, 1884.)

b Gruner, Studies of Blast-Furnace Phenomena, L. D. B. Gordon, p. 78, 1874.

c F. W. Gordon, Journ. Iron and Steel Inst., 1886, II., p. 784.

d Bell, Princ. Manuf. Iron and Steel, pp. 301–4, 1884, from Journ. U. S. Ass. Charcoal Iron Workers, III. From this number, 54·9, we should apparently deduct something like three pounds, to allow for the carbon taken up by the iron, in order to make this case comparable with the others: so that here the carbon burned is about 52 pounds per 100 of cast-iron produced.

e Bell found that wrought-iron, whose melting-point is not far from 1,600° C., was partly melted when held in a stream of slag from a blast-furnace making No. 3 pig-iron (Journ. Iron and Steel Inst., 1871, I., p. 299).

f Journ. Iron and St. Inst., 1871, I., p. 279.

$166, total $1,000: output from $40,000 worth of plant $300 \times \frac{40,000}{1,000} =$ - - - - - - - - - - - - 12,000 tons.

Siemens' Rotator: Holley's estimate that four rotators, with crusher and hammer, but without buildings, cost $40,000, with an output of 125 tons per week. Output $125 \times 52 =$ - - - - - - - - - - - - - 6,250 tons.

Blair Sponge-making Plant, to turn out 60 tons of sponge, or say 50 tons of iron in sponge, per 24 hours, $75,000, - - - - - - - - - - - - - - - 8,180 tons.

Blast-furnace 16′ × 70′, turning out say 48,000 tons per annum, and costing, excluding buildings, $180,000; $40,000 worth of plant would turn out $48,000 \times \frac{40,000}{180,000}$ = - - - - - - - - - - - - - - - - - 10,667 tons.

I infer from these numbers that any difference between the cost of installation for the direct and for the blast-furnace process is a relatively unimportant factor in forecasting the future of the direct process.

§ 315. The Difficulties of the Direct Process, some of them already touched on, are

1, Loss of iron through re-oxidation or imperfect deoxidation,

2, Heterogeneousness and carburization of product,

3, Absorption of sulphur, and

4, Heavy outlay for labor, can I think be best studied by examining certain general divisions of the direct process, to wit, those carried out at a sponge-making, a welding and a steel-melting heat respectively: at the same time we learn the characteristics of these classes.

A. *Sponge-making Processes.*—If the temperature be low, so that unmelted, unwelded spongy iron results, deoxidation is slow, the output of given plant small, and hence the outlay for labor is large. The spongy product absorbs sulphur greedily, hence it is better to use sulphurless or desulphurized fuel, for we lack the sulphur-absorbing lime of the blast-furnace: it reoxidizes readily, hence the loss of iron is likely to be excessive without special preventives, which must cost something. The gangue of the ore is not eliminated, but remains to swell the cost of subsequent operations. The phosphorus of the ore is not indeed deoxidized, but it remains in the spongy metal, and, if this is later melted in presence of an acid slag, as in the acid open-hearth and crucible processes, the phosphorus enters the iron. Here is a tremendous obstacle which many promoters of direct processes have completely lost sight of: but to-day the basic open-hearth process promises to overcome it. However, it must be clearly understood that sponge-making processes do not in themselves guard against the deoxidation and absorption of phosphorus: they are not dephosphorizing processes in any sense, nor do they help towards dephosphorization.

When the ore is heated in reverberatory furnaces, in externally heated retorts, etc., and so does not come into contact with the heating fuel, the excess of the deoxidizing fuel need not be so great as to cause more than moderate, or at most locally serious carburization, which does little harm when the product is to be used for the open-hearth or crucible process. When the ore is heated by the passage of the hot reducing gas through it, one would expect that this would deposit carbon abundantly, and might thus lead to carburization.

To purposely carburize the product, the use of hydrocarbon reducing gases (Gurlt, Blair, §§ 325, 333 A) has been proposed. Another plan is to compress the spongy iron together with carbonaceous matter (Chenot § 332), in the hope that the iron will combine with the carbon in the open-hearth or crucible process before fusion actually occurs.

I. *For Slow Deoxidation,* two remedies suggest themselves, the use of lime, as practiced by Blair (Cf. § 333, A) and that of natural gas or of artificial hydrogenous gas. The former, rich in methane, should deoxidize much more rapidly than the carbon or carbonic oxide generally used. Bell[a] found that, while pure carbonic oxide removed only 9·4% of the total oxygen from calcined Cleveland ore in seven hours at about 427° C. (800° F.), a mixture of 100 parts of carbonic oxide with 12 of hydrogen removed 68% in ninety minutes at approximately the same temperature,[b] thus acting 34 times as fast, roughly speaking. At bright redness the same mixture removed about 70% of the total oxygen in one hour.

II. *The Absorption of Sulphur.*[c]—By placing the ore within retorts, etc., it may be protected from the heating fuel, but this of course increases the consumption of fuel: this procedure should be desirable chiefly in places where sulphurous is much cheaper than sulphurless fuel. But the ore must necessarily come in contact with the deoxidizing fuel, and of this at least 16 parts must be used per 100 of iron, supposing that by some regenerative contrivance or other the ore oxidizes the whole of the carbon to carbonic acid, and at least 21·92 parts per 100 of iron if we assume that the ore cannot oxidize the carbon farther than to make the ratio $\frac{CO_2}{CO} = 1·34$.

We have two common sulphurless deoxidizing agents, charcoal, which is usually very expensive, and natural gas,[d] which is often cheap. Even if solid mineral fuel be used, the absorption of sulphur may perhaps be prevented by gasifying the fuel and desulphurizing the gas by passing it through lime or over spongy iron, as in Tourangin's process (§ 327). The practicability of this plan on a large scale is not yet shown.

III. *Reoxidation* may be *prevented* by cooling the spongy iron before exposing it to the air, as in Chenot's process, and probably as contemplated by Lucas in 1792. The sponge should then be compressed powerfully, to lessen the surface exposed to oxidation. Or reoxidation may be *cured* as in Gurlt's process by balling the sponge under strongly deoxidizing conditions, *e. g.*, in a charcoal-hearth. But we cannot re-deoxidize in the necessarily strongly oxidizing atmosphere of the puddling or other open reverberatory furnace—without adding much solid deoxidizing matter, and even then a considerable quantity of iron will remain oxidized. As already pointed out, a

[a] The temperature when the mixed gases were used was below redness; incipient redness may be taken at about 525° C.

[b] Princ. Manuf. Iron and Steel, p. 310, 1884.

[c] There is a belief that only part of the sulphur of the fuel is liable to be evolved during combustion, at least when this occurs in gas-producers. It is true that only part of the sulphur of the pyrites of the fuel is volatilized as such: but the rest will be expelled almost completely as sulphurous anhydride or otherwise by the time that the fuel itself is completely burnt, quite as in the roasting of pyritiferous ores, and relatively little will remain in the ash if the combustion of the fuel is thorough.

[d] I have met no authoritive statements about the presence or absence of sulphur in natural gas. A chemist who has paid close attention to the natural gas supply, and whose writings on the subject are well-known, informs me that he thinks the gas brought to Pittsburgh practically free from sulphur, but that he believes that the gas in certain fields has a sulpurous smell.

little reoxidation may do no harm in case of spongy iron which is to be melted in a bath of cast-iron in the early part of the open-hearth process, for the carbon and silicon of the cast-iron should take up any slight quantity of oxygen in the sponge.

The term "reducing flame" is responsible for enormous waste of energy and money in carrying out ill advised direct processes. In a certain sense it is possible to produce in a reverberatory furnace a high temperature with a reducing flame: we can reach a white heat with a flame which is reducing towards oxide of silver, of gold, or of copper; which is reducing in the sense of being relatively reducing, or less strongly oxidizing than some other flames. If in a direct-firing reverberatory we burn carbon to carbonic oxide with exactly the proportion of air chemically required, their products would reach a temperature of about 1,500° C. if no heat were lost by radiation. But of course such a combustion could not heat the furnace highly, for its heat is distributed over much matter other than its own products. If we go a step farther and burn ever so little of this carbonic oxide to carbonic acid, the atmosphere becomes oxidizing towards iron, though still reducing towards copper, for carbonic acid oxidizes iron, even in the presence of a great excess of carbonic oxide. In a regenerative or other gas furnace using carbonic oxide no combustion whatever would be possible without yielding an atmosphere which would oxidize iron slightly.

The presence of hydrogen and of hydrocarbons in the gas of regenerative gas furnaces may modify this somewhat: but I fail to see how it is possible in common gas-furnaces, Siemens or others, to obtain a high, say a welding, heat without thereby generating an atmosphere oxidizing towards iron By saying that it is possible to produce at will a reducing, neutral or oxidizing flame in the Siemens furnace, the admirers of this invaluable apparatus have, doubtless unintentionally, spread confusion on the subject. But in Morrell's and certain other gas-furnaces the ore may be heated by white-hot producer gas wholly unmixed with air, or with a slight quantity of air if desired. By a similar arrangement producer gas for reducing ore by direct contact in shafts and vertical retorts, and hence with better heating efficiency, might be intensely preheated without admixture of air. Furnaces of this class may be of great value in developing the direct process.

In Morrell's gas-furnace,[a] Figure 126, both gas and air

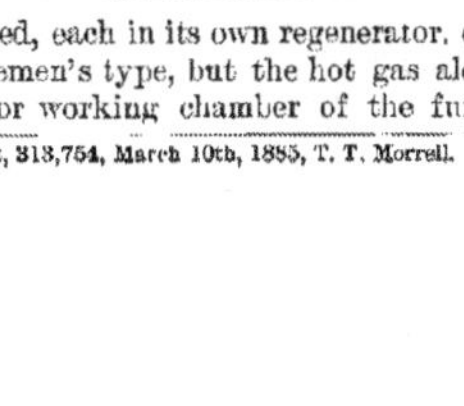

Figure 126.—Morrell's Gas-furnace.

are preheated, each in its own regenerator, quite as in the common Siemen's type, but the hot gas alone enters the laboratory or working chamber of the furnace, the hot air meeting it as at *d'*. Hot gas and hot air then burn in descending through the regenerators: in the case shown this occurs in the left-hand regenerators. On reversing the furnace the dampers F and G now shown in solid lines are moved to the position shown in dotted lines.

B. *Balling Heat Processes.*—If we use a temperature so high that the product may be welded or balled, deoxidation is more rapid, and, as the danger of reoxidation is less, it is not necessary to cool the relatively compact product before exposing it to the air: hence it would seem possible to lessen the cost of installation per unit of daily output, and the outlay for interest and labor. Further, we are saved the expense of compressing the product. Again, it is now possible to dephosphorize, but, alas, only at the cost of heavy loss of iron On the other hand, there is danger of carburizing the product, and the consumption of fuel must be greater, at least in cases of rich ores. Indeed, we directly sacrifice one chief advantage sought by the direct process, the saving of fuel due to lower working-temperature. Finally, the liability to absorb sulphur is aggravated, both because the larger proportion of fuel brings in more sulphur, and because we can hardly avoid bringing the ore into contact with the heating-fuel, or at least with the sulphurous products of its combustion.

We will now consider some of these points separately.

I. *Dephosphorization.*—If we would dephosphorize, the slag must be basic so as to hold the phosphorus as phosphate, and so fluid that it either separates from the metal before or during balling, or can be removed by hammering or squeezing; for if it remains mechanically held in the balls, its phosphorus will be deoxidized and will unite with the iron as soon as the balls are melted in contact with acid slag, whether in the acid open-hearth or in the crucible process. But it can only be made fluid by the presence of a large proportion of iron-oxide, and this of course means large loss of iron. The silicates of the alkaline earths are not fluid enough at this temperature to be squeezed out: the alkalies and manganese-oxide are too costly to be used as fluxes: iron-oxide is the only flux available under usual conditions. Strengthening the deoxidizing conditions in order to lessen the loss of iron, not only directly opposes dephosphorization by strengthening the tendency to deoxidize phosphorus as well, and thus cause it to combine with the iron, but further and indirectly by depriving the slag of base, (iron-oxide), and so removing its dephosphorizing power, and of liquidity and so preventing it from running off with whatever phosphorus it contains.

II. *Carburization* is more likely to occur if we use a balling heat, both owing to the higher temperature and to the larger proportion of fuel employed for generating that temperature. If the operation is carried out in shafts, the same fuel both heating and deoxidizing, the product is very likely to be heterogeneous, here and there absorbing a considerable quantity of carbon, unless we permit a very heavy loss of iron: this unfits it for direct use as wrought-iron, but it is not a serious disadvantage when material for the open-hearth or crucible process is sought.

If the ore is inclosed in retorts, we may add enough carbon to deoxidixe, with no excess so considerable as to cause serious carburization: unfortunately it is not practicable to bring material within a retort to a welding heat by heat

[a] U. S. Patent, 313,754, March 10th, 1885, T. T. Morrell.

applied outside it, for we have no material of which we could make a retort that could endure the temperature to which the outside would have to be exposed. Balling processes cannot be carried out in retorts.

If deoxidation occur in open reverberatory furnaces, a certain but not excessive amount of carburization may be looked for. As the atmosphere is usually strongly oxidizing towards iron, a considerable excess of carbon must be added, so that, after deoxidizing the ore, there may be enough to re-deoxidize any iron which reoxidizes. If the balls are for the open-hearth or crucible process, it is desirable that they should retain a little carbon to deoxidize during fusion any iron reoxidized after leaving the deoxidizing furnace. Now, as different proportions of this excess will be consumed, not only in different charges but in different parts of the same charge, local excesses of carbon will remain here and there, and will carburize the metal locally.

Clearly, the more difficultly oxidizable the reducing agent, the less of it will be attacked by the atmosphere of the reducing furnace, the more will persist till the metal is formed into a solid bloom or is melted, *i. e.*, till danger of reoxidization is passed, and hence the smaller excess will it be necessary to add. To this may be attributed the encouraging yield obtained in the Eames process (§ 340), in which the difficultly oxidizable graphitic anthracite or "retarded coke" is used.

III. *Heterogeneousness.*—Wrought-iron made directly from direct-process balls should be heterogeneous not only from local carburization already dwelt on, but from the presence of slag, unless excessive loss of iron is permitted, for reason already given in considering dephosphorization. The gangue of the ore can only be converted into a slag fluid enough to be thoroughly expelled by converting it into a highly ferruginous silicate, and this except with the very richest ores means heavy loss of iron. Moreover, local excesses of carbon are likely to reduce the iron here and there from this slag, and thus remove its fluidity, and make the metal unforgeable from slag-shortness. Further, if the deoxidizing conditions are so gentle that enough iron-oxide remains to make all the slag fluid, there may be enough unscorified iron-oxide to cause red-shortness. So gentle deoxidation leads to red-shortness, and heavy loss of iron, strong deoxidation to slag-shortness, local carburization, and retention of phosphorus.

IV. *Deoxidation and Reoxidation.*—As the affinity of oxygen for the carbon with which the ore is in contact increases with rising temperature relatively to its affinity for iron, so it should be easier to deoxidize at a balling heat in shaft-furnaces, charcoal hearths, etc., in which an excess of carbon is present, than at a sponge-making heat in retorts: moreover, in balling we weld the spongy metal together, close its pores, and so remove or greatly lessen its tendency to reoxidize.

In open reverberatories the higher temperature needed for balling implies a more strongly oxidizing atmosphere (unless some device such as Morrell's succeeds), and hence more difficulty in deoxidizing and greater proneness to reoxidize, than in sponge-making processes.

In short, the loss of iron should be less in balling than in sponge-making direct processes when shafts and retorts are used, but greater when open reverberatories are used.

V. *The Fuel-Requirement.*—To raise the charge to a welding temperature we clearly need more heat than in the relatively cool sponge-making process: but this disadvantage of the balling processes, while real in case of preparation for the crucible process, disappears if the hot balls are plunged as soon as formed into the bath of the open-hearth furnace, the whole of their sensible heat being thus utilized, while in the most promising sponge-making processes (Chenot's, Blair's, Tourangin's) the heat used in heating the ore is thrown away when the spongy iron cools. Be it remembered that the sensible heat thus utilized in case of balling processes has in many of them (*e. g.* those which heat by direct contact with solid fuel), been imparted in furnaces which are much more efficient transferers of heat than the open-hearth furnace, and hence represents a much smaller outlay for fuel than would be needed to raise the metal to the same temperature in the open-hearth furnace.

This consideration, in case of rich ore, still further increases the fuel-economy which we may hope that the direct process will effect over the blast-furnace; and the same is true in case of lean ores, if the balling heat be high enough and the loss of iron great enough to convert the gangue into a slag so liquid as to separate itself from the metal, so that the balls carried to the open-hearth furnace are nearly pure iron. But if, in treating lean ores, this be not done, then the advantage of the balling direct process over the blast-furnace,—that the sensible heat given the iron is preserved by plunging the hot balls into the open-hearth bath,—may be greatly outweighed by the fact that we now have to heat the gangue, in the open-hearth furnace, to a temperature much higher than than that of the blast-furnace, and that the efficiency of the open-hearth furnace as a heating apparatus is probably hardly one-third as great as that of the blast-furnace. The same objection applies to sponge-making processes as applied to lean ores. Hence, if this class of ore is to be treated by any direct process, it should be by one using a balling heat so high that the slag liquefies and separates.

C. *Steel-Melting-Heat Processes.*—If the process is carried out in a shaft furnace at a steel-melting heat we have at once a cast-iron-making and not a direct process. Hence a direct process at a steel-melting heat can hardly take place except in an open reverberatory, as in F. Siemens' process, or in crucibles, as in Mushet's.

I. *In Open Reverberatories.*—As a basic lining would be essential, we are brought pretty near to the pig-and-ore process in the basic open hearth furnace. Clearly phosphorus would be removed. The sulphur of the reducing fuel would be taken up by the iron, but later removed at least in part by the lime slag. But though, as far as fluidity is concerned, the slag does not need iron oxide, for basic lime-silicates are fluid at this temperature, yet it is hard to see how we could avoid heavy scorification and loss of iron without employing a very great excess of reducing fuel, of which at any rate a great excess should be needed to compensate for its rapid oxidation by the atmosphere of the furnace. This must be violently oxidizing to yield the extreme temperature needed to melt and keep molten the metal, which would be almost absolutely carbonless and hence extremely infusible, thanks to the continual influx of ore.

Further, this class stands at a disadvantage, compared

with the balling processes, in having to heat not only the iron but the oxygen of the ore and the products of the combustion of the reducing fuel to a steel-melting heat, in a relatively inefficient heating apparatus. The thermal capacity of chemically pure ferric oxide per degree of temperature is probably about twice that of the iron which it contains. If, in addition, the ore contains much gangue, the necessity of heating this, with its very high specific heat, (on an average probably about double that of iron) to a steel-melting heat puts the process out of the race.

II. *In Crucibles* (Mushet's process).—Here the same objections apply with greater force. Moreover, the quantity of iron in the charge of ore and charcoal which could be placed in a crucible of given size, would probably be only about one-tenth as great as when we pack the crucible with metallic iron bars, taking into account the lightness and irregular shape of the iron ore and charcoal. The cost of melting by the crucible process is about $12.00 per ton of ingots, with the cheap fuel of Pittsburgh. It would cost nearly as much for fuel, crucibles and labor to melt a crucible-full of ore and charcoal as one of iron: so that the cost of such an operation might be roughly estimated as about $100.00 per ton of metal produced, in addition to the ore and charcoal, or $0.05 per pound.[a] This should frighten the wildest dreamer, as crucible steel is quoted at 4½ cents per pound.

§ 316. CLASSIFICATION BY MODE OF HEATING.—The direct processes may be further classified, as in Tables 153–4, into those in which the heating fuel serves also for deoxidation, and those in which separate fuel is used for deoxidation.

The former class may be divided into those (A) which use solid and those (B) which use gaseous fuel; the latter into those (C) in which the ore is inclosed in externally heated retorts, those (D) in which it is heated by a current of hot gas passing through it, and those (E) in which it is treated in open reverberatories.

At the risk of repetition I will discuss these classes briefly, first pointing out that C is almost necessarily a sponge-making process, while the other classes may be either balling or sponge-making, if not steel-melting.

TABLE 155.—DIRECT PROCESSES CLASSIFIED BY MODE OF HEATING.

		Order of merit (I best, V worst).				
		Fuel-economy.	Absorption of sulphur.	Absorption of carbon.	Loss of iron.	Dephosphorization.
Heating and deoxidation by the same fuel.	A. By solid fuel	I.	III.	V.		
	B. By gaseous fuel	III.	V.	IV.		
Heating fuel distinct from reducing fuel.	C. Retorts etc., heated externally	V.	I.	I.	I.	V.
	D. Internally heated vessels	II.	IV.	III.?		
	E. Open reverberatories	IV.	II.	II.?	V.	I.

A. *Fuel Economy.*—In treating relatively poor ores, in which the proportion of gangue is so considerable that we must slag it away before further treatment, and in which consequently we must reach a slag melting temperature, the direct contact of the solid heating-fuel with the ore should give class A the best fuel-economy. D is a little worse off than A in case artificial gas is used, because of the necessarily great waste of heat in gasification; and for the same reason B, in which all the fuel is gaseous, is still worse off. But as in B and D the heating is by direct contact of gas passing *through* the charge, the fuel-economy should be better than in E, in which the heating is chiefly by radiation from flame passing *over* the charge. Last of all comes C, in which the heating is by conduction, usually through fire-clay, itself heated not by direct contact with solid fuel, but less efficiently by passing flame. The order of merit then is A, D, B, E, C.

If in treating extremely rich and almost gangue-less ores B, C, D, and E were used as sponge-making processes, the order of fuel-economy would probably be the same. I will again point out that the necessarily balling division A is only under an apparent disadvantage in having to heat the charge to a higher temperature than the sponge-making processes, because the higher temperature is a great advantage when the hot product is immersed in the bath of the open-hearth furnace.

B. *Absorption of Sulphur and Carbon.*—In both respects class C stands best. Indeed, by adding only a very slight excess of carbon over that needed to deoxidize the iron by the reaction $Fe_2O_3 + 3C = 2Fe + 3CO$, or 32%, the absorption of carbon may be practically completely prevented. In B and D a considerable absorption of carbon would be looked for, since the carbonic oxide of the gas should deposit carbon if an excess of carbon over that needed for reduction is present. But it is reported that, for reasons unknown, when producer gas made from charcoal is used, the sponge is nearly or quite free from deposited carbon. When, however, natural gas is used, it deposits carbon copiously. As in many parts of this country natural gas is very cheap, some device by which the deposition of carbon from it can be prevented is urgently needed.

The absorption of sulphur should be high and about alike in A, B, and D, since in all three the charge comes in contact with the whole of the fuel, though with less fuel in A than in D, and less in D than in B. In E it should be greater than in C but less than in the others, since part of the sulphur of the flame may be taken up by the charge.

The order of merit then as regards sulphur absorption, should be, C, E, A, D, B.

In A, D and B the opportunity for absorbing sulphur is so great that it is extremely desirable, if not almost absolutely necessary, to use sulphurless fuel, such as charcoal, natural gas, or desulphurized artificial gas.

C. *Dephosphorization and loss of iron* usually accompany each other, though it is quite possible in the sponge-making varieties of B, C, D, and E to lose much iron without dephosphorizing. Dephosphorization and loss of iron should reach a maximum under the oxidizing conditions of E, if a slag-melting heat be reached, and a minimum in C.

§ 317. THE FUTURE OF THE DIRECT PROCESS.—To sum up what has gone before: the direct process is chiefly adapted to preparing material for the open-hearth and crucible processes.

There seems little reason to expect that it can be applied to lean ores, unless they be very cheap, since it cannot remove their gangue except with fearful loss of iron.

[a] To produce 100 of iron would take say 170 of ore and 30 of charcoal by weight. Considering the greater irregularity of the lumps of charcoal and of ore than of the rectangular closely fitting pieces of iron, we may estimate that the pound of ore will occupy twice as much, and one of charcoal twenty-five times as much space as one of iron, so that we need 170 × 2 + 30 × 25 = 1,090 volumes of ore and charcoal where we would have but 100 of closely packed iron.

In case of rich ores, it holds out good hope of producing a ton of malleable iron with less fuel, but with greater outlay for labor, than is needed to make a ton of cast-iron in the blast-furnace.

It can remove phosphorus, but this implies heavy loss of iron. In any event the loss should be greater than in the blast-furnace.

The sponge-making processes are very heavily handicapped by their small output if the sponge be cooled before drawing, by the heavy loss of iron if it be not. The use of natural gas or of lime may indeed enormously increase the output: but the trouble of cooling the sponge before drawing still remains.

In the steel-melting-heat processes the fuel-consumption will probably be greater not only than in other direct processes, but even than in the blast-furnace. Moreover, the loss of iron is likely to be excessive.

The balling processes seem to hold out the most promise. Of the many processes which have been proposed and tried, only those of this class show any vitality, the American bloomary, the high bloomary (*e. g.* Husgafvel's), the Eames process. Whether the last will stand the test of prolonged use remains to be seen. This class has the advantage of getting rid of the gangue at once: of delivering hot balls ready for the open-hearth process: of dephosphorizing. On the other hand the loss of iron is considerable, the product somewhat carburetted and heterogeneous; but these last two objections are of little weight in preparing materials for the open-hearth process. If carried out in shafts, the sulphur of the fuel is absorbed by the iron, but the consumption of fuel should be small. If in open reverberatories, more fuel is consumed, but the iron does not take up the sulphur of the heating fuel.

These balling processes then should be best suited to places where ore is cheap, sulphurless fuel available at a price which does not put it out of competition with sulphurous blast-furnace fuel, and the open-hearth process at hand to consume the balls.

If direct processes offer real advantages, why, we are asked, have they failed so often, so almost universally? Knowing that the blast-furnace has defeated them in the past, how can we expect them to compete with it in the future?

First, their failure has not been so complete as many believe. Remember the steam-engine before Watt. Numberless foolish processes have failed, but even so crude and wasteful a process as the American bloomary has yielded a profit, directly or indirectly, within a few miles of elaborately equipped and apparently well-situated blast-furnaces which in the same period have failed. And, passing by the rather feeble existence of Gurlt's and of the Catalan process, we have the present increased activity of the high bloomary as modified by Husgafvel, even in face of a very great shrinkage in prices.

Next, we can see reasons why the direct process has failed in the past which apply with much less force to the future. The blast-furnace process was stumbled into, along the path of least resistance. It was developed with little comprehension of the principles on which it rests. At one end we have the modern blast-furnace: to manage this with highest efficiency demands skill, knowledge, talent. At the other we have the crudest forms of charcoal-hearths, and in these it is probably easier to make wrought- than cast-iron. But as we begin to elaborate the process and seek greater fuel-economy, greater output, and less loss of iron, it becomes easier to make cast- than wrought-iron: hence the line along which, thanks to existing ignorance, development began: and the tendency of development to follow its original lines need not be dwelt on.

As the desire to economize fuel and increase output led to lengthening the charcoal-hearth into the shaft-furnace, the difficulty of removing from beneath the overlying charge shapeless, unwieldy, pasty masses of wrought-iron and of forging them, and the ease of running molten cast-iron into easily handled pigs, led irresistibly to the development of the cast-iron-making rather than of the direct process. To-day the former has reached an extraordinary degree of efficiency: probably few human devices have so closely approached the highest perfection of which in their very nature they are capable. Fifty years ago nearly thrice as much fuel was often used as is to-day needed in our best blast-furnaces.

The direct process, on the other hand, while easy if wastefully conducted, becomes extremely difficult the moment we attempt high fuel-economy. We must guard against the absorption of sulphur and keep that of carbon within limits. If we make sponge we must guard against reoxidation: if we make balls in a furnace economical of fuel, to wit a shaft-furnace, we have the serious difficulty of forming, withdrawing and further handling them.

To do all this demands a high degree of metallurgical and engineering talent and knowledge, and just for lack of these, as I take it, direct processes have failed in the past. But to-day our knowledge is greater the amount of trained talent available for solving difficult metallurgical problems incomparably greater than formerly, and both knowledge and the quantity of available talent are increasing rapidly.

Just as the open-hearth process failed in the hands of the greater man, Josiah Marshall Heath, who realized its intrinsic merits, but succeeded later under Martin, thanks to the better technical appliances and skill of his day: just as advancing civilization constantly sees the more difficult, when capable of being made more economical, win a place beside the easier, the triple-expansion compete successfully with the single-cylinder engine, the automatic cut-off with the plain slide-valve, the railway with the coach; so may we hope that, the obstacles in the way of the direct process understood and overthrown, its disadvantages minimized, it will win a place of real importance, under the special conditions which favor it, rich ores and cheap sulphurless or desulphurized fuel.

It is clearly fallacious to reason that the process will never succeed because the past usually ill-advised attempts have failed, have wasted much iron and more gold, have used more fuel than the blast-furnace and puddling combined; because the direct process in the infancy of its intelligent life was weaker than the blast-furnace in its perfection. They failed because they did not overcome obstacles, often unseen, not understood, serious, but not in their nature insuperable. They failed not because the direct process lacked capability but because it was difficult.

But a new and most promising feature is our natural gas If with the most reckless waste it competes easily with slack coal costing \$0.80 per ton, it should compete easily with coke, which costs about $2.00 per ton even at Pittsburgh. It has enormous advantages in its freedom from sulphur (if, as reported, it be usually free from sulphur), and in its cheapness. A greater stimulus to the direct process could hardly be imagined. As we do not see how natural gas can be used to a great extent in the blast-furnace, we may expect its successful application to the direct process. It has, indeed, already given encouraging results in the Eames process: in shaft-furnaces the consumption of gas should be less and the loss of iron less, while the graphite or retarded coke of the Eames process could be replaced by natural gas, which would thus both heat and deoxidize.

If the wasteful American bloomary can exist where charcoal, labor and rich fine ores are cheap, some such improvement of it as Husgafvel's, which reduces the cost of fuel-consumption enormously, should flourish. With some quick way of cooling the sponge, some modification

TABLE 151.—GENERAL SCHEME OF THE DIRECT PROCESSES.

Group	Class	Description		Date, approximately, a: Described or patented in A. D.	Date: Used in A. D.	Date: Abandoned or not. e	Fuel consumption, b: Per 100 of	Fuel: For reducing	Fuel: For heating	Fuel: Total	Labor: Per 2,000 lbs. of	Labor: Days	Loss of iron: From ore to	Loss of iron: Per 100 of iron in ore
Ore reduced and heated by the same solid fuel: product balled.	Charcoal-hearths, balling processes.	Catalan and Corsican hearths, ore and fuel in separate columns					bars.			200 @ 307	bars.	10·7	bars.	27 @ 31%
		American bloomary, ore and fuel charged together				now in use.	blooms.			100 @ 328	blooms.	1·25 @ 1·5	blooms.	17 @ 25
	Shaft-furnaces, balling processes.	Osmund furnace, a very low shaft				now in use.								33 @ 50
		German high bloomary (stückofen), a taller shaft					blooms.			280 @ 4??	blooms.	12		
		Husgafvel's bloomary, still taller, hearth movable				now in use	"			105 @ 142	blooms.	4	blooms.	21 @ 28
		Nyhammar bloomary, spongy iron raked into charcoal hearth		1862	1862 ±		"			121			blooms.	8·15 ?
Ore reduced and heated by the same gas in a shaft-furnace or retort.	Sponge-mak'g processes.	*Gurlt's* type: carbonic oxide passed through ore, product spongy iron.	Gurlt	1856	1881		"			54 h			blooms.	19 ?
			Chenot direct-heating			probably in use.	"			99 h				
			Ramdohr	1871		abandoned.								
		Cooper's, carbonic oxide passed through ore, resulting CO_2 reduced to CO by passing through fuel, etc.	Cooper	1876 ±		"								
			Westman	1888		projected.								
		Tourangin. Hot CO from hot-blast gas producer passed through ore; residual CO burned to heat the blast		1882										
		Laureau. (Application for patent pending)		1889 ±		projected.								
	Steel-melt'g heat.	*Bull*. Ore reduced and heated and product melted by combustion of hot water-gas in shaft-furnace		1883		abandoned.	cast iron.			700				
Ore reduced by solid fuel and heated by other than the reducing fuel. Reduction in retorts, shaft-furnaces, etc.	Sponge-making processes.	*Lucas*. Ore reduced in horizontal retorts with charcoal.	Lucas	1792		"								
			Conley ? g			now experiment'g								
		Chenot's type. Ore reduced by charcoal or coke in vertical retorts heated externally; sponge cooled before removal.	Chenot	1851		abandoned.	iron in ore ingots.	45 @ 48 45 c	96 @ 137 58 c	131 @ 205 101 c	iron in ore ingots.	3·3 1·8 c	blooms. ingots	86 ± 24
			Blair	1872		abandoned.								
			Yates			"								
			Tresca			"								
		Blair's later. Ore reduced by charcoal in vert. retorts heated internally by hot carbonic oxide	Blair			"								
	Balling processes.	*Clay's* type. Ore reduced in retorts over puddling furnace; sponge dropped into puddler and balled.	Clay	1837		abandoned.								
			Renton	1851		"	blooms.	150	100 ±	250 ±				
			Wilson	1864										
			Rogers	1862		"								
		Schmidhammer. Ore reduced in shaft by charcoal and heated directly by combustion of hot water-gas; balled in forehearth		1886		projected.								
		Du Puy. Ore reduced in sheet-iron cases by charcoal; resulting sponge rolled out into bars		1878		abandoned.							blooms.	21·5
	Steel-melting heat processes.	*Mushet*. Reduction and fusion with charcoal in crucible		1800		"								
		Siemens retort type. Ore reduced in vert. retorts within open-hearth furnaces; sponge melted by bath of cast-iron in the same furnace.	Siemens	1863										
			Ponsard	1869										
Ore reduced by solid fuel and heated by other than the reducing fuel. Reduction in open reverberatories.	Sponge-making process.	*Thoma*: ore uniformly mixed with coal, heated in an open reverberatory; sponge used for copper precipitation		1845		aband'n'd within a few years.	iron in ore	45	114	159			sponge.	appar'ntly 10%
	Balling process.	*Harvey*. Ore reduced with charcoal on shelves above reverb., then balled in reverb.		1851 ±		abandoned.								
		Gerhardt. Ore bricked with tar, flux, and carbonaceous matter in a puddling furnace		1874										
		Eames. Reduction with graphite, and balling, in open reverberatory		1885-9		now in use.	balls.				balls.	1·17	ingots.	21%
		C. W. Siemens, reduction and balling in rotary puddler		1873	1881	abandoned.	blooms.	20 ? @ 138	126 @ 237	149 @ 375	blooms.	5·5	blooms.	12 @ 25
	Steel-melting heat process.	*Leckie*. Ore bricked with coal, reduced in fore hearth of open-hearth furnace, then melted on its hearth.		1868 ±		abandoned.								
		F. Siemens. Melted ore reduced by coal in open-hearth furnace		1867 ±		projected.								
		Eustis. Ore coked with coal, melted in shaft-furnaces		1880		abandoned.								

a *Dates*. No attempt has been made to trace the earliest and latest dates. I give simply those met in a superficial examination, without aim at historical methods.
b *Fuel*. In certain cases the consumption of charcoal is given in bushels; I have in these cases assumed a probable weight for the bushel; but this is only a guess.
c The quantity of fuel, etc., as used in sponge-making, per 100 parts of ing is obtained from the resulting sponge.
e "*Abandoned*" is not meant to imply that the projector has abandoned all hope, but that operations are suspended or practically so, according to such information as I have obtained.
f This process or its equivalent was in use till within a few years.
g The kind of retort used is not given.
h Fuel used in sponge-making, per 100 of blooms made in charcoal-hearth from the sponge.

of Gurlt's process should under the same conditions be applicable. Where rich ores are cheap and not charcoal but some non-blast-furnace mineral fuel is also cheap this same process should be applicable, provided the producer-gas which it uses can be cheaply desulphurized.

The pressing problems for the direct process then seem to be

1, The application of natural gas in some shaft furnace like Husgafvel's.

2, Better means of the removing the balls than in Husgafvel's process.

3, Some quick cheap way of cooling sponge for sponge-making processes.

4, An automatic compressing apparatus for sponge, so simple that a single mechanic can compress enormous quantities rapidly.

5, Some cheap way of desulphurizing producer-gas.

Let not us who have seen Thomas solve the basic problem which had long baffled the wisest, say that this goal unreached is unattainable.

SOME DIRECT PROCESSES DESCRIBED.

Under most conditions, whether in making weld-metal to be used as such or in making material for the open-hearth or crucible process, iron relatively free from carbon is sought: and I assume that it is in the following descriptions. I have pointed out in considering the sponge-making and balling processes (§§ 315, A, B) how a carburetted product may be obtained.

§ 318. In the Catalan Process ore and charcoal are charged in separate columns in a low one-tuyered hearth, the column of charcoal lying between tuyere and ore, and the deoxidizing carbonic oxide generated in it passing through the ore column. The temperature is low at first, to avoid fusion before reduction, later reaching a welding heat, when the pasty iron is balled beneath the charcoal.

The hearth is built chiefly of heavy iron plates, with a tuyere inclining downwards from 30° to 40°. The following dimensions are given:

	Area.	Total depth.	Height to tuyeres.	Charge.
Pyrenees	30″ × 20″	16″	9″	8 @ 4 cwt.
Navarre	30″ × 24″	....	16″	5 @ 6 "
Biscay	40″ × 32″	24″ @ 25″	14″ @ 15″	7 @ 9 "

After cleaning and while still hot from the last charge, the hearth is filled to the tuyere level with charcoal. On this the ore in lumps, not more than two inchbs cube, is piled, together with charcoal, the charcoal against the tuyere-side, the ore against the other, as at *b*, Figure 131, a sheet of iron (later removed) separating them. The

Figure 131.—Catalan Hearth.

talus-face *b* being plastered over with fine moist charcoal, the blast is turned on gently and reduction sets in, the gases (chiefly carbonic oxide and nitrogen thanks to the thickness of the charcoal body) passing by preference through the open pile of lump ore, and escaping at its apex. As the charcoal burns away more is charged, and with it is added fine ore, moistened to prevent blowing away and sifting down. The fine ore sinks with the charcoal, apparently reaching the zone of fusion less completely deoxidized than the lump ore.

After two hours the lump ore column is gradually pushed downwards, and the temperature raised; as successive portions of the ore become sufficiently deoxidized they are pushed into the hotter region nearer the tuyere. By the time that a given portion is pushed into the hotter region much of its iron has reached the metallic state, though much still remains more or less oxidized. The temperature in this region is so high that the unreduced part of the ore melts and forms a slag with the gangue, and that the completely reduced part, growing pasty, welds readily into a bloom.

The whole of the lump-ore reduced and balled, the blast is stopped and the bloom pried out of the hearth and hammered. It is reheated in the upper part of the same hearth while a second charge is reducing.

The slags are essentially basic ferrous silicates. To avoid carburizing and phosphorizing the iron we should (1) have plenty of highly ferruginous slag, which devours phosphorus and carbon, and should hence add much fine ore with the charcoal and tap the slag but rarely: (2) hasten the operation and so shorten the carburizing and phosphorizing exposure: (3) use much blast, to weaken the reducing and carburizing tendencies: (4) incline the tuyere downwards towards the iron, that the blast's oxygen may be less fully converted into carbonic oxide before reaching iron and ore, and the reducing conditions thus weakened. These steps increase the necessarily great waste of iron, and, in spite of them the metal is liable to be carburized and steely: it is necessarily heterogeneous, but nearly free from phosphorus.

In the *Genoese* modification of the Catalan process, which aimed at fuel-economy, a flat-bedded reverberatory received the hearth's flame at one end, delivering it at the other through a horizontal grating, on which the raw ore was piled, into a vertical chamber leading to the chimney. Roasted and somewhat desulphurized here, the ore was next made friable by quenching in water; was crushed, spread on a charcoal layer on the reverberatory's hearth, heated by the flame again and partly reduced by the charcoal on which it lay; was here mixed with cast- or wrought-iron scrap, pushed into the charcoal hearth, and further reduced and balled.

Some economic data follow.

Table 13[illegible].—Catalan Hearth Practice.

	I.	II.	III.
	Percy, 1841.	1840±, Richard, Percy.	1868, Mussy, Phillips.
Weight of bars per charge, lbs.	363 ±	384	374
Length of charge	....	3 hours,	
Men per hearth per shift	....	6 *b*	
Labor, days per 2,000 pounds bars	....	19·7	
Charcoal, tons per 2,000 pounds bars	2·75	8·66	2·00
Loss from ore to bars, per 100 of iron in ore	27·2 *a*	30·9 *a*	28·3
Cost per 2,000 lbs. of bars			
Charcoal	$42.82	....	$31.99
Ore	10.69	....	7.76
Labor	10.25	....	8.19
Repairs	1.38	....	1.22
	$65.14	....	$49.16

I. Francois, Percy, Iron and Steel, p. 316, 1864.
II. Richard, idem, p. 296.
III. Mussy, Phillips and Bauerman, Elements of Metallurgy, p. 175, A. B. 1881.
a The ore is assumed to contain 48% of iron.
b It is assumed that there were two heats per shift. There were altogether ten persons at the forge, but of these only six seem directly chargeable to bloom-making.

§ 319. The American Bloomary Process,[a] resembling the Catalan process in its general features, differs from it in that the ore is charged wholly in a fine state and mixed with charcoal, instead of chiefly in lumps and in a separate column.

The furnace, Figure 132, costing (Egleston) $550 to $600, consists of a nearly rectangular box, of thick castings. It is from 20″ to 30″ wide, and from 27″ to 32″ long, its depth being from 15″ to 25″ above the tuyere and from 8″ to 15½″ below it. It has a single D-shaped tuyere, about 1″ × 1·75″, supplied with blast heated in overhead cast-iron pipes to from 550° to 800° F., and at 1·5 to 2·5 pounds pressure per square inch.

Operation.—The hearth being filled heapingly with burning charcoal, charcoal and coarsely pulverized, washed, and nearly pure ore are thrown on at short intervals, usually one to five, occasionally 12 to 25 minutes, together with slag from previous operations if the gangue be very scanty. The ore reduces in sinking, the usually silicious gangue forms with unreduced ore a basic ferruginous slag, which is tapped intermittently. The reduced iron gradually agglomerates to a pasty ball (loup), which, after nearly three hours, is pried through the charcoal towards the tuyere for greater heat, is then drawn,[b] hammered to a bloom, reheated usually in the bloomary itself, rarely in a chamber heated by its waste gases, and rehammered.

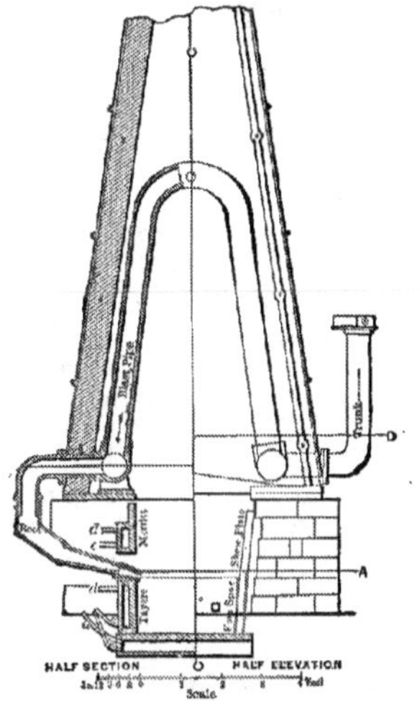

Figure 132.—American Bloomary Furnace.

The operation lasts about three hours, so that eight loups, usually of 300 to 400 pounds each, are produced per twenty-four hours, at an outlay of from 250 to 350 bushels of charcoal and 1·25 to 1·5 days' labor per 2,000 pounds of blooms, and with a yield of say 80% of the iron in the ore. Table 156 gives some numerical details.

[a] For an admirable description, see T. Sterry Hunt, Geol. Survey of Canada, Rept. Progress 1866-9, p. 274. Also T. Egleston, Trans. Am. Inst. Mining Eng., VIII., p. 515, 1880.

[b] A noted writer tells us that the bloom is dug up by the clock, but leaves us in the dark as to how the time keeping properties of this instrument are thereby affected.

Table 156.—American Bloomary Practice.

	Lake Champlain, 1880.	Lake Champlain, 1819.	Palmer.	New Russia.	Moisie, 1868.	E. Middlebury
Dimensions of hearth:	0.	I.	II.	III.	IV.	V.
Width	29″	24″ @ 30″	....	30″	30″	24½″
Length	31″	27″ @ 30″	....	32″	32″	28″
Height to tuyere	15½″	....	....	....	14″	19″
" above tuyere	25½″	....	....	....	....	
" total	41″	28″ @ 30″	....	24″	....	
Blast:						
Pressure, lbs per sq. in.	2 @ 2½	1½	....	1½ @ 1¾	¾ @ 1½	1½ @ 2
Temperature, C.	....	315 @ 427	....	....	....	288 @ 315, est.
" F.	....	600 @ 800	....	....	....	550 @ 600, est.
Size of tuyere-nozzle (one only)	2″ × 1″	1¼″ @ 1	....	....	1″ × 1½″	1″ × 1½″
Inclination of tuyere	12°	....	....	....	very slight.	
Ore, kind	Chateaugay conc'ntr'ted	magnetite	magnetite	magnetite	magnetic sands.	
" % iron	65	65	60	70 ±	55 ±	
Length of one heat	3 hours	3 hrs. aver.	....	....	3 hours.	
Labor:						
Men per hearth per shift	1	1	....	....	1½	
Length of one shift	12 hours	12 hours.	....	....	12 hours.	
Output per hearth:						
Weight of blooms per heat, pounds	400	300 @ 400	....	....	210	
Weight of blooms per 24 hours, pounds	3,200	2,500	....	2,400	1,680	
Slag:						
Composition, silica %	....	21·6 @ 26·4	....	....	8·7 @ 11	16·70
" iron-oxide %	...	48·6 @ 49·7	....	....	58 @ 67	62·06
" alumina	....	0·3 @ 1·6	....	....	....	17·33
" phos. acid	....	0·05 @ 0·06	....	....		
Outlay per 2,000 pounds blooms:						
Charcoal, bushels	310	255 @ 300	....	212 @ 255	396	230
" pounds *a*	5,425	4,640 @ 5,400	....	3,800 @ 4,550	6,240	4,160
Ore, tons	2	2 washed.	2 washed.	1·5 washed.		
Labor, days	1·25	1·5	....	....	1·8	
Loss from ore to blooms, per 100 of iron in ore	28·67	23	16·7	*b* < 7·9	48	

I. T. Egleston, Trans. Am. Inst. Mining Engineers, VIII., p. 515, 1880.
II. to V. T. Sterry Hunt, Rept. Geol. Survey Canada, 1866-9, pp. 274, et seq.
a It is assumed that a bushel of charcoal weighs 18 pounds.
b It is stated that 1·5 tons of nearly pure magnetite yield one ton of blooms. If the magnetite were absolutely pure this would imply a loss of only 7·89%; but as it never is, the loss implied is probably nearer 5%. This is intrinsically improbable: and the statement that 1·5 tons of ore yields one ton of blooms is probably intended to be only approximately true. No doubt in an occasional heat, in which a considerable quantity of rich slag from previous operations is added, such results may be reached.

Indications.—The condition of the operation is judged from the color and brightness of the flame, which should be blueish or reddish, and not brilliantly white; the appearance and consistency of the slag; and the hardness and shape of the loup, which should be moderately soft. If the loup is very soft so that a bar sinks deeply into it the hearth is too hot, and the proportion of ore must be increased: if the loup is hard the temperature is too low, and the proportion of charcoal must be increased.

The ore is so charged that a rim of iron shall form around the outer edge of the upper face of the loup, and thus form a basin which remains filled with slag, and protects the loup's face at once from the blast and from carburization.

Table 157.—Composition of American Bloomary Iron.

	1	2	3	4	5	6	7	8
Sulphur	·008	trace.	trace.	·001	trace.	trace.	trace.	trace.
Phosphorus	·015	·042	·004	·028	·023	.042	·011	·015
Silicium	·095	·280	·021	·312+	·025	·100	·016	·013
Manganese	·079	......	......	......	......	......	......	0
Carbon	·228	·170	·220	·180	·110	·155	·220	·10 @ ·30
Slag	......	....	·180	·014	·165	·075	·150	·25 @ ·50
Copper	......	......	......	......	......	......	......	......

1 to 7. Billets, Egleston, Op. Cit. 1 and 6, Saranac, Hasegawa. 2, 3, 4, Au Sable Forks, Britton. 5, Peru Iron Company, Wuth. 7, Chateaugay.
8. Bloom, A. E. Hunt, Trans. Am. Inst. Mining Engineers, XII., p. 318, 1884. Chateaugay.

The cost of making blooms in the Lake Champlain region is, I am credibly informed, about $45.00 per ton at a mill which, I understand, is closely connected with an iron-mining concern. The estimated cost, under such conditions, is in large part a matter of book-keeping, depending chiefly on the price at which the fine ore, which is to a certain extent a bye-product, is charged against the smelting works. Charcoal blooms are quoted at $52.00 to $54.00 per ton in Philadelphia.

The output of the American bloomaries is decreasing rapidly, as the following table[a] indicates: but, as it more than doubled between 1870 and 1882, it would be rash to predict the early decease of the process confidently. Yet it certainly seems moribund.

Year.	Output of blooms and billets, net tons.
1874	35,450
1876	20,784
1882	48,354
1887	15,085
1888	14,088a

a J. M. Swank, private communication.

From the following table, compiled from the "Directories to the Iron and Steel Works of the United States" for 1884 and 1888, we see that some of the bloomaries now standing are extremely old, and that the building of bloomaries continued till 1883. Between 1870 and 1880 no less than sixteen establishments were built.

TABLE 157A.—HISTORY OF THE AMERICAN BLOOMARY ESTABLISHMENTS REPORTED IN 1884 AND 1887.

Years in which the bloomaries reported in 1886 and 1887 were built or rebuilt.			Of those built in the several periods of Column 1, the following numbers were			
Years.	No. built.	No. rebuilt.	Idle or abandoned before 1884.	Abandoned between 1886 and 1887.	Idle but apparently not abandoned in 1887.	Running in 1887.
1797–1819	2	......	......	1	......	1
1820–1829	8	......	2	......	......	1
1830–1839	6	1	1	4	......	2
1840–1859	7	1	......	3	......	5
1860–1869	6	1	......	1	2	4
1870–1879	16	6	......	11	5	6
1880	3	1	......	1	1	3
1881	2	......	......	1	1	
1882	0					
1883	1	2	......	......	......	3
1884–7	0	0				

Clearly the process is applicable only where rich fine ore, charcoal, and labor are cheap. Even under these conditions it could not compete with fuel-saving processes such as Husgafvel's.

§ 320. THE OSMUND FURNACE (blaseofen, bauernofen), is intermediate between the low and the high bloomaries. It appears to be about eight feet in height. Smelting calcined phosphoric bog-ores with charcoal, it yielded 1½ tons or less of good malleable wrought-iron weekly, with a loss of from 33 to 50% "in working up the bloom:[b] the enormous loss tallies with the production of good iron from phosphoric ores.

The osmund furnace is said to be used still to a very considerable extent in Finland, apparently solely by the peasants.[c]

§ 321. THE OLD HIGH BLOOMARY (STÜCKOFEN.)—Here the height, and with it the carburizing tendencies and the economy of fuel, were carried so far that there was a strong tendency to make cast- instead of malleable-iron: indeed, cast-iron was often made unintentionally in these furnaces. They differed but slightly from the blauofen in which cast-iron was habitually and intentionally made, and in which indeed by varying the strength of the carburizing conditions wrought- or cast-iron could be made at will.

Furnace.—The old Stückofen was a shaft-furnace from 10′ to 16′ high: round or rectangular in section: say 2′ 6″ wide at top and 1′ 6″ (at Eisenerz 4′ × 2′ 6″) at bottom, usually bellying out midway to say 4′ 2″: and had one tuyere say 14″ to 20″ above the bottom, and at the bottom a drawing-hole say 2′ wide, opened for removing the bloom, but closed at other times.

Operation.—The furnace was filled with charcoal, which was lighted from below: as soon as the fire reached the top the blast was turned on, and charcoal and burden (rich slags and ore) charged. The burden was at first light, gradually increasing to the normal—one volume to four of charcoal. Descending, its iron was deoxidized, and, reaching the bottom, agglomerated to a bloom. The slags ran out constantly through a notch in the stopping of the drawing-hole. As soon as the bloom was found by probing to be large enough, charging ceased, the furnace was blown down and the bloom loosened and drawn through the drawing-hole. The furnace was then cleaned out, repaired, its bottom brasqued, and charging began again.

To guard against carburization and the production of cast- instead of malleable iron, the carburizing tendencies were purposely restrained, *e. g.* by charging a large proportion of ore to charcoal.[d]

Some economic data follow.

TABLE 158.—STÜCKOFEN PRACTICE.

	Usual.	Eisenerz.	Old Porssakoski.
Weight of blooms per charge, lbs.	448@672	1,800 ±, with 700 lbs. ± of cast-iron.	....
Length of charge	8 hrs. = 1 shift.	18 hrs.	....
Men per furnace per shift	3	......	....
Labor, days per 2,000 lbs. blooms	12±	......	....
Charcoal, tons per 2,000 lbs. blooms	4·5a	......	2·8
Ore, " " "	....	......	5·86

a At 10 lbs. per cubic foot, or say 15 lbs per bushel.

§ 322. HUSGAFVEL'S[e] HIGH BLOOMARY or continuous stückofen is a tall shaft-furnace, with double, air-cooled, wrought-iron walls, and a movable hearth.

These arrangements tend to diminish the quantity of fuel, ore and labor needed per ton of blooms, and increase the output per furnace: but this last is still very small, while the consumption of fuel is certainly moderate.

The Furnace, Figure 133.—The air-space between the double-walls serves for heating the blast, which by the spiral partitions B B is forced to travel circuitously. The lower five feet of the shaft are lined with fire-brick, the rest is naked within. The outer walls are lagged with four inches of fire-clay, to lessen heat-radiation.

A movable, air-cooled, cast-iron section is provided between shaft and hearth, as this part is relatively perishable, because its temperature is high, and because it is cut by the reduced iron which often adheres to it, and by the workmen's tools used in removing these accretions.

The movable hearth has four water-cooled tuyere-holes *s* on each of two opposite sides: four slag notches *t* at different levels: trunnions *b* for dumping: and a false bottom *u* that accretions may not form on the hearth

a Ann. Statistical Rept. Am. Iron and Steel Ass., p. 37, 1888.

b Percy, Iron and Steel, p. 320. The wording is obscure: I infer that this loss is from ore to hammered bloom.

c F. L. Garrison, Private Communication, April 10th, 1889.

d Percy (Iron and Steel, p. 330), from whose description the above as well as part of Table 158 is condensed, further says that one essential condition of obtaining malleable iron from the blauofen, (which was really a stückofen, the difference originally referring to the mode of working the furnace and the consequent product, not to construction), was to allow the slag free escape, so that it might not protect the bloom from the blast. As the slag was highly fining, containing say 51·7% of ferrous oxide, one might have anticipated that if present it would not only oppose carburization, by preventing charcoal from resting against the bloom, but would tend to decarburize the gradually arriving particles of iron.

e Cf. F. L. Garrison, Trans. Am. Inst. Min. Eng., XVI., p. 334, 1888: and Journ. U. S. Ass. Charcoal Iron Workers, III., p. 280, 1887. He refers to Husgafvel, Jernkont. Annal., 1887: Russian Mining Jl., 1887, II., pp. 398, 435. See also Eng. Mining Jl., XIV., p. 90, 1888: also Stahl und Eisen, IX., pp. 35, 121, 1889. The last has appeared since this article was written, and I have only been able to avail myself of part of its data.

proper. It rests on a lifting platform, which facilitates removal and adjustment.

From the fact that, in experimenting with slow charging and lightened burden in the Dobriansky furnace, whose internal capacity is 400 cubic feet, no cast-iron was made, it is inferred that the limits of size have not been reached, and furnaces of a capacity of 1,000 cubic feet are projected.

The Blast at a pressure of ½ to 1½ inches of mercury (3·9 to 11·8 oz. per sq. in.), is heated in passing downwards through the double walls of the shaft and of the movable section, to from 150 to 250° C. (302 to 482° F.), its temperature and to a slight extent that of the furnace being regulated by varying the proportion of blast admitted at the points f^1, f^2, f^3, f^4 and g. The tuyeres and their trunks i, counterweighted at l, m, n, o, are moved vertically to the appropriate tuyere-holes s, and have ball-joints p, permitting change of direction in all ways.

The Materials.—The ore and rich (*e. g.* puddling) slags are crushed to "quite a fine" size, apparently about ¼" to ½" cube.

The fuel is charcoal, divided into coarse and fine. Coke was used with apparent success, but for so short a while that the results are inconclusive.

The Operation is continuous, charcoal and ore being charged apparently in uniform horizontal layers: the fine charcoal is charged after the coarse, so as to close the interstices and hinder the fine ore from sifting down. The burden, descending gradually, reaches the hearth quite reduced, and probably considerably carburetted. The conditions in the hearth, contact with the ferruginous slag and exposure to the blast, appear to be decidedly decarburizing.

A fresh hearth being in place, the tuyeres are inserted in the lower tuyere-holes, and the blast turned on. The slag is apparently tapped at intervals, its level being kept somewhat above that of the top of the gradually forming bloom, so that the reduced iron, arriving little by little, sinks through a layer of molten decarburizing slag before reaching and coalescing with the iron already present. When the bloom has grown nearly to the level of the lower tuyere-holes, the tuyeres are raised to the upper holes, and the lower ones stopped. When it has reached the upper tuyere-holes the blast is stopped, the hearth lowered, and immediately replaced by a fresh one, the blast being interrupted for only about five minutes. The old hearth is now dumped, the false bottom being, if necessary, driven out by blows on the shaft x.

As false bars are not used, the charge sinks somewhat during changing hearths: to equalize this, the hearths

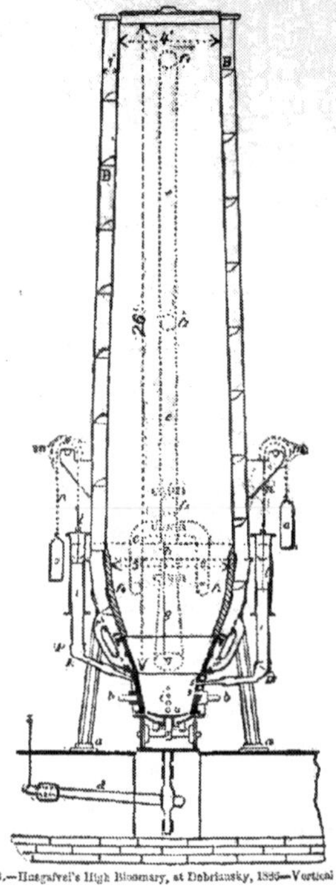

Figure 138.—Husgafvel's High Bloomary, at Dobriansky, 1885—Vertical Section.

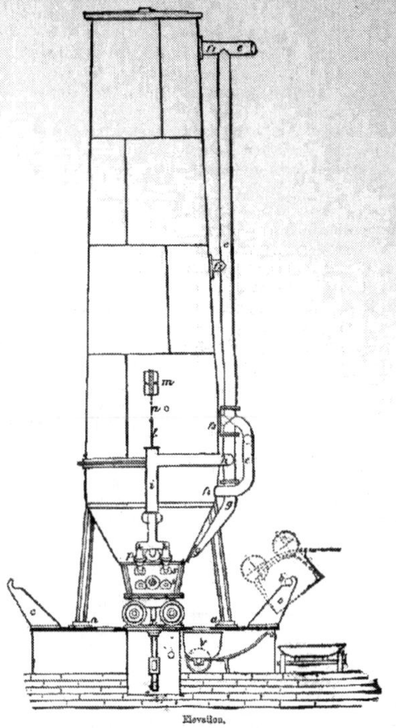

Elevation.

are changed alternately to right and left, two dumping-rests, *e*, being provided. Before running a fresh hearth into place it is filled with charcoal.

Indications.—In normal work the tuyere is clear and bright; the throat-flame lively; the slag bright and fluid; the bloom hard and slippery. A rod thrust against it heals quickly, and particles of iron adhere to it.

With too fast driving or too heavy burden, *i. e.* with insufficient reduction, the bloom is uneven and porous, the slag is very ferruginous, ultra fluid, yellowish red (*i. e.* cool) while molten, solidifying abruptly, and sub-metallic and black when cold, a "scouring cinder;" the throat-flame is thin and feeble; the tuyeres dull.

With too slow driving or too light burden, *i. e.* too strong reduction and carburization, the slag becomes less ferruginous and hence less fluid, and the metallic product steely, or even cast-iron.

When the slag is too refractory, either from faulty fluxing or because excessive reduction robs it of its ferrous oxide, scaffolds form, and the throat-flame grows blue and hot.

Remedies.—The reducing conditions are strengthened by running more slowly (lowering the blast pressure); by lightening the burden; by raising the blast-temperature through admitting a larger part of the blast through the upper part of the inter-mural space, thus increasing the heating surface, and the average of travel and length of exposure of the blast.

They are weakened by the opposite steps.

Difficulties. The product is heterogeneous, thanks partly to the irregular descent and hence varying length of exposure to the reducing and carburizing conditions. It tends strongly to adhere to the walls, especially where these are of brick.

Products. The bloom, according to the following analyses, is liable to be extremely heterogeneous: *e. g.* lines 3, 5, 8, 11, 12. The proportion of silicon is in some cases astonishingly high, and indeed hardly credible. There is a variation of 0·57% between the different parts of Number 5.

TABLE 159.—COMPOSITION OF BLOOMS FROM HUSGAFVEL HIGH BLOOMARIES.

	Made from.		C.	Si.	Mn.	P.	S.
1.	Shingled bloom } Magnetite	centre	·07	tr.	......	......	0·005
		side	·06	tr.	......	......	·03
2.	" " Ore	centre	·13	·22	......	......	·03
		side	·01	·22	......	......	·018
3.	" " Roll scale	centre	·07	·023	......	......	·015
		side	·32	·061	......	......	·015
4.	Wärtsilä "		·12@2·00	......	......	·29@·35	
5.	Shingled " fracture uneven	centre	·65	·04	......	......	·03
		side	·08	·01	......	......	·02
6.	Melted product from hot-working		1·5	·06	......	......	·02
7.	" " "		1·22				
8.	Hammered bloom, granular	centre	·06	·03			·03
		side	·19	·03	......	......	·02
9.	" " coarse granular	centre	·01	......	......	......	·04
		side	·01	......	......	......	·02
10.	" " " "	centre	·01	·06	......	......	·03
		side	·012	·02	......	......	·03
11.	Unhammered loup, hot-working	centre	·39	·65	......	......	·01
		side	·14	·40	......	......	·02
12.	Hammered bloom	centre	·01	·22	......	......	·08
		side	·01	·09	......	......	·08
13.	Unhammered loup, normal working	centre	·11	·45	......	......	·04
		side	·06	·52	......	......	·05

A. *Phosphorus.* The proportion of phosphorus eliminated of course increases with the loss of iron. When the loss of iron is small and the blooms highly carburetted, most of the phosphorus of the ore is found in the resulting metal: but when the loss is heavy and the bloom holds but little carbon, it may have only one-third of the phosphorus of the ore.

B. *Carbon.* The variation of 0·25% between the different part of bloom 3 is certainly very marked. The proportion of carbon in the bloom is said to be well under control; but it is probably only very roughly controllable.

The slag is said to contain about 52·46% of ferrous oxide, or 40·8% of metallic iron, when the blooms are but slightly carburetted; and about 9·91% of ferrous oxide, or 7·15 of metallic iron, when the reduction is strong, highly carburetted blooms resulting.

§ 323. ECONOMIC FEATURES.—Table 160 has been calculated from Husgafvel's data and from those collected by Mr. Garrison. I confess to doubts as to the value of certain numbers, chiefly because one cannot be

TABLE 160.—THE HUSGAFVEL FURNACE AND ITS WORK.

	I. Petrozavodsk, 1887.	II. Wärtsilä furnace, 1884.	III. Dobriansky furnace, fig. 133, 1886.	Dobriansky furnace, 1887. IV.	V.	VI.	VII.
Dimensions—							
Total height	>30′	....	30′ ±				
Diameter at throat	....	....	4′				
" " belly	....	....	5′				
Tuyeres, number	....	4	4				
Blast, pressure, oz. per sq. in.	....	....	0·5 @1·5	3·920@10·477	4·5 to 11·7	6·5 to 9·8	6·5 to 9·8
" temperature, °F.	....	302° @ 482° +	302°@572°	405°	446°	437 to 446°	302 to 446°
" " C.	....	150° @ 250	150 @300°	207°	230°	225 to 230°	150 to 230°
Materials and Labor—							
ORE, kind	Bog-ore.	Lake-ore and puddling slag.	Magnetites.	Raw magnetite.	Raw magnetite.	Roll scale.	Roll scale.
Percentage of iron	....	56% ±	estimate 55% ±	58%	58%		
Net tons per net ton blooms	....	1·64 ore (56% iron) 1·02 slag (49% iron) 2·66	2 tons ore 0·1 " slag 2·1 "	1·97	1·95	1·85	1·64
CHARCOAL, kind	....	Fir and pine, "Medium quality."	Fir "very inferior"	Pine.	Pine and birch.	Pine.	Pine.
Bushels per net ton blooms	....	157	150@250, average 190				
Lbs. per net ton blooms (13·4 lbs. per bushel?)	....	2,100 ?	....	2,899	2,820	2,326	2,222
" " 100 of blooms	....	105	....	945	145	116·3	111·1
Burnt lime, net tons per net ton blooms	....	0·01					
Limestone " " " " " "	....	0·12					
Cast-iron " " " " " " (for repairs)	....	0·01	0·017				
Labor, men per shift (12 hours)	....	3 +					
" days per 2,000 lbs. blooms	....	....	4·00				
PRODUCT net tons per 24 hours	....	1·62@3·00	2·46@3·08	2·95	3·23	2·94	[illegible]
Weight of each bloom, lbs	....	....	670@705				
Composition, % carbon	....	·12@2·00	·06@·82				
" " phosphorus	....	·29@·35					
" " silicon	....	....	tr. @·32				
Loss of iron, per 100 of iron in ore	....	21% *a*	23% *b*	21% *c*	21% *c*		
Slag, percentage of iron	....	7·15@40 8					

I., II. and **III.** From data collected by F. L. Garrison. **IV.** to **VII.** From Husgafvel, Stahl und Eisen, IX., p. 35, 1889.

a From the data given in this same column the loss appears to be 9%; but we cannot be sure that the data refer to the same conditions. Husgafvel states (Stahl und Eisen, 1889, p. 40) that the loss at Wärtsilä in 1885 was from 25·17 to 12%, according to whether soft wrought-iron or steely blooms were made; but that the blooms held in some cases as much as 15% of slag. If we assume that they held on an average 10% of slag, a loss of 12% from ore to bloom would, allowing for the slag contents of the blooms, rise to 21%.

b From the data about 88% of blooms appear to be recovered from 100 of iron in ore. Assuming that the blooms contain 90% of metallic iron, the loss would be 23%.

c Assuming that the blooms contain 90% of metallic iron.

sure that they refer to the same conditions. The loss of iron cannot be calculated with complete confidence, as we do not know how much iron the blooms (loups) contain. The numbers given are based on the assumption that they hold on an average 90% of iron. Husgafvel states that they sometimes contain 15% of slag. The results thus obtained tally with his further statement that the loss at the Konchozersky works at Olnetz is 20%, allowing for the slag in the loups, while in the old Finnish furnaces it was from 40 to 50%.

A Russian official table appears to show that the cost of Husgafvel blooms is the same as that of pig-iron under like conditions: but the data have a suspicious look. Thus the cost of pig-iron is only brought up to that of blooms by a charge of $2.65 per net ton for repairs. Labor costs but $0.36 per ton diem: if we assume that the cost of given repairs in Finland and in this country is proportional to that of labor, this implies repairs such as would cost here about $11.00 per ton of pig-iron, which is certainly surprisingly high.

It appears from this table that less than half as much flux, but 15% more fuel, 27% more ore and puddle slag, and 56% more labor are needed to make a ton of blooms than a ton of pig-iron. This difference in the quantity of flux must be referred chiefly to the heavy scorification of iron, which enables the bloom-maker to dispense with much of the limestone which the pig-iron-maker needs; but iron ore is a dearer flux than limestone.

On these data we might roughly put the cost of bloom-making as one-quarter greater than that of pig-iron making in a 42-foot charcoal-furnace.

The Husgafvel furnace undoubtedly gives much better economy of fuel than the American bloomary, and one would expect it to give better economy of labor. This it does not yet seem to do. As to the loss of iron, that must ever remain proportional to the degree of dephosphorization which takes place. To cut down the loss of iron we must increase the reducing tendency, and we thereby inevitably diminish dephosphorization.

In so high a furnace as the Husgafvel there should be greater liability to excessive reduction and hence imperfect dephosphorization than in the low American bloomary: and we may doubt, judging from the history of like processes, whether, even by charging an excessive proportion of ore to fuel and by rapid running, it would be possible to obtain constantly so pure a product from given ore in the former as in the latter. But direct experiment alone can answer this.

The use of coke would probably yield a highly carburetted and correspondingly impure product, indeed approaching cast-iron in composition, and rich in sulphur. We note that even with charcoal the Husgafvel furnace occasionally yields iron with 2% of carbon.

From reasoning similar to what has gone before we may infer that the cost of coke-blooms would be probably about from one quarter to one half greater than that of coke pig-iron.

In order to dephosphorize, the slag must be basic: a slag made basic by oxide of iron means heavy loss of iron. One might at first think that we could obtain a basic slag in this furnace by replacing iron-oxide with lime, and so dephosphorize without heavy loss of iron. But we must remember that to melt a basic lime slag demands a very high temperature, and such a temperature would not only imply greatly increased fuel consumption but much more strongly reducing conditions, more strongly reducing both because of the higher temperature and of the larger proportion of the reducing agent itself, charcoal. But these reducing conditions oppose the dephosphorizing action of the basic slag. In short, if we attempt to save iron we turn the furnace into a blast-furnace, and make, if not cast-iron, at least a very highly carburetted steel, containing much if not all of the phosphorus of the ore. Now charcoal blooms are marketable chiefly because of their freedom from phosphorus, and to a considerable extent on account of their relative freedom from carbon.

This ingenious direct process is certainly one of the most successful yet devised. When we consider how short a time has elapsed since these attempts to modernize the stückofen began, the progress thus far made is certainly most encouraging. The mode of dealing with the bloom is ingenious, but something much better still is needed. The output, too, is very small. One wonders whether it might not be greatly increased without increasing the tendency to carburize, or causing trouble as to the penetration of the blast, by making the furnace oblong instead of circular in plan, as in the Raschette furnace, and in the Orford copper furnaces. The Orford engineers increased the output of their furnaces enormously, with some economy in labor and fuel, by this simple expedient. In case of the Husgafvel furnace two or more hearths would have to be provided, for the bloom formed in a single long hearth would be unmanageable. Mr. Garrison informs me that Raschette furnaces are still extensively and successfully used in the Urals for making charcoal cast-iron.

§ 324. THE NYHAMMAR[s] CONTINUOUS HIGH BLOOMARY consists of a shaft 16′ high and 18″ wide, from the bottom of which covered flues lead to covered and closed charcoal-hearths. Actually there seems to have been but one hearth, but the design contemplates several attached to each shaft.

Ore and charcoal are charged in the shaft continuously, and through this the gases from the charcoal-hearths pass to heat the charge. The proportion of ore to charcoal charged in the shaft is regulated so that the temperature and reducing conditions in the shaft may be such as to deoxidize the ore and heat the resulting sponge strongly, but not to carburize or to soften it. The hot but not sticky spongy iron, together with the residual charcoal, is raked from the bottom of the shaft into one of the charcoal-hearths, through one of the flues already described. In this hearth the spongy iron is heated to the welding point and balled, fresh lots of sponge apparently being raked in as fast as the iron, balling, sinks, till enough for a bloom has reached the hearth, when raking ceases or is diverted to another hearth. The melted slag is tapped from the hearth, the iron worked into a bloom, drawn and hammered.

When it is necessary to open a charcoal-hearth (*e. g.*, for drawing), the flue which leads from it to the shaft is closed with a damper, to prevent an inrush of air into the shaft, and the consequent reoxidation of the spongy iron.

The following results were, it is stated, obtained in five

[s] Särnström, Iron, XIX., p. 467, 1882: Oest. Zeit., Aug. 12th, 1882.

apparently not successive shifts: I deduce these numbers from Särnströn's data.

TABLE 161.—RESULTS OBTAINED IN THE NYHAMMAR BLOOMARY.

	Bushels.	Pounds.[a]
Percentage of iron in ore	[illegible]	
Blooms per 100 of iron in ore	91·85	
Loss of iron	8·15%	
Charcoal per 100 of iron in ore	8·8	132
Charcoal per 100 of blooms	8·96	120·99
Blooms, pounds per furnace per shift		1083
Phosphorus in ore	0·21%	
Phosphorus in blooms	0·08 @ 0·12%	
Proportion of initial phosphorus removed	59% @ 96%	

a Assumed at 15 lbs. per bushel of 2500 cub. inches, or 10·37 lbs. per cubic foot.

The loss of iron is certainly very small, especially in view of the dephosphorization which occurs: indeed Särnströn points out that it was probably greater than it appeared.

§ 325 A.—GURLT[a] deoxidized iron ore and carburized (?) the resulting sponge in the central shaft B of the furnace shown in Figure 134, by passing through it a stream of hot producer-gas from the producers D D. Here the producer gas both heats and deoxidizes the ore, which is unmixed with solid fuel. The hot spongy iron was drawn through a doorway at the bottom of the shaft, to be

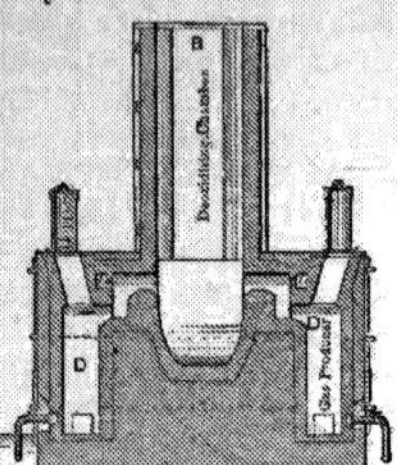

GURLT'S FURNACE
Fig. 134.

balled, or if highly carburetted to be melted, in an open-hearth furnace or in a charcoal-hearth. Apparently fearing that the producer-gas would not be hot enough to heat the ore, he would burn part of it at the points *b b* by means of a carefully regulated air-supply. By prolonging the passage of the gas he would carburize the sponge.

This process was carried on in Spain in a few small furnaces from about 1865 at least till 1884. In 1884 some larger furnaces near Bilbao were idle.[b] The process was here called Tourangin's. The furnaces were built from his design and at first managed under his direction: and the air supply for partly burning the gas before it entered the ore column was omitted. Opinions may differ as to whether this constituted a new process: it seems to me clearly Gurlt's process.

At the Alonsotegui forges in Spain, we are told, hot producer-gas made from charcoal was passed through ore in a chamber of 105 cubic feet capacity, and holding about five tons of ore. The sponge was drawn while hot, and was immediately covered with cinders. It was drawn thrice daily, the total output corresponding to about 3·2 tons of ore, so that the ore remained in the reducing chamber nearly two days. 100 pounds of ore containing about 56% of iron lost 30 to 34% in weight in deoxidizing, and the resulting say 66% of sponge yielded about 50·3% of blooms in a charcoal hearth, with a further consumption of 25 pounds of charcoal: the loss of iron from ore to blooms was thus about 10% of the iron in the ore.[c] About 84 pounds of charcoal per 100 of blooms were used in deoxidizing, so that altogether about 134 parts of charcoal were used per 100 of blooms.

The process was tried at Ticonderoga, N. Y., in 1884, apparently with little intelligence. The reduction seems to have been complete, and neither reoxidation nor carbon deposition seems to have occurred to an important extent. Four analyses of the sponge gave from 0·52 to 2·17% of oxygen.[b]

B. *Ramdohr*[d] would shower iron ore through a Stetefeldt furnace filled with carbonic oxide.

§ 326. IN EDWARD COOPER'S PROCESS,[e] which was carried out experimentally about the year 1873, at Trenton, N. J., iron ore is heated and reduced by a current of hot carbonic oxide, or carbonic oxide and hydrogen. These gases are oxidized to carbonic acid and steam by the oxygen of the ore: they are then passed through a regenerator, in which they are highly heated, and thence through a bed of coal or other fuel in which they are again deoxidized to carbonic oxide and hydrogen. Still remaining in the same closed circuit, they are then used for reducing a fresh portion of ore, a part of the carbonic oxide and hydrogen, however, being diverted to heat the regenerator already mentioned.

To simplify matters let us suppose that only carbonic oxide is used, and follow the course of the gas. What is true of pure carbonic oxide would be true of a mixture of this gas with hydrogen, mutatis mutandis.

In passing through the ore column the carbonic oxide undergoes the reaction

$$(1),\ 3CO + Fe_2O_3 = 3CO_2 + 2Fe$$

in which $3 \times 12 \times 5{,}607 = 201{,}852$ calories are developed,
and $2 \times 56 \times 1{,}887 = 211{,}344$ " " consumed.

Net consumption of heat, 9,492 calories.

We now return the resulting gas to the producer, where the reaction

$$(2),\ 3CO_2 + 3C = 6CO \qquad \text{Calories.}$$

occurs, developing	$3 \times 12 \times 2473 =$	89,028
and consuming	$3 \times 12 \times 5607 =$	201,852
Net consumption in gas-producer		112,824
Consumption in deoxidizing furnace		9,492
Total consumption of heat		122,346

We have now six equivalents of carbonic oxide, of which we may suppose that three are used to repeat reaction (1), three more being available for burning to carbonic acid in the regerator,

where they would generate	$3 \times 12 \times 5{,}607 =$	201,852
as our total deficit was		122,316
we now have an excess of		79,536

calories, or 65% of the theoretical heat-requirement as a surplus to make up for loss of heat by radiation, to use in heating the ore to the temperature of deoxidation, etc.

This, in Mr. Cooper's opinion, is not a sufficient surplus. Hence he introduces steam along with the carbonic acid into the regenerator and thence into the gas-producer, thus making water-gas, and thus increasing the quantity of gas available for burning in the regenerator, but with-

a British patent 1679, July 16, A. D. 1856 (Dec. 19, 1856; Jan. 16, 1857).

b L. G. Laureau, private communication, March 12th, 1889. The information was obtained by an agent sent to Spain by Mr. Laureau to examine the process.

c Extract from report under oath by P. Villaoz, manager of the Alonsotegui forges, October 31st, 1882.

d Berg und Hütt. Zeit., XXX., pp. 67-8, 1871.

e R. W. Raymond and E. Cooper, private communications, March 20th and May 8th, 1889.

out introducing nitrogen into the closed circuit of the reducing system. It may, indeed, be regarded as a mode of making water-gas, which is used while still hot from the gas-producer for deoxidizing iron-ore. The steam is introduced in the form of a jet, and incidentally aids the circulation of the gas through the system.

His apparatus was actually much more complex than that which I have sketched.[a]

solid fuel in the central chamber B, Figure 135 A, and through it passes a stream of carbonic oxide, generated in the gas producers DD′, which are shafts filled with charcoal or coke, hot air being blown in through the tuyeres *a a*. The waste gases (carbonic oxide and acid with nitrogen) escaping from the top of B are burned to heat the blast. The ore is heated wholly by the heat generated by the combustion of the fuel burned in the gas-producer:

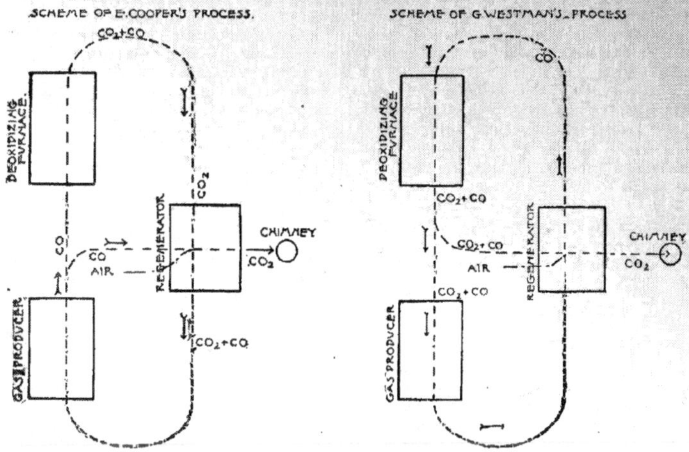

Figure 135.

Westman's process[b] resembles Cooper's, except that common producer-gas is used, and that, as indicated in Figure 135, the gas passes through the regenerator while on its way from the gas-producer to the deoxidizing furnace.

It is to be noted that by reaction (2), which is repeated indefinitely, we oxidize our carbon by oxygen derived from ore, not from the atmosphere, that is to say by oxygen unaccompanied by nitrogen. At each cycle we divert part of our carbonic oxide from the circuit to the combustion chambers of the regenerators and thence through the chimney to the outer air, and with this carbonic oxide the accompanying nitrogen. We are thus constantly eliminating nitrogen from the system, and it seems as if this might be taken advantage of to gradually remove the whole of this gas, so that we would eventually have a closed circuit of pure carbonic oxide and hydrogen, as in Cooper's process.

The course of the gases is sketched in Figure 135.

§ 327. IN TOURANGIN'S PROCESS[c] ore is charged without

part of this heat is communicated directly by the hot carbonic oxide, part by conduction through the partitions: while by heating the blast the energy in the waste gases is returned to the apparatus. In case coke is used the cham-

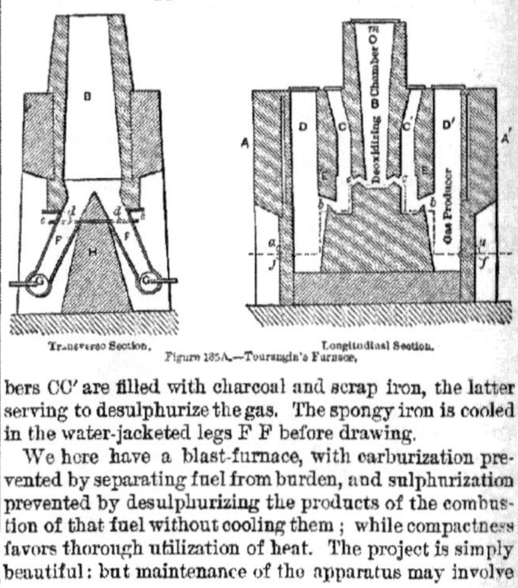

Transverse Section. Longitudinal Section.
Figure 135A.—Tourangin's Furnace.

bers CC′ are filled with charcoal and scrap iron, the latter serving to desulphurize the gas. The spongy iron is cooled in the water-jacketed legs F F before drawing.

We here have a blast-furnace, with carburization prevented by separating fuel from burden, and sulphurization prevented by desulphurizing the products of the combustion of that fuel without cooling them; while compactness favors thorough utilization of heat. The project is simply beautiful: but maintenance of the apparatus may involve

[a] Mr. Cooper would pass the gas on its way from the deoxidizing furnace to the regenerator through a second gas-producer or bed of fuel: indeed, only a part of the gas issuing from the gas-producer shown in Figure 135 goes directly to the deoxidizing furnace, part joining the gas which issues from the deoxidizing furnace, and with it entering the second gas-producer, and passing thence to the regenerator again. Further, a kiln for preheating the ore is projected. Mr. Cooper thinks the continuous passage of the current in a single direction without reversals important.

[b] G. Westman, U. S. patent 383,201, May 1st, 1888.

[c] U. S. Patent 268,840, Dec. 12th, 1882. Also "A Treatise on the Reduction of Iron Ore," by E. Tourangin, 1881. The reader is cautioned to scrutinize the heat calculations and thermal data.

very grave difficulties. If the apparatus be so compact and so well lagged that but little heat radiates, and if the blast be preheated in an efficient apparatus, a very high temperature should be developed in the gas-producer. Compared with the blast-furnace the gas-producer would be cooler in that its fuel is not greatly preheated before reaching the zone of combustion, but hotter in that it is not cooled by the constant arrival of fresh lots of burden to be heated and melted. Neglecting the losses by radiation, and supposing the blast to be cold, the gas should reach the partitions EE at the temperature theoretically due to the combustion of carbon to carbonic oxide, or about 1,500° C. (2,700° F.), the heat radiated away to the surrounding fuel being returned to the region of combustion when that fuel in turn burns. Add to this the heat brought in by the blast, and the gas at EE might reach 2,000° C. (3,600 F.). If, on the other hand, the temperature here be kept down by permitting loss of heat by radiation, by water-jacketing, etc., we diminish the heating-efficiency of the apparatus, and its chance of successful competition with the blast furnace.

§ 328. LAUREAU'S PROCESS aims to deoxidize iron-ore with natural gas, and to prevent the deposition of carbon which occurs when this fuel is passed directly through hot ore. An application for a United States patent is now pending. If the patent issues soon enough I will describe the process in an appendix.

§ 329. BULL'S SO-CALLED DIRECT PROCESS[a] was hardly a direct process at all, but rather an ill-advised attempt to replace the whole of the solid fuel of the blast-furnace with superheated water-gas. Bull indeed expected to make steel in the furnace: but these expectations do not deserve our notice. I may, however, point out that in the blast-furnace we are able to reach a temperature well above the melting point of cast- and even of wrought-iron, while preserving a reducing atmosphere, by the combustion of highly preheated solid carbon to carbonic oxide: that if we start with hydrogen and carbonic oxide, these gases can hardly be introduced into the blast-furnace while at a temperature above the melting point of cast-iron by any means of which we now know. To raise their temperature above that of wrought-iron or of the slag which accompanies cast-iron, they must burn, and in burning they must generate either carbonic acid or aqueous vapor or both, and each oxidizes metallic iron energetically: so that the use of unoxidized carbon seems a necessity if we are to obtain our iron and slag in a molten state without great loss of iron

The results obtained with the process seem to bear out these views. In a fourteen-day run at the John Cockerill works at Seraing, in an iron blast-furnace 21 feet high and 6 feet in diameter at the boshes, which appears to have used the astonishing quantity of nearly seven tons of coke per ton of white pig-iron produced, or seven times as much as in our best practice, part of the coke was replaced by water-gas. Although the quantity of coke charged in the blast-furnace along with the ore was still enormous, running from a little above one up to ten tons of coke per ton of iron, and although the total quantity of coke used in producer and blast-furnace together was still more than four tons per ton of iron, yet the partial substitution of water-gas seems to have chilled the furnace. The silicon fell from 2·3 to 0·15%, the carbon from 2·27 to 1·45%, while the sulphur and phosphorus ran from 1·6 to 0·33% and from 1·73 to 1·10 respectively. The ore seems to have held about 25% of iron.

The results obtained before using Bull's process were astonishingly bad, even for an experimental furnace. But how the promotors had the rashness to lay before investors the damning results which the Bull process here yielded: how journals of high standing could, as they did, treat them with respect, and discuss them as if they were of real technical and economic importance, passes all understanding. Verily, iron-making is the home of the charlatan.[b]

§ 330. S. LUCAS[c] in 1792 would deoxidize iron ore in horizontal retorts (the pots of a cementation furnace), and, apparently after allowing the sponge to cool within the retorts, melt it in crucibles.

Substantially similar are the processes of Hawkins[d] and Newton.[e]

§ 331. IN THE CONLEY PROCESS[f] the ore is crushed to pass a screen of about twenty meshes to the linear inch, and is then apparently dressed to remove gangue: then, mixed "with what is chemically required to free" the sulphur, phosphorus, "etc.," and enough charcoal to remove the desired proportion of the oxygen, it is gently heated and continually stirred in peculiarly constructed retorts. The partially deoxidized ore is next run into air-tight vessels and there cooled: is bricked with enough melted pitch "or other carbon" to coke and to remove the remaining oxygen but not to melt on subsequent heating, and is melted in a furnace or crucible. All conditions being rigidly fixed, complete control over the product is claimed.

Few experienced metallurgists will entertain the claim seriously. The conditions are evidently not under control. Important variations in the composition and physical condition of the ore, in the temperature of the reducing retort, in the degree of reoxidation when the partly reduced ore runs from the retort to the cooling vessel, in the temperature and in the strength of the oxidizing conditions when the bricks are remelted, will arise and will destroy the expected completeness of control. But closer control is not to-day a pressing need in our Bessemer and open-hearth practice. In the crucible process it is indeed desirable, but here the variations which arise are due chiefly to variations, not in the composition of the material charged, but in the temperature and strength of the oxidizing conditions in the crucible and in the behavior of the crucible itself; and, clearly, these variations would not be lessened by the Conley process.

Beyond this one sees no reason to expect merit in the process, unless it be in the peculiarity of the retorts and in the nature of "what is chemically required to free" the phosphorus and sulphur. What these are is beyond our present ken.

§ 332. IN CHENOT'S PROCESS[g] iron ore was deoxidized

[a] See Iron, XXI., p. 89, 1883: Ledebur, Handbuch der Eisenhüttenkunde, p. 838, 1884: Stahl und Eisen, VI., p. 578, 1886.

[b] The published account of the results is so astonishingly bad that one wonders whether there is not some clerical error, misprint, or obscurity.

[c] British patents, April 18, 1792, No. 1869.

[d] July 4, 1836, No. 7142.

[e] April 8, 1856, No. 851.

[f] Iron age, XLI., p. 722, 1888.

[g] British patent 1590, A. D., 1856. My information is taken chiefly from Percy, Iron and Steel, 1864; Grateau, Rev. Univ., VI., pp. 1-82, 189; 5Bell, Manuf. Iron and St., p. 34, 1884, and Hunt, Rept. Geolog. Survey, Canada, 1866-9, p. 288. Bell reports that the process was used in 1872 at only one establishment in the world.

by heating with charcoal in vertical retorts, whose upper part was of fire-brick and externally heated, the lower part being of sheet-iron and water-jacketed, to cool the sponge before drawing, and thus prevent reoxidation. The operation was continuous. Chenot is said to have built a large furnace for the direct process in 1831.

In his direct-heating method hot carbonic oxide was passed directly from a gas-producer through the column of ore, as in Gurlt's process.

TABLE 182.—CHENOT'S PROCESS.

	Indirect heating.			Direct Heating
	Per 100 pounds of iron in 55% ore, at Hautmont.	Per 100 of iron in 60·6% ore, at Baracaldo.	Per 100 of merchantable bar-iron, at Baracaldo.	Per 100 of merchantable bar-iron, at Larasuedo (leaner ore).
Ore as mined	......	......	300	375
Ore freed from fines	......	......	250	319
Products: Iron sponge	......	83	160	290
Products: Blooms	......	63·54	115	110
Products: Bar-iron	......	55·25	100	100
Labor, days	0·165	......	......	......
Charcoal for reducing	48	35	61	99
Coal for heating reducing-furnace	157	96	175	0
Charcoal for charcoal-hearth	......	......	88	88
Coal for last heating	......	......	100	100
Total fuel	......	......	425	287

Chenot received a gold medal at the Paris exhibition of 1855, but apparently on questionable grounds.

A. The indirect-heating process.

I. *The Furnace* contained one or two vertical rectangular retorts of the following dimensions,

	Height.	Width.	Length.	Locality.	Authority.
1.	28′ 6·63″	1′ 7·69″	6′ 6·74″	Hautmont.	Grateau, Percy, Iron and Steel, p. 338.
2.	......	1′ 7·69″	4′ 11·06″	"	" " " p. 339.
3.	38′ ±	1′ 4″	4′ 9″	Spain, 1872.	Bell, Manf. Iron and Steel, p. 84.

The upper parts were of fire-brick, and were heated by means of external flues. Below and forming a continuation of the fire-brick part of the retort were rectangular, vertical, water-cooled, sheet-iron "refroidissoirs," or coolers, which were, in the first of the above cases, 14′ 9·17″ long. The bottom of a cooler was temporarily closed with removable grate-bars 0·79″ apart. To draw a charge a wagon standing on a lift beneath the cooler was raised to the grate-bars; these were drawn, the wagon descended, and the sponge dropped into it, the grate-bars probably being replaced as soon as the wagon was full.

II. *The Process.*—Lump ore was broken to about 1·8-cubic-inch pieces: fine ore, sometimes mixed with reducing matter, was agglutinated by compression. The ore, now mixed with say 60 pounds of charcoal per 100 of iron present, was charged in the retorts and there deoxidized. The daily withdrawal of part of the spongy iron from the bottom of the cooler caused the charge to descend, so that it remained three days in the hot part of the retort, and three more in the cooler.

The sponge was worked into blooms in a charcoal hearth, or melted in crucibles. In the latter case it was first compressed into little cylinders occupying about one-third of its original bulk, together with deoxidizing and carburizing matter, such as charcoal, wood-tar, resin, or fatty matter, and these were melted in common crucibles as in the crucible process. But as the sponge cylinders were bulky and the weight of a charge consequently small (40 to 55 pounds), the cost of this fusion per pound of ingots was excessive.

While it was thought possible to reduce the iron completely, this took much time, and it was found better to reduce it partially, and to select by hand the imperfectly deoxidized pieces for further treatment.

III. *The Loss.*—At Baracaldo 100 of iron in a 60·6% ore yielded 63·54 of blooms, the loss being 36·46%, and 55·25 of bar-iron, the loss being 44·75%.

IV. *Fuel.*—For reducing 100 of iron from the ore about 48 pounds of charcoal were used at Hautmont and about 35 pounds at Baracaldo.

For heating the retorts 157 and 96 pounds of coal were used at these two establishments respectively, per 100 pounds of iron in the ore.

V. *The Labor* in producing sponge was about 3·7 days per 2 240 pounds of iron in the ore, or ·165 per 100 pounds.

Bell[a] estimates that the loss of iron is 3·5 times and the cost for fuel 2·3 times as great in producing bar-iron by Chenot's process as in making rolled steel by the blast-furnace and Bessemer processes. But it is more to the point to compare the cost of 100 units of iron available for the open-hearth process in sponge and in scrap-iron.

B. *In the direct-heating method* the heating was done wholly by the hot reducing gas, and the total fuel-consumption thereby greatly lessened: but as the reducing gas was made wholly from charcoal, somewhat more of this fuel was needed than in the indirect-heating method, in which the charcoal had merely to deoxidize: so that in the direct-heating method a given weight of coal is replaced by a much smaller one of charcoal. It would thus depend on the relative prices of these fuels whether this would effect a saving. In the cases here given one part by weight of charcoal appears to replace five of coal, which, considering that a leaner ore was used in the direct- than in the indirect-heating method, would indicate a decided advantage for the direct-heating method: but we cannot be sure that other conditions were alike in these two cases.

§ 333 A. BLAIR'S PROCESS.[b]—As the success of the open-hearth process promised a demand for iron sponge, Blair made strenuous efforts from about 1871 to 1878 to bring Chenot's process to a commercial success, introduced important improvements in heating the ore, and hastened the reduction by the addition of lime. The process has been abandoned.

I. *The early furnace*, Figure 136, like Chenot's in its general features, had three vertical retorts completely filled, above with charcoal and ore, below with spongy iron. The upper parts were made of tongued and grooved fire-bricks, and heated externally by gas introduced through the pipes OO; their lower parts or coolers were of sheet-iron water-jacketed (K). At the top was a cast-iron thimble C heated internally by gas introduced through a central pipe, and by the carbonic oxide generated by the oxidation of the carbon of the charcoal by the oxygen of the ore. At the lower end was an external sleeve LL, usually luted, but raised at intervals to allow a little of the sponge to slide out.

II. *The Process.*—The ore, in lumps two inches thick or less, mixed with 33 to 44 parts of charcoal per 100 of iron, was charged in the four-inch annulus between the thimble and the sides of the retort: here lying in a thin sheet, it was quickly raised to redness by the heat transmitted through the walls of the thimble and those of the retort. Thus one of the great difficulties,—heating a thick

[a] Prin. Manuf. Iron and Steel, p. 84, 1884.

[b] U. S. patent 126,922, May 21st, 1872: Trans. Am. Inst. Mining Engineers, II., p. 175, 1874: Journ. Iron and Steel Inst., 1878, I., p. 47, 1875, I., p. 177: Eng. Mining Jl., XVII., June 6th, 1874. Bell, Princ. Manuf. Iron and Steel, p. 84, 1884.

body of ore to the middle, was met simply: but some still more economical plan seems needed, such as preheating the ore by direct contact with fuel in a kiln, whence it could be drawn directly to the reducing retort while still red-hot.

As sponge was drawn from the bottom, the whole contents of the shaft sank, the new hot ore from the preheating annulus into the body of the retort, the sponge at the bottom of the retort into the cooler. The height and compactness of the column was thought to prevent air from entering beneath when the sleeve L was raised.

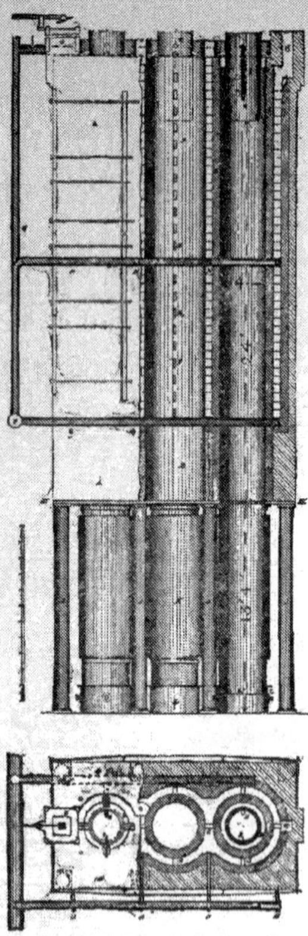

Figure 136.—Blair's Earlier Sponge-making Furnace, Heating by Transmission.

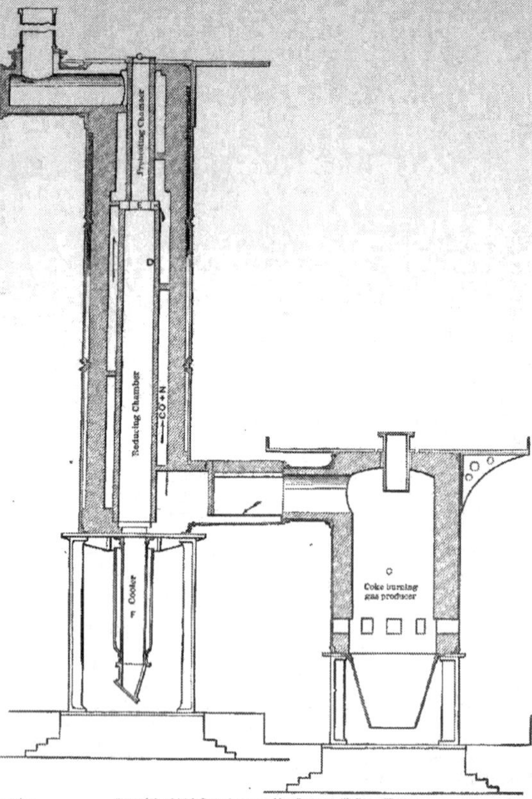

Figure 137.—Blair's Later Sponge-making Furnace with Direct Heating.

A retort 4′ 6″ in diameter and 40′ to 50′ high turned out about two tons of sponge per 24 hours. This would imply that the ore remained

in the preheating annulus about	0·5	days.
" brick retort	7	"
" cooler	4	"
	11·5	days.

The cost of a Blair sponge-making plant with a daily capacity of 60 tons of sponge per 24 hours was estimated by Holley at $75,000.

III. *The later Furnace.*—Blair discovered that the addition of say 5% of lime to the ore greatly hastened deoxidation—the alkaline earth it has been conjectured favoring the formation of cyanogen. It was now found that the thimble arrangement could not preheat the ore as rapidly as it could be deoxidized in the retort proper: to hasten heating, the single-retort furnace shown in Figure 137 was designed. In this the ore was mixed with charcoal as before, but was heated wholly by a stream of hot carbonic oxide and nitrogen from a coke-burning gas-producer C. The gas passed up around the retort D, entering at the point E where, by narrowing the retort, an annular ring was left, permitting the gas to enter the ore-column on all sides. The charcoal was relied on for the deoxidation, though doubtless the carbonic oxide took up more or less oxygen in passing through the ore. The sponge was cooled as before in a cooler, F.

Just how much the presence of lime hastened operations cannot be readily determined. Ireland stated that in such a retort 16′ high, its inside diameter being 4′ above and 6′ 6″ below, and the total height of the structure 36′, about 200 tons of ore could be deoxidized per week, which implies that about a day was occupied in deoxidizing and another in cooling, so that the presence of lime hastens deoxidation sevenfold. But Mr. Morrison Foster informs me that, "while the use of lime was undoubtedly an improvement, yet operations were not carried far enough in a practical way to justify the establishment of a basis for working."[a] I am confident that Mr. Ireland is mistaken. To increase the cooling surface he would have several narrow coolers instead of a single wide one, beneath the brick part of the retort.

Clearly most if not all the sulphur of the coke must in this arrangement be absorbed by the iron sponge: but it would seem possible to intercept it by placing between the gas-producer and the retort a thin column of some absorbent, such as lime, or iron sponge itself, through which the producer-gas would pass.

In case the producer-gas heated the ore at the point E too highly, it was cooled by diluting it with the cool gas escaping from the top of the retort at G: clearly this escaping gas, owing to the presence of the charcoal in the ore column, would be chiefly carbonic oxide and nitrogen; or, in other words, the producer-gas would be little altered in composition in passing through this column.

IV. *The product* was cold spongy iron, preserving roughly the shape and size of the original lumps of ore, and apparently unimpregnated by carbon. The temperature in the hot part of the retort was probably rather too high to favor considerable carbon-impregnation, which, as we have seen (p. 120), almost ceases when the temperature rises to bright redness: but in cooling the spongy iron must pass very slowly through the range at which carbon-impregnation occurs rapidly, and it must still be surrounded by an atmosphere of carbonic oxide. Yet, though I conducted the process for some time, I was never able to assure myself that the sponge contained carbon left by impregnation.

The deoxidation could be made very thorough: according to Blair 93 to 98% of the iron was deoxidized.

a Private communication, March 22d, 1889.

V. *Further Treatment.*—The sponge when drawn from the reducing furnace was quite cool so that it did not reoxidize. It was squeezed under a pressure of 30,000 pounds per square inch into cylindrical blooms 6″ in diameter and from 12″ to 18″ long. These could be either thrown direct into the bath in the open-hearth furnace, or preheated in an auxiliary furnace. In later practice only the fine sponge was compressed, the lumps being shovelled into the open-hearth bath either without previous preparation, or after balling in a preheating gas-furnace.

As rich ores containing about 63·0% of iron and hence about 9% of gangue were used, the quantity of gangue to be melted in the open-hearth furnace was not excessive, its heat-capacity being probably about one-quarter of that of the iron of the sponge. The consumption of fuel in melting was indeed very moderate, only about 400 pounds to the ton of steel I am informed by Mr. M. Foster.

VI. *Carburization.*—Believing sponge cheaper than cast-iron, Blair would lessen the proportion of cast-iron to sponge used in the open-hearth process by carburizing part of the sponge, either by inclosing charcoal or tar in the blooms, perhaps together with some accelerating (*e. g.* cyanogen-yielding) matter: or by passing through the reducing retort gaseous hydrocarbons, which he says would carburize the sponge.

In actual practice Blair used tar-plugs, *i. e.* cylinders of sponge compressed with 8% of their weight of coal-tar, for part and sometimes for a large part of the cast-iron of the open-hearth charge. In one case the proportion for cast-iron was only 14·05% for the average of a week's work, and in two heats it was only 10% of the whole charge.

The loss chargeable to the sponge-making process is not easily arrived at. As Table 162A shows, 100 parts of iron in the charge yielded about 91% of ingots and scrap in eleven charges selected at random by Bell, and about 85% of ingots and scrap in 428 consecutive heats. If, however, we follow the usual course and reckon the loss on the gross weight of cast-iron and scrap charged without deduction for non-ferrous substances which they contain, and on the iron actually in the sponge, the loss rises in these two cases to 14·62 and 19·90% respectively.

In the third schedule Bell finds the loss 15·83% reckoned in the former way: if reckoned in the latter way it would rise to 19·41%. Without disputing Mr. Bell's data

TABLE 162A.—LOSS IN THE OPEN-HEARTH STEEL PROCESS, USING IRON SPONGE.

	Allowing for impurities in pig-iron and scrap.									Reckoned on gross weight of pig and scrap, but on actual iron-content of sponge.								
	11 heats selected by Bell. I.			428 consecutive heats. II.			Data given by Bell, III.			11 heats selected by Bell. I.			428 consecutive heats. II.			Data given by Bell. III.		
	Gross weight.	% Fe.	Weight Fe.	Gross weight.	% Fe.	Weight Fe.	Gross Weight	% Fe.	Weight Fe.	Gross Weight.	% Fe taken as	Weight Fe taken as	Gross Weight.	% Fe taken as	Weight Fe taken as	Gross Weight.	% Fe taken as	Weight Fe taken as
Pig-iron	23,816	94	22,387	1,000,632	94	940,594	360	94	338	23,816	100	23,816	1,000,632	100	1,000,632	360	100	360
Sponge	13,255a 10,566b 8,116c	85	26,959	....	......	1,137,096	470	90	423	13,255a 10,566b 8,116c	85	26,959	....	......	1,137,096	470	90	423
Scrap-steel from previous meltings	14,161	90	12,745	843,442	90	759,098	60	90	54	14,161	100	14,161	843,442	100	843,442	60	100	60
Spiegeleisen	7,531	80	6,025	218,858	80	175,086	110	80	88	7,531	100	7,531	218,858	100	218,858	110	100	110
Ferromanganese	....	......	....	15,551	20	3,110	....	......	....	....	......	....	15,551	100	15,551			
Total	....	......	68,116	....	......	3,010,578	....	......	903	....	......	72,467	....	......	3,210,073	....	......	953
Total steel made	....	......	61,870	....	......	2,571,353	768	99	760	....	......	61,870	....	......	2,571,353	....	......	768
Loss	....	......	6,246	....	......	439,225	....	......	143	....	......	10,597	....	......	638,720	....	......	185
Loss %	....	......	9·17	....	......	14·59	....	......	15·83	....	......	14·62	....	......	19·90	....	......	19·41

a Tar plugs, *i. e.*, cylinders of sponge compressed with 8% of their weight of tar.
b Hot sponge.
c Cold sponge.
In case of the sponge, the loss here given is of course the total loss from ore to ingots.
I. "Mr. I. Lowthian Bell and the Blair Direct Process," Pittsburgh, 1875. Mr. Bell made the loss 20·01%, apparently through omitting to allow for the impurities in the sponge, which he took as 100% iron.
II. M. Foster, Vice-President of the Blair Iron and Steel Company. Private Communication, March 22d, 1889. 428 heats, between August, 1874, and Oct., 1875.
III. Bell, Principles of the Manufacture of Iron and Steel, p. 36, 1884.

I am at a loss to find what they refer to. The weight of steel scrap is but one-sixth that of the pig-iron charged, while a very different ratio exists in the data previously discussed by him and in those given me by Mr. Foster.

In formerly discussing this process Mr. Bell arrived at the loss by adding to that actually arising in the open-hearth melting *the loss previously experienced on the steel scrap charged*. While doubtless quite proper for the special conditions which he had in mind, this is wholly misleading in determining the loss between ore and ingots by the sponge-making and open-hearth processes combined. Scrap steel charged represents runners, gates, fountains, crop-ends, sloppings, skulls from previous meltings, scrap purchased in the market, and what not. The first group simply represents unmerchantable castings. The proportion of the castings which is merchantable should, with equally skillful founding, be the same whether the molten metal be made from sponge or old rails or pocket-knives. It is dependent not on the source of the materials charged in the open-hearth process, but on the mode of casting the products of that process and the skill of the workmen in casting.

In comparing the direct and indirect methods of steel-making it should be neglected quite as we neglect the loss in mining or in ore-dressing, as foreign to the subject. Whether he has included it in the data of Schedule III. I know not.

The proper way to arrive at the loss appears to be to deduct from the total loss that properly chargeable to the cast-iron and scrap used in the process, and to charge the rest against the sponge. But it is not easy to decide how much is chargeable to cast-iron and scrap, for this depends greatly on the skill with which the open-hearth furnace is managed, and, as I know well, this particular open-hearth furnace (Franks) was not well managed.

The loss in what I believe to be the first 37 heats made in this country (in 1870) by the open-hearth process, in regular working, was 16·63%.[a]

Blair claimed that the loss in using scrap, blooms and cast-iron was 18·37% in American practice at the time when the result obtained in Table 162A were obtained. M. Foster claimed that the loss by the pig and ore process was then 18·4%. According to notes which I obtained from Mr. Holley the loss at Landore by the pig and ore process was about 22% in 1874. The loss is much less at present. Bell took it at 6% for comparison with Blair's work: but I am sure that a loss of 6% represents much better open-hearth practice than Blair's, and that this number is not fair. Holley reported that the loss in the Pernot open-hearth practice was 5·94% in 1876 and 4·3% in 1878: and that the loss at Terre Noire and Creusot was 5 and 6% respectively in 1878.

The loss is usually heavier on the gross weight of cast-than on that of scrap-iron, owing to the much smaller proportion of iron initially present in the former material. From personal knowledge of the operations at Glenwood I do not believe that the loss on the cast-iron was less than 15% of its g oss weight. If we adopt this number and assume that the scrap (which in this case appears to have been especially impure, having by Bell's estimate only 90% of iron) also lost 15%, then the data given by Bell in Schedule III. of Table 162 A imply that the sponge lost 24%. Thus:

360 of cast-iron at 85% yielded	306
60 of scrap-iron at 85%	51
110 of spiegeleisen at 75%	82·5
Total	439·5
Balance of yield to be credited to sponge	320·5
Total yield	760
Sponge contained	423
Loss on sponge = 24·23%	102·5
Yield of sponge as above	320·5

TABLE 163.—BLAIR'S PROCESS.

	Indirect heating per 100 lbs. of iron in ore.		
	Blair, I.	Bell, II.	Foster, III.
Percentage of iron in ore	50	66	68
Ore used	200 lbs	....	160 lbs.
Charcoal for reducing, lbs	33	44	33 ±
Coal or coke for heating the retorts	36	150	44 ±
Labor, days	0·1±	....	1·4
Cost of compression	$0.12 ±		
Output of sponge per retort per week, tons	....	14	12 ±

I. Blair, Trans. Am. Inst. Min. Eng., II., p. 175, 1874. These are expected results.
II. Bell, Princ. Man. Iron and Steel, p. 31, 1884.
III. Report of the Blair Iron and Steel Company, January 1st, 1875. The data are given as the actual working results obtained at Glenwood, near Pittsburgh.

Comparing these numbers with those in Table 162, we see that Blair lessened the consumption of fuel for heating greatly, but not for deoxidizing. As regards loss no safe comparison can be made: for while Blair's loss from ore to ingot was much less than Chenot's, we cannot tell how much of the difference was due to better deoxidation, and how much to the smaller opportunity for reoxidation in melting in the open-hearth, in which Blair's sponge was treated, than in the charcoal-hearth in which Chenot's was balled.

The consumption of fuel and the cost of installation per unit of product were not immoderate. I have attributed the failure of the process less to its being inapplicable to existing conditions than to injudicious management, in carrying out avoidable experiments (as if the unavoidable ones were not burdensome enough), and to certain misfortunes for which the management seemed in no way to blame.

B. *Yates' process*[b] appears to be identical with Chenot's indirect-heating process.

C. *In Trosca's process*[c] ore was reduced by contact with carbonaceous matter in externally-heated vertical retorts: the resulting sponge was removed in an air-tight buggy.

D. *In Clay's*[d] *original process* walnut-sized lumps of ore were deoxidized by heating to bright redness in clay retorts, etc., with one-fifth of their weight of carbonaceous matter: the resulting sponge was immediately balled in a puddling furnace, with or without some 5% of coke, hammered, and rolled into merchant iron. The process failed, chiefly because the reduction was very slow, and because the iron was often very redshort. We may surmise that the gangue of the ore was often imperfectly

[a] From notes which I took in 1870, when attached as a student to the open-hearth plant of the Bay State Iron Company, during this early practice.

[b] Percy, Iron and Steel, p. 345, 1864.

[c] Berg. und Hütt. Zeit., XXV., p. 308, 1866.

[d] This description is condensed from Percy, Iron and Steel, p. 330. Clay's British patent was 7,518, Dec. 19th, 1837. Percy's description indicates that the sponge was taken hot to the puddling furnace: according to Kerl it was cooled before the transfer. (Grundriss der Eisenhüttenkunde, p. 206.)

fluxed, so that it formed a slag which was difficultly fusible, hence was expelled with difficulty, and, present in excess, made the iron redshort or rather slag-short. Heavy waste of iron doubtless weighed against the process.

E. *In Renton's process*[a] ore was deoxidized by heating in contact with coal in a vertical retort, at the end of a puddling furnace, by whose waste gases the ore was heated, and in which the spongy iron was balled prior to shingling. To make a ton of blooms required,

2·5 tons of ore at $4	$10.00
About 2·5 tons of coal	10.13
Welding, working, $5, shingling, $1.50, labor, $3	9.50
	$29.63

F. *In Wilson's*[b] process coarsely pulverized ore with 20% of charcoal- or coke-dust is heated to 800°@1,000° F. (427°@538° C.) for twenty-four hours in vertical retorts (C, Figure 138) at the end of a puddling furnace, by

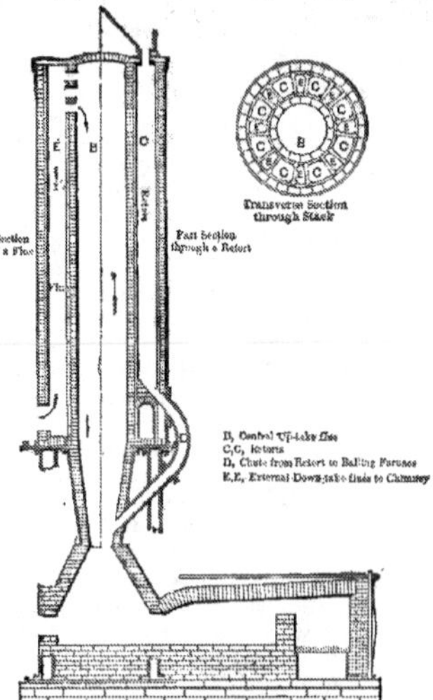

Figure 138.—Furnace for Wilson's Direct Process.

whose waste heat they are heated externally. The partially deoxidized ore is then dropped into a second hearth of the puddling furnace, and after twenty minutes more is pushed into the hearth proper, where it is balled.

G. *Rogers*[c] would heat ore with coal in a rotating retort above a puddling furnace, into which he would drop the resulting sponge.

§ 334. SCHMIDHAMMER,[d] apparently following out the idea of the Nyhammar furnace, §324, proposes the continuous stückofen shown in Figure 140. The shaft is charged continuously with ore and enough charcoal for deoxidation: the ore is deoxidized during its descent: the temperature is raised to the welding point by hot blast and hot water-gas blown through the tuyeres: the spongy iron is balled through working openings, and the balls are drawn from the fore-hearth A on lifting the door B.

The distinctive features are substitution of hot gas and air for part of the more costly charcoal; the fore-hearth A, and the door B, which permit forming and drawing the balls without allowing the superincumbent charge to slide down as in Husgafvel's furnace.

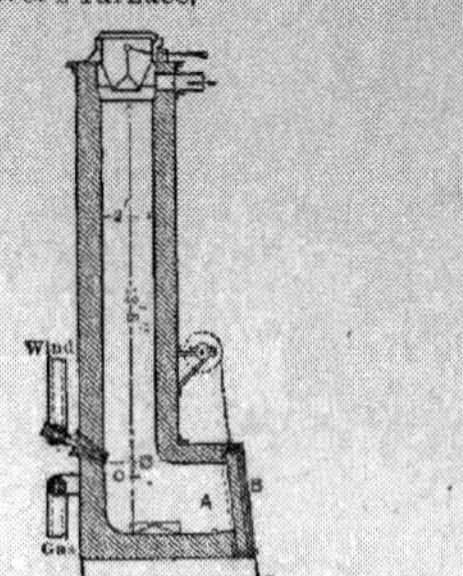

Figure 140.—Schmidhammer's Continuous High Bloomary (Stückofen).

§ 335. THE DU PUY PROCESS[e] uses a thin sheet-iron instead of a clay retort. The sheet-iron conducts heat to the charge much more readily than fire-clay, but of course lasts but a single heat. It welds to the spongy iron and is hammered, rolled, or melted with it as the case may be.

About 116 pounds of ground iron ore, mixed with carbonaceous matter for reduction and with suitable fluxes to scorify the gangue, is inclosed in annular sheet-iron (No. 26 gauge = 0·018″ thick) canisters about 13″ high, 15″ in diameter outside, 6″ in diameter inside, and weighing 6 pounds. The charged canisters are heated to bright whiteness (a welding heat) for from 5½ to 10 hours on the coke-covered hearth of a common open reverberatory furnace. The reduced metal, still in its canister, may, according to Du Puy, be converted into muck-bar by hammering or squeezing and rolling, then cut up and treated by the crucible process; may be charged at once in the open-hearth process with or without (?) cast-iron: or may be melted down with cast-iron in the furnace in which it has been reduced.

In a table of results given, from 71 to 86 or on an average 78·5 pounds of muck-bar or blooms were recovered per 100 pounds of iron contained in the ore: so that a 116-pound charge of 67% ore would yield 61 pounds of blooms: or, deducting the six pounds of canister, 56 pounds. Thus for every 100 pounds of blooms we have to sacrifice 10 pounds of thin sheet-iron on which has been put the expense not only of rolling down to No. 26 gauge, but of working into canisters. The cost of the canisters alone, judging from Mr. Du Puy's data, should have been at least $7 @ $8.50 per ton of muck-bar.

If charcoal were used the cost for reducing fuel would be considerable: if either anthracite or coke the sulphur of the fuel would contaminate the iron.

The phosphorus of the ore of course remained within

[a] Condensed from Percy, Iron and Steel, p. 834. The process was patented in 1851 in this country.
[b] W. P. Ward, Trans. Am. Inst. Mining Engineers, XII., p. 522, 1884.
[c] Berg und Hütt. Zeit., 1869, p. 341.
[d] Stahl und Eisen, VI., p. 465, 1886.
[e] Metallurg. Rev., I, p. 486, 1878. Journ. Frank. Inst., CIV, p. 377, 1877; CVI., p. 404, 1878; July, 1881.

the canister. If the mass were rolled to muck-bar and if the slag were sufficiently basic, owing to scorification and loss of iron, some of the phosphorus would be eliminated as the slag was squeezed out in rolling or hammering. But this rolling or hammering involved expense and further waste. If the canisters were charged direct into an acid open-hearth furnace, the phosphorus of the ore would enter the iron. Metcalf gives the following composition of extremely redshort wrought-iron made by this process.[a]

Silicon.	Sulphur.	Phosphorus.	Oxide or cinder.
·460	·027	·010	·796

Later, dispensing with canisters, Du Puy moulded ground iron ore with charcoal, clay and lime into pipes, 18″ × 8″, which he heated and balled in open reverberatories, with prohibitory loss of iron, 40 to 50%.

§ 337. MUSHET[b] would deoxidize iron ore with carbonaceous matter in crucibles, and immediately melt the deoxidized iron. His process has already been discussed, (§ 315, C. II).

§ 338 A. SIEMENS, in one of his early direct processes, would suspend two cast-iron retorts or hoppers AA, with fire-clay ends, above the laboratory of an open-hearth steel-melting furnace, Figure 141.

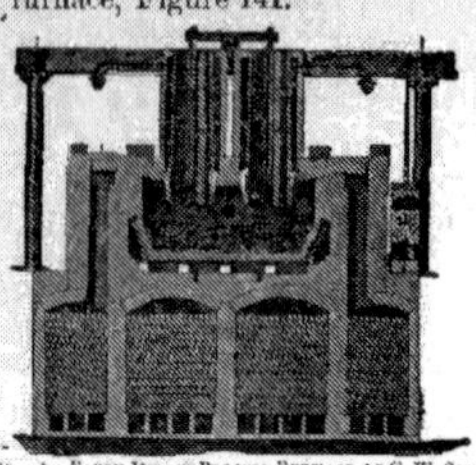

FIG. 141.—AN EARLY DIRECT-PROCESS FURNACE OF C. W. SIEMENS.

Around each hopper is a space heated by a regulated supply of flame from the open-hearth furnace: within it a wrought-iron pipe supplying producer-gas for deoxidizing the ore.

About 28 pounds of charcoal is charged through each hopper, and on this sufficient ore to fill the hopper completely. Producer-gas is then injected through the pipes in the center of the hoppers, and deoxidizes the ore which has meanwhile been raised to redness by the heat conducted through the walls of the hoppers. About half a ton of pig-iron is charged on the open-hearth: melting, it dissolves the lower end of the columns of more or less completely deoxidized iron, with a rapidity which is only limited by the time needed to deoxidize the ore in the hopper. Sufficient sponge having been thus melted off in three or four hours, charging ceases, the remaining ore in the hoppers sinks, a clay-coated cast-iron cover suspended by strong wire descending with the ore-column, so that the flame may not enter the empty hoppers. On this cover is placed the charcoal and ore of the subsequent charge, eventually lowered by cutting the wire. The charge already melted is brought to the right degree of carburization, and, after an addition of spiegeleisen, is tapped.

To-day we wonder that a man of Siemens' genius and judgment could have seriously entertained so crude a project even twenty-one years ago. To maintain these hoppers, exposed thus in an open-hearth furnace; to heat these thick bodies of ore through and to deoxidize them at their necessary low temperature in any reasonable time; to keep this open-hearth furnace waiting while the charge of ore was deoxidizing;—well, well! To-day's folly is wiser than yesterday's wisdom.

B. *Ponsard*[d] in like manner would place several fireclay retorts 8″ in diameter and 40″ high in a reverberatory gas-furnace, their mouths being fitted into openings in the roof, their lower parts open or perforated and resting on the hearth, which had gutters leading to a central sump. In the retorts is charged ore with flux and about 12% (!) of carbon for deoxidation and carburization. The reduced iron, melting, runs through the holes in the bottoms of the retorts and collects in the sump.

Ponsard claimed that for producing one ton of cast-iron in this apparatus one ton of coal sufficed for deoxidation, carburization, and melting. This process is open to the same fatal objections as Siemen's. Indeed they seem identical. Which was the prior invention I know not.

§ 339 A. FOR PRECIPITATING COPPER[e] from its solutions spongy iron was used as early as 1837, and has been used in later years. I am informed that its use is now abandoned. Three tons of "purple ore" (the residue from leaching copper from roasted cupreous pyrites), with 18 cwt. of coal which has passed a screen of eight meshes to the linear inch, is heated to bright redness in a 6″ layer on the 22′ × 8′ hearth of an open reverberatory furnace with tightly fitting doors and a very, say 4′ 8″, deep fire-box (to yield a so-called reducing flame), for from 9 to 24 hours, during which the ore is turned twice or thrice. The spongy iron is then drawn through holes in the hearth into tightly closed, wheeled sheet-iron boxes of 12 cubic feet capacity, where it cools for two days. For heating, 15 cwt. of coal are needed per ton of ore, or altogether say 159 pounds of coal per 100 of iron in ore. The composition of the copper precipitated by this sponge is given as 67·5% copper, 5·15% ferric oxide. If this is the usual composition, it would indicate that the spongy iron was surprisingly well deoxidized, probably 90% of its iron being in the metallic state.

B. *Harvey* heated coarsely powdered ore with charcoal on inclined steatite shelves connected with a balling furnace, and heated by a passing flame. The deoxidized ore was transferred to the hearth of the balling furnace and balled. The process failed.

C. *Gerhardt* bricked ore, flux and carbonaceous deoxidizing matter with tar, heated these bricks in a puddling furnace, and there balled the resulting iron, using 330 pounds of coal per 100 of finished iron.[f]

§ 340. IN THE EAMES[g] or Carbon Iron Company's process iron ore is deoxidized on the carbonaceous hearth of an open reverberatory furnace, by means of graphitic anthracite or "retarded coke,"[h] with which it is mixed.

[a] Trans. Eng. Soc., W. Penn, p. 218, Mch. 16th, 1883.

[b] British patent, Nov. 13, 1800, No. 2,447.

[c] Lecture before Fellows' Chem. Soc., May 7th, 1868.

[d] British Patent 2,334, July 24, 1868; T. S. Hunt, Geolog. Survey Canada, 1866-69, p. 292; Comptes Rendus, LXIX, p. 177, July 19th, 1868. Berg und Hütt Zeit., XXVIII., p. 415, 1869. The numbers here given are Ponsard's.

[e] Lunge, Sulphuric Acid and Alkali, I., pp. 615-21, 1879, gives drawings of the apparatus and details of the treatment.

[f] Berg und Hütt. Zeit., XXXIII., p. 183, 1874.

[g] Trans. Am. Inst. Min. Eng., XVI., p. 708, 1888. Iron Age, XLI., p. 349, 1888. A. E. Hunt, private communication. U. S. patents 318,551 to 318,554, 318,605 to 318,607, 318,609, May 26th, 1885: 396,992, Jan. 29, 1889.

[h] "Retarded coke" is coke mixed with milk of lime, so that it offers very little surface for oxidation.

These reducing agents, in that they themselves become oxidized only very slowly, indeed reduce the iron less rapidly than charcoal or common coke; but after reduction is effected they resist oxidation and so persist and remain to protect the reduced iron from reoxidation: and as the difficulty in direct processes is not so much in the reduction as in preventing reoxidation, the idea is reasonable. Indeed, I think it likely that the substitution of graphite for charcoal has diminished the loss of iron.[a]

I. *The furnace* now used is an open reverberatory measuring about 18″ from roof to hearth, and fired with natural gas at both ends, the products of combustion escaping through a flue in the middle of the roof. The hearth is about six feet wide and fifteen feet long, and has a layer of graphite from four to six inches thick on its upper surface. Eames recommends a graphite-iron bottom prepared as follows:[b]

Lumps about one foot thick of the graphitic anthracite of Cranston, R. I., are set in a single layer on the hearth; the interstices are filled with ground iron ore; the whole is covered with a layer (2″ to 4″ thick in the middle, 3″ to 6″ at the side) of wheat-grain sized anthracite: this is dried by gentle heating; on it is placed a half-inch or inch-thick layer of ground iron ore; the temperature is gradually raised during from three to five hours to 1,371° C. (2,500° F. bright whiteness) to deoxidize the ore and later to soften the mass. The hearth is then rammed solid with a heavy dolly. The iron ore, or the iron reduced from it by the surrounding carbon, is said to strengthen the hearth greatly. A graphite-clay hearth is said to be readily indented, a pure graphitic-anthracite hearth to flake and get mixed with the sponge-balls.

II. *Reduction.*—2,240 pounds of dry rich ore (say 62% of metallic iron) and 550 pounds of graphitic anthracite containing 78% of carbon, are ground to pass a screen of sixteen meshes to the linear inch, mixed with enough water to render the mass slightly plastic, and spread in a four-inch layer on this hearth. The carbon is not quite enough to deoxidize the whole of the iron by the reaction

$$Fe_2O_3 + 3\,C = 2Fe + 3\,CO,$$

so that some of it appears to be oxidized to carbonic acid by the ore. The doors are closed and luted, and the furnace is now heated with a so-called reducing flame.

20 *m.*: The charge has shrunk to a thickness of 2″; temperature incipient redness, say 538° C., 1,000° F.

1 *hr.*: the charge has shrunk to 1·3″: beads of iron are seen on its surface.

1 *hr.* 30 *m.*: the charge has shrunk to 1″: begin working into balls say 20″ in diameter, and weighing from 85 to 185 pounds each. Temperature not above moderate redness, 816° C., 1,500° F.

If the balls are for the open-hearth, balling takes but 30 to 40 minutes; if for rolling, an hour, as in this case they must be brought to a welding heat. Thus the last ball is drawn at 2 h. 40 m. and 3 h. in charges for the open-hearth and for rolling respectively. Repairs, fettling and charging take 20 minutes more, so that the total length of the operation, when balls for the open-hearth furnace are made, is three hours, and six 1,600-pound heats are made per reducing furnace per 24 hours.

III. *Further Treatment*—The sponge balls, like those produced in other processes, may be hammered or squeezed and rolled to muck-bar for use in the open-hearth or the crucible process; or they may be charged while still white-hot into a bath of molten cast-iron in the open-hearth furnace.

IV. *Loss.*—From Hunt's data I calculate the loss in one reducing heat as follows:

	Iron, pounds.
Ore charged in reducing furnace, 2,973 pounds, at 62% = - - - - - -	1,818 at 9:10 A. M.
2,010 pounds of sponge-balls resulting were charged in the open-hearth furnace at 10:45 to 11:45 A. M.	
The open-hearth charge further contained	
Of pig-iron - - - - - - - - -	870 at 9:30 A. M.
Of ferromanganese of 70% manganese	24 at 1:10 P. M.
	2,712
Ingots produced 2,150, scrap 191 - -	2,341 at 1:20 P. M.
Loss - - - - - - - - -	371
11%[c] of loss is chargeable to pig and ferromanganese - - - - - - -	98
Loss chargeable to sponge process, from ore to ingot - - - - - - - -	273 pounds,

which is 15% of the iron contained in the ore. This way of calculating the loss, I think, gives us the most valuable results, since what we seek to know is, "Assuming that the pig and ferromanganese lose the same amount when melted with sponge balls as when melted with scrap, how does the loss on the sponge-balls themselves compare with the loss on scrap?"

The loss reckoned on ore, pig and ferromanganese is 13·7% here, but in regular working the loss seems to be rather higher than this. With two 15-ton open-hearth furnaces using about 50 parts of pig-iron, 10 of scrap (both taken at their gross weight and without reduction for non-ferrous matter which they contain), and 40 parts of iron contained in sponge-balls, or altogether 100 parts reckoned in this way, 87 parts of ingots and scrap result, implying a loss of 13%.[d] If, now, we assume that the pig-iron and scrap lose 8% by weight or $60 \times \frac{8}{100} = 4{\cdot}8$ parts, we have to charge against the 40 parts of iron in sponge a loss of $13 - 4{\cdot}8 = 8{\cdot}4$ parts of iron, or $\frac{8{\cdot}4 \times 100}{40} = 21\%$ of the iron in the sponge. That is to say, in the sponge-making and open-hearths processes combined the loss from ore to ingots is 21%. This is decidedly more than in the combined blast-furnace and open-hearth processes, in which the total loss probably does not exceed 10 per cent.

In making muck-bar the loss is still greater, as at the higher welding heat to which the balls must be raised oxidation is very rapid. Hunt reports that in one week three reducing furnaces made collectively 50 heats:

Receiving altogether of ore	112,000	pounds
This contained of iron	69,445	"
There was produced of muck-bar	44,810	"
Implying a loss of 35·5%a	24,635	"

a The original contains an error, giving the loss as 29.71%.

[a] This substitution seems to about balance the excess of the oxidizing tendencies of Eames' open reverberatory over those of the charcoal-hearth and shaft-furnace, for the loss of iron is about the same as in the American bloomary and in Husgafvel's furnace. (Cf. Table 154, p. 268.) Eames' loss, 21%, is, indeed, from ore to ingots, that of these other processes only from ore to blooms, in remelting which a further loss would result. But these blooms have been made at a high welding heat, and hence with greater loss than if, as in Eames' process, the heat merely sufficed for making loose balls for the open-hearth furnace. If graphite has real advantages, a shaft-furnace like Schmidhammer's seems better for using it than an open reverberatory.

[b] U. S. Patent 396,992, Jan. 29, 1889.

[c] The loss on pig and scrap charges in this same furnace is 11%.

[d] A. E. Hunt, private communications, April 9th and 22d, 1889.

He further gives the loss as follows:

100 of iron in ore yields of blooms 6″ × 6″ × 20″	80·6	loss = 19·4%
of billets 4″ × 4″ × 24″	72·54	" = 27·46%
of muck-bar 8½″ × ½″	68·51	" = 31·49%
100 of muck-bar contains	0·015 of phosphorus.	
Ore for making 100 of muck-bar contains	0·148 "	"
100 of ore contains	0·068 "	"

In a heat described to me by a very trustworthy witness, of 100 parts of iron in the ore charged in the reducing furnace, 15·6 were removed in the slag of the same furnace, (this slag contained 57% of iron), and 19·7 more existed in the sponge-balls as oxide, so that only 6..7 of metallic iron in sponge-balls was recovered from 100 of iron in ore, a loss of 35·3%. The sponge-balls contained about 62·61% of iron as metal and 19·7% as oxide: but these numbers are only rough approximations, owing to the heterogeneousness of the sponge-balls. Had these balls been for the open-hearth furnace, part of this iron-oxide would have been deoxidized by the carbon and silicon of the bath.

TABLE 163B.—EAMES OR CARBON IRON COMPANY'S PROCESS.

Dimensions of reducing furnace.	
Length of hearth	15′
Width of hearth	6′
Height from hearth to roof	18″
Length of campaign without serious repairs	One year.
Charge for one heat.	
Ore, kind	Minnesota Y
" percentage of iron	65
" weight	2,240 lbs.
" percentage of phosphorus	0·04
Length of one heat	3 hours
Number of heats per 24 hours	6
Men employed per furnace per shift	2
Shifts per 24 hours	2
Output per furnace per heat.	
Pounds of balls per heat	1,600
" " per 24 hours	12,800
Outlay in reducing-furnace for 2,000 pounds of iron recovered as ingots in subsequent open-hearth melting.	
Ore, pounds	3,896
Labor, days	1·17
Loss from ore to ingots	21%
Composition of sponge balls.	
Iron	96%
Coke or graphite	6·
Carbon combined with iron	0·15
Gangue	8·80
Sulphur and phosphorus	0·05

These data are communicated by Mr. A. E. Hunt, of the Carbon Iron Company.

V. *Dephosphorization.*—Open-hearth steel made from these sponge-balls contains nearly the whole of the phosphorus of the ore: but muck-bar made from them is nearly free from phosphorus, having according to Hunt less than 0·015% of phosphorus from an ore holding 0·063%. The muck-bar, were there no dephosphorization, would contain 0·148% of phosphorus, so that 0·133 of phosphorus is removed per 100 of iron recovered, or 0·09 per 100 of iron in ore.

The difference between the dephosphorization in ingot and in muck-bar-making is clearly due to the general principle that in the direct process dephosphorization and loss of iron usually go hand in hand. Balls for the open-hearth are made at a low temperature, with a flame but slightly oxidizing, and with rapid balling: little iron is oxidized, the mechanically inclosed slag is chiefly an earthy silicate, difficultly fusible, pasty, and hence but little of it runs out from the balls: most of it goes with the balls to the open-hearth furnace, whose siliceous walls give rise to an acid slag, and the phosphorus of the slag within the balls is reduced by the carbon of the bath as fusion proceeds.

In making muck-bar, however, the higher temperature and the more oxidizing flame which it entails in the reducing furnace, as well as the longer heating, oxidize much iron: the slag becomes basic and hence dephosphorizing, ferruginous and hence fusible: it melts and runs away from the balls both in the reducing furnace, in shingling and in rolling, and in running away removes the phosphorus. The slag from the blooms contains, according to Hunt:

Iron	from 30 to 50%
Silica	" 24 to 30%
Phosphorus	" 0·1 to 0·15%

and is thus probably between a singulo- and a subsilicate in composition. This composition tallies fairly with the actual loss of iron and removal of phosphorus: thus, if iron and phosphorus are removed in the ratio 50 to 0·15, the removal of 0·09 of phosphorus per 100 of iron in the ore, which as we have seen occurs, implies a loss of 30% of the iron of the ore, which is very close to the actual loss of 31·49%.

The statements on page 59 imply that the silica should be near the lower of the above limits, 24%, to permit thorough dephosphorization.

Condition of the Process.—The Carbon Iron Company has eight reducing furnaces, which are running double turn all the time, and two 15-ton open-hearth furnaces running steadily, with a charge of about 50% of cast-iron, 10% of scrap and 40% of sponge-balls. A considerable part of the spongy iron is rolled into muck-bar, not for use as wrought-iron, but as a material for the crucible and open-hearth processes. The process has clearly passed to the commercial stage, and, with the cheap fuel of Pittsburgh and under the very skillful superintendence which it is so fortunate as to have, apparently to the profitable stage.

The success of the process in Pittsburgh, where the Blair, the DuPuy and the Siemens processes have failed, would be chiefly attributable to the supply of a very cheap heating fuel, natural gas; but still I think in some part to the use of special reducing agents, which lessen the loss of iron. The loss from ore to ingots is probably less than that in the DuPuy and Siemens processes from ore to blooms: while over the Blair process the Eames has the advantage of utilizing the sensible heat of the sponge when the balls are plunged into the open-hearth bath.

§ 341. A. IN THE LATE SIEMENS DIRECT[a] or "precipitation" process fine ore was reduced by coal, with which it was mixed and heated in a rotating furnace like a Danks puddler, the coal precipitating metallic iron from the molten ore. The resulting metal was balled as in puddling, squeezed to expel slag, and either used as material for the open-hearth process or worked into merchantable wrought-iron.[b] Some details are condensed in Table 165.

I. *The plant* for furnaces, crusher, hammer, etc., was estimated by Holley to cost $40,000 per 125 tons weekly capacity.

II. *The furnace*, Figure 144, differed from the common rotary puddler chiefly in being gas-fired and regenerative, the gas from the producer *d*, passing through a flue *g*, enclosed between the regenerators *h h*, direct to the rotator

a Tunner, Metallurg. Rev., I. p., 573, 1878; Holley, Trans. Am. Inst. Min. Eng., VIII., p. 321, 1880; Maynard, Idem. X., p. 274, 1881; Siemens, Jour. Iron and Steel Inst., 1873, I., p. 37; 1877, II., p. 345.

b Mr. J. Head informs me that the process was practically abandoned during the life of Sir William Siemens. The deoxidation was successful, but the reoxidation fatal. Private communication, Nov. 7th, 1888.

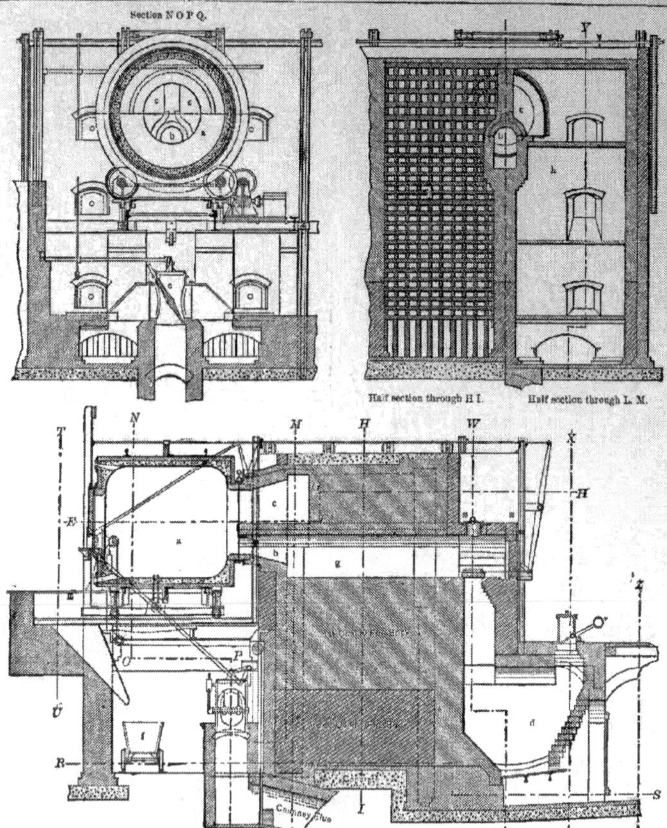

Figure 144.—Rotary Gas Furnace for Siemen's Direct Process. (Holley.)

a Rotator in which deoxidation occurs. *b* Gas-port. *c* Entrance-port for air and exit-port for products of combustion. *d* Gas-producer. *e* Reversing valve. *f* Slag buggy. *g* Gas-flue. *h* Regenerator.

a, the air alone being preheated. The entrance for gas (*b*) and air (*c*) and the exit for products of combustion were at the same end of the rotator, leaving the other end free for charging and working. The ports were small, so that the velocity of the entering gas and air should suffice to throw the flame well towards the working end.

The three inch brick lining (which lasted months) was glazed by heating with roll-scale, and fettled (say 2½ to 6 inches deep) with iron ore and a little coal, which reduces the ore slightly to a very refractory state. The ends exposed to the basic slags were sometimes lined with bauxite; thorough lining occupied from 24 to 48 hours, fettling three to four hours. To make the charge roll rather than slide the lining was roughened, *e.g.*, by ridges of fettling holding a water pipe, which cooled and maintained them; or by ridges of ore-lumps placed, after drawing the charge, in the still liquid slag, which was then chilled with water.

III. *The operation* was divisible into two periods (1) heating and partial reduction; (2), complete reduction and balling. In the first the temperature was relatively low to avoid fusion before reduction, and the rotation slow. In the second the temperature gradually became high enough for balling, and the rotation faster. In both the atmosphere was necessarily strongly oxidizing to iron and its low oxides.

Pea-sized ore, basic-slag-yielding flux (actually limestone) and small coal were heated in the slowly revolving rotator with a pretty full air-supply. After 2.5 hours, reduction being well advanced, the temperature and rate of rotation were raised, the slag began to form, accumulating till, after another hour, it was tapped. After four hours, reduction being completed, the temperature was again raised and the rotation accelerated, then temporarily arrested to permit balling by hand, and later to draw the balls successively. This done, the furnace was charged afresh. The balls contained about 70% of metallic iron, the blooms made from them it is said 99.7 per cent.

I deduce the following from Tunner:

TABLE 164.—DIARY OF SIEMENS DIRECT PROCESS: TOWCESTER.

HOURS.	MINUTES.	
0	0	Charge introduced: furnace stationary.
0	5	Rotate at 12 to 15 revs. per. min. (a) Full air supply to heat quickly.
2	0	Heat bright red. Charge still dry. Much coal yet unconsumed. Ore hard, magnetic, partly metallic.
2	30	The charge partly pasty. Heat raised. Some slag appears.
3	0	Heat raised more. More liquid slag appears.
3	30	The pasty mass begins balling. More slag forms. Rotate quicker. Tap slag, for first time, completely.
3	45	Tap again. Less slag.
4	0	Heat raised to whiteness. Rotate quicker, stopping momentarily to ball.
4	8	First ball drawn. Shape and draw remaining balls.
4	30	All drawn. Charge anew.

a This implies a circumferential speed of 380 to 400 feet per minute, or of a mile in 13 minutes. Maynard reports that the speed of the Tyrone 11-foot rotator was one revolution in 15 to 18 minutes, or a circumferential velocity of about 2 feet per minute.

charge occupied nine hours. Thus, although there was clearly an endeavor to shorten the operation, it seems to have lengthened greatly, and unavoidably.

The loss of iron was actually heavy, probably at least 20%. As the material was melted and subsequently balled in the necessarily strongly oxidizing atmosphere of the rotator, this was probably absolutely unavoidable. The rich slags given in columns I and II of Table 165 tally well with this loss. The data in column VII indeed indicate a very slight loss, for no less than 60.5 pounds of blooms were recovered from 100 of ore and scale. But this loss does not tally with the extremely small quantity of fuel used for reducing, only 23 parts per 100 of blooms, and I think that there must be some error. The heavy loss of iron of course permits dephosphorization; note the large proportion of phosphoric acid in the slags of Table 165.

The loss here given is from ore to blooms: that from ore to ingots would probably be at least 30%.

TABLE 165. DETAILS OF THE SIEMENS DIRECT PROCESS.

Number	I.	II.	III.	IV.	V.	VI.	VII.
Place	Towcester.	Towcester.	Towcester.	Towcester.	Tyrone.	Pittsburgh.	Landore.
Date	1876	1877	1877	1887	1879	1881	1881
Authority	Tunner.	Siemens.	Siemens.	Siemens.	Holley.	Maynard.	Holley.
ROTATOR.							
Diameter, outside	8′ 6″				11′	11′ 4″	
Length	9′ 6″	9′			11′	12′	
Thickness of br'k lining	9″					4½″	
Thickness of fettling	6″ @ 8″					2′	
Circum. veloc., ft. per min., initial	380′ @ 400′						
Revs. per min., initial	12 @ 15					.56 @ .67	
CHARGE.							
Ore, % Fe	44·29 d	40 ±			50		
Lbs. per charge, ore	1,950	8,860	578	500	4,000	5,025	2,240
mill-scale	504*		1,906	1,008	800		1,344
slag		162 m	784 n	784 n			
Total iron-bearing matter, lbs.	2,484	8,528	2,870	2,287	4,800	5,023	3,584
Total iron in charge, lbs.	868 a		1,812 h	1,274 h			2,156
Limestone	280	168	113	93	280	271	
Reducing coal	806	1,098	728	728	600 @ 700	1,382	504
Producer coal						6,108	2,734
Per 2,240 pounds of blooms. Ore, pounds	5,744	6,744	1,051	1,006	5,466	408	2,818
Other iron-bearing matter, pounds	1,734	339	3,258	3,598	1,086		1,888
Total iron-bearing matter, pounds	5,478	7,386	4,309	4,093	6,516		8,701
Limestone, pounds	963	589	204	101	339	235	
Coal, reducing, pounds	3,083	2,382	1,324	1,465	888	1,200	531
Coal for producers, pounds	4,592 f	4,486 e			3,900	5,302	2,624
Coal, total pounds	7,675	6,512			4,883	6,502	3,340
Labor, days					5·5		
Labor, $	10.00	3.63			10.00	9.24 l	
Repairs, etc., $						2.00	
Total cost, $		16.45	(?)		25.00	(?)	
No. charges per 24 hours	5 (?)	5 ?	5·8 ?	7 ?	3·5 ±	2·6 ±	5·3
Length of charge	4 hr. 50 m.	4 hr. 21 m.	4 hr. 8 m.	3 hr. 12 m.	7 hr. ±	9 hr. +	4 hr. 30 m. ±
PRODUCT.	a. / b. / c.	a. / b.					
Slag, composition % Fe Ox	47 / 56 / 48	47 / 56					
% P_2O_5	6·9 / 8·5 / 1·9	6·2 / 8·3					
% S	1·6 / 0·4 / 0·8	·28 / 19					
% SiO_2	24·1 / 18·8 / 12·5						
Blooms, composition % Fe	99·71	98·3 @ 99·9				87 ±	
% C	0.12	tr. @ 0·23					
% P	·074	.02 @ .138					
% S	·027	tr. @ 0·27					
Weight per charge, lbs. blooms	631	1,111	1,282	1,118	1,600 @ 1,700	2,879	2,168
Total output per 24 hours per furnace, lbs.	3,225 ?	5,550	6,580	7,791 ?	5,600 ± @ 5,950 ±	6,075 ±	11,290
Loss % of iron	23% d	19·8 i	6·07 l hj	12·6 h	15 @ 20 d	20·16	p.

I. Tunner, Metallurg. Rev., I., p. 548, 1878.
II. Siemens, 18 charges at Towcester, Jour. Iron and St. Inst., 1877, II., p. 352.
III. Idem, p. 357: Average of 27 charges.
IV. Idem, p. 359: Average of 40 charges.
V. Holley, Trans. Am. Inst. Mining Eng., VIII., p. 321, 1880.
VI. G. W. Maynard, Idem, X., p. 274, 1881.
VII. Data quoted from Holley by Maynard, Loc. Cit.
a First tapping.
b Second tapping.
c Reheating.
d Excluding mill scale used.
e Producer coal only.
f Producer and steam coal.
g Special charges only: does not include rolling the hammered blooms.
h Including scale, etc.
i Apparently including scale, etc.
j This number is incredible.
k The actual loss of iron, assuming that the blooms contained 87% of iron. It is stated that they contained 10 @ 15% of cinder.
l $9.24 per ton of blooms of 87% of iron: $10.62 per 100 of iron in the blooms. The latter seems more nearly comparable with other numbers in the same line, as in the other columns blooms apparently of 98 to 99·9% of iron are referred to. The sum, $10.62 appears to include labor for heating, for shipping, and for receiving.
m Tap-cinder.
n Undescribed cinder.
o Reheating-furnace slag.
p If, as the context suggests, the ore contained about 58% of iron and the scale about 72, the weight of blooms would exceed that of iron charged, so that the loss would be represented by the slag inclosed in the blooms.

The most important variation in the process seems to have been in its length. In 1873, Siemens reported that "the time occupied in working one charge rarely exceeds two hours." In 1880, Holley reported that the output at Tyrone had been increasing gradually, having now reached about five heats a day.[a] In 1881 Maynard reported that a

a In 1877 Holley reported that "a charge" "has been made in two hours twenty minutes. The time of the shortest operation I witnessed was 2¾ hours. At Newton, two years ago, the time was 4 to 4½ hours."

The fuel-consumption was heavy, and probably unavoidably, as the heating was indirect, and as the strongly oxidizing atmosphere of the reducing furnace both directly oxidized the reducing fuel and continually reoxidized the iron, to re-deoxidize which demanded a further excess of reducing fuel. It should hardly be possible to bring the fuel-consumption much below 200 pounds per 100 of blooms.

In addition to the compositions given in Table 165 we have the following from Metcalf, of very redshort wrought-iron made by this process[j]:

Carbon.	Silicon,	Manganese,	Phosphorus,	Sulphur,	Copper,	Dissolved Oxide.
.033	.038	0	tr.	.046	.030	.30

B. *The Cascade Furnace.*—Instead of a rotator Siemens at one time used a "Cascade" furnace, Figure 145. A lake

Fig. 145.
SIEMENS CASCADE FURNACE.

of fused ore was formed on the upper hearth, and, by piercing the intervening bank of unmelted ore, was run at intervals upon the lower hearth, upon which meanwhile a layer of equal parts of powdered anthracite or coke and ore had been spread. On stirring, the mass foamed and became pasty; in from 40 to 50 minutes the iron, precipitated by the carbon, was balled, to be melted in the open-hearth furnace or squeezed. In Siemens' published results the loss was less than 7%; but as the slag rarely held less than 15 and sometimes as much as 40% of iron, I doubt whether such results could be obtained regularly. Indeed, Siemens abandoned this method because of liability to heavy loss of iron, and because "a certain degree of manual skill and labor" was needed.[e] Truly, it is hard to understand on what kind of information Siemens and others based their statements concerning both this and the rotator process.

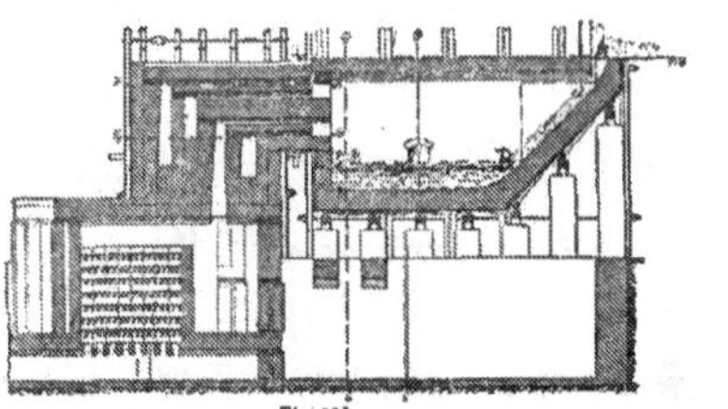
Fig. 146.
FURNACE FOR F. SIEMENS CONTINUOUS DIRECT-PROCESS.

§ 342. LECKIE[l] would brick ore with coal or peat, heat the bricks in chambers adjoining an open-hearth steel melting furnace, and when deoxidation has progressed well, push them into the bath of molten cast-iron on the open-hearth. The objections stated in § 315, C, I, apply here.

§ 343. IN F. SIEMENS'[g] DIRECT PROCESS ore, coal and fluxes are charged continuously through a slit at the end of a regenerative gas-furnace, Figure 146, which is rectangular in plan, with the entrance and exit ports at the same end, the opposite end AB being strongly inclined. The heat is so high that the ore melts immediately on entering the furnace, and so coats over and protects the coal from the action of the flame of the furnace. The melting ore trickles down the incline AB, its iron being reduced by the coal, partly during its descent, partly after reaching the bath at the bottom of the incline. Basic additions are made to the molten slag, to permit dephosphorization and the reduction of the iron. The slag runs out continuously, the metal is tapped from time to time.

For reasons given in § 315, C, I, the plan is less promising than striking.

§ 344. A. EUSTIS[m] would coke fine ore with coking bituminous coal, and melt the coked lumps in a cupola furnace, thinking that the phosphorus would escape deoxidation both in the coking and the fusion.

It would be necessary to have a great quantity of carbon present. If the product were not itself carburized, it would be so extremely infusible that an enormous quantity of fuel would have to be present in order to melt it, and this quantity of fuel would probably make the deoxidizing conditions so strong that the phosphorus would enter the iron. If, on the other hand, the product were carburized, and therefore fusible, enough carbon would have to be present to prevent its decarburization by any small quantity of reoxidized spongy metal, and to keep the slag quite free from iron-oxide, as this of course would react rapidly on the carburetted bath and remove its carbon. But in this case the slag, being free from iron-oxide, would not hold phosphorus unless made basic with lime or magnesia, and to melt a lime or magnesia slag would require so high a temperature, and hence so much fuel (the reducing agent), that here too the phosphorus would be deoxidized.

In short we have the difficult if not impossible task of dephosphorizing under the necessarily strongly deoxidizing conditions of shaft-furnace smelting.

For the rest, if cast-iron is to be made, the process is more costly than the blast-furnace; if ingot metal, the problem of melting it in a shaft-furnace is no easy one. To melt it in the open-hearth we have to preheat gas and air tremendously; to melt it in a shaft furnace would, I fear, need very hot blast and an abundance of highly preheated fuel; in short the conditions of the blast-furnace exaggerated, for the temperature must be much higher than that reached in cast-iron making.

B. IRELAND.—The same objections apply to Ireland's plan of melting sponge in a cupola furnace.[n]

j Trans. Eng. Soc. W. Penn., March 16, 1883, p. 217.
e Journ. Iron and Steel Inst. 1873, I, pp. 43, 51.
l T. S. Hunt, Rept. Geolog. Survey Canada, 1866-9, p. 236.
m Trans. Am. Inst. Min. Eng., IX., p. 274, 1881.
n Jour. Iron and Steel Inst., 1878, I., p. 52.
g Wagner's Jahresbericht, xxxiii., p. 305, 1887.

CHAPTER XVI.

Charcoal-Hearth Processes.

When steel is made from cast-iron, this material may be used without preparatory treatment, as in the Bessemer process, or it may undergo some preparatory process. The chief and normal use of some of these preparatory processes, such as pig-washing and mechanical puddling, is to prepare material for steel-making; that of others, e. g., hand-puddling, charcoal-hearth refining, etc., is to make wrought-iron to be used as such, and their use as preparatory to steel-making is only subsidiary.

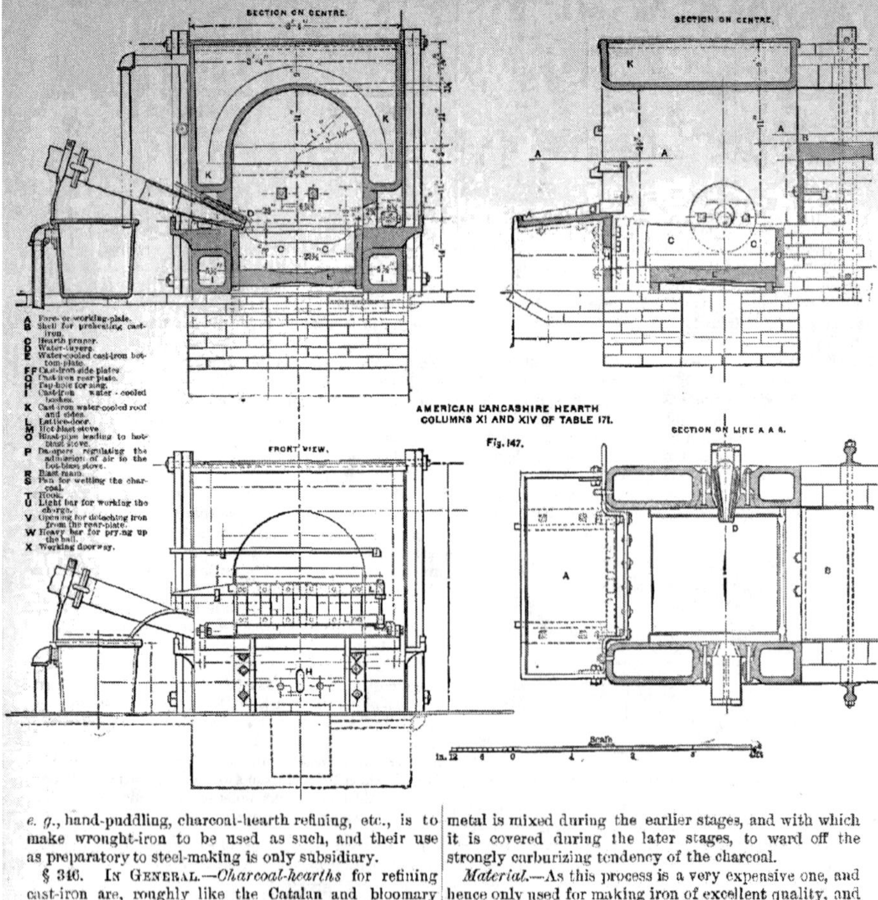

AMERICAN LANCASHIRE HEARTH
COLUMNS XI AND XIV OF TABLE 171.
Fig. 147.

§ 346. In General.—*Charcoal-hearths* for refining cast-iron are, roughly like the Catalan and bloomary hearths for reducing iron from the ore, low, rectangular chambers, Figure 149, sometimes roofed, Figures 147, 148, and with one or more tuyeres. The chief difference is that in refining cast-iron much more strongly oxidizing conditions are brought about, chiefly (1) by melting the metal down in drops before the tuyere, repeatedly if need be, so that it passes in a state of minute subdivision and with great surface exposure through a part of the hearth where the atmospheric oxygen is in excess; and (2) by the action of the basic ferruginous slag with which the metal is mixed during the earlier stages, and with which it is covered during the later stages, to ward off the strongly carburizing tendency of the charcoal.

Material.—As this process is a very expensive one, and hence only used for making iron of excellent quality, and as the quality of the product depends to a considerable extent on that of the material, *i. e.*, on its freedom from phosphorus and sulphur, so only pure cast-iron is used, and preferably charcoal cast-iron. As the length and cost of the operation increase with the proportion of carbon, and still more with that of silicon in the metal, so close gray or preferably mottled or white cast-iron is habitually

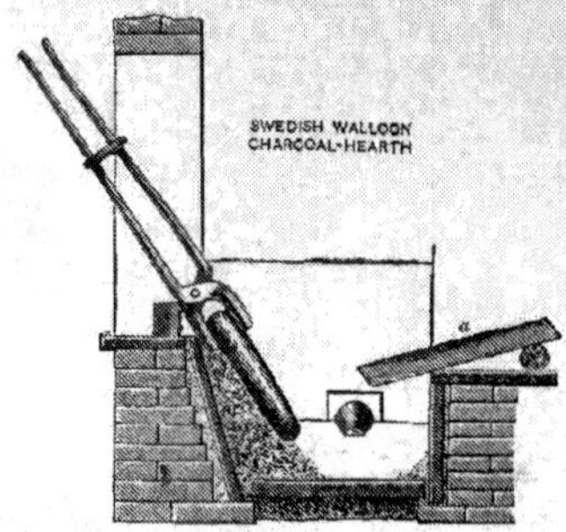

Fig. 110.

used; and, in case open gray iron is used, it is well to remove part of its silicon by a partial refining in a preliminary process.

Silicon not only greatly retards the operation by being oxidized in preference to carbon, but more especially because the silica formed by its oxidation makes the slag less basic, and so less strongly decarburizing; and the removal of phosphorus and carbon occurs in large part through the action of the basic slag. Not only does a less basic slag remove phosphorus and carbon less rapidly, but it devours iron-oxide the more readily, and thus increases the loss of iron. Indeed, we must make up our minds to a loss of over two parts by weight of iron for every part of silica, or of about one part by weight of iron for each part of silicon that enters the slag. Moreover, a very considerable outlay of labor and time is needed to work the iron-oxide into the slag.

The pigs are in many cases cast in cast-iron moulds ("chills"); if cast in sand, much of this would adhere to them and silica would thus be introduced.

The presence of manganese in the cast-iron is thought undesirable, not only because it is oxidized in part in preference to the carbon and silicon, and because the manganese slags are less strongly fining than the iron slags—thanks to the higher affinity of manganese than of iron for oxygen, and to the fact that manganese does not slide up and down in its degree of oxidation as iron does, carrying oxygen from atmosphere to metal—but also for another important reason. The manganese slags are unduly fluid, and do not adhere to the sides and upper part of the lump of iron and exert their fining influence over its whole surface like the relatively pasty iron slags, but run down and collect beneath, leaving the iron in contact with the charcoal, from which it rapidly takes up carbon.

For fuel charcoal is used, not only because free from sulphur, but because it has less ash than solid mineral fuels, and so introduces less silica into the slag. To remove sand, pebbles, etc., serious sources of silica, the charcoal shortly before use is washed in large tanks which stand hard by the charcoal-hearths themselves.

The hearths are usually of naked, unlined cast-iron plates, at least in part water-cooled. Brick-work or other clayey lining is to be avoided, because its silica would enter the slag.

§ 347. PRODUCT—THE REASONS FOR THE EXISTENCE OF THE PROCESS.

From given cast-iron the charcoal-hearth process yields better wrought-iron than puddling, perhaps in part because the charcoal lacks the sulphur which the mineral fuel of the puddling furnace contains, and of which a little may enter the metal, but chiefly for the following reason. In both processes we can decarburize the pasty metal throughout its mass only by stirring it vigorously, exposing fresh surfaces to the action of the atmosphere and of the strongly decarburizing basic slag, and this stirring intentionally mixes slag with metal to effect decarburization. We thus get a ball of stiff, pasty wrought-iron mixed with much slag. In some of the charcoal-hearth processes we get rid of most of this slag by remelting this ball; holding it aloft we allow its metal to fall drop by drop, and collect it in a new ball, which we carefully avoid touching, and which is thus relatively free from slag. In the puddling process we cannot do this, and must content ourselves with squeezing out as much of the slag as we can in hammering or rolling.

TABLE 167.—COMPOSITION AND PROPERTIES OF CHARCOAL-HEARTH IRON.

No.		C.	Si.	Mn.	P.	S.	Tensile strength, lbs. per sq. in.	Elastic limit, lbs. per sq. in.	Elongation. Per cent.	Elongation. Measured on	Reduction of area, per cent.
1	Äryd, Smaland, Sweden (Rolled)	0.07	...	...	...	...	65,669	37,397	14.1	...	49.
2	" " " "	0.18	...	...	0.264	...	...	40,185	...	...	18.
3	Hallstahammer, Westmanland, Sweden (Rolled)	0.07	...	...	...	...	50,916	27,104	16.7	...	56.
4	Lesjoforss, Wermland, Sweden (Rolled)	0.07	...	...	0.022	...	45,014	24,250	22.0	...	77.
5	Hallstahammer	0.07	...	...	...	...	47,553	...	...	...	74.
6	Lesjoforss	0.08	...	...	...	...	44,603	...	18.0	...	68.
7	"	0.07±	...	...	...	...	44,877	...	29.0	...	65.
8	"	0.06	...	...	...	...	51,058	...	...	...	66.
9	"	0.07	...	...	...	...	56,199	...	17.2	5.2"	59.
10		0.087	0.115	...	0.034	0.380					
11	From Dannemora Ore	0.054	0.028	tr.	tr.	0.055					
12		0.087	0.056	...	0.005	0.032					
13	Swedish a	.040	nil.	nil.	0.005	nil.					
14	" a	.200	.100	.054	.100	.025					
15	"	.01	.005	.005	.016	.002					
16	"	.18	.005	.02	.04	.002					
17	"	.06	.016	.01	.18	.01					
18	"	.11	.021	.07	.03	.02					
19	"	.06	.02	.005	.02	nil.					
20	"	.05	.02	nil.	.04	.006					
21	"	.05	.023	.008	.017	nil.					
22	"	.05	.02	nil.	.02	.01					
23	American	.08	.10	tr.	.05	.09					
24	"	.03	.25	.008	.01	.01					
25	"	.05	.21	.009	.01	.02					
26	"	.12	.19	.01	.01	.008					

(a) Made from cast-iron, containing carbon, 4.00 to 4.50 %, silicon, 0.20 to 0.50 %, manganese, trace to 1.80 %, phosphorus, 0.01 to 0.15 %, sulphur, 0.02 to 0.08 %.
1 to **9**, Styffe, Iron and Steel, pp. 132, 138, 140, 1869.
10 to **12**, Percy, Iron and Steel, p. 736, 1864.
13 and **14**, Bell, Princ. Manuf. Iron and Steel, p. 345, 1884.
15 to **26**, G. H. Billings, Private Communication, April 7, 1889.

Charcoal-hearth iron, then, is in a manner intermediate between common wrought-iron and ingot-iron in that it is remelted and cast while molten into a malleable mass; but instead of being cast into a slagless-mould as in true ingot-metal-making processes, it is poured upon a bath of slag of which a very little inevitably becomes mixed with the metal.

But while it is clear why charcoal-hearth iron is tougher than puddled iron, it is not so easy to see why it is tougher than ingot-iron, unless we hold that the small quantity of slag in charcoal-hearth iron promotes toughness while the larger quantity in puddled iron opposes toughness. The conditions under which the charcoal-hearth iron is melted and, as it were, cast within the hearth, are very different from those which attend the casting of ingot-iron. Charcoal-hearth iron is raised but slightly above its melting point, and for a few moments only; is cast drop by drop through an atmosphere rich in carbonic oxide and carbonic acid into a white-hot bath of slag, falling in all but a few inches: ingot-iron is held for a very considerable length of time far above its melting point, is cast in a thick stream, through a cold atmosphere of oxygen and nitrogen, usually into a cold cast-iron mould, often falling several feet. In the charcoal-hearth drop of metal follows drop in such a way that neither pipe nor blowhole nor microscopic cavity seems to form; ingot-metal is so cast that pipes or blowholes or microscopic cavities or all three arise. Charcoal-hearth iron is purposely kept as free as possible from slag, ingot-metal is purposely kept practically absolutely free from slag.

I will not attempt to say to which, if to any, of these differences the apparently very considerable difference between the properties of ingot-iron and of those of charcoal-hearth iron is due, nor even that it is due to any of these rather than to other and unnoticed differences. I will not even insist that there is a real difference in quality. We know that the properties of tough-pitch copper are influenced very greatly and obscurely by the conditions preceding and attending casting.

The apparent superiority of charcoal-hearth to ingot-iron can hardly be attributed to greater freedom from carbon, silicon, phosphorus, etc., if we may judge by the analyses in Table 167.

Uncertain whether the conditions of the charcoal-hearth give better quality than we can obtain in ingot-metal, we may not, like so many superficial observers, predict the early disappearance of the process.

Here is a case which exemplifies the curious and anomalous facts, or at least beliefs, touching the properties of charcoal-hearth and ingot-iron. For making screws charcoal-hearth iron is used because, so it is said, ingot-iron is not tough enough to endure the upsetting which arises in forming the head of the screw. But the charcoal-hearth iron used is purposely rather brittle, is intentionally made from rather phosphoric cast-iron, so that the shaving formed in cutting the thread may break off short, and not interfere with the cutting tool. Now we are told that charcoal-iron endures upsetting better than ingot-iron, and at the same time its shavings break off more aptly; in brief, it is tougher in the head but shorter in the thread! Some of these paradoxical beliefs turn out on investigation to be mere superstitions, others to be true, due now to simple now to obscure conditions. How it is with this one I know not.

Fig. 148. AMERICAN-SWEDISH-LANCASHIRE HEARTH.

It is doubtful whether the charcoal-hearth removes phosphorus as thoroughly as the puddling process, for its atmosphere seems much less powerfully oxidizing. This appears to more than outweigh the usually greater basicity of its slag, and the more thorough removal of the slag from which, as long as it is present, the iron may reabsorb phosphorus at high temperatures, as in reheating.

Thanks to the excellence of its product charcoal-hearth refining seems to hold its own pretty well, at least if we include the balling of scrap wrought-iron in charcoal-hearths. The output of charcoal blooms from cast-iron and scrap together in this country was greater in 1887 than in any of the years from 1874 to 1878; the output of the Swedish charcoal-hearths increased by about 60 per cent.

between 1860 and 1880. In South Wales the charcoal-hearth has been used very extensively for making iron for tin plates, but there mild steel is now driving it out of the field.

In the Austrian Alps and in Russia it is still used extensively, I understand. The following table gives data concerning the extent to which it is used:

TABLE 168.—PRODUCTION OF BLOOMS BY REFINING CAST-IRON IN CHARCOAL-HEARTHS.

YEAR.	United States. (Blooms from Cast-iron and Scrap.)		Sweden.	
	Number of Hearths.	Output. Net Tons.	Number of Hearths.	Output. Net Tons.
1860			1,390b	194,238
1874		35,330		
1877		28,073		
1880		34,987	729b	198,915
1882		42,989		
1884	68a	27,216		
1885		21,813		
1887		28,216		
1888		25,787		

a This does not include charcoal-hearths which make blooms for use in the plate, sheet and wire-making mills with which they are connected.
b Hearths and furnaces.
United States, from Ann. Statistical Rept. Am. Iron and Steel Ass., 1888, p. 37, and J. M. Swank, private communication.
Sweden, from Ehrenwerth, Das Eisenhüttenwesen Schwedens, p. 96, 1885, from Åkerman.

Table 169 shows that some of the American charcoal-hearth establisments existing and even running at present are extremely old, and that the development of the industry, as judged from the number of establishments built, was most rapid between 1870 and 1880.

TABLE 169.—AGE OF THE CHARCOAL-HEARTHS EXISTING NOW OR LATELY IN THE UNITED STATES.z

			Of those built in the several periods of Column 1, the following numbers were		
Years.	No. Built.	No. Rebuilt.	Abandoned apparently between 1883 and 1888.	Idle in 1887, but apparently not abandoned.	Running in 1887.
1755… 1799…	6		4		2
1800… 1819…	6		3	1	2
1820… 1829…	4		3		1
1830… 1839…	6		2		4
1840… 1849…	6		3	1	2
1850… 1859…	0	0			
1860… 1869…	7	2		3	6
1870… 1879…	10	2	4(?)		8
1880	1			1	
1883	1				1
1884	1	1	1		1
1885	1				1
1887	1				1
1888	0	0			

z One may not safely infer that the original hearths still exist in these establishments; they may have been built, rebuilt or replaced, but at least the original establishments exist.

Bell estimates the cost of making 2,240 pounds of charcoal hearth bar iron in Sweden as follows:

TABLE 170.—COST OF MAKING CHARCOAL-HEARTH IRON IN SWEDEN. *Bell*.b

2,912 pounds	Cast-iron @ $14.52 per 2,240 lbs.	$18 82
3,080 "	Charcoal @ $4.84 " " "	6 68
	Labor	5 57
	Total	$31 07

b Princ. Manuf. Iron and Steel, p. 347, 1884.

The data in Table 171 indicate that the cost of the manufacture of blooms, assuming Bell's prices, is much less, to wit:

2,575 pounds of	Cast-iron @ $14,52 per ton	$16 69
1,120 "	Charcoal @ $4.84 " "	2 42
	Labor, 2 days @ $1.25 d	2 50
		$21 61

d Bell does not give the rate of wages.

As the data in Table 171 show, important economies have been reached since the time of Percy's description of the process. Thus we see that the output of the Lancashire hearths per 24 hours has doubled, while the consumption of fuel per ton of blooms is but half as great as formerly. The loss of iron remains the same as of old.

TABLE 171.—CHARCOAL-HEARTH REFINING.

	Single-smelting.	Double-smelting process. Swedish Walloon.			Double-smelting process. Swedish Lancashire hearth. In Sweden.						United States.	Triple-smelting Process. German.	Triple-smelting Process. Franche-Comté.	Scrap-balling process, United States.
	I. Siegen, before 1875.	II. Sweden, before 1864.	III. Sweden, Dannemora, about 1873.	IV. Sweden, Dannemora about 1884.	V. Before 1864.	VI. Before 1875.	VII. Nyby, 1884.±	VIII. Ramnäs, 1884.	IX. Domnarfvet 1882.	X. Bell, before 1884.	XI. 1889.	XII. Before 1875.	XIII. Before 1875.	XIV. 1889.
DIMENSIONS OF HEARTH— Width and length	21″ × 30″	22″ @ 24″ × 32″ @ 35″		20¾″ × 17¾″			24¼″ × 22″	23⅝ × 21¼″	25¼ × 21⅛″		25¼″ × 23⅝″		25⅝″ × 20⅝″	25¼″ × 22⅛″
Height to tuyere									7⅛″		8″		9¼″	8″
" above tuyere								7¾″						
" total "	30″						7¼″							
BLAST— Pressure, ounces per sq. inch				13.6	19.5	24.7	16.9-20.4	17.9-19.1	19.1				14.2 to 15.1	
Temperature C / F		cold.		cold.	100°C 212°F	100°@200°C 212°@392°F	150°C 302°F	80° @ 100°C 176° @ 212°F	50° @ 90°C 122°@194°F	100°C 212°F	85° @ 100°C 185° @ 212°F		112° @ 125C 233.6° @ 257°F	85° @ 100°C 185°@212°F
Size of tuyere, nozzle		1.4×1.8″		.8″×1.45″		5 sq. in.	.9″×0.7″	0.7″×.91″	0.7″×0.9″		¾″		1″×1.5″	¾″
Inclination of tuyere				3°			5° @ 6°	30	12°					
Number of tuyeres	1					2	3		2					
Grade of pig-iron		White or mottled.	white or mottled.	white.		mottled.		half white, half mottled to gray			⅛% Si. mottled.	gray.		
Length of one heat		25′ @ 30′			1hr.15′ @ 1hr.30′		1 hr.	1 hr. 25′			1 hr. 15′	4 @ 6 hrs.	2 hours 25′	37′
LABOR— Men per hearth per shift		3					2	2	2	2 @ 3	2			2
Length of one shift		8 hours.					8 hrs.							
Number of heats per 24 hours		40 a c			14 c		14±	20	21		14	4	9	28
OUTPUT PER HEARTH— Weight of blooms per heat, pounds		56 a c		93 @ 84	173.5 c	130 @ 216	226	261	231		244	136	159	285
Weight of blooms per 24 hrs., pounds	1466.2	2240 a c	3123-4666 a	3685 a	2461 c	2500 to 4700	3169	5201	4903	2613 to 5600	3410	894	1582	7988
OUTLAY PER 2,000 POUNDS BLOOMS— Bushels charcoal	109.5 b	551 a	366 @ 561 a b	387 a b	157	b102 @ 146	39 b	soft 86 b	83 b	114 d		106 a b	132.5	37
Charcoal, pounds	1204.5 b	6000 a	4026 @ 6171 a b	4253 a b	1800	b1120 @ 1606	845 b	947 b	913 b	1250		1168 a b	1468.5	405
Cast-iron, pounds	2667	2500 a		2030 a	2305	2293	2229	2300	2293	2299	2299	2722	2548	2321
Labor, days		5.4 c a					2.5	1.5	1.6	1.5 to 1.7	2.3			1
LOSS— From cast-iron to blooms, per 100 of cast-iron	25%	20% e		24.2% e	13.25%	13%	13%	13.04%	12.77%	13%	13%	25 @ 28%	20 @ 23%	13.55%

a This is the consumption per 2,000 lbs. of bars, not blooms.
b It is assumed that a bushel of 2,500 cubic in. weighs 11 lbs.: then 1 m^3 = 24 bushels. The original gives the measure of charcoal, but not the weight.
c There seems to be a slight discrepancy between the output, the charge, and the loss.
d The same assumption as in b: the weight of charcoal is given, but not the measure.
e This is the loss from cast-iron to bars, not blooms.

I., Kerl, Grundiss der Eisenhüttenkunde, p. 340, 1875.
II., Percy, Iron and Steel, p. 599, 1864.
III., Kerl, op. cit., p. 338.
IV., Ehrenwerth, das Eisenhüttenwesen Schwedens, p. 32, 1885.
V., Percy, op. cit., p. 591.
VI., Kerl, op. cit., p. 338.
VII., VIII. and IX., Ehrenwerth, op. cit., pp. 27, 68, 45.
X., Bell, Princ. Manuf. Iron and Steel, p. 346, 1884.
XI., From the author's Notes.
XII. XIII., Kerl, op. cit., pp. 334, 336.
XIV., From the author's Notes.

§ 348. Classification.—The charcoal-hearth processes are classified according to the number of times that the metal is melted down before the tuyere into the single-, the double- and the triple-smelting classes (Einmalschmelzerei, Zweimalschmelzerei, and Dreimalschmelzerei or German or breaking up [Aufbrechschmiede] class).

The number of smeltings needed depends chiefly on the proportion of carbon, silicon and manganese to be removed, and also, but to a smaller extent, on the desired thoroughness of decarburization, etc. Hence the single smelting is chiefly applicable to white cast-iron and to iron already partly refined: the double smelting to mottled iron, or to white or previously partly refined iron when an extremely pure product is sought: the triple smelting to mottled or to gray iron.

The processes are also divided into the Walloon and non-Walloon classes. The ground of this distinction seems to be a little in dispute. Tunner classes as Walloon all those processes in which the bloom is reheated in a separate hearth, an arrangement which leads to a smaller consumption of charcoal, as mineral fuel, sawdust, etc., may be used for reheating. But this is not true of the Swedish Walloon process. Kerl appears to class all double-smelting processes as Walloon.

Tunner recognizes no less than fourteen kinds of wrought-iron making types of charcoal-hearth refining processes, and five more steel making: but we need concern ourselves only with those given in Table 171, which are,

Single smelting.
Double Smelting. { Swedish Walloon. / English Walloon. { Lancashire. / South Wales.
Triple smelting, e. g. Franche-Comté

Of these the Swedish Walloon (called in Sweden, plain "Walloon") is used in Sweden solely and exclusively for making bars from Dannemora cast-iron which are to be converted into blister steel. Changes in the procedure have long been and I believe are still prohibited by contract with the English consignees, lest the quality of the product be injured. However faithfully the spirit of this contract may be kept, the data in columns II. to IV. of Table 171 indicate that its letter has been violated, for the output per hearth per 24 hours has increased greatly, while the consumption of fuel has fallen off, since Percy's great work was written.

This process is more expensive than the Lancashire, using, say, four times as much charcoal and much more labor. One would naturally suppose that the excellence of the Dannemora iron was due rather to the excellence of the ore, notably its remarkable freedom from phosphorus, and to the thorough roasting which it undergoes, than to the use of the Swedish Walloon instead of the Lancashire process. The vastly greater fuel-consumption of the former should indeed be detrimental as opposing the removal of phosphorus, of which a little is reported even in the Dannemora iron (see Table 167). Moreover, the Swedish Walloon iron is probably much less homogeneous than the Lancashire-hearth iron.

Nearly if not quite all the charcoal-hearth iron made in Sweden, other than Dannemora iron for cementation, is made by the Lancashire process, and much Dannemora iron not intended for cementation is thus made. This process is also used extensively in this country. Whether it has ever been used in Lancashire I know not. It was brought to Sweden by Welsh workmen, and to this country by Swedes. The South Wales process was used extensively, and actually in South Wales, notably for making plates for tinning. But it has been driven out of that district to a great extent, if not altogether, by the Bessemer and open-hearth processes.

§ 349. Example of the Single-Smelting Process.—The white-iron pigs, much as shown at the right of Figure 149, are gradually pushed forward towards the tuyere as their hotter ends melt away, and the iron is almost completely decarburized as it trickles past the tuyere. It collects as a ball on the oxide-bottom. Imperfectly refined parts are broken off and melted again: the ball is drawn and hammered: the billets from the preceding charge are heated in the same fire.

§ 350. In the Lancashire-Hearth Process[a] three periods are distinguished:

1, the preheated cast-iron is melted down before the tuyeres (say 15 minutes);

2, the pasty mass which the collecting drops form is constantly broken up by prying from beneath, and the slag is thereby mixed with it (20 to 30 minutes);

3, the almost decarburized mass is raised above the charcoal and gradually melted down, collecting beneath in a ball which is drawn and hammered (25 to 30 minutes).

The hearth is wholly lined with naked, unprotected, cast-iron plates, the bottom and preferably the sides being water-jacketed. In American practice a bottom-plate lasts about four weeks, and the others about twice as long.

In some American Swedish Lancashire-hearths, Figures 147, 148, whose work is given in column XI. of Table 171, the whole of the roof and sides are formed by one or two heavy castings, K K, Figure 148, which are full to the top with water. Figure 148, which is from a photograph of the hearths represented in Figure 147, further shows the tools used, and the actual form of double-elbowed blast-pipe, which enables us to withdraw the tuyere readily. The products of combustion pass first into the fire-brick ells M M, in which they heat the blast, whose entrance is effected through the pipe O, and regulated by the dampers P. By shifting these dampers we can send the blast through the blast-heating pipes, or directly to the tuyeres without preheating, or in readily variable proportion through both paths simultaneously. From these ells the products of combustion pass beneath the boilers, which stand behind and beneath the blast-main R. The lattice L, designed to hold in the charcoal and to protect the workmen in some measure, was not in use at the time of my visit.

The charcoal is added and nearly all the work is done through the wide-open doorway X X, through which an enormous excess of air rushes, greatly lessening the heating power of the products of combustion.

a According to Percy this is a misnomer, as the process was imported into Sweden from South Wales in 1829. (Iron and Steel, p. 598, A.D. 1864.)

Description of Process.—I will now describe the practice which I have seen in this country; it corresponds closely to the Swedish.

Preparatory.—275 pounds of pig-iron in lumps up to one foot long are preheated on the shelf B, while the preceding charge is working. The ball being drawn, the hearth is cleaned, and the quantity of slag present ascertained. If there is not enough to cover the bottom-plate E thoroughly, slag is added. It is essential that there should be enough for this purpose, lest the molten iron should strike and attach itself to this plate.

1st Period.—The hearth is next filled to about one foot above the tuyeres with charcoal, and on this the now red-hot pigs are drawn from the shelf B. The blast is turned on; the pigs are covered with charcoal. During the whole operation charcoal is added every few minutes, and on it is thrown water by the pan S, partly that the workman may work at the hearth without excessive discomfort, partly that the charcoal and carbonic oxide may not burn uselessly at the top of the fire, and that the carbonic oxide may be preserved to burn beyond, in the flue under the boiler. The melting pigs tend to sink down as the charcoal beneath them burns away; they must therefore be lifted a little every few minutes, so that the drops which trickle from them may pass through the oxidizing core of the region of combustion. But for this they would soon sink down to the bottom of the hearth, and the fusion would lose its oxidizing character, which is due wholly to the passage of the molten metal, drop by drop, throug h the most strongly oxidizing part of the hearth.

As the mass, now considerably decarburized, collects at the bottom of the hearth, it is so far cooled by the neighborhood of the water-cooled bottom-plate that it becomes decidedly pasty; thus any given particle of metal is only fluid during the brief period when it is dropping from the still unmelted portion above to join the previously melted but now partly resolidified mass beneath.

If too much slag be present, the gradual accumulation of metal on the bottom raises the slag-level so high that the entrance of the blast is impeded; this may be recognized by a peculiar fluttering noise which the blast makes. In this case the excess of slag must be tapped out through H; but as it is not easy to judge just how much is excess, the whole of the molten part of the slag may be tapped out, and enough slag returned to cover the bottom fully when the second fusion occurs.

Up to this point one man only works at the hearth, but two are at work during the whole of the second period.

2d Period.—When the whole charge seems to have melted down and collected thus at the bottom of the hearth, the workman feels about in the charcoal with the hook T, to find any still unmelted lumps. He now begins lifting up the pasty lump with the light bar U, running its point along the face of the bottom-plate so that no scattered pieces may escape him, and from now on throughout the second period this lifting is continued with but brief interruptions; indeed, during part of the time both workmen are prying simultaneously, one at each side of the hearth. Running the point of his bar beneath the mass the workman bears down, using the inner edge of the fore-plate *A* as a fulcrum, and raises the mass by from three to five inches from the bottom-plate. Into the space thus left falls some charcoal, runs some molten slag, and pierces the blast. As the workman moves his bar from this point to another, the pasty mass gradually sinks back again, and must soon again be raised.

In prying the mass up the workman's bar cuts deeply into it, carrying some of the slag which had collected beneath the metallic lump; thus slag, cooled to pastiness by the bottom-plate, and pasty metal are intimately mixed, and thus the fining action of slag on metal is promoted. The iron-oxide of the slag gives up oxygen to the carbon, silicon and phosphorus of the metal, and when the blast again penetrates again absorbs oxygen from the atmosphere, to be again given up. The pasty mass is not only indented from beneath by this prying, but broken up here and there. It is reunited not only by the same prying from beneath, but also as the workman pries the metallic lumps horizontally from around the tuyeres towards the centre of the hearth, for pains must be taken at all times that the tuyeres are clear and that the blast issues freely. At first the metal, soft and barely pasty, is lifted readily; as fining progresses it becomes stiffer and stiffer, and soon a powerful pressure is needed to raise it.

Towards the end of this period the carbonic oxide comes off so rapidly that the fine charcoal lying above the metal seems to boil, so energetically is it stirred by the escaping gas.

The indications of progress are chiefly the consistency of the metal just noted, and the color and consistency of the slag. At first the coating of slag seen on the bar as it is drawn from the fire is sluggish and reddish, sluggish because silicious and relatively cool; reddish because relatively cool and apparently because sluggish, the outer air-cooled layer remaining outside and concealing the hotter interior. Later it grows ever thinner and whiter; thinner because more basic (with decreasing proportion of carbon and silicon in the metal, iron oxidizes more readily and is less readily deoxidized), and because hotter (the oxidation of carbon, silicon and iron as well as of the charcoal ever raising the temperature); whiter because hotter and probably because thinner, moving quickly with shifting positions of the bar, so that the hotter interior comes readily to the surface.

When the metal appears from these indications to have "come to nature," *i.e.*, to be almost wholly decarburized, the third period begins.

3d Period.—The lump is now broken into several pieces, which are lifted above the tuyere, much of the metal indeed reposing on top of the charcoal. A bar U is introduced through the opening V, behind one of the tuyeres, to break off any lumps adhering to the back of the hearth. This is the first time that the metal has been visible since charging, having meanwhile been covered with charcoal. From this point till the ball is to be pried out of the hearth, only one man is at work.

This period is essentially a remelting, and the work is

similar to that in the first period. As fast as the lumps which are to be melted sink down owing to the burning away of the charcoal beneath, they must be pried up so as to keep them well above the mass which is collecting at the bottom as fusion proceeds (call this the lower mass), and so that the metal in melting may as before drop through the current of air thrown in by the tuyeres. The workman is very careful not to touch the lower mass with his bar, lest he force slag into it, and so defeat the chief object of this period, the elimination of the slag.

During the first part of this second fusion the lower mass is so small that the molten slag protects it from the carburizing action of the charcoal; but by the time that say two-thirds of the metal has reached it, it has outgrown the covering capacity of the slag, and more slag must be added. That actually added is hammer-slag from hammering the charcoal-hearth blooms. It is thrown on the shoulders of the lower mass, and, thanks to its high state of oxidation (which the blast maintains), it is so pasty that it does not all run down, but a layer of it remains and covers the shoulders of the lower mass, and wards off the carburizing action of the charcoal.

During all this time, be it remembered, the workman is occasionally prying up the upper mass, to keep it out of contact with the lower.

The upper mass being nearly all melted, the scattered lumps are raked together and welded to the lower mass with light taps of the hook T. The blast is slackened, and the glowing bloom is pried out from the hearth by both workmen, who bear down on the heavy bar W. Nearly the whole of the slag comes out with the ball, in a layer whose lower side is nearly smooth, showing the shape of the bottom-plate, but whose thickness is naturally very irregular, being on an average perhaps three inches. The slag does not adhere so strongly but that it could be pried off in large lumps; this is not done, however. All of the slag falls off when the ball is hammered. In hammering, all imperfectly refined parts are cut off, and returned to the hearth.

The hammered ball is reheated in another furnace; we need not follow it further.

Here is the diary of an operation which I saw in March, 1889:

DIARY OF A LANCASHIRE HEARTH REFINING.

Preceding ball drawn	11h. 57m.
Hearth cleaned till	11h. 58m.
1st Period. Redhot pigs drawn from the flue from	11h. 58m. till 12h. 00m.
Blast turned on: pigs covered with charcoal; pigs lifted occasionally; charcoal added and water thrown on.	
2d Period. All melted at	12h. 14m.
Both men pry lump almost constantly; charcoal added frequently; water thrown on occasionally.	
Metal has come to nature	12h. 33m.
3d Period. The lump is broken up and lifted above the tuyeres, protruding far above the charcoal	12h. 37m.
Begins melting again	12h. 41m.
Bar introduced by one workman horizontally, to keep upper mass up; charcoal charged occasionally; water added; hammer-slag charged.	
Small pieces raked together	12h. 59m.
Loose pieces balled to main mass	1h. 00m.
Blast stopped	1h. 01m.
Ball pried up and drawn	1h. 01m. to 1h. 02m.
Begin hammering	1h. 03m.
End hammering	1h. 05m.

§ 351. IN THE SOUTH WALES PROCESS the cast-iron is first melted down in a coke refinery or run-out fire, and there part of its silicon and carbon are removed by the action of the blast. It is then tapped out into a pair of charcoal-hearths, the relatively acid slag being held back, and any which runs into the charcoal-hearth being carefully removed. The partly solidified metal is broken up and piled near the tuyere. After melting down it is repeatedly raised slightly from the bottom, apparently as in the Lancashire process. The slag is tapped off from time to time. As soon as the metal has "come to nature," *i.e.*, is thoroughly decarburized, it is withdrawn and hammered.

This process thus lacks the descorifying final melting of the Lancashire process.

I have met no late description of the South Wales process. Greenwood, indeed, states that the charge in the coke refinery is from 5 to 6 cwts. of cast-iron, and that a charge lasts a little over an hour.[1] These agree with Percy's statements made in 1864; whether they are simple copies, or whether the process has remained stationary, I know not.

§ 352. IN THE SWEDISH-WALLOON PROCESS one or two very long pigs of white or mottled cast-iron (*a*, Figure 149), are melted down drop by drop, being pushed forward as fast as their ends melt off, till enough to yield a bloom of from say 84 to 93 pounds has been melted. This may take some twenty minutes, during which the pasty metal, gradually reaching the bottom of the hearth, is worked constantly. The pasty mass is now broken up, raised above the tuyere, and melted a second time, apparently much as in the Lancashire method. During this time the bloom from the preceding charge is heated in this same hearth, held steeply inclined as shown in Figure 149.

This process differs chiefly from the Lancashire process in that the bloom is reheated in the hearth in which it is made, in that the charge is very small, and that the cast-iron, instead of being introduced all at once, is gradually pushed forward. From this last it happens that the interval between the melting of the first and that of the last part of a given charge bears a much greater proportion to the total length of the heat in the Swedish-Walloon than in the Lancashire process. Indeed, from printed and oral descriptions of the former process, I infer that the pasty mass is broken up for remelting immediately after the last of the cast-iron has melted. Hence the first-melted part of the metal is much further decarburized when the remelting begins than the last-melted part; and I am informed that the heterogeneousness thus introduced survives the remelting to a very considerable extent, *i.e.*, that the product is decidedly heterogeneous.

§ 353. IN THE FRANCHE-COMTÉ PROCESS the pigs of gray cast-iron are melted down as in the Swedish-Walloon process, Figure 149, *i. e.*, are gradually pushed forward as their ends melt off. This continues for about 90 minutes or less, during which the bloom from the preceding charge, having been cut in two, is reheated in the same hearth and forged, three heatings and forgings being needed for each half bloom. The pasty mass which has meanwhile accumulated on the hearth bottom, is now lifted above the tuyeres and gradually melted down, falling drop by drop past the tuyere. This occupies some 20 to 25 minutes more. Those parts of the mass resulting from this second fusion which are still imperfectly decarburized, must be raised up and melted down a third time.

[1] Steel and Iron, p. 223, 1884.

The hearth is usually covered, and the sensible heat of the products of combustion is utilized somewhat as in the Lancashire hearth.

The distinctive features of this process, then, are that the bloom from the preceding heat is reheated in the refining hearth; that gray cast-iron is used; that the pigs are pushed forward in melting instead of being charged all at once; that the metal or part of it is melted thrice; that the hearth is covered, and its waste heat utilized.

§ 354. MELTING SCRAP-IRON IN THE LANCASHIRE HEARTH (Cf. Table 171, Col. XIV.).—Owing to the relative prices of scrap malleable iron (steel and wrought iron) and of pure cast-iron, most of the American-Lancashire hearths now treat the former material exclusively.

The process is practically the third period of the cast-iron refining process already described. The ball from the previous operation being drawn, the hearth is cleaned and partly filled with charcoal, and cold malleable-iron scrap is thrown on it. If, as often happens, much light scrap is used, such as sheet-iron clippings, broken wire from wire-drawing establishments, etc., this is charged first, and after a few minutes whatever heavy scrap is at hand. The charge is covered with charcoal as before and melted down, the chief work being to raise the upper mass (the still unmelted part) occasionally, so that the blast may enter between it and the lower mass (*i. e.*, the metal which has melted, dropped, and accumulated on the bottom), and care is taken not to touch the lower mass with the tools, lest slag become mixed with it. As soon as all the material has reached the lower mass, this is pried out and hammered, quite as in the case of cast-iron.

In the last six months of 1888 the loss from scrap to cropped billets at an American mill was 22.75%, of which the croppings formed 0.66%, and 9.20% occurred in the two reheatings and hammerings which followed the hammering of the ball, so that the loss from scrap to hammered bloom was 12.89%. As most of the scrap was thin, with much surface, this loss is certainly small. Column XIV., Table 171, represents practice at this mill.

As the scrap is nearly free from silicon and silica, the slags are more basic than in treating cast-iron. There is thus a considerable fining, and I am informed that about 10 to 15% of the phosphorus present is removed, that the sulphur, even if initially as high as 0.10%, falls to a mere trace, and that the carbon, even if initially as high as 0.40%, usually falls to about 0.03%.

The operation is of course much more rapid than fining cast-iron, and fourteen heats are made per shift instead of seven, by two workmen.

The cast-iron plates which line the hearth last much longer, three or four times as long, as when cast-iron is treated. The difference is probably due to the fact that in the latter case the product of the first fusion, being much more fusible, and hence remaining fluid longer, penetrates to the lining-plates to a greater extent. Further, the energetic prying and scraping along the bottom during the second period of the treatment of cast-iron probably tend to wear the bottom plate out.

As the plates are less attacked, and as the addition of a little silica to the very basic slags formed in treating scrap-iron is less to be dreaded than in treating cast-iron, so the rear lining-plate is usually omitted, the brick-work of the rear wall being exposed to the heat.

§ 355. STEEL.—It is much harder to make weld-steel than wrought-iron in the charcoal-hearth, for, instead of carrying decarburization as far as it can go, we have to interrupt it at a given point, and there is little to indicate when this point is reached. Here, as in making puddled steel, the decarburization must proceed slowly in order that we may interrupt it with more certainty. Further, in limiting the final action which removes the carbon, we also limit the removal of phosphorus; hence, and because phosphorus is more hurtful to weld-steel than to wrought-iron, especially pure cast-iron should be used for making charcoal-hearth steel.

In order to retard the decarburization we use, when making weld-steel, an abundance of a liquid and less strongly fining slag than when wrought-iron is aimed at, less strongly fining through carrying less iron-oxide, and instead carrying more silica or more manganese. The slag is made manganiferous either through the direct addition of oxide or silicate of manganese, or by using manganiferous cast-iron. Manganese-silicate is less strongly fining than iron-silicate for reasons already given.

CHAPTER XVII.

THE CRUCIBLE PROCESS.

§ 356. THE CRUCIBLE STEEL PROCESS in its broadest sense consists, 1st, in melting iron of like or unlike carbon-content, and with or without carburizing or decarburizing additions, in crucibles; 2d, in tranquilizing the molten mass so that it may yield compact castings, either by holding it molten so that it may absorb silicon from the crucible walls, or by the addition of ferro-aluminium or other quieting substance; 3d, in casting or "teeming" into ingots or other forms.

Of this process the most important varieties are:—

1, *Huntsman's*, the original method, in which small pieces of blister or other highly carburetted steel are melted alone, or with a slag-making flux (*e. g.*, glass).

2, *Josiah Marshall Heath's*[a] modification of adding manganese, either previously reduced by heating its oxide with carbonaceous matter, or reduced in the process itself by the action of charcoal on oxide of manganese.

Huntsman's method thus modified, it is said, is now the prevalent one in Sheffield.

3, *The carburizing-fusion* (or cementing-fusion) method, in which the percentage of carbon in the product is regulated by the addition of carbonaceous matter (practically

[a] For an account of Heath's invention and litigation, Cf. Percy, Iron and Steel, p. 840. Percy concludes, apparently quite justly, that Heath's invention virtually covered the present method of using a mixture of charcoal and oxide of manganese, though the courts held otherwise.

charcoal), is said to have been used in the last century by Chalut and Clouet[b], and is the prevalent method in this country.

4, *Uchatius'*, or the pig and ore method, of melting granulated cast-iron with iron ore, till lately, if not now, practiced at Wykmanshyttan in Sweden.

5, The *pig and scrap method* of melting wrought-iron or steel, or both, raising the proportion of carbon by adding cast-iron.

In all the above methods the molten metal is tranquilized by killing, *i. e.*, holding it molten, so as to yield sound ingots.

6, *The Mitis method*, in which the charge originally constituted in any of the above ways, is tranquilized by the addition of ferro-aluminium immediately after fusion, and is teemed a few minutes later.

7, *The basic method*, or fusion in basic instead of silicious crucibles, while it has not been worked out so far as I know, is likely to be tried in the near future.

TABLE 178.—COMPOSITION OF SLAG OF THE CRUCIBLE PROCESS.

		SiO_2	P_2O_5	FeO.	Fe_2O_3	MnO	Al_2O_3	CaO.	MgO	S	Ca	S	Alkalies
1	L.	44.40	.....	1.08	.....	24.04	28.80	0.87	tr.	.....	.99	.93	.....
2	M.	41.24	.....	2.22	.....	18.45	35.85	.....	.....	.....	.....	.....	.....
3	M.	40.86	.....	4.06	.....	50.52	.....	.....	.....	.....	.....	.....	.....
4	B.	43.36	.....	4.41	2.66	17.43	18.05	7.74	.....	.....	.....	.....	4.11
5	B.	3.73	.80	34.10	1.51	6.40	tr.	25.73	27.43	.....	.....	.....	.....

1. Bochum, Ledebur, Handbuch, p. 856. Slag present during teeming.
2. Slag accompanying steel, No. 46 of Table 179. Lumps, gray; powder, nearly white. Insoluble in hydrochloric acid. Müller, Stahl und Eisen, VI., p. 698, 1886.
3. Slag of steel 41, Table 179; color, gray. Idem, p. 698.
4. Slag of steel 72, in Table 180; dark, brown gray, translucent; very brittle; vitreous; Sp. Gr. 3.11. Insoluble in acids. Brand, Berg und Hütten, Zeit., XLIV., p. 108, 1885.
5. Slag from No. 53, Table 180 (basic). Hardly melted, brown-gray with violet sheen, porous, with shots of iron; powder light brown. Sp. Gr., 4.11, Idem. p. 119.

§ 357. THE CRUCIBLE AND OTHER PROCESSES COMPARED.—The crucible process is on the one hand very much more costly than the Bessemer and open-hearth processes, both as to material and cost of conversion, as to labor, fuel and refractory materials. On the other hand, its product is apparently justly thought much better than that of these other processes, even for like composition. Its costliness limits it to the production of steel of high quality, designed for cutting-tools, springs, fire-arms, etc. It affords less control over the percentage of carbon in the product than either the Bessemer or the open-hearth process. Hence, when making large castings by pouring together the contents of several crucibles, to insure homogeneousness we should observe certain precautions, which are needed to a much smaller degree, if at all, in the Bessemer and open-hearth processes. When a very great number of crucible-fuls are poured together, the differences in composition probably nearly offset each other: this should be the case with Krupp's guns, which are said to be made wholly of crucible steel; but when a smaller number of crucible-fuls are poured into a single casting, it would seem desirable to mix them thoroughly, *e. g.*, by pouring into a common mixing ladle, from which the casting is teemed.

It is not easy to see why crucible should be better than Bessemer and open-hearth steel of like composition. The crucible differs from the open-hearth process,

1, In treating smaller charges;

2, In usually treating material which is not only purer but less liable to occasional serious impurity;

3, In nearly completely excluding the fire-gases;

4, In exposing the charge to a clay instead of a silica lining;

5, In being under less perfect control as to temperature, additions, time, etc. This sounds heretical, but I am convinced that it is true. In the open-hearth furnace the charge is ever open to easy inspection, so that we readily determine what additions and what changes in temperature are needed at a given instant. The closed crucible cannot, as the process is usually carried out, be thus examined readily at short intervals, and practically we are confined to a single examination; though it is not absolutely necessary that we should be so restricted. The Bessemer process is under as good control as the open-hearth.

Of these differences we summarily reject the first, fourth and fifth, as wholly improbable causes of superiority.

The second does not bear on the question of the relative merits of crucible and other steel of given composition.

The exclusion of the fire-gases, in that it prevents the absorption of sulphur from them, is in the same way beside the present point. But it may well be, as Metcalf conjectures (§ 174, p. 109), that the greater opportunity which the open-hearth and especially the Bessemer process offers for the absorption of nitrogen (and hydrogen he might add) injures their product. Whatever be the reason, there seems to be little doubt that crucible steel is better than Bessemer and open-hearth steel of like composition as actually made. However, as its superiority is unexplained, we cannot now tell whether it is due to conditions unattainable in the competing processes, or to conditions which, though as yet overlooked, are still attainable. If to the latter, we may expect that, once the needed conditions are known, the improvement of our dephosphorizing processes, basic open-hearth and Bessemer, Bell-Krupp washing, etc., will gradually bring the quality of the product of these cheaper processes up to that of crucible steel, and thus remove the reason for the existence of the crucible process.

The belief in the superiority of crucible steel of like composition rests rather on general observation than on conclusive direct evidence, and it must be confessed that the quality of much of this evidence is not of the best: this, however, from the nature of the case is almost unavoidable; but the quantity of evidence goes far to make up for its quality. Some of the evidence, however, cannot be simply ignored. Thus, eminent steel-makers assure us that Bessemer and open-hearth steel remelted in crucibles is little, if at all, better than before. A very distinguished maker of both crucible and Bessemer steel assures me that he finds much of the Bessemer and open-hearth tool-steel, of which great quantities are actually sold, almost as pure as the best crucible steel, yet hardly as good as the much less pure common grades of spring crucible steel. I am informed that the only American open-hearth tool-steel plant has lately been sold to a maker of springs.

Bessemer's assertion[a] that half the crucible steel in

[b] Gruner (Smith), the Manufacture of Steel, p. 127.

[a] Journ. Iron and Steel Inst., 1884. I., p. 397; Cf. Stahl und Eisen, V., 1885, p. 111.

Sheffield is simply Bessemer or open-hearth steel remelted in crucibles, helps not, for we do not know that this half contains any of the most excellent steel: if it does, this excellence may still be due to the remelting in crucibles.

If the foregoing be true we may conclude that, if we are to bring the quality of Bessemer and open-hearth up to that of crucible steel, while equal purity of product is surely necessary, the first step is to discover the cause of the inferiority of the former classes for given composition, the next to provide a remedy.

But, granting that there is little doubt of the superiority of crucible steel of given composition, we see causes which have probably given us an exaggerated idea of it. First, in the Bessemer and open-hearth processes we actually use, in large part, the crude product of the blast furnace, which is not only usually less pure but less uniform in purity, more subject to the occasional presence of serious quantities of impurities (phosphorus, sulphur) than the material used for the crucible process, cast-iron purified by puddling, etc., the pure iron of the bloomary fire, etc. Again, relatively little effort has been made to produce in the Bessemer and open-hearth processes the tool-steels to which the crucible process chiefly owes its high standing. From the fact that in the Bessemer and open-hearth processes we habitually and intentionally aim at a product much poorer (because cheaper and, all things including cost considered, better suited to its habitual uses) than the habitual product of the crucible process—from this fact we easily and loosely infer that the habitual great inferiority is necessary. In the Bessemer and open-hearth process we wisely habitually avoid, in the crucible process we habitually adopt, those expensive precautions which give great excellence. It is not wise, it is casting pearls before swine, to demand for a given purpose material better than the conditions of the case, cost included, warrant: to insist that rails shall have no more than 0.02% of phosphorus, taking an extreme case. While it is better to err on the side of superiority if at all, while such errors spring from the better side of our nature, to err is still to err.

§ 358. Crucibles are of two chief kinds, graphite and clay. The graphite crucibles last much longer, endure much rougher usage, at least as to changes of temperature, and hold a heavier charge than the clay ones, and are thus much more convenient and more economical of labor: they cost rather less per pound of ingots, but give up carbon and silicon to the metal to a much greater extent, and probably more irregularly than clay ones. Finally, the loss of iron is less in graphite than in clay crucibles.

In making steel of the best quality care is taken that the cover of the crucible fits tightly; this is thought less important in making steel of common grades. The cover of a European crucible, according to Ledebur, has a round hole through which a rod is introduced for examining the charge. The hole is closed with a clay plug during melting[a]. In the Mitis process the crucible cover has such a round hole, never closed, through which the ferro-aluminium is introduced; but with this exception, American crucible covers, so far as my observation goes, are always holeless.

Graphite crucibles, almost always used in this country, usually hold a charge of from 60 to 90 pounds. Heavier charges are occasionally used; in one establishment the charge was at one time 200 pounds. The objection to large crucibles is that, in order that they may be strong enough to hold the heavy charge and to endure the pressure of the tongs in drawing from the furnace while intensely hot, their walls must be made thick; this, beside increasing the difficulty of making and drying them, lengthens the time of melting, the thicker walls conducting heat more slowly to the charge. The very heavy charges possible in a cool operation like brass founding, running up to 500 and occasionally even to 700 pounds, are hardly to be hoped for; yet the attempts to increase the weight of the charge have met with a certain measure of success. The 200 pound charges above referred to were melted at the rate of three per shift like the 80 pound ones; they have, however, been abandoned, not because of technical failure, but because opposed vigorously by the labor union. As they should effect a very considerable economy, we may expect further efforts to employ them. At the Mitis works, already referred to, charges running up to 130 pounds are used.

The average life of graphite crucibles, in this country, is from four to six heats whether in gas, anthracite or petroleum furnaces. It is shorter, naturally, when making soft than making hard steel. Thus, in making soft Mitis castings in the Noble petroleum-furnace, crucibles last but three heats.

From the fact that crucibles last no longer when making hard steel in the Noble furnace than in others, although this furnace is used only for the Mitis process, in which the heat is much shorter than the common heat of other furnaces, killing being omitted, one might infer that the Noble furnace was exceptionally trying to the crucibles.

European graphite crucibles usually last only from one to three heats. But the crucibles made by Muller of Paris, have in some works an average life of from seven to nine heats in case of hard, and from five to six in case of soft steel. They contain about 50% carbon.

Use.—Graphite crucibles are usually charged quite cold in the white-hot melting furnace and are cooled off after each heat without care, being thrown out on the cold ground while white-hot, even in the dead of winter. At Mitis works, however, they are hastily refilled while still hot, and immediately returned to the furnace. They are examined, usually after each heat, to learn whether they can be used again safely.

In many works the charge is lessened slightly from heat to heat, so as to lower the slag-level, since the crucible corrodes more deeply here than beneath, where it is simply in contact with molten metal. The successive charges may be say 85, 80, 78, 75, 72 pounds, etc., in case of graphite crucibles. The reduction is heavier for clay crucibles, successive charges weighing say 50, 44 and 38 pounds. But, in many other establishments using graphite crucibles, the crucible is packed full at each heat, without attempt to regulate the slag-level.

At the Wayne works the crucibles are clay-washed within after each heat, as soon as they begin to show serious wear; this is said to increase their life to from 5 to 8 heats[a].

Manufacture.—Graphite crucibles are made[b] from a

a Handbuch der Eisenhüttenkunde, p. 843

a Jour. Iron and St. Inst., 1887, I. P., 418, from Iron Age, XXXVIII, No. 18.

b My description of graphite-crucible making is based chiefly on information given by Mr. W. F. Downs, of the Dixon Crucible Company, private communication, Jan. 12, 1889, and on an article by Dr. J. O. Booth, Journ. Am. Chem. Soc., VI., p. 288, 1884, and VII., p. 4, 1885.

mixture of graphite, fire clay and sand, say in the following proportions by weight.

TABLE 174.—PROPORTIONS BY WEIGHT USED IN MAKING GRAPHITE CRUCIBLES.

Graphite.	Air-dried Clay.	Sand.	Loss on Burning.	Authority.
50	45	5	5%	Booth.
50	43	7	10%	"
50	41	9	10%	"
50	33	17	....	Downs.

The burnt crucible pretty constantly contains about 50 to 55% carbon. The proportion of clay to sand, however, differs according to the experience of the maker and the details of the method of manufacture (Cf. Table 180, § 368).

Ceylon graphite is generally used, though some American graphite has given good results. The Ceylon graphite is nearly pure, containing (Booth) about 6%, but sometimes not more than 1%, of pyrite and quartz. The elastic-scaly or laminated variety, or the elastic-fibrous, only should be used, not the amorphous; the first two bind the matrix of clay firmly.

The graphite is crushed in "bark mills," then pulverized between common mill-stones, to from 40 to 100 "mesh," the coarser part being bolted out in a common flour-bolter; Booth recommends that none should be coarser than $\frac{1}{20}''$ to $\frac{1}{25}''$ diameter. If the graphite be too coarse the crucible is apt to become porous, and to be weakened by cleavage planes; if too fine, the crucible is too dense and is apt to crack under the extreme changes of temperature to which it is exposed, and conducts heat slowly.

The clay is usually of the best German "Klingenburg" or "Crown" brand. It is at once very fat, refractory and wholly free from grit.

The sand should be rather coarse, passing a screen of about 40 meshes to the lineal inch, and not liable to fly on heating. Burnt infusible fire-clay has been found as good, but not better: its action is mechanical, making the air-drying uniform, and acting as a skeleton to resist the pressure of the tongs.

Mixing.—The clay is made into a thin paste with water, the sifted sand and graphite are stirred in with a shovel, and the mass is then mixed thoroughly by repeated passage through a pug-mill; it is then tempered by a few days', or better weeks', repose in a damp place, covered with cloths which are moistened occasionally. During this repose any little bubbles of air are gradually squeezed out by the sinking together of the soft mass.

Moulding.—A weighed lump of the tempered mass is slapped and kneaded, thrown into the bottom of a thick, strongly banded, plaster-of-paris (or more rarely wooden) mould, whose interior has the shape of the exterior of the crucible, and centered on a potter's wheel. While this revolves, a cast-iron or steel profile of the interior of the crucible is lowered into the mass. As in moulding pottery, so here the clayey mass is pressed against the sides of the mould and raised gradually to its top, jointly by the revolution and by the moulder's hand. The very slight excess which protrudes above the top of the mould is pared off, and the inside of the lip, if any, is cut out.

This method of moulding on a potter's wheel is said to give much better results than simple pressing into shape, not only through its kneading action, but especially because it arranges the graphite flakes tangentially, so that they bind the mass very effectively.

Drying.—The crucible is left in the plaster mould about three hours, the plaster absorbing its moisture, and thus partly drying and stiffening it so that it can be handled. The mould loses during the night part of the moisture thus taken up, but by the end of a week or so it has become so wet that it must be specially dried to regain its bibulousness.

Burning.—The crucible thus partly dried is removed from the mould, and air-dried on racks in a warm room, say at 70° to 80° F., for about a week. Each crucible is then inclosed in two seggars,[a] one inverted over the other, the joint being sometimes luted for better exclusion of air.

The seggars, with their contents, are closely packed in a common pottery-kiln, which has many fire-places to insure uniform heating. In this country it is fired with anthracite, and towards the end of the firing with long-flaming pine wood, to fully heat the extreme upper parts of the kiln. To limit the oxidation of the graphite, as little excess of air as practicable should be admitted. Booth would further enclose a little coal or coke within the seggars themselves, to take up any oxygen which entered them.

Burning takes a week, of which one day is occupied in charging, three days in firing, and two and a half days in cooling down. Some kilns lately built burn much more rapidly, but perhaps not so well. The temperature reaches a strong but not dazzling white heat, say 1,350° C. (2,463° F.), but is much lower in the cooler part of the kiln.

Indications.—In burning, the graphite of the very skin is removed, leaving the crucible drab. But the graphite should not be burnt out to a considerable depth, as the strength of the crucible at low temperatures depends on it. Hence in well-burnt crucibles the black interior region, in which the graphite still remains, should lie so near the surface that it can be exposed by rubbing with the fingers. A thick drab coating means a heavy burning out of graphite and a worthless crucible. A black skin *may* be due to remarkably perfect exclusion of air. More commonly it means that the crucible is soft because not burnt enough.

The cost of graphite crucibles in this country is given approximately in the following table:

TABLE 175.—SIZE AND COST OF AMERICAN GRAPHITE CRUCIBLES.

Height Outside. Inches.	Diameter Outside.			Weight.	Capacity.	Price per Crucible. Nominal.	Actual for large lots.
	Top.	Bilge.	Bottom				
13	9⅝"	10⅝"	7⅜"	24 lbs.	80 lbs.	$1 20	$1 00
14½	10¾"	11⁹⁄₁₆"	8⅛"	32 "	100 "	1 50	1 30
16	11⅛"	12⅛"	9"	45 "	130 "	1 80	

These dimensions are given by the Joseph Dixon Crucible Company. They seem to me to be more stumpy than those of most crucibles.

The designation numbers used by different makers for a given size of crucible are far from constant.

Very poor graphite crucibles (number 4, Table 176), lasting only one heat, cost 23 cts. in Styria about the year 1878. In France graphite crucibles now cost about four cents per pound of steel which their normal charge contains.

Figure 150 shows an American 100-pound steel-crucible for anthracite shaft-furnaces. For gas-furnaces the

[a] Conical or cylindrical fire-clay vessels, which protect the crucible from the air, prevent sudden changes of temperature, and prevent the soft crucibles from crushing each other by their own weight.

crucible-walls are thicker towards the top, where the flame is sharpest, and thinner near the bottom than in this figure.

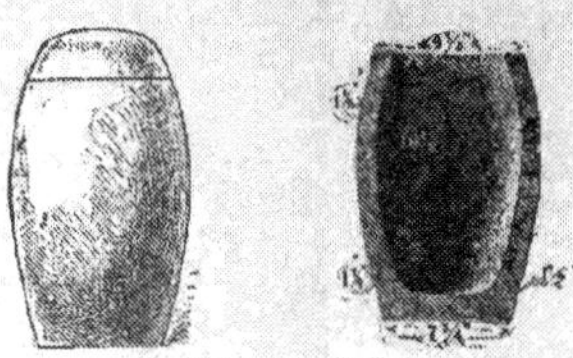

Fig. 150. Crucibles.

Clay crucibles, though decidedly tough while hot (indeed, they are thought tougher than graphite crucibles at a steel-melting heat), grow very brittle when cooled. They are therefore used continuously without cooling, being returned to the white-hot furnace immediately after teeming and inspection. Further, on account of their tendency to crack under abrupt changes of temperature below bright redness, they are heated very gradually for their first heat. They last three heats or less, while American graphite crucibles last five or six heats.

The clay crucibles always, I believe, contain a little coke, say 5%, which hastens drying, probably strengthens the crucible when hot, and hastens killing by promoting the absorption of silicon by the steel.

For the preparation of clay crucibles let two examples suffice.

Swedish Practice.—A 20-crucible batch of 540 pounds of finely-ground, sifted, dried clay, and 13 pounds of coke, is mixed, moistened and worked, rests for about twelve hours, is trodden and worked again with extreme care, and divided into 20 weighed lumps. Each is worked thoroughly to expel air-bubbles and to make it homogeneous, solid and tough. After pressing to shape, the moist crucible is dried first at 20° to 30° (C.) then at 50° to 70°, for three or even four months, and is then gradually heated for 18 hours to incipient redness. A handful of chamotte (powder of old crucibles) is thrown in, and the crucible is placed in the barely red-hot melting furnace, whose temperature is gradually raised till the chamotte partly sinters, when the crucible is filled with metal.[a]

British Practice.—The almost impalpably pulverized and carefully weighed meterials are wetted and thoroughly mixed, usually in a mill, sometimes still, and it is thought with better results, by treading systematically under men's bare feet for several hours, with periodical cutting and turning by spade. The mass is then cut into balls each sufficing to make one crucible. The ball is further hand-worked, thrown into the smooth well-oiled mould *b*, Figure 151, and squeezed macaroni-like into shape by forcing down the oiled plug *a*, centered by the pin *e*, the clay rising into and filling the annular space between mould and plug. In hand-manufacture *a* is alternately raised and pressed down, the last time being driven down by a mallet, and is then withdrawn twistingly. In machine-manufacture it is driven down and withdrawn by mechanism, the centering pin *e*, now unnecessary, being dispensed with. Its upper edge now being trimmed, the crucible and mould are placed on a post *k*; the mould is dropped; the crucible is thus bared, and its top is forced inward to the barrel-shape *m* shown, by pressing on it a conical-frustum shaped mould. The crucible is lifted with well fitting sheet-iron plates to a shelf in the pot-house; dried here for one or two days; further dried in the melting-house on a shelf next to the flues for at least ten, but preferably for 30 to 40 days; heated to incipient redness with others during some fourteen hours, mouth downward, on a bed of burning coke, and surrounded with fine coke, in a tightly luted annealing furnace Z, Figure 152, which permits but very slow combustion. It is now placed on its stand (*d*, Figure 151), in the melting hole which has previously received a little live coal, and which is now filled with coke to the tops of the crucibles. These, on reaching redness in some thirty minutes, are filled with metal,[a] if hand-made first receiving a handful of sand, which frits, closes the hole left by the centering-pin, and cements crucible to stand.

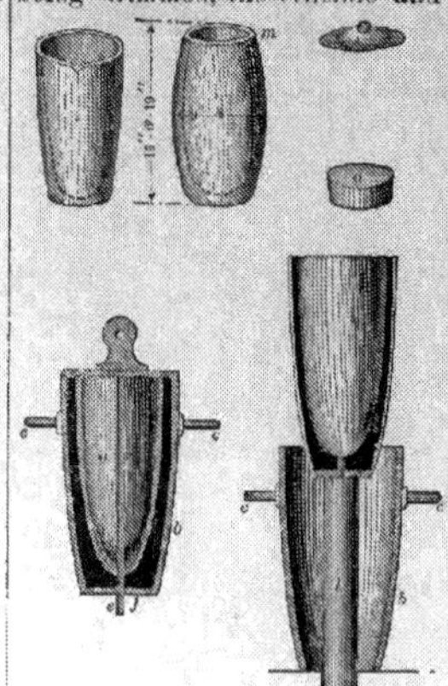

Fig. 151. British Clay Crucibles and their Manufacture. Greenwood.

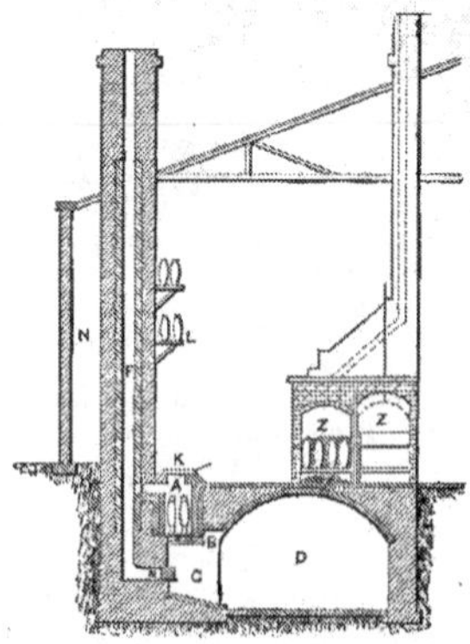

Fig. 152. Sheffield Coke Crucible Furnace. Greenwood.

Clay crucibles cost in Sheffield about \$0.15 (3d.), in 1864,[b] and about 23 to 29 cts. at present (1 sh. to 1 sh. 3d). Their present cost is thus about 20 cents in Sheffield

a Practice at Österby, Sweden. Hermelin, Stahl und Eisen, VIII., p. 340, 1888, from Jernkont, Ann. XLIII., pp. 308-343.

a Greenwood, Steel and Iron, pp. 26, 420.

b Percy, Iron and Steel, p. 835.

per 100 pounds of ingots, or about the same as that of graphite crucibles in this country. But as clay crucibles would doubtless cost more here than in Sheffield, they would be more expensive per pound of ingots than graphite crucibles.

As they are corroded more by the slag than graphite crucibles are, it is important to change the slag-level by lessening the weight of successive charges.

TABLE 176.—COMPOSITION OF STEEL-MELTING CRUCIBLES. (See also Tables 179, 180.)

A.—GRAPHITE CRUCIBLES.

	Proximate.				Ultimate.					
	Graphite. %	Coke. %	Raw Clay. %	Chamotte etc. %	C %	SiO_2 %	Al_2O_3 %	FeOx %	Alkalies. %	Other bases. %
1. Usual composition. Ledebur.	20 @ 75		33 @ 66		15@60					
2. Wedding.	44	......	12b	44	......	......	......	......	......	......
3. "	30a	......	30a	40a	......	......	......	......	......	......
			17							
4. Blomberg.	83		......	......	......	......	......	......	......	......
5. American, the author.	51		......	......	......	......	......	......	......	......

B.—CLAY CRUCIBLES.

	Graphite. %	Coke. %	Raw Clay. %	Chamotte etc. %	C %	SiO_2 %	Al_2O_3 %	FeOx %	Alkalies. %	Other bases. %
13. Mushet's.	......	12	80b	8	......	......	......	......	......	......
14. Wedding.	Charcoal	21a	31a	48a	......	......	......	......	......	......
15. Wedding.	......	4	88	8	......	......	......	......	......	......
16. Sheffield, Percy.	......	7@9	......	......	......	......	......	......	......	......

1. Ledebur, Handbuch der Eisenhüttenkunde, p. 844.
2. Wedding, Darstellung des Schmiedbaren Eisens, p. 611.
3. Döhlen Cast-steel Works, idem, p. 617.
4. Eittewald (xvii., Table 172); last 1 to 2 heats; cost 23 cents (0.48 florins); hand-made; dried at 77 to 101° F., 25 to 30 days. Met. Rev., I., p. 584, 1878.
5. A piece cut from an American 80 lb. steel-melting crucible, after long drying at a temperature well above 100° C., lost 51.17% by weight, on ignition in a platinum crucible over a blast lamp, Jan., 1889.
13. The mixture used by Mushet. Greenwood, Steel and Iron, p. 28. It is not stated explicitly that the proportions are by weight.
14. Used at Sollinger Hütte, Wedding, Darstellung des Schmiedbaren Eisens, p. 616.
15. Wedding, Idem, p. 511. The proportion of raw clay, "Rohem Thon," seems excessive.
16. Percy, Iron and Steel, p. 831.
a Proportions by volume.
b It is not stated explicitly that all this clay was raw.

§ 359. FURNACES.—In nearly all cases either direct-firing shaft-furnaces or Siemens regenerative gas-furnaces are used. Gas furnaces of other types and direct-firing reverberatory furnaces have been used to a certain extent, and Nobel's petroleum furnace is now used with success for the Mitis process.[a]

The Sheffield 2-pot coke shaft-furnaces or melting-holes, Figure 152, consist of oval chambers three feet high from the bars, by 26"x19", and three feet from center to center, arranged in rows along one or both sides of the melting-house, and lined with about six inches of fire-brick or of ganister, the latter rammed around a wooden core. In older works each hole has its own chimney-flue F, the flues of five or six holes being built into a single flat block-chimney: but in many modern works the little flues E from each hole unite in a common flue and square chimney. The draft is regulated by bricks inserted in the flues E and M. Full access is given to the grate B by the deep cellar D, so that leakage from the crucibles can be detected, and, it is said, even stopped.

The American 4-pot anthracite shaft-furnaces (usually standing in long rows on either side of boilers, which run lenthwise of the melting-house and are heated by the waste gases), have closed and luted ash-pits, into which three-inch pipes deliver low-pressure blast from a fan-blower. The compact slow-burning anthracite offers so little surface that it is necessary to have a much thicker bed of it than of coke; hence American furnaces are much deeper than Sheffield ones. On the other hand the great depth of the Sheffield ash-pit, which permits easy removal of clinkers during a heat and gives access to the crucibles from beneath for stopping leaks, is unnecessary in American furnaces, the clinkers forming more slowly with the slower burning anthracite, and the greater depth of fuel beneath the crucible preventing access from below. Indeed I do not know that it would be possible to stop a leak in a graphite crucible even if it were accessible.

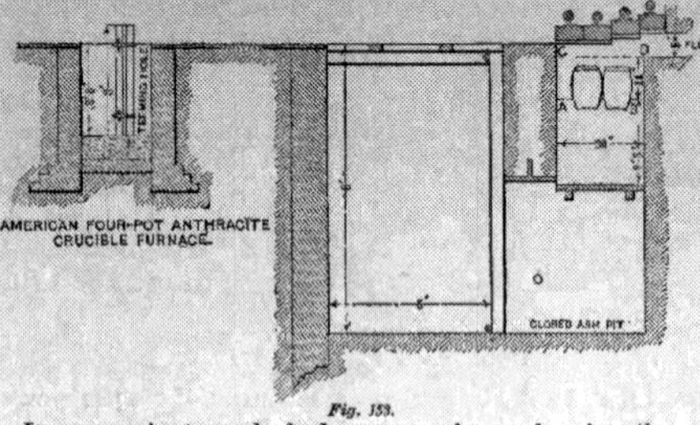

Fig. 153.

It were vain to seek fuel-economy by prolonging the shaft-furnace, so as to make the descending column of fuel intercept the escaping heat. This would lower the temperature by causing reduction of carbonic acid to oxide; further, the crucible must be near the top of the fire for examination and drawing.

Shaft-furnaces are usually run by day only, and every other day at that.

The Siemens crucible-furnace, Figure 154, is of the common Siemens regenerative type, with a pair of regenerators *a a a a* (section N P) on either side of the melting-chamber *b*, which is cut up by cross-walls *p p p* (section A B), into from two to ten melting-holes, each of which usually holds six crucibles. The flame travels so short a distance in the melting-hole or laboratory that gas and air must be mixed intimately, so as to shorten the flame. To this end the gas for each melting-hole is shot up through three small orifices *c c c* (plan and section N P) into the horizontally moving stream of air, while the velvetry *d* probably eddies and thus further mixes the streams, beside deflecting the flame downward so as to warm the bottoms of the crucibles.

Each melting-hole has a single opening above for drawing and charging, closed with clamps *e e e* (section A B), each of which covers two crucibles, and is hung by a chain to an overhead telegraph, or is lifted by a hook supported by the axle of a small two-wheeled buggy, Figure 157.

The bottom of the melting-hole has an eight-inch layer of coke-dust, and beneath this a hole *f* (section N P), temporarily closed with an old crucible-cover. Should a crucible break, a hole is forced through this, letting the molten steel run through into the vault *g* beneath. This hole is generally opened each Saturday afternoon, and all melted matter, clinker, etc., run through. The coke bottom is usually made up afresh after each shift.

The Siemens furnace is run continuously from Monday morning till Saturday afternoon. The consumption of fuel is indicated in Table 172. In one Pittsburgh mill only half a pound of slack coal was used per pound of

[a] For notices of old and rare furnaces see Kerl, Grundriss der Eisenhüttenkunde, p. 409.

steel made, in a test-run of one week; an accurate account of a year's work showed that with Wellman steam-blown producers 0.75 pounds, and with common Siemens producers one pound of slack coal was used per pound of steel.

It is very important that the flues s, s, s' beneath the regenerators, shown in section N P, should be very large, especially in the long 42 and 60-pot furnaces. The gas and air must travel through these flues the whole length of the furnace; the travel for the first melting-hole is much shorter than for the further ones, and unless these flues be very large, so as to supply the ports t and c with more air and gas than they can transmit, an undue proportion of the gas and air will enter the nearer melting-holes and the further ones will work cold. The dimensions given in section N P are standard ones, but they would be better if somewhat larger, so that the sectional area of the {air / gas} flue should be 50% larger than the sum of minimum areas of all the {air / gas} ports on one side of the furnace, or so as to make

$$2s = 9t \times 1.5$$
$$s' = 9c \times 1.5$$

s, s', t and c being the sectional areas of the passages s, s', t and c shown on section NP of Figure 154.

For larger furnaces the ratios $\frac{2s}{t}$ and $\frac{s'}{c}$ should be still larger, on account of the longer travel through the flues. Here, if we let N = the number of gas or air ports on each side of the furnace, it is well to make

$$2s = 2Nt;\ s' = 2Nc.$$

In one admirable 60-pot furnace $s' = 60'' \times 18''$ and $s + s = 60'' \times 27''$ so that

$$2s = N \times t \times 2 = 60\,t.$$
$$s' = N \times c \times 2 = 60\,c.$$

The Nobel liquid-fuel furnace,[a] Figure 155, has two chambers, a and a', each containing two crucibles, and a third a'', originally intended to hold a pair of crucibles,

Fig. 155.
NOBEL'S PETROLEUM FURNACE

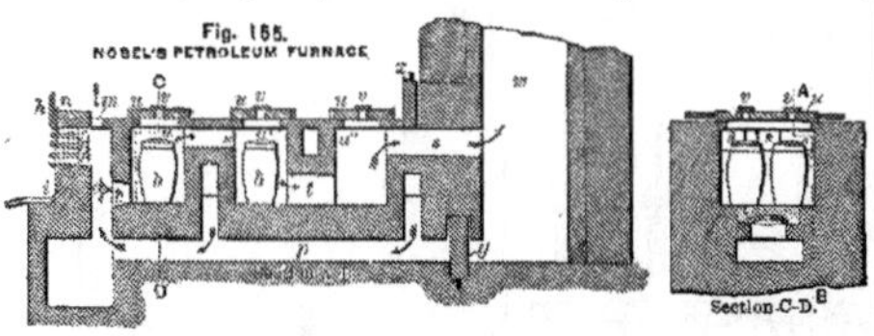

but not utilized. The fuel is a somewhat refined petroleum, costing, I am told 5 cents per gallon, while crude Pennsylvania petroleum costs about 1.6 cents per gallon. At one works attempts to use crude oil failed. I am informed that crude oil has been successfully used at another works, but I have been unable to verify this statement to my satisfaction.

The petroleum is fed from an over-head tank through the pipe h, on the upper of a series of pans f. An overflow from each pan carries any excess of oil to the next lower pan, and from the lowest back to an underground tank, whence it is pumped at intervals to the overhead tank. Air is admitted between the pans, through the slot m (regulated by the plate n), and through the passage p in the side and bridge-walls. We thus cool and preserve them, while preheating the air somewhat. The flame passes staggeringly through the passage d, the ports c, s, t, s, and the chambers a, a' a'' to the chimney w. The draft is regulated by the slide-valve x. Each chamber is covered with a large tile u, having a peep-hole v, temporarily stopped, above each crucible. When drawing and charging crucibles the tile is slid lengthwise, uncovering half a chamber at a time, while, to protect the puller-out, the flame is drawn straight to the chimney through the flue p by opening the valve g.

The staggering path of the flame, in that it impinges well on the crucibles, makes the furnace efficient as to fuel-consumption; in that it impinges sharply on the bridge-walls, it shortens the life of the furnace and increases the cost of repairs. Actually, the hottest bridge-wall is rapidly cut out by the flame.

A layer of coke is arranged at the bottom of the furnace quite as in the Siemens' furnace, for running the steel from broken crucibles into the flue p beneath. It would be well if there were a vault beneath this flue into which molten steel could be run; it should be hard to remove a mess of steel from the little flue p, without tearing the furnace to pieces.[a]

Repairs.—The Sheffield coke furnaces are relined with gannister every four weeks; their walls are rebuilt once a year; and after about five or seven years thorough repairs are needed.

Anthracite shaft-furnaces at one American works are repaired about every four months, with an outlay of one day's time of a bricklayer and helper, and 388 fire-bricks. American gas-furnaces are repaired about once in six months, with an outlay of about $350 in case of a 60-pot furnace.

A Nobel furnace runs probably about 18 days; the longest run at one American Mitis works has been 27 days.

From these data I estimate the cost of repairs per pound of steel roughly as follows:

Furnace.	Pots.	Output per month,		Output per campaign.		Repairs total.	Repairs per lb. steel.
		pots. heats. days. lbs.	lbs.		lbs.		
Anthracite..	4	4 × 3 × 12 × 75 =	10,800	10,800 × 4 =	43,200	$25.00	0.06.
		pots. hts. shifts. wks. lbs.					
Gas..........	60	60 × 3 × 11 × 4 × 75 =	594,000	594,000 × 6 =	3,564,000	$350.00	0.01
				heats. days. lbs.			
Nobel.......	2			2 × 9 × 20 × 110 =	39,600	$40.00	0.10

Comparison.—*Gas-furnaces* have great advantages over

[a] U. S. Patent 321, 840, L. Nobel, July 7th, 1885.

[a] P. Ostberg, Trans. Am. Inst. Min. Eng., xiv., p. 775, 1886, states that wrought-iron is melted in this furnace at the rate of 11 meltings in 12 hours, the last taking only about fifty (exceptionally forty) minutes, while in common furnaces to melt steel, which is more fusible, it takes four to six hours. Actually a heat occupies from three to four hours in common furnaces. As only two of the four crucibles in the Nobel furnace are drawn at a teeming, the true length of a heat is double the interval between successive teemings. Actually the crucible remains in the furnace at American Mitis works about 2 hours and 15 minutes, or just about the time required for *melting* in good American practice. Remembering that on the one hand, the time of killing is saved in the Mitis process, and that, on the other, the charge is less fusible than in the common crucible practice, the Nobel furnace seems to melt rather more rapidly than is usual with Siemens' furnaces. But the temperature in a properly designed Siemens' furnace is limited only by the refractory nature of the brickwork *and crucibles*; and it may be owing to an excessively high temperature employed in the Nobel furnace, but avoided in good Siemens' practice, that the Mitis crucibles are used only about one-half as many heats (hotter but shorter heats) as those in American Siemens' furnaces; and that there are only as many days in a Nobel furnace campaign as weeks in the campaign of a Siemens' furnace. Mr. Ostberg indeed states that in common furnaces crucibles are only exceptionally used more than thrice, while in Nobel furnaces they last six or seven heats. Actually it seems to be just the other way. In common American practice the crucibles last five or six heats; in the Nobel furnace at the Mitis works of whose practice I have direct information, they last but three.

shaft-furnaces in that they are much more convenient, the crucibles being always readily accessible; use less than half (sometimes less than one-quarter) as much fuel, and usually much cheaper fuel at that; and avoid the corrosion of the crucible by the ash of the fuel which occurs in shaft-furnaces, which probably shortens the life of the crucible appreciably. On the other hand, their first cost is much greater, and, strangely enough, the Sheffield steel-makers think that they afford less control over the temperature than shaft-furnaces. It is further objected that the crucibles next the walls in gas-furnaces heat more slowly than those in the middle; but the difference is probably unimportant. In this country gas-furnaces are habitually used, and are fast driving the shaft-furnaces out of existence. But I am informed that only one Sheffield firm of importance, Sanderson Brothers, uses the gas-furnace.

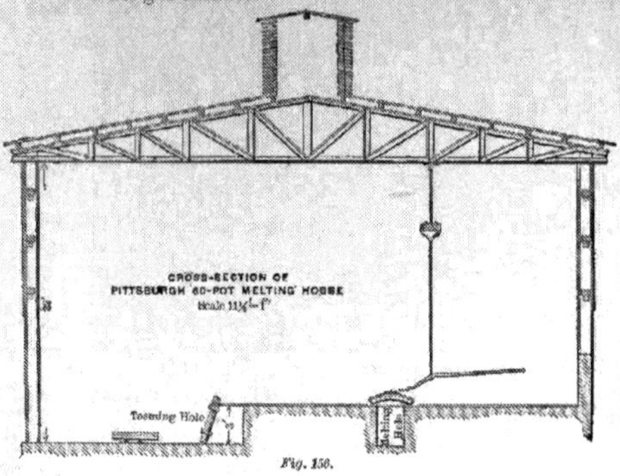

Fig. 156.

The Nobel furnace uses as much if not more fuel per ton of product than the best gas-furnaces, and of a more powerful and usually more expensive fuel at that, and it requires more labor. Its repairs, moreover, are exceedingly expensive. It is said to yield a higher temperature than other furnaces; but, while one may not estimate these high temperatures confidently, the Nobel furnace did not seem to me materially hotter than a Siemens' crucible furnace, and certainly not hotter than an open-hearth furnace. Nor can I readily believe that we cannot develop in a well-designed Siemens' furnace, as high a temperature as in this furnace. Indeed, the temperature attainable in the Siemens' furnace seems to be limited only by the melting-point of our refractory materials.

In comparing the Nobel with the Siemens' furnace we must recollect that, on the one hand, its usual product, almost carbonless steel, demands a higher temperature than the high-carbon steel usually made in Siemens' crucible furnaces; and that the Nobel furnace is run intermittently, the Siemens' continuously. On the other hand, a Nobel furnace heat is much shorter, killing being omitted, than that of a Siemens' furnace. Considering these facts, and considering that the design of the Nobel furnace, allowing the products of combustion to pass to the chimney very hot, would not lead us to expect anything like the economy of a Siemens' furnace, its fuel-consumption is surprisingly low, if, indeed, this has been trustworthily determined. The Nobel furnace is certainly much cheaper to build than the Siemens', and it uses less fuel than the shaft-furnace. It therefore commends itself for small establishments, in which castings are made only on a few days in each week; for these the Siemens' furnace is unsuited, as it must run continuously to be economical.

It is only fair to add that my direct information about

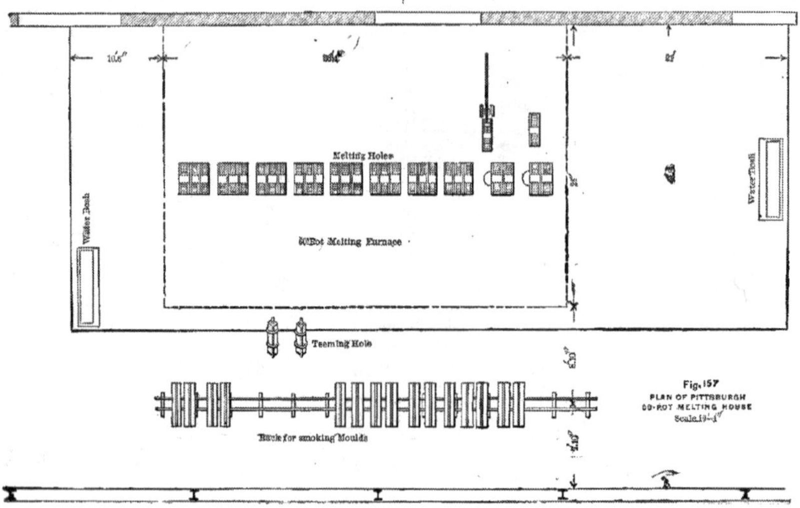

Fig. 157
PLAN OF PITTSBURGH 60-POT MELTING HOUSE

the Nobel furnace is chiefly confined to the practice of a single mill, which I am credibly informed is much less intelligently managed than several others in which the furnace is used. In spite of several endeavors, I have failed to obtain information in detail and sufficiently direct to be accepted, touching the practice in these other works.

§ 360. CHARGING.—In Sheffield the charge is introduced through a sheet-iron funnel into the red-hot (usually clay) crucible, resting on its stand in the melting-hole.

In the United States the graphite crucible is carefully filled by hand while cold. The larger pieces of metal are packed at the bottom, on these is poured the carburizing charcoal, usually with a little oxide of manganese, and often with a little "physic," such as salt, ferrocyanide of potassium, etc. Above the charcoal are packed the smaller and closer fitting pieces of metal, probably intercepting during melting nearly all the free oxygen and carbonic acid which enter from above, and thus protecting the charcoal from oxidation. The crucible is then introduced, without any stand, either into the anthracite shaft-furnace, here resting directly on the glowing coal, the several crucibles in actual contact with each other, or into the white-hot melting-hole of the Siemens' furnace, resting on the coke bottom.

The usual practice is to introduce the whole charge into the crucible at the same time; but at Österby, in Sweden, the spiegeleisen or ferromanganese is added (apparently shortly) "before the charge is wholly melted." This doubtless gives better control over the proportion of manganese in the product, and diminishes the loss of this metal.

§ 361. THE HEAT consists of two periods, "melting" and "killing."

Melting.—The crucible introduced and its cover placed, gas and air are turned on, in case of gas-furnaces, while in case of shaft-furnaces the anthracite or coke is piled up to a little above the top of the crucible, which is nearly level with the bottom of the flue E, D, Figures 152 and 153. The bulky coke burns so rapidly that it is necessary to add more after about 45 to 55 minutes, that hanging to the sides of the pots being first poked down so that we may have a solid bed of fuel next the bars, and so avoid cooling the lower part of the pots; and this is repeated at least once during the heat, so that we have at least three firings to each heat. The compact anthracite both burns away and heats up so slowly that this is neither necessary nor practicable. An anthracite fire is not replenished during the heat, for the addition of cold fuel would chill and retard the operation unduly. It is probably at least partly due to this that the crucibles in anthracite practice rest, not on stands and through these on the grate bars, but directly on a bed of anthracite so deep as to last, without replenishing, through the four hours of a heat.

When it is thought the charge is melted, the crucibles are uncovered and examined to ascertain the progress of the fusion. Care must be taken that no coke or anthracite falls into the crucible; it is said that if this happens the steel becomes very hot-short and "stares," *i. e.*, has a splendent fracture. The carbon of a pound of coal (say 34 cubic inches, a lump 3.25 inches cube), if absorbed by the metal, would raise the carbon-content of a 50-pound charge by two per cent.; were the charge initially highly carburetted, this would change it to cast-iron.

In the six-pot melting hole of a gas-furnace only the two middle pots are examined.

The melter's eye at once recognizes by the temperature whether the charge is but partially melted and therefore at the melting point, or superheated much beyond that point. In the former case it is necessary to learn how much metal is still unmelted; to this end the melter feels about in the pot with a thin iron rod, a course which is unnecessary and often dispensed with if the temperature is clearly above the melting point. If the temperature be very high, no steel adheres to the rod. According to Ledebur[a], European melters judge from the appearance of slag and metal as to the progress of operations. At first the slag is highly ferruginous, and hence black; later it grows lighter. American melters are rather close-mouthed as to the indications which they watch for; but I have never detected them in examining the slag removed by the rod.

This examination occurs at the time of the third firing in case of coke furnaces. In anthracite furnaces the crucible has by this time sunk some distance toward the bars, thanks to the burning away of the fuel beneath it. It is therefore lifted up a short distance (say 5" or 6"), through the fuel by the puller-out, just before removing its lid for examination, the melter simultaneously packing the coal down beneath the pot with a bar.

The charge now looks like slowly boiling porridge, and bright specks, probably of metallic iron, may be seen on the upper surface of the slag.

Killing.—Were the charge teemed as soon as melted, the steel would be full of blowholes. By *killing* it, *i. e.* holding it molten in the crucible, which still remains in the melting-hole, some change occurs which removes the tendency to form blowholes, and, on teeming, sound, deeply piping ingots or other castings are now obtained. Killing probably acts chiefly through enabling the metal to absorb silicon from the walls of the crucible, thus increasing its solvent power for gas, and thus enabling it to retain in solution during solidification the gas which it contains when molten. The common belief is that killing expels the gas which is present, so that less remains to escape during solidification. But, in the first place, we find that silicon is absorbed rapidly during the killing, and we have already seen that silicon seems to prevent blowholes by increasing the metal's solvent power for gas. In the second place, when the conditions are such that the metal cannot absorb silicon, holding the metal molten in this way does not kill it, *i. e.*, does not cause it to solidify without blowholes. Thus in numbers 14, 38, 43 to 45 and 47 of Table 179, we find that only from 0.006 to 0.06 % of silicon is absorbed, and here in each case the steel contains blowholes. In number 57 the metal (after-blown basic steel), though held molten for three hours, yet took up but 0.012 % of silicon; it then scattered and rose more on teeming than that which had not been thus killed[b]. It is, moreover, the experience in Mitis works that when

a Handbuch der Eisenhüttenkunde, p. 851.

b This case should pretty effectually dispose of the belief that the escape of gas during solidification is due to a protracted reaction between carbon and oxygen.

the charge is wrought-iron, the resulting metal, being nearly free from silicon and carbon, is not rendered tranquil by being held molten, or, as they put it, will not kill.

On the other hand, it is but fair to point out that in numbers 35 and 45 of Table 179, the product is relatively free from blowholes, though the metal absorbs but 0.09 and 0.11 % of silicon, or but little more than in some of those cases in which blowholes form. Again, in numbers 18 and 22, in which wrought iron is melted, 0.29 and 0.28 % of silicon is absorbed, yet porous ingots result.

If killing be unduly prolonged, the metal becomes hard and brittle, teems "dead," *i. e.*, very tranquilly, and yields very solid ingots. This, again, may be due to excessive absorption of silicon. It is very doubtful whether moderate over-killing, say of 15 or 20 minutes more than is actually necessary, produces an appreciable effect. Steel of only common grade is usually made on Mondays, because, as the furnace is not up to its normal temperature then, the proper length of time for killing cannot be readily determined.

The melter practically predetermines the length of the killing period, judging from the appearance of charge and furnace at the time of the examination already described, and from the known proximate composition of the charge, how soon it will be ready for teeming. As soon as this predetermined period (modified, of course, in case the temperature of the furnace should be changed abnormally during killing) has passed, the charge is drawn and teemed without second examination.

Killing usually lasts from 30 to 60 minutes; sometimes it does not last more than 15 minutes, and sometimes as long as an hour and three quarters. In general the hotter the furnace the shorter may killing be. It is the nearly, if not quite universal, belief of steel-melters that the better the steel, *i. e.*, the freer from phosphorus, etc., the longer killing does it need. It is said that, if the charge consists wholly of Bessemer or open-hearth steel scrap, no killing is needed.

Just what the elements are whose presence hastens killing is not known. We can understand that manganese might have this effect, since we see in § 368, D. E., that it increases the absorption of silicon. Or the presence of oxide of manganese in the slag may here, in some imperfectly understood way, promote soundness.

In the Mitis process, killing is dispensed with. A little of what is said to be ferro-aluminium is added as soon as the charge is melted, and the metal teemed a very few minutes thereafter.

Teeming.—The moulds for the small ingots usually made in the crucible process are split (Figure 158), and held together with a pair of rings and keys. Before use both halves of the mould are laid flat, with their inner faces down, and smoked from beneath by holding a pan of burning resin (used in many American works), coal-tar (British works), or birch-bark (Österby), under them (Figures 156–7). Some American steel-makers report that coal-tar yields a rather wet coating, which roughens the surface of the ingot.

Fig. 158. American Split Mould for Crucible-Steel Ingots.

Killing ended, the clamps over the melting hole are removed, *e. g.*, by a chain and telegraph as in Figure 156, or by a little buggy as in Figure 157; and the blast, or draft, or gas and air, as the case may be, shut off. In case of an anthracite shaft-furnace the fire by this time has burnt down so that most of the crucible projects above it. The puller-out, his arms and legs thickly wrapped with sacking, wet to prevent ignition, and at Mitis works with his head covered with a thick cloth and his eyes protected with dark blue glasses, now grasps the crucible with his tongs, Fig. 160, straddles the melting-hole, and with a single motion lifts the pot and swings and rests it on the melting-house floor[a], then swings it across to the teeming-hole, close to the ingot-mould to be filled. It is now grasped by the teemer with the tongs, Figure 161. The puller out or one of the moulders pries off the cover with his tongs, the slag is swabbed up by means of a mop, *i. e.*, a light iron rod with a ball of slag from previous operations attached to it. This chills the slag, and by a dexterous twisting motion is made to take up most of it.

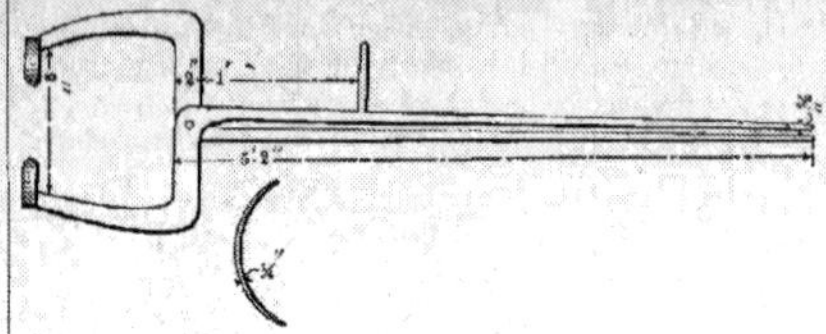

Fig. 159. Pull-out's Tongs for 130-pound Crucibles.

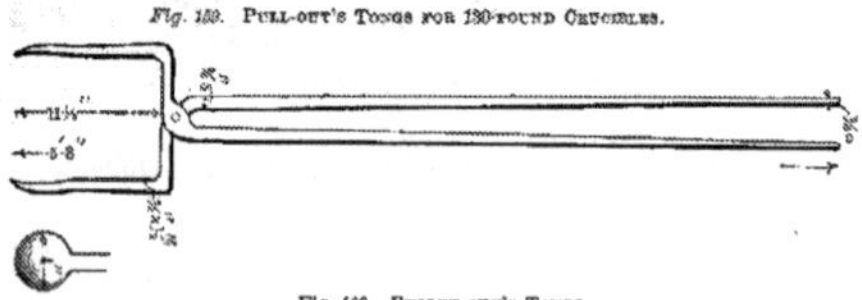

Fig. 160. Puller-out's Tongs.

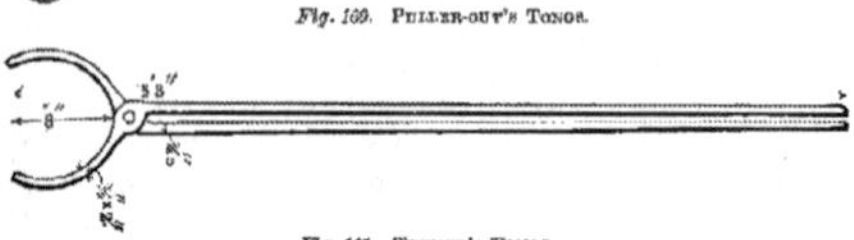

Fig. 161. Teemer's Tongs.

The teemer, his right hand and arm thickly enveloped in cloth, and standing with crucible and mould at his right, rests the tongs about midway of their length on his bent left knee as a fulcrum; raises the crucible, partly by throwing his weight on the left-hand end of the tongs, partly by lifting with his right hand, and pours the metal gently into the mould, whose top is but a few inches above the floor-level, taking care that the stream is continuous, and that it does not strike the sides of the mould; to prevent this the mould may be slightly inclined toward the teemer (Figure 156). If the stream were interrupted, the surface of the metal would crust over and a cold-shut would form; if it struck the side of the mould the metal would freeze there, and an unsound spot on the ingot's surface would result. It is that he may guide the stream more accur-

a At an American Mitis works the puller-out's tongs (Figure 159) weigh 27 pounds, the crucible 35, and the charge occasionally 130, or altogether 192 pounds. This, while a light load under favorable conditions, here clearly demands considerable strength. Actually it is swung without apparent difficulty.

ately that the teemer bears the weight of the crucible on his knee, and does not at first allow the crucible to rest on, or even touch, the mould; but later, when the ingot is nearly teemed and the stream, having but a little distance to fall, is easily guided, the teemer rests the weight of the crucible in part on the top of the mould.

Pulling the crucible from the melting-hole by hand is certainly very crude. As he straddles the hole the puller-out is exposed to almost intolerable heat, which, should a crucible break while he is pulling it out, must become simply agonizing, if not indeed dangerous. Fortunately he is only exposed to the very intense heat for from two to three seconds, as nearly as I have been able to measure it, or for perhaps three minutes collectively in a whole shift.

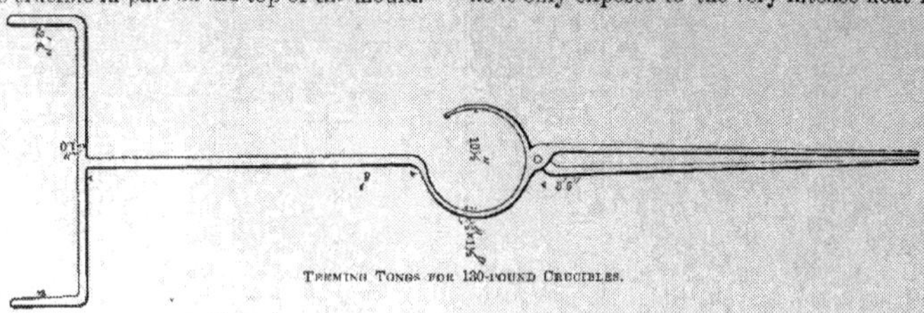

Teeming Tongs for 130-pound Crucibles.

Fig. 162.

If the weight of the ingot is to exceed that of a single crucible-charge, part or even the whole of the charge of one crucible is poured into another; or two teemers keep up a continuous stream of metal; or, finally, the contents of many crucibles are emptied into a single loam-lined wrought-iron teeming-ladle, from which the metal is teemed.

In Britain the crucible is carried from the melting to the teeming-hole with "a pair of tongs, forming a barrow mounted on a central pivot fixed to the axle of a pair of wheels, whereby the pot can be inclined for teeming, and also raised from the ground so as to be run along the iron-plated floor."[a]

The crucibles from all the melting-holes of a given furnace are teemed in rapid succession, the teemer indicating which in his judgment are ripest for teeming. If a pot is too hot when drawn from the melting-hole, it is allowed to stand by the teeming-hole till sufficiently cooled.

The moulds for the usual small ingots are unkeyed as soon as the ingot within has set, say six or eight minutes after teeming, and after teeming two or three later ingots.

Graphite crucibles are immediately thrown out and dragged away, for examination after cooling. Clay crucibles are examined while hot, and, if sound, immediately returned to the melting-hole and refilled.

During teeming the metal in the crucible is quiet, a very few bubbles escaping from it, and is said to be quite transparent to the practiced eye; this, however, I venture to doubt. I have never found a credible witness who would affirm without hesitation that he was sure that he had seen through it. I have always found it quite opaque. A very little pale flame curls slowly across the crucible. In the mould the metal gives out a very pretty shower of sparks, solidifies tranquilly, and, if highly carburized, pipes deeply.

If the metal be soft it may be desirable to stop the mould with sand, so as to chill the ingot-top and prevent rising. In American practice the mould is either not stopped at all, or a cast-iron plate is placed on the top of the mould, several inches above the ingot-top, whose chilling it probably hastens.

The 200 pound crucibles already described were, indeed, pulled out by a crane, and by it swung to the teeming-hole.

Like most hand-work, hand-pulling is surer than machine-pulling. The crucible must be grasped so firmly that it will not slip, but not so tightly that it crushes, as it readily may at this exalted temperature. The grip is more readily adjusted by hand, the feeling insensibly guiding. Indeed, it is said that the puller-out, in grasping an old weak pot, feels for the strongest points; but so rapid is he and so intense the glare, that an on-looker cannot detect this.

Grading.—The ingot after cooling is "topped," *i. e.*, has the piped upper part broken off (about 10 to 20% by weight in case of mild steel ingots, and about 20 to 35% in case of those of hard steel, Table 78, p. 153), and is graded by the appearance of the fresh fracture. It is said that a difference of 0.10% of carbon is readily distinguished, at least between the limits of 1% and 1.5%, and that an experienced eye detects even a difference of 0.05%.

Labor.—The number of men per gang and their respective duties naturally vary much. Let a few examples from current practice suffice.

Works A.—The gang for each 24-pot anthracite shaft furnace consists of seven men: 1 melter, 1 puller-out, 1 setter-in, 1 mould-tosser, 1 coal-wheeler, 1 pot-packer, 1 pot-packer's helper.

The melter is in general charge of the furnace, examines the charge when melted, decides the length of killing, teems the steel, examines the emptied crucibles, and decides whether to use them again.

The puller-out raises the crucibles at examination time, pulls them from the melting-hole for teeming, and unclinkers the melting-holes which are not running.

The setter-in places the already filled crucibles in the melting-hole, charges the coal around them, and cleans the fires after drawing and teeming. He follows the puller-out closely, charging the first melting-hole while the puller-out is drawing from the third, etc.

The mould-tosser smokes the moulds, sets them up and removes them, and draws the ingots from the teeming-hole.

a Greenwood, Steel and Iron, p. 423.

The coal-wheeler brings coal to the melting-holes.

The pot-packer and his helper fill the crucibles, swab up the slag at the time of teeming, drag away the emptied pots for examination, and bring new ones from the store-house.

Works C.—Each 12-pot anthracite furnace has 1 melter who teems, cares for the fire and takes all the labor on contract, at $6.00 per ton of steel; 1 puller-out and 1 moulder; total, 3 men.

Works E and F.—Each 42-pot Siemens furnace has 1 melter, 1 helper, 3 pullers-out and 4 moulders; total, 9.

The melters duties are the same as at Works A, except that he teems only half the pots, the helper teeming the rest.

The three pullers-out lift the pots from the melting-holes, relieving each other.

The moulders smoke, set and remove the moulds, remove the ingots, and fill the crucibles. During teeming one moulder removes and replaces the clamps above the melting hole; a second pulls off the pot-lids; a third swabs out the slag; a fourth drags away the emptied pots. This is the common Pittsburgh arrangement. Charging does not begin till all the crucibles have been drawn and emptied.

With 60-pot Siemens furnaces, drawing and teeming are done by two gangs working simultaneously, one under the melter, the other under the teemer.

In Sheffield (III., Table 172), the gang for twelve two-pot coke melting-holes is, to-day, 1 melter, 1 teemer, 2 pullers-out, 1 or 2 cellar-boys, 1 odd man, 1 yardman; total, 7.

Mitis Works.—Two Nobel furnaces, each holding four crucibles, of which two are drawn at a heat, are worked by one melter and one puller-out, the engineer lending a hand. In addition there are the casting gang and the moulders. The labor is clearly heavier than in case of Siemens' and shaft furnaces, owing to greater care required in feeding the fuel and regulating the temperature, and to the necessity of transferring the crucibles from the middle to the hot chamber, which increases the puller-out's labor by at least half; but no accurate comparison is possible, because more labor is needed to prepare and teem into the numerous small moulds for the Mitis castings than when, as in usual crucible practice, common ingots are made. I give a rough estimate in Tables 172 and 173.

The labor in the crucible process is excessively costly. The melter usually provides all the labor on contract, receiving on the eastern seaboard of this country about $6.00 and in Pittsburgh $5.50 to $6.50[a] per 2,000 pounds of ingots, though here the use of gas furnaces lightens the labor greatly. From data at hand I estimate that the melter's gangs in Pittsburgh receive on an average about $3.00 to $3.60 apiece per eight-hour shift. The melter and puller-out must have strength and judgment, but it seems to me that the price paid is wholly out of proportion to to the intrinsic needs of the case. It is rarely wise to dispense wholly with skilled men, but that one may get along after a fashion without them is shown by the experience of an American crucible steel works whose manager, discharging imported steel men in disgust, hired a sailor and a butcher, neither with any knowledge of steel-making, as melter and as puller-out. He certainly keeps his works running, though with much waste of his own issue.

a Of two thoroughly trustworthy correspondents in Pittsburgh, one assures me that he pays his melting gang $5.50; the other that he pays his $6.50 per 2,000 pounds of ingots. The difference is probably due to a slight difference in the range of duties, the higher price including topping, weighing, etc. We note in Table 172 that the labor in American mills using shaft and gas furnaces is much less per 100 pounds of ingots than in British and continental mills—0.09 to 0.13 days against about 0.20. The difference is too great to be wholly referred to the somewhat heavier charges and shorter heats of American practice.

§ 362. Time of Operation.—Shaft furnaces run one shift at a time, every alternate day, *i. e.*, one shift out of four. While not running they are unclinkered. Three heats per shift is the usual stent.

Gas furnaces run continuously from Monday morning till Saturday afternoon, with two gangs working alternate shifts of three heats apiece, each gang beginning work as soon as the third heat of the preceding shift is ended, no matter at what hour this happens. Thus they sometimes work twelve shifts between Monday morning and Saturday noon.

Melting may take 45 minutes or even an hour longer for a very soft than for a hard, *i. e.*, highly carburetted charge. The usual time is from 2 hours 15 minutes to 2 hours 45 minutes. Killing usually lasts from 30 minutes to 1 hour in this country. At Osterby, in Sweden, it is said to last only from 10 to 30 minutes. The discrepancy may be due in part to a different estimate of the time when killing begins, which is not accurately defineable. Charging and drawing usually take about 15 to 20 minutes collectively. With graphite crucibles and gas-furnaces, weight of charge and initial temperature of crucible and of furnace-walls being nearly constant, there is no very great difference between the length of successive heats, unless the degree of carburization of the charge changes considerably. But with clay crucibles and coke-shaft-furnaces the first heat of the day takes much longer than the later ones, in which the furnace walls are hotter; the crucible, returned to the melting hole immediately after teeming, is much hotter initially; and the charge much lighter. Thus the first charge may take from four to five hours, the second, according to Greenwood, about 2 hours 30 minutes.

§ 363. The Loss is generally very small, less than two per cent, and sometimes inappreciable. It is probably rather less with graphite than with clay crucibles, the carbon of the former not only lessening the oxidation of iron, but by causing a marked absorption of carbon and silicon, offsetting the loss of iron. The loss is doubtless relatively heavy when the charge consists of small and rusty pieces. In the Mitis process the loss sometimes rises to 10% when very rusty small pieces are used.

At Works A an 85-pound charge yields 84 pounds of ingots and about 66 pounds of rolled bars, so that 1.2% is lost in melting and 21% is removed by topping and in further oxidation during heating and rolling. At Österby 100 of charge yields 96.3 of ingots and 1.8 of scrap, with 1.9 of loss.

§ 364. The materials used in this country are chiefly puddled and bloomary iron, and wrought-iron and steel scrap. There is a belief that for the very best quality of steel nothing but Dannemora Swedish iron is suitable, and even that the employment of blister-steel of uniform carbon-content made from Dannemora iron is essential. Certain it is that relatively little blister-steel is made or used in this country. In 1886 only 2,651, and in 1887 only 6,265 net tons of blister, puddled, patented and apparently certain other minor classes of steel were made collectively in this country, while 80,609 and 84,421 tons respectively of crucible steel were made in these two years[a]. Of this probably nine-tenths was made from American iron,[b] so that imported blister-steel cannot have been an important component.

The only apparent explanation of the superiority of Dannemora iron is its almost complete freedom from phosphorus, of which it is reported to contain from trace to 0.034 %.[c] Åkerman reports that the ore contains about 0.003 % of phosphorus.[d]

In Sheffield, however, blister-steel seems still to be generally used. While we may have better control over the percentage of carbon in the cast-steel when using blister-steel than when using wrought-iron and charcoal, it is extremely hard to believe that, starting with a given wrought-iron, it should make any difference whatsoever in the excellence, apart from carbon-percentage, of the product whether carburization be effected by charcoal in the large crucible of a converting-furnace, or by charcoal in the small crucible of a melting-furnace. The crucible process seems to delight in and to generate an atmosphere of superstition and empiricism.

Bell-Krupp washed metal is bought, and therefore probably used, by several crucible-steel makers. If thoroughly dephosphorized it should be an excellent material.

In using scrap, especially high-carbon steel scrap, there is much uncertainty as to its quality, and hence as to that of the product, since it is absolutely impossible to make good steel from phosphoric or sulphurous materials in acid crucibles. By selecting scrap of classes for which good materials are habitually used (clinch-nails, screws, etc.), the uncertainty is greatly diminished, but is not removed. When really excellent material is needed, we must use scrap of known and guaranteed phosphorus-content, such as shearings of boiler-plate from some of the few most careful mills, etc.

The size to which the pieces of bar-iron are cut may be 6″x1″x3″. That of pieces of scrap is usually from this size down, but of course varies greatly, sometimes reaching 6″x2½″x2½″. For making very hard steel, chromium, tungsten and manganese are added (cf. pp. 48, 75, 81).

The only evident objection to the use of cast-iron and iron ore is that they usually hold much more phosphorus and sulphur than the wrought-iron and steel made from them. Where this objection disappears, as with some very pure Swedish material, the percentage of carbon of crucible-steel may be advantageously and very cheaply governed by using them.

There is a common belief that, for given composition, crucible-steel made from open-hearth or Bessemer steel is not nearly as good as that made from wrought-iron or blister-steel (§ 357).

Additions.—Besides the charcoal for carburizing the metal, a little ferromanganese or spiegeleisen is usually added to prevent blowholes and promote forgeableness; about a struck teaspoonful of oxide of manganese, to form a thin slag (it also increases the absorption of silicon and carbon); and often physics, not to say nostrums, such as salt (it may thin the slag), ferrocyanide of potassium, (it should promote carburization), sal ammoniac, etc. Without direct experimental evidence we cannot tell whether these physics have any valuable action, or whether, as one strongly suspects, they are mere gingerbread pills. The crucible-steel maker is very secretive about his mixtures; it is doubtful whether we would be much wiser than now if he told us frankly all he certainly *knew* about them.

As regards the quantity of charcoal to be added to produce steel of given carbon-content, I can give no sure rules. Probably from 60 to 75 % of the carbon of the charcoal is taken up. The charge may take up probably not more than 0.25 % of carbon from the walls of a new common graphite crucible, and probably not more than 0.15 % from those of an old one. In a coke-clay crucible the charge may gain a little carbon (say .06 %) from the crucible, but usually loses, say up to 0.23 %. Spiegeleisen, ferromanganese and oxide of manganese, and long and hot killing, increase the absorption of carbon: (see § 369).

§ 365. Uniformity.—Clearly, the percentage of carbon in the ingot depends not only on that in the charge, but on the proportion of rust and scale; on the tightness of the crucible; on the degree to which the graphite or coke of its walls are exposed to the charge, and thus on the age of the crucible and the amount of corrosion which it undergoes during melting; on the temperature; and on the length of melting and killing. So great is the uncertainty thus introduced that a well-known steel-maker informs me that, with like charges, the percentage of carbon in the ingot may vary from 0.80 to 1.50 %. This seems to me rather an exaggeration, and the statement of another and very eminent crucible steel-maker, that the carbon of the ingot may vary by from 0.15 % to 0.20 % either way from the point aimed at, seems nearer the mark.

Taking considerable numbers of heats at random, I found that, in the Bessemer process, the greatest deviation of the carbon-percentage from the average was usually from 0.01 to 0.03 % for soft steel, and only 0.04 % even for rail steel made from remelted pig. For open-hearth steel the maximum deviation was about 0.07 % to 0.08 %.[a] Doubtless the deviations would be somewhat greater in making highly carburized steel such as the crucible process usually produces: but, allowing for this, it is probable that the variations between the different ingots of a single heat in the crucible process is considerably greater than that between different heats of either the Bessemer or the open-hearth process.

With regard to silicon the crucible process stands at a still greater disadvantage, to judge from the experiments of Table 179, and from our general knowledge of the subject. I found the range of variation of silicon in Bessemer steel in no one series over 0.015 %, and in one series it was only 0.009 %.

§ 366. In the Mitis process Nobel's petroleum furnace (Figure 155) is used. It runs only one shift at a time; four crucibles are placed in the furnace, two in the middle and two in the hottest chamber. As actually practiced at one works, the charge consists solely of wrought-iron

a Ann. Statistical Rept. Am. Iron and Steel Ass., p. 30, 1888.
b Testimony of Wm. Metcalf, Rept. Select Committee on Ordnance and Warships, p. 318, 1886.
c Percy, Iron and Steel, p. 736.
d The State of the Iron Manufacture in Sweden, Stockholm, 1876, p. 13.

a Trans. Am. Soc. Mining Eng., XV. p. 347, 1887.

scrap, when the softest product is sought, mixed with more or less steel scrap and even cast-iron for harder products.

The furnace is fired the night before melting: by seven the following morning the first heat of two pots in chamber *a* is melted. This ascertained by inserting a rod through the cover of the crucible, a cold ingot said to be of ferro-aluminium (say enough 8% ferro-aluminium to introduce .05 to .10 % of aluminium) is introduced through this same hole, the lid of the melting-hole having for this purpose a little hole immediately above the crucible, usually closed. After about three minutes the metal is stirred vigorously with a little iron rod. After two or three minutes more the cover of the melting-hole is removed, one crucible is drawn, then the cover is replaced; the crucible uncovered; the abundant black glassy slag, full of shots of metal, swabbed up (I am told that sometimes a quart of it is removed), and the metal teemed. Then the second crucible is drawn in like manner. Then the two crucibles from the middle are transferred to the hot chamber *a*, and two cold ones previously filled placed in the middle chamber *a′*. From this time on a pair of crucibles is drawn about every 75 minutes till say 5 P. M., making 9 heats per shift. Table 172, and §§ 359,360 give further data. Table 177 gives the actual time of certain parts of the operation by my own observation.

TABLE 177.—TIME OF OPERATIONS IN THE MITIS PROCESS.

	I.	II.	III.	IV.	V.
Ferro-aluminium charged	....	....	— 5′ 35″	....	— 6′ 7″
Charge examined	....	....	— 4′ 10″	....	— 3′ 9″
Melting-hole uncovered	0′ 0″	0′ 0″	0′ 0″	0′ 0″	....
Crucible out	....	0′ 5″	....	....	....
Melting-hole closed	....	....	....	0′ 10″	0′ 7″
Crucible in teeming tongs	0′ 13″	0′ 37″	0′ 20″	0′ 30″	....
Teeming begins	0′ 30″	0′ 50″	0′ 45″	0′ 54″	0′ 48″
Teeming ends	1′ 40″	1′ 46″	1′ 55″	1′ 47″	1′ 28″
Number of flasks teemed	....	8	3	12	5

Watch in hand, I noted that this transferring the crucibles from one chamber to the other, and charging fresh ones, occupied 60 to 65 seconds for each furnace, excluding the time occupied in getting ready. To transfer a crucible from one chamber to the other took fifteen seconds, counting from the time of uncovering the first to that of covering the second chamber. The sliding covers of the melting-chambers permit very rapid movement.

Though it was nearly two minutes from the time of leaving the furnace to teeming into the last flask, the whole charge seemed to run out, leaving the crucible surprisingly clean and not badly corroded.

The quieting effect of the ferro-aluminium is very marked, and more sudden than that of ferro-silicon in the open-hearth process. Watch in hand, two and a half minutes after adding ferro-aluminium to a charge, which was boiling gently, I found it almost absolutely quiet. Poured within three or four minutes of this observation it lay perfectly quiet in the crucible and mould, much like cast-iron. Examining it later I found it extremely tough.

But, while the addition of ferro-aluminium quiets an almost carbonless charge effectively, there has been great trouble in getting solid castings of steel of about 0.25 per cent. of carbon, and the use of ferro-silicon for this purpose is contemplated. This accords with Davenport's observation (p. 87, foot note [c]), that the addition of ferro-aluminium, while it thinned non-carburetted iron, seemed to stiffen molten carburetted steel.

Hatchets cast by this process and wholly unforged are now selling in this country. Their polished surfaces show only a moderate number of blow-holes. But the very soft Mitis-castings are indeed remarkable. The neck of one of these, which contained 0.14 per cent. of carbon and 0.24 per cent. of silicon [a], which had not been annealed, and which was said to have been made from horse-shoe nails, was $\frac{3}{16}''$ x $\frac{3}{8}''$ and about $2\frac{1}{2}$ inches long. Fastening one end in a vise, I twisted the neck two complete revolutions (of 360°) before it broke. Nicked and broken with a sledge without heating, its fracture was fine crystalline; forged, cooled, nicked and broken, its fracture was extremely, indeed extraordinarily, silky, more like that of copper than that of iron. In both cases serious blowholes appeared.

The natural field for Mitis castings is to replace castings of common malleable-iron.

They are necessarily more costly, and actually, so far as my observation goes, much more liable to contain serious blowholes than malleable castings are. My inquiries among those who have used Mitis castings corroborates my own experience, that they are as yet very untrustworthy. Besides the serious and often fatal blowholes, there is much variation in shrinkage, so that the castings often fall short in finishing, and many of them have hard spots. On the other hand, they are incomparably tougher than malleable castings.

Thus the Mitis process has gone a step beyond the forms of the crucible and open-hearth processes hitherto used, in producing extremely tough castings, almost free from carbon: but it does not seem to have overcome the chief obstacles which the production of castings, hard or soft, by these processes has met, the liability to blowholes, uncertainty as to contraction, and heterogeneousness, whether from segregation or imperfect mixing. Nor do I see that it is more likely to overcome these difficulties than the processes with which it competes, while the very nature of the castings which it habitually produces tends to exaggerate them.

Mitis castings, then, seem to commend themselves for purposes where extreme toughness is so necessary as to compensate for greatly increased first cost, and where failure owing to presence of large cavities will not lead to serious consequences. They are used for the armatures and field-magnets of dynamo-electric machines, thanks to their extremely low magnetic retentiveness, due, of course, to their purity.

Their price, depending greatly on their size, shape and number, is not often much below 12 cents per pound in this country; that of small malleable-iron castings of usual simple shapes is commonly between 4 and 6 cents per pound.

On pages 87 and 88 I gave reasons for doubting that soft Mitis castings contained any appreciable quantity of aluminium; none had been found in them, and it seemed likely to oxidize and scorify instantly. If aluminium remained unoxidized in any of these castings it would be

a I have to thank Messrs. Hunt & Clapp, of Pittsburgh, for kindly analyzing this casting for this work.

in those which are highly carburetted, the carbon, of course, tending to prevent the oxidation of other elements present, aluminium included. But a careful analysis in Drown's laboratory, by a method which this eminent chemist has devised and believes trustworthy, failed to detect more than 0.02 per cent. of aluminium in a tool-steel high-carbon Mitis casting, to which the usual dose of ferro-aluminium had been added. The analytical method is of such a nature that this result indicates that *not more* than 0.02 per cent. of aluminium was present; while it is not unlikely that a considerable part of this 0.02 per cent. consisted of substances other than aluminium.

I am informed that the Mitis process is in actual use in five American works, in four different States; in Sheffield, in France, and in Belgium[a].

§ 367. THE COST of the crucible process is roughly estimated in Table 178. The cost of the materials varies so widely, according to their purity, that any assumed cost would be more likely to mislead than to instruct. It is, therefore, left blank.

TABLE 178.—ESTIMATED COST OF MAKING 100 LBS. OF STEEL BY THE CRUCIBLE PROCESS. SPECIAL CHARGES ONLY.

	Pittsburgh gas furnaces.	New Jersey anthracite furnaces.	Mitis process a.
Material, 102 lbs. of iron, according to quality...	....	....	....
Fuel. 100 lbs. slack coal @ 3 cts. per 75 lbs ..	$0.04	....	....
280 lbs. anthracite @ $4.25 per 2,240 lbs.	....	$0.40	....
87 lbs. petroleum @ 5 cts. per gal.....	....	....	$0.60 ($0.19)b
Labor..................	.28	.27	.33a
Repairs..................	.01	.06	.10
Crucibles..................	.22	.22	.45
Moulds, charcoal, sundries..........	.03	.03	.03
Total, excluding material	$0.58	$1.01	$1 51 ($1 10)b

a For comparison with the other processes the steel is supposed to be cast in common ingot-moulds. I assume that the puller-out's labor is half greater than in anthracite and gas furnaces, but that in other respects the labor requirement is the same for all. To allow for moulding, and for teeming many small castings by the Mitis process, the cost of labor should be increased considerably.

b Supposing that crude oil at $0.016 per gallon is used.

THE CHEMISTRY OF THE CRUCIBLE PROCESS.

§ 368. The following sketch, while partly speculative, is in large part based on and in harmony with the results of practice and of the experiments detailed in Tables 179 and 180.

The charge contains initially a moderate quantity of oxygen as rust, scale, and the slag of weld-iron. This, as well as the trifling quantity of atmospheric oxygen initially present, and free oxygen and the oxygen of any carbonic acid or aqueous vapor which may enter by leakage or diffusion, should tend to form oxide of iron and (if the charge contain spiegeleisen or ferro-manganese) of manganese. This tendency is opposed by the carbon of the crucible-walls, which, especially in case of new graphite crucibles, tends to take up the free oxygen and to reduce the carbonic acid present.

The metallic oxides, melting first to a very basic, corrosive, oxidizing slag, should collect at the bottom of the crucible and react on its walls, and later on the gradually accumulating bath of molten metal. The first action of this slag on the metal should be strongly fining, tending to oxidize carbon, silicon and manganese. As the slag-level is gradually raised by the accumulation of the molten metal beneath, the slag corrodes ring after ring of the crucible-walls, exposing their graphite or coke to the rising underlying metal, which absorbs carbon voraciously. The fining action should thus weaken rapidly as the slag grows acid, through absorption of silica from the crucible, and through the reduction of its oxides, partly by the metal's carbon and silicon, partly (in case of strongly graphitic crucibles chiefly) by the carbon of the crucible. Thus, fining probably soon gives way to carburization, the carburized metal reducing and absorbing silicon[a] from the now acid slag, and from the acid crucible-walls, from these probably the more readily the more silicious the clay which composes them.

The net result, under usual conditions, as indicated by our experimental data, is that *in graphite crucibles*, the metal gains in carbon (usually by from 0. to 0.25%), and in silicon (usually by from 0.05 to 0.20%); that, if spiegeleisen or ferro-manganese is charged before melting, much of its manganese is slagged, and the absorption of carbon is increased very greatly, rising even to nearly 2% (numbers 31 and 41), and that of silicon greatly, rising sometimes to nearly 0.50% (numbers 30 and 39), when about 3.5% of ferro-manganese is added; and that if oxide of manganese is charged, part of its manganese is sometimes if not usually reduced and absorbed by the metal. The more highly carburetted the crucible-walls, the greater will be the net absorption of carbon, manganese and silicon.

In clay crucibles the charge either loses carbon (say up to 0.23%) or gains but slightly (say up to 0.06%), while, if we may trust our scanty data, gaining but slightly in silicon, unless manganese or its oxide be present.

If the charge contains charcoal or graphite, this both carburizes the metal during heating to the melting point (probably most of its carbon is absorbed by the steel), and greatly shortens and weakens if it does not eliminate the fining period, by protecting iron and manganese from oxidation, and by reducing at least a part of their oxides.

If, on the other hand, oxide of manganese is charged, it tends to intensify and prolong the fining, to postpone and enfeeble the carburization, opposing the action of the charcoal.

Risking repetition, let us now take up the behavior of silicon, carbon and manganese separately.

THE ABSORPTION OF SILICON.—Unless basic crucibles be used, the steel always takes up silicon, the proportion absorbed in general increasing,

A, with the proportion of graphite or coke in the crucible walls;

a Private communication, The U. S. Mitis Co., Jan. 7th, 1889.

a From a basic slag iron may be reduced, as is indicated by numbers 32-4 of Table 180. The fusion in this case occurred in limeless magnesia crucibles. Ferric oxide and lime were added to the charge in the proportions 225 ferric oxide to 100 of lime. The iron remaining in the resulting slag corresponded to only 153 of ferric oxide to 100 of lime. The slag can hardly have received lime, and it can hardly have lost iron except by reduction to the metallic state. This view is favored by the presence in the slag of many globules of iron, some visible to the naked eye, others microscopic. There is, unfortunately, a possibility that the apparent reduction of iron may be due to heterogeneousness of slag, as Brand states that the slag was sintered rather than molten, and that its color was not uniform.

TABLE 179.—CHANGE OF COMPOSITION IN CRUCIBLE MELTING.

Number.	Authority.	Description of Crucible used. Proximate composition of mixture for crucibles. Graphite.	Coke.	Fat clay.	Burnt clay.	Old pots.	Percentage of carbon.	Change of composition during melting. Initial composition. C. %.	Si. %.	Mn. %.	Final. C. %.	Si. %.	Mn. %.	Gain (+) or Loss (—). C. %.	Si. %.	Mn. %.	Description of charge and product. Charge. Weight, lbs.	Description.	Product. Description.	Time of killing.	Remarks.
1	R		Bauxite				9	......	...	......	......	.14	...	......	......	......	...	Like charges, of 30% weld-steel, 70% wrought-iron.			
2	R	Clay and graphite.					28	......	...	......	......	.27	...	......	......	......	...				
3	R	"	"	"	"	"	40	......	...	......	......	.39	...	......	......	......	...				
4	L	...	....	....	....	...	28	1.29	.01	.12	1.14	.23	.10	— .15	+.22	—.02	...	Weld-steel.			
5	"	...	....	....	....	...	33	1.29	.01	.12	1.24	.24	.15	— .05	+.23	+.03	...				
6	"	...	....	....	....	...	39	1.34	.03	1.01	1.86	.46	.73	+ .52	+.44	—.28	...	Weld-steel and ferro-manganese.			
7	R	...	....	....	....	...	40	......	...	......	......	......	.101	......	......	......	...	Steel only.			
8	R	...	....	....	....	...	40	......	...	......	......	......	.211	......	......	......	...	Steel and 0.4% oxide of manganese.			
9	M	48	....	52	....	...	40±	3.59	.07	2.04	3.71	.58	1.91	+ .12	+.51	—.13	...	White cast-iron, melted thrice.			
10	"	"	....	"	....	...	....	3.71	.58	1.91	3.77	.76	1.86	+ .06	+.18	—.05	...				
11	"	"	....	"	....	...	....	3.77	.76	1.86	3.64	1.07	1.86	— .13	+.31	0	...				
12	"	"	....	"	....	...	....	.94	.02	.24	1.19	.36	...	+ .25	+.34	—.02	...	Weld-steel, melted twice.			
13	"	"	....	"	....	...	....	1.19	.36	...	1.27	.63	.22	+ .08	+.27		...				
14	"	"	....	"	....	...	...	.05	.02	.08	.25	.08	...	+ .20	+.06	......	...	Wrought-iron, melted twice.	Many blowholes.		
15	"	"	....	"	....	...	...	.25	.08	...	.35	.26	...	+ .10	+.18	......	...		Solid.		
16	"	83	....	17	....	...	70±	.91	.03	.21	1.13	.31	...	+ .22	+.28	—.02	...	Weld-steel, melted twice	....	....	Crucible pierced.
17	"	"	....	"	....	...	....	1.13	.31	...	1.45	.62	.19	+ .32	+.31		...				
18	"	"	....	"	....	...	....	.05	tr.	.11	.72	.29	...	+ .67	+.29	—.02	...	Wrought-iron, melted twice	Porous	....	" "
19	"	"	....	"	....	...	....	.72	.29	...	.67	.62	.09	— .05	+.33		...		Solid		
20	"	"	....	"	....	...	....	.91	.05	.14	1.31	.20	.56	+ .40	+.15	+.42	...	Weld-steel, melted twice, with 1% of oxide of manganese.			
21	"	"	....	"	....	...	....	1.31	.20	.56	1.62	.35	.74	+ .31	+.15	+.18	...				
22	"	"	....	"	....	...	....	.04	.02	...	.67	.30	...	+ .63	+.28	......	...	Wrought-iron, melted twice	Porous.		
23	"	"	....	"	....	...	....	.67	.30	...	1.34	.66	...	+ .67	+.36	......	...		Solid.		
24	"	...	....	....	....	...	50±	1.12	.02	.18	1.15	.35	...	+ .03	+.33	—.04	...	Weld steel, melted twice; new crucible			
25	"	...	....	....	....	...	50±	1.15	.35	...	1.11	.61	.14	— .04	+.26		...				
26	"	...	....	....	....	...	50—	.09	.02	.09	.30	.20	...	+ .21	+.18	+.01	...	Wrought-iron, melted twice; old crucible.			
27	"	...	....	....	....	...	50—	.30	.20	......	.37	.39	.10	+ .07	+.19		...				
28	"	48	....	52	....	...	....	.78	.10	1.08	1.47	.37	.88	+ .69	+.27	—.20	75.0 / 1.7	Weld-steel, with ferro-manganese.			
29	"	...	....	....	....	...	....	1.47	.37	.88	1.50	.68	.89	+ .03	+.31	+.01	....	Ingot from No. 28 remelted		3 h.	
30	"	...	....	....	....	...	40	.99	.05	2.08	2.46	.44	1.52	+1.47	+.39	—.56	34.0 / 1.1	Weld-steel / Ferro-manganese	....	1 h.±	Clay added.
31	"	...	....	....	....	...	40	.99	.05	2.08	2.92	.35	1.80	+1.93	+.30	—.28	39.0 / 1.1	Weld-steel / Ferro-manganese	....	....	No clay added.
32	"	...	....	....	....	...	40	2.46	.44	1.52	2.57	.61	1.51	+ .11	+.17	—.01	24.9	No. 30 remelted.			
33	"	...	....	....	....	...	28	.99	.05	2.08	2.24	.53	1.98	+1.25	+.48	—.10	32.0 / 1.1	Weld-steel / Ferro-manganese	....	....	Clay added.
34	"	...	....	....	....	...	28	2.24	.53	1.98	2.30	.61	1.91	+ .06	+.08	—.07	34.8	Ingot from No. 33.			
35	"	15	....	25	60		....	1.22	.05	.45	1.21	.14	.19	— .01	+.09	—.26	19.8 / 46.3	Cast-iron / Wrought-iron	Absolutely solid.	1h. 45m.	Crucible very little eaten.
36	"	"	....	"	"		....	1.49	.05	.80	1.61	.23	.42	+ .12	+.18	—.38	19.8 / 38.5 / 2.2	Cast-iron / Dannemora iron / Spiegel of 8.74% Mn	" "	2 h.	Crucible much eaten.
37	"	"	....	"	"		....	1.49	.05	.80	1.54	.24	.35	+ .05	+.19	—.45	.... / .... /	Cast-iron / Dannemora iron / Spiegel of 8.74% Mn	" "	....	" " "
38	"	"	...	"	"		....	1.03	.14	2.45	1.04	.19	1.82	+ .01	+.05	—.63	1.8 / 64.4	Ferro-manganese / Weld steel	Rather porous	15 m.	Crucible little eaten.
39	"	"	....	"	"		....	1.03	.14	2.45	1.36	.61	.83	+ .33	+.49	—1.62	....	Ferro-manganese / Weld-steel	Solid	1h. 45m.	Crucible much eaten.
40	"	"	....	"	"		....	1.04	.19	1.82	1.27	.84	.94	+ .22	+.65	—.88	....	Ingot from No. 38 remelted	....	3h. 15m.	" " "
41	"	.	...	......	......		25±	1.10	.20	2.22	2.60	.36	1.17	+1.50	+.16	—1.05	1.8 / 64.4	Ferro-manganese / Weld-steel	....	15 m.	Ferro charged before melting.
42	"	..	...	......	......		25±	1.10	.20	2.22	1.28	.33	1.60	+ .18	+.13	—.62	.9 / 32.0	Ferro-manganese / Weld-steel	....	....	Ferro charged after melting.
43	"	0	0	100			0	.94	.06	......	.49	.11	....	— .45	+.04		...	Weld-steel	Blowholes.		
44	"	"	"	"			"	......	.04	......	.14	.046	....	......	+.006		....	Wrought-iron	Many blowholes.		
45	"	"	"	"			"	.96	.09	......	.77	.15	....	— .19	+.06		....	Weld-steel	" "	45 m.	
46	"	"	"	"			"	.77	.15	......	.55	.26	....	— .22	+.11		....	Ingot from No. 45	Compact	7 h.	
47	"	"	"	"			"	1.22	.05	.45	1.20	.09	.14	— .02	+.04	—.31	19.8 / 46.3	Cast-iron / Wrought-iron	Porous	1h. 45m.	
48	..	"	5	95			....	.78	.11	.17	.70	.15	.12	— .08	+.04	—.05	....	Weld-steel.			
49	..	"	"	"			....	.45	.08	.11	.34	.10	....	— .11	+.02	....	....	Cast-steel.			
50	..	"	"	"			....	....	...	2.4±	1.46	.20	1.41	......	......	—.99±	64.4 / 1.8	Weld-steel. / Ferro-manganese.			
51	..	"	"	"			....	1.26	.20	1.41	1.03	.48	.83	— .23	+.28	—.58	....	Ingot from No. 50.			
52	..	"	"	"			....	......	...	......	.84	.12	.32	......	......	......	66.1 / 2.2	Non-manganiferous steel. / Manganese oxide.			
53	L	....	....	......	......		25±	.73	.02	.13	.75	.08	.18	+ .02	+.06	+0.5	....	Weld-steel.			
54	"	....	....	......	......		"	.92	.04	2.63	2.81	.37	1.32	+1.89	+.33	—1.31	....	Weld-steel and ferro-manganese.			
55	"	....	....	......	......		"	.94	.10	.20	.74	.10	.20	— .20	0	0	....	Weld-steel.			
56	"	....	....	......	......		"	1.14	.12	2.76	2.86	.47	1.53	+1.72	+.35	—1.23	....	Weld steel and ferro-manganese.			
57	M	....	....	......	......		..	.015	.01	P .02	.02	.02	P .03	+ .005	+.01	P+ .01	....	After-blown basic, melted 3 hours	....	3 h.	
58	B	[illegible]					...	.60	....	......	.70	......	.....	+ .10	......	......	55.1	3 like charges (steel and iron), melted successively in the same graphite crucible.	....	....	1st melting.
59	"						...	.60	....	......	.66	......	.....	+ .06	......	......	55.1		....	....	2d "
60	"						...	.60	....	......	.60	......	.....	.0	......	......	55.1		....	....	3d "
61	"	....	100@12	......	......		...	.60	....	......	.66	......	.....	+ .06	......	......	55.1	3 like charges (steel and iron), melted successively in the same coke-clay crucible.	....	....	1st "
62	"	....		......	......		...	.60	....	......	.57	......	.....	— .03	......	......	55.1		....	....	2d "
63	"	....		......	......		...	.60	....	......	.56	......	.....	— .04	......	......	55.1		....	....	3d "
64	"	....	4	......	......		...	.55	....	......	.43	......	.....	— .12	......	......	49.6 / 5.5	Wrought-iron. / Spiegeleisen.			
65	"	35	...	......	......		...	.55	...	......	.88	......	.....	+ .33	......	......		Same as No. 64.			
66	"	0	0	100			...	.50	....	......	.41	......	.....	— .09	......	......	50.1 / 5.0	Wrought iron / Spiegeleisen	....	....	Melted in 7 hours.
67	"	"	"	"			...	.50	....	......	1.50	......	.....	+1.00	......	......	....	Same as No. 66, with 0.55 lbs. graphite.			
68	"	"	"	"			..	.58	....	......	1.60	......	.....	+1.02	......	......	....	Steel, iron and graphite.			
69	"	....	100@12	......	......		...	.74	....	......	.80	......	.....	+ .06	......	......	....	3 like charges, melted successively in the same crucible.			
70	"	....		......	......		...	.74	....	......	.75	......	.....	+ .01	......	......	....				
71	"	....		......	......		...	.74	....	......	.57	......	.....	— .17	......	......	...	Steel, iron and spiegel.			
72	"	Clay (and coke?) crucible.					....	.72	....	......	1.20	......	.....	+ .48	......	......	40.2 / 14.9	Wrought-iron. / White cast-iron.			
73	"	Clay (and coke?) crucible.					....	.30	....	......	.89	......	.....	+ .59	......	......	53.4 / .8 / .5	Steel. / Spiegeleisen. / Oxide of manganese.			

1 to 3. Like charges are melted in crucibles containing different proportions of carbon, other conditions being constant. Reiser.
4 to 6. In 4 and 5 like steel is melted in crucibles made with different proportions of graphite. In 5 and 6 the same steel is melted in crucibles made with like proportions of graphite, but 2% of ferro-manganese is added in No. 6, while none is added in No. 5.
7-8. Apparently like charges melted in 7 without, in 8 with addition of 0.4% of oxide of manganese. Reiser.
9 to 11. White cast-iron is melted once (No. 9), twice (No. 10) and thrice (No. 11). A fourth melting gave fully gray iron.
12 and 13. Weld-steel (gefrischter Rohstahl) is melted once (No. 12) and twice (No. 13).
14 and 15. Wrought-iron (gefrischtes Schmiedeisen) melted once (No. 14) and twice (No. 15). The ingot from No. 14 was full of blowholes, that from No. 15 was "perfectly solid."
16-17. Weld-steel melted once (No. 16) and twice (No. 17). The crucible became perforated above the level of the steel.
18-19. Wrought-iron melted once (No. 18) and twice (No. 19). The first melting yielded a porous, the second a compact ingot. The crucible was perforated above the level of the steel.
20-21. Weld-steel melted once (No. 20) and twice (No. 21), each time with 1% of oxide of manganese. The crucible was not perforated, the part above the steel-level being made with the usual mixture of equal parts of graphite and clay.
22-23. Wrought-iron melted once (22) and twice (No. 23), yielding in the first case a porous and in the second a solid ingot. The crucible was not perforated.
24-25. Weld-steel melted once (No. 24) and twice (No. 25), each time in a previously unused crucible.
26-27. Wrought-iron melted once (No. 26) in a once used crucible, and a second time (No. 27) in the same crucible.
28-29. Weld-steel and ferro-manganese are melted once (No. 28) and then a second time (No. 29), and now held molten at the highest heat for three hours.
30-31. Weld-steel and ferro-manganese are melted once with the addition of a little fusible clay (No. 30) and once without it (31). In 30 the steel was killed for about an hour. In 31 the

crucible, where in contact with the steel, was corroded to a depth of about .31 inches (8 mm). The graphite thus set free should contain about 1.15 lbs. of carbon (520 grammes), or more than enough to account for the carbon taken up by the steel.

32. 24.25 pounds of the ingot resulting from No. 30 were remelted in a similar crucible.

33. 31.96 pounds of weld-steel and 1.10 pounds of ferro-manganese are melted with clay in a graphite crucible.

34. 24.25 pounds of the ingot from 33 are remelted in a like crucible.

35. Regular Duisburg practice: 19.81 pounds of Swedish cast-iron and 46.2 pounds of wrought-iron melted in 3 hours 45 minutes, then killed for 1 hour 45 minutes, yielding an absolutely solid ingot. The crucible was very slightly corroded, and very little slag formed.

36. 19.84 pounds Swedish cast-iron and 33.58 pounds Dannemora wrought-iron, with 2.2 pounds of charcoal-spiegeleisen containing 8.74% of manganese, were melted in 3 hours 40 minutes and killed at a high temperature for 2 hours. The crucible was much eaten, and much slag formed.

37. The same as 36, except that the crucible was lined with clay. The clay lining was destroyed and the crucible much eaten.

38. 64.4 pounds of weld-steel with 1.8 pounds of ferro-manganese of 81.3% of manganese melted in 3 hours 30 minutes, killed for 15 minutes. The ingot had some blowholes; the crucible was little eaten.

39. The same mixture melted in the same way, but killed 1 hour 45 minutes. Much slag formed, crucible much eaten, steel solid.

40. Half of the ingot from 38 was remelted in the crucible used in No. 38 in 2 hours 30 minutes, then killed for 3 hours 15 minutes at a high heat. The crucible much eaten.

41. 1.8 pounds of ferro-manganese and 64.4 pounds of weld-steel melted together, killed only 15 minutes. 8.3 pounds of slag formed and the crucible eaten .39 inches deep.

42. Charge of composition like that of 41, but the ferro-manganese was stirred into the steel after melting.

43 to **47** were carried out in crucibles so lined with clay that the charge was completely protected from the action of the graphite of the crucible.

43. Weld-steel: the molten metal was wild, rose and gave an ingot with blowholes.

44. Wrought-iron with 0.04% of silicon gave a very porous ingot.

45. Weld-steel: the gradual heating of steel and crucible occupied 9 to 12 hours; killing, 45 minutes. The resulting molten metal scattered, rose, and formed a very porous ingot.

46. The ingot from 45 remelted; killed 7 hours at the highest heat. A compact ingot resulted, with much slag.

47. The same charge as No. 35, 19.8 pounds of Swedish cast-iron and 46.3 pounds of Dannemora wrought-iron. It was melted and treated in the same way as No. 35, except that the crucible of No. 47 was lined with clay. The steel was restless, and formed a porous ingot.

48 to **51.** Fusions in clay crucibles containing only 5% of coke.

52. 66.2 pounds of weld-steel, poor in manganese, are melted with 2.2 pounds of calcined oxide of manganese.

53-56. Weld-steel is melted in clay-graphite crucibles, in 53 and 55 alone, in 54 and 56 with ferro-manganese of 72.76% of manganese.

57. After-blown basic metal, norecarburized, poured into a glowing crucible, placed at once in the crucible furnace, and held molten for three hours; on teeming, it now scattered and rose more than before killing.

59 to **63.** A charge of 33 pounds of steel, of 0.92% of carbon, 22 pounds of wrought-iron, of 0.10% of carbon, was melted in three successive fusions in the same graphite crucible: then in three successive fusions in the same coke-clay crucible. It is reasonably but not absolutely certain from the description that a new charge was taken for each fusion.

66. 7 hours needed to melt the charge.

67. The same charge as No. 66 with 250 grammes of graphite. If we suppose that the whole of the graphite was taken up by the steel, this does not account for the gain of carbon. The initial carbon, .50%, does not include the graphite.

68. 33 pounds of steel with 0.9% of carbon, and 22 pounds of wrought-iron with 0.10% of carbon and .83 pounds of graphite are melted together. The initial carbon given, 0.58%, does not include the graphite.

69-71. Like charges of 41.34 pounds of steel, 11.57 pounds of iron and 1.7 pounds of spiegeleisen, are melted successively in the same coke-clay crucible.

REFERENCES. **1** to **8**, Ledebur, Handbuch der Eisenhüttenkunde, p. 854; Stahl und Eisen, III., p. 803, 1883.

9 to **27**, also **57**, Müller, Stahl und Eisen, V., p. 179, 1885.

28 to **52**, Idem, VI., p. 695, 1886.

53 to **56**, Ledebur, Stahl und Eisen, V., p. 370, 1885.

In numbers 33, 34, 42 and 53, I have taken the liberty of correcting what appear to be errors in subtraction in the originals.

TABLE 180.—CHANGE OF COMPOSITION IN CRUCIBLE-MELTING, BRAND.

Number.	Kind.	Graphite.	Coke.	Fat Clay.	Burned Clay.	Old Pots.	Bauxite.	C	SiO_2	Al_2O_3	FeOx	Alkalies.	Other Bases.	Change of Composition.	C %	C %	Si %	Si %	Mn %	Mn %	S %	S %	P %	P %	
	Description of Crucibles Used.	Proximate Composition.						Ultimate Composition.																	
71			% 20	% 30	% 50			18.60	43.78	34.71	1.24	.87	1.23	The charge contained originally	.23		.12		.74		.03		.223		
72														Immediately after complete fusion	.38		.10		.36		.04		.223		
														Loss or gain		+.15		—.02		—.38		+.01		.0	
73														45 minutes after fusion	.44		.12				.04		.224		
														Loss or gain		+.06		+.02				.0		+.001	
74														90 minutes after fusion	.50		.25				.046		.224		
														Loss or gain		+.06		+.13				+.006		.0	
75														135 minutes after fusion	.56		.30		.28		.051		.224		
														Loss or gain		+.06		+.05		+.02		+.005		.0	
76								40.43	24.03	27.89		6.78		The charge contained originally	.23		.110				.029				
77														One hour after complete fusion	.84		.211				.035				Very slightly inclined to rise
														Loss or gain		+.61		+.093				+.006			
78														3¼ hours after complete fusion	.95		.296				.039				Perfectly quiet.
														Loss or gain		+.11		+.085				+.004			
79								0	53.92	40.57		5.28		The charge contained originally	.36		.143				.028				
80														One hour after fusion	.33		.18				.037				Strong tendency to rise.
														Loss or gain		—.03		—.013				+.009			
81														Two hours after fusion	.28		.178				.041				Slight tendency to rise.
														Loss or gain		—.05		+.048				+.004			
81.5								0	4.80	2.40	MgO 92.82		S .000	The charge contained originally	.23		.119		.74		.029		.223		
82														Sample immediately after melting	tr		0		tr.		.063		.030		
														Loss or gain		—.23		—.119		—.74		+.034		—.193	
83														45 minutes after melting	tr.		0		tr.		.065		.060		
														Loss or gain								+.002		—.040	
84														1 hour and 30 minutes after melting	.018		0		0		.077		.043		
														Loss or gain		+.018						+.012		—.087	

A mixture of puddled iron and spiegeleisen, 95% of the former with 5% of the latter in the first, second and fourth sets; 92% of the former and 8% of the latter in the third set, was melted in crucibles of four different compositions. In the first set, coke-clay; in the second, graphite clay; in the third, pure clay; in the fourth magnesia crucibles were used. In the first three sets the molten steel was held in the crucible, samples being removed from time to time through a two-inch hole in the lid, to learn the changes in the metals' composition. In the first, second, and third sets the crucibles had a capacity of 60 pounds each. The magnesia crucibles of the fourth set were inclosed in 60 pound graphite crucibles, the space between them being rammed with graphite. These magnesia crucibles were cemented with tar, which was burnt out by a five days heating in the oxidising flame of an annealing furnace. Three magnesia crucibles were used for this set, one for each of the samples Nos. 82 to 84, and to each two parts of ferric oxide and one of lime were added. Brand, Berg und Hütt. Zeit XLIV., pp. 105, 117, 1885.

B, probably with the proportion of carbon in the metal itself;

C, with the length of killing;

D, with the proportion of metallic (*i.e.*, unoxidized) manganese present;

E, the addition of oxide of manganese, however, probably usually diminishes the absorption of silicon.

A. The Influence of the Proportion of Carbon in the Crucible-Walls.—In the perfectly carbonless crucibles, 43 to 47, and in the clay crucibles with only 5% of coke, 48 to 52, wrought-iron takes up almost no silicon, and steel relatively little; with 28% of carbon or more in the crucible walls the absorption of silicon is much more marked, amounting on an average to something like 0.30% in the usually manganiferous charges of Table 179. Further increase in the proportion of carbon present in the crucible-walls seems to increase the absorption of silicon very much more when the charge itself contains but little than when it contains much carbon. Thus we find relatively little increase in the silicon-absorption by high-carbon steel as the carbon content of the crucible-walls rises from 28% to 39% in numbers 4 and 5; from about 40 to about 50% and again to about 70% in numbers 12-13, 24-25 and 16-17. Yet these same increments in the carbon-content of the crucible-walls increase the silicon-absorption greatly when the charge is wrought-iron, as Table 181 shows:

TABLE 181.—ABSORPTION OF SILICON AS AFFECTED BY THE PROPORTION OF CARBON IN THE CRUCIBLE-WALLS.

Carbon content of crucible-walls, %	0	40±	50±	70±	
Absorption of Silicon by wrought-iron, %	0.006	0.06	0.18	0.29	0.28
Number in Table 179	44	14	26	18	23

The following explanation seems to cover the ground fairly. The reduction of silicon is probably effected by the carbon of the metal and that of the crucible-walls jointly, but chiefly by the latter, thanks to the much more intimate and extended contact of the graphite with the acid and easily reduced silicates of the walls, than of the steel with the supernatant slag. (Needless to say, the presence of the molten steel is essential to this reduction of silicon: cf. § 61, p. 36.) Thus we note that when even highly carburetted steel is melted in carbonless crucibles (Nos. 43-7) the absorption of silicon is very slight, from .04 to .11%. But in order that the silicon reduced from the walls and absorbed by the metal should remain in the metal, the latter must contain a fair proportion of carbon.

Now, the metal takes up carbon from the crucible walls to a degree which probably increases rapidly with their proportion of carbon. But a given *absolute* absorption of carbon from the crucible-walls has a vastly greater *relative* effect on the carbon-content and consequent silicon-reducing power of metal initially almost carbonless, say wrought-iron, than on those of initially highly carburetted metal: *e.g.*, an absorption of 0.25% of carbon increases by 400% the carbon-content of metal holding initially but 0.05% of carbon, but that of metal with 1.00 of carbon by only 25%. Add to this the fact that the absolute absorption of carbon seems in general to be decidedly greater with charges of wrought-iron than with those of steel.

Probably more silicon is absorbed from the walls of new than of old and partly decarburized ones (cf. § Absorption of Carbon, 369 A).

B. The influence of the proportion of carbon in the metal on the absorption of silicon is illustrated in Table 182. Here we note that a charge of steel in general takes up much more silicon than one of wrought-iron; and that when the carburetted ingot resulting from the fusion of wrought-iron (in which much carbon is always absorbed) is again melted, more silicon is absorbed than in the fusion of the wrought-iron itself. This for reasons given in *A*. An exception seems to occur in numbers 16 and 18. Whether this is due to the fact that in these experiments the crucibles were perforated, thus introducing the oxidizing fire-gases, probably to different degrees in the two cases, or to some other and unnoticed factor, I cannot say. In a Mitis casting, said to be made from melted horse-nails, Hunt and Clapp found 0.24% of silicon with 0.14 of carbon; but how much of this came from the crucible-walls and how much was introduced with the ferro-aluminium, I know not.

TABLE 182.—INFLUENCE OF CARBON-CONTENT ON SILICON-ABSORPTION.

Steel	First Fusion.	Gain of Si. %	.34		.26		.23	
		Number		13		15		24
Wrought-Iron	First Fusion.	Gain of Si. %	.06		.29		.18	
		Number		14		18		26
	Second Fusion.	Gain of Si. %	.18		.33		.19	
		Number		15		19		27

C. The influence of the length of killing is illustrated in Tables 180 and 183. In the first and third sets of the latter table there is an actual loss of silicon in melting down, but the gain during killing is invariably continuous (except, of course, in case basic crucibles are used). This may be referred to the progressive acidification of the slag, already pointed out, which makes the reduction of its silicon more easy; and to the higher temperature during killing, which, raising the affinity of carbon for oxygen relatively to that of silicon, favors the reduction of silicon from slag and crucible by the carbon of crucible and steel.

TABLE 183.—INFLUENCE OF LENGTH OF KILLING ON SILICON-ABSORPTION.

	Graphite crucible.			Pure clay crucibles.	
No. in Table 179	38	39	40	45	46
Length of killing	15 min.	1 hr. 45 min.	3 hr. 15 min.	45 min.	7 hr.
Gain of carbon, %	+.01	+.33	+.22	—.19	—.22
Gain of silicon, %	+.05	+.40	+.65	+.003	+.11

D, E. The influence of manganese is shown in Table 184; here in each case the addition of ferro-manganese increases the absorption of silicon, and in two cases very greatly. The addition of oxide of manganese, however, diminishes the absorption of silicon. Thus, in numbers 20 and 21 (Table 179), in which 1% of oxide of manganese is added to a charge of weld-steel, only 0.15% of silicon is absorbed; while 0.28 and 0.31% respectively are absorbed in the parallel cases numbers 15 and 17, in which oxide of manganese is omitted; indeed, in cases 12, 13, 24 and 25 of Table 179, in which like steel is melted without oxide of manganese, the minimum silicon-absorption is 0.26%, in spite of the lower carbon-content of the crucible walls.

TABLE 184.—INFLUENCE OF MANGANESE ON THE ABSORPTION OF SILICON AND OF CARBON.

Number in Table 179		4	33	5	6	12	30
Absorption of Silicon, %	Weld-steel alone	+.22	......	+.23	......	+.34	......
	" " with ferro-manganese	......	+.48	......	+.44	......	+.39
Absorption of Carbon, %	" " alone	—.15	......	—.05	......	+.25	......
	" " with ferro-manganese	......	+1.25	......	+.52	......	+1.47
Absorption of Manganese, %	" " alone	—.02	......	+.03	......	—.08	......
	" " with ferro-manganese	......	—.80	......	—.26	......	—.56
Carbon in crucible walls, %		28±		39±		40±	

Ledebur, with hardly his usual acuteness, believes that manganese increases the absorption of silicon by increasing the steel's affinity for this metalloid, pointing out that if the excess of silicon in number 6 over that in number 5 were due to the deoxidation of silicon in 6 (Table 179) by the reaction

$$2Mn + SiO_2 = 2MnO + Si$$

then $(0.44-0.23)\frac{2\times 55}{28} = .825\%$ more of manganese should be oxidized in 6 than in 5, while actually only $0.26 + 0.03 = 0.29\%$ is. So[a], too, if the manganese simply protected the silicon from oxidation by itself taking up the oxygen present, .825% of manganese would be needed to lessen the oxidation of silicon by $.44-.23 = .21\%$.

Without denying that manganese may have such a tendency to *attract* silicon to iron, I may point out that the manganese-content of 6 exceeds that of 5 by an amount which seems hardly large enough to attract so much more silicon; and, further, that simpler explanations are at hand.

Unoxidized manganese may affect silicon-reduction in several ways:

1, *favorably*, by directly reducing silicon from slag or crucible-walls by the reaction just given;

2, *favorably*, by combining with oxygen which would otherwise have attacked silicon;

3, *favorably*, by increasing carbon-absorption. The fusible ferromanganese, melting early, gives rise to a highly manganiferous corrosive slag. This eats deeper into the crucible walls and exposes their carbon more fully to the rising molten steel, which thus absorbs more carbon than in case of non-manganiferous charges with their less corrosive slags. Note that in each case in Table 184 the carbon-absorption is very much increased by the addition of manganese. Now, this excess of carbon naturally reduces silicon vigorously from both slag and crucible walls. In harmony with this view is the fact that, in numbers 41-2 of table 179, the absorption of carbon is very much and that of silicon decidedly greater when the ferromanganese is charged before, than when it is charged after melting. In Ledebur's view one might expect the reverse, since, when the manganese is charged after melting, the resulting steel is the more manganiferous and should attract silicon the more vigorously.

4, *unfavorably*: the oxide of manganese charged as such, or formed during fusion, directly increases slag-basicity, thus opposing the reduction and favoring the oxidation of silicon.

5, *favorably*: the corrosive oxide of manganese, attacking the crucible walls, increases the quantity of slag, so that a given reduction of silicon per 100 of slag means a greater silicon-absorption per 100 of steel.

a The numbers which I give here differ slightly from Ledebur's, but not enough to affect the argument.

Of these actions (of which the last is probably relatively unimportant) the fourth should be strong relatively to the others when the proportion of manganese-oxide is very large.

While one could hardly foretell confidently the net effect of manganese under new conditions, it is not surprising that the first three outweigh the fourth consideration, and lead to a net increase of silicon-absorption when a moderate quantity of ferromanganese is charged in carburetted, well-closed crucibles, in which only a moderate quantity of manganese is likely to be oxidized; and it is very natural that, when manganese-oxide is charged as such, the first *two* actions being thus eliminated, and the fourth pronounced, the silicon-absorption should be diminished, as in numbers 18 to 21 of Table 179.

§ 309. THE ABSORPTION OF CARBON, much more variable than that of silicon, increases

A, with the proportion of carbon in the crucible-walls;

B, with the proportion of metallic manganese present;

C, probably with the proportion of oxide of manganese present;

D, usually slightly with the length of killing, in case graphite crucibles are used;

E, probably with the temperature reached, in case graphite crucibles are used;

F, the carbon of charcoal or graphite added is in large part absorbed by the metal.

A. The influence of the proportion of carbon in the crucible-walls, often masked by that of other variables, can be traced in a rough way in Table 185. It needs no explanation.

TABLE 185.—INFLUENCE OF THE PROPORTION OF CARBON IN THE CRUCIBLE WALLS ON THE ABSORPTION OF CARBON BY THE METAL.

Steel. Number in Table 179	45	43	48	51	40	58	4	34	13	19	25	24	16	17
Steel. Gain of Carbon	from —.19	to —.45	from —.08	to — .23	+.22	+.02	from - .15	to +.06	from +.08	to +.25	from —.04	to +.08	....	....
Wrought-Iron. Number in Table 179	44	....	....	....	....	....	....	....	15	14	27	26	22	23
Wrought-Iron. Gain of Carbon	+.008	....	....	....	....	....	....	....	from +.10	to +.20	from +.07	to +.23	from +.66	to +.67
Percentage of Carbon in Crucible-walls	0		5		15	25±	28		40±		50		70±	

Very experienced steel makers assure me that the charge may take up 0.25% of carbon from a new pot, but not more. This agrees with the data for normal conditions in Table 179. Here 0.25% is, with one exception, the greatest carbon absorption when the final proportion of manganese is below 0.83%, and when the crucible walls contain less than about 70% of graphite.

Thanks to the progressive decarburization of its walls (which doubtless extends for an appreciable distance beyond their inner faces), the crucible naturally imparts more carbon to the steel (and hence more silicon) during the first than during later fusions. This effect is readily traced in numbers 58 to 60, 61 to 63, and 69 to 71 of Table 179, and is well known in practice. It is, perhaps, intensified, as Böker[a] points out, by the fact that in teeming

a Wedding, Darstellung des Schmiedbaren Eisens, p. 678. Böker further points out that, thanks to this protection of the crucible-walls, the slag formed in a second and third melting is less able to take up silica from the walls, hence is more ferruginous and hence tends the more to oxidize the carbon and silicon of the underlying metal. While one may not speak positively without experimental evidence, he seems to me to exaggerate this protective action of the residual slag.

some of the slag adheres to the crucible walls. During the following heat this slag to a certain extent protects them, if not after fusion is complete, at least during fusion, from the action of the early-formed corrosive slag.

B. The influence of the presence of manganese is shown in Table 184. It is probably due chiefly to the corrosive action of the oxide of manganese formed during and after fusion, which exposes the carbon of the crucible-walls more fully to the molten metal; in part to the presence of this oxide of manganese, which, by its affinity for silica, favors the oxidation of silicon instead of carbon by what oxygen is present, and opposes the reduction of silica at the expense of carbon; and in part to the fact that the manganese unites with oxygen which might otherwise have attacked carbon.

C. Oxide of manganese, charged as such, should for the first two of these reasons favor the absorption and retention of carbon, while favoring decarburization by tending to be reduced at the expense of the carbon. We note that from 0.11 to 0.42 % of manganese is reduced from the oxide of manganese charged in numbers 8, 20, 21 and 52 of Table 179.

D. Influence of the length of killing.—Prolonging the killing should, on the one hand, tend to increase the carbon-absorption by prolonging the period of contact of steel with the carbon of the crucible-walls; on the other hand, the rise of the temperature during killing should favor the oxidation of carbon at the expense of silica and oxide of manganese. The former action should be most powerful in strongly graphitic crucibles, the latter in crucibles holding but little carbon. Further, the progressive increase in the silicon-content diminishes the steel's solvent power and probably its affinity for carbon.

We seem to find these expected results in a rough way. Thus, in the Mitis process, in which killing is extremely brief, I am informed that only about 0.05 % of carbon is taken up from a new crucible and less from old ones. I have already stated, however, that a casting selected at random and made from horse-nails held 0.14 %. In current American practice (in which, however, more highly graphitic crucibles are used) we have seen that as much as 0.25 % of carbon may be taken up. Again, in Table 183, with our graphite crucible 105 minutes' killing increases the carbon-absorption, but when the killing is prolonged to 195 minutes, the carbon-absorption again falls off. In Table 180 the carbon-absorption in carboniferous crucibles slackens as killing is prolonged, while in carbonless crucibles we have a continuous loss of carbon. Number 84 forms an exception: some coke fell into the crucible probably.

Finally in numbers 9 to 11, in which the metal is initially nearly saturated with carbon, as the silicon rises from .58 to .76 and to 1.07 %, the absorption of carbon first diminishes, then turns to a loss, and at least part of this loss very probably occurs during killing.

E. A high temperature during killing, in that it increases the affinity of carbon for oxygen relatively to that of silicon and of manganese, should lessen the absorption of carbon; in that it increases the action of the slag on the crucible-walls, and thus the exposure of graphite to steel, it should increase carbon-absorption. The experience of crucible steel makers who use highly graphitic crucibles, indicates that the second influence outweighs the first. The higher the killing temperature the greater, so it is said, is the absorption of carbon.

F. The proportion of the carbon added as charcoal or graphite which is absorbed by the metal, varies with the strength of the factors which favor carbon absorption, *e. g.*, probably declining as the proportion of carbon present from other sources (crucible-walls, initial carbon-content of the metal, etc.), increases, and as the quantity of oxygen from rust, manganese, oxides, leakage, etc., increases. A distinguished crucible-steel maker thinks that usually about 75 % of the carbon of the charcoal charged is taken up by the steel.

Comparing numbers 66 and 67 of Table 179, we find that the addition of 250 grammes of graphite to one of two like charges increased the carbon in the resulting steel by about 272 grammes, which certainly goes to show that a very large part of the carbon of the graphite was absorbed, though especially as commercial graphite is usually very impure, some unnoted variation doubtless exaggerated the carbon absorption in number 67.

§ 370. THE ABSORPTION OF MANGANESE.—In Table 179 we find that, while the manganese of ferromanganese or spiegeleisen is slagged to a considerable extent; yet when highly carburetted crucibles are used, manganese initially present in steel containing even as much as 1.52 % of manganese is but slightly affected (numbers 29, 32, 34 lose from nothing to .07 % of manganese); finally oxide of manganese charged as such is in part reduced. This harmonizes fully with the role of manganese in influencing the absorption of carbon and silicon already given. First, metallic manganese promotes the retention of silicon and carbon in part by being oxidized in their stead, and the absorption of silicon by being oxidized at the expense of this metalloid; next, oxide of manganese in part lessens the net gain of these elements by being reduced at their expense.

When the charge contains spiegeleisen or ferro-manganese, as these substances are much more fusible than the rest of the charge, the first formed bath of molten metal may contain 60 %, 70 %, or even more manganese. Its richness in manganese favors the rapid oxidation of this metal, whose oxide is greedily devoured by the acid slag. But when we charge simply manganiferous steel, even if the manganese-content reckoned on the whole charge be the same, we do not get this early highly manganiferous metal bath and resulting oxidation of manganese, because the manganese and iron of the charge melt *pari passu*. When we charge oxide of manganese, in that we make the slag both basic and manganiferous, we favor the reduction of manganese at the expense of carbon and silicon, and its transfer from slag to metal.

Table 186 illustrates the very rapid slagging of manganese when a highly manganiferous iron is melted. In the first line we have the loss of manganese on melting a mixture of ferromanganese and weld-steel. The loss when the resulting ingot is remelted, given in the second line, falls below the original loss by a far greater amount than can readily be referred to the difference in the initial manganese content.

TABLE 186.—A MIXTURE OF FERROMANGANESE AND STEEL LOSES MUCH MORE MANGANESE THAN A SIMPLE MANGANIFEROUS STEEL MELTED ALONE.

Loss of Manganese { On Melting Steel and Ferro-manganese...	—.99	—.86	—.20
Loss of Manganese { On Remelting the Resulting Ingot........	—.58	—.07	+.01
Number in Table 179..............................	50-1	33-4	38-9

So, too, in numbers 41-2 of Table 179 we note that when ferromanganese is charged before melting, 1.05% of manganese is lost, against 0.62% when, all other conditions apparently remaining constant, it is charged after melting. Numbers 30-31 of Table 179 show that the slagging of manganese is increased by acidifying the slag. Other conditions being constant, a little fusible clay was added in 30 but not in 31; in the former this addition exactly doubled the loss of manganese from the metal.

Naturally, the oxidation of manganese charged in the metallic state will be less and the reduction of oxide of manganese greater in highly graphitic than in clay crucibles; because the carbon of the crucible walls directly tends to reduce manganese, because it increases the steel's carbon-content and its tendency to take up manganese and part with carbon, and because the abundance of carbon tends to reduce silicon from the slag, which thus becomes the more basic and the readier to permit the reduction of its oxide of manganese. These are but three different faces of the same tendency. Table 187 illustrates the influence of the carbon-content of the crucible-walls on the loss of manganese.

TABLE 187.—INFLUENCE OF THE PROPORTION OF CARBON IN THE CRUCIBLE WALLS ON THE LOSS OF MANGANESE.

Steel { Loss of Manganese..	—.99±	—.63	—.90	—.26	—.28	—.20
Steel { Number............	50	38	63	6	31	28
% Carbon in Crucible-walls....	5	15	28	39	40	40±

During killing the loss of manganese should be much less than during melting, the molten metallic bath, if at first highly manganiferous, being constantly diluted by the fusion of the rest of the charge; while both the higher temperature of the killing period and the accession of carbon from the crucible-walls favor the reduction of manganese at the expense of carbon in highly carboniferous crucibles; with a high temperature the manganese may return from slag to metal (this occurs in number 75 of Table 180, even though the crucible is not highly carburetted). With crucibles relatively free from carbon and with other conditions favoring, the slagging of manganese may continue during killing, as occurs in 38-9 of Table 179.

The effect of increasing the length of killing on the loss of manganese cannot be readily traced in the data at hand, being masked by that of other variables. In 38-9 of Table 179 lengthening the killing nearly triples the loss of manganese; in numbers 72-5 of Table 180 it turns a loss into a slight gain. One would expect that prolonging killing would diminish the loss of manganese when highly carburetted steel is melted in highly carburetted crucibles, and increase it under the opposite conditions.

Sulphur, in the cases given in Table 180, increases gradually but constantly, being taken up perhaps from the pyrite of clay or graphite, perhaps from that of the fuel, very small quantities of sulphurous anhydride entering the crucible.

Copper increases very slightly in numbers 71-5 and 81.5-84 of Table 180, as shown below, doubtless because concentrated in a slightly smaller mass, owing to slight removal of other elements.

No. in Table 180.		Nickel. Cobalt.	Copper.	Phosphorus.
72.	Initial Composition...............	0.049	0.092	0.233
75.	Final "	0.047	0.094	0.234
81.5	Initial "	0.049	0.092	0.233
84.	Final "	0.050	0.097	0.243

Phosphorus, in like manner, increases slightly when clay or graphite crucibles are used, but is eliminated gradually in basic crucibles.

Nickel and cobalt once increase slightly, once decrease slightly.

CHAPTER XVIII.

APPARATUS FOR THE BESSEMER PROCESS.*

§ 371. THE ARRANGEMENT OF BESSEMER PLANTS.—According to their size these may be divided arbitrarily into the great and the small plants, or into the "big" and the "baby Bessemer."

The arrangement of large plants is a matter of the greatest importance, in view of the usually enormous quantity of material to be handled, and of the necessity of handling it not only cheaply but very rapidly: and it should therefore be studied carefully. The arrangement of small plants is much less important, and only deserves passing notice.

To fix our ideas, let us note the arrangement of the Joliet plant, Figure 163, and the path followed by the materials. We have to melt the cast-iron which is to be Bessemerized or "blown:" to blow it, removing its carbon and silicon: to re-carburize it in order to remove the iron-oxide taken up in blowing, and usually also in order to give it the desired proportion of carbon: to cast it in the form of ingots: and finally to remove these ingots. We will here follow the metal no farther.

The melting occurs in the cupola furnace I. Thence the cast-iron is tapped through the runner R into the *iron-ladle*† F, and from this a weighed quantity (say ten tons) of it is poured through the short runner below and

* This chapter treats of certain apparatus for the acid Bessemer process. The hydraulic apparatus and the cupolas, as well as the modifications of the apparatus which the basic process calls for, will be treated of in the second volume of this work.

† This ladle is called the iron-ladle to distinguish it from the casting-ladle L.

to the left of F, into one of the already highly heated converters or *vessels* Co, which for that purpose is turned about the axis of the trunnion *t* by means of the rack G, so that its length lies horizontally, and that its nose comes under this short runner.

The vessel being thus charged with cast-iron, the blast is let on through the tuyeres Q, Figures 202 and 204, and the vessel is turned upright, so that the blast is forced through the bath of molten cast-iron, throwing it into violent ebullition, and removing its carbon and silicon rapidly. The escaping gases pass through the chimney or "hood" T.

As soon as the appearance of the flame issuing from the converter's nose indicates that decarburization is complete, the vessel is again rotated about the trunnion-axis, but this time in the opposite direction, so that its nose is brought close to the runner *d*, and the blast is now stopped. Through this runner the spiegeleisen used for recarburizing is now run into the vessel, having meanwhile been melted in the one of the cupolas S, and collected in the spiegel-ladle K.

A violent reaction occurs between the spiegeleisen and the decarburized and oxygenated metal in the vessel, which is now turned so as to pour the molten steel within it into the casting-ladle L, which rides on the jib of the casting crane C. This crane now swings the casting-ladle successively over the cast-iron ingot-moulds N, standing in the casting-pit P, the steel being poured into the moulds through the nozzle in the bottom of the ladle by raising an internal stopper lifted by the stopper-rod shown.

The ingot-moulds are next lifted from the partly solidified ingots by the ingot-cranes *c*, and, by means of tongs or "dogs" hanging from these same cranes, the ingots themselves are now lifted, placed on cars and carried while still molten within to the heating furnaces in the rolling department. The removal of the moulds is termed "stripping."

But meanwhile, after discharging its steel into the casting-ladle, the vessel has been inverted to pour out its slag, inspected rapidly to see what repairs are needed, and turned back into position for receiving another charge of cast-iron, or as it is called another "heat." The oxide of iron formed by the excess of blast in immediate contact with the ends of the tuyeres gradually scorifies and corrodes these, and heat by heat the tuyeres grow shorter and the bottom thinner, so that after from 15 to 30 heats it becomes necessary to remove the bottom and replace it with a fresh one, *i. e.* to "change bottoms."

In case "*direct-metal*"[*] is used, it is brought from the blast-furnace by a ladle like F, and running on the same track, and is poured through the same runner into the vessel.

The vessels must stand at such a height that their steel pours readily into the casting ladle, and that the débris which they drop when inverted can be readily removed: the casting-crane so that it may receive the steel from the vessels and deliver it to the moulds: the moulds so that they are readily placed, and that they and the ingots cast within them are readily removed: the cupolas so that the molten metal is readily transferred from them to the vessels, and that their débris is readily removed by rail.

There are many modifications of the arrangement I have sketched; *e. g.* in the position of the cupolas and the arrangement of the runners, both cast-iron and spiegeleisen being in some mills introduced through the runner *d*: in the number of vessels, of which there are usually two, yet sometimes three or even four, while in small plants there is occasionally but one: in the number of casting-cranes, usually one, sometimes two, rarely three: in the shape of the casting-pit, which is very deep in old British mills, shallow in most modern mills, and occasionally wholly dispensed with, the moulds standing on the general level: in the number and arrangement of the ingot-cranes, etc., etc. Again, while in most mills the ingots are stripped in the casting-pit, in some they are removed with their moulds to another place before stripping. The value and object of these modifications we will consider later.

§ 372. Classification of Operations.—The operations above outlined may be divided into four groups:

1. Melting and transferring the molten metal to the converter.
2. Blowing.
3. The pit-work,[†] casting, stripping and removing the ingots.
4. Repairs, especially those to bottoms, ladles and moulds.

The following movements of materials are to be made, and for them tracks, runners, cranes, hoists, etc., are to be provided.

A. Taking cast-iron, coke and spiegeleisen to the cupolas.

B. Removing cupola-slag and "dump."

C. Conducting the molten cast-iron and spiegeleisen to the vessels.

D. Carrying the molten steel to the moulds.

E. Removing the ingots for rolling, hammering, etc.

F. Removing the moulds that they may cool, and returning them.

G. Bringing and removing ladles.

H. Bringing and removing vessel-bottoms.

I. Bringing and removing vessel- and pit-slag and scrap.

In addition to the above, which are of the nature of transportations, the following motions must be provided for:

J. Rotating the vessels.

K. Lifting the ingots from the pit.[†]

L. Setting the moulds and lifting them from the pit.

In designing a plant for small output it is usually very important that the cost of installation be kept very low, as the interest charges fall heavily on the small tonnage, and as powerful and hence costly machinery can be occupied but a fraction of the time, *i. e.*, to poor advantage. Thus a small and hence compact plant is sought; the converting building itself is small; cupolas, vessels, pit and perhaps heating furnace stand close to each other; some of the above movements are suppressed or combined, and several of them are effected by the same machine.

[*] "*Direct-metal*" is cast-iron brought while still molten direct from the blast furnace and poured into the converter. In distinction from it, cast-iron which has been cast into pigs at the blast furnace and remelted in cupolas before being run into the Bessemer vessels is known as "*cupola-metal.*"

[†] Though in certain mills there is no true pit it is still more convenient to speak of those classes of work which in most works occur in the pit, as "pit-work."

But when a large output is aimed at, *e. g.*, when rail-ingots are to made, and where operations are necessarily hurried, it is best to separate the places where the above four groups of operations are to be carried out, so that the workmen engaged in each group may not hinder those of another, and, sufficiently oppressed in hot weather with the heat necessary to their own group, may not have their working power further diminished by the heat from the other groups. Clearly this is more important in case of a large than in that of a small output, since in the former case more workmen are employed in each group, their operations and motions are quicker, and more in need of free working-space, and the evolution of heat, (whether from running streams of molten metal or the presence of hot ingots) is more constant, and its effects consequently more intense and far more trying than in the latter. Moreover, as in the case of large output there are more men in each group, so it is expedient to put in charge of each group a workman of exceptional powers of direction, and it is less important to have all the groups immediately under the eye of a single foreman. In case of large output the superintendent delegates his authority to a number of bosses (the head vessel-man, the head pit-man, etc.), and holds each of them responsible for results. In case of a small output bosses of such responsibility cannot be employed, for their wages would form too serious a charge per ton of the small product; hence, great compactness is further desirable here, in order that the superintendent, or rather in this case foreman, may be within sight and earshot of all.

Again, if we thus scatter the different groups we must have locomotives or other costly means of transporting the material from point to point; their absolute cost is relatively little larger in case of large than in that of small output, and thus forms a relatively light charge per ton of the greater product.

These considerations, of course, apply with more or less force to industries in general; but to iron manufacture with especial force, for here undue condensation not only impedes the many and rapid movements of heavy and often difficultly handled and white-hot objects, but leads to oppressive heat, which lowers the workman's efficiency, to say nothing of increasing his sufferings. Here mercy pays.

But though it is thus desirable to separate the four groups, it is best that the operations of each group be carried on in a small space, so that the men of each may have but short excursions to make, may communicate and co-operate quickly with each other, and that they and the objects in their charge may ever be well within sight and speaking distance of their boss.

§ 373. THE POSITION OF THE CUPOLAS must, as already stated, be such that the molten cast-iron can be conveyed readily from them to the vessels, and that their own débris can be readily removed.

A. *Their débris* is not only very considerable, but a very large quantity is thrown out suddenly when they dump. In order that they may dump (and dumping is by far the easiest way of removing their contents at the end of their campaign), and that the débris dumped may be readily removed, they should stand well above the ground level, not less than 8 or 9 feet; in close proximity to a broad-gauge track; and either apart from the converting-room proper, or along one of its sides, so that their débris may be delivered into an open space as free as practicable from walls and pillars, as these interfere with breaking it up, or, indeed, quarrying it as must sometimes be done.

In the older Bessemer plants, *e. g.*, Joliet (Figure 163), a chute U, beneath the cupolas, throws their débris completely out of doors. In most of the later plants the cupolas stand hardly high enough for this, but they are either removed from the converting-room (Bethlehem, Harrisburg); or their débris is carried from beneath them by a similar but shorter chute, and falls into a space encumbered only with short and smooth division walls; or both these plans are combined.

B. *Transferring the molten cast-iron.* In order that the cast-iron might run by gravity to the vessels, the cupolas in the older Holley plants stood close to and higher than the vessels, nearer even than in the Joliet type, figure 163. The cast-iron was tapped from the cupolas into stationary tipping ladles, resting on scales, and close to the cupolas; by tipping these ladles a given weight of cast-iron was run through long, loam-lined runners to the vessels. The runners in this and similar mills have a fall of about one in four or one in five. They are forked at the lower ends so as to deliver into either of two vessels, and pivoted so as to be pushed well into the vessel's mouth when delivering iron, and again withdrawn before the vessel is turned up (Figures 171 and 173).

But here a very serious difficulty arose. The cupola tappers, much of whose time was necessarily spent on the side of the cupolas nearest the vessels, were completely hemmed in by heat. In front of them were the hot cupolas, from whose shells much heat radiated; by their feet were large ladles full of molten cast-iron; while behind them rushed in a torrent of hot air, heated by the ingots in the pit and by the flame of the vessels. Their position was indeed intolerable. They stood, as it were, in a chimney conducting the hot air up from the pit and from around the vessels to the top of the cupola building. I have often known men to be overcome with the heat here, faintings, severe hemorrhage at the nose, etc.

When, as at Harrisburg, Figure 171, they sought to remedy this by setting the cupolas further back from the vessels, inordinately long runners leading from cupola to vessel resulted, in which much cast-iron solidified, and much runner scrap resulted, which had to be remelted. Further, the additional height to which it was necessary to raise the cupolas in order to give the runners sufficient fall, the additional cost of the cupola building, which had to sustain a heavy load aloft, and the additional distance through which 1,000 tons of material had to be hoisted daily, were no trifle.

Hence many builders of plants have abandoned the plan of placing the cupolas so that the molten cast-iron can run from iron-ladles standing hard by them through runners directly to the vessels, and instead have placed the cupolas in a position convenient for receiving pig-iron and coke, and for discharging their debris; and they have provided traveling iron-ladles, carried by a locomotive from the cupolas to the vessels. Here, then, it is found expedient to separate the operations of one of our four groups from those of the others.

There are three common ways of carrying the iron-ladle from the cupolas to the vessels.

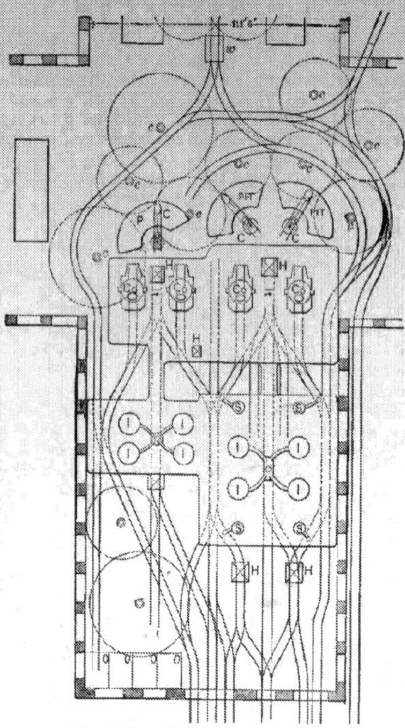

Fig. 164. Plan of Bethlehem four-vessel plant.

C Casting-Cranes. c Ingot-Cranes. Co Converters. H Hoists. I Cupola for Cast-Iron. R Track for Cast-Iron. O Ovens for Bottoms. P Casting-Pit. S Spiegel Cupolas. W Scales.

1st. It may run on a track on the general level, (Figures 164, 200,) be raised to the level of the vessels by a hoist (or on the jib of a crane as at Rhymney and Eston) standing between or beside them, and there be tipped by gearing attached to its trunnions.

2d. It may run on an elevated track at about the level of the vessels' trunnions (figures 165, 168, 169); from this track it pours the metal into the vessel, being tipped by gearing attached to its trunnions. If the vessels stand side by side this track may run either before or behind them; if opposite each other, as in the British plan, the track should run between them, as at West Cumberland.

3d. It may be carried by a crane to the vessel's mouth, and, while suspended aloft by its own trunnions, be tipped so as to empty its molten iron into the vessel by lifting its bottom with a chain (Figure 167).

In the first and third of these arrangements the cupolas need only be raised so high that their debris can be easily removed from beneath them; in the second the cupola-bottoms should be some 7 feet above the vessel floor, while in the old arrangement, in which the cast-iron ran through gutters to the vessels, the cupola-bottoms stood some 17 feet above the vessel-floor.

Of these three plans the third (carrying the ladle by a crane) is decidedly the cheapest as regards cost of installation, but is much less convenient than the others. In pouring from the ladle into the vessel four men and boys are required, one man tipping the ladle, a second racking it in towards the mast of the crane to compensate for the horizontal travel of its lip as it tips, a stage-boy regulating the height of the ladle, and another the position of the vessel. With the second arrangement (a ladle running on an elevated track) only two men are needed, the locomotive engineer and a man to tip the ladle. The first (a ladle running on a surface track) needs but slightly more labour than the second, to wit, a stage-boy to work the hoist which raises the ladle to the vessel's mouth. I think that few good judges would recommend the third arrangement for works designed for large output.

As between the first and second plans, the first may effect a slight saving in first cost, the cost of a single hoist being less than that of elevating the track, and the lower position of the cupolas effecting a slight saving. As regards lifting the metal both the first and third arrangements are at a slight disadvantage, for their two lifts, first from the general level to the cupola-charging platform, and second from the general level to the vessel, are collectively rather more, say four to six feet more, than the single lift of the second plan, allowing for the necessarily higher position of the cupolas in the second arrangement than in the others.

But the chief objection to the first arrangement is that the surface track occupies space which is, if not more needed for other purposes, at least more likely to be encumbered or obstructed than that occupied by the elevated track of the second arrangement. This may be a rather serious thing. For every heat four trips must be made, carrying the iron-ladle to the vessels and back, and spiegel-ladle back and forth. If we are blowing a heat every eight minutes, this implies a trip along these tracks every two minutes on an average. Moreover, if successive heats are to be made in vessels served by the same track and hoist, the vessel which is preparing to blow must receive its cast-iron some little time before the blow in its neighbor ceases, in order that the track and hoist may be free to bring the spiegel-ladle to the blowing vessel the instant that its blow finishes. In the Bethlehem works, with their very talented management and with their four vessels, this arrangement indeed works smoothly; but with a two, and, perhaps, even with a three-vessel plant, one might anticipate considerable delay, owing to obstructions to the track, or to interference between the movements of the spiegel and the iron-ladle.

The length of time during which the vessel is delayed in receiving the charge of molten iron is practically the same for all these plans, as the numbers in Table 188 indicate. If anything, the crane-method here gives the best results when we consider that it takes longer per ton to pour a small than a large weight of metal. And, lest it be thought that, though the crane-method pours the metal rapidly, it wastes time by swinging the metal slowly from the cupola to the vessel, I will add that in one case I saw the stream of molten iron begin running into the vessel 45 seconds after beginning to raise the ladle which held it from the scales below the cupola.

TABLE 188.—TIME OCCUPIED IN POURING MOLTEN CAST-IRON INTO VESSELS BY DIFFERENT METHODS.

Mode of Transporting the Cast-iron.	By Runners.			By Surface Track.	By Crane.	
Weight of Charge, Tons...	10	6	7½	7½	5	4
Number of Observations...	3	1	7	5	5	2
Time Occupied. Max	2' 5"	....	2'	2'	1' 5"	50"
Time Occupied. Min.....	1' 40"	....	1'	1' 15"	55"	42"
Time Occupied. Avge....	1' 55"	1' 30"	1' 38"	1' 42"	57"	47"
Seconds per Ton, Avge.....	11' 5"	13"	13"	13"	11"	12"

If direct metal, *i.e.* molten cast-iron brought direct from the blast-furnace, be used, it is necessary to combine the direct-metal arrangement with one for cupola-melted cast-iron. For not only is it important to remelt in cupolas during the week the cast-iron made by the blast-furnaces on Sunday, when the steel works are closed, but to be able to substitute cupola-metal for direct-metal in case the supply of the latter should fail, or in case its composition should suddenly become unsuited to the Bessemer process, through some temporary derangement of the blast-furnace or otherwise. For simplicity it is desirable that direct-metal and cupola-metal should be carried to the vessels through the same channels, be weighed on the same scales, etc.

§ 374. WEIGHING THE MOLTEN CAST-IRON FOR THE VESSEL CHARGE.—The iron-ladle usually stands on scales, and an exact charge is weighed into it, the stream of molten metal being interrupted at the right moment by "Botting up[s]" the cupola. But it may in some cases be more convenient to tap a larger quantity into this ladle, and then weigh out from the ladle an exact vessel-charge. When the cast-iron is conveyed by a crane, the weighing may be effected by a hydraulic weighing-machine on the trolley running on the crane-jib. This machine is a hydraulic cylinder with a pressure gauge, and the ladle is simply suspended from its plunger.

This last plan admits of many modifications. For instance, the weighing cylinder may also be a lifting cylinder for raising or lowering the ladle; when a weight is to be taken the admission and escape of water are checked, when the pressure-gauge will indicate the weight of cast-iron plus tare, *i.e.* ladle, plunger and suspending pieces. Or the pressure-gauge may be attached to the main lifting-cylinder of the crane itself. In any case the gauge should be so set that it points to zero when the water or other fluid is supporting only the weight of the tare.

§ 375. ARRANGEMENT OF VESSELS, PIT AND CONVERTING-HOUSE CRANES.—Here we have quite a different problem, to arrange matters so the several operations shall not interfere with each other, shall not hold each other back. At the same time the manœuvres and supervision must be easy, and the cost of installation must be within bounds. In approaching such a problem we must, of course, have some starting point, and probably as good a one as any is to assume a given weight of vessel-charge and given boiler and blowing engine power, so that a heat (of, say, ten tons) can be blown in given time (say eight minutes); then we must seek to arrange matters so that we shall be able to blow a heat every eight minutes, one vessel turning up to begin blowing its heat the moment that the preceding heat is finished in another, and that the vessel in which it is blowing turns down. In at least one American three-vessel plant the blowing engine often runs continuously for several hours, blowing being absolutely continuous.

After the metal is blown it is recarburized, is poured into the casting-ladle, is teemed thence into the moulds, is removed to other departments. Now, in the mill which we are designing, as soon as a heat is blown in one vessel and before it is recarburized a second is to begin blowing in another vessel; and the first vessel (or a third in case there are three) must be ready so that a third heat may begin blowing as soon as the second is blown. In like manner the casting-ladle must deliver its steel, undergo its repairs and be back ready to receive the second heat as soon as the second heat is ready to be poured into it. So, too, a second set of moulds must be ready to receive the second heat, as soon as the casting-ladle has received this second heat and swung around to where the moulds stand, and so on.

I need not here combat the belief of many European metallurgists that such extremely rapid work is prejudicial to the quality of the product. This depends chiefly on the proportion of phosphorus and sulphur in the metal, which is of course wholly independent of the rapidity of working, and further on the temperature of blowing and of casting, on care in casting, etc. Now the rapid working which has led to such enormous outputs from American mills is not due to rapid *blowing*, but to avoiding delays between blows; and it is hard to see how this is to injure the metal, unless by inducing slovenly casting. Needless to say, the arrangements for teeming must be so ample, especially when high quality is sought, that this important operation may be performed carefully. I think, however, that even in some of our quickest working mills, the ingots are as well cast, as free from blowholes and as sound as those made in the most leisurely European practice.

As regards uniformity of composition, our rapid work leaves nothing to be desired. (Cf. § 365.) On the other hand, rapid working not only lessens the interest and general charges per unit of product, but, by preventing the vessels from cooling between heats, enables us to use less coke in the cupolas, and cast-iron which has less silicon and is hence cheaper, than in case of slower working.

§ 376. NUMBER OF VESSELS, ETC., NEEDED—DISCUSSION.—From this point to § 378 follows a quasi mathematical discussion of the number of vessels, cranes, etc., needed to permit continuous blowing.

The several operations which have to keep time with the blowing are, the work in and on the vessel between blows; the work done by and on the casting-ladle; and the work in stripping and removing the ingots and replacing the moulds, or the pit-work. But for the pit-work enough time must be allowed not only for this work of the ingot-cranes, but also to permit the ingots to solidify and become firm enough to bear handling.

s To "bot up" is to stop the tap-hole of a cupola or other melting furnace, *e.g.* with a ball of clay on the end of a pole or "bot-stick."

Thus the lengths of time which we now have to consider and to adjust are:

1. The length of the blow, blowing-time .... B. T.
2. Time for the vessel-work, vessel-time .... V. T.
3. Time for the casting-ladle work, ladle-time .... L. T.
4. Time to teem, cool and strip the ingots of a heat, and to replace the moulds for a new heat, mould-time .... M. T.
5. Time for the manœuvres of the ingot-cranes, ingot-crane-time .... C. T.

With this discussion in view I have made more than 500 observations of the time occupied by the several operations connected with the production of ingots by this process.

Some results condensed from these will now be presented:

1. BT consists of the time actually occupied in blowing, plus the half minute occupied in turning the vessel up and down. The time occupied by the blow proper depends on the proportion of carbon and silicon in the metal, the weight of the charge, the number and size of the tuyere-holes and the pressure of the blast; and this last in turn on the capacity of the blowing engine. As the engine-power and the aggregate area of the tuyere-holes are usually roughly proportioned to the weight of the charge, the chief factor in determining the length of the blow is usually the proportion of silicon in the cast-iron.

Actually, Forsyth has made seven 10-ton heats in an hour and 73 in twelve hours at the Union works, or at the rate of 8.6 and 9.86 minutes per heat respectively.

At Homestead 61 five-ton heats have been made in eight hours, or at the rate of 7.87 minutes per heat[a]: and at Scranton 78 heats of 6.6 tons each have been blown in a single twelve-hour shift. As lately as 1883 Forsyth put the limit of the possible production of the South Chicago pit at one heat per twelve minutes.

Of course the output in certain single hours is likely to be much greater than the average of the day's work. It is not sufficient that the casting appliances can on an average receive and take care of the average of the vessel's output; they should be designed to receive it as it is delivered, even during the hours when its delivery is most rapid. Considering the advances made since 1883, we discount the future but little in taking BT as eight minutes, *i. e.*, in arranging our plant so that it can receive and handle a heat every eight minutes.

The little Swedish vessels, indeed, go far beyond the limit of eight minutes per heat, and, by using a very large tuyere-area per ton of charge, often blow a heat in five minutes; but it seems doubtful whether a proportionally large tuyere-area would be desirable for our great ten ton vessels.

2. VT, the time occupied by the vessel's work between heats, consists in the time occupied in recarburizing, in pouring the steel into the casting ladle, in emptying slag, in examining, and, if need be, replacing tuyeres and performing like minor repairs, and in introducing the new charge of cast-iron into the vessel. If we except time occupied in extraordinary repairs, such as changing bottoms, patching the lining, etc., VT is usually short enough. If there is any delay here, it is through charging large quantities of cold scrap steel by hand;[m] this may be avoided by charging the scrap steel through a chute during the blow.

From many observations I believe that it is not necessary that the different parts of VT should occupy more time than is indicated in the first of the following sets of numbers; I have actually known them to occupy only the intervals given in the second column.

TABLE 189.—DETAILS OF VT.

	Time probably needed.	Minimum observed time.
Recarburizing	25"	15"
Pouring into casting ladle	45"	40"
Emptying slag and turning back into receiving position	25"	22"
Receiving cast-iron and examining tuyeres	1' 50"	1' 40"
Total	3' 25"	2' 57"

I have never known the whole of VT to take so little time as this, simply because there is usually no reason for haste, as VT is readily made so much shorter than BT. There is usually more or less waiting, except when changing bottoms: then indeed matters are hurried. In one case, watch in hand, I noted that 14' 30" elapsed between the time of pouring the steel of one heat into the casting-ladle and that of running in the charge of cast-iron for the next charge, and during this time a bottom was changed. Adding 25" for recarburizing, 45" for pouring into the casting-ladle and 1' 50" for receiving the cast-iron for the following charge, VT would in this case be 17' 30". This was at the Homestead works, where the facilities for changing bottoms are not remarkably good. At the Union works VT, including changing bottoms, has been as short as 17', and 63 heats have been blown in 12 hours, using but one vessel and changing 3 bottoms!

3. LT usually consists of the time occupied by a single casting-crane in receiving the molten steel from the vessel, in swinging to the moulds, in teeming, in changing or repairing ladles and setting stoppers, and in swinging back to the vessel to receive a new charge of steel. In plants like Forsyth's, however, the time occupied in pouring from the vessel to the ladle is not part of LT, for here the casting-ladle is not put upon the casting-crane until it has received the charge of molten steel.

The details of LT should be about as follows in rapid work:

TABLE 190.—DETAILS OF TIME OCCUPIED BY THE OPERATIONS OF THE CASTING-CRANE, FOR 10-TON HEATS, LT.

	Vessel pours directly to casting-crane.	Vessel does not pour directly to casting-crane.	Minimum time observed.
Receiving the molten steel	45"	....	40"
Swinging to the moulds	28"	30"	27"
Teeming 10 tons in 8 ingots	5' 30"	5' 35"	5' 15"
Changing or repairing ladles	1' 0"	1' 0"	50"
Swinging back to the vessel	18"	13"	11"
Total	7' 50"	7' 18"	7' 11"

As LT consists chiefly of the teeming proper, its length should increase almost proportionally with the weight of the charge. For given total weight it will increase markedly with the number of ingots per charge; for a given weight of steel is more rapidly teemed into a few large than into many small ingots, as the last part of the steel poured into each mould must be added cautiously, in order that the ingot may have exactly the desired weight, and as time is lost in passing from mould to mould. But if the ingots are cast in groups, as in bottom- and other forms of multiple casting, LT increases relatively little with the number of ingots. The teeming is slower and hence LT

[a] Eng. and Mining Jl., XLIII., p. 253, 1887.

[m] *E. g.*, to lower the temperature of the blow. This may, however, be done by blowing steam into the vessel along with the blast.

is longer in case of very low-carbon steel than in that of rail-steel.

4. MT, or the interval from the time when we begin teeming into a set of moulds to the time when we can again teem into a set standing in the same place in the casting pit, consists (1) of the time needed for teeming the whole heat: plus (2) the time during which the last-teemed ingot must stand in its mould before we can strip it without danger of its bleeding, *or* the time needed for the ingot to contract and for the mould to expand so much that they separate readily: plus (3) the time needed for stripping the last teemed ingot, plus the time needed for lifting the last four ingots from the pit and placing them on cars (for it is more convenient to strip at least four ingots consecutively and then to lift them than to strip and lift one at a time): plus (4) the time needed for replacing the last four moulds, for it is hardly practicable to begin teeming into a set of moulds till the whole set is in place. We here assume that there are ingot-cranes enough to care for these moulds and their ingots.

The details of MT should be about as follows in rapid work:

TABLE 191.—DETAILS OF TIME OCCUPIED IN TEEMING AND REPLACING MOULDS, MT, FOR 10-TON HEATS OF RAIL-STEEL.

	Time probably needed.	Minimum time observed.
Teeming 10 tons in 8 ingots	5' 30"	5' 15"
Last ingot must stay in mould	10' 20"	9' 49"
Stripping last ingot	27"	23"
Lifting last four ingots	1' 50"	1' 40"
Replacing last four moulds	1' 40"	1' 30"
Total	19' 47"	18' 37"

Of these the only one as to which I feel in doubt is the most important, to wit, the time the ingot must remain in the mould before stripping. I have known ingots stripped successfully 9' 49" after teeming, but I have seen bleeding occur when a rail-ingot, cast at normal temperature, was stripped 9' 50" after teeming. On the other hand it is stated that at Darlington (Britain) half the 11-inch ingots of a rail-steel heat are stripped, removed and placed in the soaking-pit by the time that the last ingot is teeming, and that, in case of wire-steel, each ingot stays in its mould but 8 minutes. How this early stripping is made possible I know not, but it seems to imply some such expedient as the use of very cold and thick-walled moulds which, as pointed out in § 225, p. 151, is objectionable. Perhaps in addition the moulds may taper more strongly than ours. As MT consists chiefly of the time occupied by the ingots in solidifying, and as thin ingots solidify much more quickly than thick ones, so its length depends chiefly on the thickness of the ingots, and to a smaller extent on their individual weight. Further, as the teeming time forms a considerable part of it, MT must increase with the weight and the number of ingots per charge. So, too, MT seems to be somewhat longer with low than with high-carbon steel, as the former must be teemed slowly on account of its tendency to rise, and at a much higher temperature than is necessary for the latter; and this does not seem to be fully offset by the counter consideration that the former solidifies at a higher temperature than the latter, and hence quicker. The explanation appears to be that, with low-carbon steel, the difference between the temperature of fluidity sufficient for teeming and that of solidity sufficient for stripping and handling, is greater than with high-carbon steel.

5. CT consists of the time occupied by a single ingot-crane in lifting the moulds from the ingots, and placing them either on cars or in a cooling-space within the converting-room; in lifting the ingots and placing them on cars for removal, and in placing the moulds for another heat.

TABLE 192.—DETAILS OF TIME OCCUPIED BY THE OPERATIONS OF THE INGOT-CRANES, CT.

	Time Probably Needed.	Minimum Time Observed.
Lifting and removing 8 moulds	3' 30"	3' 0"
Lifting 8 ingots and placing on cars	3' 30"	3' 20"
Setting 8 moulds	3' 10"	3' 0"
Or at the rate of about 1¼ minutes per ingot.	10' 10"	9' 20"

CT clearly depends almost wholly on the number of ingots per charge, and only through this on the weight of the charge, save that heavy ingots cannot be raised and swung quite so quickly as light ones.

Table 193 condenses part of the foregoing.

TABLE 193.—TIME NEEDED FOR THE DETAILS OPERATIONS IN A 10-TON BESSEMER CONVERTING HOUSE, CASTING 8 INGOTS PER HEAT; CONDENSED.

	Probable time in rapid work.		Minimum time observed	Time depends chiefly on
	Holley and like plants.	Forsyth and like plants.		
Turning the vessel up and down	30"	......	19"	
Blowing	7' 30"	......		
Recarburizing	25"	......	15"	
Pouring into casting ladle	45"	......	40"	
Emptying slag and turning back to position	25"	......	22"	
Receiving cast iron and examining tuyeres	1' 50"		1' 40"	
Swinging casting-ladle to moulds	28"	30"	25"	
Teeming 10 tons in 8 ingots	5' 30"	5' 30"	5' 15"	
Changing or repairing ladles	1' 0"	1' 0"	50"	
Swinging back to the vessel	13"	18"	11"	
Each ingot must stay in the mould	10' 20"	......	9' 49"	
Stripping 8 ingots and setting their moulds on cars	3' 30"	......	3' 0"	
Lifting 8 ingots and setting on cars	3' 30"	......	3' 20"	
Replacing eight moulds	3' 10"	......	3' 0"	
BT or total blowing cycle	8' 0"	......	8'	% silicon in cast-iron.
VT or cycle of vessel work between blows: Without changing bottoms	3' 25"	......	2' 57"	
VT or cycle of vessel work between blows: Changing bottoms	19' 0"	......	17'	
LT or cycle of casting-ladle	7' 56"	7' 13"	17' 11"	Weight of charge and number of ingots.
MT or cycle of moulds	19' 47"	......	18' 37"	Thickness and No. of ingots.
CT or cycle of ingot-cranes	10' 10"	......	9' 20"	No. of ingots.

If, as we have assumed, blowing is to be continuous, and if we let

x = the number of casting-cranes,

y = the number of sets of moulds for which there is space in the casting pit, and

z = the number of ingot-cranes, then we must have

$$(1) \ldots . x > \frac{LT}{BT};$$

$$(2) \ldots . y > \frac{MT}{BT}; \text{ and}$$

$$(3) \ldots . z > \frac{CT}{BT}.$$

As we shall shortly see, expressions (2) and (3) require modification, and become

$$(4) \ldots y > \frac{MT}{BT} + 1, \text{ and}$$

$$(5) \ldots . z > 1.5 \frac{CT}{BT} + 1.$$

Further, there must be enough casting- and ingot-cranes, x and z, to reach the y sets of moulds.

§ 377. APPLICATION OF THE FOREGOING DISCUSSION.—1. *Number of Vessels.* For rapid work it is clearly desirable that there should be at least two vessels, so that one may blow while the other receives and discharges metal and undergoes current repairs. If we take BT as 8' and VT as 3' 25", then clearly with two vessels we can make a heat every eight minutes, while with one vessel we can only make a heat every 11′ 25″, and practically the difference would be greater than this.

But, while with two vessels blowing may be continuous as long as only minor repairs are needed, since VT is so much shorter than BT, yet when we have to change bottoms blowing must be interrupted, since in this case VT is likely to be at least as long as 18′. Assuming VT at even 19′ the course of operations is as follows: As soon as vessel 1, whose bottom is worn out, finishes its heat, the work of changing bottoms begins; even before the steel is poured into the ladle the bottom is partly unkeyed. Now while the bottom is changing, vessel 2 blows a heat taking, say, 8′; discharges and receives metal during, say, 3′ 25″ or VT; and blows a second heat, taking 8′ more, or altogether 19′ 25″ from the time when vessel 1 ceased blowing. In these 19′ the bottom of vessel 1 has been changed, it has received a new charge of cast-iron, and is ready to blow as soon as the second heat of vessel 2 ends. Thus the total interruption due to changing bottoms is only 3′ 25″.

If now a bottom last 25 heats, then on an average there will be this interruption of 3′ 25″ every 25 heats, so that the blowing, instead of being absolutely continuous, will be continuous for 25 heats, or, say, 25 × 8 = 200′, and will then be interrupted for 3′ 25″, so that the interruptions on this account will amount to 1.6% of the total time.

But occasionally, especially towards the end of the week, the lining of the vessel at points other than the bottom needs repairs, so that it may be necessary to blow three or even four consecutive heats in one vessel while the other is undergoing repairs, which would bring the delay up to 10′ or even to 14′ out of every 200′. Again, it may occasionally happen that while the bottom of one vessel is changing that of the other may give out, though this should be extremely rare in well conducted mills. Taking all these factors into consideration, it does not seem probable that the interruptions due to changing bottoms and repairing linings of vessels should amount to more than 5% of the total time.

Now by having three vessels instead of two, one may always be ready when the bottom of another is to be changed, so that, but for the inevitable occasional delay, blowing may be absolutely continuous. This naturally leads us to study

The relative advantages of two- and of three-vessel plants.

We find that the conclusion which we have just reached, that only about 5% greater output should be expected from a three than from a two-vessel plant, is born out by the results reached in practice, both as regards tonnage and the number of heats made in given time: witness the latest "record-breaking" results in table 194.

It is true that two out of the three three-vessel mills, South Chicago and Edgar Thomson, are at a disadvantage in using direct-metal, while the Union, Homestead and Scranton mills use cupola-metal. Owing to unavoidable irregularities in the conditions in the blast-furnace, the composition of direct-metal is less perfectly under control than that of cupola-metal. Mills using direct metal, therefore, are liable to have occasional heats unduly high in silicon, and hence unduly long in blowing. But the third three-vessel plant, Harrisburg, labors under no such disadvantage; its management, too, is able and energetic.

TABLE 194.—MAXIMUM OUTPUT OF AMERICAN BESSEMER WORKS.

		Tons.				Number of Heats.				Hours per shift.	Shifts per week.	Shifts in the month here given.
		Per 12 hours.	Per 24 hours.	Per week.	Per month.	Per 12 hours.	Per 24 hours.	Per week.	Per month.			
Two-vessel Mills.	Union	....	....	5,490	28,145	73	....	....	2,858	12	11	....
	Scranton	....	....	....	....	78	....	780	....	....	....	....
	Homestead. On rail-steel, 1887	477	891	4,477	16,572	91.5	170	809	3,536	8	20	71
	Homestead. Low-carbon steel, 1889	372	619	....	13,231	68	116	....	2,436	8	16	71
Three-vessel Mills.	Edgar Thomson	729	1,384	7,557	31,120	71	132	719	3,014	12	11½	Not given.
	Harrisburg	544	1,029	5,110	20,947	75	141	678	2,929	12	11	48
	South Chicago	701	1,398	6,402	27,427	60	119	556	2,441	12	11	50

Most of the results in Table 194 were given me in May, 1889, by the management of the several mills as their best record up to that time.

The Homestead shifts are of eight hours, instead of twelve hours as at the other works. To arrive at the maximum output per twelve hours at Homestead I have added one-half to the maximum output per eight-hour shift, so as to get data as nearly comparable with the others as practicable. Needless to say this is giving Homestead a slight advantage, for one may keep up a higher speed for eight than for twelve hours.

With this exception the numbers given represent actual results without qualification of any kind. Thus Union and Edgar Thomson have actually made 2,858 and 3,014 heats respectively in one calendar month.

Certainly there is nothing in our present experience pointing to a very marked difference between the capacity of a two- and that of a three-vessel plant. But the three-vessel plant has a real advantage in that, thanks to our being able to lay one vessel off for repairs without interfering with the output of the mill, the vessel-linings may be repaired more leisurely and at more convenient times, *e. g.*, during the week instead of on Sunday, by daylight instead of hurriedly at night; and in that bottoms may be changed more leisurely; needless to say work is usually not only better but cheaper when leisurely than when hurried. Finally, the superintendent's energy, spared from the frequent hurried planning of how to make vessel one last till the bottom of vessel two is changed, how to make the nose-lining last through the week, etc., is available for other matters. In a word, the three-vessel plant works a little more easily and hence a little more cheaply.

On the other hand, the three-vessel plant is necessarily a more expensive one. First we have to provide the third vessel, with its rotating mechanism, supports, hood, etc. In a mill like Harrisburg, Figure 171, or Edgar Thomson, Figure 177, we have further to provide a longer building and a second casting-crane. In a mill on Forsyth's plan, like South Chicago, Figure 168, we can have three vessels without a second casting-crane, and probably without materially increasing the size of the building; but we at least have to have an additional receiving crane.

With either the Edgar Thomson or Forsyth's plan the number and size of cupolas, the engine and boiler capacity, the number and size of ingot-cranes, and the general strength of the apparatus should be the same for a two- as for a three-vessel plant, for, as we have seen, the output is practically the same, the quantity of cast-iron to be hoisted, melted and blown, the quantity of air needed for blowing, the number and weight of ingots and moulds to be raised and lowered are all practically the same in one case as in the other. None can deny that during the hours when there is no changing of bottoms, the two-vessel plant blows as many and as heavy heats as the three-vessel plant: and that the blowing, hoisting and manipulating machinery must be designed for these hours of maximum output, not for the average of these with the slack hours. I have been surprised at the deliberate statements of eminent engineers, that the three-vessel plant must be made more substantial on account of its greater output.

Whether the greater ease of working pays for the extra cost of the three-vessel plant, is a question on which opinions are divided. If we assume that the extra cost of installation is $25,000,[h] a charge of 20% per annum for interest and amortization would amount to $5,000, or $0.025 per ton of ingots on an annual output of 200,000 tons, or of $17 per diem for a year of 300 working days.

2. *The Size of Vessels.*—There is nothing in the experience with ten-ton vessels to lead as to doubt the practicability of using larger ones. Indeed, the new vessel shown in Figures 198, 204 and 205 aims to hold from twelve to fifteen tons. If larger charges are to be blown, it will be necessary either to increase the size of ingots, so as to have fewer to cast per heat, or to provide some additional means of handling them, such as multiple casting, the use of a second or even a third casting-pit, etc. (See § 379, and the last part of § 378.)

3. NUMBER OF CASTING-CRANES NEEDED.—We saw in Table 190 that if, as in most plants, LT includes the time during which the steel is pouring from the vessel into the casting-ladle, it amounts to 7′ 56″ or dangerously near BT, which is 8′: if, however, the casting-ladle is not placed on the casting-crane till after receiving the steel, LT is considerably shorter, to wit 7′ 13″. Here LT is 47″ shorter than BT, so that a single casting-crane will perform its functions quickly enough to receive and distribute the steel as fast as it is blown. A single casting-crane then satisfies the formula $y > \frac{LT}{BT}$, which becomes $1 > 7\frac{13}{60} \div 8$, or $1 > 0.902$. This inference is in accord with the results of practice, for the work at the Union mill, with a single casting-crane which does not receive the molten steel till after this has been poured into the ladle, is practically as rapid as that at Harrisburg and Edgar Thomson where there are two casting-cranes, and as that at Bethlehem where there are three.

In short, a single casting-crane, if it has to hold the casting-ladle while the steel is pouring into it, has so little margin of time that it is liable to hold the work back at least occasionally: but if it be free to attend to its other duties during the 45″ in which the steel is pouring from vessel to ladle, it can handle the steel as fast as the vessels can produce it. If, however, the number of ingots to be cast per minute were materially raised beyond its present maximum number, whether by shortening the blow or by increasing the number of ingots per heat, a second casting-crane as in the Harrisburg type would be needed, unless some form of multiple teeming were adopted. This is true of both two- and three-vessel plants, and of Forsyth as well as of other types.

4. *Number of Sets of Moulds for which Space must be provided in the Casting Pit.*—According to (2) y must be greater than $\frac{MT}{BT}$: according to Tables 192 and 193 MT=19′ 47″ and BT=8′: hence $y > \frac{19' 47''}{8}$ or $y=3$.

In other words, if (Table 193) it takes 5′ 30″ to teem the steel of one heat; if we must allow the last ingot of the heat 10′ 20″ to cool before stripping it; and if to strip it, to remove the ingots, and to set a fresh lot of moulds in place takes 3′ 57″, we cannot begin to teem again in the place occupied by this set of moulds till 5′ 30″ + 10′ 20″ + 3′ 57″ = 19′ 47″ after the time when we began teeming the previous heat in this place. That is to say, this casting-space can receive a heat of steel only once in 19′ 47″: and in order that there may be a casting-space ready to receive a heat of steel every 8′, there must be space for at least $19\frac{47}{60} \div 8 = 2.5$ sets of moulds in the casting-pit, or, as we cannot have fractions, 3 sets. But in case of rapid working it is far better to have a spare set of moulds in the pit, or altogether four sets, so that

$$(4) \ldots\ldots y > \frac{MT}{BT} + 1.$$

This is desirable, both that the pit-men, whose labor in hot weather is extremely trying, may have an occasional breathing spell; and that, no matter what happens, there may always be moulds enough to take the steel. There is not enough margin between the temperature of the molten steel as it leaves the vessel and the melting-point of the metal, to allow us to hold it long in the ladle; moreover, the casting-crane is in constant requisition. It would, indeed, be trying to have a heat of steel blown and in the ladle, ready for teeming, and then to be forced to convert it into scrap for want of moulds.

A set of eight 14½″ ingot-moulds occupies at least 14 running feet; for four sets we need 56 running feet, and it is better to allow 60 feet. This should be measured on the arc of a circle about four feet less in diameter than the rim of the casting-pit, for the moulds come together only on the edges nearer the centre of the pit, gaping at the outer edges. In a 40-foot pit an allowance of 60 feet for the inner circle of the moulds calls for an arc of 191°.

5. *Number of Ingot-cranes Needed.*—As we have seen in Tables 192 and 193 that BT and CT are 8′ and 10′ 10″ respectively, to satisfy the formula $z > \frac{CT}{BT}$, we need more than $(10 + \frac{10}{60}) \div 8 = 1.27$, *i. e.*, we need two ingot cranes; that is, as it takes 10′ 10″ to strip and lift the ingots of a single heat and to replace their moulds for a subsequent heat, so in order that an ingot-crane may be ready to handle a set of ingots and moulds every 8′, there must be two ingot-cranes, supposing that each works continuously. But this cannot be the case, for each necessarily stands idle a considerable part of the time, *e. g.*, from the time when the moulds in its neighborhood are in place and ready for receiving steel, till they have been filled with steel, and till the steel ingots within them have so far solidified that they can be stripped safely. It is therefore found necessary in practice to have three ingot-cranes for a ten-ton plant. In addition, the crane which is used for removing the casting-ladle from the casting-crane, and for replacing it with another, and (in case it be unnecessary to change ladles) for inverting the ladle to empty the slag, though properly speaking a ladle-shifting or, as it is called, "dump" crane, is often classed with the ingot-cranes. Indeed, it is usually exactly like

h The charge of $25,000 is meant to cover simply those items which are necessitated by the addition of a third vessel to a two-vessel Forsyth or similar plant; to wit, the third vessel with its rotating gear, hood, receiving-crane, additional platforms, foundations, pit for receiving crane, etc.; but it does not cover any charge for additional engine or boiler-power, casting or ingot-cranes, cupolas, hoists, etc., which, from this point of view, remain the same as for a two-vessel plant.

them. Thus we actually need four ingot and dump cranes for rapid working with a 10-ton plant. I think that the empirical formula

$$(5) \ldots\ldots z > 2\frac{CT}{MT} + 1$$

gives a sufficiently close approximation for practical purposes. In case of a six-ton plant this formula would require three ingot-cranes.

In point of fact the American plants noted for their quick working have at least as many ingot-cranes as this formula calls for, Union, S. Chicago, Harrisburg and Homestead having four each, Scranton (a six-ton plant) having three, and Edgar Thomson five.

As the large number of ingot-cranes needed is chiefly due to their having to stand idle so much of the time, so it is clear that the number of ingot-cranes needed will not increase proportionally to the number of ingots cast from each heat.

The method I here use is less suited to the case of ingot-cranes than to the other cases to which it is applied.

§ 378. THE CAPACITY OF A CASTING-PIT is limited, 1st, by the rate at which the casting-crane or cranes can teem; 2d, by the room available for moulds within the pit; 3d, by the number of ingots and moulds which the ingot-cranes can handle.

We have seen that a single casting-crane can teem continuously at the rate of one 1.25-ton ingot per minute. I should think that it could teem 19-inch 3-ton ingots at the rate of one every two minutes, and 7-inch 750-pound ingots at the rate of two per minute. A second casting-crane would cast as much more.

If we measure the space available for moulds along the arc of a circle four feet less in diameter than the pit, the 250° of a 40-foot Forsyth pit available for moulds would give 78 running feet. If a second row of moulds were placed within the first, 70 running feet more would be available, or altogether 148 feet. In a 48-foot pit these numbers become 96 and 183 feet respectively. For a 10-ton heat of 14-inch ingots we have taken MT, or the period between beginning to teem into a set of moulds and again beginning to teem into a second set standing in the same place, as about 20 minutes; if we take MT provisionally as 30 minutes for 19-inch and 15 minutes for 7-inch ingots, and if there be a single row of moulds in case of 19- and of 14-inch ingots and a double row in case of 7-inch ingots, and if we assume that our ingot-cranes can do their share of the work, then it follows that, as far as mould-space is concerned, we could cast in a 40-foot pit 1.16 19-inch, or 2.3 14-inch, or 9.9 7-inch ingots per minute; and that in a 48-foot pit we could teem 1.4 19-inch, or 2.9 14-inch, or 12.2 7-inch ingots per minute.

Next, as regards the ingot-crane capacity. It is hardly practicable to have more than three cranes devoted solely to the care of ingots and moulds at a 40-foot pit, or more than four at a 48-foot pit, as explained in § 380 B. For each ingot three separate operations are needed, and to perform these we have seen that about 1.25 minutes are needed for each 1.25-ton ingot. Let us assume that two minutes would be needed for each 3-ton ingot and one minute for each 750-pound ingot. When casting 1.25-ton 14-inch ingots the ingot-cranes may have to stand idle half the time; but in casting smaller, say 750 pound, ingots, they would work much more nearly continuously, and I think that we may assume that each crane would stand idle only one-quarter of the time. Under these assumptions three ingot-cranes could handle 3-ton ingots at the rate of one in 1.3 minutes; 1.25-ton ingots at the rate of 1.2 ingots per minute; and 750-pound ingots at the rate of 2.25 per minute. With a fourth crane these rates would be increased by one-third.

Some of these inferences are summed up in the following table:

TABLE 193.—ESTIMATED CAPACITY OF A SINGLE PIT PER 24 HOURS.

	Number.	40-foot pit with three cranes for handling ingots and moulds.						48-foot pit with four cranes for handling ingots and moulds.					
		Casting 3-ton 19-inch ingots.		Casting 1.25-ton 14-inch ingots		Casting 750-pound 7-inch ingots: 2 rows of moulds.		Casting 3-ton 19-inch ingots.		Casting 1.25-ton 14-inch ingots.		Casting 750 pound 7-inch ingots: 2 rows of moulds.	
		Capacity for Twenty-four hours.											
		Ingots.	Tons.	Ingots.	Tons.	Ingots.	Tons.	Ingots.	Tons.	Ingots.	Tons.	Ingots.	Tons.
I.—As limited by the capacity of a single casting-crane	1	720	2,160					720	2,160				
	2			1,440	1,800					1,440	1,800		
	3					2,880	964					2,880	964
II.—As limited by the available mould-space	4	1,668	5,000					2,048	6,143				
	5			3,370	4,212					4,147	5,200		
	6					14,000	4,750					17,568	5,880
III.—As limited by the capacity of the ingot-cranes	7	1,080	3,240					1,440	4,320				
	8			1,728	2,160					2,304	2,880		
	9					3,240	1,100					4,320	1,400

These numbers indicate that the mould-holding capacity of even a 40-foot pit is far beyond the present blowing-capacity of two or three 10-ton vessels; but, before the tonnage indicated in lines 4 to 6 was reached, grave inconveniences from the excessive heat-radiation from so enormous a quantity of metal compactly stored in a single pit at one time, would arise.

It is quite otherwise, however, with the casting- and ingot-crane capacity. The former of these, even in case of 1.25-ton ingots, is barely equal to the actual rate at which a pair of vessels has turned out steel for a considerable period. On any considerable increase in the tonnage or in the number of ingots, the capacity of a single casting-crane would be exceeded. As regards the ingot-cranes, the case is not so bad, for with a 48-foot pit four ingot-cranes could, according to this estimate, take care of more 1.25-ton ingot than two or three vessels are likely to turn out. But should the number of ingots be greatly increased, *e. g.*, by diminishing their size, additional ingot-crane capacity would be needed.

In short, further increase in blowing-capacity is likely to necessitate, first an increase in the teeming-capacity, and only later in the ingot-handling capacity.

The teeming-capacity may be increased by multiple-teeming, *e. g.*, by teeming through a funnel which delivers into several moulds, and by other devices which will be considered later; or by the use of a second, or eventually a third casting-crane. The casting-cranes may all stand in the same pit; but more casting-room can be had and a greater number of ingot-cranes can be used if we have a separate pit for each casting-crane. Pits may be arranged as in Figure 175, which may be considered as the logical development of Forsyth's plan.

The use of a second casting-crane has an advantage over multiple-teeming, in that it enables us to use more ingot-cranes. For very small castings multiple-teeming seems to be a necessity, unless proportionally small charges are blown in little vessels, as a large heat would chill before it could be teemed separately into a great number of small castings.

To increase the capacity of the ingot-cranes, we must cut down the number of motions per ingot which they have to execute. Usually they have to perform three distinct manœuvres, placing the mould, stripping, and removing the ingot. The number of motions may be reduced by placing several moulds on a single plate, which with ingots and moulds is lifted from the pit by a single motion of the crane; or by lifting ingot and mould together from the pit; or by placing the several moulds of a group of ingots in a common frame, so that they are lifted from the pit by a single motion of the crane, the ingots remaining behind. In the first two cases no real saving of labor is effected, if the ingots and moulds are simply carried off to be stripped elsewhere in the way in which they are usually stripped in the pit. This simply changes the venue; but by Laureau's or Jones' mode of stripping, a saving may be effected.

§ 379. Kleinbessemerei, Small *versus* Large Bessemer Plants.—The question as to the most desirable weight of charge naturally divides itself into two quite distinct parts. 1st. Do we with large or with small charges habitually get the better product (or the more readily make a product of given excellence) from given materials? 2d. Is it cheaper to blow large or small charges? We have two distinct questions, one of quality, the other of cost.

The question of quality can be considered better in treating of the chemistry of the Bessemer process. I may here say, however, that after pretty extensive enquiries and observations, I find neither good reason to expect better product nor convincing evidence that better product is made in case of small than in that of large charges. Nor is it clear to me that soft ingot-iron is more readily or more regularly made in small than in large vessels.

As regards the question of cost, much confusion has been brought into what should be a very simple discussion, by comparing small works which run continuously with larger works which run intermittently. Nobody will deny that the more nearly continuous the work the cheaper it will be, for most obvious reasons. We have in the first place the factors common to all industries: our workmen and machines work a greater proportion of the time, charges for amortization and interest, for administration and general expenses are less per unit of product. But beyond these, we have in metallurgial operations a very important factor: the loss of heat from furnaces, vessels and what not is less in continuous than in interrupted working.

Now, some advocates of small charges have assumed that large charges cannot be blown continuously, which is untrue; for in our large American works with 10-ton vessels the blowing is habitually continuous, one vessel turning up to blow a charge the moment that the blowing of the preceding charge ends, so that the blowing-engine often runs for hours without stopping. Thus Ehrenwerth's calculation that the little Bessemer plant at Avesta is more economical than the larger ones is most misleading, for he compares a four-ton plant making only fifteen heats daily with an 880-pound plant making fifty heats daily, while our ten-ton plants make twice this number of heats. Now it is not the greater size of the four-ton plant, but the very small number of charges which it makes daily, that puts it at a disadvantage. Whatever merit there was in the Avesta work was in its continuousness, not in the lightness of its charges.

This does not really merit discussion, but if proof is needed, it is at hand in the fact that the Avesta small charges were kept up for more than five years without an imitator, and that even here it was found best to increase the charges to 3,300 pounds.

In this country the little Clapp-Griffiths vessels at first had a capacity of two tons; the later ones have three tons capacity. Indeed the American Clapp-Griffiths practice can hardly come under the term "Kleinbessemerei," which was applied to the half-ton Avesta practice in distinction to the Austrian four-ton work, termed "Grossbessemerei."

What, then, is the most advantageous weight of charge? Usually that which with continuous blowing, or with an interval of not over two minutes between blows, will yield the output which is aimed at in the establishment under consideration, supposing this establishment to run say ten months out of the year.[y] This, however, is only true within limits. I doubt whether it would be wise under most conditions to make the weight of the charge less than two tons, even when a very small output is aimed at.

What the expected output is to be must depend on many conditions, the kind of steel aimed at, whether for rails or steel pens, the supply of cast-iron, the expected demand, etc. If a mill is to be built to supply steel for fish-hooks alone, a pair of twelve-ton vessels would be absurd; no less absurd would the Avesta toy-vessels be for rail-making. I take it that the claim that steel can be made cheaper in little than in large mills does not deserve discussion. Other things being equal, *if the demand for steel will keep a ten-ton plant fully occupied*, that steel can be made cheaper in a ten-ton plant than in a one-ton or in a half-ton plant.

Many factors tend to concentrate industries into colossal establishments, ruled by giants of administration. Among these we have the increased facility of transportation, and the growth of scientific and technical knowledge applicable to industries to such an enormous

y I say ten rather than twelve months, because in case of many large manufacturing industries it is thought more profitable, if a given quantity of output is to be made in a certain year, to make that output in ten months, even if the mill be thereby slightly pressed, than to spread the work over the whole year. It is, moreover, better that the capacity of the establishment should be rather larger than the expected output, so that an unexpected demand can be taken advantage of.

volume and to such value that trained specialists, reservoirs of this knowledge, can be advantageously employed. Their salaries clearly form a smaller charge against a large than against a small output. The cost of engines, of plant, of administration,[a] clearly does not increase proportionally to the size of the establishment. Hence it occurs that, in many industries, enterprises large enough to employ the best administrative talent to their fullest capacity—but not larger, and not too large for their market—can be operated at less cost than smaller ones.

These considerations seem to apply with especial force to the manufacture of steel ingots; for the proportion of the total heat generated which is lost in case of large converters, large furnaces for heating and melting, is less than in case of small ones; the loss in scrap and by oxidation is less, the consumption of refractory materials and moulds is less per unit of product in case of large charges than in that of small ones.[b]

But it is quite in accordance with these views that small works should sometimes be profitable. Local conditions, a small local demand for steel in a region which offers the raw materials, but is remote from other markets; the manufacture of a special or even secret kind of steel, suited to certain small demands; the need of unusual knowledge and skill or extraordinary care; in short, the conditions which permit little industries to flourish all over the world without being overwhelmed by the great producers, may permit small Bessemer works to live and even thrive. But as the increased facility of transportation and indeed the whole march of civilization favors the concentration of industries into large establishments, ruled by giants of administration, so the times seem to favor larger rather than smaller steel mills.

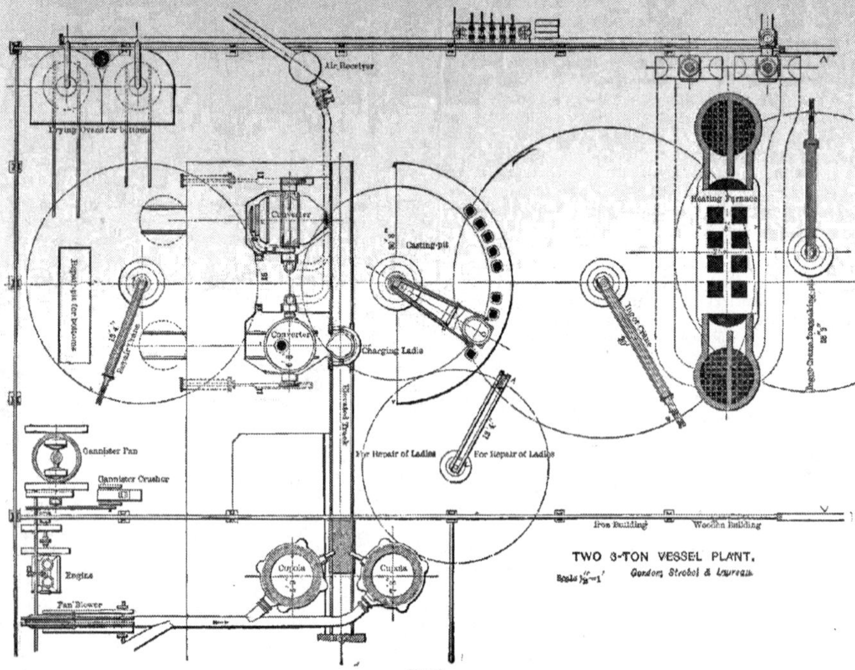

Fig. 166.

Again, while it is beyond question that well designed large works can turn out large ingots of usual sizes more cheaply than small works, most of them have not been equipped for turning out ingots, billets or slabs of a wide variety of sizes, shapes and compositions.

It may be much cheaper to make slabs for nail-plates, for instance, by making ingots in little vessels, and rolling those ingots down while they still preserve their initial heat, than to buy even cheaper but cold ingots from a large mill, pay freight and brokerage, and then heat these cold ingots at great outlay for fuel, labor, and repairs to

---

a In certain industries (*e. g.*, in making sewing machines) the cost of administration, advertisement, and collection is said to be far greater than that of manufacture proper.

b Classing as small all workshops with five workmen or less, and as large all with more than five workmen, Dr. H. Albrecht finds that in Germany, according to the trades census of 1882, 99% of the mining, smelting, and salt-making establishments are large, while the proportion is much less in other industries, running from 76% in chemical manufacture to 10% in clothing and repairing. ("The Nation," N. Y., XLVIII, P. 480, 1889, from "Jahrbuch für Gesetzgebung.")

heating furnaces. A pound of hot ingots is worth more in such cases than a pound of cold ones. This has been especially true in the past somewhat crude condition of our Bessemer industry, crude in the sense that it has been chiefly planned for turning out an enormous quantity of ingots of uniform size, to be rolled into one kind of product, rails. In this way the little Bessemer works have had a real reason for existence. As the manufacture of billets or slabs of a certain size and composition in small mills assumes serious proportions, the large mills equip themselves for making these very products, and roll their ingots, with their initial heat, into these very forms, and this special reason for the existence of the little works evaporates.

The same thing may happen in the case of little ingots. Our great mills with their one or two circular casting pits can make a thousand tons of large ingots daily; but they are not prepared to turn their product into little ingots. Let some little Bessemer works develop a valuable trade in little ingots, and the great works will establish some special form of pit or of multiple casting, swoop down and carry off the prey.

While the great works may drive the little ones from some positions readily, in others to which they are specially fitted the little mills may hold their own long, or even permanently.

This, however, belongs rather to political economy than to metallurgy. All that I can do is to point out, and indeed to insist, that the forces which make for concentration elsewhere are and will remain at work in case of the Bessemer process, in which they are reinforced by the special conditions of the process itself.

Figure 165 shows a good arrangement for a small Bessemer plant. Two cupolas deliver the molten cast-iron to a ladle which runs on an elevated track, and which in turn delivers it to the vessels. A common casting-ladle casts the steel into moulds standing along the rim of a semi-circular casting-pit. From this pit the ingots are drawn by a crane, which deposits them on end in a heating-furnace or soaking-pit, whence they are drawn later and deposited on the feed-rollers of the blooming-mill.

The refractory materials are prepared behind the vessels, in a space served by a 15 foot crane. Near here stands a small engine which drives the fan blowers for the cupola furnaces, and the crushing and pulverizing machinery for the refractory materials.

§ 380. THE GENERAL DISPOSITION OF THE VESSELS, PIT, AND INGOT-CRANES.[a]—In the early Bessemer plants, Figure 166, the vessel-trunnions were but three or four feet above the general level. This necessitated a very deep casting pit, so that the vessels might empty their slag through their noses on being inverted, that their bottoms might be removed and replaced from beneath, and that the casting-crane might raise the casting-ladle above the tops of the moulds standing in the casting-pit without having a very long lift, which would have increased its cost materially, especially as the British cranes are not supported at the top. "In this confined, unventilated and comparatively inaccessible," indeed, infernal abyss, hemmed in by red-hot ingots and moulds, bespattered by the vessel's white-hot spittings as it turned up or down, scorched by the slag which it dropped between heats, and threatened by the floods of molten steel which now and again broke through its nether parts, the salamandrine pit-men intolerably reeked and wrought.

The vessels were placed opposite each other.

In the early American or Holley[b] plants the vessels were raised, as shown in Figure 163, to nine feet above the general level, while in still later plants, *e. g.*, S. Chicago, their height has been further increased to 15', and they have almost uniformly been placed side by side. This enabled Holley to use a shallow pit, only 30" deep, though in later mills the pit is 36" deep. At the same time its

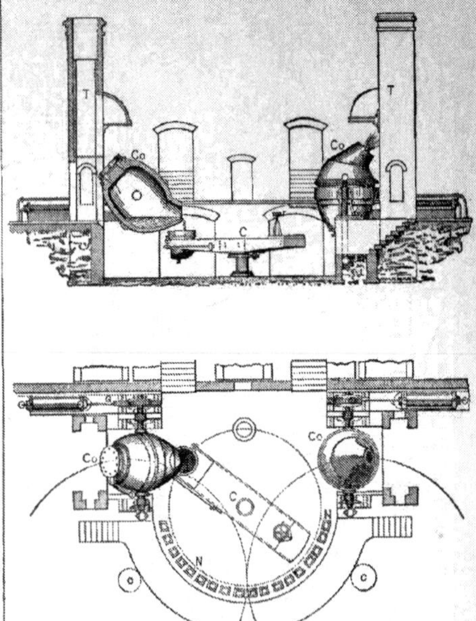

Fig. 166. STANDARD BRITISH BESSEMER PLANT. HOLLEY.

C casting-crane. c ingot cranes. Co Converter. G rack for rotating vessel. N ingot moulds. T hoods.

diameter has been increased to 40' and even to 48'. In some late British plants the vessels are supported aloft in Holley's style[c].

a For admirable descriptions of Bessemer plants see Macar, Revue Universelle, 2d Ser., XII., p. 143, 1882, from which I have borrowed several illustrations; also, Greiner, Idem, XI.; Daelen, Zeit. Vereins, Deutsch. Ing., XXIX., pp. 554, 1016, A. D. 1885. Other illustrations are borrowed from Trasenter, "L'Industrie Sidérurgique aux Etats-Unis," Rev. Univ., 2d Ser., XVII., p. 231, 1885,

b On Jan. 26th, 1869 (U. S. Patent 86,203), Holley patented supporting one side of the vessel on a beam, so that a car could be run beneath it (for removing bottoms, etc.), a hollow column for supporting this beam, and at the same time carrying the blast to the vessel-trunnion, and what appears equivalent to raising the trunnion-level high above the general level. I do not find that he patented placing the vessels side by side; indeed, he stated in 1871, that Bessemer did this in his early practice, but not in such a way as to realize the advantages of the Holley plant. (Lecture at the Stevens Inst. of Technology, 1872, p. 21: Journ. Franklin Inst., XCIV., pp. 252, 391, 1872).

c In the model of a (British) Bessemer plant exhibited at the Paris Exhibition of 1889, by J. Gjers, the vessels, pit, and cranes are arranged much as in Figure 169, save that the receiving-crane delivers direct to the casting-crane without Forsyth's transfer-track, and that the cast-iron is brought to the vessels by a hoist which stands between them, as at H in Figure 164.

A. *Raising the vessels and shallowing the pit* has had the following advantages:

1. The pit is much cooler.

2. The pit-level is so nearly that of the ground outside the works (indeed, in many works the pit-bottom is level with the ground outside, the general working-level of the converting-mill being raised some three feet above this), that the vessel-slag and the casting ladle slag, which may amount to some 150 tons daily, are readily removed by cars running on a track level with the pit-bottom, instead of being shoveled up as from the old deep pit a tremendous lift of nine feet, and then being shoveled again into cars.

3. The vessel-bottoms may be removed and replaced from the general level, and are thus readily brought by cars running on the general level to and from the repair-shop.

4. That we lift the, say, 1,000 tons of ingots and 2,000 tons of moulds handled daily only five feet in transferring them from the pit to cars on the general level, instead of eleven feet. A like saving is effected in lowering the moulds into place in the pit; and each time we raise or lower an ingot or a mould we have to lift the rising parts of an ingot-crane.

The short lift means not only diminishing the outlay for power by half, but lessening by about one-third that for labor, since the pit-men who guide the rising and falling ingots and moulds must stand in the unbearable heat about half longer for an eleven- than for a five-foot lift. Indeed I should put the saving in labor even higher than this: for with the shallow American pit the tops of the ingots and moulds are at such a level that crane-dogs and hooks can be attached to them conveniently by the men standing on the general level, and these same men swing the crane, after it has lifted the ingot or mould, around to the cars on which they deposit its burden: while they cannot readily reach down low enough, in case of the deep nine-foot pit, to attach the dogs, etc., to the ingots and moulds whose tops must be far beneath them.

5. The space on the general level occupied in the old British mills by the vessels and by the mechanism for rotating them, and by the runners through which the molten cast-iron is brought to them, as well as that which is occupied part of the time in examining and replacing the tuyeres between heats, is, in American mills, used advantageously for other purposes: for the vessel-trunnions and the working platform at their level is supported on cast-iron columns, leaving the space beneath free.

TABLE 196.—BESSEMER PLANT.

		Pit.			Vessels.						Tuyeres.						Cubic contents of vessels.	
	Number.	Diameter.	Depth.	Shape.	Number.	Cap'y, tons.	Height of axis above general level.	Diameter.	Concentric or not.	Sides straight or contracted.	No. tuyeres.	No. holes per tuyere.	Size holes.	Gross area of tuyere-square inches.	Sq. in. tuyere-hole area per 2240 lbs. of charge.	Blast-pressure, lbs. per square inch.	Cubic feet.	Cubic feet per ton cap'y.
	1	40′	5′	cir.	2	10		{10′c / 18′ 3″}	con.	con.	15	12	⅜″	19.8	1.98		650	65
	2			cir.	2	7—		6′			12	12	⅜″	15.9		20		
	3	40′	3′	cir.	3 {	10c 10.7b		10c 7′ 10⅛″f {	exc.	str.	{14 / — 4	12 12	⅞″ ⅜″	{34.7k	3.47	21 @ 25	596	59.5
	4				2	10c					18	12	⅜″	30.6	3.06			
	5		4′		3 {	9.21 10	}	10±	con.	con.	15	10	⅜″	29.4	3.35		580	62.3
	6	48′	3′	sc. ann.	2	7		8			14	7	⅜″	19.1	2.73	20		
	7				2	4}			exc.	str.	12	7	⅜″	16.5	4.12			
	8				2	5.5}			exc.	str.								
	9	40p. 14′ 0″ q	3′ 6″	cir.	2	5.	10′ 3″	7′ 6″	exc.	str.								
	10			sc.	2	7b			exc.	str.	13	12	⅜″	30.6	4.37		277	36.9
	11	34′	4′		3	7½b	16±	8′	exc.		19	12	⅜″	25.2	3.36	20		
	12				2	7½g-9h		6′	exc.	str.	18	12	⅜″	17.2	1.91		265	32.7
	13				2	6a					17	16	¼″	35.7	5.95	18 @ 25		
	14				2	6.9½d			exc.	str.	19	12	⅜″	25.2	3.15			
	15				4	8cn		8′	exc.	str.	17	12	⅜″	22.5	3.00		303	41.7
	16				2	9	14′ 6″	10′	con.	str.	16	12	⅜″	21.2	2.35	20		
	17				1	6c					8	10	⅜″	15.7	2.61			
	18		3′	ann.	2	5½b			exc.	str.								
	19				2	4c		7″										
	20				2	10			con.	str.	15	7	⅜″	11.6	1.16			
	21				2	10			exc.	con.	7	12	½″	31.2	3.12			
U. S. Clapp-Griffiths	22				2	2												
	23					3.5b					9	12				17 @ 18		
	24	42′ 11″	4′ 11″	sc. ann.	3	b11.		{10′ / 7′ 11″f}	con.	str.	19	12	⅜″	25.1	2.28	16 @ 25	588	53.4
	25					4		5′f	con.	str.							201	50.3
	26				2	3			con.									
BRITAIN—Rhymney	27				2	7												
Sheffield	28	28′	9′		2	8												
West Cumberland	29																	
Eston	30				2	8		9f	con.	con.	21						626	78.2
" New	31			r.	2	15′	20′	9′ 4″	con.									
Darlington	32				2	6c												
Brown, Bayley & Dixon	33				2	8		8′ 11″	exc.		15	13	⅜″	15.	1.87			
	34				4	8					16	13	⅜″	23.	2.87			
SWEDEN—Längsbyttan	35					2.4						1	⅜″	29.	12	10 @ 11		
Nykroppa	36					2.4		4′ 10″				1	.56	25.2	10	9 @ 17		
Bängbro	37			ann.		2.7	9′ 10″	4′ 10″	exc.			1	.50	22.	8.5	10 @ 17		
Vestanfors	38					2.2						1	.50	13.5	6.1	9 @ 11.5		
Avesta	39					39		3′ 4″	con.	str.		1	.13	1.2	3.	14.8	6	15.2
Sandviken	40				2 {	3to 6	{	5′ 7″@5′ 11″				1	.47m	20.2	3.3	17.		
Domnarfvet	41		2′		2				exc.		6	17				11.5 @ 10.8		
CONTINENT—Hoerde "old pit"	42			cir.	2	5												
Bochum "old pit"	43			cir.	3	8												
Seraing "old pit"	44			cir.	2	6		9′ 2″										
" "new pit" o	45	34′	3′ 9″	cir.	2	6		9′ 2″									261	43.4
Oberhausen	46			cir.	2	8												

6. Raising the vessels enables us to raise the level of the casting-crane, which must be able to descend low enough to receive the steel from the vessel. Raising the casting-crane enables us to support its top with tie-bars level with the roof-trusses, and thus quite out of the way. Moreover, the cylinder of the casting crane is brought to a more accessible level.

Indeed, in late works the vessels stand so high that the top of the cylinder of the casting-crane is at the general platforms, on which many tons of cast-iron, etc., may be piled, cannot be suspended aloft for nothing. Yet it is doubtful whether this really costs much in the end, because for given surface of land we have more available working space, and the area which it is necessary to give our converting-mill is thereby lessened.

Raising the level of the vessels does not necessitate raising that of the cupolas materially. For the level at which the cupolas must stand in order to deliver their iron by

TABLE 196.—BESSEMER PLANT.—*Concluded.*

		Vessel-cylinder.		Iron-cupolas.			Blowing engines.					Cranes.									
							Steam cylinders.		Air cylinders.			Casting-cranes.			Ingot-cranes.			Other cranes.			
	Number.	Diameter.	Stroke.	Number.	Diameter.	Height.	Diameter.	Stroke.	Number.	Diameter.	Stroke.	Number.	Lift.	Radius.	Number.	Lift.	Radius.	Number.	Lift.	Radius.	Water pressure, lbs. per sq. in.
	1	......	......	5	9'	......	......	......	......	......	......	1	......	20' ±	4	......	60'	1 s	......	15'	
	2	14½"	11' 3"	....	8'	......	42"	5'	2	54"	5'	1		15' 6"	2 1	9' 10'	22' 22'	1	6' 3"	10' 3"	300
	3	20"	9' 6"	....	10'	14'	54"	5'	2	66"	5'	1	9'	18' 11"	4	11'	21'	....	......	......	300
	4	......	......	....	10'																
	5	18"	9'	4	8' ±	14' ±	4' ± 3'	4' 5" 4' 5"	2	40" ± 4' 5"	4' 5 ± 4' 6"	2	6'	20' 6" ±	4	9'	20' ±	2	......	......	300
	6	16"	7' 6"	3	9'	22'	42"	60"	...	60"	60"	1	6'	24'	2 1	9' 6'	20' 30'	2	7'	20'	
	7	......	......	2	6'	......	......	......	1	......	......	....	......	......	....	......	......	....	......	......	400
	9	15"	7'	3	8'	19'	30"	5'	2	40"	5'	1	6'	19' 6" ±	4	9'	20'	1 1 1	9' 9' 9	16' 18' 22'	300
	11	......	......	4	8' ±	16'	25" 51"	70"	....	50"	70"	2	......	......	4	......	......	1			
	12	......	......	6	......	......	40"	4' 6"	1	54"	4' 6"										
Scranton	13	......	......	4	9' ±	......	54 ±	60"	2	50"	60"										
	14	......	......	4	10' 8' 6"	......	60"	60"	....	60"	60"										
	15	......	......	8	9'	19' 3"	36" 60"	60" 66"	2 2	48" 54"	60" 66"	3	......	......	6	......	......	3	......	......	300
	16	21"	......	4	9'	19'	32"	54"	2	48"	54"	1	......	16'	3	9'	22'				
	18	......	......	4	8'	24'	30"	36"	...	46"	36"	1	......	......	4	......	......	2			
	19	......	......	2	6'	16' ±															
	20	......	......	4	......	......	42"	5'	2	54"	5'										
U. S. Clapp-Griffiths............	22	......	......	....	......	......	20"	30"	2	48"	30"	1	......	......	3	......	......	....	......	......	350
	24	21"	10'	5	8'	29'	48"	72"	2	60"	72"	1	9'	18'	2	9'	30'	2 1	11' 10" 4' 8	20' 3" 13½'	
	26	......	......	2	......	......	......	......	1												
BRITAIN—Rhymney............	27	......	......	....	......	......	45"	5'	....	54"	5'	1	......	......	2	......	......	....	......	......	450
Sheffield............	28	......	......	....	7'	37'	40"	5'	2	34"	5'	1	6'	......	2 2	8' 6'	20' 12'	....	......	......	450
West Cumberland....	29	......	......	....	5' 4"	......	40"	5'	....	54"	5'	....	......	......	....	......	......	....	......	......	500
Eston	30	......	......	....	......	......	40"	5'	....	50"	5'	....	......	......	....	......	......	....	......	......	400
" New........	31	......	......	....	......	......	......	......	....	......	......	....	20'	......	2						
Darlington......................	32	......	......	2																	
Brown, Bayley & Dixon	33	......	......	....	......	......	......	......	....	......	......	....	......	......	2						
SWEDEN—Bångbro..........	37	......	......	....	......	......	......	......		46"	46"										
Avesta................	39	......	......	....	......	......	......	......	2	39"	39"										
Domnarfvet..........	41	......	......	....	......	......	......	......	3												
Hoerde "old pit"..	42	......	......	4	......	......	......	......	....			1		......	3						
Bochum acid "old pit"........	43	......	......	....	......	......	......	......	....			1		......	10						
Seraing "old pit".............	44	......	......	3	8' 3" 4' 11"	......	......	......	...			1		......	3						
" "new pit".............	45	......	......	4	8' 2"	......	......	......	....			1	10' ±	19'	3		30'				
Oberhausen..................	46	......	......	6	......	......	......	......	....			2		......	3						

a Changed from 4 tons in 1886.
b Actual.
c Nominal.
d Average of 1 month.
e Outside diameter.
f Inside diameter.
g Formerly.
h Now.
i Average.
j Usual.
k Total.

l The total number of tuyere-holes for Avesta, 90; Långshyttan, 148; Nykroppa, 91; Bångbro, 84; Vestanfors, 49; Sandviken, 117.
m .47 Upper diameter.
.94 Lower diameter.
n I am informed that the usual charge is 7¼ tons.
o "American pit."
p Casting-pit.
q Receiving-pit.
r No pit.
s Receiving-crane.

cir. Circular.
sc. Semi-circular.
ann. Annular.
In several of the works there are four vessels, but where these are grouped in pairs, each pair having a separate pit, etc., I have regarded each pit with its pair of vessels as a separate unit, and thus have given the number of vessels as two, etc. In number 15, however, I have given it as four, for here all the vessels work together, and there is much less separation of the work than in other 4-vessel mills.

level, and the little pit in which this cylinder stands, being the higher, is the more readily drained.

7. Finally, by raising the vessels a little higher than would otherwise be necessary, we can in the basic Bessemer process easily remove the vessel-shell without disturbing its trunnion-ring, and carry it off on the general level to a repair-shop in an adjoining building, replacing it rapidly with another.

It is true that these ponderous vessels and their strong means of traveling ladles into vessels whose trunnion-axes are even as much as fifteen feet above the general, is but a few feet higher than that at which they would at any rate have to stand in order to dump easily.

B. *Placing the vessels side by side* instead of opposite, has the following advantages:

1. For given diameter of casting-pit a much longer arc of its rim is available for placing ingot-moulds, to wit, about 160° instead of about 125°; or, for given space avail-

able for placing moulds, the diameter of the casting-pit may be less than when the vessels stand opposite each other. A considerable arc is occupied part of the time by the repairing and shifting of ladles, and is hence unavailable for moulds. We have already seen that we must provide space along the rim of the casting-pit for many moulds. A further reason why a long arc of this rim should be available for moulds is this: we need three ingot-cranes for plants of even moderate large output, and four in case the output is to be great, or in case many ingots are to be cast per heat. It is important that these cranes should have fairly long jibs, so that each may command two railway tracks, one for moulds, the other for ingots, and beyond these tracks a considerable space on the floor of the converting-mill for storing moulds, which are thus in readiness in case at any time it be inconvenient or inexpedient to bring others in by rail.

The areas which the several cranes command must not overlap, lest their jibs collide. In a Pennsylvania mill, in which the areas of two of these cranes overlapped, annoying and well-nigh fatal accidents occurred: *e. g.*, the lower side of one jib in descending struck on the other jib, which was rising, and unshipping fell on the floor of the mill. Now it is impossible to place four long-jibbed cranes so that they all draw from the casting-pit, and that their areas do not overlap, without giving the casting-pit large diameter. This is readily verified by experimenting with a pair of dividers, pencil and paper, or indeed, by an inspection of the plans of Bessemer works, Figures 169, 171 and 177. A pit to be served by four cranes with 20-foot jibs can hardly be less than 32 feet in diameter, and is better if 40 feet in diameter, even if it be a complete circle, and if the cranes have access to the whole of its rim.

Now the cost of the casting-crane rises rapidly as the diameter of the pit and the consequent length of its own jib increases, rising perhaps with the square if not with a higher power of the jib-length; moreover, if its jib be very long, the casting-crane becomes extremely heavy and unwieldly, so that much time is lost in manipulating it. Hence it is desirable to keep the diameter of the casting-crane, and hence that of the casting-pit within bounds, and yet to have a long arc of the rim available for moulds and commanded by the ingot-cranes; and these two requisites can only be satisfied simultaneously by having an arc of many degrees available for moulds.

2. The vessels are much more easily charged with molten cast-iron. A single runner split at its lower end (Figures 171–173) readily carries the metal from a common point to either vessel; or, in case the cast-iron is brought in a traveling ladle drawn by a locomotive, a single straight track serves both vessels if they stand beside each other (Figures 165, 169), while if they stand opposite some more complex arrangement of tracks is needed.

On the other hand, placing the vessels side by side has the disadvantage that in turning up and down they bespatter the casting space.

It must be distinctly understood that the fact that the vessels in the old British pit stand opposite instead of side by side does not limit the output directly, but only indirectly. Of course it takes no longer to blow a heat, to recarburize, to charge, or to change bottoms in case of a vessel which turns its belly than in case of one which turns its side towards its mate: the difference is chiefly in the amount of space available for ingot-cranes and for casting.

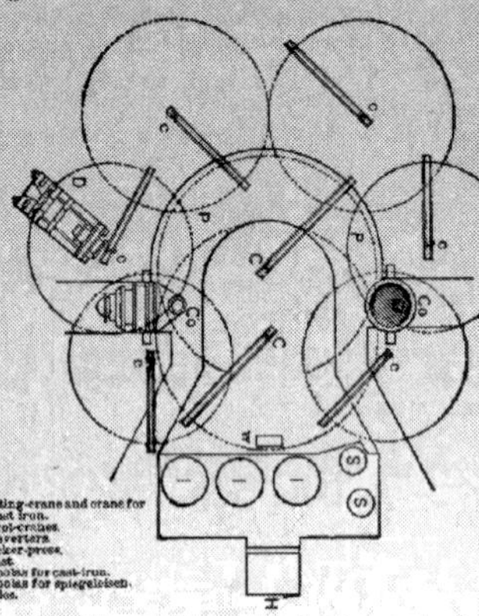

Fig. 167. HOMESTEAD BESSEMER PLANT. TRASENTER.

Thus, on the one hand, about sixty heats are now made in the Holley pit at Seraing per twenty-four hours, while in the adjoining British pit only about thirty-six heats are made. At Homestead (Figure 167), on the other hand, the vessels indeed stand opposite each other in old British style, but here the casting-space has been enlarged, the pit shallowed, and the number of ingot-cranes raised to four: and here as many heats have been made in eight hours as in the Seraing Holley pit in twenty-four. The charges are of about six tons in both cases.

Indeed Homestead has, I believe, made more heats in eight hours than any other works in the world. But this is a little deceptive, for only three ingots are made in each Homestead heat against eight in each Union heat, so that Union has for twelve hours cast more than twice as many ingots per hour as Homestead in her best eight-hours' work.

§ 381 FORSYTH'S PLAN,[q] Figures 168 and 169, adopted at South Chicago, Union and Wheeling, goes a distinct step beyond Holley's in still further removing the vessels from the casting space—a second instance of the advantage of separating the operations of one group from those of another—and in giving still more degrees of the rim of the casting pit for purposes of teeming, to wit, about 250°, while the old Holley and British types give about 160° and 125° respectively. Forsyth thus increases the casting-space by more than 50%.

The vessels stand apart from the casting-pit, and pour their steel into a casting-ladle standing on a special receiving-crane, (Rc. Figure 168), which may have a short jib. This crane delivers the ladle to a short transfer track Tr leading to the casting-pit, a hydraulic cylinder on the receiving-crane pushing it upon this transfer track, from which it is drawn upon the jib of the casting-crane, C, by the usual radial hydraulic cylinder of the latter.

[q] U.S. patent 276,384, April 24th, 1883: Trans. Am. Inst. Min. Eng., XII, p. 254, 1884.

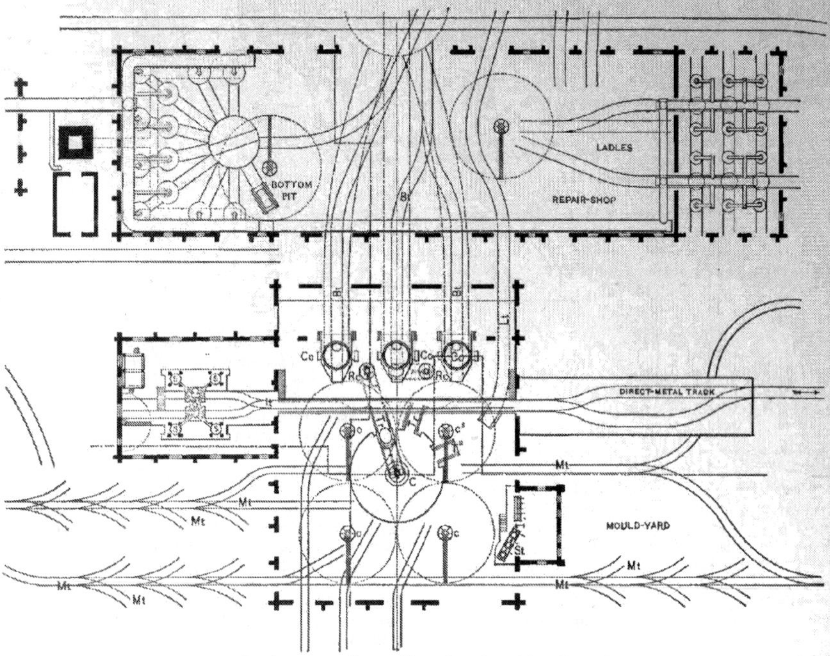

Fig. 168. PLAN SOUTH CHICAGO BESSEMER WORKS. THREE 10-TON VESSEL FORSYTH PLANT.

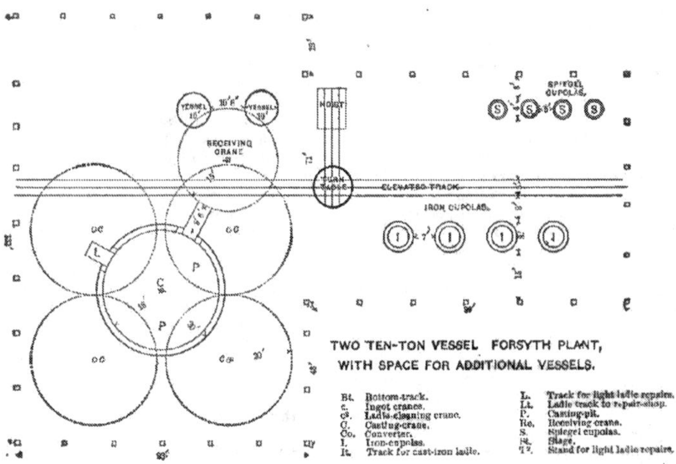

Fig. 169.

After teeming, the casting-crane delivers its empty ladle to the repair track T², and is then ready to receive a full ladle from the vessel which is blowing. Thus the casting-crane is free to attend to its other duties during the time when the steel is pouring from the vessel to the casting-ladle, a further advantage of this type. The ladle on the repair-track, inverted by the crane C³, empties its slag into a pan beneath it which is later removed by this same crane; receives a new stopper; undergoes temporary repairs, and is then swung by crane C³ to the transfer-track T, and, if need be, is taken to the further transfer-track. Slagged ladles are taken by a locomotive to the repair-shop, whence fresh ones are returned direct to crane C³.

In this same repair-shop the bottoms also are repaired. We have here still another instance of the separation of one group of operations from the rest.

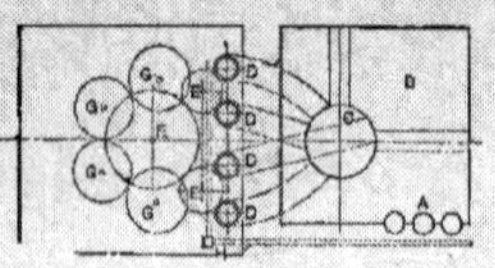

Fig. 170. PLAN OF NORTH-EASTERN STEEL WORKS.

A Cupolas. B Repair-shop. C Turn-table for vessels and ladle-cars. D Converters. E Receiving-cranes. F Casting-crane. G Ingot-cranes.

§ 382. OTHER PLANS.—Intermediate between Forsyth's and the normal Holley type is that at the North Eastern Steel Works (Fig. 170) and at Rhymney, in which the casting-ladle stands on a receiving-crane while it receives the molten steel, and is then transferred to the casting-crane, by bringing the jib-ends of both cranes together. But this does not permit us to remove the vessels as far from the pit as seems desirable, while Forsyth's transfer-track has a certain further advantage "in that it admits of adjustment, both vertically and horizontally, to suit variations in the position of the crane-jibs due to wear of top-supports, elasticity of materials," etc.

In the North Eastern plan the receiving-crane may be so arranged that it holds a receiving-ladle from which the molten steel is repoured into the casting-ladle, to insure better mixing. It is, however, doubtful whether this is needed, for the heterogeneousness formerly attributed to imperfect mixing may be wholly due to segregation.

At Eston the cast-iron ladle is or was raised to the vessels by means of the steel-casting crane; but this is very unwise, because, as we have seen, the casting-crane is fully occupied by its duty of casting the steel.

At Rhymney a receiving-crane stands, or stood, between the vessels and the casting-pit. It raises the molten cast-iron and pours it into the vessel; then at the end of the blow it raises the molten spiegel and pours this too into the vessel, then swings around and receives the steel in a ladle on its other end, and finally delivers this ladle to the casting-crane proper.

When matters are running perfectly smoothly these three operations of the receiving-crane need not interfere with each other, for, as we have seen, there is usually plenty of time during the blowing of one heat to charge in the idle vessel the cast-iron for the following heat, and this would naturally be done long before the vessel now blowing was ready to receive its spiegeleisen. But, owing to delays, we often cannot finish charging the idle vessel till just as the blow is ending in the other; and then the Rhymney arrangement would certainly cause delay.

Of the many other ways of grouping the vessels, some of them intermediate between the British and Holley's type, only the following seem to deserve especial consideration.

The converging-axed plan (Figures 174 and 176) has the advantage in case of three-vessel plants that a single casting-crane can receive steel from any of the vessels; while if the trunnion-axes are in a straight line, as at Harrisburg and Edgar Thomson (Figures 171, 177), a single casting-crane can hardly be arranged to serve all three vessels. This, however, is a doubtful advantage, for the three converging-axed vessels occupy so many degrees of the rim of the casting pit, that we can only get sufficient length of rim for the work of the ingot-cranes in the casting space, by having a very wide pit, and hence a costly and unwieldy casting-crane. For a three-vessel plant the Edgar Thomson and the Forsyth plan seem much better fitted than the converging-axed type.

When we come to two-vessel plants the converging-axed type lacks even the questionable advantage which it has in case of three vessels, for two vessels with their axes in line are readily served by a single casting-crane (Figure 173).

Further, whether there be two or three vessels, if their axes converge they bespatter not only the casting space, but what is really serious, the casting-crane, on which the man who is to rack the ladle as it receives the steel from the vessel should now be standing. Here Rothman's telescopic screen for the plunger of the casting-crane is especially needed (X Figure 163).

The Bochum plan, Figure 176, exaggerates some of these difficulties, and combines them with some of those of the British type; but it escapes part of their consequences by placing the vessels far from the casting-pit, thus going a step beyond Forsyth's plan. Here the converging-axed plan enables a single receiving-crane to serve three vessels: but the vessels are less conveniently placed for receiving cast-iron than when their axes are in line.

The Harrisburg Plan (Figure 171).—We have just seen the advantages which this plan has over the converging-axed plan for three-vessel plants. It was the natural outcome of an attempt to apply the Holley type to a three-vessel plant, for here a single casting-crane could not serve all three vessels, unless it had so long a jib as to be most unwieldy as well as expensive.

Compared with Forsyth's plan it has one disadvantage of the two-vessel Holley plant, the heat and spatterings of the vessels interfere with the casting; but in other respects it is as well if not better off than Forsyth's, for it offers a greater length of pit-rim for casting, and the length of the ladle-cycle (LT, § 376, 3), may be longer without holding the vessels back. In order that a ladle may always be ready to receive the blown steel it is only necessary that the length of the ladle cycle, LT, should be less than twice as great as the blowing-time, BT. Indeed, as we have already seen, in case the number of ingots to be cast per minute were to be materially increased, Forsyth's plan would require a second casting-crane. It will be noted that, whichever pair of vessels is in actual use, whether the two outside vessels or either outside and the middle vessel, two casting-cranes will always be available for serving them.

The diverging-axed arrangement, Figure 172, has the advantage already pointed out that the vessels do not bespatter the casting-space. Indeed, they blow so wide of it in turning up and down that the pulpit or stage (St) from which the rotation of the vessels and the rise of the cranes is governed, can be placed immediately opposite the centre of the casting-pit and thus close to the work directed, without being bespattered. It has a further advantage in that the horizontal travel of the vessel's nose in pouring the steel into the casting-ladle may be wholly compensated for by swinging the ladle-crane, without radial motion of the ladle, so that the hydraulic cylinder usually employed to move the ladle radially, and the man who controls it, are not needed. The diverging-axed plan seems hardly applicable to three-vessel plants.

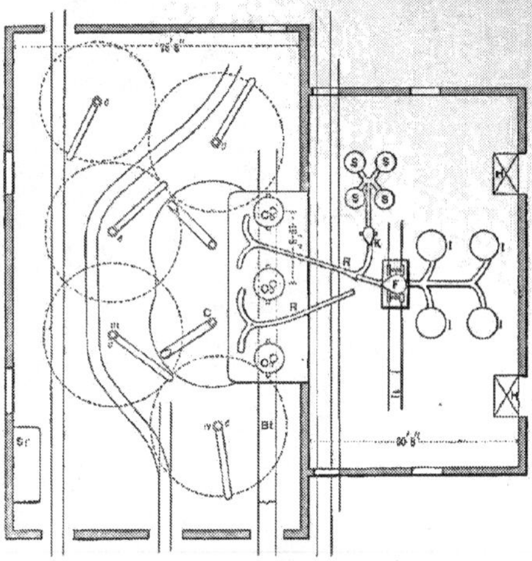

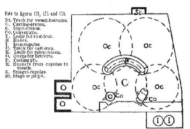

Fig. 171. HARRISBURG BESSEMER WORKS, NEW PIT. TRASENTER.

Note to figures 171, 172 and 173.

Bt. Track for vessel-bottoms.
C. Casting-cranes.
c. Ingot-cranes.
Co. Converters.
F. Ladle for cast-iron.
H. Hoists.
I. Iron-cupolas.
It. Track for cast-iron.
K. Ladle for spiegeleisen.
O. Ovens for bottoms.
P. Casting pit.
R. Runners from cupolas to vessels.
S. Spiegel-cupolas.
St. Stage or pulpit.

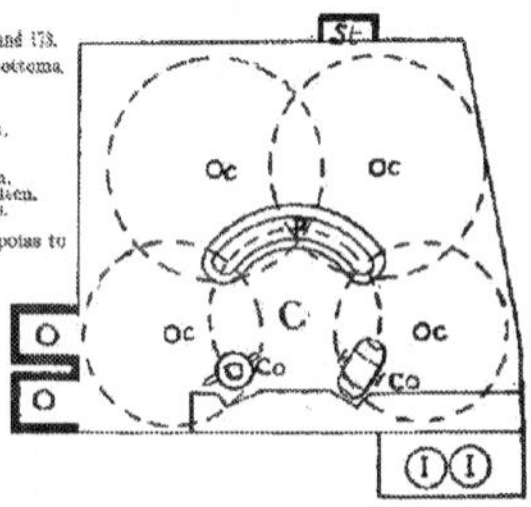

Fig. 172. BESSEMER PLANT, AXES DIVERGING.

In the Joliet modification of the Holley type, Figure 173, the vessels turn down away from instead of towards the pit to receive the charge of cast-iron. If the casting-ladle is to stand on the casting-crane while receiving the steel from the vessel, and if at the same time "direct metal" is to be used, this modification is very desirable, as explained in § 395.

But if the vessels stand back from the pit, as in Forsyth's and in the North Eastern plan, the Joliet modification is not necessary. It is, however, a wholly unobjectionable modification; it necessitates some change in the shape of the vessel, making its nose "concentric" instead of eccentric, but this change, as we shall see, seems in itself desirable.

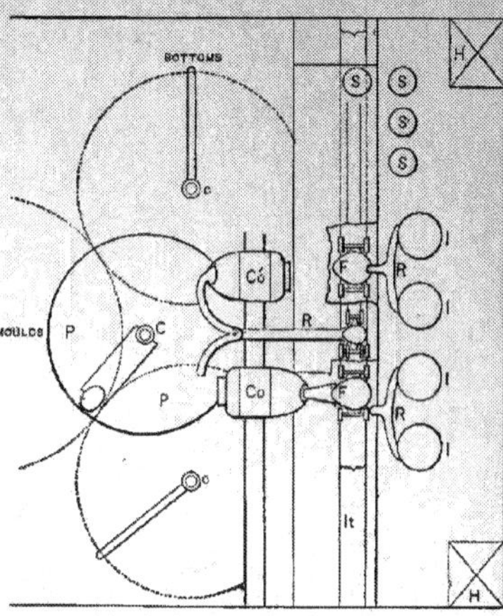

Fig. 173. PLAN OF JOLIET PLANT. TRASENTER.

§ 383. OTHER FORMS OF CASTING PIT.—Up to this point we have considered the casting-pit chiefly in connection with the arrangement of the vessels; but there are certain forms of casting-pit whose value depends relatively little on the disposition of the vessels. Let us now glance at them, and at

I. The Suppression of the Casting-pit.—In several European works the casting-pit has been wholly suppressed, the ingots being cast either on the level, or on cars running on the level. It is often said by superficial observers that the pit is a useless nuisance. A nuisance it may be, but a most useful one. First, it gives ready access to the tops of the moulds, for teeming, for stopping them with sand or water, and for attaching crane-hooks to the ears of the moulds, and crane-dogs to the ingots themselves. Secondly, it restricts the area flooded by "messes," *i. e.*, by molten steel spilt from the ladle, from ill-fitting or cracked moulds, from bleeding ingots and what not. These cannot be ignored in providing for extreme celerity.

If there be no pit, an elevated platform, A, must be provided to give access to the mould-tops in teeming, etc.,[a] unless only short ingots are to be cast. (See Figure 174.)

[a] Holley wrote in January, 1881, "Placing the moulds on the general level for casting, appeared to be very unsatisfactory. The moulds for 5 to 6 rail ingots are above 6 ft. high, so that there must a working platform about 4 ft. high around them. This platform is a series of planks laid on a temporary staging; it is narrow, insecure and inconvenient. The bursting of a mould endangers the lives of all the men about it. The steel cast when I was at the works was very rising. I saw it boil out of a mould, and drive all the men off the platform, twice in one afternoon." It is only fair to say that the platform need not be narrow and insecure.

If the ingot-moulds stand on the ground during teeming, I see no important advantage in suppressing the pit. If they stand on cars, we can remove them readily to a convenient place for stripping, and we may thus make use of some economical stripping-device, such as Laureau's or Jones', which we will consider later. But in either case we are likely to have much trouble with fouling the running-gear of the cars on which the moulds stand; and the fouling of a single wheel or of the track would detain a whole train of cars, and temporarily paralyze the establishment. Opinions are divided as to the detention which would be thus caused in actual rapid work. It is stated that this system has been used in some European works without serious trouble. But in these works the output is relatively small, and it seems to me that leaky nozzles and moulds are still common enough to form a serious menace, when such extreme rapidity of working as is common in this country is sought, and where every delay of even a few seconds is to be guarded against.

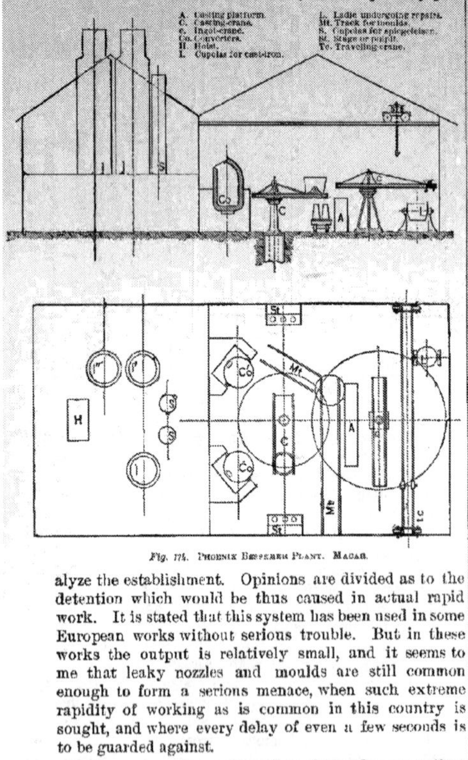

Fig. 174. Phoenix Bessemer Plant. Magab.

2. Removing the casting-place from the converting-house. In this case the casting-ladle is carried by rail from the converting-house. If, as usual, the vessel pours the steel directly into the casting-ladle, this must stand on a crane while receiving the steel, in order that its position may shift and follow the motion of the vessel's nose.

It is asserted that in practice no serious trouble has arisen from fouling the running-gear, either by the bursting of the ladle or by spilling steel over its edge; and certainly the danger seems to be relatively slight, for the ladle need not be put on the car till after receiving the steel, and may be removed from it before teeming, so that no pouring need occur in direct connection with the track and cars. The danger is certainly far less than when the six or eight ingots of a heat are teemed while standing on cars; for here an ill-fitting mould would not be detected till it had begun to leak over cars and track, and the leakage from the nozzle in passing from mould to mould, very often a considerable matter, as well as the boiling over of imperfectly stopped ingots, would have to be cared for most jealously. Indeed it is clearly less dangerous to the running-gear to teem *from* a ladle which stands on a car, than to teem *into* moulds on cars.

This plan may be regarded as carrying Forsyth's a step farther. The casting-place is certainly freer from the heat and spattering of the vessels, and the work of the pit-men is thereby facilitated; but in Forsyth's arrangement the distance between vessels and pit is already so considerable, and the quantity of heat radiated from vessels to pit seemed to me even in midsummer so slight, that I doubt whether any considerable additional outlay, for the sake of separating them still farther, would be expedient.

Fig. 175. 2-pit Forsyth Plant.

C Casting-cranes. c Ingot-cranes. Co Converters. Rc Receiving-cranes. The black circles are the casting-pits.

3. Auxiliary Pits. Taking a hint from the Oberhausen plant, one or even two auxiliary pits might be arranged as in Figure 175, if it should be desirable to cast a very great number of small ingots from each of many heats following each other quickly. The casting-ladles would preferably stand on receiving cranes while receiving the steel from the vessels, and pass thence to whichever casting-pit was ready.

4. Straight Pits instead of circular ones have been used (Figures 176 and 176 *a*). Their advantage is that the casting place may be as long as you please, so that teeming and stripping may be more leisurely and hence cheaper than in case of a circular pit or pits, the length of whose casting-space is limited by the necessity of keeping the length of the crane-jib within bounds.

The cost of installation for straight pits may be somewhat less than that for circular pits with their costly casting-cranes. But the straight pit suffers under one very great disadvantage. There is no means by which the casting-ladle can be moved from point to point, and, as is necessary in teeming very soft steel, endlessly backwards and forwards, with anything like the ease with which it is swung while resting on the jib of a hydraulic crane. Locomotive ladle-cars and simple ladle-cars moved by stationary engines have been proposed, but it seems simpler to have a plain ladle-car drawn by a locomotive. At Hoerde the ladle-car has a steam-engine for locomotion, a casting-crane moved by hydraulic pressure, generated by a pump on the car itself; a system of wheels and chains for rotating the casting-crane, and arrangements for tipping the ladle in case of accident. One naturally shrinks from the use of so complex a machine for this purpose, where the first requisite is absolute certainty. In this particular case the casting-ladle stands on its traveling car while receiving the steel from the vessel.

In another case (Peine), the casting-car carries a ten-ton hydraulic casting-crane, with pumps; two steam-engines, one for locomotion, the other to drive these pumps; a twelve-horse boiler, and the levers needed for operating these machines.

between the radial and parallel arrangement of the casting-pit would probably be chiefly governed by the extent and shape of the available ground.

It seems on the whole wiser to adhere to circular pits, having, if necessary, two or even three pits, as in Figure 175: for, as we have seen in § 378, in case we are to cast ingots even of small size and hence numerous, whose moulds need not be in place till immediately be-

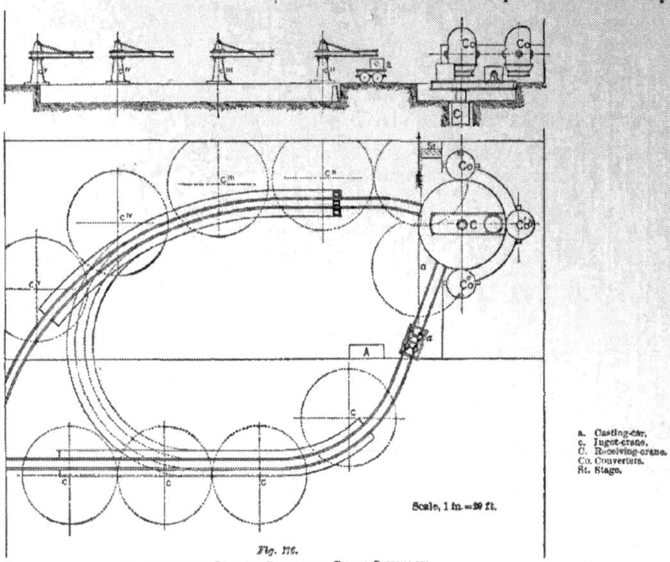

Fig. 176.
BOCHUMER VEREIN BESSEMER PLANT, WITH RADIAL CASTING-PIT.

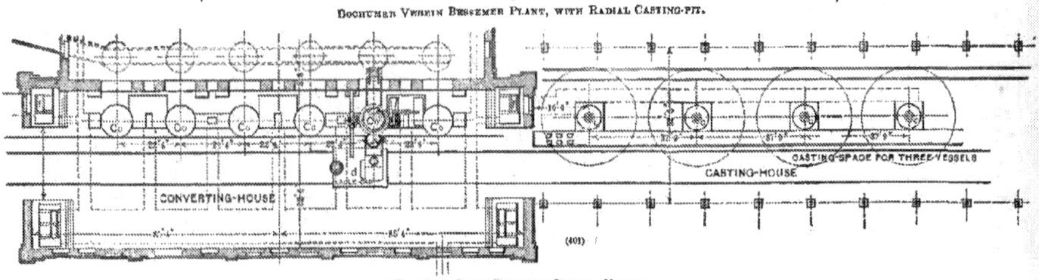

Fig. 176a. PEINE BESSEMER PLANT. MACAR.
c Ingot-crane. Co Converter. L Casting-ladle.

A straight pit may be either parallel with the vessel-axes, in case these stand in line, as in Figure 176 *a*, or it may, as in Figure 176, be radial to the orbit of a receiving crane on which the casting-ladle rests while receiving the steel from the vessel. In the former plan the ladle may rest either on a receiving-crane or on the casting-car while receiving the steel. The usual advantages of the receiving-crane, removing the casting space from the vessels and leaving the casting-car or casting-crane at liberty for its other duties while the steel is pouring from the vessel into the casting-ladle, may apply here. The choice

fore teeming, we are likely to need increase of casting-crane capacity and after that of ingot-crane capacity, much sooner than of mould-space. Now, in a radial straight pit, as in Figure 176, we can use but one casting-ladle; in a pit like that in Figure 176*a*, but two, so that these are equivalent in casting-ladle capacity to a one- and to a two-casting-crane plant respectively. In order that more ladles should be used, some mode of switching the empty ladles back past the full ones to the vessels would be needed, as for instance, by uniting the two pits of Figure 176 by a Y, or by uniting them as indicated in dotted lines so that they formed one continuous pit. In such a pit any desired number of ladles could work simultaneously.

But the numbers in § 378 show us that in a pair of Forsyth pits we can have all the casting-crane, ingot-crane and mould capacity that is likely to be needed for two or three vessels, while preserving the advantage of moving the casting-ladle by hydraulic cranes.

In harmony with these views is the experience of Mr. John Fritz.* Having seen certain advantages of the straight pit at some German works, he fitted up two straight pits for his two new vessels at Bethlehem, with every convenience, determined to give the system a fair trial. But he was unable to teem and remove even the relatively small normal output of those days.

The single hydraulic casting-crane in the circular pit connected with his old pair of vessels did more work than the two straight pits and their casting-cars. He therefore returned to the use of the circular pit, putting in two casting-cranes each with its own pit to serve his new pair of vessels, to provide for rapid working.* So, too, many if not most European metallurgists seem to have come to the conclusion that, even for their relatively small output, the straight German pits are less convenient than circular ones.

We cannot conveniently use the circular pit and the hydraulic casting-crane when the casting work is to be like that of a common foundry, *i. e.*, when we are to teem a great number not of ingots but of small sand-castings, whose moulds occupy a great extent of floor-room for given weight of casting, require long preparation, cannot be swung about rapidly, but should, during teeming, stand in the place in which they are prepared.

Here the straight pit offers weighty advantages. But it is not probable that a large part of the enormous output of many large and rapidly working plants will be used for this kind of work: ingots are their normal product.

Multiple-casting and other means of casting many small pieces from a single heat will be considered in connection with the open-hearth process.

5. Annular casting-pits have been tried at several works. They indeed give a little more floor-room, the "Island," on the general level, Figures 167, 172; but it is not clear that this room, lying as it does in the centre of the pit, is much more useful for being at the general level instead of at the pit-level. The jib of the casting-crane sweeps across it so often that it is in either case little more than waste ground. Moreover, messes are certainly removed more easily from the open circular than from the relatively confined annular pit.

If an annular pit be used, the casting-ladle cannot be lowered so far as is possible in a plain circular pit, and hence the height at which the vessels must stand in order that they may pour the steel into the casting-ladle is greater. But in the best works lately built the vessels, even in case of a plain circular pit, stand quite as high as would be necessary were the pit annular.

§ 384. Minor Arrangements.—*The ingot-cranes* (cf. § 380, B) are usually placed as close to the pit as is possible without having their orbits intersect.

Place for Repairing Ladles and Bottoms.—In the earlier works, which aimed at what now appears to be a small output, ladles and bottoms were relined on the floor of the converting-room, and spaces along its walls were reserved for this purpose. The moulds, too, were allowed to cool on the floor of the converting-room. Thus a space to the left of the lower ingot-crane in Figure 173 might be reserved for repairing ladles, and the spaces indicated for moulds and bottoms.

But to provide for the enormous product of our later mills, ten times as great as that of sixteen years ago, a correspondingly great number of bottoms and ladles must be kept on hand, and must be simultaneously under repairs. The floor-space which this requires is so great that it is found far better to make these repairs in a separate building, as in Figure 168, or at least in a separate room, as at L, Figure 177, with ample floor-space. This enables us to keep a large number of both bottoms and ladles on hand, and to dry the bottoms slowly, a point of considerable importance.

So, too, in many of the works lately built, the moulds are removed from the converting-room immediately after stripping; they cool and are examined in the open air.

These are very important steps. The attempt to repair ladles and bottoms littered up the converting-room and cramped the operations of the pit-men; while the hot moulds not only did this, but, radiating great volumes of heat, raised the temperature of the converting-room, which even without them is tryingly hot in summer. But beyond this, it is necessary to throw a stream of water on the moulds, so that they may cool quickly and be ready for use. The steam into which they convert this water not only obscures the view and thus interferes with operations, but converts the converting-room into a Turkish bath. As the perspiration will not evaporate in the atmosphere thus saturated with moisture, we cut off the human body's chief means of keeping its temperature below that of the air and of the hot objects which surround it. We mercilessly enhance the sufferings and reduce the working power of these suffering and expensive men.

§ 385. General Arrangement of Tracks, etc.—This must of course be regulated by the shape and size of the ground available; I can therefore only point out what tracks are needed, and certain desirable positions for them. All the tracks, except that which brings the pig-iron and fuel to the works, may be of narrow gauge.

1. *The Pig-iron and Cupola-fuel* may be brought by an elevated broad-gauge track, running if possible over a series of bins standing behind the cupola room, each receiving iron of a certain grade. The bottoms of these bins should be on a level with the bottom of the hoists which raise the pig-iron and fuel to the cupola charging platforms, and within reasonable wheeling distance of them. Between the bins and the hoists stand scales for weighing iron and fuel.

2. *Iron-Hoists.*—Convenient positions for the hoists for pig-iron are shown at H in Figure 173 for the Holley type of plant, and in Figures 171 and 177. It is well to have two hoists, not alone on account of the enormous quantity of material to be lifted, which may reach 1,500 tons in twenty-four hours, but also lest the whole establishment be paralyzed by the temporary disablement of one hoist. Though a general discussion of the merits of different kinds of

* Holley, Engineering, XXXII., p. 428, 1881

hoists is far beyond the limits of this work, I may point out that overwinding cannot occur in hydraulic elevators; that hydraulic pressure to drive them is always available in Bessemer works; and that there is always a number of men at hand skilled in the maintenance of hydraulic apparatus, and accustomed to guard it from freezing. In a word, hydraulic elevators are readily applicable here, and here their disadvantages are minimized.

As the cupola-charging platforms in the older works were very high, sometimes more than forty feet above the general level, it was found best to make the length of hydraulic lifting-cylinder but half the travel of the hoist-cage. This was therefore lifted by a chain running over a sheave fastened to the end of the piston-rod of the hydraulic cylinder; it is the common pulley-arrangement reversed.

3. *Track for Cupola-Débris.*—A track which may be of narrow gauge should run on the general level, and near the rear of the cupolas, for removing their débris.

4. *Track for Molten Cast-iron.*—If direct-metal is used, it may be brought from the blast-furnace in a ladle drawn by a locomotive, and by it carried up an incline, raising it to the level of the vessels. At South Chicago this incline has an average rise of 2%. It is stated that at Ebbw Vale direct metal was brought successfully a distance of six miles to the vessels.

At the head of this incline may be a siding, on which the locomotive places its full ladle or ladles, returning to the blast-furnace with one or more empty ones.

From this siding a special locomotive, which runs only on this elevated track, carries the molten iron to the vessels. The track may run either behind the vessels, as in Figures 163, 173 and 177, or in front of them, as in Figures 168 and 169, in case Forsyth's or a similar arrangement be adopted. In the former case the vessels must be concentric, in the latter they may be either eccentric or concentric. Or, finally, the track may run between the vessels, as in Figure 164.

In all direct-metal plants the cupolas should be so placed as to deliver their molten iron into ladles running on this same track. This arrangement works so admirably that it is well, even if cupola-metal only is to be used, to bring the molten cast-iron from the cupolas to the vessels by means of a locomotive. This incidentally allows us to remove the cupolas from the immediate neighborhood of the vessels, as shown in Figures 165 and 169, and as explained in § 373. This has been done in several of the best works lately built.

5. *The Tracks at and near the general level* have four chief functions; A, to remove the débris of the vessels; B, to carry moulds in and out of the converting room; C, to carry ingots away for further treatment; and D, to carry ladles and bottoms back and forth between the repair-shop and the converting-room. There are so many ingots and moulds to be carried in and out, and it is so important to remove them quickly from the converting-room, that there should be a track devoted solely to ingots, and another solely for moulds. Each track should be commanded by all of the ingot-cranes. Indeed it is better to provide two tracks for moulds, so that the removal of hot moulds may not interfere with bringing in cool ones. Admirable examples of track-arrangement are afforded by Figures 168 and 177. In the latter we have three parallel sets of tracks, a Y giving in addition a short branch. In the former works, by laying the ingot-tracks at right angles with the mould-tracks, the total number of tracks that can conveniently be laid is greatly increased. This facilitates handling, for cars standing on any one of the eight branches do not prevent bringing other cars to any of the other branches; while even with the three parallel tracks of the Edgar Thomson mill some planning and switching may occasionally be needed, *e. g.*, to bring cars to the end of a given track, at a time when its middle is occupied by other cars which are receiving ingots or moulds, etc.

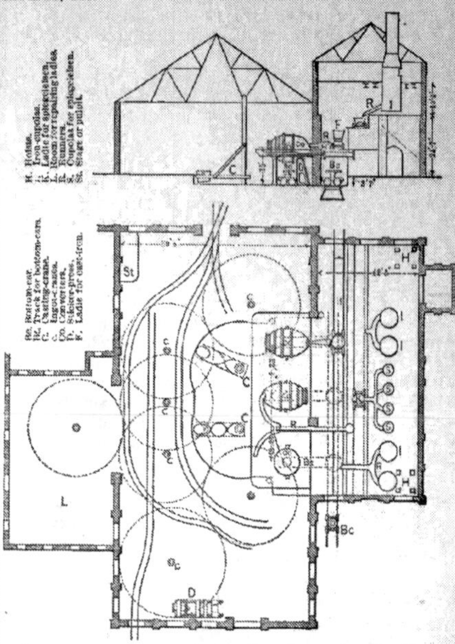

Fig. 177. Cross section and plan of new Edgar Thomson Converting Mill. Trasenter.

At South Chicago we have practically three sets of ingot- and five of mould-tracks. The latter have, in the yard adjoining the converting-room, many sidings on which the mould-cars can stand while their moulds cool and are inspected.

If the ingot-cranes, which lift the ingots from the casting-pit, deliver them directly to other cranes which place them in soaking-pits, ingot-car-tracks are of course unnecessary.

If, as at Edgar Thomson, the ladles are repaired in a room adjoining the converting-room, no track is needed for removing them, and they may be swung by a pair of cranes into this repair-room. But if, as at South Chicago, the ladles are repaired in a separate building, a track must be provided, as at Lt, in Figure 168. The bottoms at S. Chicago are removed by the tracks Bt shown in the same figure, running back from beneath the vessels. At Harrisburg (Figure 171) and many other works they are removed on a track Bt, running beneath the vessels, but parallel with their trunnion axes (Figure 163). It is evidently desirable that this bottom-track should run immediately beneath the vessels, so that the transfer of bottoms from car to vessel and back may be as direct and rapid as possible. The turn-table arrangement in Figure 177 enables us to side-track a bottom close by its vessel, leaving the main bottom-track free for bringing bottoms to or from other vessels, for removing slag, etc.

6. *The Vessel- and Pit-débris* is best removed by a track running at the level of the bottom of the pit. The cars may run directly beneath the vessels, which, after pouring the steel into the casting-ladle, are inverted and empty their slag directly into them. At South Chicago these cars run on the track which brings the bottoms to and from the vessels, a very good arrangement. At most works the vessel-slag track runs parallel with the trunnion-axes of the vessels.

§ 386. THE POSITION OF THE HEATING-FURNACES, SOAKING-PITS, ETC.—These usually stand close to the (blooming) rolls in which the ingots are to be reduced, and in a building apart from the converting-house. At Bethlehem the roll-trains, heating-furnaces and converting department are all contained in the nave of a single imposing building. There is a certain gain in facility of supervision and of communication between the superintendents of the different departments, so that they co-operate more readily. But it is doubtful whether this gain is equivalent to its cost. For the temperature in this stately hall must, other things being equal, be considerably higher than when each department stands in a separate building of its own, with abundant space for fresh (if not cool) air to blow in on all sides during summer.

The saving of time in carrying ingots from the casting-pit to furnaces in the same rather than in another building is inconsiderable, for once they are loaded on a car and once the locomotive has started, a few hundred feet more or less counts for little. I noted the following intervals in transporting ingots from the casting-pit to soaking-pits in another building at an American mill:

	Minutes.	Seconds.
Four ingots were placed on the car at the casting-pit at	0	0
They had been carried to out-door scales and had been weighed at	0	27
They arrived at the soaking-pits in another building at	1	30
The first ingot was in the soaking-pit at	1	55
The last was in the soaking-pit at	4	15

This is quicker work than I have happened to notice in mills in which the heating-furnaces and casting-pit are in the same room.

Here the length of time during which the locomotive and ingot-cars were detained because the soaking-pits were in another building instead of being in the converting-house, was less than one minute.

Another plan is to place soaking-pits so near the casting-pit that ingots drawn from the latter by one crane may be deposited by a second directly in the soaking-pits, or may even be deposited in the soaking-pits by the very crane which lifts them from the casting-pit, as indicated in Figure 165. This expedient certainly saves the whole expense of the transportation by locomotive. In a very large establishment it might wholly dispense with one locomotive by day and another by night. The number of motions of the ingot-cranes would, however, be the same as when the ingots are carried to the soaking-pits or other heating-furnaces in a separate building; for it does not take appreciably longer to place an ingot on or to remove it from a car than to set it on or pick it from the ground. From these soaking-pits[a] other cranes transfer the ingots directly to the feed-rollers of the blooming rolls. This appears to be an admirable arrangement in case of small output. Where a large output is sought we must weigh against the advantage just considered the higher temperature which must prevail both in the converting and in the rolling department, owing to their proximity to each other. This is a serious thing in case of large output, owing to the enormous quantity of hot metal at hand at once, and to the frequency with which masses of metal are brought out into the air, radiating heat in all directions.

§ 387. THE SEVERAL LEVELS.—To recapitulate these we have:

1, The cupola-charging level;
2, The cupola-tapping level;
3, The vessel-trunnion level;
4, The general level of the converting-house;
5, The pit-level; and
6, The level of the subterranean passages in which the hydraulic and other pipes lie.

Of these we have seen that 2 and 3 are identical in some of the best works lately built, while 4 and 5 are identical in some works, but to doubtful advantage.

§ 388. THE BESSEMER CONVERTER OR VESSEL[b] is essentially a chamber lined with refractory material, and suited to carrying out the Bessemer process. In this view the many vessels which are now offered to the public are all Bessemer converters; there may be a Clapp-Griffiths Bessemer converter, a Robert Bessemer converter, which we may call simply a "Robert converter," remembering that this is merely an abbreviation, and that it is essentially a Bessemer converter still.

§ 389. BESSEMER'S EARLY VESSELS.—Figure 178 shows the apparatus in which Bessemer's earliest experiments were carried out, a 40-pound clay crucible, heated in a common crucible-furnace, and provided with a tap-hole for removing the molten metal and a central clay pipe through which the blast was introduced. In this ten or twelve pounds of cast-iron were melted and then blown.

Next a rotating converter (Figure 179) was designed by Bessemer, but not built, spherical, to reduce the loss of heat by radiation to a minimum, and with a clay tuyere inserted and withdrawn, much as in Figure 178.

Next came the vessel shown in Figure 180,[c] and used for Bessemer's public experiments at St. Pancras in 1856. Its resemblance to Figure 188 is striking, while its general arrangement is much like that of Figure 216.

---

a By soaking-pits I mean those with auxiliary gas-firing. There seems little sense in constructing furnaces so that we cannot use auxiliary gas if we wish. There is no reason for tieing our hands in this matter, except that we thereby cut down the cost of installation slightly.

b As far as my observation goes, metallurgical writers almost invariably use the word "converter," while in the steel works the word "vessel" is almost always used. Vessel has, of course, a generic sense, but it has acquired a distinct specific meaning—the Bessemer converter. It seems to me high time that this unobjectionable word should be recognized. Indeed, as the briefer name, and as the one in actual use, it seems on the whole preferable to converter.

c "This fixed converter has turned out to be the father of a very numerous family, all having a strong likeness to their ancient progenitor, and inheriting but too many of his defects and shortcomings. And it therefore affords anything but an example of the survival of the fittest."—Bessemer, Journal Iron and Steel Institute, 1880, II., p. 640.

Next came the first rotating vessel, Figures 181, 182. Its trunnions were concentric with the pouring lip, so that it poured readily into moulds set beneath it. In designing it Bessemer aimed chiefly to make the metal circulate, so that all parts would be acted on alike by the blast.

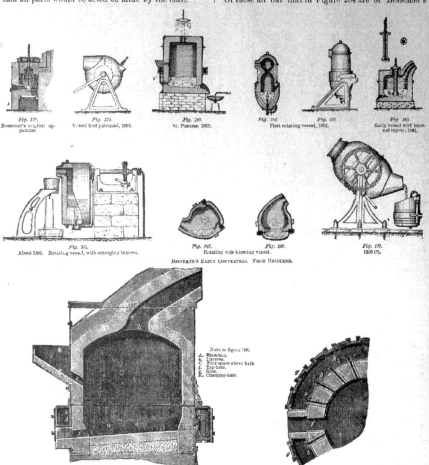

Fig. 178. Bessemer's original apparatus.

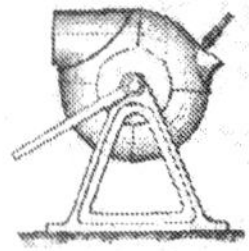

Fig. 179. Vessel first patented, 1855.

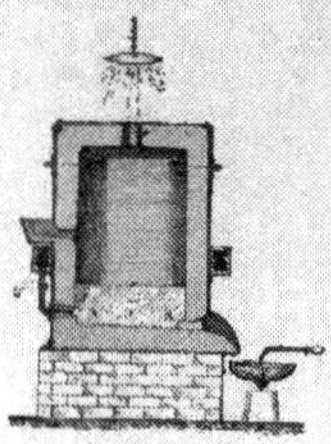

Fig. 180. St. Pancras, 1856.

Fig. 181. *Fig. 182.* First rotating vessel, 1856.

Fig. 183. Early vessel with internal tuyere, 1861.

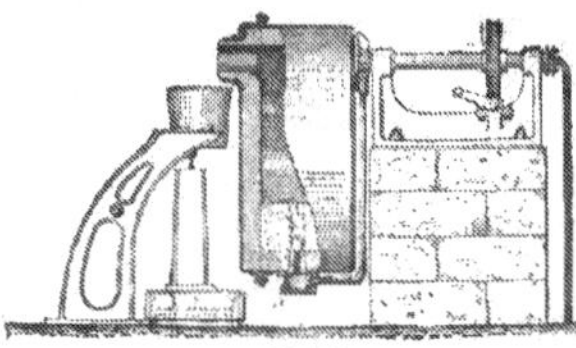

Fig. 184. About 1856. Rotating vessel, with emerging tuyeres.

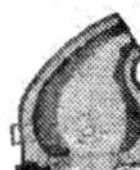

Fig. 185. *Fig. 186.* Rotating side-blowing vessel.

Fig. 187. 1858 (?).

BESSEMER'S EARLY CONVERTERS. FROM BESSEMER.

Note to figure 188.
A. Blast-box.
a. Tuyeres.
C. Free space above bath
t. Tap-hole.
D. Nose.
E. Charging-hole.

Fig. 188. OLD FIXED SWEDISH CONVERTER, WITH SIDE TUYERES. KERL.

Fig. 189. PART PLAN OF OLD FIXED SWEDISH CONVERTER WITH SIDE TUYERES.

Soon followed the rotating vessel shown in Figure 184, which also was pivoted concentrically with its pouring lip, and had in addition the advantage that, when turned for receiving molten cast-iron or for discharging molten steel, its tuyere was above the level of the metal.

Later—in 1858—we have the vessel of Figure 187. This form was used with but little alteration till within a few years, when the form shown in Figure 204 was introduced.

Later still—in 1862—we have the rotating vessels, Figures 185, 186, with side tuyeres, which were readily brought above the level of the molten metal.

Of these all but that in Figure 204 are of Bessemer's design. The rotating vessel lies with its major axis horizontal when receiving or discharging metal; before the blowing operation, or "blow" or "heat" begins, the blast is let on and the vessel then turned so that its axis is vertical, submerging the tuyeres; the vessel is then said to be "turned up." At the end of the operation it is "turned down," *i.e.*, its axis is again made horizontal,

BESSEMER WORKS AT EDSKEN, SWEDEN.
BUILT AND IN OPERATION BY THE SANDVIKEN Co IN 1858.

Fig. 191.

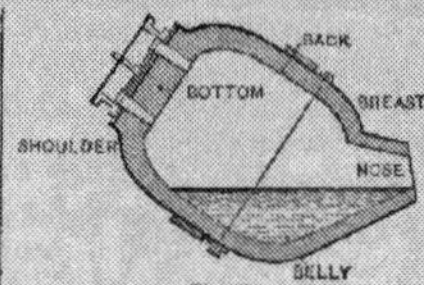

Fig. 201.

and the tuyeres emerge from below the metal. So, too, should a tuyere fail or should the charge break through the lower part of the vessel we at once "turn down."

Fig. 201 shows the names applied to certain parts of the vessel. In concentric vessels the side on which the charge of cast-iron is received is termed the "iron-side," that where the steel is discharged the "steel-side."p

§ 390. Vessels Classified. The most important classification of vessels is into the fixed and the rotating, and into the side- and the bottom-blowing. They are also divided into those with straight and those with contracted shells; and into "eccentric" and "concentric," or "symmetrical," *i.e.*, into those in which the vessel is retort-shaped, as in Figs. 197 and 202, and those in which the nose is almost concentric with the major axis (Figs. 192, 195).

§ 391. Fixed *vs.* Rotating Vessels.—Fixed vessels (*e. g.*, Figures 188-9 and 216) have four chief defects.

p This strange monster, "truly unique among organic forms," breathes through his nether parts, feeds, spits, roars and flames through his nose, which, like his breast, strangely enough grows above his back, while his shoulder lies beneath his middle.

Fig. 192.

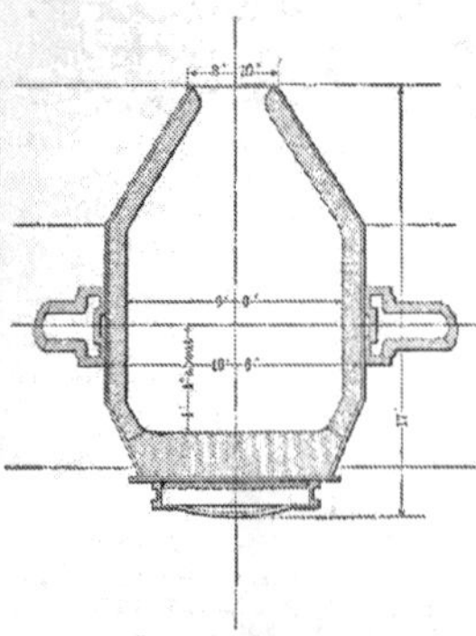

Eston, 15-ton, about 1880.

Fig. 193.

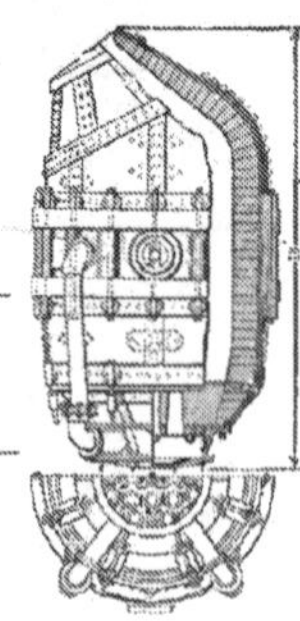

Bethlehem, 8-ton, 1881.

Fig. 194.

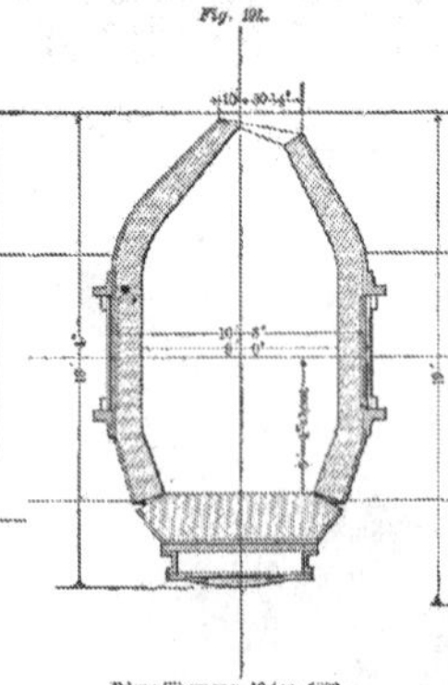

Edgar Thomson, 10-ton, 1889.

Fig. 195.

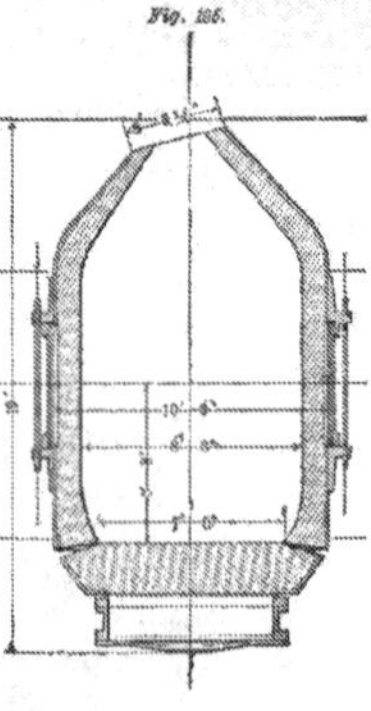

Union, 10-ton, about 1888.

Fig. 196.

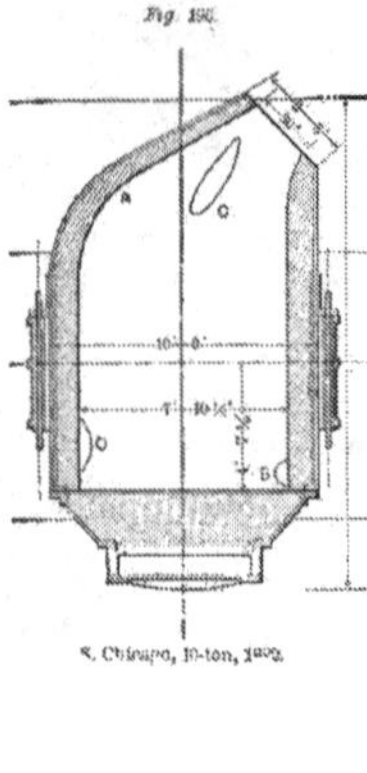

S. Chicago, 10-ton, 1892.

Fig. 197.

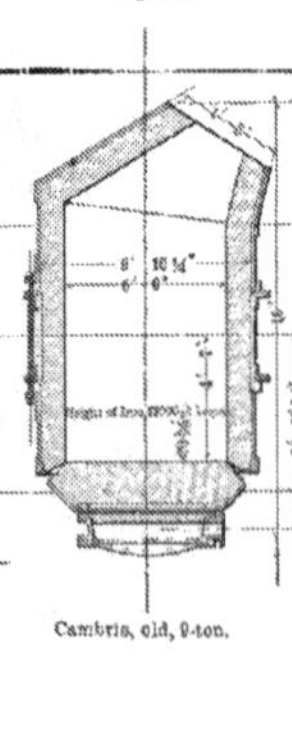

Cambria, old, 9-ton.

Fig. 198.

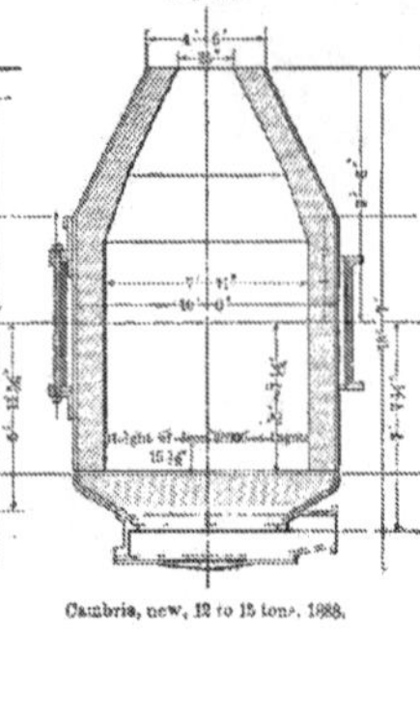

Cambria, new, 12 to 15 tons, 1888.

Fig. 199.

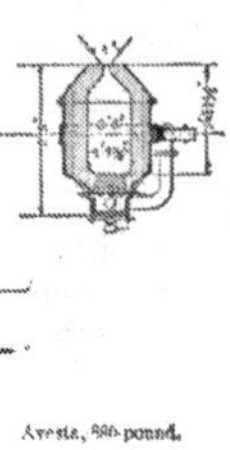

Avesta, 880-pound.

1st. They hardly permit bottom-blowing, hence they involve greater loss of iron in conversion. If the tuyeres were introduced through the bottom of a fixed vessel, the failure of a single tuyere would let the whole charge escape and might greatly injure the vessel. Should part of the charge be tapped out, it would be scrap. If a tuyere in a rotating vessel fails, the vessel is simply turned so as to bring the tuyeres above the level of the metal, when the faulty one can be repaired. The failure of a tuyere during the blow is no uncommon thing. It causes but a brief delay.

2d. Even in side-blowing the failure of a tuyere is a serious thing in case of fixed vessels, because it is then necessary to remove the charge from the vessel at once, converting it into scrap.

3d. At the end of the blow the charge has to be tapped out instead of being poured out of the vessel's nose. Formerly serious accidents were liable to arise through inability to open the tap-hole in case of a cold charge; but now that the proportion of silicon in the charge is more closely attended to, and that heats follow each other rapidly, this is of little moment. But, so far as my observation goes, the proportion of carbon in the steel is less closely under control in case of fixed than in that of rotating vessels, because the length of time taken to tap varies more than that needed for turning a rotating vessel down at the end of the blow, and for other reasons explained in considering side-blowing.

4th. It is impossible to recarburize within the vessel. This is relatively unimportant in case very soft steel is to be made, since in this case the metal may be recarburized advantageously in the ladle, but in case of rail-steel it is a serious thing.

Several minor objections, supposed greater difficulty in charging and in repairing, etc., are, I think, of little weight. The only serious difficulties, I believe, are the less complete control over the proportion of carbon in the steel; that the apparatus does not work as smoothly, as surely and as quickly as the rotating vessel; and that the loss of iron is heavier.

It must be admitted that the work done in the little fixed Clapp-Griffiths' vessels, as improved by Witherow, is extremely creditable. The difficulties which hung about the old Swedish fixed vessels, leading to their abandonment, and which caused even so broad-minded a man as Holley[c] to believe them beneath notice, have certainly been overcome to a most surprising degree. That 46 heats should be made in a pair of fixed vessels in eight hours, speaks volumes for the energy of the superintendent, and something for the possibilities of a vessel long despised and rejected.

The fixed vessel is certainly very much cheaper than the rotating one, and, where it is absolutely imperative that the cost of installation should be as low as possible, even at the cost of additional loss of iron in conversion and of some slight irregularity in the proportion of carbon in the product, it may be used with advantage. But under all common conditions the rotating vessel is to be preferred.

§ 392. Side- vs. Bottom-blowing.—The tuyeres have sometimes been placed at the sides instead of in the bottom, 1st, in *low* side-blowing (as in the old Swedish vessels, Figure 188), in which they were close to the bottom, to permit the use of a fixed and therefore cheap vessel; 2d, in *high* side-blowing (as in the Durfee vessel[d] and later in many others in which the tuyeres are raised far above the bottom), to lessen the blast-pressure needed to keep the metal from running into the tuyeres, and thus the power needed to drive the blowing-engines, and the cost of installation of these engines and of their boilers. To accomplish this object the tuyeres must be near the top of the bath of metal, or at least raised an appreciable distance above the bottom. The same object could be attained with bottom-blowing by making the bath of metal very shallow: but this would necessitate using extremely wide and hence expensive vessels.

The system has three chief disadvantages.

1st. The action of the blast is not uniform through the whole of the bath, as in bottom-blowing, but is strongest in the outer ring of metal above the tuyeres, the air bubbling up somewhat as sketched in Figure 186. Actually the whole bath is in active motion, and in tapping its different parts mix. But it is quite possible, if not indeed probable, that, at the moment of tapping, the metal immediately above the tuyeres contains considerably less carbon than the central part of the lower layer of metal does; and that this heterogeneousness is not fully removed in tapping into the ladle and thence into the moulds, so that the ingots are less homogeneous than in case of bottom-blowing. Lacking direct evidence on this point, I cannot tell how much weight should be attached to this objection.

2d. The metal immediately around the points where the blast enters becomes highly oxygenated. In case of bottom-blowing the metal is so thoroughly mixed up, and the path of the blast through the metal is so long, that this iron-oxide yields up its oxygen in great measure to the carbon, silicon, etc., of the bath. At the end of the blow, when there is but a trifling quantity of these elements present, the iron-oxide is not so fully reduced, and much of it escapes along with the blast from the upper surface of the metal, in the form of a dense, brownish red smoke, and the metal is now over-blown.

In case of side-blowing, however, the mixing is so much less perfect that the iron-oxide produced by the blast comes in contact much less rapidly with carbon, silicon, etc., and is therefore less rapidly deoxidized. This is especially true towards the end of the blow, when the small proportion of carbon and silicon in the limited quantity of metal, with which a given lot of iron-oxide comes in contact, does not suffice for its deoxidation, and we get local over-blowing in the region immediately above the tuyeres before the rest of the bath is thoroughly decarburized. But the blast must be kept up till the middle as well as the outer part of the charge is decarburized. Now, all admit that side-blown charges give off very much more red

c "As recarburization cannot be performed in such a vessel," *i. e.* a fixed one, "and as it is otherwise impracticable for a maximum production, we may properly omit its consideration" (Holley "Bessemer Machinery," p. 8). Now a pair of fixed vessels has turned out in eight hours twice as many heats as Holley then thought the normal product of a pair of rotating ones for twenty-four hours. Still, Holley was right.

d In 1863-4 Z. S. and W. F. Durfee designed and built at Wyandotte, Michigan, a side-blowing fixed vessel, with the tuyeres near the upper surface of the metal, so that light blast-pressure might be used, and with a movable bottom. Trans. Am. Inst. Min., Eng. XIII., p. 771, 1885. Let us call this high side-blowing.

smoke than bottom-blown ones at the beginning of the blow[a], and to my eye they do towards the end of the blow also.

It is, therefore, natural that the loss should be heavier in side—and especially in high side—than in bottom-blowing. From the data at hand I think that it is about 4% greater.

In order that the action of the blast might be less localized, the tuyeres in the old Swedish fixed side-blown vessels, Figures 188, 189, were placed not radially but in a position intermediate between that of a radius and that of a tangent,[c] so as to give the metal a horizontal rotation. In the Robert vessel, Figures 217, 218, the same thing is done, while to induce a vertical as well as a horizontal rotation, the tuyeres are placed on one side only.

The third disadvantage of side-blowing is that, as the bottom, and the sides near and below the tuyeres, wear away, the weight of charge remaining constant, the depth of metal above the tuyeres diminishes, so that blowing becomes more and more localized. Now, even those who prefer to localize the blowing must admit that it is important that the conditions of blowing should be as nearly constant as possible, in order that the desired degree of decarburization may be hit accurately; or, if we seek to remove all the carbon, that we may arrest the operation as soon as possible after decarburization is complete, and so overblow and oxidize iron as little as possible. Clearly, the more constant the conditions of blowing, the more accurately can we hit the point of complete decarburization. In bottom-blowing the depth of metal above the tuyeres changes but very slightly, the corrosion being chiefly on the bottom proper, and the side of the vessel slagging away but slowly.

I have no direct evidence as to how serious this effect is, for, though I have found that the composition of the steel varies more from heat to heat with side- than with bottom-blowing, yet the side-blown vessels concerning which I have data are also fixed, while the bottom-blown ones rotate, and how much to assign to the side-blowing and how much to the fact of being fixed, I know not.

In the Robert vessel this wearing away of the bottom may be compensated for by tipping the converter more.

On the other hand, side-blowing, or at least high side-blowing, has two decided advantages. If the tuyeres be close to the bottom, as in the old Swedish vessels, side-blowing merely enables us to use a cheaper because fixed vessel.

High side-blowing, however, not only lessens the blast-pressure needed, but greatly prolongs the life of the tuyeres. In good American bottom-blowing practice the average life of the bottoms is usually about 18 or 20 heats, though under favorable conditions the average life rises to 28 heats, while single bottoms sometimes last more than 50 heats; but I am informed that the average life of the bottom in some Clapp-Griffiths (side-blown) vessels is as high as 120 heats, and that a single bottom has lasted 225 heats.[d] The average life in the Robert side-blown vessel is said to be 250 heats.

This may be partly because the blast, moving relatively slowly through the tuyere because under lower pressure, corrades or abrades the edges of the tuyere-holes less as it issues from them, but chiefly because, in spite of its lower pressure, it holds the molten metal away from the tuyere-holes more fully than when there is a greater depth of metal above them (Cf. § 404).

The heavier loss of iron in high side- than in bottom-blowing naturally leads to a higher temperature, the excess of iron burnt giving out a great deal of heat; and we perhaps have a larger proportion of the carbon burnt to carbonic acid instead of carbonic oxide than in bottom-blowing, as the blast passes through a thinner layer of fuel.

Neglecting for the moment the minor disadvantages of side-blowing, that the composition is likely to vary more from heat to heat, and also more in the different parts of the metal from a single heat, we have to weigh against the greater loss of iron which it entails its advantages in saving blast-power and prolonging the life of the bottom and tuyeres.

If we assume that the loss is four per cent. greater in side than in bottom-blowing, side-blowing uses 121 pounds more of cast-iron than bottom-blowing does, per ton of ingots. If we further assume that the saving in blast-power in side-blowing is equivalent to saving half the total quantity of fuel burned under the boilers in bottom-blowing, and further if we assume that side-blown vessels need no repairs whatever to their refractory material, then side-blowing saves about 150 pounds of coal, 92 pounds of refractory materials (sand, clay, quartz), and 0.1 of a tuyere, per ton of ingots. But manifestly, even if we add a slight saving in the labor needed to make up the refractory materials, no calculation is needed to show that the value of this saving is much less than that of the 121 pounds of cast-iron with which side-blowing is charged. The data which I have

a "We have volumes pouring out at the very commencement, of brown iron-oxide smoke. The whole things looks as the Bessemer converter does when it is turned over, with air blowing across the top of the metal."—R. W. Hunt, Trans. Am. Inst. Min. Eng., XIII., p. 767–8, 1885. When a bottom-blown vessel is thus inclined so that some of the tuyeres emerge, or at least so that they are brought near the surface of the metal, enormous volumes of red smoke pour out; we thus raise the temperature by burning iron, and probably also by burning a large proportion of the carbon to carbonic acid instead of to carbonic oxide.

In the Clapp-Griffiths side-blown vessel a thick gray smoke appears the moment that the charge of cast-iron begins to run into the vessel. In about 30″, or probably at the instant that the level of the molten metal reaches the tuyeres, the smoke changes suddenly from gray to dense brownish red, and remains of this hue for about one to one and a half minutes, when the flame gradually assumes the same appearance as in bottom-blown charges. Towards the end of the blow, the reddish smoke again appears, and becomes very dense as the flame shortens. The blast is now partly shut off, and the metal is tapped almost immediately, the brownish red smoke continuing for about 20 seconds after the steel begins to run out of the tap-hole, when it ceases suddenly, probably just as the surface of the metal sinks below the tuyeres. In four observations I found that the red smoke continued from 13″ to 23″ after the steel began running, or an average of 17″.

In the few charges which I have seen blown in the Robert vessel, in which the blast enters still nearer the top of the bath, there was a great deal of smoke throughout the blow, which lasted twenty minutes. Though the smoke smelt very strongly of iron-oxide, it was less strongly red than that from the Clapp-Griffiths vessel. This difference, I think, is reasonably ascribed to a difference in the composition of the irons blown, that treated in the Robert vessel being highly silicious, and containing 1% of manganese,—a very "hot" iron.

The loss in this case is kept down by interrupting the blow very early, i. e., by "blowing young:" but I learn that in spite of this it amounts to 15%. The difficulty in getting trustworthy information about the loss is too well known to need comment here.

c It is generally stated that the tuyeres were tangential; but I believe that this is inaccurate.

d Oliver Brothers and Phillips, private communication, June 7, 1889. In another American work the bottoms of the Clapp-Griffiths vessels last only 30 heats, their maximum life being 52 heats.

In 1886 I was informed that the life of the bottoms of some Clapp-Griffiths vessels had averaged 55 heats for one week, and that for many weeks it had averaged 48 heats.

indicate that the case is really less favorable to the side-blown vessels than I have here assumed.

Beyond this, the life of the shell-linings is usually shorter in side than in bottom-blown vessels. (Cf. § 403.) Doubtless, this is because the iron-oxide is formed locally along the sides of side-blown vessels, and the lining around and above the tuyeres is thus exposed to more iron-oxide and to a locally more basic slag than in bottom-blown vessels, especially if the tuyeres of the latter be concentrated near the middle of the bottom. In this case the iron-oxide, formed in excess in front of the ends of the tuyeres, is well reduced by the carbon and silicon of the metal before it reaches the shell-lining.

§ 393. INTERNAL BLOWING.—Whether the tuyeres be in the side or the bottom, it is in their neighborhood that the lining wears out the soonest, the iron-oxide formed in abundance by the entering blast rapidly corroding the silicious lining of the vessel. To remedy this, and also to have a ready means of stopping and starting the blow at any instant without the costly expedient of the rotating vessel, Bessemer early designed a vessel with an internal tuyere, Figure 183. Indeed, as Figure 179 shows us, the internal tuyere may be considered as older than that built into the lining, whether at side or bottom. As a simple clay tube was liable to crack, and as the slightest crack would be fatal, Bessemer used the built-up tuyere of Figure 183, an iron tube coated with silicious refractory material, much as ladle-stoppers now are. But it has been found, both by Bessemer and in later experiments in this country, impossible to maintain this internal tuyere, partly because of the difference in expansion between the intensely-heated immersed part and the rest of the tuyere.[g]

§ 394. STRAIGHT *vs.* CONTRACTED SHELLS.—In the earlier vessels, Figure 187, the shell was contracted towards the bottom. The reason for this appears to be that, as the bottom is the place that wears out soonest and must most often be repaired, so it was desired to make it small in order that but little might have to be repaired and replaced. Contracting the shell at both ends, in that it is a step towards the spherical form, which has the minimum of heat-radiating surface, tended to preserve the heat generated within the vessel. Finally, the lining thus arched held firmly in place, tended less to fall out, *e. g.*, when the bottom of the vessel was removed for repairs.

But experience has shown that all this is false economy. Here, as in the case of the Siemens' furnace, it has been found best to sacrifice to other considerations part of that extreme compactness, which was at first sought in order to reduce the heat-radiating surface to a minimum. The fuel-economy thus gained was paid for too heavily in increased cost of repairs. A ring of stout angle-iron (Figures 202–204) at the bottom of a straight-sided vessel effectively prevents the well-sintered, tightly rammed, monolithic shell-lining from falling out when the bottom is removed. While contracting the lower part of the shell certainly made the bottom smaller, so that there was a smaller piece to repair, it really increased the cost of repairs, in two ways. First, it gave a greater depth of metal above the tuyeres, and this has been found by experience to shorten the life of the bottom, apparently because for given blast-pressure the metal, rich in nascent iron-oxide, is less fully kept away from the ends of the tuyeres by the blast. Next, because the shell-lining itself was liable to be eaten away near the bottom, and this is far more difficult to repair than the bottom itself. The vessels lately built have perfectly straight sides within and without. They are cheaper to build and to maintain, for the straight side within is so far from the tuyeres that it corrodes very little. With weekly repairs the linings of such vessels last a year easily.

§ 395. EXCENTRIC VS. CONCENTRIC NOSES.—When a vessel with the old excentric nose was turned down (Figure 201), a very large charge of molten metal could lie in its belly, without running into the tuyeres or out of the nose. The excentric nose was further thought to hinder slopping, *i. e.*, to lessen or to guard against the tendency of the boiling metal to be carried out of the vessel through the nose. Finally, as works were then arranged, it discharged the molten steel and the gaseous products of combustion conveniently, and received the molten cast-iron without excessive inconvenience.[d] In designing the excentric nose, however, care had to be taken that the whole bottom of the vessel should be visible through it, so that the condition of this, the most perishable part of the lining, might be readily learned between blows.

This was all very well as long as the cast-iron was melted in reverberatory or cupola furnaces, for these could be placed at such a height that the metal ran from them through long runners to the vessel turned down towards the pit, like the right-hand vessel in Figure 173 and the middle one of Figure 177.

But even in this case, the greater height which we had to give the cupolas, and the greater length which the runners needed, in order to carry the cast-iron not merely to the vessels but past their whole length, was an inconvenience, even if it was not realized.

When, however, molten metal was brought direct from the blast-furnace, it was found too serious an inconvenience to raise it so high that it would run past the length of the vessels into their noses; and, in case the metal had for any reason become cool during its passage from the blast-furnace to the converting-mill, an excessive quantity of it would freeze in the long runners.

Two expedients suggested themselves. The cast-iron-ladle could be brought to a hoist H, standing between the line of the trunnion-axes and the pit, as in Figures 164 and 209, and here raised so as to pour through a short runner into the vessel; or the nose of the vessel could be made concentric or symmetrical, so that it could receive molten cast-iron when turned down *away* from the pit, and at the end of the blow receive spiegeleisen and discharge steel when turned down *towards* the pit, as in Figures 173 and 177.

We have already seen that the surface track of the Bethlehem plan occupies space which might be utilized for other purposes, and which is likely to be encumbered, and is hence not very well suited for the extremely frequent trips of the iron- and the spiegel-ladle.

g F. W. Gordon, U. S. patent 361,624, April 19, 1887, describes a movable tuyere, with elaborate and ingenious devices for moving and protecting it. It was inserted through the side of a stationary vessel, a little above the surface of the molten metal into which it dipped. Serious if not fatal technical difficulties arose in experiments made with it.

d Holley indeed said of it "We can hardly see how the shape can be improved, or how any other would be admissible." (Lecture at Stevens' Inst., 1872, p. 9.)

Thus the concentric vessel seemed to offer a very simple solution. It allowed the spiegel- and cast-iron-cupolas to remain in their old places behind the vessels, the spiegeleisen running though the old bifurcated runner into the vessel as this lay turned down towards the pit at the end of the blow; the cast-iron running into ladles standing on a track which ran behind the vessels, and to which the direct-metal was brought over an incline by a locomotive, a special locomotive always standing on the track, ready to move both the direct and the cupola-metal ladles to and from the vessels. (See Figures 163, 173, 177.)

But the concentric-nosed vessel must be made much larger than the excentric one, in order that, when turned down, it may hold a charge of given weight without allowing it to run either out of the nose or into the tuyeres, and hence is a much more expensive vessel. The old excentric vessels had from about 33 to about 42, the new concentric ones have from about 50 to about 80 cubic feet capacity per ton of charge (Table 196). The little Avesta vessel had about 15 cubic feet capacity per ton of charge. Now this increased volume turns out to be a great, if unexpected, blessing, for very much less slopping occurs with it. The vessel is so roomy, and the height from the upper surface of the metal to the nose is so great, that the metal which is carried up by the blast from the surface of the foaming bath falls back again before reaching the nose; indeed, even some of that which issues from the nose may fall back, for the flame passes vertically from the nose to the hood. This has diminished the loss of iron greatly; indeed, many metallurgists think that, even for given volume, the concentric vessels slops less than the excentric one; but why this should be, no one can explain. With our large vessels the loss, including that in remelting the cast-iron in cupolas, is sometimes repoted as below 8% for a month at a time; and, when direct-metal is used, the loss during a whole year has been reported as only 7.5%.

Still a third expedient is to remove the vessels so far from the casting-pit that the cast-iron can be brought by an overhead elevated track running between them and the pit, as in Forsyth's plan (Figures 168, 169). In this way direct- and cupola-metal are brought to the vessel easily, while it is turned down towards the pit. But even in this case the concentric vessel is often used to diminish slopping. Perhaps it is well that this plan was not worked out till after after the advantages of the concentric vessel had been found out.

A further advantage of the concentric vessel is that its lining wears out much less rapidly than that of the excentric vessel, as explained in § 403.

One inconvenience of the excentric vessel, which has lost some precious lives, is that the hood, or chimney K (Figure 209), must stand above the rear of the vessel. Now, this is just above where the vessel-men must stand while examining the tuyeres between heats, and here they are threatened with the masses of steel sloppings which hang over their heads on the walls of the hood, giving to the eye little indication as to how firmly they hang, or when they may fall. It has, indeed, been found desirable to provide swinging platforms or awnings to shield the vessel-men from these falling masses. The hood, in case of concentric vessels, stands directly over the trunnion axis, and the vessel-men work in comparative safety when examining bottoms.

The concentric vessel has been widely adopted by American engineers, but it seems to have met with relatively little favor in Europe.

§ 396. Size of Vessel-nose.—A small nose yields a higher working temperature within the vessel for two reasons. First the radiation of heat from within the vessel is less; second, by checking the escape of the products of combustion, it leads to higher pressure within the vessel, and thus not only lessens the absorption of heat due to the expansion of the blast as it emerges from the tuyeres, but also lessens the degree to which dissociation occurs. At Eston a four-foot nose was contracted to two feet, and the temperature of the blow is said to have increased plainly. Similar results were obtained at West Cumberland by reducing a large nose.*

In case of concentric vessels a small nose has a further advantage, in increasing the quantity of molten metal which the vessel can hold when "turned down."

It is thought by some that, with the broad flame which the wide nose affords, the point of complete decarburization can be hit more accurately than if the nose and flame be narrow. Others, however, think that, if the blowing be more accurate in case of wide noses, it is because the temperature of the blow is somewhat lower than if the nose be narrow; the cooler the heat the more accurately may the point of complete decarburization be hit.

§ 397. Details of the Construction of Bessemer Converters.—To fix our ideas I shall describe two large vessels (Figures 202 to 206) lately built, and designed by distinguished engineers.

The vessel consists, first, of the iron body, and, second, of the lining; the preparation of the latter will be described in § 402.

As the region around the tuyeres (*i. e.*, in bottom-blown vessels, the bottom) wears out very much sooner the rest of the lining, so the bottom is almost universally removable. The necessity of this is seen from the fact that, while a bottom lasts on an average from twenty to thirty heats, or in rapid running only about seven hours including the intervals between heats, the rest of the lining lasts a year easily in the best American and European practice.

The iron-work then consists of the body and of a removable bottom. The former consists of the trunnion-ring A, *i. e.*, that part to which the trunnions are attached, and which carries the whole weight of vessel, lining and charge; and the shell proper B C. The shell may be made as in Figure 202 in a single riveted piece, or as in Figure 204 it may be in two pieces, a cylinder B and a cone C, bolted together.

The trunnions themselves, D, are very heavy castings, preferably of steel. An excellent form is shown in Figure 204. One of them must be hollow, and conducts the blast through the goose-neck E to the tuyere box F. In Figure 202 the blast passes to the goose-neck through a space cored in the trunnion-ring. In Figures 204 to 206 the goose-neck is carefully shrunk directly upon the trunnion itself. Instead of coring a single large hole in the un-

* Holley, Priv. Rept., 1880, II., p. 12; 1881, I., p. 58.

The shell itself is of heavy wrought- or ingot-iron plates. In Figure 202 the middle of the shell is of two plates, 1" and ¾" thick respectively, the upper part being of a single 1" plate. In Figure 204 the middle of the shell is made of two plates, each 1" thick. In another vessel lately built, with a capacity of ten tons, the middle of the shell is 1" thick for three feet of its length, and only ½" thick beyond this, and is strengthened with wrought-iron bands, 1" x 12".

The method of attaching the shell proper to the trunnion-ring is important. Formerly the trunnion-ring was part of the shell proper, but in later vessels it is a distinct piece, separated from the shell itself by an air-space, which in great measure prevents the heat and expansion of the shell from heating the trunnions and shifting their position.

As the shell grows much hotter than the trunnion-ring, so these two parts should be so attached that, while the shell is held firmly, each is free to expand and contract independently. This is effected in the vessel shown in Figure 202 by hanging the shell, by means of stout cast-iron brackets, upon the upper edge of the trunnion-ring. This, of course, only holds the vessel as long as it is upright. When it is inverted it hangs from the trunnion-ring, resting on the keys I, which in Figure 202 are at the lower end of the bolts J. The whole weight of the vessel is now borne by these bolts,

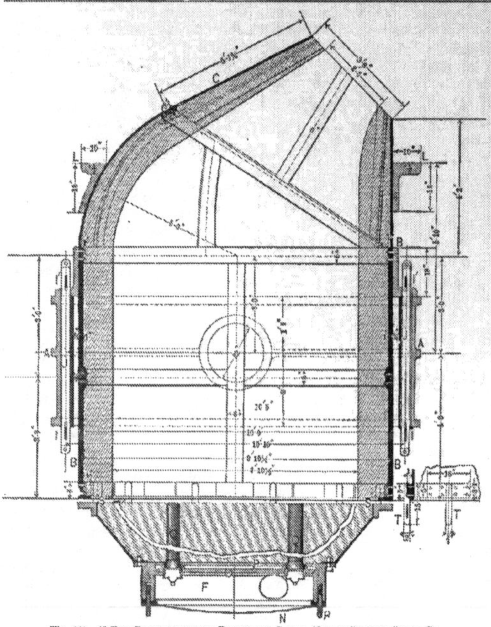

Fig. 203. 10-Ton Converter with Removable Shell, North Chicago Steel Co.

der side of the trunnion to admit the blast to the goose-neck, the blast may be taken off through a number of radial slots, as in Figure 206, and gathered by a heart-shaped box, with wings G designed to prevent the different bodies of blast from interfering with each other. This trunnion is cast solid, and then bored out; it is an expensive one, but it should be very strong for its weight, and relatively free from internal stress.

To the other trunnion the shrouded cast-iron, or better cast-steel, pinion (Figure 209), which rotates the vessel, is keyed.

The trunnion-ring A was formerly a very heavy iron casting, stoutly ribbed, and bolted firmly to the trunnions. In some vessels lately built, however, as in Figures 204 and 205, it is of heavy wrought- or ingot-iron plate, say 1½ or 2 inches thick, with flanges at either end.

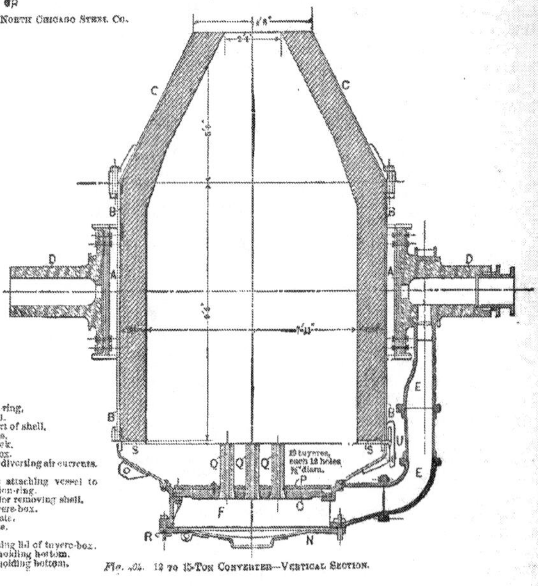

A. Trunnion-ring.
B. Main shell.
C. Upper part of shell.
D. Trunnions.
E. Goose-neck.
F. Tuyere-box.
G. Wings for diverting air currents.
I, I. Keys.
J. Key-bolts attaching vessel to trunnion-ring.
L. Brackets for removing shell.
N. Lid of tuyere-box.
O. Tuyere-plate.
P. False plate.
Q. Tuyeres.
R. Keys holding lid of tuyere-box.
T. Key-bolt holding bottom.
U. Key-link holding bottom.

Fig. 204. 12 to 15-Ton Converter—Vertical Section.

J. At the same time a series of stout radial set-screws supports the vessel when it is inclined. Here the shell is clearly free to expand and contract longitudinally, simply sliding past the points of the set-screws. And, since these set-screws need not bind the shell tightly when it is cold, a considerable amount of radial expansion may also occur, the set-screws simply denting the shell slightly. Indeed, there might be a little play between shell and set-screws when the vessel is cold. This is especially true of eccentric vessels, for the set-screws on their rear sides are never called on to support much weight.

In the vessel shown in Figures 204 and 205, two sets of cast-iron brackets, one above and one below, bolted together by the bolts, J, attach the shell to the trunnion-ring. But here we have no means of compensating for the difference in expansion between the shell and the trunnion-ring, and in many cases this mode of hanging has given much trouble. Either the bolts, J, or the brackets, K, break. Indeed, in many vessels these brackets have purposely been of wrought-iron or steel, so that they might bend rather than break, and there they stand all bent out of shape.

Holley's Shell-shifting Device.—The cast-iron brackets, LL, Figure 202, are to enable us to remove the vessel-shell by Holley's method, shown in Figure 207, so that we may carry it to the repair-shop, and immediately replace it with a newly-lined shell, whose lining may be preheated.[a] In the basic Bessemer process the apparently unavoidably rapid destruction of the shell lining must greatly lessen the output, unless we are prepared to replace the worn-out lining rapidly. This is nearly as essential to large output in the basic process as quick changing of bottoms is in the acid process.

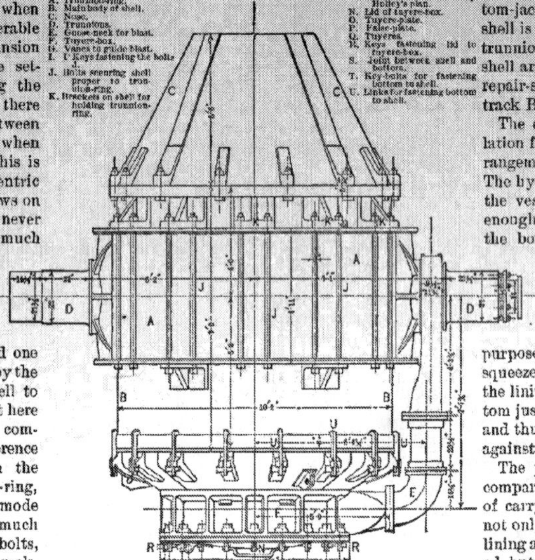

Note to figs. 202 to 206 inclusive.
A. Trunnion-ring.
B. Main body of shell.
C. Nose.
D. Trunnions.
E. Goose-neck for blast.
F. Tuyere-box.
G. Vanes to guide blast.
I. I' Keys fastening the bolts J.
J. Bolts securing shell proper to trunnion-ring.
K. Brackets on shell for holding trunnion-ring.
L. Brackets for supporting shell when removed by Holley's plan.
N. Lid of tuyere-box.
O. Tuyere-plate.
P. False-plate.
Q. Tuyeres.
R. Keys fastening lid to tuyere-box.
S. Joint between shell and bottom.
T. Key-bolts for fastening bottom to shell.
U. Links for fastening bottom to shell.

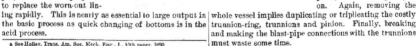

Fig. 205. New Bessemer Steel Works. 12 to 15-Ton Converter.

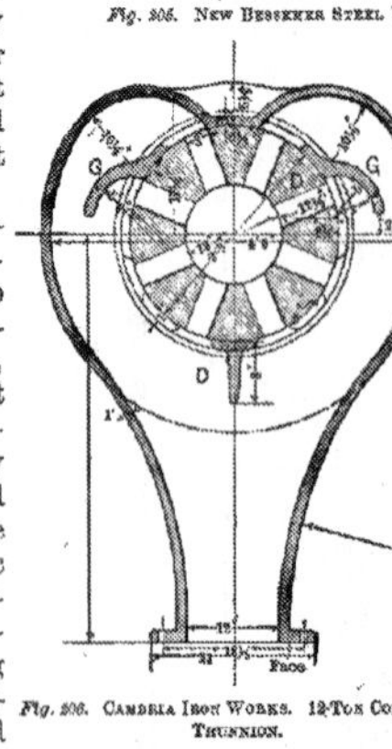

Fig. 206. Cambria Iron Works. 12-Ton Converter Trunnion.

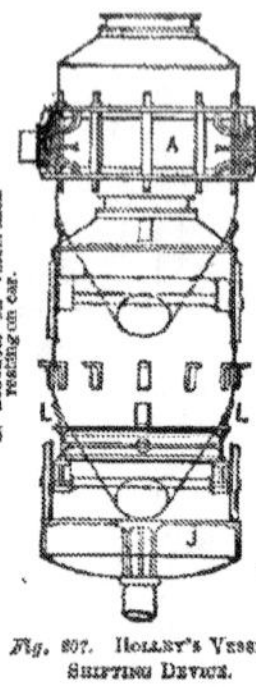

Note to figure 207.
A. Trunnion-ring.
J. Platform carried by hydraulic jack.
L. Brackets on vessel-shell resting on car.

Fig. 207. Holley's Vessel-Shifting Device.

The vessel is inverted, and a heavy car standing on the bottom-jack J (Q in Figure 163) is raised so as to sustain the shell through these brackets, L. The keys I (Figure 202), are then drawn, thus releasing the shell from the trunnion-ring, A. The bottom-jack is lowered till the shell is wholly free from the trunnion-ring, when car and shell are carried away to the repair-shop, *e. g.*, by the track Bt, Figure 168.

The extra cost for installation for this admirable arrangement is not severe. The hydraulic jacks beneath the vessels must be strong enough to lift not merely the bottom, but the shell and lining: and a few strong cars are needed. The strong bottom-jacks are useful for another purpose: they enable us to squeeze the joint between the linings of shell and bottom just so much the tighter, and thus to guard the better against leakage.

The plan is obviously incomparably better than that of carrying away for repairs not only the shell, to whose lining alone repairs are needed, but also the exceedingly heavy trunnion-ring and trunnions, by means of an over-head traveling-crane. First, the cost of such a crane, strong enough to lift the shell and trunnions, and installed at such a height, is great. Next, its motions are relatively slow and clumsy, while nothing could be simpler than the plain up and down stroke of the hydraulic bottom-jack. Then vessel and trunnions must be coaxed into place while swinging from chains, steadied, guided, and lowered little by little; the bottom car, however, brings the shell exactly under its place in the trunnion-ring, and a single stroke of the bottom-jack sets it in place, to be merely keyed on. Again, removing the whole vessel implies duplicating or triplicating the costly trunnion-ring, trunnions and pinion. Finally, breaking and making the blast-pipe connections with the trunnions must waste some time.

a See Holley, Trans. Am. Soc. Mech. Eng., I, 10th paper, 1880.

Justice[h] very slightly lessens the difficulties just mentioned by splitting the trunnion ring, so that when the vessel is turned horizontally, it, together with the then lower half of the trunnion-ring, may be lowered upon a car standing beneath, and carried off for repairs. But then the vessel cannot be relined conveniently while thus lying on its side.

The Trunnion-axis may pass through the centre of gravity of the iron-work and lining of the vessel, bottom included; but it is probably better that it should pass rather below this point, so that the vessel may be slightly top-heavy when empty, for the following reason. We need the greatest rapidity of motion when turning the vessel down after the blow, for, until we have swung it somewhere about 30°, all the tuyeres are still submerged, and all the blast is still passing through the molten metal and burning iron. But at this time, as all the metal is at the bottom of the vessel, we have not only to overcome the inertia of the vessel and bath, but to lift the bath itself. And now, when we most need quick motion, the top-heaviness of our vessel itself comes to our assistance, and helps us turn down. Many vessels have a massive hook on their breasts, to which heavy weights can be attached during the last part of the week, when the corrosion of the lining of the breast has lowered the vessel's centre of gravity.

§ 398. THE BOTTOM.—In the bottom itself we have, besides the tuyeres and the refractory matrix which we will consider in § 404, the tuyere-box, F, (Figures 202-4), which receives the blast from the goose-neck and distributes it to the butt-ends of the tuyeres.

The lid, N, which covers it, must be large, quickly removable, and very tightly fitting; large, that the ends of all the tuyeres may be easily accessible for examination and removal; quickly removable, that no time need be lost in examining the tuyeres between heats; and tightly fitting lest the blast be wasted. The importance of having it fit tightly is clear when we remember the length of the joint between lid and tuyere box, about 17 running feet in the case before us. These requirements are fully met by fastening the lid with many keys, R, and by facing it and the edge of the tuyere-box accurately, or even cutting in them a tongue and groove, as in Figure 202. In some cases the joint has been part of the surface of a sphere of long radius.

Though no gasket of any kind is provided, this joint leaves nothing to be desired. Though many bottoms are provided for each vessel, so that each may be long and carefully dried, one lid only is needed. Of course there should be a second lid in reserve, lest an injury to that in use paralyze the establishment.

A light crane, P, Figure 209, serves for handling the bottom-lid for inspection between heats, the vessel then standing turned down, as shown in dotted lines.

The tuyere-plate, O, has round openings which receive the butts of the tuyeres, and which are grooved (Figure 204) so as to make a tight joint with the luting with which the tuyere-butts are coated before they are inserted. The tuyeres are held in place, during the ramming of the bottom-lining, by dogs, clamps or screws of various designs, the important point being that they shall be quickly removable. In case of acid (silicious) linings, the tuyeres are bound so firmly by the lining rammed around them that these dogs are not needed after the bottom is rammed. In some cases, as in Figure 193, a sort of staple projects from the tuyere-plate on either side of each tuyere; a stick of wood or an iron rod is held by these staples across and tightly against the butt end of each tuyere, during the ramming of the bottom-lining, and is then knocked out, leaving the tuyere-end free for examination.

By means of the false plate, P, an air-space which communicates with the outer air is left between tuyere-box and bottom lining, for two purposes. First, if the joint between the tuyere-plate and one of the tuyeres be imperfect, the blast which works through simply escapes into the outer air, instead of cutting between the necessarily rather loose bottom-lining and the tuyere a ragged channel, and thus quickly destroying the bottom. 2nd, should a tuyere wear too short during a heat, the molten metal, instead of cutting through and filling up the tuyere-box, goes spitting out through this air-space into the outer air. The pyrotechnic effect of the escape of the first little portion of metal in this way is so striking, that the stage-boy in charge sees it at once and turns the vessel down before any harm is done. The lid or bottom-plate, N, is removed, the short tuyere knocked out, its hole rammed full of "ball-stuff" (plastic clay-balls), and the blowing is resumed with but a few minutes delay.

The sharp swift sparks, due to this escape of metal between bottom and tuyere-box, are readily distinguished from the slow droppings of white-hot metal due to leakage through the joint S, between the lining of the shell and that of the bottom, Figures 202–204. Such a leak can usually be stopped by raising it about the surface of the metal by rotating the vessel, chilling it if need be from without with the hose.

The bottom must be so attached to the shell of the vessel that it can be quickly and easily removed and re-attached. To that end it is almost always keyed on. Figures 202 and 209 show key-bolts, T, riveted to the shell, which pass through eyes on brackets on the bottom. While it is not likely that the shell can warp so much that these bolts would not enter their eyes readily, yet it may be well to avoid this danger wholly by using simple key-links, such as U in Figure 205. But others again object to these links on the ground that when the bottom is removed and the vessel is turned over, they fall off, or at least require attention. Another good form of link (W. R. Jones' design) is shown in Figure 208.

Fig. 208. HOLLEY'S EXTERNALLY RAMMED BOTTOM-JOINT.

S, Joint between bottom and shell. U, Link for fastening bottom to shell, Jones' pattern.

TABLE 197.—TOTAL AREA OF TUYERE-HOLES IN SQUARE INCHES PER TON OF CAPACITY OF VESSEL.

American, present	from	1.16 to 5.95
Swedish, 1885	"	6.1 to 12.
German, 1871	"	0.8 to 1.88
British, "	"	3.18 to 3.44
Obouchoff		3.78
England and Belgium, 1877		2.1 to 1.5

§ 399. THE SIZE OF THE TUYERE-OPENINGS still varies greatly. I condense Table 197 from the detailed data in Tables 196 and 198. It is at first very surprising that, as happens in some works, all the blast delivered by two 54-inch blast-pistons running at full speed should be squeezed through a lot of $\frac{3}{8}$-inch holes, whose collective

h Wedding, der Basische Bessemer oder Thomas-Process, p. 80, 1884.

area is less than that of a four-inch pipe. One would suppose that the consumption of power which this implies must be very considerable; yet it is hard to conceive any other arrangement by which we can have rapid and uniform blowing, without excessive loss of iron or excessive destruction of the bottoms. But as the total consumption of fuel under the converting-works' boilers is only 300 pounds and in some works only 200 pounds of coal per ton of ingots, and as a considerable part of this is chargeable to blowing the cupolas and to the movements of the cranes, hoists, etc., we can hardly charge more than 14 cents per ton of ingots for blowing-power, where fuel is of moderate price. Indeed, in some mills the fuel for generating the blast probably does not cost more than five cents per ton of ingots. And this, too, without compound engines and with but moderate expansion.

TABLE 198.—SIZE OF TUYERE-HOLES. (SEE ALSO TABLE 197.)

Authority.	Name of Works.	Capacity of the Converter in Tons.	Number of Openings in the Tuyeres.	Diameter of the Openings in Inches	Total Area of the Openings in Sq. Inches.	Area of the Openings in Sq. Inches per Ton.
1. Drown..	Königshütte...	3	49	¼	2.40	0.80
	Neuberg......	3	49	[illegible]	4.27	1.43
	Zwickau......	3	42	[illegible]	5.12	1.71
	Heft.........	2	42	[illegible]	3.66	1.83
	Crewe........	5	144	[illegible]	15.59	3.18
	Dowlais......	5	156	[illegible]	17.23	3.44
2..........	Zeltweg......	5	56	[illegible]	11.02	2.20
	"	5	84	[illegible]	14.70	2.94
	Obouchoff....	5	189	[illegible]	18.63	3.73
3. Jordan...	England & Belgium about 1877	5 to 7	77	5/16	10.5	2.1 to 1.5
4. Holley...	Brown, Bayley and Dixon, 1879	8	195	5/16	15	1.87
5. Holley...	Another British Mill, 1881......	8	208	⅝	23	2.87

1. Drown, Trans. Am. Inst. Min. Eng., I., p. 88, 1871.
2. Jordan, Jeans, Steel, p. 270, from Album du Cours de Metallurgie, 1877.

§ 400. The ROTATING MECHANISM (Figure 209), almost always consists of a heavily shrouded pinion, preferably of steel, keyed to one of the trunnions (B) of the vessel, and driven by a rack, which is keyed to the end of the piston-rod of a powerful hydraulic cylinder (D). Eccentric vessels should be able to turn through an arc of 270°; concentric vessels—at least those which receive the charge when turned down away from the pit—should turn rather farther, say 300°.

At first placed horizontally, so as to be accessible, the hydraulic cylinders were next set vertically to save floor-room, and beneath the trunnions to secure easy foundations. In this position it was found hard to give the cylinder sufficient length, without carrying it to a depth inconvenient to drain. Of course, the longer its stroke the larger could be the radius of the pinion, and the lighter therefore the stress on the rack. Accordingly the cylinder was next placed above the trunnion—standing vertically. Here it could have whatever length was needed.

The position finally adopted, however, is that shown in Figure 209. The cylinder lies horizontally beneath the platform at the trunnion-level. It is thus wholly out of the way, while the platform prevents rubbish from falling between the teeth of the rack. It is better, however, to protect the rack and pinion further with sheet-iron cases, for even a small lump of metal lodged between the rack's teeth might lead to a serious or, indeed, a fatal accident[d]. I have known a vessel to be overturned, emptying its whole charge into the pit, from such an accident.

The ports of the hydraulic cylinder, shown beneath in Figure 209, should be above the cylinder, so that the breakage of a pipe may not allow the water to leak out of either end of the cylinder. To make this clear, suppose that the vessel-bottom has been removed so that the vessel is top-heavy; that the piston has been moved to the right-hand end of the cylinder, so that the vessel's nose is turned down to the left; that the pipe leading the water to the left-hand end of the cylinder has burst or broken, and that the water has run out. Now the stage-boy, ignorant of what has happened, turns the vessel over to the right by admitting water to the right-hand end of the cylinder. The moment that the center of gravity of the vessel passes to the right of the trunnion axes, the top-heavy vessel turns down with a rush, as there is no water in the left-hand end of the cylinder to oppose its motion, and drives the piston through the end of the cylinder or breaks the rack. This has happened repeatedly.

A. Ladle for cast-iron.
B. Trunnion.
D. Cylinder for rotating vessel.
J. Runner
K. Hood or chimney.
M. Foundation of hydraulic lift for cast-iron ladle.
N. Foundation of column supporting vessel.
P. Hand-crane for removing lid of tuyere-box.

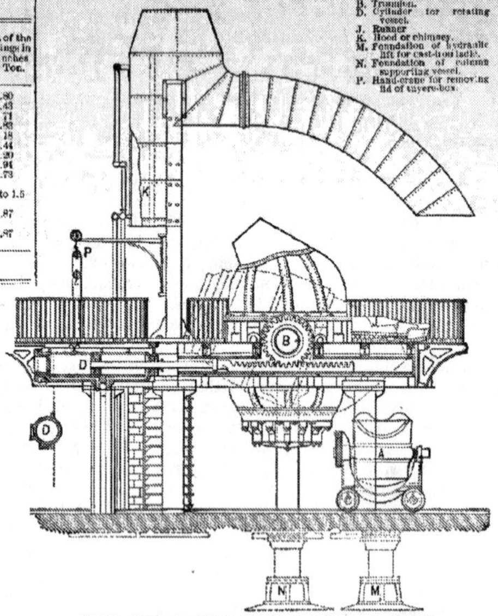

Fig. 209. BETHLEHEM VESSEL, WITH ROTATING MECHANISM. HOLLEY.

The disadvantage of the rack-and-pinion arrangement is that, however long the cylinder and rack, the vessel can only turn a certain number of degrees in one direction, be that number 270°, or 360°, or 720°. Now, it may happen that, when the vessel is inverted, it would be a little more convenient to turn it 90° farther away from the pit to receive a charge of iron on the rear side, than to turn it back 270° to reach this same position. Practically, this disadvantage is of little moment; but to avoid it the ves-

d Some have recommended placing the rack and cylinder horizontally, but so that the rack would be above, instead of below the pinion, in order that lumps of metal and splashings might not lodge between its teeth. Here, however, rack and cylinder would be badly in the way, and enclosing them in sheet-iron cases protects them fully.

sel is sometimes rotated by a worm and worm-wheel, in which case it can, of course, turn indefinitely in either direction. The worm is probably best driven by two or three hydraulic engines. While no serious objection can be made to such a design, probably the great majority of engineers prefer the simpler and wholly satisfactory rack and pinion.

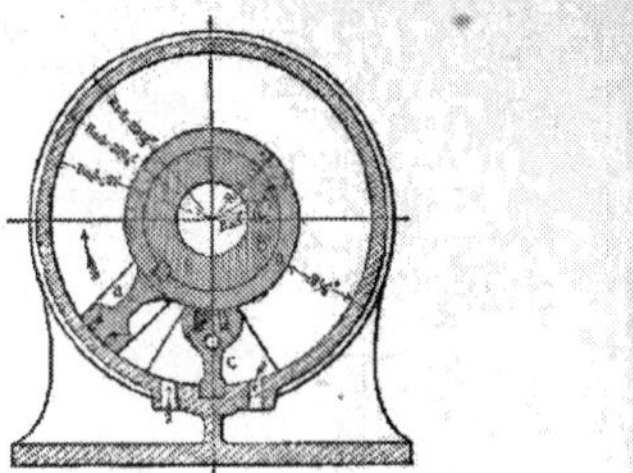

a. Wing-piston.
b. Trunnion.
c. Fixed abutment in cylinder.

Fig. 210.

Durfee[e] would rotate the vessel by means of a wing-piston, a, (Figure 210), keyed directly to the vessel trunnion b, and turning nearly 360° in a cylinder concentric with the trunnion. In this cylinder is a fixed abutment c, which takes the place of both heads of a common cylinder. Water admitted on either side of this abutment drives the wing-piston in the desired direction. The attachment is certainly more direct than in the rack-and-pinion arrangement, and there should be a saving in power as well as in cost of installation.

§ 401. The Joint Between the Lining of the Shell and that of the Bottom.—In early practice, as soon as the bottom was worn out the stumps of the old tuyeres were knocked out, new tuyeres inserted, and the space between them filled by pouring "slurry" (a semi-fluid mixture of fire-clay, quartz or ganister, and water), through the vessel's nose, and allowing it to set around them. Of course blowing was interrupted during the long time needed for drying this bottom, which, moreover, was most untrustworthy, flaky, inadherent and full of drying cracks. Another way was to allow the vessel to cool, and then make up the bottom from within by ramming "ball-stuff" (a stiff, slightly plastic mixture of clay and quartz) around the tuyeres; or better by placing a previously baked bottom within the vessel, and then ramming ball-stuff into the joint from within the vessel. But here, too, great delay arose, since for twelve or even twenty-four hours after blowing, the vessel was still too hot to enter. Cooling was sometimes hastened by removing the vessel's nose, but then this had to be replaced, and the joint thus made had to be rammed: or by pouring water into the vessel, a practice which injured the lining greatly.[x]

e Trans. American Institute of Mining Engineers, XII., p. 371, 1884.

x Even as lately as 1879 bottom-joints were made in some British works by pouring slurry through the vessel-nose, so that it ran between the shell-lining and a previously baked bottom. Setting a bottom in this way took five hours, and the bottom itself, soaked and weakened by the slurry, lasted but seven heats (Holley, Priv. Rept., 1880, No. 2, p. 30).

It is strange that Holley and Pearse's simple expedient, of ramming the joint between a previously baked bottom and the vessel lining from without, was not earlier thought of.[a] This, as improved by Holley,[b] Figure 211, lasted till lately, and is in use in some mills even now. The iron-work of the bottom was so shaped that, between the brackets by which it was keyed to the shell, lumps of

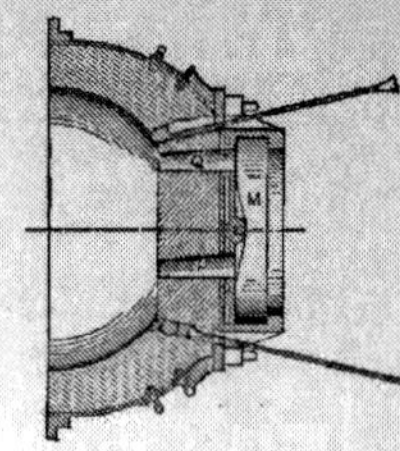

Fig. 211. Holley's Externally Rammed Bottom-Joint—Old Style.

ball-stuff could be inserted and rammed. The bottom was first keyed on while the vessel stood upright. The vessel was then turned on its side, and the balls were rammed in as shown in Figure 211. The vessel was then turned up again, and a few pailfuls of slurry were poured through its nose to fill any cracks in the ball-stuff joint.

In later practice, in the few cases in which this form of bottom is used, the vessel is held upright until a single row of clay balls has been rammed between the upper edge of the bottom and the shell-lining, and is then turned on its side for ramming the rest of the joint. This is done lest the bottom break apart by its own weight when the vessel is turned on its side.

A later form of the joint is shown in Figure 208. This joint is rammed from the pit level while the vessel stands upright. There is evidently less danger of tearing the shell-lining of the vessel in breaking this flat joint, than in pulling out the conical, tightly wedged bottom of Figure 211. I am informed that this form of joint is very frequently used in Europe.

The dish-bottom, Figures 202–204, is the form now generally used here. Its upper service is level. The joint is made by spreading on the upper side of the bottom a ring or "noodle" of ball-stuff, covering this with a little graphite, and squeezing the bottom tightly against the shell-lining by means of the bottom-jack. The graphite preserves a good parting, so that the bottom, when worn out, may be removed without tearing away the lining of the shell, instead leaving it so smooth that a sound joint is easily made with the next bottom. The powerful bottom-jacks in some recently built works exert a pressure of about 2,000 pounds per foot on the joint, which thus made never leaks. In some works which have neither bottom-jacks nor hydraulic bottom-car, the vessel is inverted, a ring of ball-stuff set on the edge of the shell-lining, the bottom placed on this by means of a crane, and merely keyed tightly. Even this uncompressed joint serves admirably.

As stated in § 376, 2, the total time between blows of a

a U. S. Patent 86,304, Jan. 26, 1869, A. L. Holley and J. B. Pearse.

b U. S. Patent 106,162, Aug. 9, 1870, A. L. Holley.

single vessel, including changing bottoms, has been as short as 17 minutes at the Union (Illinois) works.

§ 402. THE VESSEL-LININGS are usually monolithic, a mass of clay and quartz rammed solidly together and thoroughly dried: some vessels, however, are lined with blocks of stone, which give good results, but so far as my observation goes do not last so long as the monolithic lining. In either case the vessel stands inverted and without its bottom during re-lining.

The monolithic lining is usually made of a mixture of was rammed around an iron core set within the vessel, by a gang of eight or ten men, who marched slowly in the annulus between core and shell, ramming the mixture with butt-rammers like those in Figure 211, a few shovelfuls of the mixture being added at intervals.

In what is perhaps the most successful present practice (columns 17, 18 and 20, Table 199), the mixture, whose materials (quartz, sand and clay) are finely ground together, has so much water that it balls readily, and is indeed a stiff, decidedly plastic mass or "ball-stuff."

TABLE 199.—VESSEL-LININGS AND BOTTOMS (CF. TABLE 136).

	1872 1	1872 2	1871 3	1872 4	1872 5	6	7	8	9	10	11	12	13	14	15
Weight of vessel-charge, gross tons						6	6 @ 7	6	7½	9	7½	10	4	5½	3
Percentage of silicon in vessel-charge						2.2	1.15			1.25		1.45		1.5	
Diameter of vessel									8'						6'
Estimated depth of bath over tuyeres, inches								18½							3⅝
Length of blow, minutes and seconds								8' @ 10'	9' 37" @ 15'	12'		21 @ 22' 45"	11' 10"—12' 45"	13' 28"—14' 35"	
COMPOSITION OF VESSEL-LINING BY WEIGHT—															
Quartz, %	53⅓	c 41⅔–f 41⅔	71⅓ g					Ground millstone grit.	Mica-schist blocks.	66	Ground ganister.	Mica-schist blocks.	Ball-stuff.	Mica-schist blocks, c.	
Fire-sand, %	40		14⅓												
Loam-sand, %										17					
Fat clay, %	6⅔	16⅔	14⅓							17					
DURATION OF VESSEL-LINING—Months								9 @ 18			4 @ 7	5	2	12	
Heats									2,750			8,400			
Blast-pressure, pounds per square inch						18		18 @ 25		20					
Diameter of tuyere-holes, inches							⅝	⅝"	⅝"	⅝	½	⅝	½"		⅝
Gross area tuyere-holes, square inches							15.9	35.7	29.5	21.2	30.6	11.6	16.5		17.2
Kind of bottom	Holley.							dish.			1	dish.	1		dish.
Thickness of bottom, inches															
COMPOSITION OF BOTTOM—Fire sand, %	37.5		12½				Ganister bricks.	1	1			Ball-stuff.	Ball-stuff.		Holley bricks, j.
Crushed brick or chammotte, %				60	40					60					
Quartz, %	50	66⅔ h	62½ g		20 h	100 h									
Fat clay, %	12½	33⅓	25	40						40					
Calcined clay, %					40										
Length of time bottom is dried, hours									8 @ 10		24			24	
Number of bottoms kept on hand															
DURATION OF BOTTOM—															
Usual, Heats		4 to 8				14	11.45	25 @ 30	12 @ 16	18		13	24±	16	20 @ 26
Usual, Time collectively									2h. 37'	2h. 36'		6h. 57'	4h. 47'	3h. 46'—3h. 32'	
Maximum, Heats						23	22					28	36 @ 40		
Maximum, Time collectively												8h. 23'	7h. 34"		

TABLE 199.—VESSEL LININGS AND BOTTOMS.—*Concluded.*

	16	17	18	19	20	21	22	23	24	25	26	27	Bångbro. 28	Avesta. 29
Weight of vessel-charge, gross tons	10	6 @ 7		9.2	10.78	5.5	7½	7	7	11	8.5	2 q	8.7	6.39
Percentage of silicon in vessel-charge			1.95	1.8		1.4	1.5	1.6	1.75		2.0		1.08	1.4
Diameter of vessel		5'	10	10±			8'		8'	10'			4' 10"	3' 4"
Estimated depth of bath over tuyeres, inches			12¾	13.7	12½					15⅛"				
Length of blow, minutes and seconds	13 @ 14		10' 30"	16	10 @ 11		11' 30"—13'	10 @ 17			13	10'—16' 30"	5 @ 7	9'—13'.5
COMPOSITION OF VESSEL-LINING BY WEIGHT—														
Quartz, %		81	66 n	83 n		Ganister blocks.		88					5 vol.	
Fire-sand, %		16	17					Mill-stone grit, p.						
Loam-sand, %														
Fat clay, %		23	17	17									1 vol.	
DURATION OF VESSEL-LINING—Months		12	18	12		6	2	1.5 @ 2						
Heats												4000 @ 8800	200 @ 300	
Blast-pressure, pounds per square inch		20			21 @ 25		20		20	25	17 @ 18		10 @ 17	
Diameter of tuyere-holes, inches	½"	⅝	⅝	½"	½ & ⅞		⅝"	⅝	½	⅝			50	.13
Gross area tuyere-holes, square inches	30.6	15.9	19.8	20.4	34.7		35.3	25.2	17.1	25.1			22	1.2
Kind of bottom		Hol., e.	dish.		dish.	Hol.	1		dish, 1.	dish.	dish.			
Thickness of bottom, inches		18							26					8"
COMPOSITION OF BOTTOM—Fire-sand, %		12	26		12		17							
Crushed brick or chammotte, %			20	50	25 o		55							
Quartz, %		47	17		43									
Fat clay, %		41	23	50	21		27							
Calcined clay, %			16 m											
Length of time bottom is dried, hours		24 a—14 b		24	48 @ 96	48	24 @ 48	24	48					
Number of bottoms kept on hand				12			26					10		
DURATION OF BOTTOM—														
Usual, Heats		14	20.56	11±	22.24	20±	15 @ 17½	20	23		15	80 @ 120	150	7
Usual, Time collectively			3h. 38'	2h. 56"	3 h. 54"		3 h. 21'	6 h. 10'			3 h.			
Maximum, Heats		25					25		52			52 @ 225		
Maximum, Time collectively							5h. 14'							

a Usually.
b Occasionally.
c With ball-stuff, pin-rammed in the joints.
e Fine ganister.
f Coarse ganister.
g Chickies rock, fine.
h Ganister.
i Like Figure 212.
j Like Figure 213.
l Like Figure 214.
m Coke-dust.
n All materials ground fine.
o Coarse.
p In blocks.
q Clapp-Griffiths.
Hol. Holley conical bottom, like Figure 211.
1 to 5, Early American.
6. British, 1875.
7. American, 1875.
8 to **26**, Present American.
27. U. S. Clapp-Griffiths.
28–9. Swedish, about 1885.

from 50 to 66 % of coarsely crushed quartz, in pieces whose largest dimension is not over two inches, and from 17 to 25 % of finely pulverized fat fire-clay, the remainder consisting of some finely ground silicious material, such as old fire bricks, fire-sand or loam sand.

No more fat clay is used than is needed for binding the mass. As this would not be enough to fill the interstices between the large lumps of crushed quartz, some finely ground silicious substance is needed.

Formerly this mixture, only very slightly moistened, This is spread on the floor in a thick layer, and trodden under foot, but not under bare feet. It is then cut up into lumps, which a man standing within the vessel throws against its sides: he then smooths and pats them into shape with a wooden mallet. The lining thus made is dried by a fire within the vessel.

A ten-ton vessel has been lined in the same general way in seven hours. But quick and hence cheap as this way of lining is, it is so effective that at many works the vessels are relined but once a year, during which each may make 14,000 heats, or some 140,000 tons, so that the cost of relining is insignificant when reckoned on the ton of product.

In many works, however, the lining must be patched every week, and with rapid running temporary patching must often be applied during the week.

In 1872 linings made of American refractory materials lasted from 400 to 500 heats: the best British materials gave double this life, or about one-fourteenth the life of our present American linings.

The linings of the Alpine Bessemer vessels last 200 heats of 30 minutes each, according to Ehrenwerth, who estimated that the Avesta little-vessel linings would last 500 heats of 10 minutes each[c]. At Eston the linings are said to last 1,000 heats. Allowing for the difference in the length of the heats, the American linings appear to last about 25 times as long as the Alpine.

In some American works monolithic linings are made from ground ganister[b] or ground millstone grit, both of which give admirable results. The latter is said to last from 12 to 18 months.

Blocks of mica-schist and of millstone-grit are also used in this country for vessel-linings, and with good results. The life of mica-schist linings has been as long as five months, in which 3,400 heats, or 34,000 tons of steel were made in one vessel. I am informed that, at another American mill, stone blocks have lasted a year; in this case they were laid dry, and ball-stuff was rammed carefully between their joints.

In other cases the blocks of mica-schist are laid in thin mortar. They are usually about one to two inches thick, and are laid with their cleavage horizontal: but at either end of the shell a ring of these blocks or slabs is laid with their cleavage vertical, apparently so that the ends of the lining may be thus tightly wedged into place.

Blocks of mill-stone grit, roughly shaped to the circle of the vessel's shell, (10″ wide measured radially, 18″ long measured circumferentially, and 6″ thick measured parallel with the length of the vessel), are also used with fair results, lasting about six to eight weeks, or say 1,200 to 1,600 heats. It is necessary to place a layer of one-inch boards between the blocks and the shell of the vessel, for if the blocks are laid flush with the shell their expansion bursts the iron-work. After a campaign neither boards, charcoal nor ashes can be found.

Silicious brick linings are used in some European works.

The life of certain vessel-linings, the proximate composition of the mixtures used, and the ultimate composition of some of the components of these mixtures are given in Tables 199 and 200.

TABLE 200.—ULTIMATE COMPOSITION OF REFRACTORY MATERIALS AND MIXTURES FOR THE BESSEMER PROCESS.

Number.	Authority.		Composition. SiO_2.	Al_2O_3.	Fe_2O_3.	FeO.	CaO.	MgO.	MnO.	H_2O.	Na_2O.	K_2O.	NaCl	Organic Matter.
		GANISTER—												
1	Maynard	British	93.20	1.36	3.23		0.43	0.35		1.71	0.05			
2	"	" Imported in 1867	94.79	2.89	1.03		0.22	0.12			0.15	0.11		
3	Holley	" Average	84.86	8.15		3.24	0.78	0.48		2.93		0.35		
4	"	"	83.75	4.45		7.00	0.392	0.517	trace				0.73	
5	Snelus	Sheffield	89.55	4.85	0.85		0.60	0.11				0.94		
6	"	Dowlais	93.5	4.28	0.80		0.26	trace						
7	"		82.94 @ 97.31	1.61 @ 10.48	0.19 @ 4.06		0.10 @ 0.78	trace @ 0.52			.18 @ .30	trace @ .94		
8	Maynard	Chickies Rock	96.54	2.50	.93		0.09	0.30				0.12		
		QUARTZ—												
9		Lake Superior Quartz	93.18	2.37		2.74		.84		.70	.48	.08		
10	Forsyth	" " "	95.5	1.5	2.75		0.40							
11		MOULDING SAND	78.81	12.78	2.71		0.93	1.08	0.91		.18	0.11		2.30
12	Holley	Sand for Ladle, Sheffield	79.75	12.30		1.75	0.55	0.68		4.5				
13	Holley	VESSEL-LININGS, Seraing	87.	8.5			1.			3.68				
14	"	" " Sheffield	88.2	7.3		1.15	0.18	.87		2.18a				
15	Walker	" " American, 1888	81.5	13.7	3.67		0.75	0.25		2.7				
16	Holley	Ball-stuff, Seraing	78.	17.			1.6			3.5a				
17	Holley	Bottoms, Seraing	67.5	26.5			1.00			5.5a				
18	"	" Sheffield	80.3	3.5		8.6	0.67	.85		2.5				
19	Forsyth	" Illinois	85.5	6.75	2.00					2.85				
20	Holley	Cupola-lining, Seraing	97.8	1.02		.75	0	0		.5				
21	Forsyth	Bottom-bricks, baked	78.5	13.5	2.25					5.				
22	Holley	Tuyeres, Seraing	69.	23.5			2.			5.				
23	Walker	" American	58.4	37.5	5.36		0.70	0.40						
25	Snelus	Tuyeres, British	64.9	30.0	2.60		0.40	0.25				.96		
26	"	" "	58.9	39.3	trace		0.70	.36				.74		
27	"	" "	67.7	27.1	4.05		0.30	trace				.85		
28	Holley	Nozzles	70.	24.			1.2			4.5a				
29	Walker	"	59.25											

a. Water and volatile matter.
Maynard, Private Communications.
Holley, Private Reports.
9-10. Lake Superior quartz used in mixtures for vessel linings, etc.
Snelus, Jour. Iron and St. Inst., 1875, II., p. 516.
Forsyth, Trans. Am. Inst. Mining Eng., IV., p. 132, 1876.
11. Waterford (N. Y.) moulding sand.
Stoppers and nozzles are those of the steel-casting ladle.

c Das Eisenhüttenwesen Schwedens, p. 169, 1885.
b The name "ganister," originally applied to a slightly argillaceous sandstone found near Sheffield, is now applied generically to like silicious rocks containing a little clay, and indeed sometimes to an artificial mixture of ground quartz and fire-clay suitable for vessel-linings.

§ 403. WEAR OF THE SHELL LININGS.—Under certain conditions the shell-lining grows thinner, under others it grows thicker during use. In the former case it must be patched from time to time, chiefly on Sundays, but occasionally also during the latter days of the week. Where accretions form they must be cut out, or sometimes even blasted out with dynamite, so excessively hard are they. J. H. Cremer found in one of these kidney-shaped accretions,[b]

Manganous Oxide,	Silica,	Alumina and Iron-oxide,	Total,
5 %	69 %	25.5 %	99.5 %.

The lining may grow thin from actual wearing away, or from corrosion by the slag and metal. But while the slag may corrode at a given temperature, if the temperature be but slightly lower the same slag may freeze against the sides of the vessel and form accretions. Where the slag comes most in contact with the lining, there will it tend most to cut the vessel if it be sufficiently hot and hence fluid, and sufficiently basic to cut: and here will it tend most to form accretions if so cool as to stick instead of cutting. Other things being equal, the hotter parts of the lining will tend to cut more than the cooler ones.

Now the shape of the vessel, the position of the tuyeres, the depth of metal, and other factors affect the distribution and position of the slag so much, and its composition is so much affected by the proportion of silicon and manganese in the cast-iron, by the depth of metal, the rapidity of blowing, etc., and indeed changes so much during the blow, that a complete analysis of the conditions would be extremely difficult. Suffice it to point out a few considerations.

The path over which the cast-iron runs into the vessel, and that over which the steel runs out, are heated very highly by the passage of the metal, and being the more highly heated tend to cut the more. In certain cases we actually find grooves, which appear as if worn by the passage of the metal, and sometimes a sort of pocket as at A, Figure 196. It is probable that the metal does not itself wear these grooves, but merely heats the lining here so highly that it is readily corroded by the slag, or actually melted out.

This cutting is naturally more severe in vessels which receive and discharge their metal on the same side, than in those which receive cast-iron when turned away from the pit, and discharge steel while turned toward the pit: and it is especially severe in excentric vessels, as in these the blast and the rush of metal during the blow impinge more directly on this spot, which has been so highly heated and softened by the entering and departing charge.

Further, when the vessel is turned down at the end of the blow, as in Figure 201, the pasty slag lies as a placid layer above the molten metal, and has a good opportunity to attach itself to the vessel's sides. As the vessel is turned down still farther to pour the steel out, the fall of the tide beneath leaves the slag adhering to the vessel's sides, especially towards the nose, against whose sides the flow presses the slag which had been in the middle of the surface of that fiery pool, and which floats towards and in part out of the nose with the stream. In a narrow nose the slag engorges, like freshet-ice in a narrowing stream. Hence the nose-blocking so troublesome in the basic process, and hence the ridges of slag at C, Figure 196, which sometimes form even in silicious vessels along the sides, at and beneath the level of the surface of molten metal when the vessel is turned down. Slag so infusible as to be pasty during the blow, becomes hard and solid as it cools between blows.

b Private communication, A. D. 1874.

Still another place where action is apt to be serious appears to be along the level occupied by the slag during the blow itself, say at D, Figure 196.

Finally, there is often a strong tendency to form accretions near the very bottom of the bath of metal, just above the joint between the bottom and the shell lining, as at B, Figure 196. What the cause of this is I know not; but the following is a possible explanation. Just at the end of the tuyeres the metal is highly oxygenated; as we travel farther and farther from this point the proportion of iron-oxide decreases, that of silica increasing, as the silicon is oxidized by the iron-oxide. Now it may be that, at a certain distance from the tuyere-ends, at certain stages of the blow, and with iron of certain composition, there is developed within the bath a silicate of extremely infusible composition. If the swirl and eddy be such as to project this mixture in its infusible yet slightly pasty state against the lining, there it sticks, and, being of the same composition as the iron-silicate in the surrounding bath, is not fluxed or cut by it.

In acid vessels the accretions or skulls may be removed by making the slag more basic, *e. g.*, by addition of lime or of iron-ore, or by intentional over-blowing; this last is surely a costly way of introducing iron-oxide, but we get a very high temperature, while if iron-ore be thrown in it lowers the temperature of the vessel rapidly. So, too, it is thought that when direct metal is used the vessels skull less than in treating cupola-metal, because of the basic blast-furnace slag, a little of which is apt to run into the vessel along with the cast-iron. The cupola-slag on the other hand is silicious. At certain works hard silicious kidneys form, when the cast-iron is unusually rich in silicon. In others irons with much manganese and little silicon cause skulling, while those relatively free from manganese but rather rich in silicon cut the lining instead of skulling.

Again, there is much less skulling when the steel is recarburized in the vessel, than when, as in making very soft steel, it is recarburized with ferro-manganese in the casting-ladle; for in the former case the oxide of manganese, formed by the reaction between the oxygenated blown metal and the spiegeleisen or ferro-manganese, makes the slag more basic, and especially more fusible and fluid.

The linings of side-blown vessels usually endure fewer heats than those of bottom-blown vessels, because, as pointed out in § 392, the former are much more exposed to iron-oxide, or at least to locally basic slag, than the latter. The linings of British Clapp-Griffiths vessels are reported to last from 400 to 600 heats.[a] The American Clapp-Griffiths vessel-practice is much better than this; at one works the linings usually last 4,000 heats;[b] at another they are said to last 8,000 heats usually, and one lining has lasted 8,800 heats.[b]

At one French works the brick lining of a Robert vessel

a J. Hardisty, Journ. Iron and St. Inst., 1886, II., pp. 657, 660.

b Information from the management, June 7th, [illegible].

is patched after about every fifteen heats, and is almost wholly replaced after from 200 to 300 heats: in making soft steel the repairs are still heavier. But, as the blowing is confined to one side of the vessel, parts of the lining, like the greater part of that of common vessels, last indefinitely. On the whole the repairs to the linings of Robert vessels seem much more severe than those of common vessels.[c]

§ 404. PREPARATION OF THE BOTTOM-LININGS.—In this country the holes through which the blast is admitted are almost if not quite universally contained in previously thoroughly burned fire-clay tuyeres, usually bought from makers of fire-bricks, who burn them in kilns much as in making fire-bricks.

The spaces between these tuyeres may either be wholly filled with "bottom-stuff," a mixture of clay and silicious matter; or they may be partly filled with tiles standing on end, between which in turn bottom-stuff is rammed, as in

Fig. 213.
a. b. c. d. Tiles between tuyeres.
e. Tuyeres.

FROM TRASENSTER.

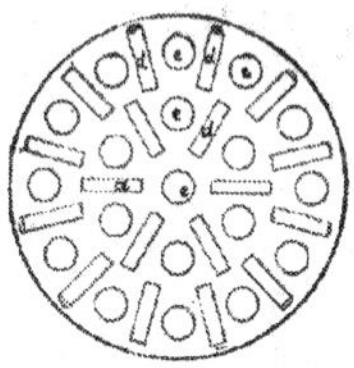

Fig. 212.

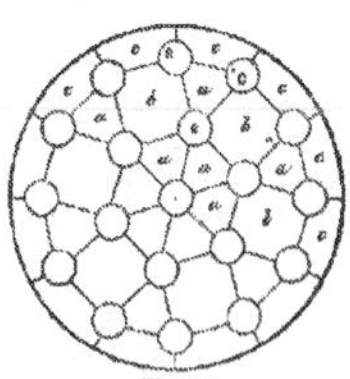

Fig. 213.

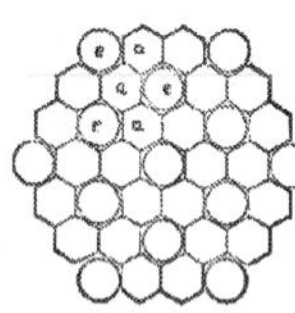

Fig. 214.

Figure 212; or they may be almost wholly filled with bricks shaped so as to fit around the tuyeres closely, as in Figures 213 and 214, a very little bottom-stuff being rammed between these bricks and around the tuyeres, to fill the slight crevices which are unavoidable.

Tuyeres may be wholly dispensed with, the bottom-stuff being rammed around pins which are withdrawn later, leaving holes for the entrance of the blast; but this system can be considered to better advantage in connection with the basic Bessemer process.

In case drying has to be wholly dispensed with, as may occur owing to the sudden unexpected failure of a large number of bottoms in succession, we may build up a bottom wholly of bricks laid with the least possible quantity of mortar, and attach it to the vessel at once. This, however, is but a makeshift.

Cone-shaped bottoms, like that in Figure 211, are made up by ramming within a conical mould. Dish-bottoms clearly need no mould.

The bottom-stuff usually contains much more clay than the vessel linings, from 20 to 40 and even 50%. At some mills all the bottom-stuff is finely ground and thoroughly mixed. In others the crushed fire brick used is in lumps, some of which are $1\frac{1}{2}$ inches long. These coarse lumps promote drying, and also bind the mass together.

Usually a few shovelfuls of bottom-stuff are added at a time, and thoroughly rammed with rammers like those shown in Figure 211, sometimes heated red-hot, that they may not adhere to the bottom-stuff, and that they may assist in drying it. It is barely moist enough to be balled with the hand; it is indeed almost dry. This is so that it may dry the more thoroughly and more quickly, and that the escape of moisture may not crack it.

The bricks and tiles inserted between the tuyeres, Figures 212 to 214, further facilitate drying, at the same time opposing any tendency to flake. Further, the kiln-burning which they receive makes them harder than the simply baked bottom-stuff. But while they probably prolong the life of the bottom, they increase its cost. In one American works these bricks are made of bottom-stuff rammed in a mould, and baked for twenty-four hours.

After thorough ramming the bottom is carefully dried. Enough bottoms should be on hand to allow us to dry each of them for forty-eight hours, though in many works the bottoms are dried but twenty-four hours or even less. Works which are to run rapidly should have at least twelve bottoms. One American works has twenty-six bottoms on hand. The South Chicago repair-shop has twelve bottom-drying hoods.

In the older works the bottoms were placed on a car which was then run into a brick chamber containing a fire-place, and here car, bottom and all were baked, to the great detriment of the running-gear of the car. An excellent arrangement is that shown in Figure 215. The bottom, when its lining is worn out, is removed by means of the bottom-car, which to that end is raised by the hydraulic bottom-jack (*e. g.*, Q, Figure 163), so as to press against the bottom while this is still attached to the vessel. The bottom-jack presses directly against the cast-iron funnel (Figure 215) which hangs down from the car, and the length of stroke which it is necessary to give the bottom-jack is thus shortened by the length of the funnel.

The keys holding the bottom to the shell of the vessel are then withdrawn, and car and bottom lowered and removed to the repair-shop. The bottom does not leave this car until it is again attached to the vessel. The car is run over a pit (see Figure 168), where the stumps of the tuyeres are knocked out, and after them the remaining bottom-stuff. New tuyeres are then inserted, wooden dummies, however, being set in three of the places left for tuyeres. The ends of the tuyeres are then covered, so that the tuyere-holes may not be stopped up by grains of bottom-stuff falling into them and lodging, and the bottom is carefully rammed as above described. It is then placed under the hood shown in Figure 215, which has above a gas blow-pipe, with air and gas supply regulated by the butterfly-valves shown. The flame from this hood passes down through the three holes left by the removal of the wooden dummies, which are knocked out as soon as the bottom is rammed up, and through the cast-iron funnel to a flue leading to the chimney. We can thus heat the bottom gradually at first, while it is still steam-

c Information from the management, July 29th, 1889.

ing, and so avoid drying it so fast as to crack it, and later thoroughly bake or even burn it, and that without first burning the iron-work of the car. We apply the heat just where it is wanted, to the bottom-lining itself, and thus with good efficiency.

After thorough baking, tuyeres are inserted in the holes left by the removal of the dummies, and the bottom, while still highly heated, is brought with its car to beneath the vessel, raised again by the bottom jack, and again attached to the vessel for blowing. It is not well to allow the bottom to cool, as its contraction during cooling may break off some of the tuyeres. In some cases as many as five or six tuyeres have been thus broken in a single bottom.

Certain data connected with the composition and life of bottoms are given in table 199.

The increase in the life of bottoms has been remarkable. In 1872 bottoms lasted but from four to eight heats. In 1875 their life had increased in at least one mill to an average of eleven heats, taken over a period of eight months. The bottoms in this case were made with bricks of baked bottom-stuff, somewhat as sketched in Figure 214.[f] There are now many works in which the average life of the bottoms is more than twenty-five heats.

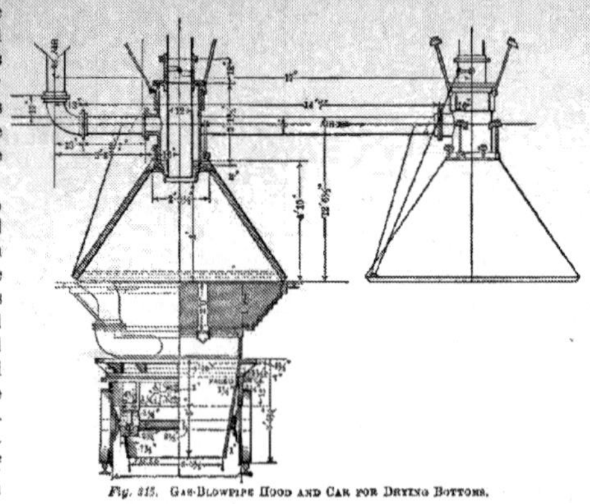

Fig. 215. Gas-Blowpipe Hood and Car for Drying Bottoms.

Heavy blast-pressure, short and cool heats, small tuyere-holes, small depth of metal above the surface of the tuyeres, as well as proper materials, careful ramming, and above all very thorough baking, all lengthen the life of the bottom. The heavy blast-pressure, small tuyere-holes and small depth of metal probably lengthen the life of the bottom by lessening the intimacy of contact of the tuyeres (and it is they that cut out before the surrounding bottom) with the bath of metal, which in the neighborhood of the tuyere-ends is highly charged with iron-oxide, a powerful flux for the silicious tuyeres. The smaller the tuyere-holes the more rapidly will the blast emerge from them, and the more will it lift the metal from them.

The direct effect of heavy blast-pressure is probably to corrade the ends of the tuyeres, but this effect is outweighed by its holding the metal away from the tuyere-ends. I have already pointed out in § 392 that the life of the tuyeres, and hence of the bottoms, is very much greater in side-blown vessels, such as the Clapp-Griffiths and the Robert, in which the blast enters near the upper surface of the metal, than in bottom-blown vessels, rising even to 250 heats.

While, in view of the many factors which influence the life of the bottom, the data at hand do not indicate decisively the most long-lived type, yet they corroborate in a rough way some of the points which I have just noted. We find in case of the bottom-blown vessels of Table 199, that, taking *the average of the average life of each class* the monolithic bottoms, rammed around tuyeres, last 17.5 heats, bottoms like Figure 212 last 21.4 heats, and those like Figure 213 last 23 heats, which indicates in a rough way that the burnt fire-bricks set in the bottoms prolong their lives. I am informed that in Continental Europe, where the space between the tuyeres is almost completely filled by burnt bricks, the bottoms usually last 25 heats of say 15 minutes. So, too, bottoms which are dried for 24 hours or less last on such a general average 15 heats, while those dried 48 hours or more last 23 heats.

In the Walrand (Robert) vessel, instead of using the common fire-clay tuyeres, the blast was formerly admitted through openings in the sides of the monolithic silicious vessel-lining, formed by ramming basic material around little wooden plugs.[g] The strong local corrosive action of the iron-oxide of the metal on the lining was thus lessened. This practice has since been abandoned.

In bottom-blowing, after a bottom has been in use for a number of heats, partly determined by experience, partly by inspection through the vessel's nose between heats, the length of its tuyeres must be determined by actual measurement, *e. g.*, by passing a wire with a hooked end through the tuyere-holes from behind, while the vessel is turned down between heats. Starting with a length of two feet, the bottom is used in some mills till the shortest tuyeres are only 4″ to 5″ long. As 2.5″ to 3″ of the length of the tuyere lie below the false-plate P, this means that the bottom is used till its lining is only from 2″ to 3″ thick in the thinnest parts.

A convenient device for learning when the bottom is worn thin is to insert in the bottom, before ramming it, a short dummy tuyere, say seven inches long, which projects only some five inches above the false-plate P, Figure 208. When the bottom is worn down to the end of this dummy tuyere, which can readily be learned by inspection through the vessel's nose between heats, the bottom may be removed, or at least the length of its tuyeres should be examined carefully by direct measurement.

In earlier practice if one or two tuyeres were worn too short while the rest of the bottom was still in condition to blow another heat, the vessel was turned down on its side, the bottom-plate was removed, the short tuyeres were cut out, and the holes thus left were rammed full of ball-stuff. There is usually time between heats to do this without delaying matters, for a tuyere can be thus "blinded" while the cast-iron for the succeeding charge is running into the vessel.

In present practice it is found better to cut out the old

f. Forsyth, Trans. Am. Inst. Mining Eng., IV., p. 132, 1875.

g J. Hardisty, Journ. Iron and Steel Inst., 1886, II., p. 660.

tuyere and insert a new one, preferably of smaller diameter and coated with wet fire-clay.

But tuyeres are still sometimes "blinded," wholly or in part, by inserting in the tuyere-holes "rat tails" of fire-clay, which are then rammed lightly; or, if we are greatly hurried, by throwing a ball of wet plastic clay against the butt of the tuyere, and covering it with a thin iron plate, which the blast-pressure and the adhesion of the clay hold in place.

When the bottom is worn out, its upper surface looks somewhat as sketched in Figure 202, with deep gougings here and there at one or more of the holes of some of the tuyeres.

§ 405. Special forms of converters.—Within the last few years several forms of converters have been brought forward, which are said by certain interested persons and by some others to produce results which are so different from those attained in the converters previously used as to constitute new processes, *e. g.*, the Clapp-Griffiths and the Robert "process." Thus the "Directory to the iron and steel works of the United States" for 1887 divides the steel works of the country into Bessemer, open-hearth, crucible and Clapp-Griffiths, implying that the difference between the Bessemer and Clapp-Griffiths process (?) is co-ordinate with that between the Bessemer and the open-hearth process. So, too, most astonishing accounts of the Robert process (?) have appeared in the non-technical papers.

A change in the shape of the vessel or in the manner of introducing the blast is likely to induce some modification in the process itself, perhaps trifling, perhaps important. But it certainly seems that those pecuniarily interested have given others, and probably themselves, a very exaggerated notion of the importance of these particular modifications. They have, in some cases through inadvertence or hasty judgment I believe, put themselves in a wholly false position, by claiming to obtain startling results by means which appear wholly inadequate, without offering sufficient evidence that these results have actually been reached. From this position they might extricate themselves by showing that the means are really adequate, or by properly substantiating their claims.

§ 406. The Clapp-Griffiths vessel,[‡] Figure 216, is essentially a high side-blown stationary vessel, with a spout H at such a level that the slag runs out of it during the boil. This slag-spout is the only real novelty.[1] Its effect can better be considered under the chemistry of the Bessemer process. Thus far I have found no jot of evidence that it accomplishes anything valuable; nor is there strong reason to expect that it should. At G is shown the tap-hole through which the steel is removed at the end of the blow. The blast enters the wind-box C through the goose-neck K, in which the valves L enable us to shut off the blast almost or quite wholly.

Arrangements have been devised for preventing the steel from backing into the tuyeres when the blast is shut off at the end of the blow. The simplest way, however, is not to shut the blast off entirely, but to admit just enough of it into the wind-box to keep the metal out the tuyeres. In practice this is found wholly effective.

For cleaning the tuyeres a readily opened door is provided in the wind-box opposite each.

The bottom section of the vessel is removable, the joint as shown being high above the tuyeres. As already pointed out, the life of the bottom is excellent.

Beneath the vessel is a hydraulic cylinder, P, for removing and replacing bottoms.

There was but one Clapp-Griffiths vessel in this country in 1884; there were 13 in August, 1886; 16 in November, 1887, and 15 at the end of 1888, one having been removed to Mexico.

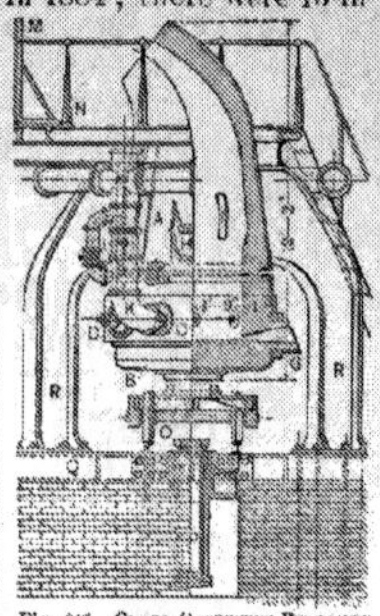

Fig. 216. Clapp-Griffiths Bessemer Converter. J. P. Witherow.

A. Shell proper. B. Bottom. C. Wind-box. D. Hand-holes for examining tuyeres. G. Tap-hole. K. Goose-neck for blast. O. Bottom car. P. Bottom-jack. R. Columns supporting vessel.

The increase in the number of other Bessemer vessels was 13 between September 1884 and August 1886; 16 between August 1886 and November 1887; and 8 between November 1887 and December 31st 1888.

In short, between August 1886 and January 1889 only three Clapp-Griffiths vessels were built, against twenty-four other Bessemer converters.

It is not easy to make a fair comparison between the rate of increase of the production of Clapp-Griffiths and of other vessels, because the great mass of the non-Clapp-Griffiths Bessemer steel goes into rails, while none of that made in Clapp Griffiths vessels does, and the demand for rails bears no close relation to that for the ingot-iron made in the Clapp-Griffiths vessels. The best approach to fairness, and it is not a very close approach, which I can make, is to compare the increase of the output of the Clapp-Griffiths vessels with that of Bessemer steel used for purposes other than rails. This class includes the soft steel made in common Bessemer vessels, which is used for the same purposes as that made in Clapp-Griffiths vessels; indeed, the two are probably wholly undistinguishable by any but transcendental tests.

Table 201.—Increase in the Number of the Clapp-Griffiths Vessels in the United States, and of their Output.

Date.		Sept. 1884.	Aug. 1886.	Nov. 1887.	Dec. 1888.
1. Vessels existing.	Clapp-Griffiths.. ..	1	13	16	15
	Other	45	58	74	82
Period.			1884 to 1886.		
2. Vessels built...	Clapp-Griffiths......	....	12	3	-1
	Other..............	....	13	16	8
Year.			1886.	1887.	1888.
3. Output	Clapp-Griffiths......	....	46,371	68,679	81,157
	Other than rail......	....	473,907	587,115	931,106
Total Bessemer............		....	2,541,493	3,288,357	2,812,500
Year.				1887.	1888.
4. Percentage of increase of output over that of preceding year.	Clapp-Griffiths..	....	....	48.1	18.2
	Other than rail..	....	....	23.9	58.6

Thus the construction of Clapp-Griffiths vessels took a sudden start between 1884 and 1886, owing, we may sur-

[1] I have heard it said that this slag-spout is no real novelty, as it was used on the old Swedish vessels (Figure 188); they certainly had such a spout, but I am informed that it was not used for removing slag. Indeed, the Swedish steel-makers wisely preferred to retain the slag, so as to keep the metal hot while in the casting-ladle. (Consul Goransson, private communication, April 13th, 1888.)

‡ Trans. Am. Inst. Min. Engineers, XIII., pp. 745, 753; XIV., pp. 130, 919, XV., p. 340. Science, VI., p. 313 1885. Stahl und Eisen, VII., No. 5, 1887. Journ. Iron and St. Inst., 1886, II., p. 654.

mise, to the remarkable claims made for the so-called process; but it seems that experience has not verified these claims to such a degree as to induce manufacturers to adopt these vessels farther. In accord with this is the great increase in the output of the Clapp-Griffiths vessels in 1887, following the completion of those built in 1886. In 1888, however, the ratio of increase in the output from Clapp-Griffiths vessels is much less than that of steel for purposes other than rails and made in other vessels (line 4, Table 201).

The fifteen Clapp-Griffiths vessels existing in 1888 had a nominal capacity of 43 tons per heat collectively, and should be able to turn out some 1,000 tons per 24 hours, or to turn out the total output reached in 1888 in some 80 days of active running. The other Bessemer converters existing in 1888 had a nominal capacity of somewhere about 500 tons per heat collectively, and should, if turning out as many heats per 24 hours as the Clapp-Griffiths vessels, have a total capacity of about 11,500 tons per 24 hours. At this rate they would turn out the total output reached in 1888 in about 175 days. This gives the Clapp-Griffiths vessels an unfair advantage, for their small heats should be more rapidly handled in the casting-pit. But even taken in this way it would seem that the Clapp-Griffiths vessels were less than half as fully occupied during 1888 as the other vessels, although the output of rails in 1888 was much below that of 1887. In other words, while the capacity per heat of the Clapp-Griffiths vessels is about one-tenth of that of the other Bessemer vessels, the actual output of the latter in 1888 was more than twenty times that of the Clapp-Griffiths vessels.

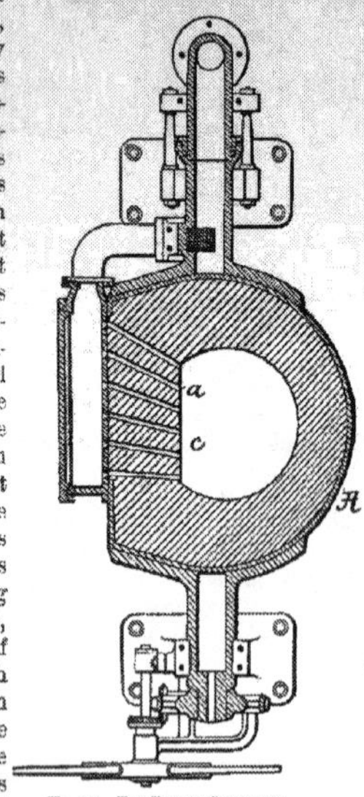

Fig. 217. The Robert Converter.

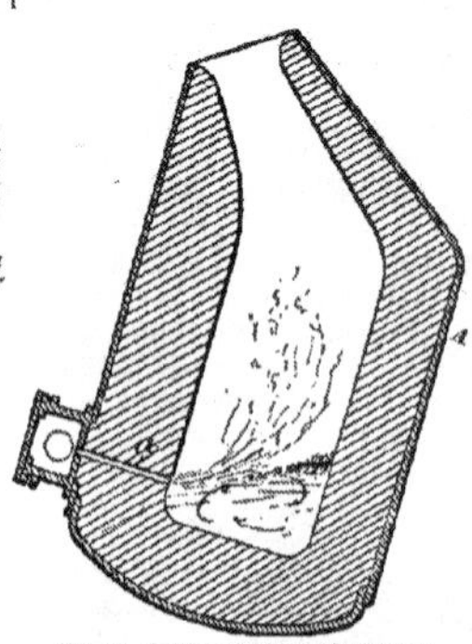

Fig. 218. Section of Robert Converter.

The Clapp-Griffiths vessels in Britain seem to be doing well, but the French ones have not been successful: several have been abandoned, and I do not learn of one now running.

Hatton's Converter seems to be essentially like the Clapp-Griffiths, except that it lacks the slag-spout.

§ 407. In the Robert or Walrand Vessel[k] (Figures 217, 218) the blast is introduced through horizontal tuyeres near the upper surface of the metal, and placed semi-tangentially, so as to give the bath a rotary motion. The vessel itself is rotary; it is tipped so that during the first part of the blow the tuyeres almost emerge from the bath, and as the blow proceeds the level of the tuyeres is gradually lowered.

Rotary motion of the bath is sought, in order that the action of the blast may be less strongly localized. This, of course, is no novelty, having been adopted in the old Swedish vessels. Great stress is laid on the highly localized "stripping" or "atomizing" action of the blast, on the gyrations of the bath, and on regulating them so that, while they may expose each particle of the metal to the blast in turn, they may not draw down into the bath of metal the "impurities" already separated.

As far as I can make it out, the idea is that in bottom-blown vessels "the impurities" eliminated from the cast-iron become mixed up with the iron, while in the Robert vessel they do not. First, bottom-blowing is not essential to the Bessemer process: the earlier successful vessels were blown from the sides. Rotary motion was induced in a way closely similar to that of the Robert "process" by setting the tuyeres semi-tangentially. High-side blowing was adopted long ago by Durfee, and later by Clapp and Griffiths. Here, then, is no novelty. It is claimed, apparently, that restricting the blowing to one side of the vessel leaves the "impurities" in a quiescent state on the leeward side of the vessel, while if the blast enters on all sides this repose is lost. What now are these impurites eliminated during the process, whose return is to be dreaded? Gases, which rush out of the vessel's nose; slag, which cannot be made to unite with the iron by any possibility; iron-oxide, the purifying substance itself, licked up voraciously by the slag, probably wholly removed by the recarburizer.[m]

Where is the evidence that injurious impurities, removable by such purely mechanical means, exist in Bessemer steel, or that one-sided blowing furthers their removal? What the reason to expect that it should? Shall in-

k U. S. Patents 395,633, Jan. 1st, 1889: 400,010, March 19th, 1889: Harper's Weekly, XXXIII., No. 1679, p. 151, Feb. 23d, 1889; Iron Age, XLIII., p. 656, 1889; Journ. Iron and St. Inst., 1890, II., p. 659. We are informed in Harper's Weekly that "the Bessemer converter must be relined after a very few blasts; the Robert after 1,000 blasts;" that the metal is heated much hotter than by the Bessemer process and is therefore more fluid. Actually the lining of the Bessemer converter lasts many thousand blows, and the difficulty usually is to keep the temperature down, not up.

In the earliest description of this vessel which I have seen (Hardisty, Journ. Iron and St. Inst., 1886, II., p. 659), it is spoken of as the "Walrand" converter. It is now always called the "Robert" vessel so far as my observation goes: and M. Robert informs me that the design is his solely. A letter of inquiry on this subject which I have sent M. Walrand remains unanswered.

m During casting, when metal and slag become cool and viscid, there is indeed danger of their becoming mixed. But this danger is not lessened by keeping them separate during the blow while molten, for then they separate automatically and need no aid. It is mixing during and immediately before their pouring, and not during the blow, that we should avoid.

The oxide of iron is the purifying substance itself, to borrow the language of the

ventors next patent stirring porridge to left instead of right; methods of making wood float and lead sink?

The chief advantage claimed for the Robert over the common converter is that it yields a better product and a higher temperature, so that it can be used advantageously for making small steel castings.

The present evidence that its product is superior is of the usual wholly unsatisfactory kind, and merits neither presentation nor rebuttal.

I see nothing in the many castings which I have seen, made from the Robert vessel, which indicates that an extraordinarily high temperature is reached; some of them were doubtless cast a a decidedly high temperature, yet not higher than can be readily attained in common vessels. I am sure that the temperature in the vessel when it was turned down after the blows which I have seen was not higher, and I think that it was decidedly lower, than that of the common vessel at the end of a normally hot blow: and so said an eminent metallurgist who was with me. Yet the conditions at hand should have insured an unusual temperature even in a common vessel, for the cast-iron was an unusually "hot" one, containing 2.4% of silicon, 1% of manganese and 3.75% of carbon; the walls of the vessel were unusually thick, about 16″ I was informed; and the charge was recarburized with only 1% of ferromanganese, so that the chilling effect of a large recarburizing addition was avoided.

Suppose, however, that we concede that an unusually high temperature may be reached thanks to these precautions, to the combustion of an excessive proportion of the iron of the charge (it is admitted that the loss is 15%, and, judging from the amount of smoke and from the well-known tendency of the siderurgical mind to persuade itself that the loss is much lower than it actually is, I should put the loss at nearer 18%, or say half greater than in common vessels), and perhaps to the combustion of an unusually large proportion of the carbon to carbonic acid, due to introducing the blast near the top of the bath—admitting all this, what follows? That these same conditions can be reproduced in the common converter, by inclining it so as to bring some of the tuyeres near the top of the bath, as has long been habitually done in case of unduly cold heats.

But as this is not patentable, while the mysterious gyrations, moderation and regulation of currents, and atomizing stripping action seem to be, the cynic readily surmises why the former simpler explanation is less palatable to the promoters of the Robert process than the latter, which, foggy, mysterious, incomprehensible, is certainly of the kind which, rightly or wrongly, we involuntarily associate with charlatanry and imposture. Therefore, while I believe that M. Robert is quite sincere though clearly mistaken as to the rationale of the effects of his particular modification of the Bessemer converter, it seems well to warn the public that wholly disinterested experts regard the extravagant statements of the promoters of his process (?) most incredulously, and are most skeptical as to its possessing any real value.

Laureau's Converter.—The corrosion of the lining is, of course, much more rapid at the tuyeres than elsewhere. In these high side-blown vessels the renewal of the tuyeres implies renewing a considerable mass of lining below them. To obviate this the tuyeres in Laureau's high-side-blown vessel lie in a separate zone or ring of the lining, quite distinct from the bottom proper. When this ring is worn out a new one is inserted, the old shell-lining and the old bottom remaining in use.

Instead of introducing tuyeres all around the circumference of the vessel, he groups them close to the plane of the trunnions, *i. e.*, just beneath the trunnions and slightly to right and left. As there are no tuyeres in the front of the vessel (*i. e.*, the part nearest the pit), we do not have to turn the vessel through so many degrees to bring the tuyeres above the surface of the metal as in Bessemer's rotating side-blown vessel, Figures 185, 186[c].

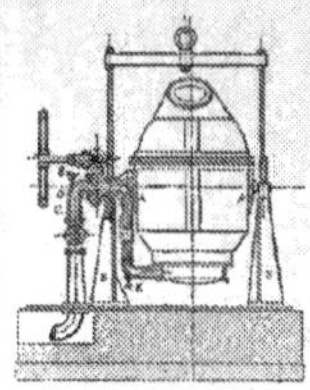

Fig. 219. Davy's 10-cwt. Portable Vessel. Hardisty.

§ 408. Davy's Portable Converter, Figure 219, is a half ton bottom-blown rotating vessel, whose trunnions rest in fixed supports during blowing. At the end of the blow the vessel is turned down by a hand- or power-driven worm, gearing into a worm-wheel on one of the trunnions. The charge is then recarburized and rabbled, and the vessel, together with its trunnions, is carried by a crane to the casting place, leaving the standards free to receive another vessel.

This arrangement aims to avoid the loss of heat which occurs when the steel is poured into a relatively cold ladle, and which is the more serious the lighter the charge. A vessel so small as to be portable is not suited to the production of ingots, while, if castings are to be made, a serious difficulty arises:—in dispensing with the casting-ladle we have thrown away the only certain way of keeping the infusible slag from running out of the vessel into the moulds, and so ruining the castings.

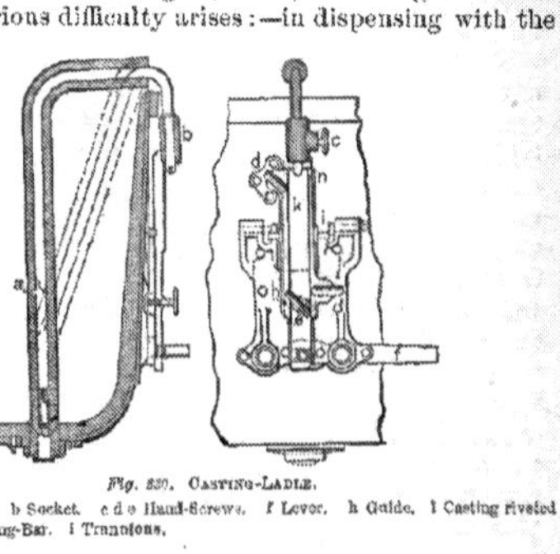

Fig. 220. Casting-Ladle.

a Stopper-Rod. b Socket. c d e Hand-Screws. f Lever. h Guide. i Casting riveted to Ladle. k Sliding-Bar. i Trunnions.

§ 409. The Ladles.—Those for cast-iron discharge their metal by tipping. They are made of boiler-plate, and

quack. It is by oxide of iron that the carbon, silicon and manganese are removed. To prevent oxide of iron from impregnating the bath, if it were possible, would be to arrest the process. Now it is only the last traces of iron-oxide that can remain mixed up with the molten metal during the blow. The great bulk of it either oxidizes carbon, etc., or separates by gravity from the metal, which is able to dissolve but a minute portion of it. As this minute portion must be and is mixed up with the metal in the Robert vessel, it profits nothing to attempt to keep the rest of the iron-oxide from the metal. Such propositions do not deserve serious consideration.

c U. S. Patent, 358,559, March 1st, 1887.

suspended from trunnions. An arrangement for tipping is shown at F and K in Figure 163.

Figure 221 shows a ladle for carrying molten cast-iron from the blast-furnace to the Bessemer converters. In tipping, as the rack into which the trunnion-pinion gears is fixed, the trunnion, and with it the ladle, shifts

Tilting Ladle-Car, with Ladle Tilted.

Fig. 221. Weimer's Direct-Metal Ladle.

towards the side to which we tip it, so that the stream of metal the more readily falls clear of the ladle-car and the tracks.

The Steel-ladles discharge the steel through a fire-clay nozzle in their bottom, as shown in Figure 220, and also at L in Figure 163. If we attempted to cast the steel over the edge of the ladle, as in foundry practice, the infusible slag which floats above the steel in the ladle, and which acts as a blanket to keep it hot, would run into the moulds. It would, moreover, be impossible to pour rapidly, much scrap would be made, and the fall of the stream of molten metal would be excessively long, cutting the mould-bottoms (stools) and agitating the metal. Still, it is necessary to provide rotating gear as shown at L in Figure 163, so that we may adjust the ladle to deliver its stream of molten steel vertically into the moulds, thus compensating for any irregularity in the shape of the nozzle. It might be thought well to provide the ladle-trunnion with a whole worm-wheel instead of only a sector of one, as shown, so that in case the steel chilled in the nozzle of the ladle it could be poured out over the upper edge, lest it freeze into a solid unmanageable mass. In this case, however, it is less easy to invert the ladle after teeming, so as to pour out the slag.

The Nozzle is stopped by a graphite or fire-clay plug or "stopper," keyed to the end of an iron stopper-rod, as shown in Figure 220. This rod may be covered with a sleeve of annular fire-clay bricks, or it may be coated with a plastic mixture of fire-clay and sand and then baked. Examples of the proximate composition of such mixtures are given in Table 202, and of the ultimate composition of fire-clay nozzles in Table 200. The stopper-rod coatings are generally richer in fire-clay than the "ball-stuff" and other refractory mixtures used in the Bessemer process, and are applied to the stopper-rod in a very soft state. After baking, the drying cracks are plastered over.

It is important that the stopper should fit the nozzle closely. We adjust the stopper-rod in one direction by turning it in the socket *b*, and then clamping it with the hand-screw *c*. To adjust it in the other direction Holley's ingenious device is used‡. In this the stopper-rod is as usual raised and lowered by the lever *f*, but the guide *h*, in which the sliding-bar *k* plays, instead of being fastened rigidly to the shell of the ladle, rests by its trunnions *s* on a casting *ii* which is riveted to the ladle. By means of the hand-screws *dd* the sliding-bar, and through it the stopper-rod, can be rocked about the trunnions to adjust the stopper. The guide *h* is then clamped by *dd*.

The stopper thus adjusted, the hand-screw *e* clamps the sliding-bar down till teeming begins, lest the molten metal buoy up the stopper-rod and allow the steel to escape through the nozzle. It is well to make the stopper-rod straight, as shown, lest its expansion when heated by the metal uncenter it, as may happen with the bent stopper-rod shown in dotted lines.

The Linings of ladles for carrying direct-metal from the blast-furnace to the vessels should be thick to diminish the loss of heat during the transit, and especially in winter. They are usually of fire brick.

The steel-ladles should have as light a lining as practicable, as their weight must be supported at arm's length by the casting-crane. Formerly lined with a more or less clayey mixture, and even now in some European works with three inches of fire-brick, in this country they are almost if not quite always lined with moulding sand about as moist as in common foundry moulding. After lining, the ladle must be thoroughly dried, and, especially in case of soft steel, well heated. This was formerly done by inverting the ladle over a coke fire, or by a coke fire within it, blown with a gentle blast. A better way to dry the ladles is that already shown in Figure 215 for bottoms. The composition and life of some ladle-linings is given in Table 202.

Table 202.—Mixtures of Refractory Materials for Apparatus for the Bessemer Process.

	Works.	Weight of Charge, tons.	Kind of product.	Proximate Composition.					Life		Life Cupola Lining.	
				Fire-sand.	Moulding-sand.	Quartz.	Loam-sand.	Fat Clay.	No. heats endured.	Period covered.	Days per campaign.	Tons melted per campaign.
Ladles	American	6 @ 7	Rail-steel				100		40 @ 50	1887		
	" d	3	"				100		25	"		
	" d	9.2	"						10	"		
	"	5.5	Soft-steel				100		8 @ 10	"		
	"	4	"				100			"		
	"	7	"				100			"		
	"	7½	Rail-steel						41	"		
	"	7	"						32	"		
	"	7¼	"						15	"		
	"			20	60			20		1872		
	"				34			66		1872		
	Seraing	6		Fire-brick lining					Sides 50, bottom 25			
Stoppers	American d	10	Rail-steel						2.25	1888		
	"	6 @ 7	"				100			1887		
	" d	10	"						2.5	"		
	"	7 @ 8	"						5	"		
	"	7	"						3 @ 4	"		
	"	7½	"							"		
	"			30	28			42		1872		
	"			44				41		1872		
Stopper-sleeves	American d	9.2	"						2.5	1888		
	"	7½	"						3.	1887		
	"	10	"						1.00	1888		
Nozzles	" d	10	"						3.25	1888		
	"	7	"						4	1887		
	"	7½	"						3	"		
	"	7 @ 8	"						5	"		
	" d	9.2	"						4	"		
	"	10	"						7.33	1888		
Cupola-linings	"	10	"	32		50		18		1885	2 @ 5	250
	"	6 @ 7	"	15		62		23		1887	1½ @ 2	219
	" d	8	"	66			17	17		1888	3	600
	"	5.5	Soft-steel	Sand-stone						1887	3	
	"	4	"	Ball-stuff						"	3	

d Direct-metal is used, *i. e.*, cast-iron direct from the blast-furnace, while still molten.

Our loam-sand ladle-linings are so trustworthy that, visiting one American mill fourteen years after it started,

‡ U. S. Patent 86,905, Jan. 26th, 1869. A. L. Holley.

I found all the original ladles still in use. I was informed that, during all this time, there had been but four cases in which a ladle had burnt through.

§ 410. CASPERSSON'S CONVERTER LADLE[m] aims to diminish the loss of heat, and consequent formation of scrap and skulls, which occurs when small charges of soft steel are poured from the vessel into a common casting-ladle, by diminishing the size of the ladle, and by allowing any given particle of steel to remain in it but a few minutes. The ladle DDD, Figure 222, is luted and firmly keyed to the mouth of the vessel, after the latter has been turned down at the end of the blow. No recarburizer is used at Westanfors where the converter-ladle is in use. If the charge were to be recarburized, it would have to be mixed before attaching the converter-ladle by rabbling, by turning the vessel up for a few seconds, or otherwise.

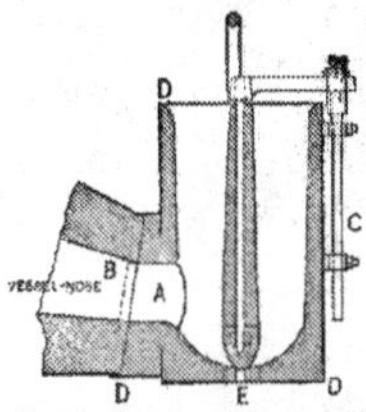

Fig. 222. CASPERSSON'S CONVERTER-LADLE. ÅKERMAN.

A. Entrance to ladle. B. Nose of converter. C. Bar for lifting stopper. D. Ladle proper. E. Nozzle.

After attaching the ladle five minutes are allowed for the luting to dry, and then the vessel is turned a little lower so as to let a little steel run into the ladle. This is purposely made very small so as to abstract as little heat as possible from the metal. Indeed, most of the metal is held back at first in the extremely hot and thick-walled converter, and only runs gradually into the ladle, passing rapidly through it into the moulds.

On raising the stopper by means of the stopper-rod, C, the metal runs through the nozzle of the ladle into moulds standing on a turn-table, which brings them in succession beneath the ladle.

Before teeming begins the tuyere-box must be opened, *e.g.*, by removing the lid N, Figure 204, so that air may enter the vessel to take the place of the steel that runs out; but for this the air would bubble in through the ladle, interfere with teeming, and cool the metal.

The small size of the ladle, and the short stay of the steel in it, give us a higher casting-temperature for given temperature of blow, an important thing especially when small ingots of soft steel (ingot-iron) are to be cast. As the steel is hotter there is less danger of its freezing in the nozzle, and thus causing scrap by preventing the stopper from shutting off the stream as we pass from mould to mould; this is especially important in case of very soft steel, in casting which we have, in common practice, to pass back and forth repeatedly to fill the mould with the foaming metal. Freezing in the nozzle also roughens the ingots, by making the metal squirt against the side of the moulds, into which it cuts, and against which it freezes in lumps which may not later unite completely with the rest of the ingot.

Moreover, we can safely pour the hotter steel more slowly without incurring risk of its chilling, and the small depth of metal in the ladle causes the steel to rush less rapidly through the nozzle. The thinner and slower-falling stream cuts the bottoms of the moulds less; causes less foaming, both because of the slower arrival of the metal and because less air is dragged down; and thus enables us to fill the mould at a single pouring, instead of going back and forth from mould to mould. Thus more solid ingots are obtained, and we avoid the surfaces of imperfect union which often occur when an ingot is filled by several separate additions instead of at one pouring.

In Sweden the use of this device seems to have reduced the proportion of scrap materially. Åkerman reports the results condensed in Table 203.

TABLE 203.—EFFECT OF CASPERSSON'S CONVERTER-LADLE IN REDUCING THE PROPORTION OF CASTING-SCRAP, ETC. ÅKERMAN.

Works.	Kind of Steel Made.	Period.	Per 100 of Cast iron (Direct-metal) Treated, there resulted: Clean ingots. Without the converter-ladle.	Scrap. Without the converter-ladle.	Clean ingots. With the converter-ladle.	Scrap. With the converter-ladle.	On using the converter-ladle. The % of ingots increased by	The % of scrap decreased by
Westanfors	Ingot iron, 22% + ingot-steel, 78%—	1878	84.48	2.60	....	.....	.....	.....
		20 weeks 1880	....	.....	88.11	0.11	3.6[illegible]a	2.[illegible]a
Westanfors		....	....	.....	88 b	0.9	....	.....
Bjornsborg	Ingot iron,	....	88	3.4	87.25±	.....	4.2[illegible]a	.....
	Ingot-steel.	....	86 to 87	.....	89.5±	.....	2±a	.....
Nykroppa.	55% of ingot-iron, 45% of ingot-steel.	....	88.74	.....	89.38	.....	0.8[illegible]a	.....

a Per 100 of cast-iron blown.
b This number is given as 80 in the original, but apparently incorrectly. I believe that 88 is the right number.

Hainsworth[n] would accomplish results like those attained by the converter-ladle, by pouring the steel from the vessel into a deep, stopperless runner, which discharges into the moulds, preferably through an intermediate stopperless funnel which has several nozzles, one over each mould. The runner and the moulds are carried by vertical hydraulic plungers, so that as the vessel turns down lower and lower in pouring, they may sink and follow its travel. The flow of metal is thus regulated wholly by turning the vessel down faster or slower, and by changing the inclination of the runner, which to that end is mounted on trunnions. It may have a dam for holding the slag back, but in spite of this one anticipates that the last part of the metal will be accompanied by slag.

m Åkerman, Jour. Iron and St. Inst., 1880, II., p. 599; 1881, I. p. 36; Hardisty, Idem, 1886, II., p. 662.

n U. S. Patent 284,005, Aug. 28th, 1883.

APPENDIX I.

SPECIAL STEELS.

§ 413. MANGANESE STEEL.[a]—Since § 86, p. 48, was written, Hadfield's extremely important papers on manganese-steel have very greatly increased our knowledge of this remarkable substance, discovered by him; yet much remains to be learnt.

Briefly, manganese-steel of the best composition, with say 14% of manganese and not more than 1% of carbon, is very fluid; solidifies rapidly and with great contraction; does not form blow-holes, but pipes deeply; does not seem subject to segregation; is forgeable, but welds poorly if at all. Naturally brittle, only moderately strong, and with very low elastic limit, it is made extremely tough and very strong and (under impact) stiff by quenching from whiteness, which neither cracks small bars of it, changes its fracture (which before forging is strongly crystalline), nor greatly raises its elastic limit; this, however, is greatly raised by cold-stretching, only to fall on reheating. Test-bars stretch nearly uniformly, like brass, instead of necking like iron. It is so hard that it can barely be machined, but is slightly softened by sudden cooling from very dull redness (V);[b] is not brittle at blueness, nor (apparently) made brittle by blue-work, but is rapidly made brittle by cold-work, ductility being restored by reheating and quenching; does not recalesce during cooling; its density (sp. gr. 7·83 for manganese 13·75), modulus of elasticity and (apparently) its rate of corrosion are about the same as those of common iron; its electric resistance is enormous, thirty times that of copper and eight times that of wrought-iron, but thrice as constant with varying temperature as that of iron; it can be magnetized very considerably temporarily, but only with most extreme difficulty, and hardly at all permanently. Now to examine some of these points in more detail.

TABLE 206.—MANGANESE-STEEL, FORGED.—Hadfield.

Numbers.	Composition.					Physical properties.									
						In the "natural state."			Air-toughened.		Oil-toughened.		Water-toughened.		
	C.	Si.	Mn.	P.	S.	Tensile strength, lbs. per sq. in.	Elongation % in 8 inches.	Contraction of area %.	Tensile strength, lbs. per sq. in.	Elongation % in 8 inches.	Tensile strength, lbs. per sq. in.	Elongation % in 8 inches.	Tensile strength, lbs. per sq. in.	Elongation % in 8 inches.	Contraction of area %.
1	·20	·08	·83	·09±	·06±	73,920	37	46							
2	·40	·15	2·30	"	"	125,440	6	7							
3	·40	·10	3·59	"	"	85,120	1								
4	·52	·37	6·95	"	"	56,000	2		47,040	2	42,560	2	51,520	3	
5	·47	·44	7·22	"	"	60,480	2		60,480	5	56,000	3	56,000	2	
6			7·50	"	"	87,360	4	9							
7	·60	·38	7·90	"	"				62,720	8	67,200	1			
8	1·00	·42	9·15	"	"						94,080	17			
9			9·20	"	"	89,600	6	19							
10	·61	·30	9·37	"	"	73,920	5		85,120	16	85,120	15	87,360	15	
11	·95	·21	10·11	"	"	85,120	5		87,360	14	91,840	20			
12	·85	·28	10·60	"	"	76,160	4		91,840	17	94,080	19	89,600	17	
13													103,040 *a*	22 *a*	
14	·72	·37	10·88	"	"								112,000 *a*	23 *a*	
15													118,720 *a*	29 *a*	
16						87,360	4	8							
17													141,120	45	
18	·85	·37	12·29	"	"								143,360	45	
19													145,600	50	
20	1·10	·16	12·80	"	"	87,360	2		82,880	11	112,000	28	126,950	27	
21			12·70	"	"	105,280	6								
22	·92	·42	12·81	"	"	87,360	5		107,520	20	129,920	32	136,640	37	
23													143,360	45	
24	·85	·23	13·75	"	"								143,360	45	
25													147,840	49	
26													136,640	48	
27	·85	·23	13·75	"	"								143,360	50	
28													145,600	51	
29	·85	·24	14·01	"	"	80,640	2		107,520	14	123,200	27	150,080	44 *b*	
30	1·15	·84	14·27	"	"								154,560	46	37
31	1·15	·84	14·27	"	"								156,990	40	
32	1·10	·32	14·48	"	"	87,360	1		109,760	5			141,120	37	
33	1·24	·16	15·06	"	"	109,760	2		105,280	2			136,640	31	
34	1·54	·16	18·40	"	"	114,240	1		87,360	1			118,720	10	
35	1·68	·26	18·05	"	"	96,320	1						123,200	5	
36	1·60	·26	19·10	"	"	118,480	1		97,440	1			132,160	4	
37	1·90	·32	19·28	"	"						51,520	0			
38	2·10	·46	21·69	"	"	80,640	0		76,160	12	79,520	11			

"Natural state" means that the metal was simply cooled slowly after forging ceased.
"Air-toughened" means that, after cooling, it was reheated to a yellow heat and allowed to cool slowly in the air.
"Oil-toughened" and "water-toughened" mean that, after forging, it cooled slowly, was then heated to a yellow heat, and quenched in cold oil or water.
The fractures of bars with from 8 to 9% of manganese were always coarse and granular: those of bars with more than 9% of manganese which had been water-toughened were silky and fibrous.
The contraction of area of the water-toughened pieces is usually from 30 to 40%.
a Lowest, highest and average results of twelve tests.
b This piece is still unbroken. Hadfield, Journ. Iron and Steel Inst., 1888, II.; Excerpt Proc. Inst. Civ. Eng., XCIII., III., 1888, p. 40 et seq.

While, as already pointed out, the effect of small proportions of manganese on the strength and ductility of steel is probably slight, that of higher proportions is astonishing. Beginning at some point now unknown, but probably at about 2·5%, further increase of manganese diminishes both strength and ductility, while conferring remarkable hardness. This effect reaches a maximum when the manganese has risen to somewhere between 4 and 6%. With further increase the strength and toughness both increase while the hardness diminishes slightly, the maximum of both strength and toughness being reached with somewhere about 14% of manganese, the hardness still remaining so high that the metal can hardly be machined.

As the manganese rises above 15% the ductility falls off

[a] Journ. Iron and Steel Inst., 1888, II.; Proc. Inst. Civ. Eng. XCIII., III., 1888. U. S. Patents 303,150-1: British Patents 200 of 1883, and 8,303 and 16,049 of 1884.

[b] It has been stated that manganese-steel is greatly softened by water-quenching. This, however, is an error. Mr. Hadfield informs me that water-quenching makes it more pliable, but changes its hardness as measured by indentation, etc., very little.

abruptly, the tensile strength remaining nearly constant till the manganese passes 20%, when it in turn falls off quickly. The effect of these high proportions of manganese is obscured by that of the accompanying carbon, which rises unavoidably with the manganese.

Steel containing from 4 to 6.5% of manganese, even if it has only 0·37% of carbon, can be powdered under a hand-hammer, yet it is extremely ductile when hot. With 11% of manganese the metal after heat-treatment has an elongation of 22% and a tensile strength of about 110,000 pounds per square inch, while with about 14% of manganese we have 51% of elongation in 8 inches and a tensile strength of 145,600 pounds per square inch. This combination of strength and elongation is far greater than any other which I have met, better even than that of nickel-steel, with the exception of one reported instance of 25% nickel-steel: and I do not know how trustworthy is the authority which gives this case.

Manganese-steel wire is reported with a tensile strength of 246,000 pounds per square inch. This, while good, is by no means remarkable, as wire with 344,960 pounds tensile strength has already been described. (Foot note to page 33.)

the strongest and toughest group of manganese-steels. Beyond these limits the influence of heat-treatment on tensile strength is not very clearly traceable in Hadfield's results, but its influence on ductility persists till the manganese reaches about 18%.

Within these limits reheating manganese-steel forgings to whiteness with slow cooling usually increases strength and ductility wonderfully, while, if quenching be substituted for slow cooling, the increase of strength and ductility is simply marvelous, tensile strength being sometimes nearly doubled, and elongation jumping from 2 to 44% in one case.

TABLE 207.—PROPERTIES OF MANGANESE STEEL AS AFFECTED BY RAPIDITY OF COOLING.

	Tensile strength, pounds per square inch.	Elongation, % in 8".
Quenched in water at 202° F.	58	32·5
" " 72° F	67 to 68	39·8 to 50
" sulphuric acid	65	50·7

These effects may be traced in Table 206, in which we note that, within the above limits of composition, oil-quenching gives better results than air-cooling, and water-quenching gives better still: while Table 207 indicates that cold water is a better quenching-medium than hot, and that sulphuric acid, represented as a still better conductor, is better yet.

Fig. 226 TESTED AS FORGED — Fig. 227 HEATED AND COOLED IN AIR — Fig. 228 WATER TOUGHENED

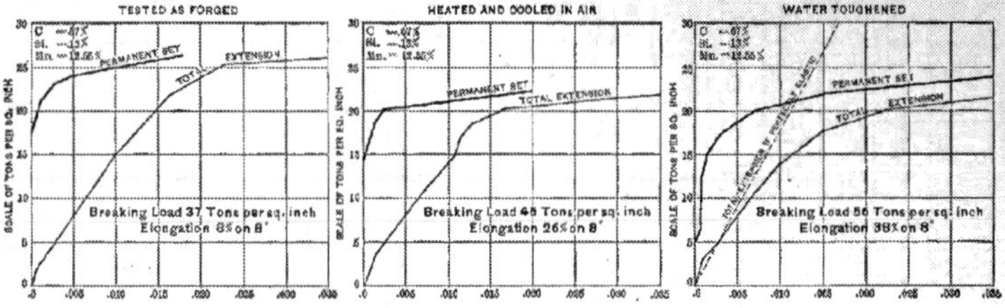

MANGANESE-STEEL UNDER TENSILE-STRESS (HADFIELD).

Manganese-steel is benefited by forging, and some varieties of it are improved wonderfully by heat-treatment.

Forging destroys the very marked crystallization of unforged manganese-steel castings, and according to Hadfield increases their strength and ductility: but he gives us no quantitative data on this point, as his transverse tests of the cast metal and the tensile tests of the forged are not readily comparable. Indeed, the "natural state," *i. e.* unquenched forgings of Table 206 seem surprisingly brittle. Even when containing as much as 21·69% of manganese and 2·1% of carbon, manganese-steel can be forged. But the engineers of Chatillon et Commentry, where manganese-steel was tried for making armor-plates, report that even when hot it is so extremely hard that the difficulty of forging it is prohibitory. If manganese-steel ingots are heated too strongly, they burst in forging.

Heat-Treatment.—Both castings and forgings are strengthened and toughened by heating to a yellow or, better, to a white heat, especially if then suddenly cooled. The higher the temperature (probably provided this is not above bright whiteness), and the more sudden the cooling, the more is the metal benefited.

The effect of heat-treatment on the tensile strength and ductility of forgings is very marked in case of steel containing from about 12 to about 15% of manganese, *i. e.*

Indeed, it seems quite necessary to quench manganese-steel rapidly in order to give it any considerable value. Fortunately, pieces of moderate size do not crack on quenching: but in attempting to quench large pieces such as armor-plates, in which the quenching-stresses would naturally be much greater than in small ones, Chatillon et Commentry found great liability to crack.

The improvement caused by quenching is partly lost on subsequent heating followed by slow cooling, such for instance as usually occurs after forging has ceased. Hence it is usually loosely stated that the improvement caused by quenching is removed by subsequent forging: but Mr. Hadfield informs me that his experience indicates that it is not the forging as such that injures the metal, but the slow cooling which habitually follows forging (Cf. § 54 A, p. 34). The injury due to slow cooling may, however, be removed by again quenching from whiteness. Still, the matter is obscure: for in this view it is hard to explain why manganese-steel forgings are improved by heating to whiteness and cooling slowly.

Heating and quenching, however, instead of increasing seems rather to lower the elastic limit, already unfortunately low, and it is possible that it may thus injure rather than benefit the metal for many important purposes (Cf. Figures 226–8).

Under stress manganese-steel acts very differently from wrought-iron and carbon-steel. As Figure 228 shows, manganese-steel with 125,000 pounds (56 tons) tensile strength may begin taking serious permanent set under stress of about 35,000 pounds per square inch, so that in this respect it is little better than common soft steel with say 60,000 pounds tensile strength.

Moreover, the enormous elongations reported may be found later to have given a greatly exaggerated notion of the metal's ductility. A test-bar of iron or carbon-steel undergoes a certain amount of elongation over its whole length, but much of its elongation occurs just at and near the point of rupture, where the metal "necks." It is owing to this that the percentage of elongation of short iron test-bars is so much greater than that of long ones. Manganese-steel, however, like brass, stretches more nearly uniformly over its entire length, without much necking. Its elongation would exceed that of equally strong carbon-steel much less if measured over a length of ⅛th inch than if, as now, measured over 8 inches. Now, elongation is indeed an index of toughness and ductility: but the relative toughness of different metals under given conditions can be safely inferred from their elongations only when those elongations occur in like manner. For certain conditions it may be better, for others worse, that the elongation should be distributed as in manganese-steel rather than concentrated as in carbon-steel. But, while we may dispute whether the toughness of manganese-steel of 25% of elongation is on the whole *greater* or better rather than less or worse than that of carbon-steel of like elongation, the important point is that it is a different toughness, which does not necessarily fit the metal for the purposes to which carbon-steel of 25% elongation is properly put.

Thus, Stromeyer found that manganese-steel, whose elongation under tensile stress led him to expect that it could be bent back and forth many more times before rupture than wrought-iron and carbon-steel, was actually rather brittle when tested in this way, enduring only 7 bendings when in its natural state and from 10 to 18 after quenching from redness, while wrought-iron and carbon-steel endured in four cases 20, 26, 12·5 and 21 bends.

Again, the results in Table 209 show that, while the shock-resisting power of manganese-steel of 12·55% of manganese is much greater than that of the best carbon axle-steel with which it was compared, yet in spite of its enormous *elongation* under static tensile stress, its ultimate *deflection* on rupture under transverse shock is less than half as great as that of the carbon-steel.

TABLE 208.—MANGANESE- AND SILICO-MANGANESE STEEL SHOWN AT PARIS BY HOLTZER. (Cf. § 83, p. 48.)

Number.	% of manganese.	Tensile strength, pounds per square inch. Natural state (forged).	Oil-hardened and tempered.	Oil-hardened and annealed.	Elastic limit, pounds per square inch. Natural state (forged).	Oil-hardened and tempered.	Oil-hardened and annealed.	Elongation, % in 7·9". Natural state.	Oil-hardened and tempered.	Oil-hardened and annealed.	Contraction of area, %. Natural state.	Oil-hardened and tempered.	Oil-hardened and annealed.
1..	·20 @ ·30	98,453	146,210	112,013	42,668	109,250	91,026	22	12·5	13	42	45	35
2..	....	87,612	149,197	131,134	49,210	110,227	98,706	14	11·9	19		44	46
3..	....	97,710	154,118	161,37[illegible]	46,860	119,706	129,235	20·8	8·5	18	42	36·5	46
4..	....	107,882	163,377	141,232	57,033	133,409	122,680	16	10	11·8	35·5	41	43·5
5..	....	102,546	173,651	154,175	57,028	146,219	133,409	19	7·5	8·5	51	81	44
6..	10 ±	98,746	176,368	148,201	55,049	155,882	121,605	23·6	8	11·5	49·2	31	40
7..	12 @ 14	115,831	132,816	131,307	58,982	61,969	52,908	22	28	41·5	24	28·5	36·5
8..	....	81,902	87,328	86,558	38,970	68,075	32,107	36	15	24·5	73	76	79·5
9..	....	96,572	136,098	128,289	47,213	19,900	106,565	14	10·5	11·2	21	42·2	46
10..	....	91,026	159,560	133,498	44,517	118,760	104,588	21·5	13	10·5	42·2	36·5	46
11..	2 ±	92,021	161,071	145,219	47,564	139,098	121,605	23	10	12·5	50·5	38·5	46

The "natural state" pieces are simply cooled slowly after forging.
The oil-hardened and tempered pieces are quenched in oil from about W, a low yellow, and slightly reheated.
The oil-hardened and annealed pieces are similarly quenched, then reheated to very dull redness, say V, and cooled slowly.
It is possible that the labels of tempered and annealed pieces have been misplaced in the show-case in certain instances. In Number 8 I have transposed them, feeling confident that they have been thus misplaced.
The compositions given are only rough guesses made at my request by M. Brustlein.

As the elastic limit and modulus of elasticity of manganese-steel are low, while its permanent set seem to increase at normal rate under increasing load, its stiffness under shock is a little puzzling. We have here another instance of the discrepancies between ductility under static stress and under shock.

TABLE 209.—EFFECT OF TRANSVERSE SHOCK ON MANGANESE- AND CARBON-STEEL (HADFIELD).

	Energy developed in foot tons	Sum of permanent deflections, inches.	
		Special carbon-steel axle.	Manganese-steel axle.
At the 5th blow,	79·888	24·983	6·591
" 10th "	208·581	69·188	19·493
" 15th "	348·582	105·248 broke.	30·212
" 20th "	497·988	....	39·491 broke.

Bars 4½" in diameter and 4' 6" long, on bearings 3 feet apart, were struck by a 20·75-cwt. ram, and reversed after each blow.

Cold-working influences manganese-steel greatly. Thus in drawing wire it is found necessary to anneal the metal by quenching from whiteness after every two draughts. As in case of iron and carbon-steel, the stretching which occurs in tensile testing raises the elastic limit so that when again tested it equals the maximum stress previously applied (Cf. § 270, p. 213), *e. g.* while the first application of a stress of 50,000 pounds per square inch gives a strong permanent set, no further set arises on repetition of this same stress. But, unlike that of iron and of carbon-steel, the elastic limit of manganese-steel in the few cases which have been described declines instead of rising during rest after stretching, so that in one case the elastic limit which had been raised to 56,000 pounds per square inch by a stress of that amount, fell in about two months to about 40,000 pounds, distinct permanent set arising with this stress.

As regards friction the statements are not easily reconciled. On the one hand Mr. C. W. Hubbard is quoted as believing that manganese-steel has the very essence of "anti-friction": on the other brake-blocks are said to "bite" manganese-steel wheels much better than cast-iron ones. This certainly seems like blowing hot and cold. The presence of grease in one case and its absence in the other may, however, cause the discrepancy.

Compressive Strength.—Under a load of 224,000 pounds per square inch, blocks one inch long and 0·70-inch in diameter, of steel (A) with 10 and (B) with 15 to 20% of manganese, shortened (A) by 25% and (B) by from 10 to 13% respectively. The compressive strength thus is lower than one would anticipate from the hardness proper.

Structure.—The fracture of manganese-steel ingots is strongly crystalline, and is not changed even by strongly reheating and quenching, though this treatment strengthens and toughens the metal. The crystalline structure is broken up by forging. The brittle group with 3 to 7·5% of manganese, if cast in a 4-inch square mould, has strongly marked brittle needles about 1·5 inches long, normal to to the cooling surface, at the outside. In the centre is a heterogeneous mass of crystals.

With 8 to 12% of manganese the fracture resembles that of "scalded" carbon-steel, and is completely covered with bundles of little, hard, and very tough needles normal to the cooling surface.

With more than 12% of manganese the acicular structure gradually gives way to a coarsely crystalline structure like that of coarse cast-iron.

According to Hadfield, the fracture of manganese-steel with less than 13% of manganese has a peculiar burnished or polished appearance, especially if metal be very hot when cast.

The ingot from which Holtzer's manganese-steel, Number 6, Table 208, appears to have been made has a most remarkable fracture, made up almost wholly of fine fibres like very fine cambric needles, normal to the cooling surface, and highly splendent. Seen through the glass show-case the central non-acicular part looked fine hackly. Around the outside is a sub-acicular fringe about 0·12" deep.

Pieces of the manganese-steel of numbers 8 and 9 of Table 208 have, after melting in crucibles and rolling into bars, been "converted," *i. e.* carburized, by the cementation process. Their fracture is very remarkable. There are long-bladed faces in it, recalling in a most striking way the prism-faces of crystals of hornblende in crystalline rocks.

Segregation.—Hadfield detected no serious segregation in 16-inch square ingots containing 14% of manganese: but it is not clear from his statements whether his borings were so taken that they would have detected segregation had it occurred.

Carbon-condition.—Manganese-steel, which by combustion showed 1·11% of carbon, gave Stead 0·90% of carbon by Eggertz' coloration test: as in case of carbon-steel, the coloration test showed less carbon in quenched than in slowly-cooled metal. This indicates that the carbon is in combination: whether its condition of combination resembles that of carbon in carbon-steel remains to be shown.

Magnetization.—Exposed to a gentle magnetizing force, wrought-iron is about 8,000 times as susceptible of magnetization as manganese-steel, but as the magnetizing force increases this difference diminishes greatly. A magnetizing force of 10,000 C. G. S. units produced in manganese-steel an intensity of magnetism of nearly 400 C. G. S. units, which is as high as the intensity commonly found in permanent magnets. This, however, was a tour de force; for practical purposes manganese-steel may be regarded as wholly unmagnetizable (Ewing).

Preparation.—Manganese-steel is made by mixing molten iron, decarburized by the open-hearth or Bessemer process, with ferromanganese in a ladle. It is less desirable to mix them in crucibles, because these are cut by the manganiferous slag. The steel usually contains about 0·5% less manganese than the ferromanganese added would imply were there no loss. It gives off a strong sulphurous smell while molten, confirming the observations recorded in §81, p. 43. But, as the composition of ferromanganese (Table 20, p. 43) had already shown, even a large proportion of manganese may not bring the proportion of sulphur below say 0·06%: this is shown by the analyses in Table 206.

Uses.—Manganese-steel is as yet used only tentatively. Among the objects for which it seems specially fitted are car-wheels, on account of its combined hardness and toughness; resistance-coils on account of its electrical resistance; and the bed-plates of dynamos on account of its low magnetic susceptibility. At first sight it seems admirably fitted for armor-plate: but, owing to its relatively low crushing strength, it may prove to have much less power of resisting penetration by projectiles than its hardness as measured by its resistance to abrasion would lead us to expect. At present its use is greatly hampered by the extreme difficulty of machining and apparently also of forging it. These and its liability to crack in quenching led Commentry et Chatillon to wholly abandon the serious attempts which they made to use manganese-steel for armor-plates. Moreover, its extremely low elastic limit is a serious defect. Indeed, ductile as it is, one is not sure that its combination of elastic limit and *useful* toughness for most purposes is as good as that of carbon-steel. Still, its combination of ductility with tensile strength is so great that it should give it some important uses, while its simply marvelous combination of ductility with certain kinds of hardness, unapproached so far as I know in any material whatsoever, unless it be nickel-steel, may well give it great value for the many purposes for which this combination seems important

The thoroughness with which its discoverer[a] has examined it, and especially the modesty with which he has described it and the candor and impartiality with which he has laid stress on its shortcomings, command admiration.

§ 413 A. EFFECT OF SMALL QUANTITIES OF MANGANESE.—An important French manufacturer is now intentionally introducing about 1% of manganese into thin armor-plates, believing that the resistance to penetration is thereby increased, without incurring brittleness under shock. So, too, St. Chamond shows steel with 0·90% of manganese and 0·85% of carbon, yet with 142,000 pounds tensile strength per square inch and 7% of elongation. Again, two armor-plates lately made by an eminent British maker have over 1·25% of manganese. Their composition follows:

No.	C.	Si.	Mn.	P.	S.
1	0·91	0·28	1·25	....	....
2	0·98	0·04	1·37	0·04	0·11

1 is a plate which a Krupp shell failed to pierce: 2 is the face of a compound plate. These facts harmonize with the conjecture expressed on page 48 that the effects of moderate quantities of manganese in causing brittleness have been grossly exaggerated.

414. SILICON-STEEL.—The ferro-silicons and silicospiegels (*i. e.* ferro-silicons rich in manganese) whose composition is given in Table 210, are shown at the Paris Exhibition. The tendency of manganese to raise and of silicon to lower the saturation-point for carbon is readily traced in this table (Cf. §§ 18, 19, pp. 8, 9).

TABLE 210.—FERRO-SILICON (Cf. p. 86).

Number.	Composition. C.	Si.	Mn.	P.	S.	As.	Cu.	Fe.		Makers.
1	1·40	12·05	2·10	·04	·01	tr.	·01	84·39	....	Gjers, Mills & Co.
2	....	12·	3@4	....	....	....	....	....	....	St. Louis.
					Silico-spiegel. S.	As.	Cu.	Fe.		
11	1·89	12·25	19·25	·05	tr.	tr.	·01	67·05	....	Gjers, Mills & Co.
12	....	12·	15@20	....	..	....	....	....	....	St. Louis.
13	1·42	17·00	18·09	·085	tr.	....	....	....	Fine gray, very bubbly, half void.	Firminy.
14	3·5	10·30	18·00	·08	....	....	....	....	Very course open gray, bubbly.	"

Ferro-silicon with about 10% of silicon and at most 2·5% of manganese is made on a considerable scale, and sells in England for less than $20 per ton.[b] Some of it has but little phosphorus, but some with 1·5 to 1·7% of phosphorus is also made, for foundry work. According to Gautier four establishments only are now making ferro-silicon.[b]

In order to make ferro-silicon in the blast-furnace, the slag should be acid, and often contains 10 or 12% of alumina; the burden must be very light, and the blast very hot. Two or even three tons of coke per day may be needed per ton of ferro-silicon produced.

Alumina, acting perhaps as an acid, is thought to facilitate the reduction of silicon. Pourcel added sulphate of baryta to the blast-furnace charge, believing that baryta was a less powerful base and would thus hold the silica less firmly than lime, and because the presence of baryta gave a more fluid slag. In England ferro-silicon is also made in the blast-furnace by charging iron-silicates with but little lime and much alumina.[b]

For making silico-spiegel in the blast-furnace we need similar conditions, save that the burden must be rich in oxide of manganese. Gautier gives the following as an example of the charge:

Coke	2,500	Combined silica	420
Ferric oxide	940	Carbonate of lime	480
Manganese oxide	570	Sulphate of baryta	190
Free silica	850		

Table 210A gives the calculated and the actual slag of another blast-furnace, making silico-spiegel of about 17% of silicon and 18% of manganese, closely like number 13 of Table 210.

TABLE 210A.—CALCULATED SLAG, ACTUAL SLAG, ETC., MADE TOGETHER WITH RICH SILICO SPIEGEL IN THE BLAST-FURNACE.

	1. Calculated Slag.	2. Probable Slag.	3. Actual Slag.	4. Fume.
Silica	50·0	39	33·2	31·6
Lime	41·5	....	50·0	37·9
Alumina	8·5	....	13·2	....
Oxide of manganese	....	....	3·0	5·5
Ferrous oxide	0	....	tr.	....

1. Calculated on the assumption that all the silica of the charge enters the slag.
2. Calculated on the assumption that enough of the silica of the charge is reduced to give the metal produced 17% of silicon, and that the rest enters the slag.
3. The slag actually made.
4. The fume found in the flues of the blast-furnace. It is thought that the fact that the ratio of silica to lime in the fume is much higher than that in the "actual slag" explains why the latter contains so much less silica than the "probable slag." The relatively high proportion of oxide of manganese in the fume recalls Jordan's statement (§77, p. 42) that 16% of the manganese charged in a certain blast-furnace could not be accounted for by the contents or the metal, the slag and the dust.

The slag actually made has in this case nearly the same composition as that which accompanies common Bessemer cast-iron, nearly all of the excess of silica charged being either reduced to silicon, or carried away in the fume.

Firminy's statement that their blast-furnace, which turns out from 110 to 120 tons of common cast-iron daily, may not produce more than from 10 to 15 tons of silico-spiegel, which sometimes contains over 20% of silicon, is instructive. Here, as in making ferro-silicon, two or even three tons of coke may be needed per ton of product.

Ferro-silicon is used in the iron foundry for softening cast-iron, and for enabling the founder to use a larger proportion of scrap. It is also used as a final addition in making ingots and other steel castings, to prevent the formation of blow-holes. Silico-spiegel is used for this latter purpose and at the same time for giving forgeableness. The choice between these two alloys depends chiefly on the relation between the composition of the bath to which the addition is to be made and that which the

a M. H. A. Brustlein informs me that he discovered the properties of these manganese-steels in 1879, but was deterred from making them by the difficulty in machining them, which he thought would effectually prevent their use. But, as he kept his discovery to himself, it is to Hadfield's wholly independent discovery that we owe our knowledge and thanks.

b Gautier, Les Alliages Ferro-metalliques, pp. 91-96 Excerpt Bull. Soc. Indust. Minérale, 2nd. Ser., III., 1889.

product should have, ferro-silicon alone being used if the bath is already rich enough in manganese. It is in general cheaper to add silico-spiegel than to add ferro-silicon and ferro-manganese separately.

In the manufacture of silicon-steel itself little progress is apparent. Holtzer indeed exhibits the silicon- and silico-manganese steels whose properties are given in Table 211, but I cannot find that they are more than curiosities.

The electrical resistance of silicon-steel is reported as six or seven times that of iron,[a] and thus almost as great as that of manganese-steel.

A paper on silicon steel is expected from Hadfield.

Gautier[b] reports that two types of silicon steel, one with about 1%, the other with from 1·5 to 1·6% of silicon, are used successfully by Hadfield in dressing steel castings. These steels are made by melting selected scrap-iron with ferro-silicon in crucibles. With caution they can be forged very well. The tools are water-quenched. Though containing only about 0·50% of carbon they are hard enough for general use in the machine-shop; hence Gautier conjectures that the silicon present intensifies their hardness, at least when quenched. I have, however, known tools made from common rail-steel, containing say 0·40% of carbon, to give tolerable results in the machine-shop.

TABLE 211.—PHYSICAL PROPERTIES OF SILICON-STEEL—HOLTZER. (Cf. Table 19, p. 48.)

Number.	Tensile strength, pounds per square inch.			Elastic limit, pounds per square inch.			Elongation, % in 7·8 inches.			Contraction of area, %.		
	Natural state.	Oil-hardened and tempered.	Oil-hardened and annealed.	Natural state.	Oil-hardened and tempered.	Oil-hardened and annealed.	Natural state.	Oil-hardened and tempered.	Oil-hardened and annealed.	Natural state.	Oil-hardened and tempered.	Oil-hardened and annealed.
1	109,855	179,349	114,067	68,705	168,967	75,940	22·5		18·5	54·5	47	54·5
2	142,226	168,977	159,722	77,087	178,854	147,068	10·8	2·3	7·8	19	10·8	31
3	97,716	170,074	159,580	65,567	152,184	131,184	22·2	10·5	14·2	59	88·5	60

The "natural state" pieces are simply cooled slowly after forging.
The "oil-hardened and tempered" pieces are quenched in oil from a low yellow, and slightly reheated.
The "oil-hardened and annealed" pieces are quenched similarly, reheated to very dull redness, and cooled slowly.
It is possible that the labels of some of these pieces have been misplaced.

Gautier[b] gives also the following siliciferous steels, and reports that their quality is excellent:

TABLE 211 A.—GOOD SILICIFEROUS STEELS.

C.	Si.	Mn.	P.	C.	Si.	Mn.	P.
0·783	0·342	0·370	0·019±	1·114	0·684	0·40	.....
0·523	0·840	0·490	0·019±	0·941	0·577	0·390	0·023
0·574	0·478	0·206	0·019±	1·050	0·299	0·410	0·015
1·015	0·675	0·520	0·023	1·188	0·515	0·400	0·018
1·091	0·600	0,370	0·019				

These examples tend to justify the doubts expressed on page 40 as to the deleterious effects of silicon.

§ 415. CHROME-STEEL.—Most of the ferro-chromes of Table 212 are shown at the Paris Exhibition. Those of St. Louis and of Firminy are made in the blast-furnace, of course with heavy consumption of fuel and small output. Some at least of those of Boucau are made in cupolas, making 5 to 6 tons per campaign we are told. There are besides those in Table 212 two other exhibits of ferro-chrome. This gives us an idea of the attention that is being paid it. Note how chromium raises the saturation point for carbon. Number 17, with only 16% of chromium, has actually 9% of carbon.

TABLE 212.—FERRO-CHROME. (Cf. Table 81, p. 74.)

		C.	Si.	Mn.	P.	S.	Cr.	
1	Boucau (St. Chamond)...	11·1	·40	4	·06	tr.	65	Not magnetic, made in cupolas.
2	" " ...	8·56	0·40	0·40	"	·01	44·80	
3	" " ...	8·75	0·32	0·40	"	"	51·10	
4	" " ...	9·10	0·56	0·35	"	"	55·50	
5	" " ...	9·38	0·45	0·50	"	"	57·96	
6	" " ...	9·35	0·60	0·45	"	"	59·85	
7	" " ...	10·95	0·40	0·42	"	"	63·10	
8	" " ...	11·90	0·38	0·38	"	"	65·20	
9	Firminy..................	3·80	4·50	2·50	·08	·02	23·00	
10	Holtzer..................	7·30	2·10	0·40	....	....	42·00	
11	"	7·50	8·20	....	....	....	32·00	Made in graphite crucible. } Silico-chrome.
12	"	5·00	9·00	....	....	....	30·00	
13	"	5·00	8·00	....	....	....	36·00	
14	"	9·00	....	....	....	....	84·00	Made in magnesia crucible.
15	"	11·00	....	....	....	....	80·00	Made in brasqued crucible.
16	"	8·60	....	....	....	....	80·00	Made in a crucible.
17	"	9·00	....	....	....	....	16·00	
18	"	2·25	....	....	....	....	15·00	
19	"	2·70	....	....	....	....	18·00	
20	"	3·20	....	....	....	....	25·00	
21	"	2·90	....	....	....	....	12·00	
22	"	4·35	....	0·80	....	....	7·00	Fractures like spiegeleisen.[a]
23	"	1·25	....	....	....	....	7·±	
24	"	5·00	0·40	0·38	..	....	7·±	
25	"	4·50	0·25	0·26	....	....	7·±	
26	"	8·46	....	....	....	....	71·5	Very magnetic.
27	Assailly (St. Chamond)...	....	....	..	..	....	42·	Made in crucibles.

[a] The fracture of No. 22 is astonishingly like that of spiegeleisen, though only 0·80 of manganese is said to be present. We have in the central vug the same broad-bladed crystals, with the same yellowish brown iridescent surface. Yet No. 24, with closely similar composition, lacks the spiegeleisen fracture.

Chrome-steel is shown by no less than ten exhibitors,[c] and has evidently become of considerable commercial importance. Thus, Holtzer has made about 5,000 projectiles, 10,000 thin plates for cuirasses, and several hundred tons of plates 0·16-inch thick for protection against musketry; Firminy has made over 4,000 projectiles, etc. The more

TABLE 213.—CHROME-STEEL, COMPOSITION. (See Table 82, p. 76.)

Number.	Maker.	Composition.						Use, etc.
		C.	Si.	Mn.	P.	S.	Cr.	
1	St. Etienne.	1·00	·30	·23	·01	·01	1·5	Razors, milling tools, wire dies, lathe-tools for white cast-iron, etc. Made in a basic open-hearth furnace.
2	Holtzer	2·00	....		..	....	12	Limit between chrome-steel and cast-iron.

important uses beside those just mentioned are (1) for tools for cutting chilled cast-iron and hardened steel without shock, (2) three-cornered files, and (3) wire-dies. There are no less than six exhibitors of chrome-steel files or of chrome-steel for files. The actual consumption for these uses is probably less than one might infer, for, though the makers have evidently convinced themselves that chrome-steel is especially adapted to them, the innumerable consumers naturally proceed cautiously. While the very hardest of the chrome-steels are so brittle that they cannot be used for tools cutting by impact the

[a] J. Hopkinson, Discussion of Hadfield's paper on manganese-steel, excerpt Proc. Inst. Civ. Eng., XCIII., III. p. 97, 1888.

[b] Les Alliages Metalliques. Excerpt Bulletin Soc. Indust. Minérale, 3rd. Ser., III., 1889, pp. 31, 32.

[c] Among them Chatillon et Commentry, Holtzer, St. Etienne, and St. Chamond of France, and Boehler of Vienna.

softer classes still have a combination of great hardness and very high elastic limit with sufficient toughness to prevent their cracking under even violent shock, such as projectiles and armor-plates are exposed to.

The thin chrome-steel armor-plates, 0·16 inches thick, are hardened and subsequently fully annealed, so that they can be bent double and hammered close. At the same time it is specified that they must not be pierced by a lead musket-ball with a velocity of about 1,500 feet, at a distance of 33 feet.

The chrome-steel projectiles, I am informed, are hardened in cold water, and only tempered by heating in boiling water, after which they are again plunged into cold water.

St. Etienne, though a maker of chrome-steel, has sought to make a material which, in the form of plates, would resist light projectiles nearly as well as chrome-steel, and would be considerably cheaper. The special plate, however, which St. Etienne makes for this purpose has to be 25% thicker than a chrome-steel plate in order to offer equal resistance to impact.

other of these shells, 16½-inches in diameter, has pierced a 21¼-inch Creusot steel plate in direct fire, but here the shell itself was broken.

TABLE 215.—TRIAL OF CHROME-STEEL AND OTHER PROJECTILES.

Number.	Maker.	Penetration, inches.	Condition of projectile after fire.		
			Broken or intact.	Shortening, inches.	Bulging, inches.
1	Holtzer, chrome.	9·87	Intact.	·12 @ ·24	·04 @ ·06
2	" "	9·45	"		
3	" "	9·76	"		
4	Krupp.	8·66	"	·47 @ ·55	·08
5	"	8·78	"		
6	"	8·90	"		
7	St. Chamond.	9·76 and 9·84	"	·08	0
8	"				
9	"	....	Broken.	Fell into the sea.	
10	"	....	"		
11	"	....	"		

Trials at Spezia, September, 1886. 79 to 82-pound projectiles 5·9 inches in diameter were fired with 40-pound charges of powder from a 5·9 inch Armstrong gun with a velocity of 1,870 to 1,980 feet, against a Creusot steel plate 13·9 inches thick, at a distance of 236 feet.

Holtzer also shows chrome-steel which he claims will drill through Mushet's tungsten-steel, and chrome-steel with 12% of chromium and 2% of carbon which can be forged, but which lies at the limit between chrome-steel and chromiferous cast-iron.

TABLE 214.—PHYSICAL PROPERTIES OF CHROME-STEEL AND TUNGSTO-CHROME STEEL—HOLTZER AND OTHERS. (Cf. Table 32, p. 76.)

Number.	Tensile strength, pounds per square inch.			Elastic limit, pounds per square inch.			Elongation, % in 7·9 inches.			Contraction of area, %.		
	Natural state.	Oil-hardened and tempered.	Oil-hardened and annealed.	Natural state.	Oil-hardened and tempered.	Oil-hardened and annealed.	Natural state.	Oil hardened and tempered.	Oil-hardened and annealed.	Natural state.	Oil-hardened and tempered.	Oil-hardened and annealed.
1	156,577	199,017	104,288	....	152,184	68,570	9·5	8	10·5	54·2	48	63
2	109,290	195,421	136,112	84,571	....	118,760	18·5	6	18	59	50·5	58·1
3	93,448	212,772	124,593	55,758	....	108,280	22·5	6·5	8	88·5	6	17·5
4	84,439	172,949	122,600	55,758	179,580	106,386	26·5	6·5	12·2	50·5	26	60
5	95,292	204,096	116,769	54,749	190,017	104,535	20·8	2·5	7	30	8	36
6	108,115	242,773	137,107	65,425	183,430	123,896	17·5	1·8	6·2	33	7	15
7	114,685	210,497	148,291	72,251	189,163	138,409	14·5	....	6	24	....	13
8	142,000 @ 156,000			113,800 @ 128,000			10 @ 12% in 3·9″			42 @ 45		
9	114,000			68,800			13·5a			....		
10	128,000 @ 142,000			....			20 @ 16a			....		

The "natural state" pieces are simply cooled slowly after forging.
The "oil-hardened and tempered" pieces are quenched in oil from a low yellow heat, and slightly reheated.
The "oil hardened and annealed" pieces are similarly quenched, reheated to very dull redness, and cooled slowly.
It is possible that the labels of some of these pieces have been misplaced.
Numbers 1 to 6 are chrome-steels; numbers 5, 6 and 7 contain both chromium and tungsten.
1 to 3, inclusive, are Holtzer's; 8 is for plates 0·59-inch thick, for the French navy.
9. Railway tire which has resisted 14 blows of a 1-ton ram falling 22 feet 10 inches. St. Chamond.
10. St. Etienne: usual properties of their armor-plates 0·16 to 1·18 inch thick.
a, the length in which the elongation is measured is not given.

St. Etienne shows a 13·4-inch chrome-steel projectile which has pierced a 15·7-inch iron plate obliquely without appreciable deformation, while Holtzer points with pride to the comparative tests of his chrome-steel projectiles with projectiles of Krupp and St. Chamond, given in Table 215.

At Firminy is shown a most instructive wooden model of a 20-inch wrought-iron armor-plate, pierced at an angle of 20°, and apparently like so much butter by a 14½-inch chrome-steel shell, which seems wholly uninjured. Another of these shells, 16½-inches in diameter, has pierced a 21¼-inch Creusot steel plate in direct fire, but here the shell itself was broken.

Most of the chrome-steel is made in crucibles, but that of St. Etienne and of another maker is made in the basic open-hearth furnace. The procedure at one mill is as follows: The carbon of the bath in the basic open-hearth furnace being brought to the desired point, enough ferro-chrome is added to give the desired proportion of chromium, allowing for a loss of 20% of the chromium added. This loss is fairly constant. Neither ferro-silicon nor ferro-manganese is added, the chromium at once preventing blowholes and giving forgeableness. As soon as the ferro-chrome is melted the charge is tapped. Chrome-steel has also been made tentatively in the acid open-hearth furnace, but I am informed that 80% of the chromium charged passed into the slag.

It is now thought that the proportion of chromium in chrome-steel should not exceed 2%, and that for most purposes it should be rather less than 2%.

Brustlein[a] gives us the following information touching ferro-chrome and chrome-steel.

The fracture of ferro-chrome depends more on the proportion of carbon and silicon present than on that of chromium. Ferro-chromes rich in carbon, or in carbon and silicon, are likely to have an acicular structure, and are always hard and brittle. As the carbon diminishes, so does the brittleness. Thus number 26, though with 71·5% of chromium, is less brittle than number 16, which has only 60% of chromium.

Chromium interferes with the magnetism of the metal much less than carbon and silicon. Thus number 26 is strongly magnetic.

Chromium has a strong tendency to oxidize. The oxidized compounds which it forms do not separate readily from the molten steel, and hence are very liable to form in the ingots ineradicable internal flaws, especially if the metal be rich in chromium and poor in carbon. Hence the successful manufacture of soft chrome-steel, say with 0·1 or 0·2% of carbon and 1 or 2% of chromium, is hardly to be looked for. For like reason chrome-steels rich in chromium weld with difficulty if at all. So, too, the employment of ferro-chrome as a recarburizer in the Bessemer and open-hearth processes is likely to cause internal flaws.

Once made, however, chrome-steel according to Brustlein requires in the forge no further precautions than carbon-steel of like hardness, though when hot, as well as when cold, it offers rather more resistance to deformation than carbon-steel. So too it is a little harder to machine than carbon-steel, but if it be well annealed the difference is not very great.

a "Le Ferro-Chrome," excerpt Bull. Soc. Indust. Minérale, 2nd Ser. III., 1889.

The effects of quenching penetrate deeper in chrome-steel than in carbon-steel. But the extreme hardness of quenched chrome-steel seems to be coupled with a disproportionate shock-resisting power: hence its special fitness for projectiles and armor-plate already pointed out.

§416. TUNGSTEN-STEEL (Cf. §141, p. 81).—The Paris exhibition indicates that the use of tungsten-steel has increased much, but decidedly less than that of chrome-steel. I found but three exhibits of ferro-tungsten, which in one case contained from 43 to 45% of tungsten. P. E. Martin reports having made ferro-tungsten of 2·% in the blast-furnace. One specimen of ferro-tungsten has a smooth conchoidal fracture much like that of "white metal," which is approximately cuprous sulphide, Cu S, and like that of chalcocite and argentite.

At least six exhibitors display tungsten-steel, at least one of whom has ceased to make it. It is recommended by most of them for cutting extremely hard metals, *e. g.* hardened steel and chilled cast-iron, but by one exhibitor for cutting soft and half-hard metals instead. Some of the best makers, who make both chrome- and tungsten-steel, believe that the latter is much the better fitted for tools for cutting hard metal, explaining its limited use by its high price, and by the scarcity of tungsten. St. Chamond recommends tungsten-steel especially for springs, stating that the carrying-power for given size of spring is about one-third greater than that of the best carbon spring-steel, and giving the elastic elongation after quenching and annealing as 0·75 per cent (0·0075). The only analysis of tungsten-steel whose results I saw gave the proportion of tungsten as about 2%. But I understand that some of Holtzer's tungsten-steels contain as much as 8% of tungsten.

Table 216 gives the properties of tungsten-steel shown by Holtzer at Paris.

§ 417. COPPER-STEEL (Cf. § 142, p. 82).—Three lots of this surprising substance are shown at Paris by Holtzer. Their properties are given in Table 217.

M. Brustlein informs me that the copper in these steels rises to three or four per cent.: that with more than one per cent they are decidedly redshort: that they have been

TABLE 216.—TUNGSTEN STEEL. HOLTZER. (Cf. Table 34, p. 81.)

Number.	Tensile strength, pounds per square inch.			Elastic limit, pounds per square inch.			Elongation, % in 7·9".			Contraction of area, %.		
	Natural state.	Oil-hardened and tempered.	Oil hardened and annealed.	Natural state.	Oil-hardened and tempered.	Oil-hardened and annealed.	Natural state.	Oil-hardened and tempered.	Oil-hardened and annealed.	Natural state.	Oil-hardened and tempered.	Oil-hardened and annealed.
1..	68,553	82,492	76,093	47,501	87,558	52,137	28·7	17·5	19·5	75·5	66	72·3
2..	71,114	71,114	93,017	50,348	48,499	—	23·5	9·2	15	60	6	29
3..	77,941	179,849	114,769	41,672	185,117	90,172	26·0	2·5	10·2	45·1	2·5	16
4..	93,017	218,185	184,406	47,504	—	104,588	17	4·5	8·5	33	4	24
5..	106,886	218,342	140,808	68,580	—	109,280	9	2·8	6·3	—	1	27

The "natural state" pieces are simply cooled slowly after forging.
The "oil-hardened and tempered" pieces are quenched in oil from a low yellow heat and slightly reheated.
The "oil-hardened and annealed" pieces are similarly quenched, reheated to very dull redness, and cooled slowly.
It is possible that the labels of some of these pieces have been misplaced.

made only as an experiment: that he believes that copper-steel has no future: that the copper does not appear to be uniformly distributed through the metal: and that it appears to favor the formation of blowholes.

The fracture of bars of Numbers 2 and 3 which have been nicked before breaking is most extraordinary. It consists of flat tables parallel with the surface of the fracture; in Number 3 a single table seems to occupy the whole surface of the fracture, which, indeed, looks as if it had been roughly ground on a grind-stone.

Note the exceedingly high elastic limit of the hardened bars, almost equalling their tensile strength, though the elongation is still considerable. The combination of elastic limit and elongation of bar Number 5 is quite as good as that of any nickel-steel which I have seen described, and of course far better than that of manganese-steel. Indeed, I know but little carbon-steel which excels it in this respect.

It has been thought that the redshortness which usually accompanies the presence of copper is due rather to the formation of sulphide of copper, the copper taking up sulphur from the furnace gases, than to the copper itself. The experiments made with copper-steel at Holtzer's works do not seem to bear out this view.

TABLE 217.—PHYSICAL PROPERTIES OF COPPER-STEEL.—HOLTZER. (Cf. § 142, p. 82.)

Number.	% of copper.	Tensile strength, pounds per square inch. Natural state.	Oil-hardened and tempered.	Oil-hardened and annealed.	Elastic limit, pounds per square inch. Natural state.	Oil-hardened and tempered	Oil-hardened and annealed.	Elongation, % in 7·9 inches. Natural state.	Oil-hardened and tempered.	Oil-hardened and annealed.	Contraction of area, %. Natural state.	Oil-hardened and tempered.	Oil-hardened and annealed.
1.	......	77,941	113,487	110,227	48,664	95,998	99,791	22·5	18·6	17·5	31·	60·	39·
2.	......	83,914	179,948	163,980	86,420	142,229	121,605	18·6	6·2	11·	50·	24·	38.5
3.	3 to 4	77,941	156,461	121,695	48,664	....	95,008	22·5	2·	14·5	51·	2·	50·

The "natural state" pieces are simply cooled slowly after forging.
The "oil-hardened and tempered" pieces are quenched in oil from a dull yellow heat and slightly reheated.
The "oil hardened and annealed" pieces are similarly quenched, reheated to very dull redness, and cooled slowly.
It is possible that the labels of some of these pieces have been misplaced.

§ 418. TITANIUM-STEEL (Cf. § 145, p. 85).—St. Chamond shows at Paris ferro-titanium in small irregular lumps, up to say one-inch cube, containing 22% of titanium, and titanium-steel containing 1·30% of carbon and 0·45% of titanium. The lumps of ferro-titanium look as if they had formed as a species of salamander in the crevices of the brickwork in the hearth of a blast-furnace, much as cyano-nitride of titanium often does.

The titanium-steel in its unquenched state looks much like carbon-steel of like percentage of carbon, but when quenched its fracture is unusually satinlike. M. Grobot[a] informs me that he is certain that the steel actually contains titanium, as he determined it himself, and that he knows of no sure way of making titanium-steel regularly. Note that, in spite of the large proportion of carbon in this titanium-steel, the proportion of titanium is small.

§ 419 NICKEL-STEEL (Cf. § 148, p. 86).[b]—Hardly have we begun to recover from our surprise at Hadfield's discoveries as to manganese-steel when J. Riley startles us with his statements concerning a probably more important and but little less remarkable substance, nickel-steel. Our information is so meagre and contradictory that the following statements are only provisional.

Nickel-steel is made in the open-hearth furnace, without especial difficulty, by the addition of metallic nickel to the bath, practically the whole of the nickel as well as that of any scrap nickel-steel added being recovered. The open-hearth heat lasts about seven hours, and a final addition of ferromanganese is made as usual. No especial care is required either in the open-hearth furnace, in casting, heating or forging, unless the proportion of nickel be very high, say 25%, when the temperature of heating must be kept somewhat lower than in case of carbon-steel of like carbon-content. When molten nickel-steel is thinner, it sets quicker, and pipes deeper than carbon-steel, with apparently little tendency to liquation, yielding ingots whose outside is clean. It forges easily, whether it contain much or little nickel: with 1% of nickel it welds "fairly readily," but with increasing nickel-content the welding-power diminishes, while the hardness and the ductility, whether as measured by elongation or by endurance of twisting, increase, the hardness reaching a maximum with 20% of nickel. The fracture is fibrous, sometimes astonishingly so. The metal takes a high polish, is sometimes highly sonorous, and becomes the whiter the larger the proportion of nickel.

With less than 5% of nickel, nickel-steels can be worked cold readily, provided the proportion of carbon be low. As the proportion of nickel rises higher, cold-working becomes less easy.

Nickel-steel has a lower combination of tensile strength with elongation but (even with only one per cent. of nickel) a higher combination of elastic limit with elongation than manganese-steel. I have met descriptions of but few carbon-steels which excel the best of these nickel-steels in this latter and more important combination.

Even when thus excelling manganese-steel in its combination of elastic limit and elongation, nickel-steel lacks the extreme hardness of the latter material: but it is still so hard that its machining will probably be expensive. I find no data for comparing the combination of hardness and toughness of the harder manganese- and harder nickel-steels.

If we confine our attention to the best specimens, a little nickel (say 1 to 5 %) seems to increase the tensile strength much and the elongation a little; much nickel, say 25%,

[a] Director of the Aciéries d'Assailly, where this remarkable product was made.
[b] Journ. Iron and Steel Inst., 1889, I.; Engineering, XLVII., p. 373, 1889; Pamphlet of "Le Ferro-Nickel" for the jurors of the Paris Exhibition of 1889.

seems to increase the elongation much while sometimes raising sometimes lowering the tensile strength. But almost any theory, except that the effects of nickel are uniform, could be deduced from the scanty and conflicting data. The effects of nickel in nickel-steel seem to vary much more than those of manganese in manganese-steel.

In the single case given annealing does not materially improve the unforged castings, but forging improves them very greatly, raising the tensile strength and elastic limit by 50%, and increasing the contraction of area and the elongation six- and seven-fold respectively. Like manganese-steel, nickel-steel seems to elongate over its entire length under tensile stress, instead of necking like carbon-steel. Its electric resistance is great, but less than that of manganese-steel, becoming 6·5 times as great as that of wrought-iron only when the nickel reaches 25%. It is much denser, and even with only 5% of nickel corrodes slightly less than carbon-steel, density and resistance to corrosion increasing with the proportion of nickel. Nickel-steel with 25% of nickel is said to be non-magnetic.

TABLE 218.—TENSILE TESTS OF NICKEL-STEEL.—J. RILEY.a

Number.	Composition.			Tensile strength, pounds per square inch.				Elastic limit, pounds per square inch.				Elongation, % in 8 inches.				Elongation, % in 4 inches.				Contraction of area, %.				
	Nickel.	Carbon.	Manganese.	As cast.	Cast and annealed.	Rolled.	Rolled and annealed.	As cast.	Cast and annealed.	Rolled.	Rolled and annealed.	As cast.	Cast and annealed.	Rolled.	Rolled and annealed.	As cast.	Cast and annealed.	Rolled.	Rolled and annealed.	As cast.	Cast and annealed.	Rolled.	Rolled and annealed.	
1	1·6	·42	·59	b	132,804	129,684	128,424	b	61,152	71,904	67,424	b					7·5	11·8	16·7	b	9·3	24·0	46·0	
2	2·0	·90	·50	Unmachinable.																				c
3	3·0	·35	·57	78,176	78,175	114,240	106,640	44,352	56,760	70,560	62,720					2·3	2·5	20·3	20·8	5·6	9·8	31·0	42·0	
4	3·0	·60	·26			115,360	96,096			63,856	67,872			9·0	7·5			10·1	9·0			9·0	12·0	
5	4·0	·85	·30	Unmachinable.																				
6	4·7	·25	·23			96,750	90,944			56,224	62,720			17·75	20·0			23·4	25·0			42·0	44·5	d
7	5·0	·30	·30			105,980	95,424			67,200	62,720			16·0	15·0			12·5	17·5			22·5	19·5	d
8	5·0	·50	·84			116,480	104,882			69,664	73,800			14·8	13·5			15·6	14·6			14·0	17·0	d
9	13·0	·50	·20	Unmachinable.																				e
10	25·0	·27	·85			115,136	109,592			85,568	28,560			10·5	29·0			11·7	30·0				28·0	
11	25·0	·82	·02			106,624	94,864			49,280	53,924			43·5	40·0			47·8	45·3			80·0	48·6	
12	49·4	·85	·01			95,774	82,880			40,320	47,040							12·0	20·8			24·0	29·0	
13				214,144 f				120,960				......				0·37				49·2				
14				419,884 f				116,502				7·8 g				....				52·4				
15				236,946 f				120,760				8·2 g				......				60·0				

a J. Riley, Engineering, May 17th, 1889, p. 574, a paper read before the Iron and Steel Institute.
b Test-piece defective.
c Too hard to machine with Mushet's steel. Good tools may be made from it by quenching from dull redness in boiling water.
d The average is reduced by the low results given by one test-piece.
e Too hard to machine. Good cutting tools may be made from it by cooling in a blast of cold air.
f We are not told how these pieces have been treated before testing.
g The length in which the elongation is measured is not given.

Let us now take up a few of these points in more detail.

The hardness depends on the proportion of nickel and of carbon jointly, nickel up to a certain percentage increasing the hardness, beyond this lessening it. Thus while steel with 2% of nickel and 0·90% of carbon cannot be machined, steel with 3% of nickel and 0·60% of carbon can. The most striking instances are summed up in Table 220.

TABLE 219.—TORSIONAL TESTS OF NICKEL-STEEL. (J. Riley.)[a]

Number.	Number in Table 218.	Composition, per cent. Nickel.	Carbon.	Manganese.	Breaking load, pounds. Hammered.	Hammered and annealed.	Load at elastic limit, pounds. Hammered.	Hammered and annealed.	Number of twists in 8 inches. Hammered.	Hammered and annealed.
Nickel-steel.										
I.	1	1·6	0·43	0·53	1,849	1,809	857	697	11	11
II.	3	3·0	0·35	0·57	1,729		685		13	
III.	6	4·7	0·22	0·23	1,493	1,443	621	652	11	23
IV.	7	5·0	0·30	0·30	1,597	1,485	677	623	24	28
V.	10	25·0	0·27	0·85	1,950	2,100	510	390	8	5
VI.		50·0	0·35		1,504		558		21	
Open-hearth carbon-steel.										
VII.			0·51		1,680		601		$14\frac{3}{8}$	
VIII.			0·51		1,697		601		$1\frac{8}{10}$	
IX.					1,229		445		3_1	

a The pieces tested were one-inch in diameter, and were twisted by means of a lever one-foot long, with the loads above given.

J. Riley, Engineering, May 17th, 1889, p. 574, a paper read before the Iron and Steel Institute.

TABLE 220.—HARDNESS OF NICKEL-STEEL. (J. Riley.)

Nickel %.	Carbon %.	Machinable or not.
3.	0·96	No.
3.	0·60	Yes.
4.	0·35	No.
5.	0·50	Yes.
10.	0·50	No.
25.	0·33	Yes.
	0·27	Yes.
49·4	0·85	Yes.

Density.—Riley reports the following determinations:

% Nickel.	Sp. gr.
100.	8·86
25.	8·08
10.	7·865
5.	7·846
0. (?)	7·84 mean of Riley's results for hammered (carbon ?) steel.
0.	7·83@7·87, usual limits for unhardened carbon steel in Table 140, p. 257.

Corrosion.—Riley states that the rich nickel-steels are practically incorrodible, and that even those with little nickel corrode less than carbon-steels, giving the following results:

TABLE 220 A.—RATES OF CORROSION OF NICKEL AND OTHER STEELS IN ABEL'S CORROSIVE LIQUID.

Metals compared. Nickel steel.	Other steel.		Ratio of corrosion of nickel steel to other steel.
5% nickel	Carbon steel 0·18% carbon.		1:1.3
5% nickel		Steel of .40% carbon and 1·60% chromium.	1:1.5
25% nickel	Carbon steel 0·18% carbon.		1:87
25% nickel		Steel of .40% carbon and 1·60% chromium.	1:116

Immersing steel said to contain 25% of nickel in fresh water in contact with carbon-steel rich in carbon, I found that the carbon-steel began to rust within a few hours, at the same time losing its polish: but even after three days the nickel-steel showed no certain sign of rusting. Immersed in fresh water alone for eighteen days the same nickel-steel showed not the least symptom of rusting.

The Fracture of a bar, said to be of nickel-steel and shown me by "Le Ferro-Nickel," nicked on one side and bent away from the nick, was astonishingly fibrous, "barking" like very tough fibrous wrought-iron (Cf. p. 196, 1st column). In another case the sheared fracture of a bar about 1·25 inches square, said to contain 30% of nickel and 1·00% of carbon,[a] was exceedingly silky, and much like that of the softest basic steel, except that its color was very much darker, indeed, almost black.

Ductility.—In the case of nickel- as in that of manganese-steel the elongation, exaggerated by the tendency of the test-piece to stretch over its entire length instead of necking, may be found to give a greatly exaggerated idea of the metal's toughness and value. Thus the contraction of area and the endurance of twisting are less than would be anticipated from the elongation, the percentage of contraction of area being actually less than that of elongation in four out of twenty cases. Number 4 of Table 218 and the rolled and annealed specimen of number 7 in the same table are very fair steels, if judged by their combination of tensile strength and elongation, but not if judged by that of tensile strength and contraction of area. These facts suggest great caution in deciding as to the value and uses of this promising alloy.

Blowholes.—A small broken ingot, about 2·25 inches square, of steel with 30% of nickel and 1% of carbon, shown by St. Chamond, has many blowholes besides the central pipe. Its columnar structure is very marked.

Source of Nickel.—It is believed that highly ferruginous nickel, which is quite as suitable as pure nickel for making nickel-steel, can be made at a much lower cost per unit of nickel than the nickel now in the market, which contains relatively little iron. M. Garnier proposes to smelt nickel ores in a common blast-furnace, obtaining thereby a highly sulphurous and ferruginous crude nickel, which he would desulphurize by repeated fusions in a cupola with a very calcareous slag thinned by fluor-spar, (Rollet's process), finally melting the desulphurized product in the basic open-hearth furnace.

Future.—I do not think that we can forecast the future of this remarkable alloy with complete confidence from the data at hand. On the one hand, apparently, even with but short experience, nickel-steels have been made which greatly surpass most of the best carbon-steel in their combinations (1) of tensile strength with elongation, and (2) of elastic limit with elongation, and are but slightly excelled in these combinations by even the very best carbon-steels which I have met: whence we might hope that, with greater experience, nickel-steel would excel the very best carbon-steels decidedly. On the other hand we must bear in mind that our data suggest that the useful ductility of nickel-steel may prove to be much less than would be inferred from its elongation: that its properties appear to vary capriciously: that those interested in it preserve an attitude of reserve, not to say concealment, which, while it is reasonably attributed to other causes, may be due to the discovery of some grave defect: that many another remarkable alloy has been discovered, for which we have anticipated a great future, only to see it play an unimportant rôle: and, finally, that the cost of nickel and the difficulty of machining are likely to be serious obstacles to the extended use of this alloy.

The claim that the properties of nickel-steel are due to the particular mode of introducing the nickel, and not to the mere presence of that element, will generally be received with extreme skepticism. Like claims are made, apparently with no supporting evidence, for most of the patented alloys offered to investors.

a Shown by St. Chamond at the Paris Exhibition of 1889.

APPENDIX II.

ANTI-RUST COATINGS.

§ 420 (Cf. § 168, p. 104).—Finding no data as to the relative protection against rusting afforded by different protective coatings, Mr. R. W. Lodge and the author have carried out a series of experiments with exposures lasting from ten months to a year, with both thin sheet wrought-iron and plates of cast-iron, under four different conditions of exposure and with six protective coatings, specimens of the same irons without protective coating being exposed simultaneously. A fifth series of plates was immersed in sea-water, but, in spite of very considerable precautions to prevent their being carried away by the water or by men, they cannot be found. To facilitate comparison with Table 44, p. 94, the results are reduced to the same standard.

TABLE 221.—LOSS OF WEIGHT OF WROUGHT- AND CAST-IRON WITH DIFFERENT PROTECTIVE COATINGS, IN POUNDS PER SQUARE FOOT OF SURFACE PER ANNUM. (Cf. Table 44, p. 94).

	Exposed to the weather inland.		Immersed.		Average.
	In Canada.	In New York State.	In fresh water.	In sewage.	
Wrought-Iron Sheets.					
Bower-Barffed	0	gain, ·000,8	·006,7	·008,6	·003,5
Tinned	gain, ·002,0	·000,1	·019,4	·007,1	·006,2
Nickel-plated	0	·000,5	·030,4	·008,1	·018,5
Galvanized	gain, ·000,4	....	·045,9	·080,5	·042,9
Barffed	·001,0	·003,1	·053,9	·117,0	·051,2
Black, i. e. unprotected	·001,3	·022,6	·181,0	·169,3	·082,5
Copper-plated	·000,2	·035,6	·179,0	·182,0	·091,6
Average	·000,02	·006,1	·074,6	·080,3	·040
Cast-Iron Plates.					
Bower-Barffed	gain, ·004,0	gain, ·003,1	gain, ·006,5	·001,4	gain, ·002,3
" " and paraffined	·000,6	·001,9	·000,2	·008,4	·002,8
Galvanized	0	0	·049,1	·061,0	·027,5
Tinned	....	gain, ·008,1	·085,5	·061,0	·041,1
Nickel-plated	gain, ·003,4	·002,5	·181,7	·088,3	·056,3
Copper-plated	gain, ·004,0	·005,0	·150,8	·119,2	·067,8
Black, i. e. uncoated	gain, ·006,8	·012,0	·148,3	·272,4	·106,6
Average	gain, ·002,0	·002,1	·077,2	·066,7	·041

A single sheet of No. 28 gauge refined wrought-iron was cut into plates 6″ × 12″ and others 6″ × 6″. Of the 6″ × 12″ pieces some were exposed without treatment of any kind, the scale being left on: others were tinned; still others were galvanized by the Rhode Island Tool Company. Of the 6″ × 6″ plates some were Bower-Barffed (Cf. § 167 C, p. 102) by the Yale & Towne Company, others were Barffed by the Pratt & Cady Company, still others were nickel-plated and copper-plated, in each case after pickling. The cast-iron pieces were skin-bearing plates, 4″ × 8·5″ × 0·187″, presented by Prof. G. W. Maynard. These were subsequently given the coatings indicated, their original skin being retained in all cases.

One set of the pieces thus prepared was exposed on the roof of a dwelling-house in the Eastern Townships of the Province of Quebec, Canada, by Mr. E. C. Hale, of Sherbrooke, Canada: a second was similarly exposed in a village in Rensselaer County, New York State: a third was immersed in the Chestnut-Hill (Boston) reservoir by Mr. Desmond FitzGerald, of Boston: a fourth was immersed in the Boston main sewer, near the pumping station, by Mr. H. H. Carter, of Boston.

Our thanks are due to these gentlemen and to the companies already named for their kind assistance in preparing or exposing the specimens.

We intend to describe these experiments in more detail in the Transactions of the American Institute of Mining Engineers. Suffice it here to say that in each of the conditions of exposure the wrought-iron pieces were in one open wooden crate, the cast-iron ones in a second, the corners of the pieces (and in case of the 6″ × 12″ wrought-iron pieces a small space in the middle of the long sides) alone being in contact with the crate; and that care was taken that the specimens should not touch each other or any other metallic substance. Though exposed nearly a year, including autumn, winter and spring, at the end of the experiments the gummed labels still adhered to twelve out of the twenty-six specimens exposed in Canada and in New York.

In brief, the Bower-Barffed pieces lost much less and the copper-plated and naked pieces decidedly more than the others: the cast-iron lost about as much as the wrought-iron: the loss was about the same in fresh water as in sewage, and slightly less in Canada than in New York.

Comparing the different conditions of exposure, immersion of course greatly accelerates rusting. Thus in ten out of the fourteen sets of cases the pieces immersed in fresh water lost at least twenty times as much as those exposed to the weather in New York. The loss is slightly but fairly constantly greater in New York than in Canada, which helps to explain the celebrated brightness of the tinned roofs of the Canadian churches. The loss in sewage is slightly greater than in fresh water, but far from constantly, for in seven out of the fourteen cases the loss in fresh water excels or about equals that in sewage, a result most unlooked for, and wholly at variance with Mallet's results with fresh water. It, however, recalls Mallet's results with sea-water, in which sewage on the whole retarded the corrosion of skin-bearing cast-iron (p. 97).

Comparing the different protective coatings the Bower-Barffed pieces win easily, undergoing no loss in five out of the eight cases, and with the single exception of the nickel-plated wrought-iron in sewage, losing less than half as much as any of the other irons in the three other cases. The copper-plated and the uncoated iron lose most heavily, copper-plating on the whole accelerating the rusting, especially in case of the wrought-iron sheets. The tinned pieces come in as a good second in case of wrought-iron, the galvanized as a bad second in case of cast-iron. As between nickel-plating and galvanizing in case of wrought-iron, and as between nickel-plating and tinning in case of cast-iron, it is not easy to decide whether the apparent difference is not due to individual peculiarities of the pieces tested.

The most surprising result is the practically identical loss of cast- and of wrought-iron, not only on a general average of the whole, but in at least three out of four of the sets of cases. It harmonizes with the belief expressed in §165, p. 98, that the slower rusting of cast- than of wrought-iron is due chiefly if not wholly to the protection which the skin of the cast-iron affords, rather than to the difference in the nature of the two substances. Just as we there saw that, when wrought- and cast-iron were brought to terms of equality by planing the skin from the latter, it ceased to resist rusting better than wrought-iron, so it does in the experiments of Table 221, in which we may suppose that the protective coatings applied put the materials nearly on equal terms. Still, even when unprotected the wrought-iron here resists rusting about as well as the cast-iron.

APPENDIX III.

Lead-Quenching.

§421. Quenching in lead instead of in oil has been adopted by the Chatillon et Commentry Company of France, especially for forged projectiles for piercing armor-plates. The metal is first heated to the desired temperature (probably the W of Brinnell and b of Chernoff), and then plunged into a bath of molten lead, in which it cools undisturbed. Owing to its density and high conductivity, lead should at first cool the piece more rapidly than oil or water, but later, as the temperature of the piece, sinking below the V of Brinnell, approaches that of the lead bath, the cooling grows slower and slower, ceasing asymptotically. Lead-quenching then should cool the metal more quickly through the higher ranges of temperature and less quickly through the lower ranges than oil-quenching. We may surmise that the fine grain acquired when the metal is heated to W will therefore be preserved better by lead- than by oil-quenching, and we would rather expect that the former operation would induce less powerful internal tension than the latter. Which of the two should the more completely prevent the carbon from passing from the hardening to the cement or non-hardening state it would be hard to judge beforehand.

At the Paris exhibition of 1889 the Chatillon et Commentry Company gives certain results of lead-quenching, which are reproduced in a modified form in Table 222.

Here the influence of lead-quenching is much milder than that of oil-quenching, the lead-quenched piece excelling the oil-quenched in elongation in 9 out of the 12 cases, and being excelled by the oil-quenched piece in tensile strength and in elastic limit in 11 out of the 12 cases. This milder quenching should be desirable for certain cases: but it can hardly be claimed that the effect of lead-quenching is absolutely better than that oil-quenching, for the oil- excel the lead-quenched pieces as much in strength as the lead-excel the oil-quenched ones in elongation. Thus, taking the last eight sets of bars, with carbon from 0·70 to 1·30%, we find that the average elongation of the lead-quenched pieces is 14% greater while their average tensile strength and elastic limit are 10% and 18% less respectively than those of the oil-quenched bars. It is not yet clear that the properties acquired by lead-quenching cannot be as readily and more cheaply given by oil-quenching followed by a more complete annealing, nor indeed that this latter combination of operations may not give higher elastic limit for given elongation than lead-quenching does.

Comparing now the lead-quenched with the simply annealed bars, we find that the former invariably excel the latter in tensile strength and elastic limit, but are excelled by the latter in elongation in nine out of twelve cases.

Finally, comparing the simply annealed, the water-quenched and the oil-quenched bars, we find that the water-quenched bars invariably excel the oil-quenched, and these in turn always excel the corresponding simply annealed pieces, in both tensile strength and elastic limit; while as regards elongation the order is as we would expect reversed, the simply annealed excelling the oil-quenched and the oil-quenched excelling the water-quenched, in either case with a single exception, in which the elongations are equal.

These results agree in a rough way with those discussed on pages 19 and 20. The fact that, although the latter indicated that oil-quenching gives high-carbon steel greater strength than water-quenching does, all the water-quenched pieces of Table 222 are stronger than the oil-quenched ones, may be due to the fact that here both have been tempered after quenching, so that some of that intense stress which water-quenching gives, and which probably directly lowers the tensile strength, has been removed.

Table 222.—Properties of Steel Annealed after Different Kinds of Heat-Treatment—Chatillon et Commentry.

Number.	% of carbon, estimated.	Tensile strength, pounds per sq. in., when annealed after				Elastic limit, pounds per square inch, when annealed (?) after				Elongation, % in 8 inches, when annealed after			
		forging.	quenching in water.	quenching in oil.	quenching in lead.	forging.	quenching in water.	quenching in oil.	quenching in lead.	forging.	quenching in water.	quenching in oil.	quenching in lead.
1	0·10	44,096	51,628	....	....	26,170	35,180	....	....	30	20	....	....
2	0·20	46,379	64,420	48,499	44,875	35,601	48,357	36,979	26,788	34	28	30	31
3	0·30	65,667	90,785	71,256	72,251	36,979	52,940	41,835	43,806	24	21	24	22
4	0·40	70,402	88,089	81,496	74,100	39,112	59,024	58,477	46,969	20	18	22	21
5	0·50	77,041	105,391	98,706	86,196	48,806	72,251	65,867	51,486	21	15	19·5	20
6	0·60	85,386	112,660	102,404	89,068	46,935	81,070	70,462	53,198	18	18	17	17
7	0·70	91,026	126,583	113,782	99,580	52,624	88,181	78,938	61,158	16	14	14	16
8	0·80	98,878	137,261	119,472	106,871	54,046	92,448	76,803	56,891	17	11	18	14
9	0·90	98,187	140,506	128,799	108,093	54,046	98,870	79,617	64,092	16	10	18	15
10	1·00	106,671	151,606	129,428	115,905	55,469	106,671	81,070	69,691	17	10·5	11	15
11	1·10	113,782	168,562	145,072	122,443	56,961	115,627	92,448	79,647	14	7	9·5	12
12	1·20	122,816	170,674	168,582	150,761	64,602	128,005	110,960	98,137	12	8	9	10
13	1·30	128,065	180,029	168,663	150,451	69,621	125,161	116,627	95,209	10	6	9	10

Thirteen sets of 1¼-inch square steel bars, apparently eight inches long between marks, each set being of constant composition, are tested tensilely in four different conditions. Those conditions are as follows:

1st, simply annealed, apparently by slow-cooling from dull redness after previous forging.
2d, quenched in cold water from about W. (b of Chernoff), then reheated to 752° F. (400° C.) and cooled slowly.
3d, the same, except that they are quenched in oil instead of water.
4th, the same, except that they are quenched in molten lead instead of water.
The proportion of carbon is approximately that given in the second column, and but little silicon, manganese, etc., is present, *i. e.* the metal is true carbon-steel.

INDEX.

ADVERTISERS' INDEX.

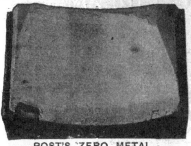

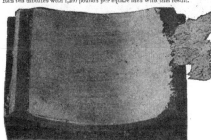

GORDON, STROBEL & LAUREAU, Limited,

ENGINEERS AND CONTRACTORS,

Works and Main Office, - - Mifflin and Meadow Streets, Philadelphia, Pa.

BLAST FURNACES AND EQUIPMENT.

Bessemer and Open Hearth Steel Plants.

Corliss and Poppett Valves,

Blowing Engines,

Feed Water Heaters,

Snort Valves,

Gas Cut-Off Valves.

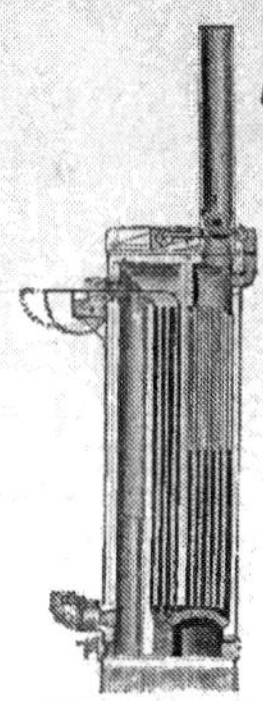

Central and Outside Combustion Chamber,

Fire Brick

Hot Blast Stoves,

Tuyere Stocks,

Bell and Hoppers,

Gas Burners.

Hydraulic Cranes,

Ingot Pushers,

Accumulators,

Hydraulic Cars,

Ladles.

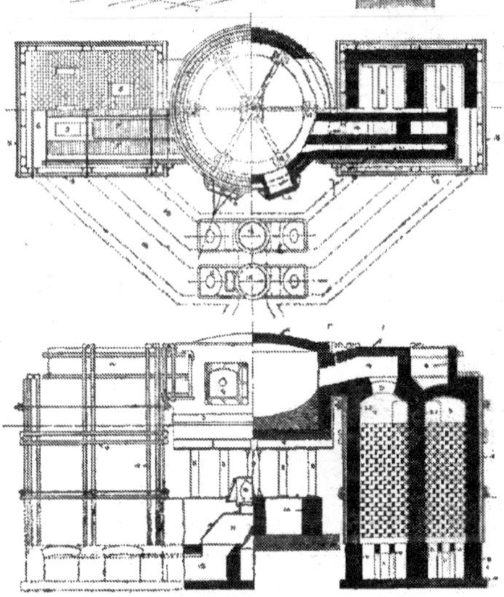

Converters,

Cupolas,

Gas Producers,

Reversing Valves.

BRANCH OFFICES:

DREXEL BUILDING, PHILADELPHIA, PA. 45 BROADWAY, NEW YORK.

PENN BUILDING, PITTSBURGH, PA.

ARCHER GAS-FUEL PROCESS

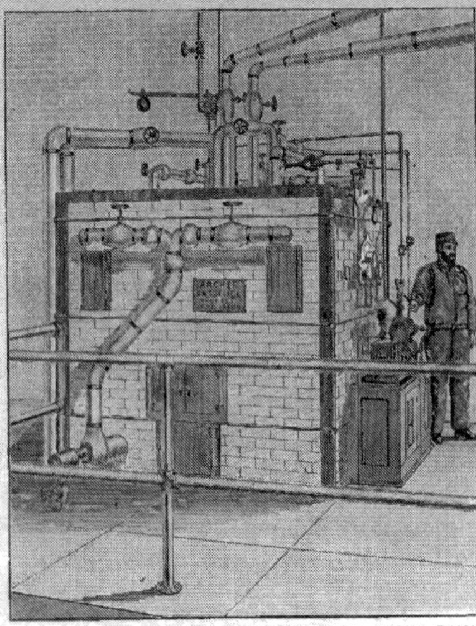

This Process solves the Problem of cheap Gaseous Fuel, meeting every requirement of Natural Gas, as to EFFICIENCY and ECONOMY. It has been in successful operation on a large scale, from 3 to 31 months, in many of the largest Iron, Steel, Glass, Pipe, Copper Works; Agate and Granite Ware Works; Iron Ship Yards, and other manufacturing establishments in the United States. ☞ IT IS THE ONLY PRACTICALLY RUNNING AND COMMERCIALLY SUCCESSFUL WATER OIL-GAS SYSTEM IN THE WORLD. ☜

We invite manufacturers and all users of fuel to the most rigid examination into the practical working of the ARCHER GAS-FUEL SYSTEM. This Process is applicable for all uses, from a RIVET and BOLT HEAD furnace to the largest OPEN-HEARTH Melting and Heating Furnaces; also for Steam Boilers, burning Brick, Lime, Cement, Pottery-tile, etc. It is ABSOLUTELY SAFE. But one man required on turn to furnish fuel for the largest Iron and Steel Works.

☞ Lima or other crude oil used. ☜

THIS PROCESS HAS BEEN RUNNING CONSTANTLY FOR OVER

31 months on a large scale in the
Bethlehem (Pa.) Iron Co. Works.

For over 24 months in the
Penna. Steel Co. Works, Steelton, Pa.

For over 23 months in the
Cleveland Rolling Mill, Cleveland, Ohio.

For over 22 months in the
Allison Mfg. Co. Pipe Works, Philadelphia.

For over 20 months in the
Oliver Iron (Chilled Plow) **Works, South Bend, Ind.**—Running Boilers, Heating, Welding, Malleable Iron Annealing Furnaces etc., etc.

For over 14 months in the
Otis & Co. Steel Works, Cleveland, Ohio.

For over 20 months in the
Detroit (Mich.) Steel and Spring Works.

For over 18 months in the
Burden (Horseshoe) Iron Co. Works, Troy, N. Y.

For over 16 months in the
Illingworth Co. Steel Works, Newark, N. J.

For over 10 months in the
Lincoln Iron Co. Works, Boonton, N. J.

For over 10 months in the
Albertson Glass Works, Norristown, Pa.

For over 9 months in the
Illinois Steel Co. (Joliet Works).

For over 8 months in the
Brookfield Glass Works, Brooklyn.

For over 7 months in the
Iron Ship Yard, West Bay City, Michigan.

For over 6 months in the
Lalance & Grosjean Agate Ware Works, Woodhaven, L. I.

For over 8 months in the
Iowa Barb Wire Works, Allentown, Pa.

For over 8 months in the
Johnson Co. Steel Works, Johnstown, Pa., superseding Natural Gas, also for House Heating and Illumination.

F. W. Wurster & Co. Iron Works, Brooklyn, N. Y.

Heberman's Granite Ware Works, Brooklyn, N. Y.

Pencoyd Iron and Steel Works, Pencoyd, Pa.

Pennsylvania Salt Mfg. Co., Natrona, Pa.

Cooper, Hewitt & Co.'s Trenton (N. J.) Iron Works.

And in many other first-class Manufacturing establishments, while new Plants are being contructed for throughout the Country.

☞ We are manufacturing the Archer Gas-Fuel Producers on a large scale for Factories, and are prepared to fill all orders at short notice, and furnish competent Superintendents to erect Plants and apply the gas.

For Domestic Fuel and for Illuminating Gas

For Towns and Cities, a FIXER is added to the ARCHER FUEL GAS PRODUCER, and any desired grade of non-condensible gas of great purity can be cheaply manufactured and stored or piped all required distances.

FOR FURTHER INFORMATION CALL ON OR ADDRESS

J. B. ARCHER, 45 Broadway, New York.

Attention Miners !

EVERETTE'S MINING OFFICE.

Pioneer Mining and Assay Office of Pacific Northwest.

Having the largest permanent brick assay furnaces, chemical laboratory and mining office on the Northwest coast, with a collection of about 4,000 samples of the ores of Alaska, British Columbia, Oregon and the Northwest Territories, and having made personal examinations of nearly every mining camp on the Pacific Slope, from California to Alaska, I am prepared to do any class of legitimate and honest mining work, such as

Examining, Sampling and Reporting on the Value of all Mineral, Coal and Fire Clay Properties, Building Stones, Earths, Assays and Analysis of Ores, Check, Samples of Ore,

Pulp "Organic Analysis" work, and, in fact, any work connected with the office of a first-class mining geologist and chemist. Any information mining men may desire to know relative to the MINERAL OR COAL RESOURCES of the entire Pacific northwest will be honestly given.

——ADDRESS——

Dr. WILLIS E. EVERETTE,

1318 E STREET,

TACOMA, WASH. TER., U. S. A.

DAVID M. FORD,

ISHPEMING L. S., MICH.,

DEALER IN

Lake Superior Gold, Iron AND Copper Stocks.

"THE RICHEST MINES IN THE WORLD."

"THE LARGEST DIVIDEND PAYERS."

CORRESPONDENCE SOLICITED.

THE JEFFREY

ELECTRIC COAL MINING

MACHINES, DRILLS AND MOTOR CARS

FOR UNDERCUTTING, DRILLING AND MINE HAULAGE.

ALSO AIR POWER COAL MINING MACHINES AND DRILLS.

Mining properties examined, estimates made, and machines furnished subject to sale after having worked on the basis of the estimate.

Send for Illustrated Catalogue.

Correspondence Solicited.

——ALSO MANUFACTURE——

Chain Elevators, Conveyers, Screens, Etc.,

FOR HANDLING COAL, ORES, GRAIN, ETC., ETC.

ADDRESS

THE JEFFREY MFG. CO.,

COLUMBUS, OHIO.

RIVERSIDE IRON WORKS,

WHEELING, W. VA.,

MANUFACTURERS OF

"Riverside" Steel Nails

Bessemer, Foundry And Forge

"Riverside" Steel Pipe,

FOR WATER, OIL & GAS.

PIG IRON.

PLATE AND BAR STEEL.

Steel Blooms, Steel Billets.

SMALL STEEL T RAILS AND FLAT RAILS.

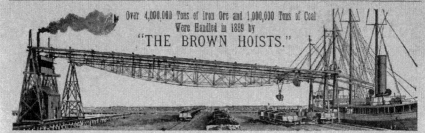

CPSIA information can be obtained
at www.ICGtesting.com
Printed in the USA
BVHW041758291019
562390BV00005B/70/P

9 780342 690121